SOCIOLOGY OF INDIAN SOCIETY

For Degree Students of Sociology and also useful for Aspirants of Various Competitive Examinations

---

C N SHANKAR RAO

Lecturer in Sociology

Canara Pre-University College

Mangalore, Karnataka

S Chand And Company Limited

(ISO 9001 Certified Company)

S Chand And Company Limited

(ISO 9001 Certified Company)

Head Office: D-92, Sector–2, Noida – 201301, U.P. (India), Ph. 91-120-4682700

Registered Office: A-27, 2nd Floor, Mohan Co-operative Industrial Estate, New Delhi – 110 044, Phone: 011-49731800

www.**schandpublishing.com;** e-mail: **info@schandpublishing.com**

Marketing Offices:

Chennai	:	Ph: 23632120; chennai@schandpublishing.com
Guwahati	:	Ph: 2738811, 2735640; guwahati@schandpublishing.com
Hyderabad	:	Ph: 40186018; hyderabad@schandpublishing.com
Jalandhar	:	Ph: 4645630; jalandhar@schandpublishing.com
Kolkata	:	Ph: 23357458, 23353914; kolkata@schandpublishing.com
Lucknow	:	Ph: 4003633; lucknow@schandpublishing.com
Mumbai	:	Ph: 25000297; mumbai@schandpublishing.com
Patna	:	Ph: 4011400; patna@schandpublishing.com

First Edition 2004
Second Revised Edition 2006, 2007, 2008, 2009, 2012
Revised Edition 2013, Reprints 2014, 2015, 2016, 2018 (Thrice), 2020 (Twice), 2021 (Twice), 2022 (Four Times), 2024, 2025 (Twice)

Reprint 2026 (Twice)

ISBN: 978-81-219-2403-0 **Product Code:** H5SIS41SOCL10ENAC13O

PRINTED IN INDIA

By Shri Shyamlal Printing Press Private Limited, Plot 20/4, Site-IV, Industrial Area Sahibabad, Ghaziabad – 201 010 and Published by S Chand And Company Limited, A-27, 2nd Floor, Mohan Co-operative Industrial Estate, New Delhi – 110 044.

DEDICATION

This Book is Dedicated to
The Memory of Those
Who Toiled and Struggled
For the Cause of
Developing Sociology in India

PREFACE TO THE REVISED EDITION

I am extremely happy to present this book entitled ***"Sociology of Indian Society"*** to all those who intend to have a glance of the Indian society. In fact, as early as in 1991 I had written a book in Kannada namely *"Bharateeya Samaja"* which was well appreciated in Karnataka region. Since then, students, teachers and many candidates appearing for the competitive examinations have been requesting and persuading me to bring out its English version. Almost after 12 years I have been able to materialise their request. And now it is being placed in your hands for solid support and encouragement.

This is neither the first book nor the only book written on "Indian Society" in English. Several books have been authored by several writers on this very topic. In regional languages of different States also sociology books on Indian Society have appeared in a large number. This present book, I am sure, will attract the attention of its intended readers because of its simple approach and wide coverage.

This book is written in simple and lucid style. Due importance is given here to provide enough explanation for each topic. For clarity and authenticity, I have given additional explanation wherever possible, in the form of footnotes. I have also tried to substantiate the explanations with the latest statistics. Wide coverage of topics would help the students in general to find sufficient reading material for the chapters contained in the syllabus. Hence, both students and teachers will find the book interesting and useful.

The book contains 22 chapters and covers various institutional, historical, economic, demographic and other aspects of the Indian society. The 22nd Chapter is on some social evils of India. The chapters selected here cover the topics that are included in the syllabi of B.A. and M.A. degree courses on the one hand and, IAS and KAS Examinations on the other. It also contains lessons that form part of MBA, Nursing and five-year Law courses. The book is thus designed to cater to the needs of people engaged in different fields of learning. The readers will soon realise that this is a book with a difference.

To get this book ready, I referred to and drew much material from the works of a number of writers, to whom I am extremely grateful. In order to be objective in the explanation of sociological concepts I have profusely quoted sentences and statements of various sociologists to whom I am greatly indebted. Hence as an author I do not venture to claim any originality for many of the ideas and descriptions contained in the book. But with all humility I can say that I have presented the matter in my own way.

It is my duty to express my gratitude to all those who have helped me in preparing this book. My thanks are due to my fellow-teachers and student-readers without whose encouragement the book would not have appeared. I am indebted to all those friends and well-wishers of mine who have given valuable suggestions in this venture. My thanks are specially due to Prof. K.S. Joseph Kalapura, Department of English, Canara P.U. College, Mangalore, who has gone through most part of the printed proof. I thank my wife Saraswathi S. Rao who has inspired and encouraged me to prepare and complete this work at the earliest. The computer services of Sri Narayana Nayak who has done the typing work neatly and impressively, cannot be forgotten.

We are thankful to the Management Team and the Editorial Department of S. Chand & Company Ltd. for all help and support in the publication of this book.

I sincerely request the readers to come out with their constructive criticisms, useful comments and valuable suggestions which will be of great help to me to further improve the book. I earnestly appeal to all the readers to give this book due encouragement, support and publicity which it deserves.

MANGALORE **C. N. SHANKAR RAO**

CONTENTS

Chapter 1

HISTORICAL MOORINGS OF THE INDIAN SOCIETY

Introduction to the Indian Society and Culture : *Indian Cultural Tradition: Characteristics - Hinduism : The Ancient Religion of India: Basic Tenets and Doctrines - Characteristics-* ***The Philosophical Literature of the Hindus :*** *Srutis and Smritis - Srutis or the Vedas : Types of Vedas and Their Socio-Cultural Importance - The Upanishads: Essential Principles and the Message of the Upanishads - The Smrities and Their Contents- Bhagavad Gita and Its Importance - Purusharthas Representing the Hindu View of Life - Meaning and Importance - Ashrama Dharma and Its Importance - Varna Dharma and Its Importance-* ***Traditional Characteristics of the Hindu Society.***

India has a long history and its cultural tradition is also very old. *"India's cultural heritage is one of the most ancient, extensive, and varied among all those which make up the cultural heritage of mankind. Throughout the ages many races and peoples contributed to India's culture. Some came into contact with her only temporarily, others settled permanently within her borders. The keynote of the distinctive culture thus evolved was synthesis on the basis of eternal values."*[1]

India's cultural heritage is not only one of the most ancient, but it is also one of the most widespread and varied. It has its own geographic, ethnic, religious and linguistic background. In its background we also observe the prehistoric Indus valley civilisation which flourished over 4,000 years ago. The Vedic civilisation had laid the grand spiritual foundation of India's culture and philosophical thought. The subsequent Jain and Buddhist movements took the accumulated spiritual wealth and spread it among the masses and classes of the country, Buddhism even spreading abroad. Thus, *"..... in these early phases of India's two ideals took shape which were to be the foundations of the whole structure of Indian culture; the spiritual nature of man, and the acceptance of all cultures as valid expressions of eternal values."*[2]

Indian society is quite old and extremely complex. Opinions of the scholars differ regarding the depth of its past. According to a popular estimate, it has covered a span of 5000 years. During this

1 Excerpts from the Introductory remarks in *"The Cultural Heritage of India."* Vol.I. Publication : Sri Ramakrishna Mission.

2 *ibid.*

long period several waves of immigrants, representing different ethnic groups, linguistic communities and religious background, have merged into its population to contribute to its diversity, richness and vitality. In the process of its evolution, Indian society has acquired a composite culture characterised by stable but varied patterns. The present day Indian culture is the result of cultural contact, cultural diffusion, cultural conflict, and cultural assimilation that took place previously between different groups. Thus the study of the evolution of the Indian society to its present form is, therefore, interesting and sometimes thrilling to the students of indology in general and sociology in particular.

Indian cultural heritage, as it is made clear from the above, consists of different systems of thought, belief and practice which have developed India from the very dawn of reflection. Though this amorphous mass appears at first sight to be highly encyclopaedic in nature, a closer second thought reveals a pervading unity which binds together the multiplicity of beliefs and practices. The different systems that we find in India *".... possess a unity of character and attitude which makes the manifold a single whole, which we might describe as the Hindu spirit. The civilisation which is inspired by the spiritual insight of our sages is marked by a certain moral integrity, a fundamental loyalty, a fine balance of individual desires and social demands, and it is these that are responsible for its vitality and continuity. To a departure from the ideals can be traced the present weakness and disorder of the Hindu civilisation."*[1]

The present chapter is only an attempt to give to the readers a glimpse of the Indian cultural tradition or heritage, a glance of the basic religion of this land, that is, Hinduism, and an introduction to the philosophical literature of the Hindus. The chapter also seeks to familiarise the readers with the Hindu society and its traditional characteristics. While some of the aspects of the Indian heritage are well known and richly documented, much of it still needs to be probed into, researched and unveiled.

INDIAN TRADITION : CHARACTERISTICS

The term ***"Indian tradition"*** virtually refers to the *Indian cultural tradition.* The cultural tradition of India is unique in the sense, it has certain special characteristics among which the following may be noted.

1. Indian Cultural Tradition is Ancient and Continuous

Indian cultural tradition has a long and continuous history. It extends over at least 5000 years. With the exception of China and Japan, in the whole world, we find only in India the most ancient and at the same time an unbroken stream of cultural tradition. This cultural tradition still continues to be the living tradition of this land. **Dr. Iravathi Karve** has rightly pointed out that in the whole of the Western world, we do not find a single country which has so extensive and diverse a cultural tradition as India has. Hence she called *"India – the epitome of the world."*

Unbroken Continuity of Indian Cultural Heritage **:** Indian heritage continued in spite of many changes that took place in it over the years. The heritage originated here and it grew till it became unalterable. It had vitality and originality of its own. It spread in all directions with speed all over India and over the eastern seas. Its stability was such that it survived repeated shocks and

1 *ibid.* Page : xxiii.

invasions from outsiders. The famous scholar and orientalist **Max Muller** writes : *"There is, in fact, an unbroken continuity between the most modern and the most ancient phases of Hindu thought, extending over more than 3000 years."*[1]

In the prolonged history of mankind which stretches beyond 6000 years, a series of civilisations and cultures have risen and fallen. **Oswald Spengler** after making a study of 30 civilisations and **Arnold Toynbee,** after a study of 19 civilisations have said that India, because of its religious dominance has been able to maintain its cultural continuity all through the history. **Sorokin** and **Dr. S. Radhakrishnan** too have said that India has withstood the foreign invasions of the Persians, Sythians, Greeks, Huns, Turks, and others and has maintained an unbroken chain of cultural tradition for at least 4000 years. Famous Indian historian **Jadunath Sarkar** has stated : *"This common Indian type has stood the test of time, it has outlined the shock of dynastic revolutions, foreign invasions, religious conflicts, and widespread natural disasters....."*[2]

Professor Macdonell also expressed the same view in his *"History of Samskrit Literature."* He writes : *"The importance of Indian literature as a whole consists in its originality. When the Greeks towards the end of the 4th century B.C. invaded the north-west, the Indians had already worked out a national culture of their own, unaffected by foreign influences. And in spite of successive waves of invasion and conquest by Persians, Greeks, Scythians, Mohammedans, the national development of the life and literature of the Indo-Aryan race remained practically unchecked and unmodified from without down to the era of British occupation. No other branch of the Indo-European stock has experienced an isolated evolution like this. No other country except China can trace back its language and literature, its religious beliefs and rites, its dramatic and social customs through an uninterrupted development of more than 3,000 years."*

2. Unity in Diversity

One feature that is most often noticed about India is its *"unity in diversity."* This stereotyped phrase has become a part of India's self-identity. *"In the past, foreign travellers – among others, Megasthenese* [315 B.C], *Fa-Heien* [A.D. 405 - 11], *Huan Tsang* [A.D. 630 - 44], *Alberuni* [A.D. 1030], *Marco Polo* [A.D. 1288, 93], *and Ibn Batuta* [A.D. 1325-51]– *observed and recorded this. After the partition of India........ this aspect has been passionately articulated both as a reality of the past and as the hope for the future......"*[3]

Reflections of Diversities : India, the **7th** largest and the second most populous nation of the world, occupying around 2.4% of the total land area of the world and possessing **15%** of the world's population – *has no doubt its own diversities* reflected in social, cultural, economic, political, religious, racial and other matters. In fact, the diversity of this land runs through various races, religions, castes, tribes, languages, social customs, cultural and subcultural beliefs, political philosophies, ideologies, and so on. Its social economic and cultural diversities are also reflected in

---

1 **Max Muller** ***in his lectures delivered before the University of Cambridge, England, in 1882 also said***– "If we were to look over the whole world to find out the country most richly endowed with all the wealth, power, and beauty that nature can bestow - in some parts a very paradise on earth - I should point to India. If I were asked under what sky the human mind has most fully developed some of its choicest gifts, has most deeply pondered over the greatest problems of life, and has found solutions of some of them which well deserve the attention even of those who have studied Plato and Kant - I should point to India. And if I were to ask myself from what literature we here in Europe, we who have been nurtured almost exclusively on the thoughts of Greeks and Romans, and of one Semitic race, the Jewish, may draw the corrective which is most wanted in order to make our inner life more perfect, more comprehensive, more universal, in fact more truly human a life, not for this life only, but a transfigured and eternal life - again I should point to India."

2 **Jadunath Sarkar** in *"India Through the Ages"* [1979]. Page - 2.

3 **S.C. Dube** in *"Indian Society."* [1990]. Page 23. *[National Book Trust of India]*

the habitat conditions in the rural, urban and semi-urban areas. There are settlements with 500 and 1000 people and also settlements with 10 to 12 million people.

The term *"diversity"* denotes collective differences reflected in the dissimilarities found among groups of people. These differences may be geographic, biological, ethnic, religious, linguistic and so on. Ethnic diversity is perceived on the basis of biological diversity. Religious diversity is visualised on the basis of religion or faith. Linguistic diversity is marked on the basis of languages spoken by a group of people. Thus, all these differences presuppose collective differences or prevalence of variety of groups and cultures.

Aspects of Indian Unity* : *Despite the diversities mentioned above, Indian culture possesses a fundamental unity, a unity the imprint of which can be found in the literature and thought of different communities of the country. The fundamental approach to literature, philosophy, traditions, and customs is typically Indian. The basis of the social and cultural unity of the country is common to every group. *"**M.N. Srinivas** is of the opinion that the unity of India is essentially a religious one. People may worship different deities but the religious scriptures – Puranas, Brahmanas, Epics and the Vedas – knit the numerous heterogeneous groups together into one religious society and give them the sense that their country is sacred. The worshippers may visit different centres of pilgrimage but all have a common goal of earning religious merit by visiting a sacred place."*[1]

The bonds of unity in relation to Indian heritage in a certain underlying uniformity of life, have been reflected in the observations of many foreigners also. The British Census Commissioner in India in 1911, **Herbert Risley**, for example, writes : *"Beneath the manifold diversity of physical and social type, language, custom, and religion which strike the observer in India, there can still be discerned....... a certain underlying uniformity of life from the Himalayas to Cape Camorin."* Unity amidst diversity is visualised in the geo-political sphere, institution of pilgrimage, tradition of accommodation, tradition of interdependence, emotional bond, etc. Therefore, in India cultural tradition could embrace and contain, absorb and assimilate people of all races, religions, castes and creeds.

The basic trait inherent in Hindu culture has influenced every Hindu. Different religions exist side by side here without causing any major conflicts or wars among them. The saints of different religions have evinced the feeling of belonging to each other, a sense of identity or purpose and emotions. People speak different languages in different regions but they have common languages such as Hindi and English to communicate with each other. Centuries ago Sanskrit was the link language. Even the caste system has provided a common cultural ideology to the Indians. Our economic, social and political philosophies are broadly based on equality, justice, liberty, rationality and secularism. The Constitution also guarantees equality to one and all.

3. Dharma as the Life-Centre of the Society

Every nation or society has its own ethos. It is often referred to as the *"national ethos"* or special attribute or character with which it is identified. As **Swami Vivekananda** has said, *"political power"* represents the national ethos of England, material and scientific progress represents the ethos of America, material pleasure and enjoyment represent the French ethos, and the like. He stresses that *religion and spirituality represent the Indian ethos.* Religious and spiritual orientation has been the characteristic feature of Indian culture since ancient times. In Indian social thought, the concept of *Dharma* has been the basic idea in different fields of society. This idea explains the functions and roles of different people, social institutions and organisations. It is the thread which ties the Indian thought together. Every thing in India contains a religious tinge. *Religion and spirituality permeate our intellectual, philosophical, artistic, scientific, cultural, social, political, economical in brief the whole of our life.*

---

1 **Ram Ahuja** *"Indian Social System"* [1993]. Page - 19.

India and Its Spiritual Life : "Spiritual life is the true genius of India. Those who make the greatest appeal to the Indian mind are not the military conquerors, not the rich merchants or the great diplomats, but the holy sages, the *rsis* who embody spirituality at its finest and purest. India's pride is that almost in every generation and in every part of the country, from the time of her recorded history, she has produced these holy men who embody for her all that the country holds most dear and sacred. Though they generally remain away from the main stream of life, kings and commoners pay reverent homage to them and take their advice in the problems of their personal lives as well as in public affairs. By their lives they teach us that pride and power, wealth and glory, are nothing in comparison with the power of Spirit. It is those who scorn their own lives that raise life above our scorn."[1]

In fact, the religious and the spiritual element of Indian culture is so deep-rooted that it has made Indians to regard their nation not merely as a geographic entity but something more than that. *They call their nation not only as their motherland, but also as their Karma Bhumi, Tapo Bhumi and Punya Bhumi.*[2]

4. Scientific Aspect of the Indian Heritage

Indian cultural heritage has its own scientific aspect and this has been unfortunately neglected. *"There is a general impression among scholars abroad, and even among educated Indians, that our heritage as enshrined in ancient Indian works is primarily religio-philosophical. There is hardly anything worthwhile to mention about our scientific and technological past. The reasons for such an impression are well known. References on science and technology are scattered in several works, whose main themes are not related to science and technology. These works are in* ***Sanskrit*** *and* ***Pali*** *that are currently not in use. Added to this is the fact that the ancient knowledge is often in a highly condensed form which can be understood only by experts in those languages."*[3]

There is much that is glorious in our scientific tradition. Some examples are worth citing here : The concept of zero, the place of value system of numeration, square roots, cube roots, and the powers of the ten were known to the ancient Indians. Brahmagupta's achievements in the field of mathematics predated the work of European mathematicians by a few centuries.

"Classical works of the Indian medical system Ayurveda, like the *"Charaka Samhita"* and the *"Ashtanga Hridaya"* on medicine, and *"Sushruta Samhita"* on surgery, are consulted even today by Indian medical practitioners."[4]

The contributions of ancient Indians in the metallurgy of iron, zinc, copper and its alloys are acknowledged the world over. Superb temple architecture, town planning including drainage systems, and the architecture associated with the construction of roads, bridges, forts and ports was well developed. Sound practices in irrigation and agriculture have been mentioned in our ancient texts. Good expertise existed in the areas of ship-building and navigation. Maritime trade with countries in South-east Asia, was very active. Ancient Indians expertise and supremacy in cotton and silk textiles is well recognised in the world. This glorious scientific tradition has contributed much to the strengthening of the science of culture in the Indian society.

---

1 *"The Cultural Heritage of India."* Vol. I. Page - xxiii.

2 **Swami Vivekananda** while praising India's glorious past writes : "If there is any land on this earth that can lay claim to be the blessed Punya-Bhumi, to be the land to which souls on this earth must come to account for Karma, the land to which every soul that is wending its way Godward must come to attain its last home, the land where humanity has attained its highest towards gentleness, towards generosity, towards purity, towards calmness, above all, the land of introspection and of spirituality. – It is India." - ***Ref*****: Swami Vivekananda's** *"Rousing Call to Hindu Nation."* - Compiled by **Eknath Ranade.** Page - 1.

3 ***Source*** : *"Science and Technology in Ancient India"* Page - xiii [Editorial Remarks]. Published by ***"Vijnan Bharathi"***, Mumbai.

4 *ibid.*

5. Spirit of Tolerance : Synthetic Approach to Religion

Religious tolerance and synthetic approach has been the characteristic of Indian religion. Hinduism which is the essence of Indian culture, has accepted many different religions into its fold and has only gained by it. Hinduism believes in universal toleration and accepts all religions as true. Hinduism believes that *"the essence of all religions is one; only their approaches are different."* *Gandhiji thus commented "religions differ only in non-essentials while in essentials they agree."*

The Hindu mind is all embracing. This is seen in the word *"manava dharma"* or *"manava samskriti"* or human culture which the Hindus gave to their culture. Indian culture is comprehensive and suits the needs of everyone, irrespective of caste, creed, colour or sex. It has universal appeal and makes room for all. It has the modesty to accept the propriety of other points of view. As the Jain theory of ***"Syadvada"*** or the theory of *"may be"* makes it evident – *"all knowledge is probable and relative the other man's point of view is as true as ours."* It, thus suggests that one must show restraint in making judgements. This is a healthy principle. We must know that our judgements are true only partially and can by no means be regarded as true in absolute terms.

The modern Indian social thinkers, social reformers and social philosophers like Sri Raja Ram Mohan Roy, Sri Aurobindo, Sri Ramakrishna Paramahamsa, Swami Vivekananda, Tagore, Gandhiji, Radhakrishnan, Bhagawandas have stressed upon the synthetic approach in Indian culture. They all exhibit an integral viewpoint in their approach towards religion. They have pointed out the contribution of each great religion to humanity and emphasised their fundamental unity. As **Tagore** has said *"These religions differ in details and often in their moral significance, but they have a common tendency. In them men seek their own supreme value which they call divine, in some personality anthropomorphic in character."* Tagore in his work *"Religion of Man"* emphasised humanism as the core of all religions. He has drawn our attention towards the essential similarity in the teachings of the pioneers of all religions.

"Live and Let Live" Policy **:** The Indian tradition has taught Indians to develop mutual understandings and mutual adjustments on the one hand, and catholicity of outlook, on the other. This attitude of tolerance and accommodation has largely been responsible for the advancement of Indian culture. This attitude has helped to bring together the divergent races with different languages and religious persuasions. From the earliest times, India followed a policy of *"live and let live."* She was not averse to contact with foreign cultures. In fact, it is her contacts with the outside elements that have added to the richness and variety of her culture. And this spirit of tolerance explains the existence of a common culture from the Himalayas in the North to Kanya Kumari in the South.

6. Harmony with Nature

Another important aspect of the Indian culture is *that nature and its various aspects* are embedded in it. It lays more emphasis on the value of all created life. Animals, birds, trees, mountains, rivers form a part and parcel of the Hindu way of life. In fact, the Gods of the Hindu pantheon are associated with animals. For example, Shiva has the Nandi or the Bull as his mount [*vahana*]; Vishnu, the *Garuda*; Brahma, the *Swan*; Indra, the *Elephant*; Surya, the *Horse*; Durga, the *Lion*; Ganesh, the *Rat*; Muruga, the *Peacock*; and so on. The Hindus have naturally invested the animals with an element of divinity. This association of Gods with the animal world indicate a healthy attitude towards nature.

Mountains, rivers, forests, lakes, land, plants, and such other things of nature also have cultural importance. The mountains of Himalayas have a great impact on the life of the Indians. As per the belief of the Hindus, Lord Shiva and His Consort Parvathi reside with Nandi [*Vahana*] on the top of the *"Gowrishankar Peak"* of the Himalayas. Referring to the role of the mountains like the Himalayas, **K.M. Kapadia** points out : *"It is not only the political life of the people of Hindustan, but the religion, mythology, art and literature of the Hindus that bear the imprint of the great* *mountain barrier."*

Not only the Himalayas, but the other mountains are also regarded as the abode of the gods and hence held to be sacred by the Hindus. Various places of pilgrimage such as Amarnath, Kedarnath, Badrinath, Kailas, are to be found in the mountains. Numerous other hills like the Tirupathi, Srishyla, Annamalai, Shabarimalai, Kodachadri, Arunadri, etc. are also venerated by the Hindus.

Rivers are also equally sacred for the Hindus. They themselves represent the Goddess Ganga, Yamuna, Saraswathi, Kaveri, Narmada, Sindhu, Godavari and other rivers are all sacred for the Hindus for a dip in the waters of a river is believed to wash off all sins. River Ganga is highly sacred for the Hindus for it continues to be the wish of every Hindu to have a dip in its holy waters. The rivers are normally addressed as *"mata"*; Ganga Mata, Yamuna Mata, and so on. The trees and plants are also sacred for the Hindus. *Ashwatha* and the *pipal* trees, and plants such as *"Tulasi"*, *"Deva Parijatha"*, for example, are venerated even today.

It is clear from the above, that the Hindus have a great concern for the nature. The Hindus' concern for the environment is genuine, because man and nature are never considered separate from one another. Nature was always considered the Mother from whom man drew his sustenance. The question of exploitation of nature was unimaginable. On the other hand, *"Mother Nature"* was considered the Goddess to be worshipped.

The Hindu tradition opposes the exploitation of nature. In fact, the word that was being used was *'milking'* and not exploitation. The attitude of the East was one of total solidarity with the entire nature. Environmental protection was the sacred duty and not a matter of expediency. The Hindu approach has been very well brought out in the **Atharva Vedic Sookta** which means *"Whenever we dig up from thee, O Mother, let it be immediately replenished; may we not cause hurt to thy vital organs. May we not harm thy heart."*

Hinduism : The Ancient Religion of India

Hinduism represents neither a dogma nor just a collection of some beliefs. It is a living religion. It denotes not only a way of life but also a way of thinking. It gives more importance to spiritual and moral principles than to religious norms, rituals and ceremonials. Hence moral and spiritual principles always encompass the Hindu view of life.

Hinduism as a religion is the most ancient and the most influential one. It has contributed in no small measure to the enrichment of the major religions of the world such as Buddhism, Jainism, Christianity, Islam and Zorostrianism. Hinduism which has a long and an unbroken tradition of wise and perfect men still continues to guide the lives of millions of its followers.

Hinduism is based on and supported by abundant literature in the form of *"srutis"* and *"smritis"*. In the vast mass of the Hindu religio-philosophical literature the *Vedas, Upanishads* and the *Bhagavad Gita* have assumed importance. The Vedas constitute the fountainhead of the entire Indian Culture, whereas the Upanishads form the basis of Indian philosophy and socio-religious thought. They are also known as the earliest treasures of knowledge. The Gita which provides the philosophical basis of popular Hinduism, seems to be very influential in guiding the lives of people.

The Hindu socio-philosophical thought also includes the theory of *"purusharthas"* which exemplifies Hindu *'life-purposes'*. The four *purusharthas – Dharma, Artha, Kama* and *Moksha* reflect the Hindu attitude towards life. The theory of *purusharthas* gets its concrete expression in the twin co-ordinated systems of social organisation namely: the *Ashrama system* and the *Varna system.* The former regulates the individual's individual life while the latter controls and systematises the individual's social life. Together they achieve individual perfection and social harmony. The *"Hindu view of life"* which is very difficult to be comprehended in its entirety covers the various aspects which are described in the following pages.

Emergence of the word *"Hindu"*

"Hinduism" is the religion of the Hindus. It is one of the oldest religions of the world. Its striking feature is that *nobody knows about its origin.* The very word *'Hindu'* is not of Indian origin. Ancient Persians [while referring to the river "Sindhu"] pronounced the word *"Sindhu"* as "Hindu".[1] The Arabs referred to it as *"al-Hind".* Thus, the people of this land [the land of river "Sindhu"] came to be known as *"Hindus", t*heir land *"Hindustan"* and their religion *"Hinduism".*

Various Names : Though *"Hinduism"* is popularly known in that name, the traditional Hindus prefer to call it *"Sanatana Dharma"*, that is eternal religion flowing from time immemorial. They also regard it as its original name. Hindu spiritualist **Sri Aurobindo** also preferred to call Hinduism *"Sanatana dharma."*[2] It is also known as *"Vaidika Dharma"*, for it is rooted in the Vedas. It is also called *"Arya Dharma"* ["Arya" means "great" or "noble"] and sometimes as *"Vedanta Dharma"*.

General Characteristics of Hinduism

1. Hinduism - An Ancient Religion : Of all the religions of the world Hinduism has been considered to be the most ancient one. It is difficult to say with precision when exactly and how exactly it came to be originated. It is the most comprehensive and influential of all the religions of the world.

2. Hinduism is a way of life : Hinduism, as **M.K. Gandhi** points out is more than a religion, *it is a way of life.* Hindu belief is a complex one combining in itself religious, philosophical and ethical notions. Hinduism consists of several streams of beliefs, practices and socio-religious institutions. These beliefs and practices pervade every aspect of the life of a Hindu. This makes Hinduism appear very complex.

3. Hinduism has no Founder and No Central Authoritative Organisation : The unique feature of Hinduism is that it was *"founded"* or established by no single person, or prophet or angel. It is not based on the preachings and thoughts of any single person.

- Unlike Christianity or Islam, ***Hinduism does not have any single central authority,*** nor a universally accepted hierarchy of religious leaders, nor an organisation to control, regulate and guide the lives of its followers.

- Further, ***Hinduism does not have a single sacred scripture*** which can be regarded as a common authority on Hinduism. Christians have *Bible*, Muslims have *Quran*, Buddhists have *"Tripitakas"* whereas the Hindus don't have a single sacred scriptural authority that way.

4. Universality and Catholicity : Hinduism is known for its broad outlook. It allows the widest freedom to its followers in matters of faith and worship. It never prescribes any particular way of worship and never imposes any belief for the devotees. There can be any number of faiths

---

1 The Greeks called the Sindhu river *"Indus"* and the people in the valley *"Indos"*. The British in course of time, popularised the word *"India"* to represent this land and introduced the term *"Hinduism"* in 1830 to represent the main religion of India.

2 **Sri Aurobindo** writes : "The religious culture which now goes by the name of Hinduism....... gave itself no name, because it set itself no sectarian limits; it claimed no universal adhesion, asserted no sole infallible dogma, set up no single narrow path or gate of salvation; it was less a creed or cult than a continuously enlarging tradition, of the Godward endeavour of the human spirit. An immense many-sided and many-staged provision for a spiritual self-building and self-finding, it had some right to speak of itself by the only name it knew, the eternal religion, sanatana dharma......"

and any type of worship within its framework. The popular saying, *"as many minds so many faiths"* reveals this freedom granted to the followers.

In fact, the **Rig Veda** stated long back that *"the truth is one and sages call it by various names."* Hinduism cherishes the value of *"sarva dharma samabhava"* [equal respect to all religions].

5. Synthesis of Many Sects : Hinduism is not a uniform monolithic [single God] religion. It allows flexibility and permits the prevalence of many sects within it. Hence, Hinduism is actually a collectivity of sects. Each may have its own distinct and independent origin. *Vaishnavism, Shaivism* and *Shaktism* are the three famous sects found within Hinduism.

(i) **Vaishnavism** is the worship of Vishnu and his ten incarnations. In its long history it has developed several groups such as *Sri Vaishnavas* and *Sri Chaitanyas.*

(ii) **Shaivism** is the worship of Shiva in his various forms. **Ex:** *Veerashaivism* of Karnataka and *Kashmiri Shaivism* of Kashmir.

(iii) **Shaktism** gives importance to the worship of *Divine Motherhood.* Here, the woman, especially the mother is assigned the highest place of honour.

In addition to the above, some cults such as *Radha-Krishna cult, Ram-Sita cult, Ganesha cult, Bhakti cult, Ayyappa cult* etc., representing different versions of Hinduism, are also found.

In case of these sects, there is what is called ***"henotheism"***. It is belief in one God without claiming that He is the only God. Thus, Vaishnavites worship Vishnu not as the Sole God, but as one among many other Gods. It may be noted that Hindus also worship a variety of lesser powers as well as village gods and goddesses. This polytheistic aspect of Hinduism does not, however, go against its basic monotheistic character.

- ***Concept of Ishtadevata*** **:** The concept of *Ishtadevata* is a unique feature in Hinduism. In no other religion this is found. In Hinduism, one can cling on to one's *Ishtadevata* with singleminded devotion to the exclusion of all others. One not only appreciates but also respects similar freedom to the devotees of every other Godhead. But the same cannot be stated about the religions that originate abroad for their philosophy was totally different. They were worshippers of a *"Jealous God."* Intolerance was inherent in such a religious attitude. To them, a believer in any other religion was a non-believer, who was to be won over by any means including violence. Aggression and conversion were part of their religious duty.

6. Idol Worship and Nature Worship : Hinduism is also associated with **idol worship**. But the worshipped idol is not uniform, but it varies according to the sect. Each sect keeps its idol [*Krishna, Rama, Shiva, Ganesh, Hanuman, Kali,* etc.] in a separate temple and worships it on specific occasions.

Nature Worship: Early Indians were simple worshippers of the forces of nature which were personified and deified. ***Example:*** *Indra* [God of wind], *Savitr* [Sun God], *Yama* [God of death], *Soma* [the Moon God] and *Prithvi* [the Mother Goddess]. The worship of these Vedic deities declined with the rise of Shaiva and Vaishnava sects in the first millennium A.D. The nature worship has declined though the basic belief in nature as a divine force still continues.

7. Concrete and Abstract Concepts of God : The God is understood in Hinduism in two ways: (i) to understand God as *an abstract entity,* that is, as *a Supreme Principle*; (ii) to understand God in terms of *images* or *symbols*, that is, through *concrete manifestations.*

(i) ***Abstract Concept of God***: According to Hindu belief, God is one only, one without a second. He is the *Creator, Conserver* and Destroyer of this Universe. He is all-knowing, all-powerful and all-pervading. He is the repository of truth, knowledge and beauty. This one Supreme God is understood in the Upanishadic language as *"Brahman"*. The Brahman is the Ultimate Reality. It is an eternal and all-embracing principle. This Brahman is formless or shapeless,

[*Nirakara Brahma*], He is beyond all earthly qualities [and hence referred to as *Nirguna Brahma*]. Only men of intellect can comprehend this abstract concept of God.

(ii) ***Concrete Concept of God*:** Hindus also believe in the concrete manifestations of God. Though Hinduism accepts in principle that God is essentially one, that is, the Brahman, it also concedes the existence of several gods or deities. God here appears with some form [*sakara Brahma*] and various qualities are attributed to Him [and hence He is referred to as *saguna Brahma*]. The Saguna Brahma takes on different forms and different *names* [*Rama, Krishna, Shiva, Ganesha, Hanuman* etc.] are assigned to these diverse forms; idols or images are made to represent them; *structures* called temples are built to install these idols and various modes of worship are developed to propitiate them. These are different modes or aspects of Paramatman, the Supreme Self or God, just as all dolls made of sugar are sugar itself.

8. Basic Theological Ideas of Hinduism : The Hindu theology is very complex. Various philosophical schools of thought have given their own interpretation regarding the Hindu theological issues. Theological ideas such as - *punarjanma* [transmigration of soul or rebirth], *immortality of atma* [soul], *papa* [sin], *punya* [merit], *Karma*[1] [deeds], *dharma* [morality] and *moksha* [salvation].

The idea of ***Karma*** teaches a Hindu that he is born into a particular social group [caste/ family] because of his actions [deeds] he performed in his previous life [*purva janma*]. The idea of ***dharma*** tells him that if he follows good deeds in the present birth, he will be born in a high social group in the next birth. The idea of ***moksha*** reminds him that his *papa* and *punya* will determine the release of his soul or atma from the necessity of *"samsara"* or the cycle of birth and death. Attaining *Moksha* means becoming one with the *"Brahman"*.

9. Major Schools of Philosophy : In India, philosophy and religion are inseparable. Hinduism in its historical development has developed different systems of philosophy or *darshanas.* These *darshanas* attempt to answer such fundamental questions as : *What is the destiny of man? What is God ? Who am I ? What is the nature of Atma ? Is there a life after death ? What is the nature*

---

1 **The Doctrine of Karma:** The Karma theory has assumed importance in the Hindu theology. According to the popular Hindu belief, *Karma is but an aggregate of man's actions in a former birth, which determines his unalterable future destiny. Its consequence is felt until it is exhausted through suffering or enjoyment. "As a man himself sows, so he himself reaps; no man inherits the good or evil act of another man. The fruit is of the same quality as the action; and whether good or bad, there is no destruction of the action." The consequences of Karma are thus inescpable. As* **Hopkins** *has pointed out "Karma struck hard against the old belief in sacrifice, penance and repentance."*

The doctrine of Karma is not found in the earliest Vedic thought, but it appears in the *Brahmanas* and the *earliest Upanishads*. In the Brahmanic thought, the doctrine of Karma has been combined with that of transmigration of soul or *punarjanma.* Accordingly, the sufferings or pleasures of an individual in this *janma* are explained in accordance with the *'Karma'* done by him is his former existence [or *janma*]. As long as the individual is caught in the bondage of the Karma there is no escape for him from the *'samsara'*, or the cycle of birth and death.

According to the Karma theory, as **Yajnavalkya** states, *an individual becomes virtuous by virtuous action and vicious by vicious action [punya vai punyena Karmana bhavati papah papeneti].* Karma is a connecting link between desires and rebirth. It is desire that binds a man to this world and things worldly and makes him liable to birth and death. The destruction of desires would, therefore, enable a man to free himself from the cycle of birth and death, to become eternal. When all the desires of a man are got rid of, the mortal becomes immortal and attains Brahman. The Bhagavad Gita provides a new approach to this problem of dispensing with the desires. *The Gita insists on the sublimation rather the eradication of desires, and that is to be done by knowing the true nature of Karma.*

It is to be remembered that "Karma" is accepted as an article of faith in all the main systems of Indian philosophy and religion. Even the Buddhists and Jains have accepted the Karma theory though they have given their own interpretation for it.

of the relationship between Brahma - Jiva and Jagat. [God-Soul and the Universe]. The answers to these questions, when formulated, become a system of philosophy. Since answers are varied, there are various systems of philosophy in India. However, their common object is to know the *Ultimate Reality.*

The systems of Indian Philosophy are grouped into two categories: *astika* [Brahmanic] and *nastika* [non-Brahmanic]. ***Astika philosophies*** accept the authority of the Vedas. **Examples:** *Nyaya, Vaisesika, Sankhya, Yoga, Mimamsa* and *Vedanta* - known as *shad darshanas*. But the ***nastika philosophies*** reject the authority of the Vedas: **Example:** *Bouddha* and *Jaina Philosophy.*

10. Concepts of Purity and Pollution : The ideas of pollution and purity are very important in popular Hinduism, that is, Hinduism as practised by the masses. The rules of pollution and purity vary from region to region and cover a wide area of life. They are important in *commensal relations, in touching or maintaining physical distance from the members of other group, in inter-caste marriages, and in personal life of an individual on occasions like birth, marriage, menstruation, death, offering prayers* etc. The concept of pollution is related *to birth* and not to cleanliness. A person has to undergo a purificatory rite, simple or elaborate, depending upon the seriousness of the violation of rules of purity. In such matters, it is the caste council that takes the necessary disciplinary action. In addition to this purificatory rites, *"samskaras"* are also prescribed in popular Hinduism. Among the 16 *"samskaras"* known as *"shodasha samskaras"* only a few such as - *namakarma, upanayana, vivaha* and *pretakarma* [funeral rites] are widely practised now. Ideas of purity and pollution and elaborate rules relating to them come under the ritual aspect of Hinduism. Many of them rarely have any theoretical justification for them.

11. The Hindu Ethics : The Hindus have an elaborate code of ethics to guide them throughout their life. The code of ethics is the subject matter of a class of sacred literature known as *"smritis"* or *"dharmashastras"*. Though there are more than 30 *dharmashastras* composed by the great Hindu Rishis and scholars at different times, three of them are regarded as significant. They are the ones composed by ***Manu, Yagnavalkya*** and ***Parashara***. *Manu dharmashastra* is much quoted for reference. The purpose of the Dharmashastras is to suggest the right and good conduct for the individual, the ruler, and different class of people. The *dharmashastras* are revised and reinterpreted from time to time. This flexibility gives dynamic character to the Hindu society to adapt itself to the new challenges. However, the rigidity imposed by them on certain areas resulted in a few problems.

12. Goals of Life : Purusharthas : According to the Hindu thinkers, human life has four main goals known as ***"Purusharthas"***. The *Purusharthas* constitute an ideal scheme of human ends. These *purusharthas* are: ***dharma*** [righteousness], ***artha*** [wealth], ***kama*** [desire or pleasure], and ***moksha*** [salvation or liberation]. Hinduism is not a life-negating religion. *Artha* and *Kama* are essential for a happy living, but they are to be realised within the boundaries of dharma. The final end for the individual is the attainment of freedom or *"moksha"*; that is, liberating one's soul from the cycle of birth and death.

13. Varnashrama Dharma : Twin Social Organisations : The Hindu thinkers developed two interrelated social organisations for regulating the individual and social life of the people. These social organisations together are called *"Varnashrama Dharma"*. They are related with the *Purusharthas* for they show the path for reaching these goals.

Ashrama Dharma: According to the *ashrama dharma* an individual's life span is divided into four phases: (i) *Brahmacharya* [the stage of childhood and adolescence meant for learning]; (ii) *Grihasta* [the stage of householder meant for leading family life]; (iii) *Vanaprastha* [the stage of hermit meant for retiring oneself from the worldly life and its responsibilites; (iv) *Sanyasa* [the stage of a wandering mendicant to prepare oneself for *"moksha"*.

Everyone according to this principle, is required to pass through the four phases: *the life of celibacy, the period of marital life, the life of retirement and finally the life of complete detachment.* This last phase is meant for attaining *"moksha"*, the supreme end of human life.

- ***Varna Dharma: Sanctioned System of Social Stratification:*** The Hindu thinkers conceived society as composing of four classes or divisions called *"Varnas"*. The individual and his society are linked together by the Varna system. The four Varnas are: *Brahmin, Kshatriya, Vaishya* and *Shudra.* According to the **Pursha Sukta** of Rig Veda, these different Varnas emerged from the four different organs of the *Virat Purusha* or *Divine Being* [Brahmins from the *mouth*, Kshatriyas from the *shoulders*, Vaishyas from the *thighs* and the Shudras from the *feet* of the Divine being. The varna system as a system of stratification has its own divine sanction. The division of society into four Varnas was based on *division of labour.* Brahmins acted as *priests and teachers,* Kshatriyas as *rulers and fighters,* Vaishyas as *traders,* and Shudras as a *servant class* [or serving class]. These are the fourfold divisions of society aimed at promoting welfare and social harmony,

14. Hinduism does not Believe in Conversions : Hinduism is not a set of unchanging dogmas. It permits greater adaptability. It very well serves the differing religious needs of the individuals. It permits a wide variety of schools of thought *[mathas]* and interpretations. This indicates a healthy freedom that is given for intellectual inquiry. *Hinduism is thus a faith that inquires.* Its inquiry is for the Ultimate Truth. It believes that truth is not the monopoly of any religion. It offers a wide variety of paths suited to each individual to attain truth on his own. Hence, it finds no reason to impose its beliefs or thoughts on the followers of other religions.

Hinduism, for the reasons cited above, does not believe in conversions or proselytization. A great philosopher **C.E.M. Joad** writes: *"Hinduism developed from the first a wide tolerance. Hindus do not proselytize: they do not claim exclusive claim to salvation and they do not believe that God will be pleased by the wholesome slaughter of His Creatures whose beliefs are mistaken. As a result, Hinduism has been less degraded than most religions by the anomaly of creed wars."*

15. Tolerant Towards Other Religions : Hinduism is a secular and tolerant religious philosophy for it not only embraces within its fold different sects and cults but also accommodates followers of other religions such as Christianity, Islam, Buddhism, etc. Throughout its history, Hinduism has maintained its stand of equal respect to other religions *[sarva dharma samabhava].* Though minor clashes have taken place among different sects they have not damaged the basic *"tolerant"* quality of the religion. In the same way, though confrontations took place between Hindus and Christians, Hindus and Muslims, Hindus and Buddhists, they have not taken the shape of any *"Crusade"* or *"Jihad"*. Hinduism still maintains this secular nature and tolerant attitude.

16. Receptivity and All-comprehensiveness : *"Receptivity and all-comprehensiveness, it has been aptly stated, are the main characteristics of Hinduism. Since it has had no difficulty in bringing diverse faiths within its ever-widening fold, it has something to offer to almost all minds.* **Monier-Williams** *in his notable work Brahminism and Hinduism dwelt on this aspect about a hundred years ago. The strength of Hinduism, he emphasized, lies in its infinite adaptability to the infinite diversity of and abstract side suited to the philosopher; its practical and concrete side attuned to the man of the poetic feeling and imagination; and man of peace and the lover of seclusion."*[1]

17. Hinduism is Neither Intolerant Nor Fundamentalistic : Fundamentalism and religious fanaticism are alien to Hinduism. Tolerance and accommodative spirit are the hallmarks of Hinduism. Hinduism is neither intolerant, nor does it believe in a theocratic state. It also makes a clear

1 *"The Gazetteer of India"* Vol. I. Page - 413.

distinction between religion and Dharma. Religion, according to the Hindu, is a strictly personal affair between man and God. There should be no external interference or compulsion. Dharma is the sum and substance of qualities that sustain the society. Hence observance of Dharma is a social duty. *Dharma Rajya* is the rule of Law. It is quite different from theocracy or even from the Rule of Law as we understand it today. Every man should be free to choose his religion, but there should be neither compulsion nor conversion; whatever the religion, Dharma is one thought depending upon the station in life, there will be variance, but Dharma Rajya will see to it that the Rule of Law prevails and that no one is above law or the ambit of Dharma.

18. Dominant Life Values of Hindu Society : The Hindu society in the course of its development has been cherishing a number of socio-cultural values. Most of these values are either originated or influenced by the Hindu religious beliefs and philosophy. Of the various values, five dominant ones which have exerted a tremendous influence on Hindu socio-cultural life may be stated here: **(i)** ***Truthfulness*** which is equated with dharma and God; **(ii)** ***Non-violence*** that is, the principle of *"Ahimsa"* which means non-injury; **(iii)** ***Respect for womanhood*** [that is, woman being considered more an embodiment of Mother Goddess than an object of beauty or enjoyment]; **(iv)** ***Respect for Nature and its various forms*** such as land, water, fire, wind, sun, moon, etc; **(v)** ***Harmony*** - that is, harmony between the individual and society, the material and the spiritual, action and knowledge and finally, between the earth and heaven.

The Elevating Power of Hinduism

Hinduism with its internal force and vitality had sought to elevate all the foreign invaders who came to India. **Jadunath Sarkar,** a famous Indian historian, writes - *"The moral transformation of savage foreigners is the greatest glory of India and a proof of the death-defying vitality of Hinduism, considered not as a dogmatic creed (which it never was), but as a social force and civilizing agency. The spirit of India has triumphed over time and change and kept the composite Indian people's mind as active and keen as in the best days of pure Aryan ascendance. The blending of races here has not led to the intellectual and moral deterioration which is found among the present-day mixed population of what was once Spanish America."*[1]

Conclusion

Thus, Hinduism is more than a religion, *it is a way of life based on justice and harmony.* Indeed, if one were to put it in a nutshell, *harmony is the keynote of Hinduism.* It signifies harmony not only among the Man, the Universe and the God, but also among the various castes, classes, creeds, peoples and their faiths, gods and goddesses. The Hindu believes that the whole world is his home and the *entire humanity is his family. ["Vasudhaiva Kutumbakam"]*

Hinduism is said to be the *earliest religion in the world* and has contributed in some measure to all the important religions of the world such as Jainism, Buddhism, Christianity, Zoroastrianism, and Islam. It is said that all religions are true, but *Hinduism condenses them all* by preserving such of their characteristics as may be acceptable to all.

Hinduism has a long and an unbroken tradition of wise and perfect men. Its vitality has never been found wanting. **Gandhiji** once wrote: *"My life would be a burden to me, if Hinduism failed me."* His glorious life was a grand testimony to the fact that Hinduism did not fail him. As **Prof. T.M.P. Madhavan** writes, it will not fail any one who in all sincerity attempts to understand its truths and practise its disciplines.

---

1 **Jadunath Sarkar** *"India Through the Ages"* [1979]. Page - 27.

THE PHILOSOPHICAL LITERATURE OF THE HINDUS
Vedas, Upanishads and Bhagavad-Gita

The authoritative sources of Hinduism are divided into two classes: (1) the *Sruti* and (2) the *Smriti.* The "Sruti" is the primary authority and the "Smriti" is the secondary authority. "Sruti" refers to that which is heard; or a form of direct but divine experience. The Srutis are also called "the Vedas". "Smriti" refers to that which is remembered or a collection of that divine experience. Sruti is revelation; Smriti is tradition. It is a recognised rule of procedure that whenever there seems to be a difference between the Sruti and the Smritis, the Sruti has to be upheld as the supreme authority and the Smriti has to be intepreted in accordance with it. The Sruti and the Smriti together constitute the whole of the traditional philosophical literature of India.

II. THE VEDAS OR THE SRUTIS

The Vedas constitute the most important philosophical literature of India. Infact, the Hindus trace the original source of their cultural life to the Vedas.

The Srutis are also called the *"Vedas"*. The Hindus have received their religious ideas through divine revelation, the Vedas. These are direct intuitional revelations and are held to be *"apaurusheya"* [not created by man] or entirely superhuman. Hence there is no particular author behind these works. The great seers [or Rishis] are said to have heard the eternal truths of religion and to have left a record of them for the benefit of others. These very records are called the Vedas.

• Vedas are the "Revealed Truth"

The Vedas represent the spiritual experiences of the Rishis. The Rishis are only the spiritual discoveries of the truth. They are not the inventors of the Veda. Unlike in other religions, in Hinduism, the Vedas do not owe their authority to any one person. Nor is the sacred message of the Vedas delivered through an angel, or a prophet, or some special messenger from God to certain chosen person. On the contrary, the Vedas themselves constitute the authority as they are eternal, as they are the knowledge of the Lord. According to **Sayanacharya**, the learned commentator on the Vedas, *"God created the whole universe out of the knowledge of the Vedas."*

• Vedas are Dateless and Without Beginning ?

By the Vedas no books are meant. They are the words of Supernatural power and not the utterances of persons. Hence the date of the Vedas has never been fixed. According to the traditional belief, the date can never be fixed for them. Their beginning in this way is not known. However, historians are of the opinion that they were written or came to be composed between 2500 B.C. and 500 B.C.

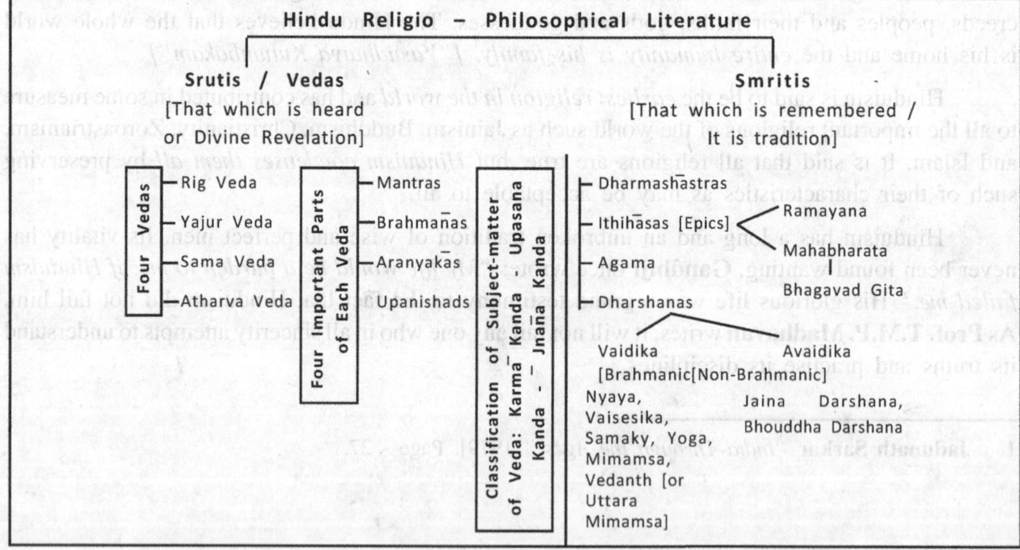

• "Veda" means knowledge

The term *"Veda"* comes from the root *"vid"* which means *"to know"*. The word "Veda" thus means knowledge. When it is applied to scripture, it signifies *a book of knowledge*. The Vedas are the fundamental scriptures of the Hindus. The Veda is the source of the other basic scriptures [such as *Dharmashastras, Ithihasas* [Epics], *Puranas, Agamas* and *Darsanas*].

Definition: The great Sayanacharya has defined Veda as - *"a book which reveals the knowledge of supernatural methods [alaukika Upaya] for the achievement of the desired object and the avoidance of the undesirable."*[1]

The Four Vedas

The Vedic scriptures, broadly speaking, comprise four great works namely: *Rig-Veda, Yajur-Veda, Sama-Veda* and *Atharva-Veda.*[2]

1. *Rig-Veda:* The Rig-Veda is the oldest and the grandest one. Its style, the language and the tone are the most beautiful and mysterious. Its immortal *mantras* contain the greatest truths of existence and it is perhaps the greatest treasure in all the scriptural literature of the world. According to the historical opinion, it was composed in between 2500 B.C. and 1000 B.C. As per the traditional belief, it evolved thousands of years ago.

The Rig-Veda is a book of prayer which contains 1,017 hymns or prayers of unequal length. They are addressed to various gods such as Agni, Indra, Varuna, Soma, Ushas, etc. These hymns were part of rituals and are in praise of nature. These hymns were sung by the priests [called the *"Hotris"*] while performing sacrifices.

The Rig-Veda gives information regarding the early life of the Aryans including their political, social and economic activities. It also provides information relating to the creation of the universe, life, birth, death, heaven, hell and such other serious topics. The commentaries written on the Rig-Veda by Sri Sayanacharya Skandaswamin and Sri Madhvacharya throw more light on these topics.

2. *Yajur-Veda:* The Yajur-Veda is essentially a prose work. It gives details about the sacrifices or Yagas which the early Aryans were conducting. It is indeed a guide book and ritual Veda. In size, the Yajur-Veda is about 2/3 of the Rig-Veda. It has 40 chapters containing commentaries and hymns. It throws light on the social life of the early Indians. It seems to be the *earliest Sanskrit prose* which was used by priests [called *"Adhvaryus"*] who used to conduct the sacrifices.

3. *Sama-Veda:* *"Sama"* means melody and Sama Samhita is a collection of melodious hymns. Sama Veda contains 1549 hymns sung in a melodious manner in praise of God. It is often called ***"sangeeta veda".*** It is mostly borrowed from the Rig-Veda and is meant to be sung by the Sama-Vedic priest [called *"Udgatri"*] in sacrifices. It is said that while performing the sacrifices a juice called *"soma"* was consumed.

4. *Atharva-Veda:* The Atharva-Veda contains 731 hymns dealing with wide range of topics such as *marriage system, burial system, house construction [vastu shilpa] selection of the king, magic spells, human diseases, medicines,* etc. Popular beliefs and superstitions of people are also highlighted in it. The Atharva Vedic Samhita is meant to be used by the Atharva-Vedic priest [called *"Brahman"*] who used to supervise the whole process of sacrifice or *yajna.*

---

1 **Sayanacharya** in his commentary on the *"Krishna Yajur - Veda"* [a part of Veda] - as quoted in *"The Cultural Heritage of India"* - Vol. I Page: 182.

2 According to the Hindu tradition, in the beginning of the Dvapara Age, Krishna Dvaipayana revived the Vedic study and classified the Vedas into four divisions. As he classified the Vedas, he became renowned by the name of **Veda-Vyasa**, that is, the classifier of the Vedas. **Ref:** *"The Cultural Heritage of India"* Vol. 1 Page: 182.

Atharva-Veda is different from the above three Vedas. The first "three Vedas represent mainly the aspect of ancient Indian civilisation dealing with *the goal of man in a future life.*" The Atharva-Veda represents chiefly the other aspect, dealing with *the life of man in this world.* The three Vedas deal with gods and sacrifices. The Atharva Veda deals with *man, his protection from enemies, destruction of foes, kings and politics, welfare in this life,* etc.

The Atharva-Veda deals with various aspects of high philosophy. Nearly all the philosophical verses in the Rig-Veda are common to the Atharva Veda. It is here the Atharva-Veda delves deep into the highly philosophical issues of *Brahman, Moksha, Rebirth, Karma, Creation,* etc. It is also known as ***"Brahma Veda".***

Divisions within each Veda

Each Veda has four parts: (1) *Samhita,* (2) *Brahmanas,* (3) *Aranyakas,* and (4) *Upanishads.* The division of the Vedas into four parts is made *to suit the four stages or Ashramas in a man's life.*

(i) ***Mantra-Samhita*** are hymns in praise of the Vedic God for attaining material prosperity here (on earth) and happiness hereafter [that is, after the death]. The *Mantra* portion of the Vedas is very much *useful for the Brahmacharins.*

(ii) ***The Brahmana*** portion of the Vedas guide people to perform sacrificial rites. They are in *prose form* and provide explanations regarding *mantras* and rituals. Since the sacrificial rites are performed by the householders, the Brahmanas are helpful to man when he is in the stage of *Grihasthashrama.* [It may be noted that the word *"Brahmana"* has nothing to do with *"Brahmins"* representing a Varna category.]

(iii) ***The Aranyakas*** are the forest books. The word *"Aranyaka"* is derived from *"Aranya"* or forest. They deal with the philosophical doctrines to be studied by those who have entered the *"Vanaprasthashrama".* They help the Vanaprasthins or hermits to prepare themselves for taking *"Sanyasa".*

(iv) ***The Upanishads*** are the most important portion of the Vedas. They contain the essence or the knowledge portion of the Vedas. They reveal profound spiritual truths. They deal with the important questions like - *the existence of God, relation between man and the universe etc.* The philosophy of the Upanishads is sublime, lofty and profound. They are specially useful for the *Sanyasins.* They are also called *"Vedanta".*

Classification of the Subject-Matter of the Vedas as a Whole

The subject-matter of all the four Vedas is divided into *Karma-Kanda, Upasana-Kanda* and *Jnana-Kanda*

(a) ***The Karma-Kanda*** or ***Ritualistic Section*** deals with various sacrifices and rituals. The *Mantras* and *Brahmanas* constitute *Karma-Kanda.*

(b) ***The Upasana-Kanda*** or ***Worship Section*** deals with various kinds of worship or meditation. The *Aranyakas* represent the *Upasana-Kanda.*

(c) ***The Jnana-Kanda*** or ***Knowledge Section*** deals with the highest knowledge. The Upanishads come under this category.

Socio-Cultural Importance of the Vedas

1. Vedas Constitute the Basis of Indian Culture : The Vedas are of tremendous importance in understanding the socio-cultural life of the Indians in general and of the ancient Indians, in particular. They constitute the earliest scriptural evidence to throw light on the inner life of the

Indians.

The Veda, taken as a whole, is the main source or the fountain head of the entire Indian Culture. The Veda is the source of the other basic scriptures of Hinduism such as *Dharmashastras, Ithihasas, Puranas, Agamas* and *Darshanas.*

2. Influence of Vedas on the Secondary Scriptures : The Vedas constitute not only the basic source of the secondary scriptures but have exerted a great influence on them. The entire mass of the Sanskrit literature such as *Dharmashastras,* the *Ithihasas, Puranas,* the *Agamas* and the Darshanas is rooted in the Vedas. The ***Puranas*** describe the lives of Vedic and pre-Vedic kings and Rishis. The entire mythology of the later period is based on the mythology of the Vedic period. All the stories narrated in later Puranas about Vishnu, Shiva and Indra and other gods have their roots in the Vedic mythology. The main philosophical doctrines are based on Vedic conceptions. Religious development is Vedic in tone from the beginning. The Vedic Rishis and kings are the starting points of *Ithihasas* and *Puranas* and the social customs that it mentions give rise to the *Dharmashastras.*

3. Vedas Constitute the Basis of the Upanishads : The Upanishads which contain high philosophy pertain to the *Jnana-Kanda* or *knowledge portion* of the Vedas. The Upanishads have only made explicit the religio-philosophic truths implicit in the *Vedic mantras.* In fact, the Upanishads frequently cite the *Mantra* texts to give authority to what they teach. *"The Vedas are the sturdy tree on which blossom the fragrant Upanishads."*

4. Vedas Glorify the Vedic Ideals: The Vedas glorify the high state of civilisation attained by the early Indians. In the whole history of India, the Vedic age has been recognised as the ideal. In all the subsequent ages, attempts have been made to approximate the life of man to the conditions of the Vedic age. *"Thus, in later periods everything that was valuable in man's life was traced back to the Vedas. Philosophy, religion, codes of conduct, all the sciences - everything was traced to the Vedas."*[1]

5. Vedas Aim at Making Man a Perfect Being ?: All our scriptures have a common source, that is, the Vedas. They have a common aim also. As the Vedas have specified the aim is *to make man a perfect spirit like God and to help him to become one with God. "With that aim in view they try to create political and social institutions which will help the spiritual development of every man according to his capacity. They rouse his imagination, they quicken his intellect and form his character and thus guide him along the steep and difficult path of ascent that leads to God."*[2]

Commenting on the Vedas, **Pandit Nehru** writes in his *"Discovery of India": "here is no idolatry in them [Vedas]; no temples for the Gods. The vitality and affirmation of life pervading them are extra-ordinary".*

The Upanishads : Their Essential Principles and Message

The Upanishads represent the sublime thought and the highest philosophy found in Hinduism. In fact, *Upanishads which form part of the Vedas are the real foundations of Hinduism.* The Upanishads are the concluding portions of the Vedas. Hence they are called *"Vedanta"*, or the

---

1 *"The Cultural Heritage of India"* Vol. 1. Page: 220]. The ancient Indians have made attempts to understand the Vedic civilisation, to revive that culture, and to model their lives after the ideals of the Vedic civilisation. The entire Sanskrit literature of the later period provides us a record of such attempts. There is no doubt that *"the Vedas satisfied the needs of the intellect, of the imagination, and of the emotion of a great nation for a long period, extending over at least 3000 years..."*

2 **D.S. Sharma** *"Essence of Hinduism"* Page: 19, Publication of *Bharatiya Vidya Bhavan.*

end of the Vedas. They represent the essence of the wisdom that is embedded in the Vedas. They are the gist and the goal of the Vedas. They are *"the finest flower of the Vedic thought."* The relationship between the Vedas and the Upanishads is like the relationship between the Old Testament and the New Testament. When we look at the great landscape of Indian culture, the Vedas appear to us as the mighty Himalayas of our cultural traditions, the Upanishads can well be described as the great peaks on the mountain ranges of the Himalayas.

The word ***"Upa-ni-sad"*** literally means *to sit down near someone for the purpose of study.* It may also mean *sitting at the feet of the teacher for learning.* It is applied to doctrines imparted by father to son or teacher to pupil. The word *"Upanishad"* also means *knowledge that helps a man to attain the supreme Brahman.* The word primarily means knowledge or philosophy and secondarily books relating to it.

Basic Theme of the Upanishads

The Upanishadic thought mostly revolves round issues such as - *Brahman, Atman, Moksha, Samsara, Karma, Upasana* and *Knowledge*. They try to answer important philosophical questions like the existence of God, relation between the man and the universe, that is, between *"Brahman-Jiva-Jagat"*. Some of the profound philosophical questions probed into by the Upanishads can be stated here. *1. Does a man's personality survive even after his death? 2. Is there a future life and a world called heaven where a man goes after death? 3. Does he return to this world? 4. What is his final goal? 5. What is the nature and goal of the world? 6. What is the nature of God and of soul? 7. What is the nature of their [God and soul] relation with each other and with the world? 8. What is the ultimate truth of existence?*

It is believed that "the Upanishads give us the last word on all such matters. Through no other means is it possible for us to get convincing answers to our queries regarding them. In fact, God has been declared in the Srutis as *"the Being that is to be known only through the Upanishads"*.[1]

The Upanishadic thought relating to the subtle philosophical questions cited above, is not a "closed" thought. *"It is open to us all to verify their statements by actual experience along the lines prescribed by them. The truths inculcated in them are not mere theories, but facts..."*

The Important Upanishads

Each Veda has many Upanishadic sections in it. With the passage of time number of Upanishads has also increased. At present, there are about 220 Upanishads out of which 108 of them are considered to be the ancient ones. There is a controversy regarding the exact period in which they were composed. However, the earliest of them were believed to be composed in between 1200 B.C and 600 B.C. According to **Balgangadhar Tilak,** they are as old as 2000 B.C. [A reference in the Maitrayania Upanishad has given him this clue]. The most important Upanishads are - 1. ***Isa***, 2. ***Kena***, 3. ***Katha,*** 4. ***Prasna,*** 5. ***Mundaka,*** 6. ***Mandukya,*** 7. ***Aitareya,*** 8. ***Taitiriya,*** 9. ***Chhandogya,*** 10. ***Brihadaranyaka,*** 11. ***Kaushitaki,*** 12. ***Svetasvàtara*** and 13. ***Maitrayania.*** These are often regarded as more authoritative. The three great Acharyas - Sri Shankaracharya, Sri Madhvacharya and Sri Ramanujacharya - too have given greater recognition for these Upanishads. The first ten are famous as ***"Dashopanishads".***

The Cardinal Principles of the Upanishads

The doctrinal aspects or the basic principles of the Upanishads can be stated in the form of five simple truths. They are as follows.

(1) *The Brahman* (God) is all pervasive: The Upanishads in an unequivocal voice declare

1 *"The Cultural Heritage of India"* - Vol. I Page: 349.

that the Brahman is all pervasive. *"Whatever exists, and wherever, is permeated by the same divine power."* [*"Isavasyamidam sarvam yatkincha jagatyam jagat"*]. The Upanishadic view is that in the ultimate analysis all manifestation [including the difference between matter and spirit, the good and the evil, the divine and the devil, and so on] is a manifestation of the divine.[1]

(2) *Atman and Brahman are inseparable:* The Brahman resides within each individual consciousness in the Atman. The Atman is not ultimately separate from the Brahman. It is a reflection of that Brahman, it is a part of it. In other words, there is the same divine spirit in every human being. Brahman, the universal spirit, is identified with *"Atman"* - self.[2]

(3) *The Principle of Oneness of Humanity: One Extended Family of Humanity:* The Vedantic concept is that all human beings because of their shared spirituality, are members of a single extended family. The Upanishadic phrase *"amritasya putrah"* [Svetasvetara Upa. II. 5] refers to human beings as *"children of immortality"*. This has given rise to the much praised concept of *"Vasudhaiva Kutumbakam"* [one extended family of humanity].

(4) *The Principle of Unity of all Religions:* A major philosophical concept of the Upanishads is the essential unity of all religions, of all spiritual paths.[3]

(5) *The Principle of the Welfare of all Beings:* The Upanishads aim at the welfare of all beings. [*"bahujanasukaya bahujanahitaya ca"*]. The Vedanta does not seek to throw one class against another class, one caste against another, one group against another. The Vedanta seeks the welfare of all the creation, not only of human beings but also of lower creatures.

Message of the Upanishads

The Upanishads are *"the finest flower of Vedic thought"*. They form the basis of Indian philosophy and socio-religious thought. The Upanishads which are known as *"the earliest treasures of knowledge"* have given to the world a rich message. The essence of this message is cited here.

1. *Upanishadic thinkers have given us the message of uncompromising commitment to truth - or reality.* The great sayings like *"Truth alone triumphs, not falsehood"*,[4] and *"lead me from unreal to real", from darkness to light and from death to immortality"*[5] - reveal the true spirit of the Upanishads.

2. Upanishads have given us the message of strength, fearlessness and hope. As Vivekananda has said, *"The Upanishads are the great mine of strength. Therein lies strength enough to invigorate the whole world through them..."*[6] They have called upon the people of the world to become free. Freedom - physical freedom, mental freedom and spiritual freedom - are the watch-words of the Upanishads."

---

1 The Upanishadic texts such as *"Tattvamasi"* [Thout art that: Chandogya. Upa., VI. 8.7] *"Sarvam Khalvidam Brahma"* [All this is verily Brahman - Chandogya Upa. III 14.1] also fortify this truth].

2 The Upanishadic texts *"Aham Brahmasmi"* [I am the Brahman: Brihadarantaka Upa. I 4.10]; *"Ayamatma Brahman"* [This "self" is Brahman. Mandukya Upa. 2] etc. also support this view]

3 The famous Rig-Vedic pronouncement *"ekam sat viprah bahudha vadanti"* ["the truth is one, the wise call it by many names"] is the basis of this principle]. The **Mundaka Upanishad** has a mantra which states that - as all streams and rivers arise in different parts of the world but flow into the same ocean, so all creeds, castes and religions that arise in different times and areas, [if they have a true aspiration] ultimately reach the same goal.

4 "Satyameva jayate nanritam"

5 "Asato ma sadgamaya, Tamaso ma jyotirgamaya, Mrityorma amritam gamaya"

6 *"Complete Works of Swami Vivekananda"* Vol. 3 - Page: 237-238.

3. ***They have stated that man cannot achieve happiness through mere physical enjoyment obtained through wealth or the goods of the world.*** Performance of sacrifices prescribed in the Vedas also cannot assure happiness. They ask us to desist from our mad search for happiness in the outside world for it rests within ourselves. Permanent happiness can be obtained only by spiritual enlightenment. *"Purity of life and a mind free from selfish desires are essential for this enlightenment."*[1] They have made it clear that *"there is no bliss in finite things, the Infinite alone is bliss"*. [**Chandukya Upa.** VII. 23]

4. ***Upanishads call upon all men and women of the world to assert their divine heritage.*** In this they recognise no limits, geographical, racial, or any other. Their appeal is universal. *"They are the greatest unifying factor in the world for all time. They break all the fetters of mankind and raise man to their true status as children of immortality".*[2] As **Prof. Paul Deussen** has said the Upanishadic thought possesses a great significance and "*....we claim for it an inestimable value for the whole race of mankind."*[3]

5. ***Upanishads highlight the importance of realising the principle of "integral humanism".*** This principle stresses the two aspects of the same reality - *Jivatma and Paramatma* ["the *Atman*" and the *"Brahman"* - the soul and the super soul]. They co-exist just as light and darkness co-exist. Brahman alone is true. He is the Supreme Soul of all. He is the human element existing in all human beings. He is the beginning and the end of the universe. His various powers function in nature. The Upanishads stress upon "self" realisation, that is, *"Atma Jnana"*. *"Know that one Atman alone, and give up all other talk. This is the bridge to immortality"* - **Mundaka Upa.** II. 2.5]

6. ***The Upanishads have stressed upon the principle of the "Karma".*** Every one should do this "Karma", his "duty". There should be no escape from it. The Upanishads provide inspiration to face the challenges of life. They never suggest people to run away from it. The famous Upanishadic saying - *"Arise! Awake! and Stop not till the Goal is Reached!!"* - emphasises courage and commitment to reach the goal of life. The goal of life is to attain *"Atma Jnana"*.

On the Importance of Upanishads...

The teachings of Upanishads have a great relevance to the modern world. **Prof. Hume** asserts that the Upanishads are *"of great present day importance."* The teachings of Upanishads are required to counter the influence of *"materiality"* which is the common enemy of the modern world. As **Mead** and **Chattopadhyaya** have said, the Upanishads as a world-scripture have a tremendous appeal *"...to the lovers of religion and truth, in all races and at all times, without distinction."*[4]

The influence of the Upanishads on Indian thought, philosophy and way of life cannot be exaggerated. The source of the entire Hindu philosophy is the Upanishads. According to **Blookfield,** *"There is no important form of Hindu thought... which is not rooted in the Upanishads."*(1)[5] **Dr. S. Radhakrishnan** also writes, *"later systems of philosophy display an anxiety to accommodate their doctrines to the views of Upanishads."*(2)[6] The various Acharyas of Hinduism like Shankara, Ramanuja and Vallabha interpreted the Upanishads to suit their respective theories.

---

1 *"Indian Inheritance, Literature, Philosophy and Religion"* - Vol. I. Page: 149-150. *Bharatiya Vidya Bhavan Pub.*

2 Sve-Upa. II. 5 as quoted in *"The Cultural Heritage of India"* Vol. 1 - Page: 364.

3 **Paul Deussen** as quoted by **R.N. and R.K. Sharma** in *"Indian Social Thought"* - Page: 11.

4 As quoted by **R.N.** and **R.K. Sharma** in *"Indian Social Thought"* - Page: 11.

5 As quoted by **P.R. Rao** in *"Indian Heritage and Culture"* - Page: 68.

6 As quoted by **P.R. Rao** in *"Indian Heritage and Culture"* - Page: 68.

Apart from the Hindus, the western philosophers and thinkers were profoundly impressed by the Upanishads. The great German philosopher of the 19th century **Schopenhauer** remarked: "From every sentence [of the Upanishads] deep, original, sublime thoughts arise... In the whole world there is no study so beneficial and so elevating as that of the Upanishads... They are the products of the highest wisdom. It is destined sooner or later to become the faith of the people." He further wrote: *"the study of the Upanishads has been the solace of my life, it will be solace of my death."* [as quoted by **P.R. Rao** - Page: 68]

The Smritis and their Contents

The sacred literature other than the Vedas is known as *"Smritis"*. The "Smritis" are collectively referred to as secondary scriptures because they derive their authority from the Sruti. Further, the main object of the Smritis is to expand and exemplify the principles of the Veda. The Smritis consist of the following: (1) *Dharmashastra* or law codes (2) *Itihasa* or epics, (3) *Puranas* or chronicles and legends, (4) *Agamas* or manuals of worship and (5) *Darshanas* or schools of philosophy.

1. *Dharmasashastras:* Dharamashastras are also known as *"Smritis"* or law codes. The laws for regulating Hindu society from time to time are codified in the Smritis or Dharma Shastras [teaching on Dharma]. They lay down the laws or norms which regulate Hindu national, social, familial and individual duties and obligations. The most important of our law-givers are **Manu, Yagnavalkya** and **Parasara**. The Manu-Smriti [The Law Code of Manu], is in many respects the most significant and influential one.

2. *Itihasas or Epics:* The Itihasas are the two well-known epics - the *Ramayana* and the *Mahabharata*. Their object is to derive home to all Hindus the laws of the Smritis and the principles of the Veda through the lives and deeds of their great national heroes. We get our earliest notions of religion from these stories.

The Mahabharatha is an encyclopaedia of, Hindu Dharma. *It is rightly called **"the fifth Veda"** [panchama veda].* It is doubly important, for it includes the famous *Bhagavad-Gita* [Song of the Blessed One]. These two epics have inspired Indian literature, sculpture, painting, dance, drama, music of all kinds.

3. *Puranas:* The Puranas are next in importance to the epics as instruments of popular education. They consist of chronicles and legends. They bring together all the four sources of popular belief - *myth, legend, history* and *prophecy.* The aim of the Puranas is to impress on the minds of the populace the teachings of the Veda. They also highlight the power and the loving kindness of God by means of concrete examples. [**Ex:** *stories of Prahalada, Dhruva, Markandeya,* etc.]

According to tradition, ***there are 18 main puranas*** and an equal number of subsidiary puranas. *Vishnu Purana* and *Bhagavata Purana* are the most popular ones.

4. *Agamas:* The Agamas are theological treatises and practical manuals of divine worship. They deal with the worship of a particular aspect of God and precribe detailed course of discipline for the worshipper. They are related to the three main sects: *Shaivism, Vaishnavism* and *Shaktism.*

The Agamas do not derive their authority from the Vedas. They are not against them also. They are very much vedic in spirit and character. Hence they are regarded as authoritative . They have succeeded in bringing religion to the hearts of common people.

5. *Darsanas* [*Schools of Philosophy*]**:** The Darsanas are based on the Vedas. Their literature is philosophical and they represent schools of philosophy. These are meant for the scholars who are endowed with wisdom, good understanding, power of reasoning and profound intellect. The

Darsanas appeal to the intellect while the Itihasas, Puranas, Agamas appeal to the heart for they are mainly meant for the masses.

There are six Darsanas called ***"Shad Darsanas"*** or ways of seeing things. They are the six instruments of true teaching or the six demonstrations of truth. Each school has developed, systematised and correlated the various parts of the Veda in its own way. Each has its own *"Sutrakara"*, that is, one great Rishi who systematised the doctrines of the school.

The six Darsanas are divided into three groups:

(a) 1. **"Nyaya"** - by ***Gautama*** and 2. **Vaisesika** by ***Kanada***

(b) 3. **Samkhya** by ***Kapila*** and 4. **Yoga** by ***Patanjali***

(c) 5. **Mimamsa** by ***Jaimini*** and 6. **Vedanta** by ***Badarayana***

Of these six Darsanas, Vedanta school is considered to be the most influential one.

Bhagavad Gita and Its Importance

The Bhagavad Gita constitutes yet another source of the Hindu philosophy. It is often referred to as the very essence of the Upanishads. The fundamental thoughts of the Upanishads are presented in practical and easily communicable form in the Gita. The Gita is said to be the most influential work in Indian thought. No single text has been more universally relied upon for daily inspiration than the Gita. It is one of the outstanding religious classics of the world. It is also known as *"handbook of Hinduism"*.

The Bhagavad Gita [or Gita, in short] literally means the *"Song of the Lord"*. The Gita forms an important part of the great Indian epic Mahabharata. This poetical work in the form of a dialogue between Sri Krishna and Arjuna appears in the Bhishmaparva of Mahabharata. It is the most popular religious poems of Sanskrit literature. The Gita consists of 700 Sanskrit verses divided into 18 chapters. It is said to be *"the most beautiful, perhaps the only true philosophical song existing in any known tongue."*[1] It is a book conveying lessons of philosophy, religion and ethics. It is looked upon as a *"Smriti"* or a tradition. It ranks high in the religious literature of the world.

Causes for the Popularity of the Gita

Next to the Bible, Gita is the most translated book in the world. There are three reasons for the greatness and popularity of the Gita. ***Firstly,*** it is a part of the great epic Mahabharata which is often venerated as the *fifth Veda*. [*Pancama-Veda*]. ***Secondly,*** the preacher of the Gita is Sri Krishna who is regarded by the Hindus as an *avatar* or incarnation of God Himself. He is an invincible warrior, a wise preceptor and Yogi par excellence. ***Thirdly,*** the Gita is one among the "three foundational works" called *"Prasthanatraya"*.[2] The other two works are *Upanishads* and *Brahmasutras.* The Hindu Vedantic tradition always considers these three works as its basis. Shankaracharya's commentary on the Gita [known to us as the earliest one] has also contributed to its popularity. Its influence on the world at large has steadily grown since its first English edition made in the 18th century.

---

1 As quoted in *"Indian Inheritance - Literature, Philosophy and Religion"* - Vol. I - Page: 152 - Bhavan's Pub.

2 **Prasthanatraya:** In the Hindu religious heritage Brahmasutras, Upanishads and Bhagavad Gita are referred to as *"Prasthanatrayas"*. The study of these is considered essential for acquiring *"Brahma Jnana"*. In the great journey of life, these "Prasthanatrayas" show us the way towards *"moksha"*. These three scriptures are considered to be fundamental for a proper understanding of Hindu Dharma.

The Context of the Gita

The Gita opens dramatically at the battlefield of Kurukshetra, just before the battle begins between the righteous Pandavas and the wicked Kauravas. The poem is in the form of a reported conversation between Arjuna, the great warrior on the side of Pandavas and his charioteer Krishna, who is the Avatar of the Supreme. Arjuna fears the terrible consequences of the war and refuses to fight. His conscience revolts at the thought of war and the large-scale murder of his own kith and kin it involves. On the opposite side, he sees many friends and relatives. Arjuna who suffers from a kind of conflict of loyalties [a kind of role-conflict] forgets his duties and shows signs of withdrawal. Thereupon Lord Krishna advises him to discharge his duties regardless of the consequences. He advances various kinds of arguments to convince Arjuna of his duties in accordance with his status in society. He urges him to fulfil them with detachment towards the result. This is the message of *"nishkama karma"*. In order to give a forceful justification to his humanistic advice, Lord Krishna indulges in a detailed analysis of man, Nature and God. This analysis is, in essence, rooted in the spiritualism of the Upanishads. *"Thus, in the Gita also, as in the Upanishads the relationship of unitariness existing between man, Nature and God has been pronounced."*[1]

Commentaries on the Gita

Various commentaries have been written on the Gita both in ancient and modern times. The earliest commentary that has come down to us is that of the great philosopher Shanakara. Other important commentaries of the ancient times are those of Bhaskara, Ramanuja, Madhav, Nilakantha, Sridhara and Madhusudana. Outstanding commentaries of modern times are those of Balagangadhara Tilak, Sri Aurobindo, M.K. Gandhi and Sarvapalli Radhakrishnanan. These modern commentaries have further added to its popularity.

Importance of Bhagavad Gita

The Bhagavad Gita assumes importance because it is the philosophical basis of popular Hinduism. Its message is universal in its scope. *"The Gita is the most precious jewel of Hindu literature. It is a universal gospel. The Gita teaches the Yoga of Synthesis. It ranks high in the religious literature of the world."*[2]

1. Bhagavad Gita highlights the message of the Upanishads: The Gita has a great philosophical importance, for it presents the Upanishadic thought in comparatively simpler terms. It is also said that the Gita functions as a commentary on the Upanishads. In his introduction to the commentary on the Gita, Shankaracharya refers to the Gita as *"a summary of the essential ideals of all Veda."* It is through the Gita, Lord Krishna summarises for us all the philosophical and ethical teachings of the Upanishads. Though the Upanishads are many, their message is brought out in a single sublime work called the "Gita". In fact, there is a popular verse which aptly compares the Upanishads to cows, the Gita to milk, Krishna to a cowherd and Arjuna to the calf. All men of purified intellect are regarded as drinkers of the nectarine milk of the Gita.[3]

2. Gita's message is universal: The message of the Gita sounds universal. It is addressed to all men without any distinction. The author of the message [Lord Krishna or the God] does not lead a missionary movement. He *"addresses no sect, establishes no school, but opens the way to all the winds that blow."* He sympathises with all forms of worship. Thus, the Gita never

---

1 **R.N.** and **R.K. Sharma** *"Indian Social Thought"* - Page: 16.

2 **Swami Shivananda** *"All About Hinduism"* - Page: 33 - *Divine Life Society Publication.*

3 *"Sarvopanishado gavo dogdha Gopalanandanah Partho vatsaha sudhir bhokta dugdham gitamritam mahat.*

breaks up culture into compartments and treat other forms of thought in a spirit of negation. The Gita appeals to us not only by its force of thought and majesty of vision, but also by its strong devotion and sweetness of spiritual emotion. *"Though the Gita did much to develop spiritual worship and undermine inhuman practices, still on account of its non-critical attitude it did not destroy altogether false modes or [ignorant modes] of worship."*[1]

3. The Doctrine of Integral Yoga: Gita is often called *"Yoga-shastra"*. Yoga is a technical term which means *union with God.* It also means spiritual discipline that leads to such union. According to the Gita, man's high objective is realisation of God. This ideal is attainable through different means or ways: ***Karma Yoga*** [*the path of work for the active persons*]; the ***Jnana Yoga*** [*for the knowledgeable persons or philosophers*]; the ***Bhakti Yoga*** *[the path of devotion for the ordinary persons and the emotional ones]* and ***Raja Yoga*** *[the path of psychic control for the psychic].* Each of these Yogas highlights the infinite faces and forms of Truth. The Gita *describes* them all. Gita *never prescribes* any particular path in a dogmatic style. Lord Sri Krishna teaches all the four yogas to the same person Arjuna and urges him to follow them at different times depending upon the requirements. Gita thus teaches integral yoga. It is a comprehensive spiritual discipline integrating into itself all the four aspects. It urges an aspirant to practise a balanced combination of all the four yogas. However, he can keep that yoga which suits his nature better, as the main discipline and adding others too in the right proportions.

4. The Doctrine of *Niskama Karma* Yoga: The teaching of *Karma Yoga* is thought by many to be Sri Krishna's special message and the very heart of the Gita's teachings. Sri Krishna insists that every individual has to do his work or duty in a dispassionate manner. He makes a distinction between *Kamya-Karmas* [or desire-motivated actions] and *Niskama-Karmas* [or desireless action] and advocates *Niskama-Karma.* What really binds one [to *"samsara"*, that is, to the cycle of birth and death] is not work itself, but the selfish desire for its fruits. Since work is inevitable for an embodied being, it is better to accept the fact gracefully and perform it with self-control. Work must be performed as a *"yajna"* or sacrifice giving up the desire for its fruits. One who performs actions thus is both a *sanyasi* and *yogi.* Alternatively, one can perform actions for the sake of the God and offer the fruits also to Him. Work done in this right spirit, thus, can also lead to Moksha [liberation] or perfection. It is in no way less effective than *Jnana* or knowledge.

5. The Projection of an Ideal Person: The Gita also aims at producing a type of character which is the loftiest that the Hindu imagination has ever conceived. **D.S. Sharma** writes in this connection: The Gita projects the ideal person [*yogin*] as one who is both a man of contemplation and a man of action. He is *"...a practical mystic whose head is in solitude, but whose hands are in society. His action proceeds out of his contemplation, and his contemplation is rooted in his love of God."*[2]

Conclusion

Thus the Gita goes beyond the ethical question with which it starts to consider broadly the nature of God and the means by which man can know him. The greatness of Gita lies in its description of both the ends and the means. It gives a synopsis of the religious thought and experience of India through the ages.

The Gita's relevance to the problems of human life and its universal approach have made it a much translated and admired book. Though it is a part of the Mahabharatha, world's longest epic poem, it can as well stand on its own as an independent work. Though taught on the battlefield

1 *"Indian Inheritance"* - Page - 154.
2 **D.S. Sharma** *"Essence of Hinduism"* - Page: 14.

of Kurukshetra urging Arjuna to fight, it has nothing to do with wars or battles or bloodshed. It only stresses the aspect of discharging of one's sacred duties of life, however unpleasant they may be. Though its messages was given by Sri Krishna to Arjuna, it can help and inspire any one of us caught by serious problems in life even now. If the Mahabharata can claim to be an encyclopaedia of Hindu religion and culture, the Bhagavad Gita can as well claim to be its quintessence. *Mahabharata is a lamp and Gita is the light in it.*

The Bhagavad Gita has inspired the thoughts and works of great men of modern times such as Swami Vivekananda, Madana Mohana Malavia, Lokmanya Tilak, Gandhiji, Tagore, Aravind, Vinobha Bhave and others. **Sri Madana Mohana Malavia** states the importance of Gita in the following words: *"I believe that in all the living languages of the world, there is no book so full of true knowledge, and yet so handy as the Bhagavad Gita..."*

Gandhiji gave to the Gita the status of the mother. He wrote: *"The Gita has occupied the place of my mother after I lost her."* He wrote in *"Young India"* [Dated 6-8-1925]: *"When doubts haunt me, when disappointment stare me in the face and I see not one ray of hope on the horizon, I turn to Bhagavad Gita and find a verse to comfort me and I immediately begin to smile in the midst of overwhelming sorrow."*

Purusharthas Representing Hindu View of Life

The Concept of 'Purusharthas'

It is very well known that Hinduism is more a way of life than a religion. For understanding Hinduism one must understand the characteristic way of life of the Hindus. Let us now try to study how the main fields of human life are ordered and organised according to the traditional Hindu conception. The Hindu attitude to life and daily conduct is oriented towards four noble ends of man. These four noble ends are exemplified in the Hindu Dharmashastras as the ***"Purusharthas"***.

Meaning of *"Purusharthas"*

The concept of *'Purusharthas'* is the fundamental principle of the Indian social ethics. The word *'Purusharthas'* implies *'attainments'* or *'life-purposes'*. According to this concept, the aim of every person is to attain four noble ends or purusharthas. They are - *Dharma, Artha, Kama* and *Moksha*. These Purusharthas govern the Hindu view of [or attitude towards] life. They are the guiding principles of life for the Hindus at all the stages of their development. The entire Hindu social organisation is built on the foundation of the Purusharthas.

The Four Purusharthas : *Dharma, Artha, Kama* and *Moksha*

1. Dharma [The Principle of Righteousness]

Dharma is the supreme principle of life. It is the major end in human life. The word *"Dharma"* is derived from the Sanskrit root ***"dhri"***, meaning *"to hold together, to sustain, to preserve."* What does dharma hold together?. It holds together the whole universe. Therefore, our *shastras* say that *"dharanat dharma ityahuh"* [It is called dharma because it holds together or sustains.] It is essential for maintaining the stability of society.

- As **Dr. S. Radhakrishnan** has pointed out *".... Every form of life, every group of men has its Dharma which is the law of its beings. Dharma or virtue is conformity with the truth of things, "adharma" or vice, is opposition to it."*
- The **Veda, Upanishad** and **Gita** equated Dharma with *Rta* or *truth* and treated it as a *cosmic principle.*

- From the point of view of **Mimamsa Philosophy,** - *dharma means moral code of conduct to be observed by all human beings in every sphere of their activity and it holds good for all times to come.*

The **Dharmashastras** also insist upon the universal form of dharma. In the words of **P.V. Kane**, *"the writers in **Dharmashastras** meant by Dharma not a creed or religion but a mode of life or a code of conduct which regulated a man's work and activities as a member of a society and as an individual..."* Dharma was intended to enable man to reach what was deemed to be the goal of human existence. [that is, liberation].

- According to **Mahabharata,** Dharma is *"created for the well-being of all creation." All that is free from doing harm to any created being is essentially Dharma..."* Thus Dharma protects all. It is capable of preserving the universe.
- According to the **Bhagavad-Gita,** *"He who protects [follows] dharma, is protected in turn by Dharma."* [*"Dharmo Rakshati Rakshitah..."*]. That is the highest ideal in the Hindu philosophy. Thus, *dharma is the holder of balance.* The basic principle of Dharma is the realisation of the dignity of the human spirit. It is the law of nature which helps man to attain the supreme end of life.

"Dharma" is Not Religion

The Sanskrit word *"Dharma"* should not be equated with the English word *"religion"*. Religion basically indicates a system of dogmas and a particular way of worshipping. *Dharma is the living experience.* It is the guiding principle of life; a complete rule of life. It leads way towards ultimate reality. It is not supernatural belief but a way of rational thinking. It consciously aims at achieving the highest perfection of human life namely *"Moksha"*.

Dharma is often connected with happiness and liberation. *"Dharma is what Dharma accomplishes."* It involves knowledge of reality and performance of duties. Non-performance of duties produces sins. The *Mimamsa philosophy* has tried to explain Dharma in terms of moral law. Philosophy with the Hindus is not a view of life; it is also a way of life. Hence, *'Dharma' means the righteous way of living.* It is intended to provide guidelines in all social actions. It harmonises relations between Kama and Artha. It is corrective of social evils. Dharma is the foundation of social structure. It has universal application. *"It enjoins the members of the society to subject themselves to obligations and responsibilities regardless of individual differences..."*.[1]

- ***Kinds of Dharma:*** Scholars have spoken of different types of Dharma. Shastrakara **Manu** speaks of what are known as *"sapta dharmas"* [seven types of Dharmas]. They are as follows:

1. ***Samanya Dharma:*** consists of general rules and duties which are almost universal in nature. ***Ex:*** truth, non-violence, non-stealing, control of senses, etc.
2. ***Raja Dharma:*** Duties and responsibilities of the king.
3. ***Stree Dharma:*** concerned with the duties, responsibilities and character of woman.
4. ***Dampatya Dharma:*** Duties of husband and wife towards each other, towards their family, children and the larger society.
5. ***Varna Dharma:*** Duties of different Varnas - Brahmins, Kshatriyas, Vyshyas and the Shudras towards each other and society.
6. ***Ashrama Dharma:*** This refers to the rules relating to different stages or Ashramas in the life of a man such as Brahmacharya, Grihasta, Vanaprastha and Sanyasa.

1 **M. Nanjammanni** *"The Study of Indian Society"* - Page: 22.

7. *Apaddharma:* This refers to certain specific rules to be followed by the individuals when they are caught in a crisis or great critical situation. These rules would act as guides and help them to overcome or face the distressing situation without sacrificing the dharma.

- ***Sources of Dharma*** : According to the Smritikars, the nature of the Dharma can be better understood only if one knows the sources from which it emerges. Smritikara Gautama, Apasthambha and others have said that Vedas constitute the main source of the Dharma. Manu who accepts the superiority of the Vedas, mentions of four other sources of Dharma in the second chapter of his Smriti.[1]

2. Artha [Wealth]

The term *'Artha'* refers to worldly prosperity such as wealth and power. It is acquiring wealth by honest means. A man is unable to conduct his life so long as the material means of living are not available. Without *'Artha'* no desire [*'Kama'*] can be satisfied. Living, means living well. It is not mere existence. Poverty is no ideal. Hungry stomach knows no virtue. Economic insecurity and individual attainments do not go together. Economic stability is the basis of social stability, individual advancement and spiritual attainment. The pleasure of giving charity comes only when there is something to give. Hence *'artha'* or wealth helps to sustain and enrich life.

The Hindu thinkers gave proper importance to this material world and to its goods. The importance of wealth in social life was fully realised by **Kautilya,** the author of *"Arthashastra".* He says that wealth is the basis of human requirements and that social well-being depends ultimately on material prosperity." He, however, insists on following the principles of the Dharma in acquiring material prosperity. Thus the early thinkers never looked down upon the worldly prosperities. They had recognised the aspirations of man for wealth and power. By providing *'artha'* a place in the scheme of life, the Hindu thinkers had recognised the pursuit of wealth as a legitimate human aspiration. But they laid much emphasis on *the path of righteousness* through which *'artha'* is to be secured.

---

1 ***Sources of Dharma, According to* Manu,** are as follows :

a. The *whole Vedas* constitute the first source of the sacred law. They constitute the supreme authority.

b. The second source constitutes *the tradition and the practices of those that know the Vedas.*

c. *Smrities or the Dharmashastras which are written on the basis of the Vedic ideas and knowledge* – constitute the third source. Though the Vedas are unchangeable the Dharmashastras are subject to change depending on the need of the time.

d. *The usages and practices of virtuous men* – constitute yet another source. Matters relating to religion could be adjudged on the basis of the life-principles and practices of the great men of our culture like **Sri Ramachandra, Sita, Lakshmana, Hanumantha, Vibhishana** of *Ramayana;* and **Bhishma, Vidura, Dharmaraya** of *Mahabharatha,* and so on.

e. Finally, *the truth and self-satisfaction of the great saintly people* – constitute one more source of Dharma.

Yajnavalkya declares the sources in a similar strain - *"the Veda, traditional lore, the usages of good men, what is agreeable to one's self and desire born of due deliberation - this is traditionally recognised as the sources of dharma."* **[P.V. Kane** in *"History of Dharmashastra"* - Vol. 1. Part 1. Page - 6.]

Of these five sources of the Dharma mentioned by Manu, which one must be considered supreme and ultimate-? whether the things stated in the Vedas are final or the interpretations given by the scholars which are often different from those of the Vedas, are ultimate-? How can one resolve this confusion-? – These questions do arise in the minds of even honest persons who follow the Dharma. As far as Manu is concerned, for all confusions and controversies relating to the Dharma, Vedas are the ultimate authority. In this way Manu has expressed complete faith in the Vedas.

3. Kama [Pleasure or Desires]

Kama refers to the desires in man for enjoyment and satisfaction of the life of the senses. It refers to some of the innate desires and urges in man. It springs in human mind, the moment one is born. It is the essence of life. With the passing of time desires increase. These desires influence and determine social action in many ways. The desire to live and enjoy becomes foremost and remains the strongest one. Without it living would appear to be very cruel and meaningless. The theory of Purusharthas makes sufficient provision for the enjoyment of life. The pleasures of life need not be discarded for the sake of the other world.

Kama does not mean only instinctive life. It involves *sexual, emotional and aesthetic life as well.* The aesthetic life expresses itself in both the creation and appreciation of all that is fine, beautiful and sublime. The healthy development of personality calls for the expression of emotions. *Kama* represents such an emotional expression. At its lowest manifestation, *'Kama'* is referred to as sex drive. It is often regarded as one of the six *"enemies"* of human beings. But it is equally true that the human beings cannot continue as a race without the realisation of *Kama* which helps the propagation of species. Therefore, the Hindu thinkers never regarded sex act as sinful. They have recognised its importance as a basic human instinct which must be satisfied in proper time. But they stressed self-control and respect for the Dharma.

4. Moksha [Spiritual Freedom or Liberation or Self-Realisation]

'Moksha' according to the Hindu thinkers, is the ultimate aim. When the end of human action is salvation or liberation from the bondage of the world, it is called *"Moksha"*. When 'dharma' becomes the absolute concept, it gets the name of *"Moksha"*. It is the supreme aspiration of man. It is the summum bonum of human existence. All our activities are directed to the realisation of this end. The other three Purusharthas namely, *Dharma, Artha* and *Kama* are called the **"trivargas"** and they constitute the means for the attainment of this, supreme end. "Moksha" alone is called the **"chaturvarga"** which symbolises the release of the soul from the bondage of 'Karma'.

Ways of Attaining 'Moksha' : Hinduism offers four ways of attaining 'moksha' or salvation. These are the paths of 1. 'Meditation' [*Yoga Marga*], 2. 'Knowledge' [*Jnana Marga*], 3. 'devotion' [*Bhakti Marga*], and 4. 'Correct action' [*Karma Marga*]. The individual is free to choose the path that suits him.

Importance of Purusharthas

1. Purusharthas signify the Hindu attitude towards life

The theory of *'Purusharthas'* is a significant contribution of the early Hindu thinkers to the field of socio-philosophical thought. Throughout the history of the Indian socio-philosophical thought the theory of Purusharthas has assumed importance. The Hindu view of life or the traditional Hindu attitude towards life is often interpreted in terms of the Purusharthas. Some thinkers have gone to the extent of equating the philosophy of Purusharthas with the Hindu philosophy itself.

2. Harmony between the Material and the Spiritual

'Purusharthas' lay stress upon the harmony between the material and spiritual aspects of life. The four ends [*dharma, artha, kama* and *moksha*] embracing material [or secular] and spiritual aspects of life are not opposed to each other, but interrelated. They lead man from *'samsara'* to *'moksha'*. The theory of Purusharthas seeks to co-ordinate material desires and spiritual life. It tries to satisfy the sex and parental instincts in man; his love of power and property and his desire for attaining salvation. It tries to comprehend the life in its entirety.

3. Co-ordination among various Desires, Needs and Interests

Man has different desires, needs and interests. The human nature is such that it involves various forces; the economic, emotional, aesthetic, intellectual, spiritual, ethical and the instinctive. These various faces may appear to be conflicting with each other; but in reality, they are not. There is no conflict between the economic and the spiritual, intellectual and the instinctive, the ethical and the aesthetic, and so on. These are quite natural to man. They get their natural expression through his activities. They are necessary for the balanced growth of his personality. Early Hindu thinkers were aware of this human need. Hence, they devised a scheme of life called 'Purusharthas' in which they have made provision for the expression of all these basic human needs.

4. No Attempt to Decry Sex and Disregard Material Aspirations

It is mistakenly believed that Hinduism glorifies spirituality and renunciation and condemns material aspirations. On the contrary, the Hindu thinkers only insisted on the proper balance among the various aspirations of life. According to them, the Dharma is the balancing factor. It means the different aspirations of life could be fulfilled only in accordance with the principles of the Dharma.

According to the Hindu thinkers, Dharma does not consist in disregarding Kama and Artha. Economic factor is an essential element in human life. The pursuit of material end is certainly necessary for life. Without acquiring some necessities of life man cannot survive. While 'Artha' constitutes the material means of living, Kama helps the propagation of species. The Hindu thinkers had viewed Artha and Kama as desirable. Man cannot reveal his spirituality when he is economically starved and emotionally strained. But artha and kama are sub-ordinated to dharma. They should be controlled by the considerations of righteousness.

The theory of Purusharthas gives maximum importance to the dharma. Dharma provides the direction to the acquisitive and emotional desires of man. The theory thus seeks to co-ordinate material desires and spiritual life. It binds together the heaven and the earth.

5. Purusharthas constitute the basis of *"Varnashrama Dharma"*

The early Hindu society had developed two co-ordinated systems of social organisation, namely: 1. *Ashrama Dharma,* and 2. *Varna Ashrama.* Of these, the former regulates the individual's conduct while the latter has a reference to the social stratification system. The principles of Purusharthas govern both these organisations. They constitute the very basis of the *"Varnashrama Dharma".*

VI. THE ASHRAMA DHARMA OR SYSTEM

The Concept of *"Varnashrama Dharma"*

The Hindu society has developed two co-ordinated systems of social organisation. On the one side, the whole human life is divided into four stages, namely, *"ashramas"*; and on the other, the whole society is divided into four strata, namely; *"Varnas"*. Ancient Hindu thinkers formulated the *"Ashrama Dharma"* to regulate the conduct of the individual's life in the world. Along with this system they formulated another system called *"Varna Dharma"* which has reference to the society. The former regulates the individual's *"individual life"* and the latter regulates the individual's *"social life"*. Both these Dharmas aim at the organisation and management of the individual as well as society. These two schemes are together called *"Varnashrama Vyavastha"*, or *"Varnashrama Dharma"* which has its own social, moral and religious importance. The "Purusharthas" constitute the guiding principles for the functioning of the Varnashrama Dharma.

The Concept of Ashrama Dharma

The Ashrama Dharma or system represents one of the well established socio-religious institutions of ancient India. It denotes the Hindu scheme of life according to which different stages [ashramas] in the life of an individual are well ordered. It is in this Hindu scheme of ashramas, the theory of Purusharthas gets its concrete expression. The ashrama system is also related to the wider social system called "*Varna System*" which regulates the individual's social life and responsibilities.

Meaning of the word "Ashrama"

The Sanskrit word *"Ashrama"* literally denotes *a halting or resting place.* The word also means *'stages', 'monastry', duties,*[1] etc. The word *"ashrama"* comes from the Sanskrit root *"srama"* which means *"making an effort"*. In this way, *"ashrama"* literally means *a step in the journey of life.* According to the Hindu ethics, the final aim of life is liberation or *'Moksha'*. Every ashrama is a step in the long journey towards the realisation of that aim.

The Four Ashramas

According to the Hindu scheme of ashramas, human life is divided into four stages or ashramas: *Brahmacharya, Grihastha, Vanaprastha* and *Sanyasa*. Every stage has it own duties and functions. Each ashrama is a stage of life in which *the individual has to get himself trained for a certain period and qualify himself for the next ashrama.* In his journey of life the individual takes rest in each of these ashramas to prepare himself for the future journey. According to the Hindu Dharmashastras, each individual should pass through these four stages or phases of life.

1. Brahmacharyashrama [Stage of Studentship]

The first stage or ashrama is *'Brahmacharyashrama'*. This stage is meant for acquiring knowledge, developing discipline and moulding character. This stage starts with the initiation ceremony called *'Upanayanam'* [means *'conducting nearer'*]. The main purpose of this ceremony is to bring the individual nearer to the life-purposes [*Purusharthas*]. This also brings him nearer to the teacher or *'guru'*. This sacrament marks the *"second birth"* of the individual, that is, birth into a higher life. Those who undergo this sacrament wear the sacred thread the *'yajnopavita'*, are known as *'dvija'* or twice-born.

- ***Beginning of Education in the Gurukula:*** With this spiritual birth, the twice-born begins his educational career with the teacher called *'guru'*. The Brahmachari [the pupil] is supposed to go to his 'guru' who lives in forest hermitage. He stays with him for study, serves him in a humble manner and makes self-study *[swadhyaya].* Here he reads books and engages himself in intellectual discussions. He acquires the knowledge of both *shastras* and *shastras* [weapons / instrument and books], *'tattwa'* and *'vyavahara'* [theory and practice[, *'siddhanta'* and *'paddhati'* [principle and its applications]. He has to lead a life of simplicity and hardwork.
- ***Development of Personality and Improvement of Character:*** This stage is useful for the development of personality. It is here the individual's character is moulded and given a shape. His behaviour, thought patterns, attitudes, feelings and instincts are channelised in the way that prepares a sound base for the years to come. He has to observe *"Indriya Samyama"* [control of senses]. Through this he develops the strength of power and perception. This helps the learning process. This stage transforms a raw, animal-like human child into an intelligent, disciplined, wise and responsible young man who is prepared in all ways to meet the challenges of life.

---

1 **V.S. Apte's** *"Sanskrit-Hindi Dictionary"* - Page: 165.

- ***Offering Gurudakshina and Receiving Final Instructions from the Guru:*** After the end of his student career, the Brahmacharin gives a present [*gurudakshina*] to his preceptor [*guru*] according to his ability and returns home to lead the householder's life. The 'guru' gives the final instruction and sends the student home. The teacher delivers a *convocation address*[1] to the students at the conclusion of their studentship. This first stage normally extends from 10 to 12 years depending upon individual efficiency and interest.

2. Grihasthashrama [Stage of Householder]

The second stage is that of the *Grihastha* or householder. This stage is entered at marriage, when the student has completed his studentship and is ready to take up the duties and responsibilities of household life. The individual in this stage gets married, earns money and begets children. In this stage, the individual pursues wealth *[Artha]* and pleasure *[Kama]* within the limits of the moral law [*Dharma*]. A householder should earn money by honest means and enjoy and distribute it in a proper manner. Marriage which is regarded as a *'sacrament'* for the Hindus provides for the enjoyment of sex life. The person has to consider his wife from his real partner in life; she is his *'ardhangini'*. He cannot do any religious ritual without her.

- ***Importance of Grihasthashrama:*** Of all the ashramas, this is the most important one for the following reasons

(i) All the other orders or ashramas exist because of the support given by Grihasthashrama. As **Manu Smriti** points out, *"As all streams and rivers flow to rest in the ocean, so all the ashramas flow to rest in the householder."*

(ii) This stage *helps the householder to perform the religious rites [Dharmasampatti]*. It also enables him to perform the basic duties of a married person namely, the *Panchamahayajnas*[2] or five great sacrifices along with the wife: *Daiva Yajna, Rishi Yajna, Pitri Yajna, Bhuta Yajna* and *Nara Yajna. [or Atithi Yajna*]

(iii) In this stage, *the individual fulfils his obligations towards the society*. He earns money, protects his own family and never makes it a parasite on the society. He begets children and assures the continuation of the race. He takes care of the Brahmacharis, Vanaprasthis and Sanyasis who are not supposed to earn their living.

---

1 **The message of the convocation address as mentioned in the Taitiriya Upanishad:** "Speak the truth. Do your duty, Never swerve from the duty of the Veda. Do not cut off the line of progeny, after giving the preceptor the fee he desires. Never swerve from truth. Never swerve from duty. Never neglect your welfare. Never neglect your prosperity. Never neglect the study and the teaching of the Vedas.

Never swerve from the duties to the gods and the forefathers. Regard your mother as a god *[Matri-devo Bhava]*. Regard your father as a god *[Pitri-devo Bhava]*. Regard your teacher as a god *[Acharya-devo Bhava]*. Regard your guest as a god *[Athithi-devo Bhava]*. Let only those actions that are free from blemishes be done and not others. Only those that are good acts to us be performed by you and not others... This is the injunction. This is the teaching. This is the secret of the vedas, this is God's word of command. This should be observed. Thus is this to be meditated upon" - **Ref:** *"All About Hinduism"* by **Swami Shivananda** - Page: 75.

2 **Pancha Maha Yajnas:**

1. ***Deva Yajna:*** offering oblations unto *Devas* with recitation of *Vedic Mantras.*
2. ***Rishi Yajna:*** study of Vedas and teaching of Vedas to students and offering of oblations to Rishis.
3. ***Pitri Yajna:*** Tarpana or ablutions to the departed souls and *'sraddha'* or annual religious rites performed for departed souls.
4. ***Bhuta Yajna:*** distribution of food to cows, crows and animals in general.
5. ***Nara Yajna [Atithi Yajna]:*** giving food to guests and honouring them, that is, extending hospitality to the guests.

(iv) It is in this stage, *the individual engages himself in all activities incidental to his "Varna"*.

3. Vanaprasthashrama [Philosophic Recluse]

After discharging all the duties and obligations as a householder, the individual enters the Vanaprastha stage. It consists of the third quarter of man's life. In this phase after retiring from active life, the individual dedicates himself to a life of spiritual contemplation.

Drinking fully from the cup of life almost upto the age of fifty, the individual has reached the stage of satisfaction, content and happiness. It is time for him to hand over his responsibilities as well as his authority to the next generation [that is, to his children]. The inner call of the *'Vairagya'* [detachment] insists on him to give up all that is his own. He gives up not only the wealth and authority but the feeling of possession also. He lives like a guest in his own house. He has the satisfaction of fulfilling all his family responsibilities and societal commitments. Hence he is a retired man both in society and in family. He indulges in the life of worship, silence and meditation. He cuts down his personal needs and turns away from the pleasures of senses.

In this stage known as the stage of Vanaprastha, the individual many a time retires to the forest, performs the rituals or yajna and observes silence and meditation. He lives like a hermit with his wife. He does not completely give up the Grihastha duties or *'atithiseva'* [service of the guest]. He is not a mere seeker of personal salvation. He gathers around him students who live with him, thus converting his hermitage into a *'gurukula'* [or residential school]. The curriculum here includes both sacred and secular subjects. The kings and leaders of the community also approach these hermits for guidance and counselling. This stage is virtually a preparation for the final stage of *'sanyasa'*.

4. Sanyasashrama [Stage of Renunciation or Wandering Mystic]

This is the last stage or phase in the life of a person. This is the time for renunciation. A Vanaprastha becomes a *'yati'* or *'sanyasi'* or an 'ascetic' on the attainment of mental serenity. When the hermit retires from the stage of Vanaprastha he is at liberty to lay down all his responsibilities and commitments and become a wandering ascetic. This final stage is designated as *'sanyasa'* or *'total unburdening'* or *'total abandonment'*. The primary goal of the Sanyasi is to attain ***'moksha'***.

The Sanyasi gives up all the bondages and attachments of this world. He gives up his name, changes his clothes, leaves his race, family and even his sect. He puts on a saffron cloth, gives up shelter in any form. He receives his food through begging. He never stays at one place for more than three days. He performs meditation and preaches Dharma. He gives himself up totally in the service of society, but does not belong to it. He belongs to the *Paramatma,* to his *Real Self.* He is thus known as *'Parivrata'* [a wanderer], *'Bhiksu'* [beggar[, *'Yati'* [restrained one] and *'Muni'* [silent mystic]. The Sanyasis' life is thus a spiritual life. He is the sacrifice incarnate.

A Sanyasi is an asset of the society. He is the spiritual wealth of society. Even though he does not possess anything *he is the spiritual master and commands respect of all.* He is the source of inspiration and founder of the path of Dharma for the society.

Importance of Ashrama System

1. Ashrama System - A Noble Socio-Philosophical System: The theory of the Ashrma system represents one of the great socio-philosophical doctrines of the early Indian thinkers. This theory reveals their attempt to understand the basic meaning of human life and its purposes. As they thought man's life is not a trivial affair. He has to live it very thoughtfully and carefully. The great seers of the Indian society have given the guidelines for the planning of man's life through the Ashrama theory. It explains the *"journey of life" in the direction of Brahman.*

2. Reveals the Planning of Individual's Life: According to the Ashrama theory, the life of an individual is divided into four stages called 'Ashramas'. The span of life being one hundred years, each stage consists of twentyfive years. These four different stages in the life of an individual according to **P.H. Valvalkar,** represent *"a kind of schooling and self-discipline".* The planning of individual's life is based on psychological study of the interests, needs, capacities, characteristics and social adjustments at the different stages of life from childhood to old age. These stages lead the individual step by step towards the realisation of *'moksha',* that is, towards final liberation.

3. Insistence on Duties and Discipline: The *"ashrama theory"* stresses the fulfilment of the special duties assigned to the individual at each stage and also on his obligations of a general nature. According to the *Smritis,* to whatever Ashrama a man may belong, he should practise the following ten characteristic features of a proper life of Dharma: *"Steadiness, forgiveness, self-control, abstention from appropriating anything belonging to others, purity, control of the sense organs, correct discernment, knowledge, truthfulness and absence from anger."*[1]

4. Interdependence of the Society and the Individual: The theory of ashrama *does not give any scope for any conflict between the individual and the society.* On the other hand, it stresses the interdependence of the two. In the ***first stage*** [*Brahmacharyashrama*], the society or the group rears, protects and gives the best of its heritage to the individual. In the ***second stage*** *[Grihasthashrama],* the individual gives his best to the group. He gives protection and supports those in the other stages of life. The ***third stage*** is a neutral stage in which the individual starts slowly his *"journey for self-search".* In the ***fourth stage,*** the individual retires from group activities and seeks to realise the self.

5. Individual Development and Social Welfare are made Mutually Complementary: The ashrama pattern of life seems to be a very sound base for the social order. The most notable feature of this pattern is that the individual development and the social welfare are not in conflict with each other. It is not that one is achieved at the cost of the other. Both go together and both can be achieved simultaneously.

The Hindu thinkers never considered man a mere cog in a social machine, sub-ordinated to social control. They never thought of man in isolation of society. They never regarded the individual and society as two different phenomena but rather the two expressions of the same Reality viz, Brahman. *"Therefore, there was hardly much distinction between individual and social welfare, individual and social development, individual and social salvation. Hence, when the ashrama system helped the individual welfare, development and salvation, it at the same time contributed to social welfare, development and salvation."*[2]

These ideals relating to the ashrama system have been again and again emphasised by Indian thinkers down from the seers of the Vedas and the Upanishads to contemporary Indian philosophers including Vivekananda, Rabindranath Tagore, Sri Aurobindo, M.K. Gandhi and others. Commenting on the Ashrama theory, the famous German scholar **Paul Deussen** writes, *"the entire history of mankind does not produce much that approaches in grandeur to this thought."*

Ashrama Dharma Under Modern Conditions

In contemporary India the ashramas cannot be exactly lived according to the details of the ancient rules as the conditions have very much changed. Today family life [Grihasthashrama] is the only ashrama that is prevalent and is of far-reaching significance, the other ashramas have either disappeared or have paled into insignificance.

---

1 As quoted by **P.H. Prabhu** in *"Hindu Social Organisation"* - Page: 92.

2 **R.N.** and **R.K. Sharma** *"Indian Social Thought"* - Page: 39-40.

The ashramas may however be revived in their spirit for the great improvement of modern life. Reviving the spirit of the ashramas virtually means insisting on all the people to do their respective duties efficiently and with a sense of moral commitment. Thus, the students at schools and colleges might lead a life of purity and simple living. The householder might lead the life of an ideal Grihastha. He might practise self-restraint, sympathy, tolerance, non-injury, truthfulness and moderation in everything. Those who find it difficult to lead the life of the third and fourth ashramas might remain in either of the first two ashramas, gradually withdrawing themselves from worldly life and practising selfless service to society and engaging in study and meditation.

Varna Dharma and Its Importance

The Varnas or Social Classes

The ancient Indian society, that is, the later Vedic Society was divided into four divisions known as *"Varnas."* Varnas which are comparable to social classes, are four in number, namely : *Brahmanas, Kshatriyas, Vaishyas* and *Shudras.* These Varnas which existed in the Vedic society, it is believed, later on degenerated into innumerable castes.

Origin of the Varnas : The division of the Vedic society into four Varnas [or four orders or classes] was based on the division of labour. The ***Purusha Sukta*** of the Rig Veda throws light on the origin of the Varnas. According to the Purusha Sukta, four Varnas emerged from the four different organs of the *"Virat Purusha"* or *"Divine Force"* or *The Lord* Himself. As per this belief, the Brahmanas were born from the mouth of the *Puruasha,* the Kshatriyas from His arms, the Vaishyas from His thighs and the Shudras from His feet. The Code of Manu also mentions of this theory of the origin of the Varnas.

Division of Labour Among the Varnas : This theory also makes reference to the division of work among people. The different organs of the Purusha [The Supreme Being] from which these four Varnas were born, represent the nature of the work each was assigned to perform. The **Brahmanas** were born out of the mouth of the Creator concentrated on learning, teaching, priesthood, etc..... They mastered the supreme knowledge contained in the Vedas. The **Kshatriyas** who were born out of the arms of the Purusha represent heroism, courage, strength, etc. They constituted warrior class. The ***Vaishyas*** who emerged out of the thighs of the Purusha came to represent the trading and commercial class. Finally, those who were born out the feet of the Purusha, namely, the ***Shudras*** pursued the task of serving the other three Varnas. *"The whole social organisation is here conceived symbolically as one human being the "Body Social" – with its organs representing the social classes based on the principle of division of labour. The same idea is expressed in the Vishnu Purana, Mahabharata and the Bhagavadgita."*[1]

This ***tradotional theory stresses the organic unity*** that was visible in the society based on work assigned to each Varna or class in the society. Varna was a uniting rather than a dividing force. Each Varna was complementary to the other. They were related to each other as the various organs of the body. Hence there was no room for conflict or class war. Each Varna performed the duties assigned to it for the common good of the society.

Varnas Were Not Rigid Classes : As it is already mentioned, Varna System existed on *the principle of division of labour.* No professional class was by itself self-sufficient. There was no rigidity of the professions, and the professions were also not hereditary. Kshatriyas could become the Brahmanas [*Example,* Vishwamitra], Vaishyas could become the teachers of the Vedas. Dharma Sutras [500 B.C.] used to permit a *Brahman* to become follower of a Kshatriya, if it was necessary. There were no restrictions on matrimonial alliances or on the commensal or social relations or even

1 **Prof. S. Nanjammanni** *"The Study of Indian Society."* Page - 32.

on the changes of membership from one Varna to other Varna. Among the *"traivarnikas"* [the first three Varnas] intermarriages were not unusual; the son of the sage **Atri** was married to a Kshatriya princess, and the wife of the sage **Agasthya**, called Lopamudra, hailed from the Kshatriya Varna. Interdining was common; only there was a taboo upon the food cooked or touched by the Shudra; if it was to be used for the sacrifice. It is interesting to note that the Sutras permit food cooked by the *Shudra* even for the sacrificial process, if he had been shaved and bathed earlier. Brahmanas, Kshatriyas and Vaishyas were still social classes and had not yet developed into castes down to the end of the Vedic period. Varna system started undergoing change particularly when it passed on from Vedic Age [4000 to 1000 B.C.] to the Brahmanical period [200 B.C. to 700 A.D.]. The four Varnas can be arranged hierarchically, with Brahmanas at the top and Shudras at the bottom. However, the growing importance of the rituals and sacrifices added to the power of the Brahmanas. Hence in course of time, they emerged as the most important *varna.*

Varna and Distribution of Guna and Karma **:** On the whole, the Varna or class division as it existed during the later Vedic period gave no room for any class to consider itself as being placed in a position of greater or lesser advantage than the other classes. Each Varna was designed to occupy a particular position in the society. Further, the Varna system provided scope for the individual to develop his personality. Each Varna depending on its own *"Satvika guna", "Rajasa guna"* or *"Tamasa guna"* was assigned a task or work. *"Satvika guna* gave the Brahmanas learning and knowledge, and the Vaishyas, intelligence and skilled craftsmenship. The *Rajasa guna* gave the Kshatriya power and action, while the *Tamasa guna* made the Shudra fit for labour and service."[1]

Social Importance of Varna System

- ***The Varna system stressed the importance of work or Karma assigned to each Varna or class.*** To engage in the work assigned to his class was *"Varna dharma"* for the individual belonging to it...... Within this fourfold scheme the individual in Vedic India followed his own nature and arrived at his possible perfection by a growth within.

- ***Varna Dharma makes it clear that a man's "swadharma"*** [a job to perform which a person has been created] ***is his only link with God.*** Gita says *"Better is one's own dharma, though imperfect than the dharma of another well discharged, better death in one's own dharma; the dharma of another is full of fear."* [Gita - 3-35]. Thus Gita emphasises the fact that man can attain perfection only through performing his allotted task. *"Worshipping Him [God] with his own duty man attains perfection."* [Gita 18-46]. Therefore, whatever be the job that falls to one's own lot, it can be converted into Karma Yoga that can take him godwards.
- ***Varna dharma would create no inequalities in society.*** In a society all the work is dignified and important. In an orderly society, neither can all people spend their time chanting the Vedas, nor can every one be a servant. For ensuring that every job of the society is taken care of, there has to be a proper arrangement for supply of workers, teachers, etc. This arrangement of Varna dharma is not for creating inequalities.
- ***Varna dharma stresses the interdependence of the Varnas.*** The four fold division of society, according to the Varna system was based upon the scientific idea of division of labour. **P.V. Kane** in this regard writes : *"The theory of Varnas as conceived by Manu and other smritikaras was based upon the idea of the division of labour, on the idea of balancing the rival claims of*

1 **Lord Krishna** also says in Bhagavadgita that the four Varnas were his own creation. He says - *"The fourfold caste was created by Me by the different distribution of guna and karma"* [the Gita 4/13]. Further He says, *"The duties of brahmanas, kshatriyas, and vaisyas as also of shudras, O scorcher of foes, are distributed according to the gunas born of their own nature."* [the Gita 18-41]. ***Reference*** **:** *"Indian Culture."* Page - 67 - Published by Vivekananda Kendra Prakashana.

various sections of the community, it laid greater emphasis upon the duties of the Varnas rather than upon their rights and privileges."[1] Therefore, all the Varnas were interdependent. The interdependence of Varnas was found in different fields such as religion, vocation and professions, education, marriage and statecraft. There was a constant upward and downward social mobility between the different Varnas, at least in theory.

• ***A Harmonious System*** **:** The Varna system prescribed by the Dharmashastras on the basis of the cultural heritage of the Vedas and the Upanishads, was very much ***a value-based system.*** *The central value was social harmony or unity in the midst of diversity.* The Western societies often call it as *"division of labour."* Social justice was a part of this system. Social justice involves fairness, equality, humanity, co-operation, freedom and harmony of various constituents. All these characteristics were very much found in the Varna system. In addition to the above, the system was designed to shoulder maximum social responsibility.

By the time of the Epics and Puranas was reached, Indian society had undergone changes and within the framework of the four classes there arose innumerable castes due to *"Varna-sankara"* or intermixture of classes."[2] It is significant to note that there was nothing like a 5th class or ***Panchama Varna,*** which is at present referred to as "untouchable caste." As **Dr. S. Radhakrishna** points out, the caste system is a degeneration of the class, or Varna system.

Traditional Characteristics of the Hindu Society

Though India is a land of multi-religions, Hinduism continues to be the major religion of Indian society. Though India as a nation has been subject to foreign invasions and servitude for several centuries, it has been able to protect and preserve its main *"Dharma"*, that is, Hinduism. Majority of the people in India, thus remain Hindus and follow the Hindu culture. The Hindu tradition still remains the dominant tradition here. *"The framework of traditional Hindu society has some broad features which are common throughout India. In fact, their influence can be seen even in communities professing religions of alien origin."* Some of the basic features of the traditional Hindu society as enlisted by **S.C. Dube**[3] can be briefly examined here.

1. Hierarchical Arrangement of the Hindu Society

Hindu society has been hierarchical. The Hindu society was based on *"Chaturvarna system."* It consisted of the four varnas which were vertically arranged and there was a fifth stratum which stood outside the Varna system. Within each of these Varnas or grades there were and still are several castes that are again fitted into a hierarchy. There could be some differences of opinion about the castes' relative position, but their basic status level is fixed. There is no dispute regarding the fact that the caste is a part of the hierarchy.

2. The Belief in the Ascribed Status

The traditional Hindu society was based on the ascribed status system. In an ascribed status system, one's status is determined not by one's capacity, achievement or performance but by certain fixed and almost unchangeable criteria. In the Hindu society which consisted of number of *"jatis"* or castes, the status of a person is determined by the accident of birth in a particular *'jati.'* Hence, upward mobility was difficult and slow, and this element of relative immobility still remains with the present day Hindu society.

---

1 **P.V. Kane** *"History of Dharmashastras"* as quoted by **R.N.** and **R.K. Sharma** in *"Indian Social Thought."* Page - 33.

2 **Prof. S. Nanjammanni.** *"Indian Society"* Page - 34.

3 **S.C. Dube.** *"The Study of Indian Society"* Page : 32 - 33.

3. Status Evaluation Based on the Criterion of Ritual

In the traditional Hindu society, economic, educational and political or other criteria were insignificant, but the criteria of status was ritual. One comes in close contact, including touch and eating together, only with those of equal ritual status, not with lower groups. The physical touch of lower-caste groups, or inter-dining with them was believed to cause pollution. The caste system as such has elaborate rules governing the maintenance of purity and avoidance of pollution.

4. *Purusharthas,* that is, "Life-Purposes" Deciding Hindu View of Life

The concept of *"purusharthas"* is the fundamental principle of the Indian social ethics. The concept refers to the Hindu *"life-purposes."* According to this concept, the aim of every person is to attain noble ends or *purusharthas.* They are : *Dharma, Artha, Kama* and *Moksha.*

- ***Dharma*** is the supreme principle of life. It is the main end or objective of human life. It holds together the whole universe. It is essential for maintaining the stability of society. It represents piety, morality, or the path of righteousness.
- ***Artha*** refers to the material possessions or pursuit of wealth and well-being. It signifies worldly prosperity such as wealth and power. It is acquiring wealth by lowest means and enjoying it in a decent manner.
- ***Kama*** signifies bodily desire including sex. It refers to the desires in man for enjoyment and satisfaction of the life of the senses. It is, however, not just instinctive. It involves sexual, emotional and aesthetic life as well.
- ***Moksha*** denotes the ultimate aim of man's life, that is, attaining salvation. It is the supreme aspiration of man. All our activities are directed towards obtaining this end.

5. *Ashrama* System as Complementary to the *Purusharthas*

The four objectives of life called *"purusharthas"* are related to what are known as ***"Ashramas"*** or stages of life. The Ashramas denote the Hindu scheme of life according to which different stages [ashramas] in the life of an individual are well ordered. There are four stages or Ashramas : *Brahmacharya, Grihastha, Vanaprastha* and *Sanyasa.*

- ***Brahmacharyashrama*** starts with the initiation ceremony called *"Upanayanam."* The main purpose of this stage is amassing knowledge. It is the life of celibacy and studenthood.
- ***Grihasthashrama*** refers to the householder's life involving earning wealth, fulfilling sexual desires and begetting children.
- ***Vanaprasthashrama*** is the stage of gradual detachment from the material life. Here the individual tries to retire from the worldly life and dedicates himself to a life of spiritual contentment.
- ***Sanyasashrama*** refers to the stage of renunciation or wandering mystic. Here the individual gives up all the bondages and attachments of world. The Sanyasis' life is thus a spiritual life. He is the sacrifice incarnate.

6. Hindu's Notion of Fulfilling Obligations / Debts / *Rins*

The Hindus believe in the debts or *"Rins"* or obligations which they owe to various people including the God. One owes a debt to the Gods, to the sages, ancestors, animals and to the society. The repayment of these debts is also a part of Dharma and is called ***panchamahayajnas*** which consists of – *Deva Yajna, Rishi Yajna, Pitri Yajna, Buta Yajna and Nara* or *Atithi Yajna.*

7. Influence of the Doctrine of *"Karma"*

The *Karma theory* has assumed importance in the Hindu theology. In the Brahmanic thought, the doctrine of Karma has also been combined with that of transmigration of soul or *punarjanma.* It is difficult to define this concept; but to the common man, it means that the deeds of one's previous lives influence the present life, and deeds in this life determine future lives. The idea of rebirth is embedded in the notion of Karma. Karma is a connecting link between desires and rebirth. It is desire that binds a man to this world and things worldly that makes him liable to birth and death. The destruction of desire would, therefore, enable a man to free himself from the cycle of birth and death, to become eternal. Karma is accepted as an article of faith in all the main systems of Indian philosophy and religion. Even the Buddhists and Jains have accepted the Karma Theory though they have given their own interpretation for it.

Conclusion

The ideological aspects relating to the social framework of the Hindu society mentioned above, have a tremendous appeal for the majority of the people. According to **S.C. Dube,** *"these features pertain to tradition and texts, not necessarily to the social reality on the ground. With the changing times they have undergone considerable modification."* [Page - 33]. Still they have a great emotional appeal. Many Hindus like to believe that these characteristics are still operative. They have their impact on Buddhism. Jainism, Sikhism, despite their dissent. The basic Indian world view could not be totally discarded even by those who got converted to Islam or Christianity. Initially, both Islam and Christianity had to adapt to the prevailing social order. Muslims and Christians continued to share many features of the regional culture in which they were located. Selectively, the Hindus also absorbed some of their traits. Modern education, the development of a network of transport and communications, and industrialisation and urbanisation provided new bases for unity.

No body can say that everything is alright in the Indian society. Some of the problems which arose previously, still persist. Problems relating to the religious misunderstandings and prejudices, caste rivalries, fanaticism in linguistic and regional matters, ethnic clashes – are still posing challenges. In the midst of these and many other challenges India hopes to forge ahead. It is banking on its rich cultural heritage to find solutions to many of the contemporary problems.

Chapter 2

INDIAN SOCIETY THROUGH THE AGES

Impact of Buddhism on The Indian Society - Impact of Islam : The Gifts of the Muslim Age to India, Evil Effects Due to Muslim Contact - Impact of the West : Negative and Positive Effects of Western Contact - Indian Society : Factors in Continuity and Change.

Indian society is one of the oldest and the most complex one. Opinions of the scholars and historians differ regarding its antiquity. Some scholars have even said that it is as old as 5000 B.C. But according to *"a popular estimate it has covered a span of five thousand years since the period of its first known civilisation. During this long period, several waves of immigrants, representing different ethnic strains and linguistic families, have merged into its population to contribute to its diversity, richness and vitality."*[1]

Any student of Indian society and its history and culture cannot help recognising one supreme characteristic of the Indian people. It is their vitality as a distinct type, with a distinct civilisation of their own and a mind as active as ever in the past. Famous Indian historian **Jadunath Sarkar** says *"The Indian people of today are no doubt a composite ethnic product; but whatever their different contituent elements may have been in origin, they have all acquired a common Indian stamp, and have all been contributing to a common culture and building up a common type of tradition, thought and literature."*[2] **Sir Herbert Risley,** a British ethnographer who was very sceptical about the Indian's claim to be considered as one people, had also been forced to admit this commonness of Indian culture. He acknowledged it when he wrote, *"Beneath the manifold diversity of physical and social type, language, custom and religion, which strikes the observer in India, there can still be discerned a certain "underlying uniformity of life from the Himalayas to Cape Camorin." There is, in fact, an Indian character, a general Indian personality, which we cannot resolve into its component elements."*[3]

Indian society has withstood the waves of foreign invasions, political onslaughts, religious experiments, natural disasters and the shocks of centuries. Its best right to live is its vital power displayed through many thousand years of shocking changes in our land.

1 **S.C. Dube** *"Indian Society."* Page - 1.

2 **Jadunath Sarkar** *"India Through the Ages"* [1979] Page : 1 - 2.

3 **Sir Herbert Risley** as quoted by **Jadunath Sarkar.** Page - 2.

It is true that each race or creed that chosen India for its home, each school of thought that has dominated human mind even in a single province of India, has left behind its own gifts and its own impact. It is a necessary duty of an historian and also of a sociologist to analyse and estimate the importance of these gifts and also of the impacts. This analysis is of great help to know how they influenced or prepared the succeeding ages and the people.

IMPACT OF BUDDHISM ON INDIAN SOCIETY

Buddhism which emerged as a challenge to the Brahmanical supremacy and caste inequality was very much promising in the beginning for it was able to get the royal support of many kings. But it could not maintain its popularity for long. The craze for Buddhism slowly came to an end within the borders of India in due course. At the same time, it became more popular outside India. Even though hardly **0.80%** of the people in India are Buddhists, the impact of Buddhism on Hinduism, on the Hindu society and on the Indian culture, in general, is indeed, very great. Here is a brief analysis of its impact on the Indian society.

1. Buddhism Indirectly Reduced the Intensity of Caste Inequality?

It is very often said that both Jainism and Buddhism rose as a challenge to the caste inequality and to assure social justice and equality. *"In a way, Buddhism and Jainism protested against some important characteristics of Hinduism like its – rigid formalism, tyrannical ritualism, value system based on hierarchy, supremacy of Brahmins, and religious orthodoxy."* Hence a large number of men and women belonging to different castes joined these new faiths. Buddhism declared that caste or varna would not come into the way of persons seeking to obtain *"Nirvana."* Had there not been that protest from Buddhism against the inequalities of varna or caste system, the caste system would have reached a stage of social explosion long back. Buddhism, thus contributed to lessen the extremity of caste inequality.

Buddha who had soft corner towards the Kshatriyas, was highly critical of the Brahmins and their self-claimed supremacy. In fact, the critical comments made and the constructive suggestions given by the Buddha, helped the Brahmins to correct themselves and to reform the Brahmin way of life. It became inevitable for the Brahmins to turn seriously towards studies and education to respond to the intellectual challenges posed by the Buddhist scholars. Buddhism even inspired them to attain greater and greater self-restraint and self-purification. Like the Buddhist monks and pandits they even turned towards educating the general masses.

2. Buddhism Enriched the Intellectual and Spiritual Life of the Country

Of all the proselytizing religions of the world, Buddhism seems to be the only religion that could spread its influence both within and outside the borders of India by virtue of its internal vitality and spiritual power. The importance of Buddhism in this context could be understood by comparing it with religions such as Christianity and Islam which often resorted to political, military and economic power to spread their faiths in India. Buddha's love towards the entire humanity, his compassion towards all the living creatures, the emphasis he laid on non-violence and peace, have all made Buddhism to acquire world-wide recognition. Buddhist monks also tried to attain the heights of spiritual life and worked sincerely to obtain for their religion positive support even at the hands of the intellectuals.

3. Buddhism Gave Us a Simple and a Popular Religion

Buddhism never gifted us a religion which is full of complications and un-intelligible rituals that could be performed only by a priestly class. *"It deliberately set itself to appeal to the masses, and wonderfully succeeded in winning their hearts by its simplicity, its emotional element, its easy ethical code, its use of the vernacular language in its scriptures, its popular method of teaching by means of parables, and its worship in congregation. It introduced a personal element into religion, in the form of a known human saviour in the place of the impersonal forces of nature to whom Vedic Aryans used to pray."*[1]

4. Buddhism Introduced Idol - Worship

As **Jadunath Sarkar** opined *"Image-worship was most probably introduced into India by the Buddhists."* [Page - 19]. In order to commemorate the memories of the Buddha as a great master and preacher statues of the Buddha were produced and soon they came to be worshipped in as representations of the godhead. *"Houses had to be built to shelter these sacred images and temples arose. Vedic Aryans had been content with offering sacrifices on altars in the open air, as was the case with the Aryans of ancient 'Persia.'"* - [Sarkar. Page - 20.]

5. Role of Buddhism in Providing an Organisational Base for Hinduism

The monastic system or the organisation of religious devotees in disciplined orders was another experiment made by Buddhism. It is true that the great sadhus and seers of Hinduism were only making lonely contemplation for they had no systematic monastic orders. Buddhism instituted the monastic orders which made the religious devotees to constitute a fraternity of monks, obeying a common head and living together under a common code of disciplinary rules.

It is said that prior to the emergence of Buddhism, Hinduism did not have any well established organisational base. The Brahmin scholars, *sadhus,* sages and *'santas'* were practising Hinduism at their individual levels. The efforts of the Buddha and his disciples in establishing the *Buddhist Sanghas, Buddhist monastic orders,* etc. impressed very much the people at the helm of affairs of Hinduism. As a result, they realised that it was necessary for them to have some sort of *"Sangha"* or *"Sanghatan"* for the preservation of their religion and to counteract the propaganda of the other religions. Perhaps, the Buddhist Sangha influenced **Sri Adi Shankaracharya** in founding the *Mutts* known as ***"Shankar Mutts"*** in four corners of the nation. Buddhist monasticism, we could say, lives in the order of Shankara's monks. In course of time, the tradition of *'mutt'* became so popular that most of the major castes of India established their own *mutts* and developed their own tradition of the monastic order.

6. Encouragement to the Development of Regional Languages

Contribution of Buddhism towards the development of the regional languages had been remarkable. The language of culture hitherto had been Sanskrit and the texts of the Brahmanical religion were in Sanskrit. Contrary to this, the Buddha preferred to preach his doctrines in the language of the common people. Buddhist texts came to be written in *Pali.* This helped the development of Pali language and literature. In the same way, Mahavira preached his tenets in *Ardhamagadi,* a form of *Prakrit* language. This helped the development of *Ardhamagadi* dialect. In this way, Buddha and Mahavira laid the foundation for the growth of vernacular literature.

Further, due to the increasing popularity of Buddhism, Indians recognised the importance of the studies of *Pali, Sanskrit, Prakrit, Tibetan* and the *Chinese* for a full understanding of Buddhism. These have influenced writers in the modern Indian languages. They have either translated Buddhist works from the original or were inspired to write independent works that reflect Buddhist thought.

7. Encouragement to Education

Buddhism gave special importance to education. *Buddha Viharas, Mutts* or monastic orders also functioned as centres for spreading education. Buddhist monks were also great scholars. Indian kings who supported and patronised Buddhism also encouraged education. Universities such as

1 **Jadunath Sarkar** *"India Through the Ages"* [1979]. Page - 19. ***Pub.***: Sangam Books.

Taxila [7th century B.C.] and **Nalanda** [4th century B.C.] had earned a good name in the ancient world. Nalanda was, in fact, recognised as a Buddhist university.

Another speciality of Buddhism was, it had extended educational opportunity for women from the very beginning. Further, Buddhism made education available for the lower sections of the Hindu society also.

8. Influence of Buddhism on Hindu Philosophy, Logic and *Vedanta* Philosophy

Brahmin scholars acquired at the hands of the Buddhist Pandits a new approach towards philosophy, logic and vedanta philosophy. Buddhism influenced Vedanta philosophy also. Both Buddhist and Vedanta philosophers assert the unreality of the material world. This doctrine is not specifically stated but implied in the Upanishads. Buddhism made possible for the Hindu scholars to give new interpretations in the light of the Buddhist thought. It is said that Adi Shankaracharya himself was influenced by the Buddhist *"Madhyamik Darshan."* Shankaracharya, no doubt, drew his inspiration from the Upanishads, but in explaining its negative aspect, that is, refutation of ideas he was surely inspired by Madhyamik philosophy.

9. Impact on the Fields of Art and Architecture

The greatest contribution of Buddhism to Indian culture is to be found in the realms of Indian art and architecture. *It is said that the history of Indian art begins from the Buddhist period.* The Buddhist monasteries were not only great centres of learning but also flourishing centres of artistic activity.

The early Buddhist monuments chiefly found at **Sanchi, Bharhut, Bodh Gaya, Amaravati** and in other places contain *stupas.* The Buddhist art and architecture that include *stupas, viharas, chaityas,* pillars, carvings, paintings, etc. are found in various places of India, like **Sanchi, Ajantha, Ellora, Nasika, Amaravathi,** and so on.

Mahayanism influenced art in another manner. It deified Buddha and introduced the cult of *Bodhisatva.* The Mahayanists considered the Buddha *"Avalokiteshwara"* and prepared the images of the Buddha and worshipped him. The Hindu worship of images was very much influenced by Buddhism.

10. Establishment of Intimate Contact with Foreign Countries

Buddhism proved to be one of the greatest gifts of India to the outer world. Through Buddhism India maintained an intimate contact with foreign countries. Buddhism was *"a universal movement, a force irrespective of country and caste, which the whole ancient East was free to accept. Indian monks and scholars carried Buddhism to foreign countries from the third century B.C. onwards, and thereafter the converts of these countries looked up to India as a holy land, the cradle of their faith, a pilgrimage to which was the crowning act of a pious householder's life."*[1]

Buddhism inspired the native Buddhist scholars to go abroad, and at the same time extended invitation to foreign Buddhist pilgrims and students to come to India. These two streams of human movement broke our isolation in that age. *"The Hindus followed this example and from the third century A.D. we have records of Hindu missionaries and colonists settling in Further India and several of the Pacific islands. The result was that, in what is called the Buddhistic Age, the fusion of foreign non-Aryan immigrant tribes and families with the Indian population became a normal occurence."* [J. Sarkar. Page - 21.]

---

1 **Jadunath Sarkar** *"India Through the Ages".* Page - 21.

11. Indianisation and Hinduisation of Foreign Races

It was during the ascendancy of the Buddhist rule or influence, number of foreign races such as **Persians, Sakas** [Seythians], **Kushans, Gujars, Parthians** and others had flocked towards India and settled down in different places of India. The accommodative spirit of the Buddhism made them to retain their un-Hindu foreign names, customs, practices in brief, their culture. *"Later, when Buddhism decayed, these foreign settlers were quietly and completely absorbed into the mass of the Hindu population, their foreign origins having been forgotten during their long stay in India. Thus Buddhism, without at first intending it, contributed very largely to the synthesis which has produced modern Hindu society."* [**Sarkar.** Page - 22.] Thus Buddhism laid the foundation for the Indianisation and Hinduization of foreign races.[1]

12. Influence of Buddhism on Modern Life

Influence of Buddhism on modern life is very great. The world has come to realise the services done by the Buddha to the mankind. The *"Panchasheela"* which govern the policy of the Government of India is based on Buddhist teachings. *Buddhism has always stood for universal peace* and it will continue to do so even in the future. Those who seek universal peace must turn to Buddhism for a better support. Swami Vivekananda has very rightly called him *"The Light of Asia."*

Japanese author **Suzuki** writes in his article : *"If the fact is one and if there is something that differentiates it from the West, the differentiation must be sought in the thought that is embedded in Buddhism....... But when the East as a unity is made to confront the West, Buddhism supplies the bond."*[2]

13. Buddhism and the Buddha's Teachings Resulted in Pessimism?

It is often commented that a sense of pessimism pervades the teachings of Buddhism. Hence it directly or indirectly made its followers to reject the material world and its prosperity and to become more and more otherworldly in their attitude.

We should remember that the Buddha was not an escapist. Though born in a royal family in the midst of material prosperity, he became an ascetic to end the miseries and evils of human life and not out of dejection and despair. But unfortunately, the effect of his teachings on people was found to be disastrous. His followers came to exaggerate the short comings of the world and even kings and emperors began to think of the *"other world."* The sudden contempt which the emperors like **Ashoka** and **Sri Harsha** developed soon after they embraced Buddhism, towards political glory and material prosperity, had disastrous effect on later history. Thus India fell an easy prey to foreign barbarians who desecrated the holy land. Even other religions of India also came under the pessimistic influence of Buddhism. *Thus the misinterpretations of Buddhist teachings and the undue importance laid on non-violence and spirituality led to a kind of political degeneration and servitude.*

Conclusion

It is significant to note that Buddhism which at one stage obtained royal patronage and support could not become popular in India. Its influence slowly faded away. It left India only to

---

1 A distinguished orientalist scholar by name **A.M.T. Jackson** in *"Indian Antiquary"* [1910] Page - 77 has rightly observed - *"The most important fact in Hindu history is overlooked [by our orthodox writers]. I mean the attractive power of Hindu civilization, which has enabled it to assimilate and absorb into itself every foreign invader except the Moslem and the European. Those Indians have a poor idea of their country's greatness, who do not realize how it has tamed and civilized the nomads of Central Asia, so that wild Turkoman tribes have been transformed into some of the most famous of the Rajput royal races."* - Quoted by **Jadunath Sarkar** in *"India Through The Ages."* Page - 27.

2 **Suzuki** in one of his articles as quoted by **I. Rebello** in *"Indian Culture and Civilisation"* [1975]. Page - 22.

become popular outside its borders that is, in **Ceylon, Burma, Nepal, Tibet, China, Japan, Korea, Vietnam, Thailand,** and other Asian nations. **Ram Swarup** has expressed the view that Buddhism also made the same experiments which Hinduism had done.[1] It could be spread to places wherein Hinduism was already introduced. Buddhism never destroyed anything to stamp its imprint. It blossomed in different places by accommodating itself with the regional peculiarities. It was not controlled by any mother organisation situated at a faraway place. Hence, *Buddhism never became an imperialist instrument to exploit people and to make them accept slavery.*

Ram Swarup is of the opinion that Hinduism and Buddhism are intimately interwined. He writes : "...... *Buddha and Buddhism form an intimate part of Hindu consciousness. Buddha was a Hindu. Buddhism is Hindu in its origin and development, in its art and architecture, iconography, language, beliefs, psychology, names, nomenclature, religious vows and spiritual discipline..... Hinduism is not all Buddhism, but Buddhism forms part of the ethos which is essentially Hindu.*"

According to **Jadunath Sarkar,** "*original Buddism was only a new form of Hinduism*" and not a separate religion as such. As he opined "*in its origin, Buddhism was not avowedly a new creed, but an appeal for holier living in the bosom of the existing Hindu religion and society.*" [Page - 25.] He writes "*As far as the original philosophy of Buddhism goes, there is, therefore, hardly any break of continuity between the Buddha and the Hindu sages who had preceded him. In the Jatakas, the Buddha says again and again that true piety consists not in the performance of rites or the repetition of set prayers, but in holy living and holy dying.*"[2]

Buddhism, though has its own independent existence, according to **Ram Swarup,** it cannot remain a total stranger to Hinduism. He writes : "........... *Buddha, his spiritual experiences and teachings formed part of a Hindu tradition. He belonged to Upanishadic heritage. He cannot be understood in any other sense......... He himself claimed no originality. He claimed to have 'seen an ancient way of life'.*"

IMPACT OF ISLAM

Islam, which is regarded as the second biggest religion of the mankind entered India in the 10th century A.D. But the Islamic culture started exercising its influence in a serious manner only after 15th and 16th centuries. Almost upto Akbar's rule, the Muslim invaders in India never made any systematic efforts to provide for India a strong and a stable political administration. They were only taking advantage of the material prosperity that India had. Great Indian historian **Jadunath Sarkar** rightly remarked : "*An important characteristic of the Muslim element in India was that from 1200 to 1580, either state or society retained their original military and nomadic character - the ruling race living merely like an armed camp in the land they ruled. It was* ***Akbar*** *who, at the end of the 16th century, began the policy of giving to the people of the country an interest in the State, and making the government undertake some social functions in addition to the mere police work it had hitherto contented itself with doing. Down to Akbar's time the Muslim settlers in India used to be in the land, but not of it.*"[3]

According to **Jadunath Sarkar** [Page - 48], the Muslims of India cannot merge into Hindu society and creed for obvious reasons. He writes: "*The Muslim conquest of India differed fundamentally from all preceding invasions in one respect. The Muslims came to India as a new element which the older inhabitants could not absorb. The Greek, Scythian, Mongolian, and Parthian invaders had, a few generations after their settlement in this land, been completely Hinduized in name, speech, manners, religion, dress and ideas.*" But Islam is a fiercely monotheistic religion. It

1 **Ram Swarup** "*Buddhism vis-a-vis Hinduism.*"
2 **Jadunath Sarkar** "*India Through The Ages.*" Page : 29 - 30.
3 **Jadunath Sarkar** "*India Through the Ages.*" Page - 50.

cannot allow any compromise with polytheism or admit a plurality of deities. the God of Islam and of Christianity - like the God of Judaism which was the parent of both these creeds - is *"a living and a jealous God."* He cannot tolerate any companion or sharer in the hearts of his adorers. *Hence, the absorption of the Indo-Muslims into the fold of Hinduism by recognizing Allah as another of the numberless incarnations of Vishnu and Muhammad as an inspired sadhu, was impossible.*

Though the triumph of Islam provided an opportunity for the intermixture of both the cultures in the beginning, it resulted in serious consequences later particularly when the Muslim invaders started destroying the Hindu and the Buddhist memorials, temples, centres of pilgrimage, study centres, educational institutions such as universities, libraries, and the like. Patronage that was being given to the priests and scholars was stopped. Royal recognition that was being accorded to education and literature also came to an end. *The cultural history of India started moving in a different direction.*

But the continued stay of Muslims in India compelled the people of both the communities [Hindus and Muslims] to develop better understandings. Slowly there took place between the two cultural exchanges, cultural borrowings and cultural intermixtures. One culture started influencing the other. The *"give-and-take"* attitude which these cultures developed resulted in the enrichment of both the cultures. Muslim ideas slowly got mixed up with the Hindu art, architecture, literature, music, dance, etc. As **Alberuni** has pointed out – *the administrative system and the styles of life of the Muslims modified the socio-economic conditions of India.*

The impact of the Muslim culture on the Indian society and culture may be briefly examined here.

1. Muslim Community Remained Mostly Urban

Since the Muslims provided more importance to the material pleasures, they preferred to settle in urban areas. They built new cities such as **Fatehpur Sikri, Aurangabad, Sikandarabad, Hyderabad, Golconda,** and so on. Muslim invaders, in particular, never showed any interest in purchasing land in rural areas to settle as agriculturists. *This made many villages to develop indigenous culture of their own uncontaminated by the invaders.* The Muslims probably felt that it was easy for them to secure political protection at the hands of their own rulers if they lived as one community in some selected towns and cities. Even today, Muslims are found in a bigger number in urban areas than in rural areas. Hence, the Muslim impact has been greater in the cities than in villages.

2. Impact of Impressive Islamic Values

Unity, uniformity, equality, fraternity, commitment to religion, and such other values associated with the Islamic community impressed Indians and provided them a new vision. *The Islamic system of administration and judicial system also had their impact on the Hindus.* The Islamic culture in an indirect manner gave inspiration for the Rajputs, Marathas, Sikhs and the Kings of Vijayanagar empire to fight against the invaders in defence of their religion and culture.

3. Attempts Towards Communal Harmony

It is true that Muslim rulers had made various attempts to convert people of other religions. But it is wrong to exaggerate this aspect and say that all the Muslim rulers resorted to forcible conversions throughout their rule. **S.C. Dube** writes : *"Thus, the alternatives for them [Hindus] were acceptance of Islam or death. Despite long years of Muslim rule, the overwhelming majority of the people remained Hindu. This would not have been possible had the requirements of Islam been strictly carried out."* Muslim rulers were aware of the fact that it was not possible for them to rule the country for long if they failed to obtain the co-operation and support of the majority community, that is, Hindus. Hence they made special efforts to develop friendly relations with the Hindus. Thus, they used to recruit a large number of Hindus into the army and also administration.

4. Emergence of *Bhakti* Cult

Islam preached universal brotherhood, social equality and rejected untouchability and idol worship. Its monotheism was a challenge to Hinduism. The only way to counter it was the *Bhakti cult.* The devotees of *Bhakti cult rejected idol worship and the caste system, preached equality of man and oneness of all religions and showed its opposition to excessive ritualism and formalities and advocated a simple faith.* But we should not infer from this that Hindus did not know the oneness of God. It was known to them long before the Prophet preached his religion. But contact with the Muslims gave an impetus to the revival of those ideas and produced a great effect on such religious leaders like **Kabir, Namadeva, Ramanand** and others. *The Bhakti movement aimed at purification of existing system and liberation of the masses from the dominance of priesthood.*

- ***Attempts to Synthesise Hindu-Muslim Thoughts* :** The Hindu saints and religious leaders made attempts to synthesise Hindu-Muslim thoughts. The **Sufi** saints, for example, adopted Hindu doctrines and followed many of their traditions. There were many common features of Sufism and Bhakti mysticism that developed in medieval India. *"The Hindu and the Sufi saints preached the unity of mankind, believed in the equality of all human beings before God, condemned caste distinctions and laid emphasis on love and devotional worship of the deity as against formal ritualism and external piety."*[1] Many Hindus were attracted towards Muslim saints and became their disciples. Some of the Muslims also followed the practice of worshipping Hindu Gods and Goddesses. In their social contacts also both the religious communities, to a certain extent, have risen above traditional barriers and religious orthodoxy.

5. Impact on Education

Education was also given some importance during the Muslim rule. Muslim children were given primary education through *"mosques"* and *"madrasas."* Every major mosque had its own educational institution attached to it. Muslim rulers used to finance such educational institutions. Universities of Agra and Fatehpur Sikri could be regarded as the great gifts of Muslim culture. Some of the scholarly Muslim kings took special interest in developing libraries and in getting some of the Sanskrit works translated into Arabic, Persian and Urdu languages. Great Sanskrit works such as *Ramayana, Mahabharata, Upanishads, Bhagavad Gita, Yoga Vasishtha, Panchatantra, Hitopadesha, Puranic stories, Jataka stories,* etc. were translated into Arabic language. Hindu writers often wrote in Hindi, Bengali and other vernaculars, often dealing with subjects of Hindu social life and religion, such as Radha and Krishna, Sita and Ram, Nala and Damayanthi, and so on. The development of Urdu language and literature provided a new meeting ground between Hindus and Muslims.

6. Influence on Art and Architecture

During the Muslim rule, there took place a harmonious combination of Hindu and Muslim art and architectural styles. Mughal architecture was an amalgam of influences of Persia, Byzantium and India. Babar had brought architects from Constantinople. In fact, the real synthesis of Muslim and Hindu features began in Mughal architecture in the days of Akbar. **Vincent Smith** called this style *"Hindu-Mohammedan."* **Taj Mahal** is the best example of this new style. Combination of Hindu-Muslim architecture could be found in the works of architecture at Fatehpur Sikri, Jahangeer Mahal, Moti Mosque, and the like. The same story is repeated in the Rampur Temple at Jodhpur. Muslim rulers with an acsetic sense built various buildings in different architectural styles some of which look like *"Jaina Basadis"*, a few others, like *"Bouddha Vihars"*; a few more, like *Hindu temples* while the remainings ones resemble the *Persian monuments.* Thus, the Hindu and Muslim

1 **P.K. Kar** *"Indian Society"* [2003]. Page - 366.

architects joined their hands to build a temple, a mosque, the palace of a King or the *durbar* of a Sultan. The services of the artists or architects whether they were Muslims or Hindus, were hired by the Hindu and the Muslim Kings alike.

Many causes led to the blending of the Hindu-Muslim art and architectures. Muslim invaders were adventurers and so they did not bring with them craftsmen and sculptors and employed the natives to construct their palaces and mosques. While conforming to the tastes of the Muslims the Hindus introduced their own techniques and thus influenced Muslim art. In the early days, palaces and mosques were built on the ruins of temples or by remodelling existing temples like replacing the *sikharas* by domes and minarets. In this way, they unconsciously adopted elements of Hindu art.

7. Influence on the Fields of Music and Gardening

In Muslim culture, there is importance even to music, dance and gardening. Muslim kings had given patronage to Arabbi, Irani and Hindusthani singers. *Hindusthani music* witnessed its hey-day in the reign of the Mughals. There took place the process of blending of Persian and Hindu music. Muslims developed new musical instruments such as – *sitar, shahanay, tabla, dilruba, sarangi* and so on. There were expert singers like **Surdas, Keshavadas, Tansen, Abul Fazl** in the court of Akbar.

Mughals took interest in developing beautiful gardens. Here also they showed their love towards variety and novelty. They had introduced Persian and Turkish styles in building gardens. *Shalimar gardens* of Kashmir, *Mughal gardens* at Delhi, *Nishat* and *Barinag gardens* stand as examples in this regard.

The Gifts of the Muslim Age to India

Jadunath Sarkar points out that the Muslim Age contributed a few "gifts" to India among which the following may be noted.

The Muslim Age led to *"the restoration of touch with outer world, which included the revival of an Indian navy and sea-borne trade, both of which had been lost since the decline of the Cholas."*

"The two hundred years of Mughal rule gave to the whole of northern India and to much of the Deccan also, *oneness of official language, administrative system and coinage, and also a popular lingua franca* [Hindustani] for all classes except the Hindu priests and the stationary village folk."

The Muslim rule led to the rise of vernacular literature. Hindi, Bengali, Marathi, Urdu and other vernacular literatures got enriched. Historical literature hitherto unknown to the Hindus, or imperfectly developed among them, was also developed. Persian, Arabic and Turkish words have entered largely in the Hindi, Bengali, and even Marathi languages. Paper was introduced by the Muslims, as its Arabic name *"Kaghaz"* universally used in India proves. Thus, books could be multiplied in a more attractive durable form.

Muslim contact led to an improvement in the art of war and also in civilisation. The art of war was highly developed by the Muslims partly by borrowing from Europe [through Turkey] and partly through Persia. The imperial Mughal army served as a model which the Hindu rajas eagerly imitated. The system of fortification was greatly improved by the Muslims in India.

"The Muslim influence was naturally most strongly felt on the system of administration, the court ceremonials and dress, the military organisation and arms, the lives of the upper classes, the articles of luxury, the fine arts, architecture [other than religious], and gardening..."[1]

The Muslims, leading generally a more luxurious life than the Hindus, encouraged several manufacturers and fine arts. Since the Muslims concentrated in cities [except in East Bengal] they were more tasteful, luxury-living and elegant than the Hindus in their daily life and even in their vices. This the richer Hindus and particularly the official class started imitating whenever they had the means.

Evil Effects Due to Muslim Contact

Hindu society could not escape from some of the evil effects caused by Muslim contact and conquests.

1. ***Enforcement of Child Marriage*** **:** The custom of child marriage among the Hindus came into practice because of the Muslim conquest. For reasons of their own, the Hindus had come to consider the birth of girls inauspicious and also a burden to the family. Muslim invasion further added to this belief. They resorted to *child marriage* as an attempt to prevent the unmarried Hindu girls from falling a prey into the hands of Muslim invaders. Even the *shastras* were revised to give legal sanction to child marriage and a marriage beyond the age of 11 or 12 was considered sinful.

2. ***Imposition of the Pardah*** **:** Prior to the arrival of the Muslims in India, there was no prevalence of the *Pardah* system in the Hindu society. Hindu women could move freely without any restriction of the *pardah.* The Muslim conquest of India imposed this unwanted practice on the Hindu women also. The *Hindu women were compelled to wear 'pardah'* like their Muslim counterparts mainly to escape from the sexy looks of the invaders and to protect themselves from being kidnapped or seduced. Practice of wearing *'pardah'* further added to the dependence of Hindu women on their menfolk.

3. ***Horrible Practices of "Sati" and "Jauhar"*** **:** The Muslim invaders after conquering different places of India, captured women and girls of the defeated, and married them. As a result of that, Hindu women, particularly Rajput women, jumped into fire to burn themselves to death prior to their husbands and nearest relatives leaving for the battle field to fight their last battle against the Muslims. This practice came to be known as *"Jauhar."* But, the *"Sati"* refers to the practice in which the wife had to be burnt in the funeral pyre of the husband. Thus, the Muslim invasions forced Hindu women to cultivate horrible practices such as *'Jauhar'* and *'Sati'* in a bid to safeguard their honour, purity and *pativratya.*

4. ***Encouragement to Slavery*** **:** *Hindus borrowed the custom of maintaining slaves,* a custom which was a recognised institution among the Muslims. It is said that **Firozshah Sultan** had made special arrangements to maintain two lakh slaves. Hindu royal harems and palaces in Rajasthan also maintained large number of slaves. Among the Rajput families women slaves were offered as dowry.

5. ***Made Caste System to Become More Rigid and Conservative*** **:** *Hindu society became more and more rigid in order to withstand the attacks made on it by the outside forces.* The conservative caste system became still more rigid. The lot of the lower castes worsened due to caste restrictions imposed by higher castes. Hence, conversion for them became an escape from politico-religious tyranny of the Muslims. *Religious conversions started taking place in a large number and as a result, Hinduism lost a sizeable number of its adherents.*

6. ***Adoption of Pleasure-seeking Attitude*** : Most of the Muslim invaders and rulers were pleasure-seekers. They loved wine, women, gambling and such other things. The Hindus, particularly the rich, adopted the vices of gambling, drinking and enjoyment of sex from the Muslim invaders. The Muslim impact also brought changes in some of the earlier games and recreations. Further, the dress patterns, food habits, social manners and daily habits of the Muslims also influenced the upper-strata of the Hindu society.

7. ***The conservative and the revivalist tendencies*** that developed within the Muslim community in India, proved to be very costly for the Hindus. **Prof. Ram Ahuja** writes : *"The great Islamic tradition, therefore, could not maintain itself with the earlier vigour and confidence. In the*

1 **Jadunath Sarkar** "*Indian Through the Ages*" Page - 62.

eighteenth century, Islam lost its earlier liberal tendencies and in its place orthodoxy and revivalism became its chief pre-occupations. The Hindu tradition became more reactive than adaptive in ethos and lagged behind in cultural change. Islamic tradition, on the other hand, got highly politicised. But in the nineteenth century, liberal and orthodox Islamic traditions began to polarise. The politico-cultural phenomenon generated by the tussle between these two cultural forces culminated in the creation of a separate Islamic nation (Pakistan)."

8. *The Gift of the Evil of Communalism* : *The greatest evil that emerged in India especially after the first half of 18th century, is communalism.* Communalism started spreading its tentacles especially when the Hindus launched various reformatory and revivalist movements during the 18th and 19th centuries. These movements made the Muslims to change their attitude towards the Hindus, and Hindus towards the Muslims. The *'divide and rule'* policy of the British further worsened the Hindu-Muslim relations giving rise to a basic prejudice between the two and a number of communal riots.

It is true that the Muslim and the Hindu cultures influenced each other. Religion was the only obstacle because of which both these communities remained hostile to each other. In spite of the close interaction between the two for more than 500 years, these two cultures never assimilated together to form one common culture, but remained as two parallel cultures. The Muslims who used to consider themselves victors, were proud of their religion, that is, Islam. They were of the belief that all the things, conceptions and practices of the victors were better than those of the defeated. This ethnocentric belief on the part of the Muslims came in the way of accepting or adopting Hindu viewpoints.[1]

Jadunath Sarkar writes : "Therefore, Hindus and Muslims - as later on, Hindus and Christians - had to live in the same land without being able to mix together. Nothing has enabled them to bridge this gulf. The Indian Muslims have, throughout the succeeding centuries, retained the extra-Indian direction of their heart. Their faces are still turned, in daily prayer, to a spot in Mecca; before English education modernized India, their minds, their law-code, their administrative system, their favourite reading sought models from outside India - from Arabia and Syria, Persia and Egypt."[2] Further, *"the Muslims would not yield on the cardinal points of their faith nor accept the few conventions necessary for entering Hindu society. They clung to the Koranic precepts. The polytheists are unclean; let them not therefore come near the Kaba."* [**Sarkar.** Page - 50].

Such tendencies and beliefs distanced the Muslims from the Hindus. The Hindus, on the other hand, were proud of their ancient heritage, their sacred texts, the Vedas, the Epics, Puranas, the Geeta, etc. The Muslim culture was always considered by them an alien culture. That is why, the harmonious mixture of both could not be achieved. In spite of these prejudices, each culture and its elements had its own impact on the other. But to talk of purities of these two cultures is sheer imagination. It is thus rightly remarked by a scholar : *"Those who seek to boast today of the purity of the Hindu and Muslim culture in India are ignorant of the history or else they lack capacity to understand the historical process."*

IMPACT OF THE WEST

India's contact with the West includes various ups and downs. This contact which is atleast five centuries old has brought about and is still bringing about a number of socio-cultural changes in the Indian society. It is difficult to assess or evaluate the exact nature of the changes and effects which this contact has brought about. The current international processes such as liberalisation, privatisation, globalisation, modernisation, etc. to which India is also exposed, have further

1 **K. Singh** *"Indian Social System"* [1972]. Page - 194.

2 **Jadunath Sarkar** *"India Through The Ages"* Page - 49.

complicated this assessment. In spite of this complication, any insider could assess that while some of the changes / effects brought about by the Western contact have proved to be extremely beneficial, some others have caused new anxieties, fears and problems. Here is an attempt to analyse the impact of the West on the Indian society.

Contact of the West Through the British

There has been direct contact of India with the West since the past five centuries. With the discovery of the sea route to the East in the 15th century, traders from Portugal, Denmark, England, and France came in contact with India. The Portuguese who were the first to visit India had contact with the Western Coast, their impact on Indian culture was not of great significance, except the fact that they managed to spread Christianity in some areas on the West coast. Though the Dutch and the French were interested in spreading their commercial and political activities in India, they were not successful in doing so. The British were the only people from the West who emerged as a dominant power in India. Therefore, the Western impact on Indian culture has been primarily that of the British.

England had established its direct rule over India for more than almost 150 years. The British brought with them not only a new system of political administration but also a new way of life. Educated Indians in the cities came under the influence of the British way of life and culture. Large number of Indians started imitating the British way of life. This imitation became a new fashion and a new trend. People in the rural areas also came under the influence of this new trend. As a result, India started witnessing a number of socio-cultural changes. Famous Indian sociologist, **M.N. Srinivas** introduced a new concept, namely, ***"Westernisation"*** to analyse these socio-cultural changes.

M.N. Srinivas has used the term *"westernisation"* mainly to *refer to the impact of British rule on the Indian society.* Srinivas has also tried to use this concept in a general manner to refer to the impact of the West on the non-western societies. Thus, he wrote: **Westernisation** refers to *"the changes that a non-Western society undergoes as a result of prolonged contact with a Western one."* (1962)

Definition of the Term "Westernisation"

1. ***"Westernisation"*** refers to *"the changes brought about in Indian society and culture as a result of over 150 years of British rule and the term subsumes changes occurring at different levels - technology, institutions, ideology, values."*[1]
2. In simple words, the term *Westernisation mainly explains the changes that have taken place in the Indian society and culture due to the Western contact through the British rule.*

The advent of the British in India and their prolonged rule led to the introduction of the Western civilisation. Those who came under the influence of the Western civilisation started modifying their life and activities in accordance with the Western standards. Western way of life became very attractive for them. The term "Westernisation" virtually indicates *the process of imitation of the Western life-styles by the Indians.*

IMPACT OF THE WEST

The impact of the Western culture and civilisation on the Indian socio-cultural system could be analysed in the following manner.

1. Impact on Institutions : Establishment of New Institutions

Western contact brought about changes in the institutional systems. Old institutions were either modified or gave place to the new ones.

1 **M.N. Srinivas** *"Social Change in Modern India"* [1966] Page 47

(a) *Impact on Education* : Western education broadened the vision and outlook of the people which made them to become conscious of their rights and freedom. In place of the *traditional educational institutions,* the Western type of formal educational institutions such as schools, colleges, technical institutes, research centres, universities, etc. were established. English became the medium of language in these institutions and gained prominence. It also served to spread English culture.

(b) *Impact on the Legal System* : Due to the British contact, India came under one system of common law and legislations. In place of the tradition, caste panchayats, and the village *Nyaya Panchayats;* the modern law, legislation, court, police and other legal systems came to stay.

(c) *Impact on the Economic System* : The modern capitalist mode of economy introduced by the British gave a fatal blow to the economic self-reliance of the village and also to the existing *"jajmani system."*[1] New commercial establishments, banks, new accounting system, partnership firms, joint stock companies, share market, co-operative societies, etc. came to be established.

(d) *Introduction of New Schemes* : In place of joint families, local communities, caste fraternities, etc. there came in new institutional arrangements, such as social welfare schemes, life insurance schemes, social security schemes, etc. in order to provide protection and security to people wherever required.

2. Miraculous Changes in the Field of Technology

The modernisation of the age-old Indian technology, agriculture, entrepreneurship and industry led to the economic advancement of the country. The new and large-scale industries introduced by the British exposed Indians to the influcncc of Western technology. Widespread use of modern technology increased the number of industries both small-scale and large-scale. Thus widespread use of Western technology led to the process of industrialisation. The process of industrialisation is normally associated with the growth of towns and cities which started attracting people from the rural areas. The cities provided a favourable atmosphere for the spread of Western influence.

Technology led to the development in the fields such as communications, post and telegraph, telephone and radio, railways, roads, canals, etc. Radical progress in the fields of transport and communication added greater speed to the spread of Western way of life.

3. Selection of New Values and Ideologies

The process of Westernisation implies *"certain value preferences"* also. Humanitarianism, rationalism, egalitarianism and secularism and such other values and ideologies are associated with Westernisation.

(a) ***Humanitarianism*** which includes in itself various other values implies *"an active concern for the welfare of all human beings irrespective of caste, economic position, religion, age, and sex"* - (M.N. Srinivas).

(b) ***Egalitarianism*** upholds the principle of equality, that is equality of sex, caste, class, colour, creed, race and religion.

(c) ***Rationalism*** upholds *"a system of belief regulated by reason, not authority",* nor dogma.

(d) ***Secularism*** is an ideology which believes *"that the state, morals, education, etc. should be independent of religion".*

1 **Jajmani System:** This refers to a system of distribution whereby high caste landowning families [called *"jajmans"*] are provided services and products by various lower castes such as carpenters *[Badagi],* barbers *[Nai]*, potters *[Kumbars],* blacksmiths *[Kammars]* washerman *[Dhobis],* etc. The servicing people called *"Kamins"* are paid in cash or in kind [grains, fodder, clothes, animal products like milk, butter, etc.] It is a system governed by relationship based on reciprocity in intercaste relations in villages. *Ref:* **Ram Ahuja's** *"Indian Social System"* - Page: 322. [For more details, see **Chapter - 7.**]

These ideologies and values had a great impact on Indians. They changed the traditional attitudes and outlook of the people. Educated Indians came under the heavy influence of these values. These values broadened their vision and made them to develop secular outlook. They realised the importance of reasoning and started appreciating the principle of equality.

4. Creation of Intense Desire to Increase the Standard of Living or Material Life

The use of Western technology and the scientific equipments and gadgets and the acceptance of the Western model of industrialism created new aspirations and ambitions in the minds of people. The *"pull"* of spiritualism became weakened and the attraction of the comforts and luxuries of worldly life got strengthened. The craving towards more and more material pleasures and economic prosperity increased. This tendency hastened the material progress of the country to a certain extent.

5. Restructuring of Political Values

The hierarchy of political values has been restructured. Though the British people left India, the Western model of democratic system introduced by them has come to stay in India. Monarchic form of government which existed in India for centuries came to an end. Then existing provincial states numbering more than 500, ultimately merged into the Indian State. Common constitutional, legislative and judicial system came to be practised. Feelings and sentiments of nationalism became stronger.

Acceptance of this new political system brought about structural changes in the social system also. For example, the feudal system, and the Zamindari systems came to an end. Practice of untouchability became illegal and unconstitutional. Social institutions such as marriage, family, caste, property, professions, etc. had to undergo major changes for the simple fact that the modern law provides for equality in all the major fields of social life. These changes provided a new scope for the middle class which became active in almost all the areas of social life.

6. Spread of New Life-Styles

The Western influence made Indians imitate the Western way of life. More than anything, the Western education had a great impact on the style of living of the people. They gave up their inhibition towards meat-eating and consumption of alcohol. They also adopted Western style of dressing and dining. Restrictions on food habits got relaxed. Carrot, beet-root, onion, garlic, cabbage, radish and such other vegetables once tabooed, became more acceptable. Modern means of transport and communication lessened the social distance between different castes. Cinemas, hotels, bars and night clubs became common. Friendly gatherings, marriages, birth-days, wedding anniversaries, new year day celebrations, felicitation programmes etc., came to be arranged on the Western model.

The impact of the Western life-style was such that there was *"a very marked tendency among the natives of India to indulge in English luxuries."* They had well furnished houses, many wore pocket watches and they were fond of horse drawn carriages and drank wine like their English masters.

As **Gandhiji** wrote in his autobiography, educated Indians undertook the task of *"becoming English gentlemen in their dress, manners, habits, choices, preferences, etc."* It included even learning to appreciate Western music and participating in ball dancing. Western education brought about a big change in the outlook of those educated.

7. Inspiration to Social Reform Movements

During the British rule and also afterwards a number of social reform movements came into being. Several traditional beliefs and practices dysfunctional to society were discarded and many new customs, institutions and social practices were adopted.

Indians who came under the influence of these values became aware of many of the existing social evils like *child marriage, taboos against widow remarriage and intercaste marriage, intercaste dining, seclusion of women, untouchability,* etc. This awareness led to the launching of a series of social reform movements right from Raja Ram Mohan Roy down to Mahatma Gandhiji. Raja Ram Mohan Roy's *"Brahma Samaj"*, Swami Dayananda Saraswathi's *"Arya Samaj"*, Swami Vivekananda's *"Sri Ramakrishna Mission"*, Dr. Annie Besant's *"Theosophical Society"*, Gandhiji's *"Sarvodaya"* and crusade against Untouchability and such other movements not only served to eradicate some of the social evils but also to enlighten people regarding modern values.

8. Inspiration to the Freedom Struggle

Western ideas and values inspired a number of freedom fighters such as Gopala Krishna Gokhale, Tilak, Bipinchandra Pal, Ranade, Gandhiji, Nehru, Sardar Patel, Subhaschandra Bose and others. The inspiration strengthened the freedom movement to a great extent. The famous movements of the West such as Italian Unification, German Unification, etc. provided inspiration for the Indians to plunge in the freedom struggle.

Negative and Positive Effects of Western Contact

Negative Effects of Western Contact

Though the process of Westernisation in the beginning brought along with it a number of positive effects, in course of time, it also led to some negative effects. Western way of life became so attractive that it made some educated Indians to imitate the West indiscriminately. Every thing from the West was considered good and worthy of being imitated, including the Western values, customs, practices, etiquettes, tastes, choices, preferences, selections, etc. In their eagerness to imitate the West, these Indians blindly picked up even the deficiencies, weaknesses, vices and evil practices of the West. In their attempts to show themselves as more forward and progressive, they started ignoring and criticising Indian cultural heritage, way of life and living. English educated Indians came more under the influence of Westernisation than others. Hence, among them a sizeable number of people have developed a soft corner towards the West and a negligent and an indifferent attitude towards India. This has also hampered the development of the spirit of nationalism in India.

The Western contact through the British had brought us not only gains but also losses. **Jadunath Sarkar** [Page - 106] draws our attention towards some of such losses.

- *The British policy served to encourage all separatist tendencies that oppose national union* and helped to widen the lines of cleavage. *"British policy consistently negatived everything that could make the Indians strong in the modern world."* They had launched an open policy for keeping Indian people as weak as possible.
- *In over one-third of the Indian soil, the British had kept feudalism alive into the very middle of the 20th century.* The primitive barbarism of Nizam's government, the defenceless political condition of Kashmir, the peasant servitude found in Rajaputana - these, and many other such things will be remembered as examples of great disservices done to India by the British.
- *The Muslim community has been kept fifty years behind the times,* thus paralysing one-third of the [then] national body.
- *Further, the old set up at home, based on the joint family has been broken up;* its effect will be felt in all aspects of our life and thought, for centuries to come.

10. Positive Effects of British Contact

The Western contact through the British had brought India some positive gains. **Jadunath Sarkar** points out a few of them.

- *The British contact led to the growth of a vast and most influential middle class.* The rise of a middle class was the natural consequence of the introduction of modern civilisation and new administration with their numberless branches of activity.
- *The recognition of the principle that the true aim of government is to uplift the people by socialistic activity, and not merely to act as a "police-state."*
- *The British rule led to the formation of a secular state with equality for all* irrespective of religion or race.
- *Women have been raised from a degraded status* by the growth of public opinion supported by state action. The freedom and education of women have doubled the effective man-power of the nation.
- *Provincial, linguistic and sectarian differences of mentality are undermined, and a uniformity of thought* is advancing throughout India thanks to newspapers, mass meetings, and a common type of literature in all our vernaculars.
- *The British rule led to the rise of a capitalist class* which started investing wealth in fruitful production and trade instead of preserving it intact in treasury.

Conclusion

Influence of the West and its culture continues unabated even today. Fascination towards Western way of life and the temptation to go to the Western countries either to get into attractive jobs or to settle down permanently there continue to govern the aspirations of our educated young people. Ever since 1990s, opportunities for higher education, especially to pursue professional courses, have been widened. These widened opportunities have opened the doors for lakhs of educated Indians to seek their prospects in the Western countries. The economic processes such as liberalisation, privatisation and globalisation let loose by the Indian Government in 1900s have further added to this tendency. Hence judged even from the present day trends the fact of the Western impact on the Indian society and culture is undeniable.

Western impact on the Indian society gives rise to a number of questions : *In which direction the Indian society is moving due to the impact of the West ? Has India really benefited ? Has it progressed ? Has it contributed to the welfare of the common people ? Can we establish the progress achieved by India objectively ? ......?* Time is ripe for attempting to find objective answers to the questions like these.

Some scholars are of the opinion that Western impact has definitely helped India in counteracting a number of socio-economic problems which India was forced to face soon after the second world war. Problems of economic backwardness, poverty, rural indebtedness, unemployment, caste conflicts, communal disharmony, shortage of capital, religious conservatism, lack of technically skilled workers, imperfect means of mobilising human and material resources, etc. have been handled with the knowledge and experience obtained through Western contact. Though these problems are not completely solved alternative solutions for them have been sought.

There are also scholars who hold the view that the Western contact has not helped India much in facing the challenges of these problems. They are of the opinion that the neglect of Indian approach in finding solutions to these problems has costed us much. Though some problems are effectively dealth with, many more have arisen in their place. Western model can never provide a permanent solution to the Eastern, particularly to the Indian problems. Independence from the British rule rather than contact with the West through the British that made modernisation possible.

In conclusion, it could be said that some truth lies in both the arguments. Western contact has definitely helped India to achieve some progress. At the same time, it has also brought some new challenges. Even while maintaining its contact with the West, India maintained its indigenous nature in some fields; especially in the non-material fields. Time tested traditional institutions, beliefs, practices, values and ideologies are still alive in India giving intrinsic strength to the Indians. **Prof. Ram Ahuja** thus rightly remarks : *"Thus, even after the impact of the West and after the modernisation of various systems, India will remain India. Indian culture will subsist and survive in the decades to come."* [***Note*** : For more details, please refer to the Chapter entitled *"Some Aspects of Social Mobility."*]

3. INDIAN SOCIETY : FACTORS IN CONTINUITY AND CHANGE

Human society involves in itself elements of stability and continuity. No society can maintain stability without allowing some changes to take place in it. Similarly, no society can encourage continuous and uncontrolled changes without endangering its stability. Some societies lay greater emphasis on stability while some others, stress the importance of change. The former ones are often branded as *"traditional and conservative societies"* while the latter ones claim themselves to be *"advanced / forward or progressive societies."*

In no society all its elements can either remain stable permanently or undergo changes in the same manner. While some of its elements struggle to maintain their existence, some others, may plan for changing their very form; further, some new elements may appear in place of old ones. It is quite natural to observe these trends especially when the process of change is actively taking place.

Let us now briefly analyse the extent of continuity and change with regard to the seven broad features of the Hindu society namely: *ascription, hierarchy, ritual purity / pollution, Purusharthas, Ashramas, Rin* and *Karma.*

Continuity and Change in Relation to the Broad Features of Hindu Society

The first three features of the Hindu society namely, ***ascribed status, hierarchy and ritual purity / pollution*** have been under attack time and again. As **S.C. Dube** has stated, *"This aspect of Hindu belief, organisation, and ritual has been mocked and ridiculed by outsiders also who found it abhorable........"*[1] In spite of these attacks, *"the system has shown remarkable resiliency; it yields some ground, but gradually returns almost to the original position. Even in the scientific temper of the contemporary world, the notions of hierarchy and ritual purity still retain some of their strength though they may be manifestly criticised."*

The ***practice of untouchability*** and several forms of gender discrimination were found unacceptable by the Hindu reformers. Gandhiji, in particular, launched massive campaigns against them. Independent Indian Government also passed legislations to abolish the practice of untouchability and to raise the position of women. But social equality in all its forms is not completely assured to them in actual practice.

The other three features of the Hindu society namely, ***Purusharthas, Ashramas*** and ***Rin*** – still remain as respectable ideologies. There are no objective indicators to measure their observance. The social system has no enforcement mechanism to ensure their observance. *"As statements of goals....... they contain nothing objectionable."* [**S.C. Dube** - 120.] What is of great interest is the fact that they, and also the doctrine of Karma, find wide acceptance. These notions seem to be very deeply ingrained in the minds of the people and no alterations for these seem to be required.

Varna system, as a form of social stratification has almost given place for the *caste* or *jati system.* After independence, *Jati* was gradually politicalised, and is believed to play an increasingly important role in elections. *Jati* has been exploited for political ends by national as well as regional political parties. Political parties always keep in their mind *"caste equations"* to achieve their political goals.

The observance of ***ritual purity and pollution*** in inter-caste relations is less rigorous, atleast in public, institutions and public transport, and in urban areas. *Jajmani relations have almost disappeared* in the rural areas. Though caste remains a strong and functional unit of social structure *caste panchayats have declined* giving place to law courts.

The ***institution of family*** is under heavy stress and bonds of kinship are no longer as strong as they used to be. What is often described as the *"joint family"* is now confined to some castes in villages and towns. Even among them, joint families beyond three or more generations are very rarely found. *Families are moving towards nuclearisation.* Modern education, new occupations, geographic mobility, impact of the mass media, and such other factors have contributed to the change in the network of family and kinship relations. Greater freedom of choice in marriage also makes living in large joint-households non-viable.

Factors Contributing to Continuity and Change

It is clear from the above description that both continuity and change co-exist in the Indian society. There are a number of factors which are responsible for continuity and change. According to **Prof. Ram Ahuja,** of the various factors which have enabled the Indian society to maintain both continuity and change, the most important ones are the following :

- Political independence and introduction of democratic values,
- Influence of industrialisation,
- Impact of urbanisation,
- Increase in education, especially at higher levels,
- Influence of legislative measures,
- Incessant social changes taking place in the caste system,
- Social movements and social awareness [relating to feminism, anti-casteism, etc.] created by them, and
- Impact of recent economic reforms such as liberalisation, globalisation, etc.

Trends Towards Modernity and Tradition

Present day Indian society is experiencing strong contrary pulls towards - modernity and tradition. On the one hand, the country has adopted and promoted the ideology of democracy, egalitarianism, secularism and social justice; on the other, primordial loyalties continue to prevail, exploitative structures have never been seriously challenged, the sentimental longing for tradition is tapped for poltical gains. Further, religious revivalism and, later fundamentalism have not been dealt with sternly. On the emotional and intellectual level, the inequality and inhumanity found in the Varna and Jati framework have been condemned, but no serious attempt is made to do away with it.

As **S.C. Dube** has pointed out, *"The politicalization of Varna and Jati has led to diverse forms of atrocities on the "lower" Jatis, who are being prevented from using their electoral strength to improve their lot. In some areas the hold of Jati has weakened, but in others it has fortified and strengthened itself. India's society, economy and polity have paid only lip service to the cause of the "degraded", the weak, the vulnerable, but they have not been able to find any viable solution to their problems. The clearly discernible results are resentment and resistance, both very understandable. Tradition has its uses, but regard for it cannot be made an alibi for the perpetuation of exploitation, inequality and injustice. There has been some change in the operation of Varna and Jati but it has been too slow and too little........"*[1]

1 **S.C. Dube** *"Indian Society."* Page - 119.

Conclusion

In conclusion, it can be said that the forces of change that are operating in the Indian society, have not only the *functional aspect* but also the *dysfunctional aspect.* People are more receptive to the changes that are taking place. The nation has made recognisable progress in certain fields such as self-reliance in food production, advancement in science, technology, industry, computer software, information technology, space research, nuclear power, and so on. It is making serious studies in the fields such as environment pollution, ecological balance, discovery of alternative source of power, and so on.

As it is already made clear, that all the changes taking place in the contemporary Indian society are not invariably functionally beneficial. Views expressed by **S.C. Dube** [Page - 123] in this regard are worth mentioning here:

"An old society undergoing massive changes is bound to encounter obstacles and setbacks........ Contemporary Indian society is undergoing a trauma of change and is confronting a series of dilemmas and paradoxes. They hurt, but they are unavoidable. It is necessary for the society to........... find solutions to the problems of economic disparities and injustice, launch a programme of enlarging mass consciousness, ... and initiate process of participatory decision-making. While some aspects of tradition will survive because of their vitality and usefulness, many of the scaly prejudices of the past will have to be eradicated and structures of exploitation and tyranny demolished. The road ahead is long, the process may be painful, but each one of us - every citizen of India - has a stake in the future."

1 **S.C. Dube** *"Indian Society."* Page : 50 - 51.

Chapter 3

Pioneers of Indian Sociology

G.S. Ghurye - Radhakamal Mukherji - D.P. Mukherji - D.N. Majumdar - K.M. Kapadia - M.N. Srinivas - S.C. Dube - M.S.A. Rao - Iravathi Karve - A.R. Desai.

Sociology as an independent social science though was born in the West in the 19th century, it emerged in a short span of time as one of the most popular disciplines today even in the East. The French, British and the American sociologists in particular, have contributed a great deal to the development of sociology on a scientific basis. Sociology had to face the challenges from other social sciences which were not ready to recognise it as one among them. Early sociologists very courageously and appropriately responded to such challenges. Sociology which imbibed the scientific perspective and accepted positivism as its article of faith forged ahead, and as a result, sociological studies and researches claimed credibility and respectability both in the academic and administrative circles.

Both sociology and social anthropology were brought to India from outside, particularly from Britain. British scholars who lived in India and later Indian scholars who were trained in Britain and the U.S.A., played a major role in the development of these two disciplines in India. Sociology came to be recognised as an independent discipline of academic study in India when a separate department of sociology and civics was started under the guidance of **Patrick Geddes** in the Bombay University in 1919. More or less during the same time, **A.R. Wadia** took initiative to introduce sociology at B.A. level at Mysore University in Karnataka. In course of time, sociology started getting warm reception in other universities also.

The Western and the Indian scholars had played an important role in the development of sociology in India. Scholars from both the sides produced literatures to the enrichment of sociological knowledge. Western scholars like – Verrier Elvin, Herbert Risley, Hutton, Nesfield, B.S. Cohn, Kathleen Gough, Sir Henry Maine, David Pocock, Charles Metcalf, Mackim Marrior – and others did contribute much to the field of sociology especially during its initial stages of development in India.

Indian scholars, though some of them often pursued anthropological, historical, indological and other approaches, contributed in no small measure for the enrichment of sociology as an academic discipline in India. Mention must necessarily be made of the intellectual giants such as – Radhakamal Mukherji, G.S. Ghurye, B.N. Seal, D.P. Mukherji, B.K. Sarkar, D.N. Majumdar, K.P. Chattopadhyaya, M.N. Srinivas, Iravathi Karve, K.M. Kapadia, A.R. Desai, S.C. Dube, M.S.A. Rao, who did a lot to provide a good foundation for the study of sociology in the Indian universities. This chapter gives profiles of a few eminent sociologists, who can be reasonably called *"the pioneers of Indian sociology."*

G.S. Ghurye [1893 - 1984]

Dr. G.S. Ghurye's name has assumed importance for he was one of the *founding fathers of Indian Sociology.* Though Prof. Patrick Geddes started the department of Sociology at the Bombay University, it was Dr. Ghurye who built and developed it on a firm foundation. He earned a permanent name as a classical sociologist of India, and also of the East, by his scholarly contributions and profound depth of sociological knowledge.

Early Life and Education

Prof. Govinda Sadashiva Ghurye was born into a Saraswat Brahmin family in Malvan, in 1893. He completed his high school and college education in Bombay, where he studied English and Sanskrit. He was throughout a brilliant student and he won the coveted Chancellor's Gold medal as the best student at M.A. Examination in 1918. After reading Ghurye's unpublished essay on *"Bombay as an Urban Centre"*, **Patrick Geddes,** who had started the department of Sociology at the Bombay University, recommended him for a foreign scholarship and Ghurye went to London. Ghurye received his sociological training in Cambridge from where he earned his Ph.D. under the guidance of **Prof. W.H.R. Rivers.** For a short time, after the untimely death of Rivers in June 1922, Ghurye was put under the guidance of Prof. A.C. Haddon, a famous Anthropologist and senior to W.H.R. Rivers.

Professional Career of Ghurye

In 1924, the University of Bombay, on whose scholarship Ghurye had gone to England, appointed him as Reader and Head of the Department of Sociology. He continued in that position, later as Professor till 1959 when he formally retired. But his association with the University continued as he was made the first professor emeritus and in this capacity he guided advanced research students till 1974. Thus, besides his own research achievements, he had a clear half a century's record as a post-graduate teacher.

Record Performance As A Scholarly Teacher

Ghurye's record as a teacher, research guide and author is unique. He guided 80 theses; 16 of these were submitted for Ph.D. after he became Emeritus Professor. During the same period of post-retirement he had 16 books published out of 31 works that were published during his life time. He wrote over 30 papers and spent considerable time in up-dating several of his books which were published in revised editions. Even his post-retirement achievements made an impressive and noteworthy record. There was a time when many sociology faculties in India had at least one of his students propagating his tradition. Ghurye attracted students from many parts of India.

An Architect of a Generation of Sociologists and Scholars

While his eminence grew to towering proportions all these years, Ghurye produced a generation of sociologists some of whom are household names in the profession now. In the long list of scholarly students which he produced mention must essentially be made of the following – M.N. Srinivas [Delhi and Bangalore], I.P. Desai [Baroda and Surat], K.M. Kapadia, A.R. Desai, Dhirendra Narain [Bombay], M.S.A. Rao [Delhi], Dr. Jaloo and K.C. Panchanandikar [Baroda], Y.B. Damle, A.C. Bopegamage [Pune], M.G. Kulkarni [Aurangabad], Vilas Sangave, V.D. Rao [Kolhapur], K.N. Venkatrayappa, C. Rajagopalan [Bangalore], G.S. Nepali [Varanasi, Khatmandu].

Some of the scholarly students whom Ghurye produced did marvellous work in the non-university spheres. Here is a list of such brilliant students. G.L. Mehta [former Ambassador], U.T. Thakur [IAS], M.N. Desai [Municipal Commissioner of Bombay, Retd.], M. Mohsin [Minister, Nepal], U.K. Jadhav [Inspector General, Prisons, Retd.], Zulie Nakhoda [Social Activist], Mabel Fonseca [Family Counsellor], K.B. Singh [Deputy Census Commissioner, Manipur], S.M. Haider and G.M. Mekhri [both in Pakistan], Devangana Desai [Archaeological Historian].

A Man of Catholic Outlook and Wide Interests

Ghurye was catholic in his outlook and systematic in his methods. In his teaching and research, he refused to make a distinction between social anthropology and sociology. A few of his students, K.M. Kapadia, Iravathi Karve and S.V. Karandikar carried his approach and material in the sacred texts and other literature in Sanskrit. He believed that India needed exploratory studies and solid data base to build up an anthropo-sociological super structure. He did field work himself in his early days in Gujarat and Sind but gave it up due mainly to ill health. He had the obsession for piling up facts from the field and other sources even to prove a small point.

Ghurye founded the ***"Indian Sociological Society"*** in 1952 and was the first editor of its journal ***"Sociological Bulletin."***

Ghurye's Approach Towards Sociological Studies

The anthropology he learnt from Rivers and Sociology from L.T. Hobhouse at Cambridge, a firm grounding in Sanskrit and a compelling sense of history which he developed from his Indian training, all these served to mould Ghurye's Sociology which he perpetuated through 35 years of post-graduate teaching. Ghurye was a prolific writer and the 25 books which he produced cover a fascinating range of topics from sociology of costume to the sociology of conflict. His books reveal a harmonious combination of sociological, indological and anthropological aspects. One wonders what would have been the course of sociology in India if Ghurye had not been trained in anthropology and Sanskrit at the same time. He put a bold hypen between Indology and Sociology, and stood against any segregation between social anthropology and sociology. Ghurye wrote : *"In India with its huge number of groups in all stages of culture there is no room for distinguishing and clearly separating social anthropology from sociology."*

A Glance of Ghurye's Books

In the task of writing books, articles and publishing them, Ghurye virtually played the captain's innings. He wrote a series of books both on sociological and non-sociological themes. Here is a glimpse of his works.

***Caste and Race in India* [1932] :** In Cambridge, caste was one of the four topics of Ghurye's doctoral research, and upon his return he was able to mould it into a comprehensive book, his first one *"Caste and Race in India"* [1932], which has now become a sociological classic. In this book he deals with the problem of caste from a deep historical perspective, delves into the Sanskrit classics and settles down to talk about the present-day complexities of the problem. Apart from shedding light on the origins of the caste system, the book brings out how caste-like features existed outside India - in Egypt, West Asia, China, Japan, Rome, Tribal Europe, etc. In the latest edition of *Caste and Race in India* [1969] he added such vital topics as the evolution of sub-castes, sub-caste and kin, caste and politics, and the then position of the scheduled castes. His concluding observations in this new edition are highly probe-worthy. He wonders if India is not moving towards a pluralistic society by *"sectional selfish appropriations and raucous demands."* The special privileges enjoyed by the backward sections have created *"vested interests in backwardness itself."* Ghurye warns us against this course of events as also the steady upsurgence of caste-patriotism at all levels of hierarchy.

The Aborigines - So Called - And Their Future **[1943] :** Closely linked with Ghurye's study of caste is his well-known analysis of the scheduled tribe problem. Though he was at the height of his intellectual powers, he did not publish any of his work for ten years. Then, he published in 1943 *"The Aborigines - 'So Called' - And Their Future"* – to refute **Verrier Elwin's** thesis of isolation of tribal groups and argued in favour of their assimilation into the larger community. In subsequent editions of the book *"The Scheduled Tribes"* [1963] he was critical of independent India's Government policies which sowed the seeds of disintegration by its internally contradicting steps of laying down the integrationist approach in the Constitution and on the other hand, promoting fission by giving importance to the idea of Scheduled Areas [**Ex.** Hill States in the NEFA region].

The Mahadev Kolis **[1957] :** Some years later, Ghurye published a study titled *"The Mahadev Kolis"* [1957], based on field data from three districts of Maharashtra. This was his first major attempt to deal with a problem at the micro-level. One can easily find the stamp of his approach in other studies under his guidance - The study of Coorgs by M.N. Srinivas was sub-titled *'a socio-ethnic study'*, while G.S. Nepali's study of Newar has the sub-title [suggested by Ghurye] *'an ethno-sociological study'*. One of Ghurye's main concerns through such studies was to find out the manner in which traditional institutions were changing.

Studies in Political Sociology

Social Tensions in India **[1968] :** In this book Ghurye examines in a historical context, the deeply divisive role of culture, language and religion in India. Social tensions, whether communal or racial engaged his concern and that led to several studies in political sociology. *Social Tensions in India* [1968] dealt with problems of national integration and Ghurye came to a pessimistic view of what was happening in India in the few decades after independence. This treatise has a fund of background material, such as a study of the articles of the Indian Constitution, an analysis of Hindu-Muslim relations during the last 500 years and a delineation of other kinds of tensions - linguistic, ethnic and regional. *"The Times Literary Supplement"* recommended this book as *"required background reading for all western students of India as she is today, as it holds the key to much that would otherwise perplex and baffle them."*[1]

Whither India **? [1974] :** Concerned about the bleak prospect of national solidarity, Ghurye expresses his dissatisfaction with the gradual amoral manipulative drift in Indian politics in his book *"Whither India ?"* [1974]. In this book Ghurye discussed the waves of political fragmentation, "Dravidian alienation" and "Muslim particularism."

India Recreates Democracy [1978] written by Ghurye on the period of Emergency also documented how the fourth requirement of culture - *free pursuit of knowledge and expression* - was being systematically scuttled by the Government.

Burning Caldron of North East India is the last contribution of Ghurye in political sociology. In fact, in the book he celebrates the restoration of democracy to India in 1977. These works show Ghurye's abiding concern with the problems of his society.

Other Works of G.S. Ghurye

Civilisation and culture, be it Indian, Egyptian or Western, absorbed him. Ghurye probed into them in his books ***Culture and Society*** [1947] and ***Occidental Civilisation*** [1949]. During the forties, more general themes and a cosmopolitan approach to sociology were exhibited in Ghurye's

---

1 Article on *"G.S. Ghurye"* issued by Sadananda Bhatkal for *"Dr. G.S. Ghurye Birth Centenary Celebration Committee"*, Department of Sociology, University of Bombay in 1993.

broader works on culture. In *"Culture and Society"* he dealt with a universal theme – *what makes a culture great* ? – In the subsequent work, *"Occidental Civilisation"*, he focussed on the reasons for peaks and clusters of creative energy. It was the evolution of 'ideas' and their expressions that engaged his attention : be it literature, painting, or costume. Thus was born his brilliant study of ***Indian Costume*** [1951] and ***Rajput Architecture*** [1948]. The former has become a valuable source book. Ghurye wrote it more than anything else to establish that there is a *Sociology of Costume* just as there is a psychology of costume. It is commented that in this book, Ghurye tried to make a historical survey to arrive at a position on the question of national dress; that is, a helpless undertaking for a country as vast and varied as India. This was again an effort aimed at finding homogeneity in extreme heterogeneity.

Another work of his that attracted attention was ***Bharat Natya and Its Costume*** [1958]. *Rajput Architecture* aimed at establishing the existence of a Rajput school of architecture from the 7th to 17th century as a distinct School.

***After Century And A Quarter* [1966] :** The growth of cities and metropolitan culture and their impact on remote regions was another sphere of Ghurye's interest. *After Century and a Quarter* [1966] is a study of Lonikund which initiated us into the growth and traditional organisation of village settlements, as available from etymological, inscriptional and textual sources.

Cities and Civilisation [1962] has a wealth of data on cities and their natural history in 14 leading countries from 1881 to 1961. In this book he also discusses the social history of Bombay, a theme which he later summarised in his last brochure *To Make Bombay Fit to Live in* [1983]. Another study ***Anatomy of a Rururban Community*** [1963] examines not only changes in the patterns in daily life but also socio-religious life in its structural aspects. Ghurye's life-long intellectual fascination with urbanism found detailed expression in these works. These works also show his intimate knowledge of Western culture.

Studies in Sociology of Religion

The "Sociology of Religion" was another of his major intellectual concerns. His book ***"Indian Sadhus"*** [1953] traced the role of ascetic organisation. The book deals with Hindu asceticism from a historical and functional perspective. ***Gods and Men*** [1961] is a sociological search for the meaning of cults and personality development of several gods and goddesses in the Hindu pantheon, based mainly on temple inscriptions, iconography and literature as sources. It is a study of the interaction between an "idolatrous" society and an "idolatrous" religion, both of which had one common evolution.

In his ***Religious Consciousness*** [1965] another major contribution, Ghurye addressed himself to the basic question : *What are the foundations of Culture* ? To him, they were : *religious consciousness, conscience, justice, free pursuit of knowledge and expression, and toleration.* In the above book, he made a searching analysis of religious consciousness in three of the oldest civilisations - Mesopotamian, Egyptian and the Hindu– their myths, speculations, cosmology, life after death, god-head, structural and architectural peculiarities of their shrines, their concept of soul and so on.

Shakespeare on Conscience and Justice [1965] gave Ghurye an opportunity to deal with the other two foundations of culture through a sociological analysis of the Western literature.

The above book, as well as ***The Legacy of the Ramayana,*** though basically studies in culture, are contributions to the literature on *sociology of Literature* as well.

***Indian Acculturation* [1977] :** Social history and social thought are the fields to which most of Ghurye's writings have notably contributed. *Indian Acculturation* is a lucid exposition of various events, anecdotes and incidents connected with Agastya and Skanda [Subramanya] to evaluate and tabulate the influence of the north on the south [India]. In his last years, he made a focussed attempt in social history taking Vedic India as his sphere.

"The Vidyas"* and *"Vedic India"* :** He had earlier written ***Vidyas [1957] where he outlined the branches of knowledge as conceived by the Hindu savants from the Vedic period. In ***Vedic India*** [1979], he gave a detailed description of the culture and people of the Vedic age, roughly counted between 2500 and 500 B.C.

One of the earlier books written by Ghurye, namely, ***"Social Process"*** [1938] attracted the attention of 'Nature'. In an abstract of the book, he says *"Scientifically, proper planning of good life must rest on the understanding of life; and the psychological study of the individual and society should precede the study of man as a political and moral being."*

Other published works of Ghurye bear testimony to the broad-based concern of this scholar to the social process. In ***Family and Kin in Indo-European Culture*** [1954], Ghurye puts forward the view that primary emphasis be laid on *'beliefs and ideas'* over economic factors as the determinants of kinship structure. This book seems to be an authoritative study of Kinship.

Sexual Behaviour of the American Female [1956] reconstructs tables from Kinsey's famous report. Actually Ghurye's research concern with this aspect of life dates back to 1938 when he was among the prime movers of the second All India Population Conference and the first *"Marriage Hygeine Conference."* He edited a volume called *"Indian Population Problems."* Two papers which he read at the conference dealt with *"birth control"* and *"sex habits of middle class people of Bombay"* based on field data. ***Race Relations in Negro Africa*** [1952] gives crucial facts for a proper understanding of movements like the *Mau Mau.*

Anthropo-Sociological Papers [1963] and *Two Brahmanical Institutions Gotra and Charana* [1973] complete the enormous volume of his literary output.

In ***"Gotra and Charana - Two Brahmanical Institutions"***, Ghurye asserts that the classification of Brahmin families into 'Gotras' and kin-units is rooted in the Vedic Aryans' knowledge of astronomy and cosmography which they gained in their new home in India.

Ghurye's Papers and Articles on Variety of Topics

Ghurye was an untiring writer. He wrote several articles and papers which were published from time to time. His papers were many and varied, covering such subjects as dual organisation in India, cross-cousin marriage, age at marriage and widowhood, Egyptian affinities of Indian funerary practices, disposal of the human placenta, salary and working conditions of clerks, megalith remains in India, sex habits of the Bombay middle class, birth control in Bombay, untouchability, explorations in pre and proto historic Sindh culture, and so on. Many are curious as to why Ghurye wrote the ***"Sexual Behaviour of the American Female"*** [1956], reconstructing tables from Kinsey's famous report, reinterpreting them, and presenting them in the framework of a critical survey of research on sex behaviour in the U.S. from 1920 to 1953. Going through this work one is struck by his knowledge of classical and modern sources on the subject. *"Very sound and just"* was how the reviewer of the *Times of India* reacted to Ghurye's analysis of Kinsey's data.

At the request of several friends Ghurye wrote ***I and Other Explorations*** [1973], an autobiographical memoir. But in this book too he could not resist the temptation of including some of his important papers in anthropology and sociology.

Two Felicitation Volumes in Honour of Ghurye

During his life-time Ghurye received two felicitation volumes. **The first one** on his 60th birthday, an eloquent tribute from Ghurye generation of thinkers with writings by stalwarts like Pitirim Sorokin, W.F. Ogburn, D.P. Mukerji, D.N. Majumdar and A.S. Altekar.

The second volume, brought out to honour Ghurye on his 80th birthday, namely, ***Aspects of Changing India*** has many contributions from Europeans who had been studying India. In both the volumes an attempt was made to analyse Ghurye's sociology by the respective editors, namely, Dr. K.M. Kapadia and Dr. S. Devadas Pillai. In 1980, a student of the Calcutta University wrote a doctoral thesis on Ghurye. In the advanced curricula on social thought, Ghurye now figures in several universities. A prize instituted by the University of Bombay some time back - Ghurye Prize for the best published work on Sociology - has so far been received by M.N. Srinivas, Veena Das, M.S.A. Rao and T.K. Oommen.

Conclusive Remarks

One abiding lesson Ghurye learnt at Cambridge, and sought to transmit to his students, was *respect for facts.* When he began his career, very little work had been done in Sociology in India, and it was salutary to insist on facts. "Ghurye's commitment to facts has both a positive and a negative side. ***Positively,*** it has given him and his students a firm empirical base, curbing the speculative tendencies that are especially tempting in the absence of concrete information. **Dr. M.N. Srinivas** rightly compliments Ghurye for conducting a one-man ethnographic survey of India from his chair in Bombay. ***Negatively,*** Ghurye's prolonged neglect of all theoretical positions, however tentative, has deprived his writings of a powerful thrust. It is puzzling that a mind so vital and aware should have remained indifferent to the fierce controversies in the West. Was this indifference a mechanism to protect himself from an interminable and seemingly profitless exercise ? If so, his accomplishments may attest to the value of his strategy."

Professor David G. Mandelbaum wrote of Dr. Ghurye **:** *"Much of his work has been on the frontiers of our knowledge. He has opened avenues of research, for better understanding, founded and advanced institutions for Sociology in India. In his example and accomplishment, he has enhanced his subject and the appreciation of its value as a necessary way of viewing men and mankind."*

Dr. Ghurye was truly the father of systematic study of Sociology in India. There is a Ghurye tradition which persists through the current generation of Sociologists in this country.

A List of the Works of G.S. Ghurye

1. 1932 : Caste and Race in India - later published as Class, Caste and Occupation, (1969).
2. 1938 : The Social Process.
3. 1943 : The Scheduled Tribes (1963) - First edition titled The Aborigines.
4. 1947 : Culture and Society.
5. 1948 : Rajput Architecture.
6. 1949 : Occidental Civilization.
7. 1951 : Indian Costumes (2nd ed. 1966).
8. 1953 : Race and Relations in Negro Africa.
9. 1953 : Indian Sadhus (2nd ed. 1964).

10. 1953 : Cities of India - Sociological Bulletin - 2, No.1; 47-80.
11. 1954 : Sexual Behaviour of the American Female, Sociological Bulletin - 3, No.2; 158-183.
12. 1955 : Family and Kin in Indo-European Culture (2nd ed. 1962).
13. 1957 : Vidyas, A Homage to Comte and A Contribution to the Sociology of Knowledge.
14. 1958 : Bharata Natya and its Costume.
15. 1960 : After a Century and a Quarter-Lonikund Then and Now.
16. 1961 : Gods and Men.
17. 1962 : Cities and Civilization.
18. 1963 : Anatomy of a Rururban Community.
19. 1963 : Anthropo-Sociological Papers.
20. 1965 : Religious Consciousness.
21. 1965 : Shakespeare on Conscience and Justice.
22. --- : The Legacy of the Ramayana.
23. 1968 : Social Tensions in India.
24. 1971 : Two Brahmanical Institutions - Gotra and Charana.
25. 1972 : I and Other Explorations.
26. 1973 : Whither India ?
27. 1977 : India Acculturation.
28. 1979 : Vedic India.
29. ---- : India Recreates Democracy.
30. ---- : Burning Caldron of North East India.

Radha Kamal Mukherji [1889 to 1968]

Radha Kamal Mukherji can be regarded as the philosopher of Indian sociology. He was one among those who laid the foundations of Indian sociology. We find in his views a harmonious combination of the Eastern and the Western thoughts. Mukherji earned a name in the West particularly for his theory of social values.

Early Life and Education

Radha Kamal Mukherji was born in a big Brahmin family on 7th Dec. 1889 at Berhampur, a small town in Murshidabad district [West Bengal]. His father was an advocate, and he grew to manhood in a house filled with books from both the East and the West. He was well grounded in Indian social philosophy. He was educated in the Presidency College, Calcutta. He was awarded the Premchand Raychand Scholarship in 1915, and Ph.D. in 1920 from Calcutta University.

R.K. Mukherji studied history with deep interest. But he gave it up for economics and sociology immediately occupied his mind. To quote his own words *"The face-to-face contact with misery, squalor, and degradation in the slums of Calcutta decided my future interests in economics and sociology."*[1] As early as in 1906, he organised and maintained continuous contact with social welfare work of various kinds, including rural credit societies and other types of village co-operatives.

---

1 **R.N. Saxena** in his obituary article on Radha Kamal Mukherji published in *"Sociological Bulletin"* Vol.XVII No.2 Sept. 1968. Page - iii.

He obtained practical experience in the adult evening schools which he started in 1906 and maintained a lifelong participation in them.

R.K. Mukherji came under the influence of Indian philosophy and particularly that of mysticism. His acquaintance with Indian philosophy helped him to add a new dimension to sociological thinking. As **W.E. Hocking** in the Felicitation Volume presented to Dr. Mukherji [*The Frontiers of Social Science,* Macmilan, 1956] points out, Mukherji added *"........ a three-fold objectivity : that of scholars scientifically trained, that of the reader widely familiar with western literature on his subject, and that of the sociologist concerned with the bearing of religion upon the health of human institutions."*[1]

Mukherji Under the Influence of Vinay Kumar Sarkar

R.K. Mukherji, even while doing his post graduation, came under the influence of the famous sociologist of Bengal, **Vinay Kumar Sarkar.** *"Mukherji pays tribute to the influence on his thinking of Prof. Vinay Kumar Sarkar "a man of great sacrifice and idealism" interested in social education and in the rehabilitation of rural village life. This contact was made more real by a visit to south India...... where Mukherji's concept of regionalism and social ecology began to take shape."*[2]

Mukherji's Professional Career

R.K. Mukherji was appointed as lecturer in Economics in the Krishnanath College, Berhampur in 1910 where he had been educated. He worked there for five years as a lecturer and spent his days in a busy manner. He also published a book entitled *"The Foundation of Indian Economics"* during that period. He was also working as the Editor of the Bengali monthly, *"Upasana".* He was arrested in 1915 and the local British administration intended to brand him as a terrorist. But his lawyer-brother was able to get him released soon. He was then sent to Punjab to work as a lecturer in Lahore College. In 1917 he returned to Calcutta University where he worked for five years during which tenure he insisted that researches in anthropology, sociology and economics should be undertaken together.

Mukherji joined the Lucknow University in 1921 as the Professor and head of the department of Economics and Sociology. He taught these subjects for 30 years [from 1921 to 1952]. He also became the Vice Chancellor of Lucknow University [1955-57] and had the opportunity of serving as the Director of *J.K. Institute of Sociology and Human Relations,* an institution associated with Lucknow university.

Influence of Three Scholars on Intellectual Thoughts of Mukherji

R.K. Mukherji's thoughts were highly influenced by three intellectual giants. **1. Prof. Brajendranath Seal** was always giving encouragement and guidance in all the major ventures of Mukherji. **2. Patrick Geddes** was motivating Mukherji to undertake studies in topics such as environmental studies, regional studies and demographic studies. **3. Narendranath Sen Gupta** was the one who instilled in the mind of Mukherji interest in social psychology. In fact, Mukherji wrote a book entitled *"Introduction to Social Psychology : Mind in Society"* [1928] with the help of Sen Gupta.

---

1 **W.E. Hocking** as quoted by **Emory S. Bogardus** in *"The Development of Social Thought"* [1969]. Page - 632.

2 **Emory S.** Page - 632.

Influence of Western Thinkers

R.K. Mukherji's thoughts also came under the influence of Western intellectuals and scholars. For example, **Robert E. Park,** who visited Mukherji in India brought home an emphasis on *"Community Studies"*. **E.A. Ross** was another visitor who was impressed by Mukherji's *"studies of regionalism."* R.K. Mukherji also had the opportunity of visiting a number of American Universities and was greatly profited by his contacts with American scholars like **Park, Ross, Ward, Giddings** and others. Mukherji had been a careful student of the writings of Ward and Giddings, Comte, Spencer, Bagehot, Hobhouse, Ricardo, Mill, Marshal, and others. *"Thus, it is seen that Mukherji's thinking represents an unusual combination of Eastern and Western thought. Perhaps, no other sociologist has been so fortunate in breadth of his mental contacts and in his approach to the interpretation of human values."*[1]

Wide Recognition to Mukherji's Talents

Mukherji's talents and services were widely recognised. As already mentioned, he was made the Vice Chancellor of the Lucknow University [1955-57]. He served as the Economic Advisor of the Gwalior State Government from 1945-47. He visited the Universities of Cambridge, Oxford, Cologne, Vienna, Harward, Columbia, Chicago, Michigan and Wisconsin for delivering lectures in Economics and Sociology in 1937, 1946 and 1948. He was nominated Chairman, Economics and Statistics Commission of the F.A.O. at Copenhagen in 1946, as a member of Indian delegation. He was also a member of the Technical Committee of the ILO for recommending names of countries for seats on its governing body. He also served as a member of various committees appointed by the Govt. of U.P. and the Union Government.

Major Trends of Mukherji's Thoughts

Mukherji had his own views about social sciences. He used to stress upon the interrelationship between different social sciences such as sociology, economics, political sciences, psychology and anthropology. *"In regional research, Mukherji found the social sciences to have a basic relation in common. In studies of regions, "the walls which keep the different social sciences in watertight compartments crumble down." Mukherji, after coming to the faculty of the University of Lucknow in 1921, introduced an integral approach in economics, sociology, and anthropology."*[2]

Special Interest in Social Ecology : Mukherji was having a special interest in social ecology. In his studies of regions, Mukherji found a regional balancing of the different forces at work. One study of this regional balance he called social ecology, which he defined as *"a synoptic study of the balance of plant, animal and human communities, which are systems of correlated working parts in the organisation of the region."* Social ecology considers human communities as an integral part of the organisation of all life – plant, animal, and human – in a region.

Concern for Weaker Sections : Mukherji had a great concern for the weaker sections of the society. He was very much moved when he came to know about the miseries and the sufferings of the famine-afflicted people of Calcutta and Tamil Nadu. Labourers get very badly affected due to urbanisation. Hence, according to him, special efforts and plans must be made in order to reform their life and promote their welfare. He insisted upon providing at least the minimum facilities of human life for the weaker sections whether they are found in the rural or urban sectors.

Theory of Social Values : Mukherji is more known for his theory of social values. *"Mukherji's theory of social values is based to a degree on his thinking regarding the regionalism and ecology.........."* According to him, values have a tremendous influence on the behaviour patterns

1 **Emory S. Bogardus.** "*The Development of Social Thought*" Page - 633.
2 *ibid* Page - 634.

of the people. Even the food habits, dress habits, greeting styles, habits, and such other small aspects are also influenced and guided by the values. Influence of values is not just limited to the field of religion and ethics. It is extended to the fields such as economics, sociology, political science, law, etc. They are not the products of the subjective attitude or thinking of the people. On the contrary, they have emerged out of the collective efforts, expectations and ambitions of a people.

General Theory of Society : Mukherji established a *"general theory of society"*. "On the bases of social value systems as created, developed, and changed by persons, Mukherji developed a general theory of society. To attain this theory he calls for a close integration of the social sciences........ Only through the close collaboration of the sciences of life, of the mind, and of society can a general theory of society be soundly based and developed. Society *"is not divisible"* and an understanding of it can be obtained only from studying *"the habits, the values, and symbols of the society as a totality"*." [**Bogardus** : Page - 640.]

Master of Science of Society : "Towards the end of his career, Mukherji was engaged in the task of envisaging a *"master science of society"*, which constituted the main theme of his inaugural Address delivered posthumously, only a week after his sad demise, to the 8th All India Sociological Conference [1968]. In this grand sweep he included the human ecological theory, sociological theory and the theory of values and symbols, with each standing on its own footing."[1]

"Mukherji envisages a master science of society. It includes *"the human ecological theory, the sociological theory, and the theory of values and symbols"* with each borrowing from and lending to the others." Together, they form what may be called a macro-scopic *"general theory of society"* that unites the various social sciences and "fills the gaps between the various islands of theoretical knowledge." It is broader *"than the science of sociology itself"*." [**Bogardus** : Page - 641].

Universality of Mukherji's Social Thought

"Mukherji's social thought has a universal tone. It is both humanly and cosmically universal. It brings the social sciences into one functioning unit of study, research and application. It brings the science of sociology and the philosophy of science together. Moreover, it views all races of peoples as one. It considers each individual and human society as one. It envisages one world community. It makes values supreme in the human universe, and the human universe an aspect of the cosmic purposeful universe, and it calls for a master science of society that will include all social science, philosophy, and religion."[2]

• Major Works of Mukherji

1. The Regional Balance of Man, 1938.
2. Indian Working Class, 1940.
3. The Social Structure of Values, 1953.
4. Philosophy of Social Sciences, 1960.
5. Flowering of Indian Art, 1964.

• Major Articles Written by Mukherjee

1. *"A General Theory of Society"*, in B. Singh, editor. The Frontiers of Social Science (London: Macmillan and Company Ltd. 1956) Page: 21-74.

---

1 **R.N. Saxena** *"Sociological Bulletin"* Vol.XVII, No.2, Sept. 1968. Page - iv.

2 **E.S. Bogardus** in *"The Development of Social Thought."* Page - 644.

2. *"A Theory of Symbols"*, Sociology and Social Research, 39: 145-50.
3. *"The Broken Balance of Man and Region"*, Sociology and Social Research, XVII: 403-8.
4. *"The Concepts of Balance and Organization of Social Ecology"*, Sociology and Social Research, XVI: 503-16.
5. *"The Dynamics of Morals"*, (London: Macmillan and Company Ltd. 1950).
6. *"Faiths and Influences"*, in B. Singh, editor, The Frontiers of Social Science (London: Macmillan and Company Ltd. 1956).
7. *"The Regional Balance of Man"* (Madras: University of Madras, 1938)
8. *"Regional Sociology"*, (New York: Century Company, 1926).
9. *"Social Ecology"*, (New York: Longmans, Green and Company, 1945).
10. *"The Social Structure of Values"*, (London: Macmillan and Co., 1949).
11. *"Sociology and Mysticism"*, Sociology and Social Research, XV: 303-10.
12. *"The Theory and Art of Mysticism"*, (New York: Longmans, Green and Company, 1937).
13. *"Toward a Sociological Theory of Ethics"*, Sociology and Social Research, 34: 431-37.

D. P. Mukerji [1894 - 1962]

Dhurjati Prasad Mukerji was one of the founding fathers of sociology in India. He was a contemporary of Benoy Kumar Sarkar [1887-1949], Radhakamal Mukerjee [1889-1968], G.S. Ghurye [1893-1983] and K.P. Chattopadhyaya [1897-1963]. He had made an attempt to analyse Indian history from the dialectical perspective of Karl Marx. He was one among those who laid the foundations of Indian sociology on a firm footing.

Early Life and Education

Dhurjati Prasad Mukerji was popularly known in the academic circle as ***D.P.*** only. He was born on 5th October 1894 in a middle class Bengali family that had comparatively a long tradition of intellectual achievements. D.P. was in close touch with the views and thoughts of the famous Bengali writers and poets such as Bankimchandra Chaterji, Ravindranath Tagore, Sharathchandra Chaterji, and others. He also came under the influence of these intellectual giants.

D.P. obtained his degree in Political Science and Economics. In fact, he was more interested in Science but finally he had to be contented with the studies in Economics, History and Political Science. He took M.A.s in Economics and History from the Calcutta University. Though he wanted to proceed to England for further studies, the outbreak of the First World War barred him from taking this opportunity.

D.P. began his teaching career at Bangabasi College, Calcutta. He very soon acquired a reputation as a brilliant young man of broad intellectual interests, artistic tastes, and social charm. Though sociology was very often mistaken during those days for social reform or socialism, D.P. took the courage of developing his career as a sociologist.

Teaching Career at Lucknow

D.P. joined the newly founded Lucknow University as a lecturer in Economics and Sociology in the year 1922. When once he joined the University on an invitation from **Radhakamal Mukerji,** the first Professor in the department, he decided to stay over there till the end of his career. In fact, he stayed there for 32 years. Both of these intellectuals *"........... shared a broad, humanistic conception of the study and teaching of Economics alongside Sociology from a comparative perspective."*[1] Within six years of D.P.'s entry into the University another promising Calcutta University Graduate and a Post-Graduate in Anthropology, **D.N. Majumdar** joined him in the Department as his colleague. All these three contributed their best to *"strengthen the comparative content of the courses."*

Intellectual Differences Between the Mukerjees

Though Radhakamal Mukerji and D.P. Mukerji worked together in the same Department of the Lucknow University, they had very little in common as intellectuals apart from the broad prospective which is already mentioned. In fact, the intellectual differences between the two widened as time passed. *"Radhakamal Mukerji moved from "Comparative Economics" to explore what he called its 'borderlands', notably, - Sociology, Cultural Anthropology, Demography, Ecology and Psychology. Eventually, he got interested in art, mysticism, religion and symbolism. The Bengal Vaishnava heritage was a major influence in his life. D.P. too was an explorer, but what he explored was the possibility of a synthesis between the Brahmanical tradition of intellectual inquiry, Western liberal humanism, and dialectical materialism. At a lower level, he searched for the unity of knowledge amidst the fragments of the social science."* [**T.N. Madan.** Page - 134.]

Two Misconceptions About the Intellectual Commitments of D.P.

As T.N. Madan has pointed out that there are two misconceptions about D.P. and his intellectual strands. *Firstly,* he was branded as a Marxist who was never able to master the theory and method of Marxism. *Secondly,* he has been described as basically a Hindu intellectual, a conservative who was only superficially modern.

D.P. – *Was He A Marxist Without A Proper Understanding of Marxism* ? : Commenting on these two misconceptions about D.P., Madan has said that D.P. had studied Marx and Hegel and their thoughts quite early in his life, but at no stage was he an uncritical Marxist. D.P. himself was jocularly remarking that he could be better described as *"Marxologist." "His deepest interest was in the Marxian method rather than in dogmas. In a short paper entitled "A Word to Indian Marxists", included in his "Views and Counterviews" [1946 b]: 166], he had warned that the "unhistorically minded" young Marxist ran the risk of ending up as a "fascist" and Marxism itself could "lose its effectiveness in a maze of slogans"."*[2] Nevertheless, it would not be misleading to say that D.P. did indeed embrace Marxism in various ways. But according to T.N. Madan, *"It was a close but uncomfortable embrace."*

D.P. – *Was He A Conservative Hindu Intellectual* ? : D.P. was a Brahmin by birth, but he was not apologetic about it. He retained a lifelong interest in classical Indian thought, which he considered essentially dynamic. He was very much impressed by the famous aphorism of *Aitareya Brahmana* which reads as *Charaiveti, Charaiveti* [Forward, Forward]. He rejected Brahmanical religious belief and ritual quite early in life. At the same time, D.P. rejected what he considered as Western fiction, namely, that *the Indian mind was "preoccupied" by religion.* However, the Charvaka Philosophy of Hinduism, was quite fascinating for him. Madan writes : *"It could be that D.P. failed to squarely face the difficulties that his triple loyalty produced; his Brahmanical intellectualism,*

---

1 **T.N. Madan** in an article entitled *"D.P. Mukerji [1894-1961] - A Centenary Tribute"* published in *"Sociological Bulletin."* 43 (2), Sept. 1994. Page - 134.

2 *ibid.* Page - 134.

liberal humanism and Marxist praxis did not mix readily. He was aware of this, and wrote to his most distinguished pupil, A.K. Saran, 'My life has been a series of reluctances'." [**Madan.** p. 135].

A Man With Analytical Mind and Critical Attitude

D.P. was a good critic. Critical attitude was, in fact, an inseparable aspect of his personality. D.P. was a good critic especially in the fields such as art, music, drama and social sciences. More than any other thing he was looking at the human life from the analytical and critical view point. He was always looking at the things from his own distinctive, but novel view point. The *"aesthetic sense"* about which D.P. was speaking of, was something new to social sciences. Even in his personal life, in his dress, in his styles and in his dealings also, D.P. had maintained the aesthetic sense, neatness and discipline.

D.P. as a Source of Inspiration and Motivation

An Impressive Teacher **:** D.P.'s direct students used to like him and love him most. In fact, there would be general agreement among those who knew him personally as students, colleagues, friends, that he had a much greater influence on others through the spoken rather than the written word. More than the printed pages, the classroom, the coffee house, the corridor or the drawing room was enough to give him freedom to explore new ideas and share them with the students and friends who were immediately available. His students were always curious to know about the style in which he would begin his lecture every time. Madan in this context writes : *"One could never be wholly sure what D.P. would speak about on a particular day – the topic addressed on the previous lecture-day, a book he had read since then........ a movie he had seen the previous evening, or a news item in the morning's papers."* [**Madan.** Page - 137]. D.P. was always stressing that there was a significant continuity between the classroom and the world outside.

Concern Towards Students **:** His students who joined him in the quest for knowledge and for life's meaning and significance became a personal concern to him. His emphasis on the aesthetic values elevated them to the level of ethical. *"He aroused their intellectual curiosity, guided their reading, stimulated their thinking, and watched over them with care and even affection."* [Madan]. D.P. used to say that *"the best thing about being a teacher was to see young minds blossom."* D.P. conveyed to his students that the life of scholarship and intellectual questing was a life of daring, and indeed a life very much worth living.

D.P.'s reputation as a teacher was not confined to the students of Economics and Sociology, but was generally acknowledged at the University level. His lectures on the history of economic and social thought, and on historical sociology [culture and civilisation], were particularly appreciated during those days. His intellectual influence was felt even outside the university campus. He was delivering lectures and writing articles for newspapers on a wide variety of topics such as – *graphic arts, music, cinema, literature and politics.*

Services Rendered by D.P. in the Non-Academic Fields

D.P. had made it a point to serve the society with the limited opportunities that he could get in his life. In 1938, he was asked to become the *Director of Information to the Government* after the Congress had formed the Ministry in Uttar Pradesh. He earned a good name in this new role. As an occupant of this new office, he took the initiative to establish the *Bureau of Economics and Statistics.* He quit this post within three years, that is, soon after the Congress stepped down from the office. However, his only other involvement with the Government was his membership of the *Uttar Pradesh Labour Enquiry Committee, 1947.*

After 20 odd years as a lecturer, D.P. was made a Reader in 1945. In 1949, the Vice Chancellor of Lucknow University, **Acharya Narendra Dev,** bestowed on him Professorship on merit basis, by brushing aside the then existing tradition [of a single professor in the department]. That gesture of the vice chancellor was widely hailed in the University and amidst intellectuals in the city. After visits to the USSR in 1952, and to the Netherlands as a visiting Professor at the Institute of Social Sciences in the Hague in 1953, D.P. was due to retire from the Lucknow University in 1954. **Dr. Zakir Hussain,** Vice Chancellor of Aligarh Muslim University [AMU] and a trained economist, invited D.P. to AMU as professor of Economics. D.P. accepted the offer and decided to leave Lucknow for Aligarh. M. Chalapathy Rao, Editor of *The National Herald* and a long time friend and admirer of D.P., described D.P.'s departure to Aligarh in the following words : *"Lucknow was letting Aligarh "take away one of its glories"."*

Major Works of D.P.

***Personality and the Social Sciences* [1924] :** D.P. had written several books and articles. His first book in English, *Personality and the Social Sciences* [1924], was described by himself as *"a personal document."* He had written the book with *"the sole purpose"* of clarifying his *"attitude towards systematised knowledge of society and life in general."*

***Basic Concepts in Sociology* [1932] :** This book was D.P.'s second major book. In this book he discussed the notions of *"progress"*, *"equality"*, *"social forces"*, and *"social control."* In this work, he had clearly stated that he was not comfortable with the contemporary Western sociological theories which seemed to him *"heavily mechanistic and ethnocentric."* On the contrary, D.P. emphasised the importance of *"comparative cultural perspectives and the historical situatedness of social reality."*

***Modern Indian Culture* [1942] :** Various factors such as the outbreak of the IInd World War 1939, the formal proposal for the partition of India in 1940, and the repression let loose by the British Raj in the wake of the Quit India Movement in 1942, had left a deep impression on D.P.'s third major work *Modern Indian Culture.* A sense of failure pervades its pages, but the concluding observations in the IInd edition are marked by a mood of purpose and hope.

D.P. believed that the immediate problem of Indian culture was – how to overcome communal hatred. He wrote : *"The immediate danger is civil hatred.... its form is likely to be Hindu or Muslim revivalism. But it can be met by a material programme in which the interests of the people, neither of the Hindus nor of the Muslims, as such, coincide. In that creative pursuit lies the hope of remaking Indian culture, thus also of the reunion of India's parts. Unity of the type created by British administration, cannot and should not survive. But union may, and should, come."*[1]

"The central theses of this book [*"Modern Indian Culture"*] was that the key to the history of India was cultural synthesis - creative responses to internal and external political and cultural challenges - and that the history of India was more than its past, notwithstanding the views of Hegel and Marx on the subject." *"India is a growing concern"*, D.P. used to reiterate in his lectures. [**T.N. Madan.** Page - 136]. He did not regard the disruptiveness of British rule as a permanent injury; it was only an interruption. He recognised the Hindu-Muslim cultural synthesis was the weakest at the level of cognitive categories. D.P. did not consider the partition of India as more than an event in its geo-politics.

1 **Mukerji** [1948]. Page - 216 as quoted by **T.N. Madan** in his article on **D.P. Mukerji.**

Other Works

Between the two editions of *Modern Indian Culture,* the first edition in 1942 and the second revised and enlarged edition in 1948, two books and three collections of papers were published. They are as follows: **1.** *Tagore, A Study* [1943], **2.** *Introduction to Indian Music* [1945b], **3.** *On Indian History : A Study in Method* [1945a], **4.** *Views and Counterviews* [1946b], and **5.** *Problems of Indian Youth* [1946a].

D.P. has left an indelible impression on the minds of the first generation of sociologists in India. But T.N. Madan regrets that due publicity is not given to D.P.'s thoughts and books. He writes : "Today, 30 years after D.P.'s death his published works are hardly known among the younger generation of sociologists. They are not a significant part of the teaching of sociology even at Lucknow University. His books are out of print and not readily available in libraries........ The ranks of those who knew him personally are getting thinner by the year. The neglect of D.P.'s work is a comment more on the character of the academy in India than on the true worth of his contributions as a social analyst and critic, and as a superb teacher."[1] Madan concludes his article with a regret – *"that there is no one among Indian sociologists today who can put us in mind of D.P. Mukerji."*

Main Works of D.P. Mukerji

Sociological Works

1. *"Personality and the Social Sciences",* 1924. Calcutta: The Book Co.
2. *"Basic Concepts in Sociology",* 1932. London: Kegan Paul, Trench, Trubner & Co.
3. *"Modern Indian Culture",* 1942. Bombay: Hind Kitabs. 2nd revised, enlarged edition in 1948.
4. *"Problems of Indian Youth",* 1946. Bombay: Hind Kitabs.
5. *"Indian Tradition and Social Change",* 1955. Presidential address to the First Indian Sociological Conference (Dehra Dun). Reproduced in D.P. Mukerji's 'Diversities'. New Delhi: Peoples Publishing House.
6. *"Diversities",* 1958. New Delhi: Peoples Publishing House.

Other Important Works

1. *"Tagore: A Study",* 1943. Calcutta: Manisha. Reprinted with an introductory note by Satyen Bose in 1972.
2. *"On Indian History: A Study in Method",* 1945. Bombay: Hind Kitabs.
3. *"An Introduction to Indian Music",* 1945. Bombay: Hind Kitabs.
4. *"Views and Counterviews",* 1946. Lucknow: Universal.
5. *"Man and Plan in India"* - Economic Weekly, 1953. Reproduced in 1958 in D.P. Mukerji, 'Diversities', pp. 28-76. New Delhi : Peoples Publishing House.
6. *"An Economic Theory for India",* 1954. Inaugural Address, Aligarh Muslim University. Reproduced in D. P. Mukerji, Diversities, pp. 228-41. New Delhi: Peoples Publishing House.
7. *"D.N. Majumdar: Scholar and Friend"* in T.N. Madan and G. Sarana (eds), 1961. Indian Anthropology: Essays in Memory of D.N. Majumdar, pp. 8-10.

D. N. Majumdar [1903 to 1960]

Dhirendra Nath Majumdar though has been well recognised as the greatest anthropologists of India, his name can be reasonably included in the list of those who are called the architects of

1 **Madan** on **D.P. Mukerji.** Pages : 140 - 141.

Indian sociology. D.N. Majumdar earned name and fame not only in India but also abroad. India has not been able to produce an anthropologist of his stature even after 43 years of his demise. He will be remembered in India for his pioneering contributions to build anthropology and sociology on firm foundations.

Education and Early Life

Majumdar was born to a Bengali couple in 1903 in Patna. He was very brilliant throughout his student career. He did his M.A. in Anthropology in the year 1923-24 with distinction. He also obtained Premchand Raychand Fellowship which was normally being awarded to the most meritorious graduates of the Calcutta University.

Majumdar's Interest in Anthropological Fieldwork

Though Majumdar got an unusual offer of becoming assistant collector even before he completed his 25 years, he refused the offer and decided to concentrate on anthropological fieldworks in Chota Nagpur of Bihar. He came under very strong influence of Sharat Chandra Roy a great anthropologist of the day. To quote his own words : "...... *I was initiated in anthropological field work by an illustrious Indian anthropologist, the late Sharat Chandra Roy.*"[1] Majumdar always used to remember Sharat Chandra Roy and the training that he had given him in anthropological fieldworks.

Majumdar's Professional Career

Majumdar began his teaching career in 1928 when he was appointed as lecturer in Economics and Sociology in the Lucknow University. The University conferred on him Professorship only after 18 years of his impressive teaching career and 22 years of fieldwork. Majumdar was at his 47th year at that time and was already famous even outside India as a great Anthropologist. He continued to be the Professor and Head of the Dept. of Anthropology of the Lucknow University till his demise in 1960. At the fag end of his service he also served as the Dean of Faculty of Arts.

Cambridge Confers Doctoral Degree on Majumdar

Majumdar had collected sufficient data through his fieldwork regarding *"Hos of Kolhan"*, a community which he had selected for his Ph.D. In 1929, he had been to Cambridge to receive Mout Gold Medal and met Hodson under whose guidance he prepared his doctoral thesis namely, *"Culture, Contact and Acculturation Among the Hos of Kolhan."* He was the first Indian anthropologist on whom the Cambridge University conferred the Ph.D. degree in 1935. He was also asked to deliver a series of lectures on topics of anthropological interests. Again he was the first Indian anthropologist to be invited to deliver such lectures in the Western Universities. He was honoured for his service by selecting him the *Fellow of the Royal Anthropological Institute of Great Britain and Ireland.* He was invited to deliver series of lectures on Indian culture at the educational conference held at Vienna in 1936-37.

Malinowski's Influence on Majumdar

When Majumdar was at Cambridge he obtained special training in physical anthropology at the hands of experts such as **G.N. Morant, R.R. Gates** and others. While in England, Majumdar was always taking interest in attending the seminars and symposia conducted by famous anthropologist Malinowski. Even after his return from England, Majumdar could never forget Malinowski, his lectures, his thoughts, his method of functioning, etc. He considered Malinowski the greatest anthropologist of the day.

---

1 **Majumdar** as quoted by **Gopala Sharan** in his article on D.N. Majumdar published in *"The Eastern Anthropologist."* Vol. XIV, No.2, May-April 1961.

On his return from England, Majumdar was invited to preside over *"Anthropology and Archaeological Research"* wing of the 26th "Indian Science Congress" held at Lahore in 1939. The 38 years young Majumdar was even made *"The Fellow of the National Institute of Science of India"* in 1941.

Majumdar Conducts the Biggest Anthropometric and Sociological Survey

In 1941, the decennial census was in progress throughout the nation. M.W. Yeatts was the Commissioner of Census and under his guidance Majumdar undertook a scheme of an anthropometric and a sociological survey which is considered one of the biggest one. Around 3000 people representing more than 21 social groups, castes and tribes were selected for this purpose and the blood groups of more than 4000 people were identified. That was probably the biggest survey ever conducted in India at that time. Dr. Majumdar was also invited by the *"Gujarat Research Society"* to conduct a similar survey in Gujarat in 1946 which he successfully did.

Establishment of Independent Dept. of Anthropology

Dr. Majumdar had established an Anthropological Laboratory in the Lucknow University in 1941 after obtaining a great experience in conducting the anthropometric and sociological survey in central India. Majumdar also undertook the task of establishing a separate and an independent department of anthropology in Lucknow University and the process was completed in 1951. Prior to that in 1945, he had established *Ethnographic and Folk Culture Society* in Uttar Pradesh and appointed Sir Sitaram as its Director. Majumdar was promoted as Reader in Anthropology in the year 1946 and the very next year he started a quarterly journal, namely, *"Eastern Anthropologist"* and worked as its Chief Editor till his death. In 1950-51, he was made Professor and Head of the department of Anthropology.

Invitations to Majumdar to Deliver Lectures

Various educational and other institutions and universities used to invite Majumdar to deliver public lectures. In 1942 he was asked to introduce anthropology to the candidates selected for Indian Civil Service [ICS]. Majumdar delivered six lectures on *"Indian Races and Cultures"* which later on were published with the title *"Races and Cultures of India"* [1944]. He was the first man to deliver such a lecture on anthropology. In 1946 the Nagpur University also invited him to deliver *Sri Mahadeo Watodkar Foundation Lectures* which were later on published with a title *"Matrix of Indian Culture"* [1947].

Dr. Majumdar visited foreign universities for delivering lectures. The Cornell University, Ithaca, New York invited him in 1952-53; *The School of Oriental and African Studies* of the London University and *"The Royal Anthropological Institute, London"* invited him to deliver lectures in 1957 and 1959. Majumdar also delivered 4 lectures on *"Indian Social Anthropology"* at The Hague, and also a series of lectures in the education institutions of Holland in 1959. He was the sole Indian representative in *"Wenner-Gren Foundation International Symposium"* held in 1952.

Honours and Awards Conferred on Dr. Majumdar

Dr. Majumdar was a member of the International Union for Scientific Study of Population [UNO] and a fellow of the American Association of Physical Anthropologists. He represented India, Pakistan, Burma and Ceylon at the International Symposium on the World Status of Anthropology, held in New York in 1952. He was a Visiting Professor at Cornell University, Ithaca, N.Y., in 1953 and Overseas Professor of Anthropology at the London University in 1957. He was a member of the Research Programme Committee of the Planning Commission, and a member of the Standing

Committee of the Central Board of Anthropology. He was general president of All India Sociological Conference, 1956.

Dr. Majumdar obtained several awards for his meritorious performances. In addition to several awards which he had obtained, Majumdar was also the recipient of the *Gujarat Research Society's Medal* for the best contribution in Physical Anthropology in 1950, and in 1958 the Asiatic Society of Bengal awarded the *Annandale Memorial Gold Medal* for his contribution to anthropology in Asia.

Dr. Majumdar was the author of a number of books. His book, namely *"A Tribe in Transition"* published in 1937 was praised by the then census commissioner of India J.H. Hutton as *"a new departure in the Indian ethnological literature."*

His another book *"Hos of Kolhan"* published in 1950 was regarded in the Indian social anthropological field as *"a classical monograph."*

"The Fortunes of Primitive Tribes of U.P." published in 1944 was another book of his, which obtained wide appreciation.

Majumdar and His Impressive Personality

D.N. Majumdar was, no doubt a man of great intellect, talent and scholarship. He was ever active in his profession and in his works. He used to inspire his students, associates and assistants in the work. He was responsible for popularising anthropology in the academic circles and personally played an important role in the establishment of the department of anthropology at Lucknow. He laid a good foundation for the department so that it could earn a good name even outside India. As **Prof. Feurer-Hiemendorf** commented, *"It has for many years been the most active department of anthropology in the whole of South Asia."*[1] Many Western scholars used to recognise the growing department of anthropology in India as *"Lucknow School of Anthropology."* He inspired a large number of students to take up careers in anthropology and to develop anthropology in India.

Main Works of Dr. Majumdar

Books

1. *A Tribe in Transition,* 1937.
2. *Races and Cultures of India,* 1944.
3. *The Fortunes of Primitive Tribes of U.P.,* 1944.
4. *Matrix of Indian Culture,* 1947.
5. *Racial Problems of Asia,* with Iravathi Karve (Book No.7), 1948.
6. *Hos of Kolhan,* 1950, [a classic monograph].
7. *The Affairs of a Tribe,* 1950.
8. *Rural Profiles,* (Editor), 1956.

Articles

1923 : "The custom of burning human effigies".
1923 : "Customs and taboos observed by an East Bengal woman from pregnancy to childbirth".
— : "Raciology of the Bhils".
1924 : "Physical Characteristics of the Hos of Kolhan".

1 **Gopal Saran** in his article on **Majumdar.**

1924 : "On the terminology of relationships of the Hos of Kolhan".

1925 : "The birth ceremonies of the Hos of Kolhan".

1925 : "Some ethnographic notes on the Hos of Kolhan".

1925 : "The significance of the totemism".

1925 : "The physical characteristics of the Kols".

1926 : "Marriage customs of the Hos of Kolhan".

1932 : "Blood Groups of the Doms".

1941 : "Report on the Anthropometric Survey of the U.P.", with Mahalanobis P.C. & C.R. Rao

1942 : "Blood Groups of the Criminal Tribes of the U.P.".

1942 : "Blood Groups of the Bhils of Gujarath".

1943 : "Blood Groups of the Tribes and Castes of U.P.".

1948 : "RG Frequency in the People of Lucknow".

1949-50 : "The Racial Status of the Nuniyas, etc. of Etah, Mainpuri and Farrukhabad, U.P. [Eastern Anthropologist], Vol.III.

1950 : "Race Realities in Cultural Gujarath".

1951-52 : "ABO Blood in India".

1955 : "Family and Marriage in a Polyandrous Society", [*Eastern Anthropologist*], Vol.X.

K. M. Kapadia [1908 to 1967]

Kaniyalal Motilal Kapadia was one of the scholarly students of Prof. G.S. Ghurye who rendered yeoman service to establish Sociology on a firm foundation in India. He was a founder member of the *"Indian Sociological Society"* and was its Secretary between 1955 and 1966. He rendered memorable service to the progress of the Society and made consistent efforts to maintain the quality of its journal *Sociological Bulletin.*

Early Life and Education

Prof. Kapadia came to Sociology with a background of Sanskrit and Indology. Even as a school boy he was very much fascinated by the Vaishnava texts in Sanskrit. He studied Sanskrit at Wilson College, Bombay from where he passed his B.A. with a First Class in 1930. He was appointed a *Dakshina Murti Fellow* in recognition of his merit.

Kapadia came from a relatively poor family and his father was an ordinary teacher. Hence he had to work his way through the odds of economic hardship and ill health. Born of a humble parentage on 17th October 1908, he had to earn and learn at the same time. While he was a Ph.D. student, he was working as a part-time teacher of Sanskrit in Bhatia High School, Bombay. He had even written a text book on Sanskrit Grammar in Gujarathi language which even today remains one of the best in the field. He was a teacher in a High School in Navsari for some years till he was appointed a lecturer in Bombay University in 1943.

Kapadia as Ghurye's Student and Successor

Kapadia took the opportunity of meeting Prof. Ghurye in 1930 with whom he discussed his plans for doing Ph.D. at the *"Bombay School of Economics and Sociology"*, University of Bombay. As advised by Ghurye, he undertook a study of Hindu Kinship on the basis of text materials in

Sanskrit. He was awarded the Ph.D. Degree in 1938 and his thesis was published in 1947 under the title *Hindu Kinship.* He became Reader in 1951 and succeeded Prof. Ghurye in 1959 as Professor and Head of the Department of Sociology.

Kapadia's Master Piece : *"Marriage and Family in India"*

Kapadia had a special interest in the study of the institutions such as marriage, family and kinship. In fact, he earned name and fame for his contributions to the enrichment of the studies in these institutions. His interest in the field became strengthened as he began teaching [in 1943] *"Indian social institutions and Indian social thought"* for the M.A. course in the University of Bombay. In 1955, he published his book *"Marriage and Family in India"* which came to be regarded as the *only text book* in the field covering diverse situations in the country. The book was so popular that the first edition of the book was sold out in less than 3 months after its publication. Subsequently, the book went for several editions and reprints. *"A singular feature of this book is that it acts as a bridge between the Indological approach and empirical approach."*[1] Commenting on this book **Leela Dube** writes : *"K.M. Kapadia's "Marriage and Family in India" [1958-66] deals with the Hindu joint family organisation through the ages, on the basis of an interpretation of historical texts, changes in legislation and empirical researches. He describes his general approach as functional."*[2]

***Kinship and Marriage* : *Topics of Special Interest For Kapadia*:** Kapadia also published many research papers with a wide coverage of the topics from tribal to caste system and upto modern industrial revolution. *Kinship and family were always the topics of his special interest.* In fact, he published from time to time small brochures and papers on these topics. He not only made a critical study of the then topical issues of the *Hindu Code Bill* and *Hindu Marriage and Divorce Bill* but also undertook an extensive survey of teachers' opinions and attitudes on different aspects of Hindu marriage and family.

Kapadia's Interest in Public Matters

Towards the last decade of his life, Kapadia started taking interest in public matters, social service and problems of society such as urbanisation, industrialisation and the general transformation of Indian society. In fact, he chose the topic *"Passing of the Traditional Society"* for the Presidential address at the Anthropology and Archaeology Section of the Indian Science Congress at its Golden Jubilee Session held at Delhi in 1963. At the time of his death, also he was working on the impact of industrialisation and urbanisation in south Gujarat, and has left behind a lot of unpublished manuscripts.

M.S.A. Rao in his obituary article on Kapadia, has pointed out that *"He [Kapadia] combined in his research both intellectual interests and a sense of social responsibility. He undertook a study of juveniles and encouraged his research students to work on different social problems."*[3]

***Struggle Against Ill-health* :** Almost throughout his life Kapadia had to fight against his own health hazards. He was a chronic patient of Asthama since 1936. His wife Mrs. Jayagauri Kapadia was not only affectionate but also sympathetic towards him and took care of him, and his four sons and two daughters attended to him dutifully. As M.S.A. Rao writes : *"He was a family man*

1 **M.S.A. Rao** in his obituary article on **K.M. Kapadia** in *Sociological Bulletin.* Volume No.XVII, March 1968, No.1. Pages : 1 - 2.
2 **Leela Dube** *"Sociology of Kinship."* Pages : 72 - 73.
3 **M.S.A. Rao** in his Obituary article on **K.M. Kapadia** published in *"Indian Sociological Bulletin."* Vol.XVII, March 1968. No.1.

in every sense of the term. Prof. Kapadia will be remembered for the affection and kindness he gave to one and all who came into contact with him. He had great regard for his colleagues and respect for his teacher, Prof. Ghurye."

Kapadia died at his residence in Bombay on October 30, 1967 at the age of 59 after a period of prolonged illness. In his death the Indian Sociological Society has lost a devoted worker, and the academic world a kind and able scholar.

A Bibliography of the Publications of K.M. Kapadia

Books

1947 : *Hindu Kinship*, Popular Book Depot, Bombay.

1950 : *The Hindu Code Bill: A Critical Study*, Popular Book Depot, Bombay.

1950 : *The Matrilineal Social Organisation of the Nagas of Assam*, Popular Book Depot, Bombay.

1953 : *The Hindu Marriage and Divorce Bill: A Crtitical Study*, Popular Book Depot, Bombay.

1954 : *Professor Ghurye Feliciation Volume*, (edited), Popular Book Depot, Bombay.

Papers

1952 : *"Criminal Tribes of India"*, Sociological Bulletin, Vol.I, No.2.

1954 : *"Changing Patterns of Hindu Marriage and Family"*, Sociological Bulletin, Vol.III, Nos. 1 & 2.

1955 : *"Changing Patterns of Hindu Marriage and Family"*, Sociological Bulletin, Vol.IV, No.2.

1956 : *"Rural Family Patterns"*, Sociological Bulletin, Vol.V, No.2.

1957 : *"Perspective Necessary for the Study of Social Change in India: A Critique on Hindu Widow Remarriage"*, Sociological Bulletin, Vol.VI, No.1.

1959 : *"Process of Education in Navsari Taluka"*, Sociological Bulletin, Vol.VIII, No.1.

1959 : *"The Family in Transition"*, Sociological Bulletin, Vol.VIII, No.2.

1961 : *"The Growth of Townships in South Gujarat - Maroli Bazar"*, Sociological Bulletin, Vol.X, No.2.

1962 : *"Caste in Transition"*, Sociological Bulletin, Vol.XI, No.1 & 2.

1963 : *"The Passing of the Traditional Society"*, Presidential Address delivered at the section of Anthropology and Archeology in the Proceedings of the 50th Session of the Indian Science Congress, Part II, Calcutta.

1963 : *"Historical Perspective for the Study of Social Change in India - The Place of Historical Method in the Study of Social Change"*, Presidential Address of the Sociology section of the 3rd Social Workers of Gujarat Conference, Ahmedabad, Journal of the Gujrat Research Society.

1964 : *"The Religious Creeds among the Patidars of South Gujarat - A Panoramic View", in Towards a Sociology of Culture in India*, (ed.) T.K.N. Unnithan et.al.

1966 : *"Industrial Evolution of Navsari"*, Sociological Bulletin, Vol.XV No.1

1967 : *"Problems of Research in India"*, in Sociology for India, (ed.) T.K.N. Unnithan et.al.

Dr. M. N. Srinivas [1916 to 1999]

Dr. M.N. Srinivas is an unforgetable name in Indian sociology. He was an internationally acclaimed Indian Anthropologist-cum-Sociologist. Dr. Srinivas who was a proud product of

Karnataka, had been instrumental in developing departments of Sociology in various universities. He dominated sociology in the country more than any other single person among his contemporaries or his predecessors. As **Andre Beteille** has pointed out in his article : *"The passing of M.N. Srinivas in 1999 marks the end of an era in the life of the social sciences in India. It is difficult to think of anyone who can fill the place vacated by him."* His influence extended beyond the boundaries of his discipline. The impact of his work was felt by historians, political scientists, economists and others. He lived for 83 years, but remained active, alert and creative till the end.

Srinivas's active career as a sociologist covers a very long span of time. When India became independent more than 50 years ago, he was a professional sociologist who had already secured a doctorate from Bombay University and was about to secure a second one from Oxford. He was there in Oxford between 1945 and 1951, he returned to India where he built successful department of Sociology in the Universities of Baroda and Delhi before leaving for Bangalore where he spent the last 27 years of his life.

Srinivas's Early Life and Education

Mysore Narasimhachar Srinivas was born to the couple M.A. Narasimhachar and Rukmini on 16th Nov. 1916. After completing his earlier education at Mysore he joined the Department of Sociology at Bombay University for M.A. degree on 17th June 1936. At that time, Prof. Ghurye was heading the Department and there were 20 or 30 students in each of the two M.A. Classes. Most of those who were studying for their Ph.D. in Sociology were part-time students. At that time, there were no scholarships or fellowships, and students registered for a Ph.D. earned their living by teaching in schools or working as clerks in firms. M.N. Srinivas obtained his Ph.D. in Bombay University and D.Phil. from the Oxford University. He was a student of Dr. Ghurye and also had the privilege of becoming the student of A.R. Radcliffe Brown and Evans Pritchard at Cambridge. In fact, we find a unique combination of Dr.Ghurye's *"untiring spirit of research"* and Dr. A.R.R. Brown's and Evans Pritchard's *"methodological skills"* in the works of Dr. Srinivas.

Impact of Oxford on Srinivas

"Oxford made a great impression on Srinivas, but Srinivas too made an impression on Oxford. It was natural for Srinivas to be impressed by Oxford; he thought that it was providential that his application to Columbia met with no response and that he was accepted by Oxford instead."[1] Srinivas was fortunate enough to be in the Institute of Social Anthropology at Oxford in the late 1940s for it was in Oxford the highest concentration of anthropological talent in the world was found. "Evans-Pritchard had succeeded Radcliffe Brown to the Chair of Social Anthropology; Fortes and Gluckman were already on the faculty; the new recruits were M.N. Srinivas and Godfrey Lienhardt who later published what many regard as the best written monograph in the history of Anthropology. When Srinivas left Oxford to return to India, he was succeeded by Louis Dumont." **[Andre Beteille].**

The Architect of the Department of Sociology at Baroda University

After his return from Oxford, M.N. Srinivas joined on June 15th 1951, the newly established M.S. University of Baroda, to start the Department of Sociology. The University at Baroda was new and small, and Srinivas was full of new schemes for the development and promotion of sociology. He was still a bachelor, and made friends easily both within and outside the university. Srinivas here took up the task of setting sociology on a new footing. "He was dissatisfied with both teaching and

1 **Andre Beteille** in his article on **M.N. Srinivas** published in *Economic and Political Weekly*, January 8th, 2000. Page - 18.

research in the subject as it then prevailed in the country, and was determined to promote the unity of sociology and social anthropology. He felt that much of the work being done by social anthropologists and sociologists in India, whether as students, teachers or scholars, had little relation to the flow of life in the real world. He felt strongly that sociology should not be used for the glorification of India's past......" [**Andre Beteille.** Page - 19].

Srinivas in the Teaching Profession at Baroda

Srinivas took the reform of teaching very seriously. At Baroda, he had the opportunity to work out his plans. He devised a new syllabus in which sociology was presented as an empirical and comparative discipline. He believed that all the students must have a close understanding of Indian society. He stressed that *"the present had to be understood on its own terms; a study of the ancient texts was not a very reliable guide to the present reality."*

Srinivas' Insistence of Research : According to Srinivas, teaching did not mean only work in the classroom with B.A. or M.A. students. According to him, it meant preparing students to do research in the field and away from the university. Research for him really meant working in the field rather than the library. Within a few years of getting started the Sociology department in Baroda, he was sending out students to do field work among tribals, among peasants and among factory workers. Srinivas had brought back from Oxford a new and a far more exacting standard of intensive field work learnt directly from Radcliffe Brown.

Srinivas believed that teaching should go hand in hand with research and publication. He found a most attractive outlet in what was then called *The Economic Weekly* to publish his and also his colleagues, articles. In fact, his famous book *"India's Villages"* consisted of a collection of articles published in *The Economic Weekly* between October 1951 and May 1954.

Good at Conducting Seminars : According to **Andre Beteille,** "Srinivas was never a very good lecturer; but he was superb at conducting seminars. He gave a very distinctive stamp to the weekly seminars which were attended by research students, teachers and visiting scholars. Under his Chairmanship the seminars were intellectually serious affairs......... He genuinely wanted to find out what people had to say even when they lacked the capacity to express themselves fluently." [Page - 20].

Srinivas in his Crowded Professional Career at Delhi

Srinivas after gaining sufficient experience at Baroda was looking forward for a wider area to operate upon. In 1959, he moved from Baroda to Delhi, and the dozen years that he spent there, were perhaps the most crowded in his professional career. Dr. V.K.R.V. Rao who was eagerly looking forward to select a scholarly person to work for the sociology department at Delhi School of Economics, finally selected M.N. Srinivas who had by then emerged as the most outstanding sociologists of his generation.

Srinivas set out to work on building a first rate department of Sociology at Delhi. By then Dr. Rao had moved out of the Delhi School of Economics to become the Vice Chancellor of Delhi University. He gave Srinivas full support to build up sociology department on a sound basis. Funds were more easily available at Delhi than elsewhere. Srinivas, however, was not in a hurry to experiment with his proposals and plans. "He wanted funds for his department, but he was more eager to build healthy conventions of teaching and research than simply to have a large department with many students and many teachers. In fact, he was keen to keep the numbers small so that the relations within the department did not become impersonal and routinised." [Andre Beteille]. Srinivas wanted "the members of the department, both students and teachers, to spend their time in the department, to make it a home away from home; in this he was trying to do what V.K.R.V. Rao had tried to do before him." For a post graduate department, Srinivas placed the highest value on tutorials and seminars.

Oxford-like Insistence on Fieldwork and Painstaking Attempts to Produce Ph.Ds : Delhi provided much scope for building up a post-graduate department on the Oxford principle of the unity of teaching and research. Srinivas had made up his mind to produce Ph.D.s of high quality in Delhi itself. So, throughout the 1960s and 70s, while the department of Economics sent most of its best M.A.s for Ph.D.s abroad, the department of Sociology kept most of them for its own Ph.D. programme. Within a short time of its establishment, research students from the department were being sent out to study plantations, sugar co-operatives, trade unions, colleges, hospitals and other organisations and institutions through the length and breadth of the country. Srinivas spent 12 precious years there in the Delhi School of Economics.

Busy Schedule of Work Both Within and Outside the University : Promoting the cause of sociology in Delhi was not an easy task for M.N. Srinivas. He was asked to be on committees both within and outside the university; U.G.C. committees, ICSSR committees and Govt. committees. In 1967, he had also become the President of the *Indian Sociological Society.* All these commitments left him with less and less time for teaching and research, and he began to worry about it. In the meantime, he had published his Tagore Lectures as *"Social Change in Modern India"* [1966]. He was so busy that he could not make any progress on his book on Rampura for which the field work was done in 1948 in his first year as lecturer at Oxford. He took the opportunity of going to Stanford [USA] in 1970 where he was struck by a misfortune. He had lost all his material he had taken to work on due to a thoughtless arson caused by some student radicals. He extended his stay in America for some time and returned to Delhi in 1971.

Back to Bangalore at Karnataka

As the Chairman of the Board of ISEC, Bangalore : After his return from Stanford in the middle of 1971, Srinivas decided to leave Delhi for Bangalore. V.K.R.V. Rao, who had brought him to Delhi in 1959, was himself building a new research institute at Bangalore and he wanted Srinivas to join him in the venture. He would have loved to go back to Mysore, but Mysore did not have the facilities necessary for his work so he decided to go to Bangalore and to settle there permanently. He concentrated all his attention and efforts to build up an institution namely *Institute for Social and Economic Change* [ISEC] at Bangalore. He served as the chairman of the Board of ISEC for a couple of years.

Thus he set a new trend of empirical research in Sociology at the time when Indological approach was very much in practice. His reputed students like **A.M. Shah, Andre Beteille, Veena Das** and others have also attained international fame. Apart from being a first-rank field worker, he had been the source of inspiration for several studies conducted by his colleagues and students during the fifties. *"India's Villages"*, edited by M.N. Srinivas bears a grand testimony to this fact.

Wide Recognition with Honours and Awards : Dr. Srinivas had the credit of having obtained many national and international honours and awards. Dr. Srinivas was the first Indian social scientist to be awarded the prestigious *"Homi Bhabha Senior Fellowship"*. He had been a *National Fellow, ICSSR, Joint Director, ISEC, President, "Indian Sociological Society"* and recipient of *"Dr. Ghurye's Award."* His other awards include the *Rivers Memorial Medal for 1955* from the Royal Anthropological Institute of Great Britain and Ireland and the *Sarat Chandra Roy Memorial Gold*

Medal for his contributions to Indian Anthropology [1958]. He had received honorary degrees from Chicago, Nice and Mysore.

Major Contributions of M.N. Srinivas

Srinivas had written several books, published several articles and presented a good number of papers. He had contributed an article on *"Hinduism"* to Encyclopaedia Britannica, and on *"Social Structure of India"* to the Gazetteer of India, Vol.1, 1969. His major works on Indian society include : **1.** *"Marriage and Family in Mysore"* [1942]; **2.** *"Religion and Society Among the Coorgs of South India"* [1952, 1965]; **3.** *"India's Villages"* (Ed.) [1955, 60, 63, 66, 69]; **4.** *"Caste in Modern India and Other Essays"* [1964, 70, 77]; **5.** *"Social Change in Modern India"* [all published by Asia Publishing House]; **6.** *"Method in Social Anthropology - Selected Essays"* by A.R. Radcliffe Brown (Ed.) 1958, University of Chicago, 1960 Asia Pub. House; **7.** *"Remembered Village"* [1976], Oxford University Press and in Paperback 1978.

His article ***"The Development of Sociology and Social Anthropology in India"*** [Co-writer M.N. Panini] published in Sociological Bulletin, 1973, Vol.22(2), 179-215, remains most valuable even today for, it provides an insight into the course of the development of these two fields in India.

Another important article that acted as an eye opener for armchair analysts and administrators about India's villages and urged for first hand field studies of the "multi-caste micro causals" was, *"Village Studies and Their Significance"* [included in his book *"Caste in Modern India & Other Essays"*, and also in A.R. Desai's (ed.) *"Rural Sociology in India."*]

Introduction of New Concepts **:** Among the considerable array of specific contributions of Dr. Srinivas to sociological literature, specific mention should be made of concepts he had introduced like *"Sanskritisation", "Westernisation", "Dominant Caste", "Secularisation",* etc. towards the growth of Indian Sociology. Most of his studies centre round his favourite topics such as – *the caste system, village communities and social change and social mobility in India.*

Dr. Srinivas was one of the few Indian sociologists, who methodically dealt with the impact of the West on Indian social structure, its stratification and mobility. His concept *"Sanskritisation"* created much heated discussion in academic circles when he refuted the stereotyped view of caste as immobile and closed system.

India's Villages - An Edited Work **:** In this book, Dr. Srinivas had edited several essays by eminent Sociologists and Anthropologists from India, U.K. and U.S.A. which present an analysis of Indian rural life and evaluate the socio-cultural changes taking place in India's villages. Each essay is the result of intensive study of a single village or a group of villages in a single region by trained observers. The area covered is vast from Himachal Pradesh in the north to Tanjore in the south and Rajasthan in the west to Bengal in the east. Many obscure strands of rural organisation came into focus and the nexus of social relationships in India's villages reveal variegated patterns. On a scientific basis, the book either confirms or dispels some of the commonly held views about Indian villages.

The Unforgetable "Remembered Village" **:** During early fifties, Dr. Srinivas conducted an intensive field study of Rampura, a village about 22 miles south-east of Mysore, that is Karnataka. The concept of *"dominant caste",* in fact, emerged from him in the study of Rampura. Prior to this no sociologist had gone and lived in a multi-caste village to study the social organisation.

In fact, his *"Remembered Village"* is a product of his study of Rampura. Reviewing this book *"The Economic Times"* wrote *"We have a monograph that cannot be too highly praised for its excellence."* This book is more than a monograph, it is almost a semi-autobiography[1] of Dr. Srinivas.

Another widely used book of the students of Indian society is his edited work along with his other colleagues of ISEC late Dr. Seshaiah and Sri Parthasarathy is, *"Dimensions of Social Change in India."*

Other Important Essays

Other important essays of Dr. Srinivas include – *"Some Reflections on Dowry"* based on his J.P. Naik Memorial Lecture, 1983, in which he had gone into the genesis of this evil and made useful suggestions to eradicate it; *"Some Expressions of Caste Mobility"* in which he used the concept *"secularization"*; and *"Some Thoughts on the Study of One's Own Society."* These are brilliant essays in which Dr. Srinivas has highlighted the complexity of Indian society.

Srinivas had delivered several lectures and written several essays. In fact, in his lectures and other writings, he was trying to explore new subjects. He lectured on *"The Changing Position of Indian Women"*, and published the lecture as a pamphlet. He also published short work on *"Dowry."* But he did not abandon his basic interest in caste. He kept a close watch on the changing fortunes of the caste, and continued to publish notes, comments and articles on it. In 1996, he edited a collection of papers which was published as *"Caste : Its Twentieth Century Avataar."* In fact, at the time of his death he was working on the paper entitled – *"Caste, A Systemic Change ?"* In the meantime, Oxford University Press had brought out four collections of his papers, beginning with *"The Dominant Castes and Other Essays"* in 1987.

Dr. Srinivas had attended a number of national and international level debates, discussions, seminars and symposiums of sociological importance and contributed a great deal for the success of all these. *"It is not enough to say that Srinivas had the vocation of a scholar; it has to be added that sociology was the chosen field of his scholarly activity. He maintained an unshakable belief in the unique significance of sociology for understanding the world in which we live."* **[Andre Beteille].**

Improvement of Science and Technology alone is not Enough. Encouragement to Sociology and Social Anthropology is Equally Required : M.N. Srinivas

M.N. Srinivas in his Inaugural Address to the 20th All India Sociological Conference held in Mangalore [Karnataka] on 31st December 1993, had said that the over-all development of the country could not be achieved by giving importance to science and technology alone. He stated that "...... a country which wants to liberalise and globalise its economy has to safeguard its long-term interests by investing considerable resources in higher education and research. It cannot hope to be continuously parasitic on research carried out elsewhere. In this connection, I must state categorically that it is not enough to invest in science and technology alone. If those who have power over us want science and technology to improve the living conditions of the people, they have to support sociology and social anthropology for these disciplines are indispensable to smoothen the transition to a situation in which the state confines its activities to certain essential areas while releasing the people's energies to help themselves. The successful and swift application of the results of science and technology requires the aid of the social sciences, in particular, those sciences which address

---

1 This book would not have been written but for a tragic accident which occurred on 24th April, 1970, when Dr. Srinivas was at the *"Centre for Advanced Study in the Behavioural Sciences"*, Stanford, U.S.A., as a fellow. All the three files of his fieldwork notes processed over a period of 18 years were reduced to ashes in less than an hour, when a fire was set by arsonists. At the very outset Dr. Srinivas writes in this book – *"I would not have thought of writing a book based entirely on my memory of my field experience. I wish, therefore, to acknowledge the part played by the arsonists in the birth of this book."*

themselves to the study of culture, institutions, ideas, beliefs and values of the people. Only when sociologists undertake to seriously study problems bearing on the rapid improvement of the living conditions of the poor and the oppressed will the discipline's relevance be appreciated by those in power. Students who opt for sociology will then have employment opportunities. This is necessary to attract able students who have an aptitude for sociology. Only then will sociology become an integral part of the intellectual discourse of this country."[1]

M.N. Srinivas : India's Best Known Sociologist

Andre Beteille in his article on M.N. Srinivas has paid a glowing tribute to his inimitable personal qualities and to the memorable contributions that he has made to the development of sociology in India. He writes : *"Over a period of half a century, Srinivas built up not only a very impressive but also a very influencial corpus of work. It would be no exaggeration to say that his work changed the face of sociology in India. His writings on village, caste and Hinduism are read by students throughout India and in many universities abroad. They have influenced many different branches of the social sciences and the humanities. In academic circles both within and outside India, he was India's best known sociologist."*[2]

More Works of Dr. Srinivas

Dr. Srinivas has written a number of books and published several articles and essays. He had been the editor of books published under *"Studies in Sociology and Social Anthropology."* The major literary works of Dr. Srinivas essentially include the following :

Books on Indian Society

1. *Marriage and Family in Mysore* [1942].
2. *Religion and Society Among the Coorgs of South India* [1952].
3. *Caste in Modern India and Other Essays* [1964].
4. *Social Change in Modern India.*
5. *The Remembered Village* [1976].
6. *India's Villages* [1955] Edited by Srinivas.
7. *Dimensions of Social Change in India.* [Edited this book along with two other colleagues of ISEC, Dr. Seshaiah and Sri Parthasarathy].

Some Important Articles and Essays

1. An article on *"Hinduism"* published in Encyclopaedia Britannica.
2. Article on *"Social Structure of India"* published in Gazetteer of India, Vol.I, 1969.
3. Article on *"The Development of Sociology and Social Anthropology in India"* [Co-writer being Dr. M.N. Panini] published in "Sociological Bulletin" 1973, Vol.22 (2), 179-215.
4. An essay on *"Some Reflections on Dowry"* [1983].
5. An essay on *"Some Expressions of Caste Mobility"*.
6. An essay on *"Some Thoughts on the Study of One's Own Society."*

---

1 **M.N. Srinivas's** article on *"Sociology in India and Its Future"* published in the Souvenir released on 27th Jan. 1995 in the First State Level Conference of "Karnataka Sociological Association" held at Shimoga.

2 **Andre Beteille** on **M.N. Srinivas** in *Economic and Political Weekly.* January 8, 2000. Page - 22.

Dr. S. C. Dube [1922 - 1996]

Dr. Shyama Charan Dube is a well known name in the realm of Indian sociology. He is considered to be one of the builders of modern sociology and social anthropology in India. He came to social anthropology from political science and almost immediately made his mark in the discipline of his choice. Very shortly he earned national and also international reputation. He is remembered in India and abroad for his celebrated village monograph namely *Indian Village* [1955]. It was, indeed, a milestone in the study of Indian society. "Prof. Dube has taught social anthropology and sociology at universities in India and abroad. His professional and popular writing, in English and Hindi, has been mainly but not exclusively on matters related to social development."

S.C. Dube was among those Indian social scientists who came into their own with the upcoming of independence. At a very young age Dube could rise to a very big height. **Andre Beteille** in his obituary article on Dube writes : *"When I first met him in late 1958 or early 1959, he already had an established reputation both in India and abroad although he was still in his 30s. I cannot think of any sociologist of my generation or the next who established so wide a reputation at such an early age. This is partly because, the discipline which he entered was still relatively young, and it had more spaces then than it has now; but Dube's own rich and vibrant personality also contributed something to his reputation."*[1]

Early Life and Education

Dube was born to M.C. Dube and Smt. Dharma in July 25th, 1922, in a place called Seoni in Madhya Pradesh. He had obtained a P.G. degree and also a Doctoral degree in sociology and got married to Smt. Leela who herself is a sociologist, and got from her two sons.

Dube joined Lucknow University as a lecturer in sociology in 1947 and taught upto 1949 in the same institution and later on shifted to Osmania University in Andhra Pradesh in the year 1949-50. He became a Reader in the department soon. He got the rare opportunity of working as the Principal and also the Director of Research of the *National Institute of Community Development* between 1960-64.

Dube's Academic and Administrative Excellence

Dube was basically a university man. He moved easily between institutions and carried his fair share of administrative burdens. He joined the Sagar University in M.P. as a Professor of Anthropology and worked there until 1972. He switched over to Shimla where he worked as the Director of *Indian Institute of Advanced Study* between 1972-77. For a brief spell of one year [1977-78], he had served the *Govinda Vallabha Pant Institute of Social Science,* Allahabad, as its Director. Apart from serving as a Professor and Director of several institutes he had an eventful tenure of office as a *Vice-Chancellor of Jammu University* in the years 1978-80. Dube's academic scholarship fetched him several precious offices. To mention a few, he was the *National Fellow of Indian Council of Social Sciences Research* - 1980; a *Fellow of Royal Anthropological Institute; a Fellow of American Anthropological Association; a Member of Commonwealth Association of Social Anthropologists;* etc. Dube was an active and outgoing person who enjoyed as much the social as the intellectual side of academic gatherings.

---

1 **Andre Beteille** on ***"Shyama Charan Dube"*** in *"Economic and Political Weekly."* March 30th, 1996. Page - 811.

Major Contributions

Dube's contributions to his discipline and his profession were many-sided. Although he had earlier published a monograph on the tribal *Kamar*, the book that brought him name and fame was his study of a village near Hyderabad, published in 1955 as *"Indian Village."* It was a tremendous success for it has been read by more people in India and abroad, than any other village monograph. Commenting on this book, **Andre Beteille** writes : *"It was the first full-length monograph on an Indian village by a professional anthropologist and it became the forerunner in a long line of monographs which were to transform our understanding of Indian society and culture. Dube was among the select few who had set the phase for those of us who entered the field in the succeeding decades."*[1]

Dube's Interest in Directed Social Change

From the very beginning, Dube took an interest in directed social change. Thus, *"Indian Village"* was followed by another of his book *"India's Changing Villages"* published in 1958. Dube was quick to respond to the changes taking place around him, and the new book was devoted to the human factor in community development. That was a period [1950-60] in which a great deal of public attention was given to community development and its role in the regeneration of the Indian village. It was Dube who took the lead in giving guidances to the working of the community development project. In fact, between 1960 and 1964, he served the *National Institute of Community Development,* as the Director of Research and as Principal. Dube like many other members of his generation, saw himself as both a scholar and a publicist. As **Andre Beteille** says, *"In India atleast, there is only a thin line between academic sociology and current affairs, and Dube seemed less troubled than others over crossing it."*

An Introductory Book on *"Indian Society"*

Dube has written a small book entitled *"Indian Society"* in a simple style, which is *"..... addressed to young readers who want to know something about the historical roots, ideological foundations, and social organisation of Indian society.... For its data and interpretations, the book draws upon such diverse sources as history, Indology, anthropology, and sociology. The insights provided by these disciplines are, ... necessary to illuminate the social realities of India."*[2]

This book which is intended for the young readers, *"........ draws upon various sources in looking at the past and the present of the Indian society. The growth of India's diversities and unities is traced through its complex history. The functioning, over the centuries, Varna and Jati and of family and kinship are examined in urban and rural contexts; and gender relations are similarly treated. Naturally, enough, this account of the creation of today's India is followed by a brief assessment of ongoing and likely changes."* The book provides a useful guide for further reading.

As an author, Dube wrote comfortably without much exertion. He addressed himself to scholars, administrators, the lay public and school children, writing in both English and Hindi, and turning more and more to his mother tongue in later years.

Author and Editor of Many Works

Dube's publications, as author and editor, make a long list, and they cover a wide range. He showed his interest in the whole process of social change in his U.G.C. National Lectures, delivered

1 **Andre Beteille** in his obituary article.

2 **S.C. Dube** in his Preface to his book *"Indian Society"* published by National Book Trust, India [1990].

in 1970 and published in 1971 as *"Explanation and Management of Change."* Later on, he continued to publish on the twin processes of development and modernisation. Accordingly, there came out the famous works **:** *Contemporary India and Its Modernisation* [1974], *Development Perspectives for the 1980s* [1983], *Modernisation and Development* [1988], and *Tradition and Development* [1990]. In addition to these, there was a stream of publications under his editorship, particularly during his tenure at Shimla between 1972 and 1977. Dube's command of language and clarity of expression was simply exemplary. He, in fact, had a literary talent as well as a talent for social science, and this is manifested in his writings, particularly in Hindi. Praising profusely his command of language **Andre Beteille** writes : *"He was enviably fluent in both speech and writing, and equally in English and Hindi. At the same time, he belonged within a tradition of Indian intellectuals whose true love was for the spoken rather than the written word. He wrote well, but not as well as he could have written.........."*

An Academician with a Public Concern

Dube's contribution to his discipline and his profession were many-sided. Although he published sociological and other works for more than 40 years, he never confined himself to the four walls of his departmental chamber. He lectured widely, and maintained an active and continuous presence at conferences, seminars, workshops and committees through the length and breadth of the country. He was not an armchair sociologist. On the contrary, he was always accessible and gave his time freely and generously to all who came to him for guidance. Students, teachers, administrators and many others with a real or imagined interest in a public cause used to seek his guidance, counsel and assistance. He liked to give of himself fully and ungrudgingly to all those who sought his participation on public occasions. He was very friendly and also very hospitable and had many friends and admirers.

Major Works of Dr. S.C. Dube

1. *Indian Village* [1955].
2. *India's Changing Villages* [1958].
3. *Explanation and Management of Change* [1971].
4. *Contemporary India and Its Modernisation* [1974].
5. *Development Perspectives for The 1980s* [1983].
6. *Modernisation and Development* [1988].
7. *Tradition and Development* [1990].
8. *Indian Society* [1990].

M. S. A. Rao [1926 to 1985]

Madhugiri Shyamrao Ananthapadmanabha Rao [M.S.A. Rao] taught Sociology at the University of Delhi for nearly 30 years and was at the peak of his professional career at the time of his untimely demise in December 1985. He had made a significant contribution to the science of sociology through his commitment to the profession and pioneering research. His contribution to the enrichment of social anthropology is also no less significant.

Early Life and Education of M.S.A. Rao

M.S.A. Rao was born on 26 Sept. 1926 at Molakalmooru of Chitradurga district [Karnataka] and grew up in Mysore during the formative years of his life. He was the last son of Shyamrao [an officer in the Forest Dept.] and Tulasi. At the age of 14, he got an opportunity to contact Dr. Raghavendra Rao, a professor of philosophy at Maharaja's College, Mysore. The scholarship and advice of Raghavendra Rao shaped the destiny of M.S.A. Rao. Raghavendra Rao became his revered *Guru* under whose guidance he studied important works on Indian philosophy. M.S.A. Rao joined the B.A. (Hons) course in social philosophy at Maharaja's College. Philosophy then had royal patronage in Mysore and the University of Mysore was able to attract eminent teachers and students for the philosophy department. M.S.A. Rao continued his studies in social philosophy of which sociology formed a part of his M.A. He secured the degree with distinction in 1949. Though he married Saroja in 1947 just before he joined the Masters programme his interest in studies never diminished.

Continuation of Academic Career in Bombay

M.S.A. Rao was attracted to the Bombay School for it had a high reputation at that time among the academic circles all over the country. Prof. Ghurye's reputation was another attraction which made him to join the Bombay School. Prof. Ghurye had a profound influence on M.S.A. Rao in terms of themes in sociology that he pursued. Sociology forged a life long bond between the *Guru* and the *Shishya*. He learnt from Prof. Ghurye the importance of hardwork, time consciousness and perseverance. Further, Prof. C.N. Vakil, a prominent economist of the day was another person who exercised a lasting impression on M.S.A. Rao during his stay in Bombay.

Research Work on Social Change and Acquisition of Ph.D.

M.S.A. Rao decided to start his research career with his study of Social Change in Coastal Kerala. He had picked up Malayalam within a year and it proved to be very useful for his fieldwork. He wrote his thesis *"Social Change in Malabar"* for which he was awarded the degree of Doctor of Philosophy in 1953.

M.S.A. Rao joined a research project on kinship undertaken by Prof. K.M. Kapadia soon after acquiring his doctoral degree. The project involved intensive field work in Gujarat and it made him to learn Gujarathi language. His exposure to fieldworks made him to become an expert fieldworker.

On completion of the project work on kinship, M.S.A. Rao was called for an interview at the Delhi School of Economics for a position in sociology. M.S.A. Rao was hesitant to obtain the permission of his *Guru* Ghurye, but finally he decided to move to Delhi with the blessings of his mentor.

Three Decades of Teaching in Delhi

The Delhi School of Economics which had an eminent founder-director Dr. V.K.R.V. Rao bestowed on M.S.A. Rao a good chance [in 1959] to work in association with well known sociologists such as Prof. M.N. Srinivas, Prof. A.M. Shah and Prof. Andre Beteille. In fact, M.S.A. Rao was one among these who first joined the faculty of Sociology headed by M.N. Srinivas in the Delhi School of Economics. Department of Sociology started growing both in terms of quality and quantity. M.S.A. Rao's academic performance grew with that of the department. In a year's time, he became a Reader and then a Professor in 1969. The Department which was started with an initial faculty strength of only four [one professor and three lecturers] in 1959, rose to ten [four professors, two readers and four lecturers] by 1969. During the initial years the department offered M.A. and Ph.D. degree courses and later started a two-year research course leading to the M.Litt. degree in 1966. M.S.A. Rao made significant contribution to the development of department into a *Centre of Advanced*

Study in Sociology in 1968 along with Prof. M.N. Srinivas. He was also instrumental in the introduction of Sociology at B.A. (Hons) and B.A. Pass levels in several constituent colleges of Delhi University during the early 70s.

Multifaceted Personality of Dr. Rao

M.S.A. Rao's multifaceted contributions may be understood by considering him a *person, teacher* and *scholar* of national and international reputation. He was known to his colleagues, friends, students as a very unassuming and a friendly person. **Chandrashekar Bhat** while describing the characteristics of M.S.A. Rao, writes : *"He was gentle, soft spoken and kind but he never hesitated to express his disagreement or displeasure if the situation warranted it. He was firm in his convictions and frank in his views. He was always an optimist by nature. M.S.A. Rao was deeply religious but, at the same time, his approach to life was highly rational. He presented a happy synthesis of tradition and modernity."*[1]

M.S.A. Rao was an excellent teacher and a conscientious scholar. He was informal with his students and his doors were always open for them, both at the office and home. He was so affectionate towards his students that he considered them a part of his family. Several of his students had the privilege of finalising their dissertation in his study under the affectionate care of his family. He used to tell his students *"to exploit"* him to the maximum in the pursuit of their research. This quality of helping, inspiring and guiding his students and research assistants was probably the one which he had acquired from Ghurye.

M.S.A. Rao was a self-made man. It was through hardwork that he earned a good name and a fame in the national and international sociological circles. Since he had only a middle class family background, he had to pursue his education beyond graduation only through the financial support of a scholarship or freeship. The *Amble Annaiah Pandit Scholarship* at the University of Mysore helped him to study for the M.A. degree and a *Research Fellowship* awarded by the University of Bombay helped him to complete his Ph.D. programme. After joining *Delhi School of Economics* he got ample opportunities to develop his abilities and talents and emerged as one of the distinguished researchers, writers and active sociologists.

Topics of Special Interest for M.S.A. Rao

M.S.A. Rao as a sociologist was more interested in sociological topics such as *social change, social mobility, social migration, social movement* and *urbanisation.* Not only did he pursue in depth sociological analysis on his familiar themes but diversified his interests to cover several new areas for investigation.

Major Works and Achievements of M.S.A. Rao

Social Change in Malabar [1957] was M.S.A. Rao's first book to be published. This book is an exposition of the changing pattern of culture as reflected in the analysis of occupational, religious, educational, and community activities in addition to leisure and family life. M.S.A. Rao was very much interested in social change and it remained central to his scholarly writings for a long time.

Urbanisation and Social Change which was published in 1970 revealed M.S.A.'s interests in the phenomenon of urbanisation. While working as a lecturer at the Delhi School of Economics

1 **Chandrashekar Bhat** in article on *M.S.A. Rao and His Work* published in *''Sociology of Development and Change''*. Page - 17.

itself M.S.A. had taken up a field study of the fringe village *Shamipur* in 1956-57 to investigate the process of urbanisation and social change.

Soon after joining the Department of Sociology he worked with M.N. Srinivas on *A Sociological Study of Okhla Industrial Estate,* funded by the UNESCO. But very soon his interest moved back to the analysis of urbanisation which he had started in 1956 particularly to understand the impact of urbanisation on rural life. Very shortly he became a visiting lecturer in Asian Sociology, *School of Oriental and African Studies,* University of London for the academic year 1966-67. In addition to the teaching of a course on *"Urbanisation in South Asia",* he conducted several seminars based on his field material and obtained very useful insights. In 1967, he went to *South East Asia Areas Centre, University of Chicago,* as a Visiting Fellow, where he completed the monograph – *Urbanisation and Social Change.* This work was totally different from the other urban studies for *its approach to the sociology of urbanisation was from a rural perspective.*

Tradition, Rationality and Change [1972] was yet another book of M.S.A. which included the essays which focussed on the problems of economic growth in the tradition-bound underdeveloped countries. In fact, after his return to Delhi, he processed the seminar papers on economic development and social change to bring out this book consisting of essays. In his book, he examined the sociological aspects of economic development in the wake of community development programmes and the efforts made to achieve an egalitarian society by reducing the gap between the rich and poor.

M.S.A. Rao as Professor and Head of the Department

In the 1960s, M.S.A. Rao started taking some interest in the activities of the *Indian Sociological Society.* In 1968-70, he accepted the Secretaryship of the Society and devoted much time for its activities. It was during this time the Department of Sociology was recognised as a *Centre of Advanced Study* and he became the Professor of Sociology. Now the department was moved from an old to a new spacious building. The decade between 1970 and 1980 brought out the best of him as an administrative head of the department, organiser of several workshops and symposia, convenor of different national committees and commissions and member of various editorial boards.

Shouldering of Several Responsibilities

M.S.A. Rao became very busy in 70s and 80s. He was the convenor during 1970-72 of the Research Group IV [Research Survey in Sociology, Social and Cultural Anthropology and Social Work] which was the part of the project on the survey of research in social sciences launched by the Indian Council of Social Science Research. He edited *A Survey of Research in Sociology and Social Anthropology* [1972 & 1974] along with Prof. Srinivas and Prof. A.M. Shah which was later published in three volumes. He participated in a project sponsored by ICSSR on *"Socio-Economic Survey of Vijayawada City"* and studied the slums of Vijayawada along with Prof. K. Ranga Rao. The findings of this survey were later published in their book *Cities and Slums* [1984]. In 1974 he edited and published another book with the title ***Urban Sociology in India*** : ***Reader and Source Book*** which proved to be the first major publication in this field. This book was especially prepared in order to supply one of the good source books on urban sociology in India.

Studies on Social Movements

M.S.A. Rao was invited by Syracuse, Pennsylvania and Duke Universities as a Visiting Professor during 1972-73. This offer gave M.S.A. Rao an opportunity to plan one of his best contributions to sociology, that is, *Social Movements.* By the time he returned to Delhi the first draft of his manuscript was almost ready. It was published with the title ***Social Movements and Social***

Transformation* : *A Study of Two Backward Classes Movements in India [1979] which won him the prestigious Ghurye Award for the best sociological work of that year.

This work was a study of two backward classes movements : *Sri Narayana Dharma Paripalana Movement* [Movement for the propagation of the philosophy of Sri Narayana Guruswamy] in Kerala and *The All India Yadava Movement. "These movements were analysed in terms of structural conditions of relative deprivation, formation of protest ideology, collective mobilisation, leadership and organisation, event structure, internal dynamics and the nature of social change in society at large."*[1]

M.S.A. Rao followed distinctive method in his studies of social movements. **Chandrashekar Bhat** writes *"M.S.A.'s study of these social movements broke new ground in more ways than one. It projected, as opposed to the imitative process approach, a different way of looking at social mobility and change in modern India. Social mobility was seen to have occurred through a process of protest and conflict and by way of wresting power and monopoly in the use of different kinds of goods and services – religious, educational, economic and political – from the forward classes."* [Page - 21]. Besides being a significant contribution to the sociology of social movements, this book brought to light the changing position of the backward classes. That throws light on the deprivations, hopes, frustrations and the ideologies of the backward classes. A second edition of this book was brought out in 1986.

Book on *"Social Movements in India"* [1978 & 79]

M.S.A. Rao's mind was fully engrossed with the *sociology of social movements* during 1970s. He had participated in several seminars and presented papers and most of the times he selected his favourite topic social movement. This persistent interest in the topic of social movements led to the publication of the book *"Social Movements in India"* [1978-& 1979] in two volumes. Both the volumes were well received by students and teachers of sociology.

M.S.A. on Various Committees

As it is already mentioned, during the decade 1970-80, M.S.A. had hectic academic and organisational activities. He was elected the President of the *Delhi Sociological Association* during 1976-78. He served on several U.G.C. committees. Some of them could be mentioned here : *"Convenor, UGC Committee on the Status of Teaching of Sociology and Social Anthropology in Indian Universities [1974-77], UGC Representative on the Syndicate of Gandhi Gram Rural University [1977], Convenor, UGC Panel on Sociology [1979-82]. He was elected an Associate Member of Current Anthropology [USA] and was honoured by the Royal Anthropological Institute [UK] as its Fellow."* [Page - 22].

Studies on *"Migration"*

Yet another topic of great interest for M.S.A. Rao was *"migration."* He was interested in analysing its role in development at the rural, urban and regional levels. When he was awarded the three year UGC National Fellowship in 1977, he commenced an exhaustive study of the *"sociology of labour migration"*, taking particularly the case of migration of graders of tobacco in and around the state of Andhra Pradesh. It was the most extensive fieldwork he had ever undertaken in terms of spatial coverage and duration. He spent more than 18 months during the 1978-79 in these field investigations and with this data he went to the University of Virginia as a Visiting Professor for the

1 **Chandrashekar Bhat.** "Sociology of Development and Change" Page - 21.

academic year 1979-80. During the tenure of his Visiting Professorship at the University of Virginia, M.S.A. conducted at various American Universities a series of seminars based on the analysis of his data on migration. On his return to India, he organised a workshop on *"Social, Economic And Demographic Aspects of Migration"* at Delhi. He prepared the manuscript of the edited papers presented at the workshop and gave it for publication in late 1985. This was posthumously published in 1986 under the title *"Studies in Migration"* [1986].

Felicitation With *"Sharat Chandra Roy Memorial Gold Medal"*

The year 1982 was very significant and memorable for M.S.A. Rao. His professional career, his writings, his scholarly papers presented at seminars, etc. got lot of appreciation. His contributions to the enrichment of sociology and cultural anthropology were well recognised when he was awarded the highly coveted *Sharat Chandra Roy Memorial Gold Medal* by the Asiatic Society.

Studies on *"Sociology of Food and Nutrition"*

In the early 1980s, M.S.A. Rao involved himself in making some studies in the field of *sociology of food and nutrition.* He was invited to be a *Member of Research Advisory Committee of Nutrition Foundation of India.* Dr. Rao conducted a workshop on *"Mother's Position in Child Feeding and Nutrition"* in Jan. 1984 in association with **Prof. I.P. Singh** of the Department of Anthropology, Delhi University. In recognition of his interest and competence in the field of Food and Nutrition, Dr. Rao was made one of the advisors in the *Research Advisory Committee of the Central Food Technological Research Institute* at Mysore. Along with **Prof. Khare,** he edited a book entitled *"Food, Society and Culture"* which was published by Carolina Academic Press in 1986. This work is regarded as the first of its kind to present a comparative study of food systems in India and Bangladesh.

M.S.A. took great interest in the study of population processes and food, and also problems of development. Studies of this kind ultimately culminated in the establishment of the *Population, Food and Development Research Institute* [PFDRI] in 1984, with its Registered Office at Delhi, and Project Centre at Mysore. Under the auspices of this institute he carried out two projects dealing with food, nutrition and infant mortality along with **Dr. Laxmi Narayana,** which were funded by Family Planning Foundation of India.

M.S.A.'s Emphasis on Interdisciplinary Approach

M.S.A. never confined his interest to the study of sociological issues and problems alone. He even *"........... moved beyond the frontiers of sociology to develop a "social sciences perspective." He laid great emphasis on an interdisciplinary approach in the analysis of any substantive social phenomenon, with equal partners belonging to different disciplines in social sciences to carry out the planning and execution of collaborative research."*[1] He was also planning to make combined studies on the issues of social change, social movements, economic changes and such other matters. But the unfortunate and untimely death of M.S.A. Rao, gave a great blow to the continuation of such projects.

M.S.A.'s Unfulfilled Project of Making on Integral Study of Indian Society

M.S.A. Rao had his own plans to analyse *the totality of Indian society* and proposed a project, in book form, to study Indian society and culture as an interconnected whole in terms of the

1 **Chandrashekar Bhat.** ''Sociology of Development and Change'' Page - 24.

major areas of religion, social stratification, kinship, economy and polity. In the meantime, the Centre of Advanced Study at the Princeton University honoured him with an invitation to spend a year at the Centre as a Fellow. Dr. Rao was making preparations to leave for Princeton in Sept. 1985. But events took a different turn. He fell ill because of sinusitis problem which ultimately turned out to be malignant. He was hospitalised and given radiation therapy. He was operated upon in the month of October 1985 and suffered silently the acute pain and discomfort till he breathed his last on 12th December 1985. Even while undergoing the treatment M.S.A. Rao was busy in revising his *"Urban Sociology in India"*, and finalising the manuscripts of *"Studies in Migration"* and the second edition of *"Social Movements and Social Transformation."* His project of making an integral study of the Indian society remained an unfulfilled dream. With his death, not only two of his sons Vasudev and Venkatesh lost their father but the sociologists in India also lost a great academician and a scholarly Professor.

A Bibliography of the Publications of Dr. M.S.A. Rao

1957 : *"Social Change in Malabar"*, Bombay; Popular Book Depot.

1966 : Along with M.N. Srinivas, *"A Sociological Study of Okhla Industrial Estate" : Small Industries and Social Change,* Delhi : UNESCO.

1970 : *"Urbanisation and Social Change,"* New Delhi: Orient Longman.

1972 : *"Tradition, Rationality and Change: Essays on Sociology of Economic Development and Social Change,"* Bombay: Popular Prakashan.

1972 : With M.N. Srinivas and A.M. Shah, *A Survey of Research in Sociology and Social Anthropology,* vol.III, Bombay: Popular Prakashan.

1974 : Alongwith M.N. Srinivas and A.M. Shah, "A Survey of Research in Sociology and Social Anthropology, vol.I and III," Bombay:Popular Prakashan.

1974 : *Urban Sociology in India: Reader and Source Book,* Delhi: Orient Longman.

1978 : *Social Movements in India,* vol.I, New Delhi: Manohar.

1979 : *Social Movements in India,* vol.II, New Delhi: Manohar.

1979 : *Social Movements and Social Transformation: A Study of Two Backward Classes Movements in India,* New Delhi: Macmillan.

1979 : *"Sociology in the 1980s" Economic and Political Weekly,* vol.XIV, No.44, November 3, pp. 1810-1815.

1984 : With K. Ranga Rao, *Cities and Slums: A Study of a Squatters' Settlement in the City of Vijaywada,* New Delhi: Manohar.

1984 : *"Some Subjective Orientations in Understanding Indian Social Reality",* in Ravindra Kumar (ed.) Philosophical Theory and Social Reality, Delhi: Allied Publishers.

1986 : With R.S. Khare, *Food, Society and Culture,* Durham: Carolina Academic Press.

1986 : *Studies in Migration,* New Delhi: Manohar.

***Unpublished*:** *"Social Science Perspectives",* unpublished paper analysing the problem of poverty.

Iravathi Karve

Dr. Iravathi Karve, a distinguished student of Dr. G.S. Ghurye, is a well recognised name to the academic world of India in general and to sociology and anthropology in particular. She is acclaimed as the first woman sociologist in India who had a great concern for developing sociology and social anthropology. She was a distinguished scholar and literatuer, apart from being known as an eminent anthropologist. The tributes that were paid to her soon after her departure in the various English and Marathi papers and journals alike bear out the impact she had made as a writer and thinker of distinction.

Academic Background of Dr. Karve

Dr. Karve who had obtained her master degree in sociology from Bombay University, and had gone subsequently to Germany to obtain a doctorate in anthropology. She had attained popularity among Marathi speaking public through her Marathi work *Yuganta* which bagged her the *Regional Sahitya Academy Award.* She was a writer with rare insight into the social problems and processes as well as the psychological factors that shape human behaviour and societies. She came from a distinguished reformist Maharshi Karve's family and she had strong views on social and political issues of the day. Like most of the Indian sociologists of her period, Karve was deeply interested in the study of the Hindu society and had the advantage of studying it as an insider.

Dr. Karve had a bright academic career. She was the head of Department of Sociology and Anthropology of Deccan College, Poona, since late 1930s. The Post-Graduate Research Institute at Deccan College, in fact, started functioning with Smt. Karve as the Head.

Karve's Good Command of Sanskrit

"Mrs. Karve belonged to that generation of Anthropologists who combined a knowledge of the rich Indological tradition with an anthropological approach. Learned in Sanskrit she was able to use her first hand knowledge of Sanskrit literature in understanding Hindu society. In combining Indology and Anthropology, she was like Ghurye and Kapadia. A deep acquaintance with the indigenous Sanskrit tradition, from the Vedas to Kalidasa, gave her a unique advantage as an Indian sociologist."[1]

A Scholar with Anthropological Approach

Dr. Karve was both a physical and cultural anthropologist. In fact, she began her research with an M.A. dissertation at the University of Bombay on her own caste, the Chitpavan Brahmins. Her interest in Anthropology was such that she used to travel widely into the interior jungles to take anthropometric measurements and blood groups of the tribals like the Bhils. She had even written a book alongwith Dandekar that deals with the topic of *"anthropometric measurements of Maharashtra."* She had a scientific frame of mind and blended anthropological theory with extensive field research, covering large areas in India.

A Pioneering Work in the Study of Indian Kinship

Iravathi Karve has done a pioneering work in *the study of Indian kinship.* It would not be an exaggeration to say that the basic focus through which she approached whatever aspect of Indian society she was studying, was *kinship.* She will be remembered for years to come for her magnificent contribution to the study of kinship in the form of a book entitled *"Kinship Organisation in India"* [1953, 1958]. In this book, she presents a macro-analysis of the major kinship systems in India. For

---

1 **Sunanda Patwardhan, New Delhi** in article on **Iravathi Karve** in *"Sociological Bulletin."* Volume XIX. No.2. Sept. 1970. Page : 156 - 157.

years she was engaged in collecting information from various parts of India and also from literature in ancient and modern Indian texts and in analysing it mainly in the ethnological-historical frame. She published a series of long papers on kinship terminology and kinship usages of Maharashtra [1940-41], Gujarath [1942-45] and Karnataka [1950]. All the significant contents of these have been incorporated in her famous book *Kinship Organisation in India.*

The book on kinship attempts a comparative picture of kinship organisation in different parts of India. The material on Indian kinship has been presented as belonging to four cultural zones - *the Northern, the Central, the Southern,* and *the Eastern.* Data presented by her have a very wide scope. They include lists of kinship terms in the major Indian languages, their linguistic content and corresponding behaviour and attitudes, rules of descent and inheritance and patterns of marriage and family. Differences between the Sanskritic North and the Dravidian South are also brought out.

As she says, her study is based on personal enquiry supplemented by readings in Sanskrit, Pali, Ardhamagadhi, Hindi, Marathi and Maithili. She also makes use of folk-literature. In the description of the Northern zone one part is devoted to the past, discussing the material found in ancient Sanskrit texts, while another part presents a generalized model for the whole of Northern India. Karve has tried to show the kinship organisation of the Central Zone, though modelled on the northern pattern, shows some very significant differences due to culture contact particularly with Southern Zone. In the treatment of the Southern zone, to quote the author's words, *"The kinship organisations in the various regions within this language area and of different castes and tribes within each region are presented as functional adjustments necessitated by culture-contact."* [P.24].

She maintains that there is something like a regional pattern of social behaviour. She is greatly interested in the process of acculturation and accommodation; and many customs, linguistic forms and kinship terms are sought to be explained through the region of their origins, migrations, settlement, contact with particular castes, functional association, and so on.

Karve's study abounds in generalizations some of which may not be anything more than tentative hypotheses, but there is no doubt that the book contains several invaluable insights into the realm of Indian kinship and offers significant hypotheses that deserve to be tested in the course of field studies. Her work makes it evident that structural-functional and formal structural studies of kinship in India must also take into account the historical processes of culture-contact and functional adjustments and not go by mere appearances of logic in the differences and similarities that are observed.

Criticisms About the Book : However, Karve has been criticised on several grounds. Dr. Ghurye was of the opinion that she has totally ignored Kathleen Gough's work on kinship and consequently Tamil kinship terms. In their article on *"Kinship"* in *"Contributions to Indian Sociology"* 1957 (1), 43-64, **Dumont. L.** and **Pocock, D.,** were very caustic about Smt. Karve for, they pointed to the looseness of vocabulary and lack of definition of terms used; an uncritical combination of sociological and historico-culturological approaches; confusion of diachronic and synchronic approaches; insufficient localization of data which makes verification or assessment difficult and uneven treatment of different regions. In Karve's book, factual data mainly serve an illustrative purpose.

Having said all this, it must be admitted that, *with all its drawbacks, Karve's book remains a landmark in the field of Indian kinship.*

In her later book ***"Hindu Society : An Interpretation"*** [1968], Karve has made use of her knowledge of Maharashtra and the Kunbi and also of the Rajput. With this she could meet the criticism waged against her by **Dumont** and **Pocock** that *"she does not present intensive treatment of any particular castes or parts of Maharashtra, although she had an enormous fund of knowledge regarding the features of kinship in this area."*

The elaborate structure of intra-caste hypergamy of the Maratha and the Rajput are regarded by her as pointing towards their composition through fusion of different tribal elements; and thus they are indirectly shown to be a proof of the agglomorative character of the Hindu society which is her main thesis and truly a provocative one in this book.

The theme of caste as extended kins was tested by Karve through her study of marital ties in two endogamous castes, namely, *Chitpavan Brahmin* and *Gangadikar-Vokkaliga.* Detailed studies of castes on these lines have been rewarding. She has enriched the study of kinship by her emphasis on the generational study of particular families, on finding out indicators for jointness and non-jointness of family and on finding out about an individual's experiences of living in different types of family units [1963, 1967].

And finally, Dr. Irawathi Karve did make her presence felt as a teacher and researcher.

Scholarly Contributions to Marathi Language and Literature

Dr. Karve was a versatile scholar in Marathi language also. She had written a number of books in Marathi. For example, **1.** *Amchi Samskriti* [1960], **2.** *Samskriti Mhanje Kayi ?* and **3.** *Marathi Lokanchi Samskriti* [1951], **4.** *Paripurti* [1949], **5.** *Bhovra* [1960], *Hindu Samajachi Samaja Rachana* [1964]. As it is already mentioned, her most outstanding contribution is *Yugant* [1967] which is now translated into English. This book can be said to be a vivid example of her creative and original contribution to Marathi literature.

She was always trying to feel at home with her own region, people and language. She had written a monograph *Land and People of Maharashtra* for the Government of Maharashtra. She also used to take interest in agitational issues such as – *the language problem, prohibition, communal tensions, eradication of untouchability,* and so on.

Mrs. Karve was a person with strong views and convictions. In her Deccan College, she was known as a rebel and a non-conformist. At the same time, she was traditional. Once she had even walked with *palkhi* from Poona to Pandarapur. As a teacher, she was not only brilliant and inspiring but also affectionate and sympathetic towards her students. She was a committed academician who took her profession as a career and worked with devotion.

"Mrs. Karve was intensely human, and a woman to the core. A fond mother and an indulgent grandmother, she was deeply involved in her family. She felt very strongly and had therefore strong attachments and loyalties as well as prejudices........ The succeeding generations of the scholars will remember her for an interest in the wider problems of man and for having brought a wide sensitivity and perception to the study of anthropology."[1]

Works by Dr. Iravathi Karve

1. *Kinship Terminology and Kinship Usages in Rigveda and Atharvanaveda,* 1940.
2. *Kinship Terminology and Kinship Usages of Maratha Country* - Bulletin of Deccan College Research Institute - 1940-41, 1(2-4), 2(1-2) and Presented the paper in 28th Indian Science Congress, 1941.
3. *Kinship Terminology and Usages in Gujrath and Kathewad* - [Bulletin of Deccan College Research Inst., 1942-43.

1 **Sunanda Patwardhan.** ''*Sociological Bulletin*'' Volume XIX, No. 2, Sept. 1970. Page - 160.

4. *Kinship Terms in Mahabharatha* - [Deccan College Bulletin - 1943-44].
5. *Kinship System and Kinship Terms in Karnataka* [Deccan College Bulletin-1950,10(1) 49-61]
6. *Kinship Organisation in India* - [Deccan College Research Institute, Poona - (1953, 1958)]
7. *What is Caste*? (i) Caste as Extended Kin - The Economic Weekly, 1958,10 Annual Number, 125-139]
8. *Succession in a Matrilineal Royal House* - Deccan College Bulletin- 1960, 20 (1- 4), 364-369
9. *'Family Through Six Generations'* - in Bala Ratnam edited "Anthropology on the March" - The book centre and the Social Sciences, Association, Madras. 1963.
10. *'Family in India'* in Baidyanath Varma (ED) Contemporary India, 1964.
11. *Analysis of Jointness and Non-Jointness of Family* - the Anthropologist, 1967, 14(1).
12. *Hindu Society : An Interpretation* - 1968.
13. *Land and People of Maharashtra* (a monograph)

Dr. Karve's Contributions to Marathi Literature

- *Paripurthi,* 1949.
- *Samskriti Mhanje Kayi* ?, 1951.
- *Marathi Lokanchi Samskriti,* 1951.
- *Bhovra,* 1960.
- *Amchi Samskriti,* 1960.
- *Hindu Samajachi Samaja Rachana,* 1964.
- *Yugant,* 1967 [a work that fetehed for Dr. Karve "Marathi Sahitya Academy Award" and also a prize from the Govt. of Maharashtra].

Dr. A. R. Desai

Dr. A.R. Desai's name finds a special mention among the pioneers of Indian sociology for the distinctive approach, that is, the *Marxist approach* which he advocated and practised in his sociological studies. Desai was also one among the students of Dr. Ghurye at the Bombay University who later on got the privilege of serving it as the Professor and Head of the Department of Sociology. He was one of the founding members of the *"Indian Sociological Society"* and a life member. He had the opportunity of serving the Society as its President between 1978 and 1980. He is known to the academic circles of India as one of the renowned rural and urban sociologists and also a political sociologist.

Contributions of Desai to the World of Books

Dr. A.R. Desai was a prolific writer and had brought out a number of books. Historical and dialectical perspectives in which he had viewed Indian society and rural India in particular, is revealed in his major works. He attained popularity among the Indian scholars through his works, *"Social Background of Indian Nationalism"* and *"Recent Trends in Indian Nationalism"* – which are considered to be significant contributions to the realm of political sociology. Through these works, Desai endeavoured to advocate and practice the Marxist approach in Indian sociology. These books became classic works not only in sociology but also in history.

"Social Background of Indian Nationalism" [1948]

Desai has dealt with the transformation of Indian society from medieval to modern times and the rise of Indian nationalism in various forms – social, cultural, religious, political and economic – in the book *"Social Background of Indian Nationalism"* [1948]. This book is an impressive contribution for an understanding of the dynamics of Indian nationalism in the historical and the cultural context. Desai was of the opinion that *the British rule had given a fatal blow to the peculiar feudal framework based on the stratificatory system of caste which provided a social matrix for the Indian society for more than 1,000 years.* He very strongly advocated the relevance of the Marxist approach in Indian sociology.

"Recent Trends in Indian Nationalism" [1960]

Desai followed the same Marxist approach in producing another major work of his, namely, *"Recent Trends in Indian Nationalism"* [1960]. In this work, he had employed the method of historical materialism in analysing structural transformation of Indian society during the British period and the nature of new forces in Indian nationalism during inter-war and post-war period. He had described the sense of nationalism as reflected in the social, cultural, religious, political, economic and educational spheres. This book seems to be a very good supplement to his earlier work.

"Rural Sociology in India" [1969]

Students of rural sociology will ever remember A.R. Desai for his noteworthy contribution to the field of agrarian sociology for the publication of *"Rural Sociology in India."* A.R. Desai has presented a brilliant analysis of rural society in this edited book. Since its publication, it has been a source book for the students of rural sociology in almost all the universities of the country. It virtually became a turning point and a trend-setter in the rural sociological studies in India.

"Rural India in Transition" [1961]

Another important major work on rural sociology by Desai is his *"Rural India in Transition"* in which he has analysed the dynamic forces operating in the Indian rural society and the process of change in the Indian rural set up. He made a systematic contribution to the study of social movements from the perspective of Marxist sociology.

Desai's Contributions to Urban Sociology : *Slums and Urbanisation*

It is unfair to brand A.R. Desai as a rural sociologist alone for he has also contributed to the other branches of sociology. He had cast his intellectual sway on urban sociology. Together with Devadas Pillai, Desai edited a book entitled *"Slums and Urbanisation"* which probes into the origin and growth of slums in Indian urban life.

Urban Family and Family Planning in India

Desai's another book *"Urban Family and Family Planning in India"* is a general commentary on family planning programme and its impact on family and society in urban India.

Peasant Struggles in India, 1978

Desai's book entitled *"Peasant Struggles in India"* [1978] published by Oxford University, provides us lot of information about the social movements launched by the peasant and the tribal communities of India. This book also presents a historical picture as to how the awareness and the unrest started growing among the peasants and the tribals. This book can be regarded as Desai's significant contribution to the fields such as social movements, rural sociology, comparative sociology and historical studies.

Desai – An Advocate of Marxist Approach

Desai's ideological commitment made him to stand at a distance from the team of the sociologists of his generation. He was so much impressed by the Marxist approach that he took every opportunity to popularise it. *"Relevance of the Marxist Approach to the Study of Indian Society"* was the topic of the presidential talk delivered by him in the annual conference of Indian Sociological Society held at Meerut in November 1980[1] reveals his basic ideological commitment.

A.R. Desai – A Multifaceted Scholar

It is an undeniable fact that A.R. Desai was one among the most brilliant sociologists of India. He had participated in several national and international seminars, symposia, academic conferences, workshops, research studies, etc. and on several occasions he had presided over such academic gatherings. He had taken part in the *First World Congress of Rural Sociology* held at France in 1964; and had visited Russia in 1971 as a member of the *Cultural Exchange* team. He had also participated in a Lecture Programme held at Columbia in 1976; and also in *Population and Economic Development,* a conference held at Bangkok in 1977. He had also obtained the privilege of making a special study on behalf of U.G.C., under the auspices of *Shastri Indo-Canadian Foundation*. On several occasions like these, he had the chance of revealing his intellectual calibre and also ideological convictions.

Major Works of A.R. Desai

1. *Rural India in Transition* - 1961.
2. *Rural Sociology in India* - (ed) 1969.
3. *'Social Background of Indian Nationalism'* - 1948,1966.
4. *'Recent Trends in Indian Nationalism'* - 1961.
5. *Slums and Urbanization* - (ed) with Devdas Pillai - 1970.
6. *'Urban Family and Family Planning in India'.*
7. *A Profile of an Indian Slum* - with S. Devdas Pillai.
8. *'Relevance of Marxist Approach to the Study of an Indian Society'* (based on his Presidential address to the annual Conference of ISS, Meerut 1980) - 1986 Mukherji : Sociological Bulletin. Vol.30 (1) 1981].
9. *'Peasant Struggles in India'* - (ed) 1978.

Other Works of Desai

1. *Essays of Modernization of Under Developed Societies* (ed) 2 Vols.
2. *State and Society in India* - Essays in Dissent.
3. *A Positive Programme for the Indian Revolution* (ed).

1 *"Sociological Bulletin"*, Vol. 30 (1), 1981. Pages : 1 - 20 and reprinted in *"Indian Sociology"* edited by **T.K. Oommen** and **P.N. Mukherji** - 1986. Pages : 193 - 213.

Chapter 4

MARRIAGE SYSTEM IN INDIA

A. Marriage Among Hindus : Traditional Forms of Hindu Marriage - Polygyny, Polyandry and Monogamy Among the Hindus - Anuloma and Pratiloma Marriages - Endogamy and Exogamy - The Hindu Marriage as a Sacrament - Aims of Hindu Marriage - Its Important Rites - The Sacred Beliefs and Values Involved in It - Recent Trends in the Hindu Marriage - Factors Affecting Hindu Marriage : Industrialisation, Urbanisation, Education and Legislation - Divorce - Definition of Divorce - Divorce in India - Causes of Divorce - Individual and Social Consequences of Divorce - Remedial Measures for Divorce. ***B. Marriage Among Muslims :*** *Marriage Among Muslims in India - Pre-conditions of Muslim Marriage - Conditions of Void Marriage - Importance of Mahr in Muslim Marriage - Divorce Among the Muslims - Importance of Iddat in Muslim's Divorce - Difference Between Hindu and Muslim Marriage.* ***C. Marriage Among Christians:*** *Objectives of Christian Marriage - Christian Marital Practice - Provision for Divorce - Position of Women in Christian Community.*

A. Marriage Among the Hindus

Marriage is one of the universal social institutions. It is established by the human society to control and regulate the sex life of man. Marriage is one of the deepest and most complex involvements of human relationships. It is a corner stone of a society and very necessary part of the Indian social system. As **Dr. S. Radhakrishnan** observes, *"Marriage is not a mere convention but an implicit condition of human society........ It is an adjustment between the biological purposes of nature and the sociological purposes of man........ It is an institution, it is a device for the expression and development of love."*[1] It is closely connected with the institution of family. In fact, family and marriage are complementary to each other. As **Gillin** and **Gillin** have said, *"Marriage is a socially approved way of establishing a family of procreation."* As **Westermarck** has remarked, *"Marriage is rooted in the family rather than the family in the marriage."* Marriage is an institution of society which can have very different implications in different cultures. Its purposes, functions and forms may differ from society to society, but marriage as such is present everywhere as an institution.

Marriage is the very foundation of civil society. It has been regarded by all religions as the basis of civilised society, sound moral system and domestic affection. Family is the most significant unit of the society and marriage is the foundation of it. Marriage and family, the two social institutions with biological foundations, are supportive of each other. Both have a long standing history of their

1 **Dr. S. Radhakrishnan** *"Religion and Society"* [1956]. Page - 147. as quoted by **C.B. Mamoria** in *"Social Problems and Social Disorganisation in India."* Page - 211.

own. In the Indian context also both the institutions have been in existence since time immemorial. Both have withstood the ravages of time and the shocks of centuries. They are the permanent elements in our social system.

In the Hindu social heritage marriage has never been looked at from the materialistic point of view. *Marriage among the Hindus is a sacrament and not a contract.* The **Rig Veda** itself [*Rig Veda - X 85*] speaks of the sanctity of the institution of marriage. The tie of marriage was regarded even at that stage as a binding force all through life. Marriage was a ritual which enjoined the husband to regard his wife as a god-given gift. The *Rig Vedic mantras,* the *Brahmanas* and the *Smriti Texts* have highlighted the importance of marriage as a sacrament or *"samskara."* Ever since the time of the Rig Veda, the marriage sacrament had attained the social and the religious sanction. The **Taittiriya Brahmana** in some context states that a man by himself is only a *half-man* and his *second half* [*"Ardhangini"*] is his wife. The *Smriti texts* have repeatedly extolled the sanctity of the matrimonial bond. The **Smritis** or the **Shastras** state that the main purpose of marriage is to enable a man to become a householder to perform *Panchamahayajnas* with the companionship of his wife, to please the *Pitris* and the Gods and to procreate sons. Centuries have rolled on since then. The Hindu marriage though has undergone vast changes has not totally lost its sanctity.

Here is a glance of the institution of Hindu marriage with a special reference to its importance and the changes taking place in it. The chapter also makes a brief survey of the Muslim marriage and marriage among the Christians in India.

THE HINDU MARRIAGE

The Hindus have been giving great importance to marriage since time immemorial. Marriage is almost obligatory and unavoidable for an average Indian. Life without marriage is almost unthinkable in this country and there is a sharp social stigma attached to those who remain unmarried for long. There is a deep-rooted, long-standing and widespread tradition here in favour of marriage as a basic ritual. Hence **C.B. Mamoria** rightly commented that *"we are a much marrying people. We marry early and we marry in large number."*[1]

Hindu Marriage - A Religious Duty and Not a Contract

Marriage is a matter of religious duty for the Hindus. Every Hindu is committed to marriage for he regards it as a great s*acrament. [sacred Vivaha Samskara]*. For the Hindus, marriage is **not** a matter of "social contract", nor is it deemed as "a licence for sex life". In the Hindu scheme of the *Ashramas,* one can enter the much praised *"grihasthashrama"* only after the marriage. With the marriage sacrament, man and woman as husband and wife establish the family, the home or *"griha". Grihasthashrama* is not merely a biological necessity but is also a well thought-out social institution. It is *"shaped, organised and idealised by human effort, ingenuity and wisdom for ages past."*[2]

Grihyasutras generally begin with *Vivaha Samskara* because it is the origin and centre of all domestic sacrifices. They presuppose that every man, in his normal conditions is expected to marry [that is, to undergo *"vivaha samskara"*] and run a family [*kutumba*]. Grihasthashrama [i.e., householder's life] begins with the *"vivaha." "Vivaha"* refers mainly to the ceremony of *"carrying away"* the bride to the house of the bridegroom [*vi + vaha* = to carry]. But the term has long since come to be applied to the whole of the wedlock ceremony. It is known that even before the period of the *"Grihyasutras"* which were composed in about 6th century B.C., the marriage ceremonies were developed and found literary expression in the *Rig Veda* and the *Atharva Veda.*

1 **C.B. Mamoria** *"Social Problems and Social Disorganisation in India."*

2 **P.H. Prabhu** *"Hindu Social Organisation"* [1998 Edition]. Page - 15.

As far as the Hindus are concerned, *vivaha* is generally considered obligatory for every person, because, in the first place, the birth of a son is said to enable one to obtain *moksha. "To be mothers were women created, and to be fathers men; therefore, the Vedas ordain that dharma must be practised by man together with his wife." Vivaha* is one of *sarira-samskaras* [sacraments sanctifying the body] each of which every man and woman must pass through at the proper age and time. **Manu** considers it as a social institution for the regulation of proper relations between the sexes.

The Hindus believe that *"one's progeny is connected with and is instrumental to happiness both in this world as well as hereafter"* [***Manu Smriti***]. Manu Smriti clearly states that *"he is a perfect man, who consists of his wife, himself and his offspring."*[1] **Mahabharatha** also stated that it was impossible for a lady *"to gain the ultimate bliss as long as she was not sanctified [asamskrita] by marriage rites."* Further, the birth of a son is conceived to be particularly contributory towards helping the father to execute his obligations which are due to the departed ancestors, called *"pitri rinas."* It is a social obligation for every Hindu to fulfil the *"pitri rinas."* **Vedas** have enjoined that dharma must be observed by man together with his wife. Sacrifices performed or pilgrimages undertaken will have no effect, if the wife is not a partner in those holy duties. **Manu** considers *vivaha* a necessary social institution for practising the *Grihastha dharma.*

Hindu *shastrakaras* have highlighted the necessity of *vivaha* for a woman though it is no less significant for men. **Mahabharatha** clearly states that a *"wife is the very source [mulam] of the purusharthas, not only of dharma, artha and kama, but even of moksa. Those that have wives can fulfil their due obligations in this world [kriyavantah]; those that have wives, truly lead a family life; those that have wives can be happy; and those that have wives can lead a full life [sriyanvita]."*[2]

Hindu *shastrakara*s have prescribed that the girls should marry as soon as they attain marriageable age. A girl who continues to stay in her father's home more than three years after attaining puberty, is called a *"Vrishala"* or a *"sudra"*, that is, a very low type, and the father or the guardian of such a girl is said to be incurring a great sin. The early *shastras* permit such unmarried girls to take the whole responsibility upon themselves of choosing their life-mates and enter into wedlock with them. They need to wait for three years only after puberty for some responsible elder to arrange for their marriage, but no more. *"**Vatsyayana** too, advises a young maiden who has attained youth [prapta-yauvana] to select a husband for herself and get married without waiting for the assistance and permission of her elders."*[3]

Some Views about Hindu Marriage

Number of Indian thinkers, writers and scholars have expressed their opinions about Hindu marriage. Let us consider a few of them.

- *"Marriage is not for sense enjoyment but to perpetuate the race. This is the Indian conception of marriage."*
- *"Marriage is a social duty towards the family and the community."*
- *"It is a social and an ethical relationship established for the purpose of begetting children and the repayment of parental debt."*
- *"Marriage is a religious sacrament which is considered primarily a complex of obligations, religious and moral, on the one hand, and social and economic on the other."*
- Among Hindus, *"marriage is a Sanskara [tradition], and a religious sacrament, not a*

---

1 **Manu Smriti** as quoted by **P.H. Prabhu.** Page - 150.

2 *Adiparva of Mahabharatha* as quoted by **P.H. Prabhu.** Page - 150.

3 Views of **Vatsyayana,** the author of *"Kama Sutra"* as quoted by **P.H. Prabhu.** Page - 151.

contract. It is a holy union of the two souls and not simply of two bodies, for the performance of religious rights. It is an indissoluble bond which could be broken only by death."

- **Dr. Radhakrishnan** observes, *"marriage is not a mere convention but an implicit condition of human society. It is an adjustment between the biological purposes of nature and the sociological purpose of man." He further says, "it is an institution, a device for the expression and development of love." Its purpose is not only the generation and nurturing of children but also "the enrichment of the personality of the husband and wife, through the fulfilment of their need for a permanent comradeship, in which each may supplement the life of the other and both may achieve completeness."*[1]

- *"Marriage was and is considered a ceremonial gift of the bride by her father, or other appropriate relative, to the bridegroom in order that both may together fulfil three of the standard purposes of human existence. The ends mentioned are : Dharma, Artha and Kama. The first, i.e., religious duty, includes the fourth end known as Moksha or salvation – we may take it that the marriage union was declared to be entered into by the two partners for the fulfilment in common of the cherished goals of human existence."*[2]

Summarising the views we may say that marriage is a union of two persons of different sexes to lifelong reciprocal "passion of their sexual qualities", which aims at the individuals' biological, emotional, social and spiritual fulfilment and development, and which canot be achieved in isolation.[3]

Traditional Forms of Hindu Marriage

The expression ***"forms of marriage"*** normally refers to the four major forms of marriage such as – *Monogamy, Polygamy, Polyandry* and *Group Marriage* – as mentioned by anthropologist **Malinowski.** But in the context of the Hindu *Vivaha* the expression *"forms of marriage"* denotes *"the method of consecrating a marriage union."* The forms of marriage that are mentioned by **Manu,** the great Hindu *shastrakara* and referred to by other *shastrakaras* are as follows – 1. *Brahma,* 2. *Daiva,* 3. *Arsha,* 4. *Prajapatya,* 5. *Asura,* 6. *Gandharva,* 7. *Rakshasa,* and 8. *Paisacha.*

The *smritis* including the *Manu Smriti* have brought together these eight forms of marriage into two main groups, namely, (i) ***Prashasta*** or *Approved* or *Desirable marriages* and (ii) ***Aprashasta*** or *Disapproved* or *Undesirable marriages.*

(A) ***Prashasta*** form of marriages include the first four types, namely, *Brahma, Daiva, Arsha* and *Prajapatya.*

(B) ***Aprashasta*** form of marriages include the last four forms, namely, *Asura, Gandharva, Rakshasa* and *Paisacha.* The *shastrakaras* have approved of *Prashasta* form of marriages while the *Aprashasta* marriages are forbidden or disapproved of.

A. *"Prashasta"* Form of Marriages

(i) ***Brahma Vivaha*** **:** Brahma vivaha is the purest form of marriage. In this form of marriage the father offers his daughter to a man of character and learning. The daughter who is decked with ornaments and richly dressed is given as a kind of gift [*danam*] to a man of good character [*srutisilavan*] and high learning. The *smritis* regard this as the most honourable type of marriage since it is free from physical force, compulsion or imposition of conditions and lure of money. This form can be traced back to the Vedic times. It is still in currency and popular in India though often disfigured with the ugly practice of dowry.

1 **C.B. Mamoria** in *"Social Problems and Social Disorganisation in India."* Page - 211.
2 *ibid.* Page - 212.
3 *ibid.* Page - 213.

(ii) *Daiva Vivaha* : In the Daiva form of vivaha the father gives away his daughter as a *dakshina* [sacrificial fee] to an young priest who officiates the *yajna* which is arranged by him. This form of marriage is called *daiva* because the girl is gifted to a priest on the occasion of a sacrifice to a *daiva* or god. These girls are maidens who are offered as *dakshina.* They are called *"vadhus."* Though this form of marriage was in practice during the early period, during the later days it was considered improper to offer a girl to a priest without taking into account his status. It was also thought that a girl could not be gifted away in this manner. Hence *daiva* form of marriage was considered inferior to *Brahma* marriage.

(iii) *Arsha Vivaha* : In this form of marriage, the father gives his daughter in marriage to the bridegroom after receiving a cow and a bull or two pairs of these from the bridegroom in accordance with the requirements of *dharma.* But this form of marriage should not be confused with the form of the bride-price or with that of the dowry. The gift of cow and bull is to be made as a token of gratitude to the man who offers his daughter to the groom to enable him to fulfil his *grihasthashrama* obligations. In course of time, with the decline of rituals, this form of marriage became out of date. *Manu Smriti* states that *"some prescribe the acceptance of one pair of cows in the arsha vivaha, but it is improper. It is a sale; it matters little whether one accepts a large sum or a small one."*

(iv) *Prajapatya Vivaha* : In this form of vivaha, the father makes a gift of the daughter by addressing the couple with the *mantram "may both of you perform together your dharma."* The girl is given as a gift with a clear understanding that the couple will perform their civic and religious duties together. This form of marriage is inferior to the first three because the bride is not a free gift but a condition is laid on both the bride and the bridegroom.

In the four forms mentioned above, the important point to be noted is that it is the father [or a person in his place] who makes a gift [*dana*] of the bride to the bridegroom.

B. *"Aprashasta"* Form of Marriages

(v) *Asura Vivaha* : Unlike the first four types of the marriage mentioned above, the *Asura* type of marriage is one in which the bridegroom has to give money to the father or kinsman of the bride. The main consideration of this form of marriage is money. The bride, in this form of marriage, is virtually purchased. The Smriti writers consider the *asura* marriage either a traditional custom or a necessary evil. According to **Manu,** the learned father of the girl should not accept even the least amount of price. If he accepts it, he comes to be regarded as the seller of children. In the present day Indian society the *asura* form of marriage mostly does not exist.

(vi) *Gandharva Vivaha* : The *Gandharva* type of marriage is the one in which a girl selects her husband by herself. The marriage of Shakuntala and Dushyantha is a classical example of this kind of marriage. Manu gives a comprehensive definition of it in the following manner – *"where the bride and the bridegroom meet each other of their own accord and the meeting is consummated in copulation born of passion, that form is called gandharva."* It can also be considered a kind of marriage wherein the mutual love and consent of the bride and the bridegroom is the only condition required to bring about the union. Neither the father nor the kinsmen need have a hand in bringing about the marriage. This type of marriage is called *gandharva,* because it was in practice in the Gandharva tribe living on the slopes of the Himalayas. During the early days it was in practice among the Kshatriyas in which the kings used to arrange *swayamvara*s inviting princes from different places so that their daughters may get a wide selection to choose their husbands. By *swayamvara* we mean the selection of the bridegroom by the bride herself. The marriage of Damayanthi with Nala, and Prithviraj Chauhan with Samyukta can be mentioned here as examples. The *gandharva vivaha* in its original style is not in practice today but it has assumed a new form called *"love marriage."*

(vii) *Rakshasa Vivaha* : The *rakshasa* form is described in the Hindu scriptures as *"the forcible abduction of a maiden from her home, while she cries and weeps, after her kinsmen have* *been slained or wounded and their houses broken."* It is the capture of bride by force. Here the bridegroom does not take the consent of the girl but simply forces her to marry him. It is to be noted that *rakshasa* form of marriage disappeared in course of time. But in its place the practice of girls eloping with heroes with whom they fall in love started taking place. The examples of Rukmini and Subhadra [in the Epic age] eloping with Lord Krishna and Arjuna respectively and Samyukta eloping with Prithviraj Chauhan [in the Medieval age], can be cited here.

(viii) *Paisacha Vivaha* : *Paisacha* form of marriage is one in which the man seduces by force a girl who is sleeping or intoxicated or disordered in intellect. Dharmashastra writers like **Gauthama** and **Vishnu** define it as *"co-habiting with a girl who is unconscious, sleepy or intoxicated."* This form of marriage, however, has disappeared altogether in India.

Of these eight forms of marriages, *Brahma vivaha* is considered to be the best form of marriage where a girl is given to a boy of merit in the same caste or in a caste of equal status. Both bride and bridegroom in this marriage are supposed to be mutually agreeable for the marriage. In the present day Hindu society also the *Brahma vivaha* is considered the most preferable one in which the father gifts his daughter to a suitable bridegroom through the ritual of *kanyadana.*

Polygyny, Polyandry and Monogamy Among the Hindus

Polygyny and Polyandry and Monogamy – all these main forms of marriage are found among the Hindus.

POLYGYNY

***Polygyny** is a type of marriage in which one man marries more than one woman.* In this form of marriage we find, what may be called *"the plurality of wives."* Though monogamy was the rule fixed by the Rig Veda and the Brahmachari entered the *grihasthashrama* with his marriage, polygyny was in practice in ancient times and persisted till the beginning of the present century. *"Until the passage of the Hindu Marriage Act in 1955, every Hindu was in theory free to marry a number of women. In fact, however, a very small percentage of Hindus were polygynous."*[1] It had become a social custom to have many wives as it increased the prestige of the man in society. It was usual for the princes and the aristocratic people and not for the common people. The Nawabs and rich landlords used to have a number of wives.[2]

Causes of Polygyny

During the early days, the barrenness of a wife or her failure to give birth to a son was generally the reason for taking a second wife. According to **Apasthamba,** a man could marry again after **10** years of his first marriage if his wife was barren, or he could marry after **13** or **14** years if he had only daughters from his wife and wanted a son. **Manu** also permitted polygyny more or less for the very same reasons.

It should, however, be noted that *during the ancient period monogamy was the prevailing practice of marriage though polygyny was permitted under specific conditions.* In the **Mahabharatha** it is said that a man who marries twice without a rational cause commits sin for which there is no penance. *Shastrakara* **Nanda** also said that a man who marries twice should not be accepted as a witness.

Among some trading and warrior castes, a wealthy or powerful man took a second wife. Among the higher castes monogamy prevailed, the ideal of having only one wife [*ekapatnivrata*]

1 **M.N. Srinivas** in article *"Social Structure"* in the *"Gazetteer of India"* Vol.1 [1965]. Page 540.

2 The Indian Muslims under the influence of the Turko-Mughal rulers, the plight of foreign origin, alien culture and the Islamic law adopted the practice of polygyny. It gained popularity at times. This practice is, however, losing its popularity, due to the changing socio-economic conditions.

being as old as the Ramayana. This applies to Jains also, but they have no religious necessity for a son. Muslims are permitted to take four wives each, even at present, provided all are treated as equals. Again, the actual incidence of polygyny among Muslims is very small; only the rich and the powerful occasionally take a second wife. Christians are forbidden to take a second wife.

Polygyny among the Hindus has become a thing of the past. It is legally prohibited. Bombay State had passed a legislation against its practice as early as in 1946 and later Madras and Saurashtra governments followed it. But ***The Hindu Marriage Act,* 1955** introduced by the Central Government repealed all the previous legislations and it strictly prohibits polygyny.

Polygyny today is not in practice for obvious reasons :

(i) People no more stick on to the philosophy that one should have a son to attain *"moksha."*

(ii) The idea that the sons are required to give support in the old age has also died out.

(iii) Maintaining too many wives is highly expensive and hence not possible for the majority.

(iv) Under the changed socio-economic and educational conditions women themselves are not ready to accept the status of a second wife at home. Most of the women are not ready to lower their social status by giving consent to polygyny.

(v) People are highly convinced that monogamy is the most ideal and at the same time, the most practicable form of marriage.

POLYANDRY

Polyandry *is a form of marriage in which one woman is married to more than one man.* It is very less common than polygyny. It is a practice involving plurality of husbands. In the Epic of Mahabharatha we have the instance of Draupadi, daughter of Drupada, the king of Panchala, marrying five Pandava brothers. According to **Dr. Keith,** *"the solitary case of Draupadi in the Epic was an exception and was so treated at that time. The father of Draupadi was shocked at the proposal of the Pandava princes to marry his daughter........"* Vyasa, referring to the case of Draupadi, remarked that it was *"against usage",* but had *"to be accepted as preordained."* **Aiteraya Brahmana** also holds : *"A woman cannot have two husbands."* In the **Mahabharatha** itself, it is said; *"to have many wives is no dharma on the part of men but to violate the duty owed to the first husband would be a great adharma in the case of woman."* It is clear from these and many other sources, that polyandry was not a prevailing practice among the Hindus during the early times.

A few Kerala castes [***Example,*** Nairs][1] practised polyandry until recently and it is not unlikely that it still continues to be practised to some extent in remote places. The **Todas** and **Kotas** of the Nilgiris, the Khasa of Jaunsar Bawar [Dehradun district] and a few other North Indian castes also practice polyandry. The Todas formerly practised female infanticide and this meant that there were fewer women than men, a condition which compelled them to practise polyandry. With the abolition of infanticide, women became more numerous and the Todas began to combine polyandry with polygyny.

MONOGAMY

Monogamy *is a form of marriage in which one man marries one woman.* It is commonly practised in our society. It is the law and the practice in our society. It is the law and practice in the country, except in case of Muslims. Ever since the Vedic times in India, monogamy has been the most dominant form of marriage being practised by the Hindus. In fact, every modern society [except the Muslim society] supports monogamy as the most suitable form of marriage.

---

1 In 1896, ***The Malabar Marriage Act*** was passed and it prohibited polyandrous unions taking place among the Nairs and stabilised marriage among them.

Monogamy produces the highest type of love and affection between husband and wife. It contributes to family peace, solidarity and happiness. **Vatsyayana,** an authority on "Kama Sutra", remarked : *"At best a man can only please one woman physically, mentally and spiritually. Therefore, the man who enters into marriage relations with more than one woman, voluntarily courts unhappiness and misery."*

Malinowski too has observed *"Monogamy is, has been, and will remain the only true type of marriage."* He also said that it *"provides a solid foundation of good home. the permanence of relationship that it guarantees, generates mutuality and oneness, loyalty and affection."* It gives, what can be best called the family protection to the old and invalid, to the grown up and growing children, and makes for family stability and equilibrium.

Most of the Hindu *shastrakaras* including **Manu** recommended monogamy as the most ideal form of marriage. The great epic **Ramayana** highlights the character of Sri Ramachandra, the hero of Ramayana, as the champion of *ekapatnivratashta* [ardent follower of monogamous marriage]. The Hindu *shastrakaras* have permitted bigamy and polygyny under some conditions but never recommended them as the best ones. It can also be said that among the higher castes monogamy prevailed, the ideal of having only one wife [*ekapatnivrata*] being as old as the Ramayana. Prior to the passing of ***The Hindu Marriage Act,* 1955,** other forms of marriage also prevailed among the Hindus. But after 1955, due to the relative stringent enforcement of the Act only monogamy prevails among majority of the Hindus.

HYPERGAMY AND HYPOGAMY OR ANULOMA AND PRATILOMA MARRIAGES

• Hypergamy or Anuloma Marriage

During the Vedic Age inter-varna [or inter-class] marriages used to take place in the form of hypergamy or *Anuloma.*

***Hypergamy or Anuloma** is a social practice according to which a boy from upper varna / caste / class can marry a girl from lower varna / caste / class.*

Anuloma marriage was recommended by the ancient Hindu law-givers for the first three varnas or classes of the then society namely, (i) the *Brahmins;* (ii) the *Kshatriyas;* and (iii) the *Vaishyas.* But marriage of a *Shudra* girl with a higher varna / caste boy was condemned. **Manu** had stated that twice-born men who wed wives of a low varna / caste would soon degrade their families and their children to the state of a *Shudra.* It was also enjoined that Gods would not eat the offerings of the men who perform rites in their honour with a *Shudra* wife's assistance.

According to the Dharma*shastrakaras*, a girl should marry in her own varna, failing which she may marry one in any of the higher varna. In the Rig Vedic period, the priests who officiated *Yajnas* [sacrifices] arranged by the kings, married *Kshatriya* girls offered to them as *"dakshina"* or fees for their services. Children born to an *Arya* [*dvija,* particularly a Brahmin] and a *Shudra* girl were known as *"dasiputras"* in the Aryan society.

"Hypergamy occurs in different parts of India; among the Brahmins of Bengal; Anavali Brahmins and Leva-Patidars of Gujarat; Rajputs in Gujarat and Rajasthan; Marathas of Maharashtra; and Nairs, Kshatriayas and Ambalavasis of Kerala."[1]

M.N. Srinivas has observed that "Hypergamy tends to occur where the structural gulf is narrow in fact, it may be said to occur among the different sections of a single caste rather than

1 **M.N. Srinivas** in article *"Social Structure"* in *"The Gazetteer of India."* Page - 543.

between castes which are widely separated." He has cited the examples of Rarhiya Brahmins of Bengal and Leva-Patidars of Gujarat among whom hypergamy is in practice.

Example of the Rarhiya Brahmins : "In Bengal, the Rarhiya Brahmins are divided into three *jatis*, Kulin, Bansaj, and Srotriya. the last mentioned are subdivided into Suddha srotriya and Kasta srotriya. The Kulins are the highest among the three *jatis* and Kulin bridegrooms are in great demand. A few decades ago, the demand for Kulin men was so great that they could [and did] demand huge dowries from the parents of girls who sought to marry them. It also gave rise to polygyny among Kulins." Among the Leva-Patidars also hypergamy is in practice but in a still more intricate manner.

Social Impact of Hypergamy

Hypergamous marriage was normally associated with polygyny.

The association of hypergamy with polygyny led to the ugly practice of dowry. "Kulin" youngmen of Bengal, for example, used to marry several girls in order to amass huge sum of money through dowry.

The urgency to find out a bridegroom of equal strata or even higher strata also contributed to the practice of child marriages.

As **Kapadia** has pointed out, hypergamy sought to fix permanently a social hierarchy in which the supremacy of the Brahmins over the Kshatriyas was categorically asserted. He has also pointed out that hypergamy helped considerably the endogamous tendency of the Brahmins.

Educated Indians are critical of the institution of hypergamy, and especially, of the large dowries associated with it. The practice of hypergamy has almost disappeared in castes such as the Nairs and Nambudiris whereas it continues to flourish in some castes such as the "Patidars."

• Hypogamy or Pratiloma Marriage

Pratiloma or ***Hypogamy*** is *a type of marital practice in which a man of lower class / caste / varna marries a girl of higher class / caste / varna.* Such cases of Shudra-Aryan connections are also recorded in the Vedic texts.

Some *Dharmashastrakaras* had even permitted the practice of *"pratiloma"* while many condemned it. By the time of *Dharmashastras,* greater disapproval was shown towards this practice. Even here, the marriage of Brahmin / Kshatriya / Vaishya girl with Shudra boy was more despised with, than the marriage of a Brahmin girl with a Kshatriya / Vaishya boy. In fact, the Kadamba king Kakustha Verma, a Brahmin by Varna, gave his daughter in marriage to the Gupta prince, who was a Vaishya.

Of the two types of marital practices, *"anuloma"* and *"pratiloma", anuloma* was considered preferable to *pratiloma* marriage. *Pratiloma* marriage was very much discouraged and even condemned. *Shastrakara* **Manu** was of the opinion that the progeny of the most hated *pratiloma* would become *"chandalas"* or "untouchables." In the ***Chandukya Upanishad*** and also in the ***"Buddhist Jatakas"*** we find vast references to *Chandalas*. In fact, the origin of the practice of untouchability is to be seen in the practice of pratiloma marriage.

Anuloma or pratiloma, as a rule of marriage is an inseparable part of the varna / caste system. **Kapadia,** thus concludes that *"the rule of anuloma and pratiloma marriages has greater significance for the caste structure of Hindu society than for the marriage pattern of the Hindus."*

ENDOGAMY and EXOGAMY

The process of mate selection among the Hindus is very much limited by the rules of marriage such as *hypergamy, endogamy* and *exogamy.*

• ENDOGAMY

Endogamy is a rule of marriage which is intimately related to the caste structure. According to this rule, *a person has to marry within his or her group or varna or caste or subcaste.* ***For example,*** Brahmins have to marry Brahmins, Rajputs have to marry Rajputs, Marathas have to marry Marathas, and so on. Further, Brahmins of Karnataka are further subdivided into Smartha Brahmins and Madhva Brahmins and these subcastes are also endogamous. In the same way, Okkaligas, i.e., one of the dominant castes of Karnataka, are subdivided into Hallikars, Nonabas, Gangadigars, Kunchudigars, and so on. Each one of these subcastes is again endogamous. Thus, an Okkaliga has to marry not only an Okkaliga girl but also in his own endogamous group whether it is Hallikar or Nonaba or any other as the case may be.

As **M.N. Srinivas** has pointed out, *"Endogamous jatis also exist among Sikhs, Jains, Christians and Muslims. The Syeds, the aristocratic Muslim caste, are divided into endogamous groups. Sometimes the endogamous group is so small that it includes only the extended families of a man's parents......... Among some Gujarathi castes there is strict spatial delimitation of the endogamous field."*[1]

• EXOGAMY

***Exogamy** is a rule of marriage according to which an individual has to select his / her life-partner outside his / her own group.* Hindus in general practise two types of exogamy, namely, (i) *Sagotra Exogamy,* and (ii) *Sapinda Exogamy.*

(i) Sagotra Exogamy

The gotra exogamy prohibits marriage between members of the same gotra. Sagotra exogamy, i.e., marrying outside one's own "gotra" is very much prevalent even today among the upper castes such as the Brahmins and Kshatriyas. In fact, as **M.N. Srinivas** points out "Gotra exogamy applies in its fullness to all the "twice-born" castes. These castes have a tradition of descent from certain sages who are believed to have lived in the remote past and two persons claiming descent from the same "gotra"....... were forbidden from marrying each other......"[2]

The gotra of a family is named after the Rishi or sage who founded the family in the immemorial past. There were only a few gotras [say, eight, according to a source] in the beginning, but in course of time, their numbers increased enormously.

Altekar pointed out that there were no restrictions on gotra marriage upto 600 B.C. Gotra exogamy, according to Kapadia, was not in existence in the Vedic period. The earliest mention of this word in its technical sense is found in the ***Chandogya Upanishad,*** where the guru asks his pupil Satyakama Jabali his gotra. By the time of Gautama Buddha, that is, 6th century B.C., the gotra system had become an established institution. It is said that Smritikara Manu imposed restrictions on marriage in one's own gotra.

"It may be added that several ambitious non-Brahmanical castes have either claimed descent from traditional *gotra-rsis* or have invented new gotras. The Lingayats of Mysore have gotras which are quite different from the Brahmanical gotras. Gujars, Ahirs, Jats and other castes in villages near Delhi have gotras but these are also different from Brahmanical gotras. Often, a non-Brahmin caste which was divided into exogamous clans with each clan claiming descent from a plant or animal changed the totem names of *gotra-rsis*. ***The Hindu Marriage Act* of 1955** *legalises marriage between members of the same gotra."*

1 **M.N. Srinivas** *"The Gazetteer of India."* Vol.I. Page - 543.
2 **M.N. Srinivas** *"The Gazetteer of India."* Vol.I. Page - 544.

Sapravara Exogamy

Pravara is closely connected with "gotra" or family. Just as the sagotra marriages, sapravara marriages are also forbidden especially for Brahmins. Persons belonging to the same pravara cannot intermarry. *People who utter the name of a common saint at religious functions are believed to belong to the same pravara.* The pravara is a kind of religious and spiritual bond. *Sapravara Exogamy,* that is marrying outside one's own pravara, has been imposed as a rule for the upper castes, especially for the Brahmins.

Sapinda Exogamy

Among the Hindus marriage within the *"pinda"* group, that is, sapinda group, is prohibited. The term *"pinda"* has two meanings : (i) Those who share the particles of the same body; and (ii) Those who are united by offering balls of cooked rice [pinda] to the same dead ancestors. In simple words, pinda means common parentage.

According to Gauthama and Brihaspathi, offsprings from five maternal generations and seven paternal generations are *"sapinda"* and they cannot intermarry. This opinion, however, is not universally accepted. Though certain exceptions are there in South India, in North India, generally, Sapinda marriages do not take place. But Sapinda exogamy, that is, marrying outside one's pinda is commonly found. Other than Brihaspathi and Gauthama, several others have narrowed the circle to permit the marriage of cross-cousins; i.e., descendants from the same pair of grandparents may marry, so long as they are not parallel cousins.

The Hindu Marriage Act of 1955 bars marriagc within five generations on the agnatic side and three on the mother's side. But it permits the marriage of cross-cousins where this is customary.

1. The Hindu Marriage - A Sacrament

Among the Hindus, *marriage is not a social contract; it is a religious sacrament.* Marriage to a Hindu is of great individual and social significance. It is a socially approved union of man and woman aiming at procreation, pleasure and observance of certain social obligations.

The Hindu ideal emphasises the individual as well as social aspects of marriage. **K.M. Kapadia** in his *"Marriage and Family in India"* has given much information in support of the view that Hindu marriage is a sacrament. His explanation can be analysed from three angles:

(a) *aims of the Hindu Marriage;* (b) *Main rituals which are involved in the Hindu marriage;* and (c) the *basic beliefs and values underlying the Hindu marriage.*

(a) Aims of the Hindu Marriage

As **Kapadia** has pointed out, the main aims of the Hindu marriage are: ***'dharma'***, ***'praja'*** and ***'rati'***. Of these aims, *dharma* is given the first place, *'rati'* or pleasure is given only the third place, and *'praja'* or progeny is given the second place.

1. *Dharma* : The Hindu thinkers regarded Dharma as the first and the highest aim of the Hindu marriage. Marriage is desired not so much for sex or for children as for acquiring a partner for the fulfilment of one's religious duties.

On marriage, the sacred fire is enkindled, and it is the duty of the householder to offer *"panchamahayajnas"* daily in the company of his wife. These obligations would cease to exist only on the death of the householder. They get disturbed on the death of the wife, and hence the householder could marry immediately a second wife. The basic aim of marriage is *Dharma* for it necessarily involves the fulfilment of a number of moral duties.

2. *Praja [Progeny]* : The desire to get issues or children is commonly felt by all the people. Psychologists call it *parental instinct.* The desire for *'praja'* or progeny is regarded by the Hindu

Shastrakaras as one of the sacred purposes of marriage. The Upanishads have aslo stressed the continuance of the line of progeny. Getting a son is essential for a Hindu, for it is believed that one can fulfil one's *"Pitri Rina"* [paternal obligations] only by getting a son. It is *'Kutumba Dharma'* [family obligation] also. In one of the important marriage rituals called *"saptapadi"* also the husband prays the wife to fetch children for the family.

3. *Rati [Kama or Pleasure]* : Though sex is one of the functions of marriage it is given the *third* place. It is the least desirable aim of marriage. To stress the lower role of sex in marriage, the marriage of a *Shudra* is said to be for pleasure only. The Brahmanic legislations enjoin that the *Shudra* wife would be taken only for pleasure. However, sex is never condemned nor degraded. It is given the third place because *dharma* is more expected of *'vivaha'* than *'kama'*.

(b) Important Rites Associated with Hindu Marriage

Among the Hindus there are certain rites which must be performed for marriage to be complete. The main rites are: *vagdana, kanyadana, homa, panigrahana, saptapadi* and *mangalyadharana.* These rites and the importance attached to them have added to the sanctity of the Hindu marriage.

(i) *Vagdana [Oral Promise]* : In the presence of the people gathered for the marriage the *names, gotras* and *pravaras* of the bride and the bridegroom are announced along with the announcement that they are ready for the marriage. This ritual is known as *"Panigrahana sankalpa"* or *Vagdana.*

(ii) *Homa* : *'Homa'* refers to the offering in the sacred fire. A number of *'homas'* or fire rituals are observed in the marriage of which *"Laja Homa"* is an important one. This *'homa'* is symbolic of fecundity and prosperity. Fried grains dipped in ghee are offered to fire [that is to *Lord Agni*] by the couple with a prayer to the God requesting him to bless them with progeny and prosperity.

(iii) *Kanyadana* : This is the most important ceremony connected with marriage. It is the ceremony of giving away the bride as a gift to the bridegroom in the presence of the sacred fire and in the presence of the people gathered. The father of the bride gifts her away to the bridegroom with a promise on his part that he would not transgress her *"in the attainment of piety, wealth and desire"*. The same promise is repeated thrice and the bridegroom affirms his promise thrice.

(iv) *Panigrahana [Holding the Hand of the Bride]* : This ritual refers to taking the right hand of the bride with the words: *"I seize thy hand for the sake of happiness that you may live to old age with me..."* With this the bridegroom takes the responsibility of looking after the bride.

(v) *Mangalya Dharana [Tying of the Tali or Mangalasutra]*: This involves the act of tying the *tali* or *mangalasutra* [which is regarded as the sign of longevity of the husband] round the neck of the bride by the bridegroom. This ritual for which there is no reference in the *Dharmashastras* is more in practice in South India than in the North. It has even influenced the Catholic Christians of the South. [In north India, particularly in Bengal, Bihar, U.P. and Orissa the binding part of the marriage ceremony is *"sindurdan"* or painting of the part of the hair on the bride's forehead with vermilion and putting lac bangles in her hands by the groom - **C.B. Mamoria** [Page: 221]

(vi) Saptapadi : This is the ritual in which the bride and the bridegroom go *'seven-steps'* together. The husband makes the bride step forward in the northern direction seven steps with the words: *"one step for sap, two for juice, three for wealth, four for comfort, five for cattle, six for seasons, friend be with seven steps united to me"*. This ritual is important from the legal point of view, for the Hindu marriage is regarded legally complete only after it is performed.

The rites cited above are performed by a Brahmin priest in the presence of the sacred fire and are accompanied by the Vedic mantras. *"They are necessary for marriage to be complete, because when they or any of them are not properly performed, the marriage may be legally questioned.*

Hindu marriage is a sacrament. It is considered sacred because it is said to be complete only on the performance of the sacred rites accompanied by the sacred formulae."[1]

(c) Sacred Beliefs and Values involved in the Hindu Marriage

The Hindu marriage is a sacrament from the point of view of the sacred beliefs and values involved in it.

(i) *Indissoluble Marital Bond* : According to the traditional Hindu belief, marital bond is said to be inseparable and irrevocable. The parties to the marriage cannot dissolve it at will. They are bound to each other until the death of either of them. The belief states that the wife is supposed to be bound to her husband even after his death.

This concept of marriage that it is indissoluble, is itself a sublime one which makes the husband and the wife to adjust their tastes, tempers, ideals, interests, choices and preferences. It thus involves sacrifices on the part of both the husband and the wife for each is called upon to bear with the other. Each individual is here called upon to make marriage a success by means of compromise and adjustment.

(ii) *Belief that marriage is a social duty towards the family and the community* : The question of conflict between the husband and the wife did not perhaps arise in the olden days for it never involved purely individual interests. The husband never expected any intellectual co-operation from his wife. The wife was more of a passive partner in the performance of religious duties than an intellectually active participant in all his affairs. *"Marriage was a social duty towards the family and the community and there was little idea of individual interest"* - [**Kapadia** - Page: 169]. The social background provided by the authoritarian joint family and the semi-sovereign caste never gave any scope for the recognition of any personal factor, individual interests or aspirations,in the relations between the husband and the wife.

(iii) *The ideal of 'Pativratya' associated with marriage* : As per the ideal of *'Pativratya'* popularised by the *puranic* writers, the wife is expected to be devoted to her husband alone. It implies that fidelity and modest service to the husband are the sole duty and main purpose in her life. As a river merging itself in the ocean loses its identity so a wife is supposed to merge her individuality with that of her husband. Her only concern in life is to provide all services to the husband, for the satisfaction of her husband is her sole joy in life. The wife is expected to prove herself as a real *"sati"* with all dedication and reverence to the husband.

***The Glorification of 'Sati' System* :** The ideal of the *'Pativratya'* was stretched too much. It made the wife to be not only attached to the husband as long as he lived, but even after his death, because a *'sati'* could never conceive of a second marriage or a second husband. Hence, on the death of the husband the wife had either to live chastely, renouncing all the joys of life, or to follow her husband by jumping into the funeral pyre. The ideal of pativratya gave rise to and glorified the practice of *'sati'*[2] or self-immolation.

With the passing of time, the ideal of *Pativratya* became so deep-rooted in the mind of the Hindu woman that immolation became not only customary but a woman's highest aspiration.

Marriage, the only sacrament for women* :** The Hindu marriage is a sacrament in another sense also. A Hindu male goes through the performance of several sacraments during the course of his life. These begin with the laying of the foetus and end with the cremation of his body. For the Hindu woman marriage is said to be essential for it is ***the only sacrament that can be performed for

---

1 **K.M. Kapadia** *"Marriage and Family in India"* - Page: 168.

2 "The practice of 'sati' seems to have been first recommended in *Vishnu Dharmasamhita* in the 2nd or 3rd century A.D." - **Kapadia** - Page: 170.

her. The Hindu women normally prefer to marry and aspire to marry for they know that the unmarried women are always put to hardship in the Indian social set up.

Does the Hindu marriage continue to be sacred ?

The Hindu marriage has undergone changes in the last few decades. These changes have given rise to two questions: (i) *Does the Hindu marriage continue to be sacred* ?; (ii) *Has it lost its sanctity, or is it to be treated as a contract ?*

Three significant changes: Three significant changes in the Hindu marriage may be noted here.

(i) The Hindu young men and women today marry not very much for performing religious duties but for *lifelong companionship*

(ii) The marital relations are no longer treated as unbreakable, or irrevocable, as *divorce* is socially and legally permissible and

(iii) The ideal of *'pativratya'* has lost its significance for there is legal provision for widow remarriage and divorce.

The Hindu Marriage Continues to be a Sacrament

The above cited changes in the Hindu marriage have not affected its main character. Widow remarriages and divorces have not become the order of the day. Though they are legally permitted, they are still looked down upon socially. Mutual fidelity and devotion to the partner are still considered to be the essence of marriage. *"So long marriage is not performed for sex gratification alone but for "living together" and "begetting children", marriage will continue to be a sacrament for the Hindus. Freedom in marriage [mate selection, etc.] does not destroy but rather confirms the stability of marriage and purifies its practice."*[1]

Changes are taking place in the Hindu marriage but they have not disturbed its universality and damaged its sanctity. As **Kapadia** writes, "*.....marriage continues to be a sacrament; only it is raised to an ethical plane. We rather go back to our Vedic ideal embodied in the 'saptapadi' formula: "I take thee to be my companion in life."* - [**Kapadia** - Page: 197]

Recent Trends in Hindu Marriage

The Hindu marriage system has undergone radical changes especially after independence. Eventhough the basic religious beliefs associated with marriage have not crumbled down, many of its practices, customs and forms have changed. The recent trends in this regard may be briefly discussed here.

1. ***Changes in the Form of Marriage*** **:** The traditional forms of Hindu marriages [as described by Shastrakara Manu] such as -1. *Brahma,* 2. *Daiva,* 3. *Arsha,* 4. *Prajapatya,* 5. *Asura,* 6. *Gandharva,* 7. *Rakshasa* and 8. *Paisacha* - are no more in practice. Polygamy , polyandry and even bigamy are also not found for they are legally prohibited. Only monogamous marriages are universally practised.

2. ***Change in the Aim or Purpose of Marriage*** **:** The traditional Hidnu marriage considers *"dharma"* as its primary object whereas the modern Hindus give more importance to *"life-long companionship"* between husband and wife. Marriage is taking place not very much for the performance of religious duties, but for obtaining *"lifelong companionship"* of the individuals of the opposite sex.

3. ***Change in the Process of Mate Selection*** **:** In the three areas of mate selection we find significant changes today.

1 **Ram Ahuja** *"Indian Social System"* - Page: 121.

(i) ***Field of selection*** has become very wide. It is wide enough to include inter sub-caste and intercaste marriages.

(ii) ***Party to selection:*** Parents do not take an active role in the selection of life-partners of their children. The practice of young men and women selecting their life-partners by themselves is becoming popular today.

(iii) ***Criteria of selection:*** Much importance is given to individual interests, preferences and considerations rather than to family considerations. This trend is reflected in the increase in the instances of love marriages.

4. *Change in the Age at Marriage* : Child marriages [at least at the level of middle and upper class people and educated people] are virtually not found now. As per the present marriage Act [that is 1978 amendment to the *Child Marriage Restraint Act, 1929*] a boy below 21 years and a girl below 18 years cannot marry. Pre-puberty marriages have thus given place to post-puberty marriages.

5. *Change in the Stability of Marriage* : Legislative provision for divorce has virtually affected the stability of the marriage. Hindu marriage is no more regarded as indissoluable. The legislative provisions for divorce and widow remarriage have undermined the importance of the value of *"pativratya".* The concept of equality of sex has also affected the value of *'pativratya'.*

6. *Change in the Economic Aspect of Marriage* : The practice of paying dowry is associated with marriage. This practice has grown into a big social evil today. Bride's parents are compelled to pay a huge amount of money as dowry. This practice has made marriage a costly affair. Marriages are often settled only on considerations of dowry.

Marriage ceremony is also becoming a costly affair since huge amount of money is lavishly spent on decorations, processions, band sets, video-shooting, music orchestra and so on.

7. *An Increase in the Instances of Divorce and Desertion* : Though the Hindu marriage is regarded as a sacrament, instances of divorce and desertion are on the increase.

Though these new trends are observed today the importance of marriage has not diminished. It is still universally practised. Though its sanctity is affected a little, it is not reduced to the level of a mere civil contract. Hindu men and women are still emotionally involved in their marriages. There is no apparent danger as such to the Hindu marriage at present.

3. Factors Affecting Hindu Marriage

Industrialisation, Urbanisation, Education and Legislation

The Hindu marriage has undergone vast changes during the recent years. Traditional values of marriage, *the form of marriage, type of marriage ceremony, the way of selection of life-partners in marriage, age at marriage* - and in such other areas significant changes have occurred. These changes have been caused by a number of factors among which the following may be noted: *industrialisation, urbanisation, education* and *legislation.*

1. Influence of Industrialisation

Industrialisation refers to the phenomenal growth of modern sophisticated industries and its consequent dominance over agriculture. *"Industrialisation is a term covering, in general terms, the growth in a society hitherto mainly agrarian, of modern industry with all its attendent circumstances and problems, economic and social."* Industrialisation directly affected the institutions of family and marriage and brought about changes in both.

Modern industries have minimised economic functions of the family and reduced its size. Nuclear families have replaced joint families. People have started *"going out of family"* for work, for eking out their livelihood. Women also have joined men in the process of finding out jobs and earning money. This has boosted the self-respect and self-confidence of women. Men could no longer boss over women and suppress their attempt to become self-reliant. This is especially true in the case of urban educated women. These developments have affected the institution of marriage.

Employed women today take an active role in the selection of their life-partners. They do not just leave it to the decision of their parents. In addition to a girl's beauty, family to which she belongs, education and character and such other considerations,due importance is given today to her job and the salary she gets before she is selected as a life-partner. Daughters' earnings in many instances have reduced the financial burdens of their parents in marriage. Daughter's job itself may function as a *substitute for dowry.* Parents who were searching a suitable match for their daughters within the narrow circle of relatives and friends are now ready to go beyond the borders of even the state, because they want to fix a suitable and a good life-partner for their daughters. Instances of young men and women working in the same industry or office falling in love with each other and getting married are also not uncommon today.

2. Impact of Urbanisation

Industrialisation and urbanisation normally go together. Industrialisation accelerates the process of urbanisation. 'Urbanisation' *refers to the* phenomenal growth of towns and cities or urban centres. It *"denotes a diffusion of the influence of urban centres to a rural hinterland."* It is *"a process of becoming urban, moving to cities, changing from agriculture to other pursuits common to cities and corresponding change of behaviour patterns."*[1]

Growth of cities and city environment has its impact on the institutions of family and marriage. Selection of life-partners, age at marriage, nature and type of marriage ceremony, expenses of marriage etc., are affected by the modern urban environemnt. Normally young men and women of cities want to select their life-partners on their own. Arranged marriages have become rarer in cities. In comparison with villagers, urban people delay their marriages. Child marriages normally do not take place in cities.

Marriage is often held in cities more as a social or a civil ceremony than a religious ceremony. Non-availability of seasoned priests, scarcity of and too expensive choultries or *'kalyana mantaps'*, difficulties involved in collecting number of items necessary for the conduct of a traditional type of marriage - all must have added to this new trend in marriage. Hence marriage ceremony in cities is tending more towards modernity than to traditionality. Huge amount is spent [sometimes running to a couple of thousands, and even a few lakhs] on the ceremony to make it a 'grand gala'. Money is spent lavishly for decorating marriage mantaps, putting up pendals, arranging grand dinner, take-home sweets, music orchestra, video shooting, photography, marriage procession, etc. The duration of marriage ceremony is also cut short in city. Elaborate customs are either avoided or shortened. Then, the whole ceremony is over within a couple of hours. It is rarely stretched over for several days.

It is generally observed that in a city a bigger number of instances of divorce, desertion, separation etc. is found than in a village. There is greater scope for developing pre-marital and extra-marital sex relations in cities.

3. Role of Education

Modern education has played its role in initiating some changes in marriage. It is through modern education that some of the modern values and western ideologies such as rationalism, individualism, equality of sex, democracy, individual freedom, secularism, etc. have influenced the outlook of our educated young men and women. Hence, they want to take their independent decisions on the main events of their life such as line of education, job and marriage. Thus our educated youths

1 **Duncan Mitchel** *"Dictionary of Sociology."*

have their own views and stand on matters like to marry or not to marry, when to marry, whom to marry, how to marry etc. They do not want their families to decide these matters.

Educated youths do not hesitate to go beyond the boundaries of family ties to select for them suitable life-partners. For this purpose they sometimes contact *"marriage bureaus"* and give advertisements in the matrimonial columns of the newspapers.

In the circle of the college educated young men and women marriage is becoming a simple ceremony losing many of its rigid traditional customs. They give more importance to personal preferences and choices in marriage rather than to the gotra rules, family traditions and rules of horoscope. Some of them are even ready for intercaste marriages and if necessary, even for registered marriages.

Modern education has influenced marriage in different ways. Parents cannot impose any unwanted marriage on their educated daughters in the name of *"family decision or prestige"*. Well educated people are expected not to insist on dowry in marriage. In India paradoxically, higher educated modern men demand a higher dowry than the uneducated or less educated. Educated and employed women are also not able to resist such a demand. They normally yield to its pressure and some of them even become victims of dowry disasters. Instances of divorce, desertion and separtion are found in a larger number in the circle of educated persons than in the midst of the uneducated.

4. Influence of Legislations on Marriage

Many of the beliefs, values, ideals and rules of marriage laid down by the Hindu *shastrakaras* have lost their original meaning and purpose now. As a result, the Hindu marriage has developed some defects. Attempts were also made by some of the social reformers to remove these defects and correct the system. During the British rule and also after independence legislations were passed in order to bring about desirable modifications in the Hindu marriage system.

The laws enacted in India relate to: (i) *age at marriage;* (ii) *field of mate selection;* (iii) *number of spouses in marriage;* (iv) *breaking of marriage;* (v) *dowry to be given and taken,* and (v) *remarriage.* The most important legislations relating to these six aspects of marriage passed from time to time could be briefly explained here.

1. *The Prevention of Sati Act 1829* **:** The glorification of the ideal of *"Pativratya"* had led to the inhuman practice of *"Sati"*. Widows were often forced to make a vow or *"sankalpa"* to die after their husbands. Some were forcibly pushed to their husbands' funeral pyres. Famous Brahmo Samajist, **Sri Raja Ram Mohan Roy** took up the cause of women and impressed upon Lord Bentinck who was the then British Governor General of India to bring out a legislation prohibiting the practice of *"Sati"*.

The Prevention Sati Act, 1829 made the burning or burying alive of widows culpable homicide punishable with fine and / or imprisonment. This legislation could save the lives of a number of widows though it could not immediately stop the practice in total.

2. *The Hindu Widow Remarriage Act - 1856* **:** This legislation was complementary to the previous legislation, that is, *'Prevention of Sati Act of 1829'*. Though widows were saved from the jaws of death they were subject to exploitation and humiliation. To remove the deplorable condition of the Hindu widows, a leading social reformer of the day, **Pandit Ishwara Chandra Vidya Sagar,** brought pressure on the British Govt. to make legal provision for widow marriages. T*he Hindu Widow Remarriage Act of 1856* was hence passed.

3. The Civil [or Special] Marriage Act, 1872 : This legislation treated Hindu marriage as a *"civil marriage"* and provided legal permission for intercaste, inter-religious and even *"registered"* marriages. [This Act was repealed by the *Special Marriage Act of 1954.* According to this Act, the parties interested in registered marriage must notify the marriage officer at least one month before the date of the marriage. It insists on the presence of two witnesses for marriage].

4. *The Child Marriage Restraint Act - 1929* : This Act came into force on April 1, 1930. The Act prohibeted the marriage of a child. According to this Act, marriage of boys under 18 and girls under 14 years of age was an offence.

***Latest Amendment* :** The Act was amended in 1978 which further raised the age for boys to 21 years and for girls to 18 years. The violation of this Act prescribes penalty. It provides punishment [three months of simple imprisonment and a fine of upto Rs.1000/-] for bridegroom, parent, guardian and the priest who are party to the marriage. No woman is, however punishable with imprisonment under this Act.

5. *The Hindu Marriage Act - 1955* : This Act which came into force from May 18, 1955 brought about revolutionary changes not only in the marital relations but also in various other social aspects. This Act applies to the whole of India, except Jammu and Kashmir. The word **"Hindu"** in the Act includes Jains, Sikhs, Buddhists and the Scheduled Castes.

- ***Conditions for valid marriage as provided in this Act* :** (1) neither party has a spouse living; (2) neither party [bridegroom or bride] is an idiot or a lunatic; (3) the groom must have completed 21 years and the bride 18 years of age as per the 1978 Amendement brought to this Act; (4) the parties should not be *'sapindas'* of each other unless the custom permits such a marriage.
- ***Conditions under which divorce is permitted as per this Act* :** (i) The spouse must have been impotent at the time of marriage and continues to be so even afterwards; (ii) party to the marriage was an idiot or lunatic at the time of marriage; (iii) consent of the petitioner or of the guardian was obtained by force or fraud; (v) the wife was pregnant by some person other than the petitioner at the time of marriage.
- ***Other conditions providing for divorce* :** The dissolution of marriage may be obtained on the grounds of adultery, conversion of religion, unsound mind,leprosy, venereal disease, renunciation, desertion for seven years and cohabitation not resumed after two years after judicial separation.
- ***Other important aspects of the Act* :** *(i) This Act gives permission for intercaste and inter-religious marriages; (ii) It provides for equality of sex; (iii) It provides equal rights for men and women in marriage, divorce or separation; (iv) Its 1986 amendment permits divorce on the ground of incompatibility and mutual consent; (v) During judicial separation and after divorce, both husband and wife have the right to claim maintenance allowance.*

6. *The Dowry Prohibition Act - 1961* : This Act which prohibits the practice of dowry was passed on May 20th 1961. The Act does not apply to Muslims. It permits exchange of gifts for not more than Rs.2000/-. It prescribes the penalty of **6** months imprisonment or a fine upto Rs.5000/- or both for its violation. This Act got amended in 1986 and thereafter its rules have become still more stringent.

The above mentioned legislations in addition to many other social legislations, have affected the Hindu marriage in several ways. These legislations, however, have not transformed it into a mere legal contract. The Hindu beliefs and values relating to marriage are still alive and legislations have only strengthened it by removing some of the anamolies associated with it.

MARRIAGE AMONG MUSLIMS IN INDIA

Marriage is Universal Among the Muslims

In the Muslim community marriage is universal for it discourages celibacy. Islam has almost made it compulsory. Prophet Mohammad also stressed that married life is preferable to unmarried life. Both the main sects within Islam called *"Sunnis"* and *"Shias"* consider marriage almost obligatory.

Main Aims and Objects of Muslim Marriage

Muslims call their marriage *'nikah'*. Marriage among the Muslims is regarded not as a religious sacrament but as a *secular bond.* The important objectives of Muslim marriage are - *control over sex, ordering of domestic life, procreation of children and perpetual increase of family, and upbringing of children.*

- For **Muslims,** *"Marriage is an institution ordained for the protection of society, and in order that human beings may guard themselves from foulness and unchastity. Marriage is not a sacrament but a civil contract, the objects of which are the promotion of a normal family life and the legalisation of children."*[1]
- ***Marriage as a Civil Contract:*** According to **Roland Wilson** [1941], *"Muslim marriage is a contract for the purpose of legalising sexual intercourse and the procreation of children."*
- ***S.C. Sarkar*** [1948] has also said that *"marriage among Muslims is not a sacrament but purely a civil contract."*
- ***Marriage is a Religious Duty Also:*** On the basis of the above statements it should not be concluded that the Muslim marriage does not have any religious significance. Marriage in the Muslim society is a religious duty also. It is a devotion and an act of *"ibadat"* [or religious duty]. It is believed that a person who does comply with it is rewarded in the next world, and he who does not, commits a sin. Hence, **Jang** [1953] has maintained that 'nikah', though essentially a contract, is also a *devotional act.*

Characteristic Features or Pre-Conditions of Muslim Marriage

The important pre-conditions or characteristics of valid Muslim marriage called *"Nikah"* are as follows.

1. Marriage Proposal and its Acceptance - Ijab and Qubul: As marriage is a civil contract in Islam, a proposal for the marriage and the acceptance of the proposal are essential. The bridegroom makes a proposal to the bride just before the wedding ceremony in the presence of two witnesses and a *'maulvi'* or *kazi* [Muslim priest]. The proposal is called ***'ijab'*** and its acceptance is called ***'Qubul'.*** These two words must be uttered clearly before the assembled persons by the bride and the bridegroom or by their agents of sound mind. It is necessary that both the proposal and its acceptance must take place at the same meeting in order to make it a *"sahi nikah"* [or "regular marriage"].

2. Capacity of a Person to Contract Marriage: This is the second condition of marriage according to which only adult persons of sound mind can enter into a marriage contract. Child marriages and marriages of people of unsound mind are not recognised. However, the marriage of a minor could be contracted by his or her guardians.

3. Observance of the Doctrine of Equality: It is a matter of tradition among the Muslims to have marriage among equals. Though there is no legal prohibition to contract marriage with a person of low status, such marriages are looked down upon. The run-away marriages called ***'kifa'*** [girls running away with boys and marrying them on their own choice] are not recognised. *Marrying idolators and slaves is also not approved.* [Among the Sunnis, social inferiority on the part of bridegroom could be a ground for the cancellation of marriage but not among the Shias].

---

1 As quoted by **C.B. Mamoria.** Page - 213.

4. Preference System in the Mate Selection: There is traditional insistence on the preferential system in mate selection. For example, a person is expected to give preferences to his cousins; and of the cousins, first preference to *parallel cousins* [*chachera cousins* or father's brother's daughter]; and next to the *'cross cousins'* [*mamera cousins* or mother's brother's daughter]. But these days no such preferences are given to cousin marriages. A person can prefer to marry his deceased or divorced wife's sister. But a widow cannot give preference to marry her deceased husband's brother.

5. Marriage should be Free From Legal Complications: Muslim marriage can be called "sahi nikah" [valid marriage] only if it is not against *'shariah'*.

Conditions of Void or Invalid Marriage

Muslim marriage held according to the stipulated Islamic rules is called *'sahi nikah'* or regular marriage or valid marriage. Marriage which is held contrary to the Islamic rules is called *'batil'* or invalid marriage or *void marriage.* Some of the conditions of invalid marriage are mentioned below:

1. Polygamy: A woman cannot marry second time as long as she has a living husband who has not divorced her. A man also cannot marry the fifth woman as long as his first four wives are alive and not divorced.

2. Marriage within the Circle of Close Relatives: Marriage with relatively close kins such as - *mother, mother's mother, sister, sister's daughter, mother's sister, father's sister, daughter's daughter, wife's mother, wife's daughter born to the first husband, son's wife* - is not allowed.

3. Marriage with Idolators: Islam opposes idolatory. Hence marriage with idolators is not permitted. However, a man can marry a non-Muslim girl if he believes that her idolatory is only nominal. The purpose is to keep idolatory out of the Islamic body politic. *But a Muslim woman under no circumstances is permitted to marry non-muslims.*

4. Marriage with People of Prematured Age and Unsound Mind: Marriage with a man of unsound mind is regarded as invalid. Marriage of immatured persons without the prior consent of their parents is also treated as invalid marriage.

5. Sisters Becoming Co-wives: As per the Islamic rule sorrate is not allowed. Sisters cannot be married simultaneously by the same person. However, one can marry one's wife's sister only after the death of the wife or only after giving divorce to the wife.

6. Marrying a Woman During Her 'Iddat' Period: No Muslim woman is allowed to marry a man as long as she is undergoing *"iddat"*.

• Difference Between Irregular Marriage and Invalid Marriage: *'Fasid'* and *'Batil'*

Muslims distinguish between two types of unacceptable marriages called *"irregular marriage"* and *"invalid marriage"*, specifically known as *'fasid'* and *'batil'*. Main differences between the two can be mentioned here.

- ***'Fasid'*** or irregular marriage, is one which could be converted into ***'sahi marriage'*** or ***'nikah'*** by removing its impediments or irregularities. *'Batil'* marriages, on the contrary, cannot be converted to *'sahi'* marriages.

(i) ***Example for Fasid:*** (i) Absence of witnesses at the time of making or accepting the proposal; (ii) Muslim man marrying the fifth woman; (iii) marriage with a woman who is undergoing *'iddat'*, etc. These *irregularities* could be corrected.

(ii) ***Example For Batil:*** (i) Marriage within the close circle of relatives; (ii) Muslim woman marrying an idolator; (iii) Muslim man marrying two-three women who are sisters, etc. These irregularities cannot be corrected and hence such marriaes become invalid.

Importance of Mahr or Dower in Muslim Marriage

Mahr or ***dower*** is a practice associated with Muslim marriage. *"**Dower** is the sum of money or other property which a wife is entitled to get from her husband in consideration of the marriage."*

- **Purpose of Mahr:** As per the Muslim law, dower is an obligation imposed upon a husband as a mark of respect for wife. Its main purposes are - (i) *to put a check on the husband to divorce wife* and (ii) *to enable a woman to look after herself after her husband's death or divorce.*

- **Proposal of Mahr before the Marriage:** Marriage proposals and Mahr discussions normally go together. The bride's relative called ***'wali'*** plays an important role in the discussion. He only keeps the account of *"mahr"*. Normally, a part of *'mahr'* [in majority of the instances 1/3 of the amount agreed upon] is paid by the bridegroom to **"wali"** [an elderly relative of the wife who may be her own father or any other such responsible person] on the third day of the marriage. The balance is generally paid when the husband dies or divorces the wife. It is her right to claim the *mahr* from her husband. She may even refuse to accompany him if the agreed-upon-instalment of *mahr* is not paid.

- **Mahr is Different from Brideprice:** Mahr is not prideprice for the wife is not purchased just by throwing away some money as it was the case centuries ago. In the modern Islamic societies, the bride's consent **[qubul]** has become a prerequisite for marriage. As it is made clear *the main purpose of mahr is to give financial security to the woman and to create responsibility in man.*

- **Determinants of Mahr:** The Muslim law does not fix the amount of *mahr*. The husband is obliged to pay some amount as *mahr*. The amount to be paid as *mahr* is normally decided before or after or at the time of the marriage ceremony. The amount of *mahr* depends upon *the social position, descent, age, intelligence, beauty and other qualities of the bride.*

The amount of *mahr* cannot be reduced but it can be increased at husband's will. A wife can voluntarily agree to reduce the amount or make a gift of whole of it to her husband or to his heirs. The amount of *mahr* varies from one **'dinar'** upwards. There is no maximum limit for that.

- **Muslim Wife's Right Over Mahr:** As per the Islamic law, the wife has absolute right over the *mahr* amount. A widow's claim for *mahr* is normally regarded as her claim over her husband's property. She can retain the property till her *mahr* is paid. She need not wait for the consent of heirs for the possession of her husband's property. In case the divorce takes place through mutual agreement or by wife's initiative, her right to *mahr* gets extinguished.

- **Specified Mahr and Proper Mahr:** When the amount of *mahr* is fixed between the two parties, it is called ***"specified mahr"***. The minimum specified amount cannot be less than ten dinars. When the amount is not fixed but is given whatever is considered to be proper it is called ***"proper mahr"***. The amount given here normally depends upon the financial position of the husband.

- **Prompt Mahr and Deferred Mahr:** The amount which is payable on demand is called 'prompt mahr'. Mahr which is payable on the dissolution of marriage [that is, after husband's death or divorce[is called *'deferred mahr'*.

Divorce Among the Muslims

Muslim marriage which is treated as a contract can be dissolved in the following ways.

1. *Divorce as per the Muslim law but without the intervention of the court;*
2. *Divorce as per the Shariah Act, 1937;*
3. *Divorce as per the Muslim Marriage Dissolution Act, 1959, that is, as per the court's intervention.*

1. Divorce According to Muslim Law: *Khula / Mubarat* and *Talaq*

According to the traditional Muslim law, divorce can be obtained directly in two ways without the intervention of the civil court. They are: (A) *Khula / Mubarat* and (B) *Talaq*

(A) Khula or Kohl and Mubarat: Husband and wife can obtain divorce by mutual consent either by *'Khula'* or by *'Mubarat'*. Difference between *Khula* and *Mubarat* is simple: In *Khula,* divorce is initiated at the instance of the wife. In *Mubarat,* since both the parties desire separation, the initiative may come either from the wife or from the husband.

(B) Talaq: *Talaq* represents one of the ways according to which a Muslim husband can give divorce to his wife as per the Muslim law without the intervention of the court. In *talaq,* the husband has the right to dismiss his wife by repeating the dismissal formula thrice. The *talaq* may be affected either orally by making some pronouncements or in writing by presenting *'talaqnama'*. *Talaq* may be given in any one of the following three ways.

(i) ***Talaq-e-Ahasan:*** This involves *a single pronouncement of talaq* followed by a period of conjugal abstinence till the completion of *'iddat'*.

(ii) ***Talaq-e-Hasan:*** This consists of three pronouncements of 'Talaq' made during three successive menstrual periods and no sexual contact be taken place between the spouses during these months.

(iii) ***Talaq-e-ul-Bidat:*** Here, *talaq* pronouncement takes place in any one of the following ways. (a) in a single sentence, for example, *"I divorce thee thrice"* or in three separate sentences: *"I divorce thee, I divorce thee, I divorce thee"* (b) in a single but clear pronouncement such as, *"I divorce thee irrevocably"*.

In the first two types cited above, there is a chance for re-establishing the marital ties but not in the thrid form.

2. Divorce as Recognised by *The Shariah Act, 1937*

The Shariah Act, 1937 provides for three forms of divorce. They are mentioned below.

(i) ***Illa:*** If the husband swears by God to abstain from sexual relations with his wife for a period of four months or more, or for a specified period, he is said to make *illa*. If he sticks on to his words, then marriage gets dissolved.

(ii) ***Zihar:*** In this type, the husband of sound mind declares in the presence of two witnesses that his wife looks like his mother to him. Though marriage is not dissolved with this, it gives scope for the wife to go to court on this ground.

(iii) ***Lian:*** In this type the husband accuses his wife of being guilty of adultery. This, however, gives an opportunity for the wife to go to court insisting on her husband either to withdraw such an allegation or prove the same.

3. Provisions for Divorce as per *The Dissolution of Muslim Marriage Act, 1939*

The Dissolution of Muslim Marriage Act, 1939 passed during the British period entitles a Muslim woman to seek the dissolution of her marriage on the following grounds.

(i) whereabouts of husband not known for **4** years.

(ii) failure of husband to provide for her maintenance for **2** years.

(iii) imprisonment of husband for **7** years or more.

(iv) impotency of husband since the time of marriage.

(v) failure of husband to fulfil marital obligations for **3** years.

(vi) insanity of husband for a period of **2** years and husband's incurable diseases like leprosy, venereal diseases, etc.

(vii) husband's physical and mental cruelty.

(viii) marriage being thursted upon her before she attained **15** years, [but in this, the wife has to seek divorce before she completes **18**th year].

(ix) any other valid ground which the Muslim law permits.

Importance of *"Iddat"* in Muslims' Divorce

"Iddat" plays an important role in Muslims' divorce cases. *"Iddat" denotes a period of awaiting.*

- ***Iddat*** refers to a period of seclusion for three menstrual periods for a woman after the death of or divorce by her husband to ascertain whether she was pregnant at the time of divorce.

- *"Iddat" ".....implies the period of waiting incumbent on a woman between dissolution of one marriage and the contracting of another."*[1] It is important to note that in this period of waiting [for three consecutive menstrual periods] husband and wife are not supposed to have sexual contact.

Legal and Social Effects of Iddat

- ***Legal Effects:*** (i) In a divorce case the wife involved is bound to wait for *"iddat"* period. (ii) During the period of *"iddat"* the husband is obliged to provide for her maintenance. (iii) The wife is not supposed to give her consent for another marriage till the *iddat* period is completed. (iv) On the completition of *'iddat'* period, the wife can legitimately demand the *"deferred mahr"*.

- ***Social Effects:*** (i) *'Iddat'* serves as a restraining influence on inconsiderate haste on the part of the husband and on the tempo of divorce. It gives time for the husband to think and act. The husband may simply take back the wife during the period of *iddat* and suspend the divorce. (ii) *Iddat* makes it clear whether the wife is pregnant or not. The fact of pregnancy sometimes brings reconciliation between them. (iii) If it becomes apparent during *'Iddat'* that the divorced wife is pregnant, the husband is recommended to take her back and treat her with consideration till the child is born. The child belongs to the husband if it is not born out of adultery. The wife also cannot marry any one else until her delivery. (iv) The *iddat* period is normally **three** months. In the case of a widow the duration is *4* months *10* days.

It may be noted that according to the **Muslim Women's Protection of Rights on Divorce Act 1986 and Iddat,** a wife can demand from her husband her maintenance during the Iddat.

Differences Between Hindu and Muslim Marriages

Main differences between the Hindu and Muslim marriages may be noted here.

Hindu Marriage	Muslim Marriage
1. ***Aims and Ideals:*** Main aims of Hindu marriage are: *dharma, praja* and *rati.* Hindu marriage is a matter of religious duty. For performing *panchamaha-yajnas* and getting a son to fulfil *'pitri-rina'*, a Hindu is obliged to marry. It is hence sacred for him.	**1.** Muslim marriage is regarded more as a *contract* than as an important sacred rite. The main purpose is to obtain *sexual satisfaction* and along with it, *children.* Religious sentiments do not characterise such a marriage.

1 As quoted by **C.B. Mamoria** in his *"Social Problems and Social Disorganisation in India."* Page 224.

2. ***Relative Permanence of Marital Bond:*** As per the Hindu belief the *marital bond is inseparable*. It cannot be dissolved, according to the tradition. Hindu males cannot indiscriminately divorce their wives. Hindus can break the marriage only through the court.	**2.** Muslims do not consider marital contract as irrevocable. Here *marital ties can be dissolved* at the whims of the males. Muslim males can divorce their wives without the intervention of the court. Only men have such right. Women can obtain it only through court.
3. ***Remarriages and Widow Remarriages***: Since the Hindus consider marriage sacred, they are are generally not prepared for remarriage or widow remarriage even though there is legal provision for that. Instances of such marriages are comparatively less.	**3.** Among the Mulsims *there is scope for remarriage and widow remarriage. There is no blemish attached for that.* One contract can be broken to enter into another contract. After completing the *"Iddat"*, a divorced woman can offer herself as a life-partner for another.
4. ***No Scope for Polygamy:*** There is no scope for the practice of polygamy among the Hindus as per the existing marriage rules. Hindus have been cherishing the ideal of monogamy right from the times of Ramayana.	**4.** *Muslims have been observing polygamy since a long time.* Even now it is in practice. There is scope for polygamy as per the Koranic rules. Koran, however, restricts the number of wives to 'four' at a time.
5. ***Mahr and Dowry:*** Among the Hindus there is the practice of bridegrooms taking dowry. But the practice is neither obligatory nor universal. The practice of taking dowry has developed into a social evil now. It flourishes eventhough it is prohibited by legislation.	**5.** Among the Mulsims, bridegroom gives some amount as *mahr* to the bride at the time of or after the marriage. The Mulsim wife has the right to demand for it if she is divorced by her husband. It is an obligatory practice. It is not considered a social evil.
6. ***The question of temporary marriage*** does not arise among the Hindus. Marriage as per the Hindu traditional belief, is permanent and irrevocable. There is no *"void marriage"* also.	**6.** Among the Muslims, at one time there was the practice of temporary marriage called *"Muta Marriage"*. It could be contracted even for a day. Among the Sunnis its practice has disappeared.
7. ***Legislations Affecting Marriage:*** Hindu marriage in its history right from the British period till today has witnessed a number of legislations affecting its nature, form, practice etc.	**7.** Muslim marriage, especially in India has not been affected much by the legislative factors. It has undergone just two or three legislations.

Types of Marriage in the Pre-Islamic Arab Society

Muta Marriage: Muslims have a system of temporary marriage which is called *"Muta marriage"*. [This type of marriage was taking shape in the days of the prophet]. This is a marriage settled by the mutual consent of the parties without the intervention of the kinsmen. A Muslim man is permitted to contract *muta marriage* with a Muslim, Christian or a Jew girl, but a woman cannot contract such marriage with a non-Muslim. A wife secured through *muta* marriage is known as *"sigha"*. This practice is not common in India or Pakistan. This marriage is lawful only among the Shias and not among the Sunnis. Two conditions for the validity of this marriage are as follows: (i) *the period of cohabitation must be stipulated or fixed;* and (ii) *the amount of the mahr should be pre-determined.* Marriage becomes void if these two conditions are not fulfilled.

Muta marriage was condemned in the Islamic law for its association with matrilocality and matrilinity. This type of marriage has almost disappeared in the Muslim world. Only among the Shias its practice is often found. It is not in practice in India.

Beena Marriage and Baal Marriage: These two represent two other types of Muslim marriage that prevailed for some time in the pre-Islamic Arab society.

(i) **Beena Marriage:** In this type of marriage a woman was free to choose her husband and cast him away at her will. She could invite a man of her selection to her own tent and stay with him for sometime and dismiss him at her pleasure. The children belonged to her and the man had no rights over the children.

(ii) **Baal Marriage:** Beena marriage in course of time gave place to *Baal* marriage. In *baal* marriage, the husband exercised the authoritarian power and correspondingly the wife lost her former freedom of dismissing her husband at pleasure. The wife here stayed with the husband who could divorce her at will. Children born by this form of marriage belonged to the husband's clan. This type of marriage continued till the days of Prophet Mohammad. Islam in its attempts to stabilise marriage had to disapprove of both these types. Today these are not in practice any where in the Islamic world.

Christian Marriage

The ***Christian community*** has got two major sects or divisions within itself, namely the *Protestants* and the *Catholics.* The Catholics are further subdivided into *Latin Catholics* and *Syrian Catholics.* Each sect and each subgroup is endogamous. Catholics marry amongst themselves and do not normally marry Protestants. Further, the Latin Catholics and the Syrian Catholics do not normally intermarry. Marriage as a social institution is common to all the sects and subgroups in the Christian community. As it has been in the case of the Hindus and Muslims, marriage is quite popular among the Christians of India.

From the point of view of Christians, marriage is considered very necessary and important. It is not established just for providing sexual satisfaction but for other purposes also. *"The Christian churches have always held that the universal institution of marriage has a special place in god's purpose for all human life."*[1]

- ***Christian marriage*** is defined as *"a contract between man and woman normally intended to be binding for life for the purpose of sexual union, mutual companionship and the establishment of a family."*

- Among the Christians, marriage has been defined as *"a voluntary union for life of one man and one woman to the exclusion of others. This type of marriage is based on monogamy and not on the religious beliefs of the partners."* [**C.B. Mamoria.** Page - 213.]

According to Christians, Marriage is a permanent and exclusive contract of love between a man and a women. Marriage is a covenant of love. Love is the basis of marriage. One freely chooses another and commits oneself to her [him]. One does not get married just to settle down or to obtain social and economic status or to legitimise the practice of sex in the eyes of the society. Love is and must be the strength and the atmosphere of the whole married life. The deeper it becomes, the more

1 *Bulletin of the Christian Institute,* Sept. 2nd, 1957.

unselfish and faithful it grows and the more continually renewed. Sex among the couple is a consequence of love. Sexual love in marriage is an extension of true love.

Christians too consider marriage as a social institution strongly supported by religion. *"In fact, United Churches of Northern India declares its belief that marriage is a holy estate instituted by God and so existing in the natural order and also that our lord's principle and standard of marriage is that a divine institution involving a life long union for better or for worse of one man with one woman to the exclusion of all others on either side and that the marriage relation signifies the mystical union of Christ and his church."*

Christian marriage is also woven around a lot of religious beliefs and ideas. Marriage, according to Christianity, is one of the sacraments. As per the Christian belief *"God himself is the author of matrimony, endowed as it is with various benefits and purposes."*[1]

Christians consider marriage as *an enduring and exclusive covenant of love between a man and a woman.* Fidelity is the essence of covenant. Covenant signifies partnership, communion, love. The Second Vatican Council preaches it when it says : *"The intimate partnership of married are qualified by his laws..... For the good of the spouses and their offspring as well as of society, the existence of this sacred bond no longer depends on human decisions alone........"*[2]

Christian marriage is very much based on religious traditions. Christians do think that marriage too has got an important place in God's purpose for all human life. They believe that marriages take place because of the will of God. The impact of Hindu marriage is also there on the Christian marriage. Hence after the marriage man and woman develop strong identification with each other. Marriage creates biological as well as psycho-religious relationship between them.

Aims or Objectives of Christian Marriage

The major objectives of Christian marriage can be specifically mentioned below.

1. ***Providing for Sexual Satisfaction* :** The main aim of the Christian marriage is to provide for the sexual satisfaction of its marital partners. The present day Christians consider sexual union of the marital partners, a necessary condition for the procreation of children.[3]
2. ***Establishment of Family* :** The purpose of Christian marriage is to help the marital partners to establish a family of their own so that they can bring up their children in a proper manner.
3. ***Stability of the Relations* :** Christian marriage provides for the stable sex relationship between the husband and the wife. It is a type of life-long contract entered into between husband and wife. Conjugal faith is the secret of marital success. This faith is based on mutual love.[4]

---

1 According to Christianity, "A sacrament is a sensible sign instituted by Jesus Christ to signify and cause justification and sanctification. It is a sensible sign because only through sensible signs can man, composed of body and soul, attain spiritual realities......... Sacraments describe the manifold sanctifying actions of God's spirit in man.......... Sacraments are instituted by Christ......... Sacraments are instituted by Christ." - **Fr. Thomas Pazhayampallil S.D.B.'s** *"Pastoral Guide : Moral - Canonical - Liturgical"* Vol. II [*Sacraments Christian Life and Sexuality.*] [1984]. Page : 5 - 6.

2 *ibid.* Page - 440.

3 Marriage comes from the Latin word "matrimonium" which means "munus matris", that is, the office of the mother. Indeed, in marriage the burden of procreation weighs heavily on the mother rather than on the father. "Matrimonium" also means "muniens matrem" that is protection of the mother. ***Source:*** *"Pastural Guide"* Vol.II. Sacraments Christian Life and Sexuality by **Thomas Pazhayampallil S.D.B.** Page - 439.

4 **Pope Pius XI** writes : "This conjugal faith .... blooms more freely, more beautifully and more nobly, when it is rooted in that more excellent soil, the love of husband and wife which pervades all the duties of married life and holds pride in Christian marriage" - as quoted in *"Pastoral Guide."* Page - 440.

4. ***Mutual Love and Co-operation*** : Development of qualities such as love, mutual co-operation, sacrifice, etc. constitute yet another purpose of Christian marriage. Love is the basis of marriage. Love pervades the whole lives of husband and wife. As it is hoped love is and must be the strength and the atmosphere of the whole of married life. **St. Paul** writes: *"Husbands, love your wives............ He who loves his wife loves himself. For no man ever hates his own flesh, but nourishes and cherishes it........."*[1]

Selection of Marital Partners

Among the Christians the selection of marriage partners takes place in three important ways –

- *Parents selecting life-partners for their children;*
- *Boys and girls selecting their life-partners by themselves;*
- *Parents and children together selecting life-partners.*

Due to the impact of modern civilisation and values, the present day Christians prefer to give freedom to the younger ones to select their life-partners. Most of the times parents and children together finalise the selection process. Unlike the Muslims, there is no such thing as *"preferential mating system"* in the Christian community.

Precaution in Selection

Christian community stresses on certain precautions to be taken by the young boys and girls before they finalise the selection of their life-partners. The main precautions are the following:-

(i) Blood relatives are to be avoided.

(ii) Social status of the partner is to be taken into consideration.

(iii) The social status and the socio-religious background of the families to be considered.

(iv) The level of education and the strength of the character of the persons to be taken note of.

(v) Finally, the physical fitness, that is, physical and mental health of the persons is to be given due weightage.

Christian Marital Practice

Among the Christians, the *"engagement ceremony"* or the *"betrothal ceremony"* is normally arranged soon after the process of the selection of the life-partner is over. The engagement ceremony normally takes place at the bride's house where the boy gives a ring to the girl. Occasionally, if not invariably, the girl also gives a ring to the boy in exchange for the one she receives. After this engagement the formalities of marriage begin. These formalities include the following conditions.

(a) *Bride and the bridegroom must provide a certificate of their membership of the church.*

(b) *They must provide a certificate relating to their character.*

(c) *Application for the marriage should be submitted to the church at least three weeks before the date of marriage.*

After the fulfilment of these conditions, the church / churches of the bride and the bridegroom invite written objections, if any, against the marriage from the concerned. If no objection is received in a specified period, the marriage is held on the day fixed for it. The clergyman performs the marriage ceremony on the specified day in the presence of certain witnesses. Even if the boy and the girl are getting married in a Civil Court, they are required to go to the church to receive the blessings of the clergyman.

---

1 **Pope Pius XI** ''*Padiral Guide*'' Page - 441.

Normally, marriage ceremony takes place in the church of which the girl happens to be the member. The Christian priest asks the bride and the bridegroom whether they accept each other as husband and wife. Depending upon their consent he solemnises the marriage by asking the couple to declare in the presence of the witnesses that *"I [A.B.], in the presence of the Almighty God and in the name of our Lord Jesus Christ, do take thee [C.D.], to be my lawful wedded wife / husband."*

Legislations Relating to Christian Marriage and Divorce

***The Indian Christian Marriage Act,* 1872** [including its Amendments upto 1928] covers various aspects of Christian marriage. *The legislation strictly prohibits the practice of polygamy and polyandry among them and prescribes strict monogamy.* Several aspects such as – who should perform marriage, the place where it is to be performed [in which church], the time of performance, the relative age of the boy and the girl concerned, etc., are all dealt with by this legislation.

Provision for Divorce

The Indian Divorce Act, 1869 lays down the conditions under which Christians can obtain or seek divorce through the court. It also deals with the dissolution of the marriage declaring the marriage as null and void on the specific grounds. It provides for judicial separation, protection to the spouses and restitution of conjugal rights.

Section 10 of *the Indian Divorce Act,* 1869 gives right to the husband to divorce his wife on the ground of debauchery. The wife can also give or demand divorce from her husband on some conditions as –

(i) Leaving of religion by the husband and adoption of another religion or to marry another wife.

(ii) Debauchery of the husband.

(iii) His marrying a second wife.

(iv) Rape, sodomy or bestiality.

(v) Cruelty.

(vi) Besides being accused of debauchery if the husband has been living away for two years.

Section 18 of the legislation provides the right to husband and wife to submit an application for the declaration of marriage as null and void. A marriage can be declared so, on the grounds mentioned below.

(i) The respondent had been impotent at the time of marriage.

(ii) The respondent is a blood relation of the prohibited degrees.

(iii) Either of the party to a marriage was insane or an idiot at the time of marriage.

(iv) Wife and husband or either of the party is living and has re-married.

(v) Some property has been acquired by coercion or fraud by either of the party to a marriage.

Section 22 of this Act provides judicial separation. Besides this, the *Act* also provides for the protection of the wife and her rights.

Law Commission in its report submitted in 1998 recommended certain changes in the Christian marriage especially relating to some of the provisions of the Indian Divorce Act, 1869. It recommended the omission of certain irrelevant things and inclusion of the new ones that suit the modern conditions. Discussions are still going on between the leaders of the Christian communities and the Church authorities on the one hand, and the Central Government on the other, to bring about a comprehensive amendment to the Indian Divorce Act, 1869 to make it more relevant to the modern conditions.

It is clear from the above, that unlike the Hindus, the Christians do not consider marital bond as an indissoluble bond. Further, remarriage of the widows is not only possible but also accepted and encouraged among the Christians. Marriage is treated as a covenant between a man and a woman in which more stress is laid on love, mutual help and friendship or companionship.

Position of Women in the Christian Community

Christian women have a comparatively better status than Hindu and Muslim women. Christian women for all practical purposes are treated on par with their men in their community. Even according to Bible, they are equal to men. Politically, economically, socially and educationally Christian women are in a better position than women of other religions in India. Christian women possess equal rights in the society which may be stated below :

(a) ***Economic Rights*** **:** Economically, Christian woman is free to have property in her name, to use it, to sell it or to deal with it in any manner she likes. She is free to join any profession of her liking and earn money to become economically independent. Large number of Christian women are found to be employed in India.

(b) ***Marital Rights*** **:** As far as marriage is concerned, Christian girls have got the final say. Since child marriage is not practised amongst them, women have their right to select their life-partners. No marriage can be performed against her wish by the clergymen.

(c) ***Status of Women in the Family*** **:** Christian woman is not a slave of the family. She is a co-sailor alongwith her husband in the ocean of family life. She cannot be confined to four walls of the house. She renders active co-operation and help for the smooth running of the family.

(d) ***Political Rights*** **:** Indian Christian woman as any other woman belonging to any community in India, has all the political rights. She can cast her vote in the elections, and herself contest elections. Christian women are politically more conscious also.

(e) ***Religious Rights*** **:** The Christian woman has almost equal religious rights on par with men to take part in religious activities. She can read Bible, go to church alongwith the menfolk, participate in common prayers, take part in religious activities, and can even become nuns and dedicate their entire lives for the cause of the religion.

(f) ***Common Rights*** **:** Christian women can move freely, travel from one area to another independently, take part in business or professional, educational or any other type of activity on par with men. Unlike their Muslim counterparts, they are not forced to wear *"Pardah."* Since monogamy is the prevailing rule of marriage among the Christians, women are well looked after, and respected.

Chapter 5

FAMILY SYSTEM IN INDIA

*Family Among the Hindus : Hindu Joint Family, Definition and Characteristics - Two Main Types of Joint Families - Illom : Patriarchal Joint Family - Tarawad : Matriarchal Joint Family - Merits and Demerits of Joint Family - Changes in the Hindu Joint Family System : Changes in the Structure of the Joint Family - Changes in the Functions of the Joint Family - Causes for the Changes in the Joint Family - Is Hindu Joint Family Disintegrating ? - **Family System Among the Muslims** - Impact of Social Legislation on Marriage and Family.*

FAMILY AMONG THE HINDUS
THE HINDU JOINT FAMILY

Joint Family As a Main Pillar of the Indian Social System

The joint family system is an inseparable part of the Indian social system. As **Panikkar** has pointed out, *the caste system, village system of life and the joint family system can be regarded as the basic pillars of the Indian social system.* The cultural roots of India have gone deep into the family system. Further, as far as the family system is concerned, the joint family system is found among the Hindus as well as non-Hindus.

The Hindu joint family and the caste system are so interdependent and interconnected that **K.M. Panikkar** consider them as constituting a common institution. He writes : *"Though in theory unconnected, these two institutions, the caste and the joint family are, in practice, interlocked to an extent which makes them in effect a common institution. The unit of Hindu society is not individual but joint family. The widest expression of this family is "sub-caste" which often consists only of a few joint families which intermarry and interdine among themselves."*

Joint family or extended family is the most common and uniform family pattern found in India. It is significant to note that the type of the joint families that we find in India are not totally unknown to the European society. **I.P. Desai** writes : *"The family is the group wider than the nuclear group is not unknown to the European society, yet strangely enough, the joint family came to be understood as the conglomeration of nuclear families for all purposes in stead of qualitatively different family."* However, it is to be acknowledged that the Hindu joint family has its own uniqueness for it has the religious sanction and the spiritual base. The family to a Hindu is a sacred institution and associated with all sorts of historical myths and legends.

Joint family in India has a long standing history of its own. It has been in existence right from the Vedic times. As **Dr. Iravathi Karve** pointed out that in the *"Indian social evolution the* *family has always meant the joint family."*[1] As against the individual family, members belonging to more than three or four generations such as grand parents, parents, children and grand children and sometimes great grand children are normally found in a joint family.

The Hindu joint family is said to be the bedrock on which Hindu values and attitudes are built. It is found in all the parts of India. Family for a Hindu, is a sacred institution deriving sanction from religion and social traditions with myths and legends. From the traditional point of view, *the unit of the Hindu society is not the individual but the joint family.*

Joint Family in the Ancient Time

Ever since the Vedic times, family has assumed importance in the Indian society. In the Vedic times, the functions of the family were mostly religious and all the *Samskaras* originated from the family. *"The Vedic family was of the patriarchal type, matriarchate being unknown to Vedic society. It was a joint family consisting of the father, the grandfather, sons, nephews and their wives. The patriarch controlled the family property and could theoretically divide it in any way he liked; but normally the division was made equitably. The stories of Sunashepa and Rjasravas suggest that the father had the power over the life and limb of the children......... The father most frequently figures as the standard of comparision when kindness is to be extolled. The father was expected to deal most kindly with the sons, who were expected to be the most obedient and courteous to their parents. The education of children was a personal concern of the father, and he initiated them into Vedic studies and family crafts. There were rituals for securing intellectual pre-eminence and success in debates."*[2]

"The striking features of the ancient Hindu family are its spiritual continuity and physical indivisibility. The Hindu home is joint in the sense that it is the dwelling place not only of the living members of the family, but also of the pitrus or the ancestors, who are remembered by offering sacrifices. The Hindu home belongs to the pitrus, the ancestors; the living members of the family are trustees of the home in the interest of the putras, namely, the future members of the family."[3]

Joint families assumed importance throughout the Vedic period, post-Vedic period, in the period of Dharmashastras, Puranas, Epics and even during the Medieval period. Literatures produced during this period throw light on the growth of the Hindu family and the changes and modifications it was undergoing.

Varnashrama system which existed during the early times also highlights the importance of the family whether it is joint family or single unit family. The Hindu thinkers enjoined that the *Purusharthas* which represent the Hindu aims of life, could be fulfilled through the *Ashrama* system. In the Ashrama scheme, the *"grihasthashrama"* which represents the life of the householder [*grihashtha*] is given more importance for the following reasons.

(i) All the other orders or *ashramas* exist because of the support given by *Grihasthashrama.* As **Manu Smriti** points out, *"As all streams and rivers flow to rest in the ocean, so all the ashramas flow to rest in the householder."*

---

1 **Dr. Iravathi Karve** as quoted in *"The Cultural Heritage of India"* - Vol. I.

2 *"The Cultural Heritage of India."* Vol.I. Page - 222. ***Pub.***: Sri Ramakrishna Mission.

3 **Prof. M. Nanjammani** *"Study of Indian Society."* Page - 128.

(ii) This stage helps the householder to perform the religious rites [*Dharmasampatti*]. It also enables him to perform the basic duties of a married person namely, the *Panchamahayajnas*[1] or five great sacrifices along with the wife: *Daiva Yajna, Rishi Yajna, Pitri Yajna, Bhuta Yajna, and Nara Yajna* [or *Atithi Yajna*].

(iii) In this stage, the individual fulfils his obligations towards the society. He earns money, protects his own family and never makes it a parasite on the society. He begets children and assures the continuation of the race. He takes care of the *Brahmacharis, Vanaprasthis* and *Sanyasis* who are not supposed to earn their living.

(iv) It is in this stage, the individual engages himself in all activities incidental to his *"Varna."*

Number of Hindu *dharmashastrakaras* or law-givers like Manu, Yajnavalkya, Vishnu, Narada, Vyasa, Brihaspathi, Kautilya, Katyayana, Parashara and others laid down norms, rules and regulations to protect the institution of family and to regulate and control family relations, family property and family activities. The Hindu customs, practices, values, institutional patterns and the whole normative system also served to safeguard the institution of family and to continue its tradition. The joint family stood firmly on the rock bed of spiritual and moral values. In such a family the individual interests were harmonised with those of the family itself. Even to this day, the Hindu sentiments are in favour of the joint family. Most of the Hindu families in many parts of the country, especially in the rural areas, are joint and agnatic.

The joint family still continues to be the characteristic feature of agricultural society. Joint families have existed in countries like China and India whose economy has been based on agriculture. Collective living, collective farming and collective share in the family wealth was the traditional features of the joint family. The joint family in modern India, is mostly patriarchal though exceptions to this are found in some parts of the country. The nature and character of the joint family, its structure and functions, and the changes that have taken place in them can be briefly examined here.

Definition and Characteristics of Joint Family

Definition of Joint Family

Joint family has been defined variously. Of the definitions cited below, **Dr. Karve's** definition seems to be more relevant to the Indian context.

1. **Dr. Iravathi Karve :** Joint family is *"a group of people who generally live under one roof, who eat food cooked at one hearth, who hold property in common, who participate in common family worship and who are related to each other as some particular type of kindred."*
2. **C.B. Mamoria :** *"Joint family is a collection of more than one primary family, the basis being close blood ties, common residence, and patrilineal descent."*
3. **I.P. Desai :** *"We call that household a joint family which has greater generation depth than individual family and the members of which are related to one another by property, income and mutual rights and obligations."*
4. **Henry Maine :** *"The Hindu joint family is a group consisting of known ancestors and adopted sons and relatives related to these sons through marriage."*
5. That household is a *"joint family which has greater generation depth, [i.e., three or more]*

1 ***Pancha Maha Yajnas*:**

- ***Deva Yajna*** : offering oblations unto *Devas* with recitation of Vedic Mantras.
- ***Rishi Yajna*** : study of Vedas and teaching of Vedas to students and offering of oblations to Rishis.
- ***Pitri Yajna*** : Tarpana or ablutions to the departed souls and *"sraddha"* or annual religious rites performed for departed souls.
- ***Bhuta Yajna*** : distribution of food to cows, crows and animals in general.
- ***Nara Yajna*** [***Atithi Yajna***] : giving food to guests and honouring them, that is, extending hospitality to the guests.

than nuclear family and the members of which are related to one another by property, and the mutual rights and obligations."

6. **In simple words :** *The joint family is one which consists of members related through blood and spread over three or more generations, live together under a common roof and work under a common head.*

Characteristics of the Hindu Joint Family

1. *Depth of Generations* : The joint family consists of people of at least three or more generations. It is a confluence of grandparents, parents, and children. Sometimes even blood relations such as uncles, aunties, cousins, etc. and adopted children also live in under the same roof. These members are normally blood relatives referred to as *"sapindas"*. According to **Mamoria,** *"the fundamental principle of the Hindu joint family is the tie of sapindaship without which it is impossible to form a joint family."*[1] The size of the joint family is relatively bigger, sometimes consisting 8-10 members or even more than that.

2. *Common Roof* : Members of the joint family normally reside together under the same household. This common residence is actually the centre of all life activities - religious, economic, recreational, social, etc. **Henry Maine** called this house a *"great home"*. Due to the scarcity of accommodation or due to educational and employment problems, members of the joint family, that is, members of individual nuclear families within the joint family, may reside separately. Still, they try to retain regular contacts and the feeling of belonging to the same family. They have emotional and economic links with the original joint families.

3. *Common Kitchen* : Members eat the food prepared jointly in the common kitchen. Normally, the eldest female member of the joint family, the wife of *"Karta"* supervises the work in the kitchen. In the patriarchal joint families, women serve the food to men at first and take their meals afterwards. All the female members of the joint family do the kitchen work. They take it as a matter of family tradition and religious duty to serve food to even uninvited guests. The house is known for its hospitality. Existence of single kitchen in the big household unites the members. Its separation, or establishment of separate kitchens under the same roof indicates the breakdown of the joint family.

4. *Common Worship* : The Hindu joint family derives its strength from religion. Hence, it is associated with various religious rituals and practices. Every family may have its own deity or *"Kula devata"* and its own religious tradition. Members of the family take part in common worship, rites and ceremonies. Even the members of the so called *"branches"* of a joint family or *"dependent nuclear families"* make it a point to join the 'great home' whenever some major religious functions take place. At least once a year they join the other members to participate in the *"pitru pooja"* or *"shradda" karma.*

5. *Common Property* : The members hold a common property. As **Melley** writes, the joint family *"is a co-operative institution similar to a joint stock company in which there is a joint property."* The head of the family that is *'Karta'*, manages the family property like a trustee. For a long time, members did not have any right to withdraw their due share in the property. The family property was almost regarded as indivisible. However, the *'Karta'* has full power over the property and to take whatever decision relating to property in the best interest of the family as a whole. The total earnings of the members are pooled into a family treasury and family expenses are met with out of those earnings.

6. *Exercise of Authority or the Karta's Authority* : In the patriarchal joint family, usually the eldest male member known as *'Karta'* exercises authority. The authority is determined on the

1 **Dr. Mamoria** *"Social Problems and Social Disorganisation in India"* Page 85.

principle of seniority. The super-ordination of the eldest member and the subordination of all the other members to him is a keynote of the joint family. His commands are normally obeyed by others. As opposed to it, in the matriarchal joint family the eldest female member in theory exercises the supreme authority. The joint family has more or less an authoritarian family structure. In this family the power to make decisions and pass judgements is in the hands of one person called *'karta'* who demands immediate obedience. Here, the power is traditionally given to him because of his age and seniority. The *'karta'* allows little individual freedom to other family members and may or may not consult them in decision-making. Decisions relating to major family affairs, property, business affairs, major purchases and sales, children's education, their occupation and marriage and such other matters, the 'Karta' takes his own independent but final decisions. He in a way exercises dictatorial power. But members never used to question his power. His decisions were believed to be rightful decisions.

During the Vedic time, the family was patriarchal, and the head of the family had absolute control over the family and family property. The head of the family could dispose of all his property under his control while performing the *"vishvajit"* sacrifice. *Taitiriya Brahmana* provides the example of Vajasravasa who actually offered the entire property as *"dana"* including his son Nachiketa who was presented to Lord *Yama* [God of Death] in a fit of anger. Rig Veda provides the example of Shunahshepa who had sold his son. These were only stray instances and not common practices. In comparison with the early Roman patriarch, the patriarch in India, very rarely used to exercise unlimited power in a reckless manner.

7. *Arranged Marriages* : In the joint family, the head considers it his privilege to arrange the marriages of the younger members. Marriages are normally arranged after providing due considerations to factors such as family tradition, *kula maryada,* [family prestige] matching of horoscope, caste rules, etc. The individual's right to select his/her life-partner is undermined. The younger members rarely challenge their decisions and arrangements. But now-a-days, the feelings of younger ones are being given due weightage.

8. *Higher Rate of Procreation* : The size of the joint family is by nature bigger. It is found to be associated with higher rate of production. It is so because in the past procreation was regarded as a religious duty. The *Grihasthashram* lays stress on the production of children. Children, that too male children are wanted to fulfil ancestral obligations. Members rarely practised birth control measures. But today the situation has changed.

9. *Mutual Rights, Responsibilities and obligations* : The members tend to identify themselves with their family. Every member has his own duties and obligations towards the family. Every family, in turn, protects the interests and promotes the welfare of all. Here, the responsibilities of the members are stressed more than their rights. Hence every member of the family is obliged to work for the promotion of family progress and prosperity. Family interests prevail over individual interests.

The joint family functions on the ideal of joint responsibility. If a father, for example, takes loan to be spent on his hospital charges, it is the responsibility of his sons to repay the loan. It is the duty of every one to help and protect every other in times of crisis and need.

Responsibilities in the joint family are not, however, equally shared. As **M.S. Gore** has observed, male members and senior members have greater responsibilities and powers than the female members and junior members in the joint family.

10. *Self-sufficiency* : There was a time when the joint family was relatively self-sufficient. It used to meet the economic, recreational, medical, educational and other needs of the members. The rural agricultural joint families were mostly self-reliant. But they can hardly depend on themselves today. No type of family is self-reliant that way today.

Two Main Types of Joint Families

The traditional joint family system in India is of two types : (i) *Matrilineal Joint Family,* and (ii) *Patriarchal Joint Family.*

1. MATRILINEAL JOINT FAMILY

Matrilineal joint family gives more importance to women. It is theoretically led and dominated by the eldest woman. Matrilineal joint families, though rare in India have existed among the Nairs of Malabar [Kerala] and the Khasis and Garos living on the Garo Hills of Assam.

Example of the Nair Matrilineal Joint Family : *"Tarawad"*

The matrilineage of the Nairs, or the Nair matrilineal family is known as *"Tarawad."* It consists of all the descendants in the female line of an ancestress. It consists of a woman who is the head of the family, her brothers and younger sisters, her children, and her sister's children and her daughter's children and her sister's daughter's children.

Main Characteristics

1. Though theoretically woman is the nominal head of the family, the eldest male member of the family called *"Karnavar"* [his wife is known as *"Ammayi"*] looks after the affairs of the family. He is the custodian of property and the manager of family matters.

2. As far as the power of the *Karnavar* is concerned, he is the absolute ruler of the family. He can sell, borrow or lend money, can give land as gift, can mortgage property. He is not accountable to any member in respect of income and expenditure. On his death, next eldest male member becomes the *Karnavar.* The *Karnavar* can be removed from the "Karnavarship" [managerial post] if he is subject to physical incapacity such as blindness, lunacy or any incurable disease such as leprosy.

3. *Tarwad* consists of the unmarried sons, i.e., they belong to their mother's *tarwad.* But married sons belong to their wife's *tarwad.*

4. All the male and female members of the *tarwad* have the right to property. It belongs to all of them. They are the co-owners of the *tarwad* property with a right to conserve it. They can therefore object to its alienation by the manager, the *Karnavar.* The *Karnavar* is subject to removal from his managerial office for mismanagement of property. [But in actual practice, it is difficult to remove him.] He cannot, however, be sued in a court of law except on the ground of fraud.

5. When a *tarwad* grows and becomes unmanageable, it often splits into smaller family units called *"Tavazhis."* A *"Tavazhis"* is a matrilineal group of persons consisting of a female, her children, and all her descendants in the female line. When a *tarwad* is divided into several Tavazhis, the property of the *tarwad* is divided equally among the *tavazhis.* They however retain their kinship ties with the *tarwad.* They also observe the rule of exogamy and marry outside the *tarwad.* Members of the *tavazhi* identify themselves with the parent matrilineal joint family.

Changes in *Tarawad* After 1912

Legislative enactments that took place after 1912 [***Example*** **:** (i) *The Travancore Nayar Regulation of* 1912, (ii) *The Kerala Act,* 1958.] led to the changes in the matrilineal joint family, that is, *tarwad,* in Kerala.

(i) Tarwad property has now become divisible; (ii) *Karnavar* no more remains as the absolute ruler of the *tarwad,* and his powers are curtailed; (iii) Members of the *tarawad* are entitled for maintenance even though they live outside the *tarwad*; (iv) Nairs' marriage has been made more stable and hence close and intimate relations prevail between husband and wife; (v) Unlike in the past, the self-earned property of a *tarwad* member goes to his widow and children after his death, or to his mother or mother's mother.

2. PATRIARCHAL JOINT FAMILY

The patriarchal joint family is father-centred. The eldest male member of the family looks after the family affairs. ***Examples*** **:** The patriarchal joint families are found among the *Nambudaris* of Malabar, the *Mundas* of Chotanagapura, and the *Angami Nagas* of Assam. The Nambudari joint family is generally called *"Illom."*

Example of the Nambudiri Joint Family : *"Illom"*

Nambudiri Brahmins lived in patrilineages or patrilineal families which were called ***Illom.*** The Nambudiris were landowners and their land was leased to Nayars on *"Kanam tenure"* [refers to 12 year lease of land]. Land was considered indivisible, and indivisibility was ensured by the rule of primogeniture.[1] Only the eldest son was permitted to marry a Nambudiri girl and the younger sons had *"liaison"* [*sambandham*] with girls belonging to the higher Nayar castes. The younger sons visited their life partners at night and the children born of the union became members of their mother's *tarawads.* The Nayars used to consider it as a matter of privilege to give their daughters in marriage to the Nambudiri Brahmin youths, though such a marital relationship was very loose. Such wives and their children were looked down upon in the Nambudiri *Illom.* Nambudiri husband had virtually no responsibility towards his Nayar wife, her children and also towards their education and marriage. Nayar *Tarawad* was taking all such responsibilities. The Nambudiri *Illom* consisted of a man, his wife or wives, his children and his younger brothers. Sometimes, the *Illom* included his old parents or his eldest son's children.

The perpetuity and continuation of *illom* property among the Nambudiris are facilitated by the custom of the eldest son marrying girl from his caste, while other sons, although not theoretically debarred from marrying women from their caste, generally do not marry Nambudiri women. It is only when the eldest son fails to have children that the next senior member marries and continues the family. The right of partition being restricted, junior members of the family have only the right to maintenance. The eldest son of the *Illom* though has absolute control over the family property, he has no power to alienate it by sale or gift without the consent of the other members. Even the female members have to give their consent in order to alienate it.

Dowry system is closely associated with the Nambudiri marriage. Dowry amount was normally very high. Much of the Illom money was being spent on dowry. The practice of paying huge amount of dowry led to polygyny. Inability to pay dowry made many Nambudiri girls to remain as spinsters. Some young girls were forced to marry old persons. Attractive dowry tempted some Nambudiri men to marry several girls. Finally, the number of girls that could be married by a Nambudiri man had to be limited to only three. *Illom* has undergone lot of changes today.

Illom : Main Differences With Other Ordinary Joint Families

As **Kapadia** has observed, the *"Illom"* system of Nambudiris is different from the typical joint families in two respects.

(i) Though *Illom* is patriarchal in nature, *the family property is indivisible.* It cannot be divided or sold without the consent of all the members since all have an authority over it.

(ii) *The Nambudiri woman has better rights* than her counterpart in the rest of the traditional patriarchal joint families in India. *She has a share in the joint family property* unlike the women of the typical joint family who have only a claim for maintenance.

---

1 ***Primogeniture*** refers to the rule of inheritance according to which only the eldest son is entitled to inherit the ancestral property of the family.

Main Differences Between Patriarchal and Matrilineal Joint Families

Main differences between the matrilineal *"Tarawad"* and the typical patriarchal joint families can be briefly stated here :

(i) In place of patrilineal descent, patrilocal residence and patriarchal authority, we find in *Tarawad, matrilineal descent, matrilocal residence and matriarchal dominance.*

(ii) Inheritance of and succession to property take place *along the female line in Tarawad.*

(iii) Conjugal relations [marital relations] are given less importance in *Tarawad* than the consanguineous relations.

(iv) The female head of the family has the power to dismiss the *Karnavar* if he is found to be incapable or dishonest.

(v) Nair's *Tarawad* has, however, either disintegrated or is on the verge of getting disintegrated. But the typical patriarchal joint families continue to exist particularly in the rural areas though lot of modifications have taken place in them.

Merits and Demerits of Joint Family

The joint family claims certain merits and suffers from certain defects. Some of them may be briefly mentioned here.

Merits of Joint Family

(i) *Stable and Durable* : The joint family is more stable and durable than the single unit family or the nuclear family. Individuals may come and go but the family as a unit stands. It contributes much to the continuation of the cultural tradition.

(ii) *Ensures Economic Progress* : The joint family meets the basic needs of its members - food, clothing and shelter - a first condition of economic progress.

Further, *it provides larger labour force* especially for the agricultural communities. It *prevents the sub-division and fragmentation of land-holdings* and *helps scientific farming.* Since about 60% of our farmers are possessing less than 5 acres of land they are obliged to live together without fragmenting their piece of land. Joint family thus protects the economic interests of the members and assures economic progress of the society.

(iii) *Ensures Economy of Expenditure* : Savings are possible here since the household purchases are done jointly. No single member has an absolute right in the family property. Everyone is bound to become spendthrift. The head of the family does not permit the members to become extravagant.

(iv) *Secures the Advantage of Division of Labour* : Here the work is distributed among the members on the basis of age and sex. Members co-operate with one another since they hold the property in common. Especially for agricultural tasks, the joint family is better fitted. As **K.M. Kapadia** has pointed out, *"The Indian farmer used to be producer, seller, labourer and investor combined. Each of these functions can be performed efficiently to the advantage of the family if it is a joint one."*

(v) *Serves as a Social Insurance Company* : For the people such as orphans, widows, the deserted, divorced, separated and the neglected, the joint family serves as a social insurance company. It gives them food, shelter and protection.

(vi) *Provides Social Security* : The joint family gives social security to the weak, the aged, the sick, the infirm, the unabled, the disabled and such other needy persons. An individual's life from cradle to cremation is looked after by the joint family. In times of accidents, crises and emergencies, one can rely on one's joint family for the needed help. Though the government has launched schemes to provide social security to the old, the sick, the disabled and such others, only a small section of our population is covered by these schemes. Majority of such needy persons are still depending upon joint family for their existence.

(vi) *Provides Leisure* : Since the work is shared by all the members on the basis of age, sex and experience, they get more leisure time. More hands at home can finish off the work with minimum time and provide enough leisure to the members to relax. Here women are the main beneficiaries of leisure.

(vii) *Provides Recreation* : The joint family is an ideal place of recreation for all the members. Childish play between the aged and the little babies, the funny talks of the old, the broken language of the younger ones, the expression of sisterly, brotherly and motherly love and the like make the joint family life a pleasurable one. Social and religious ceremonies that take place at the family bring even the relatives together and tighten the ties.

(ix) *Helps Social Control* : The joint family by exercising control over the behaviour of its members acts as an agency of social control. The individuals are taught to subordinate their individual interests to the group interests.

(x) *Provides Psychological Security* : The joint family provides psychological security to its members. By creating a harmonious atmosphere in family, it contributes to the development of social solidarity. It prevents the growth of excessive individuation inside the family.

(xi) *Promotes Co-operative Virtues* : Joint family is said to be the breeding ground of love, self-help, co-operation, tolerance, discipline, loyalty, generosity, sacrifice, service-mindedness and obedience and so on. It instils the socialistic spirit among the members. *"Work according to one's ability and obtain according to one's needs,"* and *"all for one and one for all"*, - are said to be the mottos of a joint family.

"It is because of these benefits that it is said that traditional [joint] family life in boyhood is a school, in youth a safety-device, in old age a solace, and at all times a venerable institution."[1]

Demerits of Joint Family

The Indian social environment which made the joint family a useful institution sometime ago, has very much changed today. In the present modern social structure, the joint family has either lost, or is fast losing its utilities. Some of its advantages are turning out to be its disadvantages. External agencies have taken up many of its functions and hence its utility is further undermined. Joint family itself appears to be dysfunctional in certain respects. Some of its disadvantages may be briefly mentioned here.

(i) *Retards the Development of Personality* : The joint family does not provide enough scope for the members to develop qualities of adventure, self-determination, industriousness, etc. The elder ones take up too many responsibilities and the younger ones are overprotected.

(ii) *Damages Individual Initiative and Enterprise* : The joint family does not provide proper opportunities for the members to develop their talents. Any new enterprise or adventure on the part of the young people is *discouraged* by the head of the family. This adversely affects the individuality, originality and creativity of the young members.

The youngsters in the joint family have become conscious of their rights and status and demand re-orientation of relationship within the family. But the elders, being trained in the old traditions, deny it because of which the children's initiative is damaged.

(iii) *Narrows Down Loyalties* : Joint family makes the members to develop narrow-mindedness. It is said that a member is more likely to develop a sense of loyalty to the family than to

1 **Ram Ahuja** *"Indian Social System"* - Page: 50.

the larger society. These family units develop strong opposite principles which result in *disintegration and division within the society at large.*

(iv) *Promotes Idleness* : The joint family is said to be the home of idlers and drones. Since all the members are assured of their basic necessities of life, some may not take any interest in the productive activities. The earning members get the same attention from the family as the non-earning members. As a result, the earning members lose interest in work or do it half-hearted. This leads to suspicion and misunderstanding and affects the harmonious relations of the members. Further, all the relatives may flock to the joint family with their idle habits and may become life-long parasites.

(v) *Not Favourable for Savings and Investment* : The need for saving does not arise here because all are assured of their basic needs. There is *no inspiration for the accumulation of capital and investment.* Saving is not possible also for one has to share one's income with the large family.

(vi) *The Centre of Quarrels* : The joint family is said to be the hotbed of quarrels and bickerings especially among the womenfolk. A woman whose husband earns more, agitates, revolts and demands separation. Most of the quarrels start because of the narrowminded, suspicious, conservative, jealous, superstitious, talkative and quarrelsome women. The uneven distribution of burden of work among women, the upbringing of children and the differentiation in treatment of women by the elders often become a frequent source of trouble. Since women come to the family [after the marriage] from diverse socio-economic and family backgrounds, they may find it difficult to adjust themselves properly. Quarrels very often take place between the elders and the younger members of the family.

(vii) *Denies Privacy* : Since the joint family is always overcrowded, privacy is denied to the newly wedded couple. They cannot express openly their love and affection, for the invariable presence of other members causes embarrassment to them. They rarely get an opportunity to talk about their personal matters. Hence they fail to develop intimacy.

(viii) *Affects Adversely Socialisation of Children* : Due to the lack of intimacy and privacy between the husband and wife, the socialisation of children is affected very badly. The parents cannot always give personal attention to the upbringing of their children. The children become more attached to their grandparents and often they pick up their idle habits and age-old ideas.

(ix) *Undermines the Status of Women* : In patriarchal joint families, women have only a secondary role. They lead a life of drudgery and have no voice in the upbringing of children. They are not given sufficient freedom to express and to develop their personality. Their inner feelings are never recognised. They feel repressed and suffer from emotional strains. They are made to work like servants. Women are treated as non-entities here. They can hardly resist their elders even for a just cause because obedience is enforced upon them. In such families sons are preferred to the daughters.

(x) *Encourages Litigation* : The joint family encourages litigation. Normally disputes over the common property crop up at the time of partition. Such disputes are taken to the courts which are dragged on for years leading to the waste of time, energy, money and more than that, loss of mental peace.

(xi) *Favours Uncontrolled Reproduction* : The joint family is found to be associated with higher birth rate. Members do not feel the need to adopt birth control measures. Since the joint family takes up directly the responsibility of feeding, rearing and educating the children, the married members do not experience the urgency and necessity of restricting the number of issues.

(xii) *Limits Social Mobility* : The joint family is said to be more conservative in nature. Since it is dominated by tradition, it is slow to respond to the modern trends. It does not encourage its members to go after change. Members are more concerned with safeguarding their statuses than with changing it. Hence social mobility is very much limited here.

(xiii) ***Encourages Nepotism*** : Some are of the opinion that the joint family system is the root cause of nepotism and discrimination. It is said that the public servants and officials belonging to one or the other joint family are more likely to favour their own kith and kin on public issues or in matters of providing job even at the cost of merit.

CHANGES IN THE HINDU FAMILY SYSTEM

Every thing in this social world is subject to change. Accordingly, the Indian joint family too has undergone significant changes during the recent times. Sociologists have been discussing various questions relating to these changes. Some of these changes are *"structural"* in nature, while others are *"functional"*. Both these 'structural' and 'functional' changes could be briefly analysed here.

Structural Changes in the Hindu Joint Family

The structure of the traditional Hindu joint family has undergone many changes. The *size of the family,* the *depth of its generations, ownership of property* and its *management, exercise of authority, male-female relations within the family, the marriage system* and *husband and wife relationship* and similar other structural aspects have undergone significant changes.

1. ***Size of the Family and Depth of Generations*** : The size of the joint family is decreasing. Large joint families with 15-20 people are rarely found today. It is only marginally big with 8-10 members.

Members belonging to four-five generations used to live together previously. Today's joint family consists of people belonging to two or three generations only. It provides shelter only to the nearest relatives and not to all those who are relatives and who need some protection or shelter.

2. ***Ownership of Property*** : Property rights have changed now. *The Hindu, Inheritance and Succession Act 1956* provides woman right to family property. Modern legislations have given individual members of the family the right to earn money or property and utilise it or dispose it of in any manner they like. They are not obliged to give their entire earnings to the family expenses as they used to do before. These rights have added to the economic independence of the family members. Even female members have also started earning money particularly in the urban context.

3. ***Exercise of Authority*** : The oldest male member of the family called *'Karta'* who used to exercise a lot of authority, has lost most of his power. The present day joint family is no more patriarchal in the strict sense of the term. Today women are also given much importance in the decision-making process. Employed women are given still greater importance. The *Karta's* power is now shared by his sons. The grandfather has only limited power in the present context. Though male members continue to enjoy greater power than the female members they cannot behave in an authoritarian manner.

The patriarch or parents in the family also do not want to impose their authority on the children but give them more freedom now to determine their own goals and means to achieve them.

4. ***Respectable Status for Women*** : The traditional joint family has been associated with the sub-ordination of women. The emergent trend in the joint family has changed the status of women. Abolition of child marriage system and its replacement by adult marriages, introduction of female education, extension of economic and employment opportunities for women, and such other developments have made men to treat women in terms of equality. Women now have a respectable position, if not entirely an equal position on par with men. This is more so in families of working women. In families of non-working women, however, this philosophy of equal rights for women is not much talked of. It may be noted that *no family system will grant full equality to women so long as the daily work involving house and children is regarded as women's responsibility.*

5. *Relations Among Mother-in-law, Daughter-in-law and Father-in-law* : The distance that was there between the father-in-law and daughter-in-law has been reduced now. The daughter-in-law can now directly talk to the father-in-law without hiding her face with a veil. In good number of instances, daughter-in-law is looked after affectionately by the father-in-law.

Mother-in-law and daughter-in-law relations too have improved. The mother-in-law is not found to be as dominating and dictatorial as she was sometimes ago. Daughter-in-law is not treated as a servant and is not harassed much. She is given respect in the family. Greater the educational level of the daughter-in-law, higher the respect she obtains in the family. In spite of these developments there are instances in which daughters-in-law are often harassed and ill-treated because of dowry disputes and misunderstandings.

6. *Selection of Mates and Conjugal Relationships* : In the traditional family, the marriages for the children were arranged by parents without consulting them. The emergent trend in it is that the parents and children jointly make selection of the spouses. This joint selection reduces the chances of conflict. Husband and wife relationship which was one of dominance and submission has now become almost equalitarian. Wife who could hardly talk to her husband in the presence of other members of the family, is now courageous enough to discuss things openly without much inhibition. Conjugal relationship is also treated on par with consanguine relationship.

7. *Weakening Family Norms* : The traditional joint family is known for its discipline, where the things take place in a traditional manner. In the modern families, importance is given to family adjustments and harmony rather than to tradition. Hence opportunities and rewards are distributed not according to one's membership in the family but according to one's abilities and talents. The principle of division of labour which used to take into account factors such as family membership, age and sex of the individual has lost its relevance now. Much stress is now laid on individualism. The ideals of individualism, democracy, equality of sex, etc., have weakened the traditional family values and norms.

8. *Joint Family taking the Form of Dependent Nuclear Family* : The traditional joint family which used to consist of several nuclear families living under the same roof is rarely found today. Some of these nuclear families are breaking away from the joint families and setting up separate households. Education, economic and employment opportunities have compelled young men and women of the family to go out of the family to far away places. Those who go out and prefer to settle in the places of their choice also try to maintain some contact with their original family. In times of crisis, problems, hardships etc. it tries to seek support from the original family. They are also ready to provide the necessary assistance to the original family on occasions such as marriage of girls, education of younger ones, health hazards, economic hardships, finding out job for younger ones, etc. These families can better be understood as *"dependent nuclear families"* because we find in them what is known as *"functional jointness".* Such type of dependent nuclear families is on the increase.

Functional Changes in the Joint Family

In the functional aspects of the Hindu joint family many changes have taken place nowadays. The joint family was fulfilling many of its obligations towards its members. Today, the joint family is not fulfilling many of these functions for there are well established and specialised agencies to undertake these functions. External agencies such as schools, colleges, hostels, hotels, cinema houses, hospitals, helpage homes, voluntary associations, etc. have taken over some of the traditional activities of the joint families. Various governmental agencies are also functioning as substitutes for joint families in certain areas. Some of the major changes that have taken place in the functional aspect of joint family may be discussed here.

1. *Regulation of Sex and Procreation* : These two functions are still associated with the family. Pre-marital and extramarital sex relations are severely prohibited. The Hindu joint family is regulating the sexual activities of its members through the established institution of marriage. Open expression of love and affection between husband and wife has become now common but it was suppressed previously.

Desire for children that too male children, is still being strongly felt by the members. Hence procreative activity continues to be a part of the family life though it is not regarded as a matter of religious obligation. People do not want to have large families and are contented with one or two children.

2. *Provision of Common Residence* : This function has been affected very much nowadays. After the marriage children may live for some time with their parents but soon they prefer to live separately in their neo-local residence. As urbanisation and industrialisation proceed, more and more young married couples and their families find their residence being determined by the location of their jobs. But the married sons and their wives continue to fulfil their obligations to their parents and siblings. The ties are maintained with them not only because of their obligations to them but also because of the affection and respect for them. Mutual help in various exigencies of life [like sickness, old age, accident, unemployment, etc.] and economic co-operation are found to be associated with such neo-local families which can also be referred to as "dependent nuclear families".

Sometimes, the big residential building of the joint family is portioned and the sons may convert it into an apartment house. Though they live separately under one roof and cook their food in separate kitchens they help each other in times of crisis, need, etc. There are also instances of severe conflicts and misunderstandings taking place between them.

3. *Religious functions* of the joint family have diminished. Members do not take much interest in the festivals, annual ceremonies, etc. No one marries now with the intention of performing *"panchamahayajnas"*. Most of the religious activities are held in a *symbolic manner* as a matter of *"kula dharma"* or *"kula parampara"*. Still one or the other religious activity and the *'shraddha karma'* are held annually giving an opportunity to those who live separately to go to the original family to re-establish their relationship with the family. It is an occasion for the family members and its close relatives to gather together collectively and exchange their feelings.

4. *The task of upbringing of children and socialising them* continues to be associated with the family. Parents are more concerned about it now. In the traditional joint families grandparents used to take all the responsibilities of bringing up the children and even giving them basic education. Educated parents today want to take up these responsibilities themselves and expect their parents to provide only emotional support and protection to their grand children and nothing more than that. They want to spare more time for their children to bring them up in a proper manner to face the modern competitive world.

5. *Economic functions* of the joint family have radically changed. Due to the decline in the traditional skills and household crafts, the family has lost much of its productive role. It has become a *consumption unit. Employment opportunity outside the family has freed young adults from direct dependence upon their families.* As their wages or salaries have made them financially independent, the authority of the head of the household has weakened further. In the city, in many cases, along with men their wives also have started working and earning. This has affected intra-family relations. Children have ceased to be economic assets and have become liabilities atleast in the initial stage. Since children in the modern family are to be given education for a long period, huge amount of money will have to be spent on them till they get into some jobs. In many instances, sons who go away from the family for work do not completely neglect their original family. They sometimes give a small portion of their earning to help the original family to meet its expenses.

The economic power which the *'karta'* or the head of the family was exercising all these years has diminished nowadays. One of the adult sons who stays on with the parents normally looks after the property and not the *Karta.* He does not behave in an authoritarian manner. He is not regarded as the owner of the property, but *its manager*. He cannot dictate terms to other members of the family. If the family property is very huge, all the children want to get a share in it at the time of partition. If it is too little, normally the earning members settled in a far away place, do not want to claim any share in it and leave it to those who stay back in the original family.

Changes in Some Other Functions

Family is still ***providing protection and security to its members.*** But it is sharing this task with the governmental and / or private agencies established for this purpose.

Family has almost ***transferred its recreational activities to the external commercial agencies.*** Family is not able to provide the traditional type of entertainment for its members for there is no demand for it.

It is clear from the above that the joint family system in India is undergoing both *structural* and *functional* changes. Those writers who overemphasised these developments [for instance K.T. Merchant [1935], A.M. Shaw [1961], Aileen Ross [1961], William Goode [1966], and others] have said that the joint family is going to disintegrate very soon. A few others [for instance, K.M. Kapadia [1956], I.P. Desai [1964], B.R. Agarwala and M.S. Gorc [1968] and others] have argued that the joint family system in India is successfully managing with the situation and maintaining its stability. It is relevant here to make a brief reference to the studies that have been made by the sociologists relating to the changes in the traditional joint family system.

• Sociological Studies Relating to the Changes in the Family

Sociologists have been making a study of the changes taking place in the joint family since a long time. For example, **I.P. Desai** made a study of urban families in ***Mahuwa*** in Gujarath in 1955. **K.M. Kapadia** studied rural and urban families [The percentage being 82% and 18%] that belong to ***Navasari*** town and its 15 surrounding villages in Gujarath in 1955. **Aileen Ross** conducted a study of the Hindu families in an urban settling in ***Bangalore*** [Karnataka State] in 1957. **A.M. Shah** studied families in one village in Gujarat between 1955 and 1958. **M.S. Gore** conducted a study of families in an urban [that is, in Delhi], rural and rural-urban fringe areas of ***Rohtak*** and ***Hissar*** districts in Haryana in 1960. **Ramakrishna Mukharjee** studied family in West Bengal in 1960-61. **Ram Ahuja** also made studies of families in an urban area in 1976 and the rural areas in 1981 in selected places of Rajasthan.

Studies relating to the changes [particularly structural changes] in family have revealed many things with the help of which the following inferences could be drawn.

1. The size of the traditional joint family is becoming smaller and smaller.
2. Even though the number of fissioned families is increasing, such families continue to fulfil their traditional obligations towards their parental families.
3. In the case of traditional rural communities than in the case of urban communities, we find a greater attempt to maintain the *"jointness"* with the family.
4. It could be said that as long as old cultural values persist among people so long the functional type of joint family will be sustained in our society.
5. Changes from *"traditional"* to *"transitional"* family include various trends such as – functional jointness, neo-local residence, equality of individuals, equal status for women,

weakening of family norms, increasing opportunities to individual members to fulfil their aspirations, and so on.

7. Causes For the Changes in the Joint Family System

The traditional joint system of India has undergone vast changes. These changes have not destroyed the system as such. They have definitely affected its structure and functions and also its stability. **Milton Singer** [1968] has identified five factors which have affected the family most. These are: *education, industrialisation, urbanisation, change in the institution of marriage,* specially in *the age at marriage* and *the legislative measures.*

1. Influence of Education

Modern system of education introduced by the British Government affected joint family in several ways. It has brought about a change in the attitudes, beliefs, values and ideologies of the people. Education which is spreading even amongst the females has created and aroused the individualistic feelings. While the male literacy level has increased from 9.8% in 1901 to 55.7% in 1991, and then to 75.23% in 2001, among the females it has increased from 0.6% to 39.09% and then to 54.16% during the same period.

This increasing education not only brings changes in the philosophy of life of men and women, but also provides new avenues of employment to the latter. After becoming economically independent, women demand more freedom in family affairs. They refuse to accept anybody's dominance over them. Education in this way *brings changes in the relations between the members in the family.* As the level of education rises, the percentage of those in favour of nuclear families increases and the percentage of those supporting joint family living, decreases.

2. Impact of Industrialisation

Factory system of production, new system of organisation and management and new style of life have also affected the joint family. It has made young men and women leave their joint family to far away places in search of better prospects and employment. It has resulted in the breakdown of the link between the kinship and the occupational structure. Many of the traditional skills, crafts and household industries associated with the joint family have declined because of the onslaught of factory system of production.

Some important effects of industrialisation on joint family system may be noted here.

(i) The family which was a principal unit of production has been transformed into *a consumption unit. I*nstead of all the family members working together in an integrated economic enterprise, a few male members *go out of the home* to earn the family's living. This affected *family relations.*

(ii) Factory employment has *freed young adults from direct dependence upon their families.* This financial independence of the youngsters has *weakened the authority of the head* of the household over those earning members. In many cities even women too joined men in working outside the families on salary basis. This has boosted the morale of women.

(iii) In the changed social situation *children have ceased to be economic assets and have become liabilities.* Children's educational requirements have increased. They are to be supported for a very long time till they get into some good jobs.

(iv) Industrialisation *separated the home from the work.* This has made the working members to bear themselves all the burden and headache connected with their job..Their families can hardly lend support in this regard.

3. Influence of Urbanisation

The phenomenon of urbanisation has become now widespread. Urban population is increasing steadily. In the mid-eighteenth century, around 10% of the population in India were urban residents. Their percentage increased to 25.72% in 1991, and it was projected to be 28.4% in the year 2000. The studies made by **Aileen Ross, M.S. Gore, Milton Singer** and others have revealed that the *city life is more favourable to small nuclear families than to big joint families.*

On the basis of the studies made, it could be said that the *urban living weakens joint family pattern and strengthens nuclear family patterns.* Educated persons in the urban areas are less in favour of joint family norms. Cities provide opportunities to women also for gainful employment and when woman starts earning, she seeks freedom in many spheres. She tries to break away more and more from her husband's family of orientation. Urban residence thus seems to introduce a certain measure of variation in the family pattern in our society.

4. Change in Marriage System

Change in the age at marriage, freedom in mate-selection and *change in the attitude towards marriage* have also affected our family system. Modern young men and women not only marry at a late age but also take personal decision in this matter. They do not wait for parental permission. Parents' role in mate-selection has diminished. Marriage is not very much considered a religious affair but only a social ceremony. Modern marriage does not symbolise the superior authority of the family head over the other members.

5. Legislative Measures

The impact of legislative measures on the family system cannot be ignored. Prohibition of early marriages and fixing the minimum age of marriage by the *Child Marriage Restraint Act, 1929* and the *Hindu Marriage Act, 1955,* have helped lengthen the period of education. The freedom of mate-selection and marriage in any caste and religion without the parents' consent after certain age, permitted by the *Special Marriage Act, 1954,* gave a blow to the parental authority to decide their children's marriage. Other legislations such as the *Widow Remarriage Act, 1856* which gives sanction for widow remarriage, the *Hindu Marriage Act, 1955* which permits divorce and the *Hindu Succession Act, 1956* which gives share to daughters in paternal property - all have modified *interpersonal relations within the family, the composition of the family and the stability of the joint family.*

6. Other Causes

- ***Influence of Western Values*:** The western values relating to *modern science, rationalism, individualism, equality, free life, democracy, freedom of women,* etc., have exerted a tremendous influence on the Hindu family system. The modern educated youths who came under the influence of these values took the earliest opportunity to become free from the tight grip of the joint family.
- ***Awareness Among Women*:** Increasing female education, widened freedom and employment opportunities for women created awareness among women particularly in the middle and upper classes. They also sought chances of becoming *"free"* from the authoritarian hold of the joint family.
- ***Government Jobs*:** Search for government jobs which was started in the beginning of the British rule had become very widespread. Getting into government jobs became a matter of prestige. Those who got into government service had to move from one place to another due to the usual practice of transfer. This compelled many youths in government service to go away from their joint family and to establish their separate households. Same situation continues now also.

- ***Unmanageable Size of the Family*:** Though joint family intends to accommodate a large number of people, it cannot accommodate any number of people. It has its own limitations. If the joint family grows into an unmanageable size, problems of adjustment and understanding arise, making its healthy functioning impossible. The same thing happened in the case of some of our joint families especially during the British rule. Problems of adjustment that cropped up in such families slowly led to their divisions or partitions.

Is Hindu Joint Family Disintegrating ?

Scholars have been discussing since several years the question of the disintegration of the Hindu joint family in India. No social institution can withstand change for long. The Indian family system including the traditional Hindu family system, has undergone changes. The question that is debated is whether these changes are causing the disintegration of the family or not. There are three views among the scholars relating to this question. They are mentioned below.

(i) ***The joint family system is not only changing fast but also tending towards disintegration:*** K.T. Merchant [1935], A.M. Shaw [1955-58], Aileen Ross [1961], William Goode [1963], Prameel Kapoor [1970], B.R. Ghosh [1974] - and others supported this view on the basis of their field studies.

(ii) ***Joint families are successfully continuing in India withstanding all the disintegrating forces:*** This view has been held by the scholars - K.M. Kapadia [1956], I.P. Desai [1964], B.R. Agarwala, M.S. Gore [1968] and others on the basis of their field studies conducted at Surat, Navsari, Baroda, Poona, Kheda, Delhi, Rohtak and other places.

(iii) ***Joint families though are changing fast continue to stay with relatively smaller size:*** Dr. Iravathi Karve, David G. Mandelbaum and others strongly held this opinion.

Joint family is facing changes **:** It is true that joint family system is undergoing fast changes. Some of these changes have disintegrating influence also. This disintegration is more evident in big cities and in industrial centres than in rural areas. But the disintegrating rate is slow and not fast. If some forces are at work towards the breaking up of the joint family system, some other forces are striving for maintaining its existence.

Forces of Change are not destroying the system as such **:** Since India is a land of villages, the joint family system has still scope for its continuation in the villages. The forces of mechanisation, industrialisation, urbanisation, education, etc. have not taken place to the extent of destroying all the prevailing joint families.

Joint family is not dying out **:** As **K.M. Kapadia** has pointed out, *"the general assumption that the joint family is dying out is invalid."* The rural people who desert their joint families and move to the cities due to some economic and other exigencies still want to have their connection with their parental joint families. They want to visit their native families at least at the time of marriages, festivals and such other family rites and ceremonies. Educated Indians still feel morally obliged to retain their links with the traditional joint families. They consider it their moral duty to bring up their younger brothers and sisters in the lines of education and employment. The *sentiment of jointness is very much alive* in them and they cherish it as a cultural objective. Hence joint families do not dwindle away so easily. On the contrary, they are making enough compromises with the modern trends for their survival.

Some Predictions about the Probable Changes in the Indian Family in the Near Future

On the basis of our observations and also by taking clues from various studies conducted relating to the Indian family, particularly joint family, we can make some predictions about the probable changes in it in the days to come.

1. There is no immediate threat to the existence and continuance of the institution of family as such. The family will continue to exist in spite of some forces working against its stability and security.
2. The stability of the family will probably depend more on interpersonal relations than on social pressures from outside.
3. A relatively larger number of people may go in favour of small family by resorting to birth control measures.
4. Family may have to depend more and more on community support and services in order to ensure its continuity.
5. Instances of widow and widower remarriages and even divorcee's remarriages will increase.
6. Rates of divorce, desertion and separation are likely to go up.
7. Parents and grandparents will continue to maintain their relations with their children and grand children and support them even after their retirement.
8. As the things stand today, women's position within the family will definitely improve. Women's employment outside the family will further improve their social standing.
9. Patriarchal values will continue to maintain their hold over the society, including the institution of family.
10. Indian families will remain husband-dominated family though the democratic processes are encouraging egalitarian values.

Family System Among the Muslims

The Muslim family system in India is different from the Hindu family system. Among the Muslims also family system is quite popular, universal and firmly established. The Muslim social life is very much governed by various rules, principles and values enshrined in their sacred scripture **Quran** on the one hand, and the ***"Shariat"*** [which consists of the Muslim personal law], on the other. Muslim social life including the family life is guided and directed by two important forces namely : (i) *religious belief and values dictated by the monotheistic religion and the holy Quran;* and (ii) *Islamic law called the Shariat, which decides what is right and what is wrong.* In no other religion of the world religious law plays such an important role as it does in Islam.

Muslim personal law, called the *Shariat,* thus gives guidance and directions for all human actions – individual and collective, religious and social, economic and political.

• "Marriage and Family" are Commonly Found Among the Indian Muslims

The institutions of marriage and family are commonly found among the Muslim community in India for it discourages celibacy and encourages family. Islam recognises family as the foundation of society. Family among the Muslims functions according to the patriarchal principle. Hence, Muslim families are invariably dominated by men. Prophet Mohammad also insisted on marriage and on the establishment of family. Hence, marrying, and afterwards establishing family became a religious obligation for the Muslims.

The main objective of Muslim family is *the satisfaction of biological and psychological needs of the individuals.* Equal importance is laid on *the satisfaction of sex* and *procreation of children.* Prophet Mohammad believed that by catering to these needs out of religious commitment, the family would *contribute to the stability and continuity of the Muslim community.*

Muslim families were largely joint families based on the principle of patriarch. But now-a-days their joint families are slowly transforming themselves into single unit families especially in the urban areas wherein they are found in relatively a large number. Unlike the Hindu joint families, Muslim joint families are polygamous in nature wherein a Muslim man can have more than one wife.

• Status of Women, their Responsibilities and Rights within the Family

Married Muslim woman is assigned a few responsibilities and provided with a few rights. They are mentioned below :

• Responsibilities of Married Muslim Woman

1. Maintaining good marital relations with the husband.
2. Obeying the words and orders of the husband.
3. Providing conjugal enjoyments to the husband keeping in view the principles of health and propriety.
4. Feeding the child when outsiders are not there, and looking into its welfare.
5. Following the rules of *Iddat* with religious fervour. It means when she is given *"talaq"* by her husband, she should observe sexual abstinence from that day onwards for about three months or for three consecutive menstrual periods.

• Rights Provided for Muslim Woman

1. Muslim woman has the religious as well as legal right to obtain *"Mehar"* from her husband.
2. She has the right to stay in the house of the husband permanently as long as she is not given *talaq*.
3. She has the right to claim from her husband some allowance for her maintenance, in case she is given *talaq* from him.
4. She has the right to expect from her husband more or less equal treatment, love and affection in case he has more than one wife.
5. She has the right to upbring her children in a respectable manner.

General Status of Muslim Woman in her Family

As it is made clear, Muslim family is based on the principle of patriarchy and hence women have only a secondary position in the family. Though they do not have equality with men they are not disrespected. Prophet Mohammad used to say that *"the heaven is at the feet of the mother."*. Muslims believe that women can also take part in politics, administration, education, social service, remunerative employment and such other activities. They have the right to property and to enjoy it.

• Imposition of *"Pardah"* System

Muslim women are compelled to follow the *Pardah* system. *Pardah system refers to the practice of Muslim women wearing a gown or veil to cover their face and upper part of the body.* This system is still in practice in many of the Muslim countries. This system has led to the complete seclusion of women. This is one of the factors which led to the decline in the status of Muslim women. But some nations such as Turkey took a bold decision to abolish the *pardah* system as early as in 1926.

• Domination of Patriarchal Values in the Family System

Patriarchal values rule the Muslim families. Hence, men and women cannot be equal. Muslim family cannot cherish the value of equality of sex. While the man has a right to marry several women without taking the consent of the earlier wives, the woman can marry only one. It is easy for the husband to divorce the wife, but for the wife, divorcing her husband is not easy. In case of adultery, the husband can unilaterally divorce the wife, but the wife can only divorce her husband that too with great difficulty. Wearing *pardah* is very much compulsory for married women.

• No Right to Participate in Public Prayers Along with Men

On the occasion of the Muslim festivals such as *Bakrid, Ed Milad, Ramjan, Moharram,* etc., only Muslim men are entitled to go to mosques or *dargas* for offering prayers. Muslim women can offer prayers only at home and not in public. Even during the ordinary days also Muslim women are not supposed to go to mosques alongwith their menfolk for offering prayers.

• Attitude Towards Social Change

Though the hold of tradition is still strong among the Muslims, social changes have started taking place in a slow and gradual manner. Western impact and the winds of modernism have created somewhat a favourable atmosphere for social change. As **K.M. Kapadia** has stated *"Educated Muslims have come to realise that the social legislation of Islam is in need of some change."*

Onesided divorce and provision for polygyny among Muslims complete sub-ordination of women, and such other things are very much criticised. Many have suggested that *"uniform civil code"* regarding civil matters including marriage and family is the only solution for this. Most of the Muslims are not in favour of uniform civil code for they consider it an interference in Muslim personal law, *Shariat.* Muslims have their own reasons to oppose it. They do not themselves feel the necessity of any such change. Muslims believe that Hindus are trying to impose their cultural and religious values on Muslims through the uniform civil code. Unless a consensus is evolved a legislation pertaining to the uniform civil code cannot be introduced. Any hasty decision and action in this regard may cause more damage than good.

IMPACT OF SOCIAL LEGISLATION ON MARRIAGE AND FAMILY

The Concept of Social Legislation - Meaning and Objectives

*"**Legislation** is the enactment of laws. Law is the body of rules, enacted or customary, recognised by a community as binding upon itself."* - **V.V. Shastri.**

"Laws are a form of social rule emanating from political agencies" - **J.S. Roucek.**

The main intention or object of social legislation is to ensure the security of the society and to improve its social and economic conditions. It is also concerned with assuring social justice to all without making any discrimination and to punish those who violate the laws and pose danger to the lives and activities of others.

Necessity of Social Legislation

The social philosophy of the present century is that not only individual rights are important but also social justice and protection of the social institutions are important. It is considered as the duty of the modern democratic state to protect the social interests of the communities and assure justice to one and all. Legislations undertaken with this interest can be regarded as social legislations. Social legislations are not a new phenomenon. Even during the British rule some of the social legislations were undertaken either to remove some social evils or to promote the social interests of some communities or to fulfil both. After independence, several such legislations have been taken up to protect the social interests of all the sections of the society.

Main Intentions Behind the Social Legislations

Social legislations are undertaken today to protect the social interests, to assure social justice, to safeguard individual rights and to further the ideology of equality. The main intentions behind the social legislations can be listed as below :

1. To assure social justice to all without any discrimination and to protect the social rights of one and all.
2. To give special protection to those who are weaker, poorer and without any visible means of protection.
3. To provide protection and to assure justice to all those who are weaker, the exploited, the suppressed and to the minorities.

4. To protect the human resources and to provide for proper conditions to help use these resources for the benefit of the larger society.

5. To take legal actions against social evils, to launch programmes and schemes to redress the social problems and to protect larger interests of the community.

Impact of Social Legislations on Marriage and Family

Influence of Legislations on Marriage

Many of the beliefs, values, ideals and rules of marriage laid down by the Hindu *shastrakaras* have lost their original meaning and purpose now. As a result, the Hindu marriage has developed some defects. Attempts were also made by some of the social reformers to remove these defects and correct the system. During the British rule and also after independence legislations were passed in order to bring about desirable modifications in the Hindu marriage system.

The laws enacted in India relate to the (i) *age at marriage;* (ii) *field of mate selection;* (iii) *number of spouses in marriage;* (iv) *breaking of marriage;* (v) *dowry to be given and taken* and (v) *remarriage.*

Social legislations that were undertaken both before and after independence, brought about some significant changes in our marriage system among which the following are to be noted :

1. Various inhuman practices associated with the marriage such as the practice of *sati* has been removed by law.

2. Legislations have not only abolished child marriages but also fixed the minimum marriageable age for boys and girls.

3. The legislations have also made clear the selection in marriage that is, who should marry whom. They have also legalised intercaste and inter-religious marriages and have made provision for registered marriages.

4. In the case of Hindus, Christians, Parsis, Jains and Sikhs monogamy has been made compulsory. Further, bigamy and polygyny are prohibited for these communities.

5. Legislations have made provision for divorce. Equal rights are conferred on men and women in this regard. Legislations have also specified the conditions of divorce.

6. Legislations have also made provision for remarriage. Divorced women and men could remarry if they desire so. Legislation makes provision for that.

7. Some of the evil customs associated with marriage such as taking dowry have either been removed or regulated by law.

• Details of the Legislations Affecting Hindu Marriage

1. *The Prevention of Sati Act 1829* : The glorification of the ideal of *"Pativratya"* had led to the inhuman practice of *"Sati"*. Widows were often forced to make a vow or *"sankalpa"* to die after their husbands. Some were forcibly pushed to their husbands' funeral pyres. Famous Brahmo Samajist, Sri Raja Ram Mohan Roy took up the cause of women and impressed upon Lord Bentinck who was the then British Governor General of India, to bring out a legislation prohibiting the practice of *"Sati"*.

The Prevention of Sati Act, 1829 made the burning or burying alive of widows culpable homicide punishable with fine and / or imprisonment. This legislation saved the lives of a number of widows though it could not immediately stop the practice in total.

2. *The Hindu Widow Remarriage Act - 1856* : This legislation was complementary to the previous legislation, that is, *'Prevention of Sati Act of 1829'.* Though widows were saved from the jaws of death they were subject to exploitation and humiliation. To remove the deplorable condition of the Hindu widows, a leading social reformer of the day, **Pandit Ishwara Chandra Vidya Sagar,** brought pressure on the British Govt. to make legal provision for widow remarriages. *The Hindu Widow Remarriage Act of 1856* was hence passed.

3. *The Civil [or Special] Marriage Act, 1872* : This legislation treated Hindu marriage as a *"civil marriage"* and provided legal permission for intercaste, inter-religious and even *"registered"* marriages. [This Act was repealed by the *Special Marriage Act, 1954.* According to this Act, the parties interested in registered marriage must notify the marriage officer at least one month before the date of the marriage. It insists on the presence of two witnesses for the marriage].

4. *The Child Marriage Restraint Act - 1929* : This Act came into force on April 1, 1930. The Act restrains the marriage of a child. According to this Act, marriage of boys under 18 and girls under 14 years of age was on offence.

***Latest Amendment* :** The Act was amended in 1978 which further raised the age for boys to 21 years and for girls to 18 years. The violation of this Act prescribes penalty. It provides punishment [three months of simple imprisonment and a fine upto Rs.1000/-] for bridegroom, parent, guardian and the priest who are party to the marriage. No woman is, however, punishable with imprisonment under this Act.

5. *The Hindu Marriage Act - 1955* : This Act which came into force from May 18, 1955 brought about revolutionary changes not only in the marital relations but also in various other social aspects. This Act applies to the whole of India, except Jammu and Kashmir. The word **"Hindu"** in the Act includes Jains, Sikhs, Buddhists and the Scheduled Castes.

***Conditions for valid marriage as provided in this Act* :** (1) neither party has a spouse living; (2) neither party [bridegroom or bride] is an idiot or a lunatic; (3) the groom must have completed 21 years and the bride 18 years of age as per the 1978 Amendment brought to this Act; (4) the parties should not be *'sapindas'* of each other unless the custom permits such a marriage.

The Hindu Marriage Act provides for divorce and also specifies conditions under which divorce is permitted. The Act gives equal rights for men and women for divorce under the conditions specified by law. [*Note* : For more details about ***"Divorce"***, see **Chapter 21.**]

***Other Important Aspects of this Act* :** *(i) This Act gives permission for intercaste and inter-religious marriages; (ii) It provides for equality of sex; (iii) It provides equal rights for men and women in marriage, divorce or separation; (iv) Its 1986 amendment permits divorce on the ground of incompatibility and mutual consent; (v) During judicial separation and after divorce, both husband and wife have the right to claim maintenance allowance.*

6. *The Dowry Prohibition Act - 1961* : This Act which prohibits the practice of dowry was passed on May 20th 1961. The Act does not apply to Muslims. It permits exchange of gifts for not more than Rs. 2000. It prescribes the penalty of **6** months imprisonment or a fine upto Rs. 5000/- or both for its violation. This Act got amended in 1986 and thereafter its rules have become still more stringent.

The above mentioned legislations, in addition to many other social legislations, have affected the Hindu marriage in several ways. These legislations, however, have not transformed it into a mere legal contract. The Hindu beliefs and values relating to marriage are still alive and legislations have only strengthened it by removing some of the anomalies associated with it.

Influence of Legislations on Family

The impact of the social legislations on the institution of family could be understood by means of the effects that they have brought in it. Some such effects are mentioned below.

1. Legislation has provided to all the members of the family without making any discrimination on the basis of sex, equal right to inherit the ancestral property.

2. The legislation has provided equal rights and opportunities to all the members of the family without discrimination on the basis of sex, the right to marriage, divorce, enjoyment of parental property and such other matters.
3. Legislation has provided equal opportunities even to female members of the family to work outside the family on salary or wage basis on par with the male members. There are also legislations protecting the job interests of women.
4. Legislations have also been undertaken to give special protection to women preventing the exploitation of their helplessness and weaknesses by others.
5. In order to loosen the tight grip of the patriarchal values over the joint families legislations have been undertaken providing equal opportunities, privileges, rights and facilities even to women.

Details of the Legislations Affecting the Hindu Family Life

1. *The Married Women's Property Act,* 1874 : This Act confers ownership right to women not only on their *"Streedhan"* but also on the property which they have personally earned.

2. *Gains of Learning Act,* 1930 : As a result of this Act, member of a joint family secures individual right over income or property which he or she has been able to earn by means of his or her educational attainment. This Act, has made the individual members of the family to develop personal interest in the property and this tendency has damaged the collective interest of the family.

3. *The Hindu Women's Right to Property Act,* 1937 : This Act enables a woman to have equal share to that of a son in the property of her deceased husband. If the property was joint and unseparated at the time of her husband's death, she is entitled to have the same interest therein as her deceased husband was entitled.

4. *The Hindu Succession Act,* 1956 : This Act confers on women right to property. As per this Act, not only a daughter is given a right in her father's property equal to her brothers, but also gets a share in her deceased husband's property equal to her sons and daughters. The legislation has removed the distinction between Stridhan and non-Stridhan. This Act, in course of time, led to the changes in the position of women in the family.

5. *Legislations Protecting the Economic Interest of Women*:

(i) *The Maternity Benefit Act,* 1961 provides maternity benefits [2 months maternity leave with salary] to married women.

(ii) *The Equal Remuneration Act,* 1976 does not permit wage discrimination between male and female workers.

(iii) *The Factories [Amendment] Act,* 1976 : Besides including provisions dealing with working hours, weekly rest, standards of cleanliness, ventilation, temperature, first-aid facilities, and rest rooms, the legislation provides for the establishing of creches for children [if the factory employs thirty or more women], separate toilets for females and lays down a maximum work of nine hours in a day for women and no employment of women between 10:00 p.m. and 5:00 a.m.

6. *Legislations Preventing the Exploitation of the Helplessness of Women* :

(i) *The Hindu Adoption and Maintenance Act,* 1956 permits the wife deserted by her husband to claim maintenance allowance from her husband; and it also permits women to adopt a child.

(ii) *The Suppression of Immoral Traffic of Women and Girls' Act,* 1956 gives protection to women against kidnapping and pushing them to brothel homes to do prostitution.

(iii) *Medical Termination of Pregnancy Act,* 1971 permits the termination of pregnancy by a registered doctor if it does not exceed 12 weeks on certain valid grounds [such as - pregnancy causing risk to the life of pregnant woman, pregnancy caused by rape or failure of contraceptive device, etc.]

(iv) *The Criminal Law Amendment Act,* 1983 gives protection to women against rape, violence or any other types of criminal act.

(v) *The Family Court Act,* 1984 assures women justice in family disputes and at the same time, preserves the secrecy of family matters.

Chapter 6

WOMEN IN INDIA

__Women in India - Status of Women :__ Status of Women in Ancient Age : Women in the Vedic and the Post-Vedic Periods, in the Epic Period, in the Period of Dharmashastras and Puranas and in the Buddhist Period- Status of Women in Medieval India : Problems of Women. Status of Women in Modern Period : Status of Women during the British Rule and Status of Women in Post-Independent India- Views of Manu and Gandhiji on the Status of Women - Problems of Women in Modern India - Development and Welfare of Women - __Empowerment of Women:__ A Solution to Gender Discrimination ? - Empowerment of Women and the 73rd Constitution Amendment Act, 1993 - The Rationale Behind the Empowerment of Women - A Brief Assessment of 73rd Constitution Amendment Act - Status and Problems of Women : Future Prospects.

It is customary everywhere to classify the human community on the basis of sex into groups of 'men' and 'women'. The biological fact of sex has created much difference between them. The aims and objectives, desires and aspirations, duties and responsibilities, dress styles and behavioural patterns, roles and statuses of men and women are different. No where in the history of humanity men and women were treated alike and assigned statuses alike. Women have not been able to lead a life exactly on par with men in spite of their urge for equality. This does not mean that men and women represent two different cultures as such. They represent one way of life, one culture and one heritage. This is also true of India and Indian women.

The type of the status assigned to women in any society reflect the nature of its cultural richness and the level of its civilisational standards. Hence, **Swami Vivekananda,** had said *"that country and that nation which did not respect women have never become great nor will ever in future".* The degree of freedom and respectability given to women to move about and take part in public activities gives a good idea of the nature of the society to which they belong. A study of the history of status of women is, therefore, of great importance for the students who study the Indian society.

Women in ancient India, particularly during the Vedic period, enjoyed a position which was on the whole much more satisfactory than in the later periods. Women underwent almost a kind of servitude during the Medieval period and their position went on improving during the British period and after independence. Today, Indian women are almost assigned an equal status with men. All their political, economic and educational and other disabilities have been removed legally. This does not, however, mean Indian women are completely free from problems. They do have their own problems. This chapter gives a glimpse of the status of India women right from the Vedic age down to the modern days and also reflects on the current problems haunting our women. There is also an attempt to look ahead into the future prospects of the position of women.

WOMEN IN INDIA

The status accorded to women in society symbolises its level of progress. The spirit of a civilisation can be assessed by the way in which women are treated by the members of that civilisation. Status of women is a topic of sociological studies and discussions for it mirrors the position of about 50% of the population of any society. Study of the history of human society reveals that in no society of the world women enjoyed absolute equality on par with men. Everywhere they were subject to inequality, discrimination and exploitation. In some societies, their position has been comparatively better than their counterpart in some other societies. Even in the same society the status accorded to women has never been the same all through. It has been changing in keeping with the changes in the general conditions of society. The history of the status of women in India is not different from this. It is relevant here to take a brief survey of the status of Indian women right from the ancient age till today.

The history of *"status of women in India"* can be studied in three stages namely: (i) *Status of women in ancient India;* (ii) *Status of women in Medieval India* and (iii) *Status of women in Modern India* with a reference to the modern problems with which they are suffering.

I. STATUS OF WOMEN IN ANCIENT INDIA

There are two opinions regarding the status of women in ancient India. Some scholars say that *ancient Indian women were almost "the equals of men"*, while some others argue that *women were held not only in disrespect but even in positive hatred.* These scholars have selected some passages from our classical literature to prove their point. *Examples:*

- ***Statements that reveal the higher status of early Indian women:*** (i) **Apastamba** had prescribed: *"All must make a way for a woman when she is treading a path"*; (ii) **Manu** had said: *"When women are honoured, the gods are pleased but where they are not honoured, no sacred rite yields any reward"*; (iii) **Yajnavalkya** had said *"Women are the embodiment of all divine virtues on earth..."*

- ***Statements that reveal the degraded status of early Indian women:*** (i) **Manu** who had praised women in some context had said in some other context that *women are not fit for enjoying freedom;* (ii) In **Mahabharata,** Bhishma had said in some context: *"Husband should regard his wife as an acquisition"*; (iii) In **Ramayana,** Lord Rama had said in some context: *"I can give away all my royal inheritance and even my wife and all that I value to Bharat of my own free accord."*

- ***These statements do not mirror the actual position of women.*** The statements and opinions quoted above are only *"contextual"* and it is not proper to generalise on that basis the real status of women. The real status of women could be judged by analysing the social, economic, political and religious rights they enjoyed over the years.

The status of women in ancient India can be better studied in the following stages. (i) *Vedic and post-vedic period;* (ii) *Women in the period of Dharmashastras and epics;* (iii) *Women in the Puranic period;* (iv) *Women in the Buddhist period.*

1. Women in the Vedic and the Post-Vedic Periods

The Indian cultural tradition begins with the Vedas. It is generally believed that the Vedic period is spread over from 3000 B.C. to 600 B.C. Some general observations and broad generalisations can only be made regarding the status of women during this vast period.

(i) *Freedom Enjoyed by Women:* The degree of freedom given to women to move about and take part in public activities gives a good idea of the nature of the status enjoyed by women. Literary and historical researches have revealed that women held a position of equality with men during the Vedic period. Women never observed *'purdah'* in the Vedic and the Epic periods. They enjoyed freedom in areas such as education, marriage, economic production, spending money, religious activities, etc. They enjoyed freedom in selecting their mates. They could educate themselves. Widows were permitted to remarry. Divorce was however, not permissible to them. Even men did not have the right to divorce their wives. Women were given complete freedom in family matters and were treated as *"Ardhanginis"* [better halves].

(ii) *Equal Educational Opportunities for Women:* Though male children were preferred to female children, daughters were never ill-treated. They also received education like boys and went through the *'Brahmacharya'* discipline including the *"Upanayana"* ritual. The *Atharva Veda* observes how a bride had no chance of a good match, if she had not been educated as a *brahmacharini.* The custom of *Upanayana* of girls prevailed down to the *"Sutra"* period. *"Women studied the Vedic literature like men and some of them, like Lopamudra, Ghosa and Sikata-Nivavari, figure among the authors of the Vedic hymns."*[1]

Other women scholars of the day included *Vishvavara, Apala, Shashijasi, Indrani, Sasvati, Gargi, Sulabha, Maithreye* and others. On the basis of the facts from literature **Altekar** writes: *"We may therefore conclude that many girls in well-to-do families used to be given a fair amount of education down to about B.C. 300."*[2]

(iii) *Position of Women in Matters Relating to Marriage and Family Affairs:* Though marriage was considered a religious duty, women had the right to remain spinsters throughout their life. Marriage was not forcibly imposed on them. There was no restriction on the age at marriage. Child marriages were unknown. Girls were given in marriage only after puberty, that too, after completing their education. Women had the right to select their life-partners. The practice of *"swayamvara"* would serve as an evidence for the girl's right to marital choice. Often there were also love marriages called *"Gandharva Vivaha".*

During the Vedic period, *monogamy* was generally followed though there were several instances of polygynous marriages being held in the circle of upper class and the royal class. Polyandry was, however, unknown during the Vedic times. Re-marriage of widows was allowed. There are a number of references to the custom of ***"Niyoga"*** where *a brother or the nearest relative of a deceased husband could marry the widow with the permission of the elders.* Niyoga was mostly practised to obtain a child for continuing the family tradition. The earlier *Dharmashastra* writers allowed divorce. In fact, **Kautilya** gives detailed rules of divorce. The practice of *'Sati'* is nowhere mentioned in the Rig Veda. The practice of taking dowry was there but it was only symbolic. It had not emerged as a social evil.

In family matters, Vedic women were bound by the patriarchal tradition. This tradition invested the husband with greater powers in the management of the household. Still in many

1 *"The Cultural Heritage of India"* - Vol.1 Page: 222.
2 **B. Kuppu Swamy** *"Social Change in India"* - Page: 240.

respects they were regarded as equals of their husbands. The term *"dampati"* would suggest that husband and wife were regarded as the joint heads of the household. The wife was however expected to be obedient to the husband helping him in the performance of his duties including the religious ones.

(iv) *Economic Production and Occupational Freedom:* Vedic women had economic freedom. They did not serve as occupants of some professions and earn wages only because it was not necessary for them. Home was the place of production. Spinning and weaving of clothes were done at home. Women however, helped their husbands in agricultural pursuits. Some women were engaged in teaching work.

(v) *Property Rights and Inheritance:* In property matters, there were disparities between men and women. Women's rights were very much limited in inheriting property. A daughter had no share in her father's property; but each unmarried daughter was entitled to one-fourth share of patrimony received by her brothers. Women had control over their *"stridhan"* [gifts and property etc. received by a woman at the time of marriage] but the bulk of the family property was under the control and management of the patriarch. Later vedic texts expressly declared that women had no right of inheritance as they were weak. An exception was, however, made in favour of the brotherless daughter, who was allowed to inherit the patrimony.

Stridhan was inherited only by unmarried daughters. As a wife, a woman had no direct share in her husband's property. However, a forsaken wife was entitled to 1/3 of her husband's wealth. If a wife was poor, her husband was to provide for her maintenance. A widow was expected to lead an ascetic life and had no share in her husband's property. As a widowed mother, she had some rights. Thus, *it could be generalised that the social situation was not in favour of women possessing property, and yet protection was given to them as daughters and wives.*

(vi) *Role in the Religious Field:* In the religious field, wife enjoyed full rights and regularly participated in religious ceremonies with her husband. Vedic religious ceremonies and sacrifices were performed jointly by the husband and the wife. Women even participated actively in religious discourses. The participation of *Brahmavadini* **Gargi Vachaknavi** along with many male learned exponents and representatives of the different schools of philosophy in the famous conference convened by the king **Janaka** of Videha - is an example worth mentioning in this regard. Women could offer *"sandhya"* and even perform sacrifices by themselves in the absence of their husbands. The Rishis used to teach sacred scriptures to their wives and there was no bar for women to read or study any of our sacred literature.

(vii) *Role of Women in Public Life:* There are no traces of the seclusion of women in Vedic society. They could move freely in the company of their husbands or lovers. Women could shine as debaters in public assemblies. They usually occupied a prominent place in social gatherings, lending charm to them by their graceful dress. Women of course, were not permitted entry into the *"sabhas"* [assemblies] because these places besides being used for taking political decisions, were also used for gambling, drinking and such other purposes. Women's participation in public meetings and debates, however, became less and less common in the later Vedic period.

In conclusion, it could be said that women in India during the ancient age [particularly in the Vedic age] had an honourable status. As **Romeshchandra Dutta** [1848 - 1909] wrote, *"Hindu women held an honourable place. They inherited and possessed property; they took share in sacrifices and religious duties; they attended great assemblies and state occasions; they also distinguished themselves in science and learning at their times. .... Considered as intellectual companions of their husbands, as friends and loving helpers in the journey of life of their partners,* *in their religious duties and the centre of their domestic bliss, Hindu wives were honoured and respected in ancient times."*[1]

2. Women during the Epic Period

Like women of the Vedic age, the women of Epic India held an honourable position at home. The two classical epics, *Ramayana* and *Mahabharata* have also given a respectable place for women. In fact, women are the focal points of both the epics. Sita in the Ramayana and Draupadi in the Mahabharata, are the cause for the wars which occur at the final phase of these epics. Both the epics make mention of the continuation of the marital practice of *"swayamvara"*. In both of these we find vast references of the expression of courage, strong will power, and valour of women like Kaikeye, Sita, Rukmini, Satyabhama, Subhadra, Draupadi, Savithri and others.

- *"The **Ramayana** is a glorious illustration for the Hindu ideal womanhood."* It is full of incidents of wife's devotion to her husband. Through the role of Sita the Ramayana tells us that *"in this world, the wife is the sharer of her husband's destiny; all other relatives are, each responsible for his or her own destiny only."*[2] The Ramayana glorifies the value of *"Pativratya"* and idealises womanhood as one of the most venerable aspects of our heritage.

- The ***Mahabharata*** also outlines the duties and the attitude of the wife to the husband. It makes us clear through the role of Draupadi that a woman's success was in her obedience and devotion to her husband. In the opinion of Draupadi, *"the husband is wife's god; he is her [sole] refuge..."* Mahabharata mentions of several women who could give proper suggestions, advices and guidelines to men. Mahabharata speaks of *"Sampat Lakshmi"* or *"goddess of property"* who would stay with women of chastity and strong character. Bhishma had suggested that a king without male children could be succeeded by the daughters.

- ***Women During the Period of Dharmashastras and Puranas*:** During the period of Dharmashastras and Puranas the position of women underwent a major change. Daughters were regarded as second-class citizens when freedom of women was curtailed. Sons were valued more than daughters. In the ancestral worship also sons were given more importance.

It is said that the position of women deteriorated by the time of Dharmashastras and Puranas. According to **Altekar**, *"The discontinuance of Upanayanam, the neglect of education and the lowering of age at marriage produced disastrous consequences upon the position and status of women."*[3]

Manu, the law giver, gave an injunction: *"A woman has to be under her father during childhood, under her husband during youth and under her son during old age. At no stage shall she deserve freedom."* He however, balanced this with the statement that a society in which the woman was not honoured would be condemned to damnation. The woman was not only told to accept the second position, but to accept the partner chosen for her as a gift of the heavens. In several mythological stories, wife's loyalty to the husband was very much stressed. It is in this period, masculine and priestly dominance began to take root and prevail. Girls were prevented from learning the Vedas and becoming *Brahmacharinis*.

Due to the various restrictions imposed on the freedom of women some problems started creeping in. *"In the **social field,** pre-puberty marriages came to be practised, widow remarriage*

1 **B. Kuppu Swamy** *"Social Change in India"* - Page: 240 - 241.
2 **P.H. Prabhu** *"Hindu Social Organisation"* - Page: 234.
3 **C.B. Mamoria** *"Social Problems and Social Disorganisation"* Page 623

was prohibited, husband was given the status of god for a woman, education was totally denied to women, custom of 'sati' became increasingly prevalent, 'purdah' [veil] system came into vogue and practice of polygyny came to be tolerated."[1]

In the ***economic field***, a woman was totally denied a share in her husband's property by maintaining that *"a wife and a slave cannot own property."* In the religious field, she was forbidden to offer sacrifices and prayers, practise penance and undertake pilgrimages.

• ***Factors that caused the degradation of Women:*** The main factors which caused the degraded position of women during the period of Dharmashastras are: *imposition of Brahmanical austerities on the entire society, rigid restrictions imposed by the caste system and the joint family system, lack of educational facilities for women, introduction of the non-Aryan wife into the Aryan household and foreign invasions [particularly of Greeks, Parthians, Backtrians, Huns and others] of India.*

3. Women in the Buddhist Period

In the Buddhist period, the status of women improved a little, though there was no tremendous change. Some of the rigidities and restrictions imposed by the caste system were relaxed. Buddhas preached equality. He tried to improve their cultural, educational and religious statuses. During the benevolent rule of the famous Buddhist kings such as Chandragupta Maurya, Ashoka, Sri Harsha and others, women regained a part of their lost freedom and status due to the relatively broadminded Buddhist philosophy.

Buddhism never regarded marriage as an inescapable thing for women. Widowhood was not considered disrespectful. Women could resort to an educational career if they so desired. Women were permitted to become *"sanyasis"*. Many women joined the Buddhist order, became religious sisters, wore the yellow robe and came to be known as the *'Theri-Bhikshunis'*. Women had their *Sangha* called the *Bhikshuni Sangha* which was guided by the same rules and regulations as these of the monks. The *Sangha* opened to them avenues of cultural activities and social service and ample opportunities for public life. Their political and economic status, however, remained unchanged.

II. STATUS OF WOMEN IN THE MEDIEVAL INDIA

The Medieval period [period between 500 A.D. are 1500 A.D.] proved to be highly disappointing for the Indian women, for their status further deteriorated during this period. The Muslim invasion of India changed the direction of Indian history. The influx of foreign invaders and the Brahmanical iron laws were the main causes for such degradation.

After the death of Harshavardhana [646 A.D.] the Brahmanism without the benevolence of the vedic period took hold of the Indian society with all its severe restrictions and rigidities. As far as a woman was concerned, *"her freedom was curtailed, knowledge of not only the scriptures but even letters was denied to her and her status was reduced to that of an appendage on man."*[2] Caste laws dominated the entire social life. *Mitakshara law* for the entire country and *Daya Bhaga* in Bengal, reduced women to the status of slaves. Widow remarriage and levirate were now disallowed. Women could not inherit property. Girls were treated more as burdens or liabilities than as assets.

1 **Ram Ahuja** *"Indian Social System"* - Page: 94.
2 **P. Thomas** *"Indian Women Through the Ages"*, Page: 217.

Problems of Women in Medieval India **:** Women in this period had to face a number of problems of which the following may be noted.

(i) ***Practice of Child Marriage:*** Though the practice of child marriage had emerged during the period of Dharmashastras, it had now become almost inescapable. The fear that Muslim invaders would kidnap or seduce the girls brought heavy pressure on the parents to arrange the marriage of their daughters at a very early age. Young girls had to bear the brunt of the family life, get children at an inappropriate age and bring them up, when they themselves were mentally immature. Problem of ill-health made them still weaker. Those who were unfortunate enough to lose their husbands at an early age had to spend the rest of their lives in the most pitiable manner.

(ii) ***Prohibition of Widow Remarriage:*** Dharmashastras strictly prohibited the widow remarriages. The glorification of the ideal of *'pativratya'* was another hurdle in the path of widow remarriage. Child widows had a miserable life. They were denied education, public life and most of the religious activities were tabooed for them. Their very presence on important occasions was considered to be disgraceful for they were treated as a symbol of ill-omen. They were made to work like servants throughout their lives. Prohibition of sex life for them made a few to lead an immoral life and some even became prostitutes. To prevent such sex offences child widows were forced to shave their head and forsake all types of beautification. This restriction was imposed on them to make them sexually unattractive.

(iii) ***Practice of Sati:*** The widespread practice of *'Sati'* during the Medieval period indicates the decline in the status of Indian women. *'Sati'* refers to a practice in which the married women used to jump into the funeral pyre of their husbands with the hope of attaining *'sadgati'* or *moksha.* It was actually an act of self-immolation. The glorification of *Pativratya* and the degraded and intolerable widow life made many women to become *'sutees'*. There were instances in which women were forcibly pushed into the funeral fire of their husbands. This custom was very much prevalent particularly in Rajaputana and Central India. There was also the horrible practice of *"johar"* in which the Rajput women used to immolate themselves collectively with a view to protect their chastity whenever it was very much endangered. The practice of *'Sati'* had continued even after the end of Muslim rule.

(iv) ***Pardah System:*** *Pardah system refers to the practice of women wearing a gown or veil to cover their face and upper part of the body.* It was a common practice among the Muslims [and even now] of Medieval India. Before the Muslim invasion of India *pardah* system was in practice only in the wealthy and royal classes among the Hindus. But after the Muslim invasion, the Hindu women were also forced to wear the *'pardah'* mainly to escape from the sexy looks of men and to protect themselves from being kidnapped or seduced. *The 'purdah' system led to the complete seclusion of women.* Hence the facilities of education and public life were totally denied to them. Women had to confine themselves into their own world and their progress was halted. Women became the objects of exploitation.

(v) ***Devadasi System:*** Devadasi system represents another social evil which caused the degradation of Indian women. It is a custom that denies, in the name of religion, marital opportunity to women, insisting on them to become *'devadasis'* or *'basavis'* to serve the God in the temple as dancers and singers. The devadasis and basavis were compelled by the circumstances to become prostitutes. This system grew into a social evil during the Medieval age and spoiled the prospects of many young girls.

• Equally Poor Position of Muslim Women

The social position of Muslim women was not better than that of the Hindu women, though Muslim rulers were mostly controlling Indian territories. The Muslim community which believes in the principle of male dominance could hardly give equal rights to women. Muslim men could marry four women and divorce any wife at will by giving her *"talaq"*. Muslim women did not have similar rights. They had to depend upon their men folk. Even though they had some right to property [particularly in the form of *Mahr*] they were not able to enjoy it by themselves.

Severe restrictions were imposed on the movements and activities of Muslim women. They had to wear *'purdah'* compulsorily. Availing themselves of educational opportunities, participation in public life, taking an active role in cultural and religious activities etc. were almost unthinkable for Mulsim women. Only women belonging to wealthy and royal class could enjoy some freedom to move freely at least in their own palaces, gardens, private fields etc. Hence only negligible number of Muslim women could achieve any heights during this period.

• Impact of *Bhakti* Movement On the Status of Women

Throughout the Medieval period, the status of women went on declining. However, during the 14th and 15th centuries the social situation had undergone some change. **Ramanujacharya** organised the first ***Bhakti Movement*** during this period which introduced new trends in the social and the religious life of women in India. The great saints like *Chaitanya, Nanak, Meera, Kabir, Ramdas, Tulsidas* and *Tukaram* stood for the right of women to religious worhship. Though the *Bhakti* movement didn't have the intention of radically changing the status of Indian women it unlocked the gate of religious freedom to women. As a result of this freedom, they secured certain social freedom also. The *purdah* system was abolished. Women could go out of their families to attend *pravachanas, harikathas, kirtans* [religious prayers], *bhajans, dharmic utsavs* and so on. *Bhakti* movement stressed the importance of *Grihasthashrama* and as a result, the saints were made to take to *'sanyasa'* only with the consent of the wife. This condition gave some important right to women. The *saints of the Bhakti movement encouraged women to read religious books and to educate themselves.*

The above explanation makes it clear that the *Bhakti* movement gave a new life to women. But *this movement did not bring any change in the economic structure of the society and hence women continued to hold low status in the society.*

• The Position of Women Steadily Deteriorated For Nearly 2000 Years

After making his own assessment of the status of Indian women **Altekar** concludes: *"Thus for nearly 2000 years from B.C. 20 to 1800 A.D. the position of woman steadily deteriorated though she was fondled by the parents, loved by the husband and revered by her children. The revival of 'sati', the prohibition of remarriage, the spread of 'purdah' and the greater prevalence of polygamy made her position very bad."*[1] Thus there was a vast gulf between the status of woman in the early vedic period and that in the Medieval Period and onwards.

Neera Desai observes: *"Ideologically woman was considered a completely inferior species, inferior to the male, having no significance, no personality; socially she was kept in a state of utter subjection, denied any right, suppressed and oppressed; she was further branded as basically lacking the ethical fibre. The patriarchal joint family, the customs of polygamy, the purdah, the*

---

1 **A.S. Altekar** *"The Position of Women in Hindu Civilization"* - 1962.

property structure, early marriage, self-immolation of the widows ['sati'] or a state of permanent widowhood, all these contributed to the smothering of the free development of women."[1]

III. STATUS OF WOMEN IN MODERN INDIA

Status of Indian women started radically changing during the modern period. Historically, the period after 1750 A.D. is known as the modern period. The study of status of Indian women during this period can be divided into two stages: (A) *status of women during the British rule in India* and (B) *the status of women in post independent India.*

A. STATUS OF INDIAN WOMEN DURING THE BRITISH RULE

After the fall of the Mughal Empire at the decisive Battle of Plassy [1757 A.D.] the British people established their complete political supremacy over the Indian people. The British remained the rulers of India in the 18th and 19th centuries and the first half of the 20th century. During the British rule, a number of changes were made in the economic and social structures of our society. Though the *"quality of life"* of women during this period remained more or less the same some substantial progress was achieved in eliminating inequalities between men and women in education, employment, social rights and so on. Some social evils such as child marriage, *sati* system, *devadasi* system, *purdah* system, prohibition on widow remarriage etc. which were a great hurdle in the path of women's progress were either controlled or removed by suitable legislations. After the lapse of several centuries for the first time some attempts were made on an all India basis to tackle the problems that confronted women. Social reformers with patriotic spirit on the one hand and the British Government on the other, together took several measures to improve the status of women and to remove some of their disabilities. Number of factors contributed to the change in the status of women during this period. Some important aspects or forces of that change are analysed here.

1. Change in the Attitude Towards Life

Along with the British people the western culture and its *'life-styles'* and values also came to India. The western way of life which the British represented had its impact on the Indians. The western values, their world-view, their liberal principles, rationalistic attitude towards problems, critical approach towards issues, the right to question and criticise, social equality, belief in the individual enterprise, equal importance for the rights and duties of man and such other things of the west, influenced the Indians' way of life and particularly their attitude towards women.

2. Role of Social Reformers and Reform Movements in the Emancipation of Women

The learned Indians who came under the British influence realised that immediate reform was required for the emancipation of Indian women and for raising their social status. A number of reformers led the way in launching social movements to improve the position of women.

(i) ***Raja Ram Mohan Roy,*** the founder of *'Brahma Samaj'* played an important role in getting the *'Sati'* system abolished. He raised his voice against child-marriage and *'purdah'* system. He also fought for the right of inheritance of women. It was at his behest the British Government introduced the *Prevention of Sati Act* in 1829.

(iii) ***Ishwar Chandra Vidyasagar*** launched a movement for the right of widows to remarry and pleaded for educating women. It was due to his efforts and the pressure that he brought on the British Government, the *Widow Remarriage Act* was passed in 1856.

1 **Neera Desai** *"Women in Modern India"* - 1957.

(iii) ***Maharshi Karve*** took up the problems of widow remarriage and education of women. He established the *S.N.D.T. University for Women* in Poona, the first of its kind, in 1916.

(iv) ***Maharshi Dayananda Saraswathi*** who started the *'Arya Samaj'* advocated equal rights to women as they used to enjoy the same during the vedic times.

(v) ***Maharaja Sayyaji Rao Gaekwar,*** ruler of Baroda state, worked for preventing child-marriages, polygyny and getting the right of education to women and the right of remarriage to widows.

(vi) ***Swami Vivekananda*** who launched the *"Sri Ramakrishna Mission"* gave importance to the education and self-dependence of women. He gave a call to women to come out of seclusion and bondage. He said, *"that country and that nation which did not respect women have never become great nor will ever in the future."* He took a stand for the liberation of women and equality of treatment on the basis of Vedantic ideals that *"one and the same self is present in all beings."* He emphasised that by giving good education women should be enabled to solve their own problems by thinking independently.

(vii) Other reformers like ***Dadabai Navaroji, Gopalakrishna Gokhale, Mahatma Gandhiji*** and others also played their role in improving the status of women through the Congress movement and also at their individual capacities.

(vii) Women leaders with Western background such as ***Nivedita, Annie Besant, Margaret Cousins*** and indigenous women leaders like ***Sarojini Naidu, Pandit Rama Bai, Ramabai Ranade, Torudutt*** and others tried to involve large number of Indian women in various political, social, cultural and other activities.

These reformers and their social movements succeeded in arousing the social consciousness for the liberation and equal rights to women.

3. Influence of Women Education

Education of women was neglected for more than 2000 years. Only girls belonging to rich and royal classes and those belonging to the families of dancers and *'devadasis'* could get some education, while the vast mass of women remained totally illiterate. No one felt the need for educating them for they were fed and protected by their men folk.

The idea of giving education to women emerged during the British period. The Christian Missionaries took interest in the education of girls. A girls' school was started for the first time in Bombay in 1824. By 1829 there were about 400 girls studying in that school. **Lord Dalhousie** had also said that education of female children would help the family to reap the benefits of other changes taking place in society. *The Hunter Education Commission of 1882* also emphasised the need for female education. The universities of Calcutta, Bombay and Madras did not give admission to girls until 1875. It was only in 1882, girls were allowed to go for higher education. After 1882 there has been a continuous progress in the extent of education among women. The literacy percentage among females in India increased from 0.6% in 1901 to 7.0% in 1941, 24.88% in 1981 and 39.42% in 1991.[1] It increased to 64% in 2001.

4. Role of Women Leaders and Women's Organisations

Some women leaders also took interest in women's education and welfare. Notable among them were Pandit Ramabai of Karnataka, Ramabai Ranade of Maharashtra, Bengali writer Torudutt,

1 **Source of these Figures:** *"Handbook on Social Welfare Statistics", Ministry of Social Welfare, Govt. of India 1981* - Page: 85 and Census of India - 1991.

the first Indian female politician Kamalabai Chattopadhyaya, Swarna Kumari Devi of Tagore's family, Rajkumari Amrit Kaur, a great follower of Gandhiji; Annie Besant the architect of Home Rule Movement and others.

Some women organisations tried to create awareness among women. Mention may be made of a few of these organisations.

(i) ***'Arya Mahila Samaj'*** and ***'Sharada Sadan'*** that were started [in 1887] by Pandit Ramabai Ranade and Bhandarkar gave utmost importance to female education;

(ii) ***Bharat Mahila Parishad*** which was started in 1904 had the main objective of struggling for the emancipation of women.

(iii) ***Bharat Stri Mahamandal*** was founded in 1910 to promote the general welfare of women.

(iv) ***Women's Indian Association 1917*** started by Annie Besant, strengthened and developed by the joint efforts of Annie Besant, Sarojini Naidu, and Margaret Cousins, fought for the political and educational rights of women.

(v) ***All-India Women's Conference*** established in 1947 through the efforts of Margaret Cousins and others had the following main aims: *improving the style of life of women, achieving economic self-dependence, availing of educational opportunities for women, obtaining equal political rights for women, improvement of family happiness,* etc. [By 1975, this organisation had 500 branches and more than 3.25 million members through out the nation].

(vi) ***Kasturba Gandhi National Memorial Trust*** which was started after the death of Kasturba Gandhi, has been dedicating itself to the task of uplifting women.

These women organisations and the women leaders behind them had two main purposes

(i) *Upliftment of women so as to enable them to play a more important and constructive role in society;*

(ii) *to struggle for equal rights for men and women, that is, extension of civil rights enjoyed by men in the political, economic and familial spheres to women also.*

5. Women in Employment Sector

By the end of the 19th century sizeable number of educated Indian women entered for the first time the field of salaried professions. It was, indeed, a revolutionary development at that time. *The Education Commission of 1882* had recommended the employment of women teachers in the schools and the appointment of women as inspectors of the girls' schools. It also recommended that special stipends should be given to widows who came for teaching. Accordingly, a large number of women became teachers. Many women entered the newly opened schools and colleges to qualify themselves as nurses and doctors. By the end of the 19th century, women were very much attracted towards two professions namely : (i) *medical,* and (ii) *teaching professions.* In course of time, women entered other professional fields to work as clerks, accountants, receptionists, typists and in such other capacities.

6. Participation of Women in Freedom Struggle

The armed struggle against the British hegemony launched by Rani Laxmi Bai of Jhansi [1835 - 1858] and Rani Chennamma of Kittur, [Karnataka] the two great patriotic women leaders is very famous in history. In fact, they inspired women as well as men of India to fight for the cause of freedom. But in such struggles ordinary women could hardly play an active role. It was Gandhiji who worked a lot to obtain the active participation of a large number of even ordinary women in the Indian freedom struggle. The *Women's Indian Association* also created some awareness among our women to join the freedom struggle. When Annie Besant, the leader of the *"Home*

Rule Movement" was arrested, Indian women had led processions to temples to offer their prayers for her release. Annie Besant in her presidential address at the Calcutta Session of the *Indian National Congress* had said that the strength of the Home Rule Movement was rendered tenfold greater by the admission to it of a large number of women.

Mahatma Gandhi rendered a signal service to the advancement of women's movement by making thousands of them, of all classes, to come out of their homes and participate in the political movement. He had realised that freedom movement would become a success only with the participation of women on a mass scale. He was able to persuade a large number of them to plunge into freedom struggle. In the *satyagrahas*, processions, protest meetings, demonstrations and public meetings led by him, women used to take part in a large number. For example, in the *Salt Agitation of 1930,* more than 17,000 women took part. In the *'Quit India'* agitation of 1942 and in the *'Seva Dal Camps',* women participated in a huge number.

7. Enactment of Social Legislations

The British followed the policy of non-interference in the religious and social life and activities of people. But they were compelled to take up some social legislative measures in order to do away with some of the social evils. The enacted laws pertaining to women, were related to three areas namely, (i) *marriage,* (ii) *property* and (iii) *employment.*

(i) ***Laws Relating to Marriage:*** The marriage laws concentrate on the age of marriage, remarriage, dissolution of marriage, form of marriage and freedom in mate selections. The important legislations enacted were: *The Prevention of Sati Act 1829, The Widow Remarrige Act 1856, The Special Marriage Act 1872, The Child Marriage Restraint Act, 1929* [***Note*:** These Acts have already been explained in **Chapter 4.**]

(ii) ***Laws Relating to Property and Employment:*** The property law enacted were: T*he Married Women's Property Act 1874,* and *The Hindu Women's Right to Property Act 1939.*

The legislations cited above, contributed to improve women's status to a large extent. The legislations had their own limitations for they were extremely meagre and touched only the fringe of the problem. They were lopsided and had less precision and accuracy. The machinery to implement the legislation was costly, inefficient and complicated. Hence, it might be said that legislation had not been effective in wiping out the hardships suffered by women.

Factors Responsible for the Relatively Low Status of Women During the Medieval and the British Periods

The status of Indian women throughout the Medieval period and the British period was comparatively lower. Factors such as *illiteracy, lack of the female leadership, religious prohibitions, caste restrictions, economic dependency of women, apathetic and indifferent attitude of men* were mainly responsible for that.

Everett Jana Matson [1981] has identified five specific factors responsible for the low status of women in India and also for female seclusion in our culture. These are: *Hindu religion, caste system, joint family system, Islamic rule and British colonialism.*[1]

1. ***Impact of Hinduism:*** Hinduism in its practice upholds the principle of male dominance and insists that males and females should perform different roles. Whereas women were supposed to concentrate on their roles as mother and householder, men were to be concerned with economics

1 **Ram Ahuja** *"Indian Social System"* - Page: 100.

and politics. Hindu scriptures mostly depict women as dependent on their menfolk. Hindu values stress female obedience and submission to men.

2. *The Caste System:* The caste system championed the dominance of men. It imposed many restrictions on the involvement of women in public affairs. It prescribed early marriage for girls; it prohibited widow remarriages and prescribed the practice of *'sati'*.

3. *Patrilineal Joint Family:* The superordination of men and sub-ordination of women is the keynote of Indian joint family system. The patrilineal joint family curbed women's freedom and contributed to their low status in the family by assigning status based on age, sex and kinship. Women virtually had no existence independent of joint family.

4. *Impact of Muslim Rule:* During the Muslim rule, status of Indian women further deteriorated. Under the socio-political impact of the Islamic rule, Hindus adopted the Muslim customs of female seclusion, that is, *'purdah'*. Child marriages became very common to protect girls from the evil eyes of *nawabs* and *jagirdars.* The *'sati'* system too had come to stay.

5. *Influence of British Rule:* The British rulers in the beginning pursued a policy of non-interference in the social life of the Hindus. But in the second half of the 19th century and thereafter due to the pressure of some reformers they brought about a few legislations which accelerated the women's movements. Many of the legislative measures were only half-hearted, for they were never effectively implemented. Throughout the British period, the *feelings of dependency, loss of independence, lack of self-confidence and the feeling of inferiority were haunting not only men but even the women folk of India.*

B. STATUS OF WOMEN IN INDEPENDENT INDIA

The status of Indian woman has radically changed since independence. Both the structural and cultural changes provided equality of opportunities to women in education, employment and political participation. With the help of these changes exploitation of women, to a great extent, was reduced. More freedom and better orientation were provided to the women's organizations to pursue their interests. Importance of researches, national policies and programmes focused on women came to be increasingly realised. Several commissions were appointed by the Central and State governments to study the causes of low status of women and to protect their rights in various fields. The celebration of ***"International Women's Year"*** in 1975 and the activities of **UNESCO** also created awareness of the problems of women.

The improvement in the status of Indian women especially after independence can be analysed in the light of the major changes that have taken place in areas such as *legislations, education, economic* and *employment sector, political participation* and *awareness of their rights on the part of women,* etc.

1. Constitution and Legislation in Support of Women's Cause

• ***Constitutional provision for equality to women:*** The constitution of India does not discriminate between men and women. All the men and women of India are equally entitled for individual freedom, fundamental rights including the right to participate in social, cultural, religious, educational, economic and political activities. The constitution provides for equality of sex and offers protection to women against exploitation. It has given the voting right to women and in no way treats women as second grade citizens.

• ***Social legislations safeguarding women's interests:*** The Government of Independent India undertook a number of legislative measures to safeguard the interests of women. Some of them may be noted here.

(i) ***The Hindu Marriage Act, 1955*** which prohibits polygyny, polyandry and child marriage and concedes equal rights to women to divorce and to remarry.

(ii) ***The Hindu Succession Act, 1956*** which provides for women the right to parental property.

(iii) ***The Hindu Adoption and Maintenance Act, 1956*** which gives a childless woman the right to adopt a child and to claim maintenance from the husband if she is divorced by him.

(iv) ***The Special Marriage Act, 1954*** which provides rights to women on par with men for intercaste marriage, love marriage and registered marriage. The Act has also fixed the minimum age of marriage at **21** for males and **18** for females.

(v) ***The Dowry Prohibition Act, 1961*** which declares the taking of dowry an unlawful activity and thereby prevents the exploitation of women.

(vi) ***Other Legislations:***

(a) ***The Suppression of Immoral Traffic of Women and Girls Act, 1956*** which gives protection to women from being kidnapped and or compelled to become prostitutes.

(b) ***The Medical Termination of Pregnancy Act, 1971*** which legalises abortion conceding the right of a woman to go for abortion on the ground of physical and mental health.

(c) ***The Criminal Law Amendment Act, 1983*** which seeks to stop various types of crimes against women.

(d) ***The Family Court Act, 1984,*** which seeks to provide justice to women who get involved in family disputes.

2. Women in the Field of Education

After Independence, women of India took to education in a relatively large number. *For example,* in 1901, the literacy level of the females in India was just 0.6%, it increased to 39.42% in 1991 and to 64% in 2001. Various benefits such as freeship, scholarship, loan facility, hostel facility, etc. are being given to women who go for higher education. In many towns and cities, educational institutions meant only for female children have been established. The educational performance of girl students particularly at high school and college level, is proving to be better than that of boys especially after 1980s. The performance of girls makes it evident that intellect is not the monopoly of men alone. This nation has gone much ahead in the field of education and we have today some universities exclusively meant for women. **Examples:** (i) *SNDT University for Women* [Poona]; (ii) *Padmavathi University For Women* [Tirupati]; *Mother Teresa University for Women* [Kodai Kenal, Tamil Nadu]. Girl students are getting admitted on merit basis to the prestigious engineering and medical colleges in a relatively bigger number during the recent years. Women have now realised that education makes a lot of difference in the social status of the individuals whether they are men or women. It must be noted here that even though city women are quite conscious of education and its importance, more than 70% of our rural women are still illiterate and only a negligible number of them develop their educational career.

3. Women in the Economic and Employment Fields

In both villages and cities there has been a remarkable increase in the number of women going out of the four walls of the household and becoming workers. In the *'employment market',* they are giving tough competition to menfolk. In some fields the number of women employees is steadily increasing. *For example,* women working as teachers, doctors, nurses, advocates, bank employees, clerks, typists, telephone operators, receptionists, personal assistants and so on, are to be found in almost all cities. In big cities women do not hesitate to work as bus conductors, police constables, autoriksha drivers and so on. Since 1991, though in a smaller number, women are getting recruited into armed force, air force and naval force also.

Employments have given women economic independence and the feeling of importance. They now feel that they can stand on their own legs and look after the entire family by themselves. This has boosted their self-pride and self-confidence. Employed women feel that they need not live as parasites on their menfolk.

In order to give protection to the economic interests and rights of the women folk the government has undertaken various socio-economic legislations which cover areas such as *right to property or inheritance, equal wages, working conditions, maternity benefits and job security.*

Examples

(i) ***The Maternity Benefit Act, 1961*** which gives maternity benefits such as two months leave with salary to the married women workers.

(ii) ***The Equal Remuneration Act, 1976,*** which removes wage discrimination between male and female workers.

(iii) ***The Factories Amendment Act, 1976*** which includes provisions dealing with working laws, weekly rest, standards of cleanliness, ventilation, temperature, first-aid facilities, rest rooms etc. The legislation also provides for establishing of creches for children [if the factory employs 30 or more women]; separate toilets for females and lays down a maximum of 9 hours of work a day for women and no employment of women between 10-00 P.M. and 5-00 A.M.

(iv) ***The Hindu Succession Act, 1956*** according to which not only a daughter is given a right in her father's property equal to her brothers, but a widow also gets a share in her deceased husband's property equal to her sons and daughters.

4. Women in the Political Field

The Indian Constitution has sanctioned women two important political rights: *female enfranchisement* and *eligibility for the legislature*. As early as in 1937 itself some women candidates had contested for elections to the local legislative bodies and won. After the independence, the number of women voters and women's representatives in assemblies and parliament has increased sufficiently. Women have developed sufficient political awareness and some of them have attained very high positions in political parties, legislatures and cabinets. In the Central cabinet and at the level of the State cabinets we find some ministerial portfolios being headed by women. The nation witnessed in Smt. Indira Gandhi, one of the most powerful prime ministers who gave her leadership to the country for more than a decade. In 1992, an amendment [73rd] was brought to the Constitution according to which ***one-third*** of the seats were reserved for women at the Panchayat level. Some of the all-India level political parties had declared in the 1998 Lok Sabha elections that they would get 33% reservation for women in state legislatures and in parliament, if voted to power. The proposal of reserving 33% seats for women in the legislative bodies is still at the discussion level and no legislation could be made in this regard for want of political consensus among political parties. **The Women's Bill** which requires 84th amendment to the Constitution, is still pending in the Parliament. It may be noted that political awareness is present more among the city women than among the rural women; among the middle and upper class women than among the lower class women.

5. Awareness of Women Regarding their Rights

Women in independent India have more rights than their counterparts in many other countries of the world. But most of our women are not very much conscious of these rights.

Uneducated rural women do not have any awareness of their rights. **Prof. Ram Ahuja** conducted a study[1] a few years ago in eight villages of a district in Rajasthan among 753 women belonging to different age-groups. His intention was to assess the degree of awareness and measure the level of satisfaction among women about the rights sanctioned by the Constitution of India. He concluded that the level of awareness of rights by women depends upon the following four aspects.

(i) ***Individual background of women*** which refers to their educational level, aspiration level and personal needs.

(ii) ***Social environment of women*** which includes the social expectations of kins, husband's values and family members' perceptions.

(iii) ***Economic base of women*** which refers to the level of class-membership. [that is, whether they belong to lower class, middle class or upper class];

(iv) ***Subjective perception of women*** which refers to women's own feeling and assessment of their statuses and roles.

In Prof. Ahuja's study more than 75% of women were unaware of their rights; 20% of them did not have any awareness of their political rights; less than 1/3 of women had the chance of inheriting their husband's property and only 0.5% of them got a share of the father's property.

On the basis of the above study and some other general observations made by experts, it could be concluded that even today majority of our women are being identified *not as independent individuals but only as daughters, wives, mothers or as family members. Women are also not ready for their separate or independent identification.* Hence, women are still regarded as belonging to the *"weaker section".*

It can also be said that majority of our women [surely more than 50%] are happy with their family life and do not cherish any ambition relating to the political and public life. Those earning women members also do not have the full freedom to spend their money in accordance with their own will and wish. Most of the women do not prefer to take decisions on important matters but leave them to their menfolk's discretion. Thus our women are not completely free from the hold of the customs. In the unorganised sector, exploitation of women continues, for they are illiterate, ignorant and unorganised. In most of the homes male-children are still being preferred to female children. It appears that the societal approach towards women, their role and status has not radically changed. Hence, bringing about more and more legislations to ensure better opportunities to grant more rights and concessions, is of no benefit *unless there is a basic change in the people's attitude towards women and women's role in society.*

VIEWS OF MANU AND GANDHIJI ON THE STATUS OF WOMEN

Manu and His Smriti on the Status of Women

The life of Indian woman is very much associated with the two prominent institutions namely; family and marriage. Women enjoyed considerably a good status during the Vedic period. Even during the Epic period [period of Ramayana and Mahabharatha] they had an honourable position at home. But during the period of Dharmashastras or Smritis and Puranas their position underwent a major change. The position of woman deteriorated by the time Kautilya and Manu wrote their Dharmasutras. Man made rules suppressed the freedom of women which they hitherto enjoyed. Law-givers like Manu rejected the Vedic notion that women should participate with their husbands in sacrifices.

1 **Ram Ahujas** *"Indian Social System"* - Page: 111-112.

In the Manu Smriti we find restrictions that tended to deprive woman of her traditional status. Women could no longer undergo the *upanayana ceremony* and the initiation of a person into the study of the Vedas came to be confined only to male children. The female children were entitled to only one sacrament, namely, *marriage.* Women were permitted to participate in religious rites **only** as passive partners. Naturally, then, *"a wife is not independent with regard to the fulfilment of the sacred law."* Manu ordains that *"there are no specific sacrifices for women independently of the husband, nor vratas, nor fasts without his consent."*[1] Manu imposes his new rule by exhorting Brahmins not to attend feasts given on such occasions.

Manu enunciates the ideal of wifehood which only means the negation of her personality. Manu says that *"the husband must be constantly worshipped as a God by a faithful wife [Sadhvi], even if he be destitute of character......"* A good wife desirous of living in this as well as in the next world with her husband, must never do anything that would displease him either alive or dead. A woman attains heaven not by virtue of severe penances but as a result of her obedience and devotion to her husband. Women have no right to perform sacrifices. They are not called upon to perform the *"Sraddhas."* When her husband goes abroad, the wife should live a life of restraint. Manu thus looks upon the wife as mistress in her own home and this is generally assumed to be her sphere of influence.

Derogatory Views about and Norms Imposed on Women

Manu has been very widely criticised by the modern thinkers like **Dr. Ambedkar** for having accorded a low status to women. They point out some of the views that Manu had about women and the norms that he imposed upon them. **K.M. Kapadia** quotes....[2]

1. Manu says, *"Women must particularly be guarded against evil inclinations......... for if they are not guarded, they will bring sorrow on both the families........ Even weak husbands must strive to guard their wives."*

2. *"Women do not care for beauty, nor is their attention fixed on age; they give themselves to the handsome as well as to the ugly, just for the fact that he is a man."*

3. It is the nature of women to seduce man in this world. She is able to lead astray not only the ignorant but even a learned man and make him a slave of lust. It is hence that she is called *"pramada"*, a temptress.

4. "Woman was created for infatuating man and hence there is nothing more heinous than woman."

Women do not Deserve Freedom ?

Manu who was backed by the Epic and Puranic writers assigned relatively an inferior status to women. Manu was of the opinion that due to *"their unstable temper and inherent heartlessness they become disloyal to their husbands, however carefully they may be guarded in this world"* [**K.M. Kapadia** - 254]. It is in this context he said that women must be under surveillance throughout their lives. Manu gave an injunction: *"A woman has to be under her father during childhood, under her husband during youth and under her son during old age. At no stage she deserves full freedom."* Women were told to accept the second position at home and outside.

Manu also Speaks of the Greatness of Women

It is wrong to suppose that Manu was basically prejudiced against women. He had also spoken about the greatness of women, and shown concern about women.

---

1 **K.M. Kapadia** *"Marriage and Family in India."* Page - 252.

2. *Ibid* Page - 254

Examples :

1. Though at one stage he said *"woman shall deserve no freedom"*, he balanced this view with a statement - *"that a society, in which the woman was not honoured, would be condemned to damnation."* He even wrote: *"Where the women are honoured, there the very Gods are pleased; but where they are not honoured, no sacred rite ever could yield rewards."*

2. Manu has stated that any father, brother, husband and his relatives must, for their own welfare, betterment and glory; respect women.

3. Manu has stressed again and again that only the woman can safeguard the interests of the family at large. That is why he glorified motherhood by equating mother to God. He preached what is known as *"matr devobhava."*

4. Manu is also generous in regard to women, when he says that the father should give his daughter in marriage to an excellent and handsome youth of the same varna and that it is better the girl stays at home unmarried instead of marrying a worthless man. Manu seriously cautions the father of the girl to take all the responsibilities in finding her a suitable match to escape from the outcome of the sin in the life after his death. According to Manu, a woman is empowered to choose for herself a match suited to her, if her father and guardians fail to arrange for her marriage.

"In the family, says Manu, the grihastha should regard his daughters as the highest objects of tenderness; he should bear their offences without resentment."[1]

Concluding Remarks

It seems that Manu gives a good deal of freedom to the young girls in the family at least in the matter of choosing their life partners. But at other places, Manu and other Smritikaras are not prepared to allow any kind of independent activity to women, without consultation or permission of the male members of the family. It is also a matter of fact that Manu is not prepared to give equal rights to women on par with men. He is very sharply criticised for this.

In spite of the criticisms levelled against Manu, some of the scholars have given Manu and Manu Smriti a glowing tribute. Philosopher **Fredrich Nietzsche** writes: *"I know of no book in which so many tender and kind remarks are addressed to women as in the Law Book of Manu. These old graybeards and saints have a way of being polite to women which has perhaps never been surpassed."*[2]

According to **M.N. Shankdhar,** *".... calling Manu pro-Brahmin, anti-Shudra, anti-feminist, castiest, orthodox, cruel, superstitious, and what not, is the sinister pastime of the slaves of Western scholasticism and Marxist dogma"* - [*"Indian Express"* dated 10-8-1994].

Gandhiji's Views about the Status of Women

Gandhiji had written and spoken much about the status of women. Gandhiji's writings clearly reveal that he was not satisfied with the status or position accorded to women in India during his time. Women constitute 50% of the population; they are given the responsibility of maintaining, protecting, and managing the family; and guiding the future generation of the society. In spite of all these things, women's position in India was pitiable and this aspect had disturbed Gandhiji very much. He had all the praises for **Raja Ram Mohan Roy** for what had done for the cause of women. In fact, Gandhiji decided to continue the work of Ram Mohan Roy in elevating the status of women.

---

1 **K.M. Kapadia.** ''*Marriage and Family in India*'' Page - 273.

2 *"Comparing Manu Smriti to Bible, Nietzsche says: "All things in CHRISTIANITY vents its abysmal vulgarity, procreation, for example; women, marriage, are in Manu Smriti, treated seriously, with reverence, love and trust....... How paltry the New Testament is, compared to Manu, how ill it smells"* - **F. Nietzche** as quoted by **M.M. Shankdhar** in his article in *"Indian Express"* dated 10-8-1994.

Gandhiji Advocated Equal Status for Women : Gandhiji was of the opinion that there should be no differences between men and women. He was quoting the examples of Brahmavadinis of the Vedic and the Upanishadics periods such as **Gargi, Maitreye, Nivavari, Lopa Mudra, Indrani** and others to highlight the intellectual freedom enjoyed by the early women of India. He was also citing the examples of the modern European women like **Anni Besant, Florence Nitingale, Nivedita** to point out the heights that women could reach in the modern world. Gandhiji was of the firm opinion that women should never be given inferior or a secondary position, but they be accorded a position on par with men. Gandhiji said : *"My opinion is that just as fundamentally men and women are one, their problems must be one in essence. The soul in both is the same. The two live the same life, have the same feelings. Each is a complement of the other. The one cannot live without the other's active help."*[1]

Women are Entitled for Equal Freedom : Gandhiji was opposed to the view that women are weaker. According to him, it is a sin to call them so; it is an injustice perpetrated on them by men. Women have courage, confidence, patience and dedication. Men cannot do anything without their help. It is wrong to say that only men can make achievements. Women can also reach the same heights provided the opportunities are given to them.

Women's Tasks are Different from those of Men. Gandhiji was of the opinion that men and women should be treated equally and should get equal remuneration for equal work. According to him, it is not necessary for the women to imitate men and to do the tasks of men. Gandhiji never wanted women to become men like in all respects. It is degrading both for men and women, if women are made to take to the profession of the males and vice versa. *"In trying to ride the horse that man rides, she brings herself and him down. The sin will be on man's head for tempting or compelling his companion to desert her special calling. There is as much bravery in keeping one's home in good order and condition as there is in defending it against attack from without."*[2]

Gandhiji was in Favour of Giving Equal Political Rights to Women : He desired the utmost freedom for women and favoured their right to vote and equal legal status. Gandhiji worked a lot to obtain the active participation of a large number of women in the Indian freedom struggle. He believed that freedom movement would become a success only with the participation of women on a mass scale. Because of his personal appeal and persuasion, sizeable number of women took part in the *satyagraha*'s, processions, protest meetings, demonstrations, and public meetings. For example, in the *Salt Agitation* of 1930, more than 17,000 women had taken part. In the *"Quit India"* agitation of 1942, and in *"Seva Dal Camps"*, women participated in a huge number. Gandhiji was of the opinion that many movements in India could not attain success not because of the dearth of ideology but because of the non-inclusion of women in such movements. He thought that women could play the role of a leader in *"Satyagraha"* in a better manner, since *satyagraha* required a strong heart and women were in possession of it, because it had emanated from suffering and faith. He believed that in order to make ourselves fit for the true *"Swaraj"* men must cultivate greater respect for women and for their purity.

Education Provides "Salvation" for Women : Gandhiji was a strong supporter of female education. He felt that education is of equal importance for both men and women. Educated men and women, husband and wife can understand and support one another. No woman can grow to her full capacity without education. Denial of educational opportunities for women virtually caused the downfall of Indian women. Lack of education led to their exploitation, suppression and enslavement.

---

1 **C.F. Andrews** *"Mahatma Gandhi's Ideas."* Pages : 172 73.

2 ***Ibid***

Education helps women to come in touch with the world of books. With the help of books women can develop their intellect and depth of knowledge. Gandhiji did not consider the English medium education essential for our men and women. He also believed that proper planning of education would solve many of our social problems including the problems of women.

Gandhiji's Concern about the Problems Confronting Women

Gandhiji was unhappy with the pardah system which the Hindu women were forced to accept and practise. Hinduism cannot justify that practice. In fact, it came to be practised in the Hindu society at the period of its decline. As he commented it was not in practice during the period of Draupadi or Sita. Gargi and Maitreye never argued behind the pardah. Imposition of pardah on women is not only unethical but also detrimental to their progress.

Gandhiji severely condemned the practice of dowry. He believed that the dowry system polluted the purity and the sanctity of the institution of marriage. Gandhiji had nothing but contempt for this practice which compelled many parents to give their daughters in marriage to absolutely unsuitable matches. Gandhiji gave a clarion call to the men and women of India to drive away the evil practice of dowry from the Hindu society. The system that ruined many families must be stopped at the earliest.

Gandhiji was against the practice of child marriage. He even refused to treat child marriage as marriage at all. The problem of child widows was almost the result of child marriage. Girl-children becoming widows for no fault of theirs, is not a healthy sight of a sane society. Hence, he wanted a child-widow to be treated as a maiden rather than as a widow. Gandhiji wrote : *"..... I detest child marriages. I shudder to see a child widow, and shiver with rage when a husband, just widowed, with brutal indifference contracts another marriage........ It is an abuse of the term [child-widow], abuse of language and a sacrilege.......... There is no warrant for this kind of widowhood in Hinduism."*[1]

Gandhiji favoured remarriages of child-widows. In fact, he very strongly advocated the remarriage of child widows. Though Gandhiji expected adult-widows to honour their marriage vows, he objected to their remarriages. Gandhiji gave a call to the young men of the day to come forward for marrying child widows. If widowers could re-marry, so could widows, Gandhiji argued. He thought that imposed widowhood tended to defile the home and degrade religion.

Gandhiji criticised the practice of sati. It is expected of a wife to be loyal and dedicated to the husband just as it is expected of a husband to be dutiful towards the wife. A *sati* [wife] is one who is dedicated to the husband without any selfishness. Only immatured wives think of self-immolation to become *"satis."* According to Gandhiji, they do not know the real nature of soul or *"atma."* It is immortal; it does not die with the death of the physical body. Its journey continues from one mortal body to another till it attains salvation. Experience of innumerable *sadhus* and sages has proved it time and again. In the light of these spiritual facts, suicide cannot be justified. By killing herself no wife will get back the life of her husband. Hence, Gandhiji believed that the practice of *sati* is not only meaningless but is also against the spirit of the Hindu beliefs.[1] He called upon women to give up that evil practice.

Gandhiji supported monogamy. According to him, marital life is a kind of discipline. This is not like one-way traffic. Husband and wife have an equal responsibility and a commitment to it. Marriage life is intended to promote mutual good and serve humanity. It is not just for enjoyment of sex. According to Gandhiji, Hinduism gave women absolute equality with men. He said that *"..... if the husband did not care for the wife, she could without breaking the legal tie, live away from her*

1 **C.F. Andrews.** *''Mahatma Gandhi's Ideas.''*

husband and feel as if she had never been married." However, he was not in favour of complete divorce.

Gandhiji severely criticised the practice of compelling women to work for earning their daily bread. No well established society would enforce its women to work for money. Earning the daily bread for the family members is man's task. Women's job is only to maintain the family and to look after the needs of its members. Gandhiji wanted our women to give more importance to their domestic work and to their role as mothers. He was not in favour of women working for money at the cost of neglecting the family role and the domestic responsibilities.

Gandhiji was against all kinds of disabilities of women in enjoying legal rights on par with men. But he expected women to have certain self-restraints. For example, he expected the married women not to claim their right over the ancestral properties of their parents. He advocated equality of men and women. But this equality, according to him, was relative and not absolute. Gandhiji was always trying to understand and advocate the status of women within the purview of the Hindu culture, by giving new dimensions and modern interpretations to it. For Gandhiji, Rama and Sita were the ideal husband and wife. He condemned the practice of exploiting women in the name of religion. He believed firmly that no society would achieve progress or reach greater heights by neglecting its women folk.

PROBLEMS OF WOMEN IN MODERN INDIA

Women in independent India are comparatively in a more respectable position. Some of the problems which had been haunting the community of women for centuries are not found now. Problems such as child marriage, practice of *'sati'*, prohibition on widow remarriage, exploitation of widows, *devadasi* system, *purdah* system, etc. have almost disappeared. *Development in the field of science and technology, universalisation of education, socio-political movements, modernisation* and similar developments changed the approach of people towards women to a certain extent. These developments boosted the morale and self-confidence of women. As a result, Indian women now feel that they too have their own individuality, personality, self-respect, talent, capacity and efficiency. Many of those women who could grab the opportunities extended to them, have proved that they are capable of discharging the responsibilities assigned to them. The nation which neglected almost 50% of its population for several centuries has now understood the necessity of giving equal rights and opportunities to its womenfolk.

The Constitution of India provides equal rights and opportunities to women. It does not make any discrimination on the grounds of sex. Indian women are also responding positively to this changed socio-political situation. This does not mean that our women are completely free from problems. On the contrary, the changing situation is causing them new problems. They are now beset with new stresses and strains. Some of the major problems haunting the modern women may briefly be analysed here.

IV. PROBLEMS OF MODERN WOMEN

1. Problem of Violence against Women

- ***Violence is almost universal.*** Most societies exhibit violence in one way or another. Violence against men or women is a social problem because, a large number of people are affected by it almost everyday. Each of us is affected in countless ways by the climate of violence. Violence disrupts society. Every society creates institutions designed to achieve certain ends. Violence short-

1 **M.K. Gandhiji's** *"Mahileyaru"* [Kannada version book]. ***Pub.:*** *"Gandhi Smaraka Nidhi"*, Karnataka [1969]. Page - 117.

cuts normal institutional functions. Every act of violence, from assault to armed revolution, detracts to some degree from the authority normally vested in society.

• ***Women as Victims of Violence*** : Who is most likely to be victimised by violent crime ? Women are less likely to be victimised by violent crime than men, though for some crimes and among some groups of women, victimisation is higher than men. Violence against women is not a new phenomenon in India. *"Women in Indian society have been victims of ill-treatment, humiliation, torture, and exploitation for as long as written records of social organisation and family life are available. These records are replete with incidents of abduction, rape, murder, and torture of women. But, regretfully, female victims of violence have not been given much attention in the literature on social problems or in the literature on criminal violence."*[1]

• ***Increasing Crimes Against Women*** : Crime against women is an ever-increasing problem. This problem has been growing more and more acute in India during the recent years. Crimes against women include *violence against women, rape, molestation, dowry harassment, wife-battering, kidnapping female children to be sold into brothel homes, forcible embracement, forcible religious conversion, cheating young women with a promise to marry them or fetch them a job and various types of sexual harassments and abuse of women including eve teasing.*

As per the report [1994] of the *"Crime Record Bureau"* of the Central Home Ministry,[2] crimes against women increased to a great extent in the year 1993-94. As per this report, in India on an average, (i) every day for every 6 minutes one atrocity is committed against women; (ii) for every 44 minutes a woman is kidnapped; (iii) for every 47 minutes a women is raped; (iv) every day 17 dowry deaths are taking place. The same report says that crimes against women increased two times in the last 10 years; instances of rape by 400% in the last two decades; instances of kidnapping and blackmailing women by 30% between 1974 and 1993. In 1993 alone about 82818 instances of crimes against women were registered.

Violence against women is increasing not only in the Western countries but even in India. This *violence against women, in particular, has inhibited women as a group from enjoying the full benefits of human rights.* Women have been vulnerable to acts of violence *in the family,* in *the community* and by *the State*. Women are subject to violence in the family [***Ex.*** : *battering, sexual abuse of female children, dowry related violence, incest, deprivation of food, marital rape, female genital mutilation,* etc.]; to violence in the community [***Ex.*** : *rape, sexual abuse, sexual harassment, trafficking in women, forced prostitution*] and to violence by the State [***Ex.*** : *women in detention and rape during times of armed conflict.*]

• ***Exploitation and Harassment of Women:*** Women in the unorganised sector are very much being exploited, whereas women in the organised sector are harassed in several ways. In films and T.V. shows women are more often picturised as objects of sex and nothing more than that. This type of commercialisation of sex, damages the self-image of women. Misrepresentation of women in the media definitely lowers the status of women. In the rural areas lower caste working women are sexually exploited and in the tribal areas tribal women are often kidnapped to be sold in the international market. Even today, a large number of poor rural women are working as almost *bonded labourers* in the houses of landlords.

2. *Decline in the Female Population* : Normally, in the population of any country, male-female ratio remains more or less the same, that is, 50:50. In India as the census reports reveal that female population has been steadily declining ever since 1901. It is for this reason **Neera Desai** and **Vibhuti Patel** raised the point whether the womenfolk in India represent a *"declining*

1 **Ram Ahuja** *"Violence Against Women"* [1998]. Page - 11.

2 *"Udayavani"* Kannada daily dated 27th Feb - 1994.

sex". [It was only during 1971-1981 and 1991-2001 the female population increased from 930 to 933 and 927 to 933 per every 1000 males, respectively]. Even the 2001 census report says that the female population could not be increased beyond 933 per every 1000 males. Added to this the number of women dying before they attain the age of 40 is also very much higher than that of males. This imbalance in the sex ratio will have its own social consequences.

3. *Female Children Becoming Victims of Discrimination* : In the Indian social context even today male children are preferred to female children. Hence, female children are subject to discriminatory treatment. Male preference and female negligence has almost become a working policy especially in the rural areas. Discrimination between male and female children is made in matters relating to food, dress, health, education, domestic work etc. The policy of male preference and female negligence has led to what are known as *"female disadvantages"*. In India, mothers show preferences for male children. They give them importance because - *males are wanted during their old age to offer protection, males have greater scope than women and occupational avenues are also wider for males than for females.* This male preference has led to the abuse of advanced technology. The sophisticated scanning and supersonographic equipments are being misused to find out the sex of the child; that is to go for abortion if the child is found to be an unwanted female child. These medical tests which would cost rupees between 80/- to 800/- are within the reach of the middle class and even the upper-lower class resulting in the killing of the female foetuses in large number. Between 1978 and 1982 more than 78,000 foetuses were killed mainly because of these medical tests.[1]

4. *Health Problem of Women* : Women suffer from some distinctive health problems from which men are free. Women have to undergo the distinctive biological process of pregnancy, or child-bearing, delivering, nursing, feeding, child-caring or rearing etc. These are their maternal functions. But the insistence on the family planning has posed them many health hazards. The use of contraceptives, Copper-T, sterilisation, abortion and hormonal drugs has an adverse effect on health. Those who make use of them suffer from problems such as *bodily weakness, bloodlessness, high bleeding, fatness, problems in uterus, discomfort in breast, chronic backpain,* etc. As **Neera Desai** and **Vibhuti Patel** have criticised, the advocates of family planning do not seem to bother much about these problems.

- ***Women neglecting their own health:*** Studies have revealed that our women themselves are neglecting their own health. Normally Indian women consume less food [that is, on an average 100 calories a day] and spend more energy on work. Women toil for the good of the family and children even at the cost of neglecting their own health. Women very rarely complain about their ill-health because of their virtue of *"self-denial"*. The records in the health centres reveal that women are lagging behind men [that is, 1:3, meaning one woman taking medical help for every 3 men] even in matters of availing of medical help.

- ***Women have their own reasons to neglect their health:*** *Not finding free time to go to health centres because of heavy work at home; non-availability of proper medical facility to test the health or ill-health of the mother and the child especially in the primary health centres; inability to walk a long distance to reach a well equipped health centre in the absence of proper transportation facility; non-availability of female doctors in the nearby health centres,* etc., are some such excuses.

5. *Problems of Female Education* : Social reformers and social thinkers believe that in a nation like India giving education to women in as large a number as possible can prove to

1 *Times of India,* Editorial June 1982.

be a panacea for many of the problems of women. Accordingly, much attention is paid to the education of women after independence. The female literacy level is also increasing steadily. It has increased from 18.7% in 1971 to 39.42% in 1991 and to **64%** in 2001. In spite of this change in the trend towards literacy, some problems of have cropped up. We find glaring differences between the educationality of men and women. *For example,*

- It is found ***that girls are being discouraged*** to go for higher education and also for professional and technical education.

- ***There are regional imbalances also.*** In states like Kerala, Karnataka and Maharashtra, female education is encouraged and given almost equal importance. Whereas in states like Bihar, Orissa, Madhya Pradesh etc. education of girls is neglected even today.

- ***Increasing drop-out of female children*** from schools is another problem. Though female children are getting admitted to primary, middle and high schools in a substantial number, many of them drop out of the school in the middle without completing the course. *For example,* as per the data furnished by the Ministry of Education [New Delhi], in 1984-85 the number of female children enrolled at primary school crossed the figure of 34.2 millions, and at middle school level the enrolment crossed 9.2 millions. More than 74% of these female children, between the age-groups of 6-14 years, quit schools and lapsed into ignorance.

- ***Admission to school:*** Even in the matter of admitting children to school at elementary level, female children are discriminated against male children. *For example,* in 1984-85, the admission of male children to school was around 90%, the percentage of female children was only 66.2. It means complete awareness is not there among people regarding female education.

6. *Problems of Employment and Unemployment for Women* : It is true that relatively a large number of women are entering into employment sector. An increase in the female literacy level on the one hand and extension of employment opportunities for women in the non-agricultural sector on the other, have added to the trend in favour of female employment. For example, in 1971, in the total work force of the country women's share was around 13.0% and it increased to 28.57% in 1991.[1] In spite of this increase, majority of women who are ready to work, are not finding suitable work to do.

- ***Majority of employed women are also illiterate.*** Of the every 100 women employed, 52.59% of them are illiterate and 28.56% of them have studied only up to elementary level. Of the every 100 women working in the rural areas, 88.11% are illiterate. These illiterate women in the unorganised sector are totally exploited by their employers. Women working in factories, mining industries, building construction process, in dams, bridges and road repair or construction work are not only paid less but also made to work in unhealthy surroundings.

- ***Decreasing economic participation of women:*** Technological development seems to have a negative effect on employment opportunities of women. Studies conducted between 1975-85 have revealed this fact. Application of new technology in agrarian sector, textiles, mines, jutes, pharmaceuticals, small scale industries like coir handloom, weaving, spinning, cashew, fisheries, tobacco, animal husbandry, fruits and vegetable processing etc. rendered many women jobless. Computerisation has also adversely affected the job prospects of women as clerks, typists and accountants.

7. *Decline in the Political Participation of Women* : Participation of women who constitute 50% of our total population in politics and public life is very much negligible in India. We find

1 *The Hindusthan Times,* Dated 6th April - 1993.

only a negligible number of women in prestigious positions like those of Central and State cabinet ministers, governors, secretaries and legal advisers to the governments, ambassadors to other countries, IPS, IAS, IFS officers, judges in courts, mayors of big cities, office bearers of all-India parties, etc. No political party of India has given position to women in accordance with their number in the total population. In some areas seats are reserved for women as we find in Gram Panchayat, Jilla Panchayat, University Senate, etc. Even in these areas women have not constituted themselves into a *"pressure group"*. Hence in our political life, we have caste lobbies, linguistic lobbies, capitalist lobbies, minority lobby, etc. but we do not have *"women lobby"* to bring pressure on the government.

- ***Increasing violence and terrorism in politics:*** Political corruption, criminalisation of politics, erosion of political values, disappearance of political decency, instability, lawlessness, terrorism and confusion have been increasing in our public life since 1980s. This state of confused political situation has discouraged women to take an active role in politics.

- ***Minimum representation of women in Lok Sabha:*** The representation of women in Lok Sabha has been very poor since 1962 elections. **For ex:** there were only 33 elected women members in the third Lok Sabha [out of 494 members] after the 1962 elections. In the 6th Lok Sabha out of 544 elected members there were only 19 women members and their percentage was only 3.4. In the 10th Lok Sabha [1991 Elections] there were 39 elected women members and their percentage was 7.4.

- ***In the 1996 Elections for the 11th Lok Sabha*** though the total number of women voters increased to 28.24 crores [47%], only 477 women candidates as against 14250 men candidates contested for 543 seats. [In the 1991 Elections for the 10th Lok Sabha 325 women candidates contested as against 8374 men candidates for 521 seats]. These figures reveal that only a small number of women are interested in political life.

- ***In the 1999 General Elections for the 13th Lok Sabha*** also women's participation was the poorest one. Though political parties were speaking vociferously in terms of 33% reservation for women in legislative bodies including the Parliament, no political party had given tickets to women in more than **10%.** In some parties, the percentage of women candidates was not even **2** to **3.**

- ***Poor participation of women in the party politics*** : Not only in the legislative bodies but even within the framework of the political parties also the participation of women is very poor. Political parties are still male-dominated and unwilling to give sufficient representation to women. ***For example,*** at present, [that is, in 2001] the Congress Party has only 3 women in its 20-member Working Committee. In the BJP Working Committee, out of **75** members there are only 8 women, and in its **650** member National Council, there are only **150** women. The Communist Party [Marxists] has only **12** women in its **150** member National Council, and **3** women in its **21** member National Executive. Though theoretically women's representation in politics is regarded as the first step towards women empowerment, the socio-political atmosphere has not yet become condusive for that.

V. DEVELOPMENT AND WELFARE OF WOMEN

No civilised government of any nation can afford to ignore the development and welfare of women who constitute almost 50% of its total population. Women who number 407.1 million according to 1991 census represent 48.1% of India's total population. Their number increased to 495.73 million in 2001. The development of women has always been the central focus in developmental planning since independence. Of course, there have been various shifts in policy approaches of the government towards women in the last 50 years from the concept of *"welfare"* in the 1970s to *"development"* in the 80s and now to *"empowerment"* in 90s. The Department of Women and Child Development since its very inception has been implementing special programmes designed to improve the socio-economic status of women.

The independent Indian Government has undertaken a number of measures particularly in the sectors of health, education, rural and urban development, employment, education, etc. with a view to promote the development and welfare of women. Some of them may be briefly mentioned here.

1. Welfare of Women Through Legislations

To ensure equal rights and opportunities for women and to provide for them *'justice'*, the government undertook legislative measures. **Examples:** *(i) The Hindu Marriage Act, 1955; (ii) The Hindu Succession Act, 1956; (iii) The Hindu Adoption and Maintenance Act, 1956; (iv) The Suppression of Immoral Traffic of Women and Girls' Act, 1956; (v) The Dowry Prohibition Act, 1961; (vi) The Equal Remuneration Act, 1976; (vii) The Factories Amendment Act, 1976; (viii) The Family Court Act, 1984; (ix) Medical Termination of Pregnancy Act, 1971; (x) The Muslim Women's Protection of Rights on Divorce Act, 1986. and Iddat.*

2. Legal Assistance to Assure Justice to Women

The government established a special ***'Cell'*** [attached to labour department] in 1976 with a view to provide due assistance to women in distress. The responsibility of this cell is entrusted to the *'Commissioner of Police'*. The central government has also established a separate ministry with a cabinet rank to deal with the issues and problems concerned with women. To assist judiciary in its task of ensuring judicial protection to women *"social vigilance groups"* are established. Family Courts established according to *"the Family Court Act, 1984"*, are giving legal protection to women. The Social Welfare Department has established *"Women's Bureau"* in order to look into the problems of women and to find solutions for the same.

3. Educational Development Plan for Women

The University Grants Commission had stressed as early as in 1948 the essential need for the education of women. *The Central Education Department,* the [NCERT] *National Council of Educational Research and Training,* the [NAEP] *National Adult Education Programme* and other institutions have evinced greater interest in providing educational facilities for women.

- ***Women Study Centres*** have been established with the assistance of [UGC] University Grants Commission to study the status of women and problems and issues concerned with women.

- ***Other Institutions:*** Institutions such as - (i) **UNICEF:** *United Nations' International Children's Educational Fund;* (ii) **ICSSR:** *Indian Council of Social Science Research;* (iii) **UNESCO:** *United Nations Educational Scientific and Cultural Organisation;* (iv) **CSIR:** *Council of Scientific and Industrial Research;* (v) *Ford Foundation,* etc. have shown a special interest in studying women's problems.

4. Programmes for Improving Women's Health

Various organisations, independent surveys and studies conducted by prominent individuals and private institutions brought to the notice of the Central Government at different times between 1975-85 the urgent need for improving women's health. Various governmental agencies such as

"Indian Council of Medical Research, Ministry of Health and Family Welfare, Central Government Health Services Scheme [CGHS] etc. have been paying much attention to promote women's health.

• ***In rural areas*** institutional systems such as rural *Primary Health Centres* and *Family Welfare Centres* are trying to promote women's health. *World Health Organisation, World Bank* and *Ford Foundation* are also showing concern in providing medical protection to women and children.

5. Economic Development Programme for Women

The Five Year Plans launched by the Government have paid due attention to enable women to attain greater economic participation. In some of the areas such as *factories, offices, mining, clerical posts, teaching, nursing, banking, tea and coffee plantations,* etc. women employees are found in a large number. To protect the economic interests of the employed women various legislations such as *Minimum Wages Act, 1948; Equal Wages Act, 1976; the Factories Amendment Act, 1976;* etc. have been undertaken. The Karnataka and Andhra Governments have reserved some jobs for women in government sector.

• ***Employment and Training of Women*** : The *Programme of Support to Training-cum-Employment for Women* [STEP] was launched in 1987 to strengthen and improve the skills for employment opportunities for women below poverty line in traditional sectors of agriculture, small scale industries, animal husbandry, handlooms, handicrafts, cottage and village industries, sericulture, etc. where women are employed on a large scale.

The scheme of *Condensed Courses of Education and Vocational Training* [CCE&VT] for adult women started in 1958, is implemented by the ***Central Social Welfare Board.*** It aims at providing new vistas of employment through continuing education and vocational training to women and girls, particularly to school drop-outs. During the years 1997-1999, as many as 2,000 courses were sanctioned to benefit about 50,000 women and girls.

• ***Institutes for providing Vocational Training for Women*** have been established at various places and in 1984 there were about 125 such institutes throughout the nation.

• ***Women's National Training Institute*** was started in 1977 and its regional units in places such as Bombay, Bangalore, Thiruvananthapuram, Hissar, Calcutta were also opened. *The Regional Training Institute* at Bangalore gives *"basic"* and also modern training to about 1426 girls and part-time training to about 141 girls every year.

• ***Socio-Economic Programme*** : Under this programme, the Central Social Welfare Board gives financial assistance to the voluntary organisations for undertaking a wide variety of income-generating activities, which include the production of central components in ancillaries units, handlooms, handicrafts, agro based activities such as animal husbandry, sericulture, and fisheries, and self employment ventures like vegetables or fish-vending, etc.

• ***The Dairy Scheme*** focuses exclusively on women's organisations having at least 20 women members, including *Mahila Mandals, Indira Mahila Kendras, Self Help Groups* and organisations already assisted under STEP scheme. The benefits of the scheme are meant for women whose families are below the poverty line.

• ***Mahila Samriddhi Yojana*** : This scheme was launched on 2nd Oct. 1993, through a network of 1.32 lakh rural Post Offices to promote thrift among rural women and to empower them with greater control over their household sources. After the completion of 2 years of implementation of this *Yojana* it was decided to launch a new scheme which would cover approximately 885 blocks in which about 20 lakh women would be benefited.

• ***Rashtriya Mahila Kosh* [RMK]** : The national credit fund for women called *The Rashtriya Mahila Kosh* was set up in 1992-93 with a corpus fund of Rs.31 crores with a major objective of meeting the credit needs of poor women, particularly in the informal sector. The Minister of State for Women and Child Development is the Chairperson of this *Kosh*. The RMK has sanctioned up to 31st March 1998, loans of Rs.47.85 crores to benefit 2.50 lakh women through 256 NGOs.

• ***Working Women's Hostels*** have been established in towns and cities mainly to provide boarding and lodging facilities to rural women who move on to urban centres to obtain jobs. Governmental and private agencies are taking initiative in opening such hostels. In some hostels, day-care centres for children of these women are also attached. During 1992-93 as many as 23 additional hostels were sanctioned to provide accommodation to 2,269 working women. This brought the total number of hostels to over 811 [by 1999] benefiting over 56,974 working women.

• ***The National Committee for Women Welfare*** is instituted for framing appropriate policies for women welfare to suit to the changing needs of time.

6. The Central Social Welfare Board

***The Central Social Welfare Board* [CSWB]** was set up in 1953 with the objective of promoting social welfare activities and implementing welfare programmes for women, children and the handicapped through voluntary organisations. The CSWB is unique in the sense that it was the first organisation in post independent era to achieve people's participation for implementation of welfare programmes for women and children through the Non-Government Organisations [NGOs].

The CSWB established by the *Planning Commission,* has its own women welfare programmes such as *providing housing protection to weak and helpless women, fallen women, helpless widows; creating centres of social education for women and adult education centres, condensed courses of education and vocational training courses for women and girls, awareness generation projects for rural and poor women, family counselling centres, holiday camps for children, welfare extension projects in border areas, opening centres for giving healthy entertainment to the women, giving assistance to creches and hostels for working women,* etc. The Board gives financial subsidy of Rs. 50,000/- annually to those private agencies [NGOs] which provide good service to the women. Presently, more than 18,000 NGOs are receiving financial assistance and guidance from the Board.

• ***Voluntary organisation in the service of women:*** (i) *Mobile Creches* for working mother's children aged upto 12 years; (ii) *"Annapoorna"* women's co-operative Society to provide mid-day meal to working women; (iii) *Self-Employed Women Association,* a registered trade union to organise women rag-pickers, head-loaders, junksmith, fish vendors, bamboo-workers, beedi workers, block-printers, used garment dealers has come into being to get a fair deal for women workers.

7. National Commission for Women

The National Commission for Women was set up on 31st January 1992 in pursuance of *The National Commission for Women Act,* 1990. The functions assigned to the Commission are wide and varied covering almost all aspects relating to safeguarding women's rights and promotion of their interests. The Commission has a Chairman, 5 members, and a Member Secretary, all nominated by the Central Government. The Commission continues to pursue its mandatory activities, namely, review of legislations, interventions in specific individual complaints of atrocities and remedial action to safeguard the interests of women. The Commission has accorded highest priority to securing speedy justice to women.

- ***Indira Mahila Yojana* [IMY] :** The *Indira Mahila Yojana* aims at organising women at the grass root level to facilitate their participation in decision making and empowerment, was launched on 20th August 1995, in 200 *Integrated Child Development Services* [ICDS] blocks. The strength of the scheme lies in the strength of group dynamics. The objectives of the scheme are – *awareness generation among the women from rural areas and urban slums and economic empowerment of women.*

***Conclusion* :** It is true that the Central and the State governments have undertaken various legislative and other measures for promoting the welfare of women. We cannot, however, say that the intended purpose of the Governments is fulfilled and the targeted persons have received all the benefits. The educated, middle class and upper caste women of towns and cities have taken relatively greater advantage of these measures, whereas the vast mass of uneducated, lower class and lower caste women of the rural areas are not even aware of most of these welfare measures. The deficiencies involved in these measures and the inefficient implementation of the developmental programmes by the indifferent bureaucrats have come in the way of the success of these measures. In spite of these shortcomings, the awareness of women regarding these measures is slowly growing. After the lapse of a few centuries, the society is becoming slowly aware of the historic necessity of providing women a respectable position in society and paying special attention to the problems haunting them.

EMPOWERMENT OF WOMEN

Women constitute almost 50% of the world's population. As far as their social status is concerned, they are not treated as equal to men in all the places. Though in the Western countries women are treated on par with men in most of the fields, their counterpart in the East suffer from many disabilities. The disabilities on the one hand, and the inequalities between men and women on the other, have given rise to what is known as the *"gender problem."* All over the world and particularly in South and East Asia and Africa the gender problem has assumed importance during the recent years. The gender issue has become virtually a crucial point of argument.

The United Nations, in its various declarations, has made it abundantly clear that men and women should be treated alike. Women should not be asked to wait for any more time. Their sufferings, problems, disabilities, and the humiliations perpetrated on them are historical. Hence, gender problem in the context of new forces of development, assumes vital importance.

Empowerment of Women – A Solution to Gender Discrimination

It is now widely believed that empowerment of women, that is, *providing equal rights, opportunities and responsibilities to women,* will go a long way in removing the existing gender discrimination.

Gender discrimination and gender disabilities are not uniformly found in all the countries even in the East. Further, there are regional variations also inside the big nations. For instance, in a vast nation like India, women enjoy relatively greater freedom and more opportunities in the South than in the North. Women are not allowed to move freely, to take up to education, to take up to jobs, to select their own life partners, in the North. Whereas in the South, the level of literacy among women is comparatively higher and hence, there is less discrimination against them. Women are found to be studying in educational institutions even at a higher level and working in offices, banks, public and private departments, in a relatively larger number in the South. In comparison with the Western societies, women in general in South-East Asia are discriminated against. They are considered to be a weaker section of the society. This state of affair of women warrants appropriate plan of action to strengthen and support them. Empowerment of women is a positive step in this direction.

Empowerment of Women and the 73rd Constitution Amendment Act - 1993

The 73rd Constitution Amendment Act has made an effort to give some special powers to women in all the three tiers of *Panchayat Raj.* The rationale behind this amendment was that *the social and economic status of women could not be improved much without political power.* Women in the villages as well as towns need to be given some political power. They should be given their share in the decision taking process. The new *Panchayat Raj* is the part of the effort to empower women at least at the village level.

Reservation of One-Third Seats for Women

As per the provisions of the 73rd Constitution Amendment Act, one-third of the seats are reserved for women along with Scheduled Castes and the Scheduled Tribes. This is, indeed, a very bold step towards the empowerment of women. The provisions of the Act for the women are in no way less than a revolution. Women who have been working in the fields as casual labourers, washing vessels at home, fetching water for drinking, cooking food for family members, are now legally permitted to share on par with the males, the village matters of decision-making.

Reasons for or the Rationale Behind the Empowerment of Women

Why do women require empowerment ? Is it a right step to establish equality between men and women ? Does it help them to remove their disabilities ? Will it provide solutions to many of the problems with which they are suffering ? – A series of questions like these come before us demanding an answer. The following explanation gives us some answer for these questions.

1. ***Economic Exigencies*** **:** Women are found to be economically weak all over India. They are depending on their menfolk for the fulfilment of their basic economic necessities. Only an insignificant number of women, that too in urban areas, are gainfully employed. Even in the urban areas they are culturally dominated by their menfolk and they by themselves are not in a position to take independent decisions without consulting the males. Women who are working as officers or office bosses are forced to play a subordinate role at home. Majority of women are economically dependent on men and this fact has made them to become weaker. They require economic power to stand on their own legs on par with men.

2. ***Poor Literacy*** **:** In most of the underdeveloped and developing countries, women are found to be less literate than men. The higher rate of illiteracy of women has made them to become dependent on men and to play a subordinate role. Same situation prevails in India. According to 2001 census, rate of literacy among men in India is found to be 76% whereas it is only 64% among women. Rate of literacy among women was found to be very poorer up to 1970s. Only recently, women are becoming more and more aware of education. The rate of school drop-outs is also found to be comparatively higher in the case of women. Lack of education has led to their exploitation and negligence. Only literacy can help them to understand the constitutional and the legislative provisions that are made to strengthen them. *Thus, promoting education among women is of great importance in empowering them.*

3. *Negligence of Health* : Poor health on the part of women has also added to their weakness. Women consume less food and work more. They are shy of complaining about their ill health. They prefer to suffer silently than to approach a medical practitioner for obtaining medical assistance. This is mostly true in the case of a large majority of rural women. Surveys and studies have revealed that traditional importance shown towards the male children is also one of the reasons for neglecting the health of female children. Women are found to be maintaining relatively good health in the regions wherever the rate of female literacy is higher. Kerala provides here the best example. *Thus, from the health point of view also, women folk who are found to be weaker are to be made stronger.*

4. *Atrocities Against Women* : Women represent the weaker sex. This fact is also borne by the number of crimes and atrocities committed against them. There are cases of rape, kidnapping of girls, dowry harassments, molestation, sexual harassments, abuse of women, incest sex relations and so on. Women in all walks of life are discriminated against by men. They have become the victims of atrocities in any number of ways. *They require empowerment of all kinds in order to protect themselves and to preserve their purity and dignity.*

5. *UN Declaration and Women's World Congress* : The issue of the empowerment of women no more remains a regional matter and it has become an international issue. The UN Declaration of 1975 [The International Women's Year] compelled the national government *to shift its emphasis on women's programmes from welfare to development.* It was realised that undertaking of welfare programmes for women alone would not be of help unless supported by developmental programmes. Hence, the Declaration prescribed for the development of women.

Women's World Congress held at **Nairobi** in the year 1985 released a document recommending efforts towards empowerment of women. *"In this document, the question of women political participation was highlighted and it was recommended that 35% of the total seats should be reserved for women. It was also recommended that some posts should be reserved for women at the block and village level bureaucracy. On the economic front, a number of income generating schemes were introduced for women. In addition to that provisions were also made to certain proportion of women as beneficiaries in all the developmental schemes like the IRDP, JRY, TRYCEM, and so on."*[1]

It is clear from the above that a number of national and international events have exerted their influence on the issue of status of women culminating in the reservation of 33.3% of the total seats for them at the *Panchayat* level. The need for female empowerment was never so urgent as it is today. The 73rd Constitution Amendment Act is only a step towards the development of women.

A Brief Assessment of 73rd Constitution Amendment Act

The 73rd Constitution Amendment Act came into force in April 1993. The Act has not brought about miraculous changes as expected. Though it has created some awareness among women it suffers from many drawbacks. Some of them may be noted below.

1. ***Illiteracy*** : Since females literacy rate is very poor in our villages, female members at different tiers of *Panchayat Raj* are not able to assert themselves. On the contrary, they are forced to work according to the wishes of the male members.
2. ***Non-Availability of Women*** : It is very difficult to find out adequate number of females to work as members of the *Panchayat Raj* Committee. Either we will have to make a

1 **S.L. Doshi** and **P.C. Jain** *"Rural Sociology."* Page - 341.

compromise with less qualified and totally ignorant women or be content with inadequate number of women.

3. ***Corrupt Leadership and Bureaucracy*** : Our leadership is highly selfish and our bureaucracy is totally corrupt. In this situation, it is very difficult for the women to work and to achieve progress.
4. ***Bias towards Elites and Middle Class*** : The Act focuses its attention on women and weaker sections of the society no doubt. Women who are better off in one way or another alone can take the proper benefit of this Act. It means the creamy layer of the disadvantaged groups would corner most of the benefits of the Act. As a result, the weakest of the weak the poorest of the poor would continue to suffer in the pattern of the *Panchayat Raj* also.

VI. THE STATUS AND THE PROBLEMS OF INDIAN WOMEN: FUTURE PROSPECTS

The discussion regarding the status of Indian women has been there since decades. It is an acknowledged fact that though the Indian women are given importance in society, their status is not equal to that of men. Indian women are not able to lead a free and an independent life as their counterpart do in the West. Still it is astonishing to observe that Indian women who suffered from various problems and setbacks for more than 2000 years, have been trying to come out of their traditional shells and getting themselves ready to make the best use of the opportunities offered to them.

Future Prospects

What will happen to the status of Indian women in the near future? Will they become free from the problems with which they suffered for centuries? Can we expect a better status and brighter prospects for our women in the years to come? Will they be able to lead a free and independent life as their counterparts do in the West? Or, whether their status is going to deteriorate further in future? Will they attain equality with their menfolk? These are some of the questions currently being discussed in connection with the status of Indian women. On the basis of the existing state of affairs some observations and broad generalisations could be made regarding this issue.

1. *New Problems in Place of Old Ones* : The age-old problems of Indian women such as *child marriage, sati system, prohibition on widow remarriage, purdah system, devdasi system* etc. have almost disappeared. They have disappeared only to give room for some other problems of modern times such as *atrocities against women, rape, dowry harassments and deaths, immoral traffic of women, oppression and exploitation of 'dalit' and minority women, torture and harassment of women under trials, sexual harassment of employed women* etc. These problems have made it difficult for women to lead an equal life with men.

2. *Continued Dominance of Male Supremacy* : The Indian society continues to be a male dominated society. Though sex equality has been achieved by law, it is difficult to practise it socially. The belief that the biological and cultural roles of men and women are different, is very strong in India. As long as this belief persists, and the value of male dominance prevails, male-female equality cannot be achieved in the Indian context.

3. *Regional, Caste and Class Differences* : As **Andre Beteille** has observed that there is a close link between the statuses and problems of women on the one hand and the region, religion, caste and class to which they belong, on the other. These differences may continue in the coming years also. These differences are putting some hurdles on the way of Indian women developing some *"common interests"*.

4. *Relaxed Control Over Women* : As **S.C. Dube** has pointed out there are three principal areas in which controls are exercised on women:[1] (i) *Women's sexuality is controlled much more strictly than men's;* (ii) *There are restrictions on women's movements and contacts;* (iii) *Women's resources [labour and skills] need regulation and control.* On these three issues modern Indian women are more free, no doubt; but they are not equal to men. Most of them do not bother about attaining equality with men in these areas.

5. *Women Exploiting Women* : In the Indian context, we also find social situations in which women themselves are exploiting women in one way or another. **Examples:** *'Gharwalis'* or *'lady bosses'* in the brothel homes exploiting prostitutes, mothers-in-law harassing and torturing daughters-in-law. Situation is improving in this field for the educated women are becoming quite conscious of their rights.

6. *Lack of Powerful Women Organisations and Movements* : Indian women are forging ahead in the fields of education and employment. But they have not developed powerful women organisations nor movements to safeguard their interests. Neither at the national level nor at the state level, is such a strong women's organisation found. This situation has further added to the exploitation of women.

7. *No Need for Women's Liberation Movement* ? : On the basis of the existing social situations, it can be said that there is no possibility of a ***feminist movement***[2] or a women's liberation movement emerging out in India to assert the rights of women. Since Indian women give due importance to motherhood, rearing of children and household work which they consider as *"women's tasks"*; they do not appreciate *"women's liberation movement"* of the western type which fights for equality with men in all respects. As **Romila Thapar** has observed, *"women's liberation does not have any immediate relevance to the Indian social situation."*[3]

8. *No Protection to the Interests of Lower Class and Lower Caste Women* : In all discussions and debates relating to the status of Indian women, much is said about middle and upper class women and upper caste educated women. The statuses and problems of lower class and lower caste women who constitute the majority of womenfolk, are not given due importance. This only shows that our discussions are misleading, one-sided, partial and even prejudiced. Majority of Indian women who are illiterate and ignorant are not capable of changing their life-styles, beliefs and values overnight. They take time to change themselves. Hence, no revolutionary change can be witnessed in the overall social position of Indian women at least in the immediate future.

9. *Indifferent Attitude of the Governments and Political Leaders* : The measures taken and the programmes implemented by the Central and State governments so far in the direction of raising the status of Indian women and protecting their interests, are neither promising nor adequate. Laws and legislations alone cannot bring about desired changes in the society. Consistent and honest efforts on the part of people's representatives and social leaders are required to persuade people to accept new situations and challenges. Such efforts are conspicuously absent in India.

---

1 **S.C. Dube** *"Indian Society"* - Page: 95.

2 **Feminist Movement** refers to a women's movement which started in the 60s in the western countries to safeguard women's rights and further their interests.

3 **Romila Thapar** in article "Looking Back in History" in *"Indian Women"* - Page: 5-6.

Conclusion

Women in India are not yet equal to men. There is no legal or constitutional barrier to equality. There is only the social barrier. Women in India are more after a *"respectable"* and *"meaningful"* social status which is free from all sorts of exploitation. There is no urge in them to outsmart men. They want their interests to be protected and problems solved. As long as the problems of women remain as *"women's problems"* and not as *"societal problems"*, so long, attempts at the solution of these problems do not get the required speed.

Indian women are not very much after equality with men. But they expect a change in the attitude of men towards them and their status. On the contrary, *they expect greater freedom, better education, self-dependence, decent jobs, a proper treatment of women by menfolk, and a socio-economic environment free from all types of exploitation.* Our attempts to provide such a type of socio-economic environment to women will definitely influence their social status and the socio-economic conditions in the days to come.

Chapter 7

INDIAN CASTE SYSTEM

Caste as a Form of Social Stratification - Meaning and Definition of Caste - Factors which Facilitated the Growth of Caste in India - Theories of the Origin of Caste System - Traditional Characteristics of Caste - Functions of Caste - Changes in the Caste System : Changes in the Caste During the British Rule : (i) Pre-Industrial British Period; (ii) Pre-Independent Industrial Period. Caste in Independent India: (A) Changes in the Traditional Features of the Caste - (B) Changes in the Role of Caste - Causes for the Changes in the Caste System - Merits and Demerits of Caste - Dominant Castes and Their Role - Varna and Caste : Differences - Caste System and Estates System : Differences - Caste and Class : Differences - Caste and Jajmani System - Caste Among Non-Hindus in India : Castes Among Muslims, Christians, Sikhs and Jews - Future of Caste System.

The social structure of Indian society is characterised by a unique social institution called ***"Caste."*** It is one of the ancient social institutions prevailing in India since time immemorial. Institutions similar to "caste" have been reported from Sri Lanka, Pakisthan, Nepal and certain other countries, especially where Indians have migrated in large numbers. With these few exceptions there are no parallel systems for it any where in the world. The caste system which emerged out of the Varna system has withstood the onslaughts of time and continues to exist even at present. Caste system offers interesting issues for sociological studies, debates and discussions. It is difficult to understand the complex system of caste in its entirety though attempts are being made in this direction both by the Indian and Western scholars.

Controversies prevail among the scholars regarding the origin of caste. Different theories are established in this regard. Caste was there even during the period of Buddha and Mahaveera. In spite of their attempts to remove caste inequalities, the system continued to stay with its inherent inequality. The caste after successfully passing through the Medieval period, entered the British period from where it started undergoing relatively fast changes.

It is in this modern period, the winds of modernism and the attacks of Western Culture affected the caste system very much. The myth of unchangeability of caste is exploded. The strong forces of change such as industrialisation, urbanisation, modernisation, education, secularisation, etc. have, however, only initiated changes in the system. They could neither destroy nor weaken the system. Caste is only appearing in its new roles. Its existence is still in tact.

The belief that caste is a *"closed system"* in which social mobility is impossible, has no meaning today. **Prof. M.N. Srinivas,** an eminent Indian sociologist, has convincingly established the fact that social mobility is taking place both within and outside the framework of caste. He introduced new sociological terms such as *"Sanskritisation"* and *"Westernisation"* in support of his views. The two terms have assumed importance in the analysis of the socio-cultural mobility in the Indian society.

"Caste" as a topic of sociological study has roused the enthusiasm of many scholars and accordingly volumes of sociological literature has been published on caste. Right from the days of British rule, till today caste has been able to retain the curiosity of the scholars. "A large number of people including - Nesfield [1885], S.V. Ketkar [1946], Dutt [1931], Blunt [1931], O' Malley [1931], Hutton [1946], Ghurye [1932, 1950, 1969], M.N. Srinivas [1952], Panikkar [1961], Leach [1962], Wiser [1963], Dumont [1970], Mandelbaum [1972], and a host of others have studied one or more aspects of caste."[1] Caste as an institution and a social group has also been analysed in almost all the village studies undertaken by the scholars like, Ishwaran, S.C. Dube, M.N. Srinivas, Gough, Lewis, Marriot, Andre Beteille and others in the village studies undertaken by them especially after 1950s. Further, scholars with varied background such as - indological, anthropological, social, historical, and sociological, etc. have studied the caste system with their own perspectives. These studies have enriched the sociological literature a great deal.

CASTE : MEANING AND CHARACTERISTICS

Caste as a Major Form of Social Stratification

Sociologists have recognised three major types of social stratification: *caste, estates* and *social class.* Of these, ***caste system*** with all its peculiar features is to be found only in India. ***Estate system*** as a kind of stratification system existed in Europe during the Medieval period. This is no more in existence now. But ***social classes*** are almost universal. They are found in all the civilised, industrialised and literate societies of the world today. These two stratification systems, that is, *caste* and *class* decide largely the position that a man occupies in society. The extent of social mobility is mostly conditioned by them. The range of one's social contacts is almost fixed by one's caste or class. They influence and condition to a very great extent the way of life of people or their *"lifestyles"*.

Caste System is Peculiarly Indian

The *caste system*, the *joint family* system and the *village system of life* are generally regarded as the *three basic pillars of the Indian social system.* The caste system as a form of social stratification is peculiar to India. The caste is an inseparable aspect of the Indian society. It is peculiarly Indian in origin and development. There is no comparable institution elsewhere in the world for the caste system. Traces of caste, however were found in Ancient Egypt, Japan, Rome, Burma and Persia. It is said that even the ancient Persians, Siberians, Etruscans, Mexicans, Peruvians and Spartans had their own type of caste system. Some systems resembling caste are found at present in Burma, Polynesia, Massai and Somali of East Horn. But the caste system which we understand today with all its peculiarities is found in India alone.

Origin of the Word "Caste"

The views of **S.V. Ketkar**[2] seem to be authentic regarding the origin of the word *'caste.'* According to him, the word ***'Caste'*** is of Spanish and Portuguese origin. It has emerged from the

1 **H.K. Moulesh** and **G. Subramanya** *"Sociology of Indian Society."* Page - 49.

2 **S.V. Ketkar** *"History of Caste in India"* - Page: 12-13.

Spanish word ***"Casta"*** which means *'lineage'* or *'race'*. The word 'Casta' is derived from the Latin word ***"Castus"*** which means *'pure'*. The Spaniards were the first to use it, but its Indian application is from the Portuguese.

The word ***"caste"*** however, was, not used in its Indian sense till the 17th century. The Indian usage is the leading one now, and it has influenced all other usages. In Europe this word 'caste' was loosely applied to *the hereditary classes of Europe resembling the castes of India.* The Portuguese used this word to denote the Indian institution, as they thought such a system was intended *to keep purity of blood.* It is thus clear that the derivation of the word 'caste' is rather confusing. As **S.V. Ketkar** has remarked, the *"derivation of the word (caste) does not help us to understand what caste is."*

Factors which Facilitated the Growth of Caste System in India

Among the factors that have facilitated the continued existence and growth of caste system, the following are the most important :

1. The *geographic isolation* of the Indian Peninsula for a long time made the people to foster old customs, mores, traditions and superstitious beliefs which in turn encouraged the caste system to grow.

2. The *influence of religion* is one of the main factors that caused the continuation of the caste system. The Hindu Caste system is looked upon as a divine ordained institution. Beliefs in reincarnation and the doctrine of Karma also further strengthened the caste system.

3. The existence of *many races* in the country led to the formulation of many strict laws concerning discrimination since each race endeavoured to maintain its purity.

4. The *rural social structure* has its own impact on the caste. The unchanging, static rural social structure of India favoured the growth of caste system.

5. The *unwillingness of rulers* to enforce a uniform standard of law and custom and their readiness to recognise the varying custom of different groups as valid, also facilitated the growth of caste system.

6. *Lack of education* has contributed in no small measure to the growth of caste system. Illiteracy and ignorance have made the people to become orthodox and to implicitly accept the caste rules and restrictions.

7. Further, factors such as the *hereditary occupations; the desire of the Brahmins to keep themselves pure; ideas of exclusive family; ancestor worship; the sacramental meal; the deliberate economic and administrative policies followed by the various conquerors, particularly the British, clash of races, colour prejudices and conquest,* etc., also have contributed to the growth of caste system in India.

Definition of Caste

Caste is so complex a phenomenon which is difficult to define. Writers and scholars are not unanimous in their opinion regarding caste, its emergence, definition, characteristics etc. **Bailey** and **M.N.Srinivas** have not taken the trouble of finding a suitable definition for caste. *They view castes as "structures".* **Ketkar, Dutt** and **Opler** have given the characteristics of caste instead of defining it. For the purpose of understanding the concept we may consider a few definitions of caste.

1. **Ketkar:** *"A caste is a group having two characteristics; (i) membership is confined to those who are born of members and includes all persons so born, (ii) the members are forbidden by an inexorable social law to marry outside the group."*

2. **S.C. Dube:** *"It is better to use the term Jati to denote an endogamous unity with a more or less defined ritual status and some occupation traditionally linked to it."*
3. **D.N. Majumdar** and **T.N. Madan** have said that caste is a *'closed group'*.
4. **C.H. Cooley:** *"When a class is somewhat strictly hereditary, we may call it a caste."*
5. **A.W. Green:** *"Caste is a system of stratification in which mobility up and down the status ladder, at least ideally may not occur."*
6. **MacIver** and **Page:** *"When status is wholly predetermined, so that men are born to their lot without any hope of changing it, then class takes the extreme form of caste."*
7. **Sir Herbert Risley:** Caste is a *"collection of families, bearing a common name, claiming a common descent, from a mythical ancestor, human and divine, professing to follow the same hereditary calling and regarded by those who are competent to give an opinion as forming a single homogeneous community."*

TRADITIONAL CHARACTERISTICS OF CASTE

The caste system is highly complex in nature. As **Dr. G.S. Ghurye** says, any attempt to define caste is 'bound to fail because of the complexity of the phenomenon.' He describes six main characteristics of caste in his work *"Caste and Race in India."* The following are the main traditional features of the caste system.

1. Caste - As a Segmental Division of Society

The Hindu society is a caste-ridden society. It is divided into a number of segments called 'castes'. ***It is not a homogeneous society.*** Castes are groups with a well defined boundary of their own. The status of an individual is determined by his *birth* and not by selection nor by accomplishments. No amount of power, prestige and pelf can change the position of man. The membership of the caste is hence *unchangeable, unacquirable, inalienable, unattainable and nontransferable.* Further, each caste, has its *own way of life.* Each caste has its own customs, traditions, practices and rituals. It has its own informal rules, regulations and procedures. There were caste councils or *"caste panchayats"* to regulate the conduct of members also. The caste used to help its members when they were found in distress. Indeed, *'the caste was its own ruler.'*

2. Caste - As a Hierarchical Division of Society

The Hindu society is a *gradational one.* It is divided into several small groups called castes and subcastes. A sense of *'highness'* and *'lowness'* or *'superiority'* and *'inferiority'* is associated with this gradation or ranking. The Brahmins are placed at the top of the hierarchy and are regarded as *'pure', supreme* or *superior*. The degraded castes or the so called *"untouchables"* - [Harijans] have occupied the other end of the hierarchy. All over India neither the supremacy of the Brahmins nor the degraded position of the Harijans or *'outcastes'* has been questioned. It has been taken for granted. But regarding the exact position of the other intermediary castes, there have been disputes on the part of the members.

Caste *Panchayat* and its Functions

During the early days in every village every caste used to have its own Caste *Panchayat.* It consisted of five chosen senior members who enjoyed much social privilege and respect. The caste panchayat used to perform a number of *functions* among which the following may be noted:

1. Caste Panchayat used to make the members comply with caste rules and regulations.

2. Settling caste disputes and giving its final verdict on the issues referred to it were also its functions.
3. It gave punishments to those who violated caste rules and obligations.
4. Matters such as - *breaking the marriage promise, refusal on the part of the husband to take the wife to his house, cruelty to wife, adultery on the part of wife, killing the cows, insulting the Brahmins, having illicit sex relations with other caste people etc.,* were dealt with by the panchayat.
5. It used to give punishments such as *arranging dinner party for the fellow caste-men, imposing fine, purification, pilgrimage, outcasting etc.,* for the offenders.
6. The caste panchayat was also striving to promote the welfare of the caste members. Safeguarding the interests of the caste members was yet another function of the *panchayat.* These caste panchayats have become weak and ineffective nowadays.

The castes and sub-castes together make up the Hindu social system. Still in some respects each caste is isolated from the other. It is in a way semi-sovereign. The castes are a *"complete world"* in themselves for their members. The members are expected to be loyal to the caste. *Caste feeling is hence very strong.* It is very much stronger in rural areas than in the urban area. It is because of this the amount of community-feeling is restricted.

3. Restrictions on Feeding and Social Intercourse

Restrictions on Food Habits: The caste system has imposed certain restrictions on the food habits of the members. They differ from caste to caste. *Who* should accept *what* kind of food and from *whom* is often decided by the caste. For example, in North India, a Brahmin would accept *"pakka"* food *[cooked in ghee]* only from some castes lower than his own. But he would accept *"kachcha"* food *[prepared with the use of water]* at the hands of no other caste except of his own. As a matter of rule and practice, no individual would accept *"kachcha"* food prepared by a man of an inferior caste. Generally, any kind of food that is prepared by the Brahmin is acceptable to all the caste people. This factor explains as to why the Brahmins dominated the hotel industry for a long time. Further, restrictions are also there still on the use of certain vegetables for certain castes. Even today some traditional Brahmins do not consume onion, garlic, cabbage, carrot, beatroot, etc. Eating beef is also not allowed.

Restrictions on Social Relations: The caste system puts restrictions on the range of social relations also. The idea of *"pollution"* makes this point clear. It means a *touch of a lower caste man (particularly of an "Untouchable" / "dalit" / "Harijan") would pollute or defile a man of higher caste.* Even their shadow is considered to be enough to pollute a higher caste man. In Kerala for a long time, a *Nayar* could approach a *Nambudari* Brahmin but would not touch him. Further, a *Tiyan* was expected to keep himself at a distance of 36 steps from a Brahmin and a *pulaya* [Harijan] a distance of 96 paces. In Tamilnadu, the *Shanar* toddy tapper was expected to keep a distance of 24 paces while approaching a Brahmin. *This has resulted in the practice of untouchability.* This practice has made the lower caste people to be segregated completely from the higher castes.

4. Civil and Religious Disabilities and Privileges of Different Sections

Social and Religious Disabilities of Certain Castes: In the traditional caste society, some lower caste people [particularly, the Harijans] suffered from certain civil or social and religious disabilities. Generally, the *impure* castes are made to live on the outskirts of the city or the village. In South India, certain parts of the towns or the villages are not accessible to the *"untouchables."* It is recorded that during the *Peshwa* rule in Maharashtra the *Mahars* and *Mangs* [two so called "untouchable' castes] were not allowed within the main gates of Poona before 9-00 A.M. and after 3-00 P.M. The reason was that during the time their bodies would caste too long shadows which, if were to fall on the Brahmins, would defile them.

Socially, *"dalits"* or the so called ***"untouchables"*** are separated from other members. Even today, in many places they are not allowed to draw water from public wells. During the early days, public places like hotels, hostels, public lecture halls, schools, temples and theatres were not kept open for the lower caste people particularly, the *dalits.* Entrance to temples and other places of religious importance was forbidden for them. Educational facilities, legal rights and political representation were denied to them for a long time. In South India, restrictions were imposed on the mode of constructing houses and on the pattern of ornamentation. The toddy-tappers of Malabar were not allowed to carry umbrellas, to wear shoes or golden ornaments and to milk cows. They were forbidden to cover the upper part of their body.

Civil and Religious Privileges of Certain Castes: If the lower caste people suffer from certain disabilities, some higher caste people like the Brahmins enjoy certain privileges. Nowhere the Brahmins suffered from the disabilities cited above. They are given more liberty, because they are believed to be born *"pure"* and *"superior"*. The Brahmins never saluted others, but they always had the privilege of being saluted by others. They never even bowed to the idols of the lower caste people. Education and teaching were almost the monopoly of the higher caste people. Chanting the *Vedic mantras* was a great privilege of the Brahmins. The upper caste people in general, enjoyed social, political, legal and religious privileges.

5. Restrictions on Occupational Choice

In the caste-ridden society there is a *gradation of occupations* also. Some occupations are considered to be *superior* and *sacred* while certain others branded as *degrading* and *inferior*. For a long time, occupations were very much associated with the caste system. Each caste had its own specific occupation. The caste members were expected to continue the same occupations. Occupations were almost *hereditary.*

Weaving, shoe-making, oil-grinding, sweeping, scavenging, curing, hides, tanning, washing clothes, barbering, pottery etc., were considered to be somewhat *"degrading"*. Learning priesthood and teaching were the *prestigious* professions which mostly the Brahmins pursued. Individual talents, aptitudes, interests, enterprise, abilities and achievements were neglected. But agriculture, trade and labouring in the field were thrown open to all the castes. At the same time, no caste would allow its members to take up to any profession which was either degrading or impure.

6. Restrictions on Marriage

The caste system imposes restrictions on marriage also. *Caste is an endogamous group.* Endogamy is a rule of marriage according to which an individual has to marry *within* his or her group. Each caste is sub-divided into several *sub-castes, which are again endogamous. For example,* Iyers, Iyengars, Smarthas, Madhvas, Havik Brahmins, Kota, Shivalli, Kandavara Brahmins, etc., are all Brahmin sub-castes which are endogamous. Similarly, the Vokkaliga caste consists of Morasu, Hallikar, Nonaba, Gangadigar and other sub-castes. According to the rule of endogamy, a Shivalli Brahmin, for example, has to marry a Shivalli girl, an Iyengar, an Iyengar girl, and so on. Inter-caste marriages were strictly forbidden then. Even at present, intercaste marriages have not become popular. Violation of the rule of endogamy was strictly dealt with during the early days. This rule of endogamy has resulted in close in-breeding. Some writers like *Hutton* regards endogamy as the very essence of the caste system. Exception to this rule of endogamy is seen in places like Malabar and the hill parts of Punjab.

The caste provides for some kind of exogamous marriages also. They are briefly examined here.

Sapinda and Sagotra Exogamy: *Sapinda* and *Sagotra* marriages have been generally forbidden by the upper castes and *Sapinda* and *Sagotra* exogamous marriages have been insisted upon.

Sapinda Exogamy: In Hindu society marriage within the ***"Pinda"*** is prohibited. ***Pinda*** means common parentage. According to *Brahaspathi,* offsprings from *five* maternal generations and *seven* paternal generations constitute ***"Sapinda"*** and they cannot intermarry. This opinion, however, is not universally accepted. Though certain exceptions are there in South India, in North India, generally, *Sapinda* marriages do not take place. But *Sapinda* exogamy, that is, marrying outside one's *pinda* is commonly found.

Sagotra Exogamy **:** *Sagotra* exogamy, that is, marrying outside one's own *'gotra'* is very much prevalent among the upper castes such as the Brahmins and Kshatriyas. Marriage within the *gotra* is prohibited. This restriction has been imposed since people of one *gotra* are believed to have similar blood. Similarly, ***Sapravara*** marriages are also forbidden especially for the Brahmins. Persons belonging to the same *pravara* cannot intermarry. *People who utter the name of a common saint at religious functions are believed to belong to the same pravara.* The *pravara* is a kind of religious and spiritual bond. *Sapravar exogamy,* that is, marrying outside one's own *pravara,* has been imposed as a rule for the upper castes, especially for the Brahmins.

It should be noted that the above characteristics as explained by **Prof. Ghurye,** represent *"the traditional characteristics"* of caste. These characteristics were found to be associated with caste in their typical form before the system was exposed to the influence of modern values and ideologies such as *democracy, social equality, social justice, fundamental rights, individual liberty, equality of sex* etc. Due to the influence of these values and impact of some processes such as - *industrialisation, urbanisation, secularisation, modernisation, westernisation, sanskritisation,* etc. the caste system has undergone some major changes.

Theories of the Origin of Caste

Origin of the caste system is one of the most complex issues in sociological discussions. It is very difficult to say in precise terms the exact way in which the caste system originated. Researches held in this regard have not been able to establish the facts relating to the origin of the caste system beyond doubts. Discussions and debates are still going on at the level of the scholars regarding this issue. **Dr. D.N. Majumdar** pointed out at the inability of the scholars to arrive at a consensus on this issue when he says *"..........it is evident from the fact that after a century of painstaking and meticulous research in the history and function of the social system, we do not possess yet a valid explanation of the circumstances that might have contributed to the formation and development of this unique system."*[1] In spite of the controversies prevailing over the issue of the origin of the caste system, some of the scholars have established their own theories regarding it. Some of them can be mentioned below.

1. **Traditional Theory**
2. **Occupational Theory**
3. **Racial Theory**
4. **Other Theories**

1 **D.N. Majumdar** *"Races and Cultures of India."* Page - 284.

(a) ***Political Theory***

(b) ***Theory of Cultural Integration***

(c) ***Evolutionary Theory***

1. Traditional Theory

Ancient literature of India provides the main source for this theory. The traditional theory believes that the caste system has been established by the divine ordinance or atleast with the divine approval. The main source for this is to be found in the *Purushasukta* of the Rig-Veda. According to the *Purushasukta,* the four *Varnas*[1] originated from the four different parts of the *Prajapathi Brahma* or the *Viratpurusha* or the *Divine* or the *Supreme Being.* According to this theory, the *Brahmins* had emerged from the mouth of the Supreme Being, the *Kshatriyas* from the arms, the *Vaishyas* from the thighs, and the *Shudras* from the feet. These four *varna*s or social divisions have different functions according to the places of their origin. Mouth is the seat of speech or knowledge. Hence the task of the Brahmins is to serve society as teachers, as counsellors or advisors, as priests and as thinkers and conservers of cultural heritage. The arms or shoulders stand for strength, valour and heroism. So the primary task of the Kshatriya is to serve the society as a warrior, as a king, as a protector and as a benefactor. The Vaishyas have emerged from the thighs of the Creator. The thighs of the principal repository organs nearer the stomach. Hence the primary duty of the Vaishya is to provide food for the members of society and look after its economic well-being. The Shudras have emerged from the feet of Creator and hence their duty is to serve others just as the feet serve the other parts or organs of the body.

Smritikara Manu too has supported this theory. He has also given a classical interpretation to the origin of the *Varna.* In Bhagavadgita also we find a similar interpretation pertaining to the origin of the *Varna*s. In Chapter XIV *Sloka* 13 of Bhagavadgita, Lord Krishna himself says that He only created the four *Varna*s on the basis of *Guna* and *Karma.* Traditional explanations relating to the origin of the *Varna*s are also found in the *Shatapatha Brahmana* and also in the *Taittiria Brahmana.* Apart from the Vedic texts, various legends and *purana*s also give such explanations relating to the origin of the *Varna.*

Criticism **:** The traditional theory of the origin of the *Varna* has been criticised on various grounds. ***Firstly,*** the theory is criticised as unscientific because biologically it is impossible for anyone to give rise to the birth of a child through the mouth, shoulders, thighs or feet. ***Secondly,*** the theory considers four *Varna*s as four castes. If this is accepted, it would mean that *Varna* and not caste is the unit of the caste system. The real unit of the caste system is not the *varna* but *Jati,* which is a very small endogamous group. ***Thirdly,*** **M.N. Srinivas** considers this theory of the caste, which highlights the idea of caste as the four-fold division of the society, represents a gross oversimplification of facts. ***Fourthly,*** divergent explanations offered regarding the origin of the *Varna* quoting various religious, literary and other sources, are also contradictory.

But in spite of these controversies and criticisms, this theory has its own practical importance. In the words of **Dr. D.N. Majumdar,** *"if however we take the divine origin of the Varnas as allegorical explanation of the functional division of society, the theory assumes practical significance."*

2. Occupational Theory

"The Occupational Theory of Caste" was established by **Nesfield.** This theory tries to establish connection between the castes on the one hand, and the occupations on the other. The

1 The Traditional Theory or the mythical version of the origin of the caste regards four *varna*s in a loose manner as four castes.

theory assumes that castes originated in different occupations. According to this theory, if a particular group follows a hereditary occupation it evolves into a caste in course of time.

This theory also makes a distinction between different occupations depending upon the associated idea of relative purity and impurity. Those who performed pure or better and respectable tasks or jobs came to be distinguished from the others who pursued inferior or low grade occupations. Those who followed the so called *"pure"* occupations were regarded as superior. Those who were engaged in dirty or low grade occupations were looked down upon and were considered inferior. *As per the logic of this theory, the hierarchy, castes is associated with the hierarchy of occupations.* In this hierarchy of the superior castes follow *"pure"* occupations whereas inferior castes follow *"impure"* occupations.

Nesfield, thus made it clear that the difference of occupation was responsible for difference of caste. He emphatically concluded that occupation and occupation alone is responsible for the origin of the caste system. To quote his words : *"Function and function alone is responsible for the origin of caste system."*

Criticism **:** This theory of **Nesfield** is also criticised. ***Firstly,*** this theory fails to explain the differences in the social status of various castes which practise the same occupation. ***Secondly,*** it is wrong to consider the occupational factor alone as the cause of the birth of caste system. **Hutton** in this regard comments that *"occupation is not a cause but only a factor in the evolution of caste."* ***Thirdly,*** this theory does not take into account the racial and religious factors which played their role in the formation of the caste system. **Majumdar** in this context states that *"there may not be much racial difference between the higher castes as such, there may not be great variations of physical features in groups occupying a particular geographic region or part of it but some racial difference between high and low do exist and is apparent to one who knows the country and its people."*[1] ***Fourthly,*** **D.N. Majumdar** has also criticised **Nesfield's** idea of the hierarchy of castes in terms of the superiority or the inferiority of the occupations. He is of the opinion that *"the status of castes depends not on the superiority or the inferiority of occupations but upon the degree of purity of blood and the extent of isolation maintained by the groups."* [**Ram Ahuja.** Page - 260.]

3. Racial Theory

The main argument of the racial theory is that the different castes came into being because of irremovable racial differences. Scholars such as **Sir Herbert Risley, Dr. D.N. Majumdar** and **Dr. G.S. Ghurye** are the main protagonists of this theory.

The champions of this theory contend that the division into castes is founded on an original diversity of races. These scholars are of the opinion that caste came into practice after the Aryans settled down in India. The theory believes that the so called Aryans who came from outside were comparatively fair complexioned, tall and straight postured with a prominent nose. They had conquered the Gangetic Valley and in course of time the whole of North India, and defeated the natives of the land. The natives or the original inhabitants of India who were branded as, ***Dasyus*** or Servants were completely conquered by the Aryans and made to serve them. The difference between the Aryans and the non-Aryans [or Dravidians] was so prominent that it gave birth to different caste groups. The Aryans, for example, never allowed the non-Aryans to participate in the religious activities.

The Racial Theory has been presented in a classical form by eminent anthropologists such as **Sir Herbert Risley, Dr. G.S. Ghurye** and **Dr. D.N. Majumdar. Sir Herbert Risley** gave more

1 **D.N. Majumdar** as quoted by **Prof. M. Nanjammanni** in *"The Study of Indian Society."* Page 170.

importance to the invasion of Aryans into India and their efforts to conquer North India and to make the inhabitants their servants. **Dr. G.S. Ghurye** placed emphasis on the Brahmanical aspect [i.e., socio-religious aspect] of the Aryan way of life which distinguished the Aryans from the natives. Ghurye, for example, states that *"the various factors that characterise the caste society were the result in the first instance of the attempts on the part of the upholders of the Brahmanic civilisation to exclude the Aboriginals and the Shudras from religious and social communion with themselves."*[1] **Dr. D.N. Majumdar** placed premium on the purely racial and the anthropological aspects of Aryans.

Criticism : The Racial Theory has also been criticised. ***Firstly,*** according to **Hutton,** there is no consistency between the racial interpretation of this theory and the available facts. ***Secondly,*** the theory fails to give a proper explanation for the practice of untouchability. ***Thirdly,*** **Hutton** has sought to establish that hypergamy existed not only in India but also in other countries. Whereas it gave rise to the caste system in India but not in other countries. ***Fourthly,*** **Hutton** has also tried to show that the Brahmanical influence which is believed to have played a vital role in the genesis of caste system is not uniformly found in all the places. Further, it was very much dominant in few areas while it was virtually absent in a few other areas. ***Finally,*** it is argued that the racial theory is a major weakness in the sense that it highlights the importance of purely racial factors and conveniently forgets the efficacy of other equally important factors.

4. Other Theories

a) *Political Theory* : According to some European scholars who are normally considered the supporters of the traditional theory, the caste system came to be established as a result of the Brahmins' strategy to establish and maintain their superiority over the other people. Their theory is supported by the fact that the ritual social and religious supremacy of the Brahmins still continues in many parts of India.

(b) *Theory of Cultural Integration* : **Sharatchandra Roy** is the originator of this theory. He is of the opinion that the caste system evolved due to the integration and assimilation of different cultures. He also argues that there existed variations between different ethnic groups.

(c) *Evolutionary Theory* : **Denzil Ibbetson** is the champion of this theory. According to him, the caste system originated due to the interaction of three factors, namely – (i) *tribes,* (ii) *occupational guilds,* and (iii) *religion.*

It may be noted that these theories too have their own strengths and weaknesses. It is clear from the above explanation that there is no consensus among the scholars on the issue of the origin of the caste system. It can however be said that no single factor can satisfactorily explain the complex issue of the origin of the caste system. As **Hutton** has pointed out, *"the Indian caste system is the natural result of the interaction of a number of geographical, social, political, religious and economic factors not elsewhere found in conjunction."* Hence, a *"multiple-factor approach"* alone can give a somewhat satisfactory explanation regarding the origin of the caste system.

Functions of Caste

The ***"functional theory of social stratification"*** states that any type of stratification has its own purposes or functions to fulfil. Caste as a form of social stratification has come into existence to fulfil certain functional necessities. The existence and continuance of caste in India reveals that caste has still certain functions to fulfil. Then, what are the main functions of caste ? Scholars have

1 **Dr. G.S. Ghurye** as quoted by **Prof. M. Nanjammanni.** Page - 171.

given their own explanations in this regard. British ethnographer **Hutton** has discussed the functions of caste system from three points of view. They are mentioned below.

1. *Functions of caste from the point of view of an individual.*
2. *Functions from the point of view of caste as a group / community,* and
3. *Functions of caste from the point of view of society at large.*

1. Functions of Caste from the Point of View of an Individual

(i) *Caste system provides an individual a fixed social status in the society.* Individual members in a caste-ridden society are normally recognised and identified as members belonging to some or the other caste. It means on the very birth of an individual, the caste label is pasted on him.

(ii) *Caste provides for and limits the range of relations of its members.* Individual member is provided with a permanent body of associations which controls almost all his behaviour and contacts. His choice in marriage, his selection of friends, his food habits, family customs, practices, etc. are often dictated by the caste.

(iii) *Caste provides for occupational choices of the individuals.* In the rural context, caste even fixes or determines the occupations of individual members.

(iv) *Caste also guarantees social security to the individuals* in times of crises and difficulties. Members of the caste can always look to caste for cooperation, help and support.

2. Functions from the Point of View of Caste as a Group / Community

Caste influences group / community life also. This influence which the caste exerts, can be understood in the following manner.

(i) *Caste determines the membership of the community.* Individual members are born as members of the caste. Hence membership of any caste is limited by birth. It thus cannot be increased by strategies.

(ii) *Caste system assigns social statuses to the individuals.* Every caste has a definite status in the caste hierarchy. Individual members born into the caste are likely to obtain the same status. However, the exact status of each caste in the caste hierarchy differs from village to village and region to region.

(iii) *Caste system enables members to maintain unity.* Caste is a cohesive group. It is always interested in maintaining its position in the society. Caste unity also helps its members to raise the status of the caste in the hierarchy.

(iv) *Caste safeguards and transmits culture.* Each caste has its own way of life, that is, its own culture. It means it has its own norms, beliefs, values, customs, practices, etc. which it wants to preserve and transmit to the next generation. Caste also plays its role in transmitting the specialised skills, knowledge and behaviour patterns that are very closely associated with the hereditary occupations of the caste.

3. Functions of Caste from the Point of View of Society at Large

Caste system has its advantages not only for its individual members but also for the community and the society at large. In fact, caste is the very basis of the Hindu social organisation. The main functions of the caste towards the society at large are as follows.

(i) *Caste Provides the Basis of Social Order* : As **Dr. Majumdar** has pointed out caste has rendered a great service to the Hindu community by providing for it a common basis. Caste, joint family and the village system of life are traditionally regarded as the basès of the Indian social system. Individual members of the society always try to identify themselves with one or the other caste.

Caste has provided opportunities for solidarity and mutual support and it has also served as a status system. Castes themselves constitute the hierarchy of our social organisation. In this hierarchical system castes of all shades and gradations are found. Even now caste serves as a cementing force for group formation.

(ii) *Caste Contributing to the Dynamics of Division of Labour* : It is traditionally held that caste is based on a well established system of division of labour. Different tasks or works of the society are assigned to different castes. The tasks which represent the occupations are hereditary in nature. It means each caste has its own hereditary occupation. Hence it avoids confusion for the new members regarding the occupations or professions that they must undertake. The theory of the *Karma* also states that by performing dutifully all his social labours one can rise in the next birth to the higher level of the caste hierarchy.

(iii) *Caste Contributing to Political Stability* : Caste is often regarded as the means of political stabilisation. It keeps political order free from change. It was this function of the caste system which made **Abbe Dubois** to regard *caste system as being responsible for the preservation of India from complete barbarism; to provide a defence against despotism and to serve as a means of preserving the Hindu pattern of culture under the foreign rule.*

The caste system has enabled our society to keep the social system somewhat separate from the political system. Whereas this was not so in the Western countries. **S.C. Hill** writes : *"Whereas in Europe we are accustomed to think of the political and social systems of a country as one and the same thing, the Hindus regard them as distinct and separate............"* He further writes : *"Since social life in India is entirely independent of any form of political government, it remains permanently stable."*[1]

Further, the caste system has provided a strong protection to the Hindu society against the foreign invasions and onslaughts. **Hutton** in this connection writes : *"Indian society has survived a vast number of invasions, famines, revolutions, and social upheavals of all kinds, including conquests by invaders of alien religion, essentially antagonistic to Hinduism, and there can be no doubt that this is largely due to the caste system on which that society has constructed itself, system which often survived even conversion to Islam or Christianity."*[2] Thus it is clear that the caste system has conferred an unparalleled socio-political stability to the Indian society.

(iv) *Caste Integrates Society* : One of the major functions of the caste is that it combines various groups, institutions and sub-systems into a whole. According to **Hutton,** one important function of caste is to integrate the Indian society, to weld into one community the various component competing groups in it. **Hutton** has also said that India has developed a system of caste which, as a scheme of social adjustment, compares rather favourably with the European system of warring territorial nationalities.

Changes in the Caste System

The caste system which is an integral part of the Indian system, has a long standing history of its own. To understand how the system has come to be what it is today, one has to go back through

1 **S.C. Hill** *"Origin of Caste System in India"* [1930]. Page - 120.

2 **Hutton** as quoted by **Ram Ahuja** in *"Indian Social System"* [1993]. Page - 287.

the pages of history to trace its origin, evolution and growth. It is not easy to say precisely when, how and under what circumstances and pressures the system took its birth and developed. The task of tracing the evolution and growth of this system in precise and unambiguous terms is equally problematic. For the purpose of study, three main stages in the evolution of caste may be identified. They are mentioned below:

(i) ***Caste in Ancient Age*** [The period upto 1100 A.D. which is inclusive of Vedic Age, Post-Vedic Age and Puranic Age].

(ii) ***Caste in Medieval Age*** [The period between 1100 A.D. and 1757 A.D. which includes mainly the age of Muslim Rule in India].

(iii) ***Caste in Modern Age*** [The period after 1757 A.D. which includes the Pre-Independent British period and the period after Independence].

It is not within the framework of this book to discuss in detail the developments which took place in the caste system during the first two major periods. Hence the description is confined to the third stage, that is, *Caste in Modern Age.*

Caste in Modern Age [After 1757 A.D.]

The modern period in which some major developments took place in the caste system can be divided into two stages namely: (A) *Caste during British rule,* and (B) *Caste in Independent India.*

CHANGES IN CASTE SYSTEM DURING BRITISH RULE

Prior to the coming of the British, caste had grown into a powerful social institution with the dominance of Brahmins at the top of its hierarchy. The Hindu kings also upheld this institution with the help of their civil power. With the advent of the British as the political head of the society, the traditional form of the caste started taking a different shape.

The British Intention was to Rule and not to Initiate Reformative Changes

The British brought with them their own traditional form of government which was quite different from that of the Indian monarchical system. But as Christians the British *"... could not have much sympathy with the institutions of the Hindus"* - [Ghurye: Page - 270]. As prudent foreigners they were more interested in consolidating their power over a strange land and people rather than initiating reformative changes in its peculiar institutions such as *"caste"*. They introduced a system of education which did not demand of the learners any change of caste or religion. The *policy of comparative non-interference* followed by the British made the lower castes revolt against the Brahmin supremacy. *Growth of modern industrial organisation* and the *rapid spread of urbanisation* further altered the social situation. This situation made it inevitable for people of different castes, classes and religions to live in close congregations in cities. With this background the changes in the caste system during the British rule can be studied in two stages: *(A) Pre-Industrial British Period 1757-1918 A.D., and (B) Pre-Independent Industrial Period - 1918-1947 A.D.*

(A) Pre-Industrial British Period [1757 to 1918 A.D.]
Beginning of the British Period

The **East India Company** of the British obtained from the Moghal rulers some commercial privileges in the beginning of the 17th century. It tightened its political hold over the whole of

India within 7 to 8 decades. The appointment of **Warren Hastings** in 1774 as the first Governor General of India, marked the beginning of the British Age in India.

1. Declining Hold of the Caste Panchayats

After consolidating their power the British introduced through out India *uniform legal, legislative* and *judicial systems.* The British transferred the judicial powers of the caste councils to the civil and criminal courts which affected the authority which the Panchayats had held over the members. Questions of assault, adultery, rape and the like were taken before the British Courts for decision. In civil matters such as marriage, divorce, caste-based occupational disputes, disputes between husband and wife, parents and children etc., the intention of the British was to be guided by the caste-customs. But in actual practice, various decisions of the High Courts set aside the authority of the caste.

2. Influence of Social Legislations on Caste

Some of the legislations which the British introduced shook the integrity of the caste system. Specific mention can be made of a few of the legislations such as the following.

(i) ***The Caste Disabilities Removal Act of 1850*** [which served to remove some of the disabilities associated with caste including the practice of untouchability].

(ii) ***The Child Marriage Restraint Act of 1860*** [which declared child marriages unlawful].

(iii) ***The Special Marriage Act of 1872*** [which legalised intercaste and inter-religious marriages].

(iv) ***The Hindu Widows Remarriage Act of 1876*** [which gave legal permission for widows to remarry];

These and many other socio-legal measures of the British government gave a severe blow to the tight hold of the caste system. But as **Prof. Ghurye** has pointed out, all these measures were taken by the British Government *purely for administrative convenience and it had no desire to reduce the rigidity of caste.*

3. Impact of Social Reform Movements

Some of the social reform movements launched by social reformers during the British rule also attacked the caste system and its inequalities.

(i) ***The Brahma Samaj*** founded by ***Raja Ram Mohan Roy*** in 1820 and developed by Devendranath Tagore and Keshav Chandra Sen condemned the barriers of caste divisions, idol worship, human and animal sacrifices. It advocated universal brotherhood of man.

(ii) ***The Prarthana Samaj*** launched by ***Justice Ranade*** devoted its attention to social reforms such as inter-dining, inter-caste marriage, remarriage of widows, etc.

(iii) ***The Arya Samaj*** founded by ***Swami Dayananda Saraswathi*** in 1875 repudiated the caste restrictions, protested against prohibition of sea-voyages and insisted that even the Shudras could study the Vedas. It tried to remodel the Hindu society on the basis of the Vedic ideals. It functioned as a militant force to protect the Hindu society from the *"onslaughts of Western rationalisation"*. It started the ***"Shuddhi"*** (purification) movement to re-Hinduise the converts, the fallen, the outcastes and other externals.

(iv) ***The Ramakrishna Mission*** started by ***Swami Vivekananda,*** a great disciple of Sri Ramakrishna Paramahamsa, in 1897 represents *the synthesis of the ancient or oriental and the modern or western.* Vivekananda who had imbibed in himself Raja Ram's rationalism and Dayananda Saraswathi's spirituality, was pragmatic in his approach. He condemned caste inequalities, exploitation of lower castes and women. He stressed on education, self-reliance and freedom of women. He even predicted that the Shudras ["Shramiks" or "labourers"] would dominate in the years to come.

(v) ***Other Reform Movements:*** Other social movements such as - (i) ***Jyotirao Phooley's*** (1873) **"Satyashodak Samaj"**; (ii) ***Annie Besant's*** **"Theosophical Society"**; (iii) ***Maharshi Arvind Ghosh's*** **"Divine Life Society"** - also served to loosen the hold of caste restrictions.

What is to be noted is that these reform movements *"did not succeed in removing the rigidity of the caste system in this period...."* [Ram Ahuja - Page: 277]. However, they could only affect some of the structural features of caste.

4. Spread of English Education and Influence of the Western Ideas

Spread of English education exposed Indians for the first time to the Western World. The popular Western ideas and values such as - *"liberty, equality and fraternity"*, democracy, rationalism, individualism, women's liberation, secularism, humanitarianism etc. made their inroads into India. These ideas had deeply influenced the Western educated Indians. People who had hitherto been the targets of atrocities, deprivation, exploitation and humiliation could now voice their protest by asserting their rights. Increasing influence of science and technology added greater strength to the growing awareness of the masses.

5. Birth of the Backward Castes Movement

Movements of a more militant nature against caste started with the founding of ***Satyashodhak Samaj*** in 1873 by **Jyotirao Phooley** of Poona, a man of Mali caste. The main purpose of this Samaj was to assert the worth of man irrespective of caste. Through his writings and practices he led a revolt against the tyranny of the caste system and the hegemony of the Brahmins. He appealed to the non-Brahmin castes not to engage any Brahmin priest to conduct their marriage ritual. He tried to reduce the enormous ritual system into a simple procedure. He perceived the necessity of educating the lower-caste people. He could translate his vision into practice when he opened a primary school for the so called untouchables in Poona [the very centre of orthodoxy] as early as in 1851.

Phooley's was not just a revolt against caste to cast off the domination of the Brahmins. In his writings, he demanded representation for all classes of the Hindus in all the local bodies, services and the institutions. Phooley's struggles marked the beginning of the non-Brahmin movement, which is also called *"backward classes movement."*[1]

6. Influence of Census System

The British introduced the decennial census system in 1870s, in order to collect and present information regarding the Indian population. Though this statistical information is of great demographic importance, it provided yet another chance for the British to pursue their *"policy of divide and rule"*. Census reports threw light on the numerical strength of each caste and religious group and their relative social status. Various ambitious castes quickly perceived the chances of raising their status through the census. They organised conferences of their members and formed councils to take steps to see that their status was recorded in *"honourable"* manner. *The census system thus contributed to sharpen the caste consciousness.* The census-reporter for Madras wrote as early as in 1911 that the census had witnessed *"an extra-ordinary revival of the caste-spirit*

1 According to **M.N. Srinivas**, the term *"backward classes movement"* must be understood in the Indian social context, as a kind of struggle waged by the *"lower castes"* against the supremacy of the Brahmins. It also represents a concerted effort on the part of the lower castes to improve their social, economic, educational and political statuses.

in certain aspects." Numerous caste *"sabhas"* sprang up, each keen to assert the dignity of the social group which it represented. The total result of the census had been *"a livening up of the caste spirit"* [Ghurye. Page - 279.] The grading of the caste groups in the census had provided a good rallying point for each caste to preserve the caste spirit.

(B) Pre-Independent Industrial Period [1919-1947]

The caste system underwent a few more significant changes when India stepped into the 20th century. The role of three factors in bringing about such changes is worth mentioning here.

1. Influence of Industrialisation: Decline of Caste-Based Occupational System

The advent of Industrial Revolution also affected Indian socio-economic conditions. The British brought modern machinaries and introduced factory system of production. New industries, occupations, employment opportunities, salary-based service system came to be established. The growth of industries destroyed the old crafts and household industries and provided for countless ways of earning livelihood. Introduction of railways, telegraph and laying of roads helped trade and commerce. People of all castes started making use of the new economic opportunities.

Industrialisation also resulted in occupational and geographic mobility. Movement of people from the compact ancestral village to the towns and cities started breaking down many of the caste norms. Crowded trains and buses could bring together lakhs of people of all castes and left little room for the niceties of ceremonial purity. Taboos against some foods and accepting food and water from persons of lower castes, also started weakening. Hotel system of food and hostel system of residence served to bring together people of different castes. The *"jajmani"*[1] system of economy which had made *economic interdependence of different castes, started declining. It slowly gave place to the capitalist system of economy.* These industrial and their concomitant developments made caste-members to come out of the hold of caste-based occupations and to resort to the new occupational avenues based purely on personal preferences and choices.

Influence of industrialisation was, no doubt, widespread. But its impact was not uniform and absolute on all the basic features of caste. *For example,* its impact on the endogamous nature of marriage and various marriage practices, rules and beliefs was almost negligible. Rapid industrialisation never led to the automatic dissolution of the caste system and its progressive replacement by a class system as its way believed by some Western scholars. *The economic aspects of caste underwent swift changes whereas its socio-cultural aspects never got changed with equal speed.*

2. Impact of Urbanisation

In order to reap the benefits of new educational and occupational opportunities people started moving towards towns and cities in large number. The necessities of city life relaxed the commensal taboos imposed by caste and lessened the dominance of Brahmins. As **Srinivas** has pointed out, the non-Brahmins refused to show the same respect to the Brahmins which they used to show earlier. The growth of city life with its migratory population brought about changes in

1 ***Jajmani System***: This refers to a system of distribution whereby high caste landowning families [called *"jajmans"*] are provided services and products by various lower castes such as carpenters *[Badhai],* barbers *[Nai],* potters *[Kumhars],* blacksmiths *[Lohar]* washerman *[Dhobis],* etc. The servicing people called *"Kamins"* are paid in cash or in kind [grains, fodder, clothes, animal products like milk, butter, etc.] It is a system governed by relationship based on reciprocity in intercaste relations in villages. *Ref:* **Ram Ahuja's** *"Indian Social System"* - Page: 322.

the rigidity of the caste system [Ghurye - Page: 262]. **Kingsley Davis** also *"held that the anonymity, congestion, mobility, secularism and changeability of the city make the operation of caste virtually impossible"* - [Prof. Ram Ahuja - Page: 280]

3. Influence of Freedom Movement and the Role of Gandhiji

Indian freedom struggle also altered the character of caste to some extent. The freedom struggle organised by the Indian National Congress brought together people of different castes, classes, religions and regions under one banner. The Congress led by Gandhiji launched a campaign against untouchability and roused the conscience of the people against its practice. Participation of the lower castes in the freedom struggle boosted their image.

At the fag end of the British rule, though the traditional influence of caste started declining, its organisational strength was increasing. As **Ghurye** observed, *"At about the end of the British rule in India, caste-society presented the spectacle of self-centred groups more or less in conflict with one another"*. [Ghurye - Page: 303]

CASTE IN INDEPENDENT INDIA [After 1947]

The political independence of the country, besides the process of industrialisation, urbanisation, secularisation etc. brought in a series of changes in the caste system. These changes can be classified into two categories: (A) *Changes in the traditional features of caste;* (B) *Changes in the role [or functioning] of the caste.*

(A) Changes in the Traditional Features of Caste

Caste has assumed a different form in the modern times. Some of the traditional features [described earlier] have been radically altered. Here is a brief survey of the changes that have taken place in caste system after Independence.

1. The *religious basis of the caste has been attacked.* Caste is no more believed to be divinely ordained. It is being given more a social and secular meaning than a religious interpretation.

2. *Restrictions on food habits have been relaxed.* Distinction between *'pakka'* food and *'kachcha'* food has almost vanished. Food habits have become more a matter of personal choice than a caste rule. Still commensal taboos are not completely ignored especially in the rural areas. Interdining has not become the order of the day.

3. *Caste is not very much associated with hereditary occupations.* Caste no longer determines the occupational career of an individual. Occupations are becoming more and more *"caste-free"*. Even Brahmins are found driving taxis, dealing with foot-wears and running non-vegetarian hotels, bars and so on.

4. *Endogamy, which is often called the very essence of the caste system, still prevails.* Inter-caste marriages though legally permitted, have not become the order of the day. As **K.M. Kapadia** says, *"there is an indifference to the intercaste marriages if not tacit acceptance by the society"*.

5. The special civil and religious privileges which the Brahmins enjoyed are *no more being enjoyed by them.* The Constitution of India has removed all such privileges and made all castes equal.

Most of the legal, political, educational, economic and other *disabilities* from which the lowest caste people had suffered, have been removed by the constitutional provisions. They are given special protection also. *Adult franchise* and *"reservation"* have given them a strong weapon to protect their interests.

6. *Caste continues to be a segmental division of Hindu society.* Caste with its hierarchical system continues to ascribe *statuses* to the individuals. But the twin processes of *Sanskritisation* and *Westernisation* have made possible mobility both within and outside the framework of caste.

7. *Caste panchayats, which used to control the behaviour of caste-members, have either become very weak or disappeared.* Though they are often found here and there in the village areas, they are almost non-existent in the urban areas.

8. *Restrictions imposed by the caste on social intercourse are very much relaxed.* Distinction between *'touchable'* and *'untouchable'* is not much felt especially in the community of literate people. However, instances of practice of untouchability are heard in the rural areas.

9. *Other Important Changes*

(i) Though the dominance of caste is still found in villages *it no longer depends upon its ritual status.*

(ii) *Casteism* which is associated with caste, instead of disappearing in the wake of modernism, *has become still stronger.*

(iii) The *'jajmani'* system which used to govern the inter-caste relations especially in the villages has become very weak. In many places it has vanished. In place of inter-caste dependence, inter-caste strifes are found.

(iv) *Caste has lost much of its hold over the social usages and customs* practised by its members.

(v) *Caste today does not dictate individual's life* nor does it restrict newly valued individual freedom. Hence it no longer acts as a barrier to the progress of an individual.

(B) Changes in the Role of Caste

The caste system in its attempts to adjust itself to the changed conditions of life has assumed new roles. Besides industrialisation and urbanisation, other factors such as Westernisation, Sanskritisation, re-organisation of Indian states, spread of education, socio-religious reforms, spatial and occupational mobility and growth of market economy have greatly affected the caste system. Changes in the role of caste must also be understood in the light of the influence of these factors.

1. *Decrease in the Rigidity of Caste and Untouchability* : Caste had become less rigid now. Social and religious privileges and disabilities born of caste are no longer recognised in law. They are partially practised in custom. Similarly, occupations have become more a matter of personal choice than a matter of caste rule. They are no more hereditary in character. Beliefs, practices, customs, rituals, morals, manners, food habits, dress habits, etc. associated with caste have drastically changed.

The practice of untouchability which is often called *"the hatefullest expression of caste"*, has been declared a punishable offence. The difference between *"touchable"* and *"untouchable"* is not very sharp. There is greater tolerance towards the members of lower castes. Conditional provisions such as *"reservation"* has given new strength to the lower caste people. Upper caste people are jealous of lower caste people for they are not getting lot of politico-economic opportunities.

2. *Changes in the Commensal Rules* : Commensal rules refer to the norms relating to the food habits of the people. Caste no more controls the food habits of the people. The commensal taboos, that is restrictions imposed on interdining, has been relaxed. Distinction between *"pakka food"* and *"kachcha food"* is no more found. The Brahmins' dominance of hotel industry is fading away. People give more importance today to cleanliness, service, facilities, taste of the food rather than to the caste membership of the man running the hotel. Brahmins [except the orthodox ones] and other upper caste people have the least hesitation in visiting the houses of the lower caste people and accepting the food at their hands. Brahmins also invite their friends and other important persons, who belong to the lower castes to their homes and share food along with them. Today, Brahmins are ready to interdine with *"clean"* Shudras, but not generally with members of the *"polluting castes."* Still majority of the Brahmins remain as vegetarians.

3. *Growth of Classes within Castes* : India is a caste as well as a class-ridden society. Both the types of stratification, that is, caste and class, are found working here simultaneously. At one stage in our social history, the upper castes represented the wealthy class, and lower castes, the poor class. Now the situation has changed. Today such major caste, whether lower or upper, consists of poor as well as wealthy members. Many individuals and families belonging to the lower castes have become richer today by making use of new socio-economic, political and educational opportunities. Similarly, in the circle of upper castes sizeable number of individuals and families still remain as poor. Thus, with the inclusion of the economic dimension, caste appears like a manifold class system.

4. *Increase in the Organisational Power of Caste* : Education makes people liberal, broad-minded, rational and democratic. Educated people are believed to be less conservative and superstitious. Hence it was expected that with the growth of literacy in India, caste-mindedness and casteism would come down. On the contrary, *caste-consciousness of the members has been increasing. Every caste wants to safeguard its interests. For fulfilling this purpose castes are getting themselves organised on the model of labour unions.*

Today, every caste wants to organise itself. Such caste organisations are on the increase. Mainly to cater to the educational, medical and religious needs of their members, these organisations are running hostels and hospitals, schools and colleges, reading-rooms and libraries, dharmashalas and temples and so on. These caste-based organisations are also *trying to project the leadership* of some of their members to serve as their spokesmen.

5. *Political Role of Caste* : Caste and politics have come to affect each other now. Caste has become an inseparable aspect of our politics. In fact, it is tightening its hold on politics. Elections are fought more often on the basis of caste. Selection of candidates, voting analysis, selection of legislative party leaders, distribution of ministerial portfolios etc., are very much based on caste. Even the communist parties which project the ideal of a casteless and classless society are also not an exception to this. Politics of each state, as **M.N. Srinivas** says, is virtually the politics of confrontation of its *"dominant castes"*. Thus, unless one knows the political confrontation between the dominant castes such as Lingayats and Vokkaligas in Karnataka and Reddys and Kammas in Andhra Pradesh, one cannot understand the politics of these two states. M.N. Srinivas also makes a distinction between *caste at the ritual level* and *caste at the political level.* Caste at the ritual level is a smaller unit than the caste at the political level.

6. *Protection for Scheduled Castes and other Backward Classes*: The constitution of India has made enough provisions to protect the interests of scheduled castes and tribes. They are offered more political, educational and service opportunities through the reservation policy. Seats are reserved for them from Mandal panchayat to Parliament and in all government departments. Though the reservation policy is against the declared goal of establishment of a casteless society, all political parties have supported it, mostly for political purposes. According to **M.N. Srinivas**,

"The provision of constitutional safeguards to.... scheduled castes and tribes has given a new lease of life to caste." These provisions have made some of them develop vested interests to reap permanently the benefits of reservation. They are also tempting many other castes to bring pressure on the government to declare them as belonging to the category of scheduled castes.

7. *Sanskritisation and Westernisation* : As M.N. Srinivas has pointed out, two important trends are witnessed in caste - *the process of Sanskritisation* and that of *Westernisation.* The former refers to a process in which the lower castes tend to imitate the values, practices and other life-styles of some dominant upper castes. The latter denotes a process in which the upper-caste people tend to mould their life-styles on the model of Westerners. [*Note* : For more details about these two processes, please refer to **Chapter No.8.**]

8. *Backward Classes Movement* : The non-Brahmin castes today are getting themselves more and more organised to challenge the supremacy of the Brahmins and to assert their rights. The establishment of *"Satyashodhak Samaj"* by **Jyotirao Phooley** in Poona in 1873 marked the beginning of such a non-Brahmin movement. This movement against the Brahmin supremacy by the lower castes came to be known as *Backward Classes Movement.* [*Note* : For more details see **Chapter No.10.**] In the beginning, the main aim of this movement was to limit the Brahmin monopoly in the two fields such as *education* and *appointment to government posts.*

The Backward Classes Movement has become a vital political force today. Its influence has changed the political scenario of the country. This movement has made the Brahmins politically weak and insignificant especially in Kerala and Tamilnadu. This movement has also brought pressure on different political parties to create special opportunities for the lowest caste people enabling them to come up to the level of other higher castes. Due to this pressure, *Backward Classes Commissions* were established at Central and State levels which recommended *"reservation"* for backward castes/classes.

9. *Competitive Role of Castes* : Mutual interdependence of castes which existed for centuries and was reinforced by the institutional system of *"jajmani"*, is not found today. As **M.N. Srinivas** points out, the *"vertical solidarity"* of castes has been replaced by *"horizontal solidarity"*. *"Live and let live"* policy which was once associated with the caste makes no sense today. On the contrary, each caste looks at the other with suspicion, contempt, and jealousy and finds in it a challenger, a competitor. Excessive *caste-mindedness* and *caste-patriotism* have added to this competition. The economic base of a caste and its hold over the political power virtually determine the intensity of this competitiveness. This competitive spirit further strengthens caste-mindedness.

10. *New attempts to strengthen caste-loyalty, caste-identity, caste-patriotism and caste-mindedness* : Today, caste organisations are increasing and are making every attempt to obtain the loyalty of their members and to strengthen their *caste-identity* and *solidarity.* Some such attempts can be cited here.

(i) *Though Caste Panchayats are dwindling, caste organisations are on the increase.* Some of these organisations have their own written constitutions and managing committees through which they try to preserve some of the caste rules and practices.

(ii) *Caste organisations run their own papers, bulletins, periodicals, monthlies etc.,* through which they regularly feed information to the members regarding the activities of caste organisations and achievements of caste-members.[1]

---

1 As **Ghurye** has stated [Page: 443-44] between 1950-60, there were about 913 papers in Hindi, Gujrathi and Marathi speaking areas out of which at least 85 were caste-based.

(iii) Attempts are also made to increase caste integration through the *establishment of caste based trusts and trust-units.*[1] These trusts arrange annual gatherings, get-togethers, annual dinners, occasional festival celebrations. They provide shelter to the needy members of the caste. They offer scholarships to the poor students of the caste. Some of them run schools, colleges, hostels, maternity-homes for caste members and so on.

(iv) The occupational castes are making determined efforts *to improve the economic conditions of caste members* by establishing *co-operative credit and industrial societies.*

(v) Caste organisations *collect regular subscription from the members,* arrange annual conferences, discuss matters and issues affecting caste interests and caste solidarity and organise agitations and protest meetings against the governmental policies if they were to damage caste interests. In states like Bihar, some upper and some lower castes have formed their own *'senas'* [militant groups] to protect their interests.

CAUSES FOR THE CHANGES IN CASTE SYSTEM

The caste system has undergone vast changes in modern times. Factors that contributed to the changes in the caste system are briefly examined here.

1. ***Uniform Legal System*** **:** The uniform legal system introduced by the British made the Indians feel that *"all men are equal before the law".* A number of legislations which the British introduced also struck at the root of the caste system. Independent India followed the same legal system. The Constitution of India has not only assured equality to all but also declared the practice of untouchability unlawful [Articles 15, 16, and 17]. Articles 16, 164, 225, 330, 332, 334, 335, 338 and the 5th and 6th Schedules of the Constitution provide for some special privileges to the Scheduled Castes and Scheduled Tribes to enable them to come up to the level of other upper castes.

2. ***Impact of Modern Education*** **:** The British introduced the modern secular education in a uniform way throughout India. In independent India educational facilities are extended to all the caste people. The lowest caste people are also entitled to avail themselves of these facilities. Seats have been reserved for the children of the Scheduled Castes in the educational institutions from primary to university level. Thus, modern education opened the doors of change for the caste:

(i) Modern education has *given a blow to the intellectual monopoly of a few upper castes, particularly of the Brahmins.*

(ii) Modern education provided for *wide job opportunities for the lower castes* and helped them to come out of the degrading professions to which they were clinging on for centuries. It set in motion a very high degree of occupational mobility.

(iii) It has *created an awareness among people* and *weakened the hold of caste* over the members. It does not, however, mean that the modern educated people are completely free from the hold of the caste.

3. ***Industrialisation, Urbanisation and Westernisation*** **:** During the British rule itself, Western science and technology and along with them, the modern mode of the factory system of production had made inroads into India. Introduction of Western technology led to the growth of industries. *"Industrialise or perish"* became the popular slogan in the beginning years of our

---

1 **Ghurye** has stated that he himself counted not less than 1700 caste-based trust-units in Bombay and Greater Bombay Sub-urban District in the published report of the Charity Commissioner of Maharashtra in 1954.

administration soon after independence. Heavy machineries were imported and gigantic industries were established. Development of technology resulted in the creation of vast non-agricultural job opportunities. *This new economic opportunity weakened the hold of the upper caste people who owned vast lands.*

Urbanisation, that is, growth of cities had drawn people of all castes and classes together and made them to stay together in common colonies, campuses and sometimes, in common buildings ignoring many of their caste differences. Industrialisation created attractive avenues and in order to make use of the new economic opportunities, people of different castes, classes and religions, started working together in factories, big industries, offices, workshops, business firms, service centres, hotels, banks, etc. This situation led to the relaxation in many of the caste rules.

Westernisation, particularly the Western technology has brought in the *modern means of transport and communication system.* Modern means of transport such as train, bus, ship, aeroplane, truck, etc. have been of great help for the movement of men and materials. Caste rules relating to the practice of purity and pollution and untouchability could no longer be observed. Modern means of communication such as newspapers, post, telegraph, telephone, radio, television, e-mail, internet, etc. have helped people to come out of the narrow world of caste.

4. *Freedom struggle and the establishment of democracy* : The freedom struggle waged against the British brought all the caste people together to fight for a common cause. Establishment of democratic type of government soon after Independence gave yet another blow to the caste by extending equal socio-economic opportunities to all without any discrimination.

5. *Rise of non-Brahmin movement* : A movement against the Brahmin supremacy was launched by **Jyothirao Pooley** in 1873. This movement became popular in course of time particularly in the South. It created an awareness among the lower castes and instilled in them the feeling of *"self-respect".* This movement which became a great political force, brought pressure upon the government to establish Backward Classes Commissions at the Central and State levels. The recommendations made by these commissions and their implementation provided vast scope for the lower castes to achieve progress.

6. *Other Important Causes*

(i) Social Legislations: A series of social legislations introduced by the British as well as by the Indian governments [such as the *Caste Disabilities Removal Act of 1872, The Hindu Marriage Act of 1955, The Untouchability Offences Act of 1956,* etc.] directly and indirectly altered the nature of the caste system.

(ii) Social Reform Movements: Various social reform movements [such as *Satyashodhak Samaj, Brahma Samaj, Arya Samaj, Sri Ramakrishna Mission* etc.] launched during the second half of the 19th and the beginning of the 20th centuries have been able to remove the rigidity and some of the evil practices associated with the caste system.

(iii) Impact of the West: Influence of the Western thought and particularly the ideas of - rationalism, liberalism, humanitarianism, egalitarianism etc. made the educated Indians to come out of the clutches of the caste.

(iv) Threat of Coversion: Social disabilities imposed on the lower castes made some of them to get themselves converted to either Christianity or Islam. Pressure tactics and temptations further added to this conversion process. The threat of conversion compelled the upper castes to relax many of the caste rigidities so that they could hold back the lower caste people who were getting ready for conversion.

(v) Improvement in the status of women, evolution of new social classes [working class, middle class and capitalist class] and radical changes in the system of division of labour especially in the rural areas have further loosened the roots of caste system.

Merits and Demerits of Caste

The Indian caste system which has become all pervasive and all influential has its own merits and demerits. Some of its merits and demerits may be analysed here.

Merits of Caste

1. *Harmonious Division of Society* : Caste represents the harmonious division of society based on the principle of division of labour and occupation. Occupations are normally hereditary in a caste ridden society. Since occupations are hereditary each caste provides the needed training and guidance for its members to continue the caste based occupations. Occupational skills and knowledge are transferred from elder generation to the younger generation in an informal manner.

2. *Provision of Social Security and Protection* : Caste provides security and protection to its members in times of crises, illness, difficulties, natural or economic hazards and so on. Caste has given this kind of support not only to its individual members but also to the entire Indian society particularly when it was invaded and attacked by the alien forces. Caste has given strength to the Indian society to withstand *"the shocks of politics and the cataclysms of nature."*

3. *Supports Co-operation and Co-existence* : Caste promotes the spirit of co-operation and fellow-feeling atleast within its range. It helps the poor, the needy and strengthens group sentiment. Status, power, wealth, name and fame also do not come in the way of the caste members to get united in the name of caste.

Caste has provided a pattern for numerous competing groups to co-exist side by side with little or no conflict. "There have been numerous and diverse races, religions, linguistic groups, etc. in India. The country faced many wars between local kings and also fierce conflicts among different social groups. Yet the caste system enabled the heterogeneous groups to live contentedly side by side with harmonious and stable relationships." [Ram Ahuja. Page - 292.]

4. *Caste Serves As the Constitution of the Hindu Society* : It has rendered most important services in the past and continues to sustain the social order and its solidarity. The Hindu customs, practices, festivals, ceremonies and such other things are kept alive by the innumerable castes spread over the length and breadth of this country.

5. *Caste Maintains Racial Purity* : Caste preserves the racial purity by prohibiting inter-marriages [inter-religious, inter-racial and inter-caste] and by imposing endogamy on its members. According to **Havell,** *"Such caste laws were laws of spiritual eugenics designed to promote the evolution of a higher race."*

6. *Caste Provides for Cultural Diffusion and Transmission* : Various aspects of Indian culture such as art, handicrafts, music, dance, drama, *harikathas, keerthans, bhajans,* architecture, sculpture, etc. have been in existence due to the support given by the caste system. In fact, most of these things which are associated with one or the other castes are being transmitted from one generation to another.

7. *Caste Serves as an Agent of Socialisation* : Membership in caste is based on birth. It means members are born in the families which belong to one or the other caste. Each caste has a way of life of its own which is to be imparted to the new generation. The new born members of the caste are given social training [socialisation] in accordance with caste rules, practices, customs, beliefs, etc.

Caste provides for cultural diffusion within the group. The *"caste culture"* is passed on from one generation to the next, very systematically. As **Hutton** says, the caste canalises an individual's choice in marriage, *"acts as his trade union, his friendly or benefit society, his state club and his orphanage; it takes care for him of health, insurance and if need be provides for funeral."*

8. *Caste Has Served as a Means of Political Stratification* : The caste system has served as a means of political stratification. Because of caste, the political upheavals caused by alien invaders could touch only the surface of Indian society. Caste has served as a unit of law. In fact, the caste panchayats were the real government for the individuals and they provided a framework of religious and social sanctions. It is within the caste, individuals enjoyed freedom and carried on their daily activities.

9. *Promotion of Moral Restraint* : Caste conditions and regulates not only an individuals socio-economic life but also his moral life. It brings on him tremendous moral pressure to stick on to the established norms of the caste and also of the society.

10. *Other Merits* :

(i) Caste by way of stressing on the traditions and traditional way of functioning *has contributed to social stability and continuity.*

(ii) Caste is *supportive of cultural diversities.* It has made and is still making compromises with different cultural and subcultural practices, beliefs, customs, etc.

(iii) Caste has been *encouraging noble qualities such as mutual co-operation, helpfulness, sympathy, sacrifice, service and so on.*

Demerits of Caste

Caste system has its own demerits. Some of the demerits of the caste system may be noted below.

1. *Caste System Damages National Unity* : Caste makes political and national unity almost impossible. It encourages its members to have limited group loyalties and commitments. Caste members are more loyal to their caste rather than to the larger national community. One of the most tragic results of the caste system is that it prevents the development of national consciousness among the people. It has facilitated the intrusion of foreign invaders. Even **Max Muller** too had said that *"the Indian never knew the feeling of nationality."* **Sir Lepel Griffin** had recommended to the British Government that it should make use of the instrument of caste to make permanent the British rule in India. He had said *"A nation divided against itself, is the proper description of the Hindu race."* In the words of **G.S. Ghurye,** *"It is the spirit of the caste patriotism which engenders opposition to other castes, and creates an unhealthy atmosphere for the growth of national consciousness."*[1]

2. *Caste has Created Untouchability* : Caste is responsible for the low status and unjust treatment of outcastes and low caste people. The caste system has deprived the lowest caste people of India, of the minimum human rights and privileges. In the words of **Dr. S. Radhakrishnan,** *"the caste has degenerated itself into an engine by intolerance and inequality to such an extreme extent as to give birth to the most abominable institution of untouchability. The most disgusting demerit of caste is untouchability."*

Mahatma Gandhiji who carried on an untiring crusade against untouchability, too had condemned this aspect of caste in strong terms. To use his own words, untouchability *"is the hatefullest expression of the caste, a plague and a great sin poisoning the society."* Caste encouraged the despotism of upper castes which resulted in treating a large number of people worse than animals. These people had been actually cut-off from the main cultural stream of the Indian society.

---

1 **G.S. Ghurye** *"Caste and Class in India."* Page - 200.

3. *Caste Hampers Social Progress* : Caste to a certain extent brings about unity in the society. But more than that it has brought about disparities within the society. Castes are parochial in nature and are putting obstacles in the road towards progress. Caste consciousness has brought about segregation and seclusion. Each caste thinks of its own and conveniently forgets the interests of the others. The division of society into caste has given rise to the strong ingroup feelings and ethnocentrism of the worst type. It has also made people to become fatalistic in their attitude. This fatalism has made people to become conservative in their outlook.

4. *Caste is Unfavourable for Economic Prosperity* : Caste puts limitations on the occupational choice of the members by making occupations almost hereditary. It does not give any opportunity to an able and talented person who has an aptitude for a particular job. It does not believe in the principle of *"right man for right occupation."* Hence, the result is wrong men are placed to pursue some particular jobs. Both the person and the work suffer because of this. Due to the caste system, society is not able to utilise fully the talents of its members. Caste in this way has constituted a strong barrier to maximum productivity. It disturbs technological progress by developing inertia in the individuals and by killing their initiative and enterprise. Caste has very badly damaged the prospects of geographic mobility and also occupational mobility.

5. *Caste System Encourages Caste Hatred, Enmity and Conflicts* : Caste system has unwarrantedly divided the Hindu society into countless castes and subcastes. It has prevented its members from developing healthy social contacts and friendly relations. It has generated a sense of high and low, superiority and inferiority among its members. Each caste being subdivided into innumerable subcastes, claims superiority over other castes. Caste has built up strong social and psychological barriers between members of different castes. Instead of encouraging the feelings of mutual love, affection and sympathy, respect and understanding among the members of different castes, it has created enmity, hatred and mutual distrust. It is in this way, the growth of brotherhood and solidarity within the Hindu society has been very badly affected.

6. *Caste Lowers the Status of Women* : Caste is often blamed for having imposed many restrictions on women. For example, it has not encouraged the education of women; it has not given equal participation for them in religious discussions, political activities, business endeavours. It insists on the marriage of girls at an early age and makes them confine themselves to the home and the four walls of the kitchen. It denied women the right to divorce and it put restrictions on the widow remarriages for a very long time.

7. *Caste Rigidities Encourage Conversions* : Compelled by the tyranny of upper castes a large number of lower caste people got converted into Islam and Christianity. Some of them even became permanent enemies of the Hindu community. Domination of the upper castes, suppression of the rights of the lower castes, exploitation and harassment of the so called "untouchables" virtually alienated a large section of people of the Hindu society. These persons became easy victims of the converters who belonged to different religions.

8. *Caste System Prevents the Proper Development of Individual Personality* : Caste system has a tremendous hold on its members. It controls and regulates their food habits, dress habits, morals, manners, practices, hobbies, beliefs, rites, rituals, ceremonies, language, thoughts, etc. As **Dr. Duff** criticised, *every Hindu follows the directions of his caste like a lamb or pigeon.* Western people used to make fun of Indians by branding them as the *slaves of their castes.* An individual who subordinates his individual aspirations and interests can never develop an allround personality. It only leads to self denial and imbalanced personality.

Caste has given social privileges to the members of higher castes without taking into consideration their merits or efficiency. It has often denied opportunities to the really deserving members of the lower castes. In this way, it has undermined the development of the personality of the low caste people. The talents of the low castes are unnecessarily suppressed by the caste system. In this way, it has brought social and material losses to the society.

Dominant Castes and their Role

India is a classical land of castes in which a large number of castes have been in existence since a long time and there existed mutual co-operation and harmony among them. Economic necessities also added to their interdependence. The *Jajmani system* too played its role in welding the castes into a unified system. The decline of the Jajmani system during the British rule has given a fatal blow to the interdependence of castes. These conflicts are normally witnessed wherever one caste attempts to *dominate over* others or when higher castes try to exploit the lower castes **or** when castes perceive other castes as barriers in mobility and in achieving political power. The castes are not equal anywhere in India. On the other hand everywhere in India, we find the *domination* of one or the other caste over the rest of the castes. According to M.N. Srinivas, all the castes that are found in the framework of the Indian social system are not equal in strength and their role and influence are also not equal. Some of these castes are very much disorganised while certain others are highly organised and exercise a powerful influence on other castes. It is in this context, M.N. Srinivas introduces the concept of *"dominant castes"* which is of great help in understanding intercaste relations and conflicts, particularly in the rural setup.

Definition of Dominant Caste

According to M.N. Srinivas, *"A caste is dominant when it preponderates numerically over the other castes, when it also wields preponderant economic and political power, and when it enjoys a high ritual status in the local caste hierarchy."*

NATURE OF DOMINANT CASTES

1. Determinants of Dominance

The above definition pertaining to the concept of "dominant caste" denotes the main *"determinants of dominance."* They are stated below:

(i) A caste to be called "dominant", *it should own a sizable amount of the arable land locally available;*

(ii) it should have *the strength of numbers;*

(iii) it should occupy *a high place* [*ritual status*] *in the local hierarchy;* and

(iv) it should enjoy *greater economic and political power;*

- Two other elements also add to the *"dominance"* of a caste.

(a) *number of educated persons found in the caste.*

(b) *the nature of high occupations people pursue in the caste.*

2. Decisive Dominance

When a caste enjoys all the elements of dominance [i.e., numerical strength, economic and political power, high education and high ritual status] it is said to be *dominant in a decisive way.*

Occasionally, there may be more than one dominant caste in a village, and over a period of time one dominant caste may give way to another. This happened occasionally even in pre-British India, and has been an important aspect of rural social change in the 20th century.

3. Distribution of Dominance

Different elements of dominance are distributed differently among different castes in a village. **For example,** a caste which is numerically high may be poor and lacking in political power; while a ritually high statused caste may be rich economically and lacking strength in numbers. It can also be said that when a caste enjoys one form of dominance, it is frequently able to acquire other forms of dominance also. *This however, is not true in the case of untouchable castes.* The castes [such as untouchable castes] whose members are land-less labourers, tenants or very small land-owners, are many a time exploited by the dominant castes.

4. Dominance is not Purely a Local Phenomenon

As M.N. Srinivas says no where in rural India dominance is purely a local matter. A caste group which has only a family or two in a particular village but which enjoys decisive dominance in the wider region will still be influential locally. Because, the caste members of these families maintain a network of ties with the "dominant" relatives found in the wider region. The other members of the village are also aware of the existence of this network. Contrarily, a caste enjoys dominance in only one village will realise that it has to accommodate itself with the caste which enjoys regional dominance.

5. New Factors Affecting Dominance of Caste

According to M.N. Srinivas, "New factors affecting dominance have emerged in the last eighty years or so. Western education, jobs in the administration, and urban sources of income are all significant in contributing to the prestige and power of particular caste groups in the village."

6. Dominant Castes at the State Level

At the provincial level, different dominant castes are found to be influencing the socio-economic and political life of the people. **For example,** dominant castes such as *Lingayats* and *Okkaligas* in Karnataka, *Reddys* and *Kammas* in Andhra Pradesh, *Nairs* and *Ezhavas* in Kerala, *Gounder, Padayachi* and *Mudaliars* in Tamil Nadu, *Marathas, Brahmins* and *Mahars* in Maharashtra, *Rajputs, Jats, Gujars, Baniyas* in many of the Northern states, are very powerful.

ROLE AND INFLUENCE OF DOMINANT CASTES

The dominant castes are found to be socially influential, politically powerful and economically exploitative. In different provinces, districts and villages, different dominant castes are found to be influential.

Dominant Castes as *"Models"* of Sanskritisation

In the process of Sanskritisation, the dominant castes act as *"reference groups"* or as points of reference. Dominant castes set the model for the majority of people living in rural areas including, occasionally, Brahmins. The dominant castes such as *Patidars, Lingayats* and some *Vellals,* for instance, have undergone a degree of Sanskritisation. As a result of their Sanskritisation, the culture of the area over which their dominance extends experiences a change. The *Patidars* have become more Sanskritised in the last 100 years or so, and this has had effects on the culture of all other groups in *Kaira* District in Gujarath. The *Lingayats* and the *Vellas* of South India also have a Sanskritised style of life, and from a much older period than the Patidars.

The Dominant Caste in a Village acts as a Watchdog of a Pluralistic Culture and Value System

Traditionally, the elders of the dominant caste prevented the members of one caste from taking over the hereditary occupation of another caste whose interests would have been hurt by an inroad made into their monopoly. The dominant caste probably ignored minor changes in the rituals and style of life of a low caste. But it would *punish* the low caste if it refused to perform the services, economic or ritual, which it traditionally performed or when it appropriated an important high caste symbol. ***Ex.***: It is learnt from *"the census of India Report for 1921 that when Ahirs* [cowherds] of *North India decided to call themselves Kshatriyas and donned the sacred thread, their action roused the wrath of the dominant higher castes."* M.N. Srinivas has stated, that in North Bihar such an instance resulted in violence and the matter was taken to law courts.

The role of one dominant cast was not, however, restricted to being the guardian of a pluralistic culture. It also stimuled in lower castes a desire to imitate the dominant caste's own prestigious style of life. The lower castes have to do it slowly. They had to avoid imitating in matters likely to upset the dominant castes too much. Their chances of success were much better if they imitated slowly.

Role of Dominant Castes in Political Life

During the recent years the political influence of the dominant caste has considerably increased. By making use of freedom, democracy and universal adult franchise the dominant castes have become politically strong and powerful. They have very good representation in assemblies and in the parliament. With the introduction of the *"Panchayat Raj System"* these castes have extended their area of influence even in villages, taluks, and districts. Political power has given them an opportunity to strengthen their political position and economic strength. They have used the political instruments to obtain for their caste members, particularly for young men and women, good education and prestigious jobs.

Rivalries and Conflicts between Dominant Castes

Every state has more than one dominant caste. These castes are always engaged in rivalries and conflicts for securing political power and economic opportunities. ***Example*:** Such conflicts and rivalries are found between *Vokkaligas* and *Lingayats* in Karnataka, *Reddies* and *Kammas* in Andhra Pradesh and so on. The lower and the unprivileged castes including the so called untouchables have now realised that they are getting exploited at the hands of these dominant castes. This awareness has made them organise themselves politically. The *"Bahujana Samajvadi Party"* headed mostly by lower caste leaders, is becoming popular in states such as U.P., Bihar, Punjab and Madhya Pradesh. It has given tough opposition to the leadership of the dominant castes and won a couple of assembly and parliamentary seats during the recent elections.

Social Role of Dominant Castes

The dominant castes, particularly, the non-Brahmin dominant castes have been playing a vital role in our social life. These castes are well organised. They have grabbed political power, cleverly tapped economic resources and widely made use of educational opportunities. They are found in a big number in governmental services and have been able to corner lot of favours because of their political influence. In state assemblies and cabinets, they have ample representation. Except for the religious and ritual status, they are more influential than the Brahmins.

Conflict between Non-Brahmin Backward Castes and Non-Brahmin Dominant Forward Castes

At village level, the *non-Brahmin dominant castes are found to be greater exploiters of Harijan labour than the Brahmins.* At the state level, each dominant caste is in rivalry or conflict with another for political power and economic influence. *"While the leaders of the dominant castes are sensitive to economic and political opportunities, they are socially conservative. They do not, for instance, like the condition of the Harijans to improve. They have a vested interest in keeping the Harijans poor and ignorant. At the present time, Harijans are their most important source of agricultural labour, and if they become educated and conscious of their rights they will be a threat to the position of the dominant castes"* – **[M.N. Srinivas].** The untouchables and other backward lower castes are becoming aware of this exploitative nature of the dominant castes. Hence a kind of conflict is going on between the non-Brahmin dominant castes on the one hand and the most backward non-Brahmin castes on the other.

The untouchable castes also try to resist the efforts of the dominant castes which are interested in imposing their dominance over the non-dominant lower castes. *"Sometimes the untouchables decide to give up performing services such as removing the dead animals from the houses of the higher castes, beating drums at the festivals of village deities, and removing leaf-plates on which the high castes had dined during festivals and weddings. The upper caste people become annoyed and beat up the untouchables and set fire to their huts. The attempt to dominate and resistance to dominance, thus, led to caste conflicts"* – **[M.N. Srinivas].**

It may be generalised that political leadership, economic or money power, educational proficiency and the inclination towards modernity have helped the dominant castes to preserve their dominance. As the things stand today, these castes will continue to influence our social set up in the near future also.

Varna and Jati or Caste : Differences

Varna and caste represent two forms of social stratification of India. Very often one is used interchangeably to mean the other. But the distinction between the two is of great importance in sociology. The main differences between the two are noted below.

1. *Varnas are four in number whereas castes or jatis are innumerable.* According to the *"Chaturvarna Doctrine"*, there existed four *varnas* during the Vedic and the post-Vedic period, namely; *Brahmins, Kshatriyas, Vaishyas* and *Shudras.* These four *varnas* represented the four-fold division of the then existed Hindu society.

Whereas castes are found in a very large number. It is very difficult to say the exact number of the castes existing in India. It is well known that there are more than 4,000 castes and sub-castes in this nation. The number of castes and sub-castes is also increasing.

2. *Caste system is based on birth while the Varna system is based on occupations.* Membership in the case of a caste is determined on the basis of the birth of a person. Individuals who are called caste members are invariably born in one or the other caste. *For Example,* Brahmins are born Brahmins, Reddys are born Reddys, Jats are born Jats, Rajputs are born Rajputs, and so on. Caste membership cannot be changed. No amount of power, position, influence and wealth can change the caste membership of an individual.

Varna system which existed during the Vedic period was based on occupations that is, division of labour. Membership in the *Varna* system was determined on the basis of *"Karma"* or occupation which an individual was pursuing. It was subject to change. As Lord Krishna had stated in Bhagavad Gita that the membership of the *Varna* of an individual was very much dependent on the *"Guna"* and *"Karma"* of that individual.

3. *Varna system was more or less an "open" system whereas the caste system is often regarded as a "closed" system.* *Varna* system was regarded as an "open" system because it provided opportunities for the individuals to change the membership of the *Varna* to which they belonged. It means, for example, a man who belonged to the *Kshatriya Varna* could become a Brahmin, similarly, a *Vaishya* could become a *Kshatriya* or a Brahmin. Even the *Shudras* could become Brahmins. We have the example of Vishwamitra who was originally a *Kshatriya* and later on, became a Brahmin. Similarly, Drona, Kripa, Ashwatthama and Parashurama though originally belonged to the *Brahmana Varna* pursued *Kshatriya* career. Vedavyasa, the author of *"Mahabharatha"*, originally belonged to a fishermen's family of the *ShudraVarna,* but later on pursued the Brahmin career. Many such examples are available in our ancient Sanskrit texts and also in history.

On the contrary, caste is regarded as "closed" group because caste membership cannot be changed. Opportunities for moving up and down in the caste hierarchy are virtually closed. Hence, a *Jat* who is born as a *Jat* dies as a *Jat;* a *Mochi* or *Dom* or *Chammar* or *Pasi* or any so called untouchable caste man who is born into that caste dies as either a *Mochi* or *Dom* or *Chammar* or *Pasi*, and so on. Even today, caste membership continues to be almost unchangeable.

4. *Varna system was based on the principle of equality whereas the caste system is based on the principle of inequality.* It is said that during the Vedic Period, all the four *Varna*s were considered almost equal. Equal socio-economic and educational and political opportunities were provided for the people of all the *Varna*s. Social mobility, occupational mobility and even geographic mobility were all permitted. As it is already mentioned, people could move up and down in the *Varna* hierarchy.

The caste system which is based on the principle of incquality does not permit free movement of the people from one status to another. Opportunities for social mobility are almost non-existent. As it is already mentioned, individuals are compelled to confine themselves to the caste to which they belonged.

5. *Varna system was comparatively less rigid whereas caste system is more rigid.* *Varna* system was less rigid because rules and regulations relating to the food and dress habits of the people, their occupations and religious activities, etc. were less rigid. People had more freedom in their individual as well as social life.

On the contrary, caste system is said to be a rigid system because it places restrictions on the food and dress habits of the people, their occupational and professional activities, their political, religious, educational and other activities, their morals and manners, their beliefs and practices, and so on.

6. *Varna system has the sanction of the religion, i.e., Hinduism, whereas the caste system does not have its sanction.* The origin of the *Varna* system throws light on the fact that it was divinely ordained. As it is believed by a large number of traditional thinkers that four *Varna*s emerged from the four different organs of the Prajapathi Brahma, or the Divine Being. Lord Krishna also says in Bhagavadgita [Chapter XIV, Sloka 13] that He himself had created the four *Varnas*.

The caste system, on the contrary, does not have the sanction of any divine force. In fact, caste system can be regarded as the degenerated form of the *Varna* system which existed during the ancient times in India. It means, the origin of the caste system can be traced to the *Varna* system itself. Thinkers like Swami Vivekananda and others have said that the caste system does not have the sanction of the Hindu religion. Vivekananda says *"In religion there is no caste......... The caste system is opposed to the religion of the Vedanta."*[1]

Though people speak of the *"Varna system"* and the *"Varna model"* in theoretical terms, practically they are not in existence. *Varna,* as a form of stratification, has become a thing of the past. What is in existence today, is the caste system with all its peculiarities.

Caste System and Estates System

Meaning and Nature of Estates

The term *"Estates"* represents a type of stratification that existed in Europe during the Middle Ages. Estates system has a long history. The system emerged in the ancient Roman Empire, and existed in Europe until very recent times. The estates system consisted of three main divisions – *the clergy, the nobility, and the commoners or the ordinary people.* In England and France, *for example,* these three divisions were found. In some parts of Europe, *for example,* Sweden, almost upto 1866 there were four estate divisions; *Nobles, Clergy, Citizens* and *Peasants.*

These historical estates were akin to social classes in at least two respects. (i) *Each estate, was to some extent characterised by a distinctive style of life.* (ii) *The three estates could be thought of as representing a hierarchy.* In this hierarchy, the clergy were at the top and the commoners at the bottom. The intermediary position was occupied by the nobles. It should be noted that the clergy was called the First Estate only in consonance with the medieval idea that the Church is supreme and the State is subordinated to it. Hence, in reality, there were three classes, but with the nobility (including royalty) at the top.

Characteristics of Estates

T.B. Bottomore has mentioned about three important characteristics of the feudal estates of medieval Europe. They are as follows :

1. *Legal Basis of Estates* : Estates were legally defined. Each estate had a *"status"* of its own. More precisely, in a legal sense the status was associated with rights and duties privileges and obligations. As it has been said, *"to know a person's real position",* it was first of all necessary to know *"the law by which he lived."* In comparison with the first two estates - the clergy and nobility - the third estate consisting of the serfs or commoners suffered from many legal disabilities. *For example,* the serfs had the *inability to appeal to the king for justice.* They had *no rights over their chattels or properties and holdings.* They had *the liability of paying the fines* of *'merchet'* and *'heriot',* [*i.e.,* a fine paid to a lord for the marriage of a daughter, and a fine paid to the lord on the death of a tenant.] Even different penalties were imposed on them for similar offences.

2. *Estates Representing Division of Labour* : The estates represented a broad division of labour. They had some definite functions. According to the law of the day, *the nobility were to fight and defend all, the clergy were to pray and the commoners were to pay* or provide food for all.

3. *Estates as Political Groups* : The feudal estates were political groups. An assembly of estates possessed political power. From this point of view, the serfs did not constitute an estate until the 12th century A.D. The decline of feudalism after the 12th century is associated with the rise of a third estate. The third estate behaved for a long period *within* the feudal system as a *distinctive group* before they overthrew it.

1 **Swami Vivekananda** *"India and Her Problems"* - Chapter IV.

Thus, the three estates - clergy, nobility and the commoners functioned like three political groups. As far as participation in government was concerned, the clergy used to stand by the nobility. In France, the political position was more rigid. This system of three estates remained there until 1789, that is, till the outbreak of the Revolution. In the French Parliament called *"States - General"*, these estates used to sit separately and not together. That differentiation within the estates prevailed for a long time. The political movement of the French Revolution brought about some radical changes in France.

Caste System and Estates System : Differences

The caste system of India and the estates of Medieval Europe, are not one and the same. The differences and the similarities between the two systems may be noted here :

1. *A pure caste system is rooted in the religious order whereas the estates system is rooted in the legal order.* Divisions within the caste system are an interpretation of the laws of religious ritual, the divisions of estates system are defined by the laws of man. Hence it is not necessary in the estates system to know a man's place in a ritual order. But it is significant to know the man-made law by which he lives. These laws were somewhat complicated. Still their universal characteristic was that they defined not only the rights but also the duties and obligations of the members of estates. These could be either in the courts or by military strength.

2. *Unlike the caste system the estates system has no "out-castes".* Because, at least in history, all the estates of the system enjoyed their own rights, duties and obligations. All could establish some claim on the established social order. In the caste system, the outcastes suffered from all kinds of social, political, religious, legal and other disabilities.

3. *Difference between these two systems could be observed with regard to the nature of social mobility.* Both, of course, had institutionalised barriers for social mobility. The barriers in the caste system are based on ritual impurity whereas the barriers of the estate system are legal. Since these legal barriers are man-made they can be modified in particular circumstances. *For example,* in the religious sphere, anyone belonging to any section of the community was recruited into the Church. At least in theory, anyone could attain any high place in it. Promotion within the Church indicated some kind of social mobility. In the secular sphere, however, the king could provide a distinguished servant, a noble position. In both these circumstances, changes of social position were essentially inherited.

The caste system, on the other hand, suffers from irreparable inequality created by divinity as it is believed. Hence, *no caste member could rise or improve upon his position* in the caste system even as an exceptional case.

Caste System and Social Class

"Social Class" is a principal type of social stratification found especially in the modern civilised countries. If the caste system is found to be unique to India, the class system is universal in nature. Sometimes, the word "class" is used to represent groups of professors, artists, engineers, doctors, students, etc. The word "class" is also used to refer the quality of the things whether good, better, best and so on. But the concept of *"social class"* is more used in sociology representing a kind of social stratification than anything else.

Definition

1. **P. Gisbert :** A social class is *"a category or group of persons having a definite status in society which permanently determines their relation to other groups."*
2. **Ogburn and Nimkoff :** *"A Social class is the aggregate of persons having essentially the same social status in a given society."*
3. **MacIver and Page :** *"A social class is any portion of the community marked off from the rest by social status."*

Caste and Class : Differences

Caste and class represent two main forms of social stratification. They can be distinguished on the following grounds.

Caste	*Class*
1. ***Particular*** : The caste system with all its peculiarities is unique to India. It is peculiar to India and hence it is not universal.	1. ***Universal*** : The class system is universal in nature. It is found in almost all the modern complex societies.
2. ***Ascribed Status*** : Status is ascribed to the individuals by birth. Birth is the criterion of status and not achievement. Status can neither be changed nor be improved.	2. ***Achieved Status*** : Status is achieved by the individuals. There is scope for achievement. Hence, status can be changed or improved.
3. ***Closed System*** : Caste is a closed system. It restricts social mobility, *i.e.*, the movement of people from one social status to that of the other.	3. ***Open System*** : Class is an open system. It provides for social mobility. Individuals can move from the lower class to the upper class.
4. ***Divine Origin*** : The caste system is believed to have had a divine origin. It is closely associated with the Hindu tradition.	4. ***Secular*** : The class system is secular. It has nothing to do with religion. It has been given no religious explanation.
5. ***Purity and Impurity*** : The idea of purity and impurity is associated with the caste. Some castes are called *'pure'* while others are regarded as *'impure'*. *'Impure'* castes are regarded as *'untouchables'*.	5. ***Feeling of Disparity*** : There is a feeling of disparity on the part of the members of a class. The question of purity and impurity does not arise. Hence there is no practice of untouchability.
6. ***Regulation of Relations*** : The caste system controls the activities and regulates the relations of its members to a great extent. As MacIver says, it fixes the role of a man in society. It regulates even the routine activities of the members.	6. ***Limits Relations*** : The class system, on the other hand, limits the range of contracts and communications of its members. Individuals are more free in a class. It does regulate the daily tasks of its members.
7. ***Greater Social Distance***: There is comparatively a greater distance being kept between different castes.	7. ***Less Social Distance*** : There is less social distance between different classes. Members are more tolerant towards others.

8. ***Conservative*** : The caste ridden system tends to become conservative, orthodox and reactionary. Castes become, in course of time, water-tight compartments.	8. ***Progressive*** : The class-laden system is regarded as more progressive. Classes give more freedom to the members. Class permits greater social mobility.
9. ***Endogamous Group*** : Caste is an endogamous social unit. Accordingly, every caste member has to marry within the group selecting the life partner from his or her own caste. Inter-caste marriages are not allowed.	9. ***Not Endogamous*** : A class is not an endogamous unit. The member is free to select his or her life partner from any of the classes. The class system never imposes restrictions on marriage.
10. ***Complexity*** : The caste system is a complex system. The very fact that more than 800 castes and sub-castes are found in India, makes it evident how complex it is.	10. ***Simplicity*** : The class system is known for its simplicity. Broadly speaking, there are only three classes - the upper, middle and the lower - and hence the network of relations is also simple.
11. ***Caste-consciousness*** : Caste consciousness is more dangerous to democracy. Democracy and caste, strictly speaking, cannot go together, because caste is based on inequality. Caste-feeling may also endanger the growth of national sentiments and unity. Caste restricts the amount of community feeling. Casteism has been a great hindrance to the national integration in India.	11. ***Class-consciousness*** : Class-consciousness is not inimical to democracy. Class and democracy go together. Class on the other hand, does not restrict the amount of community feeling. In spite of the Communist influence of internationalism, the class system never disturbs the growth of national sentiments.

Caste and Jajmani System

Meaning : The *"Jajmani System"* represents one of the types of exchange that prevailed in India for a long time. As **Prof. Yogendra Singh** has said *"The Jajmani system is a system governed by relationships based on reciprocity in intercaste relations in village."*

The term *"jajmani"* is derived from the Vedic term *"Yajman"* who in Vedic times conducted *"Yajna"* or fire sacrifice to appease the Gods. The term denotes a significant person and in the village context, a landowner. The people who rendered services to him, the priest, the carpenter, ironsmith, washerman, barber, potter were collectively known as *"praja"*, [and in due course, as *"Kamins"*]. Generally, the upper castes such as Brahmins and Rajputs, remained as jajmans. For their services rendered to the *Yajmans,* the *praja* or the *"Kamins"* received payment in kind [grains, cloth, fodder, buttermilk, ghee, etc.], which provided economic security.

Some Characteristics

1. *The Jajmani System Implies Traditional Occupational Obligations Between Castes* : It forges interdependence of castes. The servicing castes called *"Kamins"* and the recipients of the services called *"Jajmans"* are dependent on each other for the fulfilment of their economic needs.

2. *The System Establishes Closer Family Links* : The *jajmani* links are to be found between families rather than between *jatis. For example,* a farmer's family gets its wooden agricultural tools from a particular carpenter family, and in return, the carpenter gets a share of the farmer's crop at harvest.

3. *The Jajmani Relationship is Durable* : Here the link is inherited on both the sides. Thus the carpenter serves the same farmer family, that his father and grandfathers served. In the same manner, the farmer family gets its tools made and repaired by the descendants of the carpenter's family whose members made tools for their forefathers.

4. *The Jajmani Relationships are Exclusive* : *For example,* the farmer family is supposed to carry on transactions with a particular carpenter family only. Reciprocally, these carpenters are supposed to make tools for their own *"yajman"* families only. However, they are free to make some tools for sale in the market.

5. *The Jajmani Relationships are Multiple* : These relationships are not restricted to economic exchange alone. Economic exchange is only one facet of the *jajmani* relations. As **Mandelbaum** has pointed out, *"a family of cultivators expects help on its ceremonial occasions from most of the associated families. There is also an expectation of mutual personal support in family emergencies or fractional quarrels. Sometimes the specialist families are pressurised to support the jati of their patrons when that whole jati is embattled."*

6. *Jajmani System Adds to the Village Solidarity* : According to **M.N. Srinivas,** *jajmani system* which is based on the interdependence of castes is one of the main factors that add to the village solidarity. Indian village is based on caste system. Different castes are brought together and welded into a unity by this system. This system contributes to the *vertical solidarity of the caste system. Vertical solidarity of the caste system refers to the unity existing among different caste groups in a village.* Vertical solidarity of the caste thus contributes to the village solidarity.

7. *Coercion and Consensus in Jajmani Relations* ? : Some writers have strongly criticised the *jajmani relations* as "exploitative." According to them, the *jajmani* relationships are *"the means by which the rich and powerful exploit the poor and coerce the workers into sustaining the power of those who have the upper hand and the higher rank."*

Some other writers have argued that in spite of the coercive element in the *jajmani* relations, such exchanges *"bring solidarity and mutual benefits."* They have said that each *jati* system tries to maximise its gain and exercise as much power as it can in the matter of *jajmani* transactions. As **M.S.A. Rao** has pointed out criticism of jajmani transactions *"as brutally exploitative is too sweeping and obfuscating a generalisation."*[1]

Decline of Jajmani System

At present, in most of the villages in India, the *jajmani* arrangements are not seen in the village economy. In fact, in over all terms this system declined after the introduction of British rule in India. By now the *jajmani* relationship has been largely supplanted in many villages. In some of the villages, it has completely disappeared. Still, it persists in some way in some parts of North India. *"We may further note that jajmani relationship is now increasingly being supplanted mainly because more money is now used in village economy and also because modern transport makes market transactions more feasible."* [**Parimal B. Kar.** Page - 230.]

Caste among the Non-Hindus

It is wrong to believe that caste in India is found only among the Hindus. As Prof. Ram Ahuja has pointed out, "Several studies conducted between 1956 and 1965 by R. Gupta [on *"Muslims of a Village in North-Western Uttar Pradesh"* in 1956], G. Ansari [on *"Muslim Castes in Uttar*

1 **M.S.A. Rao** *"The Jajmani System." The Economic Weekly* - 1961, as quoted by **Parimal B. Kar.** Page - 229.

Pradesh" in 1960], Z. Ahmed [on *"Mulim Castes in Uttar Pradesh"* in 1962], U. Guha [on *"Rural Bengali Muslims"* in 1965], M.K. Siddiqui [on *Caste Among Muslims of Calcutta* in 1970], Sangare [on Jains in 1959], I.P. Singh [on the Sikhs in 1958], Schifra Strizower [on Jews in 1959], and by McKim Marriott in 1960s have pointed out the prevalence of caste system among non-Hindus [see Sinha, 1974 : 243]."[1]

S.C. Dube points out that "...... *Christianity and Islam had to come to terms with Varna and Jati and absorb some of the features which were not part of their basic tenets. It is amazing that these persist even to this day."*[2] Though a clear-cut Varna division is not found among the Christians and Muslims, a distinction is made between high-caste and low-caste converts.

CASTE AMONG THE MUSLIMS

All the religious communities in India, including the Muslims, have been very much influenced by the caste system. Caste-like divisions are found in all these communities. Varna and jati-like distinctions indicating social status and governing social interaction are present among the Muslims. Throughout the Mughal period, [and even afterwards] a distinction was made between the *"Ashrafs"* [those claiming descent from groups of foreign extraction] and *"Ajlafs"* [converts from the lower Hindu castes]. The Ajlafs definitely had a lower social position. Many of the lower groups converted to Islam continued to occupy more or less their old positions in society. Even today, it is common to speak of *"Sherif Jat"* [well-bred, an upper jati-like formation] and *"Ajlaf Jat"* [common, lower jati-like formation]. *"These distinctions determine intergroup social intercourse like marriage, inter-dining and participation in ceremonies and other functions. Origins are remembered and converts to Islam from Hinduism still largely pursue their earlier jati-linked occupations."* [**S.C. Dube** - 49.]

Islam proclaims the idea of equality of all those who profess the faith, but in India it has been characterised by caste. **Nazmal Karim**[3] points out that on the model of the Hindu caste divisions and in imitation of them social classes among the Indian Muslims are formed. Karim has also made reference to four major caste-like divisions among the Muslims namely – (i) *Syed,* (ii) *Sheik,* (iii) *Mughal,* and (iv) *Pathan.*[4] **Prof. S.C. Dube** has also expressed the same opinion.

In Mughal times, the divisions of *Syed, Sheik, Mughal* and *Pathan* were often equated with the Varna divisions of the Hindu society. In some parts of India converts from Hinduism considered it necessary to enrol themselves into one of these divisions. Whether this is true to Islam is another question, but it is nevertheless a fact – that it is being done.

*"The **Syeds** are the descendants of the family of the Prophet through his daughter; they are of Arab origin. But several higher Jatis converted to Islam claimed this status; Brahmin converts claimed that their Syed status was confirmed by the Emperor Akbar. The **Sheiks** were also of Arab descent, though they are not the descendants of the Prophet. Even first generation converts are known to call themselves Sheiks. The **Mughals,** the ruling dynasty of Delhi, ranked next. They were of Turki origin, but adopted this designation to distinguish themselves from the Ottoman rulers of Turkey. The **Pathans** were of Afghan origin, though many of them, not even remotely connected with Afghanistan, claimed this status."* [**S.C. Dube.** Page - 49.] It is also known that as per the Census reports relating to the British period, five major divisions among the Muslims, namely : *Syeds,*

---

1 **Prof. Ram Ahuja** *"Society in India."* Page - 42.
2 **S.C. Dube** *"Indian Society."* Page - 47.***Pub.***: National Book Trust, India.
3 **Nazmal Karim** *"Changing Society in India and Pakisthan"* - 1953.
4 **J.D. Cunningham** *"History of the Sikhs."*

Sheiks, Mughals, Pathans and *"others"* were widely recognised. In 1911, there were around **69 million** Muslims who belonged to these five caste-like divisions.

As **M.N. Srinivas** has stated, *"Muslim caste differs in some respects from the Hindu caste system; there are no ethico-religious ideas justifying the hierarchy or regulating inter-caste relations through ideas of purity and pollution; there are no varna categories. What we have is a hierarchy formed by several jatis."*[1] The converted Hindus of the higher Jatis – Rajput, Jat and Ahir – especially in North India, for example, retained their identity. Several jatis like *"Julaha"*, *"Bhat"*, *"Kalal"* and *"Bhishti"* were in many respects comparable to Hindu Jatis, having specialised occupations and gradations of status.

Example of U.P. [North India] : *"In Uttar Pradesh, Muslims who have a tradition of foreign ancestry [Iran, Arabia] are called **Shurafa** or **Ashraf** and are considered to be the highest. After them come converts from high-caste Hindus, such as Rajputs. Next come occupational castes such as the Weaver [Julaha], Barber [Nai], Cotton Carder [Dhuniya], Potter [Kumbar] and Oilman [Teli]. Last come the Sweepers. Among the Ashraf, the Syeds rank as the highest."* [**M.N. Srinivas** in the Gazetteer. Page - 505.]

Dr. Ghaus Ansari too has recognised such caste divisions among the Muslims of U.P.

Example of Kerala [South India] : *"The Moplah [Mapilla] Muslims of Kerala are also divided into castes. The **Thangals,** claiming descent from the Prophet's daughter, Fatima, are at the top; next to them are the **Arabs,** descendants of immigrants from Arabia. The **Pusalars,** said to be recent converts from the fisherman caste, occupy the third position while the **Ossans,** who are barbers, are at the bottom."* [**M.N. Srinivas.** *ibid,* Page - 505.]

As **Nazmal Karim** has pointed out, ***Bengal Muslims*** are very well organised as the caste groups among the Hindus. The only difference is, they do not have much rigidities due to the impact of Islam. Caste feelings and prejudices which are found among the Hindus are equally shared by the Muslims. It is said that there are more than 35 caste-like divisions among the Bengal Muslims and even Muslim reformers found it difficult to bring about desirable changes in them. What made the Muslims converted from Hinduism to retain caste order - is a perplexing question. **N.K. Bose** is of the opinion that Muslims converted from Hinduism adhered to caste patterned endogamy and hereditary traditional occupations – *because they found in it economic security.* This, of course, is not the only reason, and various other social, economic, political and other considerations must also have contributed to that.

As **S.C. Dube** remarks *"the persistence of Jati has worried Muslim theologians and social reformers, but even the recent wave of fundamentalism has not been able to do away with it."*[2]

CASTES AMONG THE CHRISTIANS

Though the British people made fun of the caste system of India the Christian religion which they had brought and propagated also succumbed to the caste influence. **Hutton** had said long back that caste seemed to have found acceptance among the Catholics of India. Christians of India today make a clear distinction between the high-caste and low-caste converts. The high-caste converts, [whether to Christianity or Islam] for example, identify themselves as Brahmin Christians or Nayar Christians or as Rajput or Tyagi Muslims.

1 **M.N. Srinivas** in article "Social Structure" in *"The Gazetteer of India"* Vol.1. Page - 505.

2 **S.C. Dube** *"Indian Society."* Page - 50.

"Caste divisions occur among Indian Christians, Catholics as well as Protestants. The Syrian Christians of Kerala, the earliest converts to Christianity in India, claim to have been recruited originally from Nambudiri Brahmins and Nairs, and caste distinctions are conspicuous among them. Caste restrictions are rigidly observed among the Christians of the West Coast. A Catholic Brahmin from Maharashtra would marry none other than a Catholic Brahmin. Some West Coast Christians have migrated to East Africa and their descendants try to marry within their particular subcaste."[1]

Scheduled Caste people converted into Christianity are not treated on par with the rest of the Christians. "In their annual meeting in January 1988, the Bishops of Tamil Nadu noted that *"the Scheduled Caste Christians, even after conversion, continue to suffer from extreme social, educational and economic backwardness arising out of the traditional practice of untouchability."* In a pastoral letter issued in February 1988, the Catholic Bishops of Tamil Nadu admitted : *"Caste distinctions and their resultant injustice and violence do still continue in Christian social life and practice. We are aware of and accept the situation with deep pain." The Indian Church now realises that approximately 60 per cent of the 19 million Indian Christians are subjected to discriminatory practices and treated as second-class Christians or worse."*[2]

In South India, caste divisions within Christianity seem to be more rigid. "In the South, Christians from the Scheduled Caste are segregated both in their settlements and in the Church. Their *cheri* or colony is situated at some distance from the main settlement and is devoid of the civic amenities available to others. *In church services they are segregated to the right wing and are not allowed to read scriptural pieces during the service or to assist the priest. They are the last to receive the holy sacraments during baptism, confirmation, and marriage. The marriage and funeral processions of Christians from the low castes are not allowed to pass through the streets of the main settlement. Scheduled Castes converted to Christianity have separate cemeteries.* The Church bell does not toll for their dead, nor does the priest visit the home of the dead to pray. The dead body cannot be taken into the Church for the funeral service. Of course, there is no inter-marriage and little inter-dining among the *"high-caste"* and the *"low-caste"* Christians. Clashes between them are frequent. The low-caste Christians are waging struggles to improve their lot; the Church is responding, but little meaningful change has come about so far. Even among higher caste Christians the Jati origins are remembered and at least covertly they colour social relationships." [**S.C. Dube.** Page - 48.]

According to **Tharamangalam** [in his *"Caste Among Christians in India"*], caste does exist among Christians but *".... without any necessary linkage with the theological ideas of purity and pollution, or karma and dharma."* He states again that *"while all major characteristics of caste are present among Christians we have seen that the ritual aspects have been considerably weakened."*[3]

"Tharamangalam has stated that under the Portuguese archbishop, "Syrians were allowed to continue practising untouchability." It is also well-known that Dalit converts to Christianity have had to sit in pews set apart from the pews reserved for higher caste converts. No wonder that Dalit Christians are protesting against discrimination in the church just as Hindu Dalits are fighting against the Hindu establishment."[4]

---

1 **M.N. Srinivas** *"The Gazetteer of India."* Page - 506.

2 **S.C. Dube** *"Indian Society."* Page - 48.

3 Quoted by **M.N. Srinivas** in Introduction to the book *"Caste Its Twentieth Century Avatar"* [1996]. Page - XXXVI.

4 *ibid.* Page - XXXVI.

M.N. Srinivas citing the examples of his own personal experiences[1] makes a concluding remark in his introduction to the book *"Caste Its Twentieth Century Avatar"* [Page : 37 - 38] says that *"Tharamangalam omits to mention how Christians have internalised the idea of caste rank even though they live and operate largely in a Christian Universe."*

CASTE IN OTHER RELIGIONS

Caste is found in one form or another in all the religions of Indian origin, namely, Jainism, Buddhism, and Sikhism. The neo-Buddhists find it difficult to delink themselves from their earlier *jati status.* The egalitarian ethos of Sikhism is blunted by the presence of Jati, and even the practice of untouchability.

Caste Among the Sikhs

"Equality is a tenet of Sikhism also, but that has not prevented the existence of castes, including Brahmins, among Sikhs. Sikhs are broadly divided into ***Sardars*** and ***Mazhabis,*** the former consisting of high castes and the latter of Sweepers.

The ***Sardars*** include *Jat* and *Kamboh* [landowners], *Tarkhan* [Carpenter], *Kumhar* [Potter], *Mehra* [Water-carrier], and *Cimba* [Washerman]. The first two castes regard themselves as superior to the others. The ***Mazhabi*** not only came from a low caste but were converted to Sikhism later than the higher caste groups. In some parts of Punjab there exist the *Sansi* [Shepherd] who were formerly included among the "Criminal Tribes"; Sansi converts to Sikhism rank even lower than Mazhabis." [**M.N. Srinivas** in the Gazetteer. Page : 505 - 506.]

Caste Among the Jews

It is surprising to note that caste is found even among the smallest religious community, namely Jews. "There are three divisions among Indian Jews : *Beni-Israel, Cochin Jews* and *Baghdadi Jews.* The Beni-Israel are to be found principally in Bombay. They are divided into two groups, *Gora* [White] and *Kala* [Black], the former being considered higher in rank. The Cochin Jews are divided into similar White and Black groups, and there is a third, descended from a White Cochin Jew claiming superiority over those who descended from a Black Cochin Jew. The third Jewish group, the Baghdadi, are later immigrants, and are found in Bombay and Calcutta." [**M.N. Srinivas.** Page - 506.]

It is clear from the above discussion, that caste is all-pervasive in India. The hold of the notions of jati are such that they transcend Hinduism, and can be seen to operate in nearly all segments of Indian society. Social reformers have not been able to change this orientation, though some of them have tried hard to do so.

---

1 "Many Syrian Christians, Goan Catholics and others have told me how they were converted originally from Brahmins. A Carmelite nun in a Cochin college chastised me for my readiness to eat fish. She became a Christian after reading the Bible, and she herself was a strict vegetarian. And finally some years ago, I happened to participate in a South Indian Bishops' Conference in Bangalore where matters of concern to the laity were discussed. And as I was about to leave the conference, one of the distinguished participants asked me, *"Professor, before you leave us will you please tell us how to get rid of caste among South Indian Christians ?" Indeed, the conference had begun with that question !"* - **M.N. Srinivas** in his Introduction to *"Caste, Its Twentieth Century Avatar"*. Page : 37 - 38.

Future of Caste : Will It Decline or Exist ?

"Future of Caste" - is one of the main topics of discussion today everywhere. The caste system which has been in existence since centuries, is undergoing radical changes. There are two main opinions about this change. (i) *Caste is fast changing and is weakening* and (ii) *Caste is undergoing slow and gradual changes and it will not die.*

(i) Caste is weakening. Early scholars of 1950s and 1970s like D.N. Majumdar, Kuppuswamy, Kali Prasad, Gardner Murphy and scholars of 1980s and early 1990s like R.K. Mukherjee, E.J. Miller, M.N. Srinivas and others hold the view that the caste system is fast changing and is weakening.

(ii) Caste is not declining, but undergoing slow changes. Scholars like I.P. Desai, Ghurye, Narmadeshwar Prasad and Kapadia and present scholars like Damle, Dumont, Andre Betille, Harold Gould, Yogendra Singh, S.C. Dube, T.N. Madan and others hold the view that the caste system is not transforming itself so fast and the changes are only gradual. These scholars are of the firm belief that caste is not going to dissolve or disintegrate. But they have made it clear that the caste today is not the same as it was half a century or a century ago. For example, Desai and Damle have said: *"The magnitude of the changes in the parts of caste system is not as great as it is believed to be. These changes have not affected the essential aspects of the caste system as a whole"* - [As quoted by **Ram Ahuja** in his *"Indian Social System"*].

Questions Relating to the Necessity and Existence of Caste: Views of M.N. Srinivas

M.N. Srinivas in his version of the future of caste, has posed two important questions: (i) *Should castes exist in India of tomorrow*? (ii) *Are they likely to exist* ?[1]

1. The Question of the Necessity of Caste

As M.N. Srinivas has pointed out, the vast majority of the population, especially Hindus, do not want caste to disappear. They find it impossible to envisage a society without caste. To the bulk of people living in rural areas, *caste is nothing but a collection of kin/ groups - agnates and affins - living in the neighbouring villages.* Joint family and caste provide for an individual some of the benefits which a welfare state provides for him in the industrialised country of the West. A man's earliest friends are frequently drawn from his caste and his kin belong to his caste. A *caste also stands for a certain amount of cultural homogeneity. Hence caste is bound to stay, it will not perish.*

2. The Question of Existence of Caste

To the question, *"Are castes likely to disappear in the India of tomorrow"* an emphatic **"No"** is the answer. It does not, however, mean that the caste system is altogether changeless. In the last hundred years, significant changes have taken place in it. There is an increase in caste solidarity and a corresponding decrease in the interdependence of castes existing in a region. The tensions existing between different castes have added to this increase in horizontal solidarity. Srinivas has thus commented: *"The horizontal solidarity of a caste is gained at the expense of the vertical solidarity of the castes of a region."* [**Srinivas:** Page - 741]

Caste no longer rigidly determines an individual's occupation. Castes are engaged in mutual competition to grab the lucrative employment opportunities offered by the new economy.

1 **M.N. Srinivas** *"Caste in Modern India and Other Essays"* - Page – 70.

Thus the economic grip of caste is weakening. On the contrary, *politically* caste has become much stronger. Castes continue to provide the *"social base"* for the candidates of any political party to contest in elections.

M.N. Srinivas is of the opinion that caste will not die in the immediate future, but inter-caste rivalries and hatreds are likely to come down as industrialisation, urbanisation and westernisation spread their influence. He has also said that *"on a short-term basis the country is likely to have more trouble with caste."* While on a long-term basis, adult franchise, industrial revolution, spread of literacy among the lower castes, and the greater Sanskritisation of the backward castes should gradually remove *"the more obnoxious features of the caste system."*

Three Broad Opinions Regarding the Future of the Caste System

Caste is not only surviving today but also showing no signs of deteriorating or dying. *What would be its future ?* Opinions of the people, particularly, educated Hindus regarding these two questions could be summarised in the following manner.

1. ***Caste Must be Abolished*** **:** The so called progressivists, leftists and atheists are of the opinion that the caste system is an evil system and it has caused enough damage to the Indian society and hence it is high time that it should go. The sooner it goes, the better it will be for the society. They even argue that it must be abolished.

2. ***Caste Must be Reinstated*** **:** There are some traditionalists who are of the opinion that the perversions of the caste must go. It has become problematic because it is totally degenerated and its original purity is gone. That is why they advocate that due steps must be taken to reinstate the traditional four orders. In fact, Gandhiji was a strong supporter of the Varna System.

3. ***Caste Must be Modified*** **:** There are many who hold the view that the caste system is basically good and hence it must be preserved. But they hasten to add that the caste system must be re-organised or modified in order to enable it to accommodate itself to the changed conditions of the modern times. They also feel that the intense inequality, practice of untouchability, commensal taboos and such other unwanted features of the caste must be done away with. They are aware of the fact that such an attempt to alter or modify the caste system would be a slow and steady process and take lot of time.

Factors Contributing to the Continuance of Caste

Most of the scholars who have studied or keenly observed the caste system are of the invariable opinion that the caste system is not going to die nor decline immediately. They have also felt that the caste which is a deep-rooted and a long standing institution is bound to continue in the future. The existing socio-religious and politico-economic conditions are more supportive and complementary than conflicting and opposing its continuation. Some of the factors that are favourable for the continuation of caste may be briefly stated below.

1. Caste as a Factor Providing a "Social Base" and an "Identity" to the People

At the social level, caste continues to provide the *"social base"* for its members. It provides an *"identity"* to the people and through their membership of one caste or the other, they get a kind of social recognition. It continues to determine the style of living as well as the rank or the position of the members in the social hierarchy. There is thus no sign of caste disappearing.

Further, caste still continues to be the basic kinship unity. Caste remains mostly endogamous even today. Intercaste marriages are not on the increase. As **Prof. N. Jayaram** has remarked,

"Caste.......... constitutes a cultural context, provides an identity marker, facilitates reference group behaviour, and regulates marriage and kinship......."[1]

2. The Adaptive Ability of Caste

Caste in its historical development has exhibited a tremendous capacity for making adjustments with the changing environment. **N. Jayaram** has stated that *"the caste system has been the most flexible of the primordial institutional arrangements anywhere in the world, and it has shown an extraordinary capacity to adapt itself to a variety of changing, and often apparently contradictory, socio-economic conditions."*[2] Caste has made compromises for the sake of its existence with many of its essential rules and practices such as restrictions on commensal taboos, practice of untouchability, imposition of restrictions on widows, observing the rule of even sub-caste endogamy, following the hereditary occupations, etc.

3. Caste Surviving as a Powerful Political Force

Caste as a Source of Vote-Bank : Political role of caste is gaining more importance today. Political parties are relying more and more on select caste groups to secure caste based votes. Political parties and politicians are making consistent efforts to create their caste based vote banks. As long as these vote banks survive, so long caste remains a powerful force in politics.

Caste as an Interest Group or a Pressure Group : All established and well organised castes are today functioning as political *"pressure groups"* or *"interest groups."* In order to protect its interest each major caste is creating a *"caste lobby"* or a caste pressure group. Caste lobbies exert a great influence on the caste members at the time of elections, and on all major political events and happenings.

4. Caste-Based Reservation

Caste-based reservation has kept alive caste consciousness and caste-discrimination. Beneficiaries of reservation tend to hold on to their caste affiliations permanently and any attempt to take away the facility of reservation will be resisisted by them. No political party has the courage to make the proposal of withdrawing the reservation facility even to those Scheduled Caste, Scheduled Tribe and backward classes people who have become financially well off over the years. Even the Supreme Court in its verdict on the implementation of Mandal Commission's report in Nov. 1992 had openly stated that *caste alone would be the basis of reservation.* Reservation facility has thus served to consolidate the positions of the lower caste people and to create in them an eternal awareness to constitute themselves into a caste-based community of backward classes.

5. Women as the Conservers of Caste System

Leela Dube in her article *"Caste and Women"* has stated that women contribute in no small measure to the - *"occupational continuity and the reproduction of caste, food and rituals, and finally, marriage and sexuality"* and such other essential aspects of caste system.[3]

---

1 **Prof. N. Jayaram** *"Caste and Hinduism : Changing Protean Relationship"* in the book *"Caste Its Twentieth Century Avatar."* Edited by **M.N. Srinivas.** Page - 71.

2 *ibid.* Page - 70.

3 **Leela Dube** *"Caste and Women"* in the Book *"Caste and Its Twentieth Century Avatar."* edited by **M.N. Srinivas.** Page - 1.

"Women's work contributes substantially to the occupational continuity of a caste group." For example, it is difficult for weavers, potters, to carry on the complex processes of their craft without the continuous help of the women and children in the household, who in turn have a well defined tasks. Similarly, *basket weaving, horticulture, tanning, oil grinding* and such other works represent the joint ventures of men and women. Further, in matters relating to food and rituals, marriage and sexuality associated with caste, *women seem to be more rigid than men.*

Women play the key role in maintaining the sanctity and purity of the home. *"The responsibility for who eats what, where and when, falls upon women within the domestic space, women's practices in relation to food play a critical role in the hierarchical ordering of castes."* [Page -7]. Significantly a woman who belongs to a caste lower than that of her husband's can often cook ordinary food for the family but is not allowed to cook for the ancestors. A woman coming from another caste cannot be fully incorporated into the husband's group and acquire the privilege of feeding the ancestors. They cling on to traditions and even remind men regarding the traditional ways of doing whenever their menfolk show indifference towards certain caste rules and practices.

6. Hinduism Will Benefit From the Survival of Caste ?

"It is well known that traditionally the ideology justifying the caste system came from such Hindu scriptures and law books as the Bhagavadgita and the Dharmashastras. Both the .... jatis [large-scale endogamous descent groups] and varnas [ranked classification of jatis], on the one hand, and the associated concepts of jatidharma and varnadharma........ on the other, were defined and interpreted in terms of the theological doctrines of Hinduism. Hence Hinduism and the caste system came to be regarded as inextricably intertwined."[1]

Dr. N. Jayaram says that *"instead of the caste system deriving operational justification from Hindu theology any more, it is Hinduism which seems to be deriving functional support from the caste system."* [Page - 74]. Sanskritisation process which has become a part of the caste system *"while structurally endorsing the caste system, contributes to the dynamic integration of Hinduism."* [Page - 75].

Hinduism has been undergoing these days a thorough change. Brahmins are no more regarded as the *sole* custodians of Hinduism. The processes of modernisation of traditional Hindu rituals, and the democratisation of Hinduism have given enough scope for the lowest castes to have close contact with the *"great tradition"* of Hinduism. Most of the restrictions imposed on the lowest castes have been removed now. The growing appeal of certain new devotional traditions such as the Aiyyappa cult, the Ganapathi Utsava, Ramalila, Devi Puja, or local cults, the growing culture of pilgrimage have further strengthened caste neutrality. It is in this context, **Harold Gould** has aptly summarised**:** *"It..... appears very unlikely that so admirable an adaptive structure as caste is in any serious danger of ever disappearing completely. Its religious basis may wane, its systematic rigour may weaken; but its social [kinship] basis will persist, and its group connotation will gain strength. As far as its interface with Hinduism is concerned, though Hinduism may lose meaning as a justificatory ideology for the hierarchy and inequalities of the system, its cultural crux will persist and crystalize. And, Hinduism will benefit more from the survival of caste than caste from Hinduism."*[2] The interdependence of caste and Hinduism is such that an intricate

---

1 **N. Jayaram** *"Caste and Hinduism"* in the book *"Caste and Its Twentieth Century Avatar."* Page - 74.

2 **Harold A. Gould** in *"Caste Adaptation in Modernising Indian Society"* as quoted by **Dr. N. Jayaram** in article *"Caste and Hinduism."* Page 84.

question such as - *"What will happen to Hinduism, when caste disappears ?"* - cannot be answered with any precision at this stage.

Some Considered Opinions of Scholars

Scholars have been expressing their opinion regarding the future of the caste system since a long time. Some such opinions may be cited here.

Max Muller, more than one and a quarter century ago [in 1869], had opined that caste cannot be abolished in India and to attempt it would be one of the most hazardous operations that was ever performed in a political body. As a religious institution, caste will die; as a social institution, it will live and improve.

D.N. Majumdar, one of the renowned anthropologists of India, also maintained in the 1950s and 1960s that just as a broken or a poisoned finger is amputated and not the whole hand, similarly untouchability, exploitation of one caste by another, and such other harmful concomitants of the caste system should be done away with and not the whole system.

Prof. K.L. Sharma is also of the opinion that the ability of the caste to adjust itself to the changing situations is a clear proof of its continuity. It will definitely survive and continue.[1]

Prof. Ram Ahuja is of the firm opinion that *"....... the caste system will continue to be a reality in the years and decades to come."*[2]

Kolenda [1997] is of the opinion that it is indeed unlikely that a social structure [such as caste] organising the political, economic and ritual life of a people for over 1,000 years could be totally expunged within a few decades.

Social scientists working in the field, report that the caste system is alive. All the existing social situations and conditions seem to be supporting the caste system and its survival. Those people who had given a call to destroy the caste system, or to oust it from the soil of India, too have now realised that caste cannot be easily done away with. Caste has become a part and parcel of our socio-religious system and the politico-economic system. Caste is making all the efforts to survive and to strengthen itself by making necessary compromises and accommodations with changing times.

1 **K.L. Sharma** in his New Introduction to **J. Murdoch**'s *"Review of Caste in India."*

2 **Ram Ahuja** *"Indian Social System."* Page - 302.

Chapter 8

SOME ASPECTS OF SOCIAL MOBILITY

*Social Mobility : Definition and Types - Social Mobility in A Caste-Ridden Society: India - **A. Sanskritisation** : Meaning and Definition of Sanskritisation - Sanskritisation and Brahminisation- An Analysis of the Process of Sanskritisation - Sanskritisation : Some Critical Comments. **B. Westernisation** : Definition of the Term - Main Features of Westernisation - Primary Westernisation and Cultural Modernisation - Effects of Westernisation - Westernisation : Some Critical Comments. **C. Modernisation** : Meaning of Modernisation - Definition of Modernisation - The Process of Modernisation - Characteristics of Modernisation - Process of Modernisation in India - Problems of Modernisation - Sanskritisation and Westernisation : Comparative Views - Westernisation and Modernisation : Comparative Views.*

Individuals are normally recognised in a society through the statuses they occupy and the roles they enact. Not only the society is dynamic but also the individuals are dynamic. Men are normally engaged in endless endeavour to enhance their statuses in society, move from lower position to higher position, secure a superior job in the place of an inferior one. For various reasons people of higher status and position may also be forced to come down to a lower status and position. *Thus people in a society continue to move up and down the status scale.* This movement is called *"social mobility."*

Social mobility is an inseparable aspect of the modern society. It does not mean that all societies provide equal opportunities for mobility. The tempo of social mobility is also not the same everywhere. Hence some societies are said to be more mobile than others. The Indian society is also experiencing comparatively a high rate of social mobility now. However, there prevailed a belief that Indian society which is having "caste" as a dominant form of social stratification system, is relatively rigid and does not favour mobility. Such unfounded views are no more relevant now. Social mobility seems to be very intense in India especially at the beginning of this 21st century.

Hence the belief that caste is a *"closed system"* in which social mobility is impossible, has no meaning today. **Prof. M.N. Srinivas**, an eminent Indian sociologist, has convincingly established the fact that social mobility is taking place both within and outside the framework of caste. He introduced new sociological terms such as *"Sanskritisation"* and *"Westernisation"* in support of his views. The two terms have assumed importance in the analysis of the socio-cultural mobility in the Indian society.

India is becoming more and more westernised. It means it is becoming modernised. Modernisation is taking place with such a speed that it has radically transformed our social, political, educational, economic, religious and other organisations. It has changed our attitudes and outlook, our world-view and our philosophy. It has provided opportunities and posed challenges. This chapter gives a glimpse of these three concepts, namely : *Sanskritisation, Westernisation* and *Modernisation.*

Definition and Types of Social Mobility

Definition of Social Mobility

1. *Wallace and Wallace* : *"Social mobility is the movement of a person or persons from one social status to another"* [in *"Sociology"*. Page : 275.]
2. *W.P. Scott* : Social mobility refers to *"the movement of an individual or group from one social class or social stratum to another"* [in *"Dictionary of Sociology"*. Page : 260].

Thus, it is clear, *"social mobility"* may be understood as the movement of an individual or group from one social status or position to that of another. *For example,* the poor people may become rich; the bank peons may become bank officers; farmers may become ministers; a petty businessman may become a bankrupt and the ruling class may be turned out of office, and so on.

Types of Social Mobility

Russian born American sociologist of great reputation *P.A. Sorokin,* distinguishes between two types of social mobility namely : (i) *Vertical Social Mobility*, and (ii) *Horizontal Social Mobility*. This typology is normally followed by other sociologists.

1. Vertical Social Mobility

Vertical social mobility refers to the movement of an individual or people or groups from one status to another. It involves change in class, occupation or power positions. It involves a change within the lifetime of an individual to a higher or lower status than the person had to begin with. *Example*: (i) Movement from the status of plumber to that of a city corporation president, or vice versa, is an example of *vertical mobility.*

(ii) Movement of people from the poor class to the middle class, from the occupation of labourers to that of bank clerks, from the power position of the opposition to that of the ruling class, etc.

2. Horizontal Mobility

"Horizontal mobility" is a change in position without the change in status. It indicates a change in position within the range of the same status. It is *"movement from one status to its equivalent"* [*David Popenoe* - 244]. *Example*: (i) A college graduate with a degree in chemistry had planned to work in the research department of a large chemical company, but after a year he finds that the work seems dull and repetitive, with no improvement in sight. He quits that job and instead becomes a professor of chemistry at a nearby university. Because the two occupations are at roughly the same level *his mobility involved no essential change of status; it was simply a move to a more satisfying job.*

(ii) An engineer working in a factory may resign for his job and join another factory as an engineer and may work in more or less the same capacity, or join an engineering college and start working as a professor. In this example also, though there is change of workplace and work, the general status of the person does not change much.

Social Mobility in A Caste-Ridden Society : India

Though the Indian society which is based on the caste system is often regarded as a *"closed society"*, it is not altogether changeless. Within the framework of the caste itself some kind of mobility is observed. Lower castes have often tried to claim higher status by imitating the life-styles of upper-castes particularly of Brahmins and Kshatriyas. M.N. Srinivas used the term *"Sanskritisation"* to denote such type of process. The upper castes including Brahmins, on the contrary, have started orienting their life-styles on the model of the Westerners. The term *"Westernisation"* introduced by M.N. Srinivas describes this process. Today not only the upper class and middle class people including upper caste and intermediary caste people are trying to orient their behaviour, attitudes, beliefs and life-styles towards those of developed societies; but also the entire mass of people are involved in this process. Daniel Lerner calls this process *"modernisation."* It denotes a process of social change whereby *"less developed societies acquire the characteristics common to more developed societies."*

Here is an attempt to understand the socio-cultural changes that have been taking place in India in terms of these processes namely, *Sanskritisation, Westernisation* and *Modernisation.* These three processes reflect an attempt on the part of the Indian masses to achieve some amount of mobility both within and outside the framework of the caste system.

A. SANSKRITISATION

Definition and Analysis of the Process of Sanskritisation

Meaning of Sanskritisation

The term *"Sanskritisation"* was introduced into Indian Sociology by **Prof. M.N. Srinivas.** The term refers to a process whereby people of lower castes collectively tried to adopt upper caste practices and beliefs, as a preliminary step to acquire higher status. Thus it indicates a process of cultural mobility that is taking place in the traditional social system of India.

Context of the Introduction of the Term *"Sanskritisation"*

M.N. Srinivas in his study of the Coorgs in Karnataka, found that some lower castes, in order to raise their position in the caste hierarchy, adopted some customs and practices of Brahmins, and gave up some of their own which were considered to be *"impure"* by the higher castes. For example, t*hey gave up meat-eating, drinking liquor and animal sacrifice to their deities. They imitated Brahmins in matters of dress, food and rituals.* These people who started calling themselves *"Amma Kodavas"*, became strict vegetarians like the Brahmins, began to wear sacred threads and arrange marriage from among themselves, on the model of the Brahmins. In fact, they started imitating Brahmin way of living in all possible ways. By doing this, within a generation or so they could claim higher positions in the hierarchy of castes. In the beginning, M.N. Srinivas used the term *"Brahminisation"* (in his book *"Religion and Society Among the Coorgs"* - 1952] to denote this process. The term *"Brahminisation"* denotes the imitation of Brahmin way of life. Later on, he replaced it by "***Sanskritisation***".

Definition of Sanskritisation

M.N. Srinivas, in fact, went on broadening his definition of the term "Sanskritisation" from time to time. Initially, he described it as follows.

1. Sanskritisation is *"the process of mobility of lower castes by adopting vegetarianism and teetotalism to move in the caste hierarchy in a generation or two"* - [M.N. Srinivas 1962]

- Prof. Srinivas redefined the term in 1966 in his book *"Social Change in Modern India"* in the following manner.

2. ***Sanskritisation is "a process by which a low caste or a tribe or other group changes its customs, rituals, ideology, and way of life in the direction of a high and frequently, twice-born caste".***

The second definition is much broader, for it includes some ideologies [such as *"Karma", "dharma", "papa"* (sin), *"punya" "moksha"* etc.] It is in currency now.

Yogendra Singh points out that the second definition cited above is broader and more appropriate in some respects:

(i) As per this definition, the imitating group need not be only a low caste group, it can be a tribal or any other group.

(ii) The imitation is not restricted to mere rituals and religious practices. It also means imitation of ideologies.

(iii) Thirdly, the Brahmins do not constitute the only model. It could be any group occupying a higher position in the hierarchy. Srinivas admits that it is the locally dominant caste which will be the model. The dominant caste could be Brahmin or Lingayat or Kshatriya or Vaisya, etc.. The criteria of dominance may be ritually higher status, education, economic strength or numerical majority.[1]

Sanskritisation and Brahminisation

The Term Sanskritisation is Preferable to Brahminisation

(i) Sanskritisation is a broader term and it can include in itself the narrower process of Brahminisation. For instance, today, though by and large, Brahmins are vegetarians and teetotalers, some of them such as Kashmiris, Bengalis and Saraswath Brahmins eat non-vegetarian food. Had the term *"Brahminisation"* been used, it would have become necessary to specify which particular Brahmin group was meant.

(ii) Further, the reference groups[2] of Sanskritisation are not always Brahmins: The process of imitation need not necessarily take place on the model of Brahmins. Srinivas himself has given the example of the low castes of Mysore who adopted the way of life of Lingayats, who are not Brahmins but who claim equality with Brahmins.

The *lower castes imitated not only Brahmins but also Kshatriyas, Vaishyas, Jats, Shudras, etc. in different parts of the country.* Hence the term *Brahminisation* does not completely explain this process. M.N. Srinivas himself acknowledged this fact.[3]

Analysis of the Process of Sanskritisation

An analysis of the process of *"Sanskritisation"* would reveal to us the following aspects.

1 Dr. M.A. Chingamani *"Sociology of Indian Society."* Page-219.

2 Reference Group: The term *"reference group"* was introduced by **Muzafer Sherif** in his book entitled *"An Outline of Social Psychology"* - 1948. As **Ogburn** and **Nimkoff** have said, *"groups which serve as points of comparision are known as reference groups". They are also groups from which we get our values, or whose approval we seek."*

3 M.N. Srinivas wrote - "I now realise that I emphasised unduly the Brahminical model of Sanskritisation and ignored the other models Kshatriya, Vaishya and Shudra..." (*"Social Change in Modern India"* - 1966 Page-7)

1. Sanskritisation as a process of imitation : "Sanskritisation" denotes *a process in which the lower castes try to imitate the life-styles of upper castes in their attempt to raise their social status.* The process seems to be associated with the role of local *"dominant caste".* Though the lower castes for some time, imitated Brahmins they soon shifted it towards the local dominant caste which in most cases was a non-Brahmin dominant caste.

2. Some Areas of Imitation or Sanskritisaion : The lower castes started imitating some of the aspects of higher castes of which the following may be noted :

(i) ***Rituals*** : Some of the "low" caste Hindus imitated the rituals of the Brahmins, such as their ways of observing festivals, chanting vedic mantras, visiting the places of pilgrimage, fixing marriages on the advice of the *"purohits"* [priests] and giving away the daughters as *"Kanyadana"* in marriage, and so on.

(ii) ***Marriage*** : The practice of pre-puberty marriages was common among the Brahmins sometimes ago. Marriage among them was regarded as an indissoluble bond and widow-marriage was not allowed. The very presence of the widow was considered a bad omen. Though such practices were not there among the lower castes, they started imitating the same on the model of the Brahmins.

(iii) ***Treatment of Women*** : Women among the high castes were assigned only a secondary position due to *puranic* beliefs and restrictions imposed by the Dharmashastras. Especially among Brahmins, women were considered to be polluting during menstruation and child birth and were expected to be subservient to their men folk in all respects. Though the low castes had given comparatively better freedom to their women folk, their imitation of *"Brahmin model"* made them to give harsh treatment and very low status to their women.

(iv) ***Food Habits and Dress Habits*** : Brahmins have been vegetarians and teetotallers since a long time. Some of the low castes imitated the food habits of the Brahmins and preferred to remain vegetarians and even gave up drinking alcohol. Some low castes also imitated Brahmin dress style such as wearing *dhoti, shalya, turban* [or rumal], *kachche panche, kachche sari* and so on.

(v) ***System of Giving Names to New Born Ones*** : Many of the low castes started giving names to new born members on the model of the Brahmins. For example, in place of the traditional and typical names such as Basava, Kariya, Kempa, Kaala, Chinna, Soma, Honni, Thimmavva, Kempi, Duggi, Beeri, Chinni, etc. they started giving names such as Parameshwara, Ramkrishna, Shankara, Madhava, Eshwara, Gowri, Parvathi, Saraswathi, Lakshmi, Rukmini and so on.

(vi) ***Imitation of Ideologies and Values*** : In their attempts to rise up in the social hierarchy the low caste people started using in their dairly conversation, ideological concepts and values such as – *Karma, Dharma, Papa, Punya, Maya, Moksha, Sansara, Paramatma,* etc. which are found in Sanskrit literature.

4. Sanskritisation indicates a process of upward mobility. In this process, a caste is trying to raise its position in the caste hierarchy not at once, but over a period of time. It would take, sometimes, a period of one or two generations.

5. Pre-conditions of Sanskritisation: A careful observation of this process would reveal to us some of its pre-conditions.

(i) The imitated caste is normally regarded as superior to the imitating caste in ritual status, economic matters, respectability and social prestige.

(ii) Castes taking part in the process of Sanskritisation must have the will to increase its social status at least by imitating the upper caste/s.

(iii) Imitating caste must have regular and close socio-cultural contacts with the imitated caste/s.

(iv) Those castes which are taking part in this process must be prepared to consider the upper-caste [the "life-styles of which it wants to imitate] their *"reference group".*

6. Sanskritisation is not necessarily confined to the castes within the Hindu community, it is found in tribal communities also. *Example,* The Bhils of Western India, the *Gonds* and *Oraons* of Middle India, and the *Pahadiyas* of Himalayan region have come under the influence of Sanskritisation. These tribal communities now claim themselves to be Hindus, for their communities represent some caste groups within the fold of Hinduism. (It should be noted that in the traditional system, a group could be called *"Hindu"* only if it was regarded as a caste group).

7. The process of Sanskritisation serves as a "reference group". It is through this process that a caste group tries to orient its beliefs, practices, values, attitudes and "life-styles" in terms of another superior or dominant group, so that it can also get some recognition. Since this term was made applicable by M.N. Srinivas even to Kshatriya, Vaishya and Shudra models (in addition to Brahmana model), it has greater relevance to function as a *"reference group".*

8. Sanskritisation does not take place in the same manner in all the places. Studies have revealed that in most of the cases the lower castes tend to imitate the upper castes particularly the Kshatriya and Brahmin castes. There are instances of upper castes imitating some of the practices of lower castes and sometimes of even tribal groups. **For example,** a Brahmin may make a blood-sacrifice to one of the local deities through the medium of a non-Brahmin friend. The Muslim cultural ways have imposed some limitations in the imitation process of some upper and lower castes. This is very much in evidence in Punjab. Thus, it can be generalised that *Sanskritisation is not a one-way process; it is a two-way process.* In this process a lower caste does not always *"take"* from the higher caste, sometimes, it also *'gives'* in return.

9. *The castes which enjoyed higher economic and political power but rated relatively low in ritual* ranking went after *Sanskritisation for they felt that their claim to a higher position was not fully effective.* The three main aspects of power in the caste system are the *ritual, the economic and the political ones.* The possession of power in any one sphere usually leads to the acquisition of power in the other two. But Srinivas opines that inconsistencies do occur.

10. *"Economic betterment is not a necessary pre-condition to Sanskritisation, nor economic development must necessarily lead to Sanskritisation.* However, sometimes a group [caste, tribe] may start by acquiring, political power and this may lead to economic development and Sanskritisation. Economic betterment, the acquisition of political power, education, leadership, and a desire to move up in the hierarchy, are all relevant factors in Sanskritisation, and each case of Sanskritisation may show all or some of these factors mixed up in different measures."[1]

11. Sanskritisation indicates only positional change. Mobility that is involved in the process of Sanskritisation *results only in "positional changes"* for particular castes or sections of castes and need not necessarily lead to a *"structural change".* It means while individual castes move up or down, the structure as such remains the same.

12. The process of Sanskritisation does not automatically result in the achievement of a higher status for the group. People will have to wait for a period of a generation or two before their claim can be accepted. Further, it may so happen that a claim which may not succeed in a particular area or period of time, may succeed in another.

1 Ram Ahuja *"Indian Social System."* Page - 355.

13. **Significant developments in the realm of material culture have accelerated the process of Sanskritisation.** Industrialisation, occupational mobility, mass media of communication, spread of literacy, advent of Western technology, improvement in the transportation system etc., have speeded up the process of Sanskritisation. Introduction of parliamentary system of democracy and universal suffrage have also contributed to the increased Sanskritisation.

14. As M.N. Srinivas has pointed out, **Sanskritisation serves to reduce or remove the gap between the ritual and secular ranking.** It is, indeed, one of its main functions. For example, if a caste, or its segment gains secular, that is, political power, it immediately starts imitating the so called *"status-symbols"* of the customs, rituals, ideals, beliefs, values, life-syles, etc. of the upper caste communities. The lower caste group which successfully gets into the seat of secular power also tries to avail itself of the services of Brahmins especially at the time of observing some rituals, worshipping and offering things to the God in the centres of pilgrimage, celebrating important Hindu festivals, fixing *"muhurtam"*(auspicious time for doing good works or starting new ventures) for some important occasions and programmes and so on.

- **Sanskritisation is not a new phenomenon as such.** M.N. Srinivas writes: *"Sanskritisation has been a major process of cultural change in Indian history, and it has occurred in every part of the Indian sub-continent. It may have been more active at some periods than at others and some parts of India are more sanskritised than others; but there is no doubt that the process has been universal"* (*Social Change in Modern India* - 1966 Page: 23).

- **Sanskritisation has often been construed as a kind of protest against the traditional caste system.** Sanskritisation is a type of protest against the caste system in which the status is ascribed or predetermined. Lower castes which are disillusioned with their predetermined statuses and impressed with the higher statuses accorded to the upper castes, naturally desire to go up in the status hierarchy. *This desire is virtually against the traditional hierarchical principle of the caste system.* Making an attempt through Sanskritisation to move up in the status hierarchy setting aside the hierarchical principle of caste, *amounts to a protest* against the caste system itself.

- *Sanskritisation,* as M.N. Srinivas himself has said, **does not denote a basic change in the structure of the Hindu society.** It should not be construed that through this process any kind of social change can be brought about in the caste-ridden society. Since membership in the caste-ridden society is based on the unchangeable factor of birth, no one can become a member of the *"reference group"* as such. However, an individual or a group may improve his or its social position within the range of one's own Varna group. Srinivas further observes that the process of Sanskritisation can only support the existing system but can never remove it. Hence, the changes that are effected through Sanskritisation, though cannot be neglected, have only limited significance.

- **The British rule in India provided a favourable atmosphere for Sanskritisation to take place.** Political independence has weakened the trend towards this change. Now the emphasis is on vertical social mobility and not on the horizontal mobility. But in this process of mobility that is, Sanskritisation, the basic unit remains only the group and not the individual or family.

Sanskritisation: Some Critical Comments

Though the concept *"Sanskritisation"* introduced by **Prof. M.N. Srinivas** has been regarded as a significant contribution to the sociological literature, it is not free from criticisms. Number of comments have been made about the term by the scholars. Some of them may be cited here.

1. According to J.F. Stall, *"Sanskritisation as used by Srinivas and other anthropologists, is a complex concept or a class of concepts. The term itself seems to be misleading, since its*

relationship to the term Sanskrit is "extremely complicated."[1]

Srinivas himself writes : *"It is an extremely complex and heterogeneous concept. It is even possible that it should be more profitable to treat it as a bundle of concepts rather than as a single concept. The important thing to remember is that it is only a name for a widespread cultural process."* It could be said that in view of the looseness of the concept, it fails to lead to any consistent theory of the social change.

2. Yogendra Singh comments : Though "Sanskritisation and Westernisation, in logical sense, are *"Truth asserting" concepts......* They *"fail to lead to a consistent theory of cultural change. Such consistency is far from realisation......."* The concepts *"contain no hypothesis"*, and in **Zetterbergs** words, *"Cannot be true or false. They can be clumsy or elegant, appropriate or inappropriate, effective or worthless but never true or false."*

3. Yogendra Singh points out that Sanskritisation did not have any pan-Indian pattern. He states : *"Neither in respect of the sources for cultural emulation nor in regard to the pattern and direction of emulation of cultural forms, has there been a universal Indian character."*

4. Yogendra Singh also opines that *"Sanskritisation fails to account for many aspects of cultural change in the past and contemporary India as it neglects the non-Sanskritic traditions".* Observing the truism of Yogendra Singh's comments in one of his studies in a village, **Mackim Marriot** observes that, we cannot establish that the process of Sanskritisation always takes place by replacing or removing the non-Sanskritic rituals. *"Sanskritic rites are often added on to non-Sanskritic rites without replacing them"* (Mackim Marriot)

5. It is also commented that much against the assumption of **M.N. Srinivas**, the *"Sanskritic influence has not been universal to all parts of the country. In most of northern India, especially in Punjab, it was the Islamic tradition which provided a basis for cultural imitation."* In Punjab, writes Chanana, *"Culturally Sanskritic influence has been but one of the trends, and at times, it could not have been the main trend. For a few centuries, until the third quarter of the 19th century, Persian influence had been the dominating one in this area"* - (as quoted by **Prof. Yogendra Singh** - Pages: 11-12).

6. **Dr. D.N. Majumdar** comments that *it is wrong to assume the process of Sanskritisation as a universal process observed throughout India.* In his study of *Mohan village* in Uttar Pradesh, he observed a strong exception to this assumption. In this village, as he noticed, the lower caste people do not have any urge or inclination to imitate the *"life-styles"* of Brahmins or any other dominant higher caste of that region. If a cobbler wears *tilak* (or *Vibhuti*), *dhoti* and the *sacred thread* and follows some of the customs of higher castes, nobody recognises him as an upper caste man. *"If Sanskritisation is really a universal process, where exactly does it stop and why ?..."* **Dr. Majumdar** questions.

7. **M.N. Srinivas** *has been changing the definition of the term "Sanskritisation" from time to time and this adds to the problem of understanding its meaning and range of operations in clear terms.* First, Dr. Srinivas used the term to mean *Brahminisation.* Later on, he extended its meaning. He used it to mean a process in which a lower caste, a tribal group or any other group attempts to imitate the *"life-styles"* of a locally dominant upper caste, mostly a twice-born caste. As per his recent interpretation, *the process includes the imitation of ideas, values and ideologies.* Here also it becomes difficult to ascertain the real meaning of the term *"ideology"*.

1 **Yogendra Singh** *"Modernisation of Indian Tradition"* Page - 10.

8. *When we try to interpret certain changes that have taken place in the field of social mobility in the light of Sanskritisation, we face certain paradoxes.* According to Dr. Srinivas, *political and economic forces are normally favourable for Sanskritisation.* But the *"policy of reservation"* a politico-constitutional attempt to elevate the status of lower caste and backward class people, presents here a different picture. Theoretically, the policy of reservation must be supportive of Sanskritisation. But paradoxically, it goes against it. Those who avail themselves of the *"reservation"* benefits have developed a vested interest in calling themselves *"dalits"* or *"scheduled caste"* people. They want to enjoy the benefits of "reservation" permanently.

9. *"As suggested by* **Harold A. Gould,** *often the motive force behind Sanskritisation is not of cultural imitation per se but an expression of challenge and revolt against the socio-economic deprivations."*

Yogendra Singh writes : *"Sanskritisation is thus a cultural camouflage for latent interclass and intercaste competition for economic and social power, typical of a tradition bound society where traditionally the privileged upper castes hold monopoly over power and social status. When the impact of the external forces like political democratisation, land reforms and other social reforms break this monopoly of the upper castes, the cultural camouflage of Sanskritisation is thrown away, in favour of an open conflict with the privileged classes based on nativistic solidarity."* – [*ibid,* Page - 12.]

B. WESTERNISATION

Meaning of Westernisation

The concept of Westernisation introduced by **Prof. M.N. Srinivas** seems to be much simpler than the concept of Sanskritisation. Like Sanskritisation, this term is also of great help in analysing the socio-cultural changes taking place in India for the past 250 years. M.N. Srinivas has used this term mainly *to refer to the impact of British rule on the Indian society.* Srinivas has also tried to use this concept in a general manner to refer to the impact of the West on the non-western societies. Thus, he wrote: **Westernisation** refers to *"the changes in technology, institutions, ideology and values of a non-Western society for a long period"* - (1962)

Definition of the Term "Westernisation"

1. "Westernisation" refers to *"the changes brought about in Indian society and culture as a result of over 150 years of British rule and the term subsumes changes occurring at different levels - technology, institutions, ideology, values."*[1]
2. In simple words, the term *Westernisation mainly explains the changes that have taken place in the Indian society and culture due to the Western contact through the British rule.*

- **M.N. Srinivas** criticises **Lerner's** concept of "modernisation" on the ground that it is *a value-loaded term.* According to him, "Modernisation" is normally used in the sense that it is good. He, therefore, prefers to use the term *"Westernisation."* He describes the technological changes, establishment of educational institutions, rise of nationalism and new political culture, etc. as almost the by-products of Westernisation or the British rule for about two hundred years in India. Thus, by Westernisation, Srinivas primarily meant the British impact.
- *"During the 19th century, the British slowly laid the foundations of a modern state by surveying land, settling the revenue, creating a modern bureaucracy, army and police,*

1 M.N. Srinivas *"Social Change in Modern India"* [1966], Page 47

instituting law courts, codifying the law, developing communications – railways, post and telegraph, roads and canals – establishing schools and colleges, and so on......" [Srinivas]. The British brought with them the printing press which led to many-sided changes. Books and journals made possible the transmission of modern as well as traditional knowledge to a large number of Indians. Newspapers helped the people living in the remote corners of the country to realise their common bonds and to understand the events happening in the world outside.

- **M.N. Srinivas** says that it is necessary *"to distinguish conceptually between Westernisation and two other processes usually concomitant with it – Industrialisation and Urbanisation."* He gives two reasons for this : (i) *Urbanisation is not a simple function of "industrialisation" and there were cities in Pre-industrial world also.* (ii) *There are cases of rural people who are more urbanised than urban people.*

Main Features of The Process of Westernisation

It is possible to identify some of the main features of *"Westernisation"* on the basis of the explanation of the term by its mentor. Some of them are listed below.

1. **Westernisation compared to Sanskritisation is a simpler concept.** As already made clear, it explains the impact of Western contact (particularly of British rule) on the Indian society and culture. M.N. Srinivas defends the uses of the term when he says that there is *"need for such a term when analysing the changes that a non-Western country undergoes as a result of prolonged contact with a Western one".*

2. **Some Main Areas Affected by Westernisation** : The process of Westernisation, according to M.N. Srinivas, mainly refers to the changes that took place in some main areas such as *technology, institutions, ideology* and *values.* The changes that took place in these areas especially during the British rule had their own impact on other areas of our social life.

3. **"Westernisation is an inclusive, complex, and many-layered concept":** Western technology, education and "life-styles" had a great impact on Indians' daily life. The Western influence made them drop out some of their traditional customs, accept many of the new practices and make a compromise between the old and the new in some other areas of life. **Example:** Urbanised Indians dropped the practice of sitting on the floor to eat food served on dining leaves. They became accustomed to dining tables, chairs, stainless steel utensils, spoons etc. Indians made use of various instruments of modern technology such as motor cars, printing press, sewing machines, typewriters, water pumps etc. At the same time, they never forgot to attribute to them the religious beliefs, and worshipped these instruments on the occasion of *Dasara* festival as they used to do it previously.

4. **Involvement of different sections of people who accelearated the process of Westernisation** : Some of the British people, and a section of people in the Indian community served to accelerate the process of Westernisation.

(A) Among the British - (i) *soldiers and high-level government officials;* (ii) *merchants and big plantation owners;* (iii) *foreign Christian missionaries* - All these exerted Western influence on those Indians with whom they had close contacts.

(B) Among the Indians - (i) People who served in the houses of British officials / citizens as domestic servants, people who got converted to Christianity; (ii) Those Western educated Indians who served in the government bureaucracy; those who worked as advocates, engineers, doctors and such others; and those highly educated Indians with almost aristocratic background such as

Raja Ram Mohan Roy, Ravindranath Tagore, Pandit Nehru, Sir Syed Ahmedkhan, Mohammed Ali Jinna and others functioned to accelerate the Westernisation process.

5. **The form and pace of Westernisation of India varied from region to region and from one section of population to another.** (Srinivas 1985): For example, one group of people became Westernised in their dress, diet, manners, speech, sports and in the gadgets they used; while another absorbed Western science, knowledge and literature, remaining relatively free from certain other aspects of Westernisation. For **example**, Brahmins accepted the Western dress habits and educational systems and also used gadgets such as radio, television, car, telephone etc. But they did not accept the British diet, dancing, hunting and such other habits. *This distinction is, however, only relative and not absolute.*

6. According to **Srinivas**, *Westernisation pervades political and cultural fields also.* He writes : *"In the political and cultural fields, Westernisation has given birth not only to nationalism but also to revivalism, communalism, "casteism", heightened linguistic consciousness, and regionalism. To make matters even more bewildering, revivlist movements have used Western type schools and colleges and books, pamphlets and journals to propagate their ideas."* [Pages 55-56.]

7. **The Concept is ethically neutral:** As M.N. Srinivas claims, *"The term Westernisation, unlike "Modernisation", is ethically neutral. Its use does not carry the implication that it is good or bad, whereas modernisation is normally used in the sense that is is good."*

8. ***Westernisation may speed up the process of Sanskritisation:*** According to Srinivas, *"the increase in Westernisation does not retard the process of Sanskritisation. Both go on simultaneously, and to some extent, increase in Westernisation accelerates the process of Sanskritisation. For example, the postal facilities, railways, buses and newspaper media, which are the fruits of Western impact on India, render more organised religious pilgrimages, meetings, caste solidarities, etc. possible now than in the past."*[1]

Preference of the lower caste people towards Westernisation ?: At present, the lower caste people feel that it is easier and more advantageous for them to elevate their social status through "Westernisation" than "Sanskritisation." Through "Sanskritisation", they could only imitate the upper caste people and their life-styles to enhance their social esteem or respectability. Whereas Westernisation provided a wide opportunity for the lower caste people to attain equality on par with the upper caste people in important areas such as education, profession, politics, financial matters, etc. Westernisation helped them to withstand and resist the dominance of upper castes especially in the fields such as education, government jobs and politics. Hence, there is a greater trend towards Westernisation than Sanskritisation. The extent, effectiveness, tempo and the urge towards Sanskritisation, seem to be diminishing giving place to the process of Westernisation.

PRIMARY WESTERNISATION AND CULTURAL MODERNISATION

The term Westernisation, as it is already mentioned, is introduced by M.N. Srinivas to denote an exogenous source of social change in India. M.N. Srinivas has also spoken of various dimensions of the process of Westernisation. Summarising the various dimensions of Westernisation discussed by Srinivas, **Yogendra Singh** states : *"Emphasis on humanitarianism and rationalism is a part of Westernisation which led to a series of institutional and social reforms in India. Establishment of scientific, technological and educational institutions, rise of nationalism, new political cultural leadership in the country, are all by-products of Westernisation."*

---

1 **Yogendra Singh** *"Modernisation of Indian Tradition."* Page - 9.

M.N. Srinivas prefers to use the term Westernisation to modernisation. He says that modernisation involves rationalisation of ends. This means that the goals chosen by a society should be rational. *"But he points out that social goals are, in the final analysis, the expression of value preference and, therefore, non-rational. The public discussion of the goals can in no way guarantee their rationality. Rationality can only be predicted of the means, but not the ends of social action. Therefore, Srinivas prefers Westernisation to modernisation."*[1]

M.N. Srinivas mentions of various dimensions of Westernisation. According to him, it is easy to identify the process when the links between the Western stimulus and the Indian response are few. But doubts may arise when the links are numerous or not visible on the surface. He writes, *"I think it will be increasingly necessary to qualify Westernisation by the prefix 'primary', 'secondary' or 'tertiary'. In primary Westernisation, unlike secondary and tertiary, the linkage is simple and direct."* [M.N. Srinivas].

Dimensions of Westernisation

Prof. Yogendra Singh who has adopted the distinction between primary and secondary Westernisation as suggested by M.N. Srinivas, elaborates the various dimensions of Westernisation. He writes : *"Following the analytic scheme we developed for the study of cultural change in India through the exogenous sources, we shall describe the ramifications of western impact both on the Little and Great Traditions*[2] *of India."* Yogendra Singh is of the opinion that the process of Westernisation occurred at different levels. He is also of the opinion that the ramifications of the Western impact can be analysed under two heads. They are :

I. *Primary Westernisation,* and

II. *Cultural Modernisation [or Secondary Westernisation].*

I. Primary Westernisation

Primary Westernisation refers to changes brought about in Indian tradition which are due to Western impact. Such changes are of two types. They are (i) *Sub-cultural Type,* and (ii) *Diffusive Type.*

(i) Sub-cultural Type

According to Yogendra Singh, the Hindu tradition which came into contact with the Western tradition, did not undergo radical and an all inclusive change all on a sudden. The Western tradition had just emerged and growing at a great speed from the days of Renaissance to those of the Industrial Revolution. The Hindu tradition was still resistant to the Western tradition. Hence, the early Western impact remained peripheral and localised. *These forms of Western impact were*

---

1 Dr. M.A. Chingamani *"Sociology of Indian Society."* Page - 226.

2 *Concept of Little Tradition* : "This term refers to the culture of the rural villager living within a civilization. The *Little Tradition* contrasts with the *Great Tradition,* which is the formal tradition of the civilization. Robert Redfield is identified with these concepts. Elements of the *Little Tradition* are continually incorporated into the *Great Tradition* through a process of universalization. Likewise, elements of the *Great Tradition* filter down to the village level, but in the process of parochialization the elements are transformed, modified, or reinterpreted to fit the rural, peasant tradition. The concept of *Little Tradition* does not apply to primitive peoples, whose culture is thought to be autonomous." ***Source*** : *"Encyclopedia of Anthropology"* edited by **David E. Hunter** and **Philip Whitten**. Page - 252.

the Little Traditions of Westernisation. A small section of the Indian intellectuals and scholars who adopted some aspects of Western culture and life-styles in a way supported its rapid expansion. As the influence of this Westernised subculture group was localised, it may be treated as a part of the primary stage of Westernisation. It forms a part of the Little Tradition. It was primarily subcultural and lacked systematic world-view, an organised structure. This subcultural pattern included in itself various aspects. Different types could be identified in this pattern.

(a) ***The Subculture of a Commercial Middle Class*** : The first manifestation of the Western impact was the emergence of a commercial middle class in the 18th century. The members of this class served as middlemen for the European traders. And it included clerks, interpreters, cashiers and petty contractors, who went from one part of the country to another to make purchases. These people were partly Westernised. They were able to speak the language of their European masters and also acquired training and ability to manage a new form of business. These middlemen were transformed into a new commercial middle class in course of time.

(b) ***The Subculture of Professional Groups*** : The middle class of the professional group emerged in India in the 19th century as a result of the British educational institutions which started functioning in India. Western educational institutions contributed to the growth of this class. This new Western educated class took to Western values and ideologies. Concepts such as individualism, equality, liberty, fraternity, democracy, etc. had a tremendous impact on them. Western education had its impact even on the attitude, outlook, morality and philosophy of this new class.

(c) ***The Subculture of New Literary Traditions*** : Westernisation had its impact on the emergence of new literary traditions in India. The subcultural group of Western educated Indians started translating several Western literary works into Indian languages. Further, the literary works of this period in various Indian languages reflected the influence of Western literary tradition.

(d) ***The Subculture of Social Reforms*** : Westernisation process led to some social reform movements in India. Brahma Samaj founded by Raja Ram Mohan Roy in Bengal represents one such movement. Ram Mohan Roy who had undergone English education was a great lover of humanity and had the belief that the Western values could be used to revitalise the Indian society and to give a new momentum to its social, cultural and economic dynamism. Subsequently, a number of other similar organisations [*Ex. Prarthana Samaj, Theosophical Society, Sathyashodhak Samaj,* etc.] were established in other parts of the country. These reform movements were led by men who were not only interested in assimilating some aspects of Western tradition and culture into the Indian society but at the same time, were particular about preserving certain basic values of the Indian tradition. These reform movements brought about many changes in the traditional social practices of the Hindu society. *Thus, a humble beginning was made towards the cultural modernisation of Indian tradition.*

(ii) Diffusive Type

Yogendra Singh states that *another aspect of the Primary Westernisation refers to the modernisation of the daily lives, customs and habits of the people in general.* This includes the adoption and the use of new technology, dress, food habits, rituals, vocabulary, material culture, mode of travel and types of conveyance and so on. Changes in dress include replacement of handloom clothes by factory made clothes. Change in the food habits refers to the introduction of new vegetables and food items in the day to day dining. Meat eating, use of eggs and vegetable oil, etc. became common. Many terms from English language such as *"law", "court", "judge", "collector", "bus", "school", "college", "party", "police station", "railway station", "injection", "post", "telegram", "phone"*, etc. became a part of the conversation of even uneducated rural people.

Diffusive type virtually differs from the subcultural types in two respects. "*Firstly,* it has its basis merely in imitation of external forms of culture and as such, there is no scope for assimilation of values. *Secondly,* it has diffused into a wider area covering both laymen and scholars, villagers and urbanites."[1]

II. Cultural Modernisation or Secondary Westernisation

The Western impact was not confined only to the Little Tradition. On the contrary, it affected the various aspects of the Great Tradition. *Cultural modernisation refers to the form of Westernisation which occurred at the national level, that is, at the level of the Great Tradition.* According to **Yogendra Singh**, some of the institutional developments which have been responsible for the creation of a Great Tradition of modernisation in India can be mentioned below :

1. *The growth of universalistic legal system.*
2. *Expansion of education.*
3. *Urbanisation and industrialisation.*
4. *Increased network of communication.*
5. *Growth of nationalism and politicalisation of the society.*

Each of the factors mentioned above, had a national character and was not a subcultural or localised process as primary Westernisation.

1. The Growth of a Universalistic Legal System

With the consolidation of the British power in India, the traditional Hindu law underwent drastic changes. In the traditional Hindu law, the norms prescribed were different for different caste groups. There was no uniform system of law. But the new laws introduced by the British were secular and were based on the principles of universalism, rationalism and individualism. *Thus, legislation became an instrument of modernisation.* Its growth, however, was slow and gradually a synthesis between the traditional and modern legal forms took place in many parts of India.

The new legal system came to be introduced due to the efforts of **Warren Hastings**. He was in favour of the decentralisation of law courts to deal with civil and criminal matters at the district level itself. For this purpose, *Civil Procedure Code, Indian Penal Code* and *Criminal Procedure Code* were enacted in 1859, 1860 and 1861 respectively. **Lord Cornwallis** was instrumental in separating the judicial powers and functions of courts from the executive ones. Around 1830s uniform system of legal rights and its administration came to be practised. In course of time, a number of social legislations[2] were introduced affecting the lives of the entire population of India. The tradition of introducing such universalistic social legislations was continued even after independence.

The universalistic legal system introduced in India brought about some basic changes. The legal system emphasised equality before the law. A number of traditional customs which had

---

1 **Moulesh** and **Subramanya** *"Sociology of Indian Society."* Page - 190.

2 ***Examples of Social Legislations Undertaken During the British Period***: **1.** The Prohibition of Sati Act, 1829. **2.** Abolition of Trade in Slaves, 1832. **3.** Caste Disabilities Removal Act, 1850. **4.** Hindu Widow Remarriage Act, 1856. **5.** The Succession Act, 1865. **6.** The Press Act, 1881. **7.** The Transfer of Property Act, 1882. **8.** Co-operative Act, 1904, etc.

lot of deficiencies were legally abolished. The new legal structure stressed on the humanistic values. The new system recognised only the individual as the unit of social and cultural participation. By the beginning of the 20th century, a uniform pattern of judicial administration was established throughout India. This created an institutional base for the process of cultural modernisation in India.

2. Expansion of Modern Education

The contemporary education system is a powerful agent of modernisation. It differs radically from the traditional educational system. Religious and spiritual matters coupled with Sanskrit literary works, constituted the main contents of the syllabi, previously. The British laid the foundations of modern education in India. India's modern education system, as on today [2003] is only 145 years old. It was started in 1857, when the first three universities - Calcutta, Madras and Bombay - were under the British rule. *"Its historical landmarks are Macaulay's Policy of 1835, Sir Charles Wood's Despatch of 1854 and the Report of the First Indian Education Commission of 1882."* Both the content of modern education and its organisational structure differed markedly from the traditional one.

(a) ***The Cultural Content of Modern Education*** : Modern education is more secular and scientific and differs from the traditional education both in its content and orientation. It is based on reasoning and free thinking. It is associated with the principles of liberty, equality, humanism and denial of faith in the dogmas. The new education is concerned with the present and the future.

(b) ***Organisational Structure of Modern Education*** : The new educational system introduced by the British was also different in its organisational structure. The *Guru-Shishya Parampara* [Teacher-Student Legacy] which existed in the traditional educational system almost came to an end. Modern education system has a cosmopolitan student structure. Education no more remained the monopoly of a few upper caste people. Modern education system extends educational opportunities equally to all the people. Children belonging to all the strata of the society have an equal chance of learning in these institutions. Teachers are appointed on the basis of educational achievements irrespective of their caste, or birth. This itself is a principle which is opposed to the traditional practice of the teachers being selected from the upper castes. The very structure of the teaching profession is secularised. The teachers at various levels [primary, middle and higher secondary level] have to undergo training schemes. English has become the medium of instruction at all levels. All these changes in the organisational structure of education have also contributed to the cultural modernisation in India.

(c) ***Rate of Growth of Educational Institutions*** : Modern education introduced by the British received tremendous support from the people. Number of educational institutions, particularly at primary and secondary level has been increasing consistently in almost all the places of India. *For example,* number of primary and upper primary schools has gone up from 2.23 lakh [1950-51] to 8.17 lakh [1998-99]; and the number of teachers in these institutions is 31.80 lakhs in 1998-99. After independence, several universities, professional colleges such as engineering colleges, medical colleges, industrial training institutes, polytechnic institutes, nursing institutes, management courses, vocational training courses, etc. have come into being throughout the nation. *For example,* at present, India has 242 universities and equivalent institutions including 146 general universities, 5 women universities, 30 agricultural and 17 medical universities. Also, there are 11,089 colleges [of these, 1260 are for women and 119 are autonomous college]. There are 7000 education / training colleges, 550 engineering and technology colleges, 170 medical colleges and 600 management institutes.[1]

The modern education has brought about its own impact. *Firstly,* it has been responsible for the creation of a class of enlightened intelligentsia. *Secondly,* it has created a subculture of students which contains elements of transition from tradition to modernity. *Thirdly,* it has contributed to modernisation by way of new educational structures such as schools, colleges, universities, professional institutions, research institutions, diploma courses, etc.

3. Urbanisation and Industrialisation

Urbanisation and industrialisation normally lead to cultural modernisation. Though cities existed in the past in India they did not provide any scope for modernisation. Cities, which sprang up because of industrialisation, have modernising effect. Industrial Revolution has changed the structure of Indian cities. The traditional cities of India started gradually changing and new industrial cities started coming up. Cities have attracted a large number of people from the villages. Today more than 25% of the people of India live in towns and cities. Industrialisation generally contributes to cultural modernisation. But compared to many other nations, industrial growth has been slow in India. Studies have shown that there are cultural and institutional factors responsible for this situation.

Historically, however, it is not possible to establish relationship between urbanisation and modernisation in India. Studies have revealed that even modern cities provide opportunities for the strengthening of caste and communal associations. It is also recognised that in the Indian context it is not easy to distinguish between rural and urban structures. Therefore, many scholars point out that urbanisation has not only a modernising impact on culture but also contributes to the survival of tradition in many respects.

Urbanisation and industrialisation support and reinforce each other. *"The two have led to the growth of commercialism, monetization of economic relationships, factory and workshop employment for many and a steady growth in the new subculture of modernised elites. There is also diffusion of urban culture and influence on the rural hinterland......... Even the physical conditions of the city life call for many compromises in the traditional mode of living and culture. New colonies, increased use of modern transport, communication facilities, mass media of education, new political culture, rational monetary transactions, etc., have created a broad foundation for modernisation of Indian tradition."*[2]

According to **Yogendra Singh**, however, *"Despite the persistence of traditional, cultural values and institutions in cities, urbanisation and industrialisation foster many cultural norms and material conditions which are macroscopic and modernising."*

4. Communication and Modernisation

India's Western contact has also led to the introduction of the modern communication system which has brought about revolutionary changes. The communication system brings the world closer and contributes to the diffusion of skills, knowledge, values, etc. within a limited span of time. The modern communication system includes the introduction of post and telegraph services, telephone, radio, television, internet, e-mail, information technology, etc.

The transportation system has also been revolutionised. Roadways, waterways, airways have made tremendous progress. In fact, space is conquered and people have regular contacts.

---

1 *Source of the Statistics* : *Manorama Year Book* - 2002. Page - 603.

2 **Moulesh** and **Subramanya**. Pages : 195 - 196.

The whole world appears like a "global village" now. *"According to Daniel Lerner, the expansion in the technological means of travel and transport and increase in the number of circulation of the newspapers as forms of media exposure, are directly associated with cultural modernisation. But in India this has resulted both in modernisation and traditionalisation as it has also contributed to horizontal unity of castes and other traditional group activites."*[1]

5. Nationalism, Politicisation and Modernisation

Nationalism and the political culture of democracy are essentially modern in ethos and have a Pan-Indian character. Nationalism results from political consensus. Nationalism and democracy as they are understood in their present form, owe their origin to the West. Indian nationalism provided the base for the establishment of a democratic structure in India. It is unfair to say that Indian nationalism is completely modelled after the Western pattern. Because, the early reformers like Raja Ram Mohan Roy, Swami Vivekananda, Maharshi Aravind, Ravindranath Tagore, Mahatma Gandhiji and other intellectuals ventured to define Indian nationalism which was rooted in the Hindu tradition. At the same time, it was noncommunal and secular in nature. Secularism, as Gandhi thought of it, does not mean a religiosity but the spirit of religious tolerance. The modern leaders who have inherited the tradition of this nationalism no doubt supported modernity. At the same time, they continued to preserve and uphold the traditional cultural identity of India.

The political culture of democracy takes pride in its secular character. But there are inconsistencies in the very growth of secularism in India. The Hindu community right from the days of British rule, has been more catholic and liberal in its attitude towards legislations. But the case of other major religious communities in India, particularly the Muslims, has been fundamentally different. This creates imbalance in the process of secularisation in India. Even though the Indian government claims religious neutrality in its dealings, it has enacted several legislations for the control and administration of temples and Hindu religious institutions. These laws regulate only Hindu religious institutions of a public character. Despite the inconsistencies, India still continues as a secular and a democratic state.

Effects of Westernisation
or
Changes in the Indian Society as a Result of Westernisation

The term "Westernisation" as it is interpreted by Prof. M.N. Srinivas denoted in general, the impact of British rule over the socio-cultural life and activities of the Indian people. The advent of the British in India and their prolonged rule led to the introduction of the Western civilisation. Those who came under the influence of the Western civilisation started modifying their life and activities in accordance with the Western standards. Western way of life became very attractive for them. "Westernisation" virtually indicates *the process of imitation of the Western life-styles by the Indians.* The process of Westernisation brought about a number of socio-cultural changes in the Indian society among which the following may be noted.

1. Westernisation brought about immediate changes in the three main areas, namely, *Technology, Institutions, Ideology* and *Values.*
2. Westernisation provided *inspiration for a number of social reform movements* such as the Brahma Samaj, Arya Samaj, Sri Ramakrishna Mission, Theosophical Society, Sarvodaya and so on.

1 Dr. M.A. Chingamani *"Sociology of Indian Society."* Page - 234.

3. Westernisation provided *inspiration for the freedom movement.* Western ideas and values also inspired a number of freedom fighters to fight against the British imperialism.
4. Westernisation has *led to a new style of life.* The Western influence made Indians imitate the Western way of life and culture in several respects.
5. Westernisation has also *brought about some negative effects.* It made Indians to imitate the West indiscriminately. In this process of imitation they blindly imitated and picked up the deficiencies, vices, and evil practices of the Western people.

[*Note* : For more details about the *"Impact of the West"* or *"Effects of Westernisation"* kindly refer to the detailed description given in Chapter 2 of this book.]

Westernisation: Some Critical Comments

Scholars have recognised and appreciated the relevance of the terms *"Westernisation"* and *"Sanskritisation"* in analysing the socio-cultural changes taking place in modern India. But they have not spared them from critical comments. A few of such critical remarks made about the concept of "Westernisation" are worth citing here.

As **M.N. Srinivas** has pointed out, *"One of the many interesting contradictions of modern Hindu social life is that while the Brahmins are becoming more and more Westernised, the other castes are becoming more and more Sanskritized. In the lower reaches of the hierarchy, castes are taking up customs which the Brahmins are busy discarding."*[1] It is true that with the Westernisation of Indian society, caste becomes more or less secular due to the new ideas introduced by the West. Westernisation as a social process has influenced the various aspects of social life of the Indian community.

Comments in Appreciation

1. The concept of "Westernisation" is considered to be *very useful in analysing the mobility taking place outside the framework of caste.* It is a simple term which denotes the impact of the British rule on Indian way of life.

2. Scholars like **Bernard Cohn** and **Milton Singer** have justified Srinivas' usage of these concepts. They relevantly commented that *"while upper caste was Westernising its style of life and religious beliefs, the lower caste was Sanskritising and assuming more traditional forms of ritual, practice and belief."*

3. As **B. Kuppu Swamy** has observed, the concept of Westernisation as used by M.N. Srinivas covers - (a) the ***"behavioural" aspects*** like, eating, drinking, dressing, dancing, etc; (b) the ***"knowledge" aspects*** like literature, science, etc., and (c) the ***"values" aspects*** like humanitarianism, equalitarianism, and secularism etc.[2] He has also said that the process of "Westernisation" represents a middle class phenomenon and as such, is very useful in understanding the major social changes of the 19th century India.

Some Comments on its Limitations

Scholars have also criticised the concept of "Westernisation". Some such critical remarks are recalled here.

---

1 M.N. Srinivas *"Caste in Modern India and Other Essays."* Pages : 54 - 55.

2 B. Kuppu Swamy *"Social Change in India"* (1975) Page: 62.

1. The concepts of Sanskritisation and Westernisation primarily analyse social change in *"cultural"* and **not** in *"structural"* terms. This denotes that these terms have a limited range of application and use.

2. *"Srinivas's model explains the process of social change only in India which is based on the caste system. It is not useful for other societies"* (Prof. Ram Ahuja - Page: 360)

3. *Though Srinivas claimed that the concept of Westernisation is "ethically neutral", it is not really so.* He himself says that it implies *"certain value preferences" such as humanitarianism, egalitarianism, secularisation,* and some degree of *rationalism.* A reference to these values definitely implies that Westernisation is, in general, good and desirable.

4. **Daniel Lerner** has raised a few objections to the use of Westernisation as conceived by Srinivas.

(i) *It is too local a label and the model which is imitated may not be a Western country, but Russia.*

(ii) *"One of the results... of prolonged contact with the West is the rise of an elite class whose attitude to the West is ambivalent".* It is not invariably positive. In this context, Lerner refers to the *appeal of Communism* in non-Western countries.

(iii) Westernisation in one area or level of behaviour, does not result in Westernisation in another related area or level. The two remain discrete.

(iv) "While there are certain common elements in Westernisation, each European country along with the U.S.A., Canada, Australia and New Zealand, represents a particular variant of a common culture and significant differences exist between one country and another."

5. Further, Srinivas equates Westernisation with the British impact on India. But, **Yogendra Singh** points out that this is too narrow, since after independence the impact of the Russian and American versions of modernisation has been considerable. Further, for many new elites in India, as also in the other new states of Asia, the term Westernisation has a pejorative connotation because of its association with former colonial domination of these countries by the West. He states : *"It is, therefore, more value-loaded than the term modernisation which to us appears a better substitute."*

6. **Daniel Lerner** who prefers to use his own concept of "modernisation" has commented that *"the term Westernisation is inadequate and parochial." According to him, Westernisation has "penetrated only the upper level....affecting mainly leisure class fashions. On the contrary, "modernisation today diffuses among a wider population"* touching not only public institutions but also private aspirations.

7. The concept has its own limitation in yet another sense. *The concept will be of little use in explaining the nature of social change taking place in post-Independent India.* Professor Srinivas is aware of this limitation. But he maintains : *"I would like to state that I am using it deliberately in spite of its vagueness and omnibus character. There is need for such a term, when analysing the changes that a non-Western country undergoes as a result of the prolonged contact with a Western one. When the entities involved, as well as the emergent processes are extremely complex, it is hardly realistic to expect that a simple unidimensional and crystal clear concept will explain them fully."*

8. *The concept has contextual limitations.* **Chanana** does not consider it to be a simple process. He says : *"As regards the present [situation in Punjab] it would be better to say that Indianisation is at work; by this we mean Westernisation to a large extent in externals and the*

reassertion of largely Indian values, mingled with the humanitarian values of the West in matters of spirit."[1]

9. It is also commented that the *Western model which Srinivas has praised has its own contradictions.* The Western model sometimes conveys values that are contrary to the ones such as rationalism, humanitarianism, equalitarianism, etc. In this context, mention can be made of the facts of Western life such as racial prejudice, colour segregation and exploitative nature of the Western economy, etc. These facts contradict humanitarian ideals, equalitarian principles and rational outlook on life.

In conclusion, it can be stated that the twin concepts of Srinivas are *"truth-asserting"* [Zetterberg - 1965] concepts. Endorsing this opinion **Prof. Yogendra Singh** writes: *"Obviously Sanskritisation and Westernisation are theoretically loose terms; but as "truth-asserting" concepts they have great appropriateness and viability."*[2]

Finally, it can be said that the twin concepts of Sanskritisation and Westernisation introduced by M.N. Srinivas in explaining the cultural changes that are taking place in India, do have their own importance. But the basic question is this : Do these twin concepts explain cultural change with all its ramifications ? Are they inclusive and universal enough to provide a satisfactory explanation to all the major cultural changes that have taken place throughout the country ? According to **Yogendra Singh**, only the concept of *"Modernisation"* can provide a satisfactory answer to these questions.

C. MODERNISATION

Meaning of Modernisation

The term ***modernisation*** *"does not denote any philosophy or movement, but it only symbolises a process of change. In fact, modernisation is understood as a process which indicates the adoption of the modern ways of life and values."* The term was used previously to refer only *"to change in economy and its related effect on social values and practices."* It was also described as a process that changed the society, from primarily agricultural to primarily industrial economy. As a result of the change in the economy, the society itself underwent changes in values, beliefs and norms. But, *today, the term is given a broader meaning.*

Today, the term, *"modernisation"* is understood as an attempt, on the part of the people, particularly those who are custom-bound, to adopt themselves to the present time, conditions, styles and ways in general. It indicates a change in people's food habits, dress habits, speaking styles, tastes, choices, preferences, ideas, values, recreational facilities and so on. It is also described as *"social change involving the elements of science and technology."* The scientific and technological inventions have brought about remarkable changes in the whole system of social relationship and installed new ideologies in the place of the traditional ones.

M.N. Srinivas, however, criticises the concept of modernisation. According to him, it is *a value-loaded term.* He says that *"modernisation is normally used in the sense that it is good. He, therefore, prefers to use the term "Westernisation" which characterises the changes brought about in Indian society and culture as a result of over 150 years of British rule."*

Yogendra Singh, on the other hand, defends the concept of modernisation. According to him, it is broader than the two processes of Sanskritisation and Westernisation. *It is, indeed a "cultural*

---

1 Dev Raj Chanana as quoted by **Prof. Yogendra Singh** in *"Modernisation of Indian Tradition"* Page12

2 Yogendra Singh *"Modernisation of Indian Tradition."*

universal" and not necessarily confined to any single society. Like science, modernity is not an exclusive possession of any one ethnic or cultural group. It belongs to the humanity as a whole. This does not mean that everywhere it should reveal the same pattern. *It need not always take place on the model of England, Germany, France or America.* It can take place on the model of Russia, India, Japan, Australia, or any other country for that matter. What is essential to modernisation is this – a commitment to *"scientific world view" and a belief in the humanistic and philosophical viewpoint of science on contemporary problems.*

Definition of "Modernisation"

1. **Daniel Lerner** : Daniel Lerner who introduced the term *"modernisation"* for the first time in his study of the Middle-Eastern societies – uses it to refer to the changes brought about in a non-Western country by contact, direct or indirect with a Western country. To quote his own words : *"Modernisation is the current term of an old process of social change whereby less developed societes acquire the characteristics common to more developed societies."*
2. **Smelser** : Modernisation refers to *"a complex set of changes that take place almost in every part of society as it attempts to be industrialised. Modernisation involves ongoing change in a society's economy, politics, education, traditions and religion."*
3. **Alatas** : *"Modernisation is a process by which modern scientific knowledge is introduced in the society with the ultimate purpose of achieving better and a more satisfactory life in the broadest sense of the term as accepted by the society concerned."*
4. **Rutow and Ward** [1964] have said that the *basic process in Modernisation is the application of modern science to human affairs.*
5. **Eisenstadt** says that *Modernisation* refers to both *(a) structural aspects of social organisation, and (b) socio-demographic aspects of societies.*

The Process of Modernisation

The key to understanding modernisation lies in thinking of it as a set of changes that affect the whole society. These changes are many and complex. Each is linked to the others. Moreover, the process is different in each country, depending on its history.

Modernisation involves a transformation of social, political and economic organisations. *"This includes the transformation indicated by **Durkheim,** from "mechanical solidarity" to "organic solidarity"; that indicated by **Becker,** the transformation from the "change-resistant sacred outlook" to the "change-ready secular-outlook"; the transformation indicated by **Weber,** from "personal bonds" to "impersonal relation" with bureaucracy; and the transformation from "status-based" relations to "contract-based" relation as indicated by **Maine,** long ago. It applies to the individualist forms of organisation of the Western model, the Communist form of organisation of the Russian or Chinese model as well as to the socialistic pattern of the Indian model."*[1]

Students of modernisation have identified many dimensions of this process. The process has its economic, political, educational, technological, military, administrative, cultural and other faces. The concept has been used in a very diffused manner. Still, some of the patterns that are common to most modern countries have been identified. **Smelser** makes a reference to them in the following way.

---

1 **B. Kuppu Swamy** *"Social Change in Modern India"* - 1972. Pages : 54 - 55.

1. *It involves a change from simple, traditional techniques such as hand-weaving towards the use of scientific knowledge and technology, for example,* powerlooms.
2. *Agricultural shifts from subsistence farming to commercial farming on a larger scale.* This means growing cash crops, buying non-agricultural products in the markets on a large quantity and often hiring people to do farm work.
3. *"In industry there is a movement away from the use of human and animal power and towards the use of machinery driven by non-human power." For example,* ploughs pulled by oxen are replaced by tractors driven by hired hands.
4. *The society changes from the farm and the village centred one to that of the industry and city centred one.*[1]

In addition to the four major patterns, other patterns of change have been observed in modernising social structure. *Traditional religious systems tend to lose influence. Powerful non-religious ideologies such as patriotism, nationalism, democracy, secularism, etc. arise.* The family changes in many ways, both in terms of its structure and functions. Its economic, educational, recreational and other functions tend to diminish. Its size gets smaller and smaller. Extended families and kingroups break up into smaller units. Personal choice becomes the basis of marriage rather than parental arrangements.

In *education,* the literacy rate increases greatly and formal educational institutions become widespread. Mass media also serves the purpose of educational resource and information channel. New form of administrative organisation such as bureaucracies develop in the political, economic, educational and other fields.

In addition to these changes in the social structure, some *psychological changes* do take place in the society's members. Studies of **Alex Inkeles** and **David H. Smith** [1974] have revealed that the modern man has become an informed participant citizen. He is highly independent and takes independent decisions relating to his personal affairs such as education, marriage, occupation, etc. He is not much carried away by the traditional influence. He is ready for new experiences and ideas. He is relatively open-minded and cognitively flexible.

Thus, the process of modernisation includes in itself the gradual development of a vast new system of social structures and psychological traits. *"As a society becomes more productive and prosperous, it also becomes more complex in social and cultural terms."*

Characteristics of Modernisation

As it has already been mentioned, the process of modernisation has different dimensions. The spirit of modernisation is expressed in different areas such as – *social organisation, culture, political field, economy, education, etc. in different ways.* Broadly speaking, the process of modernisation reveals the following important characteristics:

Modernisation includes – *"a temple of science, reason and rationalism, secularism, high aspiration and achievement orientation, overall transformation of attitudes norms and values, creation of new functional institutions, investment in human resources, a growth oriented economy, a national interest rather than kin, caste, religion or language oriented interests, an open society, and a mobile person."*[2]

According to **B. Kuppuswamy**, *"the main feature of Modernisation is the building up of an "open society" in which individuals of talent, enterprise and training can find places in the*

1 N.J. Smelser *"Sociology"* - 4th Edition. Page - 395.
2 Ram Ahuja *"Indian Social System."*

society appropriate to their achievement........ The process of Modernisation involves an increase in social unrest till the social system is responsive to the new aspirations built up by the Modernisation process." It should, however, be noted that the same process of modernisation institutes appropriate change in the social system to meet the rising expectations of the people.

Criteria of Modernity or Measures of Modernisation

Modernisation has been referred to as a process whereby less developed socieites acquire characteristics common to more developed socieites. Now our task is to identify the characteristics that are common to more developed socieites, that is, to identify the criteria of modernity.

Sociologists have not yet found out an efficient method of measuring modernisation. Because, there is no consensus among them regarding the criteria of modernity. Still, there has been some broad agreement among scholars on certain key points concerning modernisation.

Rustow and Ward [1964] have mentioned of some measures of modernisation. They include such specific aspects of changes as :

1. Industrialisation of economy and adopting a scientific technology in industry, agriculture, dairy farming, etc., to make them highly productive;
2. Secularisation of ideas – that is, a diffusion of secular - rational norms in culture;
3. A remarkable increase in geographic and social mobility which includes occupational mobility also;
4. A spread of scientific and technical education;
5. A transition from ascribed to achieved status;
6. An increase in material standard of living;
7. High proportion of working force employed in secondary and tertiary rather than primary production, that is, manufacturing and services as opposed to agriculture and fishing;
8. An increment of mobility in the society, understood in terms of urbanisation, spread of literacy and media participation;
9. High expectancy of life at birth;
10. Relatively greater measure of public participation in the polity – or at least democratic representation in defining and choosing policy alternatives.

While discussiong the criteria of modernity **Daniel Lerner** observes : *"According to this typology, the modern person is an urban literate who participates fully in the public forum, market place, political arena."*

Causes of Modernisation

What factors condition modernisation ? What conditions lead to modernisation ? What conditions hinder it ? In exploring suitable answers to these questions sociologists look within the society to discover the various factors, groups, people and agencies and instruments that contribute to modernisation. *Modernisation is not caused by any single factor.* It is the net result of a number of factors. **Myron Weiner** speaks of five main instruments which made modernisation possible : *education, mass communication, ideology based on nationalism, charismatic leadership and coercive governmental authority.*

1. Education

Education, that too higher education pertaining to the fields of science and technology, provides the basis of modernisation. Education involves a sense of national loyalty and creates skills and attitudes essential for technological innovation. **Edward Shils** has also emphasised the role of education in the process of modernisation. Still, people like **Arnold Anderson** feel that formal education is not sufficient for teaching skills. University education may increase the number of students with degrees without an increase in the number of people with modern skills and attitudes. By this we cannot underscore the importance of education in national development which is believed to be associated with modernisation. *"National development depends upon a change in knowledge – what people know, skills – what people can do, and attitudes – what people can aspire and hope to get."* This is the reason why in the recent decades education including mass communication is given utmost importance.

2. Mass Communication

The process of modernisation hinges on the phenomenon of mass communication. The development of mass communication [including the newspapers, periodicals and magazines, T.V., radio, telephone, movies, computer, e-mail, internet, etc.] is an important means of spreading modern ideas at a faster rate. The function of mass media is to open up to the large masses in society, new information, new thought, new attitude and new aspirations which lead them to a new achievement. *"The mass media is the device that can spread the requisite knowledge and attitudes quickly and widely."* The only danger with the mass media is that if these are controlled by the government, they will spread only one-sided view that suits their political ideology. But in democracies, however, the press is often given sufficient independence to express its views.

3. Ideology Based on Nationalism

Nationalism and democracy are very much linked with modernisation. Nationalism is connected with national awareness and political consensus. As far as the West is concerned, the democratic system came to be strengthened along with the development of nationalism. The nationalistic ideologies serve as a unifying influence in bridging social clevages within plural societies. They also help the political elite in changing the behaviour of masses of people. Mass media plays a vital role in democratic societies to spread modern views, ideas, values, etc., by persuading the masses. But it is argued that even though the political elite have modern ideology, their mere possession of it does not guarantee any development from the modern perspective.

4. Charismatic Leadership

A charismatic leader is in a better position to impress upon the people to adopt modern beliefs, values, practices and behaviour patterns. But the danger involved here is that this popular leader may take the undue advantage of his position and use modern values, ideas, etc., for his personal glorification rather than for the national development.

5. Coercive Governmental Authority

A strong and stable government may adopt coercive measures to compel people to accept the modern values and ways of life. It may also bring pressures on other governments and people to follow the same. The Government of America under the presidentship of George Bush [The present President of U.S.A. - 2002-03] has been making use of various tactics and strategies to bring pressure on the underdeveloped and developing countries to follow the modern ways and practices.

6. Other Factors

To the list of factors explained above, we may add two other factors: *(a) urbanisation and industrialisation,* and *(b) universal legal system.*

(a) Urbanisation and Industrialisation

Urbanisation and industrialisation are the two inter-related processes that are assumed to be invariably linked up with modernisation. These two processes can also be understood as two factors that accelerate the tempo of modernisation. *"Urbanisation" refers to the process of growth and expansion of cities.* Most of the modernised countries are either dominated by the cities or under the grip of the process of urbanisation. *"Industrilisation" refers to the unprecedented growth and expansion of industries.* It has become virtually the sine qua non of economic and technological development.

(b) Universal Legal System

In a traditional society bound by traditional values and customs the rate of change is relatively slow. But a society that functions on the basis of the universally accepted legal system is bound to be more *"open."* The *"rule of law"* is, indeed, one of the prerequisites of modernisation. The present legal system places premium on the individual protecting his rights and assuring his freedom. This role of the legal system supports the cause of *"Individualism."* The modern legal system has contributed a great deal to the scientific management of the industries.

7. Cultural Aspects of Modernisation

The above mentioned factors point out how modernisation is normally caused. They also signify the structural changes associated with modernisation. **Prof. Yogendra Singh** speaks of the nature of modernisation at cultural level. He writes : *"It symbolises a rational attitude towards issues, and their evaluation from a universalistic and not particularistic view point; when it involves an emotional response to problems, its orientation is empathic and not constrictive; modernisation is rooted in the scientific world view; it has deeper and positive association with the levels of diffusion of scientific knowledge, technological skills and technological resources in a particular society. But what may be essential to modernisation is the commitment to scientific world view, the internalisation of humanistic and philosophical view-point of science on contemporary problems, and not merely the volume of technological advancement."*

It should be noted that modernisation is a universal cultural phenomenon. But all modernised societies will not be the same in all respects. The different dimensions of modernisation described above denote its ideal typical form. No contemporary society exhibits all the features of modernisation. As Yogendra Singh states : *"There only exists degrees of modernisations and that too defined on the basis of criteria which are always partial in nature."* Further, different societies adopt modernisation differently.

Process of Modernisation in India

Modernisation in India started mainly with the Western contact, especially through the establishment of the British rule. This contact brought about many far reaching changes in the culture and social structure of Indian society. *Not all these changes could be called modernising.* The basic direction of this contact was towards modernisation, *but in the process, good number of traditional institutions got strengthened.*

There was, however, one important feature of Indian modernisation during the British period. *The growth of this process was very much selective and partial.* It never encompassed the ***micro-structures*** of Indian society such as – *family, caste, kin group* and *village community.* British people intelligently followed the policy of *"least interference"* especially at these micro-levels.

But at the ***macro-level,*** the components of modernisation such as a universalistic legal system, expansion of Western form of education, urbanisation and industrialisation, spread of new means of communication and transport and social reforms – led the way in the transformation of Indian society. Along with these, *aspects of structural modernisation* such as – rational bureaucratic systems of administration and judiciary, army and industrial bureaucracy, new classes of business elite and entrepreneurs – came into being. There was the emergence of political elite and a nationalist leadership. These modernising structures had a uniform character throughout the country.

A New Momentum to Modernisation

After independence, modernisation process in India has undergone a basic change from its colonial pattern. Discontinuity in modernisation between macro-structures and micro-structures slowly disappeared. Introduction of adult franchise and federal parliamentary form of political structure has carried new political values to all the sections of the population. Planned legal reforms in Hindu marriage and inheritance laws have tremendously influenced the Hindu family system. Community Development Projects and the *Panchayat Raj System* created a political awareness and participation in the local level management and administration of justice. Caste too has undergone a radical transformation making lot of compromises with the changed conditions.

Co-existence of Modernisation and Tradition

In spite of the British contact Indian society at the time of independence had deep-rooted traditions. Still it decided to go in the direction of modernity. There were people to support the cause of modernism and there were also people to cling on to the traditional way of life. We had to strike out a balance between the two. Thus people had to tolerate the coexistence of tradition with modernism. But, coexistence cannot last long in all the areas. Because, many a time, traditional ethos and values become irreconciliable. We were thus confronted with the practical problem of either sticking to tradition or going on along the path of modernisation.

Modernisation has not displaced traditions : Comparative studies of modernisation have revealed that traditions are not completely displaced by modernisation. This is true of the Indian situation also. In India, caste associations which are typical symbols of tradition have also been found to serve the ends of political modernisation. Advancement in the field of modern means of transport and communication not only helps in the diffusion of modernisation but also that of traditionalism. Like the earlier nationalist leaders, even the new leaders are conscious of national identity and are proud of the traditional culture of India. **Yogendra Singh** remarks : *"Consequently, it is fair to assume that and simultaneously grow the feeling of national identity and the identification with the nation's past tradition. Cultural modernisation will under this process assume a syncretic form and persist along with traditional values. Modernity will never completely supplant tradition in India."*

We decided to modernise our society at various levels. *"What aspects of life were sought to be modernised and in what manner*?*"* This question seemed to pose a serious challenge. But the Indian society sought to face this challenge in its own way. As **Ram Ahuja** writes : "At the *social level,* we wanted social relations to be based on concepts like equality, human dignity, and social values which would ensure social mobility, removal of caste disabilities, amelioration of the conditions of women, and so forth. At the *economic level,* we wanted technological growth and distributive justice. At the *cultural level,* we wanted secularism, rationalism, and liberalism. At the *political level,* we desired representative government, democratic institutions, achievement - oriented power-structure, and a greater voice and participation for Indians in the governance of the country. The *means* for *agents* selected for modernising the society were – *planning, education, legislation, assistance from foreign countries, adopting the policy of liberalisation, and the like.*"[1]

Compromise of Traditions With Modernisation ?

Commenting on the changing traditions of India due to modernisation **Milton Singer** writes : *"The height of present evidence seems to be to show that while modernising influences are undoubtedly changing many aspects of Indian society and culture, they have not destroyed its basic structure and pattern. They have given Indians new alternatives and some new choices of life style, but the structure is so flexible and rich that many Indians have accepted many modern innovations without loss of their Indianness. They have, in other words, been able to combine choices which affirm some aspects of their cultural tradition with innovative choices."*[2]

Problems of Modernisation

Prof. Ram Ahuja speaks of *five main problems* of modernisation. They can be briefly stated below :

1. Modernisation demands that society must change in all ways at once. But such a regular and co-ordinated pattern of growth cannot be planned and materialised. *Some amount of social unrest, hence, is bound to be there. **Example,** Discrepancy between mass education and employment opportunities.*
2. *During the period of modernisation, structural changes mostly remain uneven. **Example,*** Industries may be modernised but religious system, family system, etc., remain conservative.
3. *Modernisation of social and economic institutions may create conflicts with the traditional ways of life. **Example,*** Trained M.B.B.S. doctors may pose a threat to the traditional medical practitioners.
4. Another problem is that, *most often roles adopted by the people are modern, but their values continue to be traditional. **Example,*** New business firms and industrial establishments and shops, etc. are either opened or inaugurated as per the dictates of the traditional *"Muhurtam."*
5. Yet another problem is that *there is lack of cooperation among agencies which modernise and among those institutions and systems which are already modernised.* This is more or less like the problem of *"cultural lag."*
6. Finally, *though modernisation raises the aspiration of people, the social system does not provide enough chances to materialise them.* This creates frustration, disappointment and social unrest.

Sanskritisation and Westernisation : Comparative Views

Sanskritisation and westernisation help us as conceptual tools in understanding the nature of social and cultural changes that have been taking place in the Indian society. Both have their own strengths and limitations. In some respects, there are conflicts between the two also.

1 **Ram Ahuja** *"Indian Social System."* Page - 427.

2 **Milton Singer** as quoted by **Dr. M.A. Chingamani** in *"Sociology of Indian Society."* Page 240.

While sanskritisation [more precisely here Brahminisation] puts a taboo on meat-eating and consumption of alcohol, westernisation promoted meat-eating and consumption of alcohol. The highly westernised Brahmins of Kashmir, Bengal and South Kerala [who consume meat] *for example,* shed their inhibitions about these two tabooes.

As **B. Kuppu Swamy** has pointed out, *there is conflict between the two processes with respect to marriage and divorce.* "Among the "lower" castes there is no taboo against widowhood, divorce and remarriage, nor does custom enjoin on the wife to look upon her husband as a *"deity."* These customs are in line with westernisation but were all tabooed by the Brahmins. The conflict among these groups between these two sets of processes has been removed after independence by the promotion of equality of sex and legislation providing for divorce, and remarriage."[1]

Further, while sanskritisation process promoted the *"sacred"* outlook, westernisation process promoted the *"secular"* outlook. Here also the conflict has been removed by the constitution which is secular in outlook and emphasis.

"The Brahmins looked up to the British, and rest of the people looked up to both the Brahmins and the British. The fact that some of the values and customs of the British were opposed to some Brahmanical values made the situation confusing" [Srinivas - 62]. But in spite of these contradictions between Brahminism and Westernism, a section of the Brahmins adopted Westernism because of the prestige that it entailed.

But the main task of the lower castes was to catch up with the Westernised Brahmins who were well educated and enjoyed prestige in society. They soon realised that *"mere sanskritisation was not enough"* for it could only help them to improve their status in the *"immutable"* Varna system. Hence they decided to adopt westernism which would help them to move up in the social scale without the limitation of the Jati or Varna. They thus decided to obtain western education which would fetch them the fruit which they wanted. This awareness among the lower castes; and the high caste dominance in education and in new occupations provided a strong basis for the Backward Classes Movement. The *lower castes, thus, chose westernisation, that is, education through English medium, rather than sanskritisation, as the means to enable them to move up in status in the society.*

Westernisation and Modernisation : Comparative Views

The two terms namely, *Sanskritisation* and *Westernisation,* introduced by **Prof. M.N. Srinivas**, and *"Modernisation",* introduced by **Daniel Lerner** must be understood as *conceptual tools* to understand the nature and character of social changes that have taken place in the developing countries.

1. **M.N. Srinivas** writes : *"I have used....... the term "Westernisation" to characterise the changes brought about in the Indian society and culture as a result of over 150 years of British rule........." He also writes : "A popular term for the changes brought about in a non-Western country by contact, direct or indirect, with a Western country is "Modernisation""*[2]

Srinivas finds the necessity of finding an appropriate term when analysing changes that a non-Western country undergoes as a result of prolonged contact with a "Western one." But **Daniel Lerner**, "after considering the relative suitability of "westernisation" as well as "modernisation"", has opted for the latter. M.N. Srinivas, on the other hand, has criticised Lerner's concept of

---

1 **B. Kuppu Swamy** *"Social Change in India."* Page - 60.

2 **M.N. Srinivas** *"Social Change in Modern India."* Pages - 47 and 50.

"Modernisation" and felt that his term "Westernisation" is more relevant in the context in which it is used. Comparatively speaking, *the term "Modernisation" is a broader one and has a wider range of application.* The term "Westernisation" as **M.N. Srinivas** himself has recognised, *"...... is too local a label......."* to have wider range of use.

2. In a broad way it may be said that the concept of Westernisation as used by Srinivas covers : *(a) the behavioural aspects like eating, drinking, dressing, dancing, etc. (b) the knowledge aspects like literature, science, etc. (c) the values aspects like humanitarianism, equalitarianism and secularism, etc.* [B. Kuppu Swamy - 72]. The term "modernisation" *"involves a transformation of social, political and economic organisation."* As a concept it is greatly helpful to the sociologists and anthropologists who have been primarily concerned with the process of differentiation that characterised the modern societies. It helps them to know the way in which new structures arise to assume new functions, how new occupations emerge, how new complex educational institutions develop and so on.

3. It is said that *"Westernisation"* [of the 19th century] *is mostly a middle class phenomenon whereas Modernisation is a mass process involving mass media.* Thus while the 19th century Westernisation process was essentially a middle class affair involving fashions in speech, clothing, food and drinking habits, the modernisation process involves a fundamental, deep-seated and widespread change involving attitudes, the development of a rationalist and positivist spirit and the application of the new knowledge to the ways of living. It is essentially a mass affair.......... *It involves a fundamental change in social structure from the "Immutable" Varna society which is a closed society to a casteless, classless, open society........."*[1]

4. **Lerner** emphasises that the modernisation process involves the replacement of sacred revelation by secular enlightenment in the guidance of human affairs. *He considers the term Westernisation as inadequate and parochial.* As he points out modernisation is essentially based on *"a rationalist and positivist spirit."* He writes : while Westernisation *"once penetrated only the upper level......... affectiong mainly leisure class fashions, modernisation today diffuses among a wider population and touch public institutions as well as private aspirations with its diquieting positivist spirit."*

Conclusion

In conclusion, as **B. Kuppu Swamy** has said that *"the concepts of Sanskritisation and Westernisation help us only to analyse the superficial change processes which took place in the later half of the 19th century and the first two decades of 20th century. Neither Sanskritisation nor Westernisation affect the social structure. So they are entirely inadequate to help us to analyse the change processes which are currently taking place in the Indian society."* Though one cannot say that the terms Westernisation and Sanskritisation are entirely useless, one can definitely assert that the term *"Modernisation"* is more appropriate and relevant one in providing a satisfactory explanation of social change.

1 B. Kuppu Swamy [1972]. Pages : 63 - 64.

Chapter 9

THE SCHEDULED CASTES THEIR PROBLEMS, AND WELFARE MEASURES FOR THEIR UPLIFTMENT

The Scheduled Castes [SCs] - Emergence of the Term Scheduled Castes - No Precise Definition of the Term SCs - Numerical Strength and Distribution of the SCs - Problem of Untouchability: Who are the Untouchables ? - Some Ancient References to Untouchable Castes - Criteria of Untouchability - Untouchability Within Untouchable Castes - Gradations Among the Untouchables- Origin of Untouchability: Traditional Theory - Racial Theory - Theory of Ceremonial / Occupational Purity and Occupational Theory - Problems of Untouchable Castes : Social, Economic and political Disabilities of Untouchable Castes - Harmful effects of the Practice of Untouchability - Removal of Untouchability : Early Attempts - Role of Dr. Ambedkar in the Upliftment of Untouchables : A Brief Biographic Sketch of Dr. Ambedkar - Role of Gandhiji : A Brief Biographic Sketch of Gandhiji - Measures for the Welfare of Scheduled Castes: Constitutional and Legislative Measures - Other Welfare Measures - A Brief Evaluation of Welfare Schemes - Increasing Dalit Consciousness and Its Effects.

All permanently organised societies are stratified. Most societies of the world have had their type of what **Ward** calls *"the lowly"*. The Romans had their *plebeians,* the Spartans their *'helots',* the British their *villains*, the Egyptians their *slaves*, the Americans their *Negroes* and the Germans their *Jews.* Likewise, the Hindus have the ***"untouchables."*** Slavery, serfdom, villeinage have all vanished. But untouchability still exists. The practice of untouchability from which the Scheduled Caste people have been suffering is the reflection of the state of affairs of more than 1/6 of the population of this country. For no sins of theirs a large section of our population is suffering from a number of disabilities arising out of untouchability.

All sane people say that there is no rationale behind untouchability and it must go. As **Gandhiji** said, *it must become a thing of the past.* Dr. Ambedkar and Gandhiji did their best to condemn the practice and to campaign against it. The Constitution of independent India declares in an unequivocal voice that *untouchability is abolished and its practice in any manner is punishable.* Various welfare measures are also launched by the Central and the State Governments to uplift the Scheduled Castes and the Scheduled Tribes.

For ages certain groups of people in India's hilly areas and villages have suffered isolation and disability. Geographic and social factors have added to their isolation. They have lived in a state of social and economic stagnation. These people belong to certain castes and tribes listed by the President of India in pursuance of the relevant provisions of the Constitution. These castes and tribes are known as ***"Scheduled Castes"*** and ***"Scheduled Tribes."*** Together they constitute about 25% of the total population of India. These two groups along with the so called *"denotified tribes"* and *"other economically backward groups"* are sometimes referred to as ***"backward classes."***

THE SCHEDULED CASTES [SCs]

Definition of the Term "S.C." – Numerical Strength and Distribution of SCs

The Scheduled Castes occupy the bottom most rung of the social ladder. They form the majority of the *"backward"* or *"depressed"* classes. The term *"Scheduled Castes"* signifies those groups of people who were out of the caste system or the Varna hierarchy in the past. They comprise the bulk of *"untouchables"* or *"untouchable castes"*. These groups or castes have been discriminated against by the superior castes through the ages and they never had any kind of social acceptance from the majority of the people who belonged to the upper castes. They are distributed throughout India. Nowhere in India the Scheduled Castes occupy the top most position in the social, political or economic field, as a group. Their low social position continues even now though lot of measures have been taken to make them equal with others.

Emergence of the Term "Scheduled Castes"

The term *"Scheduled Castes"* is a politico-legal one. It was introduced by the British. It was first coined by the ***"Simon Commission"*** in 1928 and then ***"Government of India Act, 1935".*** The word *"schedule"* refers to a *"list"* or *"table"*. *The Govt. of India Act, 1935 "listed"* out or *scheduled* a few of the castes as the most inferior ones which required some special attention. This list of castes was designated as *"Scheduled Castes"*.[1] When India became independent, this term was adopted by the Constitution for the purpose of providing them some special facilities and constitutional guarantees.

No Precise Definition for the Term "Scheduled Castes"

The term "Scheduled Castes" is nowhere defined in the Constitution. Article 341 and 342 of the Constitution empowers the President of India in consultation with State governments to notify by an order, the castes, races and tribes which can be deemed as "Scheduled Castes".

Attempts towards a Definition

Sociologists have tried to define the term in their own way. We may consider here the definitions of *Dr. D.N. Majumdar* and *Dr. Ghurye.*

1. **Dr. D.N. Majumdar** uses the term *"Scheduled Castes* to refer mainly to the untouchable castes. He defines: *"The untouchable castes are those who suffer from various social and political disabilities many of which are traditionally prescribed and socially enforced by higher castes."*
2. **Dr. G.S. Ghurye:** *Scheduled castes are those groups which are named in the Scheduled Caste Order in force from time to time.*

---

1 It may be noted that these castes were referred to as ***"exterior castes"*** in 1931 Census. The British described them as ***"depressed classes"***. **Dr. Ambedkar** also referred to the economically, socially and religiously exploited group of lower castes suffering from "untouchability" as *"depressed classes"*.

3. In simple words, the term can be defined this way: *The term Scheduled Castes which comprises of the bulk of the "untouchable castes", includes all those groups which are subject to some disabilities in major fields of life - social, religious, educational, economic and political.*

• ***Examples for SCs:*** C.B. Mamoria has listed the following castes as the most important castes that come under the category of *"untouchables"* – Chamar, Khatik, Regar, Pasi, Kori, Dom, Dhobi, Dusadh, Balai, Mochi, Meghwal, Od, Bagdi, Bhuiya.[1]

• ***Some Scheduled Caste Groups of Karnataka:*** *Adi-Karnataka, Adi-Dravida, Holeya, Holer, Korama, Moger, Mundala, Madiga, Bhovi,* etc.

All the SCs are not Untouchables

It should be noted that all the Scheduled Castes are not untouchables. The list of Scheduled Castes also includes some *"touchable"* castes. Almost about 80% of the Scheduled Castes are *"untouchables"* suffering from various kinds of disabilities. However, people in general use the terms *"Scheduled Castes", "Untouchables", "Harijans", "Dalits",*[2] *"depressed classes"* in more or less the same way without making any difference between them. In this book also these terms are used synonymously.

Numerical Strength and Distribution of the SCs

The population of the Scheduled Castes has been steadily increasing. According to 1941 Census report, their population was about 48 million and it increased to 140 millions as per 1991 census report. This would constitute 16.48% of the total population of India. The Scheduled Caste people are not to be seen in Nagaland, Andaman Nicobar and Lakshadweep. Their number is almost insignificant in Meghalaya, Arunachal Pradesh, Mizoram, Dadra and Nagar Haveli. In the remaining states, there is not a single taluk in which Scheduled Caste people are not found.

As per 1981 and 1991 Census report, about **2/3** of the Scheduled Castes live in six states only. The highest number of Scheduled Castes is found in Uttar Pradesh [22.3%] of the total SC population in the country followed by West Bengal [11.4%], Bihar [9.6%], Tamil Nadu [8.5%], Andhra Pradesh [7.6%] and Madhya Pradesh [7.0%]. As per the 1991 Census report, in Karnataka there are 73,69,279 SCs [**5.3%** of State's total population] and majority of them live in rural areas.

Faster Growth of the Scheduled Caste Population

The number of people belonging to the Scheduled Castes has grown much faster during 1981-1991 than other people in the country put together. While the overall growth of population during the decade was 23.79%, it was much higher in the case of Scheduled Castes, that is, 30%.[3]

Concentration of the Scheduled Castes in Rural Areas

About 84 to 85% of the SC people live in rural areas and about 80% of them depend on agriculture. According to a survey report, almost 50% of the SC people are agricultural workers and they would constitute about **1/3** of the total number of agricultural workers in the country. Majority of them do not own any land. Of those who possess land, **68.8%** of them own land which is less than one hectare in size. About **2/3** of the bonded labourers are from the Scheduled Castes. Their literacy

---

1 **C.B. Mamoria** *"Social Problems and Social Disorganisation"* - 307.

2 *Dalit*: The term "*dalit*" can be used in a very broad sense to include all those people who are the victims of social, educational, economic and cultural exploitation. - Opinion of **Prof. Rao Saheb Kasabe,** Maharasthra.

3 **Ram Ahuja** *"Social System"* - Page: 365.

level is extremely low. It was 21.4% in 1981 as against the all India average of 41.3% [exclusive of SC and ST groups].[1]

The SC people who belong to the rural areas virtually live as agricultural labourers, tenants, and marginal farmers. Almost all persons engaged in jobs like *sweeping, scavenging* and *tanning* belong to the Scheduled Castes. In addition to the majority of agricultural labourers, we also find among them good number of *leather workers, weavers, fishermen, toddy-tappers, basket/rope - makers, washermen, scavengers, artisans, fruit-vegetable sellers, shoe-makers, liquor manufacturers, drummers, carpenters, iron-smiths and some others following petty occupations.*

PROBLEM OF UNTOUCHABILITY

Who Are the Untouchables ?

People who constitute the bottom most place in the Indian social stratification system are often regarded as *"untouchables"*. All of them come under the category of what our Constitution calls the *"Scheduled Castes"*. The word *"untouchable"* applies to the despised and degraded section of the Hindu population.

- According to **Dr. D.N. Majumdar,** *"the untouchable castes are those who suffer from various social and political disabilities many of which are traditionally prescribed and socially enforced by higher castes." In fact, he uses the term Scheduled Castes to refer mainly to the untouchable castes.*

- **In simple words,** *"untouchables" are those who occupy the bottom most place in the society and have been subjected to various social, cultural and other kinds of disabilities and exploitation for their very touch is regarded as contaminating or polluting the higher caste people.*

Meaning of Untouchability

Untouchability is a mass phenomenon of group prejudices and discrimination affecting about 140 million people. It is an ignoble practice associated with the Indian caste system.

- ***Untouchablity** is a practice in which some lower caste people are kept at a distance, denied of social equality and made to suffer from some disabilities for their touch is considered to be contaminating or polluting the higher caste people.*

The practice of untouchability is a stigma attached to the Indian society. It is an age-old practice and has its roots deep down in our social and religious system. **Gandhiji** regarded this practice as *"a leper wound in the whole body of Hindu politic"*. He even considered it *"the hatefullest expression of caste"*. He carried on a campaign against it throughout his life. Though the practice of untouchability in one form or another has been there in many other countries of the world, it has taken its ugliest shape in India. Millions of people have suffered from it and the suffering still continues though with less intensity.

Some Ancient References to "Untouchable" Castes

The untouchable castes were called by different names such as *chandalas, panchamas, svapachas, antyajas, atishudras,* etc. during the early days.

- **Vedic literature** also makes a mention of some *"impure"* groups which were there as early as in 800 B.C. People born of the prohibited *"pratiloma"* marriage belonged to that category and were called *"Chandalas"*, *"Svapacha"* and so on.

---

1 ***Source of Statistics:*** **Ram Ahuja** *"Indian Social Problems"* Page: 143.

Table - 1

Total Population and Percentage of Scheduled Caste and Scheduled Tribe - 1991

Sl.No	India / State or Union Territory	Total Popu- -lation ('000)	Scheduled Caste		Scheduled Tribe	
			Population ('000)	Percentage of total population	Population ('000)	Percentage of total population
	INDIA	**8,38,584**	**1,38,223**	**16.48**	**67,758**	**8.08**
	STATES					
1.	Andhra Pradesh	66,508	10,592	15.93	4,200	6.31
2.	Arunachal Pradesh	865	4	0.47	550	63.66
3.	Assam	22,414	1,659	7.40	2,874	12.82
4.	Bihar	86,374	12,572	14.56	6,617	7.66
5.	Goa	1,170	24	2.08	---	0.03
6.	Gujarat	41,310	3,060	7.41	6,162	14.92
7.	Haryana	16,464	3,251	19.75	---	---
8.	Himachal Pradesh	5,171	1,310	25.34	218	4.22
9.	Karnataka	44,977	7,369	16.38	1,916	4.26
10.	Kerala	29,099	2,887	9.92	321	1.10
11.	Madhya Pradesh	66,181	9,627	14.54	15,399	23.27
12.	Maharashtra	78,937	8,758	11.10	7,318	9.27
13.	Manipur	1,837	37	2.02	632	34.41
14.	Meghalaya	1,775	9	0.51	1,518	85.53
15.	Mizoram	690	1	0.10	654	94.75
16.	Nagaland	1,210	---	---	1,061	87.70
17.	Orissa	31,660	5,129	16.20	7,032	22.21
18.	Punjab	20,282	5,743	28.31	---	---
19.	Rajasthan	44,006	7,608	17.29	5,475	12.44
20.	Sikkim	406	24	5.93	91	22.36
21.	Tamil Nadu	55,859	10,712	19.18	574	1.03
22.	Tripura	2,757	451	16.36	853	30.95
23.	Uttar Pradesh	139,112	29,276	21.05	288	0.21
24.	West Bengal	68,078	16,081	23.62	3,809	5.59
	UNION TERRITORIES					
1.	Andaman and Nicobar Islands	281	---	---	27	9.54
2.	Chandigarh	642	106	16.51	---	---
3.	Dadra & Nagar Haveli	138	3	1.97	109	78.99
4.	Daman and Diu	102	4	3.83	12	11.54
5.	Delhi	9,421	1,795	19.05	---	---
6.	Lakshadweep	52	---	---	48	93.15
7.	Pondicherry	808	131	16.25	---	---

Note : Excludes figures of Jammu & Kashmir where 1991 census was not taken.

Source : Census of India 1991, Series 1, Paper 2 of 1992, Final Population Totals.

Ref. : **"INDIA - 1999"** - Page-13.

Table - 2

Increase in the Scheduled Caste Population in Decades

Year of Census	Total Population of SCs in Millions	Percentage of the SC Population out of the Total Population	Increase in Percentage from Decade to Decade
1941	48 Millions	–	–
1951	55.3 "	–	–
1961	64.5 "	–	–
1971	89.5 "	15.50%	–
1981	104.75 "	15.75%	0.25%
1991	140.00 "	16.48%	0.73%

Ref. : **"INDIA YEAR BOOK - 2001".**

• *Shastrakara* **Manu** was of the opinion that the *progeny of the most hated pratiloma union would become chandalas* or *untouchables*. In the vedic literature, we find the mention of *chandalas* as an ethnic group originating from inter-breeding of a higher caste or varna female [mostly Brahmin] and lower caste or varna male [mostly Shudra]. In simple words, *the chandalas who were regarded as "untouchables" were the children of the most hated union of a Brahmin female with a Shudra male.*

• **Patanjali,** yet another *dharmashastrakara* considered *chandalas* as a variety of *shudras.*

• Most of the *dharmashastrakaras* considered the *chandalas* as forming a fifth category [that is outside the four varnas] and called them ***Panchamas.*** The Panchamas were *'untouchables'*. Since they were outside the varna system they came to be known as ***"Avarnas".***

• **Alberuni** referred to these *"untouchables"* as a social group called ***"Anthyaja"*** constituting the last and the lowest position in the society. Their socio-economic life was worse than that of the Shudras [of the Varna category] and hence they were called ***"Atishudras".***

Criteria of Untouchability

Untouchability in the Indian context has become hereditary. If a person is regarded or branded as *'untouchable'* for some reason or the other, not only he would remain throughout his life as *"untouchable"* but his children also would become *"untouchables"*. Still it should be remembered that untouchability did not and does not arise by birth alone. Persons become *"outcastes"* and *"untouchables"* by being guilty of certain acts that amount to grave sins. Untouchability indicates not only a low place in the caste hierarchy together with the existence of social and religious disabilities but also a low economic position as well. Most of the scheduled castes [about 80%] are considered to be untouchables.

As **C.B. Mamoria** has cited,[1] according to ***1931 Census report***, if a caste suffers from the following restrictions, it may be termed as an *"untouchable"* caste.

(i) Inability to be served by twice born or clean Brahmins.

(ii) Inability to be served by barbers, water carriers, tailors, hoteliers, etc. who serve caste Hindus.

1 **C.B. Mamoria** *"Social Problems and Social Disorganisation."* Page 306.

(iii) Inability to serve water to the caste Hindus.
(iv) Inability to enter Hindu temples.
(v) Inability to use public conveniences such as wells, schools.
(vi) Inability to dissociate oneself from a despised occupation.

Untouchability within Untouchable Castes

Certain anomalies are found among the so called *"untouchable"* castes.[1] **D.N. Majumdar** [1948] summarised the position of the depressed [untouchable] castes in 1940s in the following way.

- These castes are not depressed in all states; the same caste may be *"depressed"* in one but may not suffer from any social or political disability in another. In Madhya Pradesh the same caste has different social rights and disabilities even in adjacent districts.
- The disabilities are more rigid where the depressed castes are numerically small and fewer or on the decline, than where they are numerically strong.
- Where the castes are all of the same ethnic stock or are largely so, social disabilities are not numerous and are usually confined to those whose function is considered degrading.
- Where the higher castes are in a minority and the depressed castes constitute the majority, the degree of ceremonial pollution observed is quite less and often we find few disabilities attached to the inferior castes.
- Individual members of the depressed castes who have succeeded in life and who are wealthy and own property have been admitted to a higher social status.

Gradations Among Untouchables

"It is not to be imagined that within the circle of untouchability, for instance, there are no sub-gradations and all untouchables are equal among themselves".(1) **Mahatma Gandhiji** himself wrote: *"All the various grades of untouchables are untouchable among themselves, each superior grade considering the inferior grade as polluting as the highest class of the caste-Hindus regard the worst grade of untouchables."*(2)[2] ***Example:*** A *Chamar* thinks that he would be polluted by coming into physical contact with a Dom or a Bhangi. Untouchable castes such as Bhuyar, Byar, Khatik and Majhwar are very particular in keeping the castes they consider *"untouchables"* at a distance.

According to **Sir Blunt,** *"Eleven castes will not touch a Bhangi, seventeen will not touch a Chamar, ten will not touch a Dhakar, six will not touch a Dhobi or a Dom."* It is said that in Tamil Nadu alone there are not less than 80 sub-divisions, those at the top considering the less fortunate of their own brothers as *untouchables.* [**C.B. Mamoria** – 307]

Origin of Untouchability

It is difficult to estimate the exact period in which the practice of untouchability originated. Still it can be said that it existed in India even 2000 years ago. Thus untouchables have been in

---

1 **C.B. Mamoria** has also cited some such anomalies. [Page: 306]. ***For example:*** *(i) There are untouchable castes with touchable sections. (ii) A caste may be regarded as untouchable by some of the "twice-born", and not by others. (iii) There are castes that are touchable to a Rajput but untouchable to a Brahmin. (iv) While in South India, the untouchables are supposed to pollute a Brahmin from a distance of as much as 32 yards, in North India, their untouchability is not so apparent.*

2 *ibid* Page - 306.

existence for the past 2000 years. There are different theories of the origin of untouchability. We shall consider briefly some of these theories.

(i) Traditional Theory

According to ***Manu,*** the *prohibited pratiloma marriage was the cause of the origin of untouchability.* Children born out of such a marriage were kept out of the Varna fold and were branded as *chandalas* who constituted an untouchable group. In the ***Chandukya Upanishad*** also there is reference to *chandalas.* In the ***Buddhist Jatakas,*** there is a mention of *chandalas* as the lowest caste people who were following the most degraded professions.

(ii) Racial Theory

Sir Herbert Risley and **Dr. Majumdar** are in favour of the racial explanation of the origin of untouchability. They say that the Indo-Aryans regarded the aborigines of India as a kind of inferior human beings and addressed them as *"dasas"* or *"dasyus"*, meaning *slaves* or *servants.* They also placed them in the lowest strata of the society and deprived them of all social and religious ceremonies. Dr. Majumdar argues that *the disabilities of the so called "depressed castes are not ceremonial, but are founded on racial and cultural differences."*

(iii) The Theory of Ceremonial/Occupational Purity

J.H. Hutton and **Prof. G.S. Ghurye** are in support of this theory. While analysing the origin of caste [also of untouchability] **Hutton** suggests that ideas of ceremonial purity were first applied to aboriginals in connection with sacrificial, ritual and certain occupational activities. According to **Dr. Ghurye,** *"Ideas of purity, whether occupational or ceremonial, which are found to have been a factor in the genesis of the caste are the very soul of the idea and practice of untouchability." Scholars* like **Laxman Shastri Joshi** have also supported it.[1]

(iv) Occupational Theory

According to **Nesfield,** association with dirty and impure occupations gave rise to the feeling of untouchability. It means low social status attached to certain occupations is the cause of untouchability. It relates to impure occupations such as removal of human waste and carcass, leather works, spinning, tanning, scavenging etc.

There are also other explanations for the origin of untouchability. It is evident from all these theories that the caste system, to a very great extent, is responsible for the development of the practice of untouchability. Conservation of the caste always supported the feeling of untouchability. The caste system also gave rise to the practice that *"untouchables" are born into untouchable castes and remain so till their death.* This feeling perpetuated untouchability. The practice of untouchablity assumed different forms and proportions in its prolonged history of more than 2000 years.

PROBLEMS OF UNTOUCHABLE CASTES

Majority of the castes that come under the category of *"scheduled castes"* are regarded as *"untouchables"*. These untouchable castes have been suffering from various disabilities throughout the history. After independence, the practice of untouchability was declared unconstitutional, but

1 "..... The entire system of caste gradation depends on the insistence on ceremonial purity, a counter part of pollution which is the main source of untouchability in various forms. The spirit of caste exclusiveness is inculcated by exaggerated notions of purity and pollution..." - **Laxman Shastri Joshi,** Chairman, Maharasthra Board of Culture - as quoted by **C.B. Mamoria.** Page 303.

the fact is that it still exists. The sufferings of the untouchables have not come to an end. This problem cannot be solved by an act of legislation.

According to **Dr. Majumdar,** *"the untouchable castes are those who suffer from various social and political disabilities, many of which are traditionally prescribed and socially enforced by the higher castes. Thus if the whole bases of untouchability are not destroyed, a simple provision for its legal status will bear scanty fruits."*

The "untouchable" castes have been suffering from various social, religious, legal, political, educational, economic and other disabilities. For centuries, they were denied political representation, legal rights, civic facilities, educational privileges and economic opportunities. During the British rule also, no proper attention was paid to uplift the untouchables to relieve them from their bondages. Even today they are not completely free from the problem which made them to suffer for centuries. These problems can be grouped into three main categories. (i) *social problems* (ii) *economic problems* and (iii) *political problems.*

1. Social Problems and Disabilities

The untouchable castes have suffered for centuries from a number of social problems and disabilities among which the following may be noted.

(i) *Lowest Status in the Social Hierarchy:* In the caste hierarchy the untouchable castes are ascribed the lowest status. They are considered to be *'unholy', 'inferior'* and *'low'* and are looked down upon by the other castes. They have been suffering from the stigma of *'untouchability'.* Their very touch is considered to be polluting by the higher caste people. Hence they have been subject to exploitation and humiliation. They have been treated as the servants of the other caste people. The untouchable castes have always served the other castes, but the attitude of other castes is of total indifference and contempt. They were kept at a distance from other caste people. In some instances (in South India) even the exact distance which an upper caste man was expected to keep between himself and the "untouchables" was specified. During the early times, they were branded as *"Panchamas, Antyajas, Svapachas, Atishudras, Chandalas, Avarnas"* etc. and were given the bottom most place in society. The distinction that arose between ***Aryans*** and ***Anaryas*** centuries ago culminated in the practice of untouchability. *Anaryas* were branded as *"dasas"* or servants and kept at a distance. They were not given any good position in the army, politics and public life, but made to follow *"unclean"* occupations such as scavenging, removing human waste and dead animals, tanning, shoe-making, spinning, washing clothes, barbering, supplying water and so on. The physical touch of these people following "unclean" occupations was considered enough to pollute the so called upper caste [varna] people. Thus the so called 'untouchables' were not only kept at a distance but also denied of various civic facilities. Several disabilities were attributed to them.

(ii) Civic Disabilities: For a long time the untouchable castes were not allowed to use public places and avail of civic facilities such as - village wells, ponds, temples, hostels, hotels, schools, hospitals, lecture halls, dharmashalas, choultries, etc. They were forced to live on the outskirts of the towns and villages during the early days. Even today they are segregated from others spatially. They were not allowed to enter the houses of the higher castes. They were allowed to work as labourers during construction or repair, storing grains, etc. But later the houses were purified by sprinkling cow urine or cow dung. In South India, restrictions were imposed on the mode of construction of their houses, types of dresses and patterns of their ornamentation. Some lower caste people were not allowed to carry umbrellas, to wear shoes or golden ornaments and to milk cows. They were prohibited from covering the upper part of their body. The services of barbers, washermen and tailors were refused to them. In the court of justice they had to shout from the pointed distance and take their chance of being heard.

(iii) *Educational Disabilities:* The untouchables were forbidden from taking up to education during the early days. Sanskrit education was denied to them. Public schools and other educational institutions were closed for them. Even today majority of them are illiterate and ignorant.

The literacy level of scheduled castes is extremely poor [21.4% in 1981]. It is less than half of the national average [41.3%]. In states like Bihar, Rajasthan, Madhya Pradesh and Uttar Pradesh their literacy level is less than 1/4 of the national average. The literacy percentage among the SCs, however, had increased to 37.41% in 1991 [SC males 49.9% and SC females 23.76%] and the corresponding national average figures were 52.21% [64.13% and 39.29%]. Female literacy is still poorer among them. In 1991, only 23.76% of SC women were literate while in Bihar, SC women's literacy level stood at the lowest minimum. At college level and university level and in professional courses, comparatively a very limited number of S.C. students are studying even after more than five decades of independence.

• ***Poor Educational Performance:*** The performance of Scheduled Caste students in the educational field is also relatively poor. The pass percentage of the SCs at the high school level is 53, at the graduate level 35, and at the post-graduate level 60. The corresponding general pass percentage figures are : 65, 57 and 76 respectively. In professional courses, their pass percentage is 60.[1] Even in the entrance tests for professional courses the poor quality of their education is very much evident. The enrolment of SCs at primary, secondary and high school levels is also far less than the national average.

(iv) *Religious Disabilities:* The untouchables also suffer from religious disabilities even today. They are allowed to enter temples in many places. Even after the successful campaign of **Dr. Ambedkar** demanding the untouchables right to enter the **Kalaram** temple at **Nasik** in 1930, things have not improved much. The Brahmins who offer their priestly services to some lower castes, are not prepared to officiate the ceremonies of the 'untouchable' castes. They do not even bow down to the deities of these 'untouchable' castes. The *Vedic mantras* which are considered to be more pure, could not be listened to and chanted by the untouchables because of the taboos. They were only permitted to make use of the *upanishadic mantras* which are considered to be less pure and more secular. Burial grounds were also denied to them in many places. However, things have started improving radically in these matters especially after 1990s.

2. Economic Problems and Disabilities

The untouchables are economically backward and have been suffering from various economic disabilities also.

(i) *No Right of Landed Property Ownership:* For centuries the untouchables were not allowed to have land and business of their own. It is only recently their ownership to the property has become recognised. The propertied people are comparatively less among them. Majority of them depend upon agriculture but only a few of them [hardly 28%] own land.

(ii) *Selection of Occupations Limited:* The caste system imposes restrictions on the occupational choice of the members. The occupational choice was very much limited for the untouchables. They were not allowed to take up to occupations which were reserved for the upper caste people. They were forced to stick on to the traditional inferior occupations such as curing hides, removing the human wastes, sweeping, scavenging, oil grinding, spinning, tanning, shoe-making, leather works, carrying the dead animals, etc. These occupations were regarded as *"degraded"* and *"inferior"*.

1 **L.M. Prasad** in the article *"Educational Policy for SCs and STs and its Implementation"* in *"The Indian Journal of Public Administration"*, New Delhi, October-December, 1996 : 908-932.

(iii) *Failure to Fill in the Full Quota of Reserved Posts:* The SCs have not been able to take full advantage of the reserved seats allotted to them in government jobs. The data collected from the Reports of the Commissioner for SCs and STs reveal that the representation in Central Government departments, public sector undertakings, and the nationalised banks in 1993 was **7%** to **10%** in **"A"** group posts, **9%** to **14%** in **"B"** group posts, **13%** to **19%** in **"C"** group posts, and **21%** to **23%** in **"D"** group posts. It is known that their [SCs] full quota positions in **"A"** and **"B"** groups is not filled in because eligible candidates are not available. The poor educational performance of the SC candidates has been the major obstacle in this regard.

(iv) *Landless Labourers:* Majority of untouchables are today working as landless labourers. More than 90% of the agricultural labourers in India belong to the depressed classes which include the Scheduled Caste and Scheduled Tribes. According to 1981 census, more than 52% of the Scheduled Caste workers in rural areas are agricultural labourers. A large number of SC families are in debts. Their indebtedness is increasing day by day. The SCs are economically exploited by the upper caste people. Even today they are the lowest paid workers. Some of them continue to suffer as *bonded labourers* at the hands of the other higher caste people. The untouchables constituted 90% of the total number of the bonded labourers found in India, according to a recent survey report. It is also observed that a large number of atrocities are committed against the untouchables because of economic reasons. **For example,** In 1977, as many as 10879 atrocities were committed against them and the figure increased to 15,053 in 1978 and then to 32,990 in 1995. Though jobs are reserved for them in government department due to lack of eligibility they are not able to get into them.

3. Political Disabilities

The untouchables hardly participated in the political matters for centuries. They were not given any place in politics, administration and the general governance of the country. They were not allowed to hold any public post. Political rights and representation were denied to them. Under the British rule, they were given the right to vote for the first time. After independence, equal political opportunities and rights have been provided for the SCs also. Politically, the SCs are yet to become a decisive force.

The untouchables or the SCs living in the city are trying to organise themselves in the form of *"Dalit Sangharsha Samithi"* and such other organisations to fight for their rights. But the vast mass of rural SCs are totally unorganised. Political parties such as *"The Republican Party of India"*, started by **Dr. Ambedkar,** *"Dalit Panthers' Party"* [of 1970s], *"Bahujana Samajavadi Party"* [BSP of 1980s] are no doubt mobilising the SCs but so far they have not been able to form a *"dalit lobby"* or *"Harijan lobby"* at the national level except in some pockets. Their political influence is mostly localised. Their total influence in the Indian politics is, so far, not very much impressive.

4. Problem of Atrocities Against Untouchables [SCs]

Another problem confronting the untouchables is that lot of atrocities are being committed against them. In fact, such atrocities are on the increase even now. According to the report of ***"Crime in India"*** [1995], *"Every 2 hours, 1 dalit is assaulted, every day 3 dalit women are raped, 2 dalits are murdered and 2 dalit houses burnt."* Further, as per the same report, in 1955, about 180 cases of atrocities committed against the SCs were registered with the police, and this number increased to 18,336 in 1991 and to 32,990 in 1995.

In some states severe caste conflicts are taking place and in many instances the targets of attack are the SCs. Bihar is notorious for caste conflicts. Bihar has sheltered several ***"jati senas"*** which take a leading role in caste conflicts. For example, *Bhoomi Sena* of Kurmis, *Lorik Sena* of

Yadavs, *Brahmarshi* and *Ranvir Sena* of the Bhumihars, *Ganga Sena* of the Brahmins, and the *Kunwar Sena* of the Rajputs, represent such *jati senas.* Further, there are also the Naxal groups of *Maoist Communist Centre* [MCC] which normally consist of people who belong to communities of the Yadavs, Koeris, and the Paswans. These jati senas and Naxal groups organised mass murders in the past. The reason for these murders was a long standing conflict between upper caste landowners and landless *dalit* farmers. The National Commission of the SCs and STs have also been regularly reporting an increase in the number of atrocities against the SCs. The central and the State governments are also seriously concerned with these crimes.

Harmful Effects of the Practice of Untouchability

The practice of untouchability gave rise not only to various kinds of disabilities but also caused damage to the Indian society. A few of such evil effects are mentioned below.

1. Untouchability *divided the Hindu society into the 'touchable'* and *'untouchable'* groups and served to develop mutual dislike, contempt and sometimes even enmity between the two. It damaged social harmony and created wide social distance between the two groups.
2. Since more than 1/6 of the total population of this land was labelled as *"untouchable"* its *socio-economic and educational progress was unwarrantedly halted for centuries.*
3. *Untouchability perpetuates inequality.* Hence it cannot support the development of healthy democratic traditions. It has affected our democratic system very badly.
4. *Untouchability provided scope for religious conversions.* Those untouchables who got disillusioned with the Hindu society got converted to other religions such as Christianity or Islam. Dr. Ambedkar himself had joined Buddhism at the fag end of his life in protest against the caste-controlled Hinduism.[1]
5. Untouchability led to *perennial conflicts between the upper castes and lower castes* for generations, sometimes resulting in loot, arson, murder, rape, molestation, burning of houses and crops and so on.
6. *Untouchability has damaged the self-image of the SCs.* It has developed in them a sense of inferiority and lack of confidence which damaged their personality development.
7. Due to the practice of untouchability, the nation was *deprived of the opportunity for making use of the talents, abilities and creative capacities* of a sizeable number of people for hundreds of years.
8. *The practice of untouchability is a black spot on the Hindu society.* It is an insult to the Hindu society. It has brought down the image of the Indians in the eyes of the foreigners.
9. Social reform movements and developmental activities could not take place in the Hindu society smoothly and effectively for it was divided vertically into *"touchable"* and *"untouchable"* castes. Even the great reformers like the Buddha, Mahaveera, Basavanna, Shankaracharya, Vivekananda, Dayananda Saraswathi, Gandhiji, Ambedkar and a host of others could not attain complete success in their attempts to remove untouchability.

Untouchability has done enough damage to the Hindu society. As **Gandhiji** said *it should become the thing of the past.* It is slowly disappearing. The earlier it goes the better it will be for the nation.

1 Such conversion of religion was reported in Meenakshipuram in Tamil Nadu in February 1981 in which about 1000 Harijans were converted into Islam.

REMOVAL OF UNTOUCHABILITY

Early Attempts of Eradication of Untouchability

Ever since the time of the Buddha and Mahavira attempts have been made to remove the social disabilities of the degraded castes including untouchability. The Buddha and Mahavira said that caste is no bar to communion with God. In fact, the Buddhism and Jainism rose as a challenge to the rigid caste system with all its evils. Thinkers and reformers like Basavanna, Kabirdas, Santa Tukaram, Guru Nanak, Tulsidas, Ramdas, Namadeva, Santa Jnaneshwar and a host of others have advocated the removal of caste distinctions, including untouchability for the good of humanity. The ***Bhakti* Cult** popularised by Purandara Das, Kanaka Das, Vadiraj and others, and the ***Veerashaivism*** established and propagated by Basavanna contributed a great deal to the removal of untouchability.

During the British rule in the 19th and 20th centuries, a number of social reformers tried to eradicate untouchability. They launched movements against untouchability and built organisations to reform the Hindu society. Swami Vivekananda's *'Sri Ramakrishna Mission',* Raja Ram Mohan Roy's *'Brahma Samaj',* Swami Dayananda Saraswati's *'Arya Samaj'*, Atmaram Panduranga's *'Prarthana Samaj',* Dr. Anni Besant's *'Theosophical Society'*, Thakkar Bapa's *'Harijan Sevak Sangha'*, Dr. Keshav Baliram Hedgewar's *'Rashtreeya Swayam Sevak Sangha',* the Indian National Congress under the leadership of Mahatma Gandhiji, Dr. B.R. Ambedkar's All-India Scheduled Caste Federation, Sri Narayana Guru and S.N.D.P. Yogam in Kerala, the Vishwa Hindu Parishad and other organisations have played an important role in the removal of untouchability.

Intellectuals like Keshabchandra Sen, Iswara Chandra Vidya Sagar, Justice Ranade, Jyoti Rao Phule, Sri Narayana Guru, Gandhiji, Sri Guruji Golwalkar and others also tried to rouse the conscience of the people against the practice of untouchability. *The Harijan Sevak Sangha, Depressed Class Union, the Social Service League, Depressed Class League, the Scheduled Classes Federation* etc. also tried to remove the caste disabilities.

Role of Dr. Ambedkar and Gandhiji in the Removal of Untouchability and Upliftment of Scheduled Castes

ROLE OF DR. AMBEDKAR

Dr. Bhim Rao Ambedkar [1891-1956] was a great modern social thinker, a born fighter, a famous advocate and a humanist. Dr. Ambedkar who was born in an *"untouchable"* or *"dalit"* community called **"Mahar"** in Maharashtra took a leading role in promoting the welfare of the untouchable castes and in elevating their status. Being the most highly educated untouchable in India, Dr. Ambedkar became the undisputed spokesman of the untouchables. He took many steps to reform the ways of the untouchables. He fought against many of the injustices done to the untouchables by establishing a political party and a couple of organisations for the upliftment of the untouchables. **Pandit Nehru** rightly described him as the *"symbol of the great revolt against all the oppressive features of Hindu society".*

1. *Dr. Ambedkar was the first man to make a scientific study of "untouchability"* : Even though Gandhiji had thought of the ways of removal of untouchability before the birth of Dr. Ambedkar, it was Ambedkar who drew the attention of the Congress Organisation and also of the entire nation towards the grave problems of the untouchables and their deplorable conditions. Ambedkar had made a detailed study of the problem of untouchability, its origin, development etc.

2. *Self-Respect Movement* : Dr. Ambedkar had made it clear that his main aim in life was to remove the practice of untouchability and to take the so called *"untouchable community"* towards socio-economic equality and justice. Through his social-movement he wanted to instill in the minds of the untouchables the ideas of self-dignity, self-confidence and self-respect. Thus his movement is often called *"self-respect movement."* Ambedkar established an institution called *"Bahishkrita Hitakarini Sabha"* which added momentum to this movement.

3. *Five Principles or "Pancha-Sutras" for the Progress of 'Dalits'*: Dr. Ambedkar wanted the untouchables or *'dalits'* to follow some principles in life so that they could attain a respectable status by their own efforts as a community. He recommended *"Pancha-sutras"* for them. They are :

(i) ***Self-Improvement:*** Making one's own efforts for one's improvement without expecting much from others;

(ii) ***Self-Progress:*** Making self-efforts for achieving progress in life;

(iii) ***Self-Dependence:*** Learning to lessen one's dependence on others and attaining finally self-reliance;

(iv) ***Self-Respect:*** Maintaining self-dignity and never sacrificing it for any reason.

(v) ***Self-Confidence:*** Developing confidence in oneself, in one's capacities and in one's efforts.

4. *Call to Reform the Style of Life* : Ambedkar made an appeal to his community people to change their style of life to suit to the needs of time. *"He urged them to stop the dragging of dead cattle out of the village. He wanted them to give up eating carrion, alcoholic drinks and begging. He wanted them to become literates and send their children to schools. Finally, he wanted them to dress well and have self-respect for themselves. Thus, one of his chief aims was to bring about a revolution in the way of life of the untouchables and in their aspirations for themselves and for their children."*[1]

5. *Three Principles of Dalit Movement: "Education, Agitation and Organisation"* : Dr. Ambedkar suggested three principles to govern the *"dalit movement"*. These principles are: *"education, agitation* and *organisation"* **:**

(i) ***Education*** is essential for helping the *dalits* to take out their mask of ignorance;

(ii) ***Agitation*** becomes inevitable to fight against all the exploiters and cheats;

(iii) ***Organisation*** is necessary to thrash out individual differences, to realise community interests and to fight for a common cause collectively.

After the ***All-India Depressed Class Conference in Nagpur*** in 1942 Ambedkar declared, *"My final word of advice is to educate, agitate, organise and have faith in yourself. It is a battle for the reclamation of human personality."*

Personal efforts to put the three principles into practice **:** Ambedkar himself worked to put these three principles into practice. Ambedkar encouraged the ***education*** of *dalits* through the organisations he established namely, *"Bahishkrita Hitakarini Sabha", "Independent Labour Party"* and *"Depressed Classes' Education Society"*.

Ambedkar organised ***agitations*** in the direction of reaching his goals. His own words reveal his faith in agitations. *"The direct action in respect of Chowder Tank in Mahad [of Kolaba District, Maharashtra], the Kalaram Temple at Nasik and the Guruvayur temple in Malabar have done in a few days what milllion days of preaching by reformers would never have done"*. He personally led the temple entry agitation at Nasik. In 1930, just 10 days before Gandhiji's *"Dandi March"*, Ambedkar launched a big temple entry movement at Nasik before the Kalaram Temple in which more than

1 **B. Kuppu Swamy** *"Social Change in India"* Page - 207.

A Brief Biographic Sketch of DR. B.R. AMBEDKAR [1893 – 1956]

Dr. B.R. Ambedkar is well known as a great thinker, a social reformer, a fearless fighter, a famous advocate and a great humanist. As a contemporary of Gandhiji he rendered a yeoman service to the nation by way of his relentless fight against untouchability, inequality, injustice and casteism. He is ever remembered for his contribution to the drafting of the Constitution of India.

☛ Ambedkar was born in an untouchable Mahar family on 14th April 1893 in the Ratnagiri district of Maharashtra. His father was Ramji an officer in the Indian Army and mother, Bhima Bai. Since he was born of an untouchable family he was as a boy humiliated by his high-caste school-mates. Ambedkar made determined efforts to continue his education undeterred by such humiliations. Awarded a scholarship by the Gaekwar [the ruler of Baroda], he studied at the universities in the United States, Britain and Germany. He entered the Baroda Public Service at the Gaekwar's request, but again ill-treated by his high-caste colleagues, he turned to legal practice and teaching. He soon established his leadership among *dalits* and became the chief spokesman of the untouchables.

☛ Ambedkar carried on his battle against untouchability throughout his life. Since he himself had suffered in his life as an *"untouchable"* at the hands of the Caste-Hindus, he had the strong urge to do away with it. He wanted to organise his community and to create awareness among his own people. He started a paper called *"Mooka Nayaka"* and organised *"Bahishkrita Hitakarini Sabha"*, a depressed classes union. He endeavoured to convene an all-India conference to bring all the untouchable castes under one banner, *All-India Depressed Classes Conference.* He was not able to achieve it due to the non-cooperation of his own community people. He however continued his campaign against untouchability, both before and after independence.

☛ In 1947, Ambedkar became a law minister of the government of India. He took a leading part in the framing of the Indian Constitution, outlawing discrimination against untouchables. "He resigned in 1951, disappointed at his lack of influence in the government."

☛ Dr. Ambedkar's thoughts, ideas and philosophy are reflected in his books. His writings such as *"Origin and Mechanism of Caste"*, *"Annihilation of Caste"*, *"Who Were The Shudras?"*, *"Who Were the Untouchables?"* etc. reveal his scholarship and the clarity of his thought. He was alegal luminary and is rightly rememberd as *"Abhinava Manu"*. He was awarded the *"Bharata Ratna"* title posthumously.

☛ Ambedkar's disappointment was growing because of the perpetuation of untouchability in the Hindu society. Finally, in great despair he renounced Hinduism and became a Buddhist in October 1956, together with his fellow untouchables at a ceremony in Nagpur in Maharasthra. He never got converted into Islam though he was tempted to do so by the Nizam of Hyderabad who was ready to offer him a huge amoung of money. He, however, died in the very same year.

☛ Dr. Ambedkar's thoughts and ideas are getting greater currency now. The number of his followers is also increasing. The struggle he carried on against inequality is also getting revived and reinforced.

15000 volunteers including 500 women, had taken part. *The programme of temple entry was more for creating social consciousness than for asserting religious rights.*

Dr. Ambedkar realised the importance of **"Organisation"** and worked to build a few of them. ***Examples:*** *"Bahishkrita Hitakarini Sabha"* [1924], *Mahad Conference or Dasgaon Dalit Conference* [1927], *"Independent Labour Party"*. As early as in 1920 he had made attempts to organise all the untouchable castes and bring them under one banner. He had organised the first *All-India Conference of Untouchables* in May 1920 at Nagpur.

6. *Call to Destroy the Caste System* : Ambedkar in his efforts to raise the status of untouchables considered the caste system one of the great obstacles. He expressed his great disappointment with the caste as well as varna system. He even gave a call to destroy the caste system in his famous book namely ***"Annihilation of Caste"*** [1936]. He wrote in **"Harijan"** in 1933 - *"The Outcaste is a byproduct of the caste system". "Nothing can emancipate the outcaste except the destruction of caste system."* As an expression of his disillusionment with Hinduism, he rejected Hinduism and embraced Buddhism with his followers in 1956. [He, however, died in the very same year, that is on 6th December 1956].

7. *Political Role of Ambedkar* : Ambedkar made use of political instruments to achieve the purpose of protecting *dalit* interests.

Demand for Separate Electorate for Dalits : In the *First Round Table Conference* convened in London in November 1930, Dr. Ambedkar who attended it on behalf of the depressed classes, spoke about the loathsome condition of the untouchables in India. He prepared a declaration of the fundamental rights of the depressed classes and submitted it to the minorities sub-committee. He demanded the abolition of untouchability and the establishment of equal citizenship. *He vehemently demanded a separate electorate for the depressed classes.* Gandhiji who boycotted the First Conference and participated in the Second Round Table Conference at London along with Ambedkar, opposed the proposal. He said *"the political separation of the untouchables and the Hindus would be suicidal to the nation."* He even said that he would resist such a proposal with his life. He declared his resolution of *"fast-unto-death"*. The conflict between the two leaders was, however, settled by the famous *"Poona Pact"* [1932][1] Ambedkar, thus, was able to get some reasonable representation for the untouchables.

Ambedkar who met Gandhiji in 1931 insisted on making the removal of untouchability a pre-condition for a person to become a member of the Congress. He supported the ***Anti-Untouchability League*** which launched a campaign all over the country to secure for the depressed classes enjoyment of their civil rights such as taking water from the village wells, admission of the children in village schools etc.

8. *Ambedkar as the "Abhinava Manu"* : Ambedkar was invited by the Prime Minister Nehru to be the Law Minister in the First Cabinet of Independent India. Ambedkar accepted the offer. He was made the *Chairman* of the *Drafting Committee* to draft the Indian Constitution. Article 17 of the Constitution abolished untouchability. Ambedkar had once declared that he would burn *"Manu Smriti"* for its failure to provide justice to the *dalits*. The same Ambedkar now could get the opportunity and the honour of giving to the people of India their Constitution. He is rightly called the *"Abhinava Manu"* [or *"Modern Manu"*]. He was awarded the *"Bharata Ratna"* title

---

1 Through the **"Poona Pact"** [1932] Gandhi ensured that the election of the SC and ST representatives would be by all the voters in territorial constituencies allotted for the purposes. As there is no constituency in which SCs are in a majority, the Pact makes sure that the elected SC candidates are in practice acceptable to the other castes and communities in the area.

posthumously. Ambedkar's ideas, views and thoughts continue to influence and inspire a number of his followers who are spread over the entire nation.

ROLE OF MAHATMA GANDHI

Mahatma Gandhi played a memorable role in uplifting the untouchables. Gandhiji popularised the word ***"Harijan"***[1] meaning *"the people of God"* - a word which was first coined and used by a Gujarathi Brahmin saint by name **Narasinha Mehta.** According to Gandhiji, the practice of untouchability is "*a leper wound in the whole-body of Hindu politic"*. He even regarded it as *"the hatefullest expression of caste"*. He made it his life mission to wipe out untouchability and to uplift the depressed and the downtrodden people. As a servant of mankind, he preached that all human beings are equal and hence the *Harijans too* have a right to social life along with other caste groups.

Gandhi's Appeal to the Conscience of the People

Gandhiji believed in the fourfold division of the Hindu society into four *varnas.* He regarded untouchables as Shudras and *not as the Panchamas* or *fifth Varna* or *Avarna.* Hence, he sincerely felt the need for bringing about a basic change in the caste structure by uplifting the untouchables and *not by abolishing the caste as such.* He appealed to the conscience of the people to realise the historical necessity of accommodating the *"Harijans"* by providing them a rightful place in the society.

Gandhi's Compassion for the Harijans **:** Gandhiji had much compassion for the *Harijans.* He said: *"I do not want to be reborn. But if I am to be born, I would like to be born an untouchable, so that I may share their sorrows and sufferings." He was of the opinion that the practice of untouchability was a moral crime. He said that "if untouchability is not wrong, then nothing in the world is wrong."* He believed that *a change of heart on the part of the Hindus was essential to enable the social and cultural assimilation of Harijans.* He was very much moved by their social distress and started a nationwide movement to remove their disabilities.

Gandhi's Campaign Against Untouchability

Gandhiji who regarded untouchability as a blot on Hinduism wanted to do away with it completely. He wrote in 1920 *"... Without the removal of the taint [of untouchability], "swaraj" is a meaningless term."* He even felt that the foreign domination of our country was the result of our exploitation of almost one-sixth of our own people in the name of religion.

Gandhiji decided to stage a campaign against untouchability and was unprepared to make any compromise with it. He advocated positive means for the uplift of *Harijans.* He addressed various public meetings reposing doctrines of *Harijan* welfare. He led several processions of *Harijans* with other upper caste people and made them participate in *"poojas, bhajans, keerthans* and *puranas*". He believed that opportunities of *education* and *temple entry* would reduce social inequalities between *Harijans* and caste Hindus. He launched movements for cleaning *Harijan* residential areas, for digging wells for them and for similar other beneficial things.

---

1 **Harijan** - "was a word used by the great saint **Narasinha Mehta,** who by the by belonged to the Nagar Brahmana Community and who defied the whole community by claiming the *"untouchables"* as his own. I am delighted to adopt the word which is sanctified by having been used by such a great saint, but it has for me a deeper meaning than you may imagine. The *"untouchable"*, to me, is compared to us, really, a Harijan - a man of God, and we are "Dhurjan" [men of evil].

Source: **M.K. Gandhi *"The Removal of Untouchability"*** - 1954 Page No: 14. Compiled and edited by **Bharatan Kumarappa** - Published by **"Navajivan Publishing House"**, Ahmedabad.

A Brief Biographic Sketch of MAHATMA GANDHI [1869 – 1948]

Mahatma Gandhiji acclaimed as the architect of Indian Independence, the *"Father of the Nation"* and the great *"messenger of peace"*, is known to the entire world. He was not just an individual but a great living force, a silent revolutionary, a man of courage, self-confidence and conviction. As **Dr. Radhakrishnan** points out, *his message is not just for the present generation but for the generations to come.* He ranks among the greatest leaders of the world of all times.

☞ ***Mohandas Karam Chand Gandhi*** was born in Porbander in Gujarath on October 2, 1869. Mohandas Gandhi, the son of Karam Chand Gandhi and Puthali Bai, did his early education in India and went to England, studied law and started practising as a lawyer in South Africa. He came under the great influence of **Leo Tolstoy** and **John Ruskin.** It was there he started his new career as an uncompromising fighter for human cause. He developed *Satyagraha* a new method of fighting against oppression. With this new instrument of *Satyagraha* he gave a severe blow to the British policy of colour discrimination.

☞ Gandhiji came to India and plunged himself into the freedom struggle in 1920s. Afterwards upto 1947 his battle against the British continued. He stood as a guiding force for the Congress Movement which had taken up the cause of freedom struggle. The nation stood as one man under his leadership. The British had to bow down and finally had to quit the land. Gandhiji could have become the Prime Minister at that stage. But he was not after power. He preferred to serve the people in his usual style without resorting to political instruments or power. Gandhiji did not have the fortune of living long to see the progress of independent India. He was treacherously assassinated on 30th Jan. 1948. Though he died, his thoughts, principles and ideals are still alive inspiring millions both within and outside India.

☞ The Gandhian views have a great value in the realm of human thought. His *"Satyagraha"*, a unique type of non-violent movement created history. It inspired leaders at the world level. **Martin Luther King, Nelson Mandela, Yaser Araafat** and a host of others derived inspiration from him.

☞ Gandhiji was an ardent believer in truth and non-violence. Search for truth was his life-mission. Where there is no truth there is no knowledge. This was not just a matter of his belief, it was his life-view. He was a strong advocate of *"Swadeshi* and *Self-dependence". Khadhi* and *Charaka* which he introduced are only symbolic. He had the ambition of establishing a *"Sarvodaya Samaja"*. His concept of *"Rama Rajya"* is only complementary to it.

☞ Gandhiji took up the cause of the removal of untouchability as his another great life-mission. But he believed in the method of persuasion and not conflict. He carried on a relentless fight against alcoholism, exploitation, casteism and religious fanaticism. He really remained a great messenger of peace.

☞ The Gandhian views, thoughts and ideals are now facing an ordeal. Has the Gandhian way become irrelevant today? Is Gandhian achievement getting defeated in his own land? These are the haunting questions. No one need spend energy to find an answer for these questions. Our own life-style and our own practice are themselves the answer.

Gandhiji wrote in *"Young India"* in April 1925. *"Temples, public wells and public schools must be open to the untouchables equally with caste Hindus."* He started two journals, *'Harijan'* and *'Young India'* through which he advocated his ideas. He started an *ashrama* where people of all castes and creeds could come and stay without any differences.

Gandhiji served the *"Harijan Sevak Sangha"* started by the social reformer **Takkar Bapa** in the year 1932 in order to promote the religious and social welfare of the Harijans. This organisation opened schools and dispensaries in various places and arranged for free educational facilities and scholarships for *Harijan* children.

Political Role of Gandhiji

As a much respected political leader of the masses, Gandhiji could never ignore the tasks of the removal of untouchability and upliftment of *Harijans.* Gandhiji entered the Indian freedom struggle in 1919. From 1920 onwards, under the leadership of Gandhiji the Indian National Congress committed itself to get the independence on the one hand, and to the removal of untouchability, on the other. In 1920 itself, he declared that *"Untouchability cannot be given a secondary place in the programme"* of Congress.

Gandhiji's Protest Against the Proposal of Separate Electorate for Harijans: Gandhiji was very much against the British policy of *"divide and rule".* He condemned the British policy of *separating the Harijans from the rest of the Hindus.* Hence he protested against the proposal of creating separate electorate for the *Harijans.* He said to Ambedkar who was in favour of the proposal, that *"the political separation of the untouchables from the Hindus would be suicidal to the nation."*

Gandhiji declared at the *Minorities Committee* of *the Second Round Table Conference* in London [1932] that *"we do not want the untouchables to be classified as a separate class. Sikhs may remain such in perpetuity, so may Muslims and Christians. Will the untouchables remain untouchables in perpetuity? I would rather feel that Hinduism died than that untouchability lived. I will resist it with my life."*[1]

Impact of Gandhiji's "Fast-Unto-Death Satyagraha: In spite of Gandhiji's protest, the British Prime Minister decided to grant separate seats for the depressed classes and the right of double vote in which they could elect their own representatives and also vote in general elections. In protest against this *"communal award"* Gandhiji decided to stage the *fast unto death satyagraha.* This declaration of Gandhiji opened the eyes of the whole country towards the problem of untouchables.

In 1932 the *Harijan Sevak Sangh* was formed and its Conference at Bombay pledged that the right to use the public roads, wells etc. would be given statutory recognition when the Swaraj Parliament met. This pledge was stressed by Gandhiji in 1932 when he said, *"There could be no rest... until untouchability becomes a thing of the past."* The *Harijan* movement gained strength throughout the country. Gandhi went on an all-India tour to collect huge sums of money for this programme.

Gandhiji Commits Congress for the Removal of Untouchability: At the behest of Gandhiji and the Congress, all the Congress candidates who contested elections in 1937 had pledged themselves to the removal of untouchability. As early as in 1931 itself at the *Karachi Session of the Congress* at the behest of Gandhiji, a resolution was adopted. It declared, *"All the citizens are equal before law irrespective of caste, creed or sex."* In 1938, the *Removal of the Civil Disabilities Act* was passed by the Madras Legislature which provided that no *Harijan* shall be disabled from any social

1 **B. Kuppu Swamy** *"Social Change in India"* Page: 211.

or public amenity. In the same year, it also passed the *Malabar Temple Entry Act* which threw open the temples in Malabar. In 1939, the temple of Madurai was opened to the *Harijans.* Thus Gandhiji's fast and his *Harijan* movement released tremendous forces throughout the country, which led to the removal of some of the disabilities of the *Harijans.*

- ***Gandhiji's personal involvement in the Harijan welfare activities:*** Gandhiji was not just a preacher. He practised what he preached. He could win the hearts of millions of *Harijans* because of his sincere approach to solve their problems. Gandhiji lived with the *Harijans* and shared their distress by inculcating in them the ideas of better social adjustment with the rest of the Indian community. He advocated equal opportunities of education and intermingling of *Harijan* students with those of the upper castes. He fought for various legal protections against several kinds of injustices done to them. He adopted a *Harijan* child and set an example for others to emulate. As a result of his sincere efforts and strong recommendations, untouchability was declared illegal under the Indian Constitution. At his behest, an opportunity was given to **Dr. B.R. Ambedkar,** leader of the depressed classes, to join the Central Cabinet and to be the chief architect of the Indian Constitution.

Gandhiji's Proposals for Harijan Welfare

Gandhiji's proposals for *Harijan* welfare include the following:

1. Those who claim themselves to be the servants of *Harijan* must serve the *Harijans* with all the dedication.
2. Awareness must be created among the *Harijans* regarding cleanliness, sanitation and health.
3. The practice of carrying human waste on head must be stopped.
4. They should be persuaded to drop their habit of eating carrion and dead animals.
5. Practice of untouchability must be immediately stopped by all.
6. *Harijans* must be provided with drinking water facility.
7. Good houses at low cost but with enough provision for lighting and ventilation must be built for *Harijans.*
8. *Harijan* children must be made to go to school and even adult education programme should be introduced.
9. Harijans must be persuaded to drop their habit of drinking alcohol.
10. Harijans must be allowed to enter all the public places and to draw water from the wells.
11. There should be no bar for the entry of *Harijans* to temples.
12. *"Harijan Day"* should be observed by all at least one day in a year.

Ambedkar and Gandhiji who fought against the problem of untouchability and served to promote the welfare of "untouchables" are not alive today. Their followers are, however, continuing their work. Untouchability has not yet become *"the thing of the past"*. The removal of untouchability requires a basic transformation in the general attitude towards it. Gandhiji was right when he wrote in his letter to Thakkar Bapa: *"The salvation of the depressed class will come only when the caste Hindu is made to think and is forced to feel that he must alter his ways. I want a revolution in the mentality of the caste Hindus."* The country is awaiting such a revolution.

MEASURES FOR THE WELFARE OF SCHEDULED CASTES

The Government of independent India has been trying to uplift the Scheduled Castes and Scheduled Tribes right from its very inception. The Governmental attempts to promote the welfare of the SCs and STs can be classified into two group. (A) *Constitutional and legislative measures* and (B) *Other welfare measures and programmes.*

A. The Constitutional and Legislative Measures

The Government of India has incorporated some special provisions in its Constitution for the removal of untouchability and to promote the welfare of SCs and STs. The constitution ensures the protection and assures the promotion of interests of SCs, STs and other weaker sections of the population in the fields such as (1) *political representation,* (2) *representation in services,* (3) *economic development,* (4) *socio-cultural safeguards* and (5) *legal support.*

1. The Preamble of the Constitution of India declares that it assures equality, promotes fraternity, guarantees liberty and ensures justice to one and all.
2. Articles 15, 16, 17, 38 and 46 guarantee that the state shall not discriminate between persons on account of their religion or region and caste or class.
3. Article 15 prohibits discrimination on grounds of religion, caste, race, sex or place of birth.
4. ***Article 17 abolishes untouchability.*** It is further provided that the enforcement of any disability arising out of untouchability shall be an offence punishable in accordance with law.
5. Article 46 promotes educational and economic interests of Scheduled Castes, Scheduled Tribes and other weaker sections.
6. Article 330 reserves representation for Scheduled Castes and Scheduled Tribes in the Houses of the People.
7. Article 334 relates to reservation of seats and special representation to cease after fifty years [Originally reservation was made for ten years and it was extended four times, the present period of expiry being 2010 A.D.)
8. Article 335 mentions the claims of Scheduled Castes and Scheduled Tribes to services and posts.
9. Article 338 empowers the Central Govt. to appoint a National Commission for Scheduled Castes and Scheduled Tribes.
10. Article 339 empowers the President to appoint a Commission to report on the administration of the Scheduled Areas and the welfare of Scheduled Tribes in the States.
11. Article 341 empowers the President to specify the castes, races or tribes deemed as Scheduled Castes in a particular State or Union territory.
12. Article 342 empowers the President to specify the tribes or tribal communities deemed to be Scheduled Tribes in a particular State or Union Territory.

Legislative Measures For the Removal of Untouchability

The Government has been taking up the required legislative measures for the removal of untouchability. In pursuance of the provision of the Article **17** of the Constitution which declares the practice of untouchability a punishable offence, the Parliament passed the ***Untouchability Offences Act, 1955.*** It was later substituted by ***the Protection of Civil Rights Act, 1976.*** According to this Act the offences of untouchability include the following.

• Offences of Untouchability as per the *"Protection of Civil Rights Act, 1976"*

(i) Committing any kind of social injustice, such as denying access to any shop, restaurant, public hospital, educational institution or any place of public entertainment.

(ii) Preventing a person, on the grounds of untouchability, from entering a place of worship and offering prayers, or from drinking water from a public well or spring.

(iii) Refusal to sell goods or render services to a person on the grounds of untouchability is an offence punishable with imprisonment for six months or a fine upto Rs. 500 or both.

(iv) Enforcing occupational, professional, trade disabilities in the matter of enjoyment of any benefit under a charitable trust, etc.

Measures to Check Atrocities Against SCs and STs

Scheduled Castes and Scheduled Tribes [Prevention of Atrocities] Act, 1989, which came into force on 30th January 1990, specifies offences, which are considered as atrocities and provides for deterrent punishments for commission of the same. Comprehensive rules were also framed under this Act in 1995 to provide relief and rehabilitation of the affected persons. All the States and UTs [except Arunachal Pradesh and Nagaland] have specified Special Courts for trial of offences under this Act. Under the centrally sponsored scheme for implementation of the Act, State Governments are funded on 50 : 50 basis and UTs are given cent per cent assistance.

- ***Scheduled Castes and Scheduled Tribes [Prevention of Atrocities] Act, 1989*** describes the following acts as punishable crimes:

1. Forcibly occupying and cultivating the land of SC / ST man.
2. Confiscating the land / property of any SC / ST person.
3. Forcing an SC / ST person to eat or drink some disgraceful substance.
4. Throwing into the house or the neighbourhood of SC / ST person any rubbish or dead animal, etc. to humiliate him.
5. Forcibly snatching away the clothes from the body of SC / ST person and making him naked.
6. Insulting a SC / ST person in some way or the other.
7. Sexual harassment of an SC / ST woman.
8. Molesting or raping an SC / ST woman.
9. Polluting the drinking water used by any SC / ST person.
10. Forcibly evacuating an SC / ST person from his house, neighbourhood or village.
11. Preventing an SC / ST person from voting or forcing him to vote for a particular person.
12. Compelling an SC / ST person for forced labour or using him as a bonded labourer.

• Special Measures Undertaken by Some States to Give Protection to SCs / STs Against Atrocities

In order to assure security and give more protection to the SCs and STs some states have resorted to some special measures among which the following may be noted.

1. Assisting the SCs in obtaining the possession of lands belonging or allotted to them;
2. Helping the SCs agricultural labourers in getting statutory minimum wages;
3. Setting up state-level communities to look after various aspects concerning the welfare of the SCs.
4. Establishing special SC cells under the DIG Police to ensure that crimes against the SCs are properly registered, investigated and quickly prosecuted.
5. To ensure quick disposal of cases pertaining to the SCs special courts are set up in some states.

6. The bureaucratic machinery is properly dealt with for solving disputes of low wages, etc., concerning the SCs.
7. Specially instructing the police authorities to treat cases of crimes against the SCs as special cases and arrange for quick trial and prosecution. Scheduled Castes

B. Other Welfare Measures and Programmes for the Upliftment of Scheduled Castes

1. Appointment of a National Commission for the Welfare of Scheduled Castes

A *National Commission for the Scheduled Castes and Scheduled Tribes* has been set up by the Central Government to safeguard the interests of the SCs and STs. It functions as an advisory body on issues and policies related to the development of the SCs and STs. The State Governments have separate departments to look after the welfare of the SCs and STs. Their administrative set up varies from state to state.

2. Educational Opportunities

Due attention is paid to extend the educational opportunities of SCs and STs and hence special provisions have been made in this regard. Free education, free distribution of books, stationery, uniform etc. giving scholarships, banking loan facilities, providing mid-day meal, arranging for free boarding and lodging facilities, reserving seats for SCs and STs in all the government and government aided institutions, etc. are some of the concrete steps which the Government has taken in this regard.

Centrally Sponsored Schemes: In addition to the above, there are some centrally sponsored schemes also for the educational benefit of both SCs and STs.

(i) ***Free Coaching and Training*** for various competitive examinations [IAS, IPS, IFS, etc.] to increase their representation in various services. Some of the coaching centres have made considerable contribution enabling SC / ST candidates to get into IAS and allied services, medical, engineering and banking services. During the year 1999-2000, Rs.2.30 crore were released for this purpose.

(ii) ***Book Bank Scheme*** : Book bank scheme is intended to provide text books required for the students belonging to SC / STs pursuing medical and engineering degree courses. From 1991-92, agricultural, veterinary and polytechnic courses have also been included under this scheme. During 1999-2000, Rs.2.43 crore were released for this.

(iii) ***Post-matric scholarships for providing financial assistance for higher education.*** Govt. spent 66.5 crore rupees for this purpose in the year 1993-94. The *University Grants Commission* [U.G.C.] and the *Ministry of Education* had earmarked 15% of their budget for this purpose during the 6th Plan - 1980-85. Beginning with mere 114 students in 1994-95, the scheme is presently covering nearly 20 lakh students. During 1999-2000, Central assistance of Rs.160.89 crore was released for this scheme.

(iv) ***Construction of hostels*** for providing residential facilities to SCs and STs studying at college and university level.

(v) ***Financial assistance*** to those SC and ST students going to reputed research institutes for research work.

(vi) ***Providing Textbooks*** to those studying in medical and engineering courses.

(vii) ***National Overseas Scholarships and Passage Grants for Higher Education*** : This scheme provides financial assistance to selected meritorious students for pursuing higher studies abroad in specified fields of Masters level course, Ph.D. and Post Doctoral research programmes in Engineering, Technology and Science only. The modified scheme would provide maintenance allowance of US Dollars 7700 per annum, or Pounds Sterling 5000 per annum per candidate in U.K. for courses covered under the scheme. From the very inception of the scheme in 1954-55, a total of 732 scholarships have been offered, out of which 532 scholarships have been availed of till 1998.

3. Expansion of Economic Opportunities

Government has taken up economic programmes also for the benefit of SCs and STs. **Examples:** Landless SC labourers are allotted land. Land reforms have been undertaken to bring benefits of land ownership for them. Poor SC farmers are supplied with seeds, agriculture implements, fertilizers, pesticides, interest-free loans, pair of bullocks for ploughing, subsidy for developing dairy farming, poultry farming, piggery, animal husbandry, handicrafts, spinning and weaving. The *"loan-mela"* programme of Rajiv Gandhi Govt. [1984-89] also provided small loans for the poorer section to help them to earn money through some secondary sources such as toy-making, basket-making, agarbatti and beedi-rolling, tailoring, shoe-making, etc.

4. Expansion of Employment Opportunities and Reservation

In order to enhance the economic position of the SCs and STs the Constitution has provided for the *reservation in services.* Reservation of jobs operates in the All-India Services, Central Government, State Governments, and Government owned and managed public sector units and institutions. Reservation exists in all these for the SCs and STs to the tune of 15% and 7.5% respectively. Several State Governments have introduced reservation for OBC's [Other Backward Classes] also.

In government services, special quotas are also allotted to them. The reservations are also extended to promotions[1] to higher positions to facilitate their adequate representation. Concessions such as relaxation of age limit, *relaxation in the standards of suitability, relaxation of the qualification and experience,* have also been provided to them.

5. Upliftment of Scheduled Castes through Five Year Plans

The welfare of the Scheduled Castes [and STs] has been given special attention in the **Five Year Plans.** The size of investment on the special programmes has been increasing from plan to plan. The expenditure of Rs. **30.04** crore in the First Plan [1951-56] increased to Rs.**79.41** crore in the Second Plan [1956-61], Rs.**100.40** crore in the Third Plan [1961-66], Rs.**172.70** crore in the Fourth Plan [1969-74], Rs.**296.19** crore in the Fifth Plan [1974-79], Rs.**1337.21** crores in the Sixth Plan [1980-85], and Rs.**1521.42** crore in the Seventh Plan [1985-90].[2] The State Governments have also been spending a sizeable amount on the welfare of these people.

• Development Strategies in the Five Year Plans

The Central Government sponsored a comprehensive three-pronged strategy for the development of the SCs during the 6th Five Year Plan [1980-85]. This consisted of three schemes: (i) *Special Component Plan* [SCPs] of the central ministries and State governments. (ii) *Special*

1 "The Supreme Court in its recent judgement on the reservation issue on Nov. 15th, 1992 adjudicated that there can be no reservations in promotions but the Central Government decided to continue them for some time. The Supreme Court also declared that reservation in certain technical posts like *scientific departments, super-specialities in medicine, engineering and defence research, professors in education, pilots in Indian Airlines / Air India,* etc. is **not advisable.**"

2 ***Source of Statistics:*** **Ram Ahuja's** *"Indian Social System"* - Page: 370.

Central Assistance [SCA] to SCPs for the Scheduled Castes of the States and (iii) *Scheduled Caste Development Corporation* [SCDCs] in the States.

(i) *Special Component Plan [SCP]*: The main objective of this plan is to assist the SC families to substantially improve their income. This plan envisages identification of schemes of development which would benefit SCs, quantification of funds from all programmes and determination of specific targets as to the number of families to be benefited from these programmes. During the 6th Plan [1980-85] Rs. 4,481 crore were earmarked for the SCPs. Till the year 1990, only eight central ministries had formulated the SCPs for the SCs.

(ii) *Special Central Assistance [SCA]*: The main purpose of this scheme is to provide additional assistance to the States from the Centre to help the economic advancement of the maximum possible number of Schedule Caste families living below the poverty line. This assistance is given through the SCPs. During the 6th plan, Rs. 600 crore was earmarked for this purpose. Later, in 1993, in one year, about Rs. 273 crore was provided as SCA.

(iii) *Scheduled Caste Development Corporation [SCDC]*: The SCDCs have been set up in 18 states and 3 union territories. These SCDCs provide money and loan assistance to these families, thereby helping to increase the flow of funds from financial institutions to SC families. These Corporations established in the States are expected to interface between the SC families and financial institutions including banks. Both the Central and the State Governments are contributing grants to these SCDCs. For example, the State Governments' contribution in 1989-90 was Rs. 19 crore and the Central Government's Rs.15 crore.

At present [2001], SCDCs are functioning in 25 States / UTs. The Centre contributes 49% to the Authorised Share Capital of the SCDC against the 51% contributed by State Governments. In 1999-2000, an amount of Rs.20 crore was released as the Government of India's contribution.

The Corporation also provides loan to the SC families upto Rs. 12,000. They not only arrange to provide financial assistance for occupations like agriculture, animal husbandry and household industry but also for small shops, industries, auto-rickshaws and many other trades and professions. Some corporations also arrange for irrigation facilities like digging wells and tubewells.

6. Other Welfare Programmes

(i) *Drinking Water Facility:* In SCs colonies and in the areas where they are found in large number, drinking water facility is provided through the construction of wells and borewells.

(ii) *Medical Facility:* Free medical check-up facility is provided for the SCs. Those who undergo family planning operations are given financial assistance for purchasing required medicine and energising tonic.

(iii) *Janata Houses:* In various States the SCs are given financial assistance to have their own houses. In States like Karnataka and Tamil Nadu, low caste houses having all minimum required facilities, known as *"janata"* houses are built for them at State expenses.

(iv) *Liberation of Bonded Labourers:* A large number of bonded labourers particularly belonging to the SCs have been liberated. As per the report of the Labour Department of the Central government in 1983 about 1.13 lakh bonded labourers [out of a total of 1.61 lakh] were liberated from their bondage with the Governmental assistance.

(v) *Sulab Sauchalaya Scheme* for the Liberation and Rehabilitation of Scavengers : This has been launched in several States for converting dry latrines into water-borne latrines in order to liberate SC scavengers and rehabilitate them in alternative occupations. During 1999-2000, Rs.70 crore was released to the States for the implementation of this Scheme.

(vi) ***Baba Saheb Dr. Ambedkar Foundation*** **:** The Foundation was set up on 24 March 1992 as a registered society initially to implement / administer four schemes, viz., (i) *Dr. Ambedkar National Public Library;* (ii) *Dr. Ambedkar National Award;* (iii) *Dr. Ambedkar Overseas Fellowships;* and (iv) *Dr. Ambedkar Chairs in Universities.* The Foundation has been reconstituted to include eminent persons in the fields of education, social work and development of scheduled castes. The scope of the Foundation has been enlarged to include more activities connected with the life and mission of Dr. Ambedkar. These, among others, include publication of books, foster academic contract, promote research, instituting awards, etc.

7. Voluntary Organisations

In addition to the Governmental schemes and instruments, some of the voluntary organisations are also playing an important role in promoting the welfare of the SCs. **Examples:** (i) *Harijan Sevak Sangh* [New Delhi], (ii) *Indian Depressed Classes League* [New Delhi], (iii) *Hind Sweepers Sevak Sangh* [Delhi], (iv) *Servants of India Society* [Poona], (v) *Indian Red Cross Society* [New Delhi], *"Ishwara Sharana Ashrama"* - Alahabad, (vi) *Sri Ramakrishna Mission* [Narendrapura, Purulia, Silchar, Puri], (vii) *Bharatiya Adimajati Sevak Sangh* [New Delhi], (viii) *Bharatiya Samaja Unnati Mandala* [Bhivandi, Maharashtra]. The Central Government has been giving financial assistance to these organisations for their Harijan Welfare activities. In 1994, the Govt. spent about Rs. 6.5 crore for giving such an assistance.

The Government also provides grants in aid to voluntary organisations of local character working among Scheduled Castes. During 1999-2000, 376 voluntary organisations were given grant in aid to the tune of Rs.26 crore.

Some other organisations which are not getting any financial help from the Government are also rendering yeomen service to the Scheduled Castes. **Example:** *"Hindu Seva Prathisthana", "Vishwa Hindu Parishad", the service units of Rashtreeya Swayam Sevak Sangha, "Dalit Organisations"* and a number of *Christian Missionary Organisations.*

A Brief Evaluation of Welfare Measures

Have the above mentioned welfare measures really contributed to the upliftment of the SCs? The answer is somewhat disappointing.

- The Scheduled Castes spend their social energy in *sanskritising* themselves on the model of the locally dominant castes. They do not gain much out of this. Their *social mobility is very much limited.* They continue to remain weak in the local power structure for asserting their rights. They still are economically insecure.
- Majority of the SCs are still illiterate and ignorant and hence they are *not able to make use of the constitutional provisions guaranteed to them.*
- The reports of the National Commission on Scheduled Castes and Scheduled Tribes reveal that *the crimes against SCs are increasing.* **Example:** The number of crimes against SCs recorded by the police in 1955 was 180; it increased to 13,884 in 1979 and to 19,342 in 1987 and further to 32990 in 1995.
- There has been a quality of *ritualistic formalism* about many welfare and development schemes formulated for the benefit of these people. *Lack of enthusiasm* and *sincerity* on the part of the Government officials and agencies have also been the cause of failure of many of the welfare schemes.

- The benefits of the SC welfare programmes have been availed of by *a few people belonging to Scheduled Castes.* This small minority has developed *vested interests* and contributes nothing for the benefit of the majority.
- The Scheduled Castes are largely concentrated in rural areas and 90% of them [including 35% agricultural labourers] derive their sustenance from agriculture. In most of the villages, they continue to suffer from residential segregation. Hence, many of their disabilities still persist.
- It is unfortunate that in spite of 50 years of consistent efforts to elevate the position of the SCs, expected success has not been achieved. Socially, economically and politically, their status has improved very little. Socially, they have not changed many of their evil customs and their status remains the same; economically, more than 30 per cent SCs live below the poverty line and their occupational mobility does not lead them to social mobility; educationally, they are very backward; politically, they are not organised and remain weak in the local power structure for asserting their rights.
- The *"dalits"* are also not satisfied with their present position. Hence, they launched a nationwide campaign for the *dalit human rights* on 10th December 1998 [that is, on the *World Human Rights Day*] which focused on three important issues : (i) *right to touch and be touched;* (ii) *"no" to untouchability in the 21st century,* and (iii) *cast out caste.*
- The *dalits* demand for the effective implementation of the *SC / ST [Prevention of Atrocities] Act and Rules,* and to provide full protection to all *dalits* who participate in Panchayat Raj and other institutions – only reveals that they still suffer from a sense of insecurity.
- The SCs are still *tradition-bound.* They suffer from *a sense of inferiority* and this takes away their *'push'* to develop further. They are not well-organised. Only in cities some *"dalit organisations"* are trying to fight for their rights. Politically also they are not a single homogeneous entity. Hence their political bargaining power is comparatively less. However, their political consciousness is growing. The younger generation among them is becoming more assertive. There is a positive change in the attitude of the caste-Hindus towards the SCs. Hence the social distance between the two is gradually getting narrowed. The social position of the SCs is comparatively better in South India than in North India. In Kerala, for example, the SCs do not suffer from the traditional type of disabilities. Greater changes are expected in their living styles in the years to come.

Increasing *Dalit* Consciousness and Its Effects

The untouchables or Scheduled Caste people are also generally referred to as *"dalits."* The term ***"dalit"*** has been interpreted in different ways.

1. According to the ***Marxists,*** *"dalits"* are those who are the victims of socio-economic and political explanation.
2. According to the ***Ambedkar School of Thought,*** *dalits* are those who are branded as *"untouchables"* on caste basis.
3. According to the ***Lohiya School of Thought,*** *dalits* are those poor caste people including the so called untouchables, who have been the victims of exploitation.

Of the three views cited above, the second one is more popular and widely prevalent. Thus, *"dalits"* are normally understood as *"untouchables."*

Increasing Awareness Among the *Dalits*

"Dalits" are becoming more and more aware of the position in the society. Various constitutional provisions that safeguard their interests, on the one hand, and the continuous exploitation of the *"dalits"* on the other, have led to an increase in what is known as *"dalit consciousness."* The continuous exploitation has made the SCs to become conscious of their separate identity. They have become more self-conscious. This growing awareness in them has led to the emergence of various SC movements and activated the process of Sanskritisation which M.N. Srinivas had spoken of. This awareness and movements have led to certain consequences :

Consequences of *Dalit* Consciousness

1. *Dalit consciousness has enabled the SCs in different parts of the country to form political groups.* ***Example*** **:** *The Republican Party of India, The Dalit Panthers Party* [Maharashtra]; and the *Bahujan Samaj Party* [U.P., M.P. and Punjab] could be cited here as examples.

2. *Dalits are becoming increasingly aware of the fact that they have a great political potentiality.* They have decided to take advantage of their numerical strength by converting it into votes. Where they cannot form their own political parties, they extend their support to the national-level political parties and demand attractive *"price"* for their support. However, in this process of political bargain only the educated and the organised *dalits* are taking an active role, but not the uneducated masses in the rural areas.

3. *The dalits are now putting pressure on the national leadership* for taking measures to remove the social disabilities of the *dalits.*

4. *They have been demanding the effective implementation of the constitutional safeguards* to protect their interests.

5. The *dalits have launched various "alienative movements"* which Dr. Ambedkar had advocated, and also a few *"integrative movements"* strongly recommended by Gandhiji. The alienative movements led to the caste consolidation of the SCs by fusion of a number of sub-castes into one caste group. ***Example*****:** In Maharashtra, more than 52 sub-castes of Mahars got fused to forge one community.

6. Apart from these movements, the *dalits*, especially the educated ones, are becoming **individually conscious of achieving social mobility.**

An anal'ysis of *dalit* consciousness and its effects invites lot of questions : Will the *dalits* ever be integrated into the main stream of the Hindu society ? Will they insist on reservation for all times to come ? Will this consciousness help them to forge ahead economically and educationally ? Or Will this lead to ever deeper conflicts with the other caste groups in the society ? Will this consciousness help them to tred the path of peace, co-operation and harmony, or the path of conflict and confrontation with the other groups ? What will be the impact of *dalit* consciousness on the larger Hindu society ? Will they wind up the practice of untouchability ? Many questions like these crop up in our mind demanding an answer.

It is difficult to find a satisfactory answer for each one of these. On the whole, the discussion could be summed up by quoting the views of **Sachidananda** [1976] : He holds that *"the combination of factors like ameliorative efforts of the government, the growing consciousness of the dalits and the liberal attitudes of caste Hindus will diminish the disabilities and discriminations with the passage of time."*[1]

1 **Sachidananda** as quoted by **Ram Ahuja** in *"Society in India."* Page - 86.

Chapter 10

BACKWARD CASTES/CLASSES [OBCs] THEIR PROBLEMS AND WELFARE

Who Form the Backward Classes ? - Definition of Backward Classes - Description of Backward Classes - Indian Constitution Does Not Define OBCs - Appointment of Backward Classes Commission : First Backward Classes Commission 1953 : Kalelkar Commission - Observations Made by the Kalelkar's Commission- Policy of the Central Government - Negotiations With the States- Decision of the Central Government - Second Backward Classes Commission 1979 : Mandal Commission - Acceptance of Its Recommendations - Reservation Policy as per Mandal Commission - Criteria of Backwardness - Weightage Given to Each Category of Criteria - Reservation for the OBCs Among the Non-Hindus ? - Four Channels for Collecting Data to Identify the OBCs - Main Recommendations of Mandal Commission - Some Other Special Recommendations - Historic Judgement of the Supreme Court and Its Impact - Arguments For and Against Reservation - Conclusion - Problems of Backward Castes / Classes and Mainly OBCs - Various Schemes and Measures for the Welfare of the Backward Castes, Particularly the OBCs.

India is a country where a large number of people are found to be illiterate, ignorant, poor and backward. India is a classical land of caste in which caste is the main form of social stratification. The backwardness of Indian people is closely connected with the type of the stratification system that it has, that is, the caste. The main disadvantage here is that the people's status is ascribed to them by birth in certain castes and tribal groups. Thus the problem of majority of the Indians can be understood, as **Prof. B. Kuppuswamy** has pointed out, "*....... only in terms of the basic character of Indian society which consists of a multitude of closed status groups with unequal ranks, each with its own privileges and disabilities supported by traditional sanctions. Thus it must be recognized at the outset that the term class is not appropriate since that term is associated with an economic category and indicates an open status group. By contrast, the backward classes in India form an aggregate of closed status groups; they belong to these groups by birth, not because of their individual economic characteristics.*"[1]

1 **B. Kuppuswamy** *"Social Change in India"* 2nd Edition [1975]. Page - 192.

Hence, it is clear from the above, that the concept of caste is more helpful in understanding the Indian stratification system rather than the concept of class. The British people too had made use of the concept of *"backward classes"* to refer to the most *"backward castes"* of India. In fact, the British Government had used the concept of *"backward classes"* as early as in 1885 in its **"Port Saint George Gazette"** dated 5th November 1885. **M.N. Srinivas** has also stated that the term *"backward classes"* represents in the Indian context, lower castes including the scheduled castes. Thus, according to him, the term *"backward classes movement"* must be understood in the Indian context, as *"backward castes movement."*

Who Form the "Backward Classes"?

The term *"backward classes"* has not been defined properly either by the sociologists or by the constitution-makers. The backward classes are a large mixed category of persons with boundaries that are both unclear and elastic. They seem to comprise roughly one-third of the total population of the country. They consist of three main categories – *the scheduled castes, the scheduled tribes* and *the "other backward classes."* The scheduled castes and scheduled tribes are comparatively better defined and they form roughly 22% of the total population according to the 1971 Census. The "other backward classes" is a *residual category.* Their position is highly ambiguous and it is not possible to give an exact statement of their numbers.

Definition of Backward Classes

Though the term *"Backward Classes"* is popularly used by sociologists it is not defined properly. Still for our purpose of study we may define it in the following way:

1. **Justice K. Subba Rao,** former Chief Justice of India, defined *"backward classes"* as – *"an ascertainable and identifiable group of persons based on caste, religion, race, language, occupation and such others, with definite characteristics of backwardness in various aspects of human existence – social, cultural, economic, political and such others."*

2. We can generally define *"backward classes" as those social groups or classes or castes which are characterised by low literacy and lack of education, poverty, exploitation of labour, non-representation in services and untouchability.*

3. In simple words, the term *"backward classes"*, can be defined as *a social category which consists of all the socially, educationally, economically and politically backward groups, castes and tribes.*

Description of the Backward Classes

The *Backward Classes Commission* in its Report [1956] described the Backward Classes as consisting of the following groups:

1. *Those who suffer from the stigma of untouchability or near untouchability.* These groups are classified as **Scheduled Castes** [SC].

2. *Those tribes who are not yet sufficiently assimilated into the mainstream of the national life.* These groups are classified as **Scheduled Tribes** [ST].

3. *Those tribes who, due to long neglect, have been forced to commit crime.* These tribes were previously known as criminal tribes [before 1953] and are presently called **Denotified Tribes** or **Ex-Criminal Tribes.**

4. **"Other Backward Classes" [OBCs]** consist of the following groups or communities :

(a) Those nomads who have no occupation of a fixed habitation and are given to mimicry, begging, jugglery, dancing, etc.

(b) Communities consisting largely of agricultural or landless labourers,

(c) Communities consisting largely of tenants without occupancy rights and those with insecure land tenure,

(d) Communities consisting of a large percentage of small land owners with uneconomic holdings,

(e) Communities engaged in cattle breeding, sheep breeding or fishing on small scale,

(f) Artisan and occupational classes without security of employment and whose traditional occupations have ceased to be remunerative,

(g) Communities, the majority of whose people do not have sufficient education and therefore have not secured adequate representation in Government services,

(h) Social groups from among Muslims, Christians and Sikhs who are still backward socially and educationally, and

(i) Communities not occupying positions in social hierarchy.

Of the four major groups that constitute the **"backward classes",** the third category of group [denotified tribes] is normally included in the 2nd category of STs. Hence, for all practical purposes, the *"backward classes"* normally consist of the following three major category of groups : (i) **SCs,** (ii) **STs,** and (iii) **OBCs.** About the SCs and STs, we have already dealt with in two separate chapters. The third category of OBCs may thus be analysed here.

Indian Constitution Does Not Define But Only Makes Reference to the Concept of OBCs

The third major category of *"backward classes"* consists of a large number of educationally and economically backward people. Though the term *"backward classes"* has not been defined by the Indian Constitution, the characteristics of backwardness are described here and there and also sometimes the categories are mentioned.

- *Article 15(4)* speaks of the socially and educationally backward.
- *Article 16(4)* uses the term *"backward class"* and speaks of inadequate representation in services.
- *Article 45* mentions free and compulsory education.
- *Article 46* mentions the weaker sections of the people and includes the expression "the Scheduled Castes and Scheduled Tribes."
- *Article 340* empowers the State to investigate the condition of the Backward Classes and to help them by grants, etc.

Thus the Constitution has accepted the following elements of backwardness; *illiteracy and lack of education, poverty, exploitation of labour, non-representation in services and untouchability.*

APPOINTMENT OF BACKWARD CLASSES COMMISSIONS

First Backward Classes Commission - 1953 Kalelkar Commission

As it is made clear, the term *"backward classes"* is vague in the sense that it includes a wide variety of lower classes as well as castes consisting of millions of people. *Article* 340 of the Constitution provides for the appointment of a commission to investigate the conditions of backward classes. Accordingly, the President [that is, the Union Government] appointed on Jan. 29, 1953, **The Backward Classes Commission** under the chairmanship of **Kakasaheb Kalelkar**. The Commission prepared a list containing as many as 2,399 communities which were treated as socially and educationally backward. Out of these, 913 communities alone had an estimated population of 115 million. The Commission adopted the following criteria for determining backwardness:

1. *Low Social position in the traditional caste hierarchy of Hindu Society.*
2. *Lack of general advancement among the major section of a caste or community.*
3. *Inadequate or no representation in Government services.*
4. *Inadequate representation in the field of trade, commerce and industry.*

Observations Made by Kalelkar Commission

Some of the major observations and recommendations made by the Kalelkar Commission and as referred to by **Prof. B. Kuppuswamy**[1] can be mentioned here.

1. One of the first recommendations of the Commission was that the 1961 census should provide caste-wise figures so that *"before the disease of caste is destroyed all facts about it have to be noted and classified in a certain manner as in a clinical record."* [Page - 11 of the Report of the Commission].

2. The Commission also pointed out the anomaly which arose when some Scheduled Caste persons called themselves *"Harijans"* but found that they were not eligible for scholarships, etc. since the term *"Harijan"* is not in the authorised list.

3. The Commission also recommended that certain sections of the Muslims, Christians, Sikhs should be included among the "Other Backward Classes" [Page : 27 - 29 of the Report].

4. The Commission prepared a list of about 2,400 castes on the basis of the position of the caste in social hierarchy, percentage of literacy and its representation in government service and in industries, etc. The Commission also revised the lists of Scheduled Castes and Scheduled Tribes on the basis of the new information available.

5. "The Commission noted that the great majority of the backward classes are ignorant, illiterate, and poor. They are easily exploited by several classes of persons like the traders, the moneylenders."

6. The Commission also noted that the administration system itself, which has to implement the Constitutional provisions, is tainted casteism; this is one of the reasons why the backward classes have no confidence in securing a fair deal even from the administration. The Commission warns that unless this is immediately remedied there would be class conflicts which would affect national solidarity. [Page - 101].

7. The Commission also draws pointed attention to the contradiction between the theory and the practice of Hinduism. While in theory Hinduism recognises the concept of universality in practice it follows the Laws of Manu which perpetuate the four-fold divisions of the social order and the superiority of the Brahmin class.

8. The Commission notes *"A complete revolution in the social outlook of the people is necessary for rendering social justice to all the backward people."* [Page - 104].

9. Dealing with the problems of educational backwardness, the Commission noted that only general figures available are the literary rates which show a very slow progress. *"The problem*

1 **B. Kuppuswamy** *"Social Change in India."* Page : 227 - 231.

of education in most of the States is chiefly the problem of the backward classes, for it is they who are extremely backward in education." [Page - 109]. Even when special scholarships and other facilities are provided the children of these classes do not study. The Commission recommends liberal budget provision to give scholarships to the students of the backward classes. The Commission recommends that 70% of the seats in professional colleges should be reserved for them; and in making selections, preference should be given to those coming from *the most backward classes* which are indicated in the lists drawn up. [Page - 125].

10. With respect to representation in government and local body services the Commission recommended the reservation of 25% of the Class I vacancies, one-third of the Class II vacancies, and 40% of the Class III and Class IV for the Other Backward Classes. [Page - 142]. This percentage has to be over and above that which has already been conceded to the SCs and STs.

11. As regards reservation in services, the Chairman of the Commission laid down : *"In this matter one clear principle must be accepted and observed. Reservations, if contemplated, must not exceed 49% whatever the total population of all the Reserved Communities be, as far as Classes III and IV are concerned. In the case of Classes I and II he recommended that "the backward classes will stand to gain both morally and materially, if they do not demand a reservation percentage in vacancies...... They should demand greatest facilities for training and education in order to fit themselves for the highest jobs, as speedily as possible"."* [Page - IX].

Policy of the Central Government

Kalelkar Commission's report was not accepted by the Central Government due to lot of criticisms and objections against it. The Government decided to find out highly objective, realistic and workable criteria to identify the real backward groups and communities of India. The Deputy Registrar General of Census was also consulted to collect through his department information regarding the jobs in which the so called socially and educationally backward people are found in a large number. Even that did not yield any fruitful results.

Negotiations with the States

The Central Government initiated talks with at least 8 State Governments to identify the castes / groups / communities which could be included in the list of backward classes. In these negotiations with the States various views came to limelight. The opinions expressed are given below :

1. Some States expressed the view that it is better to identify "backward areas" rather than backward castes / classes.

2. More than the caste, economic factor should be the main criterion.

3. Some States insisted that no change should be made in the existing caste-based list of "backward classes."

4. Central Government has no legal or constitutional obligation to prepare such a list of "backward classes." Even if the Central Government proposes such a kind of list the State Governments must have freedom to prepare their own list of backward classes.

5. Some states expressed their fear that the attempts to classify people either in the name of caste or class would not only damage the unity of the nation but also encourage divisive forces such as caste.

6. Some expressed the view that the attempts to prepare such a list of backward classes is against the principles of a secular, classless democratic socialist society. Hence, it must be dropped once and for all.

Decision of the Central Government

In the light of the expressed views as mentioned above, the Central Government decided to go forward very cautiously. It decided not to prepare a separate list of backward classes / castes other than the SCs and STs. However, it accepted in principle the right of the State Governments to find out their own criteria in order to prepare a list of backward classes. The Central Government also suggested to the State Governments that it would be better for them to find out economic criteria rather than caste for this purpose.

Preparation of a list of backward classes has become more complicated nowadays because the recent censuses do not contain statistical information about the castes. [The First Backward Classes Commission, however, had taken into consideration caste-wise statistics available in the reports of censuses held in 1911, 1921, and 1931, and also taken into account their approximate increase by 1951.] The existence of certain castes which were never taken into account in the census held prior to independence, have further complicated the process of preparing the list of backward classes. In fact, some such castes also figured in the list of backward classes prepared by the First Commission, and this led to further confusion. Hence, even though the report of the First Backward Classes Commission was published in 1955, it was not accepted by the Government. It decided to provide an opportunity for a nation-wide discussion on the issue. Finally, it instituted the Second Backward Classes Commission in 1979 under the Chairmanship of **B.P. Mandal,** an ex-judge, and a member belonging to the backward caste. The Commission submitted its report in 1980.

Second Backward Classes Commission - 1979 : Mandal Commission

The Government considered seriously the objectives of Articles 15 and 16 of the Constitution and the Second Backward Classes Commission [Mandal Commission] was appointed in 1979. The terms of reference of the Commission included (i) determination of the criteria for defining the socially and educationally backward classes, (ii) steps to be taken for the advancement of socially and educationally backward classes, (iii) desirability or otherwise of making provision for the reservation of appointments in favour of backward classes which are not adequately represented in public service and (iv) presenting a report setting out the facts as found by the Commission making such recommendations. The Commission submitted its Report on 31 December 1980.

Acceptance of the Recommendations of Mandal Commission

After long deliberations on the recommendations of the Mandal Commission, it was decided by the then Government to implement the same. The Mandal Commission in its report [1980] has listed 3743 castes and communities in the Central List whose population is estimated to be 52% of the total population of India. The Commission has recommended 27% reservation for such a large segment of the Indian population. Several Writ Petitions were filed in the Supreme Court questioning the said Reservation. All the Writ petitions were disposed off by the Honourable Supreme Court by its judgement dated 16th Nov. 1992. The Court also directed the Government and each of the State Governments to set up a permanent body for reflecting upon the request for inclusion and complaints regarding inclusions in the list of OBCs. Accordingly, a **National Commission for Backward Classes** [NCBC] was set up on 14th Aug. 1993, which had been reconstituted on 28th Feb. 1997.

As per the directions of the Supreme Court, the Govt. of India has notified the Central List of OBCs comprising in first phase, the castes / communities which are common both in the list prepared by the Mandal Commission and State Backward Classes List for 21 states and 5 Union Territories. Recently, three notifications on inclusion / amendment in the Central List of OBCs have been issued by the Government.

Reservation Policy As Per Mandal Commission

Criteria of Backwardness

Reservation facility has been provided for people who are considered to be backward. But how is the backwardness of a community decided ? At present, as we are discussing the issue of reservation in the context of Mandal Commission's recommendations, it is relevant here to mention 11 criteria for determining social and educational backwardness as used by the Commission. In the social and economic indicators, there were four criteria each, while in the educational indicators, there were three criteria. Thus, in total there were 11 indicators. These 11 indicators or criteria which fall into three categories are mentioned below :

A. Social Criteria

1. Social backwardness as considered by others.
2. Dependence mainly on manual labour for livelihood.
3. Marriage of 25% girls and 10% boys in rural areas, and of 10% girls and 5% boys in urban area below 17 years.
4. Female work Participation 25% above the State average.

B. Educational Criteria

5. Children between 5 and 15 years never attending school 25% above the State average.
6. Student drop-out rate 25% above the State average.
7. Matriculation rate 25% below the State average.

C. Economic Criteria

8. Average value of family assets 25% below the State average.
9. Families living in *Kachcha* houses 25% above the State average.
10. Sources of drinking water beyond 500 metres for more than 50% of the families.
11. Consumption loans by households 25% above the State average.

Weightage Given to Each Category of Criteria

The above mentioned 11 criteria were differently weighted. Social criteria were given a weightage of **3** points each, educational criteria **2** points each, and the economic criteria one point each. Thus the total value was 22 [4X3+3X2+4x1=22] points. Any caste getting more than 50% of the points, that is, 11 points, was counted as backward.

Reservation for the OBCs Among the Non-Hindus ?

Mandal Commission extended the reservation facility to the OBCs among the non-Hindus. The above mentioned 11 criteria are mostly applied to the case of Hindu communities, including the tribes, to decide their backwardness. Some other criteria are adopted for determining the OBCs among the non-Hindus. All untouchables converted to non-Hindu religions are considered as OBCs. If a non-Hindu community continued its traditional occupation, and if that occupation qualified a Hindu community to be treated as backward, then the non-Hindu community would be included among the OBCs.

Four Channels for Collecting Data to Identify the OBCs

The Mandal Commission found out four channels to collect data to identify castes, communities and groups that could be included among the OBCs. These four channels were :

1. Detailed questionnaires for the public advertised extensively in English and vernacular dailies;
2. Evidence from 97 MPs;
3. Extensive tours of States and Union Territories for meeting elected representatives, leaders of social and caste associations, and representatives from the public.
4. Survey of 405 of the 406 Districts of the country.

Main Recommendations of Mandal Commission

1. The Commission recommended 27% reservation of the jobs for the OBCs. It enlisted 3743 castes and communities which are entitled for this reservation. As per the Article 15(4) and 16(4) of the Constitution, total quota of reservation should not exceed 50%. Hence, the Commission recommended only 27% reservation for the OBCs though their share in the total population exceed 52%.
2. The Commission recommended that those candidates from the OBCs who were selected through open competition should not be adjusted against the reservation quota.
3. The system of reservation should apply to all levels of promotions.
4. Unfilled reservation quota should be carried on over for **3** years and de-reserved only thereafter.
5. Relaxation of upper age limit for direct recruitment from the SCs and STs should be extended to the OBCs.
6. A roster system for each category of posts should be adopted as in the case of the SCs and STs.
7. The 27% reservation to OBCs is applicable to the jobs in central government services and public sector units including the banking sector, LIC, etc.
8. This reservation is also applicable to the private sector undertakings such as educational institutions which receive financial grants from the central or state governments.
9. All the universities and colleges that receive financial assistance from the government are expected to implement this reservation.
10. Due modifications in the existing system of law, if necessary should be undertaken in order to enforce this reservation.

Some Other Special Recommendations

1. In order to improve the backward community students' cultural environment especially in the places in which OBCs reside in a large number, *special efforts must be made to give them additional coaching, vocational training and other educational facilities.* OBC students studying in professional courses may require such an assistance in order to keep pace with the other community students.

2. In all the States *rural people belonging to the OBCs must be given financial assistance* either through subsidy or cheap rate loans in order to encourage them to take more and more interest in industrial and commercial activities. If needed, the rural semi-skilled and skilled persons of these communities must be provided facilities to improve their expertise in their respective fields.

3. All the State governments are *advised to implement land reforms in a strict manner* in order to remove the dependence of the tenants, landless labourers, rural professions and the owners of small land holdings on the money-lenders and the rich farmers.

4. The *Central Government must provide financial assistance to the State governments* if they are not able to mobilise sufficient funds in order to take up the various welfare activities mentioned above, for the benefit of the OBCs. This assistance the Central Govt. must provide just as in the manner in which it is providing such an assistance to the States for the welfare activities of the SCs and STs.

Historic Judgement of the Supreme Court [15-11-1992] : Its Impact

After the fall of V.P. Singh's and Chandrashekar's ministries at the Centre, 10th Parliamentary Elections took place in 1991 in which Congress came back to power and P.V. Narasimha Rao became the Prime Minister. His Government announced in Sept. 1991 that within the 27% of the Union Govt.'s civilian jobs reserved for socially and educationally backward classes [SEBC], preference would be given to the poorer sections of such classes. He went a step further, and declared *10% reservation for the other economically backward sections of the people who were not covered by any of the existing schemes of reservation.*

The controversial issue of the implementation of Mandal Commission's Report was taken to the Supreme Court which gave a historic judgement on it on 15th Nov. 1992. The Court upheld 27% reservation recommended by the Mandal Commission but struck down the Narasimha Rao Govt.'s decision to reserve 10% jobs for other economically backward sections.

Important aspects of this judgement as enlisted by **Prof. Ram Ahuja** are : [1]

1. Caste has been accepted as a basis for identifying the beneficiaries of reservations.
2. The upper limit of reservations has been fixed at 50 per cent.
3. *"Creamy layer"* has to be excluded from reservations.
4. Reservation in certain technical posts is not advisable.
5. There can be no reservations in promotions.
6. The Union Government shall specify the socio-economic criteria to exclude socially advanced persons among the backward classes.
7. Permanent commissions should be set up by the union and state governments to examine complaints of over-inclusion and under-inclusion and requests for inclusion in the list of backward classes.

In the light of these developments which are at the background of the Mandal Commission's Report and its implementation, it is relevant here to discuss the pros and cons of the present reservation policy.

Arguments *For* and *Against* Reservation

The National Front Government's [1989-90] sudden announcement of accepting the recommendations of Mandal Commission's Report in August 1990 evoked widespread resentments and supports throughout the nation. This announcement of Prime Minister V.P. Singh was described as a political decision. The student community in particular protested against it very sharply in North India. Spontaneous agitations took place in several places of the nation. During mid-September and mid-October 1990 more than 160 young people attempted to commit suicide as a mark of their protest against the unjustifiable reservation policy. However, not a single political party openly protested the government's reservation policy.

Mandal Commission's recommendations which formed the primary bases of the reservation policy, have both positive and negative aspects. The recommendations were warmly welcomed in

1 **Prof. Ram Ahuja** *"Indian Social Systems"* [1993]. Page - 381.

some circles while they were strongly opposed in some other circles. Arguments both *in favour of* the recommendations and *against* them have been advanced. Let us now consider these arguments.[1]

Merits of Reservation OR Arguments In Favour of It

1. Providing Justice to All : Reservation policy is likely to satisfy and uplift all those weaker sections of the society which were discontented and had suffered injustice and insults for decades. If fundamental rights are to be guaranteed to all, then, they are to be guaranteed to the weaker sections also. Reservation is one of the *means* of guaranteeing such an equality. *Competition becomes just only when participants are equal.*

2. Reservations are not Made on Caste Basis alone : It is wrong to say that reservations are made *only* on the caste basis and hence such a policy is likely to perpetuate casteism. **For example,** Rajputs in Bihar are not included in the list of backward classes whereas Rajputs in Gujarat are included; similarly, the Yadavs of Bihar and U.P. are included but not the Yadavs of Haryana; Patels of Gujarat are not included but Patels of Bihar are in the list. Reservations are made on the basis of educational and economic backwardness also.

Further, **to remove inequalities of caste, actions on casteline are necessary.** Upper castes monopolised the privileges and high income occupations for centuries. To remedy this situation, jobs must be preferentially allotted to the backwards and admissions for them in education institutions must be provided, until parity is restored.

3. Economic Factor as a Criterion will Help only the Poor among the Forwards : A poor member of a forward community will definitely fare better than the poor among the SCs, STs and OBCs. This is quite natural because the forwards are mostly literate and are in touch with the latest developments. Further, they are in regular social contact with the other forwards who have already progressed. Possessing upper caste culture helps them to be at ease with the ways of those who judge merit.

4. Merit will not Become a Casuality : The argument that reservation policy damages the principle of merit is untenable. If merit were to be the sole factor for providing opportunities to the people, then the country should have progressed a lot with the leadership of the "so called merited" people. Administration by the *"meritorious"* for the last 45 years has been unable to implement land reforms and programmes to remove untouchability and backwardness among the masses of India. They have no right to speak about merit.

5. Influence of Caste is Present in the Current Product : Reservation is sought not to compensate for the past wrongs, but for removing the injustice in the present dispensation, where the forward castes continue to grab all the privileges. The handicaps experienced by the SCs, STs and OBCs are nothing but the accumulated effect of exploitation at the hands of the upper caste people who reserved all the privileges for themselves.

6. Lower Castes do not have Benefits of Connections which the Upper Castes have : Proper socio-economic and political connections are an important asset among the forward castes. Because of such connections even the poorest among the upper castes are able to get benefits without much difficulty. Whereas the lower caste people are always at a disadvantage in establishing such useful socio-economic connections.

7. Reservation is to be Made Meaningful Through other Efforts: It is unscientific to believe that reservation alone can bring about widespread changes among all the members of the

1 ***Main Source*** **: Prof. Antony P. Palatty's** article on *"Reservation and Its Implications"* published in *"Samaja Shodhana"*, Journal of the Mangalore University Sociology Teachers' Association, Vol.I, No.2, Oct. 1992. Pages : 79 - 82.

backward classes. On the contrary, various other measures such as the spread of education, increase in infrastructural facilities in the areas where the SCs, STs and OBCs live, are very much necessary. Reservation facility is to be supplemented through other efforts.

8. Social Benefits of Reservation do Spread Very Rapidly : Various studies and observations have revealed that even though only a few families are going to be benefited directly out of reservation, the social benefits of the reservation are going to spread very rapidly. It means reservation facility can create a new awareness, self confidence, courageousness, adventurous spirit and self respect among the backward castes / classes.

Demerits of Reservation or Arguments Against It

1. Gross Neglect of Merit : One of the most widely criticised aspects of reservation policy is that it affects very badly the merit. Candidates are to be recruited for jobs and admission is to be made to the educational institutions on merit basis. This is required in the interest of the concerned agencies, disciplines, individuals and also in the larger interest of the nation. Neglect of the principle of merit will bring down efficiency and lower the morale of the meritorious. This double effect is dangerous for national growth and development. As **Guha** [1990] has pointed out reservation *"mortgages the future of India."*

2. Provision of Reservation is an Insult to the Fundamental Rights and Equality of Opportunities : The Constitution should treat the people of India on equal terms. But reservation provides some special treatment for some sections of the society which is unfair. As the fundamental rights have an overriding power, reservation should not be allowed to stand in their way.

3. Providing Compensation for the Past Injustice is Meaningless: It is true that some sections of the Indian society were treated very inhumanly and were exploited in various ways. But those exploited are dead and gone. Causing injustice to the forward castes in the present generation will not restore the losses of the past generations of the backward castes.

4. Reservation Causes Great Injustice to the Forward Castes and Classes : It is very unfair to do injustice to one section of the society in order to assure justice to another section. Reservation thus does great injustice to the forward castes. The forward castes have given their own contribution to the march of society. Their members are also prepared to put forth efforts to help the nation to take a big leap towards progress. Denying them an equal opportunity is not only injustice but also unfair.

5. Poverty and Economic Criteria Should be the Basis of Reservation : Reservation is required for the people who are genuinely poor. Irrespective of the caste, class, region or religion or sex to which they belong, must be assured of help through reservation. If reservation is given in this way it can be regarded as just and appropriate. But the present reservation policy benefits only a small elite fringe among the lower castes.

6. Reservation Contributes to the Perpetuation of Caste : Modern independent India visualises a casteless society. Attempts to provide reservation on the basis of caste will only enhance the importance of caste and increase the caste mindedness and *"caste patriotism."* Reservation policy will only lead to the reversal of historical cycle by enlivening the caste. In other words, reservation will create a backward moving society.

7. Removal of Corruption should be our First Priority, but not Reservation : From the point of view of national development what is more important is an honest administration, and not an administration by the inefficient and meritless people. Reservation will only add to the corruption because people try their level best through all possible means to reap the benefits of reservation.

8. There are other Better Solutions to the Progress of Backward Classes : It is wrong to think that reservation alone is the master-fixer of solutions to the problems of backward classes. Social and educational backwardness is mostly due to the habits and attitudes of the people. These could be changed through the spread of education including what can be called a *"cultural revolution."*

9. Reservation is only a Political Game and nothing else : The haste with which the reservation policy came to be introduced during V.P. Singh's administration itself makes it evident that it is more a political gimmick than a considered scheme for the amelioration of the problems of the backward classes. Political parties and their leaders wanted to create a permanent *"vote-bank"* through the implementation of the reservation policy.

10. Fear Experienced by the SCs and STs : Reservation policy has vertically divided the Hindu population into *"forward communities"* and *"backward communities."* It has fanned the fire of animosity, ill-will, jealousy, contempt and hatred between these two communities. Instances of clashes and conflicts between the two have been on the increase ever since the policy of reservation came into force. Hence, it has created terror and horror in the minds of the poor SCs, STs and OBCs. Further, clashes between the backward castes on the one hand, and SCs on the other, have also increased. Continuous attacks on some sections of SCs by the backward caste communities in Bihar, can be sited here as examples.

Conclusion

The policy of reservation has a great implication for the Indian society. It has "........ *set in motion processes that are capable of transforming a hierarchical society into an egalitarian one. The caste system effectively restricted privileges for a few upper castes and enforced difficult menial labour on the lowest castes."*[1]

Reservation and other aspects of positive discrimination have virtually put a limitation on the actual monopoly of the forward castes on legislation, government, administration and education. The SCs, STs and OBCs have now greater fortunes to occupy positions in the legislature, posts in the administration, and seats in educational institutions.

Reservation is an attempt to provide enough opportunities to the neglected sections of the Indian society to take part in the national development processes. It is believed that "........ *native intelligence has a tendency to be normally distributed and evenly shared by all human groups. Therefore, for the development of the nation's economy, society, and polity, the best from all sections of the population, including the SCs, STs, and OBCs, should be encouraged to participate in national life."* [**A.P. Palatty.** Page - 83.]

We are now living in an age of growing liberalisation and globalisation. In the growing liberalisation of the economy, the role of the government, including regulation, is decreasing. More liberty is given to the people and to the men of talents. In this age, *"more and more talent of all sections, forward, backward and others, can be more usefully marketed in the private sector – producing more, by more and for more."*

Certain precautions are however necessary to see that reservations do not create a permanent vested interest in small sections of the group for whom reservations are provided. The present reservation system is not a fool-proof system. It has its own limitations no doubt. In spite of its limitations the policy of reservation continues to stay. It is inadmissible and practically impossible

---

1 **Antony P. Palatty** *"Reservation and Its Implications."* Page - 82.

at this stage to scrap the policy altogether. According **Roy Burman**, the policy of reservation has to be made more rational and scientific. In the given economic and political structure caste should not determine one's life chances.

B.S. Bhargava and **Avinash Samal** [1998] have given some suggestions to improve the policy of reservation.[1] According to them, – 1. Income should be given more importance in determining the backwardness of the individual and not the caste to which he belongs. 2. The concept of *"creamy layer"* should be applied to SCs and STs also. It means rich people who belong to the category of SCs and STs should not be given reservation facility. 3. Reservation should be restricted *only to the first generation beneficiaries.* Children belonging to those who have availed of the reservation facility should not be given the same facility once again. 4. Concession of scholarship may be provided to SC, ST and OBC students securing more than a prescribed percentage of marks [say, 50% and above].

If the above mentioned suggestions are implemented then the benefits of reservation will be spread more evenly and widely within the targeted growth. This will also help to reduce opposition for the reservation by the forward castes. Nation building or national prosperity is not the responsibility of any particular section alone. On the contrary, it is a collective process in which all sections of the society should play an equally important role. The purpose of reservation is to provide a chance for those sections of the society which have been neglected so far, to play their role in this collective process.

Problems of Backward Castes / Classes and Mainly "Other Backward Classes" [OBCs]

The underprivileged sections of the Indian society to which normally the SCs, STs and OBCs belong have been suffering from a number of problems since a long time. Some of the problems are commonly shared by these people with the lower sections of all the communities of India, while some others are unshared, and specifically faced by them only. Some of the socio-economic and political problems with which the *"Other Backward Classes"* / Castes are confronted, are analysed here.

1. Backward Castes [Classes] As Constituting An Indefinite, Abstract and Unorganised Category

What are the backward castes, which are the castes that come under this category – and for such other questions as these, there is no common satisfactory answer. Consensus is not formed yet. In fact, the Union Government had appointed the Backward Classes Commission under the chairmanship of **Kakasaheb Kalelkar** [on Jan. 29, 1953] to prepare a list of communities that would come under this category. Since the recommendations of this commission failed to obtain the consensus, from many sections of the society and also some of the political parties, the Government appointed the *Second Commission* under the chairmanship of **B.P. Mandal** in 1979 and it submitted its report in 1980.

The Mandal Commission listed 3743 castes and communities as belonging to the category of *"Other Backward Classes"* [These castes and communities are different from those already recognised as SCs and STs]. Some of the sections of the people belonging to the category of minorities also come under this category if they satisfy the conditions of backwardness.

1 **Prof. Ram Ahuja** *"Society in India"* [1999]. Pages : 91- 92.

The main problem here is that most of the communities, which belong to the category of OBCs are themselves strangers to one another. *The differences that exist among them are such that they do not have any common awareness regarding their own problems* and hence, uniformity in opinions about the problems is rarely formed. Conflicts do arise among themselves regarding the very issue of *"backwardness."* No single all-India level organisation has been established as yet to unify these communities. These groups are scattered over almost all the States and exhibit lot of diversities making the task of unifying them almost an impossibility.

2. Economic Backwardness

"Backward Classes" / "Castes" – as the very term indicates are economically backward. Though most of these communities are comparatively better than those of SCs and STs in economic matters, they are not self-reliant. Most of these communities are poorer than the other general populace. A large number of poor, unemployed, under-employed and only seasonally employed are found in this category. Negligible number of these people are self-employed, but majority of them are working for poor wages. Sizeable number of economically exploited people belong to this category.

3. Educational and Social Backwardness

Other Backward Classes are educationally and socially backward also. Illiterates are found in a large number in this category. Those who are interested in education are not able to continue higher levels of education for obvious financial reasons. Only during the recent years some of these have pursued their education at higher levels due to the reservation facilities provided for them.

Socially, the OBCs are not only backward but also innocent and ignorant. This is especially true in the case of rural people belonging to lower castes. The poorer sections belonging to the upper castes but get included in this category – are also suffering from inferiority complex, self complacency, lack of courage to march forward and such other weaknesses. Even though people who belong to this category of OBCs are not directly the victims of untouchability, lot of social distance prevails between these and the so called forward castes.

4. Politically Unorganised

The Other Backward Classes, in comparison with other major castes, are not very much organised. No single backward caste is numerically dominant in any province. Hence, they are politically ineffective for they cannot impose their will on the other castes or communities. They are not able to work as powerful *"pressure groups"* at the all-India level. However, in some States, they have been able to assert their existence especially after the implementation of 27% reservation. After 1990s, however, some attempts have been made in some States to unite these backward castes politically. For example, the political parties such as *"Samajwadi Party"* under the leadership of Mulayam Singh Yadav in U.P., and *"Rastreeya Janata Dal"* under the leadership of Sri Laloo Prasad Yadav in Bihar, are trying to consolidate the strength of OBCs. These parties have attained some promising success in their attempts.

5. Problem of ever Increasing Number of Backward Castes and Communities

One of the peculiar problems found in India is that the number of castes and communities belonging to the category of OBCs, is continuously increasing. Some of the lower castes, who have an eye on the attractive benefits of reservation are building up *"lobbies"* to bring pressure on the Government and also on the **Permanent Backward Classes Commission,** to include their castes into the official list of the OBCs. For example, due to such pressure, the Government of Karnataka [as per the recommendations of the Permanent Backward Classes Commission] in its notification dated

10th April 2002, included 11 castes into the State list of OBCs. These castes are : *Jangama, Namadhari Gowda, Kodagu Hegde, Nayiri, Rajabhori, Usthama, Pakanathi, Jangala, Kumbari Marathi, Baggaru,* and *Kodagu Kapala.* This kind of effort is being made in every State and hence the number of OBCs is incessantly increasing.

6. Abuse of the Facility of Reservation

Some of the castes want to claim themselves to be "backward castes", because they want to enjoy the benefits of reservation. Members of the backward castes, who have been enjoying the benefits of reservation and attained richness, want to enjoy the same permanently, and hence are not ready to give up these benefits voluntarily. Political parties, which have been successful in creating a *"vote-bank"* of the backward castes are also putting up resistance against any attempt to withdraw the facilities to those members and families of the backward castes, who have become economically forward over the years.

Backward castes and classes are engaged in a kind of extreme political rivalry and violence particularly because of reservation. Clashes between the Scheduled Castes and Tribes on the one hand and the newly declared Other Backward Classes, on the other, are on the increase especially in States like Bihar and U.P. Scheduled Castes are now inevitably drawn into permanent rivalry and violence in these States.[1] The Scheduled Castes are afraid that their interests would be endangered with the upsurge of these OBCs. The current political developments make it evident that these castes have reasons to fear about such things.

Reservation facility which has been provided for the backward castes has done more harm than good in certain areas, particularly in the area of fanning the fire of caste politics. Hence, it is argued that *as long as this facility continues so long caste consciousness, caste rivalry, caste politics, caste hatred and caste conflict will continue.* In order to grab the benefits of reservation, some of the sub-castes belonging to the upper castes are also bringing pressure on the Government and the Backward Classes Commission to declare their sub-castes as "backward castes." There is an impression among the people belonging to the lower castes and backward castes that they could come up in life and achieve social progress only through reservation, governmental programmes, schemes, concessions, facilities, etc. This kind of an attitude is damaging the self-confidence and attempts at self-dependence of these people and putting hurdles in the path towards social development.

Various Schemes and Measures For the Welfare of the Backward Castes Particularly the Other Backward Classes [OBCs]

The Central Government has launched various schemes and undertaken several measures, such as the following, for the welfare of the OBCs.

1. National Backward Classes Finance and Development Corporation

The National Backward Classes Finance and Development Corporation [NBCFDC] was set up by the Govt. of India under the then Ministry of Welfare on 13th Jan. 1992 as a company [not for Profit]. The objective of this Corporation is to provide concessional finance to the members of the

1 Clashes and rivalry between the Samajwadi Party, which has been banking on the support of mostly the OBCs and Muslims and led by leaders like Mulayam Singh Yadav and Amar Singh on the one hand; and the Bahujan Samaja Party, which is embanking the support of the Scheduled Castes and led by leaders such as Kanshi Ram and Mayavathi, on the other, in the State of U.P., could be cited here as an example.

backward classes living below the poverty line for their socio-economic development. The Corporation extends them loans for income generating schemes.

The Corporation provides financial assistance in terms of loans/ grants to the eligible beneficiaries in the following sectors : agriculture and allied; artisans and traditional occupations; technical trades; small business, small scale industries and transport services. Upto 1999-2000, the total cumulative disbursement by the Corporation has gone upto Rs.424.83 crores covering 3,09, 597 beneficiaries.

2. Various Schemes Launched

The following schemes were launched in 1998-99 for the welfare of the OBCs by the Govt. of India.

(i) Pre-Examination Coaching : The objective of the scheme is to coach candidates belonging to OBCs to enable them to compete in various competitive / entrance examinations. Candidates whose parents' / guardians' total annual income is below Rupees **one** lakh are eligible for this. Rs.23 lakhs was released to 8 organisations under this scheme in 1999-2000.

(ii) Hostels for OBC Boys and Girls : The hostels under the schemes will be constructed in States / UTs having a large OBC population but inadequate hostel facilities. The hostels will be constructed for middle, secondary, college and university level students. At least 1/3 of the hostels to be set up will be for girls. Central assistance for construction will be 50% and the remaining cost will be borne by the State Govt. An amount of Rs.4.30 crore was released under this Scheme to Bihar, Madhya Pradesh, Karnataka, Andhra Pradesh and Sikkim in 1999-2000.

(iii) Pre-Matric Scholarship for OBCs : Scholarship award will be sanctioned to students, whose parents' annual income does not exceed Rs.44,500/=. The scholarships will terminate at the end of Class X. The scholarship will be paid for 10 months in a year. The scholarship will be applicable to the institutions recognised by the concerned State Govts. / UTs. The central assistance will be 50%. An amount of Rs.5.75 crore was released under the Scheme to A.P., Bihar, M.P. and Tripura in 1999-2000.

(iv) Post-Matric Scholarships to the OBCs : The scheme provides financial assistance to the OBC students at post-matriculation / post secondary stage to enable them to complete their education. Hundred percent central assistance will be given for this. Indian nationals belonging to OBCs studying in recognised institutions and whose parents' annual income does not exceed Rs.44,500/- will be entitled for this. An amount of Rs.961.86 crore was released under this scheme to A.P., Bihar, Karnataka, M.P. and Tripura in 1999-2000.

(v) Assistance to Voluntary Organisation for Welfare of OBCs : The scheme involves voluntary sector to improve educational and socio-economic conditions of the OBCs, that is, to get them gainfully employed. Assistance will be given to establish centres and develop services which equip the OBCs to start income generating activities. The quantum of assistance is determined on merit by the Govt. of India, which may be upto 90% of the approved expenditure. An amount of Rs.1.73 crore was released under the scheme to 119 non-governmental organisations in 1999-2000.[1]

3. Reservation Facility to the Backward Classes

Reservation is a part of our Constitution which is intended to create equal in opportunities among Indians belonging to groups unequally placed in the social hierarchy. This Reservation has three principal components :

1 *Note:* Information and Statistics provided here relating to the welfare of Backward Classes, are obtained from *"India Year Book* - 2001*"*. Page : 237 - 240.

(i) Reservation of seats in legislative houses.

(ii) Reservation in jobs in Govt. and Public Sector Units.

(iii) Reservation in admission to courses in professional colleges and other institutions of higher learning.

(i) Reservation of Seats in Legislative Houses : Reservation of seats in the legislative houses on the basis of social backwardness is provided only for the SCs and STs. Explicit constitutional provision is made for seats in the Lok Sabha, Rajya Sabha, Vidhana Sabha and Vidhana Parishads. Laws relating to local bodies have incorporated it as a normal legislative practice.

(ii) Reservation of Jobs in Govt. and Public Sector Units : This Reservation operates in All India Services, Central Govt., State Govts. and Govt. owned and managed Public Sector Units and Institutions. Reservation exists in all these for the SCs and STs to the tune of 15% and 7.5% respectively. Several State Governments have introduced reservation for the OBCs also.[1] In fact, some have demanded reservation in the private sector also.

(iii) Reservation for Admission to Courses in Professional Colleges and Other Institutions of Higher Learning : Reservation of admission is found in the Govt. owned and aided educational institutions of professional and higher learning, such as engineering colleges, medical colleges. Reservation for SCs and STs exists in all such institutions. Several State Governments such as Karnataka, Kerala, Tamil Nadu, for instance, have also provided reservation for the OBCs.

1 For example, since 1990 itself reservation for OBCs exists in 13 out of 22 states. In 6 states, the total reservation exceeds 50%.

Chapter 11

SOCIAL MOVEMENTS IN INDIA

Social Movements : Definition, Characteristics and Types of Social Movements - ***A. Reform Movements :*** *The Brahmo Samaj - Resistance to Raja Ram's Reforms and the Decline of the Samaj - Arya Samaj and Its Strong Reaction to the Western Impact - Sri Ramakrishna Mission - Vivekananda as the Mighty Force of the Mission - The Theosophical Society and Its Call for the Review of the Ancient Religions of the East - Sathya Shodhak Samaj - Ideology of the Movement - The Beginning of the Non-Brahmin Movement - S.N.D.P. Yogam - Religious and Social Reforms of the S.N.D.P.* ***B. Backward Classes Movement :*** *Main Goals of Backward Classes Movement - Nature and Characteristics of Backward Classes Movement - Factors Contributing to the Movement - Non-Brahmin Movement as a Type of Backward Classes Movement : Satya Shodhak Samaj and the Non-Brahmin Movement - Justice Party and the Non-Brahmin Movement - Self-Respect Movement Under the Leadership of E.V. Ramasami Naicker- The Dravida Kazhagam and the Non-Brahmin Movement- Annadurai and the D.M.K. - Impact of the Movement - Non-Brahmin Movement in Karnataka.* ***C. Agrarian Unrest or Peasant Movements :*** *The Concept and Its Meaning - Peasant Movements in Pre-Independent India and After Independence - Types of Peasant Struggles - Causes of Agrarian Unrest - Indigo Growers' Agitation- Naxalbari Movement, 1967 - Its Causes and Factors that Caused Its Failure- Some Observations Relating to Peasant Struggles.*

Social movements have played an important role in human history. They throw light on the dynamic aspect of the human society and also of human behaviour. Members of society are not always content to be the passive playthings of social forces. On the contrary, they attempt to influence the course of human events by collective action. It does not mean, all social movements become successful in achieving their objectives. Social movements represent a powerful instrument of social change. Some movements have brought about social changes - some minor, some far-reaching. These social movements may last for years or even decades.

Social movements are comparatively well structured. Their members are not scattered, unorganised individuals but rather people consciously acting together in accordance with a shared belief system or ideology. The ideology provides a criticism of existing social conditions, a concept of the movement's purpose, a programme for action and a justification for the same. Some social movements become so organised and structured that they cease to be social movements and instead become formal organisations. Many other social movements, however, such as some short-lived religious cults, are loosely structured and relatively spontaneous and unpredictable.

Why do the social movements breakout ? *Why do people join these various types of movements* ? These two are pertinent questions for which several explanations could be offered. It could however, be said that *"Social movements arise because social conditions create dissatisfaction with the existing arrangements. People join specific social movements for an almost infinite variety of reasons - including idealism, altruism, compassion and practical considerations as well as neurotic frustration."*1

It is significant to note that social movements play a vital part in the process by which a social problem is brought to public attention. Social movements throw light on various social problems which have been in existence since decades and centuries. Modern India has also witnessed a number of social movements ever since the 18th century. Social movements have taken place here in the religious, political, economic, educational, environmental and other fields. Some of these movements had only a limited range while a few others have had a very wide range of influence. Here is an attempt to introduce some such movements that took place in India especially during the 19th and 20th centuries.

1. Definition and Types of Social Movements

Concept of Social Movement

"Social Movement" represents a social phenomenon that assumes great importance in the study of not only collective behaviour but also of social change. Sociologists have started evincing great interest in studying its role not only in bringing about changes in society but also in resisting them. A social movement is a type of collective behaviour that could be a lasting one and at the same time, an influential one. It is, indeed, *"a generator of social change"*.

Social movements of various types have been taking place in most of the societies of the modern world. In fact, they have become a part and parcel of the modern democratic societies. We hear of various types of social movements launched for one or the other purpose. There are movements to demand more and more reservation for the SCs and STs and other backward classes and there are counter movements demanding its cancellation or at least the status quo. There are movements to *"save environment"*, to *"save wild life"* and to *"save world peace"*. There are movements for and against the construction of Sri Ram Temple at the disputed place of Ayodhya. There are Fascist Movements, Communist Movements, Naxalite Movements, Tribal Movements, Peasants' Movements, Women's Movements, Youth Movements, Labour Movements, Civil Rights Movements, Human Rights Movements, Afforestaton Movements, and so on. What then do we mean by social movements?

Definition of Social Movement

1. A social movement is formally defined as *"a collective acting with some continuity to promote or resist change in the society or group of which it is a part"* - ***Turner and Killian.***
2. *"A social movement is a collective effort to promote or resist change"* - ***Horton and Hunt.***
3. Social movements can be defined as *"organised group effort to generate or resist social change"* - ***Neil J. Smelser.***

1 **Ian Robertson** *"Sociology."* Page - 532.

4. *"A social movement is a collective effort to transform established relations within a particular society"* - ***Rudolf Herberle.***

5. *"A non-institutionalised effort to change society through collective action is called a 'social movement'"* - ***David Popenoe.*** [Page - 418].

Characteristics of Social Movements

M.S.A. Rao, one of the prominent Indian sociologists, has made an analysis of the nature of social movements in the book *"Social Movements in India"*, edited by him. According to him, social movement includes two characteristics about which there is considerable agreement among the sociologists. They are as follows.

1. *Collective Action.* Social movement undoubtedly involves collective action. However, this collective action, takes the form of movement *only when it is sustained for a long time.* This collective action need not be formally organised. *It could be an informal attempt also.* But it should be able to create an interest and awakening in a relatively large number of people.

2. *Oriented Towards Social Change.* A social movement is generally oriented towards bringing about social change. This change could either be partial or total. Though the movement is aimed at bringing about a change in the values, norms, ideologies of the existing system, efforts are also made by some other forces to resist the changes and to maintain the status quo. The counter attempts are normally *defensive and restorative rather than innovative and initiating change.* They are normally the organised efforts of an already established order to maintain itself.

As **M.S.A. Rao** points out, though sociologists are almost agreeable on the above mentioned two characteristics of social movement; they differ a lot regarding other criteria – such as *the presence of an ideology, method of organisation, and the nature of consequence.*

1. *Ideology Behind the Movement.* An important component of social movement that distinguishes it from the general category of collective mobilisation, is the presence of an ideology. ***Example*:** A student strike involves collective mobilisation and is oriented towards change. But in the absence of an ideology a student strike becomes an isolated event and not a movement. On the contrary, if the strike is committed to an ideology, it may last for longer period and assume the form of a movement.

2. *Organisational Frame Work.* As **Paul Wilkinson** has pointed out, a social movement requires a minimum of organisational framework to achieve success or at least to maintain the tempo of the movement. *To make the distinction clear between the leaders and followers, to make clear the purposes of the movement, to persuade people to take part in it or to support it, to adopt different techniques to achieve the goals* – a social movement must have some amount of organisational framework.

3. *The Techniques and Results.* A social movement may adopt its own technique or method to achieve its goal. There is no certainty regarding it. It may follow *peaceful or conflicting, violent or non-violent, compulsive or persuasive, democratic or undemocratic* means or methods to reach its goal. The same thing is true of the results. It may become *successful or it may fail;* it may become *partial success* or at least it *may create a general* "awakening" in the public regarding the issue. The result of a movement has a close bearing on the ideology and the organisational framework.

Types of Social Movements

Sociologists hence classified social movements into different types on the basis of their objectives. **Wallace** and **Wallace, Horton** and **Hunt, M.S.A. Rao** and others, have mentioned of three main types of movements: (i) *reform movements,* (ii) *revolutionary movements,* and (iii) *revivalist movements.*

1. Reform Movements

Reform movements are satisfied with the existing social order but believe that certain reforms are necessary in some specific areas. The reformers endeavour to change elements of the system as it currently stands. ***Examples:*** *The Civil Rights Movement, Women's Liberation Movement, Save the Environment Movement, the Arya Samaj Movement, Brahmo Samaj Movement, Sri Ramakrishna Mission, etc.*

2. Revolutionary Movements

The revolutionary movements deny that the system will even work. These movements are deeply dissatisfied with the social order and work for radical change. They advocate replacing the entire existing structure. Their objective is the reorganisation of society in accordance with their own ideological blueprint. Revolutionary movements generally prefer not to use violence although some of them do resort to violence. ***Example:*** *the Protestant Reformation Movement, the Socialist Movement, the Communist Revolution of Russia and also of China, the Indian National Freedom Movement,* and so on.

3. Reactionary or Revivalist Movement

Some movements are known as reactionary or regressive movements. These aim at *"pulling the clock back."* Their members view certain social changes with suspicion and distaste and try to reverse the current trends. They highlight the importance and greatness of traditional values, ideologies and institutional arrangements. They strongly criticise the fast moving changes of the present.

Example: *the Catholic Counter Reformation, the Brahmo Samaj, Arya Samaj, the Sarvodaya Movement, Khadi and Gramodyog Movement of Gandhiji,* and the like.

In addition to the above mentioned three main types of movements, we can add two other types of movements as suggested by **Horton** and **Hunt.**

4. Resistance Movements

These movements are formed to resist a change that is already taking place in society. The many social and cultural changes of recent decades have been profoundly disturbing to many of the Indians who feel that our national virtues, traditional values, and cultural greatness, are being eroded by secularism, minority appeasement, sexual permissiveness, moral degradation, political corruption and sell-out of national interests for the partial political interests, and so on. Good number of contemporary resistance movements express their dismay at the directions in which our nation has been moving. ***Example:*** *Anit-Abortion Movement, Anit-Hindi Movement, Anti-Reservation Movement, the Swadeshi Movement against the movement towards Economic Liberalisation, the Movement towards Indianising Indian Education, etc.* This type of movement is not very much revolutionary in character, but more resistant in nature.

5. Utopian Movements

These are attempts to take the society or at least a section of it towards a state of perfection. *"These are loosely structured collectivities that envision a radically changed and blissful state, either on a large scale at some time in the future, or on a smaller scale in the present. The utopian ideal and the means of it are often vague, but many utopian movements have quite specific programmes for social change."* [**Ian Robertson.**] ***Example:*** the *"Hare Krishna Movement"* of the seventies, the movement towards the establishment of *"Rama Rajya"* – as envisioned by the B.J.P. and the *"Sangh Parivar"* [the community of the supporters of the R.S.S. School of Thought], the Communists' and Socialists' pronouncement of a movement towards *the classless, casteless society free from all kinds of exploitation, etc.*

A. REFORM MOVEMENTS

During the 18th century, and afterwards, a great change swept over the land of India. The Hindu mind that had been moulded for centuries by a fixed set of religious ideas and social conventions, was exposed to new ideas and new ways of thinking. It was the result of the Western impact on India. As a result of that impact, the rigid rituals in religion and traditional beliefs started losing their influence on the masses. The Western contact opened the Hindu mind to the social evils and set in motion a social reform of its time honoured institutions in the new light. Several traditional beliefs and practices dysfunctional to society were discarded and many new customs, practices, institutions and values were adopted.

Indians who came under the influence of the new values and practices became aware of many of the existing social evils like child marriage, taboos against widow remarriage and intercaste marriage, intercaste dining, seclusion of women, untouchability, etc. This awareness led to a revolt against tradition and that was the first step towards reforms in social, religious and political spheres of life. This awareness led to the launching of a series of social reform movements right from Raja Ram Mohan Roy down to Mahatma Gandhiji. Raja Ram Mohan Roy's *"Brahmo Samaj"*, Swami Dayananda Saraswathi's *"Arya Samaj"*, Swami Vivekananda's *"Sri Ramakrishna Mission"*, Dr. Annie Besant's *"Theosophical Society"*, Gandhiji's *"Sarvodaya"* and crusade against Untouchability and such other movements not only served to eradicate some of the social evils but also to enlighten people regarding modern values.

1. THE BRAHMO SAMAJ – 1822

Raja Ram Mohan Roy [1772-1833] of Bengal, often known as the *"First Modern Man of India"*, was the first socio-religious reformer of the 19th century. He was the first to see the evils that had crept into the Hindu society on account of orthodox religious practices and superstitious beliefs. He was also the first to challenge the existing religious beliefs and practices of the day. He pointed out that they were not according to the basic scriptures of the Hindu Dharma.

The Birth of Brahmo Samaj : Ram Mohan Roy showed that polytheism was opposed to the teaching of the Vedas. He attempted at the emancipation of the Indian society from the arbitrary social regulations. He advocated innumerable social reforms like – *abolition of "sati", widow remarriage, education of women, removal of caste inequalities, etc.* He wrote a number of books inspired by the Western ideals, values and models. Ram Mohan Roy not only stood for the eradication of these evils but also founded the ***"Brahmo Samaj"*** [1822] with liberal religious views. The Brahmo Samaj emerged as a powerful reform movement especially in the Bengal region.

Crusade Against Inequalities : The Brahmo Samaj launched a crusade against the inequalities of the caste system. He dubbed caste as inhuman and undemocratic. The Samaj under the leadership of Ram Mohan Roy even condemned the worship of images, the practices of "sati" and polygamy, and the abuses of caste system. Ram Mohan Roy favoured the remarriage of widows and defied the prohibition against crossing of the sea by his own example. The Samaj supported intercaste and inter-racial marriages and the abolition of child marriages.

Strong Protest Against the Practice of "Sati" : Ram Mohan Roy is known for his crusade against the burning of the widows along with the dead bodies of their husbands, a practice known as

"Sati." He was greatly responsible for the introduction of *the Prevention of Sati Act, 1829.* The Brahmo Samaj which he started released immense energy. It influenced the Hindu mind directly or indirectly. The Samaj gave shelter to the fallen, and restored Hindu worship to its pristine purity. It did not believe in the orthodox rituals and ceremonies but accepted the divine origin of the Vedas. Its object was to build up a casteless society. It awakened in the minds of the people the necessity for the reformation of the Hindu society, its social customs and conventions. By such means as these the Samaj galvanised the Hindu society and set in motion a liberalism that swept away many of the evils of Hindu society. Raja Ram as the champion of this Samaj exerted himself much for the improvement and advancement of Indian literature and culture.

Brahmo Samaj* : *The First Attempt to Reform the Hindu Society in Modern India : The Brahmo Samaj is the first organised religious institution in modern India to reform the Hindu way of life, Hindu social system and religious beliefs. The Samaj began to attract many adherents from the middle class. By 1829, Raja Ram and his supporters were able to buy a house for the new organisation, that is, Brahmo Samaj. In the very same year, his efforts resulted in the abolition of Sati.

Resistance to Raja Ram's Reforms

Raja Ram']s reformative efforts also got for him rivals and enemies. All the developments stated above, roused opposition against him from the orthodox Brahmins who now organised a rival association, *Dharma Sabha* under Radhakanta Dev. The two associations carried on a rival propaganda against each other and Calcutta was full of it. No doubt people took part in the controversy and more abuses were hurled at Rajaram Mohan Roy than against his rival.

In 1830, in the midst of this storm, Rajaram Mohan Roy formally opened his *Church.* It was laid down that the building could be used by any one for the worship and adoration of one God who is the author and preserver of the universe. No image or picture was to be admitted. So the new Church was expected to be the meeting ground of all sects for the worship of one true God. His main aim to revive monotheism on the basis of Vedanta was thus fulfilled.

Decline of the Samaj and the Continuation of the Reforms that it Launched : Though soon Brahmo Samaj became a spent force, it rendered valuable service. It popularised social reforms and did much to put down social evils like child marriage, sati, intemperance, polygamy, caste tyranny, etc. It prevented conversion to Christianity by creating a half-way house and it purified popular religion and roused the Orthodox Hindus to organise themselves and work for a revival of their religion. It did immense good by developing vernaculars and popularising education by opening various educational institutions. It advocated female education and played an important part in the re-awakening of India. Though Brahmo Samaj as an organisation declined soon the social reforms that it had launched, continued to take place for decades.

Eminent Followers of Brahmo Samaj : The principles, philosophy and practices of the Brahmo Samaj were popularised by the eminent followers of Rajaram like Dwaraknath Tagore, Devendranath Tagore, Keshavachandra Sen. After sometime, the Samaj broke into two groups on account of differences on the basic principles resulting in the formation of the Adi Brahmo Samaj led by Tagore and the Brahmo Samaj headed by Keshab Chandra Sen.

2. PRARTHANA SAMAJ – 1867

"Prarthana Samaj" represents one of the Indian reform movements that took place in the 19th century. The Brahmo Samaj entered Maharashtra as early as in 1849 and obtained some initial support especially in Bombay. Keshabchandra Sen, the creator of *"Bharatha Brahmo Samaj"*, during his organisational tour in Maharashtra initiated the **Prarthana Samaj** in the year 1867.

The Samaj's Concentration on Social Reforms : The Prarthana Samaj devoted attention to social reform. It aimed at reforming the Hindu religious thought and practice in the light of modern knowledge. It preached the worship of one God and tried to free religion from the hold of caste and priestly domination. It encouraged interdining and intermarriage among different castes. It worked to alter the religious customs and advocated widow remarriage and tried to abolish the evils in the Hindu society. It worked for the improvement of the lot of women and made efforts to improve the conditions of the depressed classes. The Samaj encouraged female education and started homes for the destitute women. For the sake of the neglected children, the Samaj established an *Asylum* and *Orphanage* at **Pandharapur.** For the benefit of the widows, it started night schools and a *Widow's Home.* It floated the *Depressed Classes Mission.* It undertook a number of service-oriented activities.

Insistence on Prayer and Worship : The Prarthana Samaj neither intended to emulate the Christian religion nor designed to oppose the Hindu religion. Its aim was to make worship a part of every one's life. It made popular a prayer suggested and advocated by reason and intelligence. In the social sphere, this Samaj was no less revolutionary than the Brahmo Samaj of Raja Ram Mohan Roy.

Inspiring Leaders of the Samaj : Social reformers like Gopal Ganesh Agarkar, Maharshi Karve, Atmaram Pandurang, Ramakrishna Gopal Bhandarkar and Justice Mahadeva Govinda Ranade and others, served the Prarthana Samaj as its leaders. The Samaj has been the centre of many activities for social reforms in Western India. Its success, especially in Maharashtra region, is chiefly due to M.G. Ranade, a great thinker and social reformer of great reputation.

3. ARYA SAMAJ – 1875

Dayananda Saraswathi [1824-1883] was another religious leader who stood for the reformation of the Hindu society and the Hindu religion. He, often *"styled as the Reforming Luther of Hinduism"*, began a puritan movement called the ***"Arya Samaj."*** Both the Brahmo Samaj and the Prarthana Samaj revealed clear influence of Western thinking on their principles, since both admittedly wanted to arrive at some synthesis between the East and the West. The Arya Samaj was staunchly a natonal organisation. It was uncompromising in its attack on the West.

Strong Reaction to the Western Impact : Dayananda Saraswathi came in close contact with Keshav Chandra Sen and other Brahmo Samajists who influenced him greatly. But Dayananda Saraswathi decided to go on in his own way. He published his work *"Sathyartha Prakash"* in 1874 and founded the ***"Arya Samaj"*** in the very next year. He reacted sharply to the anglicanising impact of the West. He called upon the people to stop self-degradation and to go *"back to the Vedas"* to obtain inspiration to forge ahead. In fact, he initiated his organisation with a fighting spirit. This spirit roused the national consciousness. As **Max Muller** remarks, *"In spite of the fact that the movement weakened during the second and the third decades of the 20th century, the Arya Samaj was one of the most progressive and dynamic forces vitally active in the earlier stages of the national resurgence in building up the new political order."*[1]

Vedas : The Source of Inspiration of the Movement : Dayananda Saraswathi drew inspiration from the Vedas which he regarded as infalliable. Since the Vedas are believed to have originated from the divine inspiration, they represent an inexhaustible reservoir of all knowledge. Since the Vedas are regarded as the result of *"divine revelations"*, Dayananda Saraswathi held them to be the bed rock of Indian culture. However, his approach had a rationalistic aspect, because the Vedas, though revealed, could be rationally interpreted by himself and others. Thus the individual reason was the decisive factor.

1 **Max Muller** as quoted by **Dr. A.V. Sreenivas Murthy** and **Dr. S.U. Kamath** in their *"Studies in Indian Culture"* [1972]. Page : 145 - 146.

***Attempts to Revive the Ancient Vedic Religion* :** Dayananda Saraswathi was in favour of improving the present day society in the light of the accepted ideals of old, and hence he accepted the Vedas as the basis of all social and religious change that he advocated. It was his desire to revive the Vedic religion. He stated that there is nothing in the Vedas to support such disliked institutions as child marriage, sati, caste ineqaulities, restrictions on widow remarriage, etc. Moreover, instead of supporting Hindu orthodoxy, he attacked it and led a revolt against it. He was opposed to idolatry, ritual and priesthood, and particularly to the prevalent caste practices and popular Hinduism as preached by orthodox Brahmin priests. He was of the opinion that all the malpractices going on in the name of Hinduism should be eliminated from the Indian society at the earliest. It was with this view, he established the **Arya Samaj** and intended to revive the ancient Vedic religion and culture. He took the oath *"to wage unswerving warfare against the dogmas and the idolatry of the Puranic faith and establish education in accordance with ancient Brahmanic tradition."*

***Study of the Western Sciences Encouraged* :** Dayananda Saraswathi was not blind to the Western views and Western sciences. In fact, he also favoured the study of Western sciences. Interestingly enough, Swami Dayananda had met and had discussions with Keshavchandra Sen, Vidyasagar, Justice Ranade, Gopal Hari Deshmukh and other modern religious and social reformers. In fact, the ideas of the Arya Samaj with its *"Sunday Meetings"* resembled the practices of the Brahmo Samaj and the Prarthana Samaj in this respect.

Service Activities of the Samaj* :** Under the leadership and guidance of Dayananda Saraswathi, the Arya Samaj started a social revolution against all the evils that could be found in the contemporary society. Some of Swamiji's followers later started a network of schools, colleges and hostels, especially in Punjab and Sindh region to impart education on the Western lines. Lala Hansaraj played a very important role in this respect. In 1902, Swami Shraddhananda started the ***Gurukul near Haridwar to propagate the more traditional ideals of education. ***Dayananda Anglo-Vedic School*** established in Lahore played an important role in imparting English education. Soon it developed into a college and became a model for all the education institutions established by the *Samaj.* Lala Hansaraj who worked as the Principal for more than 28 years contributed to its progress.

The Arya Samajists who proved to be the advocates of social reform also worked actively to improve the condition of women and to spread education among them. They fought against untouchability and the rigidities of the hereditary caste system. They repudiated the caste restrictions, protested against prohibition of sea voyages, and insisted that even the Shudras could study the Vedas. They were thus advocates of social equality and promoted social solidarity and consolidation. They also inculcated a spirit of self respect and self reliance among the people. This promoted nationalism.

Launching of the Shuddhi Movement* :** The Arya Samaj functioned as a militant force to protect the Hindu society from the *"onslaughts of Western rationalisation."* It started the ***Shuddhi [purification] movement to re-Hinduise the converts, the fallen, the outcastes and other externals. Through the Shuddhi movement it intended to prevent the conversion of Hindus to other religions. It also helped to purify the converts and to bring them back into Hindu religion. Dayananda Saraswathi and his Samaj also contributed much to the development of Hindi language and education in general.

4. SRI RAMAKRISHNA MISSION – 1897

An outstanding movement which stood for religious reformation is the ***"Sri Ramakrishna Mission"*** of Calcutta. **Sri Ramakrishna Paramahamsa** [1834-86] and his great disciple **Swami Vivekananda** [1863-1902] launched this movement which has now assumed the form of an institution.

***Message of Sri Ramakrishna* : *Unity of God - Equality of Religions and Service to Mankind*:** Sri Ramakrishna Mission was totally an indigeneous movement due to the personality of a simple and almost illiterate saint, Sri Ramakrishna Paramahamsa. He preached the unity of God and equality of religions and taught the philosophy of the Upanishads in universal language and laid particular emphasis on social service. He taught unity of God, that service to man is service to God. He taught, like Jesus Christ, truths about religion by way of parables, and gave new life to Hinduism with his braodminded ideologies.

Sri Ramakrishna Paramahamsa was a saintly person who sought religion and salvation in the traditional ways of renunciation, meditation and devotion [bhakti]. In his search for religious truth or the realisation of God, he lived with mystics of other faiths. He again and again emphasised that there were many roads to God and salvation and that service to mankind was embodiment of God.

Attempts to Stop the Advance of Western Materialism **:** Sri Ramakrishna Paramahamsa wanted *"to protect the country from the materialisation of the West. He never advocated violent change, but gradual economic and social upliftment of the people leading to spiritual reform. He actually stimulated many local socio-religious organisations and movements like the Arya Samaj, Radhaswami Satsang, Bharath Dharma, etc. which played a remarkable role in bringing about national awakening."*[1]

Vivekananda as a Mighty Force of the *"Mission"*

The greatest contribution of Sri Ramakrishna Paramahamsa was the shaping of the personality of his great disciple Swami Vivekananda. As an ardent follower of Sri Ramakrishna, Vivekananda popularised his religious message and tried to put it in a form that would suit the needs of contemporary Indian society. Vivekananda was a radical thinker, a forceful orator and staunch nationalist. He denounced the evil aspects of the Hindu society and social institutions. He stressed the need for social action. He said that knowledge unaccompanied by action in the actual world in which we live was useless. Like his Guru, he also proclaimed the essential oneness of all religions and condemned any narrowness in religious matters. At the same time, he was convinced of the superior approach of the Indian philosophical tradition. By his mastery of Eastern and Western philosophy, he showed that Hinduism was capable of adjusting itself to the latest scientific thought of the modern world. He did not preach a sectarian creed, but universal Hinduism based on *Vedanta.* He himself subscribed to *Vedanta* which he declared to be a fully rational system. He was mainly responsible for creating *"a sense of community among the Hindus."* As **K.M. Panikkar** has pointed out *"This new Shankaracharya may well be claimed to be a unifier of Hindu ideology."*

Vivekananda Heralds a Movement of Liberal Ideas **:** Vivekananda condemned caste inequalities, exploitation of lower castes and women. He stressed on education, self reliance and freedom of women. He urged the people to imbibe the spirit of liberty, equality and free thinking. He bitingly remarked **:** *"There is a danger of our religion getting into the kitchen. We are neither Vedantists, nor Pauranics, nor Tantrics. We are just "don't touchists." Our religion is in the kitchen. Our God is in the cooking-pot, and our religion is "Don't touch me, I am holy. If this goes on for another century, everyone of us will be in a lunatic asylum."*[2] He pronounced that caste had nothing to do with Hinduism and condemned the meaningless disputations about orthodox ceremonies and the *"touch-me-notism"* of the upper classes / castes.

---

1 **Dr.H.V.S. Murthy** and **Dr.S.U. Kamath** *"Studies in Indian Culture"* [1972] Page - 146.

2 **Bipin Chandra** *"Modern India - A History Textbook for Class XII."* NCERT. Page 174.

Vivekananda, like his *Guru*, was also a great humanist. Shocked by the poverty, misery and sufferings of the common people of the country, he wrote : *"The only God in whom I believe, the sum total of all souls, and above all, my God the wicked, my God the afflicted, my God the poor of all races."* To the educated Indians, he said : *"So long as the millions live in hunger and ignorance, I hold every man a traitor, who having been educated at their expense, pays not the least heed to them."*

Social Service Activities of the Mission **:** The Ramakrishna Mission which Vivekananda founded carried on number of humanitarian relief and social work. The Mission had many branches in different parts of the country and carried on social service by opening schools, hospitals and dispensaries, orphanages, libraries, etc. It thus laid emphasis not only on personal salvation but also on social good or social service. The branches of the Mission rendered ungrudging help to the people in times of distress caused by famine or flood or other types of calamity. In particular, the uplift of dumb millions of India forms the chief plank of the Mission's platform. Caste or colour or creed has no place in this organisation. The Mission has its branches even in other countries such as America, Britain, France, Ceylone, etc.

Nationalistic and Patriotic Appeal of Vivekananda **:** "The Ramakrishna Mission stands for religious and social reform but takes its inspiration from the ancient culture of India. It holds up pure Vedantic doctrine as an ideal and aims at the development of the highest spirituality inherent in man." Vivekananda who had imbibed in himself Raja Ram's rationalism and Dayananda Saraswathi's spirituality, was highly pragmatic in his approach and hence was able to give a dynamic leadership to the organisation. In Swami Vivekananda the patriotic and spiritual impulses mingled in a supreme desire to uplift the manhood of India with a view to provide for her an appropriate place among the nations of the world. He was, to quote the words of Sir Valentine Cirol, *"the first Hindu whose personality won demonstrative recognition abroad for India's ancient civilisation and for the new born claim to nationhood."*[1]

5. THEOSOPHICAL SOCIETY – 1886

The ***"Theosophical Society"*** was originally founded in the United States in 1875 by **Madam H.P. Blavatasky** and **Colonel H.S. Olcott,** who later came to India and founded the headquarters of the Society at **Adyar** near Madras in 1886. The Theosophical Movement soon grew in India as a result of the leadership and the indefatigable efforts of Mrs. Annie Besant who had come to India from England in 1893.

Call for the Revival of the Ancient Religions of the East **:** The Theosophists advocated the revival and strengthening of ancient religions of Hinduism, Zoroastrianism and Buddhism. Particularly, the Society paid greater attention to the study of Indian culture, Hinduism, and various schools of Hindu philosophy. The Society recognised the doctrines of *Karma* and *the transmigration of the soul.* It preached the universal brotherhood of man irrespective of distinctions of caste, creed, colour, race or sex. It stood for the development of national spirit among the Indians. Members of the Society held disciples of every religion in equal respect and believed in the principles of Karma and rebirth. It advocated that people of different nations should endeavour to lead the best possible life by adopting all the best qualities of every religious and social system. The Theosophists were also desirous of educating people in the study and understanding of philosophical, scientific and natural laws and in the necessity of mutual co-operation. Mrs. Annie Besant spent her life in the implementation of social reforms and made Adyar near Madras the centre of Hindu culture and

1 **J.L. Kachroo** and **Vijay Kachroo** *"Society in India."* Page - 370.

learning. The Theosophical Society stood for the development of national spirit among the Indians. The role of Mrs. Annie Besant in the struggle for independence and particularly in launching the *Home Rule movement* and creating awareness relating to the establishment of *Swarajya*, has been very significant.

Western Leadership and Indian Following **:** As religious revivalists, the Theosophists were not however, very successful. But they made peculiar contribution to developments in modern India. It was a movement led by Westerners and followed by Indian masses. The Western leadership glorified Indian religious, cultural and philosophical traditions. This helped Indians recover their self confidence which tended to give them a sense of pride in their past greatness.

Mrs. Annie Besant founded the *"Central Hindu School"* in Banaras which was later developed by **Madan Mohan Malaviya** into the *Banaras Hindu University.* Annie Besant and the Theosophical Society are very much remembered today for this significant contribution towards the development of education in India.

6. SATYA SHODHAK SAMAJ – 1873

The ***Satya Shodhak Samaj*** [Truth Seeking Society] established by **Jyothirao Phule** in Poona in 1873 represents the beginning of a non-Brahmin movement in India. This movement against the Brahmin supremacy by the lower castes came to be known as Backward Classes Movement.

Birth of the "Sathya Shodhak Samaj" **:** During the British rule, the non-Brahmin castes in India were getting themselves more and more organised to challenge the supremacy of the Brahmins and to assert their rights. Jyothirao Phule of Poona was one of the first to revolt against the tyranny of caste in general and Brahmanical dominance in particular. He had all the praise for the British and the various modern facilities which they had introduced. He started a social reform movement called the *"Satya Shodhak Samaj"* on 24th September 1873.

Jyothirao Phule as the Moving Force Behind the *"Samaj"*

Phule a son of *Mali* [gardener] was born in 1827. He was educated in a traditional Indian school upto 1838, and from 1841-1847 he was educated in a middle school run by missionaries. He was considerably influenced by **Thomas Paine's** work *"The Rights of Man."* The Enlish education which he had received also helped him to emerge as a social reformer. As **Y.M. Pathan** stated *"while all the other reformers were mostly Brahmins, Jyothirao Phule was the only non-Brahmin reformer."*[1]

Ideology of the Movement

Jyothirao Phule had stated that the sole objective of *Satya Shodhak Samaj* was – *"to redeem the Shudras and Athishudras from the influence of Brahmanical scriptures under the Brahmin priest who fleeced them, to teach them their human rights, and to liberate them from mental and religious slavery."* Main purpose of the Samaj was to assert the worth of man irrespective of caste. The movement of the *Satya Shodhak Samaj* was comparatively militant in nature and it carried on an open campaign against the Brahmin dominated caste system. Through his writings and practices he led a revolt against the tyranny of the caste system and the hegemony of the Brahmins.

Phule's Challenge to the Supremacy of the Brahmins **:** Phule tried to fight against Brahmin domination in a number of ways. He appealed to the non-Brahmin caste not to engage any Brahmin priest to conduct their marriage ritual. He tried to reduce the enormous ritual system into a simple

1 **Dr. M.A. Chingamani** *"Sociology of Indian Society"* [1998]. Page - 257.

procedure. Phule was concerned with the eradication of untouchability, illiteracy, exploitation of non-Brahmins by Brahmins, acquiring representation for non-Brahmins in services in local bodies, etc. Jyothirao extended the membership of the Samaj to all castes including the untouchables. He campaigned vigorously for social equality and abolition of caste. Phule preached against idol worship and superstitions and was interested in reviving the real Indian culture. **Dr. Ghurye** remarked, *"Phule's was a revolt against caste in so far as caste denied ordinary human rights to all members of Hindu society, and not merely a non-Brahmin movement to cast off the domination of the Brahmins."*

***Ideological Defence of the Fight against Brahmin Domination*:** Phule was searching for an ideological justification to fight against Brahmin supremacy. He realised that to unify the masses, it was necessary to attack the Brahmin domination. He used the *"Aryan Theory of Race"* which was very popular at that time for this purpose. Phule stated that the low castes were the original inhabitants of the country and they were enslaved and exploited by the conquering Aryans who formulated a caste based Hinduism as a means of deceiving the masses and legitimising their power. *"The highest rights, the highest previleges and gifts, and everything that could make the life of the Brahmin easy............. were inculcated and enjoined, whereas the Shudras and Athishudras were regarded with supreme content and the meanest rights of humanity were denied to them."*

Phule's Attempts to Spread Education Among the Lower Castes

Phule wrote number of books and ballads the important of which were – *Gulamgiri* [slavery], *Priestcraft Exposed*, and life of *Shivaji*. Phule perceived the necessity of educating the lower caste people. He believed that all the sufferings of non-Brahmins were due to the monopoly of Brahmins in education. He could translate his vision into practice when he opened a primary school for the so called untouchables in Poona [the very centre of orthodoxy], against all odds of caste tradition and time, as early as in 1848. The school was especially meant for female children belonging to the lowest castes such as Shudras, Mahars, Mangs, Chamars, etc. This attempt to educate the lowest caste female children was well appreciated by the non-Brahmin community. He was inspired to start three more schools; two were opened in 1851 and the third in 1852. To broad-base the cause of education, he organised a society for the education of low caste Hindus and put these schools under its management.

***The Beginning of the Non-Brahmin Movement*:** Phule's was not just a revolt against caste to cast off the domination of the Brahmins. In his writings he demanded representation for all classes of the Hindus in (i) *all the local bodies,* and (ii) *all the services and institutions.* In fact, he pleaded for communal representation but as **Prof. Ghurye** observes, *"Phule's demand for special representation for non-Brahmins in the services and local bodies went unheeded till the last decade of the 19th century, when the Maharaja of Kolhapur took up the non-Brahmin cause."* Thus Phule's struggles marked the beginning of the non-Brahmin movement which is also regarded as the *"Backward Classes Movement"*, the first of its kind.

Sri Sahu Majaraj's Leadership to *Satyashodhak Samaj*

The cause of the non-Brahmins and the *Satya Shodhak Samaj* movement were further carried by **Sri Sahu Maharaj** of Kolhapur. After the death of Jyothirao Phule, the Samaj received a setback and it became a mere fault finding movement with Brahmins. It was Sri Sahu Maharaj who again took up the cause of the Samaj and got for it a respectable position. He advocated social reforms and also pleaded for communal representation. Though Jyothirao Phule advocated this idea it could not be a success during his lifetime. Thanks to the efforts of Sahu Maharaj special representation through mixed electorals was conceded to the non-Brahmins in the Montague-Chelmsford Reforms. In 1923, Government of Bombay prohibited the requirement of Brahmins and allied castes to the lower services. The impact of *Satya Shodhak Samaj* movement was felt in other parts of South India also. **M.N. Srinivas** emphasises the value of Phule's efforts when he states : *"The measures which Phule advocated in the second and third quarters of the nineteenth century were to become the main items in the programme of the non-Brahmin parties of Bombay and Madras in the first half of this century."* After Phule's death in 1890, the movement spread to other areas and by 1920, the Samaj changed from a social movement to a political one.

7. SRI NARAYANA GURU DHARMA PARIPALANA YOGAM [S.N.D.P. YOGAM] – 1903

Sri Narayana Guru [1854-1928] established the S.N.D.P. Yogam in Kerala in the year 1903. The main gospel of Sri Narayana Guru was *"One caste, One religion and One God."* It was meant to be a casteless organisation open to all people. It had two important programmes.

Two Important Programmes of SNDP

1. ***Encouraging Education by Starting Educational Institutions*****:** First important programme was to uplift the Ezhavas, the community to which he belonged, that is, a depressed caste group of Kerala. As an important part of the organisational activity, Narayana Guru started a number of schools and colleges throughout Kerala to spread education on a massive scale among the community people.

2. ***Building Temples and Simplifying Rituals*** **:** Sri Narayana Guru built a number of temples, simplified the rituals regarding worship, marriage and funerals. With this he wanted to help the people of his community in secular and also spiritual matters.

Sri Narayana Guru travelled widely for about 15 years throughout Kerala and helped the community people to develop self confidence, social awareness and sense of cleanliness. He guided them to clean up their houses and streets and cultivate clean habits. He made them change their food habits and pointed out right road to reform and prosperity.

Religious Reforms of S.N.D.P. Yogam

Sri Narayana Guru undertook various religious and social reforms activities. He did not make any attempt to establish a new religion or a dogma. His approach was not propaganda oriented. He was a silent worker who had great conviction and committment in his mission and action. Sri Narayana Guru was born a Hindu and remained a Hindu until his death. He only struggled to correct some of the irregularities involved in the Hindu society. During his time, the *Avarnas* were not allowed to enter the temples and offer worships. The temples were controlled by the Brahmin priests who imposed strict rules and restrictions on the access of the *Avarnas* to the temples. Sri Narayana Guru condemned such caste rigidities and regulations and decided to change the age old practices and rituals in temple worship. He started founding temples for common people who were not admitted to the sacro-sanctum of the orthodox Hindu temples. He consecrated a Shaiva temple at **Aruvipuram** in 1888 and it represented the beginning of a peaceful and creative revolution in Kerala. Sri Narayana Guru had taken up the challenge of consecrating the temple much against the prevailing caste norms of the day. As per the caste norms only the upper caste people, particularly the Brahmins were entitled to consecrate temples. Sri Narayana Guru who became successful in consecrating the first Shaiva temple got the inspiration to go ahead and consecrated more than 60 such temples in different parts of South India during his life time. These temples proved to be the great means of emancipation for millions of people who were denied admission to the temples.

Consecration of New Temples : Sri Narayana Guru introduced three specific religious reforms alongwith the consecration of new temples. ***Firstly,*** he consecrated higher gods in place of lower ones and appointed dedicated Sanyasins from his own community to function as priests. ***Secondly,*** he suggested to his followers to build new temples in a simple and less expensive way. ***Thirdly,*** he introduced a notable change in his task of founding new temples. He never made idol worship inevitable or compulsory for his followers. He consecrated a *"silavilakha"*, a huge brass oil lamp in stead of an idol, in Karamukha Kshetram in Trichur in 1920 with a saying *"let there be light."* In another temple at Murukkunpuzha he consecrated a plain stone with the inscription *"Truth, Charity, Love and Mercy."*

Establishment of Three Types of Temples : As **K.M. Panikkar** has pointed out, Sri Narayana Guru established three types of temples : (i) There are temples with poojas or regular worship and festivals, (ii) there are temples with idols and no customary poojas or celebrations, and (iii) finally, there temples with no idols or images. It is clear that Sri Narayana Guru consecrated different types of temples to cater to the different types of emotional and spiritual needs of the people.

Social Reforms of S.N.D.P. Yogam

Emphasis on Education and Sanskritisation : "By making use of two means – *modern education* on the one hand, and *Sanskritisation* on the other – Sri Narayana Guru was able to transform the Ezhavas from an *untouchable group* in Kerala to a *"backward caste"* community within a short period of 30 years. The temple entry programmes undertaken by some Ezhava leaders in association with Nair Service Society finally led to the temple entry proclamation in 1936. **Aiyyappan** writes that C.P. Ramaswamy Iyer, the Diwan of the Travancore State, *"felt the need for consolidating the Hindus and building up the unity of the Hindus of the state as a counterpoise against the growing power and influence of the Christians. The most discontented and at the same time, the best organised among the Hindu castes were the Ezhavas. Nothing was dearer to the Ezhavas of that generation than temple entry."*[1]

Sri Narayana Guru also tried to introduce some social reforms in the ancient customs and practices of the Ezhavas. For example, he appealed to his community people to stop the expensive customs such as mock marriage [*Thalikattu Sambhandham*], puberty festival for girls [*Thirundukuli*], and a festival associated with pregnancy after marriage called *Pulikudi*.

Sri Narayana Guru vehemently opposed the practice of consuming alcoholic drinks. He campaigned against caste distinctions. He said *"All men belong to one race and one caste. There is only one religion and one God."* This seems to be the very essence of his work *"Jati Mimamsa"* [A Critique of Caste].

Opposition to the Practice of Untouchability : Sri Narayana Guru was opposed to the practice of untouchability. He preached caste equality and suggested his followers not to ask another's caste and not even to think of it. He did not appreciate the governmental procedure of seeking caste identifications in official documents. He was critical of Gandhiji's faith in the *Chaturvarna System.* During his vast tours throughout Kerala and outside, he always made it a point to mingle and live with the downtrodden masses. In fact, in his Mutt at Shivagiri he appointed a cook of low caste origin.

---

1 **Prof. B. Kuppuswamy** *"Social Change in India"* [1975], Page - 206.

The SNDP Yogam has become today a powerful organisation of the Ezhava community. It has resorted to publishing articles, booklets, books, etc. on the views of Sri Narayana Guru. Throughout his life the SNDP Yogam remained as a non-political organisation. But after his death, it was drawn into politics. The middle class of this group used to support the Congress Party and their leader, **R. Shanker** caused the first Communist Government in Kerala to be dislodged in 1958. Shanker himself became the Deputy Chief Minister in 1962 and the Chief Minister of Kerala State in 1964. However, the lower classes among the Ezhavas have been giving their solid support to the Communist Party. As Nayar writes *"the SNDP represents the Ezhava middle class which is numerically small and less influential than the Nayar middle class. The vast majority of the Ezhavas have favoured the Communist Party. Thus there is a gulf between the Ezhava middle class and the Ezhava lower class."*[1]

B. BACKWARD CLASSES MOVEMENT

The Backward Classes / Castes Movement started in the early part of the 20th century. The backward classes or castes represent the underprivileged sections of the Indian society. The concept of *"Backward Castes / Classes Movement"* virtually refers to the movement launched by the backward castes / classes [which consist of non-Brahmin caste] to fight against caste inequalities, Brahmin domination, socio-economic-religious discrimination and deprivation. The movement aims at removing or lessening the caste inequalities, promoting the economic advancement of the poor, the deprived and the low castes, and to obtain for them equal educational facilities and political opportunities. The movement also signifies a great social awakening that took place in the non-Brahmin lower castes and a determined efforts on their part to seek avenues of social mobility. The backward classes movement which first took place during the British rule in Maharashtra [in 1860 and 1870s] later on spread to various south Indian states such as Kerala, Andhra and Karnataka, still continues with different dimensions.

Main Goals of Backward Classes Movement

It can be stated that the backward classes movement started with some goals among which the following may be noted :

1. Backward classes movement is a movement launched by the lower sections of the Indian population against the discrimination of various kinds – social, political, religious, economic, educational, etc.
2. It is a movement aimed at securing greater self-respect, social recognition, prestige and status.
3. These movements are basically movements aimed at finding the avenues of social mobility.
4. These movements have been organised with the intention of unifying various non-Brahmin castes.
5. Backward classes movements are launched with the intention of promoting the welfare and well-being of the non-Brahmin lower castes.

In their attempts to achieve the above mentioned goals, they have often turned out to be *"adaptive movements,that is, movements oriented to cultural revolts and counter-cultural movements."*

1 **Prof. B. Kuppuswamy.** "Social Change in India" [1975] Page - 206.

Nature and Characteristics of Backward Classes Movement

Backward Classes Movement started in India in the early part of 20th century. According to **M.N. Srinivas,** the term *"backward classes movement"* must be understood in the Indian social context as a kind of struggle waged by the lower castes against the supremacy of the Brahmins. It also represents concerted effort on the part of the lower castes to improve their social, economic, educational and political statuses. As Srinivas has pointed out the lower castes realised that mere *Sanskritisation* was not enough to attain social mobility. They became more determined to obtain Western education in order to qualify themselves for the new jobs in administration and the new professions like law, medicine, engineering, etc. Thus higher caste dominance in education and in the new occupations provided the conditions for the backward classes movement. M.N. Srinivas has also pointed out that such a movement was inevitable in India where only one caste, the Brahmins, enjoyed preponderance in higher education, in professions, and government employment.

1. *A Caste Based Movement* : The main characteristic feature of the backward classes movement is that *it is caste based.* In the Indian context, *"backward classes"* form an aggregate of *"closed"* status groups or castes. Caste associations came into existence in different parts of the country to press their claims for new designations and occupations. Many caste-groups published journals devoted to caste welfare, collected funds for giving scholarships and building hostels for students from respective castes and undertook reform of caste customs. The qualified youths of the lower castes soon realised that it was difficult to get admission in the professional courses and in the post graduate courses. They could not compete with the upper caste youths such as Brahmins. They also failed to get jobs in the government services. They felt that they were discriminated against on the basis of caste. *This led to anti-Brahmin feelings which inspired the backward classes movement.*

2. *Backward Classes Movement is also a Political Movement* : The backward classes movement right from its inception has been political in nature. The partition of Bengal in 1905 led to the intensification of nationalism, and also to the rise of communalism, casteism, linguism and regionalism. The *Minto-Morley Reforms of 1909* conceded separate electorates to Muslims, Sikhs, Indian Christians, Anglo-Indians and Europeans. Now, the lower castes also demanded separate electorate. Dr. Ambedkar fought for it. *This made the backward classes movement to become political.* In South India, in Madras Presidency the ***Justice Party*** was formed to protect the interests of the non-Brahmins *"dominant castes."* It started newspapers in English and other languages to educate and to represent the case of the non-Brahmins. Similarly, many *periodicals* were started by caste organisations in different parts of India.

3. *Backward Classes Movement Originated in South India* : For various reasons, the backward classes movement not only originated in South India but also had become very stronger. It also assumed the character of a "Dravidian movement" and became – *"anti-north Indian", "anti-Hindi", "anti-Aryan", "anti-Sanskrit", "anti-Brahmin" movement.* In course of time, however, the movement was spread to North India also and even to the states like Bengal where the caste consciousness was found to be quite less.

4. *Backward Classes Movement was not a "Mass Movement"* : Backward classes movement was not a popular movement for a very long time. People belonging to the lower castes though were often exploited and suppressed by the Brahmins, were not ready to oppose the hegemony of the Brahmins openly. Hence, it had not become a mass movement. But in the rural areas, the forward non-Brahmin dominant castes such as the *Reddy*s and *Kamma*s in Andhra Pradesh, *Vokkaliga*s and *Lingayat*s in Karnataka, *Gounders*, *Padayachi*s and *Mudaliyars* in Tamil Nadu, were in the fore-front of this movement. Even the Muslims and Christians had joined hands with these dominant castes. This is one of the reasons as to why M.N. Srinivas preferred to call this movement a *"backward classes movement" rather than a backward castes movement.*

5. *Was Backward Classes Movement "Secular" in Nature* ? : The awareness on the part of the backward castes that education is inevitable for them to get into government jobs and political offices, helped them to resort to social mobility. They wanted to achieve social equality on par with other higher castes. In order to attain social equality it was necessary for them to resort to Western education. It is in this context, **M.N. Srinivas** considers the movement a secular movement. This movement also led to a kind of rivalry on the part of lower castes who were interested in the upward social mobility. But in any case, the movement gave a big blow to the social and cultural domination of the Brahmins.

6. *A New Polarisation within the Backward Classes* ? : It is observed that during the recent years a kind of polarisation is taking place within the category of backward classes. At present, there are two groups within the backward classes : (i) *Dominant Backward Castes,* and (ii) *Non-Dominant Backward Castes.* In order to protect themselves against the atrocities of the "dominant backward castes", the "non-dominant backward castes" are getting themselves organised. In the beginning stage [say, between 1916 and 1969], the non-Brahmin castes made an organised attempt to face the domination of the Brahmins. But now in the second stage [say, after 1969], the *more backward non-Brahmin castes* are getting organised to fight against the bossism of the more advanced non-Brahmin castes. There is justification for the more backward non-Brahmin castes to claim themselves as *"backward classes"* for they are educationally, socially and economically lagging behind and backward.

7. *Increased the Horizontal Solidarity of the Caste* : M.N. Srinivas has stated that the backward classes movement has very strongly supported the horizontal solidarity of the caste. It has helped the caste to come out of its local traditional framework. Differences between the sub-castes are becoming minimised and interdependence is increasing. Sub-castes within the bigger castes are getting united to safeguard their caste interests. *For example,* various subcastes such as *Nonaba, Hallikara, Morasu, Gangadigara, Kunchutigara, Halumata* of the ***Vokkaliga*** caste [a dominant caste of Karnataka] are getting united to reap the benefits of modern economic, political and educational system.

8. *The Backward Classes Movement – An Attempt to Achieve Social Mobility* : According to **M.N. Srinivas,** the Backward Classes Movement especially in South India, is fundamentally *a movement evolved to achieve mobility.* It was started by those groups which had lagged behind the Brahmins in Westernisation. Education, employment in the Government, and participation in the new political processes are essential for such mobility. Education is a necessary means for securing the other two involved in it. It has led to the *"Self Respect Movement."* It has assaulted the Brahmins' cultural and social dominance and exclusiveness.

Factors Contributing to the Backward Classes Movement

The backward classes movement which started as a non-Brahmin movement, ultimately degenerated into anti-Brahmin movement. This movement is the cumulative effect of several factors among which the following may be noted.

1. The Dual Effect of the Politics Pursued by the British Government

The growth of the backward classes movement is in no small measure due to the politics pursued by the British Government. The advent of the British rule in India had led to many far-reaching consequences. The consolidation of the political regime by the British, introduction of

Western-oriented educational system, opening of vast occupational and professional opportunities, produced lot of structural disturbances in the caste structure. The British rule in a way, caused two contradictory effects on the Hindu society.

(a) *British Rule Further Widened the Gap Between the Brahmins and Non-Brahmins* : The British rule led to an increase in the structural distance between the Brahmins and the rest of the castes in the Hindu society. It led to an increase in the disparities in the distribution of economic and political power. In most parts of the country Brahmins were the first to benefit from the Western education. They also increased their representation in the professional and administrative and managerial services especially in the first quarter of the 20th century. There was preponderance of the Brahmins among the literates and particularly the English knowing population in the Madras Presidency and the then princely state of Mysore. In this context, **M.N. Srinivas** writes : *"It is only in the context of English education and the fruits that it yielded that the Brahmins enjoyed an overwhelming advantage over all the others."* As **Andre Beteille** states : *"As Brahmins enetered the institutions of higher learning, the professions and the services, everywhere they formed cliques from which non-Brahmins were excluded.......... In a system which was ostensibly competitive but in which the scales must have seemed heavily weighed against non-Brahmins, the latter inevitably developed deep feelings of resentment."*

(b) *British Support to Non-Brahmin Movement to Curb Brahmin-led Revolutionary Activities* : The British, for their own benefit started supporting the non-Brahmin movement. Though the British used to favour the Brahmins in the beginning, they later realised that Brahmins were potentially dangerous. During the first phase of the 20th century, a section of the British in India believed the Brahmin to be their primary enemy. **Valentine Chirol** in his work *"Indian Unrest"* stated that *"Brahminism and Western education constituted a serious threat to the continuance of British rule in India. Secondly, the "Rowlatt Report" published in 1918 showed conclusively that the Brahmins had played a major part in the revolutionary activities in different parts of India."*

2. Role of Census System

The desire for more mobility among the backward castes came from the *census operations* also. The caste *"sabhas"* represented to the census authorities the demand of individual castes to belong to a particular *"varna"* and not to a lower one. For example, the two peasant castes of Tamil Nadu, the *Vellalas* and *Padaiyachis* wanted to be recorded as *"Vaishyas"* and *"Vaniya Kula Kshatriyas"* respectively, and not as *"Shudras."* Many such claims were made in 1931 census. The *"Sabhas"* also altered the styles of life of their castes in the direction of Sanskritisation. This included the giving up of forbidden meat [pork and carrion beef] and liquor, and the donning of the sacred thread, the shortening of the mourning period like that of the Brahmins. In the case of very *"low castes"* it included non-performance of a traditional degrading duty such as *"Carvee"* or other free labour or carrying palanquins, or beating the *"tom-tom"* on ceremonial occasions. The upper caste people were mainly indifferent towards these trends. On some occasions, they used force to make the lower caste people to perform their traditional duties. The caste consciousness created by the census system thus favoured the backward classes movement.

3. Influence of Reform Movements

During the British rule various social reform movements were initiated by the enlightened Indians. Most of these movements aimed at eliminating caste disabilities, promotion of education among women, abolition of sati, upliftment of the depressed and the down-trodden castes such as the Scheduled Castes, and so on. These movements definitely played their role in the beginning of the non-Brahmin movement. At least in the begining, these movements were generally led by the learned members of the forward castes themselves. These movements created conditions of self-awareness among the deprived sections of the society. The Brahmo Samaj was more concerned with the emancipation of women and the amelioration of the depressed classes, while the Arya Samaj had taken up the cause and the problems of untouchables. Arya Samaj under the leadership of Dayananda Saraswathi took interest in the upliftment of the untouchables by opening education institutions, hostels, etc. for their benefit. Arya Samaj even sponsored a programme of *"Shuddhi Movement"* in 1891 to re-Hinduise those low caste people who had converted into Christianity and Islam. It even gave an opportunity for the untouchables to wear sacred thread. These movements, though were led by upper caste people, particularly the Brahmins, ultimately created social awareness among the lower castes. This awareness helped them to get themselves organised.

The reform movements, in due course of time, became more militant and aggressive. Some of them even sought to reject the Brahmanical culture and dominance as in the case of the *"Non-Brahmin movement"* led by **Jyothirao Phule** in Maharashtra, *"Self Respect Movement"* led by **E.V. Ramasamy Naicker** in Tamil Nadu. The Self Respect Movement ultimately became even anti-Brahmin.

4. Role of Christian Missionaries

The Christian Missionaries too played their role in the genesis of the non-Brahmin movement. These Christian Missionaries who established their churches, convents and other institutions in different places in Madras Presidency created conditions of self awareness especially among the lower sections. They worked in the midst of lower castes and tribes spreading Jesus Christ's message of love and humanity. *"Overtly they pretended to be the benefactors of the depressed classes and yet, their ultimate aim was to convert them into Christianity. In Madras Presidency 5,000 Nadars were converted to Christianity by 1803. With the active support of British government they could expand not only the evangelical, educational, medical and welfare activities, but also secure for their new converts basic civil rights and employment in public services."*[1] The non-converts to Christianity could see their own castemen who were converted getting the benefits of modern education and employment chances in government service. This created double effect in the minds of the depressed sections. *Firstly,* it tempted a few more to get converted into Christianity. *Secondly,* it created a social awakening among the deprived castes. They realised that non-Brahmin movement was one of the powerful instruments of ameliorating their depressed conditions without necessarily getting converted into Christianity.

5. Role of Education

The non-Brahmin movement was to a very large extent the result of the general awakening under the impact of British education. The British introduced English education on a uniform basis throughout India. Though they were reluctant to introduce English education in India, *Lord Macaulay's Minute of* 1835 made them to promote European learning in India through the medium of English.[2] The new education which was introduced by the British was not only secular in nature but also egalitarian in outlook. Educational opportunities were extended to all the sections of the society

1 **H.K. Moulesh** and **G. Subramanya** *"Sociology of Indian Society."* Page - 218.

2 **T.B. Macaulay** in *"Minute of Education in India"* [2.2.1835] stated that "...... it is impossible for us with our limited means, to attempt to educate the body of the people. We must at present do our best to form a class who may be interpreters between us and the millions of whom we govern; ***a class of persons, Indians in blood and colour, but English in taste, in opinions, in morals, and in intellect.***"
In the same minute he had also stated : "..... it is possible to make natives of this country thoroughly good English scholars and to this end our efforts ought to be directed." – as quoted by **Dharampal** in *"Despoliation and Defaming of India" The Early 19th Century British Crusade."* Pages : 201 - 202.

including the so called untouchables. Liberal ideas, egalitarian values, democratic views, rational and scientific perspectives could be spread through this education. This new education never remained as the monopoly of the Brahmins, nor set any traditional bars for the lower castes to avail of its benefits. The introduction and the spread of modern education helped the non-Brahmin movement to challenge the supremacy of the Brahmins.

6. Growth of National Movement

The national movement that was going on in India challenging the British imperialism also contributed to the strengthening of the non-Brahmin movement. The Brahmins who had taken the advantages of modern education came to dominate the national movement in the beginning. But the establishment of Indian National Congress and the entry of Mahatma Gandhi into the freedom struggle changed the situation. Under the leadership of Gandhiji, the Congress gave a clarion call to all the people of all the sections to join the freedom struggle and fight against British supremacy. Gandhiji was successful in persuading the lower sections of the Indian society including the untouchables to join the national struggle. He in fact stood for the emancipation of Harijans. He supported their temple entry movement. He made the Congress to commit itself for the removal of untouchability. Many organisations and their leaders at this stage tried to improve the depressed and the degrading conditions of the downtrodden in the society.

7. Economic Factors

In the traditional economic system, the Brahmins enjoyed a favourable position. The Brahmins in the Madras Presidency areas owned sizeable landholdings, although they did not constitute the dominant element of the landed gentry. The Brahmins particularly in the South India were successful in converting their landed resources into more paying resources of the government service and profession. Sizeable number of Brahmins became absentee landlords and exploiters of lower caste people who were working as tenants. The social and economic conditions of the backward castes were miserable and they were exploited at all levels. The Brahmins in fact dominated government service, prestigious professions and political leadership. The Brahmins occupied *"the storm centre of political debate"* for many years.

8. Provision of Modern Facilities

The British during the course of their rule established countrywide communication networks like post and telegraphs, railways and mass circulation of newspapers. These facilities made strong inroads into the isolated caste structure and enabled the similar caste groups to form caste associations. These changed situations, to a very great extent, diluted the sub-caste distinctions. The caste now assumed a new role much different from what was envisaged in Hindu ethics.

Modern communications facilitated sanskritisation, and even militant social reforms. Introduction of adult franchise and provision for mass participation played an important role in the development of backward classes / castes movement.

NON-BRAHMIN MOVEMENT AS A TYPE OF BACKWARD CLASSES MOVEMENT

Beginning, Growth and Course of the Non-Brahmin Movement

Sathya Shodhak Samaj and the Non-Brahmin Movement : *The First Phase*

The foundation for the non-Brahmin movement was laid by the great social reformer of Poona **Jyothirao Phule.** He was the first to have revolted against the tyranny of caste in general and

Brahmanical dominance in particular. He established the *"Sathya Shodhaka Samaj"* in 1873 which spearheaded the non-Brahmin movement. Phule undertook the social reforms by establishing schools and hostels for the low caste people, etc. in order to elevate the status of the low caste people. He appealed to the non-Brahmin castes and particularly the depressed castes to liberate themselves from mental and religious slavery. He preached against idol worship and superstitions. He also pleaded for communal representation. **Prof. Ghurye** observes, *"Phule's demand for special representation for non-Brahmins in the services and local bodies went unheeded till the last decade of the 19th century when the Maharaja of Kolhapar took up the non-Brahmin cause."*

Sri Sahu Maharaj as the Leader of "Sathya Shodhak Samaj" **:** "Sathya Shodhak Samaj" movement was further carried by **Sri Sahu Maharaj** of Kolhapur after the death of Jyothiba Phule in 1890. Sri Sahu Maharaj who was a prince, appreciated the cause of Phule and decided to continue the same. He started schools and hostels for exclusively non-Brahmin students. He had shown inclination towards Arya Samaj and decided to carry the message of the Vedas to the down-trodden castes. He raised some basic questions relating to caste, laws of caste membership, sanctions of the Shastras for the caste in its present form, etc.

Sri Sahu was more interested in getting *"communal representation"* to the depressed and the downtrodden castes. Thanks mainly to his efforts, special representation through mixed electorals was conceded to the non-Brahmins in the *"Montague-Chelmsford Reforms."* Due to his efforts certain percentage of posts for non-Brahmins was reserved. Sri Sahu separated judiciary from the executive functions in his home state.

The greatest contribution of Sri Sahu Maharaj is the fact that he supported and inspired many of the non-Brahmin organisations such as *Somavamshi Arya Kshatriya Jnana Vardhak Samaj, Gujarati Untouchables Depressed Classes Mission Society, Kurmi Kshatriya Samaj, Maratha Samaj, Mohammedan Samaj, Lingayat Samaj* in Mysore, Justice Party in Tamil Nadu, and so on. He gave all the support to these organisations and helped them to be united as one single Non-Brahmin Movement.

Justice Party and the Non-Brahmin Movement : *The Second Phase*

The discontentment of the non-Brahmins began to express itself through various efforts to organise the non-Brahmins in the city of Madras. A Vellala medical student by name **Natesh Mudaliar** established a *Dravidian Association Hostel* in Madras in June 1916 with the help of non-Brahmins. He also started a joint stock company called *"South Indian People's Association Ltd."* for the purpose of publishing English, Telugu and Tamil newspapers to express the grievances and problems of the non-Brahmins.Dr. J.M. Nair, Sir P.T. Chettiar and T. Mudaliar also joined this association and made it stronger. This association which advocated the cause of the non-Brahmins started dailies in English by name *Justice,* in Tamil by name *The Dravidian,* and in Telugu by name *Andhra Prakashika.* Finally, they set up the *South Indian Liberal Federation* which later on came be called the **The Justice Party.**

The "Non-Brahmin Manifesto" of the Justice Party **:** The Justice Party released the *"Non-Brahmin Manifesto"* in December 1916. It was directed against the Brahmins who had dominated the fields of education, public service and politics. It revealed an extremely high concentration of the Brahmins in all the important positions who constituted only 3% of the total population of the Madras Presidency. The chief leader of Justice Party Movement, **Dr. J.M. Nair** announced that without a provision for communal representation the reforms would be a failure. He made known to his people through the Manifesto that the Brahmins had secured 94% of the positions in Madras Provincial Civil Service between 1892 and 1904. He also said that in 1904, 77 out of 140 Deputy

Collectors were Brahmins and in 1913, 93 out of 128 permanent district Munsifs wer Brahmins; 450 out of 650 registered graduates of the Madras University were found to be Brahmins in 1914. The non-Brahmin Manifesto which highlighted these statistics demanded a provision for communal representation. The Justice Party with this slogan contested elections and captured polls and formed its ministry in 1920-23. It was defeated in 1926 but it acquired power once again in 1930. But the Congress Party dislodged the Justice Party in 1937 by successfully winning the elections. According to **Dr. S. Saraswathi,** the Justice Party had played a notable role during 1920-35 as a ruling party.

***Justice Party – A Party of Elites and Not Masses* ? :** It should be noted that though the Justice Party claimed to represent the non-Brahmins as a whole, in practice the depressed castes and Muslims were considered separately. As **Andre Beteille** has pointed out *"The Justice Party was in a very real sense an elite party dominated by urban, Western educated, landowning and professional people. It contained a number of Rajas, Zamindars, industrialists, lawyers and doctors. It was by no means a mass party and it is doubtful whether any serious effort was made to draw peasants and workers into the organisation."*[1]

The "Self Respect Movement" or *The Dravidian Phase* : Leadership of E.V. Ramasami Naicker

The non-Brahmin movement assumed the form of the Self Respect Movement when **E.V. Ramasami Naicker** became its leader. Ramasami Naicker, a Baliya Naidu had begun his political career with the Congress. But he was unhappy with the way in which the non-Brahmins were treated within the Madras Congress organisation and hence he decided to come out of it. He was also very much annoyed with Gandhiji's support of a purified *Varna* ideology. He left the Congress Party to start the *"Self Respect Movement"* [1925].

***Call to Reject the Brahmanical Culture and Religion* :** The Self Respect movement aimed at the rejection of the Brahmanical culture and religion. It rejected the caste system and the supremacy of the Brahmins in all respects. It considered the Brahmanical religion and culture as the main instrument of enslaving Tamilians. Naicker as a leader of this movement publicly ridiculed the *puranas* as fairy tales, not only imaginary and irrational but also totally immoral. He carried on an active propaganda in an attempt to rid people of *puranic* Hinduism. He condemned religious ceremonies which required the priestly services of the Brahmins. In strong words he denounced caste rules, child marriage, enforced widowhood and attacked the Laws of Manu, which he regarded as totally "inhuman." According to Naicker, the Laws of Manu were designed to maintain the supremacy of the Brahmins and to enslave the other caste people to them.

***Attempts to Advocate Dravidian Culture* :** Ramasami Naicker championed a new system of values in which all people could enjoy self respect. By directly attacking the Brahmins and making fun of their religious culture he sought to obtain the support of a large number of lower caste people. Naicker claimed that the lower classes and the lower sections of the Tamilian society represented the Dravidian culture. He considered Dravidian culture superior to Brahmanical Aryan culture. Formulation of the Dravidian ideology as opposed to Aryan ideology was the very basis of Self Respect Movement.

***Anti-Brahmin, Anti-Sanskrit, Anti-Aryan, Anti-North Indian, Anti-Hindi and Anti-God Movement* :** Ramasami Naicker represented a new type of leader. He did not have English education

1 **Dr. M.A. Chingamani** *"Sociology of Indian Society."* Page - 263.

and was able to speak in Tamil only. Unlike the Justice Party which drew support from middle and upper-middle class Hindus in both Tamil and Telugu areas, the Self Respect movement concentrated almost entirely on Tamil districts and on groups low in the caste hierarchy including the untouchables. He used Tamil as the medium of communication. Tamil newspapers reflected his thoughts which were *anti-Brahminical, anti-Aryan, anti-Sanskrit and anti-North Indian.* As a result of that the movement got the support of the uneducated, untouchables, the depressed and the exploited sections of the community, women and rural youth. The movement took a violent turn when a copy of the *Manu Smrithi* was burnt by the supporters of the movement in 1920.

As **M.N. Srinivas** points out, this movement was explicitly anti-Brahmin. It encouraged non-Brahmins not to call upon Brahmin priests to perform wedding and other rituals. Its followers were required to use the Tamil language for all political and other purposes. These followers were claiming themselves to be Dravidians and members of a sovereign independent state. As **M.N. Srinivas** writes *"the movement was anti-Brahmin, anti-north, anti-Hindi, anti-Sanskrit and finally anti-god. It included an attempt to rid Tamil of long-established Sanskrit words, and to introduce the singing of exclusively Tamil songs at public concerts."*

***Demand for Dravidasthan* ? :** The Self Respect movement became very radical and violent. The movement demanded the establishment of the *"Dravidasthan"* on the same lines as Pakisthan. Naicker at this stage was able to find out an effective young leader by name **C.N. Annadurai,** a Tamil Vellala, who was very fluent in both English and Tamil. Impressed by Annadurai's ability and talent, Ramasami Naicker gave him an important role in the activities of the Self Respect movement.

The *"Dravida Kazhagam"* [D.K.] and the Non-Brahmin Movement

In December 1938, Naicker was elected president of the Justice Party. As a leader of this party he raised the slogan *"Tamil Nad for Tamilians"* [or non-Brahmins]. In 1944 the Justice Party formally changed into the ***Dravida Kazhagam*** [D.K.] under the leadership of **C.N. Annadurai.** Its main aim was the realisation of a separate Dravidian or non-Brahmin country. Thus the Self Respect movement which arose as a protest against Aryan culture turned into an explicit political movement.

The Dravida Kazhagam under the leadership of Annadurai continued to pursue anti-Brahminism in the social and cultural fields. This expressed itself in assaults on individual Brahmin priests, destroying images of Hindu deities, trying to burn copies of the epic *Ramayana*, insulting the *puranas,* epics, *Manu Smrithi*, Sanskrit literature and so on. The epic *Ramayana* was regarded by DK as an expression of Aryan racialism.

Annadurai and *"Dravida Munnetra Kazhagam"* [DMK]

The differences of opinion between Annadurai and Ramasami Naicker led to a split in Dravida Kazhagam leading to the establishment of the ***Dravida Munnetra Kazhagam*** [DMK] in 1949 under the leadership of C.N. Annadurai. The primary objective of DMK was to establish *"Dravidanad."* During the initial years, the DMK was also an advocate of Tamil separatism and was anti-north, anti-Hindi and anti-Sanskrit. But in course of time there was a softening of its stand. As **Oommen** notes : *"Once the Brahmin dominance in Tamil Nadu declined, it became imperative for the movement to shift its goal from anti-Brahminism if it were to survive. Thus, after a short period during which the movement pursued the goal of establishing a sovereign Dravidian state, it settled for the objective of moderating north Indian domination - economic and linguistic - and for greater authority for states within the federal set up and promotion of Tamil nationalism and culture within the framework of the Indian Union thereby becoming a regional movement."*

The DMK proclaimed a casteless society, an egalitarian Dravidanadu to which the depressed and the down-trodden could pledge their allegiance. As in Self Respect movement, the DMK also claimed to remove all superstitious beliefs based on religion and tradition. No member of this party was allowed to wear the sectarian marks of faith across his forehead. Members were urged to boycott the use of Brahmin priests in ceremonies. The movement campaigned vigoursly for widow remarriage and intercaste marriages. The "reform" marriage rites of the DK and the DMK gained wide acceptance among non-Brahmins of Tamil Nadu.

Impact of the Non-Brahmin Movement

According to **Andre Beteille,** the non-Brahmin movement led to some important consequences.[1]

1. According to him, the most important consequence of the movement was the introduction of *"communal"* or *"caste"* idiom into south Indian politics. It created an impression that in virtually every political contest it was very important whether a person was Brahmin or non-Brahmin.
2. Secondly, it created alliances which cut across linguistic and cultural divisions.
3. Other than the above ones mentioned by Beteille, the movement led to some other consequences.
   (i) The movement made the leaders to extol the virtues of Dravidian gods and culture as against the Aryan gods and culture.
   (ii) The leaders adopted a secessionist strategy to achieve their independence and self respect.
   (iii) The combined Dravidian religious ideology with political separation.
   (iv) The movement had a tremendous appeal to the lower middle classes, lower castes and untouchables.
4. The movement was by no means a mass movement. As M.N. Srinivas pointed out *"The opposition to Brahmin dominance did not come from the low and the oppressed castes but from the leaders of the powerful, rural dominant castes such as the Kammas and Reddis of the Telugu country, the Vellalas of Tamil country, and the Nayar of Kerala."*[2]

Non-Brahmin Movement in Karnataka

The non-Brahmin movement which took place in Madras had its impact on the princely state of Mysore. ***Lingayats*** and ***Okkaligas*** the two dominant castes of Mysore, in addition to the minority community, the Muslims felt that they were also dominated and bossed over by the Brahmins. The Okkaligas and Lingayats established their caste associations in 1906 and 1909 respectively. By 1917, different ethnic and cultural groups in Mysore formed a common association called the *"Praja Mitra Mandali."* This Mandali made an appeal to the Maharaja of Mysore in 1918 requesting him to reserve posts in public services and education institutions for the non-Brahmins. The Maharaja appointed the *"Miller Committee"* to look into the demands of the Mitra Mandali. The Miller Committee of Mysore State finally recommended all the demands of the Mandali. Because of this recommendations the Okkaligas and Lingayats have availed themselves of maximum benefits in the fields of education, employment and politics. They have also been able to excel and oust the Brahmins from their position of command and control in different fields.

---

1 **Dr. M.A. Chingamani.** "Sociology of Indian Society" Page - 265.

2 **B. Kuppuswamy** *"Social Changes in India."* Page - 225.

However, the non-Brahmin movement in Mysore was different from the one that has been taking place in Madras. ***Firstly,*** unlike the Dravidian movement of Tamilnadu, the movement in Karnataka did not alienate the backward classes and the Muslims. ***Secondly,*** the anti-Brahmin ideology in Mysore has not assumed the form of a pro-Dravidian and anti-Aryan, anti-north or anti-Sanskrit image.

C. AGRARIAN UNREST OR PEASANT MOVEMENTS

Agrarian Unrest is Not a Recent Phenomenon

"Rural India, contrary to the general belief, is not inert. It is seething with discontent and conflicts. The old stable social structure of the village community with its varied institutions had experienced a severe jolt during the British period and is undergoing a very rapid, almost hectic transformation after independence. The impact of elections based on universal franchise, of increasing competitive profit-oriented production by peasants and of the emergence of various new institutions and associations - political, economic, social and administrative, on various classes and castes, has resulted in a mobility and created a tension which is, in its intensity and depth, unparalleled in the history of Indian rural society."[1]

Agrarian unrest or peasant unrest is not a new phenomenon in India for it has been in existence since a couple of decades. As **Bipin Chandra** has pointed out peasant movements had been a part of national movement against the British supremacy. Even now the unrest has not subsided in spite of various rural development activities and programmes. The growth of green revolution and the spread of education along with the development of agriculture have only added to the problem. The tribals who have taken to agriculture of late have also started asserting their rights and demanding the government to concede their demands. Since agriculture and land are regarded as state-subjects, the issue of *"agrarian unrest"* is to be taken up and handled carefully by the state governments. It is a known fact that a number of issues related to the peasantry of our country are not settled and still hold their sway. As **S.L. Desai** and **P.C. Jain** have pointed out *"the root of peasant unrest, therefore, lies in the social structure of the peasantry, its history and processes of agricultural modernisation."*[2]

Concept of Agrarian Unrest

Rural sociologists have tried to analyse the phenomenon of "agrarian unrest" in their own way. ***For example,*** **N.G. Ranga** uses the expression *"struggle of the peasantry"* to refer to the agrarian unrest. **A.R. Desai** also uses the term *"peasant struggle"* to refer to the *agrarian unrest.* **Kathleen Gough** terms it as *"peasant uprising",* while **Hamza Alavi** prefers to use the expression *"peasant revolution."* According to the Marxian sociologists, it represents a type of *"class struggle"* or *"class war."* **Prof. D.N. Dhanagare** from a liberal view point considers the peasant agitation a *"peasant movement."*

Agrarian Unrest - A Concept With a Wide Meaning

As **Prof. H.V. Nagesh** has pointed out, the expression *"agrarian unrest"* could be used as a broad concept to include in itself various types of struggles which are often described as - *agrarian*

---

1 **A.R. Desai** *"Rural Sociology in India"* - 5th Edition [1990]. Page 389.

2 **S.L. Doshi** and **P.C. Jain** *"Rural Sociology"* [1999]. Page - 223.

revolution, farmer's revolt, farmer's agitation, peasant movement, farmer's strikes, etc. But, farmer's agitations which are more *"fundamental"* and widely spread over as witnessed in the nations such as Soviet Russia, Communist China, Cuba, Mexico, Algeria, Vietnam, etc., can better be termed as *"peasant revolutions."* Peasant revolutions are normally full-fledged struggles and they are intended to bring about changes which are not just agricultural but more fundamental.

A Few Agitations Representing Agrarian Unrest

Not only in foreign countries but also in India, some of the peasant agitations have taken place in different places mostly for one or the other local causes. Some of these agitations are branded or labelled as *"farmers' revolts", "farmers' strike", "peasant revolution", "peasant movements",* and so on. While some of these had taken place prior to Independence and a few others took place after the Independence. Some of them are mentioned below.

Peasant Movements in Pre-Independent India

During the first quarter of the 20th century, the peasant movements became much more violent in India. These movements were deeply influenced by the struggle for national freedom. Peasants of the country began to develop political consciousness only after 1918. They started taking part in national struggles and rose in revolt with their own problems. It is also true that a few of the peasant movements also had taken place before 1918. The hardships and misery caused mostly by the severe famines that gripped the country especially between 1870 and 1900 triggered a few of the agitations. Some of them were targeted against the Zamindars, money-lenders and the government. Of the various struggles, which the Indian peasants had undertaken prior to the Independence, the following may be noted as significant ones.

1. Santhal Insurrection [1855-56].
2. Peasant Revolt in Punjab [1930].
3. Champaran [Bihar] Movement [1917-18].
4. Kheda Peasant Struggle [1918].
5. The Bardoli Satyagraha [1920].
6. Moplah Rebellion in Malabar [1921].

Peasant Movements After Independence

Of the peasant movements that took place after independence the following may be noted:

1. Telangana Peasant Struggle [1947-51].
2. Naxalbari Peasant Struggle [1967].

Present Peasant Struggles Under the Leadership of Peasant Organisations

Peasant struggles have not become a thing of the past. They are still in currency. But they have taken an organisational form today. Some of the peasant struggles are controlled by some well established organisations, whereas a few others are controlled by some powerful leaders. A few examples of such struggles are cited below.

1. *"Bharatiya Kisan Union"* [BKU] led by Mahendra Singh Tikayat of U.P.
2. *"Karnataka Rajya Raita Sangh"* led by Prof. M.D. Nanjunda Swamy.
3. *"Bharatiya Kisan Union"* led by Ajmir Singh Lekanlal, Babir Singh Rajawal and Bhupinder Sing Man of Gujarat.

4. *"Tamilnadu Farmers' Sangha"* [TVS] led by Narayan Swamy Naidu.
5. *"Shetkari Organisation"* led by Sharad Joshi of Maharashtra.

Types of Peasant Struggles

Though the peasant struggles were taking place in India for the past 225 years they are not uniform in nature. The *Santal insurrection* [1855-56] was of one variety whereas the *Bardoli Satyagraha* [1920] represented another variety. The *Naxalbari peasant struggle* was actually a violent armed struggle. In the *Mopla Rebellion of Malabar* [1921] there was the influence of Muslim religious leaders. The *Champaran Movement* [1917-18] which was led by Gandhiji was absolutely a peaceful non-violent struggle. It is in this manner the peasant struggles in India differ significantly depending upon their purpose, ideology, organisational base, working style, etc.

Kathleen Gough's Classification of Peasant Struggles

Kathleen Gough in one of her articles, has classified peasant agitations or struggles into five important categories, which are mentioned below.

1. Restorative Rebellions.
2. Religious Movements.
3. Social Banditry.
4. Terrorist Vengeance.
5. Mass Insurrections.

Dr. Dhanagare, a renowned Indian sociologist has added the 6th variety to this list, which is mentioned below.

6. Liberal Reformist Movements.

1. Restorative Rebellions

These types of struggles though appeared to be intending to drive away the British from the Indian soil, their basic purpose was different. They virtually had the intention of re-establishing monarchy or kingship and the associated social system. Agitations of this type usually consist of an attempt on the part of the agitators to fight for the restoration of the one time existed privileges, statuses, etc. They were very rarely initiated to fight against the foreign domination. ***Example*:** Santal Insurrection. The Santals fought against the British not very much for driving them away from India, but for restoring their traditional rights. According to Kathleen Gough, as many as 29 such rebellions took place in India prior to the national freedom struggle of 1857.

2. Religious Movements

Many a times, agitations took place in India with the guidance and sometimes with the active leadership of religious leaders. People joined these agitations with the belief that there would be the re-establishment of *"Rama Rajya"*, wherein social equality, justice and brotherhood would be assured for all. ***Example*:** The Mopla Muslims of Malabar, for example, revolted against the Hindu landlords and also the British, from 1836 to 1921 at least 50 times under the leadership of **Thangal**, a local Muslim religious leader.

3. Social Banditry

"Social Banditry" represents a type of social oriented robberies in which the leaders plunder and loot the property of the rich and later on claim to distribute it among the poor. ***Example,*** the banditry led by Narasimha Reddy of Karnool in Andhra Pradesh; the dacoity carried on by a few of the Kollar Community in Madras; the Sanyasi-Fakir banditry that took place in Bengal - can be mentioned here as examples.

4. Terrorist Vengeance

Agitations or struggles in which the agitators make a frontal attack on the opponents who are regarded as their enemies, belong to this category. Capturing the people who are dubbed as enemies, torturing and tyrannising and finally killing them, and such other violent activities are common here. Agitations of this kind are different from that of other categories for there is a scope for violence and armed revolt. ***Examples***: Naxalite agitations and agitations conducted by the Marxist extremists known as *"People's War Group"*, etc.

5. Mass Insurrections

Agitations which are called *"mass insurrections"* take place suddenly and come to an end abruptly. They take place as *"mass explosions."* They erupt out of the prolonged problems for which solutions are not found out. These explosions take place sometimes as an attempt to find solutions for these long pending problems. ***Examples***: The so called *"Deccan revolts"* that took place in Poona, Ahmed Nagar, Satara, Solapur belong to this category. These types of agitations suddenly arise without having any leader or any organisational base. When once they breakout they start spreading in different directions. Whenever they get a solution, however temporary it may be, the agitations may come to a sudden end. Sometimes, such agitations are suppressed with political heavy handedness.

6. Liberal Reformist Movements

These liberal movements which may not be of any use in bringing out any basic changes in society often prove to be useful in removing some of the dangerous or at least harmful laws / legislations. There is no scope for the use of violence, bloodshed or atrocities. These agitations / movements do not have the intention of creating any conflict or enmity between different communities. In some respects these may prove to be movements launched in support of status quo. ***Examples,*** peasant agitations staged under the leadership of Gandhiji, Sardar Patel, such as *"Champaran Satyagriha"*, *"Bardoli Satyagriha"*, *"Kheda Satyagriha"* in Bihar, Gujarat, etc.

Causes of Agrarian Unrest or Peasant Struggles

Agrarian unrest is not an unfamiliar thing in India. In a traditional society like India, peasant struggles have been taking place for the past 225 years. In spite of the expressed views of **Barrington Moore** and others - that Indian peasants are basically traditionalists, and god-fearing people who are tied down tightly to the caste system and hence cannot float any type of peasant struggles - these struggles have taken place. As **Kathleen Gough** has pointed out, upto 1912, as many as 77 major peasant revolts had taken place out of which 34 revolts were initiated by the different Hindu castes themselves. **S.R. Maheshwari** too has expressed the opinion that after Independence, particularly after 1960s, large number of peasant struggles took place and about 65% of them were found to be violent. These struggles clearly reveal that our rural development programmes and activities have failed to bring about peace and harmony in the rural areas. Hence it is necessary to find out an explanation for the serious issue of increasing instances of agrarian unrest in peasant struggles after Independence. Agrarian unrest was there even during the Mughal period and afterwards during the British rule. Even after Independence they have been alive and are taking new dimensions. Number of factors have contributed to this unrest among which the following may be noted.

1. *Feeling of Relative Deprivation* : During the British rule, *zamindars, jahgirdars, inamdars,* and higher level government officials and the rich in general enjoyed several facilities and privileges. The common people, including the ordinary peasants, were deprived of such privileges. The feeling of relative deprivation made these peasants agitated and disillusioned.

2. *Foreign Invasion, Atrocities and Exploitation* : Prior to our independence, foreign invasions, atrocities and exploitation of different kinds had instigated our people to fight against such things. The spirit of patriotism was also there in these struggles. The peasants too had joined hands with other people to fight against the British officials, their agents and their henchmen.

3. *Destruction of Cottage Industries of the Farmers* : The industrial system of economy and the factory system of production, introduced by the British, led to the destruction of cottage and home industries of our farmers. Many of the handicrafts, home industries, in which children, women, and even old people could take part, had to be stopped because of the unfavourable import and export policy of the British.

4. *Exploitation of the Tribals* : The tribals, who were leading a peaceful life in the midst of forests and mountainous regions, were not only disturbed but were even exploited by the British. The Munda, Oraon, Chauri, Ho, Kola, Tamara of the Bihar region; the Koli and the Varli of Maharashtra; Khasi, Dafla, Lusha, Kukinaga of Assam; Khoya, Palegara, Gondakolan of Andhra Pradesh; Bhil and Nayika of Gujarat; Juvanga and Khonda of Orissa; Dhundia of Karnataka; and many other agricultural tribal communities, which were exploited by the British, had revolted against the British.

5. *Coercion Exercised to Grow Commercial Crops* : Some of the zamindars, plantation owners and British supported jahgirdars brought heavy pressure on the farmers to grow commercial crops, such as cotton, jute, rubber, coffee, indigo, sugarcane, etc. They never looked into the farmers willingness and the convenience in growing these crops, but just imposed their will on them. Farmers, who were upset by this kind of pressure and coercion, were ready for any kind of a fight against their bosses. The explosion of Bengal indigo growers agitation is an example in this regard.

6. *Increasing Burden of Debt* : Economic incapacity and increase in debt also made the Indian farmers become restless. The farmers were deprived of various sources from which they could earn money. This situation even led to the unwanted system of *'bonded labour'*. Farmers, who had borrowed money had to pay heavy debts. Money lenders and zamindars who had given loans to the farmers charged exhorbitant rate of interest. In fact, revolts such as *"Deccan Revolt"* sparked off against such heavy rate of interest.

7. *Increasing Number of the Landless and the Unemployed*: Various tribal farmers and low caste Hindus, who had possessed some pieces of land, had to surrender the same to the landlords, zamindars and money lenders, due to their failure to repay the debt. This led to an enormous increase in the number of landless labourers and unemployed people. For instance, in 1961, of the total number of labourers, 22% constituted agricultural labourers; and in 1971, this number increased to 37%. Rural unemployment, poverty and dissatifaction in general, contributed to rural unrest.

8. *Organising Power of the Farmers* : Farmers started organising themselves in order to safeguard their interests. Accordingly, many farmers' organisations, such as *sugarcane growers' organisation, tobacco growers' organisation, coffee growers' organisation,* came to be established. Organisations of this kind arose in different parts of the country asserting the farmers' rights.

9. *Illegal Eviction of the Tenants* : Large number of the tenants, who were forcibly evicted from the land which they had been cultivating, were forced to join the farmers' agitation. Some of them had even taken part in *'land grab movements'*. For example, in 1970 around 12,000 farmers in

Tamil Nadu, and 6,000 farmers in Andhra Pradesh, were arrested for having taken part in such movements.

10. *Anti-Farmers' Measures of the Government* : Many a times Central as well as State Governments take decisions without taking into consideration the interests of the farmers. For example, in revising the electricity rates, prices of fertilisers and interest rates on farmers' loans, water tax, etc. the State Governments have often offended the interests of the farmers.

11. *Increasing Political Awareness and the Village Becoming the Hot Bed of Politics* : Political ideology and political commitments and affiliation with the political parties have also inspired farmers' agitation. The recent political developments have brought about greater political consciousness among the farmers. This consciousness has very often made them to make a collective effort to protect their interests. The villages, which have hither to been away from politics, have now become the hot bed of politics. Political parties working at the state as well as national level have got their own *Kissan* [farmers'] wings. These political parties have often themselves instigated farmers' agitations.

12. *Use of Modern Technology* : The introduction of rapid means of transport and communication have helped the farmers to organise themselves in a better manner to fight for their rights and to protect their interests.

Conclusion

It is clear from the above description that the farmers' unrest or agrarian unrest in India has been caused by various factors. The various economic and political developments that have taken place at the national and international levels, especially during 1990s, have caused new anxieties, fears and threats for the farming community. The economic processes of liberalisation, privatisation and globalisation have only added to the helplessness of the farmers. Indian farmers at the beginning of the 21st century, are faced with the toughest challenges. They are not able to compete with their counterparts in the West and also in the developed nations and are thereby suffering a great deal. They have demanded the Governments to fix the minimum prices for their produces. For example, farmers of Karnataka have demanded the Government recently to fix the minimum price for their produces, such as, arecanut, coffee, rubber, copra, etc. A large number of the Indian farmers who depend only on agriculture are now finding themselves in a very difficult situation. In this context, it seems that farmers' agitations are bound to aggravate.

INDIGO GROWERS' AGITATION / MOVEMENT

• Indigo Growers' Agitation : The First Agitation of Indian Farmers

Among the various agitations, which the Indian farmers have staged, the Bengal Indigo Growers' Agitation assumes historic importance. This agitation can be considered the first agitation or struggle or strike led by Indian farmers. This agitation broke out in 1860 in Bengal, about 60 years prior to the *"Champaran Strike"* that was led by Gandhiji in Bihar. The farmers of Bengal for the first time rose in revolt against their exploitation and suppression. Without resorting to violence, they were able to register their protest against the plantation owners, mostly the British, and the local zamindars.

Background of Indigo Growers' Agitation

Behind the Bengal indigo growers' agitation, there is a long story of peasant exploitation. Its brief description is given here.

About 150 years ago, there was no practice of manufacturing and using blue powder or liquid to whiten the white clothes that we wear. On the contrary, there was the practice of preparing the blue out of a bush plant called *"indigo fera."* Since there was no alternative for this plant product, there was a very good demand for it in the European market. Since, the cotton textile industries in Britain were making use of this blue in the manufacture of white clothes, it was highly profitable to produce and sell it. Hence, Indian farmers were pursuaded, pressurised and compelled to grow this plant. Though the farmers were made to grow this indigo, they were not given any extra benefit for that. Nor any share of the profit of selling this indigo went to the farmers. The indigo growers of Bengal region started feeling that they were being exploited in this issue. This feeling of exploitation, on the one hand, and various atrocities committed against them on the other, contributed to what is known as *"Indigo Growers' Agitation."*

- ***Craze for Indigo Crop*** : Since, growing indigo was highly profitable the *East India Company* and its retired officials started acquiring and even purchasing fields in which indigo was being grown, and made the farmers work as wage-earners for growing indigo. These people also started purchasing land from the local *zamindars* and started making arrangements to grow indigo in these lands. The American brokers, who were selling the Negroes in the European market, also joined hands with the British officials in this trade. These officials and traders compelled the farmers to grow indigo and indigo only. Growing indigo and preparing blue from the plant was a very laborious and unpleasant task. For undertaking this strenuous task, the farmers were given no extra remuneration. The plantation owners brought in all sorts of pressure and even used coercive techniques to make the farmers grow indigo. In fact, the indigo crop was proving to be a golden egg for the plantation owners, but the farmers got no profit out of it.

The Mounting Exploitation of the Farmers

The Bengal indigo growers were reduced to the level of European slaves. They had no courage to oppose the plantation owners, nor could they resort to other employment avenues. Hence, they were inevitably trapped into the games of these plantation owners. Those who opposed these owners, were subject to ill treatment, violence and cruelty. Those, who had received loans at the hands of these plantation owners and failed to return the same with due interest on the promised date, were sent to jails. When this exploitation reached beyond tolerable limits, the farmers started protesting it. The farmers, who were growing indigo in different places of Bengal region, complained to the British Government about these atrocities and suppressions. The Hindu and Muslim farmers joined hands forgeting their differences in protesting against the plantation owners' atrocities. The Commissioner of Nadia region himself made an enquiry into these complaints and submitted a report to the Secretary of the Government of Bengal. He had cautioned the Bengal administration about the manner in which indigo growers were getting themselves organised to protest against their exploitation.

The Beginning of the Agitation - 1860

Indian farmers of Barasath sub-division of Bengal blew the trumpet of the first Indian peasant strike in the year 1860. The farmers of this sub-division collected together and took a unanimous decision that *they would never grow indigo.* In Ninasapur, thousands of farmers from the nearby **52** villages collected together and *gherao*ed the blue manufacturing factory. They encircled the military official, who had arrived there to give protection to the factory. The farmers shouted slogans against the plantation owners, factory owners, British traders, British administrators and also against the British Government. They were giving ventilation to their pains, sufferings, agonies, exploitations, etc. Even though the atmosphere of the agitation was very tense, the farmers never lost their patience nor they resorted to any kind of violence.

The message of Ninaspur agitation reached various other places of Bengal, such as, Jessore, Khulna, Rajashahi, Dacca, Malda, Dinajpur, etc. wherein farmers were growing indigo. Entire Bengal was awakened and the plantation owners received a shock. They felt as though the entire Europeans were faced with a danger in Bengal region. They suggested and appealed to Bengal Government to arrest, punish and suppress the farmers, who were taking part in the agitation. The Government, which had a bitter experience in using force against the Santal Revolt, decided not to use force once again. They knew that sizeable number of farmers had taken part in the 1857 freedom struggle. They never wanted to give an opportunity to them to convert this farmers' agitation into a freedom struggle. Added to that, a few of the freedom fighters had already joined these farmers' agitations. Reports started pouring into Bengal about the various protests made by the Indian citizens in several parts of the nation against the suppression of the Bengal farmers. At this juncture, the Government wanted to take a decision at the earliest and settle the issue. The Government instituted an *enquiry commission* and assured the farmers that justice would be given to them and their interests would be safeguarded.

Victory of the First Peasant Struggle : Farmers, who appeared before the enquiry commission, boldly justified their decisions and actions. They reiterated that they would never grow indigo for the sake of European traders. They also brought to the notice of the commission about the unjustifiable atrocities committed against them by the plantation owners and others. In the meantime, the European Christian Missionaries, who were carrying on their missionary activities, also received a mild shock by this agitation. In a sarcastic manner, the agitators suggested to the missionaries that they should first preach Jesus Christ's message of love, peace and compassion to the Europeans. Since the entire episode had damaged the interests of the British imperialism and their religion Christianity, they decided not to resort to coercive measures, but to accept the stand of agitators. Thus, the indigo growers obtained glorious victory in their agitation.

What is very significant with regard to this agitation is that, no all-India level leader had taken part in this. There was no big publicity for this, even in the Congress circle. It was not a well organised agitation like the Champaran Agitation or the Bardoli Satyagraha or the Kheda Satyagraha. It assumes importance in the history of the peasant struggles in India, because it was the first of its kind and also because it obtained a jubiliant victory for the farmers.

NAXALBARI MOVEMENT - 1967 : A Violent Peasant Agitation

The ***Naxalbari peasant struggle / agitation*** was launched in March - April 1967 in a place called ***Naxalbari*** that belongs to Darjeeling district of West Bengal. The Naxalbari region, all of a sudden attracted the attention of the world in 1967 by giving rise to the Naxalite Armed Struggle. Various newspapers of the world gave publicity to it in the front pages, radios broadcasted the news with a big bang. The Peking Radio, for example, called it the *"Beacon light for the revolutionary struggle in India."* The Chinese newspaper *"People's Daily"* in its editorial dated 5th July 1967 referred to this peasant struggle as *"A peal of spring thunder crashed over the land of India."* This Naxalbari revolt spread to almost **82** square mile area in a record speed. Various tribals, such as Santals, Oraons, Mundas, etc. numbering around 42,000 had taken part in this agitation. These tribals, who were residing in forests, tea plantations, and agricultural lands, were made to go out of the land in which they were living, and pay heavy interests for the loans that they had borrowed from the money-lenders. Conflicts were going on regularly between the forest officials on the one hand, and the tribals on the other. The entire peasant community in this Himalayan region, spread over more than **60** villages of the Darjeeling district, was totally agitated. Their dissatisfaction and frustration culminated in the Naxalbari Agitation of 1967.

Movement with a Difference : The Naxalbari agitation is totally different from those of the peasant agitations, which had taken place earlier. The main reason was that various political purposes were clubbed together in this movement. In fact, *"The prime objective of this movement was to change the whole society, not the conditions of the peasants only. Then the Naxalbari movement was highly charged by the ideology of violence. The idiom of the movement was that power comes from the barrel of the gun and not by slogans and non-violence. The movement was aimed at the total annihilation of the big farmers, landlords and jahgirdars. Nothing short of it could change the structure of the society."*[1]

'Naxalbari' is a police sub-station in the Darjeeling district of West Bengal. It is in the name of the police sub-station that the movement is known all over. At a later stage, it took an ideological flavour. Naxalite leaders like **Charu Majumdar, Kanu Sanyal, Punjab Rao, Jungal Santhal, Kumar Kishan, Jail Singh, Vinod Mitra,** and others had played a key role in this movement. These leaders had taken up the cause of the farmers only to fulfil their political objective of capturing power through armed struggle. *The main feature of this agitation is that the farmers never fought for their land nor for a better price for their products; but, they fought for political power.* This was the opinion of Charu Majumdar, the main architect behind this agitation.

Causes for the Naxalbari Agitation

Various political, economic, and other factors have contributed to the Naxalbari agitation. A brief explanation of these factors is given below:

(i) *Economic Dissatisfaction* : Economic dissatisfaction is said to be the primary cause of this agitation. The tribals of this region were comparatively poorer in relation to the farmers in other areas. Even though, their population was increasing, they were not able to feed the growing population due to the poor productivity.

(ii) *Demand for Reasonable Distribution of Benami Lands* : Another cause that led to this movement was the demand for the regulation and distribution of *benami* lands in an appropriate way. The zamindars, landlords and money-lenders had forcibly acquired the lands of the tribals and poor farmers, who had taken heavy loan, but failed to repay the same. These people had transferred the ownership rights of these acquired lands into the names of some anonymous people. The leaders of the agitation wanted the proper redistribution of these lands.

(iii) *Nationalisation of the Forests* : When the State Government started nationalising the forests, tribals of this region were deprived of their right over forests and to collect and enjoy forest products. It became an offence to cut the wooden logs and collect forest products without the permission of the Government. Tribals who were resorting to shifting cultivation had to stop it. In a way, the tribals had become refugees and parasites in their own original homeland.

(iv) *Partiality of the Judiciary* : The judiciary of this region was charged of being partial towards the landlords and money-lenders. The poor farmers and tribals, known as the *praja*, felt that they would never get justice at the hands of the judiciary.

(v) *Exploitation by the Money-lenders* : The tribals in their attempt to find a solution to their economic difficulties, approached the landlords and got into their traps. These landlords levied exorbitant rate of interest and made the tribals mortgage their lands with them. When the tribals

1 **S.L. Doshi** and **P.C. Jain** *"Rural Sociology."* Page - 256.

failed to repay the debts with interests the landlords confiscated their lands mortgaged with them. Thus, the tribals who lost the ownership of the land got terribly disappointed.

(vi) *Removal of Peasants from the "Bhakshis Land"* : When the tribal agriculturists started agitating against the landlords with the help of communist extremists, the landlords resorted to another technique. The landlords used to give some land as *Bhakshis* land to the agricultural labourers for the services rendered by them. Now the landlords started insisting on these agricultural labourers to return the *Bhakshis* land. They even resorted to violence in evicting the tribal agricultural labourers from the *Bhakshis* land. This virtually led to the direct clash between the *adivasis* on the one hand, and landlords on the other.

(vii) *Propaganda of the Marxist Extremists* : The Naxalbari movement was admittedly a movement of the peasants, but above all, a major cause of the movement was the class war, between the big farmers [landlords] and the ordinary peasants [mostly the tribals]. The communist extremists took the opportunity of fanning the fire of tribal dissatisfaction. They carried on a powerful propaganda in that region that only through armed struggle the tribals could get justice. They even gave a call to the ordinary peasants and tribals to loot the food stocks lying in the Government godowns and also the food stocks of the landlords.

(viii) *Role of Farmers' Organisations* : When the West Bengal Government started implementing *Land Ceiling Act* in a strict manner, the zamindars resorted to the manipulation of land records and *benami* transfers. The farmers who got disillusioned with that approached the *Krishik Samithi* of the Communist Party and started organising themselves to fight back. The *Krishik Samithi,* which was working in the area since 1951, launched its *land grab movement* in the year 1967, which was supported by a large number of tribals and ordinary peasants. This incident virtually paved the way for the Naxalbari movement.

Situation that Triggered the Naxalite Agitation

An incident that took place in May 1967 in the Naxalbari region of West Bengal, virtually triggered the Naxalbari revolt. When a landlord tried to evict a poor farmer from his farm house, in spite of the judicial protection, which he had obtained, the other farmers in the area got infuriated and forcibly stopped the process of eviction. More or less at the same time, similar incident took place in the plantation field of a plantation owner. There also the farmers had physically protested against the eviction process and guarded the interests of the afflicted poor farmers. When the police rushed to the spot, the farmers stopped them on the way. Strong verbal exchanges took place between the police and the farmers. When the situation became tense, there took place a violent incident which cost the life of a police officer. The very next day, the police rushed to the spot with heavy reinforcement and fired recklessly killing atleast **9** people and causing lot of injuries, even to women, children and old people. This episode instigated the community of the farmers in that region, which led to Naxalbari revolt.

The Naxalbari revolt was actually a movement mobilised against the landed, propertied class. It can be safely said that the broad based peasantry, inclusive of all its strata, was involved in this struggle. The violent leaders of the movement went to the extent of killing a money-lender within the jurisdiction of Naxalbari police station. This murder was followed by a series of other murders, and one after another the *jotedars, sahukars* were killed by the participants of the movement.

The revolt was spread to the whole area of Naxalbari region. Farmers from different villages of that region responded to it positively. They started executing the orders of communist naxalite leaders, such as Charu Majumdar, Kanu Sanyal, Punjab Rao and others. They started looting the houses of the zamindars with the help of communist workers and distributed the grains and other things to the poor people. They even tore into pieces the promissory notes, documents relating to the loans obtained, and captured schools and panchayaths into their hands. They even formed a security force comprising of the local youngsters to give protection to the farmers. The message of the movement was given through several slogans. In course of time, the movement got ablaze in different parts of West Bengal. The college students, including girls, participated in this movement. The movement, thus posed itself to be not only a movement of peasants, but also of the society at large.

This incident and the struggles going on in this region, secured wide publicity in the media, both within India and in the foreign countries. The Marxist Communists started making tall claims and said that the Naxalbari agitation was a model to the whole nation. Mao-Tse-Tung, the then President of Communist China, also declared his open support to this revolt. But the Communist Party of India [CPI], which was the ruling party of West Bengal at that time and supported by Communist Russia, took this as a prestige issue. The Central Government also expressed its total dissatisfaction about the way in which the agitation was handled by the State Government.

The West Bengal Government, which was upset by the Naxalbari developments, finally decided to suppress the movement. It resorted to police action and started arresting the leaders of the movement. Punjab Rao, Charu Majumdar, Pancham Sarkar, Kanu Sanyal, and most of the leaders were kept behind bars. The leaderless movement could not be persuaded. It came to an end within a short period of time. Though there was no immediate gain of the struggle, it definitely influenced the course of peasant movements of the country. The Naxalbari movement was a specific struggle, ideologically oriented to Marxian Socialism. The rank and file of the Communist Party [Marxist] had taken part in this agitaion. The agitation was a big failure because of various factors.

Causes for the Failure of Naxalbari Movement

Various factors contributed to the failure of the Naxalbari movement. Some of them may be noted here.

1. *Selfish Political Interests* : The Communist extremists had taken undue advantage of this agitation *to subserve their selfish political interests.* Their prematured decisions resulted in its failure.

2. *Too Much Faith in Violence* : The movement unfortunately went into the hands of naxalite communist leaders like Charu Majumdar, Panchnam Sarkar, Kanu Sanyal, and others, who had faith only in armed revolts. When the agitators obtained initial victory, they jumped to the conclusion, the whole of West Bengal and later on the whole of the country would stand by them and support their cause.

3. *Lack of Consensus Among the Leaders* : Misunderstandings and the personal maladjustments that existed among the leaders of the Naxalbari movement also caused its failure. Within the time span of 5 years, its leadership got divided into several factions.

4. *Illusion of Heralding a Revolution* : The leaders of the movement were under the illusion that they were spearheading a revolution, which would bring about overall changes in the society. They failed to safeguard the interests of ordinary peasants and tribals, who stood with them all the way through the revolts. Virtually they had forgotten the very purpose of the movement.

5. *Too Ambitious a Movement* : The "........... *Naxalbari movement was like other movements of the country, it did not stand for or put the demand for structural changes in the old feudal system.*

Instead, the movement, ideologically and operationally too, stood for a systemic change which could end exploitation and operation inherent in the semifeudal system."[1]

Conclusion

Though the Naxalbari episode came to an end by July 13th, 1967, naxalites as such have been carrying on their struggles in different places of the country. For example, in Srikakulam of Andhra Pradesh [1970], Midnapur and Purulia of West Bengal [1969], Kerala [1968], Muzafferpur, Dharbhang, Singhbhum of Bihar [1968-69], Lakhinpur-Khed forest areas of U.P., Golpara, Kamaroop, Nadia, Virbhum of Assam and in other places the naxalites had staged their armed revolts at different times. In course of time, the naxalite struggles spread to urban areas also. The naxalite struggles are still going on here and there, wherever the extremist - leftist communists are powerful. But today, they rarely remain as agrarian struggles.

Some Observations Relating to Peasant Struggles

Various peasant struggles / agrarian agitations, farmers revolts/ satyagrahas have taken place in different places of India, both before and after independence. An analysis of these agitations or struggles help us to make the following observations.

1. ***Most of the Farmers' Agitations Are Caste Based*** **:** It has been observed that most of the peasant struggles that are taking place in India today, are the struggles staged not by the deprived and exploited landless labourers or untouchables or tribals, for the real benefit of the peasant community. On the other hand, most of these struggles are caste-based.

2. ***Peasant Struggles Floated to Protect the Interests of the Rich Farmers*** **:** It is also observed that the rich farmers, ex-jahgirdars and ex-zamindars are behind the contemporary peasant struggles. These struggles are mobilised to fulfil the vested interests of the better off segments of the country.

3. ***The Present Peasant Struggles Rarely Protect the Interests of the Poor Farming Community*** **:** The study of contemporary peasant struggles reveals that the demands of the peasant struggles revolve around the interests of the rich farmers who have marketable surplus. It is this segment of the peasantry which has become caste conscious. These [rich] farmers demand remunerative prices for their produce. These agitations or struggles rarely take up the causes of the poorest sections of the farming community.

4. ***Greater Influence of Left-Oriented Political Parties on These Agitations*** **:** It is also observed that a large number of peasant struggles are either instigated or supported by left-oriented political parties. The objective of these parties is to gain political power by mobilising the peasant masses as their support base. Now there is a claim that the national politics in India has been dominated by urban leadership and hence time is ripe for providing such leadership to the rural based leaders.

5. ***Peasant Struggles as a Reaction to Exploitation, Persecution and Atrocities*** **:** It is argued that the present day ills of the country manifesting themselves in poverty, famine, unemployment and economic inflation can be solved only by a peasant backed revolution. As **Kathleen Gough** has pointed out that the peasantry in India is not passive today and for more than 200 years, *"it has repeatedly arisen against landlords, revenue agents and other bureaucrats, money-lenders, police and military forces. The uprisings were responses to relative deprivation of unusually severe character, always economic, and often also involving physical brutality or ethnic persecution."*[2]

1 **S.L. Doshi** and **P.C. Jain** *"Rural Sociology."* Page - 259.

2 **Kathleen Gough** as quoted by **Doshi** and **Jain.** Page - 262.

Chapter 12

TRIBAL LIFE IN INDIA

*TRIBE : Its Other Equivalent Terms and Usages - Definition of Tribe - Limitations of the Anthropological Definition of Indian Tribe- Characteristics of Tribe - Tribals' Relationship with Hinduism - Tribe and Caste : Differences - Tribe and Clan : Differences - Geographic Distribution of Tribals in India - Difficulties Involved in Estimating Tribal Population - The Tribal Zones : The North and North-Eastern Zone, The Central or the Middle Zone, The Southern Zone, The Small Zone Consisting of Andaman and Nicobar Islands- B.K. Roy Burman's Classification of Tribes - Elwin's Classification Based on Cultural Difference and Development - Contact of the Tribals With Civilisation - Adivasis Under the Influence of Caste ? - Effects and Problems Due to the Contact With the Civilisation - **Problems of the Scheduled Tribes** - Tribal Movements : Causes of Tribal Unrest and Discontent - Measures for the Upliftment of Scheduled Tribes - Three Views to Solve Tribal Problems : Policy of Isolation, Policy of Assimilation, Policy of Integration - The Tribal Panchasheela- Tribal Welfare Programmes and Projects- Brief Assessment of the Welfare Programmes : Their Deficiencies and Failures - **The Changing Face of the Tribal Life.***

The tribal communities represent an important social category of Indian social structure. The tribals are said to be the original inhabitants of India. India is a country of multiracial stock. Different types of groups occupy different parts of India, having their own cultural characteristics and levels of development. A number of groups are still in primitive stage and they are very often referred to as *"tribals", "primitives", "adivasis"* and so on. The tribal population in India, according to the 1991 census, was **67.76** million. This was almost equal to the population of Britain. At present, India has the second largest tribal population in the world next only to Africa. Tribals in India are spread over the length and breadth of the country.

"Tribes" in the Indian context today are normally referred to in the language of the Constitution as *"Scheduled Tribes."* It was **Dr. B.R. Ambedkar**, the chairman of the drafting committee of the constitution, who preferred the concept of Scheduled Tribe to *"Adivasis"* for it enumerates the tribes and hence has a specific meaning. The *"Scheduled Tribes"* constitute the second largest group of the backward classes that come under what is known as the *"unprivileged section"* of the populace. The scheduled tribes, generally known as *"tribes"*, constitue **8.8%** of the total population [1991 census report] of India. The tribal people who are regarded as the earliest among the present inhabitants of India have survived here with their unchanging ways of life for centuries. Many of them are still in a primitive stage and are far from the impact of modern civilization.

TRIBE : Its Other Equivalent Terms and Usages

The term *"scheduled tribe"* or *"tribe"* has been explained variously. For example, *Scheduled Area* and *Scheduled Tribes Commissioner,* in this regard observes – *"The term "tribe" is nowhere defined in the Constitution and, in fact, there is no satisfactory definition anywhere. To the ordinary man the word suggests simple folk living in hills and forests; to people who are a little better informed, it signifies a colourful people famous for their dance and song; to an administrator it means a group of citizens who are the special responsibilities of the President of India; to an anthropologist it indicates a special field for study of a social phenomenon. In their own way, all these impressions are correct. No standard term has been accepted to denominate the people who are classified as of tribal origin."*[1] S.C. Dube has also commented that *"the term tribe is used indiscriminately."* A few examples of the use of the term "tribe" can be cited in this regard.

1. Tribals are very commonly referred to as *"Adivasis".*
2. **Risley, V. Elwin** and others used the word *"aboriginals"* to mean tribals.
3. **Sir Bains**, a Census officer called the tribal community *"the Hill Tribes".*
4. **Dr. Hutton** preferred to use the term *"primitive tribes".*
5. **Takkar Bapa**, an indigenous social reformer, called the tribals *"Adi praja".*
6. **Dr. G.S. Ghurye**, a senior sociologist, called the tribals *'Backward Hindus'.*
7. **International Labour Organisation** [ILO] used the expression *"indigeneous people"* to refer to the tribals.
8. **M.K. Gandhiji** popularised the word *"Girijan."*
9. Tribes are also known as *"Vanavasis", "Aranyavasis", "Vanya Jatis"* etc.
10. **The Constitution of India** has accepted to use the term *"Scheduled Tribes"* [ST], which was introduced for the first time by ***Simon Commission*** in 1928.

[*Note*: In this book the terms such as Scheduled Tribes, Tribes, Adivasis and Girijans are used as synonymous terms]

The *"Backward Classes Commission"* which was asked to revise the list of the scheduled tribes, states that *"the scheduled tribes lead a separate excluded existence and are not fully assimilated in the main body of the people. Scheduled Tribes may belong to any religion. They are listed as scheduled tribes because of the kind of life led by them."* At another place it said that *"the scheduled tribes could be recognised by their way of living, the way of their living being peculiar."* [C.B. Mamoria. Page - 170.] This definition puts emphasis on the peculiarity of the mode of life.

There is no Definition but Reference only in the Constitution for the Term "Scheduled Tribe": The term *"tribe"* is nowhere defined in the Constitution. Though the Indian Constitution has not defined clearly the term *'tribe'*. Article 366 (25) of the Constitution says that Scheduled Tribes are the tribes or tribal communities or parts of or groups within such tribes or tribal communities which the Indian President may specify by public notification under Article 342(1).

It is relevant here to know the sociological meaning, definition and characteristics of the word *'tribe'* before studying the problems of the Scheduled Tribes and finding solutions for the same.

DEFINITION AND CHARACTERISTICS OF TRIBE

Definition of Tribe

There is no agreement among the sociologists and anthropologists regarding the definition of the term *"tribe."* Some of the definitions may be examined here:

1 C.B. Mamoria *"Social Problems and Social Disorganisation."* Page - 170.

1. D.N. Majumdar: A tribe is *"a collection of families bearing a common name, members of which occupy the same territory, speak the same language and observe certain taboos regarding marriage, profession or occupation and have developed a well assessed system of reciprocity and mutuality of obligation."*
2. Imperial Gazetteer of India: *A tribe is a collection of families bearing a common name, speaking a common dialect, occupying or professing to occupy a common territory and is not usually endogamous, though originally it might have been so."*
3. S.C. Dube: Tribe is *"an ethnic category, defined by real or putative descent and characterised by a corporate identity and a wide range of commonly shared traits of culture."*
4. Gillin and Gillin: *"A tribe is a group of local communities, which lives in a common area, speaks a common dialect and follows a common culture."*
5. W.J. Perry: A tribe can be defined as *"a group speaking a common dialect and inhabiting a common territory."*
6. **Andre Beteille**'s revised definition of a tribe runs like this : *"We have described the tribe as a society with a political, linguistic and a somewhat vaguely defined cultural boundary; further, as a society based upon kinship, where social stratification is absent."*

Limitations of the Anthropological Definition of Indian Tribe

Andre Beteille is of the opinion that when applied to the tribal situations in India the definitions mentioned above [including his own] appear to be inadequate in many respects. He identifies some of the limitations of the anthropological definition of a tribe when applied to the Indian tribes.

1. *No Separate Political Boundary* : No tribe in India has a completely separate political boundary. In some cases, in the NEFA for instance, a certain amount of political separateness has been retained within the wider structure. In most cases even this is absent. The larger *tribes of Chhota Nagpur,* the *Oraons* and the *Santals* are territorially dispersed. In several instances, the boundaries of different States cut across the tribal divisions.

2. *Changing Linguistic Boundary* : The linguistic boundary which is supposed to be more explicit, has also been gradually changing. The linguistic boundary has been relatively more explicit. But even this has been gradually changing. The *Bhils* who constitute one of the largest tribes in India, have been using a dialect of Hindi for many years. Several tribes in Middle and South India, speak Dravidian languages, which have close affinities with the languages spoken by the advanced communities of South India. The abandonment of tribal dialects in favour of one of the regional languages appears to have accelerated during the last few decades.

3. *Vague Cultural Boundary* : Cultural boundary of the tribe is also not explicit in the case of Indian tribes. In the culture of the tribal people there are many elements of continuity with the more advanced regional cultures. It cannot, therefore, be considered distinctive in a rigid and clear cut way. As Dube remarks : "Keeping in mind the cultural processes of India, where *"little traditions"* of the tribal people have gone into the making of the classical tradition of the land and where elements of the classical tradition have percolated back to the tribal people, the criteria of isolation and special cultural emphasis cannot be emphasized beyond a point."

4. *Vanishing Homogeneity of the Indian Tribe* : According to Beteille, even regarding the absence of stratification, the situation in India is distinctive. Large sections of tribal population have been entering into the productive system of the country. This has resulted in the breaking down of the homogenous nature of the tribal society. Some elements of stratification have been observed in most of the larger tribes of Chhota Nagpur and Central India.

According to him, therefore, in contemporary India, tribes which exhibit the features associated with the anthropologist's conception of the *"ideal type"* are rarely found. Hence Beteille remarks: *"In India, we cannot have a ready-made definition with which to go into the field and locate a tribe. The greatest emphasis has to be placed on an historical perspective. The process by which tribes have been transformed is an historical process. And only by going into the antecedents of a group can we say with any confidence whether or not it should be considered as a tribe."*[1]

CHARACTERISTICS OF TRIBE

Definitions of tribe cited above point out some of the characteristics of tribe. Tribal community including the tribals of India generally reveals some of the characteristics of which the following may be noted.

1. *Common Territory* : A tribe is a territorial community. It means the tribe has a definite territory in which its members reside. For example, the *Naga, Rengma Naga, Sema Naga* and other tribals reside in Nagaland; *Garos, Khasis, Khasas* live in Assam; *Bhils* in Madhyapradesh; *Soligas* in Mysore; *Thodas* in Niligiri Hills of Tamil Nadu, and so on. In the absence of a common locality or territory a tribe would lose its uniqueness.

2. *Collection of Families* : As the definitions of tribe cited above clarify, tribals constitute a collection of families. These collections may have various sizes. These families which normally have blood relationships among themselves could be matriarchal or patriarchal in nature.

3. *Common Name* : Every tribe has its own name. Each tribe is known to other tribes by its distinctive name. ***Example of some Indian Tribes*:** *Garo, Khasi, Khasa, Naga, Rengma Naga, Sema Naga, Limbu, Santal, Munda, Gond, Kota, Badaga, Urali, Thodas,* etc.

4. *Common Language* : The members of a tribe speak a particular language. Different tribes speak different languages. These languages are not only different from the language of the civilised people, but they themselves differ from one another. Common language contributes much to the development of community feeling. Since these languages do not have a script of their own, education of the tribals has become problematic.

5. *Common Ancestor* : The tribals claim that they have a common ancestor. A major cause of the sense of communal unity in the tribe is *"the tie of blood relationships"* between its members arising out of common ancestry. The tribals are bound by kinship bonds.

6. *Common Religion* : Religion plays an important role in the tribal organisation. The members of a tribe usually worship a common ancestor. Also, nature worship is common among them. In addition to the ***ancestral worship*** and ***nature worship*** the tribals practise other types of faith such as - ***fetishism, animism*** and ***totemism***.[2] Magic is also widespread among them. The tribal social and political organisations are based on this religion. Participation in common religious ceremonies,

---

1 Dr. M.A. Chingamani *"Sociology of Indian Society."* Pages : 281 - 282.

2 Fetishism is nothing but the adoration of material things because of their mysterious power. It is an attempt to find divine power or mysterious power in the fetishes or inanimate things such as a leaf, a feather, a horn, a stone or any such thing.

- Animism or Animatism: According to Tylor, animism is essentially a belief in the spirit of the dead. It is a belief in the existence of some supra-physical being within the body of every living or non-living being.
- Totemism: This is an extension of fetishism. "A totem is a species of animal or plant; or part of an animal or plant, or a natural object or the phenomenon of the symbol of any of these which signifies distinguishing features of a human group as against other groups similarly represented, in the same society." - H.D. Munro in *"Dictionary of Sociology"*. Totemism is associated with the tribal organisation. The relation that exists between the totem and the people is sometimes taken to be one of blood relationship. Hence totemism has to be crossed in marriage. The totem may be *wolf, bear, turtle, hawk, fox,* etc.

functions and festivals contributes to the unity of the group. A sizeable proportion of Nagas, Mizos, Santhals, Oraons and Munda, etc., have embraced Christianity while some tribals such as *Butia, Lepcha Chakma* have largely identified with Buddhism.

7. *Common Culture* : Each tribe has a way of life of its own. Each tribe has its own way of behaving, thinking, feeling and acting. Each has its own customs, traditions, morals, values, its own peculiar institutions in brief, its own culture. The very peculiarities of a tribe reveal that it has a distinctive culture of its own.

8. *Common Political Organisation* : Each tribe has its own political system. The tribal chief normally exercises authority over all the other members. The chieftainship is normally hereditary. He occupies an important position in the tribal society. The tribals do not possess a government in the modern sense of the term. But they do have their own tribal government, tribal council and tribal court or judicial system. *Santhal,* for example, an advanced tribe, has a village council the members of which are democratically elected. Nagaland emerged on the first of December 1963 as the 16th State of the Republic of India and Meghalaya in the month of April 1970.

9. *Feeling of Unity* : The members of a tribe always feel that they are united. This sense of unity is essential for them to retain their identity. Tribals are normally cohesive and they fight against common enemies as one man. They are ever ready to avenge the injustice done to the group or the individuals.

10. *Common Economic Organisation* : As against 73% national average, 91% of the tribal workers are engaged in agriculture. About 3% of tribals are engaged in manufacturing against the national average of 11%; and 5% in tertiary servicing [against the national average of 16%.] Just 1% tribals are engaged in forestry and food gathering. Their economic position is very poor. Though they are poor, against the national average of 43%, nearly 57% of tribals are economically active. In spite of that, they get very poor returns for their efforts.

11. *Organisation of Clans* : The Clan or sib is an important part of tribal-organisation. *The clan includes all the relatives of mothers or fathers and the children of one ancestor.* People belonging to a clan trace their origin to one ancestor. The descendants of a clan are of either matrilineal or partilineal lineage. The tribal society may include in itself many clans. There exists mutual helpfulness among the members of different clans.

12. *Prevalence of Dormitories* : Tribal community has a peculiar feature which is evident in the form of *common sleeping chambers* or dormitories. Such organisations train the youth in the tribal ways of life. These are the centres which preserve tribal legends, music, dance, paintings, etc. Young boys and girls spend much of their time in the night in these dormitories and often they are vested with the responsibility of giving protection to the community people. Till they get married they continue to become the members of the dormitories and are supposed to maintain secrecy relating to their activities. After their marriage their membership of the dormitories get cancelled. Members of the dormitories are expected to follow the rules and regulations strictly.

13. *Simplicity and Self-Sufficiency* : A tribal society is not complex but simple in character. Hunting, fishing and collection of roots, fruits, nuts, berries, honey and forest products are their main means of subsistence. Some have taken to cultivation also. They do not possess, neither do they enjoy the facilities of civilised people. There was a time when the tribals were self-sufficient. Due to the increase in their population and changed economic conditions, their self-sufficiency has gone. They are becoming more and more dependent on the civilised community and also the government help. They are simple, honest, frugal and some of them very hospitable also. They are not educated, neither are they interested in it.

14. *The Need for Protection* : The tribals always experience the need for protection. Hence they are a *cohesive group.* The tribe is a *homogeneous* group also. There is less diversity and more unity and uniformity. Ethnic, political, religious and other kinds of prejudices and mutual distrust between the civilised and the tribal people have made the tribals feel insecure. Hence they experience the need for protection. Their political organisation is established mainly to protect themselves.

15. *Endogamous Group ?* : Though not always, the members of a tribe generally marry among themselves. *Marrying within one's own group is called endogamy.* Each tribe has many clans within itself and these are *exogamous in nature.* The tribals practise endogamy probably to maintain the purity of blood and cultural peculiarities and to preserve the property within the group. But today, due to the influence of the civilised people and increased contacts, *exogamy* is also practised. The tribe is not necessarily an endogamous group, though originally it might have been so says *Imperial Gazetteer of India.* All known tribal societies have laid stress on the rule of exogamy. An individual is not allowed to marry inside a definite set of his own kin-group, that is, clan. In conclusion, it can be said that taken together as a unit, each tribe is largely endogamous, but various sub-groups that it consists, namely clans, are mostly exogamous.

Tribals' Relationship with Hinduism

Tribals are normally found to be associated with various types of religious practices such as – *fetishism, animism, totemism, ancestral worship, nature worship,* etc. Due to cultural diffusion and impact of civilisation some of the tribals came into contact with Islam, Christianity, Buddhism, and Hinduism. Majority of the tribals in India are either basically Hindus, or have come under the influence of Hinduism. Religion-wise speaking, 89% tribals are Hindus, 5.5% Christians, 0.3% Buddhists, 0.2% Muslims, and 5% others. All those who consider themselves Hindus do not have the same type of loyalty towards Hinduism.

Four Types of Relationships and Four Types of Groups

According to Prof. Ram Ahuja,[1] on the basis of the influence of Hinduism on the tribals and the type of relations the tribals have with the Hindus, the tribals can be classified into four groups :

1. *Those Tribals who have Accepted the Hindu Social Order* : It is estimated that around 89% of the tribals have accepted the Hindu social order including the caste system. *Example, Bhils, Bhumijs.*

2. *Those who are Positively Oriented towards the Hindu Social Order* : There are some tribals who accept and adopt the ethos and symbols and the world view of the Hindus, but are not ready to include themselves in the framework of caste. *Example, Santhals, Oraons, Mundas, Gonds.*

3. *Those who are Negatively Oriented towards the Hindu Social Order* : Some tribals do not accept the Hindu social order; on the contrary, they oppose it mostly because they are already converted into Christianity.

4. *Those who are Indifferent towards the Hindu Social Order* : Some tribal groups in Arunachal Pradesh, for example, are not at all bothered about the Hindu social order. They are that way indifferent towards Hinduism.

---

1 Prof. Ram Ahuja *"Society in India."* Page - 275.

Tribe and Caste : Differences

One speciality about the Indian society is that in its huge population, we find a large number of groups which are called *"Hindu castes"*, and a large number of communities which are called *"tribes."* But there are no specific criteria by which we may distinguish a tribe from a caste. Though it is difficult to speak of the differences between the two, some attempts are made to speak of the differences.

1. ***Difference in the Definitions of the Concepts : Tribe, Caste*** :

- ***A tribe is a group of local communities, which lives in a common area, speaks a common dialect and follows a common culture.***

- As S.C. Dube has said ***"it is better to use the term Jati to denote an endogamous unity with a more or less defined ritual status and some occupation traditionally linked to it."***

2. ***Territorial Basis*** : Tribals normally live in geographically isolated places like hills, mountains, forests, etc., whereas Hindus live in plains, that is, in villages, towns and cities. Max Weber has stated that when an Indian tribe loses its territorial significance, it assumes the form of a caste. Thus, tribe is regarded as a local [territorial group] whereas caste is a social group.

This difference cannot be taken as absolute but only a relative one. Because in this age of technology and mass communications, no group or community ever lives in total isolation. It is thus argued that geographic isolation cannot be accepted as a criterion for differentiating tribe from caste.

3. ***Religious Basis*** : On the religious basis, it is argued that the religion of tribals is mostly *Animism* or *Totemism*, and that of the caste Hindus, is *Hinduism*. As Dr. D.N. Majumdar opined, the tribes look upon Hindu ritualism as something foreign to them, though they often indulge in it and worship Hindu Gods and Goddesses. Whereas in the caste, ritualism forms a necessary part of religion itself.

- The religious basis of difference between caste and tribe is also criticised. It will be wrong to say that the Hindus, [particularly the lower caste Hindus] do not believe in *"spirits"*, *"ghosts"*, magic and the like. In the same way, there are also tribals who worship Hindu Gods and Goddesses and celebrate Hindu festivals; observe Hindu customs, practices and so on.

4. ***The Criterion of Language*** : It is known that each tribe has its own dialect, but not a caste. *Even regarding this criterion also there are objections.* Because there are tribes which do not have a specific dialect of their own. Further, there are some castes which have a specific dialect of their own.

5. ***The Factor of Economic Backwardness*** : It is said that the tribals represent the poorest or economically the most backward section of the Indian population. Some have even said that they are poorer than the low caste Hindus.

- This criterion of difference is also criticised because we find poverty in both the communities. Some of the caste Hindus are equally poor. At the same time, some tribals have attained richness in some areas. Economically also the tribal economy is not entirely different from the regional or national economy.

6. ***Similarity and Consciousness of Status*** : Max Weber has pointed out that the status of all people is more or less similar in a caste whereas much differentiation of status and rank is found in the tribe.

- This view of Weber cannot be accepted completely because this view does not apply to all the castes. Differentiation of rank and status can be found in many castes also.

- But another difference between the two is that *there is greater consciousness of such differences in status and rank in the caste than in the tribe.*

7. *Occupational Factor* : In the traditional caste system, occupations are mostly hereditary. Under the caste system, each caste in assigned a particular occupation which its members are expected to follow. But in a tribe, though occupational choice is limited, individuals are not very much compelled to follow a particular occupation.

- This factor has also been criticised because during the recent years occupations have become dissociated with the caste due to the spread of education and advent of industrialisation, modernisation and urbanisation.

In conclusion, it can be said that the differences between caste and tribe are getting reduced during the recent years for various reasons. Some of the tribes are getting themselves converted into castes. This process of transformation may take place by any one of the ways as mentioned by Risley:

(i) *By changing one's lineage,*
(ii) *By accepting the principles of any school of Hinduism,*
(iii) *By joining Hinduism,* and
(iv) *By entering into relations with Hindus without changing one's name.*

From an anthropological point of view, tribes in India appear to be gradually merging with the caste system. Dr. Ghurye has said that some of the Hindu castes living on the plains are not at all different from the Hindu tribes in terms of language, economy and religion. In fact, he calls them *"backward Hindus."* Castes and tribes, thus represent two ends of the same scale, the scale of continuum.

CLAN AND TRIBE

Clan represents an important type of group which constitutes a part of the kinship system. This is of special importance in the tribal society. In fact, a tribal community is often understood as an organisation of different clans.

Definition of Clan

1. William P. Scott: Clan refers to *"a unilateral kin-group based on either matrilineal or patrilineal descent"* [*'Dictionary of Sociology'* - Page: 49].
2. R.N. Sharma: *"A clan is that collection of unilateral families whose members believe themselves to be the common descendants of a real or mythical ancestor"* [*'Indian Social System'* Page 108].

Clan is a kinship group of fundamental importance in the structure of many societies. Membership of clan is socially defined in terms of actual or purported descent from a common ancestor. This descent is unilineal, that is, derived only through the male or female line. A clan is an extended form of lineage constituted by the blood relations. It includes all the relatives of either the father's side or the mother's side.

Characteristics of Clan

1. *Clan - An Exogamous Group*: Normally, but not always, clans are exogamous for marriage within the clan being forbidden and regarded as incest. Since the clan members believe themselves to be the descendants of the common ancestor they do not intermarry among themselves.

2. *Common Ancestor*: Clan membership is defined in terms of actual or purported descent from a common ancestor. In fact, the very organisation of the clan is based on the conception of a common ancestor. This ancestor could be real or mythical.

3. *Unilateral*: Clan is the most widespread of the unilateral groups. It consists of blood relations of one side only who are grouped into an exogamous group. A clan would consist of either the collection of all families on the mother's side or of all families on the father's side.

4. *Totemic Worship*: Members of a clan normally worship a totemic object or god. Members of a clan believe in some totemic object.

5. *There are Clanless Tribal Groups Also*: Though the organisation of clans is common to the world of tribals, there are some tribal groups wherein the clan system is not found. *Examples*: (i) Andaman Islanders, and (ii) Kadars of Kerala.

6. *Clans having their Own Names*: Clans may have their own names. *Example of some Indian Clans*: Shandilya, Kaundinya, Bharadwaj, Kunjam, Naagsori, Jaunpuriya, Mahanadiya.

Types of Clan

There are two types of clans: (i) *Matriclan*, (ii) *Patriclan*.

(i) Matriclan [Matrilineal Clan]: This type of clan consists of all the offsprings of one woman. Her sisters and brothers also belong to it. A matrilineal clan includes the woman, her offsprings, her sisters and their children. But it does not include the children of the brothers.

(ii) Patriclan [Patrilineal Clan]: In this clan are included the man, his children, his brothers, and sisters and the children of the brothers but not of the sisters.

Distinction Between Clan and Tribe

As it is already mentioned, each tribe consists of smaller kinship units called *"Clans."* It is difficult to describe all the clans found among more than 40 major tribal groups of India. One or two examples may be cited here. *Ex. Santhal* tribe has more than 100 clans, while the *Ho* tribe has 50, the *Bhils* 38, and the *Munda* 65. These clans are related to wild animals, trees and plants. Majumdar and Madan have spoken of 8 clans in *Kharia* tribe. They are : *Khoren* [a stone], *Myur* [crocodile], *Samad* [deer], *Barliha* [a fruit], *Charad, Hansad, Mail* and *Tepna* [all birds]. Among the *Tamarias,* the clan name is related to a ghost, animal or plant. The clan history of any tribe is, however, very mysterious. Main differences between clan and tribe are :

- Clan is an exogamous unit and its members do not marry among themselves. A tribe is largely endogamous. Only during the recent years the tribe started losing its endogamous character.
- A tribe normally speaks a common dialect. Whereas a clan has no definite language as such.
- A tribe occupies a common territory and its members normally concentrate there. But the clan has no definite geographic area.

2. GEOGRAPHIC DISTRIBUTION OF TRIBALS

According to 1991 census, there are about 67.76 million tribals in India, who form 8.08% of India's total population. This is more than the population of Britain. India, in fact, has the second largest tribal population in the world next only to Africa.

As far as Karnataka is concerned, the tribals' share is around 5% of the state's total population. Though in the beginning our Constitution gave recognition to [in 1956] only 414 tribal groups and termed them as *"scheduled tribes"*, the number of such groupings now runs to a few more hundreds. At the national level, in 329 thaluks the tribals are in a majority. More than 65% of the tribals live in the areas in which the tribals form more than 50% of the population of those areas. From the point of view of their numbers, the tribals are a *"dominant group"* in many local areas.

Geographic Distribution of Tribals in India

The tribes in India are spread over the length and breadth of this country. They vary in strength from a few hundreds to several lakhs. About 2/3 of the total tribal population of the country are found in the five states of Madhya Pradesh, Orissa, Bihar, Gujarath and Maharashtra. The highest number of tribals according to the 1991 census are found in Madhya Pradesh [15.4 million], followed by Maharashtra [7.3 million], Orissa [7 million], Bihar [6.6 million], and Gujarath [6.1 million].[1] In states like Rajasthan, West Bengal and Andhra Pradesh tribes with more than 20-25 lakh population are found. In four states and Union Territories such as Mizoram, Nagaland, Meghalaya, and Arunachal Pradesh the tribals constitute 70% to 95% of the total population of the state territory. In Mizoram, the tribal population constitutes 95% of the total population, in Meghalaya and Arunachal Pradesh 80% each, in Tripura 70%, in M.P. and Orissa 23% each, in Gujarath 14%, in Rajasthan 12%, and in Assam and Bihar 10% each. [*Note* : For more details about State-wise distribution of Tribals, please refer to Table No.1 in Chapter No.9.]

Difficulties Involved in Estimating Tribal Population

For a very long time definite figures were not available about the numerical strength of tribals. Dr. Davis had rightly observed that the *"most inaccurate figures on religion in India are those covering the "tribals" or "animists" as they were called prior to the 1931 census."*[2] Whatever data that are available show great variation from census to census. Three main reasons are given for this :

1. *Firstly,* the criteria in the classification of people have changed from census to census;
2. *Secondly,* most of the tribal areas are inaccessible which made the collection of accurate data rather difficult;
3. *Thirdly,* the deliberate misrepresentation of the people contributes to swell their numbers.

Though doubts were raised about the reliability of the figures, the tribal population has been continuously increasing. It is estimated that the total tribal population in 1921 was around 16 million. It increased to 22.4 million in 1931, to 24.7 million in 1941 and then to 67.75 million in 1991.

The Tribal Zones

The tribes in India are not found in any one particular region alone, but distributed among the various states. For example, the *Gonds* whose population is around 4 million are found in M.P., Maharashtra and A.P. The *Bhils* too have a strength of about 4 million and are distributed in Rajasthan, Maharashtra and M.P. These two tribes have a high number of tribals. *Santhals* who have a strength of 3 million are spread over Bihar, Orissa and West Bengal. The *Andamanese* is the smallest community with a strength of only 19 people. Dr. B.S. Guha has given a three-fold territorial distribution of the tribals which is as follows :

(i) The North and North-Eastern Zone,

(ii) The Central or the Middle Zone, and

(iii) The Southern Zone.

C.B. Mamoria adds to this list the *fourth zone* a small one, consisting of Andaman and Nicobar Islands.

---

1 *Source* : *The Hindusthan Times,* July 11, 1995.

2 C.B. Mamoria. "*Social Problems and Social re-organisation*" Page - 176.

1. The North and North-Eastern Zone

This zone consists of the sub-Himalayan region and the hills and mountain ranges of North-Eastern frontiers of India. It includes Himachal Pradesh, northern U.P., Sikkim and seven states of the North-East consisting of Arunachal Pradesh, Assam, Meghalaya, Mizoram, Nagaland, Manipura and Tripura. The tribals of this zone mostly belong to the *Mongoloid race* and speak languages belonging to the Tibeto-Chinese family. This zone is inhabited by the tribes such as - Gurung, Limbu, Lepcha, Aka, *Mishmi, Mikir, Rabha, Kachari, Garo, Khasi, Chakma, Naga, Angami, Sema, Pham, Chang* and so on. It is estimated around 12.50% of the total tribal population is found in this zone.

2. The Central or the Middle Zone

The tribal groups of this zone are scattered all over the mountain-belt between the rivers Narmada and Godavari. It includes West Bengal, Orissa, Bihar, Southern U.P., Southern Rajasthan, Gujarath, Madhya Pradesh and Maharasthra. The main tribes of this area are the *Gonds, Munda, Kandh, Baiga, Bhil, Bhuiyan, Bhumji, Koli, Savara, Kharia, Oraon, Ho, Santal, Juong,* and so on. The tribes living in this region form the largest assemblage of India's aboriginal population contributing to almost 81% of the total tribal population.

3. The Southern Zone

This zone falls south of the river Krishna. It includes Andhra Pradesh, Tamil Nadu, Karnataka, Kerala and the two union territories, Andaman and Nikobar Islands and Lakshadweep. The tribals of this zone are regarded as the most ancient inhabitants now living in India. This zone consists of the tribes like *Chenchu, Kota, Kurumba, Badaga, Toda, Kadar, Malayan, Muthuvan, Urali, Koya, Soliga, Kanikkar, Paniyan, Yerava,* etc. This zone contains around 6.50% of the total tribal population.

4. The Small Zone consisting of Andaman and Nicobar Islands

This is the smallest but isolated zone consisting of only 27,000 tribals [1991 census] who form around 9.54 of the total population of these two islands. The main tribes living in this zone are the *Jarawas, Onge, North Sentinelese,* the *Andamanese* and the *Nicobarese.* The Andamanese seem to be the smallest tribal community and their total strength is 19. Though separated from the main body of India's aboriginal tribes, they are ethnically connected with them. Though they are numerically the smallest tribes, they are anthropologically very important.

B.K. Roy Burman's Classification

B.K. Roy Burman divides the tribal communities into five territorial groupings, taking into account their *territorial, ethnic* and *socio-cultural relations.*

1. ***The North-East India*** comprising Assam, NEFA, Nagaland, Manipur and Tripura. Some of the tribes of this area are : the *Ahoms, Garos, Khasis, Mizos, Nagas, Kukis,* etc.
2. ***The sub-Himalayan region*** of North and North West India - comprising Northern Uttar Pradesh and Himachal Pradesh and as a whole. Some tribes of this area are : *Gujjars, Bodh, Kinnaurs, Swanglia,* etc.
3. ***Central and East India*** comprising West Bengal, Bihar, Orissa, Madhya Pradesh and Andhra Pradesh. Some tribes of this area are : the *Santals, Ho, Munda, Oraons, Gonds, Chenchu, Koya, Kolam,* etc.
4. ***South India*** comprising Madras, Kerala, and Karnataka. The tribes of this area are *Irula, Kurumba, Kadar, Hakki Pakki, Jenu Kuruba, Kadu Kuruba,* etc.
5. ***Western India*** comprising Rajasthan, Gujarat and Maharashtra. Some tribes of this area are : *Mina, Bhils, Kumbis, Mario Gonds, Mahadev Kolis, Gonds,* etc.

It is necessary to note that, though some of these tribes are generally associated with one particular zone, in reality many of these tribes are spread over many states. *Ex.* The *Gonds* are found in Madhya Pradesh, Karnataka, Orissa and West Bengal. Similarly *Bhils* are found in Madhya Pradesh, Andhra Pradesh, Gujarat, Karnataka, Rajasthan and Tripura.

According to **Verma**, among these the seven major tribes which have a population of 9 lakhs or more are : the *Gonds,* the *Bhils,* the *Santhals,* the *Minas,* the *Oraons,* the *Mundas* and the *Khonds.*

Elwin's Classification Based on Cultural Difference and Development

Verrier **Elwin** classifies the tribal groups into four classes according to their cultural development.

1. Class I refers to those *tribes which have been protected from contacts with other groups* on account of geographical conditions. They have retained their social organisation, culture, etc., in their pure form.

2. Class II refers to those *tribes which have been experiencing contact with the other groups* and consequently have been undergoing change. This group, though retaining their tribal mode of living, exhibits changes due to contact with the non-tribal groups.

3. Class III includes *tribes which are in a peculiar state of transition.* They are tribals only in name, but have become backward Hindus, constituting a sizeable section of the lower rung of the Hindu society.

4. Class IV denotes *a minority, which have secured the benefits of civilisation without injury to themselves.* They retain their old tribal name, their clans and totem rules, and observe elements of tribal religion, though they have also adopted the Hindu faith. According to Elwin, tribals of this class have won the battle of culture contact.

Ghurye's Classification

Based on cultural factors and cultural contacts, **Ghurye** classifies tribes into three classes. He writes : "***Firstly,*** such sections of them as the Raj Gonds and others who have successfully fought the battle, and are recognised as members of fairly high status within Hindu society; ***Secondly,*** the large mass that has been partially Hinduized and has come in closer contact with the Hindus; and ***Thirdly,*** the hill sections, which have exhibited the greatest power of resistance to the alien cultures that have pressed upon their border."

According to A.R. Desai, the classifications mentioned above suggest that the problems of tribal population belonging to various categories are qualitatively different and demand different solutions.

Contact of the Tribals with the Civilisation

Tribals live away from the civilised life and are mostly found in remote areas such as forest areas, hilly areas, mountainous regions, deep forests, dense valleys and so on. There was a time when one could travel over vast areas of the world exclusively inhabited by savage and semi-savage peoples who had never come into contact with the civilised races. In the case of India, there were many tribes who lived in secure asylums in hills and forests, lived on fruits, nuts, berries, etc. and wore leaves or rags round their loins. Today, most of these tribes have come into contact with the advanced community and have learnt cultural traits of their neighbours. They have borrowed the patterns of their dress and developed an intricate material economy. Some of these tribes have progressed at a tremendous speed, effecting in a few years, changes which have taken centuries to achieve in other areas.

The Ways of Contact of the Tribals with the Civilised People

The tribals came in contact with the civilised people in a number of ways. D.N. Majumdar points out at some of these ways[1] :

1. Existence of mineral resources in and around the primitive tracts helped the immigration of the outsiders who influenced the culture, the way of life of the tribals in a number of ways.
2. The administrative officers introduced significant changes in the cultural life of the primitive tribes everywhere. They introduced to the tribals various aspects of the civilisational amenities.
3. The Christian missionaries who entered these places to spread the religion and convert the tribals into Christianity also influenced the tribals.

   "The tribal beliefs in mysterious and impersonal forces, or in other words, in the concept of *mana,* or the *bonga* or *aren* has endowed officers of the government and missionaries with unlimited power for good or evil, and in many areas the tribal people have learnt to imitate the ways of these foreign elements in the population." [Majumdar. Page - 371].
4. The itinerant vendors of imported toys and trinkets, the shawl merchants and travelling agents who tour with modern medicines, imported textiles and brass and other metal utensils have gone into the most inaccessible parts of hills and jungles.
5. The tremendous development of transport and communication has led to the infiltration of foreign traits of culture.
6. The displacement of the tribal people in many areas from their hereditary possession of *jhums* lands has led to a change of occupation. Some tribals used to go out of their place to the far away tea gardens and plantations to work for small cash earnings which do not even supply their primary material needs. Yet they bring back with them traits of culture which are passed on and accepted by the community on account of the prestige they possess.

• *Adivasis* under the Influence of Caste ?

Most of the primitive tribes have come under the influence of the caste system and have increased the number of "depressed" communities; while others have been converted to Christianity and have escaped the tyranny of caste rules. *"Where the tribals have lived for long in association with the lower castes and where the tribes do not suffer from much discomfort or exploitation at the hands of the alien groups, the tribes have gradually entered into the social economy of the caste system."* [Majumdar. Page - 372]. However, the line of demarcation between popular Hinduism and tribal religions is thin and it is difficult to know when a tribe crosses into Hinduism. As Majumdar has pointed out, where there is a clash of interest between the tribal people and the Hindu landlords the tribals have been subjected to hardships or have been dispossessed of their rights to land or have been reduced to servitude, and where the middlemen have forced them into the grip of moneylenders, Christianity has proved a great friend of the tribes. Majumdar cites the example of the rapid spread of Christianity in Chota Nagpur where 98% of the Indian Christians have been recruited from the tribal population. This conversion is due more to the secular benefits, the Christian converts enjoy, than to the spiritual side of the new religion.

---

1 *Source* : D.N. Majumdar *"Races and Cultures of India"* 1973. Page - 371.

The Effects and Problems due to the Contact with Civilisation

The contact with civilisation has brought about a series of changes in the tribal areas and also in the tribal way of life. At the same time this contact has been responsible for some of the tribal discomforts and disadvantages. **Majumdar** [Pages : 372 - 374] makes a mention of some of the effects and problems of this contact.

1. The excise laws of the government in the primitive areas are hitting them hard. This policy has led to an increase of drunkenness and immorality in the tribal areas. The government is accused of making money by these means. Liquor has become cheap and the tribals who had been preparing it in their own way find it now highly uneconomic to do so. This has led to their economic downfall and misery.

2. The displacement of the tribal officers by those who are nominated by the state for administrative efficiency has disorganised the tribal life in various ways. These young officers from outside show scant respect to the tribal way of life, values, morals and culture. Tribal people have found it extremely difficult to accept these young officers as their own.

3. The tribal land used for *jhumming* is held to be *"unclassed state forest"* and the possessors of these lands could be ousted without giving any compensation. This annoyed the tribals very badly.

4. Quarrying stone, gravel and ores for private use is forbidden to the owner of the *jhum* land where there may lie. The licence fee demanded for quarrying has further complicated the issue.

5. *Jhumming* or *Dahiya* cultivation has been prohibited by the State. This has forced the primitive tribes to a kind of agriculture which is unsuited for them.

6. *"Marriage by capture"* practised amongst the primitive tribes is often treated as abduction and the offenders are punished under the provisions of *The Indian Penal Code*. The primitives have been prevented from practising this type of marriage which used to help them to escape from the clutches of the practice of the heavy bride price.

7. Tribal ceremonies, festivals and dances have been replaced or superseded by fairs and weekly markets which attract the people by their novelty, but ultimately bring about financial ruin.

8. The system of education which has been introduced in the tribal areas, either through the missionary efforts or by the local governments, is mostly unsuited to their life and ideals. The tribals have not completely realised the relevance and the importance of these new types of education.

9. Tribal customs and practices are often at variance with the complicated system of law and legal procedure. Hence, the tribals had to suffer and endure discomforts due to the fact that the judges and magistrates who never knew the languages, customs and mentality of the tribals, are to give judgements many a time against the tribal spirit.

10. Missionary influence has not been all the while good as far as the tribals are concerned. The new converts to Christianity who started despising the tribal way of life have disturbed the traditionalists.

11. Finally, the occurrence of the diseases, through the contact of especially the foreigners, has invaded the security of the tribal life. The medical aid available is too insignificant to cope with the situation.

Thus, the contact of the tribals with the civilisation has brought them some good things, it has also led to the new problems, anxieties and challenges.

3. PROBLEMS OF THE SCHEDULED TRIBES

The tribals who constitute 8.8% of the total population of India, are distributed in various states of the country and are facing many problems. Some of these problems are peculiar to some areas while some others are common to tribals of all the areas. Many of these problems are the direct outcome of the changes that are taking place in the tribal community. These changes are also not uniform. Hence it is not easy to understand the tribal problems in their true perspective.

Tribals in India, in general, are facing some common problems such as *problem of geographic separation, economic problem, cultural problem, social problem, educational problem and health problem.* These problems are briefly discussed below.

1. Problem of Geographic Separation

Most of the tribals of India are in a way geographically separated from the rest of population. Some of them are living in the unapproachable physical areas such as deep valleys, dense forests, hills, mountains, etc. It is difficult for them to establish relations with others, and hence, socially they are away from the civilised world. This kind of physical as well as social isolation or seclusion has retarded the tribal development. The welfare programmes and developmental projects undertaken by the government many a time do not reach the tribals because of this geographic isolation. Hence the tribals need to be protected from leading an isolated life away from villages, towns and cities. Regular contact should be maintained with them through the network of roads and communication system.

2. Cultural Problem

The tribal culture is entirely different from the way of life of the civilized people. The tribals fail to understand the civilised people, their customs and practices, beliefs and attitudes and so on. They are suspicious of the civilised people. They are clinging tenaciouslsy to their customs and traditions. During the British rule some foreign Christian missionaries made an attempt to propagate their religion in some of the tribal areas, particularly in the North-Eastern provinces. They even tried to impose their culture on them. Even today such an attempt is going on.

"In several tribal areas, mass conversion to Christianity had taken place during the British period. While the missionaries have been the pioneers in education and opened hospitals in tribal areas, they have also been responsible for alienating the tribals from their culture. Christian missionaries have many a time instigated the tribals to revolt against the Indian government."[1]

On the other hand, the Ramakrishna Mission, R.S.S. [Rasthreeya Swayamsevak Sangh] the Vishwa Hindu Parishad and other organisations are spreading Hinduism in some of these areas. Further, some of the tribal leaders have now started popularising the tribal religion. These different propagandas have created a great confusion and conflict for them. The cultural gap between the civilised and the tribal people is coming in the way of the assimilation and integration of the tribal people into the mainstream of the national life of India.

3. Social Problems

The tribals have their own social problems. They are traditional and custom-bound. They have become the victims of superstitious beliefs, outmoded and meaningless practices and harmful habits. *Child marriage, infanticide, homicide, animal sacrifice, exchange of wives, black magic* and other harmful practices are still found among them.

1 Prof. Ram Ahuja *"Social Problems in India"* - Page: 137.

Hinduisation of tribals has led to problems such as dowry, divorce, untouchability, child marriage, etc. Various studies on tribal communities in India have provided information about the impact of Hinduisation. Studies on the *Konds* of Orissa, *Kotas* of the Neelagiris, *Bhumji* in West Bengal, *Bhotias* of Uttar Pradesh and *Santhals* of Bihar indicate the general trend of change owing to cultural contact with the neighbouring Hindus. *Example* : "A recent study of *Botia* women of Pithoragarh district of U.P. by **Dharmaveer** and **Manral** [1990] reveals that the status of *Botia* women has changed for the worse. Traditionally, they had a fairly high status and enjoyed considerable freedom in different spheres of life. But their status has declined significantly due to Hinduisation, Sanskritisation and modernisation."[1]

Christianisation of tribals has led to problems of separatism, alienation, religious conflict and cultural confusion. Christianity has been an important factor of tribal change in India. "Many tribals have become Christians during the last 100 years. Thus there are a large number of Christians among the *Khasis* and *Garos* of Meghalaya, *Oraons* of Chota Nagpur, *Bhils* of Madhya Pradesh, *Mizos, Nagas* and many other tribals of North East. *According to one estimate, the tribal Christians constitute about 1/6th of the total Christian population of India.* The traditional tribal cultures and institutions have been adversely affected under the impact of new ideas, ethical values and a new style of life........ **Vidhyarthi** [1977 : 460] is of the opinion that Christianity has provided the first model of Westernisation to the tribals in the shape of "Church Organisation", western education, and above all, western values and morals."[2]

Many tribals still believe in ghosts and spirits. They have a keen desire to maintain their own practices, beliefs, etc. Hence, it is said that *"the tribals are tribesmen first, the tribesmen last and the tribesmen all the time."*

4. Economic Problems

The tribal people are economically the poorest people of India. Majority of them live below the poverty line. The tribal economy is based on agriculture of the crudest type. The main economic problems of the tribals are explained below.

(i) *Exploitation:* The innocence, illiteracy and helplessness of the tribals are exploited by the outsiders. The British policy, in particular, had led to ruthless exploitation of the tribals in various ways as it favoured the zamindars, landlords, money-lenders, forest contractors and excise, revenue and police officials.

(ii) *Unprofitable Agriculture:* About 90% of the tribals are engaged in cultivation and most of them are landless and practise *"shifting cultivation."* They need to be helped in adopting new methods of cultivation. The tribals possess uneconomic holdings because of which their crop yield is very less. A very small percentage of the population participates in occupational activities in the secondary and tertiary sectors.

(iii) *Problems of Land Ownership:* A good portion of the land in the tribal areas has been legally transferred to non-tribals. Tribals demand that this land should be returned to them. In fact, the tribals had earlier enjoyed much freedom to use the forest and hunt their animals. They are emotionally attached to the forests for they believe that their gods, spirits live in forests. The tribals who are *"deprived"* of their rights to the land and forest have reacted sharply to the restrictions imposed by the government on their traditional rights.

---

1 **Dr. Y. Ravindranath Rao** *"Tribal Social Transformation"* published in *"Samaja Shodhana"* Vol.1, No.2., Oct. 1992. [Page - 62.] Journal of the Mangalore University Sociology Teachers Association.

2 *ibid.* Page - 63.

(iv) *Unemployment and Underemployment:* A large number of tribal young men and women are either unemployed or underemployed. They are unhappy for they are not able to get jobs that can keep them occupied throughout the year. They need to be helped in finding secondary source of income by developing animal husbandry, poultry farming, handicrafts, handloom weaving, etc.

(v) *Non-Availability of Banking Facilities:* Banking facilities in the tribal areas are so inadequate that the tribals have mainly to depend on the money-lenders. The tribals, therefore, demand that *"Agricultural Indebtedness Relief Acts"* should be enacted so that they may get back their mortgaged land.

5. Educational Problems

Illiteracy is a major problem of the tribals. More than 80% of them are illiterate. Literacy among them has increased from 0.7% in 1931 to 11.30% in 1970 and to 16.35% in 1981 to 29.60% in 1991. Compared to general literacy rate of 52.21% in the country, this is very low. Even now almost 70% of the tribals are illiterate. Further, the growth of literacy rate in the past three decades in the country as a whole was 28.21%, but among the STs it was only 11.7% [*The Hindustan Times,* July 11, 1955]. Even though tribal literacy rate in Mizoram is 82.71%, and between 57 and 61% in Nagaland, Sikkim and Kerala; there are regions [example, Orissa, U.P., Bihar] wherein their literacy level is extremely poor.

Tribals, who are far away from the contact of the civilised world have no faith in formal educational organisation. Many of them do not know any thing about education, schools, colleges, universities, degrees, etc. They feel no urge to educate their children. Since most of the tribals are poor, education appears to be a luxury for them. Tribal people who are engaged in agriculture want their little children to work along with them either in the fields or at home. The illiterate parents do not consider it as their primary responsibility to give education to their children.

The Problem of Language: The medium of instruction is another hindrance to the promotion of education among the tribes. Most of the tribal languages do not have a script of their own. Hence the children are obliged to learn things in a language which is foreign to them. Even in tribal areas the number of tribal teachers is very less and hence communication problem always arises between the students and the teachers.

The Curriculum of Education is another Main Problem : The existing curriculum, as experts rightly have pointed out, is not suited and has little relevance to the tribal people.

6. Problem of Health and Sanitation

Due to illiteracy and ignorance the tribals are not able to appreciate modern concept of health and sanitation. They do not take much care pertaining to their own health. They believe that diseases are caused by hostile spirits and ghosts. They have their own traditional means of diagnosis and cure. Good number of them fall a prey to the diseases such as skin disease, forest fever, typhoid, T.B., leprosy, malaria, venereal diseases, small pox, etc. Contact with outsiders further added to a few more diseases in the tribal areas. Example: *It is observed that the Thodas of Niligiri Hills have been suffering from some modern diseases like venereal diseases, diabetes, blood pressure, etc. after coming into touch with the British who made Niligiri Hills one of their summer resorts.* These diseases take a heavy toll of tribal life. Their suspicion and lack of faith in modern doctors have made them not to avail themselves of the modern medical facilities.

7. Problem of Separatism

The *"divide and rule"* policy adopted by the British did a lot of damage to the tribal community of India. The British had superimposed their own administrative patterns in tribal areas and deprived the tribals of their traditional methods of interacting with people. The *"Criminal Tribes Act"* which the British had introduced gave an impression that the tribals were either *"criminals"* or *"anti-social beings"*. The tribal groups such as *Kolis, Mundas, Khasis, Santals, Nagas,* etc, who fought against the British were branded as *"dactoits"* and *"robbers"*. The British government which wanted to humble these tribals and *"correct"* them gave direct encouragement to the foreign Christian missionary activities especially in the Central and the North-Eastern Zone. These activities which went on for more than 200 years, alienated many of the tribals and developed in them separatist tendencies.

Relations between tribals and non-tribals have started worsening. In states like Mizoram, Nagaland, Meghalaya, Bihar, Manipur, Tripura, and Arunachal Pradesh, demand for separate state for tribals took the shape of insurgency, revolt, terrorism and so on. Neighbouring countries which are unfriendly to India, have instigated the tribals to rebel against the establishment. They have exploited the anti-Indian sentiments of the tribals to their advantage.

8. Tribal Revolts and Uprisings

Numerous revolts and uprisings of the tribals have taken place beginning with the one in Bihar in 1772, followed by many other revolts in Andhra Pradesh, Arunachal Pradesh, Assam, Mizoram and Nagaland. During the recent tribal uprisings the *Nagas,* the *Mizos* and the *Bodos* took part in them in a large number and created serious law and order problem.

Smuggling, Infiltration and Drug Addiction: The foreign infiltrators especially from Bangla Desh, Pakisthan, Burma and China are entering the borders of India through what are known as *"tribal belts"*. Some of them take undue advantage of the tribals' innocence and ignorance for their *smuggling activities.* Prohibited drugs and unlicensed weapons are smuggled inside the land and beyond the borders of India through the tribal areas. Some of the tribals have been made the victims of drug addiction also. Hence, tribal areas in the borders have become extremely sensitive areas.

Causes of Tribal Unrest and Discontent

Tribals in India led a comparatively contented and peaceful life prior to the coming of the British. Along with the British rule there came in series of social changes. Some of these changes affected tribal life also. Exposure of the tribals to the modern civilisation also resulted in their exploitation at the hands of the non-tribals. Conversion activities of the Christian missionaries encouraged by the British, especially in the tribal areas, further added confusion to the tribals. Tribals reacted very strongly when their religious beliefs were mocked at, when their rights over the forests were removed and when their very way of life was disturbed.

Even now, tribals in India are not happy and are agitated over several things. Ever since the days of the British rule they have been revolting against the establishment, for various reasons. The important tribes involved in revolt in the 19th century were *Mizos* [1810], *Kols* [1795 and 1831], *Mundas* [1889], *Daflas* [1875], *Khasi* and *Garo* [1829], *Kacharis* [1839], *Santhals* [1853], *Muria Gonds* [1886], *Nagas* [1844 and 1879], *Bhuiyas* [1868] and *Kondhs* [1817]. After independence also many tribal revolts took place. The continuing state of discontent among the tribals is revealed through the contemporary tribal movements. Some of the contemporary movements are – ***the Jharkhand movement, Gond movement, Naga movement, Mizo movement, Bodoland movement,*** etc.

Some Major Types of Tribal Movements

It is possible to identify some of the major types of tribal movements.

1. *Religious and social reform movements.*
2. *Movements for statehood within the Indian Union, or for autonomy for tribal areas.*
3. *Insurgent movements for independence from the Indian Union,* and
4. *Movements for asserting cultural rights.*

It is significant to note that there are lots of variations in tribal movements from region to region. In the North East, the tribals are in an overwhelming majority in some of the states. ***Example*** : Meghalaya, Mizoram, Nagaland. Their tribal economy and social systems are relatively stable. The tribal movements in this areas are essentially ***political in nature.*** Here, some of the tribal groups [*Ex.* Nagas in Nagaland, Mizos in Mizoram] demanded autonomy and for that sake carried on continuous agitations some times back.

The situation in Middle India is far more complex. The tribals have been reduced to a minority in many areas in which they were dominant numerically at one time. Further, they have been exposed to the process of rapid social change. The tribal movements in this region have essentially an ***agrarian character*** and are often related to the exploitation of forest resources.

In some regions the tribal movements have a ***cultural dimension*** in the sense that they are related to language, tribal art and religion. Tensions have often prevailed in these regions on account of religious conversions and linguistic tussles.

Tribals in South India are either too backward or too few in number or widely dispersed over a large area to organise any movement in spite of their exploitation and discontent. *"However,* Mishra [1982] *says that there is evidence of incipient political mobilisation among the tribals in South India. In fact, political consciousness among the tribals of Kerala may be the highest in the country."*[1]

The study of the tribal movements is relatively recent in the field of social anthropology. Tribal movements may be seen as an aspect of social change. The policy of the colonial administration regarding forest and land, later on alienation of the tribal land, the immigration and settlement of an increasing number of non-tribals, the slow pace of industrialisation and modern developments – have been some of the reasons for the emergence of various tribal movements in the North Eastern states of Manipur, Mizoram, Meghalaya, Arunachal Pradesh and Assam.

According to A.R. Desai, the fundamental problems of the tribal population are economico-political such as the security of a job, a decent standard of living, easy accessibility to the resources of civilised life, the acquiring of education, which can enable them to decide what customs, what rituals, and what aesthetic and cultural elements they should retain, or eliminate or absorb from their culture and various other cultures. He is of the opinion that the violent and militant struggles which are being launched by the tribal populations are revolts against various inhuman conditions to which they have been subjected and which are being perpetuated even after independence. He points out : *"The tribal problem is a problem which raises the fundamental issue – the issue of the establishment of a social order founded on equality of opportunities and the elimination of exploitation."*

The Causes of Tribal Unrest

Tribal unrest and discontent are a cumulative effect of a number of factors. The factors or causes that led to the tribal revolt, unrest and discontent may be listed here.

1 Dr. Y. Ravindranath Rao *"Tribal Social Transformation."* Page - 63 published in *Samaja Shodhana.*

1. *Governmental Failures* : The failure of the Government to take appropriate measures to rehabilitate the tribal population both before and after independence had disappointed the tribals. Independent India's Constitution envisages a comprehensive and well designed scheme of action for the tribal protection and development. The State Governments are vested with the responsibility of implementing the Constitutional provisions. Unfortunately, these Constitutional provisions have remained non-operational. Land continues to pass out of the tribals to non-tribals. Money lenders continue to exploit them. There has been a heavy influx of outsiders into the tribal areas and they have grabbed most of the opportunities.

2. *Irresponsibility and Lack of Accountability of the Agencies of Tribal Development* : Indifference, irresponsibility, lethargy and lack of sympathy on the part of the administrators and bureaucrats in dealing with the tribal problems and grievances have been obvious. There are a number of agencies to look after and supervise the implementation of the tribal welfare programmes and schemes. At the level of the Central Government, for example, there are five major agencies namely; (i) *the Welfare Ministry,* (ii) *Commissioner for Scheduled Tribes and Scheduled Castes,* (iii) *National Commission for Scheduled Castes and Scheduled Tribes,* (iv) *Secretary in Cabinet Secretariat,* and (v) *the Planning Commission*. In addition to these, the development and administration of the tribal affairs is spread over a number of ministries and departments. Such multiplicity of agencies divides the responsibility and leads to irresponsibility and unaccountability.

3. *Unjust Forest Policy* : Inconsiderate and unsympathetic forest laws and regulations damaged the tribal emotionality. Lands traditionally owned and cultivated by the tribals have been branded as *"forest lands"* under the new Forest Policy. As a result, the tribals have become strangers and encroachers in their own land.

4. *Alienation of Tribal Land to the Non-Tribals* : Lack of legislation to prevent the passing of the tribal land into the hands of non-tribals has added to tribal unrest. Due to some loopholes in the existing system of law the tribal land continues to be alienated to non-tribals for their own exclusive uses. The state governments have also acquired tribal land for industrial, irrigation, power, mining, and other projects. As a result, the tribals have been deprived of their rights over the land.

5. *Political Indifference* : Lack of interest and dynamism among the political elite to solve the tribal problems made them to become disgusted. National level political parties have not paid due attention to the genuine problems of the tribals. They have been speaking of the tribal development and the tribal welfare only for the name sake. Tribals are remembered only at the time of elections. The political indifference has made the tribals to organise their own political parties at local level. Because of their groupism they have not been able to forge a unity to fight for their own cause.

6. *Absence of Efficient Tribal Leadership* : Tribals should be able to develop their own leadership to fight against exploitation and to secure justice. But unfortunately, various vested interests have prevented the emergence of powerful tribal leadership. There is virtually a vacuum of tribal leadership. This has very badly affected their development.

7. *Forceful Cultural Impositions* : Tribals are trying to come in touch with civilised people. Leaders of various religious communities such as the Hindu, Christian and the Muslim, are trying to approach them and influence their way of life. Tribals who want to retain their original culture are bewildered at this. The Hinduisation, Christianisation and also the Islamisation of the tribals have caused lot of anxiety and a sense of insecurity for them.

It is clear from the above, that various social, political, economic and legal factors have contributed to the problem of tribal unrest.

3. MEASURES FOR THE UPLIFTMENT OF SCHEDULED TRIBES

Independent India has been paying due attention to the problems of the scheduled tribes and attempts are being made to deal effectively with those problems. Before the independence, the British Government was only discussing the issues and problems of tribal development and practically did nothing either to face them or to solve them. The only thing the British did was that, they kept the tribals away from the contact of the civilized people. Through their *"policy of indirect rule"* they wanted to "protect" them from the neighbouring dominant communities.

The British followed their so called *"policy of giving special protection"* to the tribals till the *Government of India Act, 1935* came into force. Afterwards, though the elected provincial legislative bodies were established, some tribal areas known as *"the excluded areas"* were brought under the direct control of the British Governor.

The British policy of separating the tribals from the rest of the people created suspicion in the minds of the nationalists. They severely criticised the British policy and charged the British with preventing a large section of our countrymen from joining the mainstream of national life. *"In practice what happened was that the tribes were isolated and then left to stagnate, halting the evolving process of cultural fusion."* - [S.C. Dube][1]

This brings us to the questions *whether the tribals should be assimilated into the mainstream or, whether they should be kept separately from the rest of the communities and protected? And in what way they will benefit from the developments taking place in the country?* Let us consider the different approaches or view-points which the scholars have developed regarding the tribals and their development.

Three Views or Approaches to Solve Tribal Problems

Various solutions have been presented for dealing effectively with the tribal problems. The tribal problems have been approached from three viewpoints. They are as follows:

1. Policy of Isolation

Hutton, who was a Commissioner for Census of 1931 and **V. Elwin** have suggested that the tribals must be kept at a distance from the rest of the society. **Hutton** and others condemned too much of isolation as also of complete assimilation of tribals. **V. Elwin** wanted a revivalist policy to be adopted. He proposed a scheme of *"National Parks"* for the tribals and pleaded for the complete non-interference of the British forces and their withdrawal from the tribal areas. Keeping the tribals in isolation in some "National Parks" or "reserved areas" would solve two problems: (a) *the tribals would be in a position to maintain their independent identity,* (b) *they would be free from the exploitation of outsiders.* The champions of this approach are of the view that sufficient time must be given to the tribals to assimilate themselves with the rest of the community.

- The ***limitation of this approach*** is that when once the tribals are kept in isolation, they are likely to develop vested interests and keep themselves permanently away from others. **G.S. Ghurye** and others criticised this approach and advocated complete assimilation of the tribals.

2. Policy of Assimilation

"Assimilation is the process whereby individuals or groups once dissimilar become similar and identified in their interests and outlook" [Ogburn and Nimkoff]. Assimilation is one of the ways of dealing with the tribal problems. Assimilation or the *"missionary solution"* has been advocated

1 S.C. Dube *"Encyclopaedia of Social Work in India"* - Vol. III.

by Christian missionaries, Hindu social reformers and voluntary organisations. According to this solution, assisting and encouraging the tribals to assimilate themselves with the mainstream of national life, can alone permanently solve the tribal problems. Thus, according to this approach, we cannot deal with tribal problems on the basis of tribal culture and life but by changing them into the frame of new community. **Prof. G.S. Ghurye**, a senior sociologist made a case for the complete assimilation of tribals with the rest of the people in India. He said that it was misleading to call the tribes *"aborigines"* as they were actually only *"backward Hindus"* and the solution of all their problems cultural as well as economic and social lay in their complete assimilation into the Hindu society. The Christian missionaries on the one hand, and the Hindu social reformers like **Thakkar Bapa** on the other, have been trying to assimilate them into Christian and Hindu community respectively.

- ***This approach has its own limitations.*** Complete assimilation is a difficult task. The tribals are not prepared to give up all their traditional tribal beliefs, practices and ideas. Any attempt to impose the external cultural practices on them, creates in them guilt feelings, confusions and mental conflicts. This solution may even create economic, religious and moral degradation among them. Tribal culture has many happy and useful aspects and the same must be preserved. **D.N. Majumdar** opines that the best policy about tribes would be for their controlled [planned] and limited assimilation. By limited assimilation he implied the need and desirability of preserving their useful institutions, customs, practices, etc. though these are tribal in origin and character.

3. Policy of Integration

The third view, which is actively followed in the recent years, is that of *integration*. The policy of isolation is neither possible nor desirable and that of assimilation would mean imposition. Hence integration alone can make available to the tribes the benefits of modern society and yet retain their separate identity. ***This view recommends the rehabilitation of the tribals on the plains along with the civilised people, but away from their native places such as hills, mountains, forests, etc.***

This suggestion has also been criticised. It is said that this suggestion has been advocated in order to further the interests of the industrialists and capitalists. This solution is not appreciated on the ground that it may create economic and moral decadence to those who are separated from their beloved land to plains. Still, the policy of integration which aims at developing a creative adjustment between tribes and non-tribes has been supported by thinkers and writers like **Pandit Jawaharlal Nehru**.

Conclusion

The solutions to the tribal problems mentioned above, have their own merits and demerits. Tribal problems are simple but very delicate to handle. No solution can be experimented with before winning the confidence of the tribals. The modern culture must not be imposed on them. It is essential to establish a harmonious compatibility between the tribal mode of living and the material advancement of culture. The integration of the tribal society into the Indian society takes time and it has to be promoted while retaining the good points of the tribal culture. Only those elements of new culture which may vitalise them for material advancement must be infused in them. **Pandit Nehru** observes that, *"Tribal people possess a variety of culture and they are in many ways certainly not backward. There is no point in trying to make them a second rate copy of ourselves"*.[1]

With regard to the tribal development and welfare, Pandit Nehru observes that our duty

1 Quoted by **C.B. Mamoria** *"Social Problems and Social Disorganisation"* - Page: 203.

which comes *"First is to preserve, strengthen, and develop all that is best in tribal society, culture, art and language. The second is to protect the tribal economic rights. The third is to unite and integrate the tribes in a true heart unity with India as a whole, so that they may play a full part in their life. And the last is to develop welfare and educational facilities so that every tribesman may have an equal opportunity with the rest of the fellow citizens who work in the fields, factories, and workshops in the open country and the plains"*.

• The Tribal *'Panchasheela'*

Pandit Jawaharlal Nehru in 1957 in his foreword to Verrier Elwin's *"The Philosophy for NEFA"*, laid down five principles known as *"Panchasheela"*, as a part of the policy of integration. The tribal *"Panchasheela"* as has been enunciated by him are as follows.

(i) *Nothing should be imposed on the tribal people. They must be allowed to develop along the lines of their own genius. We should try to encourage in every way their own traditional art and culture.*

(ii) *Tribals right on land in which they are living and also on the forests must be respected.*

(iii) *Attempt must be made to train and build up a team of their own people to the work of administration and development. Some technical personnel from outside will be of great help for them in the beginning. But too many outsiders must not be sent to the tribal territory.*

(iv) *Over-administering the tribal areas or overwhelming them with too many schemes must be avoided. We should not work in rivalry to their own social and cultural institutions.*

(v) *The results of the work must be adjudged by the quality of the human character that is evolved and not by statistics or the amount of money spent.*

The Ministry of Home Affairs and the Ministry of Community Development (under the Article 46 of the Constitution), set up 43 sub-multipurpose tribal blocks in the various States of India to promote the welfare and the integration of the tribals. Two committees were set up, one in May 1959 under the chairmanship of the anthropologist Verrier Elwin and the other in April 1960 under the presidentship of U.N. Dhebar, to examine the programmes and projects of these blocks. Both the committees submitted their reports in 1960 and 1961 respectively. The reports have emphasised and amplified the five fundamental principles enunciated by Nehru in 1957.

Welfare Programmes and Projects for Scheduled Tribes

The tribals constitute a sizeable proportion [8.8% in 1991] of the total population of India. The tribals are also the citizens of India and hence promotion of their welfare is of equal importance. Not only the Central and the State Governments have undertaken various steps in this regard, but also various voluntary organisations have evinced interest in this task. Organisations such as the *Bharatiya Adim Jati Sevak Sangh, the Bhil Seva Mandal, Kasturba Gandhi National Memorial Trust, the Indian Red Cross Society, the Vishwa Hindu Parishad, the Vanavasi Kalyanashrama, The Ramakrishna Mission, The Rastreeya Swayam Sevak Sangh and several Christian organisations* carry on welfare activities among the tribals. The Government through its *Department of Tribal Welfare* and through its Five Year Plans has been trying to elevate the tribals from the state of ignorance, illiteracy and poverty. Some of the tribal welfare measures of the Government may be examined here.

1. Constitutional Safeguards

The Constitution of India has made various provisions to safeguard the interests of the tribals.

1. *Article 15* of the Constitution provides equal rights and opportunities to all the citizens of India (including the tribals) without any discrimination.
2. Reservation in employment is made for the tribals under *Article* 16(4), 320(4) and 335.
3. Seats have been reserved for them in the legislatures (in Lok Sabha and State Vidhana Sabhas) under *Articles* 330, 332 and 334.
4. Under *Article* 19(5) the tribals can own property and enjoy it in any part of the country.
5. According to the *Article* 275 a large amount of money can be taken from the *Consolidated Fund of India* to be spent on tribal welfare activities.
6. *Article* 338 empowers the President of India to appoint a Commissioner to look after the tribal welfare activities.
7. Under *Article* 339(2) the Central Government can give directions to the States in the formulation and execution of tribal welfare plans, projects and programmes.
8. Under *Article* 275(i) the Centre is required to give grants-in-aid to the States for approved schemes of tribal welfare.
9. *Article* 164 empowers the State Governments to appoint a separate minister to look into the welfare of the tribals.
10. *Article* 46 consists of provisions that protect the economic and educational interests of the tribals.
11. *Article* 224 gives instructions to the administration to take special care to protect tribal interests in *"Scheduled Tracts"* or *"areas"*.
12. *Article* 342 gives power to the President of India to declare on the recommendation of the Governor some groups or communities as *"scheduled tribes"*. It also gives details on the basis of which new groups could be recommended as *"scheduled tribes"* entitling them for all the constitutional benefits.

Committees and Commissions

In addition to the constitutional provisions mentioned above, the government appoints committees, commissions and study teams from time to time to look into the way in which the target groups are making use of the constitutional provisions, the problems faced by them and to suggest measures for further improvement. ***Examples of Some Commissions and Study Teams:*** *(i) Backward Classes Commission [1953-55], headed by* **Kaka Kalelkar**; *(ii) The Study Team of Social Welfare and Welfare of Backward Classes [1958-59] headed by* **Renuka Ray**; *(iii) The Scheduled Areas and Scheduled Tribes Commission - 1960-61 under the chairmanship of* **U.N. Dhebar**; *(iv) The Second Backward Classes Commission [1979-80] under the chairmanship of* **B.P. Mandal**, *etc.]*

2. Special Central Assistance [SCA]

Special Central Assistance is given to States and Union Territories to supplement their efforts in tribal development. This assistance is basically meant for family oriented income generating schemes in the sectors of agriculture, horticulture, minor irrigation, soil conservation, animal husbandry, forests, education, co-operatives, fisheries, village and small scale industries and for minimum needs programme. During 1999-2000, an amount of Rs.400 crore was released to the States / Union Territories [UTs]. Grants are given to States / UTs to meet the costs of the projects for tribal development [as per the provisions of Article 275(1)]. An amount of Rs.100 crore was provided as grants to States / UTs during 1999-2000.

3. Economic Programmes and Facilities

Majority of the tribals are extremely poor and economically backward. Various economic programmes and projects have been undertaken to improve their economic position.

(i) *Development through Five Year Plans:* The Government spent Rs. 30 crores, Rs. 80 crores, Rs. 101 crores, Rs. 172 crores and Rs. 257 crores on tribal welfare activities during the 1st, 2nd, 3rd, 4th and 5th Five Year Plans respectively. *Integrated Tribal Development Projects* [ITDPs] evolved for the tribal development during the 5th plan [1974-79] cover today 19 States / Union Territories and 374 lakh tribal population.

The amount allocated for the tribal sub-plans in the **5th plan** was Rs. 1100 crores, in the **6th** plan [1980-85] it was Rs. 5,535 crore and in the **7th Plan** [1985-90] it was Rs. 10,500 crore.

Specific objectives set forth under the tribal sub-plan strategy were: *(i) raising production in the field of agriculture, small industries, horticulture and animal husbandry; (ii) elimination of exploitation of tribals in money lending, bondage, forest, liquor vending, etc; (iii) development of education and training programmes; (iv) development of tribal areas; (v) upgradation of environment of tribal areas.*

(ii) *Establishment of "LAMPS": Large-sized Multi-Purpose Co-operative Societies:* These co-operative societies are established in the tribal areas for giving productive and unproductive loans, for sale of surplus produce and purchase of necessities of life to the tribal people. Through these societies the tribals are supplied with improved seeds, modern agricultural equipments, chemicals and fertilizers, pesticides, etc. These societies are striving to relieve the tribals from the exploitation of middlemen, contractors and money-lenders.

(iii) *Tribal Co-operative Marketing Development Federation of India* [TRIFED] : The *Tribal Co-operative Marketing Development Federation of India* was set up by the Govertment of India in 1987 with a prime objective of providing marketing assistance to ST communities. The TRIFED also provides remunerative prices for the minor forest produce and surplus and agricultural produces of the tribal communities so as to protect them from the hands of the exploitative private traders and middlemen. The authorised share capital of TRIFED is Rs.100 crore and its paid-up capital has gone upto Rs.99.98 crore in 1999-2000. The Govt. of India's contribution is Rs.99.75 crore in that.

(iv) *The 20 Point Programme* focussed its attention on the development of the scheduled tribes, including assisting the tribal families economically to enable them to cross the poverty line.

(v) *Vocational Training in Tribal Areas* : This scheme under the Central Sector introduced in 1992-93 aims at developing skills of the tribal youth in order to gain employment / self-employment opportunities. The scheme envisages setting up of *Vocational Training Centres* [VTCs]. During 1999-2000, an amount of Rs.375 lakh has been released for 19 VTCs.

(vi) *Encouragement to Crafts and Home Industries:* Encouragement is given to the existing crafts and home industries among the tribals and such new endeavours are also encouraged. **Example:** (i) In West Bengal, tribals are encouraged to develop silk industry. A training institute is established in Darjeeling to give proper training to those engaged in sericulture. (ii) In **Bihar, M.P., Orissa** and **West Bengal**, wax industry is encouraged among the tribals of these provinces. (iii) **Madhya Pradesh** Government is helping its tribals to prosper in their economic pursuit of collecting beedi leaves. (iv) **Bihar** Government has established a Woman's Co-operative Society for its tribal women to give encouragement to them to pursue their handicrafts.

(vii) *Agriculture made Stable:* The tribals are persuaded to give up their system of *"shifting cultivation"* and to settle permanently in a place of their selection by making agriculture their occupation. Thousands of tribals in Assam, Bihar, M.P., Orissa and Tripura, have been made to settle down permanently for agriculture. *Thodas* of Niligiri Hills and *Soligas* of Biligiri Rangana Hills in Mysore provide two other examples in this regard.

(viii) ***Promotion of Labour Interests of Tribals Engaged in Mining Industry and Tea Plantations:*** Attempts have been made to protect the labour interests of the tribals in Bihar, West Bengal, Mandhya Pradesh and Orissa who are engaged in mining industry and of the tribals such as Santals, Gonds, Khondas and others who are working in tea plantations of Assam.

4. Educational Facilities

Measures to provide educational facilities to the S.T. have been taken by the Government. Schools are established in some tribal areas. In the First Five Year Plan itself about 4000 schools were opened in the tribal areas. Education upto 10th standard has been made completely free for them. The students belonging to S.T. are getting various concessions such as free tuition, stipends, scholarships, free supply of text books, stationery and other equipments. In some places mid-day meals are also supplied. Free boarding and lodging facilities are provided for them. For the S.T. and S.C., 20% of the seats are reserved in technical education and relaxation is made in respect of age limit and qualifying marks.

- ***Education of ST Girls in Low Literacy Pockets*** : This scheme launched in 1993-94 aims at raising the literacy level of tribal females in 48 identified tribal districts in 8 states with female literacy below 2%. This scheme was revised in July 1998. This scheme envisages residential educational complex from 1st to 5th standards. The scheme is to be implemented through the voluntary organisations and State Governments / UTs. During 1999-2000, an amount of Rs.183.76 lakh was released for 75 complexes.

- There are ***Ashrama Schools*** for providing basic education and vocational training for S.T. In these schools education and training is given in areas such as agriculture, forestry, animal husbandry, poultry, farming, bee-keeping, handicrafts, etc. There are 600 Ashrama Schools of residential character situated in Andhra Pradesh, Gujarat, Himachal Pradesh, Madras, Karnataka, Orissa, Rajasthan and Tripura.

- ***Ashrama Schools in Tribal Sub-Plan Area*** : This centrally sponsored scheme was started in 1990-91 to provide assistance to the states and Union Territories on 50 per cent and 100 per cent basis, respectively. During 1999-2000, Rs.532.28 lakh have been released for the construction of 36 Ashrama Schools.

- ***Pre-Examination Training Centres for S.C.s and S.T.s*** are established in some places to help them to appear for UPSC Examinations and for I.A.S. and I.P.S. Examinations. The 1971 Census Report indicates that literacy has gone down in some tribal areas, while it has registered a slight progress in some other areas. Even in 1981 the literacy campaign could reach only 16.35% of the tribals.. In some cases 100% of the expenses of the students may have to be met by the Government.

- ***Girls / Boys Hostels for STs*** : Girls hostel scheme was started in the Third Five-Year Plan with the aim of providing residential facilities to tribal girls in pursuit of education. For this scheme, the central assistance is about 50% of the cost of construction of the hostels. During 1999-2000, an amount of Rs.393 lakh has been released for 29 hostels. ***Boys hostel scheme*** was started in 1989-90 under the same pattern of the scheme. During 1999-2000, an amount of Rs.698.43 lakh has been released for the construction of 77 hostels.

5. Medical Facilities

Various medical facilities have been provided for the tribals in the tribal areas. In some places, hospitals are established and in many places mobile hospital facilities have been provided.

Many preventive and curative measures to combat the diseases like malaria, leprosy, forest fever, monkey fever, typhoid, small pox, skin diseases etc. are undertaken. Medical camps are organised in the tribal areas to enable the tribals to realise the importance of modern medical facilities.

6. Research Work into the Problems of the Tribals

Tribal Research Institutes, which undertake intensive studies of tribal art, culture and customs and problems have been set up in Bihar, Madhya Pradesh, Orissa, Gujarat, Kerala, Maharashtra, Tamil Nadu, Andhra Pradesh, U.P., Rajasthan and West Bengal. The research work done in this field has thrown light on the tribal life and problems.

The research institutes are engaged in providing planning inputs to the State Governments, conducting research and evaluation studies, collection of data, conduct of training, seminars and workshops. Some of these institutes are also having museums exhibiting tribal artefacts. During 1999-2000, a sum of Rs.105.53 lakh was released to the State Governments for this purpose.

7. Role of Voluntary Organisations

The tribal welfare is not the concern of the government alone. Private organisations and individuals interested in the task of tribal upliftment must also be given due encouragement in this regard. Takkar Bapa and Gandhiji have shown that individuals and voluntary organisations with social commitment can do a lot for the welfare of tribals. Organisations such as – *Sri Ramakrishna Mission, Vanavasi Kalyanashrama, the Rastreeya Swayam Sevaka Sangha and a number of Christian Missionary Organisations* are already working in the field. Such organisations can help the tribals to develop better interaction with the neighbouring people.

- *Aid to Voluntary Organisations Working for the Welfare of the STs*: The ministry gives grant in aid to voluntary organisations working for the welfare of the scheduled tribes for projects like residential schools, hostels, medical units, computer training units, short-hand and typing training units, balawadis / creches, libraries and audio - visual units. The grant is generally restricted to 90% of approved total cost of the project and the balance 10% is borne by the grantee organisations. During 1999-2000, an amount of Rs.14.74 crore was released to 137 NGOs [Non-Governmental Organisations].

• Brief Assessment of the Welfare Programmes : Their Deficiencies and Failures

The Government of India which claims itself as a welfare state has no doubt made several constitutional and legislative provisions for the development and the welfare of the tribals. In almost all the Five Year Plans crores of rupees had been earmarked for undertaking tribal developmental activities. All the Ministries in the Central Cabinet had their own wings to look into the needs of the tribals and to promote their welfare. Various committees and commissions were constituted from time to time to recommend new programmes and schemes for the tribals. State Governments are also being encouraged to take initiative in help solving the problems of the tribals.

In spite of all these attempts to improve the living conditions of the tribals and promote their welfare, tribals of India have not benefited much. They continue to suffer from the same age-old problems though their intensity is somewhat reduced now. Governmental efforts to promote tribal welfare have not attained the expected success. On the contrary, many of these programmes and projects have proved to be a failure. S.C. Dube in his article in *Encyclopaedia of Social Work in India* Vol.3 points out various defects and deficiencies involved in the tribal development and welfare programmes. The views expressed by S.C. Dube in this connection can be briefly mentioned here.

1. The planners of the Tribal Developmental Projects have *failed to understand the diversities that exist between different tribal groups.* On the contrary, they treated the tribal community as *"a monolithic and undifferentiated entity."* Hence most of them ended in failures.

2. The planners *never took into account the relative numerical strength of different tribal groups.* There are tribal groups which have lakhs of members, while there are certain others which have only a couple of hundreds which are struggling for their existence. This difference is ignored by the planners.

3. The planners resorted to the *"omnibus planning, with a generalised conception of tribal problems"* and this led to *"misdirection of efforts."* When the tribals have got so much of cultural and physical diversities no single plan or project could be deemed as all comprehensive or all inclusive.

4. Most of the projects and schemes that were launched by the government *never took into account the felt-needs of the people.* Priorities were never fixed taking into account the immediate needs of the tribals. On the contrary, what the planners considered important was imposed on the tribals. Needless to say, they met cold reception.

5. A major portion of the money allotted for developmental programmes was *spent on the establishment of the plans and projects.* The amount of money that was really spent on the tribals was the least one. Much of it was spent on the salaries of the planners, the bureaucrats, employees of different cadres, on buildings, offices, employees' quarters, vehicles and their maintenance, roads and bridges, and so on.

6. The type of the services such as educational, medical, etc. that is being given to the tribals in the name of "tribal welfare" is found to be of very *poor standard.* This has annoyed the feelings of the tribals.

7. *Tribals are not supplied with enough foodgrains.* There are many tribal groups residing in the distant corners of the forests who are not even supplied with pure drinking water. In some areas, tribal women and children are made to walk miles of distance eveyday to fetch drinking water. This picture has not changed yet.

8. There are tribals who *do not have proper and enough dresses to wear, and good houses to live in.* Some of the tribals are so poor that they do not have erven a second pair of clothes to wear when the first one is kept for drying after wash.

9. The new economic system has posed new problems and challenges for the tribals. It has neither provided them *a job for the entire year nor enough salary to make their both ends meet.* Unemployment and under-employment coupled with poverty have made them borrow money at the hands of money lenders. Their economic helplessness compel them to get trapped in this vicious circle.

10. Education has been considered a panacea for all social problems including the tribal problems. *But the educational programmes launched by the governments are found to be disappointing. Ashrama* schools which posed themselves to be attractive in the beginning have failed to get enough children. Teachers who are appointed in the schools in the tribal areas are also found to be insincere having no concern for the tribal children.

11. It appears as though the central and the state governments are treating the tribals as things that could be "paraded" or "exhibited" to the dignitaries who visit national or state headquarters. Tribals are slowly becoming aware of the fact that they are being paraded to the so called dignified visitors as "show-pieces" of indigenous culture. This has hurt their self-respect.

12. It has also been found that several state governments have miserably failed in making effective use of the central financial assistance given for promoting the welfare of the tribals. There are also instances in which the funds that were allotted for the tribal welfare were diverted to other departments. In some other cases, the unutilised funds came back to the centre.
13. Indifference, irresponsibility, and lethargy on the part of the government employees have made many plans to meet with miserable failures. Hence, Dube cautions that one should *"....... not have an illusion that good plan necessarily produces good results."*

Conclusion

Though the Central and the State Governments have taken much interest in the tribal welfare programmes, projects and schemes, much remains to be done. The progress achieved in this field is far from satisfactory. The Sixth Plan document notes with concern that *"three decades of development have not had the desired impact on the socially, economically and educationally handicapped section"*. The Welfare programmes have not been effective due to the "inadequacies in the administrative machinery, lack of sensitive trained management, lack of general preparedness for large investments, deficiency in accounting systems, procedural delays and lack of proper monitoring and evaluation...." The plan document admits [in its clause 26-10] that *"no positive steps were taken to ensure that S.C. and S.T. obtained their share of the benefits of public distribution."* Even after the completion of the 9th Plan things have not radically improved. It is necessary that in the current plan and in the years to come due attention is to be paid for the over all improvement of the tribals.

S.C. Dube is of the opinion that in the absence of *"strong political will"* and *"bureaucratic commitment"* all our plans and projects are bound to become failures. He bitterly criticises the manner in which the list of the Scheduled Tribes is prepared. The process of preparing the list has become a matter of *"political policy"*, and hence cultural, economic, sociological and ethnic criteria are conveniently ignored. In order to provide the real benefit of the welfare programmes to the needy persons *"an economic criteria will have to be introduced"* in the process of the preparation of the list of Scheduled Tribes. Dube has warned about the political interference in the implementation of welfare programmes. He was also aware of the difficulties involved in de-politicalising the developmental programmes. Hence he suggests *"It is not possible to de-politicise the development process, but institutions will have to be built to take over the responsibility of this programme ultimately."*[1]

Dube has also recognised the need to harmonise the national and tribal interests. He states : "........ let it be understood that the tribal problem cannot be isolated from the broader national problems. Its solution will have to form part of the overall strategy for the regeneration of Indian society and polity........" Dube has stated that there are certain problems which are uniquely tribal. These problems are to be studied in detail sympathetically and scientifically. The studies must help us to find out a long lasting solution for these problems. He concludes : *"The tribes have to find themselves a place in Indian society consistent with their conception of honour, but this must be done without detriment to the integrity or strength of India as a nation."* At the same time, it is also necessary to appreciate and retain the distinct cultural ethos of the tribal communities.

The Changing Face of the Tribal Life

The *Adivasis* or aboriginals lived in this country and witnessed the rise and fall of several empires. They had the occasion to participate in several battles that took place over the years either

1 S.C. Dube *"Welfare of Scheduled Tribes"* in *Encyclopaedia of Social Work in India.* Vol.III.

supporting the local rulers or opposing them. They could no longer confine themselves to their so called unapproachable territories. The flood of socio-political, religious and economic changes has made them understand the realities and face the challenges of the modern world. Hence, social change has become the companion of tribals in India, as it has been the case all over the world. Social change as such is not a challenge, but to find the equilibrium between their indigenous culture and the borrowed culture, is a tough task.

Inevitable Exposure of the Tribals to the Influence of the Modern World: In the process of massive social change tribals too have experienced vast transformation. Hence, it is unfair to portray them as savage, uncivilised and pitiably backward. On the contrary, tribal communities in different parts of the world are coming in close contact with the modern world, its civilisation, its economy, its religion and politics. Some have already become *"modernised"*, and many others are becoming *"Westernised"* in the Eastern world. **Eriksen**'s observations are very relevant here. *"In any corner of the world today – whether tribal or non-tribal – it is not possible to live without regular contact with the world market and the state. The fact is that the tribals today cannot escape from state and its citizenship. The state, on the other hand, is in close relationship with the civil society. Money has become a dominant medium. The subsistence economy of the tribals has taken to capitalistic economy. Tourism, migration and other factors of transport and communication have brought the tribals closer to the wider society. It is in this context that we look at the changing tribal India."*[1]

Government's Policy Towards the Tribals

The Govt. of India for the purpose of its governance administratively defined the *Adivasis* or tribals as *"Scheduled Tribes."* But it has not been able to resolve the ethnic relations between the tribal society and the caste Hindu society. The secular government is not much bothered about it also. Ethnographers like **Hutton,** for example, maintained that *"Caste system and many cultural traditions of Hinduism have organic links with the tribal cultures."*[2] **Ghurye** who called the Indian tribals *"backward Hindus"*, also held more or less the same view. The Government, instead, wants that the tribals should be given benefits of development and protective safeguards. These are necessary because the tribals have suffered enough from exploitation, discrimination and oppression by the rest of the society. They remained poor, illiterate, ignorant and backward.

Social Change in Tribal India

After independence, lot of changes have taken place in the Indian society at large. As **Prof. Yogendra Singh** observed, *"Major occupational and techno-cultural changes have taken place in our society due to the political, social and economic developments. These changes have promoted linkages and interactions among castes, tribes, religious groups and cultural regions. We notice significant magnitude of the spread effect of these cultural changes across the regions and ethnic boundaries......... The process of cultural integration on a national scale has grown but with simultaneous increase in search for cultural autonomy."*[3]

It is true that the tribals have become conscious of the fact that their ethnic identity is invaded by Christianity and Hinduism. Tribals are at a confusion now. Some among them have raised the slogan *"Return to the tribal religion"* despite the religious conversion. Tribals are also engaged in some of the movements in their search for tribal identity and cultural protection.

1 **Eriksen**'s Views as referred to by **S.L. Doshi** and **P.C. Jain** *"Social Anthropology"* [2001]. Page - 379.
2 **Hutton** as quoted by **S.L. Doshi** and **P.C. Jain** *"Social Anthropology"* [2001]. Page - 379.
3 **Prof. Yogendra Singh** in his presidential address to the *"Indian Sociological Society"* [1994]. As quoted by **Doshi** and **Jain**. Page - 381.

The various social and cultural changes that have taken place among the tribals during these decades may be briefly discussed here.

1. ***Changes in Tribal Social Stratification*** : Some of the studies conducted in the tribal areas have revealed that slowly a kind of change is taking place in the tribal social stratification. The tribals seem to have attained *the status of class from that of ethnicity*. For example, the *Mundas* of Chotanagpur area, have formed themselves into social classes [**S.D. Badgaiyan**]. A similar kind of class stratification has taken place among the *Chaudhari* tribe of southern Gujarat [**Jan Bremman**]. It is also said that the class formation among the tribals in this part of the country has developed to the level of Marxian class consciousness.

2. ***Tribals Taking to Non-Agricultural Occupations*** : Tribals in India in general resorted to agriculture during the first quarter of the 20th century. They had enough land in their possession at this stage. Because of the British intervention and their forest policy, the caste Hindus started making their entry into the tribal hinterland as a result of which the tribal land slipped into the hands of these non-tribals. Tribal population started increasing on the one hand, and on the other, they experienced land alienation. This situation forced the tribals to migrate to the neighbouring villages in search of jobs. For example, a section of the tribals in Orissa, Bihar, and Madhya Pradesh have migrated from their parent villages. They became job workers in the migrated places. This process of the tribals taking to non-agricultural occupations is often referred to as *"depeasantization."*

As **Bremman** has pointed out that *the tribals have not only been depeasantised but also have become proletarianised.* He cites the example of *Halpatis* and *Chaudhras* of Bardoli taluka of Surat who have become proletarianised. As he remarks, this fall is very serious.

3. ***Migration*** : Social anthropologists have picturised the tribal people as immobile people. According to them, they confine themselves to a particular territory ["common territory"] from which they hardly move out. But the search for employment in the case of the Indian context, has made many tribals to move out of their villages. Some have even gone to the big cities and a few others to Gulf countries. A large number of tribals are working as migrant groups outside their parent village. Reservation facility which has helped the tribals to obtain government jobs, also encouraged them to move from one state to another or outside their own state. Migration is thus a powerful factor in the transformation of the tribals.

4. ***Political Awareness and Participation*** : Political factors and forces do work among the Indian tribes. As **Rajani Kothari** has pointed out *"The universal right for voting, party functioning, social activism have all initiated a strong process of political socialisation among the tribals. They have become shrewd enough to make compromises and alliances at the regional, state and central levels."*[1]

5. ***Diversified Economy*** : Tribal economy for a very long time depended on the forests and forest produce. Tribals were experts in wood cutting and collecting fruits, nuts, berries, medicinal plants available in forests, etc. Along the coastal belt they are good in fishing. *But unlike the caste Hindus, their occupations are not hereditary as such.* Hence, they have the freedom to switch over from one occupation to another. This factor has enabled the *"subsistence economy"* of the tribals to get transformed into a *"diversified economy."*

6. ***Tribals From Local to Global Plane*** : In this modern era of globalisation no single community can keep itself in isolation for a long time. This factor has affected the tribals also. The tribals are also able to establish their links with the outside world. The small tribal homelands, for example, are linked with the region, state, nation and the world. *"The world problems, for instance,*

1 Doshi and Jain *"Social Anthropology."* Page - 383.

environment pollution, endemics of malaria, cancer and AIDS have become the larger problems of a tribal village also." The modern mass media has helped the tribals to be in touch with the rest of the world though a large number of them are still residing in the remote areas.

"The tribals are no longer an encapsulated mass of people restricted to hills and forests. They have become a part of the larger process of globalisation. The process is a vigorous and continuous one, and the tribals have to decide which direction they have to march in. The future of the tribals rests on their own rational and cultural decision."[1]

Modern Factors of Tribal Transformation

As it is made clear from the above explanation that the tribal world is in transformation. Various factors have contributed for this transformation. Some of them may be examined here.

1. Christianity and its Missionary Activities

Christianity has been an important factor of tribal change in India especially from the time of the establishment of British rule. The Christian Missionaries who were indirectly supported by the British rule converted a large number of tribals during the last 100 years. We find sizeable number of Christians among the *Khasis* and *Garos* of Meghalaya, *Oraons* of Chotanagpur, *Bhils* of Madhya Pradesh, *Mizos* of Mizoram, *Nagas* of Nagaland, and among many other tribals of the North-East. *"According to one estimate, the tribal Christians constitute about one-sixth of the total Christian population of India. The traditional tribal cultures and institutions have adversely affected under the impact of new ideas, ethical values and a new style of life......... Vidyarthi [1997 : 460] is of the opinion that Christianity has provided the first model of Westernisation to the tribals in the shape of "church organisation", Western education, and above all, Western values and morals."*[2]

2. Factors of Industrialisation and Urbanisation

Industrialisation and urbanisation have brought about revolutionary changes in some parts of tribal India. Especially after the launching of the Five Year Plans, the process of industrialisation started taking a new momentum. Industries were established even near the forest and the tribal areas. The tribals residing in these areas started making use of this new economic opportunity. For instance, the mining and mineral based industries in Chotanagpur have provided employment to thousands of tribals. Tribals of Bihar, M.P., and Orissa took to wax industry. Tribals in West Bengal resorted to sericulture. Bihar government encouraged tribal women to take part in handicrafts. Tribals of M.P. became the collectors and suppliers of *beedi* leaves to the big *beedi* industries.

"Thus, the once isolated homogeneous and primitive communities are now exposed to the forces of industrial urbanisation and face the prospects of assimilation into the global network of urban-industrial civilisation. A new line of change is seen also in tribal occupation, economy and social life." [Dr. Ravindranath Rao. Page - 64].

3. Factor of Education

The level of literacy is very poor among the tribals. In fact, according to the Census of 1991, literacy rate among the tribals is as low as **29.6%** [males 40.65%, females 18.19%]. Prior to independence no systematic efforts were made to promote literacy among the tribals. This situation changed after independence with the introduction of many measures for tribal uplift. In the Five Year Plans due attention was paid to the establishment of schools in the tribal areas. Residential schools

---

1 S.L. Doshi and P.C. Jain *"Social Anthropology."* Page - 384.

2 Dr. Ravindranath Rao *"Tribal Social Transformation"* in *"Samaja Shodhana"* Vol.1, No.2, Oct. 1992. Page - 63.

known as the *Ashrama Schools* also came in. Freeships, scholarships, free boarding and free lodging facilities and free tuition classes and such other facilities were provided to the tribal children to promote education among them. Though these efforts have not brought about the desired results, they have definitely created an educational awareness among the tribals.

4. Change in the Government's Attitude Towards the Tribals

Before independence, the policy of the British government was to let the tribals live in isolation. The administration was, therefore, regulatory in character and dealt with such matters as revenue, regulation of land, and law and order. *People had to go to the administrators in order to find solutions to their problems.*

After independence, through the introduction of various welfare measures, the government expressed its great concern in the development and progress of the tribals. *Now the administrators are required to go to the tribal areas to meet the tribals in order to find out their problems.* The government expects the administrators to be honest and humane in their approach towards the tribals. It is unfortunate that such a change in the attitude of the bureaucrats has not taken place. Hence, expected progress has not taken place in the tribal world. Still, the gap between the tribals and non-tribals is not bridged. The gap between the rich tribals and the poor tribals is also not minimised. Much is to be done in this regard. *"Nevertheless, at the all India level, it cannot be denied that the tribal development schemes have broken the stagnation of tribal societies and have initiated the process of tribal transformation."* [Dr. Ravindranath Rao. Page - 65].

5. Tribal Elites as Agents of Modernisation

Tribal leadership is an important aspect of the tribal transformation. It is widely recognised that the tribal elites have been effective human agents in the tribal system. They can keep in touch with the outside world on the one hand, and on the other, they can maintain their leadership among their own tribes. Dedicated tribal elites can play a vital role in transforming the tribal society. But the question is, whether in actuality, they are doing this. This is because some studies have shown that in some cases, the tribal elites are involved in the economic exploitation of their own fellow tribals. As Sah [1985] has pointed out in his study of the *Bhotias* of Uttar Pradesh, the benefit of the developmental schemes have been largely reaped by the already well to do members of the community and the poorer sections continue to remain backward. In the present context, it appears as though the role of the tribal elites is very much limited mainly because, *they have not been organised to become agents of social transformation.*

Chapter 13

RURAL LIFE IN INDIA

PART I : RURAL INDIA

NATURE, FEATURES AND PROBLEMS

***India A Classical Land of Villages** - Indian Villages Through the Ages - Village Studies - Some Important Village Studies and The Main Issues Involved in Them - Importance and Limitations of Village Studies - Definition of Village - Traditional Characteristics of Indian Village - Agrarian Class Structure - Daniel Thorner's Classification : Landlords, Working Peasants and Labourers - Village Solidarity : Factors Favourable for Solidarity - Manifestation of Village Solidarity : Critical Comments - Village Settlement Patterns : Nucleated and Dispersed Villages - A.R. Desai and J.B. Chitambar's Classification - **Land Tenure System and Land Reforms After Independence :** Systems of Land Tenure in Pre-Independence India : The Zamindari Tenure and Its Defects: The Mahalwari System; Ryotwari Tenure and Its Evil Effects - Land Reforms After Independence - Land Reform Measures : Abolition of Intermediaries, Tenancy Reforms, Ceilings on Land Holdings and Its Advantages - Consolidation of Land Holdings and Its Advantages - Co-operative Farming - Progress of Land Reforms in India A Brief Assessment - Causes for the Poor Performance of Land Reforms Programme - **Problems of Indian Villages :** Agricultural Problems, Economic Problems, Social Problems.*

The present world is still dominated by the villages. In spite of the craze towards city life majority of the people in this globe prefer to stay back in their villages in the midst of nature. Hence the world population is predominantly rural. More than 2/3 of the world's population still lives in villages. India is basically a land of villages. In spite of the increasing trend towards urbanisation more than 3/4 of the population of India resides in more than **5.58** lakh villages. The study of the Indian society becomes meaningful and fruitful only if its villages, and their problems are studied carefully. It is the task of *"rural sociology"* to delve deep into the phenomenon of village life. Even in India, rural sociology, that is sociology of rural life is becoming a full-fledged academic discipline with a firm foundation.

Villages existed in India even during the Vedic period and also prior to that. Some even described these villages as *"self-contained little republics"*. The autonomy, independence and self-sufficiency which the Indian Villages enjoyed for centuries came to an end during the British Period. But under the British rule they were slowly exposed to the modern trends. Scholars started making some systematic studies of the villages especially after Independence. These studies though have their limitations, are of much importance in understanding our own rural society and its dynamics. They started throwing much light on village solidarity, village settlement patterns, rural class structure, land reforms and their impact, agrarian unrest and so on.

It is true that the Indian Villages are undergoing a fast change now. These changes have not always brought the positive results in all the spheres of village life. There are a large number of villages which suffer from major problems such as *poverty, unemployment, illiteracy, indebtedness, superstition* and the like. Progress of the nation can be ensured only if these rural problems are dealt with carefully and efficiently. Sociologists have time and again emphasised this point.

This part of this chapter gives only a glimpse of the Indian rural society, its nature, character and its problems.

India a Classical Land of the Villages

The social life of man has undergone different stages of development. The earliest human communities were perhaps the loosely organised aggregations of a few families who carried on mutually interdependent activities in gathering food and defending themselves against their enemies. These primitive bands were migratory. Gradually, man acquired skill and knowledge in agriculture. Then began the settled life of man. With the development of agriculture and the consequent stabilisation of the source of food, human communities became more permanent. These communities came to be known as *Village Communities.* The village is the oldest permanent community of man.

All early communities were basically rural in character. As **Kropotkin** points out, *"We do not know one single human race or single nation which has not had its period of village communities."* **Bogardus** says, *"Human society has been cradled in the rural group."*

India is a land of villages and villagers constitute the backbone of the country. Since time immemorial India has been cherishing the village life. Villages continue to dominate the Indian way of life as they have done before. Villages constitute one of the basic elements of our social structure. It is the village which has sheltered the two other elements of social structure, namely: *caste* and *joint family system.* An overwhelming majority of India's population live in more than **5.58** lakh villages. According to 1991 Census, the village population in India is about 74.28%. In the previous 1981 Census, the village population stood at 76.7%. The urban population of India was 10.8% in 1901; it increased to only 23.3% in 1981, and 25.72% in 1991 and is projected to be at **28.4%** in the year 2000. In absolute terms, the urban population in India is projected to be **285** million in 2001 compared to **217.17** million in 1991. In the time span of around 100 years [1881-1991] India's urban population increased only by 10%. Thus the dominance of villages continues.

Varied Size of the Villages

According to 1991 census, India has 5,58,088 villages. But the size of the villages has always varied. However, a large number of villages are medium sized. Details of village size and their percentage to the total number of villages, according to 1991 census, are given below :

Population Size	*Percentage to Total Number of villages*
Less than 500	26.5
Between 500 - 2000	48.8
Between 2000 - 5000	19.4

Obviously, medium size villages constitute about half of the number of total villages. Besides population size, the number of villages found in different states also varies. For instance, the largest number of villages, i.e., 1,12,566, are found in Uttar Pradesh, followed by 71,352 in Madhya

Pradesh, 67,546 in Bihar, 46,553 in Orissa, and 39,354 in Maharashtra. In the states of Sikkim and Nagaland the smallest number of villages, that is, 440 and 1112 respectively, are found. People normally prefer to settle in villages where they get some land for cultivation, some source of drinking water and more or less a friendly physical environment.

Indian Villages through the Ages

Indian villages have a prolonged history of their own. They existed in all the major stages of our socio-political history. As an important unit in the Indian social polity the village has played a prominent role. It finds significant mention in the classical texts of the land.

Villages in the Vedic Period

The Rig Veda denotes *"grama"* [or village] as an aggregate of several families sharing the same habitation. According to Rig Veda, society is divided into many dynamic hierarchical groups. Smallest unit of the society is the family. A *grama* consists of several such families. A group of *gramas* constitute one *"vish"*. Many such *vishas* taken together constitute one *"jana"*, and several such *janas* together make one *"desha"* [nation]. It is clear that in the Rig Vedic period village was a unit of social and political organisation of India. Each village or *grama* was headed by a *"gramani"*.

Villages in the Epic Period

Ramayana makes a mention of villages. According to Ramayana, *gramani*, the head of the village who was appointed by the King, was working strictly as per the advices of the village elders who were chosen by an assembly of the village. *Gramani* was assigned the duty of looking after village defence. It was also his duty to collect state dues and to maintain records relating to such collections. He was in charge of important papers and records. Finally, he was vested with some judicial functions.

Mahabharatha mentions several types of habitations and settlements. It refers to the village as the most fundamental unit of administration having *"gramani"* as its leader and chief spokesman. It was the concern of the *gramani* to arrange for the defence of the village within certain demarcated area. Villages were grouped together and a group of 10 villages [*dasha grama*] had a leader called *"Dasha gramani."* Two groups of *dasha grama* was headed by its leader *"Vinshatik."* The one who was the head of 100 villages was known as *"Shathagramani"* and the one in charge of 100 villages was called *"Adhipathi."*

Villages in the Buddhist Period

We have enough literature to speak of the position of the villages during the 5th and 6th Century B.C. the period in which Jainism and Buddhism emerged. Self governing village communities existed during this period. Buddhist literature give us information about the arrangement of villages, towns and forts. *Jataka Stories* often mention of *Gana, Nigama, Kula* and *Nagarika.* The Jain texts also provide us references relating to the settlements such as *Ghosha, Kheta, Kharvata, Grama, Palli, Pattana, Samvaha,* etc. The *Jataka Stories* refer to the village as a unit composing of 1,000 families. Each *grama* was organised as a socio-political unit under the authority of the headman. The headman was vested with the authority of collecting the revenue and protecting the village from thieves and robbers. The most significant aspect of the village organisation during this period was that the village affairs were completely managed by the villagers themselves. It means in several respects each *grama* was independent and autonomous.

Villages in the Mauryan Period

"Arthashastra" of **Kautilya** provides us specific details about the village and its administration during the Mauryan period. *"Arthashastra"* states that a unit of 10 villages was called *"Samgrahana"*, of 200 villages a *"Karvatika"*, of 400 villages a *"Dronamukha"* and of 800 villages a *"Mahagrama."* Each village had a wonderful administrative system. Village administrative staff consisted of the *"Adhyakhsa"* [headman], *"Samkhayaka"* [accountant], *"Sthanikas"* [officials of different grades], *"Anikastha"* [veterinary doctor] and *"Jamagha Karika"* [village couriers]. In addition to these staff, there were also persons to look after village sanitation, horse training, etc. and these people were granted non-alienable rent free land.

Analysing the nature of village communities in the Mauryan period **Dr. Satya Ken Vidyalankar** writes : *"Every village was self-governed and absolutely free in all matters relating to itself. The village had its own assembly [Sabha] which discussed all matters relating to the village, framed rules for the entire community and punished offenders after regular trials. The assembly made provisions for the religious and social welfare of the community. It also arranged for recreation........ whoever may be the ruler of the country, it affected little to these village folks. They were governed by their own assembly. The Indian people lived independently in these self-governing village republics."*[1]

Villages during the Gupta Period

After the decline of the Mauryas, the Guptas in course of time emerged as a powerful political force. Even during the Gupta and post-Gupta period, villages and village councils continued to enjoy importance as local administrative units. Sometimes the members of the village council were elected and some other times selected. The village councils were in charge of all major affairs of the village such as public works, village defence, temple management, village disputes, charities, etc. It is significant to note that **Dr. Majumdar** and **Altekar** have stated that these village councils especially during the rule of *Vakataka Gupta* discharged almost all the functions of the government.

Villages during the Mughal Period

Even during the period of the Muslim rule, villages remained as political units having a network of relations with other political units such as town, city, *paragana* and province. The Mughals were more interested in their administration of the cities rather than the villages. Muslims also concentrated much in the cities. The Mughal rulers showed no interest in the development of the villages. Hence the administration of village *panchayat* was left in the hands of the local village *panchayat.* The village *panchayat*s were themselves looking after security, education, sanitation and other essential matters. The head of the village was exercising power in his own way to control the village and village activities. In fact, each village had a *Chowkidar* who used to look after village defence and discipline. The Mughal administration did not interfere in the internal affairs of the village and only under special circumstances was giving directions.

Villages in the British Period

It is here under the British rule the dominance, autonomy and self-sufficiency of the Indian villages almost came to an end. As **John Mathi** remarks, *"The village organisation lost much of its internal cohesion, many of the administrative duties left to be done by the village community were*

---

1 **Dr. Sathya Ken Vidyalankar** as quoted by **H.K. Moulesh** and **G. Subramanya** in *"Sociology of Indian Society"* [1997]. Page - 130.

taken up into the hands of the Central Government and its subordinate agencies." The village community lost its autonomy and its administration now became centralised. Centralised British administration was controlling the villages through an army of bureaucratised officers. Indian village administration had never experienced such a kind of ruthless centralised administration in the past. Hence, it was not able to cope with the new situation. Villages started declining thereafter. Number of factors contributed to the disappearance of the erstwhile village administration. Some of them may be noted.

Causes For the Decline in the Importance of Villages

1. ***Denial of Financial Assistance*** **:** The British administration never provided any grant to the village fund from the village revenue for the developmental activities. This very badly affected the financial position of the local administrative unit.

2. ***Centralisation of Administration*** **:** The British by establishing centralised and uniform legal system put an end to the power and authority of village administration. The village elders and headman could no more exercise their power and prestige to control the village affairs. All types of civil and criminal matters and disputes came under the British courts.

3. ***Impact of Urbanisation*** **:** During the British rule the process of urbanisation got a new momentum. As a result, large number of people started moving towards urban centres for various purposes. Cities became more attractive than the villages. Villages which lacked all kinds of avenues and opportunities got relegated into insignificance.

4. ***Introduction of the Exploitative Zamindari System*** **:** The British introduced the zamindari system and through that it wanted to establish a new system of revenue collection and land settlement. This new system which the British introduced to their advantage virtually ruined the villages. Class and caste hatreds also started because of that.

5. ***No Sincere Efforts to Revive Village Panchayats*** **:** The British administration passed certain *Panchayat Acts* in certain states to revive the village *panchayat*s only for the name sake. Virtually, the administration did nothing in concrete to revive the *panchayat* system. The Acts remained as dead letters.

6. ***Impact of Industrialisation and Technology*** **:** The process of industrialisation, technological advancement, improvement in the system of transport and communication and modern education which the British introduced, resulted in rural-urban migration. The Western culture which the British brought along with them made Indians to become egoistic and individualistic. The ugly fruits of egoism, individualism, hedonism, etc. also crept into the villages. This led to group conflicts, feuds and factional strifes, caste and class conflicts at the cost of village harmony. Thus, the self-sufficiency, self-reliance and the autonomy of the Indian villages were sacrificed at the altar of the British rule.

Village Studies and their Significance

Though systematic study of the Indian villages have been made only recently, available records would tell us that even during the British rule some studies were made about them. As **Doshi** and **Jain** have pointed out that on the basis of the available information, village studies that have been made right from the days of British Raj to the present day could be categorised into the following three divisions :

Statewise Distribution of Villages

According to Population - 1991

States / UTs	Less than 1,000	1,000 to 1,999	2,000 to 4,999	5,000 to 9,999	10,000 & over	Total
INDIA[1]	**390,093**	**114,395**	**62,915**	**10,597**	**2,779**	**580,781**
1. Andhra Pradesh	11,586	6,433	6,510	1,474	313	26,586
2. Arunachal Pradesh	3,538	82	25	3	1	3,649
3. Assam	17,784	4,988	1,793	111	9	24,685
4. Bihar	45,164	12,768	7,647	1,604	330	67,513
5. Goa	156	78	94	31	1	360
6. Gujarat	8,528	5,432	3,418	575	75	18,028
7. Haryana	2,627	2,021	1,703	364	44	6,759
8. Himachal Pradesh	16,361	495	136	5	-	16,997
9. Karnataka	17,113	5,861	3,422	570	100	27,066
10. Kerala	7	16	102	252	1,007	1,384
11. Madhya Pradesh	56,568	11,426	3,264	261	7	71,526
12. Maharashtra	24,111	10,632	4,715	762	192	40,412
13. Manipur	1,834	192	135	16	3	2,182
14. Meghalaya	5,316	129	38	1	-	5,484
15. Mizoram	616	61	19	2	-	698
16. Nagaland	929	170	108	8	1	1,216
17. Orissa	39,309	5,761	1,812	103	4	46,989
18. Punjab	7,447	3,130	1,628	209	14	12,428
19. Rajasthan	27,123	7,060	3,255	420	31	37,889
20. Sikkim	336	79	29	3	-	447
21. Tamil Nadu	4,915	4,625	4,764	1,247	271	15,822
22. Tripura	195	203	648	94	15	855
23. Uttar Pradesh	74,866	24,523	11,949	1,336	129	112,803
24. West Bengal	22,701	8,065	5,819	1,117	208	37,910
25. A & N Islands	445	44	15	-	-	504
26. Chandigarh	7	6	8	3	1	25
27. D & N Haveli	27	17	25	1	1	71
28. Daman & Diu	9	6	6	2	1	24
29. Delhi	29	44	86	19	21	199
30. Lakshadweep	2	-	4	1	-	7
31. Pondicherry	174	48	38	3	-	263

1. Excludes the population of Jammu & Kashmir where the 1991 census could not be conducted due to disturbed conditions.

Source : **India Year Book 1999.** Page - 15.

(i) *Studies / reports brought out by administrators;*[1]

(ii) *Studies conducted by economists;* and

(iii) *Studies prepared by sociologists and anthropologists.*

Of these types of studies, studies made by social anthropologists and sociologists have started assuming importance today. **Yogesh Atal** [1969] in this regard has aptly pointed out that *"...... both sociologists and anthropologists are jointly exploring the village community with a largely common methodology. Rural India provides a good meeting ground for the two disciplines. This effective communication is indeed a healthy trend and one should welcome this happy 'merging'."*[2]

M.N. Srinivas in his book *"Caste in Modern India And Other Essays"* has made an attempt to stress the importance of anthropological studies of Indian villages for other disciplines such as economics, history, comparative religion and for the practical tasks of social and agricultural reconstruction.

Some Important Village Studies and the Main Issues Included in Them

Village studies conducted during the British rule were made mainly for consolidating the British Raj in India. But in the post-independent era these were held basically for two reasons namely; (i) *to help village development or reconstruction,* and (ii) *to consolidate Panchayat Raj.* It is in this context, village studies became an urgent task for nation building.

Some of the most important village studies which were undertaken especially after 1955 may be mentioned here. In fact, the year 1955 itself witnessed a flood of sociological literature on villages.

1. S.C. Dube's *"Indian Village"* [1955], for example, gives a traditional account of a village located in the Telangana region of Andhra Pradesh namely; **Shamirpeth.** The village exhibits integration in spite of the fact that it has more than a dozen castes in its range.

2. M.N. Srinivas's edited work *"India's Villages"* [1955] for which Indian, British and US scholars like M.N. Srinivas, S.C. Dube, David Mandelbaum, Eric J. Miller, Kathleen Gough, McKim Marriott and others have contributed – takes into consideration the totality of village life. The concept of *"dominant caste"* makes its first appearance in this edited work in which M.N. Srinivas has given his explanation of **Rampura Village** near Mysore.

3. McKim Marriot's *"Village India"* [1955] which is also an edited work, includes both foreign and Indian anthropologists and it looks at the Indian villages from the complexity of Indian civilisation.

4. D.N. Majumdar's edited work *"Rural Profiles"* consists of the contributions of sociologists and anthropologists. The contributing authors of this work have made an attempt to re-examine the concepts such as *"Sanskritisation"*, *"Dominant Castes"*, etc. introduced by M.N. Srinivas.

5. F.G. Bailey's *"Caste and the Economic Frontier"* [1957] as a study of two villages of Orissa highlights the problem of caste and class formation.

---

1 Some of the important British writings of Indian village are as follows :

(i) W.F. Firminger's *"The Fifth Report from the Select Committee of the House of Commons on the Affairs of the East India Company"* [1812].

(ii) Charles Metcalfe's *"Minutes on the Village of Delhi"* [1830].

(iii) H.S. Maine's *"Village Communities in the East and West"* [1871].

(iv) B.H. Baden-Powell's *"The Land Systems of British India"*[1892] 3 Vol.

2 **Yogesh Atal** as quoted by **S.L. Doshi** and **P.C. Jain** in their *"Rural Sociology."* Page - 61.

6. A.R. Desai's edited work *"Rural Sociology in India"* [1969] is another major study in the field of rural sociology. Different anthropologists and sociologists who have contributed for this work, have highlighted the historical aspects of village life, its stratification system, land reforms, agrarian unrest and such other topics.

Other Important Village Studies

(i) **D.N. Majumdar's** [1958] study of *Mohana Village* in U.P.

(ii) **G.S. Ghurye's** *"After a Century and a Quarter"* [1960].

(iii) **Andre Beteille's** study of *Sripuram.*

(iv) **Lewis's** study of *"Village Life in Northern India"* [1958].

(v) **Edrian Mayer's** *"Caste and Kinship in Central India"* [1960].

(vi) **A.R. Desai's** *"Peasant Struggles in India"* [1979].

Importance of Village Studies

Village studies may have their own limitations but they have definitely enriched our knowledge regarding the Indian society in general and rural India, in particular.

1. Rural Studies Help in Planning Rural Reconstruction

M.N. Srinivas is of the opinion that the village studies provide detailed information regarding various aspects of rural life such as the extent of sub division and fragmentation of holdings, the nature of rural credit, the conditions of landless labourers, etc. They also highlight how these aspects are related to other social aspects. As Srinivas remarks : *"Thus for instance, a survey of rural credit cannot ignore the existence of elaborate marriage and funeral rites and ideas regarding how they ought to be performed."* In this connection Srinivas describes how his study of Rampura helped him to understand the various dimensions of the cattle problem of India.

2. Village Studies Provide Useful Information to Other Disciplines

The data collected by the anthropologists and sociologists are more accurate and unbiased and hence, are highly useful for other social scientists. It is true that the data collected by village officials appointed by the government, many a time are used by economists, political scientists and others. It is in this context, M.N. Srinivas states that *"These officials do not, as a rule, have either the training or the interest to collect accurate information and besides in a majority of cases, they have a vested interest in supplying wrong information."*[1]

Further, the studies of villages also provide the future historian with lot of information about rural social life. M.N. Srinivas thus writes : *"These studies constitute, therefore, valuable contributions to the social, political, economic, and religious history of the country. And these studies are specially valuable in view of the fact that we have only a few more years to record facts about a society which is changing fundamentally and with great rapidity."*

Village studies throw light on an important aspect of Hinduism. M.N. Srinivas is of the opinion that though Hinduism does not believe in religious conversions, a peculiar type of conversion is going on within Hinduism. He writes : *"It is true that Hindus do not try to convert Christians and Muslims, but in a sense conversion is going on all the time within Hinduism. The lower castes and tribal people have been undergoing Sanskritization all the time, and sects, Brahmanical and non-*

1 **Chingamani** *"Sociology of Indian Society"* [1998]. Page - 185.

Brahmanical and Vaishnavite and Shaivite, have actively sought converts........"[1]

3. Village Studies Provide Useful Knowledge about Indian Social Reality

It is true that an understanding about different aspects of Indian social reality is highly influenced by the Indological literature, that is, by the *"book-view."* There could be a lot of difference or incongruity between the 'book-view' and the empirical reality. Hence **M.N. Srinivas** argues that *"The only cure for this marked literary bias lies in doing field research. The field worker confronted by the bewildering variety and complexity of facts as they actually are, is forced to relate what he sees to what he has assumed it to be, and the lack of correspondence between the two results in his attempting to reassess the written material."* M.N. Srinivas is aware that all sociological problems cannot be studied in the villages.

The significance of the village studies is such that sometimes their value may extend beyond national boundaries. According to Srinivas, *"To the anthropologist, the villages are invaluable observation centres where he can study in detail social processes and problems to be found occurring in many parts of the world. An anthropologist goes to live in a village for a year or even two not because he wants to collect information about curious and dying customs and beliefs but to study a theoretical sociological problem and his most important aim is to contribute to the growing body of theoretical knowledge about the nature of human societies."*

Commenting on the value of village studies **S.C. Dube** also remarks : *"There can be no doubt that village studies in this country have a future. Our teething troubles are over, we have now to devote ourselves to the task of developing a proper conceptual frame of reference testing our methodological tools, formulating clear hypothesis, and the going into the field for a spell of good solid field work. In doing this we shall not only satisfy our overdeveloped sense of curiosity and make valuable theoretical advances, but shall contribute our bit towards understanding of the emotional integration of India, and will provide the requisite background data from which more purposeful planning can emerge."*[2]

Main Drawbacks of Village Studies in India

"Village studies" have assumed sociological and socio-anthropological importance no doubt. They still continue as popular area of sociological studies. According to **S.C. Dube**, one should be very critical about their validity, and be aware of their limitations. He speaks of a few limitations of such studies among which the following may be noted.

(a) Village Studies are not often Representative in Nature

Indian society is complex and diverse that many a times the village studies do not add anything to our knowledge about Indian society for they do not constitute a representative sample. **Yogesh Atal** further add to this view when he cautions that *"In every village in India, there is something which distinguishes it from the village of the other countries in the world. If the two villages of different countries are to be examined, at least this could be easily said that both these villages do not belong to the same country and culture."*[3]

---

1 **Chingamani.** ''*Sociology of Indian Society*'' Page - 186.

2 **S.C. Dube** as quoted by **Prof. Chingamani.** Page : 187 - 188.

3 **Yogesh Atal** as quoted by **Prof. Chingamani.** Page - 183.

M.N. Srinivas who admits this view also states that the anthropologists must become aware of this problem and take proper precautions[1] to overcome it.

2. Exaggerating the Unity and Self-Sufficiency of the Village

One of the tendencies of the anthropologists is to consider the village as an isolated entity and to ignore or underscore its links with the wider social system. As a result, the unity or solidarity of the village is overemphasised and its connecting links with other units of society are conveniently forgotten.

Dube criticises that some of the village studies in India do suffer from this limitation. But he makes an optimistic observation when he says that the anthropologists and sociologists are becoming aware of this problem, and hence they have started studying single villages in the background of the wider universe of Indian civilisation.

3. Influence of Alien Concepts and Categories

It is very often commented that most of our social researchers, including those who undertake village studies, blindly imitate Western methods, styles and models. It is observed that most of the Indian village studies have been often modelled on similar studies done elsewhere in the world. **S.C. Dube** also comments : *"While our descriptive categories are satisfactory our analytical categories leave much to be desired."* Dube states that these limitations are natural to the initial efforts in any field of study. But he agrees that it is necessary to build up concepts and hypotheses derived from the Indian culture.

Definition of Village - Traditional Character

Village consists of people living in a limited physical area who have common interests and common ways of satisfying them.

- According to **A.W. Green,** *"A village community or rural community is a cluster of people living within a narrow territorial radius who share a common way of life."*
- The Census of India has defined a village in the following manner : – *"The basic unit for rural areas is the revenue village which has definite surveyed boundaries. The revenue village may comprise several hamlets but the entire village has been treated as one unit for presentation of census data. In unsurveyed areas, like villages within forest areas, each habitation area with locally recognised boundaries within each forest officer's beat, was treated as one unit."*
- In simple words, the Indian **rural community** may be defined as *a group of about 5000 people depending on agriculture and allied occupations, permanently residing in a geographic area and participating in common socio-economic and cultural activities.*
- A rural community may also be defined as *"a group of people permanently residing in a definite geographic area who, having developed a certain community consciousness and cultural, social and economic relations feel that they are separate from other communities."*

The rural community has a long history of its own. It has become almost natural with the human life. No known community was started on purely urban character. Urban community is a

---

1 **Precautions Suggested by M.N. Srinivas to those who take up Village Studies :** (a) He must not speak of Indian villages as a whole until a sufficient number of villages in the different cultural areas have been studied. (b) He also takes care to see that the villages he studies is typical of an area or is suitable for the study of a particular theoretical problem.

phenomenon of recent development. Rural life has preceded the urban life. It is said that *God made the village and man built the city.* In spite of the growth of cities, the population of the world has largely rural. In India alone more than 50 crores of people live in villages. More than 74% per cent of Indians live in more than **5.5** lakh villages in India. The urban life still depends on the farm and what it produces.

Traditional Characteristics of Village

As it is already referred to, India is known to the world as one among the village dominated nations. Villages are found in the nook and corner of India. Study of the Indian society immediately and invariably leads us to the study of villages. There are about **5.58** lakh villages in India spread over more than 500 districts. The pattern of village community has never been the same everywhere. It differs in different parts of the country. However, the undercurrent of the socio-cultural life in its essence has been the same throughout India. As **R.K. Mukherjee** rightly points out *"India is predominantly one physically and culturally"*. It is true of her villages also. The main characteristics of the traditional Indian villages are described below.

1. *Small Size of the Village Community* : Indian villages are comparatively smaller in size. Its population is quite limited. In the Indian context, a community with a population of about 5000 people is called a *"village"*. If it exceeds that, it is called a *"town"* or *"an urban community."* As and when the village population increases, villages grow into towns. In India, normally village people reside either in the midst of their land or very much adjacent to the land.

2. *Intimate Relations* : *"Primary relations"* which we normally observe in a typical village context, are also found in the Indian village. Here we find *face-to-face relations* among people. Every person knows every other and hence everyone is interested in the welfare of all. Since the village is small in size members frequently meet and maintain regular contacts. The relationship is informal, personal and inclusive. Community spirit prevails over the individual interests. People are free and frank in their expressions. *A sense of belonging to the community* holds them together.

3. *Social Homogeneity* : Indian villages are homogeneous. Diversity which we find in her own cities are not found here. Indian rural life is simple and smooth going. Unity and uniformity in social life are largely visible. We find similarity in the ways of thinking, behaving, dressing, acting and living. We find consensus among people with regard to habits, opinions, morals, values, religious beliefs, dress and so on. This consensus, especially on political matters has been adversely affected during the recent days mainly due to the impact of *caste-based power politics.*

4. *Informal Social Control* : Indian villagers normally respect the rules. They are custom-bound. Customs, traditions, group standards and morals are themselves effective as social pressures. Any kind of social disobedience is easily noticed and the disobedient is put to gossip and slander. Hence they are hesitant to go against the customary way of life. The ***Caste Panchayats*** on the one hand, and the ***Village Panchayats*** on the other, used to look into the instances of social disobedience. The effectiveness of village control, however, deteriorated during the periods of Muslim and British rule.

5. *Dominance of Joint Family* : The rural community is built around the institution of family. This is true of the Indian villages. Families in Indian villages are mostly *joint families.* Their size is normally big. Agricultural operation requires a large labour force. The village families meet such requirements. Indian village families are patriarchal in nature and are controlled by the senior male members. The Indian rural family is very cohesive. It lives together, eats together and works together as a unit. Family members are bound by family customs and traditions. Wealth and property belong to the family, the eldest male member manages it. Members of the family obey the head of the family called *"Karta"*. There is less scope for individuality in the family. Generally, there is less individual question and rebellion in a family.

6. *Status of Rural Women* : Women in the Indian rural context, are very much dependent on their men folk. They require the support of the institutions like marriage and family. Most of the time rural women engage themselves in indoor activities but often they work in fields along with their men folk. They look after children and the domesticated animals. They are sentimentally attached to their husbands and their families. They have implicitly accepted the ideal of *"pativratya"* which is glorified in the Indian tradtion. Women adjust themselves to the family conditions and are ready to make any kind of sacrifice for its smooth running. Women are less *educated* and do not bother about their *career.* They play a *sub-ordinate role* in the family. Instances of desertion, divorce and separation are comparatively less in the rural context, for the women do not relish such things.

7. *Occupation* : *Dominance of Agriculture* : India is a land of villages and also of agriculture. Almost about 40% of our national income is obtained through agriculture and more than 66.5% of the people still depend on agriculture.

Agriculture is associated with different crafts like pottery, carpentry, smithery, basket-making, toy-making, brick-making, shoe-making, beedi-rolling, spinning, weaving, tanning, oil-grinding, barbering, house-building and repairing, curing hides, stone-cutting, and so on.

There is less scope for division of labour and specialisation in the village. There is no wide scope for specialisation in a village. Villagers are not equipped with sufficient qualification to pursue varied tasks nor is there a scope for them. On the contrary, the villager at times performs the role of an *all-rounder.* He is often called a *"jack of all trades but master of none."* During the recent years, an increasing number of rural youths are moving towards nearby towns and cities either for higher education or in search of jobs. Higher educated rural youths normally prefer to stay in cities pursuing one or the other salaried profession.

8. *Role of Neighbourhood* : In a village, neighbourhood is of great importance. *Neighbourhood refers to a community in miniature.* All the essentials of community life are found in it. Neighbours share the joys and sorrows together. They have the spirit of comradeship. Since they do not cherish individuality they rarely disregard the feelings, interests and expectations of the neighbours. In times of festivals, marriage and other religious ceremonies and in times of ill-health, accidents and other crises, neighbours support each other. Feeling of dependence on the neighbours is always present in the village.

9. *Faith in Relgion* : Indian villagers are highly religious. They have deep faith in religion, God and in religious traditions. Religiosity has become a virtue for them. They have *faith in Nature Gods* also. They believe that Nature Gods will have to be pleased through various means to help them in agricultural operations. This deep faith in religion and God has minimised their mental tensions and disturbances.

Each village has *its own deity* called *"Gramdevata"*. People of all castes normally worship it and at least once in a year they celebrate fairs or *'utsav'* or yearly religious festival in honour of that God. In addition to this common deity, each dominant caste may have its own deity and a temple built in honour of it. Villagers' faith in religion is often mixed with their faith in magic, sprits, and ghosts.

10. *Conservative Attitude and Unfavourable Environment for Social Mobility* : Indian villagers are said to be extremely conservative and even dogmatic in their approach. *They go by majority opinion, and belief.* They do not accept policies, plans, programmes, principles, values, ideals, etc. which the majority disapproves. They are basically skeptical in their attitude. They are not ready for immediate change. They are *'status quoists'*. For the very same reason they are often branded as *"conservatives"* and *"opposers of progress"*. Readiness to consider or accept change is not there in them. New ideas and things are looked at with suspicion. It is because of this mentality ruralites are less mobile.

11. *Indian Villages and Self-Sufficiency* : Indian villages are often described as self-reliant. It is also said, for centuries in the past the Indian village functioned as a self-reliant *"little republic."*[1] It is argued that the vertical solidarity of the castes and the *"jajmani system"* were complementary to the so called self-reliance of the villages. This self-suffciency of the Indian villages did not last long, for it was given a fatal blow during the periods of Muslim and British rule.

The above view has been contradicted by many scholars. **A.S. Altekar** points out that *"our village communities were never in historic times 'republics'..."* **S.C. Dube** in his *"Indian Society"* writes: *"Contrary to the much published view, the Indian village is not 'a self-contained little republic'. Even in the past it had to depend on outside resources in some respects at least."* There was inter-village trade in common salt, bangles and several other items. Market centres attracted visitors from several villages. Local and regional fairs, drawing crowds from far-off places, find mention in old religious books and travellers' accounts. There was a tradition of inter-village Panchayats. Hence, the Indian village was not self-sufficient as such, argues S.C. Dube.

Thus, it can be said that though during the Vedic period village community was like an independent republic, it was not so throughout the historic period. The rural community was always sub-ordinated to and was a constituent element of larger political units.

12. *Widespread Caste System* : Indian village life is inextricably mixed up with the caste system. There is no village without the castes. Each village has several caste segments which have their own ties in some spheres. The necessities of village life have brought together different castes. This inter-dependence of castes could be seen in the exchange of specialised occupational services. The *"jajmani system"* has further strengthened inter-caste dependence.

The village life has been controlled by two types of *panchayat* system. (i) ***Village Panchayat*** [which normally consists of representatives of different castes residing in the village] and (ii) ***Jati Panchayat*** [each caste having its own caste panchayat consisting of normally elderly and influential persons of the caste]. Caste is inseparable from caste identity, caste patriotism and casteism. **Dr. Ambedkar** who had his contempt for the caste called villages the *great centres of casteism.* Caste conflicts often do take place in the village disturbing village peace. Caste feelings mixed with politcal rivalries lead to groupism in the village. These developments are becoming very much evident now-a-days.

Indian villages have undergone vast changes especially after independence. The traditional characteristics of villages described above too have undergone significant changes. Hence, these features are to be understood in their dynamic perspective and in a relative sense.

Agrarian Class Structure

The concept of *"agrarian class structure"* refers to the type of the class structure that prevails in an agricultural society or set up. Scholars such as **S. Bhargava, D.R. Gadgil** and others have stated in their studies that the agrarian classes did exist in pre-independent India. The agrarian social structure consists of agrarian classes which represent different social groups in rural India.

1 *"The village communities are little "Republics" having nearly everything they can want within themselves and almost independent of any foreign relations..."* – **Charles Metcalf.**

An analysis of the post-independent Indian rural set up reveals the existence of four classes. They are – (i) *landowners,* (ii) *tenants,* (iii) *labourers,* and (iv) *non-agriculturists.*

As **A.R. Desai** has stated (i) the land-owners constitute about 22%; (ii) tenants about 27%; (iii) agricultural labourers about 31%; and (iv) non-agriculturists about 20%.

It is also found that a large majority of the cultivators [about - 60%] are marginal cultivators with less than 2 hectares of land, followed by small cultivators [about 16%] with 2 to 5 hectares land; medium cultivators [about 6%] with 5 to 10 hectares land, and big cultivators [about 18%] with more than 10 hectares land.

Daniel Thorner's Classification of Rural Classes into Three Social Categories

Daniel Thorner classified rural classes into three social categories namely; (a) *maliks,* (b) *kisans,* and (c) *mazdoors,* on the basis of three criteria which are as follows :

(i) ***Income Obtained from the Land*** that is, through rent, one's own cultivation or wages.

(ii) ***The Nature of Rights*** that is, ownership rights, tenancy rights, share-cropping rights, or no rights at all.

(iii) ***The Extent of Field Work Actually Performed*** that is, doing no work at all, doing partial work, doing total work, and doing work for others to earn wages.

The three agrarian classes which Daniel Thorner spoke of are (a) *Malik,* (b) *Kisan,* and (c) *Mazdoor.* According to **Thorner,** the prevalent agrarian relations can also be analysed in terms of three specific terms.

(a) Maliks or Landlords

The term *"Maliks"* refers to the big landlords and considerably rich land owners who constitute the relative affluent class in the village set up. The *Malik* obtains his agricultural income mostly, but not solely, from property rights in the land. It means, a share of the produce of land, [i.e., the land over which he has his rights] is realised by him either in cash or in kind, or sometimes both. The *Maliks* sometimes cultivate lands personally by making use of hired labourers. They may employ managers to supervise the cultivation of land.

The *Maliks* can be grouped into two groups, namely, the big absentee landlords, and the rich resident land owners.

(i) *Absentee Landlords,* that is, those who do not stay in the village but in a far away town or city and get the cultivation done through the managers or supervisors. These *Maliks* are normally big landlords who have their rights over lands spread over several villages. They are absentee landlords for they do not have any personal interest in the land, and get it managed by supervisors.

(ii) *The Rich Resident Land Owners,* that is, those *Maliks* who reside in the village in which they own land. These people also do not work in the land personally but get the cultivation work done by others.

(ii) Kisans or Working Peasants

The term *"Kisans"* refers to the working peasants. They occupy the intermediary position in the three-tier agrarian class structure. This class consists of small landowners or tenants. In comparision with the Malik, the Kisan owns land which is smaller in size and unlike the Malik, the Kisan and his family members actually take part in the cultivation work that goes on in the field. Some of these Kisans secure relatively poor income and hence in order to compensate it they, along with their family members often work as agricultural labourers. They very rarely employ outside labourers, but often invite others to work in their fields on exchange basis. It is also probable that most of the *Kisans* belong to what are known as *"intermediary castes."*

(iii) Mazdoors or Labourers

The term *"Mazdoors"* refers in the rural context to the landless villagers who work as labourers on wage basis. They obtain their livelihood primarily from working on other people's land. The class of *Mazdoors* may consist of poor tenants, share croppers and landless labourers. The *Mazdoors* receive wages in cash and sometimes in kind also. These *Mazdoors* are often forced to migrate to the neighbouring villages, to other districts or states, particularly when they fail to find enough work in their own villages. Some of them even turn out as construction or industrial workers.

Dhanagare's Model of Agrarian Classes

Prof. D.N. Dhanagare has commented that **Thorner's** *classification of agrarian classes* suffers from its own limitations for it is not based on any specific theoretical assumptions. Dhanagare himself has suggested yet another model of agrarian classes. Dhanagare's model consists of five categories or classes which are as follows : (i) *landlords, (ii) rich peasants,* (iii) *middle peasants,* (iv) *poor peasants,* and (v) *landless labourers.*

Agrarian Classes Based on the Size of the Cultivated Land

On the basis of the size of the land possessed by the peasants and the other sources of income which they obtain, one can speak of a five-fold classification of agrarian classes. It is as follows :

(i) Big-farmers who hold more than four hectares of land.
(ii) Medium-farmers owning 2 - 4 hectares of cultivable land.
(iii) Small-farmers possessing 1 - 2 hectares of land.
(iv) Marginal-farmers having land whose size is less than one hectare.
(v) Agricultural-labourers who may [or may not] possess a small piece of land, and who mainly relies on wage labour as their source of income.

Conclusion : The above mentioned classifications of agrarian classes signify that a few more classifications are possible. It is very difficult to make a clear identification and analysis of agrarian classes in the Indian rural set up for it is highly varied and complex.

VILLAGE SOLIDARITY

In their discussion on Indian village scholars generally give much importance to the *"solidarity"* or *"unity"* of the Indian village. Village unity has its own historical importance. Indian villages saw the rise and fall of various dynasties throughout the historical period from the Greeks to the British. They also witnessed the fall of the British imperialism in India and the rise of the independent Indian Republic. The Indian village *"has contributed more than to any other cause to the preservation of the people of India, through all revolutions and changes they have suffered."*[1] The village communities suffered a lot from isolation for they had no facilities of the modern times. Withstanding all the hardships they have survived. As **Mamoria** further says, centuries of village living has made our villagers *to develop common viewpoints, beliefs, attitudes and practices that have become an integral part of their very being.* The very word *"solidarity"* implies such commonness and at the same time strong sense of unity and cohesion.

---

1 **C.B. Mamoria** *"Social Problems and Social Disorganisation"* - Page: 1200.

Factors Favourable for Village Solidarity

Solidarity that is evidenced in the Indian village has been strongly supported by certain factors.

1. *Physical Unity* : M.N. Srinivas maintains that the village is a unity in several senses of the term. According to him, it is a physical unity in the sense, people living in a particular physical or geographic boundary feel that they are united. For example, if monsoon fails, it fails for everyone. Similarly, if diseases break-out, they cause hardship for all. This is how they think and feel.

2. *Village Homogeneity and Common Life-Styles* : Indian village is known for its homogeneity. Differences and disparities are ignored here and common ways of thinking, believing and behaving are pursued. The small size of the community, its geographic limits, and the intimate relations found among the members add to the village solidarity.

3. *Religious Factors* : Common religious beliefs, practices, values etc. contribute to village unity. Any village community composed of Hindu castes regard the earth as *Mother Earth,* and the deity that represents the crops is regarded as *Lakshmi,* the goddess of wealth. The domestic lamp, granary, a heap of grains, a grain measure, etc., are all objects of ritual importance. A caste has a ritual attitude towards the tools, implements or objects associated with its occupations. Each village has its own deity [Grama Devata] which is believed to look after the welfare of the village. Festivals, fairs, *'utsavs', bhajans, kirtanas,* etc. that are held in honour of the deity give scope for the people for collective participation.

Ritual Unity : Religious unity is virtually the ritual unity. "The village boundary has a religious significance. Formerly when there was an attack of epidemics like cholera, plague or small pox, the entire village acted as one, and moved to a different place. They all joined together to propitiate the deities presiding over these diseases. It could be said that the disease was ritually driven out of the village.......... *"It was believed that the moral lapse of any member of the village would result in the rest of the village suffering the consequences of such a lapse."*[1]

4. *Interdependence of Caste-Jajmani System* : Indian villages are inseparably associated with the caste system. Each caste follows its own traditional occupation with the exception of agriculture which is common to all. Each caste in a way has a monopoly over its occupation. **Ex:** Potter makes pots, washerman washes clothes, waterman supplies water, barber does the hair-dressing, carpenter does wooden works, chamar makes shoes and so on. Each caste depends on the other for the service it requires. This interdependence of the castes add to the village unity.

Jajmani System : The *jajmani system*[2] is a system of traditional occupational obligations. The term *jajman* [*Yajman*] refers to the *'patrons'* or receipient of specialised services at the hands of servicing castes. The patrons are the families of *"clean castes"* while the suppliers of services are the families of lower and sometimes *"unclean castes"*.

It could be said that the jajmani system is a system of distribution whereby high caste land-owning families are provided with services and products by various lower castes such as carpenters [Khati or Badagi], barbers [Nai], potters [Kumbars] blacksmiths [Kamaras in Karnataka, Lohars in North India], washerman [Dhobis], sweepers [Chuhra], etc. *The servicing castes are called **"Kamins"** while the castes served are called **"jajmans"***. For the services rendered, the servicing castes are paid in cash or in kind [*grains, fodder, clothes, animal products like milk, butter,* etc.]. This system also indicates economic, social and ritual relations existing among different caste groups in a village.

1 **Prof. Chingamani** *"Sociology of Indian Society."* Page - 192.

2 **Jajmani System** is a system governed by relationships based on reciprocity in inter-caste relations in village. - **Prof. Yogendra Singh.**

5. *Threat of External Danger* : M.N. Srinivas is of the opinion that the village unity is *"normally not visible, but some incident suddenly and strikingly reveals its existence. When the village is threatened with an epidemic or drought or floods or fire or when the government passes an order which the villagers regard as unjust or on certain religious occasions, or in a fight with neighbouring village, the unity of the village reveals itself in an unmistakable manner."*[1]

6. *Role of Gram Panchayat and Jati Panchayat* : As ***S.C. Dube*** points out, the village used to have two kinds of Panchayats - a *Jati Panchayat* and a *Village Panchayat.* The Jati Panchayat used to have elderly and influential leaders of a particular caste. But in the Village Panchayat elders from nearly all jatis were represented. The Jati Panchayat heard property disputes, family disputes and internal jati disputes. The Village Panchayat settled disputes between two or more jatis. Village Panchayats used to function as *'Nyaya Panchayats'* assuring justice to the parties to the dispute and preserving the unity of the village. [In some states, after independence "Nyaya Panchayats" got statutory judicial power to administer quick and cheap justice in minor cases].

Manifestations of Village Solidarity

M.N. Srinivas says that the feeling of unity on the part of the villagers gets expressed in diverse ways and contexts. He gives examples also.

(a) *When Comparisons are Made* : The village solidarity is expressed particularly when the villagers compare themselves as a community with members of other villages. They normally consider themselves as superior to members of other villages in some respects.

(b) *When Clashes Take Place* : Village unity is invariably manifested when there is a fight between two neighbouring villages. Srinivas describes in detail a fight between the people of *Bihalli village* and the people of *Kere village* during the Madheswara festival.

(c) *When Villagers' are Threatened* : The village proves itself to be united particularly when its interests are threatened. Srinivas gives details as to how the people of *Rampura village* [of Mysore district] opposed a government order relating to auctioning of the fishing rights in their tank. They managed to see that no one from their village or from any of the neighbouring villages attended the auction.

(d) *When Festivals are Celebrated Collectively* : Village unity becomes apparent when the festivals, fairs, and ceremonies are collectively celebrated. Holi, Raksha Bandhan and Diwali are the main festivals of northern villages while Ganesha festival, Nagara Panchami, Pongal [Sankranti], Onam, and Deepavali are the main festivals of southern villages. These festivals provide occasions for the rural people not only to meet but also to express their sense of unity. Sometimes, Muslims and Christians too take part in their own way in these festivals.

Village unity does not mean that there are no factions in the village. A few divisive forces have definitely forced their entry into the village. These forces tend to weaken the village unity by promoting inequalities and diving the society on class, caste and reservation lines. Anyone who looks only at these forces would get an impression that the future of village unity is very bleak.

Srinivas concludes *"I have said enough to show that the unity of the village has several aspects, most members of the village, whatever their caste, consider themselves to be villagers in certain contexts. There are seventeen sub-castes in Rampura. Each of these sub-castes has a distinctive tradition with strong ties with the same sub-caste in villages nearby. That is, the village is a vertical*

1 **M.N. Srinivas** *"India's Villages"* - Page: 8.

unity of many castes whereas caste is a horizontal unity, its alliances going beyond the village."[1]

Critical Comments Regarding the Concept of "Village Solidarity"

1. ***Solidarity of the village - An Exaggerated View:*** **Dr. M.N. Srinivas** is of the opinion that the idea of village solidarity is much exaggerated. According to him, *"the solidarity of caste is so great that it nullifies the unity of the village community in those villages in which more than one caste live..."*[2] He writes: *"the unity of the village is not then an axiom to be taken for granted, but sometimes that has to be shown to exist."*[3]

2. ***Village Solidarity is not a Permanent Phenomenon:*** Villagers in India do not confine the range of their relations to their village only. They do have socio-economic ties or connections outside the village.[4] In times of crises they do take the help of outsiders. Further, within the village, caste-rivalries, conflicts and property disputes are quite often found endangering the unity of the village. It is in times of external threats or dangers, as **M.N. Srinivas** said that the so called village solidarity is evidenced and it cannot be taken for granted as a permanent feature of the village.

3. ***Horizontal Solidarity of the Caste is Unfavourable to Village Solidarity:*** Two kinds of solidarity are observed in caste: *horizontal solidarity* and *vertical solidarity.* ***Vertical solidarity of the caste*** *refers to the unity existing among different caste groups in a village.* ***Horizontal unity*** *of the caste refers to the unity existing among the same caste people within and outside the village.* It is said that the increase in the horizontal solidarity of the caste leads to a decline in the solidarity of the village, because for the caste members the caste becomes more important and protective than the village.

4. ***Growing Economy Undermines Village Solidarity:*** **Dr. Bailey** has expressed the opinion that *"as the village gets more closely integrated with the larger economy of the country, it becomes less of a unity.* Such integration is increasing everyday and widespread industrialisation and growing paternalism on the part of the state will increasingly reduce this sense of unity."[5]

5. ***Village is Becoming Just a Unit of Neighbourhood?:*** **Dr. Gough** is of the opinion that due to the gradual shift of educated ruralites towards the cities, transfer of land to the middle-class trading families of the towns, domination of urban type of labour in the village, the village is losing its traditional integration and is becoming *"little more than a unit of neighbourhood".*

Conclusion

It is true that the solidarity of the Indian village is fast declining. Factors such as *increasing dependence of the villages on the cities, increasing caste rivalries and conflicts, increasing influence of caste-based power politics in the rural areas, increasing trend towards urbanisation and greater impact of modernisation* have a negative effect on the preservation of village solidarity.

Village Settlement Patterns

Indian villages though exhibit some common characteristics are not altogether uniform. They assume different patterns or forms. Attempts were made during the early past to classify the

---

1 **M.N. Srinivas** in *"India's Villages."*
2 *ibid* Page: 6.
3 *ibid* Page: 6.
4 "These ties are so powerful that a few anthropologists have been led into asserting that the unity of the village is a myth and that the only thing that counts is caste." - **M.N. Srinivas** *"India's Villages"* - Page - 6.
5 **Dr. Bailey's** views as referred to by **M.N. Srinivas** in *"India's Village."* Page : 9 - 10.

Indian villages into different types. **Kautilya's** *"Artha Shastra"* gives details of different types of early Indian villages such as *Sangrahana, Karvatika, Dronamukha* and *Sthaneeya.* These early classifications do not help us to understand the modern type of villages. Hence we have to refer to the modern attempts at classifying the villages.

1. Nucleated and Dispersed Villages

Indian villages are generally classified by the sociologists into (A) *"nucleated villages"* and (B) *"clustered villages."* This classification is based mostly on the pattern of settlement.

A. Nucleated or Clustered Villages

In a nucleated village the farmers live in the middle of the village whereas their land lies at some distance. The very word *"clustered"* indicates that the villagers are living as a *"close group"* in a small physical proximity. Since the villagers make their small physically compact area the nucleus of their dwelling place and all their social activities it is also called *"nucleated"* village.

In a clustered or nucleated village, the farms or cultivated lands are spread around the dwellings. People work on the fields which lie outside the village site. If the land is far away from the dwelling place much time is consumed for travelling the distance. Since the villagers dwell together in a single habitat they develop a compact life and their sense of belonging is also quite strong. Such villages exist almost all over India.

Depending on the distance between the land and the settlement area or dwelling area, people approach their land either on foot or by cycle, bullock-cart, or by bus and so on. If the land is very far away, then it becomes difficult for the farmers to take the best use of the land and to have complete control over all agricultural operations and also on crops. Good roads and the availability of required vehicles reduce this problem in a few of the villages, but in many villages the problem continues.

In nucleated or clustered village, usually the houses are built mostly with mud walls and sometimes with bricks. Country tiles are used for the roofs, with wooden beams and bamboo rafters. The houses are often so close to one another that there are often common walls between two houses. Tea shops cigarette shops are also found in the centre of the village.

Nucleated villages are often cosmopolitan in character composing of the Hindu, Muslim and Christian population. Places of worship - the temple, mosque and the church are situated in such villages in suitable places. Every village has a *'grama devata'* [village deity] to protect the village from evils. On occasions like festivals, *utsavs,* fairs people congregate in festive mood. Children from the villages where the schools are not found go to the neighbouring village.

Many of the villages are still custom-bound. The chamars, bhangis and the scheduled caste people, the sheperds and the landless labourers of the low castes generally live in small huts on the outskirts of the village. The people who are well of have their houses in the centre of the village.

People in a nucleated village draw water for drinking purposes from the wells located in different parts of the village. In some villages nearby ponds, lakes and small rivers also provide water facility to the residents. Round about the village are the thrashing-floors and hay-stacks. Villagers have their own recreation such as folkways, folk songs, etc. Since the villagers are living together they are able to develop strong unity to fight against odds and the common enemies or dangers.

B. Dispersed Village

In dispersed type of villages, the farmers live separately on their respective farms. The dwellings of the people are scattered according to the farm areas owned or cultivated by each farmer.

Dispersed villages are found on the Western Ghats of India, in Kerala, Karnataka and Maharasthra states. In Karnataka, in Malnad areas such as Shimoga, Chikmagalur and Kodagu, farms and estates are normally scattered. Here, often five-ten houses constitute a village.

In dispersed villages, the dwelling houses are connected with the country service road. Adjacent to the dwelling houses, the farmer keeps his live stock and farm equipments. In this type of village, families are normally isolated. People are forced to find services such as markets, stores, hostels, shops, schools, primary health centres and such other things in the nearby towns. Since people are scattered over the area their social life may assume different forms. The dispersed villages are such that one often finds it difficult to make out where one village ends and another starts.

The people of dispersed villages, have their own difficulty in defending their common interests against odds or external dangers. Each family has to do it by itself. The nucleated village in this respect has a greater advantage for it can defend its common interests collectively. The problem of self-defence of the dispersed villages has made some communities such as Nayars of Malabar and Coorgs of Kodagu to grow into martial races.

2. A.R. Desai's Classification based on Degree of Permanence

On the basis of the degree of permanence of living of the people in a settlement area, villages are classified into three types. **A.R. Desai** makes a mention of such a classification. **Prof. H.V. Nagesh** in his book *"Gramantara"* also mentions of the same.

(i) Migratory Agricultural Villages: These are the villages where the people like tribals and semi-nomadic people live in fixed abodes for some fixed time. After that, they leave it and go to other places.

(ii) Semi-Permanent Agricultural Villages: Here, the people mostly the tribals, live in a fixed place for about 5 - 10 years, build their houses, carry on their agricultural work and when the soil becomes impoverished, they leave that village and go to another.

(iii) Permanent Agricultural Villages: Here, the settled human groups live for generations and even for centuries. The villager here is invariably a farmer earning his livelihood through the land. This type of villages are found throughout the world. In India also most of the villages belong to this category.

3. J.B. Chitambar's Classification

J.B. Chitambar is his book *"Introductory Rural Sociology"* mentioned about seven types of settlement patterns which can be briefed here.

1. ***Isolated Farmsteads*** **:** In this type, the individual lives on his farm land surrounding him. He keeps his live stock, barn, farm equipments, harvested produce and such other things adjacent to his dwelling. This pattern is particularly found in the state of Kerala.

2. ***Villages*** **:** Here, the dwelling units of the rural people are concentrated in a particular area and their farm land is spread around the dwelling units. The number of dwelling units will vary depending upon the size of the village. This type of villages are commonly found in the entire Eastern world. All over the country in India this pattern is visible.

3. ***Line Villages*** **:** In this type, houses are located along a road or a waterway each with adjoining strips of farmland. Houses are close to one another and are located on their respective farms. This pattern of settlement is seen more in France, Germany and Canada than in India. In Kerala, this type of houses can be located in some areas.

4. ***Round Village or Circular Pattern*** **:** In a round village, houses are arranged in circle in the central area. Houses are closer together without creating much length in the tract of farm land. This pattern is common in Israel where irrigated land is very much limited.

5. ***Cross Roads and Market Centre Settlements*** **:** Here, houses are located adjacent to cross roads or market centres and are mainly inhabited by merchants who handle agricultural products, bankers and shopkeepers. Farmers normally do not reside in such centres unless their farmland is adjacent. These settlements also provide needed products and commodities such as prepared foodstuffs, refreshments, services such as petrol stations, garages, workshops, barber shops, etc.

6. ***Hamlets*** **:** These settlements are small villages and are found away from the main villages or on the border of larger villages. These villages do not possess adequate supplies and service facilities that are normally available in the larger villages.

7. ***Others*** **:** These are other types of settlements serving one or the other specific functions. ***Example*** **:** In India, at points of religious pilgrimage or at the centres of historic or tourist interest, settlements have been formed.

These different patterns of rural habitat have come into being for different causes in different areas. According to **Sorokin,** three main features such as (i) *natural conditions,* (ii) *social conditions,* and (iii) *the nature of agricultural economy* are very significant in influencing the pattern of settlements.

LAND TENURE SYSTEM AND LAND REFORMS AFTER INDEPENDENCE

Villages in any corner of the world depend on agriculture. Though we often make references to *"industrial villages"*, such villages are very rare in the Indian context. Hence, naturally cultivated land assumes importance. Progress of the village depends much on the progress of agriculture. Agricultural progress depends on issues such as *the agriculturist's relationships with the land, who cultivates it, how it is cultivated, how the agricultural products are distributed and enjoyed, and so on.* The present topic is to be analysed in the light of these questions.

Meaning of *"Land Tenure"*

Agricultural reforms or land reforms depend very much on the very nature and type of the ownership of the land, that is, *"land tenure system."* The term *"tenure"* means *to hold.* ***"Land tenure"*** means how land is held and managed by a person. The system of land tenure includes two conditions : (i) *the conditions under which the land is held by a person from the state,* and (ii) *the conditions on which the land is given by the landlord to the actual cultivator for the purpose of cultivation.* It, therefore, denotes as to who owns the land and who cultivates it.

Systems of Land Tenure in Pre-Independent India

The land tenure system has a prolonged history of its own. There are references to it even in the *"Arthashastra"* of **Kautilya.** As it is stated in *"Arthashastra"*, the king was the sole proprietor of the land, and he often used to give some land in charity or as *"gift"* to those individuals or families which served him or his kingdom. For other lands, some amount payable to the king or his treasury as his share, was fixed. Though, theoretically, king was regarded as the owner of the land, most of the *"shastra"* books tell us that the tiller of the land was practically regarded as the real owner of the land. The kings, of course, had the power to increase or decrease the land tax.

The ancient system of land tax continued even during the Muslim rule with some modifications here and there. During the Mughal's period, particularly during the fag end of their regime, an attempt was made to collect land documents and to systematise them. An effort was also made to classify land into different categories on the basis of the fertility of the land. It was at this stage new systems of land tenure started emerging out in place of the old ones.

It could be generalised that at the fag end of the Mughal rule and at the beginning of the British rule in India, the old land revenue systems which the Hindu rulers were following disappeared and in their place, new systems came to be practised. The three types of land tenure systems which prevailed in the country at that period are mentioned below :

1. *Zamindari Tenure.*
2. *Mahalwari Tenure.*
3. *Ryotwari Tenure.*

1. The Zamindari Tenure

The ***Zamindari Tenure*** system which existed during the Mughal period and which had taken a definite shape during the British rule, consisted of the following characteristics.

According to the Zamindari system, the cultivated land belonged to the Government and all those who were making use of it were expected to pay tax to the Government. Since the Government felt that the task of collecting tax from the users of the land individually was a hazardous task, it entrusted the responsibility of collecting land tax from the people of a fixed region to a few known individuals. These individuals came to be called the *"Zamindars",* sometimes as *Inamdars* and also as *Jagirdars.* The ordinary peasants or tenants who were actually using the land had to pay heavy dues to Zamindars. Though the Zamindari system assumed different forms in different places its essential principle remained the same everywhere.

The Zamindari system was created by **Lord Cornwallis** who entered into *"permanent settlement"* with the landlords in 1793, with a view to increasing the revenue of the ***East Indian Company.*** *"Zamindar"* means normally a non-cultivating landlord. In this system, ownership of the land is separated from the managerial and labour function. Under the *"settlement",* the landlords [known as Zamindars] were declared full proprietors of large areas of land. In return for this honour, the task of collecting rent from the farmers was entrusted to them. [Zamindars were also known as *"Talukdars"* in U.P.]

The Zamindari system was thus introduced by the East India Company to create vested interest in land and thereby cultivate a privileged and loyal class. The various forms of tenure such as *Zamindari, Jagirdari, Inamdari,* etc., were artificially created. The revenue collectors were raised to the status of landowners. Earlier they were responsible for collecting the land revenue for which they received a commission. The Zamindari settlements [*The Bengal Permanent Revenue Settlement,* 1793] made them owners of land, thereby creating a permanent interest in land.

Two Types of *Zamindari* Settlements

This new Zamindari system consisted of two types, namely (i) *Permanent Settlement,* and (ii) *Temporary Settlement.*

(i) *Permanent Zamindari Settlement* : The permanent settlement fixed land revenue on a permanent basis. This system prevailed in Bengal, Bihar, Orissa, North Madras, Banaras and in some parts of Assam.

(ii) *Temporary Zamindari Settlement* : Under temporary settlement, land revenue was assessed for a period ranging between 20 and 40 years in various states. This system made provision for the revision of revenue. This was prevalent in the remaining areas of Bengal, Uttar Pradesh, Punjab, Rajasthan, Madhya Pradesh and Oudh. Since the period of assessment was pretty long, temporary settlement was not really temporary. More than any other thing, the primary object of the East India Company was to fix the responsibility for the punctual payment of land revenue.

Main Defects of Zamindari System

The British government justified the Zamindari system with its own logic. It said that the Zamindars represented the most enlightened section of the rural population and hence they would help the improvement of land and agriculture. But the expectation of the British government was never fulfilled. The system as such suffered from a number of defects. Some of the defects are mentioned below.

1. *Quality of Cultivation Suffered* : Much against the expectations of the British administrators, the Zamindars never took interest in the improvement of either land or cultivation. They concentrated their attention on the collection of revenue and enjoying the luxuries of life. That's all.

2. *Problem of "Absentee-Landlordism"* : This system created a unique agrarian structure in the villages, which conferred a right of the sharing the produce of the land on a few without participating personally in the productive process. It means it gave rise to what is known as *"absentee landlordism."* The very creation of the section of absentee landlords, resulted in the decay of the agriculture. *"Historically, the landlords as a class are known for their extravagance on women, wine and vices. The landlords of India were no exception. Thus the money extracted from the cultivators by these parasites did not result in capital formation but increased conspicuous consumption."*[1]

3. *The Zamindari system itself was based on exploitation* as it conferred unlimited rights on the Zamindars to extract as much rent as they wished. *"According to* **Bhavani Sen,** *approximately 25% of the produce was taken away by the intermediaries in the form of rent. This would mean that out of the income of Rs.4,800 crores from agriculture in 1949-50, the share of the intermediaries was as high as Rs.1,200 crores."*[2] The grabbing of such a high proportion of income by a parasitic class was thus socially unjust. The Zamindari system only added to the helplessness of the farmers. The actual cultivator was left with no surplus to invest in better implements, improved seeds or fertilisers. There was no incentive for him to increase agricultural production and productivity.

4. *Another great evil of the system was sub-renting.* The Zamindars subdivided the land and rented it out to other small Zamindars, who failed to give rent to the main Zamindars. The ultimate result was the reduction in the number of actual cultivators possessing occupancy rights.

5. *The Zamindari system led to a mass of litigation and agrarian discontent.* Large number of tenants who got disillusioned with the system took land disputes to the court. The number of such litigations in the court went on swelling.

---

1 **Ruddar Datt** and **K.P.M. Sundharam.** ''*Indian Economy*'' Page - 532. S. Chand & Co. Ltd.

2 **S.K. Misra** and **V.K. Puri** *"Indian Economy"* - 2000. Page - 419.

6. *The Zamindari system created a kind of insecurity in the minds of farmers.* The farmers were under the impression that, however, much they might work in the field with all sincerity, one day or the other, they would be evicted from the land by the selfish and cruel zamindars.

7. *Torture of the agents of Zamindars* : The agents of the Zamindars, who were given the power to collect the rent, used to behave inhumanly and indecently with the farmers. They used to exploit the humble farmers in countless ways. But the farmers had no means of taking the matter to the court for seeking justice.

8. *Service without returns* : The tenants in the Zamindari system had to work freely on some important occasions [on the occasion of religious festivals, social ceremonies, marriages, and various other types of programmes taking place in the houses of the Zamindars] without expecting any return.

9. *Farmers lost interest in the land* : The farmers in the Zamindari system showed no interest in modernisation of agriculture or in prevention of the evils of fragmentation. Consequently, agriculture production went on decreasing from 1880s almost upto 1940s.

The Abolition of the Zamindari System

The Zamindari system, as it is made clear from the above description, was a failure. It did not positively contribute to the development of Indian agriculture. The independent Indian government, after realising the evil consequences and the defects of the Zamindari system, took a bold decision to abolish it.

2. Mahalwari Tenure or Mahalwari System

This kind of the tenancy was first introduced during the British rule by the then Viceroy, **Lord William Bentinck.** It was first started in Agra and Oudh and was later on extended to Punjab. Under the Mahalwari tenure, the village lands were held jointly by the village communities, the members of which were jointly and severally [individually] responsible for the payment of the land revenue. A typical example of the Mahalwari tenancy system was widely prevalent in Punjab. It was a kind of joint landlordism and distinguished from individual landlordism under the Zamindari system. This system is said to be the product of Muslim tradition and development particularly in Punjab.

In this system, the whole village was treated as a unit as far as the payment of the land revenue was concerned. The responsibility of collecting the land revenue and depositing it in the treasury was the duty of the village headman [or a co-sharer appointed for the purpose]. A certain sum was assessed as land revenue for the whole village for which the whole body of co-sharers were jointly and severally responsible. The village *"lumberdar"* [village headman] collected revenue for which he received *"panchortra"*, that is, 5 per cent as commission.

Under the Mahalwari system, the land ultimately belonged to the State. The land belonging to the state was held by *Mahals* [that is, villages or village communities] and not by individuals. As the land was held by the village communities, the village communities were made jointly responsible for the payment of the land revenue to the state. The lands held by the village communities were either cultivated by the members of the village communities themselves, or were leased out to others on rent. According to the *Congress Land Reforms Committee,* the ownership of land under this system was collective. Period of 'settlement', fixation of the land revenue, etc. were different in different mahalwari areas.

Under this system also there were certain intermediaries. Hence, this system also contributed to the presence of absentee landlords. This system also came to an end soon after independence. Today, it is not at all found anywhere in North India.

3. Ryotwari Tenure or System

The Ryotwari system was introduced by **Sir Thomas Munro** in 1792. It was initially introduced in Tamilnad and was later extended to Maharashtra, Andhra Pradesh, Mysore, Kerala, Gujarat, Punjab, Himachal Pradesh and even to Jammu & Kashmir and to a few places of Manipur.

Under the Ryotwari system, the responsibility of paying land revenue to the Government was of the cultivator [or individual ryot] himself and there was no intermediary between him and the state. Under this system, the registered holder of the land was recognised as its proprietor. Since he was paying the revenue directly to the government, he had the liberty to sub-let his property or to transfer it by gift, sale or mortgage. He could not be ejected from his land till he paid the revenue. Actually, these rights were not available to the cultivators under the Zamindari system.

The Ryotwari system too had its own advantages. Absence of sub-infeudation and the cultivator's direct relation with the government was the main advantage of this system. Further, there were no intermediaries or middlemen between the state, to whom the lands ultimately belonged and the ryots or the actual cultivators. It means it was successful in abolishing intermediaries. Yet another advantage of this system was that the proprietor of the land took all interest for improving the land and its irrigation facilities.

Evil Effects or Defects of Ryotwari Tenure

The Ryotwari system, however, had its own inherent drawbacks. The main defects of this system are as follows :

(i) *Problem of sub-letting* : In Ryotwari system also there was provision for sub-letting the land to the landless persons. In the long run, the Ryotwari system created a group of peasants who were subordinate to the proprietor of the land. It did not put an end to the practice of absentee landlords and tenant cultivation, as the ryots who owned the lands could let out their lands to others for cultivation.

(ii) *Undesirable Opportunity for mortgaging the land* : Another major defect of this system was that the money-lenders and the *mahajans,* who granted loans to the cultivators or ryots, could mortgage their lands. Thus, substantial portions of the land slipped out of cultivators' hold and became the property of money-lenders and *mahajans.* The latter started giving land for cultivation on lease and soon a new zamindar class, with all its exploitative practices, developed.

(iii) *Problem of fixing appropriate rent* : Yet another defect of this system was that it created a great deal of problem for the settlement officer [rent settlement] to fix an appropriate rent for the land at the time of assessment. Every periodical revision of the rent was utilised as an opportunity for the enhancement of the rent. Hence, this system of *"peasant proprietorship"* did not bring the expected results.

When the defects of the Ryotwari system went on swelling, the *"Bengal Land Revenue Commission"* appointed in 1940 under the leadership of **Flaud,** also enlisted the deficiencies of the system and recommended to the British Government the abolition of this system.

LAND REFORMS AFTER INDEPENDENCE

India is basically an agricultural country. Hence, the progress of the nation depends very much on the progress of agriculture. The independent Indian Government decided to give priority to the agricultural sector. The Central Government also gave suggestions and directions to the State Governments to take all the possible steps to help the Indian agriculture to grow towards greater heights. The Government of India and the various state governments have taken up several measures towards the Land Reforms under the Five-Year Plans. As far as the land reforms are concerned, the Central Government could ***only*** give suggestions and directions to the state governments. The task of implementing the land reforms is, however, vested with the state governments.

Meaning of Land Reforms

The term ***"land reforms"*** refers to *the legislative measures or reforms, initiated by the government to bring about changes in the pattern of land holdings to solve the tenancy problems, to increase the size of the land holdings, and to effect improvements in agriculture.*

The land reforms virtually include various programmes of action, such as – *abolition of Zamindari and Mahalwari systems of land tenure, tenancy reforms, ceilings on land-holdings, consolidation of the land-holdings, creation of economic land-holdings, etc.*

Objectives of Land Reforms

Land reforms in India have been undertaken with many objectives, among which the following may be noted.

1. The land reforms are the measures *to bring about institutional changes in the agrarian structure.* Accordingly, they include various institutional reforms such as the redistribution of land ownership in favour of the actual cultivators, improvement of the size of farms, provision of security of tenure to the tenants, etc.
2. *To abolish the intermediaries* and to ensure social justice by distributing the surplus lands taken from the intermediaries and the excess lands taken over under the land ceiling legislation from the owners, among the landless cultivators.
3. *To prevent the exploitation of the tenants by the landlords* by fixing fair rent providing security of tenure to the tenants and conferring ownership rights on the tenants.
4. *To ensure rational or scientific use of the limited agricultural* lands through ceiling on land holdings, consolidation of land holdings, and creation of economic land holdings.

Land Reform Measures

Various land reform measures undertaken by different provincial governments in India, could be listed below :

A. Abolition of intermediaries.
B. Tenancy reforms.
C. Ceilings on land-holdings.
D. Consolidation of land-holdings.
E. Compilation and updating of land records.
F. Co-operative farming.

A. Abolition of Intermediaries

The first step in the land reforms programme undertaken by the government is the abolition of the zamindars, jahagirdars and others, who used to function as intermediaries between the government and the tenant farmers. Even before independence, it was widely recognised that the main cause of stagnation in the Indian agriculture was the very existence of the institution of zamindari system, which was patronised and promoted by the alien government. Approximately 40 per cent area of the country was under the Zamindari system on the eve of independence. The existence of the Zamindari system gave rise to tenancy cultivation of the worst type. The government wanted to abolish the intermediaries or the Zamindari system. Although steps were taken earlier, the actual abolition of intermediaries started in 1948, with enactment of legislation in Madras. Afterwards, between 1955 and 1960 most of the states in India had abolished the intermediaries through suitable legislations. The lands held by these intermediaries were taken away by them, by giving compensation. The land, thus acquired, was redistributed among the landless cultivators. As a result of the conferment of rights, about 30 lakh tenants and share croppers acquired ownership rights over a total cultivated area of 62 lakh acres throughout the country.

Unlike communist countries, abolition of intermediaries was not done in India without paying compensation to the landlords. In Russia, China, Yugoslavia, etc., landlords were driven out of their land without any compensation. They were reduced to the position of wage earners at the collective farms. But the Government of India decided to make payment to the landlords as compensation for handing over the ownership right of the land to the actual cultivators. The basis and rate of compensation, however, differed from state to state. The compensation was, however, to be paid in cash or in bonds. The ex-intermediaries have been given a compensation amounting to Rs.670 crores in cash and in bonds.

B. Tenancy Reforms

The state governments were forced to enact tenancy legislations in order to remove the evils of the tenancy system. The tenants of India, broadly speaking, could be divided into three categories – 1. *Occupancy or permanent tenants,* 2. *Tenants at will,* and 3. *Sub-tenants.* Occupancy tenants enjoy permanent rights, like the owner, and do not face the fear of eviction as long as they pay rent on time. However, the two other categories, *tenants at will* and *sub-tenants,* are in a precarious position. Their very existence depends on the mercy of landlords and this make them prone to various exploitative practices adopted by the landlords. The tenants in India had three important problems. They are as follows :

1. *The tenants were forced to pay high rents for the lands they cultivated.*
2. *The tenants enjoyed no security of tenure.*
3. *They did not have the right to become the owners of the land they were cultivating.*

As a result of these problems mentioned above, the Indian tenants took no interest in cultivation. The problems of the tenants virtually halted the progress of the Indian agriculture. Therefore, special laws and legislations had to be instituted in order to protect these tenants. Accordingly, after independence, all the State Governments took necessary steps to pass tenancy laws to overcome the evils of the existing tenancy system.

The tenancy laws passed by various state governments included the following aspects – (i) *regulation of the rent,* (ii) *security of the tenure,* and (iii) *right of ownership.*

(i) *Regulation of Rents* : During the pre-independence period, rents were fixed either by custom or were the result of market forces of demand and supply. Due to the increasing population, there has been a continuous demand for the land, which led to a continuous rise in rents. The decay of handicrafts increased the dependence on land further and thus pushed up rents. Rack-renting was a common feature of the Indian agrarian structure. Even the rates of rent were not uniform throughout India. In Gujarat, Maharashtra and Rajasthan, 1/6th of the gross produce has been fixed as maximum rent. In Punjab, 1/3rd of the produce has been considered as a fair rent, while in Tamilnadu, it has been between 33.3 and 40 per cent of the gross produce. In Assam, Karnataka, Manipur and Tripura, maximum rents varied between 1/4th to 1/5th of the gross produce. The tenants had no voice to protest against the exorbitant rate of interest levied by the landlords.

The legislations passed in this direction have fixed fair rents for the lands. They have also made provisions to pay the rents in cash rather than in kind. Historically, rents were paid in kind only. This is in fitness with the requirements of the rural economy changing rapidly from barter to money exchange.

(ii) ***Security of Tenure*** : To protect tenants from ejectment and to grant them permanent rights on lands, legislations have been enacted in most of the states. Legislation for security of tenure had three essential aims.

1. Ejectments do not take place except in accordance with the provisions of the law;
2. Land may be resumed by an owner, if at all, for personal cultivation only; and
3. In the event of resumption, the tenant is assured of a prescribed minimum area.

The legislations also include two other aspects : (a) Even if the tenants give away their lands voluntarily to the landlords, the officials should confirm whether such episodes consist in themselves any element of compulsion or use or threat of coercion. (b) The legislations also assure the tenant the right over the land in which he lives, the cattle that he possesses and the grazing land of the cattle in addition to the land which he is cultivating.

(iii) Right to Become Owner [Right of Ownership] : The Plan documents have repeatedly emphasised that the ownership rights should be conferred on tenants, that is, they should be made owners of the land they cultivate. Under the tenancy laws, the tenants could acquire the ownership of the lands they have been cultivating by paying some amounts in instalments. Accordingly, some states have passed the legislations to confer the right of ownership on the tenants. West Bengal, Karnataka and Kerala have achieved more success than the other states in this regard. However, on the whole, the progress with regard to the legislation has not been very satisfactory. In fact, it was envisaged in the Sixth Plan that legislative measures to confer the ownership right to the tenants would be introduced in all the states by 1981-82. This is still an issue that has to be tackled.

C. Ceilings on Land Holdings

Ceilings on Land Holdings means the fixation of maximum limit on the individual land holdings. This maximum limit has two aspects: (i) ***the maximum limit [or the ceiling limit] on the present holdings,*** and (ii) ***the maximum limit on the future holdings.*** The concept of ceiling on land holdings has now attained much importance because it decides how much land would be held by a farmer and his family.

Main Objectives of Ceilings on Land Holdings

1. To reduce the inequality in the ownership of lands.
2. To reduce the glaring inequality in the agricultural income of the people.
3. To increase the opportunities of self employment by distributing the surplus lands [that is, the lands in excess of the ceilings] among the surplus landless cultivators.
4. To satisfy the desire of the landless cultivators to own lands.

Advantages of Ceilings on Land Holdings

1. *The social justification* : The basic rationale for ceilings on agricultural holdings rests in social field. It is argued that a poor economy like ours, where the supply of land is limited, it is socially unjust to allow a small number of people to hold a large part of land. It is also unjust to subjugate the interests of millions of labourers to the interests of this handful minority. Putting ceiling limits on land holdings is thus upheld as a right step in assuring social justice.

2. *Improving the position of the poor* : The income of the poor who receive land as a result of redistribution is expected to rise above the poverty line. According to Food and Agricultural Organisation [FAO] of the U.N.O. *"Redistribution of only 5% of farmland in India, coupled with improved access to water, could reduce rural poverty level by 30%* .... "[1]

3. *The efficiency argument* : Many economists argue that small farms can be more efficiently managed in comparison to large farms, especially in the Indian context. For example, **C.H. Hanumath Rao** has pleaded for the redistribution of land after careful examination of the Farm Management Data. According to Rao, small farms also offer more opportunities for employment because they are less capital intensive in comparison with the large farms.

4. *Inculcating the spirit of co-operation* : It has also been said that the redistribution of the excess land among the beneficiaries would forge a co-operative spirit in the management of the land. This practice will help the landless labourers and petty peasants to learn the technics of social management and joint cultivation.

Legislation on Ceiling on Land Holdings

The National Government of India has realised the need for and the importance of ceiling on land holdings. Hence, as early as in 1950, legislation had been passed on ceiling on land holdings. All the states in India, had passed legislation prescribing ceiling on agricultural land holdings. The ceiling on land holdings deferred from state to state. Again the ceiling on land holdings differed from land to land, depending on the nature and the quality of the land, its location, irrigation facilities available, etc. Certain categories of lands, such as tea, coffee and rubber plantations, certain orchards and specialised farms were exempted from the ceilings.

The ceiling laws enacted in 1950 were modified by all the states in 1972 on the basis of the recommendations of the Central Land Reforms Commission of 1971. As per the revised ceiling laws of 1972, the ceiling on land holdings is prescribed not for individual, but for family of 5 members. The 1972 legislation prescribed 3 categories of ceilings. They are :

1. For *irrigated land* the ceiling limit is 10 to 18 acres.
2. For *partly irrigated land* the maximum limit is 27 acres.
3. For *dryland* the upper limit is kept at 54 acres.

Progress of this Measure

"According to the Annual Report [1997-98] of the Ministry of Rural Areas and Employment, since the inception of ceiling laws on agricultural holdings, upto 31st December 1997, total quantum of land declared surplus in the entire country was 75.49 lakh acres out of which about 65.90 lakh acres have been taken possession of and a total area of 52.73 lakh acres has been distributed to 54.16 lakh beneficiaries, of whom around 36% belong to the Scheduled Castes and around 14% to the Scheduled Tribes. But as facts stand, the progress of distribution of surplus lands was palpably slow. Between March 1990 and December 1997, a span of 7 years, only 6.26 lakh acres could be distributed.[2]

D. Consolidation of Land Holdings

Consolidation of Holdings means bringing together the various small plots of land of a farmer scattered all over the village as one compact block, either through purchase or exchange of land with others. This measure is designed to solve the problem of fragmentation of land holdings.

1 **S.K. Misra** and **V.K. Puri** *"Indian Economy"* [2000]. Page - 427.

2 **Ruddar Datt** and **K.P.M. Sundharam** *"Indian Economy"* [2001] S. Chand & Co. Ltd. Page - 539.

Initially, the programme of consolidation was started on a voluntary basis, but was later made compulsory.

Advantages of Consolidation of Land Holdings

Consolidation of land holdings has several advantages, of which the following may be noted :

1. It prevents the endless subdivision and fragmentation of land holdings.
2. It saves the time and labour of a farmer, since all his lands are brought together as one compact block.
3. It encourages improvements on land, such as bunding, fencing, etc.
4. It is condusive for mechanisation and large scale cultivation.
5. It is very helpful for irrigation.
6. It brings down the cost of cultivation and reduces litigation among farmers.

Progress of this Measure

Various state governments have passed legislations making provisions for consolidation of holdings. But however, progress under the programme has been very slow. So far, only 60.2 million hectares of land has been covered under consolidation, which is nearly 1/3rd of the total cropped area in the country. The bulk of the land consolidated has been in Punjab, Haryana, Maharastra, Uttar Pradesh, Bihar and Orissa. In some other states [*Ex:* Andhra Pradesh, Tamilnad, Kerala, Pondicherry, North Eastern states], no beginning has been made in this direction.

Though consolidation of land holdings is a very useful instrument to solve the problem of fragmentation, the task is not completely accomplished unless laws are passed to prevent fragmentation in the future. In the absence of such laws, land can be subdivided and fragmented again and again on account of factors such as law of inheritance, pressure of population, etc. Keeping this point in view, some state governments have passed legislations to fix a minimum limit for subdivision and fragmentation beyond which it cannot be made. This minimum limit is known as the *"standard area"* and has been fixed at different levels by different state governments. Even in this regard, the implementation of the legislations, are not satisfactory.

E. Compilation and Updating of Land Records

Compilation and updating of the land records are an essential condition for effective implementation of land reform programmes. Land records such as – the survey number of the land, the total size of the land, the name of its owner, information regarding irrigation facility, the level of fertility of the land, the types of crops raised in the land, and other information are very much necessary for classifying the land and to attempt its improvement. It is unfortunate that most of our farmers do not have proper records in this regard. In government offices also proper records are not maintained. During the recent years, efforts are being made to maintain the land records through computerisation.

F. Co-operative Farming

Co-operative farming constitutes one of the aspects of land reforms. This reform has been advocated to solve the problems created by subdivision of holdings. The idea is that farmers having very small holdings should join hands and pool their lands for the purpose of cultivation. Though the lands are pooled up the farmers retain their ownership right on their land and are free to withdraw their membership at anytime. The pooled land is cultivated commonly and the produce is distributed among the farmers according to the size of their land. In addition, the farmers working on the land will get wages for their labour. The whole process depends on the willing co-operation and the voluntary participation of the members.

Co-operative farming was proposed for India on various grounds, such as the following : (i) Co-operative farming would solve the problem of subdivision and fragmentation of holdings. (ii) It would facilitate extensive cultivation and mechanisation of agriculture. (iii) It would encourage better methods of cultivation and contribute to higher agricultural productivity and production. (iv) It would provide more income to the farmers and improve their standard of living.

Progress of Co-operative Farming : By and large, co-operative farming has not made much progress in the country. By 1981, only 9,000 co-operative farming societies were formed in the country with a membership of 42.4 lakhs covering 475 lakh hectares of land. Moreover, a large number of these societies are not genuine co-operative societies started by small farmers. Some of them are found to be bogus societies started by families of big landlords to circumvent land ceiling.

Progress of Land Reforms in India - A Brief Assessment

Land reform measures undertaken by independent Indian government had been conceived as the most important instrument of revolutionising agriculture and improving rural areas. The state governments too have passed suitable legislations to implement the land reforms. The land reform measures have, no doubt, brought about some immediate positive effects.

1. A large number of tenants or farmers have now become the owners of the land that they are cultivating. The slogan *"land to the tiller"* has been effectively translated into action in a few states.
2. The tenancy rights are more secure now.
3. The Zamindari, Ryotwari and the Mahalwari systems of exploitation which were in existence during the British period, have almost been abolished. Thus, the intermediaries have no place in our agricultural system.
4. Eviction of the tenants from the land which they have been cultivating, is not easy now.
5. Most of the states have fixed ceiling limits to the land holdings that could be possessed by the farmers. This is a step in the direction of assuring social justice.
6. Land reform legislations have regularised the rent payable by the farmers.
7. The evil of absentee landlordism associated with the Indian agriculture is almost eradicated.

Though the land reform measures were undertaken with great enthusiasm, they have not brought much justice to the large number of ruralites. Various measures associated with land reforms have not made much progress in the country. Great agricultural economist **Prof. M.L. Dantawala** has rightly observed : *"By and large, land reforms in India enacted so far and those contemplated in the near future........ are in the right direction; and yet due to lack of implementation the actual results are far from satisfactory."*[1]

Causes for the Poor Performance of Land Reforms Programme

The much expected land reforms programme has not attained a great success for obvious reasons. The Planning Commission Task Force headed by **Mr. P.S. Appu** mentions the following as the principal reasons for poor implementation of land reforms : *"Lack of political will; absence of pressure from below because the poor peasants and agricultural workers are passive, unorganised*

1 **Ruddar Datt** and **K.P.M. Sundharam** *"Indian Economy ."* S. Chand & Co. Ltd. Page - 541.

and inarticulate; lukewarm and often apathetic attitude of the bureaucracy, absence of upto-date land records, and legal hurdles in the way of implementation of land reforms."[1]

Some of the important reasons for the poor progress of the land reform measures can be briefed here.

(i) *Lack of Strong Political Will* : A strong political will is necessary for the successful implementation of land reform measures. Due to vested interests in the political system, the land reform measures were not implemented by various governments sincerely and seriously.

(ii) *Transfer of Lands to Family Members* : To escape the laws relating to land ceilings, the Zamindars indulged in large scale transfer of land to their family members. For quite sometime, there was no law in some states to prevent such transfers.

(iii) *Absence of Strong Pressure from Below* : For the successful implementation of land reform measures, there must be pressure from below, that is, from the beneficiaries of land reform measures like tenants, landless agricultural labourers, and others. Unfortunately, the unorganised tenants and landless agricultural labourers could not bring sufficient pressure on the government to demand speedy implementation of land holdings.

(iv) *Legal Hurdles or Difficulties* : Judiciary should not be involved at any stage in the implementation of land reforms. This suggestion was given at the very beginning of land reform programmes. But in the Indian context, number of legal hurdles came in the way of the implementation of land reforms.

It was alleged that in most of the instances courts and land tribunals gave judgements mostly in favour of the rich landlords. The complicated and the complex land reform laws and legislations also contributed to the very defeat of its purpose.

(v) *Lack of Uniformity in Land Reform Laws* : The land reform laws are not uniform throughout India. They are different in different states. This variety with regard to land reform laws is also responsible for the slow progress of land reform measures.

(vi) *Absence of Updated Land Records* : The beneficiaries of the land reforms must produce evidence of their rights in order to get the benefits of land reforms. Unfortunately, they are not able to produce correct and updated land records because such records are not properly maintained.

(vii) *Problem of 'Voluntary Surrender'* : Landlords often forced their tenants to voluntarily surrender the land being cultivated by them. For this purpose, tenants were often threatened and even beaten up. The poor tenants had no strength to match the force of landlords and often *"voluntarily"* surrendered the lands under such pressure.

(viii) *Limits for Retention of Land for Personal Cultivation*: The very definition of 'personal cultivation' was defective. Hence, intermediaries took the chance to retain substantial areas of land for personal cultivation. This enabled Zamindars to resume large areas of land for cultivation defeating the very purpose of the abolition of Zamindari system.

(ix) *Helplessness of the Central Government* : The Central Government could only give suggestions and directions for the implementation of land reforms, for it has no right to impose its will on the state governments on this issue. Nor did it take any interest in pressurising the state governments to implement it seriously.

(x) *Role of the Corrupt, Ineffective and Inefficient Administrative Machinery* : Land reform measures could be successful only if the administrative machinery concerned would take interest in

---

1 Planning Commission, *Report of the Task Force on Agrarian Relations* [1973], Pages : 9 - 10 as quoted by **Ruddar Datt** and **K.P.M. Sundharam** in *"Indian Economy."* S. Chand & Co. Ltd. Page - 541.

the effective implementation of the land reform measures. But the ineffecitve, inefficient, indifferent, corrupt administrative machinery contributed to the failure of the land reforms.

Conclusion

There is no doubt that in an agricultural country like India, land reforms constitute an important aspect of rural development. Our experience with regard to the implementation of land reforms has revealed that it is highly a complex issue. By 1994, more than 16 lakh legal cases relating to land reforms were pending before the courts. Any programme to become a success requires people's support. Land reform programmes also require active and whole-hearted support of all the sections of people. Unfortunately, the land reform programmes could not get the support of all the sections concerned. In many instances, it only furthered ill-will and antagonism between the Zamindars on the one hand, and the tenants / farmers on the other.

In the Eighth Five-Year Plan, the Central Government had ear-marked 1,087 crore rupees for the effective implementation of the land reforms. The Plan had the intention of providing tenancy rights, ownership rights to the farmers and updating the land records. But, the desired results could not be obtained even after the Eighth Plan. As a ritual, the Ninth Five-Year Plan [1997-2002], has devoted just two paragraphs on land reforms. It states **:** *"All possible efforts would be made to detect and redistribute the surplus land and to enforce ceiling laws with firmness........ Absentee landlordism must be eliminated........ Rights of tenants and share croppers need to be recorded and security of tenure provided to them.......... Preference should be given to the poor, especially women, with respect to waste lands and common property resources."*[1]

PROBLEMS OF INDIAN VILLAGES

Though India is known as the classical land of the villages her villages are not free from problems. Ever since the Muslim rule the Indian villages have been receiving one or the other setbacks. The Muslim rule and later the British rule brought enough hardships to the villages. The villages could no longer preserve their self-sufficiency and autonomy. The centralised administration of the British and their industrial economy including the factory system of production brought untold miseries to the Indian villages. The villages gradually became the centres of problems. The problems of the villages continued even after the independence. Some of the major problems with which the Indian villages are confronted are analysed here.

1. Agricultural Problems

(i) ***Traditional and Unscientific System of Cultivation:*** Even today [i.e., in 2000] more than 65% of our people are depending on agriculture and what it produces. Agriculture is the largest industry that provides employment to the biggest number of people. Since most of the farmers are uneducated and custom-bound they follow traditional methods of agriculture. Agricultural operations such as ploughing, planting, putting chemicals and fertilizers, taking out seeds, cutting crops, separting seeds from the plants, cleaning the grains - are carried on through human or animal power. The farmers are not able to follow the modern scientific mode of cultivation and this is reflected in the relatively poor agricultural production.

(ii) ***Lack of Irrigational Facilities and Dependence on Nature:*** A large number of Indian farmers still depend on monsoon. In many places dams and tanks are built and canal water facility is

1 Planning Commission, Ninth Five Year Plan [1997-2002], Volume II. Page - 448, as quoted by **Ruddar Datt** and **K.P.M. Sundharam.** S. Chand & Co. Ltd. Page - 543.

provided. But this is not in tune with the demand. For example, before Independence about **18%** of the land was irrigated. In spite of all our efforts to provide better irrigation facilities the ratio of irrigated land to total cultivated land is now [in 2000] about 33% per cent. Majority of the villages thus continue to suffer on the one side, by the onslaughts of famine, and on the other, by the floods. Vast land lies unutilised due to lack of water facility.

(iii) *Sub-Division and Fragmentation of Land-Holdings*: The size of the land-holdings in the Indian context, is very small. As per the *Agricultural Census Report - 1975,* more than 51% of the total land holdings [that is about 35.7 million land-holdings] in the country are smaller than one hectare. The average size of la nd holdings in India is very low, less than **2** hectares or **5** acres. As and when partition takes place in the family, land also gets partitioned and fragmented. Small-sized holdings lead to great waste of time, labour and cattle power, difficulty in proper utilisation of irrigation facilities, wastage of crops in the absence of fencing, etc. Thus, the small land holdings have their own practical difficulty and hence are not amenable for scientific farming.

Official data about land distribution indicate that **61** per cent of the rural households either own no land or small fragments of land or marginal uneconomic holdings of less than **1** hectare. Taken together, **61** per cent of households own barely **8** per cent of cultivated area. Out of them, **22** per cent households own no land at all; another **25** per cent own less than half a hectare [1.2 acre]. Since these landless labourers subsist at the border of the poverty line, they have been gradually slipping below poverty line.

2. Economic Problems

(i) *Burden of Loans or Rural Indebtedness:* It is often said that *"the Indian farmer is born in debt lives in debt and finally dies in debts."* Village economy gives little scope for saving. The poor position of the Indian farmer compels him to borrow money from the local money lenders who charge exorbitant interests and squeeze their clients to the maximum. It is a kind of vicious circle. When once a person gets into that he finds no way of coming out of it. They become ultimately the bonded labourers of these money-lenders who are, in many instances, big land-lords. Absence of banking facility, and the procedural delay involved in the sanctioning of the loan also make many to go to money-lenders for immediate financial benefit.

It is true that due to the operation of institutional financial agencies especially after independence, the rural money-lenders are losing ground. For instance, according to the ***"All India Rural Credit Survey"*** undertaken in 1951, the money-lenders accounted for nearly 70% of all rural credit. In 1991, they accounted for only **17.6%** of rural credit. Further, as it is made clear in the **Table 1,** given below, that for all rural groups the average debt per household has risen steadily from Rs.500 to Rs.1906 between 1971 and 1991. [However, this increase is partly due to the process of inflation that has been taking place consistently.] This only shows that rural indebtedness is still having its hold on the rural people.

Table - 1

Average Debt of Rural Households

In Rupees

Year	*Cultivators*	*Non-Cultivators*	*All*
1971	605	223	500
1981	803	205	661
1991	2,294	1,151	1,906

Source **:** *Reserve Bank of India Bulletin,* May 1999.

(ii) ***Helplessness of Small Farmers:*** As it is made clear large number of our farmers are small farmers. Their land can fetch them limited income. Unless they earn some more through one or the other means, they cannot survive. For centuries together, such small farmers were depending on handicrafts, and home industries such as pottery, basket-making, mat-making, toy-making, brick-making etc. The factory-made goods have destroyed their market. Hence they struggle a lot for finding out alternate source of income and finally fall a prey into the hands of local money lenders.

(iii) ***Problem of Landless Labourers:*** All those who live in the villages are not the owners of the land. Only a few own the land but many work as landless labourers in the field. In many instances, the upper caste people own the land and the low caste people toil in their land as agricultural labourers.

According to the *"Second Agricultural Labour Enquiry"* published in 1960, agricultural labour families constituted nearly **25** per cent of all rural families. According to this, more than **85** per cent of the rural workers are casual, serving any farmer who is willing to engage them and only **15** per cent of agricultural labourers are attached to specific landlords. More than half of the workers do not possess any land, and even the rest of them own only very little of land. Agricultural labourers predominantly belong to the Scheduled Castes, Scheduled Tribes and Other Backward Classes. According to one estimate, between **75** and **80** per cent of all agricultural labourers belong to the Scheduled Castes. According to the data provided by *The Census of India* [1991], the number of agricultural labourers increased from **27.5** million in 1951 to **74.6** million in 1991.

Bonded Labourers **:** It is well known that the landless labourers who live in the rural areas depend upon agriculture and majority of them are found to be Scheduled Caste people. Many of these people have become *bonded labourers.* Bonded labourers are - *"persons who are forced to work for the creditors for the loan incurred, either without wage or on nominal wage."* **[*Commission for Scheduled Castes and Scheduled Tribes*].** Surveys held in the year 1978-79 by the *Gandhi Peace Foundation* [GPF] and *National Labour Institute* [NLI] have revealed that more than **87%** of the labourers belonged to Scheduled Castes and Tribes. *It is also said that around* ***5.7%*** *of the total agricultural labourers working in India, constituted bonded labourers.* Many of them have become bonded labourers due to their inability to pay back the loan borrowed from the land-owning money-lenders. Of the existing bonded labourers, around 90% of them are found to be Scheduled Caste and Tribe people who are exploited in several ways. Some of these labourers do not even get an annual income of Rs.1,000/=. [***Note*** **:** For more details about the problem of ***"Bonded Labourers"*** please refer to **Chapter No.22.**]

(iv) ***Defective Marketing System:*** Small farmers can lead a comfortable life only when good marketing facility is provided and minimum rate for their produce is assured. This cannot be expected in the Indian rural context. Lack of transport and storage facility and absence of systematic marketing facility have damaged the economic strength of the people. *For example,* the storage facilities which are available in the village at present are so poor that **10** to **20** per cent of the produce is eaten away by rats. The small farmers have the feeling that they are not getting the right value for their produce. Due to the lack of the marketting facility the agricultural surplus reaches the intermediaries or middlemen which results in exploitation of villagers. At the time of purchasing the agricultural produces the illiterate farmers are cheated in weights and measures. Only recently the government has taken serious steps to improve this marketing condition. Co-operative Marketing and Regulated Market facilities are only the recent developments. It is stated in the First Five Year Plan document that *"the purchase of the agriculturist's requirements and the sale of his produce are key activities in the business of farming and their importance is likely to be even more crucial in* *a socially regulated economy....... Due to his inability to secure a fair deal at these two stages, the average agriculturist is denied the full fruits of his industry."*[1]

(v) ***Lack of Transport and Communication Facilities:*** Transport and communication systems in society are like the circulatory system in human body. Unfortunately, these facilities are not available to a sizeable number of our villages. There are villages which are almost like islands. There are villages with no proper roads, bridges and transport facilities. Hence the farmers find it extremely difficult to take their produce to a market where the prices are comparatively attractive. Farmers are made to walk miles together to reach a town to obtain news papers, postal, banking, medical and telephone facilities.

(vi) ***Poverty and Unemployment:*** Poverty has become an inseparable part of our rural life. More than **37%** of our farmers are living below the poverty line even today [2001]. The following Table gives us a glimpse of the estimate of poverty in Inida.

Table - 2

Number and Percentage of Population Below Poverty Line

[*Modified Expert Group Methodology*]

	Rural Number of Persons	***%***	***Urban Number of Persons***	***%***	***Combined Number of Persons***	***%***
ALL INDIA						
1973-74	2,613	56.4	600	49.0	3,213	54.9
1977-78	2,642	53.1	647	45.2	3,289	51.3
1983	2,520	45.7	709	40.8	3,229	44.5
1987-88	2,319	39.1	752	38.2	3,071	38.9
1993-94	2,440	37.3	763	32.4	3,203	36.0

Source : Planning Commission, *Ninth Five Year Plan* [1997-2002]. Vol.1, p. 29.

Though more than 70% or our people depend upon agriculture, agricultural output accounts for less than 40% of our national income. Our land distribution system is one of the reasons for this. About 10 to 20% of landholders hold 70% of the total land and 50% of the landholders are marginal farmers with less than one hectare of land. This disparity has added to rural poverty. There are poor householders in the rural areas which are called *"destitutes"* [by the *Ministry of Rural Development*] with an annual income of even less than Rs.4000/- [at 1991-92 price-level]. The decline of the traditional skills and handicrafts, slow disappearance of home industries and the increasing industrialisation have deteriorated the economic conditions of our farmers. Poverty has adversely affected the standard of living of the ruralites.

Unemployment is another serious problem of the Indian villages. For example, open unemployment was around 1.91% in the rural areas in 1983 and this increased to 3.07% in 1987-88. Destruction of village crafts, and cottage industries have virtually thrown lakhs of farmers out of job. Due to their illiteracy, and lack of experience in other fields these unemployed people are not able to find alternative job. The only job that is known to them is snatched away making them unemployed. Rural youths are also not able to get any job opportunities in the villages. Self-employment opportunities are also not being availed of by many youths due to lack of education, confidence and

1 **Ruddar Datt** and **K.P.M. Sundharam.** *''Indian Economy''* S. Chand & Co. Ltd. Page - 584.

proper guidance. We find total unemployment, seasonal unemployment, under-employment also in the villages. For example, ***"Committee of Experts on Unemployment"*** [1973] has estimated that 8.5 million persons were working less than 14 hours per week; and 23.50 million persons [15.9% of the rural labour force] were working less than 28 hours per week. They were all severely underemployed. This problem of underemployment continues even today though with some less intensity.

3. Social Problems

(i) *Illiteracy:* Indian villagers are mostly illiterate. As per the 1991 Census report, about 52.1% of the people in the total population are literate. Though this rate of literacy increased to 65.38% in 2001, literates are found in a bigger number in cities and not in villages. There are villages wherein not even 10% of the people are literate. Lack of reading and writing ability has made our farmers to turn their back to the progress in modern science and technology. Illiterate parents who do not know the value of education are unfortunately denying education to their own children. Those children who join the school also drop out in the middle. As far as female children are concerned, no one is bothered about their education. Though the village people of the present generation give relatively more importance to education, the performance of the rural children is not that impressive.

(ii) *Traditionalism, Conservatism and Superstitions:* Indian ruralites are known to be conservative, traditional, dogmatic and superstitious. Rural people are under the grip of caste, customs, traditions and superstition. They are unprepared to change their way of life and outlook. They are slow to change and very often resist changes. They are in a way status quoists. New things and novel ideas are looked with suspicion by them. They lack initiative, and the urge to prosper. Their fatalistic attitude does not allow them to take risk and experiment with new things.

(iii) *Casteism and Untouchability:* Indian villages are in a way controlled by the caste system. It is the dominant factor that decides almost all aspects of rural life. During the early times there were caste councils which used to rule or govern the social life of the caste members. Even today in remote villages such *'caste panchayats'* are powerful. Since caste constitutes the social base and the source of individual's identity, no one is able to ignore it in the village. Caste identification leads to casteism also. Strong identification with the caste and the increase in the horizontal solidarity of the caste lead to caste conflicts damaging the unity of the village.

Untouchability and ***casteism*** often go together in the village. The practice of untouchability is more alive in the village than in the town. The difference between the *"touchable"* and the *"untouchable"* is more apparent here. The untouchables who are mostly working as landless labourers are exploited to the maximum and put to various hardships. Their literacy level is also very low. Crimes and different types of atrocities are committed against them by the upper-caste people. The Harijan farmers who own small size of land are always harassed and put to inconveniences by the large-farmers belonging to the upper-caste. ***Ex.*:** By 1978, about 15 lakh crimes were registered in the country out of which about 3 lakhs were connected with land disputes. In these disputes, in many instances the upper-castes were found to be guilty of harassing and exploiting the lowest caste people, that is, Scheduled Castes. Since the *dalits* are unorganised they are not able to put up resistance. *"Crimes in India"* [1995] reports that there is an increase in the number of crimes against SCs which is evident from the fact that as against 180 cases registered with the police in 1955, the number of cases increased to 18,336 in 1991 and to 32,990 in 1995.

(iv) *Low Status of Rural Women:* Women in the Indian villages have a very low social status. They are confined to kitchen work and to look after the children. They are treated as non-entities and also as the servants of menfolk. Their education is neglected. They are subject to early marriages. They are not consulted in taking any major decision regarding family matters and all the decisions are enforced on them. They do not have any individuality. Due to their illiteracy they are not able to give proper social training to their children.

(v) ***Lack of Civic Facilities:*** Many of our villages are deprived of the basic required civic facilities such as - medical facilities, schooling facility, banking facility, postal services, bus and other transport facility, and so on. While the villages that exist near the towns and big cities have access to all these facilities, those that exist in the remotest corners are deprived of them. Lack of these facilities has halted their progress.

(vi) ***Rural Ill-health:*** Rural people are facing the problem of ill-health. The rate of birth and also rate of death are relatively higher in the village. Due to their illiteracy the rural people neglect their health and do not take proper medical advice when required. Rural women very rarely complain of diseases and prefer to suffer than to go for medical check-up and advice. The ill-equipped primary health centres are also not able to give medical assistance whenever it is required. Though the government has spent huge amount of money for improving rural health, the progress achieved in this field is far from satisfaction.

It is evident from the above that the Indian villages are faced with a number of problems. The problems are not, however, equally found in all the villages. There are villages quite advanced. In such villages many of the problems mentioned above are not found. But villages in the remote corners are full of problems. It is necessary to study these problems in a scientific manner to find suitable solutions for them. Study of the Indian villages is a need of the hour especially for the rural sociologists and rural economists. It is a matter of regret that no systematic and comprehensive study of the problems of the Indian villages on an all-India basis has been made so far.

Chapter 14

RURAL LIFE IN INDIA

PART II : RURAL DEVELOPMENT AND RURAL CHANGE

A. Rural Development : *Meaning and Essential Aspects of Rural Development - Important Rural Development Programmes - Community Development Programmes: Aims, Achievements and Evaluation of CDP - The Establishment of Panchayat Raj System - Poverty Alleviation Programmes [PAPs]: The IRDP : Integrated Rural Development Programme : Objectives and Progress - NREP: National Rural Employment Programme - TRYSEM : Training Rural Youth for Self-Employment - Other Important Rural Development Programmes : RLEGP: Rural Landless Employment Guarantee Programme - JRY : Jawahar Rozgar Yojana- Antyodaya Programme - SFDA : Small Farmers' Development Agency - FFWP: Food For Work Programme - DDP : Desert Development Programme- PMRY: Prime Minister's Rozgar Yojna - DPAP : Drought Prone Area Programme - Scheme for Providing Self-Employment to Educated Unemployed - EAS : Employment Assurance Scheme - JGSY : Jawahar Gram Samriddhi Yojna - SGSY : Swarna Jayanthi Gram Swarozgar Yojna - Impact of Development Programmes : The Green Revolution - Its Effects, Limitations and Social Consequences - Other Impacts of Development Programmes.*

B. Rural Change in India : *Major Trends in Rural Social Changes : Transformation From Subsistence to Market Economy - Rural Transformation by Technology - Transformation by Abolition of Intermediaries - Emergence of Various Associations and Institutions - Conclusion.*

It is well known that India is a classical land of the villages. Villages constitute the backbone of the country. Villages continue to contribute 40% of our national income. Villages, therefore, play a vital role in the life of the nation. If villages grow and develop, the country shall automatically develop. These villages were once self-sufficient units, but now they have become the victims of innumerable problems such as illiteracy, casteism, untouchability, conservatism, economic backwardness, and so on. The British people did nothing to develop our villages. On the contrary, villages lost their autonomy, self-reliance and importance during the British period. They not only mismanaged the villages but even destroyed the cottage and home industries that existed in the villages. The economic structure of the villages was shattered, their social fabric was disturbed.

Gandhiji, Vinobha Bhave, Jaya Prakash Narayana and all other frontline leaders of the nation and right thinking people reiterated that the development of country and its prosperity depend on its villages. They also had warned that the negligence of the villages would ruin the future of India. Needless to say rural development, that is, development of villages became a priority issue soon after independence. It was decided to counter the problems confronting the villages in a methodical manner. The government soon after independence decided to launch various developmental programmes and welfare activities to improve the villages and increase the standard of living of the people.

The developmental programmes which the country has been implementing for the past 50-55 years represent a concerted attempt to give a proper direction to the change. Plans and programmes which are especially meant for rural development *have the objective of changing and improving the quality of lifestyle of the rural people.* Though the development efforts are not a new phenomena, plans, programmes, schemes and projects that are launched today assume special significance because, they are mostly designed, on the one hand, to fulfil the immediate and "felt-needs" of the people, and on the other, to meet the challenges of the modern conditions.

This chapter gives a glimpse of the rural development programmes. It also provides us a picture of the changing scene of the rural society. The chapter dispels our doubts regarding the dynamic nature of our rural society. It provides necessary explanation relating to the changeability of the village society.

RURAL DEVELOPMENT : MEANING AND ESSENTIAL ASPECTS

Meaning of Rural Development

- *Rural Development virtually means development of villages including agriculture.*
- *Rural development is a comprehensive socio-economic process undertaken by the government for the purpose of improving the economic and social conditions of the people living in rural areas.*
- *It represents planned programmes to change and to improve the quality of the life-style of rural people.*

Main Components of Rural Development

Rural development includes some major elements or componenets among which the following may be noted.

Firstly, the rural development is concerned with the development or improvement of all the sectors of rural economy, namely, *the primary sector, the secondary sector* and *the tertiary sector.*

Secondly, it is concerned with the improvement of the social conditions of the rural people through the provision of drinking water, education, vocational training, medical facilities, etc.

Thirdly, it is concerned with the improvement of the socio-economic conditions of the weaker sections of the rural areas such as the Scheduled Castes, Scheduled Tribes, the landless agricultural labourers and the marginal and small farmers.

Essential Aspects of Rural Development

Programmes of rural development should necessarily satisfy certain conditions among which the following may be noted :

1. *Agricultural development is the most significant aspect of rural development.* Hence, it is necessary to give the highest importance to agricultural development. Agricultural

development can be ensured through mechanisation of agriculture, consolidation of land holdings, effective implementation of land reforms, use of good varieties of seeds, adequate fertilisers, pesticides, adequate supply of water, proper crop planning, proper harvesting and so on.

2. *Rural development must necessarily include proper plans to change the socio-economic structure of the rural set up.* The change in the socio-economic structure refers to changes in socio-economic institutions. These changes would ensure maximisation and equitable distribution of income among rural people.

3. *Rural development programmes must be politically independent.* Political interference through political parties and leaders is going to spoil the very purpose of the programme. The required political freedom should be given to the people in charge of these programmes to go ahead with their plans and programmes of action.

4. It is essential that all the *rural development programmes must have co-operative orientation.* Co-operation seems to be a powerful instrument of uplifting the poorer sections of the rural society. Co-operative societies should be set up performing, production in cottage industries, marketing, finance or credit and even for the supply of consumer goods.

5. *Programmes of rural development demand the active participation of the rural people.* No programme should be imposed forcibly on the ruralites. The programmes should always be framed on the basis of the felt needs of the people. Further, rural people must be motivated properly to take an active role in the programmes. In this respect honest and respected leaders of the rural areas must come forward and give proper guidance to the masses.

Important Rural Development Programmes

As it is made clear, rural development is a very complex process. It cannot be achieved through any one organisation or by any one person. As such it consists of a large number of programmes among which the following are important.

1. Community Development Programme [CDP - 2nd October 1952].
2. National Extension Services [NES - 2nd October 1953].
3. Integrated Rural Development Programme [IRDP - 1978].
4. National Rural Employment Programme [NREP - 1980].
5. Antyodaya Programme [1972].
6. Jawahar Rozgar Yojna [JRY - 1989].
7. Rural Landless Employment Guarantee Programme [RLEGP - 1983].
8. Training Rural Youth for Self-Employment [TRYSEM - 1979].
9. Tribal Development Programme [TDP - 1959].
10. Drought Prone Area Programme [DPAP - 1979].
11. Desert Development Programme [DDP - 1977].
12. Food For Work Programme [FFWP - 1977].
13. Nehru Rozgar Yojna [NRY - October 1989].
14. Prime Minister's Rozgar Yojna [PMRY - 2nd October 1993].
15. Employment Assurance Scheme [EAS - 2nd October 1993].
16. Swarnajayanthi Gram Swarozgar Yojna [SGSY - April 1999].
17. Jawahar Gram Samriddhi Yojna [JGSY - 1st April 1999].

Special programmes for providing rural employment such as –

(i) Command Area Development Programme [CADP].
(ii) Employment Guarantee Schemes.
(iii) Small Farmers' Development Agency [SFDA].
(iv) Marginal Farmers' and Agricultural Labourers' Development Agency [MFAL].
(v) Crash Scheme for Rural Development [CSRD].
(vi) Pilot Intensive Rural Employment Programme [PIREP].
(vii) Development of Women and Children in Rural Areas [DWCRA].
(viii) Scheme for Providing Self-employment to Educated Unemployed.

RURAL DEVELOPMENT PROGRAMMES

Independent Indian Government has launched various developmental programmes to assist the rural sector to march towards progress. Though the general purpose of all these programmes remains the same, that is, achieving rural development and promoting rural welfare, the specific purposes and the main thrust of these programmes are not the same.

Firstly, some of the developmental activities were production-oriented. ***Example*** : Community Development Projects -1952 [CDP]; Land Reforms [1950]; Poverty Alleviation Programmes [PAPs] such as IRDP : Integrated Rural Development Programme [1978], etc.

Secondly, some of the activities are undertaken not for the productive purposes but for improving the living standards of people. ***Example*:** Food For Work Programme [1977]; Tribal Development Programme [1959]; National Rural Employment Programme [NPEP]; Training Rural Youth for Self-Employment - TRYCEM [1979], etc.

Thirdly, some programmes were intended to increase assets and benefit people economically. ***Example*:** Rural Employment Programme; Minimum Agricultural Wage; IRDP; etc.

Fourthly, some programmes are basically aimed at alleviating poverty and unemployment. ***Ex*:** NREP; TRYCEM; DPAP [Drought Prone Area Programme - 1979]; and so on.

Fifthly, some programmes were announced as a matter of political exigencies under which category we may include, for example, *"Garibi Hatao"* and *"Twenty Point Programme."* They were announced by the late Prime Minister Indira Gandhi during the period of emergency [1975-77].

Let us now take a glimpse of these various developmental activities which the Government launched for the benefit of the people.

Community Development Programme [CDP - 1952]

The *Community Development Programme* [CDP] launched on 2nd October 1952, constitutes the first organised effort at rural reconstruction. The Government of India has launched a number of programmes to eradicate poverty and unemployment in India. Community Development Programme [CDP] represents one such programme. It may be noted that exactly after one year, that is, on 2nd October 1953, *the National Extension Services* [NES] was launched. Both these programmes were intended to promote agricultural and rural development. The only difference between the two was that the former [CDP] was a more intensive programme than the latter [NES]. Both these schemes virtually worked hand in hand. Both these schemes were extolled by Pandit Nehru as *"the armoury of our nation's toiling spirit."*

Meaning of Community Development Programme

Community Development Programme was a programme which sought to change the economic, social and cultural life of the rural population, and to transform the stagnant villages into progressive rural communities.

According to *International Co-operation Administration,* community development is a *"Process of social action in which the people in a community organize themselves for planning and action define their common and individual needs and problems; make group and individual plans to meet the needs and solve their problems; execute these plans with a minimum reliance upon community resources; and supplement them with services and material from governmental and non-governmental agencies."*

Aims and Objectives

The main objectives of the CDP are mentioned below :

1. The programme was intended to create an interest among the rural people for better economic, social and cultural life and make them satisfy their interest by self help.
2. It intended to increase agricultural production by means of good irrigational facilities.
3. It intended to provide safe drinking water facilities and to make the villagers conscious of water contaminated diseases.
4. It aimed at improving transport and communication facilities and promote cottage and small scale industries in the villages.
5. It aimed at generating progressive outlook among the rural people and to make villages self sufficient.
6. It also aimed at encouraging community thinking and collective action.
7. It intended to promote rural welfare through the improvement of education, public health and sanitation, medical facilities, housing, drinking water, hospitals, community centres and sports and cultural activites.
8. It also intended to increase people's participation in developmental programmes.
9. It aimed to provide a single multiple agency for rural development.
10. Community development projects and programmes intended to improve the many-sided development of rural life.

Implementation of Community Development Programme

The Community Development Programme was implemented in units of blocks. Initially, this project was launched in 55 selected blocks. By March 1979, it was extended to 5,123 blocks covering a population of about 47 crores spread over all the five lakh villages in the country. Each block covered an area of about 400 - 500 Sq.kms. in about 100 villages and a population of about 1 lakh. It was implemented through project officers, block development officers, technical experts, and *gram sevaks.*

Achievements

The Community Development Programme started in 1952 covered almost all the villages of India. The expenditure incurred on CDP during the First Five-Year Plan was Rs.233.1 crore. During the Second Plan the government spent a sum of Rs.267.3 crores. During 3rd, 4th, and 5th Plans, Govt. of India spent a sum of Rs.26.7 crores, Rs.115 crores, and Rs.150 crores respectively. Even during the Sixth Plan, a sum of Rs.150 crore was spent. During the Seventh Plan the total expenditure on the C.D. Programme was Rs.416 crores. By 1969 the whole nation was covered under the C.D.P. with 5011 blocks.

Evaluation of the Community Development Programme

The CDP attained some success in the beginning. But gradually it started loosing its importance. It failed to obtain effective participation of people in the programmes. The Government too lost its interest in the programme and finally replaced it by IRDP [Integrated Rural Development Programme] from 1978-79. Various factors contributed to its failure.

1. The CDP was not well planned and *it failed to cater to the "felt needs" of the people.* The needs of the people were perceived by the project personnel themselves, that is, by those who were at the planning level. The real needs of the people remained unidentified by the government.
2. Government *failed to provide proper training to the personnel who were in charge* of the implementation of the programme.
3. The programme *did not contain clearly defined priorities.*
4. The *project became highly bureaucratised.* It was a development of the village people from the above and not from the below. There was least involvement of the masses of people.
5. Absence of functional distribution of responsibility among the government personnel connected with the implementation of the programme.
6. The CDP *failed to obtain proper response from the beneficiaries, that is, the rural people.* The programmes were implemented uniformly and hence they failed to cater to the needs of diverse situations at the local level.
7. *Indifference, irresponsibility, lack of commitment, administrative inefficiency and corruption* at the level of the bureaucracy contributed to the failure of the CDP. People had the impression that the whole bureaucracy was corrupt. Only a meagre part of the budgetary allocation was spent for the people.
8. The *benefits of the CDP went to the rich and big farmers* at the cost of small and marginal farmers.
9. The CDP *lacked co-ordination very badly* among different development departments. As a result, there was much overlap in the programmes.
10. In spite of the huge expenditure being incurred on CDP, agricultural development did not take place as per the expectation and food production also did not increase.

The Establishment of Panchayat Raj System

The Central Government launched the CDP with the main intention of obtaining people's participation in the development projects. Towards the end of the Five Year Plan period an evaluation of the working of the NES and CDP revealed that these have not succeeded in getting the participation of the people which was one of the most essential requirements. So the Central Government appointed a Committee headed by **Balwant Rai Mehta** in January 1957 to revive the working of the CDP and the NES.

The Mehta Committee which submitted its report by the end of 1957, strongly recommended the establishment of *"Panchayat Raj."* [*Note*: For more details about the ***Panchayat Raj System,*** please refer to **Chapter No.20.**] The meaning of *"Panchayat Raj"* is – *"democratic decentralisation".* The basic argument given for the establishment of *"Panchayat Raj"* was, people should be given power to rule over the villages. The Committee has also said that the *Panchayat Raj* system would establish *"........ a lineage between local leadership enjoying confidence of the local people and the government, and translate the policies of the government into action."* With this initiation in mind the *Mehta Committee* made its recommendations to fulfil three major objectives. They are :

(i) *To represent the "felt needs" of the village community;*

(ii) *To give power to the non-officials for the development of village communities; and*

(iii) *To give power of implementation or execution of programmes to the people.*

The above explanation makes it clear that the *Panchayat Raj* system came into being with the main intention of ensuring the involvement of people in the development of villages. Keeping in view the role of *Panchayat Raj,* the Third Five Year Plan was also revised. Thus Planning Commission in the Third Plan suggested several new strategies for the development of villages. The new form of development programmes included the following :

(i) *Increase in agricultural production.*

(ii) *Area development programme,* and

(iii) *Programme for special target groups.*

The Government launched various programmes in order to fulfil the above mentioned three targeted objectives. A glimpse of such programmes is given below.

Poverty Alleviation Programmes [PAPs]

A. THE IRDP : INTEGRATED RURAL DEVELOPMENT PROGRAMME

*The **Integrated Rural Development Programme** is a programme or scheme for improving the living standards of the poorest of the poor living in rural areas and for making the process of rural development self-sustaining.*

A large number of rural development programmes had been introduced in different states with different funding patterns often creating confusion and problems of administration and effective implementation. Hence, the Government of India decided to replace all these programmes by a single *Integrated Programme* for the entire country. It is in this background the *Integrated Rural Development Programme* [IRDP] was launched.

The Integrated Rural Development Programme initiated in 1978-79 was a major attempt to attack poverty. In the beginning, it was limited only to 20 districts, but, by 1982, it was extended to 5011 blocks. The programme is based on *"the local needs, resources, endowments and potentialities."* Its major objective is to enable selected families to cross the *"poverty line"* through *"a strategy of productive assets and endowment."*

Objectives of IRDP : The objectives of IRDP are mentioned below:

1. The first objective of the IRDP is to improve the economic and social conditions of the poorest sections of the rural society and to help them to cross the line of poverty.
2. The IRDP aims at developing agriculture and raising the productivity in agriculture by providing agricultural inputs and credit facilities.
3. The IRDP is equally concerned with the development of the secondary and tertiary sectors of the rural economy especially to help the landless labourers.
4. Another thrust of IRDP is to generate employment opportunities in the rural areas and to enlighten the rural masses to exhibit their capacity for fuller development.

5. The IRDP is concerned with the task of promoting self employment in rural areas by providing productive assets, skills, inputs and credit facilities to the poor. The TRYSEM [*Training for Rural Youth for Self Employment*] and DWCRA [*Development of Women and Children in Rural Areas*] are launched with this intention.

The Central and State governments provide financial resources for the programme and lay down broad guidelines for its implementation. The main administrative unit for its implementation is the **District Rural Development Agencies (DRDAs).** At the block level, number of extension officers are provided for programme implementation. The total allocation for IRDP including state's share for the year 1988-89 was Rs.687.95 crores. This programme considers family as the basic unit of development. Under this programme, during the Sixth Five Year Plan [1980-85], about 16.5 million families were assisted against the target of 15 million families. The Seventh Plan had earmarked an outlay of Rs.2643 crores and targeted to cover about 20 million families.

As per this programme, upto the end of 1985, [during the Sixth Plan] a family was considered *"poor"* if it had an annual income of Rs.3500/=. This definition was changed in December 1985, and as per the new definition, the families with an annual income of Rs.6,400/= are eligible to take advantage of the assistance provided by the Programme. The quantum of assistance was raised from Rs.300/= to Rs.6,000/= per family.

Progress of IRDP

The progress of IRDP was quite impressive. The target set for the ***Sixth Plan*** was reached. During the Sixth Plan, as against the target of 15 million families, 16.56 million families were

Table -1

Performance of IRDP during the Seventh Plan and Thereafter

	Item	*Unit*	*Seventh Plan Achievement*	*1990-91 to 1991-92*	*1992-93 to 1996-97*
1.	Total expenditure	Rs. crores	3,316	1,582	4,875
2.	Total term credit mobilised	" "	5,372	2,337	7,567
3.	Total investment	" "	8,688	3,919	11,541
4.	Families assisted	Lakhs	182	54	108.2
5.	SC / ST beneficiaries	" "	82	27.5	54.1
6.	% of SC / ST to total	" "	45	51	50
7.	Women beneficiaries	Lakhs	34.3	17.4	36.4
8.	% of women to total	%	19	32	34
9.	Per capita subsidy	Rs.	1,824	2,930	3,673
10.	Per capita credit	Rs.	2,956	4,328	6,993
11.	Per capita investment	Rs.	4,780	7,258	10,666
12.	Subsidy as % of total per capita investment	%	38	40	34

Source **:** Compiled from Planning Commission, *Eighth Five Year Plan* [1992-97] and Ministry of Rural Development *Annual Report* [1992-93] and [1996-97] and *Ninth Five Year Plan* [1997-2002]. As quoted by **Ruddar Datt** and **K.P.M. Sundharam** in *"Indian Economy"* [2002]. Page - 389.

actually assisted under this programme. Nearly 6.46 million families of SCs and STs were covered under this programme. The total investment under the IRDP during the Sixth Plan was Rs.4762.78 crores as against the target of Rs.4,500 crores.

"The progress of IRDP during the ***Seventh Plan*** reveals that 18.2 million families have been assisted and Rs.3316 crores have been utilised. Besides this, term credit of Rs.5,372 crores was mobilised by financial institutions. Thus, a total investment of Rs.8,688 crores was made to help 18.2 million beneficiaries. As per official records, 45% of the families assisted, belonged to SCs and STs. It is heartening to note that investment per beneficiary improved to Rs.4,780/= [gross], out of which Rs.1,824/= [38%] represented subsidy and the balance of Rs.2,956/= [62%] was in terms of credit. Further, 19% of the beneficiaries were women."[1]

During the ***Eighth Plan*** [1992-97], a total investment of Rs.11,541 crores was made to cover 108.2 lakh families out of which 50% belonged to SC / ST categories. Thus, the per family investment works out to be Rs.10,666/=. The percentage of women beneficiaries was only 34% as against the target of 40%. The Government set a target of reaching an investment level of Rs.12,000/= per family, which was achieved during 1996-97 by reaching per capita investment of Rs.15,036/=.

In order to observe the implementation and assess the relative success or failure of this programme, institutions such as – **RBI :** *Reserve Bank of India;* **NABARD :** *National Bank for Agriculture and Rural Development;* **IFMR :** *Institute of Financial Management and Research* [Chennai]; **PEO :** *Programme Evaluation Organisation of the Planning Commission* – have done some studies and recommended a number of suggestions. But the main problem with these studies is that they have not looked into the real utility of the programme.

Main Defects of IRDP

(a) *The Poorest People are Neglected.* There are leakages in the programme and all assets created under IRDP are not with the poor. It is surprising to note that this programme has excluded the poorest people. The poor people also have their own suspicion towards this programme. The cumbersome procedure involved in availing of this facility also keep them away from taking the benefits of the programme.

(b) *Widespread Corruption.* There is lot of corruption, misuse and malpractice in the implementation of this programme. Facilities have been abused, funds have been misused and the beneficiaries of the programme have been wrongly selected. Political considerations in the implementation of the programme could only add to the prejudices of the people.

(c) *Not Integrated with Development Needs.* The IRDP programme is household based and is not integrated with the development needs or resource base of the area. Thus, the IRDP loan neither raises the living standards of the beneficiaries nor does it have any impact on rural poverty.

(d) *IRDP has no Impact on Poverty.* Serious doubts have been raised whether IRDP would increase the standard of living of its beneficiaries and bring down poverty. Studies conducted in Rajasthan, Gujarat, West Bengal, etc., have given sufficient rooms to support these doubts.

Though the IRDP has its own limitations, it has the potentiality of helping the poor. Hence the scheme need not be dropped down, but it has to be thoroughly revised and honestly implemented.

B. NREP : NATIONAL RURAL EMPLOYMENT PROGRAMME

The NREP, the *National Rural Employment Programme* was launched in October 1980 and it became a regular programme of our Five Year Plan from 1981. In the beginning, it was called

1 **Ruddar Datt** and **K.P.M. Sundharam** *"Indian Economy."* S. Chand & Co. Ltd. Page - 389.

FFWP [*Food For Work Programme*]. It came to be known as the NREP from October 1980. It is continued as an important component of the anti-poverty strategy.

The main purpose of NREP is to *generate additional gainful employment opportunities, to create durable community assets and to improve the overall quality of life in rural areas.*

Features of NREP : 1. The scheme sought to provide employment to the unemployed and under-employed labourers in villages. 2. The scheme intended to raise the minimum level of wages of the rural workers. 3. Under this scheme, the workers were paid partly or fully in the form of foodgrains like rice and wheat supplied by the central government. 4. The scheme worked as a relief measure for the poorer sections of the rural areas in times of droughts and famines, and thus, has become a major instrument of rural employment and development.

This programme is implemented through DRDA [District Rural Development Agencies]. The expenditure of this centrally sponsored scheme is to be borne by the Centre and the States on 50 : 50 basis. During the Sixth Plan period [1980-85] totally Rs.1843 crore was spent on this scheme. During the same period, about 4.69 lakh irrigation and group-housing wells, 54,000 village tanks and 2.23 lakh schools and balwadi centres were constructed. In the Seventh Plan [1985-90], the scheme assisted about another 20 million families.

The NREP allocated about 10% of its budget to provide drinking water facility for Harijan colonies and to undertake community irrigation schemes in Harijan areas. In the same manner another 10% was earmarked for social forestry and fuel plantations. This scheme paid attention only to those works which are durable in nature. The State Governments were expected to take up the responsibility of maintaining the assets created under this programme. Further, the *"Panchayat Raj"* institutions were expected to involve themselves actively in this programme.

The NREP was merged with the Jawahar Rozgar Yojna [JRY] from April 1989.

C. TRYSEM : TRAINING RURAL YOUTH FOR SELF-EMPLOYMENT - 1979

This scheme was started on 15th August 1979 to provide technical skills to the rural youth and to help them to get employment in fields such as – *agriculture, industry services and business activities.* Youths of the poor families belonging to the age-group of 18-35 are entitled to avail of the benefits of this scheme. Priority is given to persons belonging to ST and SC and ex-servicemen. Almost one-third of seats are reserved for women.

The rural youths trained under this TRYSEM programme are also assisted under the IRDP and are provided with loans from financial institutions. The trainees under this scheme are given a stipend which ranges from Rs.75/= to Rs.200/= per month. This scheme is aimed at training 2 lakh rural youths a year. The Sixth Plan had a target of training 10.5 lakh youths but actually 9.4 lakh youths received training and of these 4.64 lakh youths are self-employed. This programme was continued in the Seventh and Eighth Plans also. During the Seventh Plan this scheme covered about 8.73 lakh youths. Between 1990-91 and 1995-96, this scheme has benefited about 17.03 lakh rural youths.

This programme has also been criticised. 1. It is criticised because it provides a very small coverage in relation to a big need. 2. Further, the skills provided through this programme have not been co-ordinated in any manner with the rural industrialisation process. The skills that are imparted are also found to be of very low level. 3. Finally, this scheme is criticised for the stipend that is given to the youth is too inadequate to motivate them for any kind of good training.

Other Important Rural Development Programmes

(i) ANTYODAYA PROGRAMME

"Antyodaya" is a special programme for the upliftment of the poorest of the society. This programme was launched for the first time by the then Government of Rajasthan on October 2, 1972. As per this programme, every year five poorest families of every village are identified and selected, and efforts are concentrated on these families for their economic upliftment.

Some conditions were laid down to select the poorest families as beneficiaries : (i) *Families which are under the grip of utter poverty and the families which do not have any visible means of subsistence are to be selected for this;* (ii) *Families with no single member in the age group of 15-59 years capable of economic production, are to be preferred;* (iii) *Families which do not have any productive assets such as land, cattle, etc., but may have one or two persons working as labourers but whose income does not exceed Rs.20/= a month, are entitled for obtaining this benefit;* (iv) *Families which have, on an average, Rs.40/= as per capita income could also be included in this programme.*

The responsibility of identifying the poorest families was assigned to the *"Gram Sabhas."* This scheme helped these poor families in various ways. The help was given in the form of allotting land for cultivation, monthly pension, bank loan or help in getting employment, etc. Further, each selected family was given a pension of Rs.30/= to 40/= per month. The scheme helps the beneficiaries to obtain bank loan for purchasing bullocks, carts, buffaloes, cows, goats and pigs; to help basket making, purchasing carpentry tools, opening a tea-shop, or a tailor's shop, barber's shop, etc.

The Rajasthan Government's experiment with *Antyodaya Programme* inspired the Governments of Uttar Pradesh and Himachal Pradesh to launch the same programme in 1980. But due to the political changes the experiment with this programme in these two states was adversely affected. It is almost a failure in these states.

At the district level, the district collectors were given the responsibility of looking after the administration of this scheme, and at the state level, the *Agriculture Department* itself administered it. The scheme was reintroduced by the Rajasthan Government in Sept. 1990. Political changes leading to the change of government at the state level affected the performance of this scheme. At the beginning of the year 2000, the scheme was hardly found to be functioning.

(ii) RLEGP : Rural Landless Employment Guarantee Programme

The *Rural Landless Employment Guarantee Programme* [RLEGP] was launched on 15th August 1983 with the objective of generating gainful employment, creating productive assets in rural areas and improving the overall quality of rural life. It aimed at providing guarantee of employment to atleast one member of the landless household for nearly 100 days in a year.

Main Features of RLEGP : 1. The scheme was launched with an intention of guaranteeing gainful employment to the people in rural areas and of raising the overall quality of rural life. 2. Under this scheme, preference in the employment is given to the landless labourers, women, SCs and STs. 3. As per the scheme, the workers are paid wages according to the provisions of *Minimum Wages Act*. 4. Under this scheme a part of the wages was to be paid to the workers in the form of foodgrains at subsidised rates. 5. This scheme includes in itself various rural development programmes such as construction of wells, roads, houses and social forestry. 6. Another speciality of this programme was that the entire scheme was financed by the Central Government. However, the programme was to be implemented by the state governments. 7. Various schemes such as *"Million Wells"*, *"Indira Awaas Yojna"* and *"Social Forestry"* are covered under RLEGP.

Evaluation of the Working of RLEGP : RLEGP programme was found to be working satisfactorily in the Sixth Plan. The programme was continued in the Seventh Plan with an allottment of Rs.1,744 crores. But the actual expenditure was about Rs.2,500 crores. The target was to generate 1,013 million mandays of employment during the Plan period. During the first four years it was possible to generate employment to the tune of 1,154 million mandays.

The overall performance of the RLEGP has not been found to be satisfactory. Certain factors have been responsible for the unsatisfactory functioning of this scheme. Some of these factors are – 1. *Absence of systematic selection of workers for employment under this scheme.* 2. *Failure to guarantee minimum of 100 days of employment to workers.* 3. *Open cheating resorted to by the contractors under this scheme contributed to its failure.*

This programme too has now been merged alongwith **NREP** *into the* **JRY.** The merger is based on the premise that the objectives and implementation in the field of these two programmes are by and large similar.

(iii) THE JRY : JAWAHAR ROZGAR YOJNA

Prime Minister Rajiv Gandhi announced on 28th April, 1989 the launching of the *Jawahar Rozgar Yojna* [**JRY**]. All the existing rural wage employment programmes were merged into JRY. This implies that *National Rural Employment Programme* [NREP] and *Rural Landless Employment Guarantee Programme* [RLEGP] have been merged so as to be brought under this umbrell programme referred to as Jawahar Rozgar Yojna.

Main Features of JRY

1. The JRY intends to help atleast one member of each poorest family by providing employment for about 90 to 100 days in a year at his own work place or residential area. 2. This scheme was sponsored by the Central Government. 3. The scheme was funded or financed by the Central and the State Governments on 80 : 20 ratios respectively. 4. Contractors or middlemen were not permitted to operate for executing the works under this programme. 5. About 60% of the funds allocated for the scheme were spent for wage employment. 6. Under this scheme, 2 Kgs. of foodgrains per day was given to every worker employed at subsidised rate. 7. A part of the funds allocated for this programme was spent for housing under the *Indira Housing Scheme.* 8. The entire scheme was implemented through the Village Panchayat. 9. About 80% of the funds obtained by the Centre and State are to be utilised through the *Gram Panchayats* for helping the targeted beneficiaries. 10. At least 30% of the employment is to be provided to women under JRY.

In the year 1993-94, the JRY was modified and split into 3 streams. The ***first stream*** consisted of general works along with two sub-schemes, namely, *Indira Awaas Yojna* [IAY] and *Million Wells Scheme* [MWS]. The ***second stream*** comprised of intensified works in 120 identified backward districts. The ***third stream*** consisted of special and innovative projects.

As per the provision of this Yojna, *Panchayats* with a population ranging between 4000 to 5000 persons are given an annual financial assistance from Rs.0.80 lakh to 1 lakh. But 30% of the money goes for women only. In the year 1990-91, about Rs.500 crore was spent under this Yojna. It covers about 46% of the population.

In the Eighth Plan, about Rs.30,000 crore is allotted for rural development out of which JRY gets about Rs.18,400 crores. Apart from this Central assistance, the JRY gets the state assistance of about Rs.400 crore.

This scheme has been implemented in 2,20,000 villages all over the country. Between 1989-90 and 1993-94, about 4,283 million mandays of employments was generated as against the

Table - 2

Expenditure Under Different Heads in JRY

	Head	1989-90 to 1995-96 [Rs. crores]	Per cent of total
1.	Minor irrigation [including wells]	915	9.1
2.	Rural roads	3,332	33.0
3.	House sites and house construction	389	3.8
4.	School and Community building	1,084	10.7
5.	Social forestry	584	5.8
6.	Other items	3,792	37.6
	Total	10,096	100.0

Source : Ministry of Rural Development, *Annual Report* [1996-97] as quoted by **Ruddardatt** and **K.P.M. Sundharam.** Page 395

target of 4332 million mandays.

To sum up, JRY has been conceived with laudable objectives. Its focus on SCs / STs / freed bonded labourers / women living below the poverty line is indicative of the intention to help the weaker sections of our society. Although it has made some headway in providing employment, its target of providing 90 to 100 days employment for every registered person is a distant goal judged by the achievement made so far. Hence, JRY needs reconsideration and greater intensification of implementation.

As a result of the expenditure incurred in JRY, the following principal physical achievements could be claimed for the period 1989-90 to 1995-96.

Table - 3

Physical Achievements Under JRY

[1989-90 to 1995-96]

	Item	Unit	Achievements
1.	Construction of wells under MWS	Lakhs	10.0
2.	Development of house sites	Nos.	69,374
3.	Construction of houses	Lakhs	4.2
4.	School buildings	Nos.	2,01,017
5.	Rural Roads	000 Kms.	690
6.	Drinking water wells	Thousands	589
7.	Construction of Village Tanks	Thousands	76
8.	Area covered under social forestry	000 Hectares	768

Source : Ministry of Rural Development, *Annual Report* [1996-97] as quoted by **Ruddar Datt** and **K.P.M. Sundharam.** Page - 395.

"The overall impact of the JRY in generating employment has been much below the target laid down. JRY has helped the weaker sections to acquire a house or provided access to drinking water or improve sanitation, but yet much remains to be done to make a perceptible improvement in the quality of life. Obviously, this necessitates larger devolution of resources – both financial and human."[1]

(iv) Small Farmer's Development Agency [SFDA] - 1971

This Agency was set up in accordance with the recommendations of *All India Rural Credit Survey.* It was in operation since 1971 covering 1,818 blocks in the country.

Among the various activities of SFDA, the most important one was that it made the provision of easy and cheap credit facilities to small farmers and in all, 25% of the total amount involved has been sanctioned as a subsidiary and the rest as loans. At present SFDA has become a part of the Integrated Rural Development Programme [IRDP] and it is renamed as *District Rural Development Agency.*

(v) Food For Work Programme [FFWP] - 1977

This programme which was introduced in 1977 aimed at making payment of wages in kind, that is, in foodgrains either in full or in part to the persons living below the poverty line. It aimed at - (i) *generating additional gainful employment for both men and women in rural areas;* (ii) *creating durable community assets and strengthening the social infrastructure; and* (iii) *utilising surplus foodgrains for the development of country's human resources.* This scheme was started at a time when the government had a huge buffer stock of foodgrains.

(vi) Desert Development Programme [DDP] - 1977-78

The Desert Development Programme was launched in 1977-78 on the recommendation of the *National Commission on Agriculture.* This programme aims at raising the level of income, production and employment of the people in the desert areas of Rajasthan, Haryana and Gujarath in hot and arid regions and in Jammu & Kashmir and Himachal Pradesh in cold and arid regions.

(vii) Drought Prone Area Programme [DPAP] - 1979

This programme was started in the year 1979 for drought prone areas. Almost two-thirds of the cultivated area in the country is rain fed and has low productivity, though bulk of the foodgrains, pulses, oil seeds, etc. comes from here. This programme has been launched with an intention of helping the farmers in the drought prone areas to get sufficient income even in the condition of drought. During the Seventh Plan, Rs.237 crores were spent on this.

(viii) Scheme for Providing Self-employment to Educated Unemployed - 1983

This programme was introduced in 1983. It intends to provide a loan of Rs.25,000 to the educated unemployed residing in areas other than cities with a population of 10 lakhs or more. A subsidy of 25 per cent of the loan was provided under the scheme for all the loans granted by the banks to the unemployed youth. This programme was continued in the Seventh and Eighth Plans.

(ix) Employment Assurance Scheme [EAS] - 1993

The main objective of this scheme was to provide gainful employment in manual work to all able bodied adults in rural areas during the lean agricultural season. Under this programme, a maximum of two adults per family could be provided with gainful employment. Under this scheme, 416,533 lakh man-days employment was generated by spending Rs.2,819.76 crores upto 31st March 1999.

---

1 **Ruddar Datt** and **K.P.M. Sundharam.** "*Indian Economy*" Page - 396.

This scheme was launched on 2nd October 1993 initially covered 1778 blocks of 23 states. As on 31st March 1999, the scheme covered all the rural blocks of the country. The Centre and the States provided the needed funds for this programme in the ratio of 75 : 25.

(x) Jawahar Gram Samriddhi Yojna [JGSY] - 1999

The Jawahar Gram Samriddhi Yojna [JGSY] launched on 1st April 1999 represents the previously existed but restructured and streamlined scheme called *the Jawahar Rozgar Yojna* [JRY].

This programme is concerned with the development of rural infrastructure at the village level. This porgramme is to be implemented by village panchayats. The cost of this programme will be shared between the Centre and the States in the ratio of 75 : 25, and in the case of programmes undertaken in the Union Territories, the entire cost of the programme will be met by the Centre.

(xi) Swarnajayanthi Gram Swarozgar Yojna [SGSY] - 1999

This programme aims at establishing a large number of industries through bank credit and subsidy and bringing the assisted poor families above the poverty line in three years.

This programme launched in April 1999 replaces earlier programmes like the IRDP, the TRYSEM, etc. It is the single self-employment programme for the rural poor.

(xii) Prime Minister's Rozgar Yojna [PMRY] - 1993

The Prime Minister's Rozgar Yojna [PMRY] was launched on 2nd October 1993. In this PMRY the Jawahar Rozgar Yojna [JRY] and all other similar schemes sponsored by the Central Government were merged together. This scheme covered both rural and urban areas. This scheme aimed at providing sustained employment to about 10 lakh educated unemployed youths in small industries, services and small business ventures during 8th Five-Year Plan.

IMPACT OF RURAL DEVELOPMENT PROGRAMMES

Various rural development programmes, projects, plans and schemes which the government has launched have brought about some impact. It must be noted that the impact of these programmes has not been uniform throughout India. As far as the programmes are concerned, some of these programmes are directly sponsored by the Central Government, while some others are sponsored and supported by the State Governments. In some states, a particular programme gets an encouraging and healthy response while in other states, it proves to be a failure. Of these various programmes, some are able to elicit a relatively good response from the public while many others fail to obtain the positive support and co-operation of the people. While making an assessment of the impact of rural development programmes, these observations should be borne in our mind.

It may also be noted that most of these development programmes beginning from Community Development Project [CDP] to Integrated Rural Development Programme [IRDP] have stressed on the development of agriculture and irrigation. Some of these programmes have no doubt emphasised the importance of education, public health, sanitation, veterinary and housing. It appears that the basic content of all these programmes seem to be the same. But specific programmes give more emphasis on one or the other needs of the people. As **Doshi** and **Jain** have pointed out, *"Generally the impact has to be seen at two levels. If we look at any particular programme we would find that either it falls in the individual beneficiary programme or community beneficiary programme............ Any evaluation of the impact of development programmes on the village life should take stock of both individual and community beneficiary programmes."*[1]

---

1 **Doshi** and **Jain** *"Rural Sociology."* Page - 287.

Let us now make a brief analysis of the impact of the rural development programmes *on the village life of people in general* :

A. The Green Revolution

The concept of ***"Green Revolution"*** refers to *"the introduction of new species of crops and new techniques leading to greater crop yields. This began in Mexico in the 1950s, and from the mid-1960s new high-yielding varieities of rice and wheat were introduced in many Third World countries. The most noticiable applications were in the Indian subcontinent.........."*[1]

The term *"green revolution"* denotes the well-marked improvement in the agricultural production in a short period and the sustenance of a high level of agricultural production over a fairly long period of time.

Green Revolution in the Indian Context

Since the mid 1960s, the traditional agricultural practices have gradually been replaced by modern technology and farm practices in India, a veritable revolution, namely *"green revolution"*, is taking place in our country. Initially, the new technology was tried in 1960-61 as a pilot project in about seven districts. Later on, the *"high-yielding varities programme"* [HYVP] was extended to cover the entire country. It must be admitted that the HYVPs revolutionised the agricultural production. Hence, it came to be known as ***"green revolution."***

The main aspect of "green revolution" consists in agricultural production and extensive use of technology. The revolution also basically encouraged private investment in agriculture. Noted economist **K.M. Raj** has rightly observed : *"What the new strategy can be expected to achieve is not so much a sharp acceleration in the overall rates of growth of agricultural output as in giving considerable stimulus to private investment in the bigger sized farms in region which have the necessary climate and soil conditions, as well as source of water supply for adopting the new technology."*[2]

The "green revolution" has taken place in India in 1967-68 and continued for about 10 years. It is expected that the general trend is likely to continue in the future also. It has occurred in the States such as Punjab, Haryana, Gujarat, Maharashtra, Andhra Pradesh and Tamil Nadu. The high-yielding varities have been tried in the case of wheat, rice, jowar, sugarcane, maize, millet, etc. This trial has provided a high boost to our production especially in the case of wheat and rice which is ascertainable in the Table No.4 given below.

Table - 4

Progress in Foodgrains Production Due to Green Revolution

[Units of Production in Million Tonnes]

	1960-61	1990-91	1998-99	1999-2000
Rice	35	75	86	88
Wheat	11	55	70	69
(a) Total Cereals	69	162	188	185
(b) Total Pulses	13	14	15	14
(c) Total foodgrains (a+b)	82	176	203	199

Source **:** Economic Survey, 1999-2000 as quoted by **Ruddar Datt** and **K.P.M. Sundharam** in *"Indian Economy"* - 2001. Page - 499.

1 *Collins Dictionary of Sociology.* Page - 271.

2 **K.M. Raj** as quoted by **Doshi** and **Jain** in *"Rural Sociology."* Page -288.

Relatively High Production of Rice and Wheat

It is interesting to observe that the ratio of wheat to rice [Table No.**5**] has steadily increased from 1/3 in 1960-61 to 85% in 1996-97. It was 78% in 1999-2000. The production of wheat which was **11** million tonnes in 1960-61; increased to 70 million tonnes in 1998-99. The yield per hectare increased from 850 Kgs. to 2580 Kgs. per hectare, signifying three times rise in the last 40 years. The following Table No.**5** makes it clear that though rice continues to be the most important cereal in the country, wheat is catching up fast.

Increase in the Production of Commercial Crops

Though the green revolution was mainly directed to increase the production of foodgrains it also led to significant improvement in the production of other cash crops such as oil seeds, cotton, sugarcane, potatoes, etc. But this improvement was not such as to be called a revolution. See Table No.**6**.

Table - 5

Production of Rice and Wheat in India Between 1960-61 and 1999-2000

Year	Rice (million tonnes)	Wheat (million tonnes)	Percentage of wheat to rice
1960-61	35	11	31
1970-71	42	24	57
1980-81	54	36	67
1990-91	74	55	74
1998-99	86	70	81
1999-2000	88	69	78

Source : Plan Documents and Economic Surveys as quoted by **Ruddar Datt** and **K.P.M. Sundharam.** Page - 500.

Factors Contributing to Green Revolution in India

Several factors contributed to the green revolution that has taken place in India in 1967-68. It is expected to continue in the years to come. The main factors contributing to it are mentioned below.

1. The *use of high-yielding varieties of seeds* has contributed to increased production.
2. The *use of chemicals, fertilisers, pesticides* have also played a key role in boosting agricultural production.
3. The *use of modern agricultural machines* like tractors, harvestors, threshers, pump sets, sprayers, etc. has led to a great increase in agricultural output.
4. The *adoption of better methods of cultivation* like the Japanese methods, has also improved the productivity.
5. More and *more irrigational facilities* are being made available for the farmers and these have added to the agricultural output.
6. The *adoption of double or multiple cropping* has also helped the cause of increased agricultural production.
7. More and *more credit facilities* made available to the farmers by several institutions like co-operative credit societies, land development banks, regional rural banks or *grameena* banks,

Table - 6

Production of Cash Crops in India

	1960-61	1990-91	1998-99	1999-2000
Sugarcane [m. tonnes]	110	254	296	315
Cotton [m. bales]	6	10	12	12
Jute [m. bales]	4	8	9	10
Oil seeds	7	19	25	22
Potatoes	3	15	23	23

Source : Plan Documents and Economic Surveys as quoted by **Ruddardatt** and **K.P.M. Sundharam** in *"Indian Economy."* Page - 500.

commercial banks, State Bank of India, etc. have also helped the farmers to grow more output.

8. The *government's incentive price policy* also induced the farmers to grow more.
9. The *soil conservation schemes* have helped the conservation of soil fertility and thereby contributed to increased output.
10. The extension of marketing facilities for agricultural products by the *co-operative marketing societies, regulated markets,* etc. has also contributed to increased output.
11. The *implementation of land reforms* including the abolition of intermediaries, security of the tenure, conferring of ownership rights on the tenants, consolidation of holdings, regulation of rent, etc. has contributed in no small measure to augment the output.
12. The community development projects, national extension services and various rural development programmes have also helped the cause of the green revolution.

Effects of Green Revolution

Beneficial Effects : It is undeniable that the green revolution in India has resulted in several beneficial effects. It has contributed to an increase in agricultural production. It has improved the financial position of the farmers. It has provided better employment opportunities in the rural areas. It has created an awareness among the farmers to make use of modern techniques of cultivation. It has raised the status and standard of living of the farmers. In general, it has contributed to an overall growth of the Indian economy.

Major Limitations of Green Revolution : Though the green revolution brought about some beneficial effects it has its own limitations. The *impact of the green revolution was very much short lived.* Only for about 10 years its effect was evident. The *impact of the revolution has been confined to a few states* such as Punjab, Haryana, and some parts of Gujarat, Maharashtra, Andhra Pradesh and Tamil Nadu.The remaining states have not been benefited much out of this revolution. Only the big farmers and landlords have been able to reap the benefits of the revolution. The impact of the revolution has been very much impressive mainly in the case of wheat production. Hence, it is often referred to as *"wheat revolution"* rather than green revolution.

Social Consequences of Green Revolution

Green revolution has brought about number of social consequences among which the following may be noted :

1. The green revolution has resulted in *a dramatic increase in the production of foodgrains* on a scale that would have been unimaginable before the advent of the new technology in agriculture. This increased production boosted the morale of the farmers.

2. Green revolution *produced a number of by-products.* The massive agricultural production has improved transport system, widened educational network and above all, introduced rural electricity. These things have made the villages to forge ahead towards progress.
3. Some economists are of the opinion that in the long run, *green revolution would discourage the rural population to migrate to urban areas.* The villages that have undergone through the process of green revolution have the facilities of urban life-style. Electricity, tap water, cooking gas, roads, modern toilet facilities, supply of newspapers, television, radio and telephone facilities, and such other facilities of urban dwellers are also available to the villagers now. Non-migration to urban centres would save congestion in the overcrowded cities.
4. Green revolution has *prevented the rural artisans to migrate towards urban slums.* Because agricultural prosperity turns villages into expanding markets not only for the products of agro industries but also for a growing range of consumer goods.
5. The impact of the green revolution has not always been positive. The increased food production *has not improved the quality of life of people.* It has only increased the gap between the big farmers and the small farmers. It means the *"haves"* have got more than the *"have-nots."* The growth in agriculture definitely gives self-sufficiency in foodgrains but it is highly unjust as far as social justice is concerned.
6. It is normally believed that the green revolution would bring the *"trickle-down effect."* The logic behind this belief is that if the higher segments of rural life develop, its impact would also go to the lower segments. But this, however, did not happen. The growth in the economy did not necessarily lead to the improvement in the quality of life of all the people. On the other hand, it only widened the gap between the rich and the poor.
7. It is said that the new strategy initiated along with the green revolution has created three kinds of conflicts, namely, (i) *between large and small farmers,* (ii) *between owners and tenant farmers,* and (iii) *between employers and employees on agricultural farms.*
8. The *Economic and Social Survey of Asia and the Pacific* [ESCAP] report has stated in categorical terms that *the rural poor have been by-passed in the green revolution.* The report has also stated that the poor peasants with very meagre resources in their possession, could not benefit by the introduction of high yielding varieties. They were obviously deprived of the trickle-down effect.

Suggestions to Overcome the Limitations of Green Revolution

In order to remove the limitations of the new agricultural strategy the following suggestions have been made.

1. The range of green revolution is to be extended to all the regions where it has not taken place so far.
2. A better land and land-use policy should be framed so as to maximise agricultural production.
3. The tempo of green revolution is to be maintained for a longer period.
4. Provision should be made to provide better irrigation and marketing facilities to the farmers.
5. The impact of green revolution should be extended to all the important crops, both food crops and cash crops.
6. It is necessary to resort to intensive research work in the field of agricultural production. Agricultural education programmes should be conducted to inspire rural people.
7. To inspire the small farmers to take to green revolution special efforts are necessary.
8. A better cropping pattern should be developed to suit to the climatic and fertility conditions of the land.

The adoption of the new technology depends on the level of literacy of the farmers. **D.P. Chaudhri** in his study, *"Education and Agricultural Productivity in India"* has shown that large farmers, invariably are always the early adopters of yield-raising, cost-reducing innovations, while small farmers, who are generally illiterate, are among the laggards. The spread of the new technology, therefore, depends upon the extent of the information, and this in turn, depends on the level of literacy. A programme of removal of illiteracy can, therefore, become the chief vehicle of the spread of green revolution.

C.H. Hanumanth Rao is of the opinion that *"participation in the modernisation process is usually greater in regions which have shed the feudal and semi-feudal structures and attitudes and where the inequalities in wealth and status are not conspicuous."*[1] Mr. Rao cites the examples of Punjab, Haryana and Western U.P. where the technological change did not result in perceptible social tensions, because real wages had risen in these regions. But such was not the case in Thanjavur in Tamilnad. The landlords in Thanjavur district tried to counter the demand for higher wages by bringing in farm labour from outside. Therefore, it is necessary that for the success of green revolution one has to make a frontal attack on feudal and semi-feudal land relations.

Green revolution cannot become a success on its own. Agricultural productivity cannot increase automatically. *"Ultimately, yield is a product of interaction between the genetic efficiency of the plant and the management efficiency of the farmer. It is the dedication, hardwork, innovativeness and enthusiasm of the farmers which have been the catalyst of change in India's agricultural destiny."*

B. Other Impacts of Development Programmes

The *"green revolution"* had its impact no doubt. In addition to that, various other developmental programmes have also brought about their own effects. Let us now take a glance of the other impacts which the development programmes have brought in.

1. Predominance of Political Interests

Most of the village development programmes undertaken by the Government have been politicalised. Developmental programmes and schemes were often launched more to benefit the ruling political party, its workers and supporters than to cater to the *"felt needs"* of the people. It has been observed that political leaders, Panchayat Raj leaders and members of dominant castes have reaped most of the benefits of the development programmes. In many places, the poor villagers continue to remain in poverty-stricken condition.

2. Development Disparities

One of the noble intentions behind the development programmes was to bring forward the backward areas and backward people almost on par with the advanced areas and advanced people. But when we take stock of the performance of these programmes we get astonished to note that these programmes have in no way contributed to the fulfilment of this objective. Much against these noble intentions, the backward areas have become further backward and neglected, whereas the advanced areas and people have gained more prosperity and progress.

3. Creation of Cleavages Between Stratas ?

Wide disparity between the rich and the poor was not there in economic matters in most of the villages of India. It means that the existing stratification never made a sharp difference between

---

1 **C.H. Hanumanth Rao** as quoted by **Ruddar Datt** and **K.P.M. Sundharam** in *"Indian Economy"* [2002]. Page - 504.

the rich and poor. However, religion and tradition have served as the main bases of inequality. The development programmes have worsened the situation by increasing the gap between the village poor and the village rich. Most of the development projects have gone in favour of the village rich. These programmes have even created "classes" within the caste. ***For example,*** we find now a sharp cleavage between a poor *Okkaliga* [a dominant caste of Karnataka] and a rich Okkaliga in the rural set up. Rich Okkaligas who want to maintain their "class-status" are not prepared to give their daughters in marriage to the poor Okkaligas. The development programmes have only contributed to the creation of new classes, but the traditional structural aspects of caste continue to remain unchanged.

4. A New Momentum to Urbanisation

Rural development programmes have provided a new infrastructure and many individuals took the benefit of many of these programmes. These developments have thus given a new direction to the rural change. Some of these villages have now evolved into towns. It is true that these development programmes have given sufficient encouragement and the necessary infrastructure for sizeable number of villages to get transformed into urban centres. Once villages get transformed into towns, people get tempted to move further into big cities. For example, the proportion of the population living in class IV, Class V and Class VI towns[1] has come down sharply from 47.2% in 1901 to merely 10.7% in 1991. Further, the number of Class V and Class VI towns is also decreasing, that is, from 1124 in 1951 to 725 in 1991, and from 569 to 185, respectively.[2] These figures indicate that the rural development programmes, in stead of entieing the rural people to stayback in the rural areas by providing them the necessary avenues of a comfortable living, are only encouraging the people to move towards big cities.

5. Rural Development Programmes – A Grand Failure ?

Ever since the launching of the Community Development Project in 1952, crores and crores of rupees have been poured into a large number of village development programmes. A huge army of officials has been vested with the responsibility of implementing these programmes. Political leaders, legislators, village officials and engineers have been working out any number of plans and projects to be experimented at the village level. Innocent rural people have been anxiously awaiting the miracles to happen through these plans and projects. But paradoxically, these development programmes brought disappointment to many and prosperity only to a few. Though crores of rupees were spent they could hardly reach the needy hands. In this context, **Doshi** and **Jain** have observed : *"It could be guessed that out of the money spent for the village development programmes the larger beneficiaries are big farmers, village money-lenders, village officials, development personnel, engineers and political leaders. Much money has been invested and little has been harvested in terms of the real improvement in the life of the village people. "*[3]

Conclusion

It is clear from the above analysis, that the rural development programmes failed in many respects to fulfil the intended objectives. It does not mean the programmes have not achieved anything. It only means that in comparision with the amount of money that is spent, and the time that is taken, performance of the programmes is not upto satisfaction.

---

1 ***Class IV*** city consists of 10,000 to 19,999 people; ***Class V***, between 5,000 to 9,999, and ***Class VI*** town, less than 5,000.

2 ***Source of Statistics*** : *"Registrar General of India."*

3 **Doshi** and **Jain** *"Rural Sociology." Page* - 291.

Rural development programmes, in general, have created an impression among the ruralites that the Government wants to do something for the development of villages. The programmes have created socio-political consciousness among people. Empowerment of rural people through the Panchayat Raj system has given them fresh hopes for the future. The exploitative Zamindari system is abolished. Attainment of self-sufficiency in food production has boosted the morale of Indian populace, in general. These development programmes have created job opportunities for many young men and women. The weaker sections, particularly, the SCs and STs are given importance in these programmes and hence their exploitation has become now minimised. Though clashes do take place between the forward castes and backward castes, the weaker sections can be hopeful of getting the legal protection. These programmes have introduced to the villages various avenues of city life - for example, supply of electricity, medical help, telephone connection, transportation facility, establishment of educational and banking institutions, community centres, reading rooms, postal facilities, co-operative societies, and so on. Still it is a long way to go. Rural self-sufficiency still remains our dream. Gandhiji's vision of *"Gram Swarajya"* and *"Ram Rajya"* is still far away from us.

B. RURAL CHANGE IN INDIA

Domination of Rural Population Continues

Change is an ever present phenomenon everywhere. Human society is also subject to change. Most of the civilised nations of the world are moving faster in the direction of industrialisation, urbanisation and modernisation. Nations such as U.S., England, France, Germany, Israel, etc., have already become the most urbanised nations of the world. More than **60** to **70** per cent of the people in these nations are living today in cities. In comparison with these nations India presents a different picture. Even at present [2003 A.D.] around 74% of the people in India live in villages. Urbanisation has, no doubt, made its impact, but has not yet revolutionised rural life in India. Numerical domination of rural population is sure to continue for many more years.

High Hopes about Indian Villages

Indian rural life is not stagnant. It has also been undergoing fast changes. The changes that have been taking place in the rural set up seem to be more rapid during the last three-four decades. The architects of modern India and also others who fought for the freedom of the country like Gandhiji, Vinobha Bhave, Jaya Prakash Narayan, Vallabha Bhai Patel, Ravindranath Tagore and others, were clear about the direction of the change. They knew that the development and progress of India would very much depend upon the development and progress of the villages. Gandhiji's message of freedom struggle, non-co-operation with the British administration, non-violence, peaceful co-existence had already reached the villages. Gandhiji wanted rural India to undergo rapid change for it was infested with the evils of conservatism, casteism, untouchability, alcoholism, illiteracy, superstition, etc. The Constitution-makers too had emphasised the importance of rural change and rural progress. **Pandit Nehru** who took the reins of administration into his hands was more interested in industries rather than in agriculture. *"Industrialise or perish"* became the popular slogan. Industries were expected to become the *"centres of pilgrimage."* In spite of this initial setback, Indian villages proved to be promising in undergoing changes.

Changing Rural Life

If we look at the rural scene, we find that there is a marked change in the condition of rural women, landless workers, Scheduled Castes and Tribes, public health, education, agricultural output, transport and communication, etc.. The change has not taken place on its own automatically.

Government of India has spent crores of rupees in the development of villages. In fact, it is not in India alone but in almost all the Third World countries, much amount has been spent on rural development. In this process of development the national governments have placed premium on certain areas of rural life such as education, industry, co-operatives and entrepreneurship. Sociologists in India also took a keen interest in the study of the changes taking place in the rural sector. *"It would not be wrong to say that about half of our sociological literature in India belongs to the study of rural society. The economists who concentrate on macro studies have also come down to district level studies."*[1] What is very important here is that while studying the village society one must not ignore the socio-historical perspective with which it has to be studied. Scholars like **Chitra, Shiva Kumar** and **S.S. Shiva Kumar** have stressed this aspect in the following words :

"Rural social change has been among the most important subjects of study in the Third World countries since 1950, partly because major national efforts in these countries have been directed towards economic development and partly because such efforts have been located in predominantly, agrarian social settings. The entire future of development efforts rests on what happens in rural areas. While this is well known, the fact that all changes, including rural changes, are historical process, is ignored. We say "ignored" because the research efforts of various statistical and planning organisations in many countries [including the Planning Commission in India] are characterised by an absence of historical perspective. All share a historicity in their efforts."[2]

Major Trends in Rural Social Changes

Rural changes taking place in India have been studied from various angles; economic, statistical, historical, sociological, etc. But the basic questions that haunt us here are : — *In which direction the social changes are taking place in the rural society ? What are the main trends of rural transformation ? Does the change imply only economic change*? – As a reply to these questions, one of the prominent rural sociologists of India, **A.R. Desai** has sought to identify four major trends of social changes.[3] They may be stated below :

(i) *Transformation of agrarian society from subsistence economy to market economy;*

(ii) *Transformation followed by the introduction of modern technology;*

(iii) *Abolition of intermediaries such as Zamindars , Jagirdars, etc.*

(iv) *Emergence of various associations and institutions having linkages with urban national organisations.*

1. Transformation from Subsistence to Market Economy

Historically speaking, village economy has been a subsistence economy. Caught between the dual processes of modernisation and urbanisation the village economy has become now a market-oriented economy. It does not mean that there was no market in the subsistence economy. But it was only rudimentary and served its primary function of supplying consumer goods to all the people of a village living in its remotest corners, and sometimes to the neighbouring villagers. It had never induced people to produce for a market. Due to the introduction of modernisation by the British, the subsistence economy of the village got transformed into a new kind of capitalistic economy. Land came to be treated as a kind of property and *growing commercial crops became more fashionable.* It

---

1 **Doshi** and **Jain** *"Rural Sociology."* Page - 345.

2 **Chitra, Shiva Kumar, S.S. Shiva Kumar** in their essay *"Rural Change, Social History and Participant Observation"* - as quoted by **Doshi** and **Jain.** Page - 346.

3 **A.R. Desai** as quoted by **Doshi** and **Jain.** Page - 346.

means that the villagers now grow not only for their own consumption but a part of it for market too. *Market now constitutes the central part of the economy.* Markets are also systematically expanding. They have stretched their hands to the villages also. Hence, even in the remote villages tooth-pastes, toilet soaps, powder, snow, razor, shaving blade, soft drinks, beverages, biscuits, chocolates, etc., of various brands produced by national and sometimes by even multinational companies are available. Further, milk, eggs, fruits, vegetables, etc. of even simple remote villages have reached metropolitan markets. Day in and day out buses, trucks and other means of transport shuttle between towns and villages making the marketing tasks easier for the villagers. All these markets are not, of course, uniform. Depending upon various factors they do differ significantly.

Social Consequences of Market

The spread of markets into non-market societies has been accelerated by political conquests and colonialism. Hence the Third World countries have come under the heavy influence of the market. In the study of these societies the *"market"* has occupied important concept of analysis. Market has been influencing the nature of stratification and the style of living of people in these societies. **Jean Baudrillard** who is regarded as one of the renowned post-modern sociologists also speaks of such consequences.

(a) *Market Influences the Ways of People* : According to Baudrillard, market is the crucial variable in the development of hyper capitalism. The contemporary capitalist European society is branded by him as the *"consumer society."* He says that *"in the consumer society market is the predominant determinant of the ways people consume things."* He argues : *"When we consume objects we are consuming signs and in the process, are defining ourselves."*[1] It is possible to identify the status of people with the things that they consume. **Baudrillard** writes : "....... *people are what they consume, and are differentiated from other types of people on the basis of consumed objects."* For example, no family of average income can afford to have a refrigerator, a colour television, a motor cycle or motor car, or a mobile phone.

(b) *Market Influences and Increases Consumption* : The post-modern society which is becoming more and more capitalistic, is concentrating its attention on the expansion of market. Hyper technological development has added momentum to this expansion. Europe and U.S. consider the Third World countries a fertile ground for expanding their market. India is, indeed, a *"giant"* market for them.

Taking advantage of the changed conditions, India is also expanding the horizons of its industrial market. In this expansion process, the rural society is not spared, but caught. *The local rural market is fast becoming a consumer market.* Mass media and technology, advertisements through print and electronic media have been able to approach the local rural market. Hence, the remote corners of our villages, even the high lands and forests, have been able to receive the new commodities of different brands. This network of new market has also provided opportunities to the rural markets to send their products [example, milk, raw fruits, raw materials, etc.] to the towns and big cities. The villages in the remote corner, are thus brought into close contact with the regional, provincial and national markets.

***Higher Levels of Consumption* :** The markets have created a new class in the rural society. This new class consists of big traders, big peasants, petty officials, political workers, and others who are known to consume objects of new culture. Their consumption level is so high that it represents a new style of life which differentiates them from the other rural groups. Importance of this type of

1 **Jean Baudrillard** as quoted by **Doshi** and **Jain.** Page - 348.

consumption is so much emphasised that *"the Marxian stress on production relations has been replaced by consumerism."* [Page - 350].

(c) *Market Creates Various Facilities* : Development of market in any society for that matter, has created a large number of facilities for the people. As **Doshi** and **Jain** have said, *"In these markets which are also making their entry in the rural areas, all objects, services, bodies, sex, culture and knowledge, are considered to be items of exchange. Portraying the image of this new market **George Ritzer** observes : Consumer society is a place where everything is for sale. Not only are all commodities, but all signs are commodities. Given the latter all "objects, services, bodies, sex, culture, knowledge" are produced and exchanged"."*[1]

2. Rural Transformation by Technology

Technologies have made the new world system possible. Technologies were not limited to tools of trade such as the compass, the machine gun, mechanised boats, etc. They also included organisation techniques for bringing land, labour and local currencies into the larger market economy. They included new financial and accounting systems. These systems led to the creation of institutions such as banks, co-operative societies, companies, corporations, etc.

As far as the Indian agrarian society is concerned, it had resorted to traditional methods of cultivation. Our farmers made use of local breed of bullocks and never used chemicals, fertilisers and pesticides of the modern type. Hence they did not have much surplus to be taken to the markets. But when modern technology was used it proved to be highly beneficial. It brought about far-reaching effects on the society.

(a) *Improved Implements* : Introduction of the new technology in the rural area helped the peasants to attain greater level of self-sufficiency. Improved ploughing materials, hybrid seeds, chemicals, fertilizers, tractors, tillers, trucks, threshers, spraying machines and other modern equipments were introduced to the agrarian society as a result of technology. In States such as Maharashtra, Punjab, Gujarath and Haryana, tractors and tillers are more popular than the bullock-carts.

(b) *Enormous Increase in Agricultural Output* : Our agricultural output has tremendously increased. Construction of dams - major and minor, borewell and tank water facilities have added to improve irrigation facilities. Fertilisers radically improved the crops whereas insecticides saved the crops from the clutches of insects, and plant diseases. The *"green revolution"* has added to the radical increase in the output. India today has attained self-sufficiency in food production.

(c) *Improved Cattle* : Though India is an agriculture dominated country, it used to suffer from the scarcity of milk. Nourishment of improved cattle today has led to vast dairy produce. The country is now poised to witness a ***"white revolution."*** By-products of milk have added to our export items.

3. Transformation by Abolition of Intermediaries

Abolition of the system of intermediaries consisting of the *Zamindars, Jagirdars, Jotedars,* and others in 1950s brought about a structural change in the rural society. In States such as Rajasthan, Punjab, Gujarath, and Karnataka where there were princely states, there took place a structural change in the rural society. Exploitation of the peasants by the landlords almost came to an end. That was indeed a second freedom for the peasants. **K.L. Sharma** has analysed the impact of abolition of the system of intermediaries on rural society in the following words. *"Thus, the abolition of the*

1 **Doshi** and **Jain.** Page - 350.

jagirdari system affected not only the land-owners and the tenants, but a whole lot of rural people. This has provided a ground for the emergence of a new social formation. It is not that the entire change has emanated from the initial land reforms alone. Several other subsequent factors have equally been responsible for social transformation including education, migration, adult franchise and electoral politics, electrification and rural development programmes."[1]

4. Emergence of Various Associations and Institutions

Rural transformation includes the emergence of new associations and institutions in the rural society, in addition to the changed roles and forms of the already existing institutions such as caste and class.

(a) *Changes in Caste* : Some major changes that have taken place in the caste in rural India are as follows :

(i) *Caste no more puts restrictions on economic mobility.* Occupations have become mostly secular. Though some are still clinging on to the hereditary occupations, they are doing it not as a matter of caste rule, but either out of convenience or due to their failure to switch over to other occupations.

(ii) *Urbanisation holds its sway over caste-members.* There is a clear-cut drift of rural people towards cities and towns. Though upper-caste people are more responsive to the call of the cities, there are no institutional restrictions for the movement of other caste people towards urban centres.

(iii) *Caste continues to provide the "social base" for the people,* in spite of the changes taking place in it. It still remains *a mark of their social identity.*

(iv) Though caste is weakening institutionally, it is *assuming new political dimensions* to strengthen its hold over the people.

(v) *Empowerment of women* due to the introduction of *Panchayat Raj,* has brought about structural changes in the rural society. It has affected the role of women in caste. Caste associations have lost much of their power with regard to marriage and family matters. Modern courts have replaced *caste panchayats,* and *Village Nyaya Panchayats.*

(b) *Changes in the Class System* : Changes have started taking place in the caste-class nexus in the rural society. Caste and class are not the opposite poles. They even go together. As **Doshi** and **Jain** have pointed out the whole rural society is polarised into two categories of classes; namely, (i) *"classes emerging out of the higher castes who have benefited from rural development programmes"*, and (ii) *"classes belonging to weaker sections who have cornered a larger portion of the benefits from the programmes of rural development."*

(c) *Associations and Institutions* : Rural society is exposed today to the operation of various types of associations and institutions such as – co-operatives, religious organisations, political parties, caste associations, peasant organisations, youth organisations, educational organisations, etc. Most of these are non-governmental organisations. These organisations advocate programmes of rural social change. Some of these organisations are urban-based and have a wide network. There are also national level organisations other than the political parties influencing the ruralites and their life through a network of their workers.

Conclusion

Indian villages are today undergoing a fast change. The process of industrialisation, urbanisation, modernisation, sanskritisation, universalisation of education etc. have changed

1 **K.L. Sharma** as quoted by **Doshi** and **Jain.** Page - 352.

the mode of village life. The facilities of civilised life such as - science, technology, education, modern medicine, electricity, transport and communication have reached a large number of villages and as a result, the gap between the city and the village is getting reduced.

Modernisation has exerted its influence on many of the traditional characteristics of the Indian villages. For example, the message of modern education has reached the villages. Rural literacy rate is increasing. Modern transport facilities such as buses, taxies, trucks, bicycles, motor bikes, etc. are found connecting the villages with the towns. There are villages with the facilities of community centres, public reading rooms, libraries, primary health centres, post office, school, etc.. Rural people have become more mobile today. They are prepared to go out of their villages for the sake of better jobs and opportunities.

It is also significant to note that the cultural content of the village life is changing fast. At the regional level, the self-consciousness of each group such as caste, tribe, minority group, linguistic group, etc. is increasing. But fortunately, this regional consciousness also leads to the growth of a *"holistic consciousness."*

The tempo of rural change is such that the very way of life of ruralites has changed. Their lifestyles and leisure time activities have changed. Their manner of conversation, style of dress, modes of consumption, means of transport and communication, hobbies and habits, have changed. The twin revolutions [the green revolution and the white revolution] have enhanced confidence in the rural people and brought about new attitudes and outlook.

Prof. Yogendra Singh while referring to the contemporary social change taking place in India, has observed that there is a profound significance of culture in these changes. In spite of being traditional, the rural society, according to him, has taken to new cultural ways of life. He points out that the much publicised view that Indian culture being other worldly in nature could *"hinder the growth of a modern economy and democratic polity, has been proved to be erroneous. Castes, tribes, family institutions and religions as illustrated by sociological studies, have richly contributed to the growth in agricultural and industrial entrepreneurship, and modern systems of profession, education, technology and science."*[1]

Indian villages are marching ahead. It would be wrong to think that the path to change is only for economic growth. Villages have changed in all walks of life. A historical view of these changes would tell us that Indian ruralites do respect their traditions and at the same time, welcome changes. It is true that the challenges of globalisation have brought them new fears and anxieties. For the first time, a new trend called *"Globalisation"* has posed a big threat to their age-old skills and time-tested occupations. Currently, they are a bit worried about it. Indian villages have successfully witnessed many such ups and downs in the past. This time also they are hopeful of facing the new challenges in a successful manner, and marching ahead in the path of progress and prosperity.

---

1 **Prof. Yogendra Singh** in Presidential Address in XXI *All India Sociological Conference,* New Delhi on the topic *"The Significance of Culture in the Understanding of Social Change in Contemporary India"* as quoted by **Doshi** and **Jain.** Page - 355.

Chapter 15

URBAN LIFE IN INDIA

Urban Life : Meaning and Definition - Characteristics of Urban Community - Advantages and Disadvantages of the City - Factors of Urbanisation - Concepts of Urban, Urbanism and Urbanisation - Urbanisation in India - Some Trends in Urbanisation in India - Some Demographic Dimensions of Urbanisation in India - Factors or Causes of Urbanisation in India - ***Problems of Urbanisation - Solutions to These Problems*** *- Urban Influence on the Village - Urban-Rural Contrast : Differences Between Rural Community and Urban Community - Rural-Urban Convergence - Rural-Urban Continuum.*

Urbanisation, that is, unprecedented growth of cities, is one of the most significant trends in the modern world. Human beings have inhabited the planet for well over a million years, yet our ancestors lived in small primary groups for about 5 to 6 thousand years of that time. The growth of large cities that contain the bulk of a society's population is a very recent development. But this growth of cities is taking place all over the world at an astonishing speed. Our new and highly urbanised social environment offers opportunities and challenges that are without precedents in the history of humanity.

Urbanisation is a part of the development process. In backward and stagnant societies, the process of urbanisation, that is, growth of cities, is rather slow, because cities fail to offer employment opportunities to the people living in the countryside. But urbanisation process is faster in rapidly growing economies where newly established industries and other commercial establishments provide jobs to the people. The economic attractions of the cities in this phase of development become particularly strong if industrial growth is fast. The process of urbanisation slows down only when the proportion of urban population to total population in a country becomes very high. This stage has been reached in some 30-odd countries which are regarded as *developed industrialised countries.* India is definitely not in this list for it is regarded as a *developing nation.*

Though India is traditionally regarded as the land of villages, towns and cities are not strange things to India. India has long standing tradition of urban living and has been a land of cities from pre-historic times of the Indus Valley, going back to nearly 6000 years. The two cities of Harappa and Mohen-jo-daro of Indus Valley are known for high standards of town planning and architecture. The process of industrialisation and urbanisation obtained new speed especially after Independence. By 1991, there were about 21.8 crores of urban dwellers in India. It means around 25.7% of the people are living in towns and cities according to 1991 Census report. Some of the economic reform measures such as liberalisation, privatisation and globalisation initiated by the

Government have further added to the process of urbanisation and made it more complex. The already existing big cities are getting overcrowded and becoming centres of congestion, confusion, indefiniteness and insecurity. There is a simple attempt here in this chapter to take a glimpse of the city life in India.

1. URBAN LIFE : MEANING AND CHARACTERISTICS

The City or Urban Area or Urban Community

The terms such as *"city"*, *"urban area"*, *"city community"*, etc. are all often used interchangeably in sociological literature.

The City : The *"urban community"* means the city community. *"The history of every civilisation is the history not of its countryside, but of its cities and towns. Civilisation means the city, and the city means civilisation. Man originally built the city, and the city, in turn, civilised man."* Man became a citizen when he became a member of a city-state. With the rise of the world-city, as **Spengler** tells us, *"there were no longer noblesse and bourgeoisies, freemen and slaves, Hellenes and Barbarians, believers and non-believers, but only cosmopolitans and provincials. All other contrasts pale before this one, which dominates all events, all habits of life, all views of the world."*

The city is culture par excellence; it is the epitome of culture. It is mankind's greatest work of art - and of artifice - because it contains all others. Culture, a manufactured environment, surrounds the city man. *"It is an environment of bricks and steel and mortar and cement, of bridges and tunnels, of sidewalks and streets, of monuments and buildings, of elevators and subway platforms."* The city is the product of man and his own achievement. The city *"has everything that is 'tardy' and everything sublime. It holds both hope and despair. It encompasses millions of people, and it can be the loveliest place on earth........ It is a vital centre of every civilised society...... It is both a place and a state of mind."*[1]

Meaning of Urban System or Community

By *"urban system"*, we mean urban community. Urban Community life represents the city-life. Though the term *"urban"* is popularly used, it is not properly defined. There is no single all-inclusive definition of a city or urban community.

1. The urban sociologist **Howard Woolston**, in his *"Metropolis"*, defines the city as a *"limited geographic area, inhabited by a largely and closely settled population, having many common interests and institutions, under a local government authorised by the State."*
2. **Robert Park** in his *"The City"* says that the city far from being a mere collection of individuals and of social conveniences, is rather a *"state of mind, a body of customs and traditions, and the organised attitudes and sentiments that inhere in these customs."*
3. **James A. Quinn** in his *"Urban Sociology"*, views the city as a *"phenomenon of specialisation"*, as a population aggregate whose occupations are non-agricultural.
4. **Adna F. Weber** in his *"The Growth of Cities"*, defines the city as any incorporated place with a minimum of 10,000 inhabitants.
5. **Louis Wirth** in his essay *"Urbanisation as a Way of Life"*, writes : *"For sociological purposes a city may be defined as a relatively large, dense and permanent settlement of socially heterogeneous individuals......."*
6. **Ian Robertson** : *"A city is a permanent concentration of relatively large number of people who do not produce their own food."*

1 **Robert Bierstedt** *"The Social Order."*

Though some sociologists have tried to define the concept of *"urban"* no one has given satisfactory definition so far. **Bergel** writes, *"everybody seems to know what a city is, but no one has given a satisfactory definition."* ***Kingsley Davis** writes, "much ink has been wasted in trying to make sharp demarcation to tell where the city ends and country begins."* Every village possesses some elements of the city while every city carries some features of the villages. Different criteria are used to decide a community as urban. Some of them are, for example, *population, legal limits, types of occupations, social organisations.*

Characteristics of Urban Community

1. *Social Heterogeneity* : An urban society is heterogeneous. The city is complex and manysided. Wide difference is found in the ways of living of the people. Uniformity and similarity are rarely found. It is more characterised by diversity. As **Louis Wirth** in his *"Urbanism as a way of life"*, points out "the greater the number of individuals participating in a process of interaction, the greater the potential differentiation between them ...." Louis Wirth further says that *"the city has been the melting-pot of races, peoples and cultures, and a most favourable breeding ground of new biological and cultural hybrids."* He also says that the city "has brought together people from the ends of the earth *because* they are different and thus useful to one another, rather than because they are homogeneous and likeminded." The ways of thinking, behaving, acting, the habits, morals, religious beliefs and practices, food and dress habits, occupations, etc., of the people differ significantly. Differentiation is potent in urban life.

2. *Secondary Relations* : The urban community is characterised by secondary relations. A city by virtue of its size cannot be a primary group. It is a secondary group. People are indifferent towards one another. Face-to-face, friendly or intimate relations may not be observed among people. Mass media of communication such as telephone, radio, press, post and telegraph, etc. are often resorted to by the urbanites for contacts. In cities people rarely take personal interests in others' concerns. Superficial form of politeness and manners are commonly found. Physical contact rarely results in intimacy and closeness. Even the neighbours are often found to be strangers. Private interests prevail over the common interests.

3. *Anonymity of City Life* : The city is an ocean of strangers. Heavy concentration in a limited space makes it impossible for people to know one another. Every one appears to be a stranger for every other person. There prevails a state of namelessness in which the individual identities remain unknown. This kind of namelessness that is found in the city is often referred to as *the anonymity of city life.* The anonymity of city life makes the problem of social control more complex.

4. *Secondary Control*: Control of social behaviour is more difficult in a city. Predominance of secondary relations makes it more complex, the social control. The social behaviour of the people is no more regulated by customs, traditions, religion and group standards. Instances of social deviation are commonly found in a city. As the city is the ocean of strangers, violations of standards of behaviour may pass unnoticed and unchecked. In this way, informal means of social control are not very effective. Regulation of social behaviour is largely done through the specialised agencies like law, legislation, police, court, etc. The larger the city, the greater it becomes the problem of control and more complex the agencies of secondary regulation.

5. *Large-scale Division of Labour and Specialisation* : An urban community is known for its large-scale division of labour and specialisation. Specialisation is visible in every walk of life. The larger the city, the greater is the specialisation. Hence we find different people in society engaging themselves in different kinds of activities like mechanical, commercial, educational, political, recreational, artistic, literary, scientific and so on. There are skilled, unskilled and semi-skilled workers, the artisans, the technicians, the *"paper expert"*, the *"white-collar"* employees, the

financiers, the businessmen, administrators, the politicians, the artists and others in society specialising themselves in some particular kind of activity or the other. City depends on large-scale division of labour. Work is divided among people on the basis of interests, talents, efficiency, opportunities, age, sex and so on. Division of labour and specialisation are possible because of co-operation.

6. ***Large-scale Social Mobility*** : An urban community is characterised by intense social mobility. *"Social Mobility" refers to the movement of people from one social status to another, from lower status to higher status or from poor position to rich position.* An individual's position in an urban community is determined more by his achievements than by his birth. *The status is not predetermined.* High stress is laid on accomplishments. Urban life in this way is highly competitive. The city with its elaborate division of labour, its competitiveness, its impersonality, has a tendency to emphasise the achievements of people. A city judges status according to what the individual does and how he speaks and what he accomplishes.

An urban society provides for social mobility in countless ways. It provides for *occupational mobility and geographic mobility* on the one hand, and *horizontal social mobility and vertical social mobility,* on the other. Individuals are busily engaged in improving their *"career."* An element of chance is always present in city. **MacIver** and **Page** write - *"An accident, a lucky contract, a sudden opportunity seized or missed, a change of style or fad, a happy or unhappy forecast of some event far beyond his control, may revolutionise his prospects in a day."*

7. ***Individuation*** : In an urban community, people are more individualistic in their attitudes. As **Kingsley Davis** points out, *"the secondary and voluntary character of urban association, the multiplicity of opportunities and the social mobility all force the individual to make his own decisions and to plan his life as a career."*

The concentration of people in a limited space has the effect of emphasising individuality. The city dweller takes his independent decisions on such matters as education, marriage, occupation, enterprise, adventure, and so on. *He is more selective in his choice and more individualistic in his preferences.* He is guided by his own whims and fancies. *He is detached except for the attachment of his own choice.* He is not tied to any particular relationship or any particular cause. As **Davis** points out, *"the individual stands over against the whole city, never completely absorbed by any one social group."* The city provides wide opportunities for the adventurous spirit of the individuals. **Simmel** observes, *"the city person is free in behaviour, less restrained, more individualistic, more formal and less sympathetic, and less of a conformist than the country person."*

8. ***Voluntary Association*** : An urban community is the breeding centre of a number of voluntary associations. The size of the urban population, its close proximity, diversity, and easy contact, make it the proper ground for voluntary associations. *"No matter what a person's hobby or vocation, national background of religion, age or colour, he can always find others with a similar basis of interest."* As a result, new kinds of groups arise based on extremely specialised interests. The group must organise or its cause will perish. People normally become members of a number of associations which may be called *"secondary groups"* in order to fulfil their varied interests.

9. ***Social Tolerance*** : Social tolerance characterises city life. Diversity of population, impersonality of contacts and heterogeneity in living style make it almost inevitable for the city people to develop the spirit of tolerance. *"People rub elbows with and become indifferent to extremes of all kinds - extremes of opinion and interest, extremes of poverty and wealth, extremes of education and background."* The spirit of tolerance gives the strength of unity in diversity to the life in a city. *"Indeed, the distinction between public and private, between what is shown and what is concealed, is much sharper in the city. It is the public behaviour that the city regulates, the private behaviour*

that it ignores. Its control is impersonal and general, that of the country, personal and particular" - **Kingsley Davis.**

10. *Spatial Segregation* : Due to its very nature, the city is bound to be overcrowded. It attracts a large number of people from the village areas. It is found that various types of business tend to concentrate in different spots of the city. Occupational groups of people also prefer to live together in distinct zones of a city. That is to say, some kind of *functional segregation* is found there. Commercial activities in the form of big departmental stores, showrooms, fancy stores, legitimate theatres, fine hotels, jewellery stores, etc. are located in the centre. The same is true of high-priced professional services - *e.g.* clinics, law offices, accounting firms, government offices, etc. Retail grocery establishments, filling stations, cleaning and pressing shops, shoe repair shops, garages, drug stores, etc., may be found at the cross-roads of the entire city. In the city, land is so costly that the buildings expand vertically, filling the centre of the city with skyscrapers.

11. *Unstable Family* : It is said that the urban family is not firmly organised. Many of the traditional functions of the family are transferred to the external agencies. Family is no longer the economic, educational, protective, recreational and affectional unit. Family has lost much of its control over its individual members. Individualism is developing even inside the family. Even the women are getting employed outside the family. Relations between the husband and wife, parents and children are strained to some extent. Some sociologists have even remarked that the urban family is much more disorganised.

2. FACTORS OF URBANISATION IN THE INDIAN CONTEXT

Concepts of *"Urban"* or *"City"*, *"Urbanism"* and *"Urbanisation"*

Concept of *"City"*

As it is already stated the city in the words of Louis Wirth refers to *"a relatively large, dense and permanent settlement of socially heterogeneous individuals."*

The term *"city"* is defined as a small community characterised by a large heterogeneous population, large scale division of labour, a high degree of specialisation, predominance of non-agricultural occupations, wide opportunities for social mobility, heavy dependence on formal social control, and a formalised system of local government.

Determinants of City as Prescribed by 1991 Census

The 1991 Census has defined a city or urban place on the basis of certain determinants which are mentioned below.

1. An urban area to be called so, must have a minimum of 5000 people.
2. At least 75% of its male workers' population is engaged in non-agricultural pursuits.
3. A density of population of atleast 400 persons per square Km [or 1000 persons per square mile].
4. All places with a municipality, corporation, cantonment board or notified town area, are also regarded as *"urban."*

As far as the *"determinants of city"* are concerned, 1961 basis was adopted in 1971, 1981 and 1991 censuses also for defining an urban area or town. The definition of the *"urban area"* is still not comparable with the definition of urban area provided in other countries. For instance, in **Japan**, a place having 30,000 or more inhabitants, is classified as *"urban."* This number is fixed at 3500 in **U.S.A.**, 20,000 in **Netherlands** and **Holland**, and just 2000 in **Austria**, **Germany** and **France**. Sociologist **Mark Jefferson** fixed this at 10,000. Sociologists, however do not attach much importance to the size of the population in the definition of city. They give importance to the characteristics of the city such as - *heterogeneity of population, complex division of labour, prevalence of impersonal secondary relations, dependence on formal social controls, predominance of non-agricultural occupations,* and so on.

Classification of Cities on the Basis of Size

After 1961, taking into consideration population strength towns and cities come to be distinguished on the following :

Class IV 1. *Small Towns* : Urban areas with population between 5,000 and 20,000.

Class III 2. *Large Towns* : Urban areas with population between 20,000 and 50,000.

Class II 3. *Big Cities* : Urban areas with population between 50,000 and one lakh.

Class I 4. *Metropolitan Cities* : Urban areas with 10 lakh and above population.

Concept of "Urbanism"

The concept of *"urbanism"* represents a way of life. The term generally denotes the diffusion of urban culture and the evolution of urban society. The term urbanism can be defined in the following way :

- C.B. Mamoria is of the opinion that *"Urbanism is a cultural - social - economic phenomenon which traces interaction between the social and technological processes."*[1]
- Louis Wirth has mentioned four characteristics of urban system or urbanism : *heterogeneity of population, specialisation of function, anonymity and impersonality, and standardisation of behaviour.*
- Prof. Ram Ahuja says that *urbanism is a way of life which is characterised by certain elements such as transiency [short-term relations], superficiality, anonymity and individualism.*

As a result of urbanism a market economy grows, innovations that take place come to conflict with traditions, complicated type of division of labour is introduced and more than any other thing, a new way of living gets evolved. Urban way of living may even spread to villages.

Concept of *"Urbanisation"*

The concept of *"urbanisation"* generally refers to the concentration of people in towns and cities. This has become a continuous and almost a universal process in all the modern societies. The term indicates the movement of people from the less concentrated areas to the more concentrated ones. As urban sociologists have noted this process need not take place in the very same manner, but can take place in diverse ways in different places. Sociologist Munro is of the opinion that *the process of urbanisation or unprecedented growth of cities stands out as one of the greatest developments of the recent one hundred years.*

Definition of *"Urbanisation"*

1. C.B. Mamoria : *"Urbanisation refers to a process by which the urban values get diffused, behaviour patterns are transformed and movement from villages to cities occur."*
2. Wallace and Wallace : Urbanisation refers to *"the movement of people from rural areas to city."*
3. Anderson is of the opinion that *"urbanisation involves not only movement of population to cities but also change in the migrants' attitudes, values, and behaviour patterns."*
4. Ram Ahuja : *"Urbanisation is the movement of population from rural to urban areas."*

1 C.B. Mamoria *"Social Problems and Social Disorganisation in India."* Page - 459.

5. **Thompson Warren** : *"Urbanisation is the movement of people from communities concerned chiefly or solely with agriculture to other communities generally larger whose activities are primarily centred in government, trade, manufacture, or allied interests."*

Urbanisation - A Global Trend

Urbanisation has become a global trend. Large scale urbanisation had occurred since 1800, particularly after the Industrial Revolution. In 1800, there were only 21 cities in the world each with a population of one lakh or over; and all these cities were in Europe. This figure increased to 859 in 1950, that is, within 150 years. The total population of these 859 cities was estimated to be 313 million. Of these, 364 cities were in Europe alone. In 1950, the world had more than 49 cities each with a population of more than one million people.

Until 1850, not more than 5% of the global population was urbanised, and no society had more than half of its members living in cities. In 1850, only one city, **London**, had more than 1 million inhabitants. Yet today all the industrialised societies of the world are heavily urbanised, and over 140 cities contain more than 1 million people. **Kingsley Davis** predicted in 1965 that – if the present trends continue, there will be 500 cities with over 1 million inhabitants by the end of the 20th century, several of them containing more than 25 million people. By then, more than 80 per cent of the world's population will live in cities. Fortunately, the global population has not become urbanised to that extent by the close of the 20th century.

Importance of the Study of Urbanisation

The study of urbanisation has its own importance and **C.B. Mamoria** mentions four important factors in this regard.

1. The cities, once established, tend to develop into centres of political, economic, industrial and other activities.
2. The cities have proved themselves to be not only centres of heavy concentration of people, but also as places of intellectual, scientific, artistic, educational, political and other achievements.
3. The development of cities has been a recent trend in human history and it has contributed to changes in various other fields.
4. Urbanisation has been a product of economic and technological development. Once it sets in, it goes on influencing the rural people, their lives and activities.

URBANISATION IN INDIA

Towns and cities are not new things for India. In fact, India has a tradition of urban living and has been a land of cities from pre-historic times of the Indus Valley Civilisation. The famous cities of **Harappa** and **Mohen-jo-daro** existed in the Indus Valley more than 6000 years ago. These two represent the earliest examples of the well planned and best maintained cities of the ancient world. *"These cities were centres of rich and varied urban culture and a progressing order of social life. They were well laid out with wide streets, market places, public offices, religious halls, community baths and drainage and sewage systems."*[1] The people in these cities had attained high standards of town planning and architecture.

The urban tradition of living continued for centuries in India. For example, in the ***ancient period*** during the rule of the **Magadha Dynasty** [5th and 6th centuries B.C.] Ayodhya, Kashi,

1 C.B. Mamoria. Page - 459.

Indraprastha, Pataliputra and other cities had attained prominence. During the **Buddhist Period**, cities such as Nalanda, Taxila, Kaushambi, Mithila, Vaishali, Shravsthi and others, assumed importance. In the **Gupta Period**, Pataliputra, Kanauj, Banaras, Mathura, Ujjain, Prayag, Nasik and other cities were the main centres of political, religious, educational and other activities.

In the ***Medieval Period,*** there was a considerable growth of many small and big cities which attained importance because of their flourishing handicrafts and trade. ***Example*** : Dacca was known for fine muslins, Murshidabad for silk, Krishnanagar for clay modelling, Golconda for diamond and jewellery, Agra for perfumes and marble works. Agra and Fatehpur Sikri the two great cities were not only much greater than London, but also more populous. Vijayanagar was one of the largest cities of the world. Ahmedabad was regarded as one of the biggest cities of India. Delhi and Agra rivalled Paris in beauty, extent and in the number of inhabitants.

During the medieval period, the kings who belonged to the great dynasties of Chalukya, Rashtrakoota, Chola, Hoysala, etc. also built a few good cities. Hampi, Kanchipuram, Vijayanagar, Bangalore, Mysore, Calicut, Cambay and other cities of the south, assumed importance at different times.

During the ***Mughal period,*** cities such as Fatehpur Sikri, Shahajahanabad [the present Old Delhi], Lucknow, Lahore, Golconda, Hyderabad, Bijapur, Srirangapattanam, came to prominence. All these cities bear the impact of the Muslim rule.

During the ***British regime,*** a few other cities such as Calcutta, Bombay, Madras and New Delhi assumed importance. The British administrators had made these cities the centres of their administration. These cities also emerged as great centres of learning and socio-political activities.

After independence, some of the old cities became enlarged and some new cities also emerged. Some cities came to be known as ***industrial cities. Examples*** : Rourkela, Durgapur, Bhilai, Chittranjan, Roopnarayan Nagar, Sindri, Nangal, Neyveli, Vishakpatnam, etc. Cities such as Faridabad, Rajpur, Nilokheri, Ulhasnagar, Kalyani and others were developed to rehabilitate the refugees who came from Pakistan during partition. Some cities evolved into ***port cities. Examples*** : Kandla, Haldia, Paradeep, New Mangalore, Tuticorin, etc. Some cities were developed as ***Capital cities. Examples*** : Chandigarh, Bhuvaneshwar, Bhopal, Hyderabad, etc. Some cities became centres of attraction due to the vast employment opportunities available in them. ***Example*** : Mumbai, Chennai, Kolkota, Kanpur, Ahmedabad, Pune, Dhanbad, Bangalore, etc.

Some Trends in Urbanisation in India

1. There is a Growing Trend Towards Urbanisation

Urban population is slowly but steadily increasing in India. It increased from about 26 million in 1901 to 62 million in 1951 and then to 218 million in 1991. During the decade 1981-1991 alone urban population increased by 57 million which indicates a growing trend towards urbanisation. [*See* Table - 1].

2. There is a Trend Towards Concentration of People in Big Cities

A glance of ***Table*** - 2 [page 459] shows that the proportion of urban population in Class I [With a population of over one lakh] has increased from 25.7% in 1901 to 65.2% in 1991. It only confirms that there is a greater trend towards concentration of people in bigger towns. The Table also shows that the relative proportion of urban population in Class II and Class III towns taken together, has remained practically constant, that is around 26 - 28% in 1990-91. In contrast to this, relative proportion of population in Class IV, Class V and Class VI towns has come down sharply from 47.2% in 1901 to barely 10.7% in 1991.

Table - 1

Relative Growth of Urban and Rural Population

	Population in millions			*Percentage of total population*		*Percentage increase in urban population during the decade*	*Urban-Rural Ratio*
	Total	*Rural*	*Urban*	*Rural*	*Urban*		
1901	232.9	207.3	25.6	89.0	11.0	-.-	1 : 8.1
1911	246.0	220.4	25.6	89.6	10.4	0.0	1 : 8.6
1921	244.3	216.6	27.7	88.7	11.3	+8.25	1 : 7.8
1931	270.8	237.8	33.0	87.8	12.2	+19.1	1 : 7.2
1941	309.0	265.5	43.5	85.9	14.1	+32.1	1 : 6.1
1951	361.1	298.7	62.4	82.7	17.3	+43.2	1 : 4.7
1961	439.2	360.3	78.9	82.0	18.0	+25.3	1 : 4.5
1971	548.2	439.1	109.1	80.1	19.9	+38.0	1 : 3.7
1981*	685.2	525.7	159.5	76.7	23.3	+46.8	1 : 3.3
1991**	844.3	627.1	217.2	74.3	25.7	+35.6	1 : 2.9
2000***	1000.0	716.0	284.1	71.6	28.4	-.-	-.-

* Includes projected population of Assam.

** Includes population projection for Jammu & Kashmir.

*** Projected Figures included by the Author.

Source : Registrar General, India.

3. Degree of Urbanisation in India - A Comparison

In comparison with the developed countries of the world, the level of urbanisation in India is far behind the high income countries. The proportion of urban population to total population in India was 25.7% in 1991, whereas it was 74% in Russia [in 1972], 76% in U.S.A., 77% in Japan, 85% in Australia and 89% in U.K. The experience of other countries would reveal that creation of employment opportunities can bring about the much desired change towards urbanisation.

4. Population of Large Cities with 10 Lakh or more Population

According to 1991 Census, there are now 23 large cities [mega cities] accounting for 70.7 million people. The population of these 23 cities was about 33% of total urban population. Greater Bombay ranked first with a population of 12.6 million, followed by Calcutta with a population of 10.9 million. The population of Delhi was only 5.7 million in 1981, it has jumped to 8.4 million by 1991. The overall decaded increase in population in 23 mega cities was about 68% during 1981-91. Hyderabad witnessed the highest rate of population growth [67.0%], followed by Lucknow [63.0%]; Jaipur [49.2%]; Pune [47.4%] and Delhi [46.2%]. [*Note* : See *Table* 3 in Page 460.]

5. Regional Pattern of Urbanisation

Urbanisation has not taken place uniformly in all the states. It reveals regional variations. The rate of growth of population in various states between 1981 and 1991 reveals that the poorer states like Orissa, U.P., M.P., Rajasthan, A.P. have urbanised faster than the old industrialised states

Table - 2

Trend of Urbanisation in India

	Towns with different population size-classes						
	Class I 1,00,000 *& above*	*Class II* (50,000 to 99,999)	*Class III* (20,000 to 49,999)	*Class IV* (10,000 to 19,999)	*Class V* (5,000 to 9,999)	*Class VI* (*Less than* 5,000)	*All Classes Total*
Number of Urban Agglomerations / Towns							
1951	76	91	327	608	1,124	569	2,795
1961	102	129	437	719	711	172	2,270
1971	148	173	558	827	623	147	2,476
1981	216	270	738	1,053	739	229	3,245
1991	296	341	927	1,135	725	185	3,609
Urban Population (in Lakhs)							
1951	275	61	97	84	80	19	616
1961	399	87	132	99	53	6	776
1971	612	117	171	117	48	5	1,070
1981	945	182	224	149	56	8	1,564
1991	1,388	233	281	165	55	6	2,128
Percentage Distribution of Urban Population							
1901	25.7	11.3	15.8	20.9	20.1	6.2	100.0
1951	44.6	10.0	15.7	13.6	13.0	3.1	100.0
1961	51.4	11.2	16.9	12.8	6.9	0.8	100.0
1971	57.2	10.9	16.0	10.9	4.5	0.4	100.0
1981	60.4	11.6	14.3	9.5	3.6	0.5	100.0
1991	65.2	10.9	13.2	7.8	2.6	0.3	100.0

Note : *Excludes Assam and Jammu & Kashmir.*
Source : *Registrar General of India.*

like West Bengal, Gujarat, and Tamil Nadu. Among the rich states Maharashtra and Haryana are the only exceptions where the growth rate of urban population is as high as in some of the poorer states, In Orissa and M.P. rates of growth of urban population have remained consistently high. In other poor states like U.P., A.P. and Rajasthan, the growth rates have risen over the period. Urbanisation was faster in old industrially advanced states than in some poorer states during the fifties, but the process in the former did not get accelerated over the years as it happened in the latter.

6. Relatively High Stability of Urban Settlements

It has been observed that the urbanisation process in India is very closely associated with the relatively high stability of urban settlements. Since the very beginning of the 20th century, the urban population of the country has grown 8 fold, and yet the number of towns has increased significantly and thus they have grown in size. The number of villages developing into town status over the period is not very large. The stability in the structure of urban settlements reveals built in resistance to change in the socio-economic structure of the country.

Table - 3

Population of Large Cities with a Population of 1 Million and Above

	Population in 1991 *(in millions)*	*Population in* 1981 *(in millions)*
Greater Bombay	12.6	8.2
Calcutta	10.9	9.2
Delhi	8.4	5.7
Madras	5.4	4.3
Hyderabad	4.3	2.9
Bangalore	4.1	2.5
Ahmedabad	3.3	2.5
Pune	2.5	1.7
Kanpur	2.1	1.7
Nagpur	1.7	1.3
Lucknow	1.6	1.0
Jaipur	1.5	1.0

Source: Ruddar Datt and K.P.M. Sundharam's *"Indian Economy."* Page - 58.

7. Migration of Rural Population to Urban Areas

It is observed that the urban population is steadily increasing in India. One of the main reasons for this is the migration of rural population towards the urban areas. It has been estimated that around 45% of the annual increase in urban population is due to migration. *Example*: The population of Bangalore increased by 75.6% during 1971-81. Similarly, population of Asansol in West Bengal increased by 108.7%, of Faridabad in Haryana by 85.5%, of Guwahati in Assam by 188.3%, of Thane in Maharashtra by 105.9%, of Vishakapatnam in A.P. by 75% and of Bhuvaneshwar in Orissa by 87.7% during 1981-91. Because of this shift in population Class I cities with a population of 1,00,000 and above accounted for 65.2% of the total urban population in 1991 as against 44.6% in 1951.

At present, India's urban population [21.8 crores] is larger than the urban population of all countries except China. In absolute terms, India's urban population is quite large and its significance must be properly understood for the future development planning in this country.

Some Demographic Dimensions of Urbanisation in India

1. As it is already made clear, though India is regarded as a classical land of villages, it occupies the second place in terms of possessing the highest number of urban dwellers. The first place is occupied by China in this regard.

2. As per the 1991 census, there are about 21.8 crores of urban residents, who constitute 25.7% of the total population and it was projected to be 28.4% [285 million] in 2001.

3. Between 1901 and 1981 India's rural population got increased by 2 $^1/_2$ times whereas during the same period the urban population got increased by 6 times.

4. Out of 3,287,762 square kilometre land area in this country, only 43,600 square k.m. area is regarded as urban area and in this area the density of population is consistently increasing.

5. Between 1971 and 1981 the population of urban area increased at the rate of 3.4% per annum. As per the records of 1991 census, the growth rate of population of the cities with an average population of one lakh or over, was found to be 4.68% per annum.

6. As per 1991 census report, around 217.6 million people are living in 3768 cities.

7. 1991 census records reveal that the largest number of towns / cities are found in U.P. [704] followed by Tamil Nadu [434], M.P. [327], Maharashtra [307]. But in Andaman and Nicobar Islands, and in Dadra and Nagar Haveli, only one town is found in each of these states. Tripura, Sikkim and Nagaland have 10, 8 and 7 towns / cities respectively.

8. *Urbanisation in India is taking place relatively in a slow manner.* For example, in 1901, there were around 1916 cities and this number was increased to 3768 in 1991. It means in the time span of 90 years the number of towns / cities in India increased almost by 3 times whereas the urban population increased by more than 8 times. The urban population, during the same period increased from 26 million to 217 million. This only shows the increasing concentration of people in cities.

9. In 1981, there were 12 large cities in India, each with a population of more than one million. The combined population of these cities was around 42.1 million then. In 1991, both of these almost got nearly doubled. The number of large cities got increased to 24 and their combined population to 7 crores in 1991.

10. As far as the mobility is concerned, it is greater in the cities than in the villages. In 1991, of the 225 million migrants in the country, 17.7 had migrated from rural to urban areas, 11.8% from urban to urban areas, 64.5% from rural to rural areas, and 6% from urban to rural areas [*Manpower Profile, India,* 1998 : 26]. This reveals that mobility in urban areas is more from one city to another city than from villages to the cities.

11. According to 1991 census report, of the 74.27% population living in villages, 36.57% villages have population of less than 2,000, 21.37% between 2,000 and 5,000, and 13.33% more than 5,000.

On the other hand, of the 25.73% population in urban areas, 0.72% urban areas have less than 10,000 population, 5.27% between 10,000 and 50,000, 2.75% between 50,000 and 1,00,000, and 16.4% above 1 lakh.[1]

12. As per 1991 census reports, the population of four major cities of India is as follows : Mumbai - 125.7 lakhs, Kolkota - 109 lakhs, Delhi - 84 lakhs, and Chennai - 54 lakhs.

13. In 1950, Kolkota was the only city to be included in the 15 largest agglomerations in the world. In 1995, Mumbai and Delhi were added to the list. The U.N.O. defines mega-city as the one with a population of 10 million or more. In 1950, only New York was classified as a mega-city. By 1995, the number rose to 14 mega-cities and Mumbai, Calcutta and Delhi were included in the list. Population projections indicate that by 2015 Hyderabad will also become a mega-city. Bangalore is also in the race.

FACTORS OR CAUSES OF URBANISATION IN INDIA

Urbanisation has been taking place incessantly in India. The process assumed greater momentum soon after independence. As reflected by the figures the old cities are growing and new cities are coming up. In 1901, only 10.8% of the total population of the country lived in towns and cities and this percentage has increased to 25.72 in 1991 and it was projected to be 28.4% in the year 2000. In the time gap between 1901 and 1981 the rural population in India increased by 2 $^1/_2$ times

1 These figures exclude population of Assam and Jammu & Kashmir. - *Manpower Profile, India,* 1998 - 23-24.

whereas urban population increased by 6 times. By 1991, there were as many as 3768 cities with a combined population of more than 217.6 million and it was projectecd to be at 285 million. Though the rate of growth of cities is said to be comparatively very slow, the growth is witnessed consistently for the past five decades.

Various factors have contributed to the rapid growth of cities in India. A.N. Agarwal[1] in this regard, speaks of the role of a few factors which are mentioned below :

1. Natural increase in population.
2. Continuous migration of people towards cities :
   (a) the "push" factors, and
   (b) the "pull" factors which include :
      (i) the "pull" of the job opportunities, and
      (ii) the "pull" of city attractions.
3. Changes in City-Boundaries.

1. Natural Increase in Population

Population is consistently increasing in the country. Naturally, the urban population is also increasing. The natural cause for the increase in urban population is that, in the urban areas always the number of birth exceeds the number of death. *Example*: The birth-rate in the urban areas in 1971 was estimated at 30.1 [per thousand] with death-rate at 9.7 [per thousand]. In 1978, the birth-rate declined to 27.8. The death-rate fell slightly to 9.4. This caused the growth rate to be high because of large differences between the two rates. Availability of better medical and health services, good drinking water supply and sanitation, higher rate of literacy, etc., must have been the reasons for the relatively low level of death rate in the urban areas. The rate of growth of population per annum in the urban areas was 3.4% in between 1971-81, but it increased to 4.68% per annum in 1991.

2. Continuous Migration of People Towards the Cities

Both economists and non-economists are of the opinion that the economic and non-economic forces have been playing their role in driving the people from the rural hinterland to the urban areas. Of the total rise in urban population, while a major contributory factor is the natural growth, a part is also contributed by immigrations from rural areas. Their exact number at the moment is not properly known. It can only be guessed. The factors that induce people of the rural areas to shift towards the cities are of two types, namely : (a) the *"push"* factors, and (b) the *"pull"* factors.

(a) Role of *"Push"* Factors

People from the rural areas are moving towards the cities for economic reasons also. A large number of agricultural workers, small and marginal farmers depend upon agriculture for their subsistence. Many of these people who possess small holdings are not able to ensure productive employment to all the adult members of the family. Added to this, there is also the disguised unemployment. These people all the time feel pressure to migrate to towns / cities. Most agricultural workers find only seasonal work and the wages they earn from this work are not sufficient to maintain them throughout the year. Hence they look forward to some other work in their own village or nearby villages. If they are not able to get any one, then the economic forces *"push"* them out of the village, mostly towards towns and cities in search of better opportunities.

1 A.N. Agarwal *"Indian Economy - Problems of Development and Planning."* 22nd Edition - 1996. Page - 83.

(b) Role of the *"Pull"* Factors

If certain factors are forcibly *"pushing"* the villagers towards the cities certain attractions of the cities are also *"pulling"* or drawing the ruralites towards them. These *"pull"* factors are of two types : (i) *The "pull" of the better job opportunities,* and (ii) *the pull of city attractions.*

(i) ***The "Pull" of Better Job Opportunities*** : The comparatively better job opportunities that are available in some cities, are attracting people towards them. All cities do not have such attractions. Cities or towns where heavy public investments in industry and mining and other establishments are made as we find in Ranchi, Dhanbad, Bokaro [of Southern Bihar], Durgapur, Bhilai, Raipur [of M.P.], people tend to concentrate. In the same manner, industrially advanced cities such as Bangalore, Mumbai, Khanpur, Ahmedabad that belong to the industrially developed states of Karnataka, Maharashtra, U.P. and Gujarat respectively are attracting ruralites towards them with the promise of better wages and salaries. Urban wages are generally higher as compared to rural wages. Therefore, the *"pull"* of relatively high urban wages is quite strong and a large number of people, particularly the young men and women, keep on migrating to the cities.

(ii) ***The "Pull" of City Attractions*** : The city is a centre of attraction. From the beginning the city has been attracting a large number of people especially from the village areas. The city is pulling people from various corners towards its nucleus. The rural people who are faced with various economic problems, burdened with a large number of children, bored with the monotony of the routine life, and attracted by the glamour of the city, have started moving towards the cities. The city is tempting the rural people with its employment opportunities, educational facilities, medical facilities, recreational facilities, such as movies, dramas, night clubs, cabarets, gambling centres, horse race, library, public parts, museums, orchestra, zoo, circus shows, etc.

In comparison with the village, the city provides ample opportunities for personal advancement. The city is a centre of brisk economic, commercial, artistic, literary, political, educational, technological, scientific and other activities. The rural people who come in contact with the city for a brief spell of time get themselves impressed by its appearance, glamour, comfort and luxuries. They are likely to develop rosy imaginations of the luxuries of the city life. They have come to believe that money-making is easier in the city. The city men and women, their dresses, fashions, habits, styles, tastes, interests, intelligence, talents, comforts, luxuries, etc., have great impact on the rural people. As a result, they have started flocking towards the cities in a big number. This has contributed to the process of urbanisation. Urbanisation resulted in urban concentration on the one hand and rural depopulation, on the other.

3. Changes in City-Boundaries

For various reasons and at different times the boundaries of the towns have been extended. As cities get expanded, the semi-urban or entirely rural areas that are found in the outskirts of the cities also get included in the urban areas. It is not that these rural areas suddenly become urban areas. They may even continue to retain some of the characteristics of villages. But their inclusion in the expanding cities put them under the areas classified as towns. The people living in these areas start acquiring the features of urban life. The rural population that gets included in these areas increase the number of urban population.

It is clear from the above explanation that the process of urbanisation continues to take place even today. It has acquired new momentum at the fag end of the 20th and in the beginning of the 21st centuries. Expansion of educational facilities, technological and industrial development, availability of employment opportunities, and such other factors continue to play their role in accelerating the process of urbanisation.

Advantages and Disadvantages of the City

Advantages or Merits

1. The city offers *opportunities and facilities* for making full use of one's abilities and talents. City is a centre ever ready to welcome talents from any corner. It is a laboratory for experimenting various plans, projects and schemes.

2. It can make life *joyful and comfortable.* Major *service agencies are centralised* in the city to satisfy various interests of the people such as work, education, health, recreation, religion and politics.

3. It *encourages new ideas and inventions.* People of the city are said to be broad-minded and ready to welcome divergent ideas, views, plans and projects. It is even ready to accommodate conflicting ideas, attitudes and philosophies.

4. It *quickens social movements* and enlarges social contacts. Social mobility is relatively easier in a city. People move up and down the status scale relatively with greater speed. Consolidating public opinion and mobilising people either in favour of or against something, is not very problematic due to the availability of modern means of communication.

5. There is less *social distance* being kept among people of different castes, races and religions. Hence there is *more tolerance* towards others.

6. The city is *dynamic.* This dynamism contributes to social changes. Life is not static but dynamic here. Things are always in flux and flow. Accepting the new and rejecting the old, embracing modernity and keeping tradition at a distance is not a big problem here.

7. The city has *liberated women* from the exclusiveness of domesticity. It has made women to stand on an equal footing with men. City has made women to become aware of the multifarious facilities which the modern society has offered them. It has boosted the status of women in various respects. City has contributed to the emancipation of women from the bondage of the tradition.

8. The city provides various means of *recreation.* In a city there is *scope for personal advancement.* The multifarious associations of the city cater to the multiple needs, interests and tastes of the people. By providing various avenues the city can add to the intellectual delight, artistic ecstacy and scientific urge of the educated people.

9. That is why, as Quinn says, *"the great civilisations of antiquity - Mesopotamian, Egyptian, Greek, Roman, - were cradled in cities, that urban communities typically have led in the creation of art, the advancement of science, and the dissemination of learning."*

10. The city *functions as a laboratory for human genius.* It is in the city that man tries to explore the different dimensions and horizons of knowledge. City poses a permanent challenge to human genius and at the same time provides ample opportunities for developing it.

Disadvantages or Demerits

The city has its dark or the ugly side too.

1. The city makes life *materialistic* and *mechanical.* It takes away from man his human aspect. In a city everything becomes a means to means and for no values beyond. City encourages the hedonistic outlook which makes man to think in terms of obtaining maximum advantage for minimum efforts.

2. *Secondary relations* are dominant in the city. People are *indifferent* to one another. Superficial forms of politeness and manners are commonly found. There is lack of *intimacy* and

privacy in the city. Individuals are always interested in themselves, in their interests, aspirations, ambitions and achievements. Individual interests prevail enormously over the collective interests.

3. The city makes the people to become *individualistic, selfish, rationalistic* and *calculative.* Relations are commercialised. All relations are means to means and to no final ends. Individuals are so much occupied with themselves and their aggrandisement that they have scant respect for others and for their interests. Often, family and even community interests are sacrificed at the altar of personal glorification.

4. The city poses a *challenge to family.* The urban family is in doldrums. It is less balanced and more unstable. Individualism is ripening within it. We find clashes of interests of husband and wife, of brothers and sisters, and of parents and children. The rate of *divorce, desertion* and *separation* is increasing. Joint family has disappeared in the Western cities and is on the verge of total collapse in the Indian cities. Urban family is cut to size.

5. *Social control is complex* and *less effective* in the city. Informal means of social control such as family, neighbourhood, morality, religion, education, etc. have become less effective in exerting a restraining influence on the behaviour of the individual members. Further, agents of socialisation are also not able to exercise the required moral influence on the behaviour of the children. Hence, instances of *social deviance* are more in the city.

6. *City makes human life to become uncertain, insecure and competitive.* It is true that city provides ample opportunities for the adventurous spirit of the individuals. For the very same reason he feels unrestrained. New adventures, new inventions, new experiments, new plans and projects may yield materialistic benefits, but at the same time they may bring lot of pressure on our nerves. Rate of speed of social change is so fast in city that it may rise the status of the individuals and at the same time reduce it to nothing.

7. *The city is said to be the centre of problems* of economic, social, political, psychological and religious nature. The problems of the city such as economic insecurity, mental illness, gambling, prostitution, drunkenness, drug addiction, corruption, nepotism, environment pollution, crime, juvenile delinquency, dowry, violence against women, and so on.

8. Concentration of people in the *city gives rise to the problem of providing basic civic amenities to the people.* The city administration, especially in a densely populated nation like India, fails miserably to cater to the fundamental needs of civilised living. Cities are normally faced with the problems such as housing, lack of water supply, failure of power supply, poor drainage facility, overcrowdedness, insanitation, ill health, etc.

The cities are thus condemned as *"abnormal seed-beds of sin, scepticism, greed, crime, misery, filth and congestion."* It is branded as the centre of *crime, vice and misery.*

Urban - Rural Contrast

The city and the country [village], the town and the land, the capital and the province [this despite Spengler's exaggeration] is one of the most widespread and important of all kinds of social differentiation to be found in all human societies except the most primitive, and in most uncivilised societies of human history. *"Soil and cement, the land and the pavement, the lane and the street – these are symbols of two different ways of life, two different cultures."*

"The city man and the country man do indeed have two different views of the world, have different rounds of activity, sustain in different ways the progression of the seasons, indulge in different kinds of work and play, and spend their span of life in different surroundings." The city and the village are very often construed in their *"ideal form"* and the differences between them are

very often exaggerated. Such exaggerated differences between the rural society and the urban society can be elaborated in the following way :

Rural Society	Urban Society
1. The rural society is ***homogeneous.*** It is marked by unity and uniformity. Here likeness is more stressed and differences are undermined.	1. The urban society is ***heterogeneous.*** It is known for its diversity and complexity.
2. It is dominated by ***primary relations.*** It is hence more cohesive and united. Face-to-face relationship forges friendship and a sense of community feeling.	2. It is dominated by ***secondary relations.*** It is not united. Urbanites pursue divergent interests, cherish different values, ideas, careers, and so on.
3. People here are known for their ***simplicity and hospitality,*** frankness and generosity. Co-operative spirit is very strong here.	3. The urban people are known for their ***artificiality,*** narrow-mindedness and selfishness.
4. ***Informal means of social control*** such as customs, folkways, mores, conventions are sufficient to regulate interpersonal relations.	4. ***Formal means of social control*** such as law, legislation, police, court, etc. are needed in addition to the informal means of regulating the behaviour of the people.
5. It is ***less mobile.*** Opportunities for social mobility are comparatively limited. Status is mostly "ascribed." Further, mobility in rural areas is more from villages to villages, and villages to cities. ***Ex.*** In 1991, of the 225 million migrants in our country, 64.5% migrated from rural to rural areas and 17.7% had migrated from rural to urban areas.	5. It is ***more mobile.*** It is an "open" society. It provides more chances for social mobility. Here status is "achieved." Further, mobility in urban areas is more from one city to another. ***Ex.*** In 1991, only 11.8% of the people moved from urban to urban areas and hardly 6% of the people from urban to rural areas.
6. The main occupation of people in the rural community is ***agriculture.*** Only a negligible number of people are engaged in non-agricultural pursuits. In fact, agriculture is the backbone of the rural economy. The rural society provides ***limited scope for division of labour and specialisation.*** Occupations are mostly unspecialised.	6. Urban community is known for ***non-agricultural pursuits*** like manufacturing, trade and commerce, service and professions. Here occupations are more specialised. There is wide spread division of labour and specialisation, and opportunities for pursuing occupations are, numerous.
7. It is ***built of family*** units. Family is a very influential and dominant institution. People are bound by the family traditions.	7. Here, the family is said to be ***unstable.*** More than the family, individual is given importance. Joint families are comparatively less in number.
8. ***Women are mostly tradition bound.*** They are passive, meek, submissive and obedient. They work in the field as well as in the kitchen. Women are ***not career-conscious.*** They cannot live without family.	8. ***Women have almost an equal status with men.*** Many are employed outside the family. They are more free, and have their individualistic ideas. They are very much career-conscious.
9. Rural areas are stratified, especially in the Indian context, ***more on caste and less on class basis.*** Cleavages between the strata are also not that sharp here.	9. Urban communities, on the contrary, are stratified more on class basis. Sharp cleavages do exist between the rich and the poor or the upper classes and the lower classes.

10. Rural people are poorer. Still they are **not class-conscious**. Class conflicts are unknown to them.	10. Chances are greater for people to become rich. People are **more class-conscious**. Class-conflicts often paralyse the city life.
11. People are more **conservative**, orthodox and dogmatic. They are for *status quo,* not for change.	11. *People are progressive.* They welcome changes. They are exposed to the modern developments in the fields of science and technology.
12. The rural community has a **small number** of people. According to the 1991 Census figures, of the 74.27% population living in villages, 36.57% villages have population of less than 2,000 each, 21.37% between 2,000 and 5,000 and so on.	12. Urban community consists of a **big number** of people. Of the 25.73% population in urban area, only 0.72% urban areas have less than 10,000 population whereas 16.4% of the areas have population above 1 lakh. Thus, cities are normally bigger in size.
13. It is a "**simple unigroup society**" for the interests of people are common and limited, and not multifarious.	13. Urban community is a "**complex multigroup** society." People form multifarious groups and associations to satisfy their divergent interests.
14. The rural community is known for its ethnocentrism and its correlative, suspicion towards outsiders.	14. Here, the growing contacts with outsiders make the people to become tolerant with them.
15. It is relatively *free from conflicts, frictions* and *tensions.* It is characterised by common **consensus**. The social organisation is well defined and there is little scope for mental illness and anomie [lawlessness].	15. The urban community replaces consensus by *common dissensus.* The social organisation is atomistic and illdefined. It is characterised by dis-organisation, mental illness and anomie.
16. There is **less stress on education** in the rural system. Scanty formal education pervades the village. Education is largely informal.	16. **Mass education** is widespread in the city. Increasing democratisation of the organisations and institutions demand formal education.
17. The **average size of household** in rural areas in 1991 was 4.9 members, which means rural households have relatively larger membership.	17. The **average size of the household** in urban areas in 1991 is 4.4 members. It means urban families are relatively smaller in size.
18. Rural communities are **closer to nature** and natural environment. Since they are associated with agriculture, green atmosphere is found everywhere.	18. Urban communities are **far away from the nature** and natural environment. They are surrounded more by man-made environment and are isolated from nature.

Some Other Differences

In addition to the differences between the city and rural community mentioned above, some other differences can also be observed between them.

1. *Number of working children* [child labourers] in the rural communities is found to be 10 times more than in the urban areas. In 1991, the difference between the rural and the urban areas in this particular aspect was found to be 10.26 to 1.03 million.
2. *Labour force participation rate* in the rural areas is more than 3 times than that found in urban areas. *Ex.* In 1993-94, it was 294 million in rural areas against 85.7 million in urban areas.

3. It is also found that the *infant mortality rate* in rural areas is one and half time more than the rate found in urban areas.
4. Speaking from the perspective of **Tonnies**, rural community is dominated by *gemeinschaft relationships,* whereas urban community is characterised by the predominance of *gesellschaft relationships.*
5. Viewing the rural - urban contrast through the **Durkheimean** concepts of mechanical and organic solidarity, it may be said that the *rural community is based on mechanical solidarity* whereas the *urban community is characterised by organic solidarity.* Rural community places premium on the homogeneity of values, behaviour patterns and ways of living. On the other hand, urban community is characterised by unity based on the interdependence of a large number of highly specialised roles, complex division of labour and so on.

Rural - Urban Convergence

Though the communities are normally divided into *"rural"* and *"urban"*, the line of demarcation is not always clear as **MacIver** has remarked, between these two types of communities *"There is no sharp demarcation to decide where the city ends and country begins."* Every village possesses some elements of the city and every city carries some features of the village. The concept of *"rural-urban convergence"* refers to the striking similarities between the village and the town in some aspects of community life.

Cities are growing in number and size everywhere. It is true that the urban culture is diffusing at a very fast rate in the rural areas. As **Kingsley Davis** has said, *"the city effects are wider than the city itself."* The influence of the city varies with its size also. The urban way of life can be carried far beyond the city boundaries and can thus characterise people who do not actually live in cities.

With the diffusion of urban culture to the rural areas, the extreme differences between rural and urban cultures have diminished. The growing transport and communications, the radio, press, television, telephone, etc., the growing circulation of the urban newspapers in the rural areas have changed the attitudes and outlook of the ruralites. Medical, educational, commercial, recreational and other facilities are also being enjoyed by the rural people. The automobile has played an important role in the rural areas. It has ended the secluded life of the ruralites. People prefer to reside near the highways now. Villages in a way are closely linked with the cities. Buses, trains, taxies and motor cycles, etc., have helped the city people to go out and stay in the fringes of the city.

Everywhere big cities are characterised by sub-centres or sub-urban areas. In structure and function they are like cities. Too much concentration in the city contributes to an opposite process of decentralisation. The sub-centres or sub-urban areas resemble the city in several respects. A single city may have a number of small *sub-urban* areas. These sub-urban areas may retain in them some of the features of the city. They are like *satellite cities* built around a major city. *Sub-urban areas represent the rough amalgam of rural and urban ways of living.* Here, we may find the urban way of life being mixed with the rural way of life. In these areas we find the *"rural-urban convergence."*

The Rural-Urban Continuum

Some sociologists have used the concept of *"rural-urban continuum"* to stress the idea that there are no sharp breaking points to be found in the degree or quantity of rural urban differences. The impact of urban life over rural life is evident in many ways. With regard to birth rate, age at marriage, infant mortality, church affiliation, divorce, suicide, etc., rural indices are moving nearer to urban indices. In this way, rural areas can become highly urbanised.

As the contacts of the city become closer, as transportation and communication become more rapid, the rural community tends to assume more closely the urban social structure. We may even speak of different degrees of *"urbanness"* or *"ruralness."* One country can be demographically more urban and yet socially more rural than another. ***Example*** : Chile has a greater percentage of its population living in cities than does Canada, but its people, by almost all sets of indices, are less urban.

Urban Influence on the Rural Community

In the recent years it has been evident everywhere that the city is growing in population at the expense of the village. It has also been observed that urban culture is spreading to the rural areas. As Davis says that *"The city effects are wider than the city itself."* McKenzie has proved conclusively that *"the influence of a city varies with its size and that it tends to wane with distance outward."* The growing transport and communications, the increased urban newspaper circulation in rural areas, advancement in science and technology, etc., have gone a long way in diffusing a wide variety of urban attitudes, ideas and habits from the city to the village.

The rural - urban interaction is very widely recognised today. In fact, it is an important aspect of urbanisation. It is quite understandable that urbanisation and urban growth do have their impact on the rural areas and activities. Similarly, rural areas do have their effect on the nearby towns and cities. A few studies have been made on this rural - urban interaction. These studies have highlighted three important aspects:

(i) *Urbanisation has impact on the economy of the surrounding villages. Ex.* There is an increase in farm productivity due to the availability and utilisation of fertilisers, better seeds, pesticides, modern agricultural implements, tillers, tractors, and so on. These things could be purchased from the nearby towns.

(ii) *Level and pattern of migration has been affected.* There has been a continuous migration of the people from rural to the urban areas.

(iii) *Villagers have imbibed several urban characteristics.* City culture is spreading to the villages. People in the villages look to urban models in various fields.

1. Extension of Urban Facilities to the Rural Areas

Some of the *facilities and the comforts* of the city like electricity, radio, newspapers, hotels, libraries, post offices, schools and even colleges, games and sports facilities and various electrical appliances are now diffused to the rural areas. The newspapers carry the stories and editorial comments about politics, sports, prominent persons and a host of ideas about religious, civic, economic, artistic and other interests and events. As readers of these newspapers the people in the rural area share these interests.

2. Urban Impact on the Rural Family

Urbanism or the urban way of life, has affected the size and character of the rural family. The *size of the family* in the village is decreasing. Joint families are slowly disappearing. The family is losing its control over its members. The younger generation wants to enjoy more freedom like its counterpart in the city.

3. Extension of Modern Means of Transport and Communication Facilities

The *modern means of transport and communications* are introduced in many villages. Cycles, scooters, motor cycles, taxis, are also found in many villages which are equipped with post and telegraph. Radios and transistors are commonly found in villages. Many villages have even phone connections. Further, rural occupations and agricultural operations are slowly being *mechanised.* The blacksmiths, goldsmiths, silversmiths, coppersmiths, barbers, carpenters and others are now using modern tools in their work. The city as a market for rural products, and as a centre of trade and financial control over the rural regions, provides for the increasing dominance over the village.

4. City Affecting the Character of Rural Recreation

The *mode of rural recreation* has changed due to the urban influence. Radios and gramophones and tape recorders have changed the tastes of rural people. Football, volleyball, cards, chess and such other plays also becoming popular. The cricket is equally interesting for the rural youth. The fashions of the ruralites have changed.

5. Urban Community Serving as a *"Reference Group"* for the Village

City normally serves as a model for the villages. Changes are quick to take place in the cities. Villagers, particularly the rural youths are always looking to the city for novelty. The rural youth are slowly becoming *career conscious.* Education is becoming popular among them. The rural people take interest in political and cultural activities. They look to the city for guidance and imitation.

6. Migration of Ruralites Towards the Cities

Throughout the world the cities are proving to be the centres of multifarious activities. Hence the tendency of the rural people to move towards cities. The *"push"* [mostly economic pressures] factors and the *"pull"* [the attractions of the city] factors have made the rural people to rush to the cities. This has resulted in *urban concentration* and *rural depopulation* in many places. The city has continued to absorb the people from the hinterland. The process will be faster, the more the city is linked with its rural hinterland.

7. Ugly Impact of the City on the Village Life

The *rural people have also acquired some of the evil habits of the people of the cities.* Drunkenness, gambling, prostitution, smoking, crimes, etc. have made inroads into the villages. Morality has fallen, costly fashions and expensive habits are acquired. Life in the country is slowly becoming more and more individualistic, materialistic, rationalistic, commercial and calculative.

8. Interdependence of Urban and Rural Communities

In spite of the rural - urban contrast, there is an inevitable interdependence of rural and urban communities. The ruralites are dependent on the urbanites for their banking and credit needs, for the purchase of agricultural equipments and other supplies, for marketing of farm products, and even for commercial recreation. In the very same manner, urban communities are also dependent on the rural sector for their food supply, for cheap labour, and for vast market of their manufactured goods. Further, urban professionals like advocates, doctors, mechanics, repairers, electricians and others, draw a large number of their clients, patients, customers from the rural masses. A good harvest in the village side leads to an increase in marketing activities whereas a bad harvest leads to a dull and discouraging market.

9. Dominance of the City Continues Unabated

It is true that the city continues to dominate the country. Even with respect to birth rate, death rate, age at marriage, infant mortality, divorce, suicide, church affiliation, etc., rural indices are moving nearer to urban indices. The dominance of the city over the country is regarded by some sociologists as a dangerous trend. Oswald Spengler in his *"Decline of the West"* points out that *"the city destroys the solidarity of the kin, the family, the "blood", the nation and with its competitive stress fosters the disintegrating attitudes of individualism, socialism, rationalism and cosmopolitanism."* However, sociologists like MacIver, are of the opinion that there is no need to be pessimistic about the city as such. Man is gradually making the urban environment more suited to his needs. In spite of the widespread urbanisation, more than two-third of the population of the world is rural in character.

Cleavages and Conflicts Between Rural and Urban Sectors ?

The above description makes it evident that there exists co-operative relationship and functional interdependence between rural and urban communities. However, possibilities of rural - urban conflicts cannot be ruled out. Such conflicts often do erupt open violence. Nagpaul in his study identified three factors which promote cleavages and conflicts among the rural people for the urban people. They are – (i) *contrasting environmental subcultures,* (ii) *modernisation,* and (iii) *urban bias.*[1]

(i) *Contrasting Environmental Subcultures* : Rural and urban environments are not the same. If the former is more natural the latter is more artificial. Rural work is mostly decided by seasons and weather factors, and most of it is done outside the dwelling place. On the contrary, urban work is carried on under predictable conditions mostly within the building structures. Though rural people are bigger in number they are not able to dominate or boss over the urban people. In economic matters, in political issues, in educational fields, in employment sectors and in various other areas, urban people ride over the rural people and their views and opinions are simply brushed aside. This has created a kind of ill will towards the city, city life and city dwellers.

(ii) *Modernisation* : Modernisation is said to be another major factor that fosters conflict. Four important consequences of modernisation programmes undertaken by the government for the benefit of the rural people have been – "(a) *increasing pace of urbanisation and concentration of power in the urban sector,* (b) *political democratisation,* (c) *weakening of traditional institutional structure based upon caste and religion,* and (d) *wide spread emergence of revolution of rising expectations.*" [Nagpaul. Page : 160 - 161].

Modernisation has made rural people to move toward the cities in a large number particularly draining off young males from the rural sector. Rural people feel jealous of the material comforts enjoyed by the city people. Increasing contacts between city and village promote more and more cleavages and conflicts between the villagers and the city dwellers. Political democratisation has brought new tensions and anxieties. Increasing involvement of women in the newly introduced democratic processes has produced some conflicts and strains. The introduction of modernisation programmes has weakened traditional institutions such as caste, family, religion, etc. Agitations and movements which were unheard of in the past have become almost common today in the rural areas.

(iii) *Urban Bias* : Urban bias also acts as a source of conflict between rural urban sectors though the government has been giving much importance to rural development, rural reconstruction and poverty alleviation programmes. In actuality, very less has been done to improve the lot of the rural people. Rural people very strongly feel that rural income and funds are diverted toward the cities to develop urban infrastructure of education, health, housing, road, transport, communication, sanitation, etc. Partial attitude of political leaders and bureaucrats towards the cities and city dwellers has been very much criticised by the rural people.

---

1 Nagpaul [1996] : 158 - 160 as quoted by Prof. Ram Ahuja in *"Society in India"* [1999]. Page 348

However, scholars like B.R. Chauhan, N.R. Seth, and others have highlighted the intimate relationship between urban and the rural sectors. Conflicts and cleavages between the sectors should not be exaggerated to the extent of undermining the co-operation between the two. *"A town and a city, by and large, act as service centres for their surrounding village communities. L.K. Sen [1971] has shown that like a town and a city, a large village also performs central-place functions for the city as well as surrounding smaller villages."*

Problems of Urban Society or Urbanisation

The process of urbanisation has been taking place continuously in India. Migration of rural people towards the cities continues unabated. Once the rural people move towards the cities either in search of job or better prospects, they rarely go back to the villages. They become permanent residents of the city. Thus, urban concentration is taking place consistently. This uncontrolled and limitless concentration of people in the city areas has led to several problems. Some of them are : *problem of overcrowdedness, problem of urban housing, problem of drinking water, problem of drainage, transport and traffic problem, problem of power shortage, problem of environment pollution, problem of slums, and problem of social evils such as drug addiction, alcoholism, crime, juvenile delinquency, gambling, commercialised recreation, beggary, and so on.* Let us now analyse in brief the gravity of some of these problems of urban society.

1. Problem of Overcrowdedness

Heavy concentration of people in a limited place has led to the problem of overcrowdedness. Due to the attractions of city life [*pull factors*] men have started flocking towards the cities. Lack of educational job and other opportunities in the rural areas [*push factors*] also forced people to desert villages and start moving towards the cities. This has led to urban concentration which has added to overcrowdedness in the city. People are forced to live in large number in small residential houses. Some houses are so overcrowded that 5 to 6 persons live in one single room. Urban neighbourhoods are also heavily crowded.

Overcrowding has its own adverse effects. It damages privacy, disturbs intimacy, spoils mental peace and health and encourages deviance. It also leads to the spread of diseases and creation of conditions that are favourable for developing bad habits such as drinking and drug addiction.

2. Problem of Urban Housing

Growth of population in cities is so fast that it has become impossible to provide adequate residential accommodation to all. Hence housing problem or what is known as *"houselessness"* has become one of the serious problems of the city. The pressure on space in cities is so tremendous that large number of people are forced to live on roads, bus stands, railway stations, slums, and in poorly equipped houses. It is said that around half of the city population are either ill-housed or pay more than 20% of their income on rent. According to 1991 census report, around 27.4% of the city houses are *kachcha* houses, 30.9% of the houses are *semi-pakka* houses and only 41.7% of the houses are *pakka* houses. According to one estimate [as reported in *The Hindustan Times* dated 9-5-1988], around 50% to 75% of the people living in urban areas are either residing in temporary houses or slums. The rate of overcrowding is so high that in a city like Delhi, the population has increased from 2 millions in 1957 to 9 million in 1990. Hence, every year Delhi is forced to provide accommodation for 60,000 people. According to paper reports, more than 70% of the people in Delhi are not residing in "safe houses."

Mega cities like Mumbai, Kolkota, Delhi and Chennai are suffering from acute housing problem. In a heavily concentrated city of Mumbai more than 77% of the houses are found to be single room houses wherein on an average more than 5.3 persons are living. A survey conducted in 53 cities in addition to the four mega cities revealed that more than 44% of the people are living in single-room houses in the urban areas.

Not only good houses are not available for living but also exorbitant rent is charged. Housing boards such as the *HUDCO, the Housing Development Finance Corporation Ltd. [HDFC], the Apex Housing Financing Co-operative Societies, the State Housing Boards,* and various co-operative housing boards and nationalised banks are helping people to go for their own independent houses, the problem of housing is not solved yet.

3. Problem of Slums

Increasing industrialisation and urbanisation have created slums in the city. Slums consist of substandard, ill-ventilated, insanitary and poorly lighted houses. They consist of houses which are unfit for human habitation. Slum dwellers live in horrible areas. Their living conditions are really horrible. The low-paid workers normally live in these slum areas. The facilities that are generally found in the cities are not found in these slums. The *Ahatas* of Kanpur, *Bastis* of Delhi, *Chawls* of Mumbai, *Cheries* of Chennai, and *Kolegeri* of Bangalore are stigmas on the face of India. According to **Dr. Radhakamal Mukherji**, *"In the thousand slums of India's industrial centres manhood is unquestionably brutalised, women dishonoured and childhood is poisoned at its very source."* **Pandit Nehru** was so moved emotionally on seeing slums that he wanted them to be burnt down and the persons responsible for them to be hanged.

Slums are a black spots on our cities. Their number and the number of people living in them are cosistently increasing. According to 1991 report, the country's slum population stood at nearly 40 million. Slum dwellers form 44% of the population in Delhi, 45% in Mumbai, 42% in Kolkota and 39% in Chennai. All the major cities such as Bangalore, Hyderabad, Ahmedabad, Pune, Nagpur, Kanpur, Lucknow, Jaipur are faced with the problem of slums. Slums which are often called *"living dustbins"* have also become centres of filth, immorality, alcoholism, gambling, crime, beggary, prostitution, juvenile delinquency and so on. They have also become the breeding centres of various diseases such as cholera, T.B., typhoid, AIDS, venereal diseases, etc.

4. Problem of Drinking Water

Water is an essential requirement for living beings. But it has become a scarcity in various cities. In the whole nation there is no big city in which water supply is assured all the 24 hours a day. Cities like Chennai, Hyderabad, Rajkot, Ajmer and Udaipur get water from municipal sources for less than an hour a day. Most towns and cities which normally get good rain every year, have been undergoing the agony of acute water shortage in the last 90 years. Unfortunately, we do not have a well planned and an efficiently workable national water policy. States like Tamil Nadu and Karnataka, for example, clash between themselves almost every year on the water issue. It has been estimated that atleast 30% of the people living in cities are consuming *"unsafe"* water. However, the 1991 census report says that only 18.59% of the people living in cities are not supplied with "safe" drinking water.

5. Problem of Drainage

Water problem is closely associated with the drainage problem. Continuous water supply is necessary to maintain cleanliness. Continuous flow of water in the drainage pipes helps the maintenance of drainage system. But in the Indian context, shortage of water supply has added to the drainage problem. Efficient sewage or drainage system is essential for the maintenance of cleanliness in any city. But unfortunately, drainage system is deplorably bad in India. There is not a single city in India which is completely sewered. Even the so called planned city of Chandigarh is not an exception to this. Due to the inefficient or non-existent drainage system, stink water gets collected everywhere, spoiling cleanliness and spreading diseases. In fact, we need to have a national and also a provincial drainage policy.

6. Problem of Transportation and Traffic System

Continuous increase in population in cities puts heavy pressure on a good transportation and traffic system. Such a system is very unsatisfactory in the Indian cities. Vast majority of people use buses, mini buses, tempos, while a few use train as transit system. Large number of middle class people and a few upper class people use scooters, motor cycles, mopeds, cars, vans, jeeps, which make the traffic system very worse. ***For example,*** in Mumbai automobiles have trebled [from 3.1 lakh to 8.73 lakh] between 1986 and 1996 [*The Hindustan Times,* 29-11-1996]. These vehicles also add to pollution. In Mumbai alone daily pollutants let out into the air are about 3,000 tonnes, of which 52% come from automobiles, 2% from domestic fuels, and the remaining 46% from industries.

City bus services, metro train service and other private service systems are also not able to meet the transportation requirement of the people. Hence, even in vehicles we find heavy load and overcrowdedness. Road accidents are also found to be very high in the Indian cities. In addition to the regular residents of the city, people who shuttle between cities and their nearby native places also add to the overcrowdedness in the city traffic. It is also observed that most of the vehicles that are being used for meeting the city traffic requirements are found to be very old and hence they also add to the pollution problem.

Table - 4

Households Having Drinking Water, Electricity and Toilet Facility (Percentage)

	1991*	1981*
Households with Safe Drinking Water	62.72	37.91
Rural	55.92	26.34
Urban	81.59	74.13
Households with Electricity	42.98	25.74
Rural	31.10	14.29
Urban	75.93	61.60
Households with Toilet Facility	23.55	*n.a.*
Rural	8.84	*n.a.*
Urban	63.58	57.44

* Excluding Jammu & Kashmir in 1991 & Assam in 1981.

Source : Statistical Outline of India - 1995-96. ***Pub.*** : Tata Services Ltd., Department of Economics and Statistics.

7. Problem of Power Shortage

Power shortage is becoming a major crisis in the urban areas today. Use of electricity and electrical gadgets has become a part and parcel of city life. Hence, city people want 24 hours power supply. Even after 55 years of independence we have not been able to provide adequate power supply to the people though they are ready to pay the charges for the same. Slums and poor people's houses are not completely connected with electricity. According to 1991 census report, only 75.93% of urban houses are supplied with electricity. [See ***Table*** 4]. The demand for electricity is consistently increasing in spite of the attempts that are being made to supply power. ***For example,*** the difference that was there between electricity supply and demand increased from 6.1% in 1993-94 to 13% in 1994-95. It means the demand for electricity is increasing at a greater speed than the attempts at supplying it.

8. Problem of Environmental Pollution

The city atmosphere is highly polluting. As **Margaret Mead** pointed out long back, environment pollution is the worst problem which the modern industrial and city-centred civilisation has created. This is often highlighted as a *"rape on environment."* Most of the Indian cities have become the victims of environment pollution. The cities themselves are polluting the environment. Several cities discharge 40 - 60% of their entire sewage and industrial effluents untreated into the nearby rivers. These rivers get polluted. Urban industry pollutes the atmosphere with smoke and toxic gases from its chimneys. The city of Delhi is branded as the 4th most polluted city in the world. The vehicular emissions in Delhi account for 64% of Delhi's air pollution load, power plants are responsible for 16% and industries account for 12%. The poison we put in to the environment [by way of carbon monoxide, smoke, garbage, solid wastes, etc.] comes right back to us through our air, water and food, slowly seeping into our bodies and showing up as cancer, immune disorders or as hormonal system disorders. Doctors are of the opinion that the chances of getting caught by cancer by the residents of the cities of Delhi, Mumbai, Bangalore and Chennai are as high as 7 - 11% during a life time. More than the rich the poor people always suffer most from the polluted atmosphere of the city.

9. Other Social Problems

Problem of Privacy : Lack of privacy and intimacy are the natural outcome of the city life. Due to the indirect and impersonal relationships, closeness and intimacy will not develop. Life becomes mechanical, competitive and charmless.

Problem of Individuation : The urban community encourages *individuation.* Individuals are moved by their own aspirations, ambitions, aims, and interest. They have become more and more *career-conscious.* They are invariably caught in the competitive race for a successful career. The competitiveness of the city, places one over against everyone else. The materialistic outlook that a city-dweller develops may often result in what is known as the *"loss of community."* An individual may become *"alienated"* from his own community, his own people, his own profession. This state, when it reaches the extreme, may drive a depressed and an *"alienated"* man to commit suicide.

Problem of Vices : The city is a centre of economic insecurity, mental illness, gambling, prostitution, drunkenness, crimes, juvenile delinquency, alcoholism, environment pollution and such other vices. There is poverty in the midst of plenty. The city life endangers the physical, mental and moral health of the people.

Adverse Effects on the Rural Areas : Cities often provide a wrong model to the villages. Villagers who are in touch with the cities get influenced by the hedonism, individuation, self-centredness and such other ugly aspects of the city life. The tendency of the rural people to move towards the cities often leads to rural depopulation. Western countries are faced with such a situation. Further, the rivers that pass through the industrial cities often spread diseases in the rural areas also for the river water contains lot of industrial wastes and effluents which are poisonous in nature.

Heavy Pressure on Municipal Administration : Most of the Indian towns and cities are heavily crowded. Hence, it has become a big challenge for the city municipal administration to provide the basic civic facilities to all the urban residents. City budget is not sufficient to meet with such requirements. Hence, most of the cities are known for ill-administration.

Encouragement to Beggary : It is a known fact that the city atmosphere is conducive for begging. We find a large number of beggars in cities rather than in village areas. It is easier for the lazy people, unemployed persons, work-evaders and public cheats to eke out their livelihood by means of begging. City environment also tempts social parasites and public cheats to plan what is known as *"organised beggary."*

It is clear from the above, that Indian cities are suffering from various problems. Though cities have their own positive aspects they have their ugly side also. Life is not a bed of roses in a city. It poses problems, challenges, breeds diseases, encourages ill-will in spite of all the attractions that it has at its command. The quicker these problems are solved the better it will be for the cities and for the city dwellers.

Some Suggestions to Face and to Solve Urban Problems

There is no city in the world which is free from problems. Indian cities are not an exception. It does not mean that these problems are beyond solutions. Efficient urban planning and effective implementation of the same can bring about positive results. A few suggestions to face and to solve the urban problems can be mentioned here :

1. *Efficient and Integral City Planning* : Lack of proper planning is one of the major causes of urban problems. Hence, city administration has to take sufficient care in making a comprehensive planning for the improvement of the city. The city planners must have far-sightedness and must take into account the probable growth of the city in atleast another 50 years. There should be co-ordination among the city administration, the state administration and also the central administration. While drafting a plan for the improvement of the city, advices and suggestions of the experts must be sought. It is equally important to make use of the latest technological know how in preparing the plan for the future. Political interference should not be there in the implementation of the plan.

2. *City Administration to Become Financially Independent* : It is essential that the municipal administration must have sufficient financial resources to undertake developmental programmes for the benefit of the city dwellers. City administration cannot always depend upon the state and the centre for finance. It has to find its own financial resources to meet its requirements. By revising property, water and electricity taxes money can be collected and more money per head per annum can be made available for providing necessary facilities. City administration is to be toned up and bureaucrats must be made to commit themselves to the service of the people.

3. *Creation of More Job Opportunities* : We have been concentrating on the rural areas to provide more job opportunities for rural people through IRDP, NREP, JRY and such other programmes to hold back people in rural areas. It is time now to do something for creating better job opportunities for the urban people. This will not only help jobless urbanites but also add to the urban income. By spreading out various economic activities and by increasing income in the city it is possible to pay more attention to the requirements of the people.

4. *Providing Better Transportation Facility* : Most of the cosmopolitan cities of India are overcrowded and are not able to provide the necessary transportation facility to the people. Hence, it is necessary to make proper arrangements to face this problem. Private transport system can be encouraged along with the existing public transportation system. Healthy competition between the two systems can help solve the problem to a great extent.

5. *Adopting an Efficient and a Workable Housing Policy* : People who migrate to the city face the housing problem. Existing residents of the cities are also not having satisfactory housing accommodation. Hence, city administration must make it a policy to encourage housing industry. It can give encouragement to the private builders, relax the rigid rules for the construction of houses

and the private, public and the co-operative housing boards may be given all the necessary help to construct as many houses as possible. Employees, government servants and private individuals who want to construct houses for self-occupation must be helped in getting loans from the nationalised banks, housing boards, co-operative societies, etc. The National Housing Policy which the central government presented in 1988 to the Parliament should be made more workable. The existing Rent Control Act must be amended so as to give courage to the owners of houses to give houses on reasonable rent to the needy people.

6. *Environment Pollution to be Checked* : Environment pollution is becoming a major problem in the mega cities. Sufficient care is to be taken to control this pollution. New industries should not be given permission to start their establishments near the residential areas. On the other hand, industries should be established far away from the cities. Scientific arrangement is to be made to dispose of the solid waste including the garbage . People should be educated properly in order to maintain cleanliness in the city. Voluntary organisations and the media can play a vital role in this regard.

To conclude, it may be said that urbanisation wherever it takes place, is bound to create socio-economic problems. These problems are to be countered in a planned and in a scientific manner though they cannot be completely solved. However, we can keep them under control and find effective solutions for some of them. City administration or government alone cannot do that. City dwellers themselves should take an active role and must be prepared to co-operate with the administration in the removal of these problems.

Chapter 16

ENVIRONMENT POLLUTION

Meaning of Environment and Environment Pollution - Environment Management - Causes of Pollution - Different Types of Environment Pollution - Air Pollution, Water Pollution, Sound [Noise] Pollution, Soil [Land] Pollution and Solid Wastes Pollution, Nuclear Radioactive Pollution and Their Adverse Effects - Prevention of Environmental Pollution : Some Suggestions - Environment Movements in India.

"Environment Pollution" has become today one of the biggest menaces of the modern civilised world. Due to ever increasing human population the pressure on the environment is continuously mounting. The developed countries are engaged in abusing the limited natural resources for their pomp, splendours and luxury, while the underdeveloped countries are tapping these resources for their existence and to achieve some development. In both the cases the natural environment is the target of attack. Preserving the natural resources for the future generations has become a big challenge.

Our vital and fragile eco-system is today increasingly threatened by commercial exploitation, growing population demands and industrial pollution. Our mother Earth's rivers and oceans, forests and plain lands, grasslands and wet lands are fighting for survival. Great efforts are necessary to protect the natural environment threatened by over-population and misguided technology. Though the problem of pollution is as old as Industrial revolution, it has attained new proportions today.

Pollution has invaded all the three states of matter we are familiar with - *solid, liquid* and *gas.* Nay, there are new forms of pollution also. There is *"noise pollution"* and *"nuclear pollution."* Pollution is causing a great danger to human existence. Not only human beings but even plants, trees and animals are affected by pollution. Petrol or diesel fumes from lorries, buses and cars contain certain chemicals which on coming in contact with sunlight, are transformed into poisonous substances. These poisonous substances can affect sensitive plants like tobacco, tomato and potato, some varieties of beans and spinach, some cereal crops and certain flowers. Smoke from factories manufacturing plastic produce chemicals which injure cotton and rose plants. Factories processing metal ore produce silver dioxide which has destroyed tens of thousands of hectares of timber plantations.

The problem of pollution is spreading its tentacles in different fields. The *land* in which we live, the *air* that we inhale, the *water* we drink and the *sound* that we hear – are all polluted. Economists, sociologists and presently the environmental scientists and administrators are very much worried about this menace and are seeking to find a solution for the same.

The key to man's ill-health lies largely in his environment. In fact, much of man's ill-health can be traced to adverse environmental factors such as water pollution, soil pollution, air pollution, poor housing conditions, presence of animal reservoirs and insect vectors of diseases which pose a constant threat to man's health. Often man is responsible for the pollution of his environment through urbanization, industrialization and other human activities. In 1972, the *UN Conference on the Human Environment* focussed world-wide attention on the environmental hazards that threaten human beings. To facilitate work in this area, the *World Health Organisation* [WHO] has compiled a wide-ranging survey of environmental hazards to human health.

In the past, sanitation was centred on the sanitary disposal of human excreta. Even now, to many people "sanitation" still means the construction of latrines. In actual fact, the term sanitation covers the whole field of controlling the environment with a view to prevent disease and promote health. Man has already controlled a number of factors in his environment, ***e.g.,*** food, water, housing, clothing, sanitation. These controllable factors are those included in the *"standard or living."* It is the control of these factors that has been responsible for considerable improvement in the health of the people during the past century in the developed countries. As old problems are being solved, new problems are arising. Air pollution is of growing concern in many urban centres. Industrial growth has given rise to the problem of environmental pollution by industrial wastes. Advances in nuclear technology have produced the problem of radio-active pollution of the environment. The demographic growth and fast urbanisation all over the world are bringing profound social and environmental changes. Therefore, the attainment of a healthy environment is becoming more and more complex. The term *environmental sanitation* is now being replaced by *environmental health.* Proper environmental health now requires the services of the public health qualified doctor, the epidemiologist, the public health engineer, the town planner, the sociologist, the economist, and the health inspector. A purely medical or engineering approach by itself is no longer sufficient; a combined multi-disciplinary programme of action is needed to achieve a healthy environment.

MEANING OF "ENVIRONMENT" AND "ENVIRONMENT POLLUTION"

Meaning of Environment

The term ***environment*** implies *all the external factors – living and non-living, material and non-material – which surround man.* In its modern concept, environment includes not only the water, air and soil that form our environment but also the social and economic conditions under which we live.

The term ***"environment"*** etymologically means *"surroundings"* which comprise of air, water and land. Environment creates favourable conditions for the existence and development of living organisms. The term environment can be defined in various ways. For example –

1. *The term environment refers to anything that immediately surrounds an object and exerts a direct influence on it.*
2. *Environment is the sum of all social, economic, biological, physical or chemical factors which constitute the surroundings of man, who is both creator and moulder of his environment.*
3. **C.C. Park** defines the term in the following way : *"Environment refers to the sum total of conditions which surround man at a given point in space and time."*

For descriptive purpose, environment has been divided into three components, all closely related :

(i) ***Physical*** **:** Water, air, soil, housing, wastes, radiation, etc.
(ii) ***Biologic*** **:** Plant and animal life including bacteria.
(iii) ***Social*** **:** Customs, culture, habits, income, occupation, religion, etc.

Environment Management

Environmentalism is a fairly new movement in the world in the recent years. It is getting a top priority in the national policies among the developed and developing countries. The environmental experts, during project planning give due consideration to social, cultural and environmental impacts. It is in this context, the Govt. of India, in the Sixth Five-Year Plan [1980-85] had formed the following policy : – *"It is imperative that we use our renewable resources of water, soil, and vegetation to sustain our economic development. Over exploitation of these is visible in soil erosion, floods, deforestation, siltation, floral and wild-life resources. The depletion of these resources tends to be irreversible and since the whole population depends on these natural resources to meet their basic needs i.e., fuel, fodder and land, it has meant a deterioration in their standard of life."*

Objectives of *"Environment Management"*

Environment management has become an important aspect of the modern economic planning. It has got its own aims and objectives. The main objectives of environment management are stated here.

1. Maintenance of environmental quality.
2. Balancing the ecosystem.
3. Restrict and regulate the exploitation of natural resources.
4. To protect the environment from degradation.
5. To renew natural resources and reduce natural disasters.
6. To adopt engineered technology without creating adverse effects on the environment.
7. To formulate laws and regulations to control pollution.

Meaning of *"Environment Pollution"*

The environment we live in is a complex and dynamic one in which all forms of life are interdependent on each other. But in his quest to improve the quality of his life man has changed this balance in nature by adding some of the essential components. This very human act of spoiling or contaminating the environment and disturbing the ecological balance can be called *"environment pollution."* The concept can be better be defined in the following ways.

1. *Contamination of the environment by the addition of undesirable substances produced by human activities which cause damage to the living organisms is called "environment pollution."*

The undesirable substance that is added is called *"pollutant." **Ex.*** Carbon monoxide is an air pollutant, sewage is a water pollutant.

1. *Pollution is the contamination, unfavourable alteration or desecration of any part of the environment by products produced by human activities.*
2. *Pollution is an undesirable change in the physical, chemical or biological characteristics of air, water and land that may harmfully affect living organisms, industrial processes or raw materials.*
3. *"Pollution is the release of harmful substances or energy into the environment by man in quantities that damage health and resources"* **[Edwards** - 1972].
4. Pollution is viewed as – *"the release of substances and energy as waste products of harmful activities which result in harmful changes within the natural environment"* **[National Environmental Research Council,** 1976].

CAUSES OF ENVIRONMENT POLLUTION

Pollution of the environment is one of the most horrible ecological crises to which we are subjected today. We know that three basic amenities for living organisms are ***air, land*** or ***soil*** and ***water.*** The earth is the only object known in the entire universe capable of supporting life. The amenities of life such as air, land and water are found in our mother earth. Unfortunately, all these amenities are polluted and this pollution has posed a very serious threat. Pollution is caused by so many factors among which the following may be noted.

1. According to **Write** [1970], *human greed and ignorance* have allowed our culture to develop an ecological crisis like pollution.

2. According to **Southwick** [1976], *human population explosion is the main cause of pollution.* He pointed out that with more people there is more sewage, more solid wastes, more fuel being burnt, more fertilisers and insecticides being used to produce more food for hungry mouths.

3. The root cause of environmental pollution has been *man's misbehaviour with the nature under the false ego that he is the master of the nature.* This undesirable situation created by man has threatened the survival of man himself and other living beings on the earth.

4. Modern ecologists have pointed out some important factors of environmental pollution. They can be stated here. Factors such as – *human population explosion, rapid industrialisation, deforestation, unplanned urbanisation, scientific and technological advancement, etc.* are mainly responsible for the pollution crisis on earth.

Industrialisation is the Greatest Menace of Pollution. Man is forced to set up more factories to provide the clothes we wear. We have to use more insecticides and fertilizers, and to make a large number of tractors to cultivate the land to supply food for ever increasing number of people. Hence more factories are built and more oil and coal are burnt. Burning of both adds to pollution.

Coal is called the *"Black Diamond"* and oil *"Liquid Gold"* since both are valuable fuels in producing energy that is required to run factories. *"Unfortunately, these valuable fuels are among the world offenders in the pollution of air. Over the past 50 years nearly **half** the known reserves of coal and oil in the world have been burnt. Industrialisation is taking place so rapidly that it won't be surprising if the **remaining half** is exhausted within the next twenty-five years."*[1] One can imagine how much more pollution will be caused by that time.

5. *Industrialised countries are mainly responsible for the environmental pollution.* For example, the United States with its vast infrastructure of industries is one of the leading polluters of the world. The worst pollution occurs in countries where there have been the greatest scientific, technological and industrial advances. Developing countries such as India, Thailand, Philippines and others have been caught in the spiral of industrial growth. But they are not aware of the dangerous consequences of pollution. ***For example,*** pollution in the textile city of Kanpur in Uttar Pradesh is six times more than that of the famous cotton city of Manchester in England in the latter half of the nineteenth century. In Kanpur, the factories alone contribute as much pollution as that from all the inhabitants. Bombay is another case in point. Within the next twenty years, the number of factories in and around Bombay will have increased threefold. But even today more than 1,000 tonnes of poisonous chemicals, soot and dirt are emitted into the atmosphere over Bombay.

6. *Thoughtless burning of agricultural wastes and destruction of forests can cause pollution.* Rich industrialised countries are not the only culprits in causing pollution. Recent investigations indicate that tropical grassland fires and the burning of agricultural wastes contribute almost as much pollution as do factories all over the world. There are 2,000 million hectares of burnable land in the world in the form of cultivated land, permanent meadows and pastures. These areas are often

1 **N. Sheshagiri** *"Pollution."* Page - 24.

subjected to seasonal burning. It is estimated that more than 6,000 million tonnes of agricultural wastes and other vegetation are burnt every year, and dust and soot is being continuously injected into the atmosphere. [**N. Sheshagiri.** Page - 39].

6. *Rapid population growth combined with modern technology has caused a serious environmental crisis.* This is because of the fact that in well developed countries, citizens consume more food, use more fertilisers and pesticides, fuel, minerals, automobiles [cars, scooters, vans, trucks, etc.] and other manufactured products of all kinds. Almost all of these products are manufactured in one or the other kinds of the industries. These industries are responsible for adding pollutants to our environment [land, soil, water and air] and hence cause pollution.

7. The environmental pollution seems to be the necessary evil of all man-made progress. It is not only the industrialised countries which are threatened with the environmental pollution, *but the developed countries are also contributing to it and at the same time struggling to face it.* The developed countries dump lot of affluents into the environment polluting the whole globe. The newly developing countries are also adding to it. For example, New York in U.S.A. is the most polluted city of the world and New Delhi is the fourth most polluted city. India occupies **7th** place among the industrialised developing countries of the world. Hence its contribution to environmental pollution is not insignificant.

TYPES OF ENVIRONMENT POLLUTION

The environment in which we are living is being polluted in various ways. Many a times man himself is responsible for this pollution and consequently suffer from his own misdeeds. Environment pollution assumes different forms : *air pollution, water pollution, sound pollution, land pollution and pollution by radioactivity.*

1. AIR POLLUTION

The phenomenon called *"pollution"* is an inescapable consequence of the presence of man and his activities. The term *"air pollution"* signifies the presence in the surrounding atmosphere of substances [*e.g.,* gases, mixtures of gases and particulated matter] generated by the activities of man that interfere with human health, safety and comfort. The direct effect of air pollutants on plants, animals and soil can influence the structure and function of ecosystems, including self regulation ability, thereby affecting the quality of life. In the past, air pollution meant smoke pollution. Today, air pollution has become more subtle and recognizes no geographical or political boundaries. Air pollution is one of the present day health problems throughout the world.

Air is a mixture of gases existing as a thin layer around the earth. ***Air or atmospheric pollution*** refers to *the contamination of the air by the addition of unwanted solid wastes or gases produced by human activities. Air is polluted when it is contaminated by poisonous gas, smoke, fly ash, fuel, malign water, etc. given out by the factories, automobiles, etc.*

"Excessive release of air pollutants in the atmosphere by anthropogenic activities disturb the dynamic equilibrium in the atmosphere and thereby affect man and his environment."[1]

The **World Health Organisation** [WHO] has defined air pollutants[2] as *"substances put into air by the activity of mankind in concentration sufficient to cause harmful effect to his health, vegetables, property or to interfere with the enjoyment of his property."* Air pollution may consist

1 **S.S. Dara** *"A Text Book of Environmental Chemistry and Pollution Control"* [1998]. *Pub.* S. Chand & Co. Ltd., New Delhi. Page - 23.

2 **Pollutants :** Pollutants are by-products or waste products, which when released into the environment cause pollution.

of (i) Smoke and fog, together called *Smog,* and (ii) the second category that consists of *dust, fumes, gases,* etc.

A large portion of the pollutants released into the air come from the exhaust pipes of automobiles. The major chemical component of this exhaust is carbon monoxide, known to be highly toxic. Also found in exhaust fumes are nitrogen oxides, which give the air a brown tinge. Gasoline also contributes to the level of lead found in the air.

Air pollution is caused mainly by smoke from automobile exhaust and gases released by industrial plants. The most important air pollutants are gases like carbon monoxide, carbon dioxide, sulphur dioxide, oxides of nitrogen, hydrogen sulphide and particulates like dust, smoke and lead particles.

Air pollution is the greatest threat to our health in the future. Factories with chimneys throwing out smoke into the air are not the only sources of this air pollution; a major offender is the automobile - cars, vans, lorries, and buses. The smoke belching from the exhausts of lorries and buses is a familiar sight everywhere in big cities. For example, the big five cities - Mumbai, Kolkota, Delhi, Chennai and Bangalore - spew daily into the air we breathe more than *one crore* kilograms of smoke.[1] Residents of the heavily industrialised and thickly populated city of Mumbai are hard hit by air pollution. It is said that every moment Mumbaiyites breathe air containing so many poisonous chemicals that 10% more of them suffer from *asthma, bronchitis, coughs, colds and headaches* than citizens of almost any other city or town in India.

Badarpur and **Indraprastha** Thermal Electric Plants [both in the State of Delhi] produce on an average per day 180 tonnes of fly-ash and 70 tonnes of sulphur dioxide which contaminate the atmosphere. A number of monuments close to Rajghat and Indraprastha Power Stations in Delhi are turning black due to the fumes and smoke.

The **National Environmental and Engineering Research Institute** [NEERI] has also pointed out that many monuments in India are being affected by the fumes emitted by industries. For example, the Government-owned Oil Refinery, 4 kms. away from Taj Mahal, spews out 24 tonnes of sulphur dioxide daily.

In **Bhatinda** of Punjab the Thermal Electric Plant produces on an average per day 1200 tonnes of fly-ash which pollute the nearby atmosphere.

The NEERI which has conducted a study in **Kolkota** has stated that in the city on an average 1299 tonnes of polluted things join the atmosphere everyday. It is because of this atmospheric pollution 60% of the citizens are suffering from disease connected with lungs. Further the marble of Albert and Victoria Memorial in Kolkota are attacked by stone cancer.

Air Pollution

Air quality in Latin America's most major cities threatens human health. In Sao Paulo and Rio de Janeiro, air pollution is estimated to cause 4000 pre-mature deaths a year. The average ozone concentration in 1995 in Mexico City was about 0.15 parts per million, ten times the natural atmospheric concentration. The region, nearly 75% of whose population is already urbanised, is responsible for 4.3% of the world's total carbon dioxide emissions from industrial processes and 48.3% from land-use changes.

Toxic air pollutants may also do immediate damage to human health and life. The accidental leak of deadly gas at a Union Carbide Plant in **Bhopal** [M.P.], in 1984 cost 2,000 lives and thousands were injured. Similar accidents have happened in United States and also in the then U.S.S.R. causing lot of damage to large number of people. More frightening is the deliberate pollution of the air with toxic chemicals because it is the part of the manufacturing process of many industries.

1 ***An illustration of the smoke emitting out of vehicles*** **:** If hundred diesel lorries throw out smoke for five minutes continuously, together they would produce one kilogram of smoke.

Adverse Effects of Air Pollution

About **1.3** billion urban residents worldwide are exposed to air pollution level above recommended limits. Air quality in the developed countries has generally improved in the past two decades, but in many developing countries air quality has deteriorated because of rising industrial activity, increasing power generation, and the congestion of streets with poorly maintained motor vehicles that use leaded fuel. Air pollution can affect by two ways.

(i) Air pollution affects the health of the human beings adversely. It causes diseases like heart disease, lungs disease, high blood pressure, nervous debility, eye sore, paralyses, throat irritation, chronic bronchitis, lung cancer, bronchial asthama, emphysema, respiratory allergies, etc. It may even cause death. Epidemiological studies have shown that a sudden increase in the air pollution has often been associated with immediate increase in morbidity and mortality.

- Heavy release of carbon monoxide alone causes – headache, decrease in usual perception and paralysis. It affects the cardio-vascular system. It reacts with haemoglobin of blood and thereby reduces oxygen carrying capacity of haemoglobin.
- Lead itself poisons many systems in the body and is particularly dangerous to children developing brain and nervous system. Elevated lead levels in children have been associated with impaired neuropsychologic development as measured by loss of IQ, poor school performance and behavioural difficulties. ***Table*** **1** shows the major air pollutants, their source and adverse effects on health.

Table - 1

Major Air Pollutants, their Sources and Adverse Effects

Noxious Agent	*Sources*	*Adverse Effects*
Oxides of nitrogen	Automobile exhaust, gas stoves and heaters, wood-burning stoves, kerosene space heaters	Respiratory tract irritation, bronchial hyperactivity, impaired lung defences, bronchialitis obliterans
Hydrocarbons	Automobile exhaust, cigarette smoke	Lung cancer
Ozone	Automobile exhaust, high altitude aircraft cabins	Cough, substernal discomfort, bronchoconstriction, decreased exercise performance, respiratory tract irritation
Sulphur dioxide	Power plants, Smelters, oil refineries, kerosene space heaters	Exacerbation of asthma and COPD, respiratory tract irritation, hospitalization may be necessary, and death may occur in severe exposure
Lead	Automobile exhaust using leaded gasoline	Impaired neuropsychological development in children

Source : As quoted by **K. Park** in *"Park's Text Book of Preventive and Social Medicine"* [2002]. Page - 515

(ii) It affects the growth of plants and trees. It causes corrosion of metals, damages buildings, leads to high cost of cleaning and maintenance. It also causes repairs and aesthetic nuisance.

(iii) It results in the formation of smoky atmosphere which is dangerous to vehicular traffic. Air pollution reduces visibility in towns. It can soil and damage clothings.

(iv) It affects the weather adversely, raises the temperature, reduces the humidity and adversely affects the rainfall.

2. WATER POLLUTION

Water is essential for the survival of any form of life. On an average, a human being consumes about 2 litres of water everyday. Water accounts for about 70% of the weight of a human body. About 80% of the earth's surface [that is, 80% of the total 50,000 million hectares of area] is covered by water. Thus a great quantity of water exists on the earth, but only a fraction of it is usable, and that fraction is shrinking due to pollution. As usual, the combined pressures of the population growth and industrial development have imperilled the world's water supply.

Meaning of *"Water Pollution"*

- The term ***water pollution*** refers to *the contamination of water by toxic pollutants that may either eliminate some living organisms or all forms of life.*
- *"Any human activity that impairs the use of water as a resource may be called water pollution. With exploding population and increasing industrialisation and urbanisation, water pollution by agricultural, municipal and industrial sources has become a major concern for the welfare of mankind."* [**S.S. Dara.** Page 64]
- *Water is polluted when it is contaminated by sewage, malign water, chemicals, affluents of water given out by factories, automobiles, etc. When all these substances flow into the river water, or lake water, or well water, or sea water, pollution of water takes place.*

Water can purify itself of a certain amount of pollution. But if pollution becomes too great, it cannot purify itself. Water pollution comes from three major sources – (i) *Sewage,* (ii) *Industrial waste,* and (iii) *Agricultural waste.* Today, industry contributes more to water pollution than do household users.

Even if the source of water supply and its treatment are of a high standard, water pollution may still occur as often happens, due to corrosion of pipe lines, leaky joints and cross connections between water supply pipes and sewage drainage pipes. Surveillance has to be exercised at every point in the distribution system to ensure supply of safe water to the consumer.

Rivers and Lakes are Polluted **:** The nation's rivers and lakes have long been the dumping grounds for many industries. The rivers such as Ganga and Cauvery, the lakes such as the Dal and Nagin [Srinagar], Loktak [Manipur], Chilka [Orissa] and many others are becoming the dumping grounds for poisonous chemicals, factories, agricultural wastes, insecticides and even acids. *"Major industries – paper, steel, automobile, cotton textile, leather industry, etc. depend on water in their production processes. They take water from the rivers and return it polluted and heated, thus doubly affecting aquatic life. Pollutants that industries discharge into rivers and oceans are many and various : solid wastes, sewage, non-degradable byproducts, synthetic materials, toxic chemicals, and even radioactive substances. Added to this are the polluting effects of sewage systems of towns and large cities, detergents, oil spills, pesticide run-off from agricultural areas, and acid run-off from strip-mined lands and the enormity of the problem is even clearer.*[1]

"***Even oceans have not been spared.*** More than half the oil produced in the world is transported across oceans by ships and oil-tankers. One part in a thousand of this is lost by spillage and leakage. In fact, into the oceans encircling India alone is spilt more than 1 million tonnes of oil annually. Much of this oil will not leave the ocean because unlike water it does not evaporate easily and year after year it accumulates."[2]

---

1 **F.R. Scarpitti** and **M.L. Andersen** *"Social Problems"* [1989] Page 544

2 **N. Sheshagiri** *"Pollution"* [1994]. Page : 4 - 5.

India receives about 1,400 - 1,800 mm of rainfall annually. It is estimated that 96% of this water is used for agriculture, 3% for domestic use and 1% for industrial activity. An analysis conducted in 1982 revealed that about 70% of all the available water in our country is polluted. [**S.S. Dara.** Page - 65.]

Damage Caused by the Industries and Sewage Systems **:** Most of the rivers in India are polluted either by industries or by sewage systems. For example, the **Hoogly river** flowing through **Kolkota** is polluted because 350 factories are spread over on both the banks of this river within a distance of about 100 Kms. The river **Damodar** supplies water to all the families and industries in the two major industrial cities of **Durgapur** and **Asansol.** In between these two cities there are about 70 big factories and 250 coal mines. These factories and mines have made the Damodar water almost poisonous. The river **Vrashabhavathi** that flows near the city of **Bangalore** is so polluted that its colour has completely gone black.

Polluted water can cause damage not only to the human beings but also to the cattle, fish, plants, trees and other forms of living beings. Experiment of Malappadu Villagers of Guntur district of A.P. reveals that polluted water can create a serious problem for the people.[1]

No Arrangement for Purifying Polluted Water **:** A study conducted in 1989-90 has revealed that out of 3119 major cities in India, only in 8 cities there is arrangement for purifying the polluted water; there is partial arrangement in 209 cities. But virtually there is no arrangement to purify the polluted water in any manner in the remaining 2902 cities. The polluted water in these cities directly flows down and joins various rivers thereby polluting them. The extent of water pollution is such that around **60%** of the diseases in India are caused due to the consumption of the polluted water.

Adverse Effects of Water Pollution

(i) Water pollution *causes number of diseases* like cholera, typhoid, dysentery, jaundice, and viral diseases. Typhoid and cholera are very big killers. It is estimated that during a nine-year period in India [1898 and 1907] about 3,70,000 people died of cholera alone. [In 1947 in a wide spread epidemic of cholera an estimated 10,000 people died in Egypt. ***Table* - 2** shows that a large number of people in

Table - 2

Population with access to safe water and adequate sanitation in South-East Asia countries 2000

Countries	***Safe Water*** **(%)**	***Adequate Sanitation*** **(%)**
India	88	31
Bhutan	62	69
Bangladesh	97	53
Indonesia	76	66
Maldives	100	56
Mynmar	68	46
Nepal	81	27
Sri Lanka	83	83
Thailand	80	96

Source : *"Science Today"* Oct. 1970 as quoted by **K. Park.** Page 489

1 ***The Case of Malappadu Village*** : Malappadu village is in Guntur district of A.P. "This village is situated on the banks of the river-stream Chappadibagu. Less than 1,000 people known as Lambadas live here with their cattle. The cattle drink water from this stream. Around 1977, this peaceful village became the victim of a strange disease. The cattle developed diarrhoea and within a few days suffered paralytic strokes. This was followed by more complications and ultimately death. Scientists who investigated the disease found that the stream was polluted with lead-based chemicals and the cattle had died of lead poisoning. The Government of Andhra Pradesh immediately ordered a nearby factory to stop poisoning the stream." [**N. Sheshagiri.** Page - 13].

many of the South-East Asia countries do not have access to safe water and adequate sanitation.

(ii) It adversely *affects the growth of plants and trees* and also animal life.

(iii) It *takes away the lives of fish and other animals* that live in water.

(iv) It also *affects the marine transport* and inland waterways.

(v) Water is absolutely essential for maintaining cleanliness. When water itself is polluted, the question of maintaining cleanliness is to be dropped once and for all.

(vi) Water pollution can cause damage to the nervous system and can cripple people, especially children. It may even affect adversely the unborn children in their mother's wombs.[1]

While pollution seems to be an inevitable consequence of modern industrial technology, the problem now, is to determine the level of pollution that permits economic and social development without presenting hazards to health. The evaluation of the health effects of environmental pollutants is currently being carried out as part of the WHO Environmental Health Criteria Programme.

3. SOUND (NOISE) POLLUTION

Noise is often defined as *"unwanted sound."* This definition is subjective because of the fact that one man's sound may be another man's noise. Perhaps a better definition of noise could be stated in the following words:

- Noise is *"wrong sound, in the wrong place, at the wrong time."*
- *"The term* **noise** *may also be defined as an unwanted sound at a wrong time and at a wrong place."*

Man is living in an increasingly noisy environment. The previous 20th century has been described as the *"Century of Noise."* Noise has become a very important *"stress factor"* in the environment of man. The term *"Noise Pollution"* has been recently coined to signify the vast cacophony of sounds that are being produced in the modern life, leading to health hazards.

Although noise is undesirable, it could be meaningful or meaningless. An irresponsible or meaningless noise is disturbing and annoying. Prolonged and loud sound is generally considered as noise which is mostly caused because of industries, vehicles, trains, loudspeakers, aeroplanes, etc. Since such a noise is found to cause some kind of physical, physiological or psychological harm or stress to human beings, it is also considered as a pollutant. Noise is a byproduct of human activity. Excessive noise can result in loss of hearing, increase in accidents, and decrease in productivity. Hence, it is essential to take suitable precautions to reduce noise pollution particularly in urban and industrial areas.

Table - 3

Acceptable Noise Levels (dBA)

Residential :	Bed room	25
	Living room	40
Commercial :	Office	35 - 45
	Conference	40 - 45
	Restaurants	40 - 60
Industrial :	Workshop	40 - 60
	Laboratory	40 - 50
Educational :	Class Room	30 - 40
	Library	35 - 40
Hospitals :	Wards	20 - 35

1 ***Polluted Water Adversely Affects Even the Unborn*** : Example of Japan is worth citing here. "A chemical factory in Japan was pouring its mercury into Minamata Bay. All those who ate fish from this bay got a terrible illness now popularly known as the "Minamata disease." This is a strange ailment of the nervous system. It killed many and crippled numerous others. Children were the worst affected. Even unborn children in their mother's wombs were afflicted. The worst of it was that this particular factory had been throwing out this poison into the waters for fifty years without anyone being aware of the hazard. The danger is, therefore, our ignorance of the poisonous materials around us." ***Source*** : **N. Sheshagiri** *"Pollution."* Pages : 58 - 59.

Sources **:** The sources of noise are many and varied. These are automobiles, factories, industries, air-craft, etc. Noise levels are particularly acute near railway junctions, traffic roundabouts, bus terminuses and airports. Use of pressure horns, recreational noise of loudspeakers with full volume during festivities particularly at night are other sources of noise production. The domestic noises form the radios, transistors, T.V. sets – all add to the quantum of noise in daily life. Noise has two important properties **:** *loudness* or *intensity;* and *frequency.* The loudness of noise is measured in decibels [dB]. ***For example,*** normal conversation produces a noise of 60-65 dB; whispering, 20 db; heavy street traffic, 60-80 dB; and boiler factories, about 120 dB. A daily exposure upto 85 dB is about the limit people can tolerate without substantial damage to their hearing.

Table - 4

Sound Levels of Some Noises

Sources of Noise	*Sound Level* **(dB)**
Wishper	10
Speech, 2 - 3 people	73
Speech on radio	80
Music on radio	85
Children shouting	79
Children crying	80
Vacuum cleaner	76
Piano	86
Jet take off	150

Noise pollution or environmental noise is one of the new killers of our society. If we live near a busy airport or big industry we come to know what noise pollution is. As civilisation grows noise pollution also grows. It is said that Julius Caeser banned chariots from the Cobblestone streets during evening hours because of the noise they made. Noise pollution has become the subject of study for our scientists very recently. They have cautioned about the undesirable consequences of noise pollution. The scientists at the Indian Science Congress in 1991 also discussed at length the consequences of sound pollution and the ways and means of reducing it.

Effects of Sound Pollution

(i) It has adverse effects on a human life. *It damages man's hearing,* reduces his age, causes loss of mental peace and results in emotional upsets.

(ii) *It has also an adverse effect on animal life.* It retards their growth and effects their working ability.

4. SOIL POLLUTION OR SOLID WASTE

***Soil pollution** is desecration of soil by man-made substances that alter its physical, chemical and biological characteristics.*

• *"Any unwanted or discarded material from residential, commercial, industrial, mining and agricultural activities that cause environmental problems may be termed as solid wastes. Solid waste management comprises of purposeful and systematic control of the generation, storage, collection, transport, separation, processing, recycling, recovery, and disposal of solid wastes."* [**S.S.Dara.** Page 100]

• *Solid wastes can be broadly defined as those wastes which have been rejected for further use and which can neither be transported by water into streams nor can readily escape into the atmosphere. They include all the discarded solid materials from municipal, agricultural and industrial activities.*

Among the world's most serious environmental problems is how to dispose of its wastes. From Kashmir to Kanyakumari tonnes of garbage are produced everyday, including paper, yard wastes, glass, metals, food, plastic and wood.[1] This garbage which is termed as *"solid wastes"* includes – food wastes, rubbish things consisting of metal, plastic and glass, demolition products such as bricks, masonry and pipes, sewage treatment residues, dead animals, manure and other discarded material. The output of daily waste depends upon the dietary habits, life styles, living standards and the degree of urbanisation and industrialisation. The per capita [that is, per head] daily solid waste produced, ranges between 0.25 to 2.5 K.G. in different countries.

Not only the processes of urbanisation and industrialisation are causing land pollution, but each family is contributing to it in one way or another. ***For example,*** "In India, there are more than 100 million families. They account for as much as 50 million buckets of solid waste every day. In a year, nearly 20,000 million buckets of these wastes find their way to garbage yards. If such garbage yards are not provided, people throw garbage wherever it is convenient for them."[2] In the absence of proper arrangement for the disposal of solid wastes, each family is adding to land pollution in one way or another.

Solid waste, if allowed to accumulate, is a health hazard. Because it decomposes and favours fly breeding. It attracts rodents and vermin. The deadly bacterias present in the solid waste may be brought back to man's food through flies and dust. Heaps of refuse here and there present an ugly scene and a nuisance, and contribute to intolerable bad odours. Studies have revealed that there is a correlation between improper disposal of solid wastes and incidence of vector-born diseases. Therefore, in all civilised countries, there is an efficient system for the periodic collection, removal and final disposal of solid wastes without risk to health.

The solid waste is typically disposed of by burying it in landfills, burning it, and sometimes even recycling it. In some cases, it is dumped into the ocean. Except for recycling, all of the traditional disposal methods create problems of air, land or water pollution. They also create potential public health risks and spoil the beauty of the land and seascape.

The industrialised nations, with their higher standards of living, consumption and disposal face increasingly serious problems of waste management and control. All over the world, people throw away 1,000 crore tonnes of solid wastes every year. *"All over the world, every year we throw away 15,000 crore cans and 8 crore tonnes of bottles and 15 crore tonnes of paper and plastic, creating larger and larger mountains of garbage whose disposal we are leaving to the future."*[3] What to do with this, and where to deposit this and how to get away from their evil effects – these questions are haunting the environmentalists.

Sources of Soil Pollution

1. ***Industrial wastes*** thrown out by paper, chemical, rubber, cement, sugar, fertiliser, textile, and other industries. The fly-ash thrown out by furnaces pollute not only the soil but also air and water.
2. ***Agricultural wastes*** include artificial fertilisers, pesticides, farm wastes, etc. Some of these are biodegradable.
3. ***Radioactive wastes*** are those released during nuclear explosions, and those released from nuclear power plants, and by institutions using radioactive substances.

---

1 "The quantity of domestic and municipal solid wastes generated in some major cities of India is 300 - 600 grams per person per day. Since the quantity of waste generated depends on the affluence of the society, the per capita waste produced in India is naturally lesser as compared to that produced in affluent western countries. The amount being spent in municipalities in India for solid waste management is estimated to be 805 to 1200 million rupees annually which accounts for about 10% of their total budgetary provisions" **S.S. Dara.** Page 102

2 **N. Sheshagiri** *"Pollution."* Page - 8.

3. *ibid.* page 57

4. ***Domestic Waste or refuse*** which consists of ash [residue from cooking and heating], rubbish [including paper, clothing, bits of wood, metal, glass, dust, etc.] and garbage [consisting of waste food, vegetable peelings and other organic substances] also add to solid waste.
5. ***Street Refuse*** consisting of leaves, straws, paper and plastic pieces, animal droppings, and litter of all kinds collected by the street cleansing agency, especially in the towns and cities.
6. ***Market Refuse*** that is collected from markets consists of a large proportion of putrid vegetable, packing materials and animal matter.

Adverse Effects of Soil Pollution

(i) Soil or land pollution *reduces the fertility of the soil.*

(ii) Due to the excessive use of chemicals and fertilisers our *land is losing its natural capacity to support growth of plants and trees.*

(iii) *It adversely affects animal and human life.* The accumulation of the pesticides in the soil on the one hand, and the accumulation of tonnes of garbage on the other, pose a serious threat to our health. Such accumulations contaminate the plants and animals that are consumed by human beings. Human health is also endangered due to the diseases caused by heaps of the garbage.

Solid waste is posing a serious problem. Every cubic meter of garbage can foster about 750,000 flies, not to mention rats, mice, mosquitoes, cockroaches, etc. It becomes the breeding ground for disease-bearing bacteria. It spoils the landscape and devours our living space. Every passing day brings in more solid waste which cannot be destroyed easily. Today's industry is greatly contributing to this menace.

5. NUCLEAR RADIOACTIVE POLLUTION

***Radioactive pollution** results out of atomic radiation during which there is a spontaneous emission of particles [electrons] and rays [electromagnetic].* These radiations are invisible and penetrate living tissues.

Nuclear power plants are becoming one of the biggest sources of radioactive environmental pollution. The reason is that they produce a large quantity of nuclear waste. It remains radioactive for thousands of years. It cannot be stored without the risk of leakage. Developed nations dump the waste in the oceans in closed containers. Radioactive particles can get into the food chain and can create an extremely alarming situation.

Adverse Effects of Nuclear Radioactive Pollution

(i) High doses of *radiation can cause death.*

(ii) In lower doses *it can cause serious effects,* impairing the functioning of organic systems.

(iii) Repeated and long exposure can cause cancer.

(iv) Embryos of man and animals are highly sensitive to radiation. It has been observed that handicapped children were born to persons exposed to atomic radiation.

(v) The deadly and the disastrous effects of radioactive pollution could be found in atomic explosions. During the second world war, when America exploded the first nuclear device by dropping a bomb on **Hiroshima** [Japan] on 6th August 1945 more than 1,47,000 people were killed. The second bomb that was exploded on **Nagasaki** on 9th Aug. 1945 killed more than 67,000 people. In 1986, the leakage of nuclear reactor plant at Chernobyl [USSR] also caused the death of large number of people.

PREVENTION OF THE ENVIRONMENTAL POLLUTION

Governmental Efforts

Environmental purification is the need of the hour today. Environmental purification means purifying the environment which has been polluted in various ways. Therefore, it refers to the prevention and control of environmental pollution through various measures. Like all other developing countries, India entered the area of environmental protection in the 1970s itself. It has taken some measures in the direction of stopping or reducing environmental pollution. Some of the legislative measures taken by the Government are worth mentioning here.

1. In 1974 the *Water [Prevention and Control of Pollution] Act* was passed by the Central Government in order to prevent water pollution.
2. The *Air [Prevention and Control of Pollution] Act* was passed in 1981 with the intention of controlling air pollution.
3. At the state levels the State Governments have also enacted water and air protection Acts and set up *State Pollution Control Boards.* These are strengthened by the formation of *Central Pollution Control Board* [CPCB] at the national level.
4. The CPCBs made a study of polluting industries and evolved guidelines to reduce pollution by introducing *Minimum National Affluent Standards* [MINAS] in respect of selected industries.
5. The Central Government has established the *Department of Environment* - DOE - in order to co-ordinate and integrate various schemes and projects which have been undertaken with an intention of preventing environmental pollution.
6. The Central Government has realised that the environmental protection and economic development of the country are closely related. Hence, it has started working in this direction as per the advices and suggestions given by the environmental scientists.

Major Legislative Measures Undertaken Since 1972

1927 The Indian Forest Act
1972 The Wildlife (Protection) Act
1974 The Water (Prevention and Control of Pollution) Act
1980 The Forests (Conservation) Act
1981 The Air (Prevention and Control of Pollution) Act
1986 The Environment (Protection) Act
1991 The Public Liability Insurance Act
1995 The National Environmental Tribunal Act
1997 The National Environment Appellate Authority Act Policies
1988 National Forest Policy
1992 National Conservation Strategy and Policy Statement on Environmental Development
1992 Policy Statement on Abatement of Pollution

Prevention of Environmental Pollution : *Some Suggestions*

Pollution of our environment is increasingly posing problems for man's survival on earth. This has not happened in a day or two. Continuously we have been contaminating and damaging our environment. Man has been continuously ignoring *"the laws of nature"* and disturbing the ecological balance. Scientists and environmentalists have already warned about the impending tragedy if the environment is continuously contaminated. **Dr. Einstein** said, *"All our technological progress –*

our very civilisation – is like the axe in the hand of the pathological criminal. So like pathological criminals we have mercilessly destroyed the forest and converted fertile land into desert."[1] There should be a final stop for this creeping paralysis. We must think in terms of protecting our environment which protects us in turn. Some suggestions could be given in this regard.

1. *It is necessary to undertake an appropriate National Industrial Policy* so as to protect our national interests including the environmental interests. It is a known fact that unregulated industrialisation has been causing environmental pollution. Hence it is necessary to implement very strictly the National Industrial Policy.

2. *Uncontrolled urbanisation is to be stopped.* Urbanisation has been taking place in an unprecedented manner. Existing cities are growing and new cities are coming up. There is no regulation nor any control over the growth of cities. These cities are spoiling the nearby environment. Only through proper regulations and control the unwanted effects of urbanisation on the environment could be stopped.

3. *Owners of motor vehicles are to be instructed strictly to use pollution control gadgets.* The use of these instruments can help to reduce pollution caused by vehicles.

4. *The sewage system of the cities is to be revised.* Sewage wastes let into streams, rivers, lakes and coastal waters are causing several problems. Hence sewage water is to be purified before it is allowed to join rivers, lakes or coastal waters.

5. *A separate arrangement is to be made to collect and transport the inorganic and non-degradable garbage wastes to a distant place.* The unwanted inorganic substances like tins, plastic bags, boxes, bottles, etc. are to be deposited separately in the dustbins so as to help the municipal administration to collect and take it to a distant place. People should also learn to minimise the use of such things. The Government can also think of banning the use of plastic bags at least in some specified fields and areas.

Recycling non-degradable materials. It is necessary to minimise the use of non-degradable materials. We must also make necessary arrangements to recycle and reuse discarded materials. People must help organisations which recycle such materials.

6. *Regular removal of the garbages.* The municipal and city administrations must take steps to remove the garbage, dust and other thrown away articles deposited in the dustbins. People also should learn the art of depositing the garbage only in the dustbins and not throwing it everywhere.

7. *Launching of save environment campaigns and movements.* Since sizeable number of Indians are still illiterate, it is necessary to educate them to keep the environment neat and clean. They must also be educated regarding the adverse consequences of pollution. A national level campaign or movement to *"save environment"* could be launched with the active participation of political leaders, labour leaders, peasant leaders, student leaders, and leaders of various religious and cultural organisations.

8. *Encouragement to conservation of forests.* It is necessary to awaken the people about the importance of forests in preserving the purity of our environment. Appropriate steps should be taken to conserve the existing forests. Special efforts should also be made to develop gardens, parks, within the premises of hospitals, educational institutions, industries, government offices, etc. *"Vanamahotsava"* should not become a governmental ritual. There should be active participation of the people in it. *"Plant a tree before cutting one"* should become a meaningful and a practical slogan.

As far as forests are concerned, they now comprise of about 64 million hectares, or about 19% of land area of the country. Roughly 33% probably represents primary forest. About 10 million

1 **Dr. Einstein** as quoted by **Biswanath Ghosh** in *"Contemporary Social Problems of India"* [1988]. Page - 95.

hectares are managed as *"Protection Forests"* for ecological stability, 15 million for production of timber, and 25 million as social forest to meet the demand for the fuel wood and fodder. About 14 million hectares lie within national parks and wildlife sanctuaries. This forest area is to be preserved and expanded.

There are schemes to protect wildlife and its habitat. A wide network of 83 National Parks, 447 Wildlife Sanctuaries, 25 (+6) Project Tiger areas, 200 zoos and 8 Biosphere reserves have contributed towards conservation of these species. As per the Tiger Census carried out in the Tiger Reserves, the total number of tigers recorded was 3750. There are about 1500 to 2000 elephants settled in more than 15 states' isolated forest areas. They are under severe ecological stress. Because, more than 250 elephants have been killed in the past 3 years.

At present, the wildlife protected area network comprises 84 national parks and 447 wildlife sanctuaries covering 4.5% of the total geographical area of the country. There are also over 200 zoos, 23 Tiger reserves in the country.[1] The National Wildlife Action Plan adopted in 1983 provides the framework of strategy as well as programme for conservation of wildlife.

9. *A Special Care is to be Taken to Protect the Ozone Layer* : Between heights of twenty and thirty kilometres from the ground the earth's atmosphere is covered by what is called the *"ozone layer."* A few kilometres thick, this layer is spread over the entire globe and shields all living things below from ninety-nine per cent of the sun's ultra-violet rays. Destruction of this layer could create a suicidal effect. It is, therefore, absolutely essential to protect the thin, sensitive ozone layer. Hence, it is necessary to ban S.S.T. flights,[2] stop atmospheric nuclear explosions [at present only France and China have stopped this], and ban aerosol containers [such as aerosol cans like hair-dye or perfume-spray containers].

Environment Movements in India

Chipko Movement : People of Mandal village of Chameli district, U.P. started their struggle against deforestation in 1973. The movement obtained the leadership of Gowra Devi, Sundarlal Bahuguna and Chandi Prasad Bhat.

Silent Valley Movement : An environmental movement against a 75 Mega Watt Hydro-electric project on **Kuthipuzha** [a tributary of Periyar river] on the dense ever green forest region of Western Ghats. It is a home to many rare species of plants and fauna which would otherwise have been destroyed by inundation.

Narmada Bachao Andolan : A movement for proper rehabilitation of over 100,000 people being evicted for building Rs.1,000 crore multipurpose project over Narmada river. The movement is led by Baba Amte and Medha Patkar. The Oct. 19, 2001 decision by Supreme Court allowing the Gujarat Govt. to proceed with the construction was a heavy blow. But the movement is still simmering.

Baliyapal Movement : Baliyapal Movement was against taking over of the thickly populated Baliyapal village's fertile land for testing of missiles. [***Source*** : *Manorama Year Book* - 2002. Page - 592.]

Successful Protest Against Cogentrix Company : Villagers, students, particularly Akhil Bharatiya Vidyarthi Parishad [ABVP] activists, and local environmentalists successfully fought against an American company namely "Cogentrix Company" which had obtained legal permission from the Karnataka Government to establish a hundred Mega Watt thermal power project at the cost of Rs.4000 crores, in Nandikoor village near Mangalore [Karnataka]. The company was legally and physically not allowed to start its construction work. Environmental scientists and the National Environmental Engineering Research Institute [NEERI] had cautioned against the establishment of such a big thermal project in this eco-sensitive coastal area of the Western Ghat.

---

1 ***Source*** : *Manorama Year Book* - 2002. Page - 592.

2 ***S.S.T. aeroplanes*** are those that fly at speeds exceeding that of sound. S.S.T. is a source of pollution of the upper atmosphere.

9. ***Special financial assistance for protecting the environment.*** In our national budget there should be a provision for a special fund to give financial assistance to the local bodies to safeguard the environmental interests.

10. ***Creating Environmental Awareness Among the Children*****:** Special arrangements must be made to create environmental awareness among the children and the young people. Training given to the children in this direction at an early age especially in schools and colleges go a long way in creating awareness to protect the environment.

11. ***Launching of Environmental Education Programmes*** **:** It is necessary to educate the people to take proper precaution to save our environment. A specialised body of the U.N.O. namely UNEP [*United Nations Education Programme*] has stressed the importance of such a kind of education long back in 1977. The environmental education programmes should include the following–

(i) ***Environmental education and training*** at school, college, and university level.

(ii) ***Environmental sciences,*** which deal with advanced science and its effect on air, water, and soil degradation.

(iii) ***Environmental engineering,*** which includes the study to assess the impact of engineering science on environment.

Mrs. Indira Gandhi, the late prime minister of India had told : *"Modern man must re-establish his unbroken link with nature and with life. He must again learn to invoke the energy and to recognise, as did the ancients in India centuries ago, that we can take from the earth and atmosphere only so much as one put back into them."*[1]

1 **Mrs. Indira Gandhi** in her speech at U.N. Conference on Environment at Stockholm [Sweden] on June 14th, 1972 as quoted by **B.K. Sharma** and **H. Kaur** in *"Air Pollution"* [1993-94 Edition]. Goel Publishing House, Meerut. Page - 15.

Chapter 17

ECONOMIC FACTORS IN MODERN INDIA

*A. **Economic Development and Its Determinants** : Meaning of Economic Development - Factors in Economic Development - Role of Economic and Non-Economic Factors in Economic Development - Social Determinants of Economic Development - Barriers of Economic Development - India As a Developing Economy*
*B. **Market Economy** : Market Economy and Its Social Consequences - India's Attempts Towards Economic Reforms - New Economic Policy : Liberalisation / Privatisation / Globalisation- Liberalisation - Main Features of the Policy of Liberalisation - Privatisation - Definition of Privatisation - The Global Trend of Privatisation - Privatisation in India - Arguments in Favour of and Against Privatisation - Some Remedies for Reforming the Indian Economy - Globalisation-Concept of Globalisation - Definition of Globalisation - Main Purposes of Globalisation - Some Features of Globalisation - Effects of Globalisation : Positive Effects and Negative Effects - Multinational Corporations and Their Impact on the World Order-Criticisms Levelled Against the Functioning of the Multinational Companies.*

Economic Development : Its Social Determinants

Sociology and Economics are very closely related as social sciences. There are certain common topics of interest for both. On certain issues and areas the studies of these two disciplines coincide. *"Study of economic development"* is one such area in which one normally crosses the border of another for obtaining more authentic information. The question of economic development is closely connected with the issues such as – socio-economic meaning of economic development, social infrastructure, need for economic development, the pre-requisites or preconditions for economic development, factors accelerating and hindering the rate of economic development, socio-cultural factors putting obstacles for economic development, social consequences of economic development, and so on. These issues are socio-economic in nature and are interconnected. It is in this way, the study or analysis of "economic development" has a close bearing on sociology.

Meaning of Economic Development

The concept of *"economic development"* has been understood differently by different scholars. One or two such views held by the experts in the field may be cited here :

The concept of economic development, unlike the term *"economic growth"*[1] is more comprehensive in nature. *"Economic development implies progressive changes in the socio-economic structure of a country, viewed in this way, economic development involves a steady decline in agriculture's share in GNP [Gross National Product] and a corresponding increase in the share of industries, trade, banking, construction and services. This transformation in economic structure is invariably accompanied by a shift in the occupational structure of the labour force and an improvement in its skill and productivity."* [**Misra** and **Puri.** Page - 7].

The concept of "economic development" can also be understood by means of simple definitions like the following.

- Economic development implies *the process of securing levels of productivity in all sectors of economy and this, in turn, is a function of the levels of technology.*
- According to **Robert Faris** [1964], economic development may be understood as *"any growth in real income per capita from whatever source."*
- **Jaffe** and **Stewart** have opined that economic development refers to the process of *"rationalisation of economic production."*
- **Novack** has said that economic growth refers to the *"continuous substantial increase in per capita consumption of goods and services."*
- Sometimes, the term economic development is used in a loose manner to refer to the *"general economic prosperity of a nation. It is also often used synonymously with "economic growth."*

Factors in Economic Development

Economic development is a complex process. It depends on the levels of technology. It is indeed, a process of stepping up the rate of capital formation. But it must be noted that capital, though necessary, is not a sufficient condition of economic development which depends on such non-economic factors as social attitudes, political conditions, human endowments and efficient governance. It is clear now, that two types of factors, *i.e.,* (A) *economic factors,* and (b) *the non-economic factors* influence the economic development of any country. The relative influence of these two factors may be briefly examined here.

A. Economic Factors in Economic Development

Economic development depends upon factors such as – *capital formation, capital-output ratio, marketable surplus of agriculture, conditions in foreign trade, economic system, growth of population and finally, building human capital.* It is the task of the economists to study to what extent these factors influence economic development.

Pre-requisites of Economic Development : Views of Robert Faris

It is generally acknowledged that the factors such as – *natural resources, labour force, capital accumulation, technology, sources of power, manpower, characteristics of population, nature of economic organisation, social setting or social environment of the economy, etc.* – play a vital role in contributing to the economic growth of a society.

1 "The term ***economic growth*** refers to increase over time in a country's real output of goods and services – or more appropriately product per capita. Output is generally measured by gross or net national product, though other measures could also be employed." **– S.K. Misra** and **V.K. Puri** *"Indian Economy"* [2000]. Page - 7.

Robert Faris is of the opinion that economic development of any society is based on certain pre-requisites. He mentions some major pre-requisites which can be stated below.

1. Institutions or normative complexes, that unanimously accept and follow the rules of conduct.
2. Values or ideology that exercise a tremendous influence on behaviour.
3. Nature and type of the policies of the government, that is, whether the government wants to promote public sector or private sector or both.
4. Motives and incentives pertaining to profit / prestige.

B. Role of Non-Economic Factors in Economic Development

It is now widely recognised that various non-economic factors and forces also play a vital role in the economic development of a country. The non-economic factors provide the requisite social climate in which the seed of economic development can germinate to full bloom. Therefore, it would be unwise to underrate the importance of the sociological and psychological factors. **Professor Cairncross** emphasizing the non-economic factors, writes : *"Development is not governed in any country by economic forces alone and the more backward the country, the more this is true. The key to development lies in men's minds, in the institutions in which their thinking finds expression and in the play of opportunity on ideas and institutions."*[1]

Social Determinants of Economic Development

It is an established fact that economic development cannot take place in vacuum. It has to take place in one or the other social framework, that is, social system. The nature and character of the social system definitely affect the rate of economic development. Hence, it is necessary at this stage to take into account various social factors that act as the determinants of economic development.

1. Nature of Human Resources : Role of People's Ability, Experience and Knowledge in the Realm of Economic Production

Economic development depends upon the way in which the four factors of production – *land, labour, capital* and *organisation* – are efficiently and effectively used. But the mere existence of these factors of production does not assure economic development. Factors of production are very much *"conditioned by cultural factors."* The people must have the ability, experience and knowledge to make the best use of the natural and other kinds of facilities that are made available. Work culture and economic rationality are moulded by cultural and social factors which have a close bearing on economic rationality........" *"Economic development is, therefore, not a function of economic resources alone, but of social and cultural factors as well."*[2]

2. Adoption of Appropriate Technology

There is a direct relationship between the nature and character of technology that is used in the productive process on the one hand, and the economic development on the other. Adoption of technology is not governed by simple mechanical considerations. Technology can fetch results only when appropriate social conditions are present. A technology which is very much useful in one society may prove to be dysfunctional in another. Technological development becomes meaningful only under appropriate social conditions. All types of technology do not suit all types of societies.

---

1 As quoted by **Ruddar Datt** and **K.P.M. Sundharam** in their *"Indian Economy"* [2002]. Page - 12.

2 **Parimal B. Carr** *"Sociology - The Discipline and Its Dimensions"* [1990]. Page - 250.

For example, introduction of computer may help economic development in an industrialised country but not in an *adivasi* society, nor in a society which is still dominated by crude agricultural techniques.

As regards the adoption of an appropriate technology **Galbraith** makes an observation in the following way : *"The borrowing of technology is....... a subtle matter. In principle, it is highly desirable....... One must know, however, when the thing was worked out. Was it a step forward in process of product of universal application ? Or, was it an adaptation to the requirements of advanced economic development itself ? .... They [the first type] are as appropriate and important for the less as for the more developed country. But much of the technology of the more advanced countries represents an accommodation to labour shortages or reflects the three special requirements of the more advanced economy."*[1]

R.T. Gill has stated in this connection that the modern under-developed countries have a tendency to borrow the modern Western technology without taking into account the fact whether such a technology would suit their socio-economic environment at all. He writes: *"...... Lacking it, the modern under-developed country typically tries to import the "latest" Western methods. With the consequence that it takes acute shortages in certain areas [capital and trained personnel] while it has idle surpluses [large numbers of unemployed, unskilled workers."*[2]

3. Innovative Personality

Another major requirement of economic development is the presence of sufficient number of persons with innovative ability. The formation of creative and innovative personality is largely a function of early socialisation. It also depends on the nature and contents of education to which the child is exposed from the primary stage onwards. There are countries in which sufficient encouragement is given right from the childhood to solve problems independently and in a creative manner. But in the traditional societies much emphasis is laid on conformity and the children are instructed to accept the things uncritically and asked to obey the elders implicitly. Children in such societies simply accept the lore and practices handed down to them from previous generations. Innovative personality cannot blossom under such rigid conditions. Hence, it is quite natural that economic development in these societies would naturally be slow and halting.

4. Time Gap Between the Introduction of Technology and Cultural Support for the Same

It is true that technology grows faster in society where it obtains a favourable cultural support. People normally take sometime to accept a new technology. For example, even though computer system came to India in 1970s itself, it has come to be accepted by the people of India only 1990s. It means a time gap between preparation and adoption normally exists. If the time gap is too wide, then, economic development is hampered. The Western countries have realised this. Hence, for *"....... several decades the cultural traits and social conditions appropriate to technology were developed prior to the actual discovery and adoption of sophisticated technology."* But as **R.T. Gill** has pointed out the problem in the underdeveloped countries is *"to accomplish simultaneously both the industrial revolution and the preparation for such a revolution."* Added to this, the mass media of communication carry lot of advertisements about the products turned out by the advanced technology of the West. As a result, people start cherishing high expectations about the government which is ruling them to invite and adopt such advanced technology. No democratic government can

1 **J.K. Galbraith** *"Economic Development in Perspective"*; The United States Information Service. Page - 1.

2 **R.T. Gill** as quoted by **Parimal B. Carr.** Page - 251.

ignore the rising expectations of the people and it is compelled to go in for sophisticated technology even in the absence of appropriate cultural and social support. This situation creates complications for smooth economic development.

5. Explosive Growth of Population

Rapid growth of population is considered an important determinant of development. Since economic growth is measured in terms of an increase in per capita income, a part of the increase in additional income is utilised to maintain the additional population. In other words, in terms of per capita income, on account of a rise in population, the country experiences a very thin spread of the benefits of growth. This highlights the need for a large and active programme of family limitation so that the benefits of the massive development effort are not dissipated.

As it is clear from the above, that explosive growth of population especially in the Third World countries must be taken into account in our discussion of economic development. It is highly dysfunctional for economic growth. **Prof. Gill** makes this point when he says : "........ *population growth is not a stimulant to development....... but a depressant. Because of the lack of industrial capital the growing labour force cannot find jobs in the city and therefore adds itself to the already congested rural areas. Rapid population growth in such "labour surplus" economies may mean that despite the attempts to increase industrial employment, the absorption rate is insufficient, and that open and disguised unemployment increases as a percentage of the labour force – the reverse of successful development.*"[1]

It is significant to note that economic development and population growth are interconnected. Whereas population hinders economic development, the latter, as it gathers momentum, leads to the creation of more appropriate conditions to control population.

6. Nature of Social Organisation

For the acceleration of the economic growth it is necessary that people must participate in the developmental programmes in a large number. People show interest in the development activity only when they feel that the fruits of growth will be fairly distributed. Experiences from a number of countries suggest that whenever the defective social organisation allows a small section of a people to amass the benefits of growth, the general mass of the people develop apathy and indifference towards the State's development programmes. India's experience for the past few decades has proved that the economic power is concentrated in the hands of a few monopoly houses, individuals and the so called elite groups. The new agricultural strategy has given rise to a class of rich peasantry creating widespread disparities in the countryside. These things prove that India's social organisation is far away from providing for social equality and justice. Hence, it is not surprising that there is widespread apathy towards development planning in this country.

7. Political Freedom

It is now known to everyone that nations such as India, Pakistan, Bangladesh, Sri Lanka, Malaysia, Burma, and a few other countries which were in the past British colonies, are still lagging behind in achieving economic progress. Similarly, countries such as Algeria and Indo-China which were once the colonies of France are yet to attain economic advancement. It was a common practice for the imperialist countries to exploit their colonies and to suppress the political freedom of the people of these colonies in all the possible manner. Hence, the economic development of the countries

1 **T.N. Gill** as quoted by **Parimal B. Carr.** Pages : 251 - 252.

which were one time the colonies of some other imperialist forces, always depends on their present relationship with either the previous imperialist forces or the other nations. It is in this way, we have to understand the economic development or underdevelopment of Latin American countries in terms of their relationship with the U.S.A. It is only in a period of political freedom a country can think in terms of attaining economic progress. We do not find any good example of economic development of any nation under the colonial rule from history. Political freedom is an essential condition for economic development of any country.

8. Desire to Develop

Economic development is not a mechanical process. It depends to a very great extent on people's desire to develop. A nation wherein corruption is rampant and political and economic exploitation is at its height, and where its people lack the spirit of adventure and achievement, economic development cannot take place rapidly. **Richard T. Gill** has rightly remarked, *"The point is that economic development is not a mechanical process; it is not a simple adding up of assorted factors. Ultimately, it is a human enterprise. And like all human enterprises, its outcome will depend finally on the skill, quality and attitudes of the men who undertake."*[1]

Barriers of Economic Development

If certain factors promote and strengthen economic development certain other factors hamper and put obstacles to economic development. **Jacob Viner** makes a mention of six factors which act as barriers to economic development. They can be stated here : 1. *Unfavourable physical environment.* 2. *Low quality of working population.* 3. *Scarcity of technical knowledge.* 4. *Scarcity of capital.* 5. *Rapid growth of population, and* 6. *Defects in agrarian structure.*

Yet another scholar **Novack** has maintained that certain factors impede economic growth especially in underdeveloped areas. According to him, factors such as – 1. *Lack of sufficient quantity of innovation.* 2. *Lack of agrarian reforms.* 3. *Lack of discipline.* 4. *Population growth,* and 5. *Foreign exchange shortages* – put obstacles to economic development in various ways.

Barriers to Economic Development in India **:** India which is regarded as *a developing nation* is also confronted with various factors which disturb the process of its economic growth. **Thomas Shea** has spoken of four important barriers to economic development in India. They are– 1. *Caste system,* 2. *Pattern of land tenure,* 3. *Population growth,* and 4. *Property laws* [which lead to fragmentation and subdivision of land holdings].

Role of Health in Economic Production **:** Physically strong and health-wise sound people are always an asset to any country for increasing its economic production. People with poor health, and having very low life-expectancy cannot contribute much to the productive process. The health consequences on production are severe. People with poor health die younger and suffer more from disability. They are exposed to greater risk from unhealthy conditions at home at work. Malnutrition and the legacy of the past illness mean that they are more likely to fall ill and slower to recover especially if they have little access to health care. ***Table* - 1** shows that there is a close link between income on the one hand and life-expectancy at birth and infant mortality rate [two health factors], on the other.

1 **Richard T. Gill** as quoted by **S.K. Misra** and **V.K. Puri** *"Indian Economy"* [2000]. Page - 24.

Table - 1

Per Capita GNP, life Expectancy at Birth and Infant Mortality Rate in SEAR Countries

Country	*Per capita GNP US $ (1999)*	*Life expectancy at birth (2000)*	*Infant mortality rate (2000)*
India	450	62.3	69
Bangladesh	370	59.4	54
Bhutan	510	62.0	77
Indonesia	580	66.2	35
Maldives	1160	65.4	59
Myanmar	220	56.0	78
Nepal	220	58.6	72
Sri Lanka	820	72.1	17
Thailand	1960	70.2	25

GNP : GNP is gross income generated from within the country as also net income received from abroad.
Source : *UNICEF* [2001] and *UNDP* [2002] *Human Development Report* 2002 as quoted by **K. Park.** Page 486.

India as a Developing Economy

Indian economy is not stagnant but a dynamic one. It is often regarded as an underdeveloped economy. But the recent progress which India has attained in various areas of economic life gives us an impression that it is trying to forge ahead. Hence, it is more appropriate to call Indian economy *"a developing economy"*, rather than an underdeveloped economy. India has started progressing in the direction of modernisation. The tempo of economic progress has increased since 1951 with the adoption of the Five Year Planning system. During the past 50 years the country has made much progress in agriculture, industry, science and technology, particularly in the fields of computer science and information technology, health and education, and in various other fields. The changes that have taken place in the Indian economy for the past 50 years clearly prove that *India is a developing economy*.

1. ***Increase in National Income*** **:** National income is the sum total of all incomes in cash and kind accruing to factors of production in a given period of time for a country. The national income of the country has increased significantly over the past 5 decades. India's national income at current prices has grown up from Rs.8,574 crores in 1950-51 to Rs.7,18,639 crores in 1994-95. This has further increased to Rs.12,65,167 crores in 1997-98. This is a clear proof of India's economic attainment. [***Table*** - 2 reveals this increase.]

2. ***Increase in Per Capita Income*** **:** Per capita income of the country has been increasing. It has increased from Rs.239/- in 1950-51 to Rs.7,950/- in 1994-95. This has further increased to Rs.13,193/- in 1997-98. Of course, the per capita income in India has not grown at a pace at which national income has risen over the past 5 decades. [**Table** - 2 reveals the same.]

3. ***Substantial Increase in Investment*** **:** Increase in national income has been due to the increasing investment during the period of economic planning. The amount of investment, both in the public and private sectors, has increased considerably over the past 50 years. The total investment under private and public sectors was Rs.3,360 crores during the First Five Year Plan [1951-56]. This

Table - 2

National Income and Per Capita Income

(At Factor Cost)

At Current Prices	*Net National Product (NNP)** *Rs. Crores*	*Per Capita NNP* *Rs.*
1950-51	8,574	239
1960-61	14,242	328
1970-71	36,503	675
1980-81	1,10,685	1,630
1985-86	2,06,133	2,730
1990-91	4,18,057	4,983
1991-92	4,79,001	5,596
1992-93**	5,43,566	6,234
1993-94**	6,15,273	6,929
1994-95	7,18,639 ***	7,950 ***

* National Income. ** Provisional. ***Non-Official Estimates.

investment under the 8th Five Year Plan [1992-97] was Rs.7,98,000 crores. The investment during the 9th Five Year Plan [1997-2002] was estimated to be around Rs.20,04,000 crores. This increase in the investment has contributed to considerable improvement in agriculture, industry, mining, power, irrigation, trade and transport and so on.

4. ***Impressive Increase in Agricultural Production*** : Agricultural sector too has shown sufficient progress. The agricultural production was 50 million tonnes in 1950-51 and this has increased to 199.3 million tonnes by 1996-97. Tremendous progress has been made in the use of fertilisers, improved seeds, pesticides and agricultural equipments, and so on. Land reforms have been introduced and ownership rights have been conferred on the peasants. Considerable area of waste land has been brought under cultivation. Various multipurpose dams were also built to reduce the dependence on rainfall.

5. ***Sizeable Increase in Industrial Production*** : Indian economy's achievement in the field of industry has also been impressive. The general index of the industrial production [with 1970-71 as the base] increased from 18.3 in 1950-51 to 253.7 in 1994-95. Prior to the adoption of economic planning, India was industrially very backward. But after the introduction of the Five Year Plans, there has been spectacular growth in the heavy industries like iron and steel, cement, fertilizers and chemicals. Many technological developments have been introduced in the field of industries, and a large number of industries have been modernised. It is because of these developments India is moving towards self-sufficiency in industrial goods. In fact, a number of industrial goods, which were in the import list, have now entered the export list. In certain areas, for example, computer software, information technology, cotton textile, leather products, jute products, sugar industry, milk products, manufacture of sewing machines, ceiling fans, bicycles, and such other things, India has maintained a clear lead over majority of the nations of the world.

6. ***Progress in the Field of Science and Technology*** : There has been a significant progress in the field of science and technology over the past 5 decades. In some specific areas, India is able to produce sophisticated machines and instruments with assured quality and precision with indigenous science and technology. In many areas, Indian scientists and technologists have proved themselves to be very efficient and second to none in the world. Particularly after the successful nuclear tests at Pokhran, and the launching of various multipurpose satellites, on the strength of indigenous scientific talent, the image of India has very much gone up. In fact, there is a good demand for Indian engineers and scientists abroad.

7. *Appreciable Increase in Social Overheads* : After independence, we have witnessed an enormous increase in the social overheads. There has been a considerable improvement in the provision of infrastructural facilities and social security services. For instance, transport and communication facilities have been extended. Improvement in power supply has been impressive. Banking and financial facilities have been extended even to the remote villages. Educational facilities have been widened and as a result the rate of literacy has gone up to **65.38%** in 2001. The public health and medical facilities have been improved considerably. As a result, the death rate has now gone down from 49 per thousand in 1950-51 to 9 per thousand in 1999-2000. The life expectancy has gone up from 36 years in 1950-51 to 62 years in 1999-2000. Various social and labour legislations have been enacted to give adequate protection and security to the weaker sections.

8. *Increase in the Standard of Living* : Standard of the living of the people has improved a lot. This has been made possible due to continuous increase in national income and per capita income. Technical and vocational education has enabled people to enjoy a better standard of living. The nationalised banks are also taking sufficient interest in launching various programmes to improve the quality of the life of the masses.

Though the standard of the living of people is increasing we cannot be self-complacent about it. ***Table* - 3** gives us a comparative picture of the standard of living of the Indians in relation to that of the people of a few selected countries of the world.

9. *Provision of Better Opportunities for the Backward Classes* : The government has made special provisions for not only protecting the interests of the backward classes but also promoting their welfare. Various Constitutional and Legislative provisions including the policy of reservation, have given a big boost to the neglected and exploited sections of the Indian populace. As a result, the socio-economic gap between the forward communities and the backward communities has been considerably reduced.

10. *Desirable Changes in the Indian Society* : Caste ridden Indian society which was once branded as a stagnant and a *"closed society"*, is marching ahead towards modernisation. It is getting itself ready to face the challenges of globalisation. India is exposed to the various processes such as urbanisation, industrialisation, modernisation, westernisation, privatisation, liberalisation and globalisation. The age old customs, beliefs, practices including untouchability are on the decline. Science, rationality and technology have now become attractive forces.

Conclusion

On the basis of the above explanation, we can reasonably conclude that India is a fast developing economy. Improvements that have taken place in this land over the last 50 years have changed the very face of the nation. India is a recognisable economic force in the world. No advanced nation in the world can take India for granted. It does not mean that India can have self-complacency. Much has been done no doubt. But many more things are to be done in order to make India a strong and a formidable economic force. As things stand today, it appears as though India is going to take a big leap in the economic, scientific and commercial fields in the coming years.

Table - 3

Some of the Standard of Living Indicators in Selected Countries

Countries	Per Capita GNP US $ 1994	Per Capita daily intake (1993)			Enrolment ratio in primary schools (%) 1993*	Per Capita annual consumption newsprint 1993 (kg)	Physicians per 100,000 population (1993) (No.)	Per 10 person (1992-93)			Access to safe drinking water % of population	Electricity generated (Bn. kwh.) 1990
		Fats gms	Proteins gms	Calories kcal				Radio	TV	Telephone		1991
India	320	38	55	2395	102	0.6	48	8.0	5.0	1.1	75	286.0
Sri Lanka	640	45	47	2275	107	1.1	23	20.0	5.0	1.0	60	3.2
China	530	46	64	2729	121	0.7	115	18.0	23.0	2.3	71	621.2
Pakistan	430	57	62	2316	46	0.5	52	9.0	2.0	1.0	50	49.9
Bangladesh	220	20	43	2019	77	0.4	18	4	0.5	0.2	78	6.1
Japan	34630	81	95	2921	102	29.8	177	91	64.0	68.3	100	856.3
Singapore	22500	79	88	3121	107	36.4	147	65	38.0	47.3	100	15.6
UK	18340	142	94	3270	104	32.2	164	114	45.0	48.9	100	319.2
USA	25880	154	110	3642	104	47.6	245	212	79.0	59.5	100	3031.0

* In several countries it is more than 100% because the actual number of primary students exceeds the population in the age group 6-11 years to which it is related.

Source **:** *(i) Statistical Outline of India* [1995-1996]; *(ii) WHO* [1997] *The World Health Report* 1997; *(iii) World Bank* [1995] *World Development Report* 1995 as quoted by **K. Park** in *"Park's Textbook of Preventive and Social Medicine."* Page - 487.

MARKET ECONOMY AND ITS SOCIAL CONSEQUENCES

Economic Reforms : *Liberalisation - Privatisation - Globalisation*

The Concept of Market

1. According to **Kornblum,** *"Markets are economic institutions that regulate exchange behaviour."*
2. According to **Allan G. Johnson,** *"A market is a social mechanism for exchanging goods and services."*[1]

A hallmark of an industrial society is the production of commodities and services to be exchanged in markets. In a market, different values or prices are established for particular goods and services. These values which vary significantly depending upon the levels of demand and supply, are normally expressed in terms of a common measure of exchange, or *"currency."*

A market is not the same thing as a *market place.* As an economic institution, a market governs exchanges of particular goods and services throughout a society. That is what we mean, for example, when we speak of *"the housing market"*, or *"employment market"*, etc. A market place, on the other hand, is an actual location where buyers and sellers make exchanges.

Market can have a concrete existence in a particular time and place, such as village market, or a stock market. It can also refer to a general pattern through which exchanges are made, such as a *"labour market"*, or even a *"marriage market"*. Markets are based on certain principles such as competition, a fair deal, profit and gaining advantage over others, etc.

MARKET ECONOMY

The historical emergence and growth of market economies are of great interest to sociologists because of their profound influence on social life. Evolution of market is an important stage in the development of economic system. Due to industrial revolution family lost its economic importance and in course of time productive processes reached national and international levels. By the end of the 20th century, the world had reached a stage in which *the economic strength of a country could be judged or assessed on the basis of its market performance.* Among the hunting and food-gathering communities and in relatively isolated agrarian societies before this century, markets in the modern sense of the term did not exist. There existed only the barter system of exchange.

The spread of markets into non-market societies has been accelerated by political conquests and colonialism. Even the tribal groups and the farming classes which had been living far away from the market economy also started showing inclination to purchase and use the modern industrial products.

"In the late 15th and early 16th century, there came into existence what we may call a European world economy......... It was not an empire yet it was as spacious as a grand empire and shared some features with it. But it was different and new. It was a kind of social system, the world had not really known before........ it encomposses....... empires, city-states. and the emerging nation-states."

Political Empires as Primitive Means of Economic Domination

Before the beginning of this Modern Age, and since almost 500 years big empires did exist in the world situation. But most of these were basically political in nature rather than economic. The

1 **Allan G. Johnson** *"The Blackwell Dictionary of Sociology."* Page 164.

political empires required a huge military and civil bureaucracy, which absorbed much of the imperial profit. In the case of India also much of the expenses of the British bureaucracy and military force were being met by the Indian community. Thus *political empires could be viewed as primitive means of economic domination.*

Technology - A Great Achievement of the Modern World

"It is the social achievement of the modern world to have invented technology that makes it possible to increase the flow of the surplus from the lower strata to the upper strata, from the peiphery to the centre, from the majority to the minority." Technologies indeed made the new world system possible. Technologies were not limited to tools of trade such as the compass, the machine gun, mechanised boats, etc. They also included organisation techniques for bringing land, labour and local currencies into the larger market economy. They included new financial and accounting systems. These systems led to the creation of institutions such as banks, co-operative societies, companies, corporations, etc. The term technology referes not only to tools but also to the procedures and forms of social organisation that increase human productive capacity.

Technology Converting the Whole World into One Single Market

The diffusion of technology has been widespread because of improved worldwide transportation and communication. In a real sense the world is not as large as it once was : one can travel from one end of the globe to another, or reach someone a continent away by phone. *One major result is that the world can now be concieved of as a single market place.* There is even evidence of a certain commonality in buyer's preferences around the world. The manufactured goods that appear in the stalls and markets of Bombay, Delhi, Madras are no longer markedly different from goods available in London, Toronto or New York. The plastic bags, tins, plates have replaced the age old banana leaves, earthern pots, etc. Electric batteries have taken over many of the functions of kerosene, wood and vegetable oil.

While the marketplace is gradually being unified in terms of space and tastes, the profits of business are not equally shared. There remains a substantial disparity between the world's *"haves"* and *"have-not"* nations. For example, *"the **140** developing nations accounted for 75% of the world's population but possessed only 20% of all wealth........ Two forces are particularly responsible for the domination of the world marketplace by a few nations;* (i) *the legacy of colonialism and* (ii) *the advent of multinational corporations."*[1]

The Hold of the Multinational Corporations [MNCs] Over the Newly Born Countries

The European colonial powers often used political and military force to bring isolated societies into their markets in the 20th century and maintained economic control over them. This occurred because the economies of the colonial societies had become dependent on the technologies and markets controlled by the European powers. Today some former colonies are beginning to develop independent economic systems, but their ability to compete effectively in world markets is limited by the increasing power of multinational corporations or companies. These companies [MNCs] are economic enterprises that have headquarters in one country and conduct business activities in one or more other countries. They have their business networks throughout the world. Since they have a powerful command over sophisticated production technology and a mastery over business

---

1 **Richard T. Schaffer** *"Sociology - International Edition"* [1989]. Page - 419.

and marketing technology no newly established nation can compete with these companies effectively. Newly independent country like India is also finding it extremely difficult to face the challenges of these MNCs. It is in this context the Government of India undertook to certain economic reforms so as to enable itself to face the economic challenges posed by the multinational companies. The economic reforms launched during the decade 1990s and onwards in the form of *liberalisation - privatisation* and *globalisation* must be understood in this background.

Situation that Triggered the Privatisation Wave in the World

During the 1980s, the disillusionment witnessed in the socialist economies accelerated the process of dissatisfaction with the public sector in the mixed capitalist enterprise systems in the world. The wave of economic reform under *perestroika* started in the U.S.S.R., swept the economies of the eastern Europe. Communist China in the beginning suppressed the move towards democracy in its domain. But it has itself introduced economic reforms since it felt that the public sector could not work with efficiency in its economy. In quite a large number of developing countries in Asia and Africa, the occurence of continued losses in public enterprises forced governments to change their views about the virtues of the public sector. As a reaction to the inefficient working of the state owned enterprises, the wave of privatisation spread all over the world. The dependence of the developing economies on the advanced capitalist economies of the West, especially U.S.A., hastened the process of economic reform. The continuous pressure from the U.S.A. and other capitalist economies on the World Bank, I.M.F. and other international financial institutions to help them to come out of economic crisis also forced them to accept privatisation as the new philosophy for economic rejuvenation.

India's Attempts Towards Economic Reforms
New Economic Policy : *Liberalisation / Privatisation / Globalisation*

In 1990s the Government of India in order to come out of the economic crisis decided to deviate from its previous economic policies and lean towards privatisation. In July 1991 when the devaluation of the Indian currency took place the Government started announcing its new economic policies one after another. Though these policies pertained to different aspects of the economic field they had one thing in common. The common element was to orient the Indian economic system towards the world market. It is in this context the Government launched its new economic policy which consisted of among other things three important features. They are: (i) *Liberalisation,* (ii) *Privatisation,* and (iii) *Globalisation.*

Main Objectives of New Economic Policy - 1991

The main objectives behind the launching of the *New Economic Policy* [NEP] in 1991 by the then Union Finance Minister Dr. Man Mohan Singh, could be stated as follows :

- The main objective was to plunge Indian economy into the arena of "globalisation" and to give it a new thrust on market orientation.
- The NEP intended to bring down the rate of inflation and to remove imbalances in payment.
- It intended to move towards higher economic growth rate and to build sufficient foreign exchange reserves.
- It wanted to achieve economic stabilisation and to convert the economy into a market economy by removing all kinds of unnecessary restrictions.
- It wanted to permit the international flow of goods, services, capital, human resources and technology, without much restrictions.

LIBERALISATION

The term *"liberalisation"* in this context implies economic liberalisation. *"Economic liberalisation"* constitutes one of the basic elements of the **New Economic Policy [NEP]** which the Indian Government launched in the middle of the year 1991. The other important aspects of the policy are - *privatisation of the public sector, globalisation and market-friendly state.*

The main thrust of the New Economic Policy is *"liberalisation."* The essence of this policy is that greater freedom is to be given to the entrepreneur of any industry, trade or business and that governmental control on the same be reduced to the minimum.

The belief behind the policy of liberalisation is that the government instead of keeping with itself all the power and authority to take decisions on economic matters must share the same with the private entrepreneurs so that better control be established on the market.

The main purpose of the process of economic liberalisation is to set business free and to enable it to run on commercial lines. The underlying belief is that commerce and business are not matters to be contained to fixed national boundaries; they are global phenomena. Hence, artificial government restrictions which hinder economic and commercial activities and flow of goods and services must be removed. Governmental restrictions on areas such as – *import and export duties, financing, licensing, foreign investment and dealings in foreign currencies, qualitative restrictions on commercial things, etc.* have been now relaxed. On the contrary, governmental policies and procedures are now expected to provide incentives to investments and accelerate the process of liberalisation and globalisation. Thus, *"liberalisation" intends to liberate commerce and business and trade from the clutches of controls and obstacles.*

Main Features of the Policy of Liberalisation

1. Lessened Government Control and Freelance to Private Enterprises

The main feature of liberalisation is that governmental control over industries, trade and business goes on lessening and in those fields the participation of non-governmental agencies and individual entrepreneurs goes on increasing. The government no more believes in nationalisation as the only solution for all problems in trade and business. On the contrary, *"nationalisation"* of any thing is discouraged and private enterprises are encouraged.

2. Simplification of Licensing Policy

Liberalisation has led to the total review of and simplification of licensing policy. Licences are no longer needed to start a business as has been the case earlier. The government only lays down certain guidelines and puts forward some simple conditions for the private enterprises to be observed while they attempt to start new economic ventures.

3. Capital Markets Opened for Private Entrepreneurs

As a result of the "liberalisation policy" the capital markets too have been freed and opened to the private enterprises seeking capital. Any new company can now be floated with new issue of shares and debentures, etc., without seeking the prior consent or permission of the government.

4. Opportunity to Purchase Foreign Exchange at Market Prices

Liberalisation policy has become so liberal that if an imported-equipment is needed for an industry, the entrepreneur need not approach the government for foreign exchange or seek import license. The entrepreneur can buy foreign exchange in the market at the market-rate.

5. Right to Take Independent Decisions Regarding the Market

The new economic policy which has relaxed many of the rules and regulations, helps the entrepreneurs to make their decisions themselves. Without the interference of the Government, the entrepreneurs can take their own decisions taking into consideration market related prices and profits.

6. Better Opportunity for Competition

Present day economy is virtually market-oriented and hence the entire economic environment provides better opportunities for competition. Due to this competition between the entrepreneurs, quality of the products would be improved. Talents, capacities and good qualities are needed for achieving success in trade.

7. Widened Liberty in the Realm of Business and Trade

In brief, it could be said that the process of economic liberalisation provides maximum liberty to the private entrepreneurs in the realm of business and trade. For example, it removes export restrictions and quantitative restrictions, allows direct foreign investments, permits Indian companies to go global. Liberalisation removes import restrictions by taking out licenses and by reducing customs duty on imports, allows buying or selling of goods, technologies and services from or to any country in the world. Further, the process of liberalisation removes licenses and permits to industry and commerce, it imposes very reasonable taxes and duties to encourage industry and flow of goods. It also liberalises the labour laws permitting free flow of labour. Finally, it allows the free conversion of currency.

Brief Evaluation of Liberalisation

From the Indian point of view, it is very difficult to say at this stage whether the process of economic liberalisation taken up by the Government of India in 1990s has really brought big economic gains to India. The process has no doubt brought some benefits, though suffers from some deficiencies.

The Gains **:** The liberalisation process has helped the free movement of goods and services. It has led to better industrial performances. Industrial organisations have now become more efficient and market responsive. Country's exports are on the increase. Sectors such as information technology and computer software have registered tremendous progress. The annual rate of inflation came down in the previous decade. Bank interest rates have come down. Commercial banks have become more responsive to the financial needs of the industries. Indian industrial sector has become fully aware of the global competition. Labour laws have become highly liberal and this has accelerated the process of globalisation.

The Deficiencies **:** Liberalisation process has its deficiencies also. The economic reforms including liberalisation were introduced all on a sudden and proper background was not created to take their full advantage and to face their consequences. It is alleged that these reforms supported the interests of only the rich and the big business companies. Liberalisation has proved to be a costly experiment for the small scale industrialists and the poor labourers. Proper steps were not taken to equip and enrich human resources. Development strategies are not properly setforth as yet to take the full benefit of the reforms. It has proved to be harmful for the interests of the agriculturists. The pace of liberalisation is also not found to be active, but sluggish.

PRIVATISATION

"Privatisation" is also one of the aspects of the New Economic Policy which came to take shape in the decade 1990. The term "privatisation" connotes wide range of ideas. But the broad meaning of privatisation is that in the economic field much broader role is to be given to the private individuals and agencies and the role of the public sector activities is to be limited.

Definition of Privatisation

1. **Steve H. Hanke** refers to privatisation as – *"the process whereby the public operations are transferred to the private sector."*
2. **Collins Dictionary of Sociology** refers to the process of privatisation as – *"the sale or transfer of "nationalised", publicly owned industries into private ownership and control"* [Page 522].
3. **D.R. Pentse** is of the opinion that – *"any process which reduces the involvement of the state or the public sector in the economic activities of a nation is a privatisation process."*
4. **Barbara Lee** and **John Nellis** define the concept in this manner : *"Privatisation is the general process of involving the private sector in the ownership or operation of a state owned enterprise. Thus the term refers to private purchase of all or part of a company. It covers "contracting out" and the privatisation of management- through management contracts, leases or franchise arrangements."*

The Global Trend of *"Privatisation"*

The disillusionment witnessed during the eighties [1980s] in the socialist economies accelerated the process of disenchantment with the public sector in the mixed capitalist enterprise systems in the world. The wave of economic reform under ***"perestroika"*** started in Russia swept the economies of Eastern Europe. Communist China was also forced to introduce economic reforms for it felt that the public sector did not optimise efficiency and productivity of capital. Excessive bureaucratisation and centralisation in decision making resulted in unwanted delays and escalation of costs in the public sectors in a number of mixed economies including India.

As a reaction to the inefficient working of the state-owned enterprises, the wave of privatisation spread all over the world. The dependence of the developing economies on the advanced capitalist economies of the West provided a chance for these Western countries, particularly the USA to hasten the process of privatisation. The continuous pressure from the USA and other capitalist economies of the West on the World Bank, IMF and other international financial institutions to bail them out of economic crises also forced them to accept privatisation as a new economic philosophy for revitalisation.

It can also be said that the global trend towards privatisation began with the coming into power of Mrs. Margaret Thatcher in Britain and Ronald Reagan in the United States. By 1980s the world economy was taken over by *"Thatcherism"* and *"Reagonomics."* President Reagon [1980-88] of the USA was an advocate of free market economy the world over. This free market economy, he felt, would make enterprises competitive and efficient. Mrs. Thatcher of Britain also favoured radical measures towards privatisation of industry and services. Rest of the European countries such as Germany, France, Italy, Greece, Portugal, Norway, Spain, etc. followed the example set by USA and Britain.

Privatisation in India

The privatisation wave that swept the world did have its impact on India. But in India the wave of privatisation that was generated during the Eighties [1980s] became more powerful when Rajiv Gandhi assumed office as the Prime Minister of India. The issue of privatisation in India has to be understood in the context of – *the relative inefficiency of the public sector industries, dearth of financial resources, defective competition system, continuous labour problems and so on.*

When India became independent it embarked upon planned economic development. In order to accelerate the economic development it started giving more importance to the public sector on which the Government had its control. *The Industrial Policy Resolution of 1956* also gave importance to the public sector industries. *"The need for achieving planned targets, creation of necessary infrastructure, the necessity of achieving the socialistic pattern of society and the inability of the private sector to enter into several critical areas of production"* – also made the public sector to become an integral component of the economic policy of the government. Government's investment in public sector went on increasing from 129 crores in 5 enterprises in 1951 to about 20,000 crores in 250 state enterprises till the middle of the decade 1990-2000.

The growth of the public sector assumes importance in the Indian economy. It contributed to employment opportunities, capital formation, development of infrastructure, increase in exports over the years, and to many other areas. But it failed in certain respects. *It failed to generate adequate surpluses to support sustained growth. The public sector was also a failure in obtaining consistent profits, fulfilling labour demands and interests, encouraging industrial researches, reducing the cost of production, achieving technical expertise, and in successfully facing the competition at the hands of the private sector.* The poor performance of some of these enterprises made them to obtain the label of *"sick enterprises."* As a result of that they were left with large deficits which were covered by funds provided by the public exchequer resulting in budgetary deficits. This issue triggered a public debate on the alternative to public enterprises. During the later years of Mrs. Indira Gandhi's regime a search for the new policy options began. Gradually, a new industrial policy started taking its shape. The essence of this policy is this **:** *The Governmental control in the industrial field must be reduced to the minimum, and the market forces must be allowed to play their role in shaping the economy.* With the announcement of new economic policy on 24th July 1991 by **Dr. Manmohan Singh,** the then Union Finance Minister, India opted for a radical change.

The Particular Context of Privatisation

Ever since the days of independence Indian Government concentrated on Public Sector Undertakings [PSUs] for they were considered to be effective instruments of industrial advancement. In addition to about 400 Central PSUs, the State Governments too have their own PSUs. Even up to 1970s, their role in industrial progress was not very much disputed or questioned. But these PSUs which had turned into governmental agencies over the years, started declining. Production went down, profitability, quality levels of service, etc., were adversely affected. Labour strikes further added to the losses. Not only India, but many countries in the world also experienced the same situation. Some countries started privatisation of these companies on an experimental basis especially after 1980s. Seeing the positive effects, as many as 80 countries went ahead with privatisation, each following its own particular way. India also followed the example of these countries in 1990s particularly when Dr. Manmohan Singh, the Union Finance Minister in the then Cabinet headed by the then Prime Minister Sri P.V. Narasimha Rao, proposed the great economic reforms in the form of the **LPG,** that is, *Liberalisation, Privatisation* and *Globalisation.*

Main Objectives of Privatisation

1. The process of privatisation has been triggered with the *main intention of improving industrial efficiency and to facilitate the inflow of foreign investments.*

2. It also intends *to ensure efficient utilisation of all types of resources* including human resources.

3. *It wants to make the PSUs strong, able and efficient companies.* It recommends a change in the role of the government from that of the *"owner-manager"* to that of a mere *"controller"* or *"regulator"*.

4. Privatisation insists on the government to concentrate on the areas such as education, administration and infrastructure, and to give up the responsibility of looking after business and running industries. It is expected to strengthen the capital markets by following appropriate trade policies.

Arguments in Favour of and Against Privatisation

The *"policy of privatisation"* has become a topic of hot discussions and debates nowadays. It is being defended by a few as an essential and an inevitable step *"to revitalise the Indian economy"*; while a few others have severely criticised it as *"a total sell out"* to the private sector. The idea of the relative merits and demerits of the policy of privatisation is also woven around these arguments. Let us now try to analyse these arguments before taking a final decision regarding the relative propriety of this policy.

• Arguments in Favour of Privatisation

1. *Privatisation is Necessary to Revitalise the State Owned Enterprises* : Indian economy has been struggling to come out of inefficiency, irresponsibility and unregulated growth. Control over the economy has virtually become the concentration of power in the hands of bureaucracy and politicians. A large number of projects are ending in failures because of inefficiency, corruption, delay in the progress of work and enormous amount of loss of resources by way of time and cost. Privatisation is suggested as the panacea for all these perils.

2. *Privatisation is Necessary to Face Global Competition* : The public and the private sector units must function with the positive spirit of competition. Only then, progress could be found in both. These units will be able to face global competition successfully only if privatisation is implemented as a matter of economic policy.

3. *Privatisation is Needed to Create More Employment Opportunities in Future* : Many of the public sector units which are running under loss and labelled as *"sick units"* are not able to generate vast employment opportunities either at present or in the near future. Maintenance of *"sick industries"* itself has posed a big challenge and hence the question of creating new avenues for jobs is beyond imagination. Privatisation is often suggested as a way out for this problem.

4. *Helpful for Mobilising and Investing Resources* : Privatisation is better suited for the mobilisation and proper use of resources. Privatisation is helpful for the recovery of vast resources blocked in the public exchequer for more investment. Consequently, resources available can be utilised for social development, that is, development in important sectors such as – education, housing, health, water supply, sanitation, improvement of transport and communication and so on. If the Government which has the monopoly right over the public sector units is not able to protect the social interests of a large number of employees, the future will be much more jeopardised.

5. *Recognition of Talents and Good Performance of Work*: It is only the private sector which is ready to recognise, encourage and reward the talents, efficiency, honesty and the good performance of its workers. It is ready to give incentives for encouraging good workers. But in the public sector the promotion policy is more guided by the *"seniority principle"* than by the principle of merit or efficiency. The trade unions in the public sector units which demand various incentives for their members organise protests against the management if it takes disciplinary action against the inefficient, dishonest and corrupt employees. This attitude of the trade union damages the dynamism of the public sector managements.

• Arguments against Privatisation

1. *Profitability Alone Should Not Become the Sole Yardstick to Measure Efficiency* : Profitability is very often taken as a yardstick to measure efficiency of public sector enterprises. Those who oppose privatisation strongly criticise this point and assert that the performance of the public sector enterprises covers wide range of things such as – *contribution to development goals of the country, financial viability, optimum utilisation of the resources for research and development, etc.* Public sector units in this way makes greater contribution than mere profitability.

2. *Role of Public Sector Undertakings From the Socio-Economic Angle Also Cannot be Ignored* : Public sector enterprises have a social commitment. *Public sector enterprises incur social cost for the benefit of their employees; payment of higher wages, and provision for education, medical and housing.* The private sector units do not have this kind of social commitment. Hence, most of the workers oppose the very idea of privatisation for they equate it with exploitation. Very few firms in the private sector provide better working conditions and assure reasonable pay scales and retirement benefits.

3. *Protection of the Interests of the Weaker Sections* : It is generally believed that public sector is credited with the social welfare function. Public sector enterprises have the obligation to employ people of the scheduled castes, scheduled tribes, ex-servicemen, political sufferers, the physically handicapped, economically backward and such other weaker sections, sometimes by even relaxing service conditions. Public sector is bound by the *reservation policy* of the government, whereas the private sector units do not have any such commitments or restrictions.

4. *Price-fixing Policy Here is Not Profit-Oriented* : Public sector units are not always guided by the *"profit-making principle." They are influenced by social considerations* rather than strict economic conditions. In many cases, they fix the prices of their products on the basis of *"no profit no loss"* principle.

5. *Argument that the Private Sector is More Efficient than the Public Sector is Not Right* : Empirical evidence about the functioning of the public and private sectors reveals that it would be incorrect to think that the working of the private sector is definitely superior to that of the public sector. "The stark reality is that 2.48 lakh units were sick in the private sector by the end of March 1992, out of which 2.46 lakhs were in the Small Scale Sectors and 2,149 units were in the non-Small Scale Industrial Sector. The total bank credits locked in these units was Rs.11,530 crores. Incidentally, it may be pointed out that in December 1980, the total number of sick units was only 24,550 in which a total bank credit of Rs.1,830 crores, was locked up. Obviously, both in relative and absolute terms, *there is growth of industrial sickness in the private sector."*[1]

6. *It is Improper to Neglect the Truth that in the Beginning the Public Sector had Contributed to the Growth of the Private Sector* : *"In the initial phase of development when the private sector was not in a position to undertake investments in infrastructure and heavy industry, it was the public sector which acted as the leading sector. The public sector, despite all the*

1 **Ruddar Datt** and **K.P.M. Sundharam** *"Indian Economy"* - 2001. Page - 228.

inefficiencies associated with it, did provide irrigation, energy and power at subsidized rates by underpricing of public utilities and other intermediate goods produced by the public enterprise. In that sense, the public sector has contributed to the rapid growth of the private sector."[1]

Conclusion

The experiment of privatisation undertaken in the European countries has been given a lot of publicity in the media. The privatisation programmes implemented in Britain, Mexico and the previously existed East Germany had attained good success. This success has inspired many nations to go in that direction. India is also one among them. *What about the Indian experience of privatisation ? Has it been beneficial or harmful to Indian interests* ? Answers to these questions differ a lot. Economists differ in their view regarding the relative success or failure of privatisation in the Indian context. It is however, widely held that privatisation could achieve notable success only if it is solidly backed by the political authority, effectively implemented by the bureaucracy and implicitly supported by the public. Privatisation becomes successful only when it is made socially and politically acceptable. In a nation like India wherein there is widespread poverty and unemployment and where a large number of people depend for their very existence on the government and its public welfare activities, it is not an easy task and also most impossible to make the policy of privatisation acceptable to the people. It is also recognised that privatisation is complicated and its efficient management is a competent task.

A big country like India which is still in the stage of development, private and public sectors must exist side by side in it. Those who support and those who oppose privatisation have their own strong and weak points. Indian economy at this juncture cannot afford to favour any one of the two at the cost of the other. It is necessary to have a reconciliation between the two [*market-oriented private sector and centrally controlled public sector*] systems and find an effective way of combining market mechanisms and government planning.

Some Remedies for Reforming the Indian Economy

1. *Healthy Competition* : It is suggested that in India both the public and the private enterprises should be mutually complementary and supportive. In order to enhance the efficiency and overall improvement of both, they should develop healthy competition between them.

2. *Some of the Industries must be Left to the Private Sector*: Though the public sector has played the role of the *"senior partner"* in the realm of industries, it is high time that it leaves a few areas to the private sector, that is, the areas in which private sector can function in a better manner than the public sector. Tourism, road transport, education and such other areas could be mentioned here as examples.

3. *State Intervention only to Protect Industrial Interests* : It is wrong to say that the state intervention is always inimical to the growth of industries. Sometimes such intervention may prove to be helpful. For example, the process of industrialisation could be carried on successfully in the post-war period in the nations such as Japan and Korea with the due support of the Governments of these nations.

4. *Successful Handling the Crises of Management* : What the Indian economy requires urgently at present is the evolution of an efficient management culture, because there is a serious

1 **Ruddar Datt** and **K.P.M. Sundharam.** Page : 228 - 229.

crisis of management and that has plagued the public sector.[1] In fact, the issue of privatisation becomes irrelevant if our industrial experts master the art of management.

5. ***Industrial Sector should be Freed from the Stranglehold of the Bureaucrats*** **:** One of the basic problems found in the management of the economy is the excessive hold of the bureaucrats. *"The basic issue here is this : How can we free the private sector from the excessive state control ? Or, how can we bring about de-bureaucratisation ? This implies simplifying rules and procedures and speeding up approvals and wherever controls are not essential, they should be done away with. In the new environment, free of bureaucratisation, the private sector would be able to improve its economic performance."*[2]

6. ***Removal of Poverty and Attainment of Technological Progress- these are our Ultimate Purposes and Not Privatisation*** **: Dr. V.V. Ramanathan** refers to this issue in his own way : *"In view of the historical background of public enterprise in India, it is inconceivable that privatisation in this country will be accepted by the society as an end in itself..... The real issues centre on the alleviation of poverty and the upgrading of technology..... This implies that privatisation will have to be viewed essentially as the best possible means of achieving pre-determined ends, and ensuring that it does not distort the parameters of such ends."*[3]

GLOBALISATION

"Globalisation" represents one of the aspects of the new economic policy launched in the decades of 1980s and 1990s. The new economic policy has also made the economy outwardly oriented such that its activities are now to be governed both by the domestic market and the world market. This will mean unification or integration of the domestic economy with the world economy. The measures taken by the Government of India added momentum to this progress.

Concept of Globalisation

The process of *"globalisation"* has become today one of the important issues of politico-economic discussions. In the media and also in the press this issue is getting lot of propaganda and publicity. In the first half of the 20th century, *the process of industrialisation, urbanisation and modernisation* were considered to be significant while at the fag end of the same century *the processes of computerisation, liberalisation, privatisation and globalisation* became the most fashionable ones. Particularly since 1990s, the issue of *"globalisation"* has become the most crucial one and almost every nation is directly or indirectly influenced by it.

Definition of Globalisation

1. ***Collins Dictionary of Sociology*** **:** *"Globalisation of production refers to the integration of economic activities by units of private capital on a world scale."* [Page - 230.]

2. ***The Blackwell Dictionary of Sociology*** **:** *"Globalisation is a process in which the social life*

---

1 How to make the economy more efficient is the question. *"Punjab, Haryana, Delhi Chamber of Commerce and Industry has put the problem in the correct perspective. The point is that there is a serious crisis of management that has pledged the public as well as private sector. Privatisation of the public sector undertakings would not be of any help so long as there is this crisis of good management....."* – As quoted by **Ruddar Datt** and **Sundharam.** Page - 229.

2 **Ruddar Dutt** and **Sundharam.** Page - 229.

3 **Dr. V.V. Ramanathan** *"Privatisation in Developing Countries"* [1990] - as quoted by **Ruddar Datt** and **Sundharam.** Page - 230.

within the societies is increasingly affected by international influences based on everything from political and trade ties to shared music, clothing styles and mass media."

3. **S.K. Misra** and **V.K. Puri** : *"Stated in simple terms, globalisation means integrating the economy of a country with the world economy."*[1]

4. ***Manorama Year Book* 2002** : *"Globalisation is the process of integration of world's economies in conditions of freer flows of trade and capital and movement of persons across borders, facilitated by new technologies for instant communication of information."* [Page - 63.]

5. ***In simple words,*** the term *"globalisation refers to a process of increasing economic integration and growing economic interdependence between countries in the world economy."*

Main Purposes of Globalisation

The word "globalisation" is now used to sum up the contemporary world order. But the influence of the process of globalisation is directly visible in the economic field and hence the term is very often taken to mean *economic globalisation.* Economic globalisation means *"globalisation of production"* and *"globalisation of market."*

The main purpose of globalisation *is to integrate international market across the geographic and political boundary, so that goods, commodities, services, capital, labour and human population can move freely.* It means expansion of free flow of international trade without any barrier and restriction. "The term globalisation has four parameters **:**

(i) Reduction of trade barriers so as to permit free-flow of goods across national frontiers;

(ii) Creation of an environment in which free flow of capital can take place among nation-states;

(iii) Creation of an environment, permitting free flow of technology; and last but not the least,

(iv) From the point of view of the developing countries, creation of labour can take place in different countries of the world."[2]

The supporters of globalisation especially from the developed countries, limit the definition of globalisation to only three aspects, namely: (i) *unhindered trade flows,* (ii) *capital flows,* and (iii) *technology flows.* They insist on the developing countries to accept their definition of globalisation within the parameters set by them. However, several economists in the developing world believe that this definition is incomplete. They argue that in case the globaliser's ultimate aim is to look upon the world as a *"global village",* the fourth component, that is, unrestricted movement of labour cannot be left out.

Some Features of Globalisation

1. Globalisation is not Entirely a New Concept

The term *"globalisation"* which has come to limelight after 1980s is not entirely a new concept. It had expanded immediately after the industrial revolution and thereafter during the period of colonial rule. The imperialist nations during the 18th, 19th and 20th centuries, for example, had also emphasised *"capital and technology flows"* into the colonial countries. But at that time, they could force their will on the colonial countries because they were the *"ruling bosses."* Two consecutive

1 **S.K. Misra** and **V.K. Puri** *"Indian Economy"* - 2000. Page 738.

2 **Ruddar Datt** and **K.P.M. Sundharam.** Page - 753.

world wars and the events that followed these wars, had stopped the pace of globalisation but it was re-opened in the past couple of decades.

2. Globalisation also Means Globalisation of Production

As it is made clear the most powerful form of globalisation is *"economic globalisation"* in which planning and control expand from a relatively narrow focus to a broad global focus. At the global focus level, the entire world serves as a source of labour, raw materials and markets.

When business is conducted on a local level, for example, problems of dealing with workers, obtaining raw materials and other goods, transportation, and selling the final product – all take place within the same socio-economic framework. In a globalised economy, production also becomes globalised. The *Trans-national corporations or multinational corporations* [MNCs] operate in many different countries at once and exploit variations in local conditions for their own advantage. If workers in a more affluent industrial society such as Britain or the United States, for example, go on strike in order to improve salary or working conditions, a multinational company can simply shift work to another country where workers are more obliging and have lower expectations. The utility of the MNCs to harmonise, integrate and to make their production flexible, is simply tremendous. This ability has been enormously enhanced by the new technologies of communication and robotics. In fact, internationalisation of production has been taking place over the last few decades through these MNCs, which operate with tens of thousands of affiliates.

3. Importance of Export Sectors in Globalisation

In the economy of globalisation the export sector gets the prominence. When export forms an important economic aggregate, the industrial growth to a very great extent becomes dependent upon the export sector. When the industrial production is attached to the export sector, indirectly all the services [including banking, insurance, etc.] get integrated with the export sector. *The total sales of the MNCs in 1998, for example, were of the order of two trillion dollars, almost 1/3 of the world trade in merchandise.*

4. Dependence of Domestic Economy on the Global Economy

Another important aspect of "globalisation" is that it is not an independent process taking place on its own without affecting the nations taking part in it. In fact, the participant nation in it becomes virtually a part of it. As it is made clear, globalisation is linked with and dependent upon exports. The exports themselves are dependent upon the Gross Domestic Production [GDP] growth of the major trading partners. It is in this way, the growth of the domestic economy inextricably gets linked up with the global economics.

5. Globalisation has to take Place within Certain Limits

It is true that globalisation has widened the market economy to the global level and made materials, services and human resources to move freely from one end of the world to any corner in the world. Still the process has to take place within certain limits. "However vocal the advocates of free trade be, still less than 1/4th of the total world production is exchanged through international trade [*Financial Times,* Jan.2001]. Globalisation cannot ignore the question of nationalism or national politics. No country would be willing to participate in world trade without its national interest. The present day export process for development is an area of political economy. Obviously spread of globalisation would be different from situation to situation and from country to country."[1]

1 **Sujit Sikidar** and **Debabrata Das** *"Third Concept"* - October 2001 Issue. Page 11.

Effects of Globalisation

A good lot of discussion and debate is going on regarding the differential roles, dimensions and effects of the process of globalisation. Some defend the process very strongly while a few others criticise the same very severely. Whatever may be the views of these scholars the effects of the process have started emerging out. These effects could be classified into two categories : (a) *the positive effects,* and (b) *the negative effects.*

(a) Positive Effects of Globalisation

1. ***Size of the World has Shrunken*** **:** The process of globalisation has narrowed down the size of the world. Nations of the world are able to come out of their national boundaries and take part in the global economic affairs. Miraculous developments that have taken place in the world of the media and communications, have brought the nations of the world much nearer. This has led to the development of the concept of a *"global village."* The whole globe appears like a "village" now.

2. ***An Increase in the Wealth of the World Due to Globalisation*** **:** Globalisation accelerates the process of exchange of materials which have great economic value, and also helps the exchange of talented persons, education, science and other institutional matters, cultural instruments, etc., between the nations. Such exchanges lead to the scientific, technological, intellectual and cultural enrichment of the world.

3. ***Encouragement to World Peace and Co-operation*** **:** The protagonists of globalisation argue that the process would not only bring the nations of the world together but also motivate them to forge better political, economic and other types of co-operation. Globalisation is regarded as the first step towards establishing *"world peace", "world government", "world parliament",* and so on.

4. ***Advantages of the Healthy Competition*** **:** Due to the pressures of globalisation, goods are to be manufactured with sufficient care and responsibility for a global market. The very presence of a global market creates a healthy competition among the producers. This competition compels them to improve the quality of the products and reduce the prices. The customer also becomes free to select a commodity of his choice. The desire to become successful in the competitive race makes the producers to search for and to patronise good talents and capacities.

5. ***Economic Advantages of Globalisation*** **:** The process of globalisation is supposed to bring various economic advantages among which the following may be noted.

- *Globalisation accelerates the process of industrial growth.* It becomes easier for the industrial units to move from developed countries towards developing countries, from forward countries towards backward countries.
- It helps upgradation and improvement of technology. Borrowing and lending of technical know-how from one country to another, also becomes easier.
- Along with industries and technical knowledge, *capital movement also gets facilitated.* It can move from countries where it is in surplus towards countries, where it is deficient.
- *It helps the speedy production and free flow of goods.* Goods can be produced in the countries where the cost of productions is very less, and supplied to any corner of the world at competitive prices.
- *Globalisation gives impetus to consumption.* Due to the application of sophisticated technology goods can be produced and supplied to the market at competitive prices in attractive styles. Modern media of advertisement also adds to the quantum of consumption. In brief, *it facilitates consumerism.*

- *Globalisation contributes to higher standard of living.* It familiarises international standards. Globalisation has greater employment potentiality. It can fetch greater income to the employees. Hence, human welfare can better be promoted and balanced growth of human personality can be achieved.

(b) Negative Effects of Globalisation

It is said that the disadvantages or the negative effects of globalisation outweigh its advantages or positive effects. Hence, the process of globalisation is very severely criticised in some circles. The main arguments against globalisation may be mentioned here.

1. ***Globalisation Widens the Gap Between the Richer and Poorer Nations*** **:** Critics of globalisation have argued that the process is partial towards the richer nations. Due to this process the rich or the developed nations have become richer, while the developing nations like India are in financial crises; and the poor nations, on the verge of becoming bankrupt. The rich nations by the help of the sophisticated instruments of production, by attracting the talented human resources towards them, and by resorting to powerful advertisements, are able to establish their hold over the market. Hence, the developing countries are not able to face the competition at the hands of these developed countries. Their inability to compete, forces them to withdraw from the world market.

2. ***Disadvantages of the Developing Nations*** **:** Due to the pressure from the international financial institutions such as World Bank, I.M.F., W.T.O., [International Monetary Fund, World Trade Organisation] etc. the developing countries and the underdeveloped or poor countries were compelled to keep open their national markets. But at the same time, the rich and the developed countries are either delaying or reluctant in opening their own domestic market for international trade. This unwillingness or indifference of the developed nations has created problems for the underdeveloped countries. Some underdeveloped nations have started rethinking about their decision of actively participating in the process of globalisation.

Globalisation is Inimical to the Existence of Small Scale Industries [SSIs]

Globalisation which came into force in India in 1991 has been consistently hammering the very existence of the small scale industries. More than 3 lakh small scale industries and more than 3 lakh handloom and powerloom units had to be closed down within the time span of 10 years [1991-2001]. Despite government's commitment to give priority to small scale industries their share has always been low in the banking sector. It means the years of globalisation have affected very badly the SSIs in terms of bank loans. The below mentioned table makes it clear that there has been a consistent fall in the number of loan accounts of SSIs and also in terms of loans. The table reveals a fall in lending to SSIs by public sector banks from Rs.6,344 crores in 1997-98 to Rs.3,454 crores in 1999-2000. The situation in private sector should be worse than this. Further, the SSIs due to their failure in competing effectively with the MNCs are becoming not only weak but also sick. Number of such sick units increased from 2,21,472 in 1991 to 3,06,221 in 1999.[1]

3. ***Exploitation of Poor Nations and Workers by the Multinational Companies*** **:** The multinational companies [MNCs] through the globalisation of production have not only established their supremacy, but also exploited the poor nations. With the entry of MNCs in areas which were the monopoly of the informal sector, large number of artisans – like the basket maker, the potter, village blacksmith, carpenter, spinner, weaver, oil grinder, and a host of others – are being marginalised, driven out of their occupations, and converted into environmental refugees.

1 ***Source of Statistics*** **: Dr. Ashwani Mahajan** *"Globalisation and Small Scale Industries."* Pages 13 & 15 published by Swadeshi Jagaran Prakashana.

Table - 4

Public Sector Banks Loans to SSIs

Year	*Net Lending (Rs. Crores)*	*Percentage in Total Loans*
1997-1998	6344	17.50
1998-1999	4720	17.30
1999-2000	3454	15.63

Year	*Number of SSIs Loans Accounts (in Thousands)*
1997	3059
1998	2484
1999	2425
2000	2241

Source : Report on Trend and Progress of Banking in India [Reserve Bank of India] as quoted by **Dr. Ashwani Mahajan** in his book *"Globalisation & Small Scale Industries"* published by Swadeshi Jagaran Prakashan, New Delhi. Page - 12.

4. *Cultural Invasion through Globalisation* : Globalisation does not merely mean economic globalisation, it has also led to cultural globalisation. Cultural globalisation is often branded as *"cultural invasion."* The *"drinks-drugs and dance"* culture of the West has invaded the whole globe. The media, especially the T.V. media which has added momentum to the process of globalisatin is virtually making the children and youth, total strangers to their own culture. Speaking from the point of view of the Asian countries, it is said that the process of globalisation is proving to be another type of Westernisation, which has made the nations strangers to their own motherlands.

5. *Globalisation is Eating Away the Vitals of the Poor and the Developing Countries* : In the developing countries, MNCs are allowed to feast on natural resources, human resources and national wealth. They displace farmers from their land, workers from their jobs, and communities from their roots. They are responsible for the breaking up of communities and the destruction of environment to serve the human needs and raw material requirements of global production for the global market.

6. *Ecological Effects* : The "ecological effects of globalisation are strikingly catastrophic. Under the fiscal pressures imposed by capital movements, the third World state, in particular, sells off more and more of its public resources – forests, mining regions, natural reserves, and maritime resources. In this context, it is obvious that greater the external integration, greater the exploitation of domestic resources to fuel overseas expansion."[1]

7. *Intensification of Human Insecurity* : One of the main consequences of increasing globalisation has been the intensification of human insecurity. *"The key contributory factors for economic insecurity are – intensified competition, internationalisation of production, changes in the methods of production, surges of financial speculation, and rapidity of technological innovations. Even people with jobs have experienced a deterioration in conditions of employment,*

1 **Dr. D. Jeeval Kumar** in article *"Understanding Globalisation"* in *"Karnataka Journal of Politics."* Issue No.1. Jan. 2001. Page - 7.

as reflected in – the decline of employment security, the increase in casual and part-time work, the increase in work pressure from employers, and the need for constant adjustment to rapidly changing circumstances."[1]

8. *Globalisation Policy has Created a Pool of "Surplus Labour"*: Hence, increasing number of people are forced to migrate in search of work. Migrant workers have long been used by the MNCs as a source of cheap labour and a tool for driving down the rates of pay. They are doubly discriminated – as aliens and also as the lowest paid workers. Further, the migrants frequently work and live in inhuman conditions and are invariably subject to racist scape-goating, especially during the times of high unemployment. The misery of the unemployed and the low skilled in the developed countries is painfully visible in the great cities, nearly as painful as the poverty of the developing countries.

Added to this, full employment has been abandoned as the goal of governments. Governments just leave it to the people the task of finding their jobs except perhaps, recreating a few for carrying out essential services.

9. *Feminisation of Labour* : Another impact of globalisation is the feminisation of labour. As more and more women are forced to look for employment, an overwhelming majority of this labour is being concentrated in low-wage industries like textiles, footwear production. These industries are notorious for exploiting their workers by denying them job security, and their right to organise, etc. They are subject to long working hours without even being provided with basic amenities.

10. *Impact of Globalisation on Agriculture* : The impact of globalisation on agriculture is increasingly being felt. Industrialisation of agriculture which is being imposed on the developing world is posing a serious threat to the livelihood of traditional farmers. The social and environmental consequences of the Green Revolution with its emphasis on intensive irrigation, chemical, fertilisers and pesticides and abandoning of traditional and sustainable practices – are proving to be dangerous.

11. *Violates Human Rights* : Globalisation enriches only a small minority within nations, and within the international system. It marginalises and violates the human rights of millions of people. *"Very specifically, globalisation violates human kind's basic human rights – the right to work, the right to food, the right to livelihood, the right to adequate housing, the right to health, the right to education and the right to development."*[2]

12. *Globalisation Leads to Commercial and Political Exploitation* : Globalisation gives opportunities to the rich countries to establish their industrial units in under-developed countries which ultimately leads to their commercial exploitation. Commercial and business hold which the rich countries establish over the poor countries often culminates in political colonisation. This is how Great Britain made India its colony. Many European countries have such a kind of commercial and political hold over several Asian and African countries.

***The Problem of the Transfer of Natural Resources* :** Rich countries exploit poor countries in yet another manner through globalisation. The developed countries make it a point to establish production units wherever it is advantageous for them to bring down the cost. This leads to the transferring of natural resources from one place to another to the total neglect of the interests of the poor countries where the resources are plenty.

Conclusion

It is clear from the above, that the adverse effects of globalisation outweigh its positive effects. It is true that globalisation brings in its wake great inequities, mass impoverishment, and

1 **Dr. D. Jeevan Kumar.** Page - 7.

2 *ibid* Page - 10.

misery. It fractures society along the existing fault lines of class, gender and community. It almost irreversibly widens the gap between the developed and the developing nations.

What we learn from this process of globalisation is that it is more harmful for the developing and the underdeveloped countries. *"The choice for developing countries like India lies not in total global integration, but less of global integration and more of self-reliance and self-sustenance with an emphasis on indigenous and traditional production and knowledge systems."*[1] Without running away from globalisation and without being caught in its vicious circle, India has to find ways and means of taking advantage of this process.

Multi-National Corporations [MNCs] and their Impact on World Order

The third type of the economy which is growing at a fast rate [almost at an annual rate of 10%], in the world today is no other than the *"multinational corporations"* or *"companies."* They are potentially the most influential and are perhaps the most controversial economic units in the world today.

"A multinational corporation is simply one which owns or manages businesses in two or more countries."[2]

Normally, in their pure forms the multinationals manufacture various goods in many countries, sell to world markets, draw management from several nations, and are owned by shareholders around the world. ***Examples*** : Shell Unilever, IBM, Nestle, Coco Cola, ITT [International Telephone & Telegraph]. At present, multinational company is likely to be centred in one home country.

Mighty Economic Forces

Multinationals have emerged as very powerful economic forces. ***For example,*** the ITT which has diversified into hundreds of industries, now employs 400,000 workers in 68 countries.

Many multinational corporations are richer than some of the countries in which they operate. Already, they account for more than $^1/_4$ of the total economic production. This share is likely to rise over one-half in the next 25 years.

They Represent a New Independent Politico-Economic Force

It is difficult to deny the fact that multinationals constitute a major new and independent force in the world's politico-economic scene. By crossing the national boundaries, these multinational corporations gain independence. ***For example*** : Nestle company of Switzerland [which is one of the world's thirty largest corporations, does 98% of its business outside Switzerland. Hence the Switzerland government can hardly exercise any control and authority over this company.

• Criticisms Levelled against the Functioning of the Multinational Companies

(i) ***Political Interference*** : Multinational companies have drawn criticism during the recent years. To safeguard their interests they have started interfering in the internal political affairs of the countries in which they have their business activities. ***For example*** : (i) The ITT attempted to

1 **K. Kanti Kumar Reddy** in article *"Globalisation and Environment - A Third World Perspective"* in the Journal *"Third Concept"* [October 2001].

2 **Wallace** and **Wallace** *"Sociology."* Page - 510.

sabotage in 1970, Chilean Presidential election to protect its 160 million dollars investment in that country. (ii) It is said, that the Fire Store Company, United Fruit Company, and the Royal Dutch Shell Company had instigated internal conflicts in Liberia, Latin American countries and Sumatra respectively leading to the establishment of military governments. (iii) It is also reported that the American intelligence agency called the CIA had made use of the multinational companies to create political anarchy in nations such as Namibia, Philippines, Nigeria and Morocco.

(ii) *Encourage Corruption* : The multinational companies are prepared to spend any amount to pay towards bribe to protect their interests. ***For example* :** "The ITT secretly requested the Nixon administration to overthrow the government of Chile, offering upto Rs. One million dollars to the federal government as a contribution towards the expenses involved." [**Simpson**].

(iii) *Myth of Employment Generation by MNCs* : Supporters of MNCs have created a myth that they provide large-scale employment to our educated youth. But, in reality these MNCs do not believe in providing employment rather they believe in reducing job opportunities wherever possible. Figures of employment provided by some major MNCs speak the truth themselves.

Ex. : (a) **Nestle India Ltd. :** Though the net sales of this company increased by 55% between 1990 and 1994, the total number of the people employed by the company increased only by 1.5%. In 1994, there were 2,692 persons employed with the company, whereas the total sale was Rs.710 crores. (b) **Sandoz India Ltd. :** In 1984, total number of people employed by this company was 1,960, which declined to 894 in 1995, whereas for the same period profit of the company increased from Rs.194 lakhs Rs.1,856 lakhs. (c) **Hindustan Lever Ltd. :** This company, considered to be the largest MNC in India, with more than Rs.10,000 crores of sales, provide employment to ***only*** 36,000 people.

The MNCs which are motivated by only profits destroy employment opportunities. Even in their own countries of origin they reduce jobs on a very large scale. During the period from 1982 to 1993, MNCs of America, instead of increasing employment, reduced the same by 7.50 lakhs. *The jobs in the largest 500 MNCs of the world have been reduced by 2,62,000 in just one year, i.e., in 1994.* Thus, MNCs whether in India or elsewhere, do business not for promoting job opportunities or generating employment, but only to maximise their profits.

(iv) *Cause Unemployment* : It is clear from the above statistics that MNCs do not provide for more job opportunities, on the contrary, they take off the existing jobs of their own employees thereby they only add to the problem of unemployment. Hence, conflict theorists have branded multinationals as irresponsible exploiters who export jobs from the home country to the poor countries, where they can exploit the unorganised labour of the people. ***For example* :** The Wimco Company manufacturing match boxes made 55,000 families in Shivakashi and other places in Tamil Nadu lose their jobs.

(v) *MNCs Destroy the Small Scale Industries* : The MNCs with their huge capital, wide business network and attractive advertisement techniques provide a tough challenge for the small scale industries. As a result, the small scale industries find it very difficult to sustain themselves. The MNCs which play on the economic weaknesses of the small scale industries ultimately destroy them. It is said that these MNCs have been directly or indirectly responsible for the closure of more than **3** lakh small scale industries and another **3** lakh handloom as well as powerloom units. By destroying a number of small scale industries, and by way of their sales network, these MNCs take home every year, on an average, more than Rs.50,000 crores. About 200 years ago, there was one MNC by name

East India Company, and today there are more than 4,000 MNCs actively engaged in weakening the indigenous industries and looting the country's wealth by way of profit.

(vi) *Consumerism and Cultural Invasion* : These companies have made people to become crazy after new things. They manufacture certain luxurious commodities such as chewing gums, soft drinks, cleaning synthetics; cosmetics such as face cream, shampoo, hair oil, lip stick, etc., and through attractive advertisements bring heavy mental compulsions on people to purchase these. This tendency has led to unwanted consumerism. Further, by introducing Western styles, practices, values, etc., wherever they do their business, they have virtually launched a type of cultural invasion against the national cultures.

(vii) *Danger of Aid and Death Trap* : The multinational companies are making huge profits. They are trying to trap the poor countries by giving them financial and other types of aid. They now represent a disturbing concentration of unscrutinised political and economic power that they may have adverse social impact. The type of financial and other help which these companies are giving for the poor countries has been proving to be a death trap from which they find it difficult to come out. India too is experiencing such an unfortunate situation.

Chapter 18

DEMOGRAPHIC DYNAMICS IN INDIA

Meaning of Demography - World Population Trends *- Growth Rate of World Population - Salient Features of World Population Growth - Demographic Trends in India - Is India Over-populated? - Population Explosion in India - Some Important Aspects of the Growth of Indian Population - Population Explosion - Tests of Over-population - Causes for the Rapid Growth of Population in India -* ***Major Demographic Trends in India :*** *1. Growth Rate of Population, 2. Uneven Distribution of Population, 3. Age Composition, 4. Sex Composition, 5. Density of Population, 6. Life Expectancy, 7. Dependency Ratio, 8. Population and Urbanisation, 9. Birth and Death Rates, 10. Literacy Structure - Occupational Distribution of Population in India - Effects of Over-population - National Population Policy 2000-* ***Family Planning and Its Achievements*** *- Difficulties Involved in the Implementation of the Family Planning - Karnataka Population Highlights-2011.*

Population of the world has been consistently increasing especially after the II world war. In demographic terms, the world is experiencing a period of population explosion. Even India also experienced unprecedented and accelerated growth of population. Its population has already crossed the alarming mark of one billion. Prior to 1921, the population growth in India was insignificant; between 1921 and 1951 it was rapid, and after 1951, it has become ***"explosive."***

Population, itself is not a problem, qualitatively good population with a manageable size, represents the strength of a nation. But if the size becomes unmanageable, the same population invites unwanted problems. It not only halts economic progress but also poses innumerable challenges to the social system. India is unfortunately caught in such a precarious position.

No social problem is beyond human control and solution. A serious problem like *"the problem of over-population in India"* requires an immediate solution. Though it cannot be solved by an act of legislation or by the Presidential promulgation, it can very well be handled skilfully and efficiently.

The Government must be sincere and efficient in tackling this problem. But more than the Government, people must be made to realise the need for controlling the size of their population. A strong *"political will"* on the one hand, and creation of *"general social awareness"* on the other, can alone provide a lasting solution to this problem. This chapter highlights the recent demographic situation in India.

Meaning of Demography

Demography, as understood today, *is the scientific study of human population.* It focuses its attention on three readily observable human phenomena : (a) *changes* in the size of population [growth or decline], (b) the *composition* of the population, and (c) the *distribution* of population in space. It deals with five *"demographic processes"*, namely *fertility, mortality, marriage, migration* and *social mobility.* These five processes are continually at work within a population determining size, composition and distribution. The main sources of demographic statistics in India are population censuses, National Sample Surveys, registration of vital events, and ad-hoc demographic studies.

1. WORLD POPULATION TRENDS

The world population is continuously increasing. Several nations of the world are gripped by the problem of overpopulation. Most of the developing countries are experiencing this problem. At the beginning of the Christian era, nearly 2,000 years ago, world population was estimated to be around 250 million. Subsequent estimates of the world population, and rates of increase are given in ***Table* 1.**

Table - 1

World Population

Year	*Population (million)*	*Average Annual Growth Rate (%)*
1750	791	–
1800	978	0.4
1850	1262	0.5
1900	1650	0.6
1950	2526	1.1
1960	3037	1.79
1970	3696	1.92
1975	4066	1.89
1980	4432	1.72
1987	5000	1.63
1991	5385	1.7
1998	5884	1.6
2000	6054	1.4

***Source* : Park's** *"Text-Book of Preventive and Social Medicine."* Page - 325.

It required all the human history up to the year 1800 for the world population to reach one billion. The second billion came in 130 years [around 1930], the third billion in 30 years [around 1960], the fourth billion in 15 years [in 1974], the fifth billion in 13 years [in 1987], and the sixth billion in 12 years [1999]. On October 12th, 1999 world population became 6 billion. It is expected to reach 8 billion by 2025.

Growth Rate is Faster in the Developing Countries

About three fourths of the world population lives in the developing countries. The UNO has estimated that world's population grew at an annual rate of 1.4% during 1990-2000. But China registered a much lower annual growth rate of population [that is, 1%] during 1999-2000, as compared to India [1.93%]. In fact, the growth rate of China is now very much comparable to that of USA [0.9%].

India, Indonesia and Bangladesh, the three countries of the South-East Asia Region [SEAR], are recognised among the most populous 10 countries of the world. According to UN projections, India's population will reach 1.53 billion by the year 2050, and that will be the highest population in the world. The trend of population increase in the SEAR countries is shown in ***Table* - 2.**

Table - 2

Trends in Increase of Population of South East Asia Region (SEAR) Countries

(In thousands)

Country	*1985*	*2000*	*2005 (Projected)*
India	797940	1008937	1082184
Bangladesh	99310	137439	139911
Bhutan	1451	2085	2313
DPR Korea	18942	22268	25416
Indonesia	167332	212092	226938
Maldives	184	291	355
Myanmar	37544	47749	53479
Nepal	16503	23043	27439
Sri Lanka	16060	18924	19858
Thailand	51128	62806	62612
Total	1176394	1535634	1640505

Source : WHO - World Health Report - 2001.

Growth Rate of World Population

The growth rate is not uniform in the world. There are many countries in the world [*Ex.* European countries] where the growth rate is less than 0.5 per cent per year. In developing countries, the growth rates are excessive - it is around 2.8 per cent in Africa, 1.5 per cent in Latin America, 0.5 in Europe and 1.9 per cent in Asia. A population growing at 0.5 per cent per year will double in about 140 years, a population growing at 3 per cent per year will double in 20-25 years. These differences in growth rates are largely the result of fertility and mortality patterns.

Salient Features of World Population Growth

The salient features of the world population growth at a glance are as follows :

(i) Approximately 95 per cent of this growth is occurring in developing countries.

(ii) Currently, one third of the world's population is under the age of 15 and will soon enter the reproductive bracket, giving more potential for population growth.

(iii) The UNFPA estimates that world population is most likely to nearly double to 10 billion people in 2050, peaking at 11.6 billion reaching 20.7 billion a century later.

(iv) The expected number of births per women, at current fertility rate, is : Africa 6.1; Asia, 3.2; Latin America 3.4; North America 2.0; Europe 1.6.

(v) World population is currently growing at 176 people per minute; 10,564 people per hour; 253,542 people per day; and 92,543,000 people per year.

The world population is indeed, increasing at an alarming rate. This speedy growth of population is one of the greatest obstacles to the economic and social advancement of the majority of people in the underdeveloped world.

2. DEMOGRAPHIC DIMENSIONS IN INDIA

India has a vast population, that is, **121.02** crore in 2011. With a huge population of **121** crore [April 1st 2011] India is the second most populous country in the world, next only to China, whereas seventh in land area. With only 2.4 per cent of the world's land area, India is supporting about 17.5 per cent of the world's population. The population of India since 1901 is shown in ***Table* - 3.** In 2001, India accounted for 19.96% of the estimated population of developing countries.

Table - 3

Growth of Population in India, [1901 - 2011]

Year	*Total Population (in million)*	*Average Annual exponential growth rate (%)*	*Decadal increase or decrease [in crores]*	*Increase in Population during the decade [in percentage]*
1901	238.4	—	------	------
1911	252.1	0.56	+ 1.6	5.7%
1921	251.3	(-) 0.03	- 0.1	0.3%
1931	279.0	1.04	+ 2.8	11.0%
1941	318.7	1.33	+ 4.0	14.2%
1951	361.1	1.25	+ 4.2	13.3%
1961	439.2	1.96	+ 7.8	21.5%
1971	548.2	2.20	+ 10.9	24.8%
1981	683.3	2.22	+ 13.5	24.8%
1991	843.9	2.14	+ 16.1	23.5%
2001	1027.0	1.93	+ 18.4	21.34%
*2011	1210.02	1.76	+18.15 **(crore)**	17.64

Source : Govt. of India - 2001 Census of India 2001. Provisional Population Totals, Paper 1 of 2001.

* As per the first set of data from the 2011 Census (as on March 31st)

Is India Overpopulated - ?

Population, if manageable and efficient, is an asset to any country. It is the index of its inner strength. It leads to a better and fuller exploitation of its natural resources. But if it becomes unmanageable, it eats into the vitals of the nation and becomes an evil. A large size of population by itself must not be confused with overpopulation. A country is over-populated or under-populated in relation to its *area, resources,* and *their utilisation.*

At the present stage of her economic development, there is little doubt that India is over-populated. India's population is about *one-fifth* of the total world population. Population has become a socio-economic problem for India. The following facts would fortify this.

Population Explosion in India !

India is the 2nd most populous country in the world. Its population has been steadily increasing since 1921. Having crossed the mark of **121.02 crore** in 2011 A.D., India's population is currently increasing at the rate of **18.15 million** each year and its annual growth rate is 1.76% as per 2011 census report. India's population is consistently increasing in all the States. State-wise break-up of India's population along with variation in sex-ratio is given in ***Table* - 4.**

Alarming growth of population has become one of the most formidable problems of India today. Massive population is seriously threatening our economic development. ***Tables* 3 - 4** make clear the abnormal growth of population which is, indeed, the population explosion.

India's population numbered 238 million in 1901, doubled in 60 years to 439 million [1961]; doubled again, this time in only 30 years to reach 846 million by 1991. India's population was projected to cross 1 billion mark on 11 May 2000, and to reach 1.53 billion by the year 2050. This will then make India the most populous country in the world, surpassing China.

Some Important Aspects of the Growth of Indian Population

- As per the 1991 census, India's population was 844 millions, and it increased to 1027 millions in 2001, and to 1070.3 million [107.3 crore] in 2004, and 121.02 crore in 2011.
- The land area of the country is only 2.4% of the total land area of the world. But its population is about 17.5% of the total population of the world as per 2011 census.
- At the present rate of growth, India is adding every 10 years a number of people more than double the total population of the U.K., or equal to the entire population of Pakistan or Brazil or more than the half the population of the USA or of the USSR.
- India is just two-fifth of the USA, but India's population is more than 2 and a half times the population of the USA and USSR put together.
- India's population is equal to the total population of 55 countries of Africa and Latin America.
- India's present population [121.02 crore] is equal to the combined population of USA, Indonesia, Japan, Brazil, Bangladesh and Pakisthan.
- In India today, 30 babies are born every minute, 55,000 babies are born everyday and about 13 million babies are born every year as per 2001 census.
- India, it is remarked, adds one Australia [that is the population of Australia] to its population every year.

The Reality of Population Explosion

It is clear from ***Table* - 3** that the population of India has increased by 21.5% during the decade 1951-1961, by 24.8% during the decade 1961-1971, by 24.8% during the decade of 1971-1981, by 23.5% during the decade of 1981-1991, by 18.5% between 1991-2001 and by 17.64 in 2011. ***Table* - 3** shows that the increase in population of India was rather slow upto 1921. The year 1921 is called *"the year of the great divide"* as the growth rate after this has been very sharp. After 1911-21, the decade between 2001-2011 is the first decade to witness a reduction in the rate of population growth. This reduction, however, is only marginal. Hence the rate of growth of population as well as the size of the population of India is definitely very high. On the basis of the rate of growth and the size of population, one can certainly say that there is population explosion in India.

Tests of Over-Population

The following tests make it evident that India is over-populated :

1. The rate of population growth in India is abnormally high, that is 1.76% per annum according to 2011 census report.
2. The rapid increase in population is eating away the fruits of the Five-Year Plans.
3. Per capita income of India is extremely low in comparison with that of many other countries.
4. The country is not able to provide for the minimum requirements of its people for the population is too large and the production too less.
5. Population growth has created problems such as unemployment, illiteracy, poverty, beggary, housing problem, ill-health, etc., which are not met with.

3. CAUSES FOR THE RAPID GROWTH OF POPULATION IN INDIA

Various factors have contributed to the rapid growth of population in India among which the following can be noted :

(i) ***Peaceful Conditions*** **:** For nearly a century [1860-1960] India enjoyed comparative peace without involving herself in major inter-conflicts or wars especially after the establishment of British rule. Peaceful conditions provided an impetus for over-population.

(ii) ***Excess of Birth Over Death*** **:** Growth of population depends on the excess of births over deaths. Death rate has been declining rapidly in India. It was 42.6 per 1000 in 1911 and it decreased to 807 per 1000 in 2001. The birth rate is still high in India. It was 49.2 per 1000 in 1911 and it decreased to only 26.1 per 1000 in 2001. The gap between birth rate and death rate has widened leading to an increase in the population. [The average annual rate of increase of population in India is 1.76% at present [2011] whereas it is only 1.2% in U.S.A., 0.4% in U.K., 1.1% in China, 0.4% in France and 0.3% in Japan.]

(iii) ***Progress in Medical Knowledge*** and its application has considerably reduced the death rate. It has helped us to control the spread of diseases like Malaria, T.B., Cholera, Plague, Influenza, Smallpox, etc., and protected the lives of people from the jaws of death. Positively, it has contributed to greater population, because, those persons saved from the death also produced children to add to the existing numbers.

(iv) ***Improvement in Transport Facilities*** has helped people to avail of medical and health facilities without much difficulty. These have saved countless lives and added to the size of the population.

(v) ***Improvements in the field of Agriculture and Industry*** also contributed to an increase in population. Uncertainties in the field of agriculture have largely been removed with the help of science and technology. Food production has considerably increased. Industries have been providing employment opportunities to thousands of persons. These developments have given people the confidence that they can afford to feed more people if they beget.

(vi) ***Certain Social Factors like Universal Marriage, Child Marriage, Early Marriage*** have also contributed to the problem. Indians consider marriage as a social obligation and almost all marriageable persons are in a married state. Life-long bachelorship is looked down upon. Particularly for women marriage is almost an inescapable obligation. Further, the number of children born per couple is also large.

(vii) ***Social Attitudes of Indians*** also favour an increase in population. Poverty, illiteracy, ignorance, absence of recreational facilities, attitudes of conservatism, orthodoxy, feeling of dependence on God, a sense of resignation towards life, looking upon children as old age pension, etc., are all responsible for the rapid growth of population.

(viii) ***Lack of Conscious Family Planning*** **:** There is the lack of conscious family planning on the part of the married people. The use of contraceptives is unknown to the illiterate masses. People feel that more children are wanted for economic purposes. Further, blind faith in fate and the existence of joint family system induce thoughtlessness in the matter of begetting children.

(ix) ***The Climatic Conditions of India*** are also very conducive to the growth of population. The tropical climate stimulates sex urge. **Montesquieu** said that people of warm land are more sex-indulgent. Further, girls become physically mature at an early age ranging from 11 to 15 years of age. Immediately after puberty they are pushed into marriage and they begin to bear children. Child-bearing capacity of women lasts in the tropical places.

(x) Added to this, during the earlier days the ***Government did not take much interest in introducing family planning*** to slow down the rapid growth of population. Though family planning

Table - 4

Population Size of States / UTs As Per 2001 Census

S. No.	India / State / Union Territories	POPULATION PERSONS	MALES	FEMALES	Population Variation 1991-2001	Sex Ratio (Females per 1000 males)	* Population Share of Some states in 2011 in %
	INDIA	**1,027,015,247**	**531,277,078**	**495,738,169**	**21.34**	**933**	
1.	Andaman & Nicobar Is.*	356,265	192,985	163,280	26.94	846	
2.	Andhra Pradesh	75,727,541	38,286,811	37,440,730	13.86	978	7
3.	Arunachal Pradesh	1,091,117	573,951	517,166	26.21	901	
4.	Assam	26,638,407	13,787,799	12,850,608	18.85	932	3
5.	Bihar	82,878,796	43,153,964	39,724,832	28.43	921	9
6.	Chandigarh*	900,914	508,224	392,690	40.33	773	
7.	Chhattisgarh	20,795,956	10,452,426	10,343,530	18.06	990	2
8.	Dadra & Nagar Haveli*	220,451	121,731	98,720	59.20	811	
9.	Daman & Diu*	158,059	92,478	65,581	55.59	709	
10.	Delhi	13,782,976	7,570,890	6,212,086	46.31	821	1%
11.	Goa	1,343,998	685,617	658,381	14.89	960	
12.	Gujarat	50,596,992	26,344,053	24,252,939	22.48	921	5
13.	Haryana	21,082,989	11,327,658	9,755,331	28.06	861	2
14.	Himachal Pradesh	6,077,248	3,085,256	2,991,992	17.53	970	
15.	Jammu & Kashmir[2, 3]	10,069,917	5,300,574	4,769,343	29.04	900	1%
16.	Jharkhand	26,909,428	13,861,277	13,048,151	23.19	941	3
17.	Karnataka	52,733,958	26,856,343	25,877,615	17.25	964	5
18.	Kerala	31,838,619	15,468,664	16,369,955	9.42	1,058	3
19.	Lakshadweep*	60,595	31,118	29,477	17.19	947	
20.	Madhya Pradesh	60,385,118	31,456,873	28,928,245	24.34	920	6
21.	Maharashtra	96,752,247	50,334,270	46,417,977	22.57	922	9
22.	Manipur	2,388,634	1,207,338	1,181,296	30.02	978	
23.	Meghalaya	2,306,069	1,167,840	1,138,229	29.94	975	
24.	Mizoram	891,058	459,783	431,275	29.18	938	
25.	Nagaland	1,988,636	1,041,686	946,950	64.41	909	
26.	Orissa	36,706,920	18,612,340	18,094,580	15.94	972	3
27.	Pondicherry*	973,829	486,705	487,124	20.56	1,001	
28.	Punjab	24,289,296	12,963,362	11,325,934	19.76	874	2
29.	Rajasthan	56,473,122	29,381,657	27,091,465	28.33	922	6
30.	Sikkim	540,493	288,217	252,276	32.98	875	
31.	Tamil Nadu	62,110,839	31,268,654	30,842,185	11.19	986	6
32.	Tripura	3,191,168	1,636,138	1,555,030	15.74	950	
33	Uttar Pradesh	166,052,859	87,466,301	78,586,558	25.80	898	16
34.	Uttaranchal	8,479,562	4,316,401	4,163,161	19.20	964	1
35.	West Bengal	80,221,171	41,487,694	38,733,477	17.84	934	8
							Other States-2%

Notes : 1. The population of India includes the estimated population of the entire Kachchh district, Morvi, Maliya-Miyana, and Wankaner talukas of Rajkot district, Jodiya taluka of Jamnagar district in Gujarat and the entire Kinnaur district of Himachal Pradesh where population enumeration of the Census of India 2001 could not be conducted due to natural calamity.

2. For working out density of India, the entire area and population of those portions of Jammu and Kashmir that are under occupation of Pakistan and China have not been taken into account.

(*Source* : *Provisional Population Totals* : *India.* Census of India, 2001, Paper 1 of 2001 as quoted by ***"India Book of the Year 2002"*** published by *Encyclopaedia Britannica (India) Pvt. Ltd.* & *The Hindu.* **Page 253-254)**

* As per the provisional data of 2011 census as published on 1st April 2011.

programme was started under the Five Year Planning system, proper attention was not given to popularise it in the beginning. People also failed to recognise its importance. The result is the phenomenal growth of population.

(xi) ***Lack of Entertainment Facilities*** **:** It has been observed that people especially in the rural areas, have been forced to find *entertainment in the sex-play* in the absence of proper entertainment facilities. This has further aggravated the problem.

4. MAJOR DEMOGRAPHIC TRENDS IN INDIA

India, as it is made clear, is the second most populous country in the world. Its total population crossed the mark of 121.2 crore by March 2011. Its population is currently increasing at the rate of 18.15 million per year. The average annual exponential growth rate of India's population is 1.76% in 2011. The salient demographic features or trends of India's population may be noted below.

1. Growth Rate of Population

The population of India grew at a slow rate prior to 1921. But its population has started growing at a fantastic rate of speed particularly after 1931. The population growth rates in India are presented in ***Table*** **- 3.** The average annual growth rate of India's population was 0.56% in 1911 and it reached the record height of 2.22% in 1981. However, it has come down to 1.9% in 2001, and further to 1.76% in 2011.

2. Uneven Distribution of Population

Population of India is not equally distributed among all the states. On the contrary, we find heavy concentration of people in some states rather than in others. ***Table*** **- 5** shows the ten most populous states in the country by rank. As per 2011Census, the state of Uttar Pradesh comes first with about 200 million people followed by Maharashtra with 112 million, Bihar with 103 million and so on. It is significant to note that these 10 states account for about 76.34% of the total population of India.

3. Age Composition

As per 2011 Census, the population of children [0-to-6 years] has declined by 5 million over the 2001 Census. In general, the proportion of population below 15 years is showing decline, whereas the proportion of elderly people in the country is increasing. This trend may continue in the time to come.

Table - 5

Ranking of Most Populous States by Population Size in 2001 and 2011

Rank	*State*	***Population 1-3-2001 (million)***	***Per cent to total population of India 1-3-2001***	****Population March-2011 (Millions)***	****Percent in to Total population of India***
1.	Uttar Pradesh	166.05	16.17	200	16%
2.	Maharashtra	96.75	9.42	112	9%
3.	Bihar	82.87	8.07	103	9%
4.	West Bengal	80.22	7.81	91	8%
5.	Andhra Pradesh	75.72	7.37	84	7%
6.	Tamil Nadu	62.11	6.05		6%
7.	Madhya Pradesh	60.38	5.88		6%
8.	Rajasthan	56.47	5.50		6%
9.	Karnataka	52.73	5.14	611	5%
10.	Gujarat	50.59	4.93		5%

Source : Census of India 2001. Provisional Population Totals, Paper 1 of 2001.

* Provisional statistics Relating to 2011 censes.

The increase in the elderly population will impose a greater burden on the already outstretched health services in the country.

The age composition of India's population according to National Family Health Survey - 2 [NFHS-2] done in 1998-99 is shown in ***Table* - 6.** The age composition of people in any country is very much related to components of population change like *fertility, mortality, age at marriage, migration, etc.* Its distribution also has its important socio-economic effects. A large number of people under the age group of 0.14, that is, 37.3% in 2001 would lead to certain effects such as – allocation of large amount of fund to provide for health, medical and educational needs for children; more dependents on working people and low productivity of labour.

Table - 6

Percent Distribution of Population by Age and Sex From the NFHS - 2, India, 1998-99

Age	*Male*	*Female*
0 - 4	11.2	11.1
5 - 9	12.8	12.4
10 - 14	12.1	11.8
15 - 19	10.4	10.3
20 - 24	8.5	9.3
25 - 29	7.8	8.7
30 - 34	6.7	7.1
35 - 39	6.6	6.4
40 - 44	5.1	4.7
45 - 49	4.5	4.2
50 - 54	3.4	3.1
55 - 59	2.6	3.3
60 - 64	2.9	3.0
65 - 69	2.0	2.0
70+	3.3	2.8
Total	100.0	100.0

Source **:** Govt. of India [2000] Annual Report 1999-2000

Table - 6(A)

Percentage Distribution of India's Population by Age Groups

Year	*Age Gourp*		
	0-14	**15-60**	**60 and above**
1911	38.8	60.2	1.0
1921	39.2	59.6	1.2
1931	38.3	60.2	1.5
1951	37.4	57.1	5.5
1961	41.0	53.3	5.7
1971	41.4	53.4	5.2
1981	39.7	54.1	6.2
1991	36.5	57.1	6.4
2001	37.3	55.4	7.3

Source **:** IAMR, Fact Book on Manpower, Census of India 2001.

4. Sex Composition

Sex ratio is one of the characteristics of the population. It has an important bearing upon marriage rate, death rate, birth rate and even migration rate. The sex ratio is defined as *"the number of females per 1,000 males."* In any study of population, analysis of the sex composition or sex ratio plays a vital role. The major trends in the sex ratio in the country from 1901 onwards are represented in ***Table* - 7.** According to the 2001 census figures, there are 933 females per 1000 males in India. This sex ratio recorded a slight increase from 933 in 2001 to **940 in 2011.** There are various reasons for this imbalance in the sex ratio. Factors such as *female infanticide, neglect of female infants, early marriage, bad treatment and hardwork of women, craving for male children, practice of dowry, dominant patriarchal values, etc.* have been instrumental in reducing the number of females in India. It is also significant to note that the sex ratio is higher in the urban areas and among the educated, than in the rural areas and among the uneducated. It is also observed that there are 13 States with sex ratio above the national level and 12 States with sex ratio lower than the national level. Kerala and Pandichery the only states wherein women outnumber men, and there are **1084** and **1038** women per 1000 men in 2011 in these states respectively.

1901-2011 Table - 7

Sex Ratio in India

Year	*Females per 1000 Males*
1901	972
1911	964
1921	955
1931	950
1941	945
1951	946
1961	941
1971	930
1981	934
1991	927
2001	933
2011	940

Table - 8

Density of Population in India 1901-2011

Year	*per sq. km.*
1901	77
1911	82
1921	81
1931	90
1941	103
1951	117
1961	142
1971	177
1981	216
1991	267
2001	324
2011	382

5. Density of Population

Density is also a major factor in the study of population. In the Indian context, *density is defined as the average number of persons living per square kilometre.* The trends of the density of population in the country from 1901 onwards are shown in ***Table* - 8.** The density of population was found to be 77 in 1901 and 324 in 2001and it increased to the record mark of **382 in 2011**. Dehli with 11297 persons per sq. km in 2011 is the most densely populated state in India. Arunachal Pradesh with just 17 persons per sq. Km is the least densely populated state. Comparatively, China has a density of population of 135 persons, whereas Canada, Australia and America have 3, 2, and 31 persons respectively.

6. Life Expectancy

Life expectancy or expectation of life at a given age is the average number of years which a person of that age may expect to live, according to the mortality pattern prevalent in that country. Demographers consider it as one of the best indicators of a country's level of development and the overall health status of its population.

***Table* - 9 & 10** present life expectancy at birth in India and those in selected countries. Japan leads in life expectancy for both males and females, 77 and 83 years respectively for the year 1998.

Table - 9

Expectation of Life at Birth – India

Year	*Males*	*Females*
1901	23.63	23.96
1911	22.59	23.31
1921	19.42	20.91
1931	26.91	26.56
1941	32.09	31.37
1951	32.45	31.66
1961	41.89	40.55
1971	46.40	44.70
1981	50.90	50.00
1991	58.10	59.10
2000	62.80	63.80

Source : Park's *"Text-book of Preventive and Social Medicine"* [2002]. Page - 331.

Table - 9(A)

Rural and Urban Population 1901 - 2001

Census Year	*Population (m.)*		*Percentage of (m.)*	
	Rural	*Urban*	*Rural*	*Urban*
1901	213	26	89.2	10.8
1911	226	26	89.7	10.3
1921	223	28	88.8	11.2
1931	246	33	88.0	12.0
1941	275	44	86.1	13.9
1951	299	62	82.7	17.3
1961	360	79	82.0	18.0
1971	439	109	80.1	19.9
1981	524	159	76.7	23.3
1991	629	218	74.3	25.7
2001	741.7	285.4	72.22	27.78

Source : Census of India, 2001

Table - 10

Expectation of Life at Birth in Selected Countries - 2000

Developing Countries	*2000 Male*	*2000 Female*	*Developed Countries*	*2000 Male*	*2000 Female*
Nepal	58.8	58.3	UK	75.2	80.2
Bangladesh	59.4	59.5	USA	74.1	79.9
Myanmar	53.7	58.5	Sweden	77.2	82.2
India	62.8	63.8	Switzerland	75.6	82.0
Sri Lanka	69.5	75.3	Russian Federation	61.0	73.0
Thailand	67.3	73.2	Japan	77.4	84.4

Source : **Park's** *"Text-book of Preventive and Social Medicine"* [2002]. Page 331.

As far as India is concerned, in the year 1901, the life expectancy of males and females at birth was found to be 23.63 years and 23.93 years, respectively. These figures have increased respectively to 62.80 years and 63.80 years in 2000.

Trends in life expectancy show that people are living longer, and they have a right to a long life in good health, rather than one of pain and disability. Health policy makers need to recognise this changing demographic pattern, and plan for prevention and control of diseases associated with old age.

7. Dependency Ratio

The proportion of persons above 65 years of age and children below 15 years of age are considered *to be dependent* on the economically productive age group [15 - 64 years]. *The ratio of the combined age groups 0 - 14 years plus 65 years and above to the 15 - 65 years age group – is referred to as the total dependency ratio.* The dependency ratio reflects the need for a society to provide for their younger and older population groups.

In terms of dependency ratio, we can also speak of *young age dependency ratio* [0 - 14 years]; and *old age dependency ratio* [65 years and more]. These ratios are, however, relatively crude, since they do not take into consideration elderly or young persons who are employed or *working age persons* who are unemployed. ***Table*** **- 11** shows the trends of dependency ratio in India.

Table - 11

Trends in Dependency Ratio in India (per 100)

Year	*Total Dependency*	*Child Dependency*	*Old-age Dependency*
1985	71.5	64.3	7.2
1995	65.5	57.8	7.6
2005 (projected)	55.5	47.2	8.3

Source : WHO [1999] Health Situation in the South East Asia Region 1994-97.

8. Population and Urbanisation

Growth of population in most of the developing countries is closely associated with growing urbanisation. Urbanisation is taking place at a relatively greater speed in India. The proportion of urban population in India increased from 10.84% in 1901 to 17.3% in 1951, to 25.7% in 1991, and to

27.8% in 2001 and was projected to be 32% in the year 2011. In absolute terms, the urban population in India was 285 million in 2001 compared to 217.17 million in 1991. See ***Table* - 9(A).**

The percentage of population residing in urban areas has increased marginally. The number of urban areas and towns increased from 3,378 in 1981 to 3,768 in 1991. In 2001, three major cities of India - Mumbai, Kolkota and Delhi - attained the status of **mega-cities** each with a population of more than 10 million. The pace of urbanisaion is relatively due to predominance of agriculture, slow rate of industrialisation, low rate of literacy, slow growth of towns and cities, slow rate of social and occupational mobility, shortage of capital, etc.

9. Birth and Death Rates

The birth and death rates are important components of population growth. The birth and death rates in India are shown in ***Table* - 12.** A look at ***Table* - 12** shows that whereas the death rate considerably declined from 42.6 in 1911 to 8.7 per thousand population in 2001; and the birth rate declined niggardly from 49.2 in 1911 to 26.1 per thousand in 2001.

The birth rate in India was 26.1 per thousand in 2001 and the death rate was 8.7 per thousand for the same period. This widened the gap between the birth rate and the death rate. As a result, the net rate of increase of population in the country is 1.9%. This is the most significant factor behind the population explosion in India.

India like many other developing countries is faced with the problem of a high birth rate and a declining death rate. ***The causes of high birth rate are*** – (i) universality of marriage, (ii) early marriage, (iii) early puberty, (iv) low standard of living, (v) low level of literacy, (vi) traditional customs and habits, (vii) absence of family planning habit, etc.

Declining death rate has been attributed to – (i) mass control of diseases such as smallpox, plague, cholera, malaria, etc. (ii) better health facilities, (iii) impact of national health programmes, (iv) absence of natural checks as found in the instances of famines, floods, large scale epidemics, etc., (v) improvements in food supply, (vi) international aid in different ways, (vii) development of social

Table - 12

Birth and Death Rates in India

Year	*Birth Rate*	*Death Rate*
1911	49.2	42.6
1941	39.9	27.4
1951	41.7	22.8
1961	41.2	19.0
1971	37.2	14.8
1981	33.9	12.5
1991	29.5	9.8
1995	28.3	9.0
1996	27.5	9.0
1997	27.2	8.9
1998	26.4	9.0
1999	26.1	8.7
2001	26.1	8.7

Source : Govt. of India [2002], Annual Report 2001-2002, Ministry of Health & Family Welfare, New Delhi.

Table - 12 (A)

Birth and Death Rates in India

Census Year	*Percentage of total Population*		*Urban - rural ratio*
	Rural	*Urban*	
1901	89.0	11.0	1:8.1
1911	89.6	10.4	1:8.6
1921	88.7	11.3	1:7.8
1931	87.8	12.2	1:7.2
1941	85.9	14.1	1:6.1
1951	82.7	17.3	1:4.7
1961	82.0	18.0	1:4.5
1971	80.1	19.9	1:3.7
1981	76.7	23.3	1:2.9
1991	74.3	25.7	1:2.9
2001	72.2	27.8	1:2.6
2011	68.0	32.0	
2026	63.8	36.2	

Source : Register General, India.

consciousness among the masses. The demographers are of the opinion that in future rapid decline in India's death rate may not be continued.

10. Literacy Structure

As far as the literacy structure of the country is concerned, in 2011, on an average, around **74.04%** people are found to be literate [**82.14%** males and **65.46%** females]. Kerala is a state wherein we find the highest literacy rate, that is **93.91%** and Bihar has the lowest one, that is, **63.82%.**

Of the total literate people in India in 1991 [846.3 million], 56.7% had less than 3 years education, 23.8% 3-6 years education, 11% 7-11 years education, 6.8% 12-14 years education and 1.7% more than 14 years education. It is evident that we find a very limited number of people with college education. While the literacy rate for males rose from 75.26 to 82.14% marking a rise of **6.9%** it increased by **11.8%** for females to go from 53.67 to 65.46 per cent.

If we look at the State-wise break-up of the literacy rate, we find that Kerala continues to occupy the top rank in the country with about 93.91% literates (2011). Ten states and union territories, including -Kerala, Lakshdveep, Mizoram, Tripura, Goa, Damun and Diu, Puduchery, Chandigarh, Delhi, Andaman and Nicobar Inlands - have attained a literacy rate of above **85%**, one target set by the planning commission to be achieved by 2011-12.

Table - 13 (A)

Literacy Rates in Major States of India – 2001

State	*Male*	*Female*	*Total*
U.P.	71	44	58
Bihar / Jharkhand	62	35	49
Rajasthan	76	44	61
M.P.	77	51	64
Haryana	79	56	69
Assam	72	56	64
Gujarat	80	59	70
Orissa	76	51	64
Maharashtra	86	68	77
Punjab	76	64	70
West Bengal	78	60	69
Karnataka	76	56	67
A.P.	71	51	61
Tamil Nadu	82	65	73
Kerala	94	88	91
India	76	54	65.38

Source : Govt. of India [2001] Census of India 2001. Provisional Population Totals, Paper 1 of 2001.

Table - 13 (B)

Literacy Rates in India : 1951 - 2011

Year	**Total** *Persons*	*Males*	*Females*
1951	18.33	27.16	8.86
1961	28.30	40.40	15.35
1971	34.45	45.96	21.97
1981	43.57	56.38	29.76
1991	52.21	64.13	39.29
2001	65.38	75.85	54.16
* 2011	74.04	82.14	65.46

Source : Census of India, 2001.
* Povisional Statistics, census 2011

Occupational Distribution of Population in India

Occupational distribution of population or occupational pattern in India refers to – *the proportion of total working population engaged in different broad sectors of the economy.* These broad sectors are – **1.** ***Primary sector*** which includes occupations like agriculture, mining, fishing, animal husbandry and forestry, **2.** ***Secondary sector*** which consists of occupations like manufacturing, construction, electricity, etc., and **3.** ***Tertiary sector*** which consists of occupations such as trade, transport, communications, banking, insurance, personal services, and both government and non-governmental services, etc. This sector is supposed to meet the needs of both primary and secondary sectors.

It is quite significant to note that the occupational distribution of population in the country remained almost constant over the last 90 years. ***Table* - 14** reveals the same. Even after the vigorous efforts by the Central and the State Governments to develop industries, trade, transport and communication, banking, insurance, etc. the majority of our working population are still dependent on agriculture for their livelihood. During the recent years, that is, after 1991 sizeable number of educated piople have been able to get jobs with attractive salaries in the service sector.

The occupational distribution of population in India is imbalanced. It shows that India is still backward in the field of industries and depending too much on agriculture. Inadequate and lop sided growth of secondary and tertiary sectors is another fundamental cause for this imbalance in the occupational distribution. The performance of public sector industries is not that satisfactory, and the tertiary sector too has failed to absorb the excess population.

In order to forge a balance in the occupational distribution of the people, it is necessary for us to give more importance to industrial growth. Industry should be able to attract and accommodate a sizeable number of people from the rural areas to lessen their dependence upon agriculture. Further, the tertiary sector which consists of trade and commerce should be developed to absorb increasing number of unemployed youths.

Occupational Distribution of Working Population in India [in %] **Table - 14**

Year	*Primary Sector*	*Secondary Sector*	*Tertiary Sector*
1901	72%	12%	16%
1951	72%	11%	17%
1971	72%	11%	17%
1981	68.7%	13.5%	17.8%
1991	65%	15.0%	20.0%
1999-2000	60.4%	15.8%	23.8%

Source : Census of India, 1981 - 1991. For 1999-2000, NSSO 55th Round

5. EFFECTS OF OVER POPULATION

If the size of population of the country reaches the optimum level, it will not pose any problem. If the growth exceeds the reasonable limits, problems will crop up and that has happened in India. It means population in excess of demand or need proves to be a great liability to the society. The unprecedented growth of population in India during the recent years, has brought about a series of serious consequences. Some of the main effects of population may be described here.

(i) *Population and Poverty* : Poverty and population very often go hand in hand. In fact, poverty is both the cause and the effect of rapid growth of population. The mass poverty of our country is due to the rapid growth of population. It is estimated that about 26% [1999-2000] of the people of India still live below the poverty line. They are ill fed, ill clothed and ill housed. Thus, mass poverty is due to rapid growth of population.

(ii) *Unemployment and Under Employment* : Not only new born individuals are to be fed and sheltered but they are also to be provided with jobs. New jobs are to be created for new hands. It is not easy to create jobs. There is already unemployment coupled with under employment.

Every year more than 5 million people who attain the working age join the group of job seekers. Job opportunities that are created during the course of the Five Year Plans are not enough to meet the demand. For instance, the number of the unemployed increased from 12 million at the end of the Third Plan to 16 millions at the end of the Fourth Plan, and to 21 millions at the end of the Fifth Plan. The percentage of the people who did not get employed as per 1991 census was 42.3%. As per the figures for 2003, about 41.39 million individuals were waiting [for jobs] in the live registers of 945 employment exchanges scattered over the whole nation. [Bhagavati Committee etimate]. As per the estimates of the 8th and 9th Plan, there would be 106 million job- seekers in India by 2000 A.D.

(iii) ***Low Per Capita Income*** **:** During the past 50 years of planning, the national income of the country has increased by about 3.6% per annum. But the per capita income has increased only by 1.5% per annum. This low per capita income of the people in India is attributed to the rapid growth of population.

(iv) ***Shortage of Food*** **:** The rapidly growing population in India has led to the problem of shortage of food supply. In spite of the fact that more than two-third of its population engaged in agriculture, people do not get even minimum necessary amount of food. Even though we have attained self-sufficiency in food production, due to improper distribution, all the people do not get sufficient food to sustain their health. As a result one out of every four is suffering from malnutrition and two out of every four get only half of the daily required quantum of energising food.

(v) ***Increased Burden of Social Overheads*** **:** When there is rapid growth of population in the country, the government is required to provide the minimum facilities for the people for their comfortable living. Hence it has to increase educational, housing, sanitation, public health, medical, transportation, communication and other facilities. This will increase the cost of the social overheads. Government finds it difficult to find sufficient funds to meet these *"unproductive expenses."*

(vi) ***Population and Labour Efficiency*** **:** Since an increase in population reduces per capita income, the standard of living of the people deteriorates. This affects very badly the health and efficiency of the workers. The physical and the mental efficiency of the workers naturally comes down. Labour inefficiency reduces productivity and the nation at large loses very heavily.

(vii) ***Population and the Standard of Living*** **:** The standard of living denotes the way in which people live. It reflects the quantity and the quality of the consumption of the people. Due to the rapid growth of population standard of living of the people has been adversely affected.

(viii) ***Population and Pressure on Land*** **:** Overpopulation inevitably leads to heavy pressure on land. Since land is limited and fixed in supply, an increase in population can only bring more pressure on it. Hence the new born people will have to share the land with the existing people. With the exception of Rajasthan and Madhya Pradesh, in all the other states heavy density of the population is to be found. Further, the per head availability of the land for cultivation in the 1911 was 1.1 acres, and this has declined to 0.3 acres in 1992. On the contrary, the average size of the agricultural land that each person could get is 2.59 acres in Russia, and 2.68 acres in America.

(ix) ***Increased Unproductive Consumers*** **:** When there is a rapid growth of population in a country like India, there will be large proportion of unproductive consumers. In fact, today about 51% of the total population of India is unproductive. Rapid increase in the population contributes to an increase in the dependency ratio. [See ***Table*** - 11].

(x) *Slow Economic Development* : Economic development is bound to be slower in a country in which the population is growing at a very fast rate. Absence of savings results in low capital formation. The shortage of capital has restricted investments and contributed to the slow economic growth of the country.

(xi) *Political Unrest* : Unmanageable population size may contribute to political instability and unrest. The failure of the government to provide the basic minimum facilities to the people contributes to agitation and unrest among the masses.

It is true that India is gripped by the problem of over-population. It has shaken the stability, integrity and the security of the nation. The progress that has been made is being eaten up by the growing population. A careful study of the adverse effects of population leads us to realise the need to control it. We cannot destroy or remove our large population so as to bring it down to the optimum level. We can only control it. *"If population is not checked our progress would be like writing on sand with waves of population growth washing away what we have written."*

6. NATIONAL POPULATION POLICY, 2000 [NPP-2000]

It is an undeniable fact that India is over-populated. How to face this problem of over-population ? India must make planned efforts to control the growing population for which she should have a well-thought out population policy. A more positive and more effective policy of population control is the need of the hour.

Population policy in general refers to the policy intended to *decrease the birth rate or the growth rate.* Statement of goals, objectives and targets are inherent in the population policy.

India formed its first *"National Population Policy"* in April 1976. It called for an increase in the legal minimum age of marriage from 15 to 18 for females and from 18 to 21 years for males. The policy was, however, modified in 1977. The new policy statement emphasised the importance of the small family norm without compulsion and changed the programme title to – *"Family Welfare Programme."*

National Population Policy 2000 **[NPP-2000]** – is the latest in the series. It was announced on Feb - 15th 2000 A.D. It reaffirms the commitment of the government towards target free approach in administering family planning services. The NPP-2000 is not just a matter of fertility and mortality rates. *It deals with women education; empowering women for improved health and nutrition; child survival and health; the unmet needs for family welfare services; healthcare for the under-served population groups like urban slums, tribal community, hill area population and displaced and migrant population; adolescent's health and education; increased participation of men in planned parenthood; and collaboration with non-governmental organisations.*

The object of NPP-2000 is to bring the total fertility rate [TFR] to replacement levels by 2010. The long term objective is to achieve requirements of suitable economic growth, social development and environment protection. It contains the goals and the target to be achieved by 2010. They can be briefed here.

1. Giving rewards to panchayats and Zilla Parishads for promoting small family norm.
2. Reduce infant mortality rate to below 30 per 100 live births.
3. Reduce maternal mortality ratio to below 100 per 1 lakh live births.
4. Achieve universal immunisation of children against all preventable diseases.

5. Achieve 80% institutional deliveries and 100% deliveries by trained persons.
6. Achieve 100% registration of births, deaths, marriage and pregnancy.
7. Prevent and control communicable diseases.
8. Promote vigorously the small family norm to achieve TFR.
9. Contain the spread of AIDS [Acquired Immuno Deficiency Syndrome].
10. Address the unmet needs for basic reproductive and child health services, supplies and infrastructure. Strict enforcement of 'Child Marriage Restraint Act'.
11. Make school education up to age 14 free and compulsory, and reduce drop-outs at primary and secondary school levels to below 20% to both boys and girls.
12. Health insurance cover of Rs. 5000 fer couple below the poverty line with two living children, who undergo sterilisation.
13. Achieve universal access to information / counselling and services for fertility regulation and contraception.
14. To take appropriate steps to make family welfare programme a people-centred programme.
15. Setting up of a National Commission on Population, headed by the Prime Minister.

The planning of the population must also include the improvement of quality of population. Further, life expectation has to be increased. If the NPP-2000 is fully implemented, it is anticipated that in the year 2010 the population will be 1,107 million instead of 1,162 million projected by the Technical Group of Population Projections. Similarly, the anticipated crude birth rate will be 21 per thousand population, infant mortality rate 30 per thousand live births and total fertility rate 2.1. The NPP-2000 is to be largely implemented and managed at *panchayat* and *nagarapalika* levels in co-ordination with the concerned State / Union Territory administration.

Ninth Five Year Plan Objectives

The planning commission observed that given the present demographic situation in the country, the achievements are lagging behind the proposed goals for the year 2002. Against this background fresh targets were formulated to be achieved by the end of the Ninth Five Year Plan. The goals are revised to slightly lower levels. These are as follows:

Infant Mortality rate per 1000 live births	56-50
Crude birth rate per 1000 population	24/23
Crude death rate per 1000 population	9
Maternal mortality rate per 1000 live births	3
Life expectancy	
Male	62 [1996-2001]
Female	63 [1996-2001]
Couple protection rate (%)	51 - 60
Growth rate (%) annual	1.6 / 1.5
Total fertility rate	2.9 / 2.6
Immunization	Universal
Pregnant mothers receiving antenatal care (%)	90
Delivery by trained personnel (%)	45
Institutional deliveries (%)	35

7. MEASURES FOR CONTROLLING THE RAPID GROWTH OF POPULATION

Need For Controlling the Growth of Population

Overpopulation is, indeed, a serious socio-economic problem of India. This problem has adversely affected the progress of the economy and the standard of the living of the people. The problem is an urgent one and needs immediate solution.

The problem of overpopulation is to be tackled immediately. There is an absolute need to contain the rapid growth of population. If this growth is not checked it is going to affect adversely the various aspects of our economy. It brings down per capita and national income, brings down standard of living of the people. It becomes difficult to face the challenges of poverty, unemployment and underemployment. Basic needs of the people cannot be met with, political unrest and immorality cannot be efficiently dealt with.

Overpopulation is related to *the size of the population and the utilisation of the countries resources.* The problem should be tackled from both the sides. *Firstly,* production should be increased to meet the needs of the people. *Secondly,* size of the population should be controlled and reduced.

(A) Measure to Increase Production

Growing population of the country can be supported through increased production. Agricultural and industrial productions are to be increased for this purpose.

1. *Increase in Agricultural Production* : It is necessary to resort to modern scientific cultivation in order to increase agricultural output. Use of irrigation, high yielding seeds, rotation of crops, utilisation of chemicals, fertilisers, manures and such other means are to be adopted for this purpose. *Production should keep pace with increasing population, if possible, should outstrip it.*

2. *Increase in Industrial Production* : The process of industrialisation is to be accelerated. Modern sophisticated technology must be made use of for industrial production. The industrial strategy should be such that it should be able to increase production and at the same time provide job facilities to a sizeable number of people. Industries are to be established in different places by making use of the locally available raw materials and human resources.

3. *Development of Trade and Commerce* : The development of trade and commerce will contribute to additional income and help the country to support the growing population.

(B) Measures to Control and Reduce Population

The problem of overpopulation can be effectively dealt with only if the rapid growth rate of population is contained. Various measures are to be undertaken in this regard.

1. *Family Planning Measures* : Family planning is nowadays considered an indispensable method of controlling population. The motto of family planning is – *"child by choice and not by chance"* or *"child by desire not by accident."* The size of the family must be limited voluntarily. It can be done in two ways : (*a*) *Birth control methods,* (*b*) *Other family planning methods.*

a) ***Birth control methods*** include – use of rubber contraceptives by males, use of pills by females, use of loops by females, sterilisation for both males and females [that is, vasectomy for males and tubectomy for females], abortion, *i.e.*, medical termination of pregnancy.

b) ***Other family planning methods*** include – practice of celibacy [that is, practising *brahmacharya* or self-restraint], postponement of marriage [or resorting to late marriage], observance of moral or self-restraint.

2. *Providing Education Facility to the People* : Illiteracy is one of the factors of overpopulation. It is to be countered in order to contain the population growth. Spread of education among illiterate masses is a significant step in reducing the birth rate. People must be educated regarding the benefits of small family and late marriage. Education helps to increase the earning capacity of males and females. It improves the status of women, it creates awareness regarding family planning.

3. *Rise in the Age of Marriage* : In order to reduce the child-bearing period of women [reproductive span of women], it is necessary to rise the minimum age of marriage from 18 to 20 for females and from 21 to 24 for males. Child marriages should be strictly prohibited.

4. *Improving Status of Women* : Experience in the West has shown that high status of women is closely associated with a low birth rate. The desire to rise in the social scale develops a strong feeling for a smaller family. The educated, employed urban women exhibit a desire for a small family. Efforts must be made to impress upon the rural women to go in the direction of a small family.

5. *Propaganda in Favour of Small Family* : Enough publicity is to be given in a country like India regarding the benefits of a small family to the general masses. Mass media of communication like the press, radio, television and movies are of great help in this regard.

6. *Provision of Incentives* : Incentives such as cash payments and promotion in jobs, free education, preference in admission to technical courses, etc. could be given to the people who accept and adopt family planning.

7. *Increasing the Standard of Living of the Masses* : People with higher standard of living normally opt for small family. Hence, it is necessary to increase the standard of living of the masses.

8. *Providing Enough Recreational Facilities* : It has been observed that lack of sufficient recreational facilities has often contributed to the problem of overpopulation. People must be provided with sufficient recreational facilities to relax and to refresh. This will prevent them from resorting to sex play whenever they feel like refreshing themselves.

9. *Internal Migration* : Unequal distribution of population in different parts of the nation can be dealt with if internal migration is allowed. It means people must be encouraged to move from the densely populated areas towards the thinly populated areas. This is not, however, easy. As **Adam Smith** observes, *"Of all sorts of luggage, man is the most difficult to be transported."*

10. *Provision of Social Security* : In the absence of comprehensive social security [especially, in old age, sickness, unemployment and accident] people have tended to depend on large families for security. The poor, in particular, consider children as their wealth. It is necessary to introduce various social insurance and social security schemes to help the poor to develop confidence to face the future.

11. *Reduction in Infant Mortality* : By resorting to suitable medical steps the rate of infant mortality is to be reduced. If it is reduced, then parents will definitely feel that their children will survive and live long.

12. *Changes in the Tax Structure* : **Dr. S. Chandrashekhar,** a noted Indian demographer, is of the opinion that by introducing a change in the taxation policy, especially that of income tax, the problem can be reduced a little. In stead of giving concessions to married people with more children, he has suggested, it is better to give such concessions to the unmarried, and also to those couples without children or with only one child.

8. FAMILY PLANNING AND ITS ACHIEVEMENTS

Family Planning and Its Meaning

Family planning basically means planning the number of children in the family. It is *"limiting the size of the family by conscious efforts."* The motto of family planning is *"child by choice, and not by chance"*. Family planning can be defined as an instrument of social transformation which aims at creating better parents, healthier children and happier homes. It seeks to inject social responsibility into married life.

Family planning is described by an ***Expert Committee of the WHO*** in the following manner. *"Family planning refers to practices that help individuals or couples to attain certain objectives*:

(a) *to avoid unwanted births,*

(b) *to bring about wanted births,*

(c) *to regulate the intervals between pregnancies,*

(d) *to control the time at which births occur in relation to the ages of the parent; and*

(e) *to determine the number of children in the family."*

Family Planning as a Basic Human Right

The United Nations Conference on Human Rights at Tehran in 1968 recognised family planning as a basic human right. *The World Conference of the Women's Year in 1975* also declared – *"the right of women to decide freely and responsibly on the number and spacing of their children and to have access to the information and means to enable them to exercise that right."*

Scope of Family Planning Services

It is unfair to think that family planning is just equal to birth control. In fact, it is something more than mere birth control. WHO Expert Committee [1970] has stated that family planning includes in its purview the following aspects – **1.** *the proper spacing and limitation of births,* **2.** *advice on sterility,* **3.** *education for parenthood,* **4.** *sex education,* **5.** *genetic counselling,* **6.** *premarital consultation and examination,* **7.** *carrying out pregnancy tests,* **8.** *marriage counselling,* **9.** *preparation of couples for the arrival of their first child,* **10.** *providing services for unmarried mothers,* **11.** *teaching home economics and nutrition,* **12.** *providing adoption services.* These activities vary from country to country according to national objectives and policies with regard to family planning.

The Renaming of "Family Planning Programme" as *"Family Welfare Programme"*

The Government of India evinced greater interest in controlling population growth in 1976. During the emergency [1976-78] compulsory sterilisation was carried on at great speed through coercive measures in various places in North India. For example, in 1976, more than 76 lakh sterilisations were carried out against a target of 43 lakh. Coercive methods adopted for the implementation of the programme during this period resulted in people's discontentment. Hence the Janata Government, which came to power soon after emergency, wanted to follow a soft policy. It announced a comprehensive population policy in that year. Family planning programme was renamed as *"Family Welfare Programme."* This welfare programme has experienced several ups and downs in its performance over time.

Achievements

Government's efforts at controlling population through family planning / welfare programme has not yielded consistent results. The programme has experienced several ups and downs in its performance over time. *For example,* the number of sterilisations increased from around 7000 on 1956 to 1.84 million in 1970-71. This figure increased to 2.19 million during 1971-72 but it came down to 0.94 million during 1973-74. This decline was particularly due to abandonment of camp approach. During the emergency period [1975-77] sterilisation performance of sterilisations was really good [about 8.26 million sterilisation cases in 1976-77 alone]. The performance of sterilisation came down particularly after emergency. But the trend nowadays is slowly changing in favour of family welfare programme. Particularly, in the nineties the total programme seems to have greater acceptance among the public.

The Central Government has been investing more and more money for the implementation of the family welfare programmes through its five year plans. The Government, for example, spent a meagre amount of Rs.65 lakhs for this purpose in the First Five Year Plan. The Government, however, started spending more and more money towards the programme in the other Plans. For example, it spent Rs.27 crores in the Third Plan, Rs.497 crores in the Fifth Plan, Rs.1,010 crores in the Sixth Plan, Rs.3,221 crores in the Seventh Plan and Rs.6,792 crores in the Eighth Plan. The Ninth Plan allocated Rs. 14,194 crores for this programme.

Uneven Response of the States for the Family Welfare Programme

A state-wise break-up of the figures indicates that while some states notably Punjab, Gujarat, Maharashtra, Karnataka, Haryana and Tamil Nadu are forging ahead in the direction of family planning, some other states such as Bihar, Uttar Pradesh, Assam, Rajasthan, West Bengal, Jammu Kashmir, etc. are lagging behind.

Difficulties Involved in the Implementation of the Family Planning

(i) Birth control is associated with a high standard of living, but in India it is very low.

(ii) The available contraceptives are not safe, cheap and easily available.

(iii) Due to administrative and organisational defects, the message of family planning programme has not reached properly the remotest corners of the country where it is all the more needed.

(iv) Illiterate and ignorant people have failed to understand the significance of the programme.

(v) Traditional-minded Indians look at the programme with disfavour and suspicion. This, they feel, strikes at the very root of their belief or faith in God.

(vi) The use of contraceptives requires privacy in the houses, which is not found in some large joint families.

(vii) Finally, the success of the programme depends upon the integrity, sincerity and honesty of the officials engaged in the programme. It is unfortunate, that these officials themselves are not much serious about it.

Karnataka Population Highlights – 2011

- *Total population of Karnataka* in 2001 was 52850562, and it increased in 2011 to 6,11,30,704 [Men – 3,10,57,742 as against 2,68,98,918 in 2001, and women 3,00,72,962 as against 2,69,51,644 in 2001].
- *Sex Ratio:* For every 1000 men, there are 968 women [as against 965 in 2001], in the case of children, sex ratio is 943 [as against 965 in 2001].
- *In Bangalore city*, the state capital, there are only **908** women for every 1000 men.
- *Rate of population growth* has declined in Karnataka from **17.5%** during 1991-2001 to **15.7%** between 2001-2011.
- State retains its **9th** place in the total population of India as it was in 2001.
- Between 2001-2011, there was 15.46% increase in the population of men and in the case of women, the increase was 15.88%.
- The average literacy of the state in 2011is 75.60% , and it was 66.64% in 2001, and this reveals an increase of 8.96% over the previous decade.
- The State witnessed much increase in literacy over the previous decade. There were 3,04,34,962 literates in 2001 and the number increased to 4,10,29,323 [Men - 2,28,08,468 and women – 1,82,20,855] in 2011 by making 1,05,94,361 people literate.
- In 12 districts of the State, literacy rate is higher than the State average. Dakshina Kannada [D.K.] district has the highest literacy [88.62%] and it is lowest in Yadgiri district [52.36%].

- As far as *female literacy* is concerned, in 8 districts, it is less than 60%, in 12 districts it is between 60-70%; in 7 districts it is between 71-80%, and in 3 districts it is above 80%.
- Population growth has increased in Bangalore by **37%** over the previous decade and the share of Bangalore in the population of the state is 15.69% [95,88,910 people]. Belgaum stands second with 7.82% [47,78,439]. Mysore occupies third place with 4.90% [29,94,744]; Gulbarga [4.20%] and Bellary [4.14%] secure the fourth and fifth places respectively.
- Kodagu district has the least share in the State's population [0.91% with 5,54,762 people] and the second place in this regard is occupied by Bangalore (Rural) and its share of population is 1.61% [9,87,257 people].
- As far as *the number of children* between the age of 1 to 6 years is concerned, there has been a positive development. Their number was 71,82,100 in 2001 and it got reduced to 68,55,801, denoting a decline in the growth rate by **4.54%.** Out of these 68,55,801 children, 35,27,884 are males [that is, 1,63,114 less than what it was in 2001], and 33,27,957 are females [that is, 1,63,185 les than what it was in 2001.]
- *Density of Population:* There were 276 people per k.m. in 2001 and the number has increased to 319 in 2011, indicating an increase of 15.58%.
- Udupi and DK are the two districts wherein women outnumber men in 2011. For the first time in 110 years of demographic history of these two districts, there has been a slight decrease in the sex ratio of men and women. In Udupi, there were **1130** women for every 1000 men in 2001 [1107 women in 1991] and their number decreased to **1093** in 2011. In the same way, in D.K. district, there were 1029 women for every 1000 men in 2001 [and 1029 women in 1991] and their number decreased to 1022 in 2011.
- Three other districts in which women outnumber men are Kodagu [1019], Hasan [1005], and Chickmagalur [1005]. The corresponding numbers of women in these districts for 2001 are – 996, 1004 and 984 respectively.

***Source*:** As per the press statement released by the Directorate of Census, Karnataka and published in *"Udayavani"* Kannada Daily, Dated: 07.04.2011, Udupi-Manipal, Karnataka.

POPULATION BY RELIGION IN INDIA [1971 - 2001]

	1971		1981		1991		2001*	
Religious Group	***Number (million)***	***%age to total***	***Number (million)***	***%age to total***	***Number (million)***	***%age to total***	***Number (million)***	***%age to total***
Hindus	453.4	82.7	549.7	82.6	672.6	82.4	827.50	80.5
Muslims	61.4	11.2	75.6	11.4	95.2	11.7	138.18	13.4
Christians	14.2	2.6	16.2	2.4	18.9	2.3	24.05	2.34
Sikhs	10.4	1.9	13.1	2.0	16.3	2.0	-	-
Buddhists	3.9	0.7	4.7	0.7	6.3	0.8	-	-
Jains	2.6	0.5	3.2	0.5	3.4	0.4	-	-
Other	2.2	0.4	2.8	0.4	3.5	0.4	-	-
Total	548.2	100.0	665.3	100.0	812.3	100.0		

Source : INDIA Year Book - 1999. Page - 16. *Census Report 2001

Chapter 19

Religion and Society

Religious Groups in India, *Their Size, Growth and Distribution- Buddhism and the Buddhist Community - Jainism and the Jain Community - Sikhism and Sikh Community - Parsis or Zoroastrians - Islam and the Muslim Community - The Muslim Social Outlook - Christianity and the Christian Community - Hinduism and the Hindu Community -* ***Religious Minorities in India*** *- Concept of Minority - Problems of Religious Minorities - Some Problems of Minorities in India - Welfare of Minorities - Secularism and Its Definition and Characteristics - Secularism in Practice - Impediments in the Practice of Secularism.*

Man is not only a social animal but also a spiritual being. Religion is a major concern of man. It is one of the earliest and the deepest interests of the human beings. Religion is one of the universal, permanent, pervasive and perennial interests of man. Man not only, has biological, economic and social needs, but also, what is known as a *religious need.* He has a *religious quest* which makes him to become restless even beyond the satisfaction of his basic physical needs. Hence the Biblical saying, *"Man cannot live by bread alone".* It is also true that man from the earliest times, has been *"incurably religious".*

Religion is not a phenomenon of recent emergence. Its beginning is unknown. It is dateless. Some artifacts and evidences of the burial practices of Neanderthal man indicate that human being was a religious creature long before history began. The institution of religion is *universal.* It is found in all the societies, past and present. Religious beliefs and practices are, however, far from being uniform.

Religion is a powerful instrument of social control. Laws, customs, conventions and fashions, etc. are not the only means of social control. Overriding them all, are *religion* and *morality* which formulate and shape all of them. They are not only the most influential forces of social control, but also *the most effective guides of human behaviour.*

Religion represents one of the main social facets of man: The social life of man in addition to its economic, political, philosophical, scientific and other aspects, has also the *religious* aspect. Not only religion has been in existence from the beginning but also it has been exerting a tremendous influence upon other institutions. Religious dogmas have influenced and conditioned economic endeavours, political movements, property dealings, educational tasks, ideological fervours, scientific inventions and artistic developments. Religion, which is based on the cultural needs of men, has added new dimension to human life and human development.

Religion revolves round man's faith in the supernatural forces. Religion is a concrete experience which is associated with emotions, especially with fear, awe, or reverence. Many societies have a wide range of institutions connected with religion and a body of special officials, with forms of worship, ceremonies, sacred objects, tithes, pilgrimages, and the like. In modern civilised societies, religious leaders have developed elaborate theories or theologies to explain man's place in the universe. Religion is closely associated with morality and has elaborate rules of conduct. Further, well established world religions – *Hinduism, Buddhism, Confucianism, Judaism, Christianity,* and *Islam* – are really centres of elaborate cultural systems that have dominated 'whole' societies for centuries.

Definition of Religion

1. ***Durkheim*** in his book *The Elementary Forms of the Religious Life* defines religion as a *"unified system of beliefs and practices relative to sacred things, that is to say, things set apart and forbidden".*
2. **MacIver** and **Page** have defined religion in the following words: *"Religion as we understand the term, implies a relationship not merely between man and man but also between man and some higher power".*

Table - 1

Religions	World Population
Christians	1,974,181,000
Roman Catholics	1,044,236,000
Protestants	337,346,000
Orthodox	213,991,000
Anglicans	78,574,000
Muslims	1,155,109,000
Hindus	799,028,000
Chinese folk religionists	381,632,000
Buddhists	356,270,000
Ethnic religionists	225,421,000
New-Religionists	101,406,000
Sikhs	22,837,000
Jews 14,313,000	
Spiritists	12,184,000
Baha'is	6,932,000
Confucians	6,253,000
Jains	4,151,000
Shintoists	2,778,000
Zoroastrians	2,486,000
Mandeans	38,000
Other religionists	1,019,000
Non-religious	762,640,000
Atheists	149,723,000

Source : The World Almanac, 2001 As quoted in **Manorama Year Book 2002.** [371]

3. According to **Ogburn**, *"Religion is an attitude towards superhuman powers".*
4. In simple words, it can be said that – *religion is a system of beliefs, rituals and values concerned with the sacred or the divine forces.*

Religions of the World

People of the world pursue and practice religion in their own way. Religions of the world which people practice "may be grouped into three broad classes – (i) *Leading religions,* (ii) *Lesser religions,* and (iii) *Primitive religions.* The Leading religions are Buddhism, Christianity, Confucianism, Hinduism and Islam. The Lesser religions include Jainism and Sikhism of India, Judaism of Palestine, Shintoism of Japan, Taoism of China and Zoroastrianism originally of Persia. The Primitive religions count by the thousands. They are all very small communities, each with a handful of votaries."[1] [*Note*: To know the numerical strength of each religion, please refer to **Table No.1** in Page No.**549.**]

1. RELIGIOUS GROUPS OF INDIA : SIZE, GROWTH AND DISTRIBUTION

India is known as a land of many religions though the Hindus constitute the major religious community. Existence of many religions, sects, and cults have added a new dimension to the Indian social structure. Right from the beginning of Buddhism till today multi-religious character of Indian society has not been affected. Census held as early as in 1931 had classified the Indian community into ten religious groups such as – *Hindus, Muslims, Christians, Buddhists, Jains, Sikhs, Zoroastrians, Jews, other religious people* [people who belong to tribal religions] and *others* [those who do not belong to the tribal groups].

The 1961 census, however recognised and classified only **7** religious groups in India. They are **:** *the Hindus, Muslims, Christians, Sikhs, Buddhists, Jains,* and *other religious people.* The relative numerical strength of these different religious groups as recorded in the 1991 census is mentioned below in **Table No.2.**

Some basic information about the nature and character of these religious groups, their numerical size, and growth over the years and their distribution in different places and provinces of India, could be briefly presented here.

Table - 2

Population by Religion In India

	1961		*1971*		*1981*		*1991*	
Religious Group	***Number (million)***	***%age to total***	***Number (million)***	***%age to total***	***Number (million)***	***%age to total***	***Number (million)***	***%age to total***
Hindus	366.5	83.5	453.4	82.7	549.7	82.6	672.6	82.4
Muslims	46.9	10.7	61.4	11.2	75.6	11.4	95.2	11.7
Christians	10.7	2.4	14.2	2.6	16.2	2.4	18.9	2.3
Sikhs	7.8	1.8	10.4	1.9	13.1	2.0	16.3	2.0
Buddhists	3.2	0.7	3.9	0.7	4.7	0.7	6.3	0.8
Jains	2.0	0.5	2.6	0.5	3.2	0.5	3.4	0.4
Other	1.6	0.4	2.2	0.4	2.8	0.4	3.5	0.4
Total	**439.2**	**100.0**	**548.2**	**100.0**	**665.3**	**100.0**	**812.3**	**100.0**

Source **: INDIA Year Book** - 1999. Page - 16.

1 **Manorama Year Book 2002.** Page - 371.

BUDDHISM AND THE BUDDHIST COMMUNITY

Buddhism is one of the most ancient religions of India, though the followers of this religion constitute, as per 1991 census report, only 0.77% of the total population. Buddhism originated in India but became more popular outside the borders of India, mostly in Asia, than within the physical boundary of the Indian society. It is adjudged as one of the major religions of mankind. In the whole world, more than 356 million people are Buddhists today.

Buddhism originated in India in the 6th century B.C. as a reform against Brahminism. It spread rapidly in Magadha where Brahmanic influence was less predominant and where *"Kshatriya"* was regarded as superior to the *"priest"*. The Buddha whose original name was Siddhartha was the founder of Buddhism. *"Buddha"* means *"the Awakened One"* or the *"Enlightened One."* Though the Buddha was born in the royal family of king Shuddhodhana he lost interest in leading a royal life. When he got the first opportunity to come out of the royal palace he could visualise the extent of human suffering [*dukka*]. He decided to renounce the worldly pleasures and dedicate his life entirely to discovering the cause of human suffering and finding out ways and means of removing it. He went out of the palace, travelled across a number of villages and towns in search of a teacher. After studying under various teachers, he realised his own path and attained Enlightenment under the Bodhi tree in Gaya. He thus became the *"Buddha"* [the Enlightened One] in the real sense of the term. He later on took to the career as a preacher.

After becoming enlightened, the Buddha moved towards a Deer Park near Varanasi where he delivered his First Sermon which came to be known as the *"Turning of the Wheel of Law."* Soon his name became well-known throughout the Ganga plain. Large number of people became his followers. The Buddha left no written records of his teachings. His disciples preserved teachings by means of their memory and transmitting the same from generation to generation.

The **Four Noble Truths**[1] and the **Eight-Fold Path**[2] virtually summarise his teachings. The final goal in Buddhism is *"Nirvana."* It is the final result of the end of desire. The Buddha stressed the moral way of attaining it. He pleaded with the people to avoid the extremes of luxury on the one hand and asceticism on the other. He advocated the Middle Path, which consists of moral principles such as - *truthfulness, charity, purity, control over passions, love, compassion, non-injury to living creatures,* etc. Because of the excessive stress on Nirvana [salvation or *"Mukti"*] Max Weber regarded Buddhism as a religion which is more *"other worldly"* in its orientation.

Buddhism found ready patronage from the ruling monarchs of the day. Bimbasara and Ajatashatru patronised it. Later on, great rulers like Ashoka, Kaniska, Sri Harsha and others gave it full support and took pains to popularise it. Ashoka made special efforts to spread the message of the Buddha even outside the borders of India. At one time it seemed to capture the entire population. But its popularity did not last long. It started declining and various factors accelerated its downfall. Among them the following may be noted :

(1) The Original Buddhism or Hinayana was merely a monastic sect and not a mass movement. Hence it could not flourish.

(2) Secondly, the restoration of Hinduism by Kumarila Bhatta and Sri Adi Shankaracharya gave a great blow to the spread of Buddhism.

---

1 (i) *The Noble Truth of Suffering,* (ii) *The Truth of the Cause of Suffering,* (iii) *The Truth of the Ending of Suffering,* and (iv) *The Truth of the Path leading to the End of Suffering.*

2 ***Eight-Fold Path***: 1. Right Understanding, 2. Right Aspiration, 3. Right Speech, 4. Right Action, 5. Right Livelihood, 6. Right Effort, 7. Right Mindfulness, 8. Right Concentration.

(3) Thirdly, Buddhism failed to obtain the royal patronage of the later kings.
(4) Disunity and spiritual decay within the Buddhist Sangha also led to its downfall.
(5) The uncompromising attitude of the Buddhists to the redemption of man who lived a married life also caused its decline.
(6) Buddhism received a strong blow from the Huna invasion of India, who destroyed Buddhist monasteries and temples and massacred a large number of Buddhist monks.
(7) A further and a final blow to Buddhism came from the Muslim invaders.

It is not correct to say that Buddhism vanished from the land of its birth. Rather the Hindus imbibed the essential teachings of Buddhism. Hindus had included the Buddha in the Hindu Pantheon where he came to be regarded as the Ninth Avatar of Lord Vishnu. This catholicity of Hinduism in a way proved to be disastrous for Buddhism. By the 10th century AD, it virtually disappeared from India. Though Buddhism failed to become popular in India, it attained a great success outside the borders of India, especially in Nepal, Burma, Tibet, Ceylone, Korea, Japan, China, Vietnam and other countries.

Numerical Strength and Regional Distribution of the Buddhists

In the land of the birth of Buddhism there are only 6.3 million Buddhists consisting 0.77% of the total population [1991 census]. About 85% of the total Buddhist population lives in Maharashtra only. In Assam and Sikkim too they are found in a sizeable number. They are also found in a small number in West Bengal, M.P., Jammu & Kashmir. Numerically, they increased from 180,823 in 1951 to 3256,036 in 1961. This enormous increase has been due in part to the neo-Buddhist movement during 1951-61. A sizeable number of the Scheduled Caste persons converted themselves into Neo-Buddhist. This factor might have contributed to this extra-ordinary growth. But after sometime some converts from the SCs to Buddhism preferred to return to Hinduism since they were not entitled to obtain concessions available to the SCs.

Buddhist temples and monasteries that are found in Buddha Gaya, Kushinagar, Saranath and Sanchi have been attracting Buddhist pilgrims. The *"Mahabodhi Sangha"* of the Buddhists is actively functioning and is looking after the three main Buddhist temples that are there in Delhi. The headquarters of the *"Bouddha Sangha"* of the South is found in Chennai.

The Buddhists are slightly better educated than the Hindus. They have high fertility rate, and as such they tend to reproduce about as rapidly as the general population. They have a very low proportion of widows but a high proportion of single women.

The Buddhists due to their insignificant numerical strength have not emerged as a strong political force. Never in future, they could emerge so. They do not constitute a majority community in any village, town or city. They are a silent going people.

JAINISM AND THE JAIN COMMUNITY

Along with Hinduism and Buddhism, Jainism is one of the ancient religions of India. It still has its own limited following. Jainism preaches a path to spiritual deliverance through a disciplined way of life founded upon the principle of non-violence. In the course of its history, it evolved into a well developed cultural system. The Jain cultural tradition made a significant contribution to Indian civilisation in various areas such as philosophy and logic, art and architecture, mathematics, astronomy and astrology, and literature. Though Jainism as a religion makes use of several religious concepts that are commonly found in Buddhism and Hinduism it has its own identity.

Birth of Jainism

Jainism was founded by **Vardhamana Mahavira** regarded as the 24th and the last *Tirthankara,* in the 6th century B.C. It originated in the Ganga basin of North India, the scene of intense religious speculations, meditations and activity at that time. Buddhism too appeared in the very same region. Both the religions questioned the authority of the Vedas and rejected the ritualistic Brahmanic School. Jainism, thus developed as a protest against the exclusion of all but the Brahmins from the ascetic fraternity. The founders of both the religions though never met each other, travelled mostly in the same regions [Mithila, Sravasthi, Magadha, Vaishali, Kaushambi and other places of the day] for the propagation of their faith.

Vardhamana Mahaveera, who was born in a Kshatriya family, received the training and education generally given to princes of the day. He soon realised the futility of worldly life and turned an ascetic at the age of 30. He practised hard penance and meditated for 12 years. At last he attained the True Knowledge while meditating under the sal tree. He then became a *"Jina"* [conqueror] and Tirthankara. Afterwards he began to preach his doctrine and popularised *"Ahimsa"* and on it he built an ethical code for householders as well as for monks. He preached what he had realised for about 30 years and died at the age of 72 at Pavapuri in Patna District of Bihar.

Main Teachings

Like the Buddha, Mahavira also held that the world was full of sufferings. The misery of *"Samsara"* was regarded as universal. Hence, he recommended a *"moksha-marga"* [path to salvation] which consisted of three principles known as ***"Ratna Trayas"*** [Three Jewels]. These principles are :

Right Faith [*Samyak Darshana*],
Right Knowledge [*Samyak Jnana*], and
Right Conduct [*Samyak Charita*].

Mahavira also stressed upon the moral conduct. The *Anuvrata* or the moral code which he prescribed consists of the five important principles.

(a) ***Ahimsa*** [non-violence],
(b) ***Satya*** [truth],
(c) ***Asteya*** [non-stealing],
(d) ***Brahmacharya*** [control of sex],
(e) ***Aparigraha*** [free from greed].

Mahavira laid great emphasis on non-violence. In fact, all the religious rites of Jains are centred round non-violence. In no other school of philosophy do we find the application of non-violence as comprehensive as in Jainism.

Jainism, in course of time, got divided into two sects known as the ***Digambara*** and the ***Svetambara.*** Digambaras who are usually found in South India held that the monks should not wear any clothes, and the Svetambaras insisted that they should. Jainism, however in both forms is one as far as its philosophy is concerned.

Unlike Buddhism, Jainism did maintain good relationships with Hinduism. It employed Brahmin priests as its domestic priests who officiated at their birth rites and often acted as officials at their death and marriage ceremonies. It had a place for the Hindu Gods like Rama and Krishna in their temples. Mahavira's organisation took refuge in Hinduism whenever persecuted. To the outside conquerors Jainism appeared only a part of the greater system, that is, Hinduism.

Jainism received royal patronage at the hands of some of the Indian rulers. It is said that Chandragupta Maurya became a follower of Bhadrabahu and accompanied his guru to

Shravanabelagola. In the 2nd century B.C., Kharavela of Kalinga popularised Jainism and set up several images. During the 5th and 12th centuries A.D. several southern ruling families like the Gangas, Kadambas, Chalukyas and Rashtrakutas of Manyakheta extended their patronage to Jainism. About 1100 A.D. Jainism became popular in Gujarat where the Chalukya kings, Siddharaya and his son Kumarapala openly professed Jainism and encouraged literature and building activities of the Jains.

Contributions of Jainism to Indian Culture

1. *Jains played an important part in the linguistic development*: While the Brahmins established their supremacy over Sanskrit and Buddhists used Pali for the purpose of writing and preaching, the Jains used the local languages for their religious propaganda as well as for preserving their knowledge. The early Kannada classical works were written by Jain poets. Most of the major and minor epics in Tamil were also composed by the Jain authors.

2. *Jainism has contributed to Indian art* : The Jains erected *stupas* in honour of their saints. Jains built temples cut in rocks. The Jain marble temples at Mount Abu in Rajasthan display some of the finest examples of sculpture. The huge stone of Bahubali, known as Gomateshwara at Shravanabelagola and Karkala in Karnataka State are among the wonders of the world. The numerous Jain temples are found in Parshvanath Hills, Pavapuri, and Rajgir in Bihar and Girnar in Palitana in Kathiawad in Gujarat.

3. *Jains gave great importance to Ahimsa or non-violence* : All the acts prescribed by the religion are centred round *"ahimsa"*. The Jain philosophy of *Ahimsa* was responsible for ending *"himsa"* in Yajnas and other Vedic rites. It inspired millions of people to adopt vegetarian diet.

4. *Glorification of Human Heritage* : Jainism holds that heaven is the privilege of man alone. The pleasures of even the Gods should come to an end one day or other unless they become men. This embodies an important truth namely, *man's heritage as man is far superior to any other riches in the world.* The main message of Jainism to mankind is that : *"Be a man first and last, for the kingdom of God belongs to the son of man." It is the same truth that is proclaimed in unmistakable terms by the upanishadic text* : *"Tat tvam asi"* [Thou art that].

Jains do not believe in the Creator of the world and hold that man's emancipation from the Karma is a personal effort. Man is the architect of his own destiny.

Geographic Distribution of Jains

Jainism once held a wide sway in India, but now the followers of Jainism are numerically very small and they are found in both the northern and southern states. They do not constitute a majority anywhere in India. They constitute 0.4% of the population of India and their number hardly exceed 3.4 million [1991 census]. The Jains are found relatively in a large number in states such as Maharashtra, Rajasthan, Gujarat, M.P., Karnataka, U.P. In fact, 90% of them are found in these states only.

The Jain population is not growing fast in India. The population of all the six major religions of India has increased but Jains have increased only marginally, that is, by 4.42%, whereas the average rate of increase in the case of the other five religions was 26.77%.[1] Its growth is almost stationery or only marginal. There are a few causes for that :

1. Jains do not allow widow remarriages. Comparatively, Jains have a low percentage of their women married in the age group of 15 to 39 years. For example, during 1911-31 almost $^1/_5$ of

1 **Manorama Year Book - 2002.** Page - 547.

their women in this age group were widows. It goes without telling that the enforced widowhood cut down Jain population to a large extent.

2. It is also said that Jains have a low fertility within the circle of marital relations. The number of married women is also said to be very low next only to the Parsis.

3. Jains are mostly urban dwellers. They are largely literate and hence have a liking for small families.

4. Jains do not believe in conversions. Unlike the Muslims and Christians the Jains do not resort to conversion activities to acquire new converts. Jainism also does not get new entrants who join its fold voluntarily.

*"The Jain community, according to **Sangave,** a modern Jain sociologist, had an open class system : people could move from one class to another according to their aptitude. Untouchability is not practised among them and interdining is allowed. However, the Jains have endogamous Jatis. A 1314 document mentioned 87 Jatis in one branch of the community; of these, 41 had a population of less than 500. A more recent [1953] study estimates nearly 60 endogamous groups with a population of less than one hundred each."*[1]

SIKHISM AND SIKH COMMUNITY

The ***Sikh*** religion traces its origin to its first *"guru"* or preceptor **Guru Nanak** who was born in Punjab in **1469.** It developed into a full-fledged religion in the 16th century. *"Prior to 16th century, the Sikhs formed a part of the Vaishnava sect, and retained the Hindu pantheon as well as the Indian social system and the doctrines of Karma and incarnation."*[2]

Though **Guru Nanak** [1469 - 1538 A.D.] is regarded as the founder of Sikhism he did not overtly contribute much to the development of his new faith. He led a worldly pious life as a married person and could not do much to organise his followers and to provide an organisational network for them. But he was successful in appointing **Angad,** to succeed him as *"Guru."* Angad and his three successor *"Gurus"* led saintly lives as religious teachers. During the lifetime of these "gurus" [1539 - 1606] the sacred book of the Sikhs namely *"Adi Granth"* ["Original Book"] almost took its final shape. It was written in the Punjabi language and in the Gurumukhi script which is used only for the Punjabi. This consists of the teachings of the Gurus' and devotional hymns by them and by other devotees, both Hindu and Muslim, most notably the poet-saint Kabir. Sikhism has elevated the *"Granth"* to the status of religious preacher [*Guru Granth*] and the Sikhs address this Granth as ***"Granth Sahib."***

Sikhism evolved itself into a *militant sect* for it came into conflict with the Mughal power. The 5th Guru, Arjun Dev was executed in 1606 by emperor Jahangir. The **6**th Guru, Hargobind clashed with the Mughal forces several times. The ***10th Guru,* Gobind Singh** [1675-1708] completely transformed the Sikhs into a Sikh Military order known as *"Sikh Khalsa"* [*"Order of the Pure"*]. Men initiated into the Khalsa are pledged to wear the five symbols of Sikh identity and militancy:

1. *Kesha* = Unshaven hair,

2. *Kangha* = a comb,

3. *Kaccha* = undershorts,

---

1 **S.C. Dube** *"Indian Society."* Page - 26, published by National Book Trust, India.

2 **C.B. Mamoria.** Page - 148.

4. *Kara* = a steel bracelet, and

5. *Kirpan* = a long knife.

Mr. Rose writes *"The Sikh creed involves belief in God, condemning the worship of other deities; it prohibits idolatry, pilgrimage to the great shrines of Hinduism, faith in omens, charms or witchcraft and does not recognise ceremonial impurity at birth and death. As a social system it abolishes caste distinctions, and, as a necessary consequence, the Brahmanical supremacy and usages in all ceremonies, at birth, marriage, death, and so on. But this creed is probably accepted and acted upon by a very small number even of those who call themselves true Sikhs."*[1]

The early Sikh Gurus lived in harmony both with the Hindus and Muslims. But Sikhism rejected the caste system of the Hindus and borrowed the monotheistic idea of Islam. Sikhism has an uncompromising belief in monotheism. The key note of the Sikh religion is as follows: *"There is but one God. He is Supreme Truth, Sikhism believes with Hinduism in the doctrines of the immortality of the soul and transmigration. Meditation on God, utterance of the Name [Nam], the guidance of the Guru, the company of the saints, righteous living, and the service of humanity are the means of salvation."*

The **Golden Temple** at **Amritsar** [Punjab] is the holiest temple for the Sikhs and ***Granth Sahib*** is the holy scripture of the Sikhs. Other important temples are - *Nankona Sahib* and *Dehra Sahib* in Lahore; *Panja Sahib* near Taxila and *Dera Baba* Nanak in Punjab. The Sikh temples are normally called *"Gurudwaras."*

Sikhism does not pursue conversion as its main religious activity. But it accepts converts to its faith. Such converts comprise members of the depressed classes and castes, agriculturists, washermen, tailors, carpenters, masons, and others. Sikhs are not against widow remarriages and marriage among them takes place quite late. Sikhism emphasises equalitarianism. Still, it has not been able to remove some of the unwanted elements of the caste system. For example, the lower castes converted to Sikhism are known as *"Mazhahirs"* who live in separate hamlets. In their own villages, they are not addressed with the common title *"Sardar."* The Jats, the Kshatriyas, the Brahmins, and the artisan castes have their separate identities within the Sikh community and they continue to be endogamous.

Sikhs are very hard-working people. Their contribution to the strengthening of the Indian armed forces is well recognised. They are excellent sportsmen, good cultivators and highly enterprising. They have shown considerable enterprise in venturing abroad. They are good colonists, in the sense they make small colonies of their own wherever they are whether it is for business or for any other purpose. They have developed, for example, wonderful colonies or Sikh centres in Canada, U.S.A., Great Britain, East Africa, Japan and in other places.

Numerical Strength and Geographical Distribution of Sikhs

There are around 16.3 million Sikhs in India and they constitute 2% of the total population of India [1991 census report]. Before 1947 they were mostly scattered over Northern India. Along with the partition of India, partition of Punjab also took place. This resulted in considerable redistribution of the Sikh population. Of the total population of Sikhs in India, more than 60% live in Punjab only. Rest of the people live in Haryana [6.29%], Rajasthan [1.33%], Jammu & Kashmir [2.29%], Delhi, M.P. and other places.

---

1 **Mr. Rose** *"Census Report of the Punjab"* - 1901, Vol.I and Part I, as quoted by **C.B. Mamoria** in *"Social Problems and Social Disorganisation in India."* Page : 148 - 149.

The Sikhs as a community are increasing fast numerically. For example, in 1881 the Sikhs constituted 0.74% of our total population, and their percentage increased to 1.89 in 1971 and then to 2% in 1991. Various factors contributed for this increase in population. Some of them are mentioned below :

(i) Sikhs have a strong community feeling and they want to retain their separate identity.
(ii) Sikhs are ready to accept converts to their fold. There has been a high rate of conversion to Sikh community especially from the side of the low castes.
(iii) Sikhs do not prescribe any taboos on widow remarriages.
(iv) The Sikhs have exceptionally high fertility.
(v) Because of the nutritious food, which they consume, they have a low mortality. They are economically better placed and hence can afford to have good food.
(vi) Sikhs have a greater number of married women [15 to 39] than any other religious groups.

The Sikhs indeed, have contributed a great deal to the enrichment of Indian culture. They are a big force in the armed forces even today. The Sikhs in the army have proved on several occasions their valour, heroism and patriotic spirit. The Sikhs by means of their hard work, have made Punjab one of the richest states of India.

THE ZOROASTRIANS OR THE PARSIS

The ***Parsis*** or the fire worshippers who constitute a small community have played an important role in India's industrial development. They came to India from Persia in the 8th century A.D. to avoid conversion to Islam and to seek refuge from persecution. After their arrival in India on the Western Coast, it is said that their leaders met the local ruler and the elites of that region. It is believed that the leader of the Parsi group in the course of his discussion with the ruler had promised in the following manner : *"As the sugar dissolves in the milk and imparts sweetness to it, we shall mix in your society and the result will be sweet."*[1] As per this promise the Parsi community harmoniously blended itself with the Indian community, without giving rise to any type of separatism. The Parsis made use of the freedom and open avenues provided for them and emerged as a successful mercantile community. Almost up to the middle or end of the 18th century, Surat, Navsari and the neighbouring parts of Gujarat were their main headquarters. But slowly, the Parsis shifted towards Bombay which provided lot of industrial and commercial opportunities. From Bombay they have now spread all over India.

Parsis have two main sects namely *"Kadimi"* [older] and *"Shenshai"* [royal]. Parsis also believe in heaven and hell. They give much importance to morality and moral way of behaving. *"Ahura Mazda"* is their supreme God and Zarathustra is His main prophet. The prophet is highly respected and often worshipped. Among their socio-religious rites the most important one is the exposure of the dead on the so called *"Towers of Silence."*

Parsis have their own system of belief and philosophy. But Zoroastrianism does not advocate either Brahmacharya or *"Sanyasa"* or asceticism. Their sacred book *"Zend Avestha"* criticises Sanyasi and encourages family life. Parsis do not observe penances and liquor is consumed even in the religious ceremonies. The essence of Parsi ethics can be stated in three words, namely, ***"Humata"***, ***"Hukkta"*** and ***"Huvarshta"*** [*"good thought"*, *"good words"* and *"good deeds"*].

Geographic Distribution of the Parsis

Numerically, the Parsis constitute a very small group. During the time of 1951 census, their number was around one lakh. Good number of these people have high level of education. But they

1 **S.C. Dube** *"Indian Society."* Page - 27.

seem to have low level of fertility. Their population strength decreased from one lakh in 1951 to 71,360 in 1981. More than 70% of the Parsis population is concentrated in Greater Bombay. Rest of them are scattered in big cities like Poona, Surat, Ahmedabad, Navsar, Daman, Diu, etc.

The total fertility of Parsis is the lowest one because the community has the greatest number of single-women in the age group of 15 to 39. It means they have the smallest percentage of married women in the reproductive ages. They have also the lowest reproduction per married women.

In spite of their smaller percentage in the population their contribution towards education, industry, commerce has been appreciable. In the fields in which they have worked they showed recognisable performance. Field Marshal Manek Shaw, a great name in the Indian armed forces and Nani Palkhivala, an advocate of international reputation, for example, belong to the Parsi community.

The speciality of the Parsis is that they have maintained healthy and harmonious relationship with the people among whom they are living. They have become a part and parcel of the Indian national community and on no occasion took any chance to assert their minorityism. They have not created any political controversy on account of their religious minority status. They constitute a rich community leading a peaceful life and there seems to be no danger in the near future to the Parsis' interests as a religious minority community in India.

ISLAM AND THE MUSLIM COMMUNITY

Islam is one of the major religions of the mankind. More than one-fifth of the people of the world are Muslims. They are found in a big number in nations such as Indonesia, Bangladesh, Pakisthan, Iran, Iraq, Kuwait, Saudi Arabia, Yemen, Libya, Morroco, Tunisia, Algeria, Turkey, Sudan, Albania, Abyssinia, Afghanisthan, Yugoslovia, Lebanon, Russian Turkomania, Philippines, China and India. According to 1991 census report, as many as 11.7% of the people [about 9.52 crores] in India are Muslims. The Muslim community as the biggest minority group in India has played historically and socially an important role in the emergence of modern India. Hence it is relevant to take a glimpse of the Islamic community in general with a particular reference to the Muslim social outlook.

Islam is the second biggest religion in the world. Judged from the point of view of its followers it is next only to Christianity with all its sects. In India also the Muslims constitute the biggest religious community next only to the Hindus. Prior to the partition of India, Muslims constituted almost 25% of the total population and now their share in the total population is 11.7% [as per 1991 census report]. With the exception of Indonesia and Bangladesh it is only in India, and not in any other country, we find the highest number of Muslims. India which has declared itself as a *"secular state"* has provided all the constitutional protection to the Muslims. They are not treated as *"second class"* or *"second grade"* citizens as the Islamic countries like Pakisthan, Bangladesh and many of other countries do treat their non-Muslim citizens. Muslims here enjoy equal socio-economic opportunities and are guaranteed fundamental rights on par with the people of other community. Muslims are found throughout India though they are not evenly distributed in all the provinces.

Social Conditions of Pre-Islamic Arabian Society

In order to have a better understanding of the main principles of Islam and the Muslim community, one must take into account the nature of pre-Islamic Arab society. Islam has its roots and beginnings in the tribal society of Arabs of the 7th century A.D. The main features of the then existing Arabian society which influenced some of the basic principles of Islam, are as follows.

1. "The pre-Islamic Arab society *did not* recognise the individual as it was centred round a tribe or a kindred." [*Kapadia].* Hence the group claimed all the rights, not the individual.

2. It was a society characterised by *tribal wars and conflicts.* It included harsh social customs in tune with its tribal character. For example, it avenged any injury done to any member of the group, or received forcibly due compensation for it.
3. Kinship was recognised on the father's side. Mother's side was ignored.
4. *Women had no recognition* or *status* in society.
5. Marriage in the Arab society was *contracted* on payment of bride-price.
6. The wife *"bought"* in this way was, therefore, looked upon as a chattel or an article which could be disposed of at will. Chastity was not regarded as a virtue. A wife could be *lent* to a guest as a mark of hospitality. *"She could be handed over to a friend for sexual intimacy when a man went on a journey."*[1] No wonder if such a society at such a time evolved values of life in terms of war, wine and women.
7. *The Arabs were not deeply religious.* They were idolators and offered prayers to idols and stones. Though they believed in a Supreme Being, *they indulged in polytheism* to which each tribe contributed its deities.

Emergence of Islam

It is in this background, Islam emerged in Arabia during the 7th century A.D. Prophet Mohammad, the architect of Islam, was very much perturbed by the decadence in the religious life of the Arabs. He sought an opportunity to stabilize their political life, improve their religious life and chasten their moral life. He placed before them new values of life. He tried to unite them into a community of faith. He preached the Arabs *"to forget the pride and arrogance of ancestry."*

Meaning of Islam: The new community came to be known as the community of ***'Islam'***. In the religious sense the word *'Islam'*[2] means *'surrender'* or *'submission'* to the will of God ['Allah'] and obedience to His Law. Islam postulates only *One God,* that is *'Allah',* and only *one Holy* and authoritative Book, that is, *'Quran'* [Kuran']. The God had been sending now and then his messengers to guide the humanity to correct its mistakes and to find the right way to live. Muslims believe that Prophet Mohammad was the last and the ablest of all the messengers. Hence his teachings and messages should be regarded as authoritative and final. The message of Allah got delivered to Mohammad through the angel **Gabriel.** This message made known to the world through the Prophet's revelations are contained in the noble Book, ***the Quran.***

Mohammad, not the Founder but the Consolidator of Islam

It is important to note that Muslims consider Mohammad not the founder, but the consolidator or stabilizer of Islam. According to them, the original founder of Islam is none other than God, ***Allah*** Himself. Hence the date of the founding of Islam goes back still earlier.

The three Sacred Principles: The Muslims consider three principles very sacred for them.

(i) Belief in the God *Allah,* the *Supreme Lord* of the Universe, Omnipotent and Omnipresent and the sustainer of the world and mankind;

(ii) Acceptance of the *supremacy of Prophet Muhammad* and his teachings and

(iii) The *Holy Quran* which consists of the sacred views and teachings of Mohammad. One who does not accept these principles or any one of these cannot be called a Muslim.

---

1 **K.M. Kapadia** *"Marriage and Family in India"* - Page: 38.

2 The word 'Islam' is derived from the Arabic word *'slm'* which means peace, purity, surrender or submission and obedience.

Fundamental Practices and Institutions of Islam

Five Pillars of Islam

During the earliest decades after the death of the prophet, certain basic features of the religio-social organisation of Islam were singled out and formulated as the *"Pillars of Islam"*.[1]

1. *Profession of Faith* [Belief in one God Allah {Iman)]: The first pillar is the profession of faith: *"there is no God but the God Allah"*; Mohammad is the prophet of this God. The membership in the community depends on this faith. This profession must be recited at least once in one's life time, aloud and correctly. All faithful Muslims believe in the sole God *"Allah"*, who is viewed as Supreme, Eternal and Merciful and Creator and Provider.

2. *Reciting Prayers* *[Salah]:* The second pillar consists of five daily congregational prayers. Every Muslim male and female must offer prayer [*namaz*] five times a day. *[that is before sun-rise, between midday and afternoon, in the later afternoon, immediately after the sunset and before retiring to bed].* According to Islam, prayer strengthens the belief in the existence and goodness of God.

3. *Alms Giving* *[Zakat]:* The third pillar is the obligatory tax called *"Zakat"*. The literal *meaning of the word* "Zakat" is purification. Every Muslim must give a portion of his wealth to the needy and the poor and this is called *Zakat.* Such a payment makes the rest of one's wealth religiously and legally pure. It is also believed that by giving *Zakat* a man's own self becomes purified. [According to Quran, Zakat could be given to the following type of persons: 1. *to the poor Muslims;* 2. *to the needy Muslims;* 3. *to the new Muslim converts;* 4. *to the Muslim prisoners of war;* 5. *to the Muslims in debt* and 6. *to the Muslims in service of the cause of God by means of study or propagation of Islam]*

4. *Fasting* *[Sawn]:* A Muslim is expected to observe *'fast'* during Ramzan, the 9th month of Islamic Calendar. Fasting means abstaining 'completely' from food, drinks, intimate intercourses and smoking from the break of the dawn till sunset. Fasting is insisted upon in order to *remain fresh in one's thoughts and actions, to protect oneself from committing sins, to cherish goodness by developing a god-fearing attitude and to abstain oneself from lying.* Daily feeding of a poor person is also prescribed "for those who can afford it."

5. *The Pilgrimage* *[Hajj]:* A true Muslim is expected to go on a pilgrimage or *Hajj* to Mecca, the birth place of Mohammad at least once in his life time. The performance of Hajj is obligatory for every Muslim male or female who is mentally, physically and financially fit.

Islam as a way of life

'Islam' is not merely a religion. It is something more than that, it is a way of life. Islam does not make a clear distinction between the religious and secular matters, nor between religion and state. Mohammad himself was playing dual roles - *the role of a religious leader and the role of a political leader or administrator,* particularly when he was in Madina. The 'Caliphs' who ruled over the Arabian territories also followed his example after his death. In the Islamic thought, State and religion, state and society are almost indistinguishable. Hence, Quran deals with political, economic, social and administrative matters. Thus, the influence of the Islamic thought was all pervasive.

1 To these five, the Khawarij sect added a sixth pillar, *"the jihad"*, which however was not accepted by the general community" - Encyclo-Brita - Vol. 22 - Page: 12

The Socio-Religious Character of Islam

During its early period, "Islam acquired its characteristic ethics as a religion uniting in itself both the spiritual and temporal aspects of life..." It sought *"to regulate not only the individual's relationship to God* [through his conscience] *but human relationships in a social setting as well."* Thus, there is not only an Islamic religious institution but also *an Islamic law, state and other institutions governing society.* Not until the 20th century, were the religious [private] and the secular [public] distinguished by Muslim thinkers and separated formally, as in Turkey."

Two Directive Forces of Islamic Social Life

Every Muslim's social life is guided and directed by two important forces namely (i) ***Religious belief** dictated by the monotheistic religion* and (ii) ***Islamic law** which decides what is right and what is wrong, what should be done and what should not be done.* It is often said that in no other religion of the world law played such an important role as it did in Islam.

The Muslim Law and its Sources

The socio-cultural life of the Muslims is very much guided, directed and conditioned by the Muslim law. *Total and unqualified submission to the will of Allah [God] is the fundamental tenet of Islam. Islamic law is, therefore, the expression of Allah's command for Mulsim society.* In its application the law constitutes a system of duties that are incumbent upon a Muslim by virtue of his religious belief.

Shariah - The Muslim Law and its Nature

The Muslim law is called *'Shariah'*. The word 'Shariah' literally means *'the road to the watering place'*, or *'the path to be followed'*. It prescribes a path or a way of behaving for all the Muslims. It gives guidance and directions for all human actions - individual and collective, religious and social, economic and political. It is basically a *'doctrine of duties'* and a *'code of obligation'*.

The Evolution of Shariah: The Shariah was taking its shape in the beginning of the Islamic era called *Hijrah.* Two hundred years later after the death of the prophet, attempts were made by his great followers to give a final shape to the Islamic law and to his teachings. This historical process was regarded as completed by the end of the 9th century A.D. Throughout the medieval period this basic doctrine was elaborated and systematised in a large number of commentaries. The voluminous literatures thus produced constitutes the traditional textual authority of Shariah law.

Differences between Shariah and the Western Systems of Law

The Shariah differs from the Western systems of law in two main respects.

(i) ***The scope of Shariah is wider:*** It regulates man's relationship not only with his neighbours and with the state but also with his God and his own conscience. Ritual practice such as the daily prayers, alms giving, fasting and pilgrimage are an integral part of Shariah law. The Shariah is concerned with the *legal rules* as well as *ethical standards.* The legal rules indicate not only *what man is entitled or bound to do in law* and the ethical standards denote *what he ought to do* or *refrain from doing in general.* Thus the Shariah is not merely a system of law, but a comprehensive code of behaviour that embraces both *private* and *public activities.*

(ii) ***Shariah - as the expression of the divine will:*** The Islamic law 'Shariah' belongs to the category of the *'sacred law'* and not to the category of the secular law of the Western type.

It is not created by man, but is believed to have emerged from God through Mohammad. The will of God is contained in it. *With the death of the Prophet in 632, communication of the divine will to man came to an end.* Hence, the terms of the divine revelation were considered to be *fixed and unchangeable.* It is for this reason Shariah law became *a rigid and static system.*

The secular legal systems grow out of society and change with the changing circumstances of society. Unlike the legal system, *Shariah law is imposed upon society from above.* In Islamic jurisprudence *it is not society that moulds and fashions the law, but it is the law that precedes and controls society.*

"Such a philosophy of law clearly poses fundamental problems of principle for social advancement in contemporary Islam. *How can the traditional Shariah law be adapted to meet the changing circumstances of modern Muslim society*? This is now the central issue in Islamic law."[1]

Sources of Islamic Law and Social Views

Islamic doctrine, law and thinking in general are based upon four important sources. 1. *the Quran,* 2. *the Sunna* and *the Hadith,* 3. *the Ijma* and 4. *the Qiyas.*

1. ***The Quran*** is the first source of law which is divinely ordained. It is unchangeable and authoritative.
2. ***The Sunna*** and ***Hadith*** refer to the second source of law. **"Sunna"** means custom or usage. It refers to the usage or the practice of prophet and also his *"mode of behaviour".* The usage of the prophet had replaced the usage of the ancients.

   The ***Hadith*** refers to the story of particular occurrences or events that took place in the life of the prophet as quoted by the eye witnesses.
3. ***The Ijma*** refers to the consensus of opinion among the learned Muslims in the community.
4. ***The 'Qiyas'*** represent the last source of Muslim law. It refers to the collection of rules deduced from the first three sources. It implies reasoning by analogy. It was Abu Hanifa [699 - 766 A.D.] who recognised **'qiyas'** as a source of law when the Book [Quran] did not provide a categorical solution to meet the new conditions.

The Principle of Movement within the Mulsim Law

Though Islam was often regarded as changeless, it was not altogether changeless. It had to imbibe in it *"the principle of movement"* to accommodate itself to the changing conditions of space and time.

Abu Hanifa [A.D. 699 - 766] **Ash-Shafi** [A.D. 767 - 820] and many other religious leaders within the community tried to introduce the principle of greater freedom in the realm of Islamic law without violating the social implications of Islam. As **Kapadia** has pointed out, *"...contact with non-Muslim peoples, economic and political conditions of the Islamic empire, ancient custom, alien ideas and usages - all have in a certain measure influenced the Muslim law in its evolution."*

The Islamic law which was once considered unchangeable and unalterable has undergone remarkable reforms in the 20th century in nations such as Egypt [1931], Albania [1928], Lebanon [1932], Syria [1953], Iraq [1953], Tunisia [1957] and in Pakisthan in 1961. In Egypt and Tunisia, the Shariah courts as a separate entity, have been abolished. In 1926 itself, Turkey took a radical step in abandoning the Shariah and replacing it with the Swiss family law. No other Muslim country, however, has yet followed this example. Instead, Shariah law has been adapted in a variety of ways to meet the present social needs.

1 **Ref:** Encyclopaedic Britannica Vol. 22 - Page: 31

Factors Reflecting Muslim Social Outlook

1. ***Religious and the Moral Factors*** **:** The Muslims believe in only one God, that is, Allah. He is powerful and at the same time very merciful also. All those who surrender themselves to his *"will"* are blessed and protected. Those who obey the dictates of Allah will be rewarded with and those who do not, will be punished on the last day, the *"day of Judgement."* Islam places high premium on leading a moral and a righteous life.

2. ***Family and Marital Affairs*** **:** Islam recognises family as the basis of society. The Muslim family upholds the patriarchal tradition. The man looks after almost everything while the woman confines herself to the tasks of domestic affairs.

Marriage is universal among the Muslims. Still it is regarded as a contract and not a sacrament. Islam lays down the conditions of *"sahi nikah"* [valid marriage]. Islam recommends monogamy though Quran permits a Muslim man to have four wives at a time. Both men and women have the right to divorce though it is comparatively easier for men than women to resort to divorce.

3. ***Status of Women*** **:** Since Islam upholds the patriarchal principles women have only a secondary position in the society. Still they have a respectable position. Prophet Mohammad used to say that *"the heaven is at the feet of the mother."* Islam does not consider women as *"wicked"* and *"impure."* It permits even the widow to remarry. Women have the right to property, politics, education and occupation. Islamic law recognises Muslim woman's right to the inheritance of property.

Pardah System has been imposed on Muslim women. It refers to the practice of Muslim women wearing a gown or veil to cover their face and upper part of the body. This system has curtailed some of their freedom. It is still in rigorous practice in many nations including India.

4. ***Festivals and Rituals that Strengthen the Social Ties*** **:** Of the various festivals the Muslims observe Bakrid, Edh Milad, Ramjan and Moharam are important. These festivals act as means of strengthening their social ties. On the festival days, the Muslims normally wear new dresses, exchange greetings, go to Mosques and offer prayers collectively. But in all these, the role of women is very much limited.

Muslims undergo various rituals during the course of their life. Naming, initiation to learn Arabic and to read Quran, the practice of "Sunnah."[1] Muslims follow their own funeral rites. Among them, the dead body of a person is not burnt but normally kept in a coffin and buried. The religious practices of the Muslims such as collective prayers, the Zakat, fasting, the Hajj pilgrimage also add to the communal solidarity among the Muslims.

5. ***Attitude towards Social Change*** **:** Social changes in general take place at a relatively slow rate in the Muslim community. The hold of tradition is still strong among them. ***Examples*** **:** (i) Islam has elevated the status of the slaves but it has not completely done away with that institution. (ii) Though Turkey has abolished the Shariah law and the Pardah system in most of the other Muslim dominated nations they are still in practice. (iii) The patriarchal principle is still dominant. (iv) Muslim women cannot offer prayers along with their menfolk in Mosques but should do so on their own at home.

The Advent of Islam into India

Islam took its birth in the 7th century A.D. in Arabia. Soon after its birth, the followers of Islam started moving towards India and spread the message of Prophet Pygambar. It means, India had received the message of Islam much before the Muslim rule in India. Politically speaking, *"In* **712,**

1 ***"Sunnah"*** is an important ritual which the Muslims, particularly the Sunnies undergo. This has the purpose of guiding the individual in order to lead a disciplined civic life.

the sword of Islam reached India, and Sind was occupied. But the Arab rule in India did not last long. It was almost 200 years later that serious attempts were made to establish Islamic rule in India."[1] The Turks coming from Afghanistan were the early conquerors. Mohammed of Ghazni invaded India 17 times. His main aim was to plunder the wealth of India and not to establish any Islamic empire here. *"His campaigns were so disastrous that the Hindus cherished, "the most inveterate hatred of all Muslims," says* **Alberuni,** *a traveller, who had accompanied his army."*[2]

The real founder of Muslim power in India, was Mohammad Ghori, again a Turk from Afghanistan. He captured Delhi in 1193 A.D. by defeating Prithviraj Chauhan. Thereafter the Muslim rule continued in India until it was conquered by the British in 1757. For more than 500 to 600 years India came under the Muslim rule.

Causes for the Muslim Invaders Settling in India

Various explanations have been offered for the question as to why the Muslim invaders permanently settled in India. Some such explanations can be stated here :

1. Islam was spread by the strength of the sword.
2. Indian society was degenerate and disunited that it could not resist the might of Islamic arms.
3. A long confrontation that took place between Islamic rule and Hinduism helped the spread of Islam for the Islamic rule was imposed on Hindus in many places of India.
4. Under Islamic rule, all the Muslims were in a privileged or superior position compared to the non-Muslims. Naturally, non-Muslims were attracted towards Islam. This led to conversions.

According to **S.C. Dube,** each of the above explanations is *"either incorrect or at best only partially correct."* He is of the opinion that *"Islam first came to India by peaceful methods, often with the encouragement of Hindu rulers"* [Page - 14].

Islamic Invasion was Different from the Previous Ones

Before the invasion of Islam, India had experienced various other conquests at the hands of the Greeks, Persians, Sythians, Hunas, Shakas, Kushanas and others. These invaders who had come mostly from Central Asia, were almost totally absorbed in the Indian society after initial confrontations. *"The confrontation with the Islamic invaders was longer and more bitter as they brought with them their own theology and considered only their religion as true. A divide was created, but at the same time, forces to bring about conciliation were also in operation. The Muslim rulers were in India not only for the spread of Islam, but had other interests also. Some of them took upon themselves the mission of Islamizing society more seriously than others; discriminatory practices such as the imposition of jizyah [poll tax], in addition to kharaj [tax on land and property], were pursued more vigorously by some rulers, while others were relaxed about them."*[3]

Options Kept Open for the Non-Muslims

According to the Islamic doctrine, theoretically three options were open to the non-Muslims under the Islamic rule. They are mentioned below:

1. Accepting the religion of Islam and getting oneself converted into that.
2. Accepting the Muslim rule, becoming *"Dhimmis"* and paying *"jizyah"* and *"kharaj"*.
3. Fighting against the Muslim rule.

---

1 **Dr. H.N. Sreenivasa Murthy** and **Dr. Suryanath U. Kamath** *"Studies in Indian Culture"* [1973]. Page - 58.

2 **Sreenivasa Murthy** and **S.U. Kamath.** Page - 58.

3 **S.C. Dube.** Page - 18.

As per this doctrine, the alternatives left for the Hindus were – *"acceptance of Islam or death"*. As S.C. Dube points out *"Despite long years of Muslim rule the overwhelming majority of the people remained Hindu. This would not have been possible had the requirements of Islam had been strictly carried out. The army, state administration and trade and commerce - all depended on the direct and indirect support of the Hindus."* [**S.C. Dube** - 19]. Further, the internal strength of Hinduism and the rigid caste system also must have prevented Hindus from being converted into Muslims in a large number.

Numerical Strength of the Muslims

Throughout the Muslim rule in India, Muslim population went on increasing incessantly. In 1881, there were about 4.99 crore Muslims [19.97% of the total population] in India and this number increased to 9.44% crores [24.28%] in 1941. From 1881 till 1941, the Muslims grew steadily in numbers. This growth is attributable not solely to conversion of lower caste Hindus into Muslims but to higher fertility among the Muslims. The Muslims are more fertile because they permit widow remarriages. But after 1941 their population got reduced to relatively a low level due to partition that took place in 1947.

The increasing trend in the Muslim population continued even after partition. For example, the Muslim population in 1951 was 35.4 million [9.93%] and it increased to 61.4 million in 1971 [11.20%], to 75.5 million in 1981 and then to 95.2 million in 1991 [11.7%]. Between 1951 and 1961 Muslim population in India increased by 25.6%, while the national average increase was around 21.5%. By 1971, this rate of increase in Muslim population further increased to 30.8%. It means their decennial growth was about 5% higher than that of the total population in 1951-61, as well as in 1961-71, so that their share in total population rose to 10.7% in 1961 to 11.2% in 1971 and to 11.7% in 1991.

Geographic Distribution of Muslims

Muslims are found in almost all the states though they are not equally distributed in all the states. About half of the total Muslim population is distributed in three states, Bihar, U.P. and West Bengal. Muslims in Jammu & Kashmir accounted for about 2/3 of the population in the state. Due to Pakistan instigated terrorist activities and heightened atrocities on the Hindu minorities, mass exodus of the Hindus from Kashmir to other states has taken place. This has further added to the numerical domination of the Muslims in the state. The states in which the population of Muslims exceed the national average of 11.7% in 1991 are - Assam [28.4%], West Bengal [23.6%], Kerala [23.3%], U.P. [17.3%] and Bihar [14.8%]. They constitute 11.6% of the population of Karnataka, 9.7% of that of Maharashtra, and 8.9% of Andhra Pradesh.[1] These figures make it evident that the Muslim concentration varies between 8% to 29% in different states. There are two Muslim majority pockets in India. Jammu & Kashmir [66%] and Lacadiva and Minicoy Islands [94%]. About 5% of Indian Muslims speak Urdu and all those who speak Urdu are not invariably Muslims.

Patterns of Muslim Concentration

It is quite interesting to note that the Muslims in India prefer to live in areas in which their community people are found in a relatively large number. There are some causes for this :

(i) *Muslims feel secure* in areas in which they have their domination.

(ii) *They are able to preserve their culture* particularly when they concentrate in a common physical area. It helps easy communication and better co-operation especially in times of emergencies.

1 *The Hindustan Times* dated 8.7.1995.

(iii) *Finally, the Hindus, in general, do not like to take Muslims as tenants and also as their neighbours.* In areas in which both Hindus and Muslims live we find separate clusters.

It can also be observed that wherever Hindus and Muslims live together in a common area, there is very limited social exchanges, such as exchanges of invitations. *"Hindus and Sikhs, however living in one neighbourhood exchange things and even attend each others, marriages, etc. It requires liberalism and flexibility so that individuals can spontaneously enter into spontaneous relationships with others."*[1]

Caste like Groups within the Muslim Community

It is indisputable that Islam has been in existence in India for the past one thousand years. Islam was more used as a political weapon by the foreign settlers such as Turks, Afghans and Mughals, than as an instrument of social service. These foreign settlers always maintained a distance and caused a distinction between themselves and the converts. They called themselves ***"Ashrafs"*** or *nobles,* and the converts from the lower Hindu castes were regarded as ***"Ajlafs"***. The latter definitely had a lower social position. The Ashrafs were known as ***"Saiyads"*** and ***"Sheiks"***, *"men of pen"* and *"men of sword"* respectively. The rest of the Muslims were the Hindu converts with whom the Ashrafs had limited social contacts. They remained *"divided into numerous groups on caste lines."* The leadership throughout remained in the hands of the religious and the political elite who were generally of the alien origin. This religious and political leadership pursued the Central Asian tradition in ethics and morality, language and literature, and culture and communication. This tendency virtually caused alienation and ultimately resulted in the partition of the country. In spite of this partition, the Islam that is surviving in our country is very much Indian in nature. Many of the practices and features which the Muslims of Muslim majority nations are having, the Indians are not having. Some of the features are associated with only Indian Muslims. *For example, the features such as the worship of saints differentiates Indian Islam from the Islam of Arabia and other countries.*

Muslim Law in India and Need for Change in it

Muslims in India, and their socio-religious life is governed not by the whole of the Islamic law but only a certain part of it. Therefore, Muslim law in India is meant *"that portion of the Islamic law which is applied in India to Muslims as personal law."*

Muslims at different places in India were following for centuries different practices and customs which were believed to belong to the domain of Shariah. The then Indian Government introduced the ***Muslim Personal Law [Shariah] Application Act of 1937*** in order to bring about some uniformity. It was an attempt to integrate all varieties and diversities found among the customs of Indian Muslims into a uniform pattern without violating the basic principles of Shariah.

Need for a Change

"Educated Muslims have come to realise that the social legislation of Islam is in need of some change...." [**Kapadia** - Page: 44] for two reasons: **Firstly,** the law that was given to the desert nomads cannot serve the needs of an agricultural community or of an industrial civilisation; **Secondly,** the contact with the Western civilisation has provided a new pattern and ideal of marriage relationships. The radicals are also aware that any *"reform in this direction is always met with stubborn resistance."*

The modernists therefore employ another device. They go back to the Quran to show that some of the Muslim practices are against the spirit of Quranic teaching. They try to impress

1 **Prof. Ram Ahuja** *"Society in India."* Page : 241 -242.

upon the community that their mission is to present the Quranic ideal in all its purity and loftiness. This new device serves two functions (i) *It restores faith in Islam among the doubting Muslims by demonstrating the great ideals of their religion;* (ii) I*t persuades the "old fashioned" Muslims and makes them understand that they, by their social conservatism and their stand upon the letter of the law, are "sinning against" Quran.* It remains to be seen how far the sentiments of nationality and the implications of democracy render possible the evolution of Muslim society on a rationalistic and equitable principle.

Protection to Muslim Community and Culture

The Constitution of India protects the interests of all the minorities including the Muslims. All the governments which have ruled the country have taken proper steps to protect the Muslim interests and to promote their culture. Since the Muslims have considerable numerical strength [11.7% in 1991] they are in a position to form themselves as a strong political pressure group.Muslims are also having equal political rights to contest elections on par with other communities. They have been making use of this right to elect the candidates of their own community, to support candidates of the political parties of their choice and also to defeat candidates of the political parties which they dislike. Both at the Central and at the State levels, Muslim candidates are getting elected to the legislative bodies in a relatively big number. **Table - 3** shows the strength of the Muslim Parliamentarians in different Lok Sabha Elections. Muslims as constituting a political pressure group have been able to influence the governance of the country. Since Muslims constitute a very strong minority group all political parties are wooing the Muslim community to obtain support to fight elections. Unlike their counterpart in Pakisthan and Bangladesh, Muslim minority people are comparatively well protected both at the national level and at the states level. Governments at both the levels have taken various measures to promote their welfare and protect their interests.

Table - 3

Number of Muslim Members in the Lok Sabha [1957-1996]

Different Lok Sabha Elections	*Strength in Parliament*
1957	19
1962	20
1967	28
1971	21
1977	31
1984	44
1989	27
1991	25
1996	21

Source **: Asghar Ali Engineer,** *Mainstream,* 22 June 1996. Page - 19, as quoted by **Dr. Parvathy Appaiah** in *"Hindutva Ideology and Politics"* [2003]. Page - 198.

CHRISTIANITY AND THE CHRISTIAN COMMUNITY

Christianity is the biggest religion of the mankind judged in terms of its followers. It was founded in the first century A.D. by Jesus of Nazareth [the Christ]. The religion has 2000 years of history and is spread over all the parts and corners of the world. However, there are several sects and groups within Christianity. In addition, there are several independent churches of eastern Christianity and numerous sects throughout the world. The total membership of the Christian Church is **1869** millions [1993] spread over 270 countries, and constitutes 33.5% of the total population of the world. In India, there are 18.8 million Christians forming 2.32% of the population [1991].

Christianity entered India during the first century A.D. itself. One of the 12 Apostles of Jesus Christ by name **St. Thomas,** and **St. Barthalomew** are believed to have brought Christianity to India in 50-52 A.D. St. Thomas reached the southern coast of Malabar and started his missionary activities right from that place and that period. Because of this grand old relationship of India with Christianity, Pandit Nehru was referring to it as *"an old and honoured religion of the land."*

According to a well-established tradition, **Judas Thomas** [St. Thomas] was reluctant to go to India to convert its people. He hesitated because he felt that he did not have strength enough for it. He felt that he was not equipped to teach Indians, who were known to be more proficient in the fields of religion and philosophy. But, as it is believed that the Lord assured him of His Grace. Thomas embarked upon his journey to India. It is said that Thomas visited the court of the king of Punjab and even tried to convert him. St. Thomas became more successful in the South, particularly in Kerala where he could convert a large number of people. When the Portuguese arrived in India, Christianity was found to have spread to the seventeen kingdoms in which Kerala was also included. In Kerala, Christians had several churches and more than one lakh followers.

***The Spread of Religion through Compulsions and Persuasions*:** The carly Christians, however, were held in high esteem by the Hindus. Things began to change with the arrival and establishment of the Portuguese in India. Portuguese made it a compelling religion in Goa. The persecution of non-Christians has caused some friction on that Christian missionaries of the West used various means of attracting people to their faith. The Italian Jesuit **Roberto de Nobili**, who reached Goa in 1605 and died in Madras in 1656, resorted to unconventional methods of spreading the faith. *"He lived like a Hindu ascetic, dressed in saffron robes, and observed the rules of ritual purity in his food and social contacts..... He was familiar with Hindu philosophic and religious thought and was attempting to win over Hinduism from within. de Nobili was keen to get convinced converts from the top of Hindu society to facilitate the rapid spread of Christianity. He avoided contact with Christians of lower caste origins, including their priests. By the end of the 17th century, de Nobili and his associates had made 150,000 converts...."*[1]

The association of the Church with the foreign powers such as - the Portuguese, the Dutch, the British and the French - helped the later development of Christianity in India. Considerable humanitarian work was done by Christian missionaries of different nationalities and denominations. Besides Kerala and Tamil Nadu, there were pockets of Christianity in most of the Indian states. In the north-eastern states also they are widespread. At least three such states have substantial Christian majorities. In spite of the various service oriented activities of the Christians, they had been distanced from the mainstream of the Indian society to a certain extent because of their association with the European rulers.

Geographic Distribution of the Christians

According to the 1991 census report, there are about 18.8 million Christians in India consisting 2.32% of the total population. They are widely scattered over. Various Christian sects include the Syrian, Roman Catholic and the Protestant. Of the total Christians in India, about 2/5th

1 **S.C. Dube.** Page - 13.

are Roman Catholics; 1/8th Romo-Syrians, 1/9th belong to the Anglican body; 1/11th are Jacobites and 1/12th Baptists. The other sects include the Lutherans, Methodists and the Presbyterians.[1]

Speaking about the geographic distribution of the Christians, about 2/3rd of the total Christians are found concentrated in South India, particularly in the states of Andhra Pradesh [2.09%]. The southern states of A.P., Tamil Nadu and Kerala together account for nearly 60% of the Christian population in India. In Goa [32%] and Maharashtra also they are found in a sizeable number. In Assam [7.15%]; Orissa [1.73%] and Bihar [1.17%] also they are concentrated in some areas. In the north-eastern territories they are a dominant force. In Meghalaya [67%], Nagaland [67%] and Mizoram, they constitute the majority community.

The census of India makes a distinction between Christians of three categories: (i) *Europeans and allied races,* (ii) *Anglo-Indians, that is descendants of mixed unions,* and (iii) *Indians, consisting of the converts.* Since 1891, the number of the first two categories has steadily gone down while that of the third has risen considerably. *The Indian Christians are said to be more fertile compared with the non-Indian Christians.* The Christians have been increasing at comparatively higher rates. For example, they constituted only 0.71% of the total Indian population in 1881, and their share in the total population increased to 1.77% in 1931; and to 2.60% in 1971. However, it slightly came down to 2.32% in 1991.

HINDUISM AND THE HINDU COMMUNITY

Hinduism is one of the major religions of the world and is said to be the most ancient one. *"Hinduism"* is the religion of the Hindus who constitute the major religious community in the Indian population. Nobody knows about its origin. In fact, the very word *"Hindu"* is not of Indian origin. Ancient Persians [while referring to the river "Sindhu"] pronounced the word *"Sindhu"* as "Hindu".[2] The Arabs referred to it as *"al-Hind".* Thus the people of this land [the land of river "Sindhu"] came to be known as *"Hindus"*, their land *"Hindustan"* and their religion *"Hinduism"*.

Traditional Hindus prefer to call their religion *"Sanatana Dharma"*, that is, eternal religion flowing from time immemorial. They also regard it as its original name. It is also known as *"Vaidika Dharma"*, for it is rooted in the Vedas. It is also called *"Arya Dharma"* ["Arya" means "great" or "noble"] and sometimes as *"Vedanta Dharma"*.

Hinduism represents *neither a dogma nor just a collection of some beliefs.* As **M.K. Gandhi** has pointed out, it is more than a religion, *it is a way of life.* Hinduism consists of several streams of beliefs, practices and socio-religious institutions. These beliefs and practices pervade every aspect of the life of a Hindu. This makes Hinduism appear very complex. [***Note*** : For more details about Hinduism, refer to **Chapter - 1.**]

Hinduism is unique in certain respects. It was *"founded"* or established by no single person, or prophet or angel. It is not based on the preachings and thoughts of any single person. Unlike Christianity or Islam, *Hinduism does not have any single central authority,* nor a universally accepted hierarchy of religious leaders, nor an organisation to control, regulate and guide the lives of its followers. Further, *Hinduism does not have a single sacred scripture* which can be regarded as a common authority on Hinduism.

---

1 **C.B. Mamoria** *"Social Problems and Social Disorganisation in India."* Page - 147.

2 The Greeks called the Sindhu river *"Indus"* and the people in the valley *"Indos"*. The British in course of time popularised the word *"India"* to represent this land and introduced the term *"Hinduism"* in 1830 to represent the main religion of India.

Hinduism is known for its broad outlook. It allows the widest freedom to its followers in matters of faith and worship. It never prescribes any particular way of worship and never imposes any belief for the devotees. There can be any number of faiths and any type of worship within its framework. The popular saying, *"as many minds so many faiths"* reveals this freedom granted to the followers.

Hinduism is not a uniform monolithic [single God] religion. It allows flexibility and permits the prevalence of many sects within it. Hence, *Hinduism is actually a collectivity of sects.* In addition to the prevalence of these sects there is what is called *"henotheism."* It is belief in one God without claiming that He is the only God. It means the polytheistic aspect of Hinduism does not go against its basic monotheistic character.

Hinduism is also associated with idol worship. But it varies with the sect for it is not uniform. Hindus also worship the forces of nature. Further, God is understood in Hinduism in two ways: (i) to understand God as *an abstract entity*, that is, as *a Supreme Principle*; (ii) to understand God in terms of *images* or *symbols*, that is, through *concrete manifestations.*

Hindus have developed over the years two types of philosophy : (i) ***astika*** [*Brahmanic*] and (ii) ***nastika*** [*non-Brahmanic*]; the former accept the authority of the Vedas while the latter reject the authority of the Vedas. The Buddhist and the Jain philosophy belong to the latter one. The Hindu theology is very complex and is woven around abstract spiritual concepts such as – *atma, paramatma, punarjanma, karma, papa, punya, brahma, dharma, moksha,* and so on.

The theory of *purusharthas* consisting of *dharma, artha, kama* and *moksha* which represent the aims of Hindu life, is also an essential aspect of Hinduism. This theory is related to the theory of *"Varnashrama dharma."* The theory of *"ashramas"* regulates an individual's individual life while the *"theory of the Varnas"* regulates an individual's social life.

Hinduism has its own *system of values to exert a moral and a spiritual influence* over the behaviour of the people. Of all the religions, Hinduism is said to be *more tolerant* towards other religions. Further, it *does not believe in conversions.* It permits greater adaptability for it is not a set of unchanging dogmas. It believes that truth is not the monopoly of any religion. It offers a wide variety of paths suited to each individual to attain truth on his own. Hence it finds no reason to impose its beliefs or thoughts on the followers of other religions. Philosopher **C.E.M. Joad** writes : *"Hinduism developed from the first a wide tolerance. Hindus do not proselytize: they do not claim exclusive claim to salvation and they do not believe that God will be pleased by the wholesome slaughter of His Creatures whose beliefs are mistaken. As a result, Hinduism has been less degraded than most religions by the anomaly of creed wars."*

Conclusion **:** Thus, Hinduism is more than a religion, *it is a way of life based on justice and harmony.* Indeed, if one were to put it in a nutshell, *harmony is the keynote of Hinduism.* It signifies harmony not only among the Man, the Universe and the God, but also among the various castes, classes, creeds, peoples and their faiths, gods and goddesses. The Hindu believes that the whole world is his home and the *entire humanity is his family.* [*"Vasudhaiva Kutumbakam"*] Hinduism is not static but dynamic. It had undergone many changes maintaining its essential elements and characteristics. Its influence on the Hindu social life and also on the other religions has been very significant.

Geographic Distribution of the Hindus

Hindus constitute 82.4% of the total population of India as per the Census Report of 1991. All the states except Assam, Jammu & Kashmir, Kerala and Punjab, have more than 75% Hindu population. Majority of the Hindus are concentrated in the States such as Himachal Pradesh, Karnataka,

Orissa, M.P., Gujarat, Maharashtra, Rajasthan, U.P., Bihar, Andhra Pradesh, Tamil Nadu and Haryana. In these states, the percentage of the Hindus in the total population exceeds 80 to 90%.

Although Hindus have been increasing in absolute numbers since 1881 to 1941, they had been steadily declining, that is, in proportion to their number in the total population. **Kingsley Davis** has given three reasons for this.[1] (i) *Secularisation because of the Western influence;* (ii) *the alteration of the social system,* and (iii) *the growth of other equally important religious groups.*

The Hindu community often gains in strength by absorbing tribal people here and there, but more than that it loses heavily particularly when its members [chiefly from lower ranks] get converted to other religions such as Islam and Christianity. During 1941-51, the proportion of the Hindus increased as a result of partition when about 2.5 million Hindus migrated from Pakistan to India. At that time, they formed about 84% of the total population. In the succeeding generations, the strength of the Hindus went on declining. For example, it declined from 84.8% in 1941 to 83.5% in 1951, and then to 83.5% in 1961, 82.7% in 1971, to 82.06% in 1981 and then to 82.4% in 1991.

There are several causes for this decline in the Hindu population : (i) *The conversion of low caste Hindus to Christianity and Neo-Buddhism;* (ii) *The Hindus have a low fertility rate in comparison with tribal people, Sikhs or Muslims.* This low fertility is mainly due to the fact that the Hindus have a high proportion of widows who are forbidden to remarry. Hence, a large number of women are found to be unproductive. Further, among the Hindus, in comparison with others, a relatively larger number of people are found to be unmarried between the ages of 15 and 32. This has also added to low fertility among the Hindus.

RELIGIOUS MINORITIES AND THEIR PROBLEMS

India is a multi-lingual and a multi-religious country. Indian society is pluralistic in character from the religious and other point of view. Since a very long time people belonging to various religious communities have been living together in this nation. Though majority of the people living in this land are **Hindus** [82.41%], people belonging to other religious communities such as **Muslims** [11.67%], **Christians** [2.32%], **Sikhs** [2%], **Buddhists** [0.77%], **Jains** [0.41%] and **others** [0.43%] are also living along with the Hindus by enjoying on par similar rights and opportunities. By virtue of their numerical strength the Hindus constitute the majority while the rest of the religious communities come under what is known as *"religious minorities."*

Concept of *"Minority"*

- The dictionary meaning of the word *minority* is that it signifies *"a smaller number" in opposition to the other party that is, the majority group or party.*
- *"A minority is a category of people singled out for unequal and inferior treatment simply because they are identified as belonging to that category."*[2]
- Minority group refers to *"any recognisable racial, religious, or ethnic group in a community that suffers from some disadvantage due to prejudice or discrimination."*[3]
- *"The most common general description of a minority group used, is of - an aggregate of people who are distinct in religion, language, or nationality from other members of the society in which they live and who think of themselves, and are thought of by others, as being separate and distinct."*[4]

1 **Mamoria C.B.** in *"Social Problems and Social Disorganisation."* Page 140

2 ***The Blackwell Dictionary of Sociology.*** Page - 179.

3 **W.P. Scott** in *"Dictionary of Sociology."* Page - 258.

4 ***The New Encyclopaedia Britannica*** Vol. 27. Page: 356.

Speaking about the concept of *"minority"* in the Indian context, it can be said that the term has not been properly defined anywhere in the Indian Constitution. But *"minority status"* has been conferred on many groups.

- According to the ***Article 29*** of the Constitution, *any group living within the jurisdiction of India is entitled to preserve and promote its own language, script or literature, and culture.*
- ***Article 30*** states that a minority group *"whether based on religion or language shall have the right to establish and administer educational institution of their choice."*
- ***The preamble of the Indian Constitution*** guarantees for all of its citizens *justice, liberty, equality* and *fraternity.* There is no discrimination against the minorities on any ground whatsoever.

Problems of Religious Minorities

Minority groups of ethnic, religious, racial or linguistic character are found in several countries of the world. The recent history of these minority groups reveals that most of these groups are faced with two main types of problems, (i) *the problem of prejudice and discrimination,* and (ii) *the problem of preserving the distinct social and cultural life.*

1. Prejudice and Discrimination

Prejudice and discrimination are found in any situation of hostility between racial and ethnic groups and divergent religious communities. The two terms are often used interchangeably in ordinary speech, but in fact, they refer to two different, but related phenomena :

(a) ***Prejudice*** refers to a *"pre-judged" attitude towards members of another group.* These groups are regarded with hostility simply because they belong to a particular group, and they are assumed to have the undesirable qualities that are supposed to be characteristic of the group as a whole.

(b) ***Discrimination,*** on the other hand, *refers to action against other people on the grounds of their group membership.* It involves the refusal to grant members of another group the opportunities that would be granted to similarly qualified members of one's own group.

Speaking about the Indian context, ***discrimination** especially in providing opportunities to people of different religious communities* ***is, not at all in practice.*** The Preamble of the Constitution itself declares that all people irrespective of their caste, class, colour, creed, sex, region or religion will be provided with equal rights and opportunities. *Article 15(1) and 15(2)* prohibit discrimination on grounds of religion. *Article 25* promises the right to profess, propagate and practice religion. It is clear that there is no legal bar for any religious community in India to make use of the opportunities [educational, economic, etc.] extended to the people. It is true that some religious communities [for example, Muslims] have not been able to avail themselves of the opportunities on par with other communities. This situation does not reflect any discrimination. It only reveals that such communities are lagging behind in the competitive race.

As far as ***prejudices*** are concerned, prejudices and stereotyped[1] thinking are common features of a complex society. India is not an exception to this. Commonly used statements such as – *"Hindus are cowards and Muslims are rowdies; Sikhs are dullards and Christians are converters"*, etc. – reflect the prevalent religious prejudices. Common people who are gullible in nature never bother to find out the truth behind these statements, but are simply carried away by them. Such prejudices further widen the social distance among the religious communities. This problem still persists in India.

1 ***Stereotypes*** : "Prejudiced thought always involves the use of a rigid mental image that summarises whatever is believed to be typical about a group. This kind of image is called a ***stereotype.***" - **Ian Robertson** in the book *"Sociology."* Page - 275.

2. Problem of Preserving Distinct Social and Cultural Life

India is one among the very few nations which have given equal freedom to all the religious communities to pursue and practise their religion. *Article 25 of the Constitution* provides for such a right. Added to this, *Article 3D(1) states all minorities whether based on religion or language shall have the right to establish and administer educational institutions of their choice.* They are given the right to preserve their socio-cultural characteristics. It has set up a *"Minorities Commission"* to help the minorities in seeking justice. No minority community can have a grievance against any government particularly in this matter.

Some of the Problems of Minorities in India

In spite of the provisions of the constitutional equality, religious minorities in India often experience some problems among which the following may be noted.

1. *Problem of Providing Protection* : Need for security and protection is very often felt by the minorities. Especially in times of communal violence, caste conflicts, observance of festivals and religious functions on a mass scale, minority groups often seek police protection. Government in power also finds it difficult to provide such a protection to all the members of the minorities. It is highly expensive also. State governments which fail to provide such protection are always criticised. For example, (i) the Rajiv Gandhi Government was severely criticised for its failure to give protection to the Sikh community in the Union Territory of Delhi on the eve of the communal violence that broke out there soon after the assassination of Indira Gandhi in 1984. (ii) The Gujarat state government was criticised for its inability to provide protection to the Muslim minorities in the recent [Feb. Mar. - 2002] communal violence that burst out. (iii) Similarly, the Government of Kashmir's inefficiency in providing adequate security to the Hindu and Sikh minorities in that state against the atrocities of Muslim extremists, is also widely condemned.

2. *Problem of Communal Tensions and Riots* : Communal tensions and riots have been incessantly taking place since independence. However, there are ups and downs in the incidents of communal riots. [Please see **Table - 4** given below.] Whenever the communal tensions and riots take place for whatever reason, minority interests get threatened; fears and anxieties become widespread. It becomes a tough task for the government in power to restore the confidence in them. The Delhi [1984] and the Gujarath [2002] episodes of communal riots as stated above clearly reveal this situation. [*Note* : For more details about *"Communalism - Its Causes and Effects"*, please refer to **Chapter 22.**]

Table - 4

Communal Riots 1992-96

Years	*No. of Communal Incidents / Riots*	*No. of Persons Killed*	*No. of Persons Injured*
1992	1601	1681	10417
1993	2292	952	2989
1994	179	78	794
1995	203	73	1050
1996	161	39	612

Source : **Organiser,** 272 April 1997, as quoted by **Dr. Parvathy Appaiah** in *"Hindutva Ideology and Politics"* [2003]. Page - 238.

3. ***Problem of Lack of Representation in Civil Service and Politics*****:** Though the Constitution provides for equality and equal opportunities to all its citizens including the religious minorities, the biggest minority community, that is, Muslims in particular, have not availed themselves of these facilities. There is a feeling among them that they are neglected. However, such a feeling does not seem to exist among the other religious communities such as the Christians, Sikhs, Jains and Buddhists, for these are economically and educationally better than the majority community.

4. ***Problem of Separatism*** **:** Some of the demands put forward by some of the religious communities in some areas are not acceptable to others. This has widened the gap between them and others. ***Examples*****:** The separatist tendency present among some Muslim extremists in Kashmir and their demand for the establishment of Independent Kashmir is not acceptable to others. Such a demand is regarded as anti-national. Similarly, some of the Christian extremists in Nagaland and Mizoram are demanding separate statehood for their provinces. Both these demands are supportive of *"separatism"* and hence cannot be accepted. Supporters of such demands have been causing lot of disturbances and creating law and order problems in the respective states.

5. ***Failure to Stick on Strictly to Secularism*** **:** India has declared itself as a *"secular"* country. The very spirit of our Constitution is secular. Almost all political parties including the Muslim League claim themselves to be secular. But in actual practice, no party is honest in its commitment to secularism. Purely religious issues are often politicised by these parties. Similarly, secular issues and purely law and order problems are given religious colours. These parties are always waiting for an opportunity to politicalise communal issues and take political advantage out of it. Hence the credibility of these parties in their commitment to secularism is lost. This has created suspicion and feeling of insecurity in the minds of minorities.

6. ***Problem Relating to the Introduction of Common Civil Code*****:** Another major hurdle that we find in between the majority and minority relations is relating to the failure of Governments which have assumed power so far, *in the introduction of a common civil code.* It is argued that social equality is possible only when a common civil code is enforced throughout the nation. Some communities, particularly the Muslims oppose it. Even though some progressive Muslims are in favour of the Common Civil Code, the orthodox Muslims have been opposing it very strongly.Pressure is mounting on the Government to introduce such a uniform code. The Supreme Court itself had issued directives to the Government to take necessary steps to introduce such a Uniform Civil Code. Some intellectuals have, for example, cautioned that the Government must be very careful in introducing it. **Prof. M. Mujeeb** has stated : *"A uniform Civil Code is a good idea, but the necessary integration of different communities should be achieved first through judicial decisions and practical government measures."*[1]

The traditional Muslims who are not in favour of this proposal argue that the imposition of common civil code will take away their religious freedom for it is opposed to the *"Shariat."* The Governments which ruled over the country so far have not dared to take the risk of introducing it for fear of losing Muslim votes. Intellectuals like **Justice Krishna Iyer** too have cautioned the Government to be very careful in taking steps in this direction. Sri Iyer had stated in one context: *"Hurried remedies, enthusiasts and Chauvinists, will aggravate the malady; for in the socio-political field one wrong step forward is two regrettable steps backward and a policy of principal compromise, not of doctrinaire as sectarian rigidity, moving up in zigzags, may be, is the right approach."*[2] The

1 **Prof. M. Mujeeb's** views as quoted in *"Encyclopaedia of Social Work in India"* Vol.II.

2 **Justice Krishna Iyer** as quoted in *"Encyclopaedia of Social Work in India"* Vol. II. Editor **S.C. Dube.**

very issue of Common Civil Code has become controversial today. It has further widened the gap between the religious communities.[1]

It is important to note that though the major political parties [except *Bharateeya Janata Party* (BJP) which has kept provision for uniform Civil Code on the top of its agenda] and politicians are hesitant to take up the issue of Uniform Civil Code and legislate on it though majority of the people seem to be supporting it. Some of the survey reports also confirm this. See **Table - 5.** Of the people surveyed in 1996, around **77%** expressed their support in favour of the Common Civil Code. Of the men took part in the survey 53%, and of the women 46% were in favour of a Common Civil Code.

Table - 5

Survey Topic : Do You Support a Uniform Civil Code - ?

Yes	77%
No	12%
Can't say	11%

Source : *"India Today"*, 28-12-1996. Page - 26, as quoted by **Dr. Parvathy Appaiah** in her *"Hindutva Ideology and Politics"* [2003]. Page - 249.

It is true that communal disturbances, religious conflicts, group clashes are taking place frequently. In spite of these disturbances the nation has maintained its secular character for the past 56 years. Further, the government has been making special efforts to safeguard the interests of the

1 ***Supreme Court's Support Towards the Common Civil Code*** : It is significant to note that though the major political parties are not ready to take the *risk* of initiating and supporting a Bill on the politically controversial issue of the Common Civil Code, the Supreme Court in the context of giving a judgement [dated 23rd July 2003] on a case relating to Section 118 of *the Indian Succession Act*, has observed that the Common Civil Code *"would help the cause of national integration."* The **Chief Justice S.N. Khare** has said in his Judgement that *"It is a matter of regret that Article 44 of the Constitution has not been given effect to. Parliament is still to step in for framing a Common Civil Code in the country. A Common Civil Code will help the cause of national integration by removing the contradictions based on ideologies."* **Mr. Justice S.N. Sinha** and **Mr. Justice A.R. Lakshmana** who concurred through their separate judgements also said : *"We would like to state that Article 44 provides that the State shall endeavour to secure for the citizens a uniform Civil Code throughout the territory of India.* The aforesaid provision is based on the premise that there is no necessary connection between religious and personal law in a civilised society." It is **Mr. Justice Khare** who discussed the need for a common civil code. This topic was not discussed by the other two judges who gave separate judgements concurring with the Chief Justice on the constitutionality of the Succession Law provision. – ***Source*** : *"Deccan Herald"* English Daily [Bangalore] dated 24-7-2003.

Previous Judgements of the Supreme Court : As early as in 1985 itself, [that is during Congress rule headed by Rajiv Gandhi], in the much controversial ***Shabano Case,*** the Supreme Court Bench headed by Chief Justice **Chandrachud**, in its judgement had clearly stated that the absence of Common Civil Code would be dangerous for the national integration, security and protection. It also stated that it would be unfair to discriminate among the citizens of a country. It stressed the need for introducing the Common Civil Code.

Court's Reiteration of the Need for the Uniform Code in 1995 : Further, in 1995, the divisional bench of the Supreme Court had taken the Congress Government headed by Narasimha Rao into task for not having taken any step towards the introduction of the said Civil Code. It even issued directive to the Government to inform the court about the steps taken by the Government in that direction within one and a half year and also to appraise the court frequently about the Government's attempts to fulfil the requirements. It is a pity, that Narasimha Rao's Govt. lost its power within that specified period. The Governments which came later also failed to take any measures in this direction.

religious minorities. Some of the governmental efforts in promoting the welfare of the minorities are mentioned below.

WELFARE OF THE MINORITIES

Government of India has notified 5 communities, viz. *Muslims, Sikhs, Buddhists, Christians* and *Zoroastrians* as religious minorities at the national level. As per the Census of 1991, population of the minority groups constitutes 17.17% of the total population of the country. The Constitution of India protects the interests of the minority and recognises their rights to conserve their languages, scripts or culture and establish and administer educational institutions of their choice.

National Commission for Minorities

The Govt. of India had set up a *"Minorities Commission"* in January 1978 to evaluate the working of the various safeguards in the Constitution for the protection of religious minorities and to make recommendations to ensure effective implementation of enforcement of all the safeguards and laws.

The National Commission for Minorities Act, 1992 was passed by the Parliament with the intention of providing protection to the minority community. Under this Act, the National Commission for Minorities was constituted on 17th May 1993, with a statutory status replacing the previous Commission. The Commission has a Chairperson, a Vice Chairperson and five members to be nominated by the Central Government. The National Commission has been reconstituted with effect from 21st January 2000.

The Commissioner for Linguistic Minorities appointed under the Article 350-B of the Constitution investigates all matters relating to the safeguards provided for the linguistic minorities. He looks into representations and complaints received from various associations and individuals belonging to linguistic minorities. The Commissioner has his headquarters at Allahabad, with regional offices at Calcutta, Belguam and Chennai. So far [upto 2001], 35 reports have been laid before the Parliament.

For improving the employability of the minorities in the public employment and increasing their intake in the professional courses, a pre-examination coaching scheme is being implemented by the *Ministry of Social Justice and Empowerment,* since 1992-93. During the Ninth Plan, provision of Rs.12 crore was made of which Rs.5.51 crores was released for training 13,150 candidates of the weaker sections among minorities upto March 2000. The Government has approved area-based approach for socio-economic development of the minority concentration areas. In the first phase, 41 districts identified on the basis of 1971 census would be taken up.

National Minorities Development and Finance Corporation

The Government has set up a *National Minorities Development and Finance Corporation* with an authorised share capital of Rs.500 crores. The Corporation would provide economic and developmental activities for the benefit of the backward sections among the minorities. Preference is given to the occupational groups and women among minorities. The Govt. of India has raised the level of contribution from Rs.125 crore to 300 crore subject to pro-rata contribution from the State Governments and UTs towards the share capital of the Corporation. During 1999-2000, Corporation disbursed Rs.60.78 crore as loan covering 22,510 beneficiaries. The cumulative assistance provided by the Corporation since 1994-95 amounts to Rs.224.34 crore for 66,891 beneficiaries.[1]

1 *Source* of the statistics : **India – 1999** and **2000.**

SECULARISM

The concepts of ***"secularism"*** and ***"secularisation"*** which are closely related to contemporary Indian politics are subject to lot of criticism. Heated discussions and debates are still going on throughout the nation about these concepts. These discussions are still inconclusive.

The spirit of our Constitution is *"secular"* though originally the word "secular" did not occur in our constitution. ***The Constitution [42nd Amendment] Act, 1976*** added the term *"secular"* to the Preamble of our Constitution. Accordingly, now India is a *"Sovereign, Socialist, Secular Democratic Republic."* As per the provisions of the Constitution, the Indian State cannot establish, recognise or patronise any religion. It does not discriminate against its own people in the name of religion. Hence India is called a *"secular state."* It is surprising that endless discussions are going on even today about the very secular nature of the Indian polity. These discussions however, point out two important things :

(i) The concept of *"secularism"* still continues to be a controversial one for it has not been properly and unambiguously explained;

(ii) Though India has been declared as a *"secular state"* constitutionally, the governments which have ruled over the country have failed to develop or to shape India as a *"secular state"* in the real sense of the term.

Concept of Secularism

It is generally felt that the growth of modernism and modern civilisation has affected religion, its functions and the religiosity of the people. Developments in the fields of science, technology and education have also adversely affected religion and its traditional functions. There is a growing trend towards secularism and secularisation today.

The term secularism is given a variety of meanings as it implies different aspects to different people. For some, the word *"secular"* means pertaining to this world or the present life, or dissociation from religion and religious teachings.

Meaning and Definition of *"Secularism"*

Meaning of Secularism

The word *"secularism"* can mean different things to different nations, society and people.

(i) *It means generally the separation of religion from the state.*

(ii) *But it also means equal treatment of all religious communities* or *equal distance from all religions* and particularly the religious freedom that is granted to many communities.

(iii) In communist states, it may mean even *the absence of religion in the functioning of the state* and concentration on economic or material welfare of citizens.[1]

Definition of Secularism

1. *"Secularism is a system of social or political philosophy that rejects all forms of religious faiths"* – ***Random House Dictionary.***
2. *"Secularism....... means liberation of politics from the hegemony of religion"* – **Sri Asghar Ali Engineer,** [*Indian Express* dated 30-4-1991.]

1 **Dr. Parvathy A.A.** in article on *"Secularism Vs Communalism"* in the Journal *"Third Concept"* – July 2003. Page - 28.

3. ***Secularism*** **:** *"Belief that morality, education, etc. should not be based on religion" –* ***Oxford Advanced Learner's Dictionary.***

4. **Dr. S. Radhakrishnan :** *"Secularism does not mean irreligion or atheism, or even stress on material comforts. It proclaims that it lays stress on universality of spiritual values which may be attained by variety of ways."*[1]

5. **A.P. Avasthi :** *"Secularism is a way of life and conduct guided by material considerations devoid of religion and spirituality."*

Meaning and Definition of *"Secularisation"*

1. **M.N. Srinivas :** *"The term 'secularisation' implies that what was previously regarded as religious is now ceasing to be such, and it also implies a process of differentiation which results in the various aspects of society, economic, political, legal and moral, becoming increasingly discrete in relation to each other."*[2]

2. **Ian Robertson :** *"Secularisation is the process by which traditional religious beliefs and institutions lose their influence in society."*[3]

3. ***In simple words,*** *"secularisation means separation of matter ecclesiastical from matters temporal."*

Main Features of Secularism

It can be said in a general manner that there are three kinds of secular states :

(a) ***Secular States of the Western Type*** in which the governments remain completely neutral in religious matters. They do not discriminate among people and treat people of all the religions as equal. In such states, politics is free from the hold of religion. Religion is not supposed to interfere in the affairs of the government in any manner.

(b) ***Communist States*** claim themselves to be *"secular states."* They are religionless states. **Karl Marx,** the father of communism, called religion *"the opium of the masses."* He spoke in terms of materialism. According to communists, materialism is another name for secularism. It means that matter is the ultimate reality. There is no life beyond or after the world. Hence, there is no scope for believing in spiritual things.

(c) ***Secularism in a Multi-religious States like India*** **:** India is trying to imitate the Western model of secularism by making certain modifications. For example, secularism in the Indian context is expected to establish harmony between religious communities and forge national integration. Whereas Western secularism does not have such commitments.

Secularism of whatever model is, in general, expected to possess the following characteristics.

1. ***Religious Neutrality*** **:** Secular should not meddle with religion. It is supposed to show equal respect and treatment to all.

2. ***No Proposal of Religion*** **:** It does not establish, recognise or endow any religion.

3. ***Religious Freedom to All*** **:** It assures full religious freedom to all of its citizens. Citizens are allowed to follow their religion, build and maintain places of worship and other institutions. It treats alike adherents of all religions.

---

1 **Dr. S. Radhakrishnan** as quoted by **Prof. Parvathy A.A.** in *"Secularism and Hindutva – A Discursive Study"* [1994]. Page - 15.

2 **M.N. Srinivas** *"Social Change in Modern India."*

3 **Ian Robertson** *"Sociology."* Page - 384.

4. ***No Proposal to Promote the Welfare of any Particular Religion*****:** In what it does for the welfare of its citizens, it is guided by worldly reason and considerations of worldly happiness. It is not guided by the dogmas of any particular religion or consideration of other worldly happiness. It does not take responsibility for the promotion of religious or spiritual welfare of its citizens. For all practical purposes, religion is not considered as the domain of the State.

5. ***Secularism is Founded on Scientific Knowledge*** **:** Secularism connotes secular knowledge which is considered as scientific. This knowledge is founded upon experience of this life and can be tested by reason and experience. Secularism always deals with the known world whereas theology interprets the unknown world. *"It is the province of this worldly endeavour and neither subscribes to nor denies a transcendental sphere."*

6. ***Secularism Promotes Humanitarian Values*** **:** Secularism is based on humanitarian values and *not on the spiritual beliefs or values of any particular religion.* It looks at citizens as *"human beings"* and not as adherents of any particular religion. "Secularism" is not just the ideology of the state, it is the ideology of the individual also. Secularism in this way aims at universal humanism.

7. ***Secularism is niether against Religion, nor Morality*** **:** It is wrong to believe that secularism strikes at the very root of religion and questions its existence. In fact, *"Secularism does not subscribe to irreligion or atheism. It does not deny spiritual quest. What it subscribes is that there are different paths of such quest."* [**Prof. Parvathy A.A.** Page - 17.] *"It only denies the rationale and appropriateness of religious way of life."*

It is equally significant to note that *secularism is not against morality.* It does not deny ethical and moral values. In fact, they are reasserted. However, man is capable of arriving at or devising the same.

8. ***Secularism does not Recommend State Religion*** **:** A secular state does not have an official religion of its own. It gives equal importance to all religions. Government officials and those who rule the country in the capacity of ministers, legislators, etc., *are not supposed to take part in the religious activities of any particular religion as a matter of official programme.* Secular state is not supposed to sponsor or prevent any religious programme.

9. ***Secularism as an Aspect of Modernisation*** **:** Progress of modernism can be assessed by means of secularism also. Modernisation gives importance to individual freedom and as a result of that religion becomes more a matter of individual belief and practice than a collective endeavour. In fact, modernisation undermines the importance of religious organisations and collective participation in religious practices.

10. ***Secularism Purports to be a Cultural Environment*** **:** Secularism as an ideology can exist only when it becomes a practising ideology. It can succeed only when the cultural environment is favourable to it, and only when it becomes a part and parcel of people's life.

Secularism in Practice

Secularism is our Constitutional commitment. The spirit of our Constitution is secular. The Preamble declares that India is a ***"Sovereign Socialist Secular Democratic Republic."*** The Indian State does not establish, recognise or endow any religion. It gives special protection to the minorities.

- *Article 15 (1) and 15 (2)* prohibits discrimination on grounds of religion.
- *Article 25 (1)* guarantees freedom of conscience and the right to profess, propagate and practice religion.

- *Article 27* bars compelling anybody to pay any taxes for the task of promoting or maintaining any particular religion or its denomination.
- *Article 30 (1)* lays down that all minorities whether based on religion or language shall have the right to establish and administer educational institutions of their choice.

Though the spirit of Indian Constitution is secular, secularism in its practice, is very much distorted. The idea that Indian society has become secular is easy to grasp but complex to demonstrate. Though the *framers of the Constitution had their own differences relating to the very meaning and definition of secularism*[1] *they had consensus regarding India remaining as a secular state.* It is significant to note that no political party which ruled the country could escape from the criticisms levelled against it by the opposition parties in its task of implementing the principles of secularism. Parties which have accepted secularism as one of their basic political ideologies too have not remained sincere to its philosophy. Hence, secularism still continues to be one of the topics of heated discussions. The most controversial Ayodhya issue has further complicated the theory of *"secularism"* especially in the Indian context. Several impediments come in the way of effectively implementing the principles of secularism.

Impediments in the Practice of Secularism

The practice of secularism has been encountering many problems in India. Some of the main impediments in the implementation of secularism may be briefly discussed here.

1. Problem of Communalism

The greatest hurdle for practising secularism in India is communalism. Communalism is virtually the negation of secularism. Communalism has bedevilled India for long both before and after independence. It is regarded as the most serious challenge facing the secular nature of the state.

Communalism as a term has several interpretations. Generally, as a term, *"communal"* is referred to as something pertaining to a community as a whole or relating to a "commune." In the current English usage, it does not have any adverse connotation. But in the Indian usage it has acquired a negative meaning. In the Indian usage, communalism usually implies a conflict ascribed to religious communities. This conflict or antagonism or tension usually leads to and often anticipates a sense of fear, superstition and hostility. As **C. Subramanyam** pointed out, *"Religion when used for political purposes degenerates itself into communalism."* Extreme loyalty which people show towards their caste and religious community often negates the basic purposes of secularism. As a result of

1 ***Some of the Divergent Opinions which the Framers of Our Constitution had*:**

(i) **Prof. K.T. Shaw :** "The State in India being secular shall have no concern with any religion, creed or profession of faith."

(ii) **Tejamual Hussain :** "........... that this is a secular state [it] should not have anything to do with religion........"

(iii) **K.M. Munshi :** "A secular state is not a Godless state. It is not a state which is pledged to eradicate or ignore religion.......... Any state that seeks to outlaw God will very soon come to an end."

(iv) **Shri Loknath Mishra :** "..... that the secular state of partitioned India was the maximum generosity of a Hindu dominated territory for its non-Hindu population..... that our secular state is a slippery phrase, a device to by-pass the ancient faith and culture of the land....... Justice demands that the ancient faith and culture of the land should be given a fair deal if not restored to its legitimate place after a thousand years of suppression......"

(v) **Shri Damodar Swarup Seth :** "Recognition of minorities based on religion or community is the very negation of secularism."

Source : Prof. Parvathy A.A. *"Secularism and Hindutva - A Discursive Study"* [1994] Page : 32 - 36.

that, religious loyalty often turns out to be religious rivalry and religious conflict. In a multi-religious country like India, religious conflicts in the form of communal riots have been taking place between two or more religious communities or castes. These communal riots have caused lot of damage in terms of human lives and property. Neither the Central Government nor the State Governments have been successful in handling these riots in an impartial manner. Hence the trust in secularism has been shaky.

2. Communal Based Parties

"The greater danger to secularism in our country is that communal political parties are allowed to exist and openly participate in the political process........."[1] Indian Muslim League and Akali Dal, for example, are existing and functioning on the basis of the support given to them by religious communities such as Muslims and Sikhs respectively. It is quite natural that these parties have a greater commitment to their religious communities than to secularism. Similarly, some political parties are banking on the support of some particular caste communities. In a situation like this, the State claims to follow secularism on the one hand, and on the other, enters into agreements and makes compromises with communal parties.

3. Religious Bigotry

Religion plays a significant role in Indian elections. Parties select their candidates taking into consideration with an eye on the religious composition of various constituencies. The leaders of all political parties keep aside their commitment to secularism and seek the support of religious leaders to mobilise the votes of common people who belong to their respective religious communities.

Even at the time of forming the ministries, both at the Centre and at the State level it is regarded as almost obligatory to give adequate representation to every powerful community. Political experience and administrative ability are thought to be secondary considerations. Secularism has become a mockery at the hands of these political leaders.

4. Problem of *"Vote-Bank"* Politics

What is very commonly observed in the Indian politics is that even those political parties and their leaders who claim themselves to be *"secular",* conveniently sacrifice the principles of secularism for the sake of obtaining votes at the time of elections. The practice of such type of secularism is often branded as *pseudo-secularism.*[2] Even those political leaders who are known to be *"honest"* also extensively practice casteism and communalism and accuse political leaders of opposite parties for being communal. **Ram Ahuja** thus observes : *"It may, thus, be said that secularism for political parties has implied the creation of a vote bank comprising Muslims, the Scheduled Castes, the Scheduled Tribes and OBCs."*[3]

The communal - secular card is now being played for political motives only. Sincere commitment to secularism is found nowhere and in no political party. The bogey of communalism is

---

1 **A.P. Avasthi** *"Indian Government and Politics."* Page - 603.

2 "In India, with the rise of Hindutva forces in the 1990s, there is a new interpretation of secularism, i.e., pseudo-secularism which is considered to be fake-secularism as practised by the Congress party. Usually when such a reference is made it implies that the party in power speaks of equal distance from all communities but practices appeasement of certain communities just to ensure their votes in the elections. It is referred to as *"vote-bank politics."* Such a secularism is regarded as unnecessary for any state, therefore, such a pseudo-secularism is culled out to be communalism." – **Dr. Parvathy A.A.** Page - 28.

3 **Prof. Ram Ahuja.** Page - 270.

being kept alive not for checking national disintegration but with a view that *"minority vote bank"* does not dissipate itself into the larger Indian ethos. The power-seekers in India are using secularism as a shield to hide their sins thereby ensuring that people remain polarised on the basis of religion and India remains communalised.

5. Disharmony Caused Due to the Inability to Introduce a *"Common Civil Code"*

Failure to introduce a common civil code throughout the nation has posed a big challenge to secularism. Though the adherents of Hinduism, Islam and Christianity are considered citizens of this nation with equal rights and opportunities, they are governed by different inheritance laws, marriage laws, etc. Though the Directive Principles of the State Policy of the Constitution has stressed the need to have a Common Civil Code as applicable to all the citizens of India; so far we have not been able to have one, for want of support from the minorities, especially from the Muslims. Muslims who give importance to the provisions of Muslim Personal Law called *"Shariat"* are not prepared to accept the introduction of Common Civil Code. As long as it is not introduced, so long the differential treatment of people on the ground of religion would continue and so long achievement of national integration becomes impossible. This will only add to the mutual prejudices between the religious communities.

6. Interference of the Government in the Hindu Religious Institutions

Hindus though constitute the majority community, have neither an all-acceptable leadership nor an all-commanding single organisation to obtain the obedience of all. In the absence of these things, as **Donald Eugene Smith** has pointed out, the Government claims that it has the right to intervene in the Hindu religious matters in order to bring about suitable reforms in them. It has established the *"Hindu Religious Endowment Department"* through which it is trying to regulate the administration of the Hindu temples. **C.P. Ramaswamy Iyer Commission** also reported long back that there is the *"danger"* of the government officials getting more and more involved in the reformative activities of the Hindu religious institutions including the temples. Not only at the provincial level, but also through the central legislations, the interference of the Government officials in the internal administration and management of the Hindu religious institutions is likely to be increased. This tendency of the government is very much against the spirit of secularism.

This tendency of the government and many other practices have made a few to consider the principle of secularism as an unwanted Western concept "which is unnecessarily leading to communal riots." *"Many claim that secularism is natural for India and need not be imposed by the state machinery since the basic term itself is misunderstood by many. Tolerance, freedom, pluralism are all values which are inherent in the Hindu history and heritage. Therefore, ... that special efforts need not be made to incorporate the secularism of the Western kind which is not suitable to India."*[1]

Conclusion

The theory of secularism has become highly controversial today. It is under heavy attacks from all sides. Political parties openly proclaim themselves to be *"secular"*; but in practice prove to be highly *communal.* No single party is sincerely committed to this ideology in its actual practice. Hence people's faith in it is slowly dwindling.

---

1 **Dr. Parvathy A.A.** Page - 28.

Theoretically, *"secularism in the Indian context has tried to enhance the power of the state by making it a protector of all religious communities and an arbiter in their conflicts. It checks patronising any particular religion by the state."*[1]

When we take into consideration the present day Indian politics especially in the light of Ayodhya dispute, it becomes clear that we have given undue importance to secularism. *"Nirbhai Singh has maintained* [1994 : 111] *that the present crisis in India is partially due to over-emphasis on secularisation and politicisation of religion by the fundamentalists and politicians."*[2]

Secularism does not mean atheism. The process of secularism should not lead to the devolution of religious values. At the same time, it should not pose a challenge to the religious plurality of India. What is needed today is new insights and openness of mind towards other religious faiths – to appreciate other faiths is to guarantee freedom to them. As **John F. Kennedy** once remarked – *when one's loyalty towards one's religion comes into conflict with one's loyalty towards one's nation, one should lean towards one's nation and not otherwise.* It is with this spirit secularism is to be understood and religion is to be practised.

---

1 **Ram Ahuja** - 269.

2 Views of **Nirbhai Singh** as quoted by **Prof. Ram Ahuja.** Page - 271.

Chapter 20

POLITICAL SYSTEM IN INDIA

Democratic System in A Traditional Society *- Democratic Decentralisation or Panchayat Raj - Concept of Panchayat Raj and Its Evolution - Panchayat Raj After Independence - Critical Appraisal of the Panchayat Raj System - Panchayat Raj and Nagarapalikas in Karnataka State - Gram Panchayat : Its Structure- Committees and Functions - Taluk Panchayat - Its Formation and Functions - Zilla Panchayat System - Its Composition, Committees and Functions - Nagarapalika System in Karnataka - Corporations- Their Composition and Functions - Composition of City and Town Municipalities and Their Functions -* ***Gandhiji's Theory of Sarvodaya****- Concept of Sarvodaya - Political, Economic, Social and Religio-Moral Characteristics and Functions of Sarvodaya.*

India plays an important role in the world political affairs today. It proudly claims itself as *"the world's largest democracy."* On the eve of India becoming independent, and deciding to form a democratic political setup, some foreign observers had expressed their own doubts whether India would attain success in its democratic experiment. *"They argued that India was used to authoritarian and paternalist rule and had no tradition of democracy; its leaders had not the experience of operating the complex apparatus of the State; its national cohesiveness was fragile because of religious and Jati differences; and its electorate was steeped in ignorance and superstition. It is a major achievement that the democratic experiment has survived in India, though it has had to face several crises, both internal and external."* [**S.C. Dube.** Page - 112.]

As **S.C. Dube** has remarked *"India has had its teething troubles, but has given a reasonably good account of itself and demonstrated its viability."* [Page - 112]. It is true that Indian leaders lacked experience in running a government when they assumed office. But Indian leaders within a short period proved their statesmanship and their ability to lead a nation politically. In spite of their shortcomings, *"The illiterate electorate and the inexperienced leadership have many plus points to their credit. The freedom movement had created a degree of national consciousness and independence raised the hopes of India's people."* These two factors held in check, at least for a while, all divisive forces and fissiparous tendencies.

India's polity is not without problems, in fact, it is under considerable stress. It has been struggling to maintain its unity on the one hand and to fight against the internal and external enemies, on the other. It seems very astonishing to think at this stage as to how India, a tradition bound country, with its deep-rooted monarchic heritage could take a bold decision to go on democratic lines. India is still on its democratic track even after 55 years of its Independence. The old political traditions have given place to the new ones. Democratic traditions are taking comparatively strong roots now. India's successful experiment with democracy must be understood in its ability to make compromises and adjustments with its age-old traditions, beliefs and practices.

1. DEMOCRATIC SYSTEM IN A TRADITIONAL SOCIETY

India after its independence preferred democracy to all other types of government. India successfully experimented with democracy for more than 50 years after independence and is now forging ahead as the world's largest democratic state. Democratic institutions have taken relatively strong roots here. But historically speaking, democratic institutions and processes such as elections, political institutions, political offices, legislative bodies, etc. were in existence in India prior to Independence much before the British rule. But these had not yet acquired the aroma of Indian tradition. During the British rule, they were based on British norms and were elitist in composition. Soon after independence the introduction of full fledged democracy provided an opportunity for the full play of the deep rooted national traditions. Political elites of the country exploited these political opportunities for their own advancement. Such attempts greatly influenced the working of the political polity. This influence contains both the good and the ugly elements. Here is an attempt to analyse the manner in which our national traditions have influenced the democratic political system.

1. Charismatic Leadership and Its Influence

Indian mind is highly amenable to charismatic leadership. Hero worship has been a historical legacy here. People had been cherishing the view that the "king is the real representative of the God" [*"Raja Pratyaksha Devata."*] Right from the days of Epics down to the modern days our people have been looking to their honoured leaders for model and for guidance. Sri Ramachandra of Ramayana, Yudhisthira and Bhishma of Mahabharatha, and such other epic personalities on the one hand; and Pauras, Chandragupta Maurya, Ashoka, Prithviraj Chauhan, Rana Pratap Sinha, Shivaji, and such other historical figures on the other, represent such reference persons worthy of emulation. In the religious field also we have any number of towering personalities – such as Buddha, Mahaveera, Basava, Sri Shankaracharya, Kabir, Nanak, Ramdas, Vivekananda, Sri Narayana Guru who always identified themselves with the people and who provided guidance and leadership to the people.

Hence, it has been the tradition of our land to look to the *"reference persons"*, or in other words, the charismatic persons. The Bhagavad Gita also states : *"Whatever a great man does the same is done by others as well. Whatever standards he sets, the world follows."* This deep-rooted and strongly ingrained tradition soon dominated the working of the democratic system. Gandhiji though was not in power position in politics, emerged as a charismatic leader and maintained his hold over the people till his death. Nehru too by virtue of his charismatic leadership maintained his command over the masses. In fact, all political parties tried to encash this tendency of *"hero worship"* of the people to serve their political interests especially in elections. People with this tendency vote not for the political programme and ideology of the party, but for the leader. Thus, the *"image building cult"* has become a common practice of our political leaders.

2. Participation in Decision Making Process

Even in the decision taking process there was the practice of common people taking an active role in it. We hear of *"Sabha"* as a great political institution in the later Vedic period, whose elected members could speak with effect. The practice of people's participation in decision making process was well recognised in the country. Several Buddhist kings, kings of the Magadha Empire, Raja Nrupatunga and Sri Krishna Devaraya of Karnataka and such other kings had provided opportunities for the common people to express their views in appropriate forums. But unfortunately, the institutions that provided opportunities for such participation either faded away or remained ineffective. When the entire society got into political oblivion, the great tradition was lost. The present day democracy, has however, restored this tradition and the appropriate institutions like the Parliament, State Assemblies and the Panchayats are established for this purpose only. In practice, however, decision is reached through the intervention of the higher leadership and arranged consensus.

3. Democratic Elections and Traditional Group Associations

India has adopted the parliamentary form of Government. It is a common practice in a parliamentary form of democracy for the majority party to form the cabinet or the council of ministers. The chosen members of the majority party get the chance to enter the cabinet. The same process is repeated at the State level.

As a matter of democratic procedure, elections take place after every five years. The representatives are assumed to be elected on party lines, and to act on party lines in respective legislatures. But in practice what happens is that the candidates for the elections are selected on the basis of their caste and religious affinities. During the election campaign the candidates very often make appeals in the name of caste and religion. It means *"the practice of traditional group appeal is not allowed to die."*[1] For example, the Vokkaligas or Lingayats in Karnataka frequently respond to political appeals as a group. In a similar manner, Muslim candidate contesting elections makes an appeal on a religious ground to obtain the support of the community votes. It is not uncommon to find the Gurudwaras working as the political base of the Akalidal, mosques functioning as the base of the Muslim League, and the Muslim candidates. Churches as the support base of the Christian candidates. Caste-based Hindu Matts also mobilise caste-votes in favour of the candidates of their selection.

4. Caste Politics and Social Mobility

Struggling to achieve social mobility is quite common everywhere. Lower castes have been trying to enhance their social status through Sanskritisation, that is, by imitating the life-styles of the upper castes. But the democratic system provides for "equality" and treats all the people equal. It works on the principle of *"one vote for one person."* Naturally, number of votes assumes more importance here than the caste. The lower castes are not forging a unity to increase their numerical strength, that is to improve their vote-catching ability. Lower castes also have now realised that they would get greater benefits by making combined efforts to get elected their representatives than by simply imitating the upper caste people. This has also made the higher castes which are in minority to join hands with the lower castes which constitute a majority in some particular constituencies.

5. Dominance of Numerically Strong Caste Groups

Caste is basically a hierarchical system. Traditionally, the *Dvijas* [Brahmins and Kshatriyas] occupied the top most position in the hierarchy. *"The democratisation and politicisation of social structure, along with land reforms and industrialisation has changed this configuration of power and influence of caste."* [**Kachroo** and **Kachroo.** Page - 218.] Due to the introduction of the adult franchise system the locus of power has shifted from ritually higher castes to numerically stronger castes. The lower caste groups which are numerically stronger in some regions have emerged as dominant castes through political mobilisation. ***Example*** : Lingayats and Okkaligas in Karnataka, Reddys and Kammas in Andhra Pradesh, Nairs and Izhavas in Kerala, Jats, Minas and Gujjars in Rajasthan, Patidars and Kshatriyas in Gujarath, Gounder, Padayachi and Mudaliars in Tamil Nadu,

1 **Kachroo** and **Kachroo** *"Society in India."* Page - 218.

represent such politically dominant castes. The increased mobilisation of caste is used for gaining secular objectives such as governmental positions, obtaining jobs and promotions, sanctioning permissions for starting new medical and engineering colleges, and so on. Caste organisations have come to play an important role in the political process, particularly in elections from *Panchayat* to the Parliament levels.

6. Caste Association and Their Role

Though caste is losing some of its functions and influence, politically caste associations are becoming a big force. They constitute a strong *"pressure group"* in the local politics. In this context, the caste association has begun to take on the features of the voluntary association. Membership in caste associations is not purely ascriptive; birth in the caste is necessary but not a sufficient condition for membership.

7. Panchayats and Tradition

Panchayat is an age-old institution. With the introduction of the *Panchayat Raj* it has become all the more central to the village community and is expected to play an appropriate role. The abolition of the privileges of the intermediary such as the Zamindars and others has brought about a great change in the ex-tenant groups. The new democratic environment has motivated them to compete with the traditional powerful groups to get into power positions. The traditional village leadership has now realised this situation and has become persuasive in its approach.

Conclusion

Democratic processes are in force in India today. It cannot however, be said that the process is fully matured. Traditional force which has been in existence in this land though has become weaker still remain, as a force. The expanding educational opportunities, widespread development of science and technology, increasing industrialisation and urbanisation, growth of new leadership, economic advancement and all such developments are bound to have their impact on the democratic system. Hence this system may be obliged to acquire a national character and content. It is hoped that this system in the long run, will prove to be more impersonal, institutional and functional.

2. DEMOCRATIC DECENTRALISATION OR PANCHAYAT RAJ

Democratic decentralisation in the Indian context assumes the form of *"Panchayat Raj System."* This system which came into existence in 1960s has a history of its own. *Panchayat Raj* is directed towards democratisation of administration at the village, block and district level. It is essential to know the very concept of *"Panchayat Raj"* and its evolution in the Indian set up.

Concept of *"Panchayat Raj"*

- The word *"Panchayat"* literally means a committee of five elderly and experienced persons elected by the people of a village.
- The self-governing institutions which are set up in the rural areas are commonly called *"Panchayat Raj."*
- *"Self-governing rural local bodies are described in the Indian context as institutions of democratic decentralisation or Panchayat Raj."*[1]

According to **Rudramurthy,** *"The essence of Panchayat Raj consists of the constitution and working statutory democratic institutions at the local levels and the decentralisation and*

1 **A.P. Avasthi** *"Indian Government and Politics"* - 2001. Page 516.

devolution of power and resources to these institutions to enable them to function effectively as local self-governing units assuming responsibility for planning and development of the people and area in their jurisdiction."

The Constitution of India has a reference to the organisation of the Village Panchayat. Article 40 which is related to the ***"Directive Principles of State Policy"*** clearly states...... *"The State shall take steps to organise Village Panchayats and endow them with such powers and authority as may be necessary to enable them to function as units of self government."*

A Glance of the Evolution of *"Panchayat Raj"* System

The idea or the concept of *Panchayat Raj* system is not new to India. Village Panchayats have been the basic units of administration in India since the Vedic period. There are numerous references made in Kautilya's *"Arthashastra"* which depict the set up of the administration at a local level. Even in Ramayana, Mahabharatha, and in the *"Jataka Stories"* of the Buddhists we get information relating to the type of local self-governments that existed during the ancient times.

During the period of **Muslim rule,** local self-governments did not receive any encouragement. The Muslim rulers, however, did not destroy the system as such. Since these rulers concentrated in cities only their attention was not shifted towards the rural system of life. Hence, the rural self-governments continued to function without much disturbance. The urban governance was, however, disturbed by them.

The Panchayats were the thriving local self-governing institutions in the country till the advent of the **British.** The Village Panchayats started steadily disintegrating during the British rule. Centralised system of administration and uniform system of legislation which the British introduced proved to be fatal for the *Panchayats.* The development of *Panchayat Raj* received serious attention at the hands of popular government after independence.

"Panchayat Raj" after Independence

Panchayat Raj system received special attention of the Government soon after independence. Even before independence many national leaders wanted to improve the local institutions. In this connection Mahatma Gandhi wrote in 1947 : *"Independence must begin at the bottom. Thus, every village will be a Republic or Panchayat having full powers. It follows, therefore, that every village has to be self-sustained and capable of managing its affairs even to the extent of defending itself against the whole world."* The present day *Panchayat* administration owes its debt more to Mahatma Gandhi than to anyone else.

The existing system of *Panchayat Raj* in India owes its origin to a study team constituted for the purpose of studying the working of National Extension Services [NES] and Community Development Projects [CDP]. Towards the end of the Five Year Plan period an evaluation of the working of the NES and CDP revealed that these has not succeeded in getting the participation of the people which was one of the most essential requirements. So the Central Government appointed a Committee headed by **Balwant Rai Mehta** in January 1957 to revive the working of the CDP and the NES.

Recommendations of the Mehta Committee : The Mehta Committee submitted its report by the end of 1957. The Committee prepared the plan for the establishment of *Panchayat Raj.* Its recommendations were accepted by the National Development Council.

The Committee observed, *"So long as we do not discover or create representative and democratic institution which will supply the local interest, supervision, and care, ... we will never be able to evoke local interest and excite local initiative in the field of development."*[1]

To achieve the above objective the Committee recommended a scheme of *"democratic decentralisation"* known as *Panchayat Raj* system. The Committee remarked about the philosophy of *Panchayat Raj* that *"Panchayat Raj system established a linkage between local leadership enjoying confidence of the local people and the government, and translate the policies of the government into action."*

The three-tier structure of the *Panchayat Raj* recommended in the Balawant Rai Mehta Committee consists of three self-governing institutions namely :

1. ***Village Panchayat** – at the Village level,*
2. ***Panchayat Samithi** – at Block level, and*
3. ***Zilla Parishad** – at the District level.*

The Committee also recommended that regarding the developmental administrative spheres these governments should be given certain definite powers and entrusted with clearly defined functions.

The National Development Council gave its approval to the recommendations made by the committee in 1958. As a result the state governments came to be vested with the powers of establishing the local self governments. The state governments began to implement these recommendations in stages.

Main Recommendations of Mehta Committee

The major recommendations of Mehta Committee on democratic decentralisation were **:**

1. There should be the three-tier structure of the local self-government from the village to the district. The village occupies the bottom position and the district assumes the top position with its intermediary link institutions.
2. There should be genuine transfer of power and responsibility to these institutions of local government.
3. Adequate resources should be transferred to these bodies to enable them to discharge these responsibilities.
4. All socio-economic developmental programmes to be formulated and channelled through these institutions.
5. The whole system of *Panchayat Raj* should facilitate further devolution and dispersal of power, responsibilities and resources in the future.

Acceptance of the Recommendations by the *"National Development Council"*

The recommendations of the Mehta Committee were accepted by the National Developmental Council in Jan. 1959. The Council, however, agreed that there should be insistence on a single rigid pattern and left it to the states to work out a pattern suited to their requirements. But it insisted that the basic principles such as the three-tier structure, the transfer of adequate power and responsibility, leaving adequate resources at their disposal, entrusting development work to these bodies at each level, etc. will be facilitated.

Emergence of *"Panchayat Raj"* throughout the Nation

As per the recommendations of the Balwant Rai Mehta Committee, the three-tier *Panchayat Raj* system came into existence with great fanfare in many parts of the country. Rajasthan and

1 **A.P. Avasthi** *"Indian Government and Politics."* Page - 52.

Andhra Pradesh were the first states to adopt the system in 1959. Other states slowly followed their examples. Till the end of 1975, there were 219892 *Gram Panchayats,* 3863 *Panchayat samithis,* and 201 *Zilla Parishads* in the country. After the implementation of the ***Constitution 73rd Amendment Act, 1992,*** about 2,26,108 *Panchayats* at the village level, 5,736 *Panchayats* at the intermediate level and 457 *Zilla Parishats* at the district level were constituted in the country. These are being manned by about 345 lakh elected representatives of the *Panchayats* at intermediate level and 15,395 persons at the district level.[1]

Panchayat Raj System in Different States

The Mehta Committee report has been interpreted by scholars in different states in different manner depending upon the conditions prevailing in their own territories. There emerged in Tamil Nadu a two-tier system. In West Bengal there is a four-tier system. Assam has a three-tier system without a body which can be compared with the Zilla Parishad at the district level.

In Gujarat and Maharashtra, the Zilla Parishads are the stronger of the three tiers. In Maharashtra, the President of Zilla Parishad is virtually *"the District Chief Minister"* with monthly salary and the car allowance, heading a full-fledged administrative structure to serve him.

In Rajasthan, on the contrary, the Panchayat Samithi at the Block level is the strongest. It is entrusted with the task of the rural development. The Zilla Parishad is an indirectly elected body performing as a co-ordinating and supervisory body. In some states like Haryana, Punjab and Karnataka, the Zilla Parishad is the main advisory and co-ordinating body.

As it is clear from the above, there was no uniform pattern of *Panchayat Raj* throughout India. It came into existence in different states with all kinds of variations in its structure of decision making, implementation, resource allocation, staffing pattern, training and recruitment of staff and devolution of power at different levels. It may be said that *Panchayat Raj,* that was introduced with a lot of enthusiasm failed to fulfil the expectations. Only in Gujarat and Maharashtra it was successful in certain respects and in all other states particularly in Hindi-speaking belt it virtually failed. In some states it completely collapsed.

Critical Appraisal of the Panchayat Raj System

The *Panchayat Raj* system as a decentralised form of administration looks very viable and workable. It constitutes a training ground for democracy. It was introduced to encourage popular participation not only in the management of local affairs but also in the implementation of development programmes. It was believed by the framers of the Constitution that without popular participation no democratic system of government can be successful in the real sense of the term. From this point of view, the establishment of *Panchayat Raj* is really a laudable endeavour. But the experiment has not been as successful as it was hoped to be. Some factors contributed to its deficiencies. They may be briefly examined here.

1. Mixed-up Functions

One major problem with the *Panchayat Raj* system is that local government functions and development functions have been mixed up. Development functions require expert knowledge and a certain measure of centralised planning and control. On the other hand, the management of local affairs requires maximum freedom of action. The mixing up of the two functions has created a lot of confusion.

1 **Sources India Year Book** - *1999.* Page - 360, as quoted by **A.P. Avasthi** *"Indian Government and Politics."* Page - 521.

2. Insufficient Autonomy

The lower levels in the *Panchayat Raj* system do not enjoy sufficient autonomy. The higher bodies dominate lower ones. Zilla Parishad dominating the *Panchayat Samithi* and the *Panchayat Samithi* dominating the *Village Panchayat* have been the common scene everywhere.

3. Inadequacy of Financial Resources

Paucity of funds is a major problem of the *Panchayat Raj* system. The three bodies of the system have very limited powers to levy taxes and cesses, and the funds allotted to them by the State Government are very meagre. The *Panchayats* are generally reluctant to raise necessary funds through taxes for fear of losing popularity with the masses.

4. Institutions in the *"Panchayat Raj"* System are Dominated by the Government Officials

Panchayat Raj system was introduced with the intention of obtaining people's participation in the management of the affairs that primarily concern them. But in reality the key administrative and technical positions are manned by government officials who are under the administrative control of the State government and care very little for the people. In order to make the system a success it is necessary that the administrative personnel should be under the direct control of the local institutions themselves.

5. Undemocratic Character of the *"Panchayat Raj"* Bodies

Panchayat Samithi and the Zilla Parishads are packed with ex-officio, associate and co-opted members. This clearly vitiates the very working of the system. The very inclusion of large number of non-elected members destroy the ideal of democratic decentralisation.

6. Tight Control Exercised by the State Government

Excessive control of the State Government over the *Panchayat Raj* bodies retards their healthy growth. *"The State government constitutes the Panchayat Raj institutions, delimits their jurisdiction, assigns them specific powers and functions and has the ultimate power of abolishing them. It may remove the President or any member of any Panchayat Raj body. It arbitrates in all interlocal disputes that is, disputes between Panchayats, Panchayat Samithis, and Zilla Parishads and also between rural and urban local governments."* [A.P. Avasthi. Page - 528.] The deputy commissioner and divisional commissioner also exercise powers over the Panchayat institutions. Thus, the State control over the *Panchayat Raj* institutions is too much.

7. Party Politics Spoils the *Panchayat Raj* Institutions

Self-centred political parties have spread their tentacles to *Panchayat Raj* institutions and vitiated their working. Political leaders and parties are poking their noses in the day-to-day functioning of the local bodies. Caste and communal factors are also let loose in their working. These tendencies have destroyed the unity and harmony of the village communities.

Conclusion

"The story of Panchayat Raj has been a story of ups and downs. It seems to have passed through three phases : the phase of ascendancy [1959-64]; the phase of stagnation [1965-69]; and the phase of decline [1969-77]."[1]

Regarding the very functioning of the Panchayat Raj institutions the Report of the Committee

1 **A.P. Avasthi** *"Indian Government and Politics."* Page - 529.

of Panchayat Raj institutions has rightly observed, "......... *the activities of Panchayat Raj institutions were meagre, their resource base weak and the overall attention given to them niggardly. The functioning of the Panchayat Raj system has become discouraging. As if this was not enough, some of the state governments would postpone the holding of elections or supersede some of the important tiers of Panchayat Raj institutions for one reason or the other.......... In the ultimate analysis, all this led to a weakening of political support to Panchayat Raj institutions and of administrative will to work through them.*" [A.P. Avasthi. Page - 529.]

Renewed Interest in *"Panchayat Raj"* System in 1977

Panchayat Raj system which was heading towards a grand failure became once again the subject of interest particularly when Janata Party [Undivided Janata Party] under the leadership of Morarji Desai came to power at the Centre in 1977. It appointed a Committee under the chairmanship of **Ashok Mehta,** to review the working of the *Panchayat Raj* set-up and command ways and means of streamlining it. The Committee submitted its report consisting of 132 recommendations in 1978. Many State Governments including Karnataka tried to implement the recommendations. But these attempts also ended in failure.

Recent Trends Since 1985

Some attempts were made to revive the *Panchayat Raj* system particularly after 1980s. In 1985 and also in 1986 two committees were constituted separately, one under the chairmanship of **G.V.R. Rao** [1985]; and the other, under the Presidentship of a famous jurist **L.M. Singhvi** [1986]. An attempt was made to introduce *Panchayat Raj Bill* in the Parliament in 1989 by the Rajiv Gandhi led Government, but for want of the required support in the Rajya Sabha it could not be moved. But the Congress Government headed by P.V. Narasimha Rao was able to reintroduce it in the Parliament and obtain a tremendous support. In this context, the Government had to bring the *Constitutional [73rd and 74th] Amendment Acts* which were passed by the Parliament on 22nd December 1992. It is argued that these Acts seek to enshrine democracy at grassroots, as they intend to give power to the people. *The 73rd Amendment is concerned with the structure of the Gram Panchayat or rural self-government while the 74th Amendment deals with the urban local self-governments.*

3. PANCHAYAT RAJ AND NAGARAPALIKAS IN KARNATAKA STATE

"Panchayat Raj" System in Karnataka

During the year 1985, Karnataka saw a tremendous change in the *Panchayat Raj* system in terms of real decentralisation. Radical amendments were brought to the then existing *Mysore Village Panchayat and Local Boards Act, 1959.* These amendments were meant to establish an elected body at the district level and to decentralize administrative as well as financial powers from state capital to the district and further down to the Mandals. These radical amendments brought about unprecedented changes in the area of decentralization and ushered in a new era of decentralisation in Karnataka.

In 1983, in Karnataka, Janata Government was voted to power and the Government under the leadership of **Ramakrishna Hegde** formed the *Panchayat Raj Bill.* This proposed Bill was formulated in accordance with the recommendations made by **Ashok Mehta Committee** report. With a few changes in both the houses, this Bill came into force as the ***"Karnataka Zilla Panchayat, Taluk Panchayat Committee, Mandal Panchayat and Nyaya Panchayat Act - 1983"*** in the month of March 1984. After obtaining Presidential consent on July 10th, 1985, this Bill came into force as a law. Elections were held in 1985 for the *Zilla Panchayat* and *Mandal Panchayat* and the rural local self-governments came into being.

Thus, in the field of *Panchayat Raj* system, thanks to Sri Ramakrishna Hegde, the then Chief Minister of Karnataka, and Late Abdul Nazir Saab, the then Rural Development and Panchayat Raj Minister, *Karnataka became a role model in the entire country.* The then Prime Minister Rajiv Gandhi took cue from Karnataka and replicated Karnataka model at the National Level by bringing amendment to the Constitution which is called *73rd Amendment* which gave constitutional status to the *Panchayat Raj Institutions* in the country. Thus Karnataka became a pioneer state as far as real decentralization is concerned and considered more progressive as the state had brought about these changes 8 years prior to the 73rd Amendment.

The newly constituted Panchayats functioned for sometime. After the fall of Ramakrishna Hegde's Janata Government, the Congress Government came to power in the State and it did not take any interest to promote the rural local self-governments. The elections to these bodies which were scheduled to be held in 1990, were never conducted. In the meantime, the Central Government which was inspired by the experiment of the Karnataka Government brought about the 73rd Amendment to the Constitution to give constitutional status to the *Panchayat Raj* system. This Amendment to the Constitution made it mandatory for the Karnataka Government to bring about *Panchayat Raj* system in Karnataka also. Hence, to fulfil the objective of democratic decentralisation of political power, the State Government adopted ***The Karnataka Panchayat Raj Act, 1993.*** This Act was similar to the 1983 Act in some respects. The main difference was that the previous Act had provided for only two-tier rural local self-government called : (i) *Zilla Parishad,* and (ii) *Mandal Panchayat.* But the 1993 Act, keeping in view with the 73rd Amendment to the Constitution made provision for three-tier rural local self-government system. These three-tiers or local bodies are as follows :

1. ***Grama Panchayat** – at the Village Level,*
2. ***Taluk Panchayat** – at the Intermediate Level,*
3. ***Zilla Panchayat** – at the District Level.*

GRAM PANCHAYAT – Its Formation and Functions

As per the provisions of *Karnataka Panchayat Raj Act* - 1993, the Deputy Commissioner is empowered to declare a village or a group of villages having a population of not less than 5,000 and not more than 7,000 as constituting ***"Gram Panchayat."***[1]

Formation of Gram Panchayat

A *Gram Panchayat* consists of elected members at the rate of 1 member per 400 people. A fixed number of seats are reserved for the people belonging to Scheduled Castes [SCs], Scheduled Tribes [STs], Other Backward Classes [OBCs] and women. The term of office of the democratically constituted Gram Panchayat is 5 years. The members of Gram Panchayat elect from among themselves one as the President and another as the Vice President. The Gram Panchayat is supposed to hold its sessions atleast once in 2 months. However, the President is empowered to summon special sessions

1 But for the areas that come under some Zilla Panchayats such as Belgaum, Chickmagalur, Dakshina Kannada, Dharwad, Hassan, Kodagu, Shimoga, and North Kanara, a minimum population of 2,000 is enough to constitute Gram Panchayats.

if emergency arises.

Standing Committees for the Gram Panchayat

The Gram Panchayat consists of the following committees. Each committee consists of 3 to 5 elected members including the President and the Vice President.

(a) *Production Committee* : This committee performs functions related to agricultural production, animal husbandry, rural industries and poverty alleviation programmes.

(b) *Social Justice Committee* : Promotion of educational, economic, social, cultural and other interests of the people belonging to SCs, STs and OBCs and protecting them from any exploitation and thereby assuring them of social justice – are the main functions of this committee. It also has to work for the welfare of the women and children. Atleast one woman and one person belonging to SC or ST are appointed as members of this committee.

(c) *Amenities Committee* : This committee performs functions related to education, public health, public works and such other matters of the Gram Panchayat.

Gram Panchayat Fund

A Gram Panchayat requires a separate fund known as *"Gram Panchayat Fund"* to meet its expense and to carry out its functions. The Gram Panchayat Fund contains the following :

1. The Gram Panchayat Fund consists of the amount sanctioned to it as grants-in-aid by the respective Taluk Panchayat or Zilla Panchayat or the State Government.
2. The amount earned by the Gram Panchayat by levying taxes and collecting fees.
3. Consists of the loans or gifts of any individuals or institutions or the Government.
4. Consists of income earned from the rent or sale of properties of Gram Panchayat.

Functions of Gram Panchayat

The main functions of the Gram Panchayat are as follows :

(a) *General Functions* : General functions of the Gram Panchayat include – preparation of annual plans for the development of the panchayat area, preparation of annual budget, providing reliefs in case of natural calamities, removal of encroachments on public properties, organising voluntary labour and contribution for community works and maintenance of essential statistics of the village.

(b) *Other Functions* : A Gram Panchayat undertakes a large number of functions among which the following may be noted. — Promotion of agriculture; improvement and promotion of animal husbandry, dairy farming and poultry; development of fisheries; promotion of village and cottage industries; distribution of houses and sites; supplying drinking water to the people in the area; providing for electricity facility; construction and maintenance of roads, buildings, culverts, bridges, water-ways and other means of communication; creating awareness regarding primary and secondary education; maintenance of public health, general sanitation and family welfare; promotion of women and child development; promoting social welfare including the welfare of weaker sections and the physically and mentally handicapped; maintenance of public parks, play grounds, public libraries, reading rooms, dharmashalas, choultries and similar institutions; construction and maintenance of cattle sheds, cart and stands; regulation of fairs and festivals; and promotion of social and cultural activities.

TALUK PANCHAYAT – Formation and Functions

As per the provisions of *Karnataka Panchayat Raj Act* - 1993, every taluk has a ***"Taluk Panchayat."*** With the exception of the areas that come under the jurisdiction of the municipality or municipal corporation or town panchayat of the corresponding taluk, the rest of the areas come under the jurisdiction of the Taluk Panchayats.

Composition of Taluk Panchayat

A Taluk Panchayat consists of the following members.

(a) Taluk Panchayat consists of elected members at the rate of one member per every 10,000 people. The Panchayat consists of a minimum of 11 members for the Taluks with a population of not more than 1 lakh.

(b) Taluk Panchayat consists of members of the Lok Sabha and State Legislative Assembly whose constituencies cover the respective taluk completely or in part.

(c) Members of the Rajya Sabha and State Legislative Council who have enrolled themselves as voters in that taluk.

(d) One-Fifth [1/5] of the Presidents of the Gram Panchayats of that taluk, who are elected by Assistant Commissioner for a period of one year on rotation basis.

As per the provisions of the Act some specified seats are reserved for the people belonging to SCs, STs, OBCs and women. Taluk Panchayat sessions are held atleast once in two months. If need arises special sessions could be held with the prior notice of atleast 10 days to the members. The President and the Vice President are elected from amongst the elected members of the Taluk Panchayat immediately after elections. The term of the office of a newly constituted Taluk Panchayat is 5 years.

Standing Committees of Taluk Panchayat

Every Taluk Panchayat has the following committees. (a) *General Standing Committee;* (b) *Finance, Audit and Planning Committee;* and (c) *Social Justice Committee.* The elected members of the Taluk Panchayat elect from among themselves 6 members including the President, as the members of each committee.

Taluk Panchayat Fund

In every Taluk Panchayat, the *"Taluk Panchayat Fund"* is established to provide for the financial requirements of the Taluk Panchayat. The Fund contains — the grants in aid or loans provided by the State Government / Zilla Panchayat; income from taxes and fees; grants provided by Government and other institutions; and income from the rent or the sale of properties of the Taluk Panchayat.

Functions of Taluk Panchayat

The Taluk Panchayat performs some general functions in addition to some specific functions. They are as follows :

(a) *General Functions* : The general functions consist of preparation of annual plans, preparation of annual budget; consideration and consolidation of the annual plans of all the Gram Panchayats in the taluk and submission of the same to the Zilla Panchayat; providing relief in natural calamities; and performing such functions as entrusted to it by the Government or the Zilla Panchayat.

(b) *Other Functions* : The other functions of the Taluk Panchayat include the following : Promotion of agriculture; providing assistance in minor irrigation and water management; maintenance of animal husbandry, dairying and poultry farming; construction, repair and maintenance of public streets, school buildings and minor irrigation works; promotion of fisheries development of rural and cottage industries; providing for social and farm forestry, minor forest produce, fuel and fodder; implementation of poverty alleviation programmes; promotion of primary and secondary education, rural artisan and vocational training; distribution of fertilisers and improved seeds; promotion of health and family welfare programmes, programmes relating to the development of women and children, programmes relating to the welfare of the handicapped and the mentally retarded persons; promotion of libraries and improvement of means of communication; promotion and welfare of the people belonging to Scheduled Castes and Scheduled Tribes and other weaker sections; acting as a link between Village Panchayat and Zilla Parishad; granting licenses, regulating fares and festivals and establishing markets and regulating trades; removing encroachment and obstruction on public roads, lands and buildings.

ZILLA PANCHAYAT

As per *Karnataka Panchayat Raj Act, 1993* there is provision to establish Zilla Panchayat in every district of the state. The Zilla Panchayat can have its own office in any place which it finds suitable or convenient.

Composition of Zilla Panchayat

(a) The Zilla Panchayat consists of elected members at the rate of one member representing every population of 40,000.[1]

(b) Zilla Panchayat includes members of Lok Sabha and State Legislative Assembly whose constituencies cover the district completely or in part.

(c) Members of Rajya Sabha and State Legislative Council who have enrolled themselves as voters in that district.

(d) All the Presidents of the Taluk Panchayats of the respective district.

(e) It consists of not more than 15 government officers working in the district.

- Seats are reserved for the representatives of Scheduled Castes, Scheduled Tribes, Other Backward Classes and women.

- The tenure of office of the Zilla Panchayat is **5** years. Sessions of the Zilla Panchayat are held atleast once in 2 months.

- ***President and Vice President*** **:** The elected members of the Zilla Panchayat elect from among themselves, one as the President and another as the Vice President. They are called *Adhyaksha* and *Upadhyaksha* respectively. They hold their offices till their membership of the Zilla Panchayat lasts.

- ***Zilla Panchayat Fund*** **:** Zilla Panchayat Fund is established in every Zilla Panchayat and the Fund consists of the following : (i) All grants, loans and contributions made by the Government; (ii) Amount transferred to the Zilla Panchayat from the consolidated fund of the State Government; (iii) All fees and penalties imposed and collected by the Zilla Panchayat; (iv) The rents Zilla Panchayat earn from its properties and lands; (v) All types of amounts which the Zilla Panchayat receives.

Standing Committees and Their Functions

Every Zilla Panchayat has the following committees : (i) *General Standing Committee;* (ii) *Finance, Audit and Planning Committee;* (iii) *Social Justice Committee;* (iv) *Educational and Health Committee,* and (v) *Agricultural and Industries Committee.*

---

1 However, in the districts such as North Kanara and Chickmaglur, for every 30,000 population one member is to be elected, and in Kodagu for 18,000 people one member is to be elected.

Functions of the Standing Committees

1. *General Standing Committee* : This committee looks after building, rural housing, village extension and relief against natural calamities, etc.

2. *Finance and Planning Committee* : Looking after the finances of the Zilla Panchayat, preparing its budget, reviewing the proposals for increasing the revenue, assessment of receipts and expenditure statement, assessing the plan priorities, etc. are the main tasks of this committee.

3. *Social Justice Committee* : (i) Promoting educational, economic, social, cultural and other interests of the weaker sections such as STs, SCs, OBCs and women. (ii) Protecting these people from all sorts of exploitation. (iii) To work for promoting the general welfare of STs, SCs, OBCs and women. These are the main tasks of social justice committee.

4. *Education and Health Committee* : The functions of this committee are as follows : (a) The Zilla Panchayat takes up all the responsibilities relating to the educational activities under its jurisdiction. (b) To survey and evaluate the educational activities of the Zilla Panchayat. (c) To execute all educational projects within its framework of the national education policy and national and state level projects. (d) To carry on activities such as adult literacy, cultural activities, etc. (e) Looking after health services, hospitals, water supply, family welfare and other matters.

5. *Agriculture and Industry Committee* : The main tasks of this committee are as follows : (a) Looking after agricultural production, animal husbandry, co-operation, village and cottage industries. (b) Promoting the industrial development of the district. (c) Any other functions assigned by the Zilla Panchayat.

Functions of the Zilla Panchayat

Zilla Panchayat has two types of functions : (i) *General Functions,* and (ii) *Other Functions.*

(i) *General Functions* : These functions include the overall supervision, co-ordination and integration of developmental schemes, plans and projects at the taluk and district levels. It also prepares the plan for the development of the district.

(ii) *Other Functions* : The Zilla Panchayat undertakes a number of *'other functions',* which may be noted below.

Promotion and maintenance of agricultural and horticultural farms; planning and implementation of land improvement and soil conservation programmes; promotion of small scale industries, rural and cottage industries, animal husbandry, dairying, and poultry farming; promotion of rural housing programme; development of fisheries and irrigation works; promotion of drinking water and rural sanitation programmes; construction and maintenance of district roads, buildings, bridges, waterways and other means of communication; establishment of rural artisan and vocational training centres; promotion of adult and non-formal education programmes; promotion of programmes relating to the welfare of women and children, STs, SCs and OBCs; promotion of social welfare of the physically handicapped and mentally retarded people; promotion of social and cultural activities, libraries, sports, etc.; implementation of health and family welfare programmes; improvement of rural distribution system, rural electrification, etc.; and performing any task or function assigned to it by State Government.

NAGARAPALIKA SYSTEM IN KARNATAKA

As per the ***74th Constitution [Amendment] Act, 1992*** it became necessary for the Karnataka Government to bring about suitable changes in *Karnataka Municipal Corporations Act, 1976* and *Karnataka Municipalities Act, 1964.* If the *Gram Panchayat system* is concerned with the rural areas, *the Nagarapalika System,* which includes Municipalities and Corporations, is concerned with towns and cities. The 74th Amendment to the Constitution has brought about changes in the administration of the local bodies and urban areas. We shall now discuss the composition, powers and functions of the Corporations and Municipalities of Karnataka State in the light of the new provisions made in this Constitutional Amendment.

CORPORATIONS – Their Composition and Functions

The administrative task of the Corporation is shouldered by three authorities :

1. *Corporation* [*Corporation Council*],
2. *Standing Committee,* and
3. *Commissioner.*

1. Corporation or Corporation Council

Corporation or Corporation Council is the supreme authority whose elected membership should not be less than 30 and more than 100. The elected members are called Councillors. [The State Government is empowered to take decision regarding the exact strength of the membership of any Corporation from time to time.]

- The *State Government nominates five members* to the Corporation who are residing in the Corporation area and are experienced in *municipal administration or health matters or town planning or education or social service.* [However, these nominated members do not have the voting right.]
- The members of the Legislative Assembly and members of the Parliament who are enrolled in that area and whose constituencies cover the area of that particular Corporation partially or completely.
- Members of the Rajya Sabha and Legislative Council who have enrolled themselves as voters in that area also become the members of the Corporation by virtue of their elected position.
- The members belonging to STs, SCs, OBCs and women get a particular percent of the total seats of the Corporation as reserved ones.
- The term of the office of elected councillors is five years. The five nominated members also remain in power for five years but the State Government has the right to remove them from the membership.

• ***Mayor and Deputy Mayor*** : Every Corporation in its very first meeting elects one of its members as Mayor and the other as the Deputy Mayor.

Standing Committees

In Karnataka, the Corporations consist of the following Standing Committees.

1. The Standing Committee for Taxation, Finance and Appeals,
2. The Standing Committee for Public Health, Education and Social Justice,
3. The Standing Committee for Town Planning and Improvement, and
4. The Standing Committee for Accounts.

Corporation in its very first session of every year elects members of the above mentioned four standing committees. Here also reservation is there for STs, SCs and OBCs. The Mayor and the Deputy Mayor act as the ex-officio President of these committees. However, other than the ex-officio president, each standing committee is empowered to have its own elected president.

Commissioner

The Commissioner with the status of K.A.S. [Karnataka Administrative Service], of the Corporation looks after the executive works. He is appointed by the State Government for a period of two years. However, his tenure of office could be increased by the State Government.

• ***Sources of Corporation Fund*** : The Corporation has some main sources of income. These sources include – (i) various types of local taxes; (ii) income from corporation trading and corporation property, such as Corporation markets; (iii) receipt of fees for providing drainage, scavenging and sanitation facilities; (iv) grants given by the State Government; and (v) loans raised from the public and donations given by individuals and parties.

• ***Functions of the Corporations*** : [***Note*** : Please refer to the next two pages for details about the ***"Functions"***.]

MUNICIPALITIES : Their Structure With Reference to Karnataka

As per the provisions of the ***74th Constitution [Amendment] Act, 1992*** some modifications were brought about in *the Karnataka Municipalities Act, 1964.* Accordingly, City Municipalities and Town Municipalities can be established.

In Karnataka, cities with a population of more than 50,000 and less than 3 lakhs, are considered to be ***City Municipalities.*** On the other hand, towns with a population of more than 20,000 and less than 50,000, are considered to be ***Town Municipalities.***

Composition of City Municipalities and Town Municipalities

(a) Every Municipality, either town or city, will have Municipal Councils. The Municipal Councils consist of elected representatives called ***Councillors.*** The number of councillors is determined on the basis of the population. The table given below gives us an idea of the strength of the Municipal Councils in Karnataka.

Population	***No. of Councillors***
20,000 to 40,000	23
40,000 to 50,000	27
50,000 to 1,00,000	31
1,00,000 to 3,00,000	35

(b) The Council consists of five members nominated by the State Government. It is essential that these nominated members must be residing in that municipal area and must be recognised as persons having some special knowledge of municipal administration or health matters or town planning or education. They do not have the voting right.

(c) Members of the Lok Sabha and State Legislative Assemblies who are enrolled as voters in that town or city are also entitled to become the members of the council.

(d) Members of the Rajya Sabha and State Legislative Councils who are enrolled as voters in that town or city are also entitled to become the members of the council.

(e) The term of the office of the members is five years.

(f) *President and Vice President* : Every Municipal Council elects in its very first meeting one member as the President and another as Vice President and their elected position lasts till the completion of their membership.

(g) *Standing Committee* : A committee is appointed by the Council to look after tax, finance, public health, education and social justice, town planning and all developmental works.

(h) *Sources of Finance* : The sources of finance of the Municipalities are also more or less like the sources of Corporations.

Functions of Corporations and City and Town Municipalities

The functions[1] of Corporations and City and Town Municipalities can be divided into two types of functions. (i) *Compulsory or Obligatory Functions,* and (ii) *Optional or Discretionary Functions.*

(i) Compulsory or Obligatory Functions

The compulsory or obligatory functions of the Municipality include the following :

(1) Lighting of public streets and buildings;

(2) Cleaning of public streets and places;

(3) Collection, removal, treatment and disposal of sewage, garbage and rubbish things;

(4) Constructing, altering and maintaining public streets, municipal boundaries, culverts, markets, slaughter houses, latrines, urinals, drains, drainage works, tanks, drinking fountains, wells, dams, and the like;

(5) Registration of births and deaths;

(6) Public vaccination;

(7) Fire protection and protection of the lives of those who are injured in fire accidents;

(8) Maintenance of an ambulance service and service for cremating the dead;

(9) Naming streets and numbering houses;

(10) Providing for public hospitals, dispensaries and medical reliefs and also prevention of diseases and epidemics;

(11) Providing for public parks, gardens, play grounds and recreation;

(12) Prevention of environmental pollution and making provision for planting trees on both sides of the roads and in the suitable public places;

(13) Construction, maintenance and improvement of public streets, bridges, sub-ways and the like;

(14) Maintenance of corporation office and all public monuments and open spaces that are considered the property of corporation.

(ii) Optional or Discretionary Functions

The following are the optional or discretionary functions :

(1) Encouragement of local arts and industries by granting loans;

(2) Making surveys and taking statistics;

(3) Protection of destitutes and cripples;

(4) Improvement of cattle, livestock;

(5) Maintenance of maternity homes and art galleries;

---

1 Since the functions of the Corporations and the City and Town Municipalities are more or less the same, they are explained together.

(6) Giving protection to refugees and orphans during famine or flood or earthquakes;

(7) Reservation of places for swimming pool;

(8) Granting licences to markets, etc.;

(9) The organisation, maintenance of chemical or bacteriological laboratories for the examination or analysis of water, food or drugs;

(10) The provision of music for the people;

(11) Construction or maintenance of infirmaries or hospitals for animals;

(12) The organisation or maintenance, in times of scarcity of shops or stalls for the sale of necessaries of life;.

(13) Any other measures for the welfare of corporation servants;

(14) The building or purchase and maintenance of suitable dwelling for the poor and working classes;

(15) The provision of shelter to destitute or homeless persons and any form of poor relief.

GANDHIJI'S THEORY OF *"SARVODAYA"*

Concept of *"Sarvodaya"*

The concept of *"Sarvodaya"* assumes importance in the Gandhian thought. Gandhian views contained in the concept of Sarvodaya emerged into a movement known as *"Sarvodaya movement."* The Sanskrit word *"Sarvodaya"* basically means *"rise or progress of all."* According to Gandhiji, the highest aim of any govenment as well as the individual is to promote this concept. Gandhiji took special pains to distinguish his idea of Sarvodaya from the utilitarian philosophy, which propagated *"the greatest good of the greatest number."* Gandhiji called this a heartless doctrine that promotes the supposed welfare of 51 percent but sacrifices that of the 49 per cent. Gandhiji writes: *"The only real dignified human doctrine is the greatest good of all, and this can be only achieved by uttermost sacrifice."* He is, therefore, an absolutist and not a utilitarian.

Gandhiji's ideas of *Sarvodaya*

- *Sarvodaya means the welfare of all, and not the welfare of only one class or section of society.*
- *In Gandhiji's Sarvodaya society "there will be freedom for all and utmost equality, there will be no classes and castes; no exploitation nor injustice; and equal opportunity for each for fullest development. Man will be the centre of such a society, but self-interest will not be the basis of social organisation. Life in such a society will be integrated and whole, so that work, art and play will form a unified pattern making possible the growth of an integrated human personality."*[1]
- *Thus it is clear, Gandhiji's concept of Sarvodaya signifies an ideal society which strives to move towards the highest of mankind as a whole.*

Source of Inspiration for Gandhiji's Vision of *"Sarvodaya"*

Gandhiji drew inspiration for his Sarvodaya or the ideal social order immediately after reading **John Ruskin's** book *"Unto This Last."* Gandhiji acknowledged this in his autobiography in the following words: *"The book marked the turning point in my life."* Gandhiji got the chance of

1 As quoted by **A.C. Kapoor.** Page - 708.14

reading that book when he was travelling in a train between Johansberg and Durban. After reading the book Gandhiji decided to orient his entire life towards the realisation of the ideals and values contained in it.

When Gandhiji wrote the Gujarati Version of Ruskin's *"Unto This Last"*, he used the title *"Sarvodaya"* for the work.[1] It became later an ideology very dear to him. The gist of *"Unto This Last"* could be summarised by means of three points:

1. *That the good of the individual is contained in the good of all.*
2. *That the lawyer's work has the same value as the barber's in as much as all have the same right of earning their livelihood from their work.*
3. *That a life of labour, that is, of the tiller of the soil and the handicraftsman is the life worth living."*[2]

Gandhiji was very much impressed by these three ideals and accepted them and incorporated them in his concept of *"Sarvodaya."*

Political - Economic - Social and Moral Characteristics of *"Sarvodaya"*

• Political Characteristics of *Sarvodaya*

1. Sarvodaya society is free from political dictatorship of all kind.
2. Here, we find the democratic decentralisation and not centralisation of power. There will be no party system and majority rule, and society will be free from the evil of the tyranny of the majority.
3. Sarvodaya society is self-regulated and self-managed in small communities, rural or urban. Coercion is not the basis of a such a society.
4. Politics will not be the instrument of power but an agency of service and *Rajniti* will yield place to *Lokniti.*
5. Sarvodaya society involves the idea of a strongly built *Gram Swaraj.*
6. Sarvodaya society does not require strongly built army for it is only a big but loose federation of self-governing villages. There is almost self-sufficiency in each village.
7. Sarvodaya society requires minimum politics and armed forces, that too, for name sake, to ensure security to the political system.

• Economic Characteristics of *Sarvodaya*

1. Sarvodaya society believes in economic equality. But much against what Marx said physical force is not resorted to for establishing equality. People voluntarily come forward to share whatever things they have among themselves.

2. Here the difference between the bourgeoisie and the proletariat, or the owner and the worker is not found. All industrial and economic activities are carried on, on the basis of the trusteeship principle. All land belongs to God, and human beings are to hold it in trust.

3. Sarvodaya society is a village-oriented society and hence village and cottage industries and handicrafts are more encouraged than the big industries.

4. Big land-lords come forward with a voluntary socialist spirit to offer the excess of land they have to the needy ones through Bhoodan programme.

---

1 It is also said that Gandhiji picked up this word *"Sarvodaya"* from a Jain saint Sumantabhadra who lived during the first century B.C.

2 **M.K. Gandhi,** *"Sarvodaya".* [1958] Page - 3.

5. There is no scope in a Sarvodaya society for heavy industries, foreign technology and labour-saving machines. Swadeshi technology that suits to the needs of rural areas is mainly resorted to.

• Social Characteristics of *Sarvodaya*

1. *Sarvodaya society is an egalitarian society* wherein there is no difference between the rich and poor, upper and lower, propertied class and propertyless class, and so on.

2. *Sarvodaya society is free from class differences, caste differences* and there is no room for unwholesome competition, exploitation and class hatred.

3. *Sarvodaya stands for the progress of all.* All individuals should do physical labour and follow the ideal of non-possession. Then it will be possible to realise the goal of: *"From each according to his work and to each according to his needs."* There will be no private property, which is the instrument of exploitation and the source of social distinctions and hatred.

• Moral - Religious Characteristics of *Sarvodaya*

1. Sarvodaya society is basically a society based on morality and religion. Moral values are widely recognised and respected here and they constitute the very basis of the society.
2. All people here are imbued with the spirit of love, fraternity, truth, non-violence and self-sacrifice Society functions on the basis of non-violence.
3. Sarvodaya society is free from seven social sins. They are:

1. Politics without principles,

2. Possession of wealth without the involvement of labour,

3. Business without morals,

4. Education without Character,

5. Luxury and pleasure without "conscience",

6. Science without humanity, and

7. Worship without sacrifice.

Social Programmes and Functions of *Sarvodaya Society*

According to Gandhiji, Sarvodaya society engages itself in various types of programmes and activities. Some of them are mentioned below:

1. Development of Agriculture and Cottage Industries

A nation with abundant man power like India must always search for labour-oriented industries. Gandhiji supported the development of agriculture and cottage industries which would provide job opportunities to a large number of people. Gandhiji was not against mechanisation; but he was against the introduction of industries that would take away the jobs of men.

2. Encouragement to *Khadi*

Gandhiji advocated Khadi for it symbolises nationalism. *"Khadi"* is based on *"swadeshi"* principle. It indicates self-reliance, economic independence and also social equality.

3. Basic Education

Gandhiji believed that the all-round development of the individual is possible only when education is imparted through a profitable job. Gandhiji called such a type of education *"basic education", "life education", "job-centred education"*, and also as *"new education"* [*Nayi Talim*]. This type of education must incorporate the values of truthfulness, non-violence, co-operation, equality, social justice, dignity of labour and so on. Gandhiji also called it rural - national education.

4. Removal of Untouchability

Gandhiji gave utmost importance to the removal of untouchability. He called that practice great national stigma. The lowest caste people of the Indian society who were subject to suppression, exploitation and untouchability were referred to by Gandhiji as *"Harijans",*[1] *meaning the children of God.* He appealed to his followers to take a pledge for the removal of untouchability. He urged that *"there could be no rest.......... until untouchability becomes a thing of the past."*

5. Prohibition of Alcoholic Drinks

There should be no scope for drug addiction and alcoholism. If alcoholism is removed then gambling, untouchability and prostitution will automatically come down. Gandhiji considered alcoholism the enemy of the poor, the low and the so called *"untouchables."*

6. Harmony Among Religious Communities

Gandhiji who proudly called himself a *"Hindu"* was a staunch advocate of religious harmony. Sarvodaya society does not make a distinction between religious communities. On the contrary, it aims at religious harmony.

7. Rural Cleanliness

Sarvodaya society is actually village-centred and village-based society. Hence it pays attention to the task of rural cleanliness, rural sanitation, rural health, and all-round development of the rural community. Gandhiji himself used to take part in the rural-cleaning campaigns to set an example for others to emulate.

8. Improvement of the Status of Women

In Gandhiji's Sarvodaya society men and women are equal. If husband is called *"swamin"*, then the wife must be called *"swamini."* Women are not the servants of men; but are respectful companions and partners in pursuits. The roles of men and women are only complementary and supplementary and not contradictory. This was the belief of Gandhiji and hence he gave equal importance to men and women in his Sarvodaya society.

9. Other Programmes of *Sarvodaya Society*

In addition to the programmes and activities mentioned above, the Sarvodaya society as visualised by Gandhiji would also engage in various other functions among which the following may be noted:

---

1 **Harijan** - "was a word used by the great Gujarathi saint **Narasinha Mehta,** who belonged to the Nagar Brahmana Community and who defied the whole community by claiming the *"untouchables"* as his own. I am delighted to adopt the word which is sanctified by having been used by such a great saint, but it has for me a deeper meaning than you may imagine. The *"untouchable"*, to me, is compared to us, really, a ***Harijan*** - a man of God, and we are ***"Dhurjan"*** [men of evil]. ***Source:*** **M.K. Gandhi** in ***"The Removal of Untouchability"*** - 1954 Page No: 14. Compiled and edited by **Bharatan Kumarappa** - Published by ***"Navajivan Publishing House"***, Ahmedabad.

(i) Promoting the welfare of Harijans and Girijans [tribal people]
(ii) Organising students for constructive activities
(iii) Launching *"swadeshi campaigns"*
(iv) Advocating education through the mother tongue / regional languages
(v) Making the national language Hindi popular among people
(vi) Establishment of non-violent democratic set-up
(vii) Formation of *"peace squads"* [*'Shantidals'*] to prevent communal riots from taking place
(viii) Giving encouragement to Ayurveda, and naturopathy
(ix) Special programmes be launched to look after leprosy patients and to remove leprosy
(x) Propagating family planning by the practice of *"brahmacharya"* or self-control.

Evaluation of *Sarvodaya*

Main Merits

The following are the main merits of *Sarvodaya.*

1. *State is made an agency of service for common welfare*: Sarvodaya sets its face against the politics of power and exploitation. The state is regarded as an agency of service, and not an agency of power.

2. *Promotes high ideals*: Sarvodaya stands for the good of all, and not for the good of any small or particular group with vested interests. It promotes equality, freedom, fraternity and social justice. It believes in non-violent methods entirely free from bitterness, fanaticism and hatred. It lays great emphasis on moral and spiritual values.

3. *New social and economic values*: Sarvodaya seeks to create new socio-economic values. The concept of private property gives place to the concept of trusteeship. People will work for the good of all with family - feelings. There is no mutual ill-will and hatred.

4. *Sarvodaya provides a model of a good Society*: Sarvodaya projects the model of an ideal society, a society which resembles Plato's *"Republic"* and the Hindus' Concept of *"Rama Rajya."* It shows the direction in which the human societies must work in order to overcome the deficiencies that they have.

Demerits or Defects of *Sarvodaya*

1. *Not practicable*: Sarvodaya ideals will remain as ideals for they are not practicable. The ideals, objectives and methods of functioning of Sarvodaya are laudable, but in the actual world they will be found wanting. It will be almost impossible to establish a society strictly on the basis of the great principles upheld by Gandhiji and others.

2. *Change of heart is not easy*: It is very difficult to change the heart and soul of the people. Average people are basically narrowminded and selfish. Only broadminded, self-less people with cosmopolitan approach may appreciate and cherish Gandhian ideals and not ordinary people.

3. *Sarvodaya not Possible in any one country alone*: The present day world is highly competitive and hence no country can face this cut-throat competition single-handed if it is given to practice Sarvodaya. A group of nations must decide together to practice it. Only then it may become a success. Hence the chances of practising it in a single country like India are very remote.

4. *Human world has not seen such a Society so far*: It is an acknowledged fact that an ideal society such as "Sarvodaya Society" never existed in the past. There is no guarantee that such a society will come to be established in the future. The concept of *"Sarvodaya"* will remain only as an *"utopian"* concept. **Dr. Usha Mehta** writes: *Sarvodaya "especially in its political aspect is more of an idea which has not yet taken a practical shape. This is mainly because the utopia of the Sarvodayites flounders on the dock of human nature as it fails to take account of the "lower" and "baser" elements of human nature in its over-enthusiasm to emphasise the "higher" and the "better."*[1]

1 **Usha Mehta** as quoted by **A.C. Kapoor** *"Principles of Political Science."* Page - 713.

Chapter 21

Education in India

***Meaning and Definition of Education** - Society and Education - State and Education: Totalitarian State and Education - Democratic State and Education - The Ways in Which the State Can Propagate the Cause of Education - Education in the Traditional and the Modern Indian Contexts - Education in the Traditional Contexts : Education in Ancient and Medieval Period - Education During the British Period - Education in the Modern Context - Development of Education After Independence - Main Defects of the Present Educational System - Literacy and Education - How to Define Literacy ? - The Problem and the Magnitude of Illiteracy in India - Causes for the Widespread Illiteracy - Measures for the Eradication of Illiteracy : National Adult Education Programme - Rural Functional Literacy Programme - National Literacy Mission - Total Literacy Campaign - Literacy Position in India - 2001 Census Highlights - Issues Related to Primary Education- Directive Principles of State Policy and Primary Education - Importance of Primary Education - Problems of Universalisation of Primary Education - Educational Problems of the Disadvantaged Groups - Progress of Education in India : A Brief Mention of Educational Institutions of India - Elementary and Secondary Education- Multifarious Educational Establishments for Promoting the Cause of Education - Education and Social Stratification - Education and Social Mobility - Equality of Educational Opportunities - Education and Modernisation.*

Education has been and continues to be one of the major concerns of the modern as well as the traditional society. It is a powerful instrument that decides the destiny of mankind. It is a major force behind the continuity of cultural tradition. In social control and social change the contribution of education is immense. Hence no sociologist can afford to neglect its role in society. The modern day sociologists are more interested in studying the social functions of education and its effectiveness in bringing about desired changes in society.

Education is one of the basic activities of people in all human societies. The continued existence of society depends upon the transmission of culture to the young. It is essential that every new generation must be given training in the ways of the group so that the same tradition will continue. Every society has its own ways and means of fulfilling this need. *"Education"* has come to be one of the ways of fulfilling this need.

"Education" very simply means providing profitable experience. Learning is gaining through experiences. For efficient learning, education is necessary. Giving education to young means providing such experiences to them which may help them to grow physically, mentally, and spiritually.

Education is being given much importance in India today though it was much neglected for centuries. Education in India has not been planned properly and hence it has its own weaknesses. Millions have become literate after independence, still millions remain as illiterate. Problem of illiteracy is a big menace for India's progress. The present chapter gives some details about the relative position of Indian education, its literacy level, problems involved in the removal of illiteracy, and the governmental measures in promoting the cause of education.

Meaning and Definition of Education

Meaning of *"Education"*

The term *"education"* is derived from the Latin *educare* which literally means to *"bring up"*, and is connected with the verb *"educare"* which means to *"bring forth."* The idea of education is not merely to impart knowledge to the pupil in some subjects but to develop in him those habits and attitudes with which he may successfully face the future. The Latin author Varro wrote, *"The midwife brings forth, the nurse brings up, the tutor trains and the master teaches."* Plato was of the opinion that the end of education was *"to develop in the body and in the soul [of the pupil] all the beauty and all the perfection of which they are capable."* It means, in short, *"a sound mind in a sound body"*, [*mens sana in corpore sano*]. According to the Aristotelian conception, the aim of education is *"to develop man's faculties, especially, his mind, so that he may be able to enjoy the contemplation of the supreme truth, goodness and beauty in which perfect happiness essentially consists."* The Arabic equivalent of education is *"Talim"* which means – *"the process of providing and acquiring knowledge."*

As **Peter Worsley** says, *"A large part of our social and technical skills are acquired through deliberate instruction which we call education. It is the main waking activity of children from the ages of five to fifteen and often beyond...."* A large part of the budget of many developed and developing countries is set apart for education. Education employs a large army of people. Sociologists are becoming more and more aware of the importance and role of educational institutions in the modern industrialised societies. In recent years education has become a topic of major interest for some sociologists. As a result, a new branch of sociology called *Sociology of Education* has become established.

Definition of Education

(1) **Durkheim** conceives of education as *"the socialisation of the younger generation."* He further states that it is *"a continuous effort to impose on the child ways of seeing, feeling and acting which he could not have arrived at spontaneously."*

(2) **Sumner** defined education as the attempt to transmit to the child the mores of the group, so that he can learn *"what conduct is approved and what is disapproved....... how he ought to behave in all kinds of cases: what he ought to believe and reject."*

(3) **F.J. Brown and J.S. Roucek** say that education is *"the sum total of the experience which moulds the attitudes and determines the conduct of both the child and the adult."*

(4) **Samuel Koenig** : *"Education may also be defined as the process whereby the social heritage of a group is passed on from one generation to another as well as the process whereby the child becomes socialised, i.e., learns the rules of behaviour of the group into which he is born."*

(5) **Swami Vivekananda**, an eminent thinker and a great social reformer of India, understands education in the following way : *"Education is the manifestation of perfection already in man."*[1]

Vivekananda further says *"Education is not the amount of information that is put into your brain and runs riot there, undigested all your life. We must have life-building, man-making, character-making, assimilation of ideas. If you have assimilated five ideas and made them your life and character, you have more education than any man who has got by heart a whole library."*[2]

(6) **Dr. S. Radhakrishnan**, a great philosopher and educationist of India, has said thus : *"Education to be complete, must be humane; it must include not only the training of the intellect but also the refinement of the heart and the discipline of the spirit."*

(7) **M.K. Gandhiji** : *"By education I mean an all round drawing out of the best in the child / man's body, mind and spirit."*

In simple words, education means *"developing of and cultivating the various physical, intellectual, aesthetic and moral faculties, in an individual."* It is, according to **Durkheim**, "the action exercised by the older generation upon those who are not yet ready for social life. Its object is to develop and awaken in the child those physical, intellectual and moral states which are required of him both by his society as a whole and by the milieu for which he is specially destined."

Broad Objectives of Education

Regarding the main objectives of education, ancient Greek philosopher **Plato** said long back thus : The end of education is "to develop a sound mind in a sound body." It is widely held that education fulfils three main objectives. They are as follows :

1. Education helps man to know himself and the universe. It also enables him to understand the way in which he is related to the social world in which he is living.
2. Education by providing for transmission of culture establishes a connecting link between the past - present and the future, and
3. Education by contributing to the development of both the individual and society, enhances human progress.

SOCIETY AND EDUCATION

Education has become one of the pre-requisites of modern society. Education is both a modern and a traditional social force. Though education assumes modern forms and enacts a role that suits the requirements of the modern society, it has a long standing history of its own. Mutual dependence of these is such that one cannot exist without the other. The present society is very much based on modern education, and education as such is a part and parcel of the modern society. *"Given a purposive orientation, education can be a powerful instrument for reshaping and modernising the society."* Education provides necessary knowledge and skills which enable an individual to operate efficiently in the society and also to contribute to its successful functioning.

Education is One Among the Main Social Institutions

Education has been functioning as a powerful means of cultural transmission. This is, in fact, one of the basic functions of education as a social institution. But educational institutions do not exist in a vacuum and do not function in isolation. They are an integral part of society. No educational system can operate without being influenced by the norms and values of society.

---

1 *"Complete Works of Swami Vivekananda"* Vol. IV. Page - 490.

2 *ibid.* Vol. III, Page - 302.

Education "is firmly entrenched in the wider social network and is reciprocally related to other social institutions. Among the principal social institutions which are influenced by education and which in turn have influenced it mention may be made of family, economy, politics, religion, and social stratification. In view of the crucial position that education occupies in relation to these institutions it seems to have immense potentialities for social change and modernisation."[1]

Education and Family

Education and family are inextricably mixed up. The role of the family as a social institution engaged in the transmission of culture is well recognised. Family has been appropriately described as the *"incubator for culture"* [Goldschmidt - 1971 : 195][2] Though the processes of industrialisation and urbanisation have considerably reduced the educational role of family, it continues to be a centre of informal education.

Both family and education have one purpose in common, that is, the socialisation of the younger generation. The family provides the first and the easiest context for socialisation. The role of socialisation by school starts later. Particularly when the child has reached five or six years of age. Thus, the socialisation of the child in its crucial formative years takes place in the family itself. In fact, the child enters the school with some mould of socialisation. Even after entering the school the child normally continues to live with its parents and to be deeply influenced by the behaviour and the attitude of its family members. As and when the child grows and proceeds to higher stages of learning the influence of the family slowly gets diminished.

Education and Economy

The level of economic development of any society is closely linked with the level of educational attainment of its people. Certain level of educational attainment is absolutely necessary for preparing economic planning. Scholars have recognised that *education is an important instrument in the national development.* The growing complexity of urban-industrial society has necessitated the interconnection between economy and education.

The relationship between education and economy is reflected in the close link that has developed between education and occupation in modern urban-industrial societies. Education influences economic development in two distinct but related ways. ***Firstly,*** the education system provides the labour force that matches the needs of the economy. This is called *"the manpower allocation function of education"*, and is broadly discussed as *the problem of human resource development.* ***Secondly,*** education is a pre-requisite of economic development in the sense economic development assumes a particular set of attitudes and values, or broadly a new culture of its own. Education seems to be an important agency for fostering such values and attitudes among the people and preparing them for economic development. *Education, thus, is capable of generating "a climate for growth."*

Education and Politics

The relationship between education and political life has been the subject of discussion among philosophers and social scientists since a long time. The relationship between the two, that is, education and politics, is reciprocal. Education not only influences the political process and environment of a given society, but it also in turn gets influenced by political dynamics. As far as the political functions of formal education are concerned, we may point out the importance of the following : 1. *Political socialisation,* 2. *Selection, recruitment and training of leaders,* 3. *National integration,* and 4. *Political input role.*

1 N. Jayaram *"Sociology of Education in India."* Pages : 43-44.

2 As quoted by N. Jayaram in *"Sociology of Education in India."* Page - 31.

Education and Religion

Religion is closely embedded in the social life of man. It has its own traditional links with education. Throughout human history religion has played a prominent role in the socialisation of the younger generation. In some societies, the importance of religion as an agency of socialisation has been next only to that of family. The history of the development of education reveals that in most of the countries of the ancient world educational institutions were invariably associated with the religious institutions. Type of education, its content and course, etc. were all very much influenced by religion. Most ancient Indian universities like Nalanda, Takshashila, Nagarjuna and Kanchipura, for example, imparted religious education.

As regards the influence of education on religion, it is interesting to note that in modern society education has been called upon to perform a task which is almost the opposite of the one which it had done in the past. Most of the modern societies claim themselves to be secular and hence they expect their educational system to train people for secular occupations. In multi-religious societies, education is expected to be highly secular, free from all religious touches.

Education and Social Stratification

There is a close link between these two. The nature of social stratification has its own impact on the type of education. During the early days educational facility was available and extended only to the *"privileged sections."* During the period of *Dharmashastras* and *Puranas*, for example, educational facilities were extended only to the *"Dvijas"* [Brahmins, Kshatriyas and Vyshyas] and not to the *Shudras.* Education in fact, widened the gap between the privileged and the unprivileged. It added to social inequality. Today, this role of education is totally reversed. *Education is, today, a great equaliser.* It is one of the powerful means through which the lower classes can improve their social statuses. *Education is recognised as a generator of upward social mobility and a solvent of inequalities.* All the developing and the underdeveloped countries seem to have understood this changed role of education. Hence, they have been struggling to provide all the available educational facilities for the underprivileged sections of the society so that they come up socially and economically.

STATE AND EDUCATION

As educational system is so influential in the life of society it is not surprising that the State has always taken a special interest in it. The State has begun to take interest in education not in very distant past. In Europe as late as 19th century, the principle of assigning the responsibility of the education of the citizen upon the State, had become acceptable. In the ancient times, the State was giving financial assistance for the spread of education, yet it was not at all interfering with education. The modern State, however, takes full responsibility of the education of its citizens. It actively participates in the planning, organisation, expansion and control of education. But these functions are performed differently in two types of State – ***Totalitarian State*** and ***Democratic State.***

Totalitarian State and Education

In a totalitarian state the individual freedom cannot be demanded in the form of individual right. It can be bestowed upon the individuals, if the State so desires, for its own good. Therefore, in such a State, ***the philosophy of education lays much emphasis on the values such as harsh discipline, self sacrifice, absolute loyalty to the State, and obedience to the administrators, etc.*** Nazi Germany, Fascist Italy, and Communist States represent a few examples of such a State.

Education to Serve the Cause of the Regime and Teachers are Made Its Paid Agents : As soon as a totalitarian regime gains control over a nation one of the first things it does is to bring under its control the whole system of education and to transform the teachers into paid agents of the regime. The philosophy of education in a socialist country like Russia [or a Communist Country like

China] is considered akin to the philosophy of education of a totalitarian state. Thus, "the principal of a secondary school in Moscow, not long ago stated : *"The prime duty of the Soviet teacher is to train our younger generation for the work of building Communism."*"[1] "It is thought that the leadership in the communist countries is of the same type as was existent in Fascist Countries. Therefore, in these countries the State extols those very qualities which subjugate the will of the individual to the will of the State."[2] It is unfortunate that this unhealthy tendency is spreading in various forms even in the democratic countries.

Democratic State and Education

In a democratic state also it is very much emphasised that one should be loyal to one's own State and obey its laws. It is considered that this obedience of laws is not because the State is all-supreme but from the feeling that it is for serving the interests of the individual citizen. In a democratic country, all the institutions are not run by the government. Non-governmental agencies are given much liberty and they undertake variety of welfare activities including educational activities. The democratic state does not direct the children to read this or that, to follow this method or that, but gives a lot of freedom to the educational institutions. It is now widely believed that *"State monopoly of education, or discrimination against any type of educational institutions is incompatible with true democracy. The granting of the charters to the universities and other educational institutions, which is still common in many nations, is one of the best guarantees for ensuring a living and adoptable system of education.'*[3]

What Role State Should Play in Education ?

As far as the role of the State in educational matters is concerned, there are two major opinions. *One opinion is that the State should not interfere in the education of its citizens.* Renowned thinker like **Herbert Spencer**, felt that the national education should be given by private bodies. Similarly, **Raymont** also says, *"The function of the State is to protect and promote, not to absorb or take the place of the family and the individual.'*[4]

The other opinion is in favour of complete control over education by the State. Here, the State has the responsibility of not only establishing educational institutions but also running and regulating them. This responsibility includes the task of preparing the syllabus, appointing teachers, giving training to them, conducting examinations, and awarding degrees.

These two opinions reflect the existing situation in the two types of States. The confusion is still existing in many minds about the relation between the State and education. The best method seems to be that *the State should keep control over the organisation of education but must not meddle with the day to day business of the educational institutions.* Education is basically a social function and the State must make arrangements for its fulfilment. Hence, it should give sufficient freedom to the educationists so that they can chalk out their own educational programmes without any interference by the State. The State should keep a watch over the spread of education and the measures for the social upliftment of the citizens. Wherever it finds deficiencies in the developmental works the State must take adequate measures to rectify them.

The Ways in Which the State Can Propagate the Cause of Education

All modern educationists of the democratic states are of the opinion that the *State's control over education should be minimum and moderate.* They also believe that *"education cannot be*

1 As quoted by P. Gisbert in *"Fundamentals of Sociology."* Page - 234.
2 Dr. S.S. Mathur *"A Sociological Approach to Indian Education"* [1976]. Page - 116.
3 P. Gisbert. Page - 235.
4 As quoted by S.S. Mathur. Page - 116.

regarded only as a mere way of training a man for a job, but of bringing him up also as a citizen of his country and one who shares her ideals." [P. Gisbert. Page - 236.] ***What is to be taught, how is it to be taught, who should teach it, and why should it be taught ?*** These questions are addressed to the educationists and not to the State. Still, the State can take an active part in the educational process to spread literacy and also to uplift the condition and state of education. Some of the ways in which the State can help the cause of education, can be stated below :[1]

1. The State must see that *schools of every type are established* according to the needs of the locality. For example, primary, secondary, technical and professional institutions, degree colleges, universities, etc. are to be set up wherever they are required.
2. The State should *ensure that each citizen is provided an opportunity for education.* It is necessary especially in the underdeveloped and the developing nations, that compulsory free education till the secondary stage must be provided with.
3. The State should *keep control over all the educational institutions established by it.* At the same time it should appoint talented and efficient staff in the department of education.
4. The State must *undertake the responsibility of giving training to the teachers and pay them adequately.* "As the teacher is the soul of the educational apparatus he should be well trained and paid." This is necessary in order to attract talented people to the teaching field.
5. The State should *take a firm decision regarding the centralisation or decentralisation of education.* But such a decision must be based on the needs of the society than anything else. Mere political exigencies should not lead the State to take the decisions in matters of education.

Education – A Concurrent Subject in the Constitution of India

In the modern Indian context, education has been given importance by the State. But the responsibility of providing education to the people is shared between the Centre and the States. Under the Constitutional scheme, *"education"* is in the *concurrent list,* and the Union Government and the States exercise joint responsibilities. As a result, while the role and responsibilities of the States in regard to education remains unaltered, the Union Government accepts a larger responsibility to reinforce the national and integrated character of education. The Centre also takes up the responsibility to maintain quality and standards, to study and monitor the educational requirements of the country as a whole in regard to the manpower for development. The Centre also caters to the needs of research and advanced study, to look after the international aspects of education, culture and human resource development. In general, the Union Government ventures to promote excellence at the tertiary level of the educational pyramid throughout the country. The coordination and cooperation between the Union and the States is brought about in the field of education through the *Central Advisory Board of Education* [CABE]. This body needs strengthening.[2]

EDUCATION IN THE TRADITIONAL AND THE MODERN INDIAN CONTEXTS

Education in the Traditional Context

Education in Ancient India

Education has been a major concern of the Indian thinkers ever since the times of the Vedas. The commitment of the Indian thinkers towards knowledge and education was such that they were ready to welcome it without any prejudice from whatever source it might have stemmed. Thus the

1 S.S. Mathur. Page - 117.

2 *Source* : *"Selected Reading Material"* issued at *National Seminar on Internationalisation of Indian Higher Education - Quality Dimensions* [24 - 25 April 2003, Bangalore]. Page - 18.

Rig Vedic hymn states : *"Let noble thoughts come to us from all sides."*[1] The theme of higher knowledge and higher education was fashioned in India by the ancient Rishis and sages in the Vedic Age; the date of which is uncertain but is supposed to be traceable to great antiquity. Thus, higher knowledge, education, and the philosophy of education which we inherit has come down to us from the days of the Vedas and the Upanishads. Quest for the highest knowledge or the knowledge of self may be said to be the essence of this philosophy. This quest for the highest knowledge should pilot all our educational activities.

"India has had a long tradition of inquiry and articulation of concepts of universe, self, role of state, economy, social order and other related matters. The methodologies adopted were both subjective and objective and included observation, conceptualisation, verification, articulation and teaching.

As a result, India had gone further in science than any other country before the modern era – specially in mathematics, astronomy and chemistry, metallurgy and physics. Indian scientists discovered and formulated and anticipated by force of reasoning or experiment some of the scientific ideas and discoveries which Europe arrived at much later. Ancient India was well equipped in surgery and its system of medicine survives to this day. A vast literature is also available on *"vriksha Ayurveda"* [Herbal Medicine]. In literature, in philosophy, and in systems of yogic knowledge not only ancient India but medieval and modern India reached highest levels of achievement. The higher education system flourished in ancient India well; and it continued to influence developments during its subsequent ages, in spite of diverse forms that developed under the impact of changes in religion, and in social, economic and political life."[2]

Early Educational Institutions : During the Vedic and the Upanishadic periods, educational institution was in the form of *"the Gurukula system."* The *"house of the teacher"* itself was the centre of learning. In course of time, numerous educational towns such as **Takshashila, Mathura, Pataliputra, Ujjain, Amaravathi** and others, came to be established. A huge university came to be set up at **Takshashila** in the 6th century B.C. Two other universities, namely, **Nalanda** and **Vikramashila** were established in the 4th and 5th centuries A.D. respectively. In fact, the Buddhist monasteries developed into educational institutions. In addition to Nalanda and Takshashila other institutions such as **Vallabhi, Jagaddla,** and **Odantapuri** also earned wide recognition. These were the institutions of higher learning, attached to temples or monasteries. Numerous disciplines were taught here.

Importance to Primary Education : Special emphasis was given to primary education during this period. This was done through *"agrahara villages."* In these villages there were arrangements to look after the basic needs of the teachers so that they could completely devote themselves to the task of educating the pupils. Local monasteries also had taken up the cause of education on their own. Children's education began at the age of 5 and they were taught reading, writing, simple mathematics, logic and grammar. Particularly, during the periods of rule of the Kings such as the Guptas, education had become mass education, remarkable literature, philosophy and culture.

Education in the Medieval Period

During the Muslim period, education suffered a set back due to the changed political circumstances. But, in spite of the social distresses, educational work was carried out in the villages

---

1 *"Aano Bhadraha Kratavo Yantu Vishvataha"* - Rig Veda.

2 ***Source*** : *"Selected Reading Material"* Issued on the occasion of National Seminar on *"Internationalisation of Indian Higher Education – Quality Dimensions."* Page - 29.

and towns by private individuals and institutions. Muslim rulers also established institutions to teach theology but these institutions were not open to all. Only during the period of Akbar some educational institutions were thrown open to the Hindus. Sanskrit, Arabic or Persian were the mediums of instruction. Teachers' remuneration was paid by the rulers through grant of land, presents of pupils, allowance paid by wealthy citizens, and payment in the form of food, cloths or other articles. There was no emphasis on physical education, developing thinking ability or teaching craft. Education in a way was provided to only a small section of the people. Neither culturally nor socially it had any appeal to the common people, other than the elite and the *ulemas*.

Education During the British Period

During the British period, educational sector received some importance. But the British did not have any intention of seriously developing the educational institutions of India. [*Kindly refer to the details given in box at the end of this Chapter.*] British education in India was mainly aimed at producing clerks. Education was student-centred rather than teacher-centred. Christian missionaries took more interest in spreading education which helped their conversion process. Education during the British period never aimed at equality, national cohesion, individual freedom and excellence. It was not productive and never aimed at making Indians, masters of technology.

The British education in India hardly contributed to the cultural revival of India. Wide gap existed between the British system of education and the traditional system of Indian education. ***"Throughout the national movement, there were attempts at bringing about a synthesis between western education and the values and the traditions of Indian society."***

Education in the Modern Context

Beginnings of Modern Higher Education During the British Regime

The modern higher education system is only 140 years old, when the first three universities were set up in 1857 under the British Rule. Policy guidelines given by Macaulay and Wood's Despatch [1854] shaped the scope and the role of universities in India. To begin with, colleges set up in India were affiliated to British universities. In 1857, for the first time, universities were set up in India. Existing colleges got affiliated to these universities.

The period from 1857 to 1947 was the period of slow development of institutions of higher education in India. They were set up mostly in administrative headquarters and port towns. They provided education in literature, history, philosophy, political science, social science and natural sciences. The thrust of development was mainly on liberal arts education. Science education occupied a very small proportion. The rate of development was slow in a period of 90 years. Only 18 universities were set up in the country. Most of these followed the model of the three leading universities in Bombay, Calcutta and Madras. Along with liberal arts, some engineering and medical colleges were also set up. Most of the colleges imparted education as formulated by the universities. The universities also acted as examining and degree granting bodies. The initiative in the hands of college teachers in terms of curriculum development was, therefore, very much limited.

The guiding principles of colonial rulers were slightly modified by Indian scholars who desired to blend Indian culture with western thought. They felt this would make Indians appreciate knowledge both from the Indian and the British point of view. These two philosophical approaches simultaneously operated during the colonial period.

During this colonial period, particularly after 1906, the desire for a national system of education and need for imparting knowledge of India's philosophy, art and literature also gained momentum. Some of the leading persons attempted to establish indigenous educational institutions with the support of the community. A National College was set up by nationalist leaders in 1906 in

Calcutta under the principalship of **Sri Aurobindo**, and some other institutions too came to be established, such as **Viswa Bharati** by the great poet **Rabindra Nath Tagore**.

Development of Education After Independence

Education today is oriented to promoting values of urban, competitive consumer society. Role of education in accelerating the processes of modernisation and industrialisation can hardly be exaggerated. Formal education has become an absolute necessity today. Education is not confined to simply literacy but is used a means to prepare the individuals to face the challenges of the modern society. Education could no more follow its elitist approach nor could it be associated with religious institutions such as temples, churches, mosques and monasteries. Education has become secular both in its content and in its approach. The architects of independent India visualised this changed role of education and accordingly started placing premium on it.

After independence, India adopted the approach of planned development of the country. The First Five Year Plan focused on agriculture, the Second Five Year Plan on industry and the Third Five Year Plan again attempted to focus on agriculture and agro-based industry for the development of the country. This approach for development called for development of the education system in the subsequent Five Year Plans, to meet the challenges of development and the needs of agriculture, industry and society in general.

With independence in 1947, India inherited a system of higher education which was not only small but also characterised by the persistence of large intra / inter-regional imbalances. Determined efforts were made to build a network of universities, and their affiliated colleges which provided tremendous out reach to a country of vast diversities in language as also in the prevailing standards of education at the lower levels. The feeder schools differentially impacted on the higher education system leading to significant qualitative imbalances within it.

When India became independent, it had only 20 universities and 500 colleges located in different parts of the country. It enrolled around a hundred thousand students in higher education. Participation of women was limited and those who graduated annually were no more than a couple of dozens or so. The policies and aspirations of people influenced the development in the following decades.

Wide Network of Educational Institutions : India, today, ranks very high in terms of the size of the network of educational institutions. The number of pre-primary schools has gone up during the period from 1961 to 1998, by about 21 times, of the primary schools has almost doubled, of higher secondary schools by about 6 times and of the universities by about 5 times.[1] The number of teachers has also increased significantly. The number of teachers in primary schools has increased by about 2.5 times from 1961 to 1997; of the teachers in the higher secondary schools by about 5 times, of the degree and post-graduate colleges by about 12.5 times. The number of educational institutions and also of the teachers has been consistently increasing.

Main Defects of the Present Educational System

Though educational institutions have increased tremendously and lakhs of students are taking up to education, the present educational system in India has its own drawbacks. Some of the main defects may be mentioned here.

1. Present system of education is *not very much linked with the socio-economic needs* of the society.

1 *Manpower Profile,* India, 1998 : 70 as quoted by **Prof. Ram Ahuja** in *"Society in India."* Page 219.

2. The *budgetary allotment* for education for a vast nation like ours is very meagre [less than 6%]. [*Note* : For comparisions, please see *Table No.4*.]
3. The present education *does not generate the type of knowledge that is relevant to adjust ourselves with changed conditions of society.*
4. The *employment potential of our education is very inadequate* for it is not associated with a particular body of the knowledge, which is necessary for meeting the challenges of the technological world.
5. *Our education is not value based.* It does not have the necessary tinge of Indianness. It has failed to provide the value framework which may prepare committed leaders, professionals, technocrats, bureaucrats, businessmen and others.
6. The present education *largely focuses on the individual material gains, it neglects the non-material aspects* which are necessary for developing a healthy personality.
7. It is alleged that the present educational system *has failed to inculcate the spirit of nationalism* among the children of the new generation.
8. Our education system still continues to be *urban biased.* It has failed to cater to the needs of the villages and also of agriculture which is the backbone of the country.

Conclusion

That the deficiencies and the short-comings that are found in our educational system will have to be removed. Education must be made an effective instrument of economic development and social change. It must be able to produce an army of skilled personnel with social sensitivity that will address itself to the problems of the society with a sense of commitment.

Educational system must strike a balance between the economic, political, social and other aspects and must guarantee the basic cultural ethos of the Indian society. The role of education as an agent for transmission of culture should never be forgotten. Our education system is often criticised on the ground that it gives more importance to the borrowed Western ideas and foreign cultural elements than the Indian cultural heritage and its values. As Vivekananda's disciple Bhagini Nivedita has said, *"In a true education the place of foreign culture is never at the beginning. All true development must proceed from the known to the unknown, from the familiar to the unfamiliar, from the near to the far."*[1] Hence, the normative character of education which stands neglected, should not be lost sight of. It is by attending to these fundamental needs that the real ground can be prepared for the promotion of the "welfare of people by securing and protecting as effectively as it may, a social order in which justice, social, economic and political, shall inform all the institutions of national life."

LITERACY AND EDUCATION

The 1948 *Declaration of Human Rights* stated that everyone has a right to education. Yet, even today, this right is being denied to millions of children. Education is a crucial element in economic and social development. Without education, development can neither be broad based nor sustained. The benefits that accrue to a country by having a literate population are multidimensional. *Spread of literacy is generally associated with modernisation, urbanisation, industrialisation, communication and commerce.* It forms an important input in the overall development of individuals enabling them to comprehend their social, political and cultural environment better, and respond to it appropriately. Higher levels of education and literacy lead to greater awareness and also contribute to improvement of economic conditions and is a prerequisite for acquiring various skills and better use of health care facilities.

1 Bhagini Nivedita as quoted in *"Vivek Hamsa"*, monthly magazine, Jan. 2003.

How to Define Literacy ?

How is literacy defined ? Who is literate and who is illiterate ? Generally, a person who can read and write, is regarded as *"literate"* ? But the *Census Commission of India, 1991* made the definition of literacy specific. It was decided in 1991 Census to use the term literacy rate for the

Table - 1

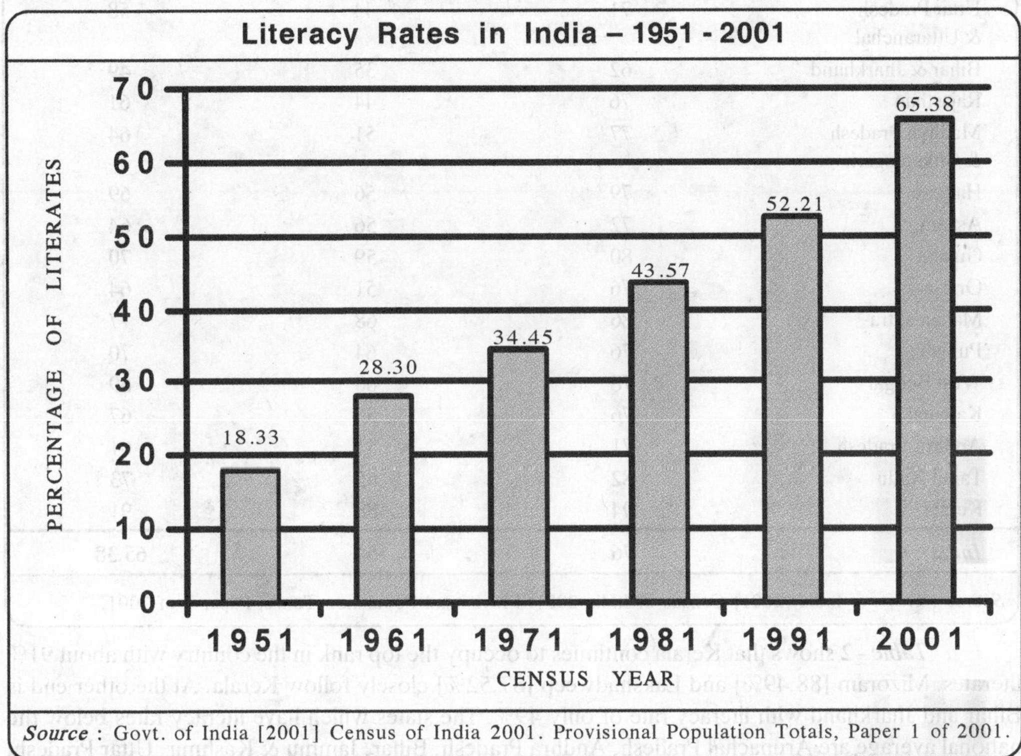

Source : Govt. of India [2001] Census of India 2001. Provisional Population Totals, Paper 1 of 2001.

population relating to seven years of age and above. ***A person is deemed as literate if he or she can read and write with understanding in any language.*** A person who can merely read but cannot write is not considered literate. Further, formal education in a school is not necessary for a person to be considered *"literate."* The same concept has been continued in census 2001 also.

The significant milestone reached in census 2001 is that the total number of illiterates has come down from 328.1 million in 1991 to 296.2 million. Thus for the first time since independence, there is a decline in the absolute number of illiterates in the country. This is a major step forward in improving the literacy status of India. ***Table*** - 1 shows the literacy rates from 1951 to 2001.

The national average of literacy rate is misleading as wide variations exist between the states. ***Table*** - 2 shows the literacy rates in different major states in India. The literacy rate has improved since 1991 census but there is a clear difference between literacy rates among males and females. The national percentage of literates in the population above 7 years of age is about 65.38, with literate males about 76% and females lagging behind with about 54%.

Table - 2

Literacy Rates in Major States of India – 2001

State	*Male Literacy Rate*	*Female Literacy Rate*	*Total Literacy Rate*
Uttar Pradesh & Uttaranchal	71	44	58
Bihar & Jharkhand	62	35	49
Rajasthan	76	44	61
Madhya Pradesh & Chhattisgarh	77	51	64
Haryana	79	56	69
Assam	72	56	64
Gujarat	80	59	70
Orissa	76	51	64
Maharashtra	86	68	77
Punjab	76	64	70
West Bengal	78	60	69
Karnataka	76	56	67
Andhra Pradesh	71	51	61
Tamil Nadu	82	65	73
Kerala	94	88	91
India	76	54	65.38

Source : Govt. of India [2001] Census of India 2001. Provisional Population Totals, Paper 1 of 2001.

Table - 2 shows that Kerala continues to occupy the top rank in the country with about 91% literates. Mizoram [88.49%] and Lakshadweep [87.52%] closely follow Kerala. At the other end is Bihar and Jharkhand with literacy rate of only 49%. The states which have literacy rates below the national average are Arunachal Pradesh, Andhra Pradesh, Bihar, Jammu & Kashmir, Uttar Pradesh, Rajasthan, M.P. and Orissa, etc.

THE PROBLEM AND THE MAGNITUDE OF ILLITERACY IN INDIA

Largest number of illiterates are found in India. Even up to 1991, there were as many as 328.1 million illiterate people in the country and the total percentage of literacy for the whole nation stood at 52.1%. Though by 2001 the number of illiterates in the country came down to 296.2 million, it is not a small number. Illiteracy in India has, since long before independence, been regarded as one of the greatest obstacles for development. It is a fact known to everyone that India cannot achieve expected progress without eradicating or at least reducing substantially the extent of illiteracy. No nation in the world has attained advancement in science and technology or in agriculture, industry, trade or commerce without achieving substantial rate of literacy. Hence, education in general, and the spread of literacy in particular, will have to be given high priority in the development process of our country.

Causes for the Widespread Illiteracy

Various factors contributed for the widespread illiteracy in India among which the following may be noted.

Table - 3

Literacy Rates Among Males and Females in India : 1951 - 1991

Year	*Persons*	*Males*	*Females*
1951[1]	18.33	27.16	8.86
1961[2]	28.31	40.40	15.34
1971	34.45	45.95	21.97
1981[3]	43.56	56.37	29.75
	(41.42)	(53.45)	(28.46)
1991[4]	52.21	64.13	39.29
2001[5]	65.38	75.00	54.00

Source : *India Year Book* - 1999. Page - 10.

1 Excluding the population of J & K, Pondicherry and NEFA, D.N. Haveli and G.D. and Diu.

2 Excluding Goa, Daman & Diu, NEFA.

3 Excluding Assam.

4 Excluding J & K.

5 Inserted by the Author.

1. *Foreign Conquests* : Incessant foreign conquests of India particularly by the Muslims and later by the British gave a fatal blow to the most widespread educational system of India.

2. *Exploited State of Affairs of the People* : Due to the total exploitation of the resources of India by the British during their rule, Indians had become poor. In the absence of material prosperity, and in the condition of their exploited lot, they could not pursue their educational endeavour. Thus, illiteracy started spreading its tentacles everywhere in India.

3. *Neglect of Education* : India was overwhelmed by the extremity of poverty at the time of its independence and hence educational sector failed to become a priority issue. Spread of literacy was neglected for several years, particularly during the first three plan periods. Money that was earmarked for education was negligible. [See *Table* No.3].

4. *Lack of Educational Awareness Among People* : Indians lacked very badly an awareness regarding the value of education. Hence millions remained illiterate throughout their lives. Only recently, that is, after 1990s, educational awareness has been slowly spreading among the people.

5. *Prevalence of Child Labour and the Provision of Poor Educational Facilities* : A large number of children [11.28ml, according to 1991 census] are still working as child labourers. Uneducated rural people consider education as a luxury item, an unproductive venture. They prefer to send their children for earning a few rupees as labourers than to learn at school as students. Though this tendency is slowly changing today, it maintained its grip for over 50 years.

Facilities given to the children at schools are also disappointing. Schools without trained teachers, proper buildings, drinking water and toilet facility, play ground, blackboard, furniture, etc. present only a horrible picture.

6. *Indifference of the Government Servants and Lack of Community Spirit on the Part of the People* have also added to the widespread illiteracy found in India.

Measures Adopted for Eradicating Illiteracy

The spread of literacy is of vital importance for achieving progress in all the spheres of life. Hence, appropriate steps are to be taken up for the eradication of illiteracy. As far as the Government of India is concerned, it has adopted over the years, three important measures : (i) *National Adult Education Programme;* (ii) *Rural Literacy Programme;* and (iii) *National Literacy Mission [NLM].*

(i) National Adult Education [NAE] Programme

This programme represents a joint and collaborative effort of the Central and State Governments, UT administrations, voluntary agencies, universities, colleges, and youth centres. Having the main aim of providing education and promoting literacy among all illiterate persons, particularly in the age group of 15-35 years, the programme was launched on October 2, 1978. The programme lays special emphasis on the education of women, SCs, STs, and other weaker sections in India.

International Literacy Year [I.L.Y.] - 1990 : In order to generate public awareness about the need for the relevance of literacy, the UNESCO declared the year 1990 as the *International Literacy Year.* In India also, the Prime Minister launched the ILY at Delhi on 22 Jan. 1990 in which he gave a call to the student and non-student volunteers to plunge themselves to the task of spreading the message of literacy throughout the nation.

(ii) Rural Functional Literacy [RFL] Programme

The RFL programme was launched as a sub-programme of the *Adult Education Programme* in May 1986. The programme which is fully funded by the Central Government and implemented by the States and UTs. The programme was designed to involve the NSS and other student volunteers in colleges and universities on the principle of *"Each One Teach One".* Its broad objectives are : (i) *to develop abilities in the learners to read and write,* and (ii) *to create awareness among learners about their rights and duties and the benefits that they can obtain from various schemes of socio-economic development which the Government launches from time to time.*

The RFL programme which was launched in 1986 included in the beginning 2 lakh volunteers and the number went up to 4.50 lakhs in 1990 covering over 4.10 lakh learners. Under this Programme, the Government undertook another venture in 1987 to involve both students and teachers of schools and colleges to spread literacy among the illiterates keeping in view the needs and languages of the learners. To begin with, the Government selected only 50 districts to improve the quality of adult education. Only after considering its impact, the Government intended to extend it to other areas to spread literacy in the minimum possible time.

(iii) National Literacy Mission [NLM]

The NLM was launched by the then Prime Minister in May 1988 to achieve the goal of imparting *"functional literacy"* to 80 million illiterates in the 15-35 age group. It intended to make 30 million literates by 1990 and an additional 50 million by 1995. This was also designed to involve the youth and voluntary agencies in the programme. In 1990, there were 513 projects in operation in various States and Union Territories.

Eradication of illiteracy plans and programmes launched by the Government did not yield much results. But things started improving especially after 1981. The number of illiterates came down considerably.

Total Literacy Campaign [TLC]

Illiteracy eradication programmes launched by the Government did not yield any satisfactory results even up to 1991. On the contrary, the number of illiterates went on increasing from one census to another. At the beginning of the year 1991, there were as many as 328.10 million illiterates in the country. The NLM launched in the year 1988 did not achieve its targets. This made the Government to formulate a new strategy for the spread of literacy. The spread of literacy campaign now came to be known as *"Total Literacy Campaign."* It consisted of the following :

(i) Closure of Adult Education Centres [AEC]
(ii) To introduce radical changes in the scheme of financial assistance to voluntary agencies for adult education
(iii) To organise *"Total Literacy Campaign"* in selected places
(iv) To make the district collectors as the personnel in charge of the TLC.

The State of Kerala was selected for starting this campaign to achieve total literacy. The trial began in 1988-89 with the help of the NSS [National Social Service] units of the Mahatma Gandhi University in **Kottayam Municipality** area. Within 100 days the city was declared as the first total literacy city of India. Due to the initiative taken by the Kerala State Sahitya Parishad [KSSP] another similar campaign was organised in Ernakulam district. The District Collector who was the Chairman of this campaign sanctioned the sum of Rs.80 lakhs and the campaign was also a success. As a result, in 1990, Ernakulam was regarded as the first Total Literacy District in India. The example of Kerala inspired South Kanara [Dakshina Kannada] in Karnataka, Burdwan in West Bengal, Union Territory of Pondichery, Sindhudurg in Wardha in Maharashtra which in due course achieved [almost near] total literacy.

Total Literacy Campaign now covers about 401 district in the country. Now the concentration is on the Hindi-speaking States of U.P., M.P., Rajasthan and Bihar where millions of illiterates are found. The campaign covers around 163 districts out of 200 districts in these states. Though the main aim is to achieve 80-85% literacy in these areas, the report of the achievement is not that encouraging. In the absence of a well equipped adult education project of a permanent nature with proper infrastructure at the local level, the campaign may not fetch the desired result in the fixed time limits.

Literacy Position in India : 2001 Census Highlights

After a very long time after independence an impressive rise in the literacy rate has taken place, that is, from 52.21% in 1991 to 65.38% in 2001. The salient features of the increase in the rate of literacy in 2001 can be noted below.[1]

1. As per 2001 census, 75% of males [that is, 339,969,489 males] and 54% of females [that is, 226,745,947 females] are found to be literate in India. This brings down the gap between male-female literacy rates from 28.84% in 1991 to 21.70% in 2001.
2. Kerala has maintained its lead in the literacy level. But its annual growth rate dropped to 0.90 in this decade [1991-2001].
3. Tamil Nadu registered an annual growth rate of 1.06% and Andhra Pradesh 1.30%.
4. Highest rate of literacy is found in Kerala, that is, 90.92% whereas Bihar recorded the lowest literacy rate of 47.53%.
5. At the national level more than 203 million people including 95.6 million females turned literate in the decade 1991-2001 and the total number of illiterates in the country came down to a little over 296 million [which includes 190 million females].
6. There are 56.67 crore literates in India which include 33.99 crore males and 22.67 crore females.
7. Of the four major Hindi-speaking states of U.P., M.P., Bihar and Rajasthan, significant improvement in male literacy is reported from Rajasthan followed by M.P. In female literacy, Chhattisgarh occupies the first place, with an increase of 24.87% during the decade ending 2001, followed by Rajasthan.
8. A very interesting finding in the field of literacy is increase in female literacy at a faster rate than male literacy rates in all States and Union Territories except Dadra and Nagar Haveli.
9. Of the various states, U.P. has the highest number of illiterates [57.8 million] followed by Bihar

1 ***Source***: *Manorama Year Book* - 2002. Pages : 74 - 75.

[34.9 million] and Andhra Pradesh [25 million]. Bihar, probably is the only state where we find an increase in the number of illiterates, both male and female, during the decade 1991-2001.

10. Of the southern states, Andhra Pradesh has the least literacy rate, that is, 61.11% which is below the national average. Almost one-third of its population is illiterate. Kerala has the literacy rate of 90.92% followed by Tamil Nadu 73.47% and Karnataka 67.04%.
11. For the first time after independence, the absolute number of illiterates have shown a decline. The decline is as large as 31.96 million during 1991-2001 which includes 21.45 million males and 10.51 million females.

National Policy on Education [NPE] - 1985-86

In 1980s the Central Government showed great interest in bringing about some important changes in the system of education. Hence, it expressed its eagerness to formulate a *New Educational Policy* for the country. The 119 page document namely *New Educational Policy* [NEP], prepared by the *Ministry of Human Resources Development* was presented to the Parliament in Aug. 1985. The NPE was however, announced in 1986. This Policy laid much emphasis on matters such as the following : (i) *reorganising the educational system,* (ii) *improving the quality of education,* (iii) *promoting national integration,* (iv) *inculcation of moral values,* (v) *stressing the importance of science and technology,* and (vi) *to develop good citizenship qualities in the younger generation.*

The NPE - 1986 contained many proposals among which the following may be noted :

1. Introducing throughout India one common form of educational structure consisting of 10+2+3 years of study.
2. Implementing adult education programme and also vocational education.
3. Imparting value education.
4. Increasing teachers' responsibility and accountability.
5. Delinking degrees from jobs.
6. Bringing about reforms in examination system.
7. Giving importance to sports, games and physical education.
8. Extending equal educational opportunities for women, SCs, STs and OBCs.
9. Redesigning of the higher education courses to suit to the needs of the society.
10. Launching of open university system.
11. Encouraging technical and management education and introducing agriculture-related courses.
12. Promoting technological research.
13. Providing more resources to implement effectively universalisation of elementary education and adult literacy.
14. Making provision for access to education to all the students irrespective of caste, class, religion, or sex.

Critically examining this NPE-1986, Dr. N. Jayaram[1] writes : "As far as education is concerned we are already on the threshold of the 21st century. We educate now to reap the benefit 20 years hence. Any measure to change the educational system should therefore be in tune with the vision of a society that we would like to create. This vision must essentially be a politico-ethical one, and not just a demographic or technical one. Among other things this vision has to take into account such issues as appropriate technology, developmental priorities and strategies, national income and wage policy, and a definition of a minimum standard of life. We now have an opportunity to debate

1 Dr. N. Jayaram in the book *"Sociology of Education in India"* writes in the concluding paragraph under the title *"New Educational Policy : A Critique"* [Pages : 225 - 226]

on "the desirable society" and work out strategies for realising it. If we let this opportunity pass, we may well be faced with a similar situation in the year 2001 discussing another document prepared by another set of bureaucrats."

Issues Related to Primary Education

Directive Principles of State Policy and Primary Education

It is increasingly being recognised that education is one of the pre-requisites of social change and social development. All the modern countries have placed high premium on education. India, soon after its independence took great interest in education. The Constitution makers had foreseen the importance of education and accordingly through the 45th Article of the Constitution insisted that India should introduce free and compulsory education before 1960. Independent Indian Government had also shown great enthusiasm to provide compulsory and free education for all boys and girls between the ages 6 and 14.

Insistence on the Compulsory Primary Education by the Directive Principles of the State Policy of the Constitution : The Directive Principles of the Constitution of independent India [Article 45] emphatically stated in 1950 : *"The state shall endeavour to provide, within a period of 10 years from the commencement of the Constitution, for free and compulsory education for all children until they complete the age of 14 years."* The Kothari Commission in its report [1964-66] had also insisted that free and compulsory education should be provided as a matter of state policy for all the children below 14 years. The National Education Policy - 1968 in its resolution had also laid down that universalisation of primary education was the need of the hour. It also laid down the time limit [1988] for the introduction of such a policy. The 7th Five Year Plan extended this time limit to 1990.

***Emphasis Laid on Compulsory Primary Education by the National Policy on Education* 1986** : The National Policy on Education - 1986 which highlighted the importance of universalisation of primary education reiterated its resolve that *"by 1995 all children would be provided free and compulsory education up to 14 years of age."*

Importance of Primary Education

The Government of India by resolving and repeatedly reiterating its resolve to provide elementary education to all the children below 14 years free of cost, has implicitly recognised the *"public good"* of the nature of primary education. All educationists, social reformers, statesmen with farsightedness have stressed upon the importance of primary education especially in the underdeveloped and the developing countries. The importance of primary education can be briefly examined here :

(i) The contribution of primary education to all the spheres of development – social, economic, industrial, agricultural, commercial, scientific, etc. – is significant. In fact, *it provides the general basis for the overall development of the society.*

(ii) *Primary education has its own intrinsic value,* it enhances human capabilities to enjoy life, instils better habits in the individual, and develops in him a new approach to life so that he can improve the quality of his life.

(iii) Primary education is a significant component of human capital. *It is an essential instrument of economic development at personal level* for it enhances the productivity of labour force in the labour market. Studies have revealed that labour force with primary education, more than doubles its earnings in comparison with the illiterates. It has also been estimated that primary education enhances individual earnings at least by 20%.

(iv) *Primary education has also several non-monetary benefits.* It changes the habits of the people, makes them ready for changes, prepares them to accept challenges, and equips them to adopt new methods of farm / industrial practices of production.

(v) The World Bank in its 1993 report stated that *"On the national economic front, primary education is found to contribute to miracles in transforming nations from poor underdeveloped societies to rapidly developing or industrialised tigers."*

(vi) *In the developing countries, primary school education is enabling the whole population to do things they would never have been able to do before.* Literacy helps them to read labels on cans, bottles, tins, to read signboards, newspapers, birth control leaflets, small booklets containing information about new crops, new ways of cultivation, etc., and also to move around the strange town or city independently. These events though look very simple, definitely lead to changes.

(vii) *Primary education is also found to contribute towards the improvement of health.* People are able to understand the need for maintaining good health and seek modern medical advice whenever the health is upset. The awareness of health has led to an improvement in the rates of child survival and life expectancy.

(viii) *Primary education is a big boon for women.* It has elevated their status and made them to play a responsible role at home. They have realised the importance of family planning measures and hence insist on their menfolk to have small family.

(ix) *Primary education contributes to reduction of fertility rates* by indirectly increasing the rate of participation of women in labour force. It has created awareness among men and women regarding the minimum age for marriage. It makes them to adopt better approaches to family planning and development and thereby reduces population growth.

(x) Primary education *is of tremendous importance in the process of socialisation of young children.* It helps the parents to resort to modern approaches to bring up the children.

(xi) Universal primary education is of great importance in yet another manner. *Universal access to education can reduce class, caste and social status barriers to individual advancement.* It can help to equalise earned incomes by educating people and leading to the mobility of people from one status to another, and from one area to another.

(xii) *Primary education creates political awareness among people and helps them to take a greater participation in the political process.* This helps wider distribution of power and enables people to develop greater tolerance towards others.

(xiii) Primary education in general, *helps people in their effective participation in social, cultural, political and economic spheres of development.*

Problems of Universalisation of Primary Education

To attain 100% literacy, it becomes mandatory for any nation to introduce the policy of universalisation in a strict manner. This is not an easy task for the underdeveloped and the poor countries. The experience of the developing nations like India, is also not very much different from it. In spite of Governmental insistence on the compulsory introduction of elementary education, it has not been successful in its efforts. In 1970-71, there were as many as **4.8 lakh** primary schools in the country in which around 57 million students [76.4%] were admitted. The number of schools increased to **5.7 lakhs** in 1991, and the number of students admitted in them also increased to 108.2 million. Still it was not 100%. The percentage of enrolment at the primary stage had gone up to 92.14% in 1998-99 and around 31.80 lakh teachers were teaching in primary and upper-primary schools.[1]

1 *Source* : *Manorama Year Book 2000.*

Various problems come in the way of effectively implementing the policy of universalisation of primary education. The main problems are : (i) *shortage of budgetary allotment,* (ii) *shortage of essential facilities in schools,* (iii) *problem of admission of students,* (iv) *problem of drop-outs.*

1. Shortage of Budgetary Allotment

In an over-populated country like India, providing for educational facilities for the children of educable age, is a very expensive task. It requires huge fund, judged purely from the economic point of view, money that is spent on education, is unproductive for it yields no immediate results. Only in the long-run it fetches immense wealth. The Government which was more interested in immediate returns, naturally showed its indifference towards education. This is reflected in the poor budgetary allotment it made towards education. In comparison with countries, for example, India spent just 3.6% of its total annual budget on education in the year 1981, whereas during the same year America spent 19.9%, Japan 19.6%, France 17.8%, Canada 17.3%, Russia 11.2% of their respective annual budgets. More details are given in ***Table*** - 4.

Table - 4

Percentage of Budget Spent on Education [1981] in Some Selected Cities

	Country	*Budget Spent on Education*	*Literacy*
1.	U.S.S.R.	11.2	98.5
2.	U.S.A.	19.9	99.5
3.	Japan	19.6	99.0
4.	England	13.9	99.0
5.	France	17.8	97.0
6.	Australia	14.8	98.5
7.	Canada	17.3	99.0
8.	Germany	10.1	99.0
9.	India	3.6	36.2
10.	Pakistan	2.1	20.7
11.	Bangla Desh	2.1	25.8
12.	Sri Lanka	3.5	86.5
13.	Burma	1.6	65.9
14.	Nepal	3.0	23.3
15.	Bhutan	1.9	18.0
16.	Singapore	N.A.	84.2
17.	Egypt	5.5	68.6

Source : Myron Weiner [1991], *The Child and the State in India,* Princeton University Press, p. 159, and *Frontline,* April 27 - May 10, 1991, p. 55.

It is clear from the above, that the attainment of the goal of universal elementary education seems to be very difficult with this meagre fund being spent on education.

2. Shortage of Essential Facilities in Schools

The population in India is increasing at a fast rate and we have not been able to provide for the educational facilities for all the people newly born. Thousands of villages in India do not have schools. The existing schools do not have good buildings, proper blackboards, chalk-pieces, furniture, toilet facility, playground, library, drinking water facility, etc. Only a few schools have permanent buildings. Many do not have any permanent structure. Hence classes are held in temporary tents, open fields, under the shades of trees, in huts, in the corridors of some temples, etc. As the NEP document [1985] itself pointed out *"Forty per cent have no pucca buildings, 39.72% have no blackboards, and 59.30% have no drinking water. 35% schools have a single teacher to teach three or four different classes."* [Page - 35][1]

Example of Karnataka* : *"Dr. M. Nanjundappa Commission" in its survey report [2002-2003], has stated that out of 983 *Primary Schools* [1st to 5th standards], which it surveyed on a random basis, 817 schools [83%] do not have electricity supply; 857 schools [87%] do not have toilet facility; 692 schools [70%] do not possess even drinking water facility and 622 schools [63%] do not provide playground facility for their children. Same story repeats in the case of *Higher Primary Schools.* Of the 1510 schools surveyed, 651 schools [43%] do not have electricity; 741 schools [49%] do not possess drinking water facility; 935 [62%] do not have toilet; and 666 schools do not have sufficient space for their students to sit comfortably in the class-rooms.

Educational surveys conducted in various States have also revealed that in most of the States there is a great dearth of school teachers. There are schools in which there are no teachers. There are a number of single-teacher schools in which one person is forced to handle four / five classes in spite of the relatively good strength of the students. Many teachers are not ready to go to rural areas for service. Even if they are forced to go and serve them, they do not go to the schools and take classes regularly. Lack of service-mindedness and commitment to the cause of teaching on the part of the teachers has also added to the indifference of the children towards joining to schools for education.

3. Problem of Admission of Students

It is true that over the years education is becoming more and more popular. For example, the number of pre-primary schools has gone up during the period from 1961 to 1998 by about 21 times [from 1909 to 40553]. During the same period, the strength of primary schools has almost doubled [from 3.3 lakhs to 6.107 lakhs]; of the middle / senior schools, it increased by 3.5 times [from 49663 to 1.85 lakhs] of higher secondary schools by about 6 times [from 17,257 to 107,200 and so on].

This increase in the number of the student strength does not assure that all the children of the school-going age are going to schools. Children belonging to SCs, STs and poor sections, especially in the rural areas are not going to schools in an expected number. In rural areas of the States such as Assam, M.P., Orissa, Bihar, Rajasthan, and U.P. the rate of admission of children of school-going age was less than 80% in 1982-83. On an average in 1984-85 at the all-India level the admission of male children to school was around 90% and the percentage of female children was 66.2. The atmosphere of admitting children compulsorily to schools as soon as they attain the age of eligibility [that is, 5 year 10 months], is not there in many States. Attempts to motivate the parents to send their children to schools have not been completely successful in many places and in many States.

4. The Problem of Drop-out of Children

In many States the number of schools and the number of students, both have increased tremendously. At the same time, our attempts to make the children studying without discontinuing or dropping out, have not been successful. A very high number of students drops-out of the schools in the middle of their studies for reasons of their own. Available statistics show that the percentage of such drop-outs was as high as 38% to 41% in 1996. According to the *Human Resources Development Ministry,* in 1997-98, around 38.23% of the boys and 41.34% of girls left the school system before reaching the 5th standard. By the time, the remaining children reach the stage of 8th Standard more than half [54.14%] drop out. Of these drop-outs, 50.72% are boys and 58.61% are girls.[2] Different

1 NEP document as quoted by N. Jayaram. Page - 217.
2 As quoted by Ram Ahuja in *"Society in India."* Page - 222.

States have designed different schemes to reduce considerably the number of school drop-outs. *For example,* Karnataka Government is giving textbooks, uniforms, umbrella, etc. free of cost to the needy students. In Government Schools and Government aided Schools. Children were also given freely 5-to-6 KGs of rice every month as incentive if they maintain the required minimum attendance at school. The Government now [from 2003] started providing mid-day meal to all the children in the Government schools. In spite of such attractive schemes on the part of the States, 100% success has not been attained.

5. Other Problems

(i) *Negligence of Primary Education* : Financial constraint is not the sole justification for poor performance though this is often highlighted for poor literacy performance. Many countries such as Burma, China, Sri Lanka, Indonesia have achieved better literacy and primary education levels with lower percentage of GNP spent on education. The difference is that these countries spared large portions of their education budgets on primary education while in India it is primary education that is neglected and higher education is given prominence. Only during the recent years, say after 1990s, much attention is paid towards primary education.

(ii) *Prevalence of Child Labour* : In spite of the legislations [*The Child Labour (Prohibition and Prevention) Act*] against the practice of child labour, it still persists. According to 1991 census, the total number of working children in the country is 11.28 million.[1] Prevalence of child labour is found to be one of the strong causes of either non-admission to schools, or school drop-outs. According to one estimate, about 25% of the children in the age group 6-11, and around 70% of the children in the age group 12-14; are not either enrolled in the schools or drop out of them, for they are compelled to work for improving the economic position of the family. Various survey reports too have revealed that more than 50% of the boys and around 40% of the girls drop out of schools due to the economic pressures and the domestic drudgeries.

(iii) *Lack of Active Participation of the Community* : Universalisation of primary education necessarily demands the active participation of the whole community in it. Local people, voluntary organisations, government servants, school teachers all must work with a community spirit to see that all children of school-going age get admitted to school and continue their education without dropping it in the middle. Unfortunately, such a community spirit is lacking in India.

Educational Problems of the Disadvantaged Groups

Though independent Indian Government has made it a policy to extend educational opportunities to all the citizens of India without making any discrimination on the ground of sex, class, caste, colour, religion, region, and so on. It does not mean all the groups and all the sections have been able to avail of this facility equally. Some sections have gone too far educationally while others are very much lagging behind. *Education of women and Scheduled Caste / Tribe people has been neglected in India since a long time.* In fact, these two groups [women and SC and ST people] can be regarded as educationally disadvantaged groups.

A. Educational Problems of Women

1. *Poor Literacy Level of Women* : The literacy level of women is comparatively very low. In 1901, their literacy level was just 0.6%, it increased to 10% in 1951, 29.75% in 1981, 39.29% in 1991 and to 54% in 2001. In states like Bihar, M.P., U.P. and Rajasthan female literacy rate is found to be very low even in 2001. The literacy rate of females among the SCs in India was 23.76%, and that of the females of the STs was 18.19% in 1999.

---

1 *Ref*: *India Book of the Year 2002 Encyclopaedia Britannica and The Hindu.* Page - 307.

2. *Increasing Drop-out of Female Children* : Increasing drop-out of children from schools is another problem. Though female children are getting admitted to primary, middle and high schools in a substantial number, many of them drop out of the school in the middle without completing the course. *For example,* as per the data furnished by the Ministry of Education [New Delhi], in 1984-85 the number of female children enrolled at primary school crossed the figure of 34.2 millions, and at middle school level the enrolment crossed 9.2 millions. More than 74% of these female children, between the age-groups of 6 and 14 years, quit schools and lapsed into ignorance.

3. *Admission to School* : Even in the matter of admitting children to school at elementary level, female children are discriminated against male children. *For example,* in 1984-85, the admission of male children to school was around 90%, the percentage of female children was only 66.2. It means complete awareness is not there among people regarding female education.

4. *Majority of Employed Women are Also Illiterate* : It was found that in 1991, of every 100 women employed, 52.59% of them were illiterate and 28.56% of them had studied only up to elementary level. Of every 100 women working in the rural areas, 88.11% were illiterate. These illiterate women in the unorganised sector were totally exploited by their employers. Women working in factories, mining industries, building construction process, in dams, bridges and road repair or construction work were not only paid less but also made to work in unhealthy surroundings.

• Causes For the Low Educational Status of Women

1. *Neglect of Female Education Due to Gender Inequality* : Ever since the days of Medieval Period, female education has been totally neglected in India. Foreign rulers never took any interest in female education. Even after independence things did not improve immediately. "Girls are neglected since their birth or even before due to our patriarchal society that prefers sons. *"Girls are withdrawn from education once they attain puberty due to the conservative cultural values of the parents and society. Girls' education is cut short by early marriage."*

2. *Imposition of Domestic Responsibilities on Girls* : Unlike the boys, girls are made to assume domestic responsibility from an early age. They are expected to do domestic work in order to make free their mothers to go out of home for undertaking economically rewarding activities. At home, *"Girls not only sweep, wash, collect water, fuel, fodder, mind younger siblings and animals, but also work in the fields and help their mothers in beedi-rolling, gem-polishing, or any other home-based piece rate work they may be engaged in." Girls belonging to poor class are also made to work in the houses of the well-to-do people as "domestic servants."*

3. *Lack of Educational Facilities Especially in the Rural Areas* : For a very long time we were not able to provide educational services to the remote places in the village areas. Parents of female children were reluctant to send their children to far away places for educational purposes. Acute shortage of women teachers working in rural areas also prevented parents from sending their daughters to the schools where there were no female teachers. Though things have improved much, even today female children in the rural areas have greater problems than the male-children. For example, they have hesitation to go to co-education schools. Hostel facilities for girls are not available in the rural areas. Schools exclusively meant for girls are very meagre in the rural areas and so on.

4. *Historical and Traditional Factors* : For centuries together female education in this land was neglected and hence *tradition-bound people came to believe that the education of women is unworthy of any serious consideration.* Since most of the mothers themselves were uneducated they never felt the need for getting education to their female children. In the beginning of the 20th century, that is, in 1901 hardly 6 women out of 1000 were literate. As per 2001 figures, more than 46% of women remain illiterate in India. It is not easy to inspire them to take up the responsibility of giving education to their children, particularly, female children.

• Strategies, Measures and Schemes to Improve Girls' / Women's Participation in Education

Of late educationists and administrators are very much concerned about improving the educational status of women. Hence, various strategies have been suggested to overcome the problem of low educational status of girls, particularly in the rural areas. Specific steps taken in this direction may be mentioned below.

1. The Government launched the *"Operation Blackboard"* scheme in 1987-88 under which it intended to create one lakh posts of primary school teachers mainly to be filled by women. By 1992, 75000 posts were filled in, out of which 45000 [60%] posts were filled in by women teachers.
2. Under *the rural literacy programmes,* illiterate adult women were enrolled in a large number. Their enrolment was about 55% in 1995.
3. Special attention is given to *enrolment of women in adult education centres.*
4. In *Navodaya Vidyalaya* also a minimum of 28% admission of girls is ensured.
5. A new attempt was made to mobilise rural women for education through the *"Mahila Sanghas."* This project called *"Education for Women's Equality"* [*"Mahila Samaikhya"*] was launched in 1989 and the entire expenses of this project are to be borne by the Government of Netherlands. U.P., Gujarat and Karnataka have availed of the assistance for this project.
6. Various incentives and special concessions such as freeships, scholarships, free boarding and lodging facilities have also been provided for the girl students who are in absolute need of them.

7. *Other Measures and Strategies* : Various economic measures are also undertaken to reduce poverty and generate employment opportunities so that for economic reasons girls' education is not neglected. Attention is also paid to provide more primary and secondary schools in remote areas; recruit a larger number of female teachers for schools in rural areas; to make school-timings more flexible so as to enable rural girls to attend schools without neglecting their domestic responsibilities. Direct incentives such as scholarships, stipends, freeships, free supply of library books, mid-day meal, etc., are also offered to make it more attractive for the parents to send girls to schools.

B. Educational Problems of the Backward Classes [OBCs], the Scheduled Castes [SCs] and the Scheduled Tribes [STs]

It is well known that the poor and the under-privileged sections of the Indian society including the OBCs, SCs and STs are lagging behind in education. It is reflected in the literacy level achieved by these sections. For example, the average literacy rate for the general population in India, according to 1991 census, was 52.21% whereas it was 37.41% [that is, 15% less than the average] in the case of SCs and only 29.60% [that is, 23% less than the average] in the case of the STs. The state-wise position of the literacy level of the SCs is the highest in Kerala [79.66%, that is, very much above the national average] and lowest in Bihar, that is, 19.49%. In the case of the STs also, highest literacy rate is found in Kerala, that is, 57.22%, whereas the lowest rate is observed in Andhra, that is, 17.16%.[1]

• Measures Recommended to Improve the Educational Status of SCs and STs

Even during the British rule under the leadership of Gandhiji a programme for social, educational and economic improvement of the SCs, STs and backward classes had been taken up as early as in 1937 when the popular Ministries came to be established in the Provinces in British India.

1 *Source* : *Manpower Profile, India* 42-43, as quoted by Prof. Ram Ahuja in *"Society in India."* Page - 235.

Independent Indian Government took up various measures to continue the Programme by adding to it several other dimensions as an attempt to pursue and put into practice some of the relevant provisions of the Constitution.

The Central Advisory Board of Education [CABE] as early as in 1976 recommended certain measures to improve the educational status of the SCs, STs and OBCs. Some of them are as follows :

1. Special care should be taken *to implement the programme of universalisation of elementary education in some selected areas* where the level of literacy or SCs, STs and OBCs, has been found to be very poor.
2. *Different types of programmes are necessary to popularise literacy improvement activities* for the SCs, STs and OBCs do not represent one single homogeneous community.
3. Wherever educational institutions are not found, especially in tribal areas, *a network of educational institutions in the form of Ashrama Schools or residential schools, single-teacher schools, free hostels,* etc. are to be established.

• Measures Adopted to Extend Opportunities for the Educational Development of SCs and STs

Due attention is paid to extend the educational opportunities of SCs and STs and hence special provisions have been made in this regard. Providing free education, free distribution of books, stationery, uniform etc.; giving scholarships, bank loan facilities, providing mid-day meal, arranging for free boarding and lodging facilities, reserving seats for SCs and STs in all the government and government aided institutions, etc., are some of the concrete steps which the Government has taken in this regard.

In addition to the above, there are some centrally sponsored schemes also for the educational benefit of both SCs and STs. The Central Government sponsored the following schemes to facilitate the educational improvement of SCs and STs :– (i) *Free coaching and training for these candidates to appear for the competitive examinations*; (ii) *book-bank scheme*; (iii) *post-matric scholarships for providing financial assistance for higher education*; (iv) *construction of hostels*; (v) *financial assistance to do research work*; (vi) *supply of text books free of cost*; and (vi) *national overseas scholarships and passage grants for higher education.* [*Note* : For more details please refer to *Chapter No.9 - Scheduled Castes.*]

• Recommendations of National Policy on Education [NEP], 1986

The NEP - 1986 recommended certain measures to be undertaken to improve the educational status of the SCs and STs. Some of them are mentioned below :

(i) Giving special incentives to SC families to send their children to the schools at least up to 14th year;

(ii) Maintaining a proper record relating to the enrolment of SC and ST children, and their attendance in schools and their performance in the examinations;

(iii) Pre-matric scholarship scheme for children of families engaged in low occupations such as scavenging, sweeping, curing hides, tanning, oil-grinding, shoe making, etc.;

(iv) Appointing teachers from the category of SCs and STs;

(v) Providing for as many hostel facilities as possible;

(vi) Encouraging educated tribals to take up teaching in tribal areas;

(vii) Establishing educational institutions in the remote places like hilly areas, mountainous forest areas;

(viii) Designing instructional materials in tribal languages at least at the initial stages.

Deficiencies Involved in These Educational Programmes

In spite of the special measures undertaken to improve the educational position of the SCs, STs and OBCs, expected results have not come. Because, the measures themselves are not free from defects. Some such deficiencies can be listed here : (i) reservation rules and their implementation are defective; (ii) scholarships, stipends, hostel facilities that are given are inadequate; (iii) the rate of drop-out of children of these three communities is still very high; (iv) teachers appointed in the remote areas are not attending to their duties regularly and in a responsible manner; (v) cultural gap in the case of the tribal children is not yet effectively bridged; (vi) medium of instruction, that is, regional language often creates problems for the tribal children; (vii) proper awareness is not created among the SCs and STs regarding the importance of education.

PROGRESS OF EDUCATION IN INDIA

Education system in India has a prolonged history of its own. As it has already been referred to, education was given very high importance during the ancient period. Even during the medieval period elementary education was very popular, for the community itself had taken up the cause of education. But at the end of the medieval period and in the beginning of the British period, education reached its lowest ebb. The British with their own imperialistic motives introduced some educational measures mainly to produce an army of English knowing clerks to run the British bureaucracy in India.

Though not in tune with the actual demand, education has been given due importance after independence. The Directive Principles of the State Policy of the Constitution of India strongly recommended universalisation of primary education. In the Five Year Plans also some serious interest was shown towards the progress of education. The progress of education in India started with a low profile almost up to 1970s, and afterwards it took a little greater speed. By the end of the year 2000, the literacy rate in India went up considerably [65.38%] and the number of educational institutions increased substantially catering to the educational needs of millions of students.

A Brief Mention of Educational Institutions in India

India's modern education system which is as old as almost 140 years has made a tremendous headway nowadays. In 1857, there were only 3 Universities – Calcutta, Madras and Bombay – under the British rule. At present the number of schools, colleges, universities, technical and research institutes has increased considerably. The following statistics gives us an idea of the tremendous increase in the number of educational institutions in India.[1]

India at present has —

- *242 Universities and equivalent institutions.* These include the following -
  - 146 General Universities
  - 18 Science and Technology Universities
  - 5 Women Universities
  - 8 Open Universities
  - 30 Agricultural Universities
  - 17 Medical Universities
  - 18 Language Universities
  - 16 Central Universities
  - 40 Deemed Universities
  - 169 State Universities, and

1 *Source of Statistics and Information* : *Manorama Year Book* 2002.

- 11 Institutes of National Importance
- *11,089 Colleges,* which include
  - 1,260 Women Colleges, and
  - 119 Autonomous Colleges
- 7,000 Education / Training Colleges
- 600 Management Institutes
- 550 Engineering and Technology Colleges
- 1100 Polytechnic Institutes
- 170 Medical Colleges

We find in our educational institutions a large army of students. Enrolled strength of students in higher education is around 7.418 million and the teachers number about 0.342 million. As many as 74,000 have been enrolled for research and nearly 10,000 are awarded Ph.D. every year.

Elementary Education

There is a substantial increase in the number of students studying in the primary institutions today. The enrolment ratio, for example, at the primary stage has gone up from 42.60% [1950-51] to 92.14% [1998-99]. The number of primary and upper primary schools has gone up from 2.23 lakh [1950-51] to 8.17 lakh [1998-99], and the number of teachers in primary and upper primary schools is around 31.80 lakhs in 1998-99. The National Policy on Education envisages that free and compulsory education of satisfactory quality should be provided to all the children up to the age of 14 years before the beginning of the 21st century. As a result today, 94% of the rural population have been provided with primary schools within one kilometre and 84% have upper primary schools within 3 Kms.

Non-Formal Education [NFE] : In addition to the formal educational centres as mentioned above, there are as many as 2.97 lakh NFE centres that have the sanction of the government and cater to as many as 74.25 lakh children. Of these NFE centres, about 1.17 lakh centres are exclusively for girl students. About 58,788 centres are being run by 816 voluntary agencies.

Secondary Education

Secondary education caters to the needs of the students of age between 14 to 18 years. It serves as a bridge between elementary and higher education. In 1999, there were 1.10 lakh secondary and senior secondary institutions, 272 lakhs enrolment, 101 lakh enrolment of girls and 15.42 lakh teachers.

Multifarious Institutional Establishments for Promoting the Cause of Education

In order to promote the cause of education a large number of institutions have been established by the government a glimpse of which is given below.

1. NCERT [*National Council of Educational Research and Training*] : This institution established on Sept. 1, 1961 has the objective of assisting and advising the *Ministry of Education and Culture* in implementing policies and major programmes in the field of education, particularly school education. Among other activities, the Council takes up the task of revision of secondary level syllabi and textbooks in association with the *Central Board of Secondary Education* [CBSE].

2. NTSS [*National Talent Search Scheme*] : The NTSS is a part of NCERT. The NCERT through its NTSS, awards about 1,000 scholarships including 775 for general category, 150 scholarships for SC and 75 for ST candidates each year. The main purpose of the scheme is to identify brilliant students at the end of Xth standard and give them financial assistance towards getting good education.

3. *Teacher Education* : As envisaged in the *National Policy on Education* [NPE] and *Programme Of Action* [POA] - 1986, a scheme provides for continuous upgradation of knowledge and competence and skill of the teachers. More than 12 lakh teachers have been given orientation training under this scheme.

NCTE [*National Council for Teacher Education*] : This institute established in 1995 aims to achieve planned and co-ordinated development of teacher education system. There are 4 *Regional Colleges of Education* under NCTE at – Ajmer, Bhuvaneshwar, Bhopal, and Mysore. Yet another namely, the North-Eastern Regional Institute was established at Shillong in 1996-97 for the same purpose.

4. CBSE [*Central Board of Secondary Education*] : *The Board of High School and Intermediate Education* which had been functioning ever since 1929, assumed the present name of CBSE in 1952 by a Resolution of the Government of India. At present, the schools affiliated to this Board are located in all parts of the country and even abroad. The schools affiliated to CBSE are expected to provide uniform school education cutting across State borders and linguistic areas. This institution is expected to promote national integration through interstate mobility of students besides helping children of transferable persons to continue their education uninterrupted.

5. COBSE [*Council of Boards of School Education in India*] : The COBSE is a voluntary association of all the Boards of Secondary Education. It gives academic assistance to its member Boards on – setting and maintenance of educational standards, planning of curriculum, preparing curriculum materials, evaluation in schools and public examinations. The COBSE works in association with the Ministry of Human Resources Development, NCERT, and NCTE.

6. *Kendriya Vidyalayas* [KVs] *or Central Schools* : The Govt. of India approved the scheme of Central Schools or Kendriya Vidyalayas in Nov. 1962. The scheme started by the take over of 20 regimental schools during 1963-64. Subsequently, Kendriya Vidyalaya Sanghatan was set up as an autonomous organisation to establish and run the Kendriya Vidyalayas. There are 874 such Vidyalayas in the country catering to 7.5 lakh students [1999]. Two units of the KVs are opened abroad, one in Kathmandu and another in Moscow.

7. *Navodaya Vidyalayas* [NVs] : There are at present 423 Navodaya Vidyalayas covering 30 States / UTs with over 12.7 lakh students. These institutions are residential and co-educational and are primarily for children from rural areas. About 25,000 new students are admitted every year. At least 1/3 seats are reserved for girls. Admission seats for children from urban areas is restricted to 25%. The Navodaya Vidyalayas aim to provide free education upto +2 level to the talented children. It intends to develop in the children their full potentialities and to promote national integration. These institutes are affiliated to CBSE.

8. NOS [*National Open School*] : Autonomous educational organisation such as the NOS was set up in 1989. Its primary purposes are to provide quality education to the children who are either school dropouts or those who cannot attend formal schools. This school is given the power to examine and certify students registered with it upto the pre-degree level. The certificates issued by the school have got official recognition. The students have the freedom to select the set of subjects depending upon their requirement. In 1998, admission to the various courses of NOS reached an all time record of 0.3 million. This institute conducts examination twice a year [May and November]. As a matter of its admission policy, it gives preference to the marginalised groups.

9. *Universities* : Under an Act of the Parliament, the Government established the University Grants Commission [UGC] to coordinate and determine the standards in the universities. The UGC has powers to allocate and disburse grants to universities for their maintenance and development.

- *Central Universities* : The Central Government under Acts of the Parliament have established some national agencies for promotion and coordination of research efforts in specialised fields. They are – 1. *The Indian Council of Social Science Research*, 2. *The Indian Council of Historical Research*, 3. *The Indian Council of Philosophical Research*, and 4. *The Indian Institute of Advanced Studies.*

• *The main Central Universities are as follows* : 1. Aligarh Muslim University, Aligarh; 2. University of Delhi, Delhi; 3. Jamia Milia Islamia, Delhi; 4. University of Hyderabad, Hyderabad; 5. Jawaharlal Nehru University, New Delhi; 6. Indira Gandhi Open University, New Delhi; 7. North-Eastern Hill University, Shillong with campuses in Shillong, Mizoram and Nagaland; 8. Viswabharati, Santiniketan; 9. Benaras Hindu University, Varanasi; 10. Pondicherry University; 11. Assam University, Silchar; 12. Tezpur University, Tezpur; and 13. Nagaland University, Kohima.

10. I I Ts [*Indian Institute of Technology*] : There are now 7 Indian Institutes of Technology [at Kharagpur, Bombay, Chennai, Khanpur, Delhi, Guwahati and University of Roorkee] at the national level to provide adequate facilities for post-graduate studies and research especially in the field of engineering. These institutes conduct undergraduate as well as Master courses and Ph.D. programmes in different branches of Engineering, Science, Humanities and Social Sciences. The Indian Institute of Science [I.I.Sc.], Bangalore is a premier centre of education in engineering and applied sciences.

11. I I M [*Indian Institute of Management*] : The Government of India has established 6 Indian Institutes of Management at Ahmedabad, Calcutta, Bangalore, Lucknow, Indore, and Kozhikode [Kerala]. The primary objective of these institutes is to provide education, training, research and consultancy in Managerial Science.

12. *Regional Engineering Colleges* [RECs] : The Central Government in collaboration with the State Governments has set up Regional Engineering Colleges, one each in the major states. The country at present has 17 RECs. Of these, the KREC [Mangalore - Karnataka State] which is presently known as NITK [National Institute of Technology Karnataka] has assumed the status of a deemed university [technical]. The RECs provide facilities for Post Graduate and research courses [Ph.D. level]. Most of the RECs have now been raised to NITs.

13. *Correspondence Education* : Continuation of higher learning through correspondence has become quite popular in India. Facilities for correspondence education have been expanded since 1962 in 50 more universities offering a number of courses for as many as 5 lakh students all over the country.

• *Open Universities* : Continuation of education through correspondence is carried on through open universities. There are at present 9 open universities. 1. B.R. Ambedkar Open University, Hyderabad; 2. Kota Open University, Kota; 3. Nalanda Open University, Bihar; 4. Yashwant Rao Chavan Maharashtra Open University, Nasik; 5. Madhya Pradesh Bhoj Open University, Bhopal; 6. Ambedkar Open University, Ahmedabad; 7. Karnataka State Open University, Mysore; 8. Netaji Subhash Open University, Kolkata; and 9. Rajrishi Tandon Open University, Allahabad.

• IGNOU [*Indira Gandhi National Open University*] : The recently launched and offering the most sophisticated teaching method in distance education is the IGNOU. Through a separate satellite channel, it offers facility for clearing the doubts instantly by using a hot-line attached to the Delhi centre. This university through its 50 programmes has so far provided 604 courses. MBA is the most popular course sought after. During the year 2000, over 1.96 lakh students have registered for various programmes of study. It has established its network with 26 regional centres [at state levels] and 504 study centres across the country.

14. *Adult Education* : The purpose of adult education programme is to make 100 million people in the age group of 15-35 totally literate by 2005. Since the inception of National Literacy Mission [in 1988], 556 districts have been covered and 57.96 million persons have been made

literate under adult education scheme. Around 60% of the learners under this scheme are found to be women, over 22% are SCs and over 13% STs.

15. ***Scientific Institutions*** : The Govt. of India has been providing due encouragement for the progress of science. The world of Indian science is dominated by 3 academies. 1. *Indian National Science Academy,* Delhi, 2. *Indian Academy of Science,* Bangalore, and 3. *National Academy of Sciences India,* Allahabad.

EDUCATION AND SOCIAL STRATIFICATION

Education - As a Criterion of Social Stratification

In technologically advanced countries education has become the most important criterion of social stratification. In such societies occupation is the determinant of income. It is also found that recruitment to various occupations in these societies is determined by the educational levels of individuals.

Education - As a Determinant of Social Placement and Social Stratification

In the technologically advanced countries normally the status gradation is defined by the occupational and educational levels. "*Briefly, in view of the close relationship between education and occupation, and to the extent that occupation is an important if not the only avenue for income and social status, education acquires significance as a determinant of social placement and social stratification.*"[1]

It is noticeable that in the industrial societies the most prestigious jobs tend to be not only those that yield the highest incomes but also the ones that require the longest education. The more education people have, the more likely they are to obtain good jobs and to enjoy high incomes.

The Complex Relationship Between Education and Social Stratification

Though education acts as a generator of upward mobility it does not invariably do that. Empirical evidences suggest that in the reciprocal relationship between education and social stratification it is stratification that affects education primarily. This effect is greater than the effect of education on stratification.

In many societies the facilities for education leading to higher levels of occupations and professions like medicine, engineering, management, etc., are limited. But the number of aspirants to make use of such facilities is very high. Since the cost of higher education is very high and several constraints govern admission to such educational courses, only a select section of the society can manage to enter such courses. This section is normally the privileged section of the society, which occupies a top position in the stratification system. Such a system of higher education with all its constraints etc., is often defended *on meritocratic grounds. Thus education instead of being a generator of upward social mobility is forced to function as an agency of stratification to function as an agency of "status retention."*[2]

Social Stratification Affecting Lower Levels of Education : Social Stratification affects lower levels of education especially in the rural areas. In many of the developing countries wastage and stagnation in school education is found to be very high. This problem seems to exist even in the advanced countries to a certain extent. It is found that generally students belonging to the lower stratum background drop out of the school in a large number. Even though education is provided free and additional incentives are given, the situation does not seem to improve much.

---

1 N. Jayaram *"Sociology of Education in India"* (1990) Rawat Publications, Delhi - Page – 42.
2 *ibid* Page – 43.

It is clear from the above that *the relationship between education and social stratification is more complex than what it appears to be.* It is true that education has enough potentiality for changing the system of stratification. But this potentiality itself seems to be governed by the existing system of stratification.

In conclusion, it can be said that *from the point of view of an educational system those who are already at the upper strata of the society are likely to gain more.* They have higher achievement motivation and their environment helps them. If we wish to provide equality of educational opportunities we will have to keep this aspect in mind.

EDUCATION AND SOCIAL MOBILITY

Education as a Promoter of Upward Mobility

In the context of urban-industrial society education functions as a promoter of upward social mobility. In such societies occupation is the principal channel of social mobility. Occupations that help social mobility require certain educational qualifications. It is in this context education acquires significance as a promoter of upward social mobility. Sociologist Reid Writes : "*The functions of the educational system are to provide people with the qualification and aspirations to meet society's occupational needs. Built into the system is that assumptions that people will or should want to be upwardly mobile. Underlying such reasoning is, then, the belief that social mobility is a desirable characteristic of that society and that the educational system exists to promote and facilitate it*" - [Quoted by N. Jayaram - Page : 121.]

Peter Blau and Otis Duncan (1967), in their study of social mobility in America, found that the important factor affecting whether a son moved to a higher social status than his father's was the amount of education the son received. *A high level of education is a scarce and valued resource,* and one for which people compete vigorously.

Due to the increased awareness regarding the importance of college-level education, large number of persons are trying to avail of the same to increase their social standing. As a result, the number of new college graduates is now far greater than the number of "*college-level*" jobs available to them. Hence, in India, we find a large army of educated unemployed people. "*In fact, it has been calculated that only 15% of the increase in educational requirements for jobs during the course of this century can be attributed to the replacement of low-skill jobs by new jobs requiring greater expertise* [Collins - 1971]". What has *actually happened is that the "educational threshold" has risen : people need higher qualifications to get jobs that previously required much lower educational credentials*"[1]

Lack of Educational Qualification Restricts Social Mobility

In developed nations people want to attain higher level of education to equip themselves to obtain more prestigious jobs. What is observed is that people want to receive extra years of education even if it is not necessary for some of the jobs or occupations that they are seeking for. There is evidence that *educational achievement has no consistent relationship to later job performance and productivity*. What is significant, however, is that the *lack of educational qualifications restricts social mobility of those people, who for one reason or another, have been unable to obtain them.*

Education as a Solvent of Inequalities - ?

Education serves as a solvent of inequalities to certain extent especially in societies where the traditional systems of stratification did not permit large scale social mobility. Here the introduction of formal education [as was done by the British in India] gave an opportunity for people who were

1 Ian Robertson - Page 354.

hitherto confined to lower or intermediary statuses in the traditional system of stratification [say, caste] to try for attaining a higher status in the changed situation. That is what the scheduled caste and the scheduled tribe people and the people belonging to the backward classes have done and are doing in India now. Thus, *education under conditions has the potentiality of radically altering the previous system of stratification.* Thus, education has often been hailed as a solvent of inequalities.

Education and Internal and External Constraints on Mobility

There are a number of factors which impede mobility of the individuals in a social structure. They are referred to here as *constraints on mobility.* These constraints may be internal or external. The internal constraints are *values, aspirations and personality patterns of the individuals.* The external constraints are the *opportunity structure of a society* with which the individual is influenced.

(i) *System of Beliefs and Values* : The major constraint in the upward mobility is a system of beliefs and values prevailing in social structure. **H.H. Hyman** in his study[1] regarding - class differences in educational values, motivations for economic advancement and perceptions of the opportunity structure - found that the lower socio-economic groups place less emphasis upon college education as necessary for advancement, and are less likely to desire college education for their children. This holds true in the Indian situation also.

Further, *opportunities for education to the lower classes are very limited, particularly in the rural areas.* Thus the prevalent value system governs their aspirations and actions. Hence they may lag behind the upper classes in this regard.

(ii) *Family Influcnce* : Upward mobility is also restricted due to the family influences. In a study made by **Stephenson**[2] it was found that both occupational plans and aspirations are positively associated with the prestige ranking of father's occupation. If the family itself lacks initiative it is reflected in the child's desire for not moving out of the family bonds. The child develops a tendency to take up a job which the parent wants him to take up in his hierarchical set up. The child also does not show much interest in education because the parents are least concerned about it. This influence is very much visible in joint families in India.

(iii) *Factors in Individual Personality* : Individual's personality structure may also contribute to his immobility. It has been found in a number of studies that achievement motivation, intelligence, aspirations and values are related with mobility. In one study[3] it was found that I.Q. [Intelligent Quotient] plays an important role in the school performance in the early years of an individual's life. But as the person grows older he begins to shape his performance according to certain values that he learns from his family and friends. Here desire to go to the college is taken as an aspect of mobility. One who performs well is expected to go to college and thus is mobile in upward direction.

In the above mentioned study it was found that upper - status boys learn that good performance in school is necessary, and that they are expected to do well enough in secondary school to get admitted to college. On the other hand, a boy from a lower status home is taught that college is either not meant for him or at best a matter of indifference to his parents. The boy's friends are not interested in college nor in high school. Consequently, even a bright boy among them gets discouraged. This indifference towards studies spoils the prospects of many in the rural areas in India.

---

1 **H.H. Hyman's Study** : *"The Value System of Different Classes*: A social psychological contribution to the analysis of stratification".

2 **Richard M. Stephenson** : *"Mobility Orientation and Stratification* : *A Study of One Thousand Nineth Graders"* - Unpublished doctoral dissertation, Columbia University, New York - as quoted by **Dr. S.S. Mathur** in *"A Sociological Approach to Indian Education"* (1975) - Page : 260.

3 Study of **Joseph A. Kahl** : *"The American Class Structure"*, Holt, N.Y. 1960 – as quoted by **Dr. S.S. Mathur**. Page - 261.

Various findings have revealed that the strength of the achievement motive is clearly related to upward mobility. It seems that youth from upper strata of society may not need strong personal motivation for mobility. Such youth get good advice, they live in such environment where 'looking-up' is encouraged and where they are provided with wise decisions for setting up their careers. This is not the case of lower class youth. They have to learn a great deal to make these decisions.

Equality of Educational Opportunities

It is an accepted working policy of all the democratic nations to make provision for equal opportunities. As **Dr. Radhakrishnan** had pointed out long back *"Democracy only provides that all men should have equal opportunities for the development of their unequal talents".* The Indian Constitution also as per the articles 15, 16, 17, 38 and 48, guarantees that the State shall not discriminate between persons on account of their religion or region and caste or class. The Preamble of the Constitution also assures equality to all the citizens. It means that our constitution is committed to the principle of equality and accepted it as an article of faith.

It is in tune with this spirit of the constitution *the Education Commission* has observed thus: *"One of the important social objectives of education is to equalise opportunity, enabling the backward or underprivileged classes and individuals to use education as a lever for the improvement of their condition. Every society that values social justice and is anxious to improve the lot of the common man and cultivate all available talent, must ensure progressive equality of opportunity to all sections of the population. This is the only guarantee for the building up of an egalitarian and human society by which the exploitation of the weak will be minimised."*[1]

Need for Equalisation of Educational Opportunities

The equalisation of educational opportunities is essentially linked with the equality notions in the social system. The social system which intends to provide equal opportunities for the advancement of all has to make provision for equal educational opportunities also. The need for emphasising the equality of opportunity in the education arises for various reasons. They may be cited here.

1. Equality of educational opportunities is needed for the establishment of an egalitarian society based on social equality and justice ;
2. It contributes to the search for talents among all the people of a nation ;
3. It is essential to ensure rapid advancement of a nation ;
4. It is needed for the successful functioning of a democracy. Educated and enlightened people alone can ensure a meaningful democracy, and
5. It helps to develop a closer link between manpower needs of a society and the availability of the skilled personnel.

Role of Education in Equalising Opportunities

It is now widely held that provision for equality of education has become an absolute necessity for improving one's social status or standing. In modern society achieving merit and ability is possible only through education. Though education does not guarantee high status and high positions to all people, yet without education, an individual is unlikely to achieve social mobility.

---

1 *Report of the Education Commission, 1964-66. Govt. of India, Ministry of Education,* New Delhi - 1966 - as quoted by Dr.S.S. Mathur - Page : 267.

M.S. Gore is of the opinion that education plays the role in equalising opportunities in three important ways.[1] They are as follows :

(i) By creating opportunities which should be made available for all those who have the desire and the ability to be profited by it.

(ii) By preparing a content of education which endeavours to promote the development of scientific and pragmatic outlook.

(iii) By establishing a social environment based on religion, language, caste, class, etc. to provide equal opportunity to secure good education.

It is true that education is not the only channel to social mobility. At the same time, it is equally true that lack of education is bound to prove a great obstacle in mobility. Studies have revealed that the disadvantaged people in our society, that is, the SCs, STs, OBCs, women, and others have been exploited because of their illiteracy. At the same time, they have also revealed that education has proved to be an effective instrument of equality especially for the SCs, STs, OBCs and women.

Problems Concerning Equality of Opportunities in Education

Education is of great help in establishing equality and ensuring social justice no doubt. But the system of education itself can add to the existing inequalities, or at least perpetuate the same. This has been the major problem in providing equal educational opportunity for all. Inequalities of educational opportunities arise for the following reasons.

Causes for the Inequalities of Educational Opportunities

1. Inequalities of educational opportunity occurs due to the poverty of a large number of people. The poor cannot afford to meet the expenses of education ;
2. Children in rural areas studying in poorly equipped schools have to compete with the children in urban areas where there are well-equipped schools. The poor exposure of rural children may lead to their poor performance.
3. In the places where no primary, secondary or collegiate educational institutions exist, children do not get the same opportunity as those who have all these in their neighbourhood.
4. Wide inequalities also arise from differences in home environments. A child from a rural household or slum does not have the same opportunity as a child from an upper class home with educated parents.
5. There is wide sex disparity in India. Hence, girls education at all stages of education is not given the same encouragement as boys.
6. Education of backward classes including scheduled castes and tribes and economically backward sections is not at par with that of forward communities or classes.

Suggestions for Reorganising Educational System for Providing Equality of Educational Opportunity in India

The Government of India has been striving to achieve the target of providing equal educational opportunities to all the people. Some suggestions could be cited in this regard. These suggestions may be of some help in reaching the target.

1. In order to reap the fruits of education and also to remove the prejudices and biases, adult illiteracy has to be removed by launching appropriate programmes.

1 M.S. Gore *"Education and Modernisation in India."* Page - 30.

2. By following a "*policy of protective discrimination*" all efforts must be made to increase the opportunities for education to all the weaker sections of the society like the scheduled castes, scheduled tribes, backward communities and even women.

3. Honest attempts be made to provide compulsory education to all the children at least up to 14 years. No one should be made to suffer for want of educational opportunity and facilities.

4. The higher educational chances should be extended to all on merit.

5. *Education Commission* suggests that for equalisation of educational opportunity the following measures may be adopted :

(a) Education should be made tuition free for all immediately at the primary and secondary levels and in course of time, at the university level at least for the needy deserving students ;

(b) Free text books and writing materials should be supplied at the primary stage ;

(c) Transport facilities should be provided to reduce cost on hostels and scholarships ;

(d) Facilities for the students to earn a part of their educational expenses, that is, *"earn while you learn"* schemes should be developed ;

(e) There should be liberal schemes for scholarships ;

(f) Wide differences that are found in the educational development in different states and districts must be minimised to a desirable extent.

In the industrialised countries the idea of equality of opportunity is very firmly rooted. Halsey believes that the principle of equality has a powerful and a persistent appeal. He further points out that "*its influence is reinforced in advanced society by the impersonal demands of the economy for efficiency, for a fluid labour force, and for rational allocation of jobs by tests of fitness to fill them.*"[1]

EDUCATION AND MODERNISATION

Education has become today an essential aspect of the modern industrial society. It is more regarded as an agent of social change than an instrument of social control. It has become increasingly secular. All the nations of the world are investing huge amount of money on education for it has become an essential condition of advancement.

Education for Promoting the Cause of Science and Technology: Education, modernisation, advancement in science, technology and industry normally go together. Formal professional education has become an absolute necessity today. Education is not just needed to read, write and do simple calculations but, it is essential to earn one's living. It is the main source of supply of trained and technical persons to industry. The job that one gets today depends largely on the type of education that one has secured.

Modern schools, colleges and universities do not give much emphasis upon transmitting a way of life to the students as was given by the earlier forms of education. This is due to the fact that traditional education was meant for an unchanging and static society, a society not marked by rapid changes associated with industrialisation. Modern society, on the other hand, is a changing society. In such a society education aims at communicating empirical knowledge, that is, knowledge about science, technology and other types of specialised knowledge. A transformation in the contents and methods of education has taken place to meet the demands of the changing society. This transformation has led to some far-reaching consequences. Some of them are mentioned below :

1 H.H. Halsey "*The Sociology of Education in Sociology*" (1967) Page : 434 - as quoted by **Dr.S.S. Mathur.** Page : 273.

(i) Heavy Study Materials : Modern education includes heavy study materials on modern science and technology into the syllabus. Due to this inclusion and over emphasis on this, courses of study on classical language and literature had to be abridged, or altogether dropped. This has prevented the modern learners from knowing their own past traditions and cultural heritage. "*It is argued that in such circumstances an individual would be cut off from his 'roots' and his creative faculties, particularly his emotional and spiritual talents, would languish for want of nourishment.*"[1]

(ii) Values Losing their Importance : Due to the impact of modern science and technology many of the cherished values of the past have lost their previous importance. There is no attempt to persuade people of the younger generation to accept these values uncritically. At the same time, new set of values have not been developed to occupy the place of the old ones. This situation has created confusion both to the individual and to the society. In the absence of meaningful human values the life of modern educated man has become more mechanical and materialistic. In the absence of consensus regarding some basic questions as to what is right and what is wrong, what is desirable and what is not - the society has to face conflicts.

(iii) Dangerous Face of Science and Technology : Science and technology are growing today at a fast rate. Modern education has accelerated this growth. The uncontrolled growth of technology and the directionless development in science have today added much to human tension, anxiety and misery. **Francis Bacon** at one stage had said that "*knowledge is power.*" But today many eminent scientists have reluctantly come to the view that "*knowledge is unfortunately power.*" The manufacture of deadly war weapons has created fear in the minds of people about science and technology. This only calls for rethinking and reappraisal in the field of educational planning as part of modernisation.

Education for Spreading the Values of Modernisation

In the Indian context, education came to be more and more used as an instrument for spreading the values of modernisation especially from 1960s and 1970s onwards. Modernisation of India demanded certain changes in other value system. Adoption of modern sophisticated technology for increasing the efficiency of industries and agriculture; greater involvement of all sections of people in the decision making process; giving due importance and representation to women, SCs, STs, OBCs and other neglected sections, adoption of the principle of social justice in the distribution process, and such other changes in our social system were regarded as essential and almost inevitable for modernising the Indian society. These changes were to be brought about by education. The range of modernisation was not restricted to the economic field alone, but was extended to social, political, cultural and religious fields also. Education was selected as the obvious instrument for the spread of modernity.

Confusion Regarding the Values of Modernisation ?

Modernisation as such incorporates in itself values such as *secularism, individualism, socialism, egalitarianism,* etc. The confusion and the conflict in the Indian context is that whether all these values should be accepted and propagated or some of the traditional cultural elements be retained. What should be the role of education in spreading the values of modernisation ? Who should impart the values of modernisation ? Are they really equipped to play that role ? Though the Education Commissions and the New Policy of Education 1986 have very much stressed the importance of India forging ahead in the direction of modernity, they have not made clear about the nature of the path of modernisation. Hence, time is ripe to think seriously about the precise role of education and the extent to which it can be used as an instrument for the spread of modern influences and modern values.

1 **Parimal B. Kar** "*Sociology - The Discipline and Its Dimensions*" - Page : 284.

Was India Educationally Backward Prior To the Coming of the British ?

Sri **Dharampal**, one of the contemporary Indian writers, in his book ***"The Beautiful Tree"***, tries "to explode two misconceptions" which are widespread among the learned people about the state of education prior to the coming of the British in India. These misconceptions are as follows : (i) *Education was in a bad shape prior to the coming of the British in India;* (ii) *Education was confined to the higher castes, i.e., mainly to the twice-born, and the Shudras were denied of it.*

Sri Dharampal draws his conclusions based mainly on the following British documents : (i) *Survey of Indigenous Education in the Madras Presidency* 1822-26, (ii) **W. Adam**'s report on *State of Education in Bengal* 1835-38, (iii) **G.W. Leitner**'s report on *History of Education in the Punjab since Annexation and in 1882* [first published in 1883].

1. ***Education was Widespread in Pre-British India*** : Dharampal has stated that education was universal and widespread in India prior to the advent of the British. He quotes the reports of **W. Adams** : Referring to the Elementary schools, W. Adams reports – "that there are 1 **lakh** such schools in Bengal and Bihar and assuming the population of those two provinces to be 40,000,000 there would be a village school for every 400 persons." [p. 267]. **Sir Thomas Munro**, Governor of Madras Presidency, gave evidence in the House of Commons that *"every village had a school."* Senior official G.L. **Prendergast** reports from Bombay in 1820 : *"that there is hardly a village, great or small, throughout our territories, in which there is not at least one school, and in larger villages more"* [p. 12]. And **Dr. G.W. Leitner** observes that the spread of education in the Punjab in 1850 was of a similar extent [p. 12]. Sir Thomas Munro, the Governor of Madras Presidency, observed in March, 1826 that the boys between the age of 5 to 10 years *"who receive school education to be nearer to one-third than one-fourth of the whole."* [p. 20].

• *Comparative Position of Education in England and India* : In 1822 to 1825 the number of those in ordinary schools in the Madras Presidency was put at over 1,50,000 for a population of 1,28,50,941. The population of England in 1811 was estimated at 95,43,610. While the difference in the population was not significant, the number of children attending various types of schools [Charity, Sunday, Circulating] in England was around 75,000 – *about half of that in Madras Presidency*! [p. 62].

In January 1797, the famous public school at Shrewbury did not have "above three or four boys", but after some major reorganization it had about 20 pupils a year later [Adamson]. It was only during the next 50 years that primary education got a big thrust in England. The number of those attending schools in England, were estimated at around 40,000 in 1792, at 6,74,000 in 1818, and 21,44,377 in 1851. Even as late as 1834, *"the curriculum in the better class of national schools was limited in the main to religious instruction, reading and writing, and religious arithmetic; in some country schools writing was excluded for fear of evil consequences."* (A.E. Dobbs.) [p. 5-6].

As for the quality and content of education in India in 1800 does not in any way appear inferior to that obtained in England. The duration of study of a pupil was more prolonged in India. The method of teaching was certainly not inferior. [The *monitorial method* used by Joseph Lancaster and Andrew Bell around 1800 was said to have been borrowed from India; where it had prevailed for centuries!] The school attendance in Madras Presidency even in the decayed state of 1822-25 was proportionately far higher than the numbers in all variety of schools in England in 1800. The conditions under which teaching took place in the Indian schools were less dingy and more natural. And the teachers were generally more dedicated and sober than their English counterparts [p. 14]. In the early 19th century England, *"the teachers were seldom competent"* and *"Lancaster insinuates that the men were not only ignorant but drunken"* [Adamson] [p. 5].

2. ***Education was Not Denied to the Shudras*** : Sri Dharampal's book explodes yet another myth. It is generally assumed that education in India, whether in the ancient period, or at the beginning of British Rule, was mainly confined to the higher and middle strata of the society [that is, it was limited to the twice-born], and that the *shudras* were denied of education. The book provides extensive data collected between 1822-25 which effectively

Continued on next page.........

refute this notion. For example, in the Malabar area the proportion of the twice-born in the schools was below 19%, that of *shudras* and other castes was 54%, and Muslims nearly 27%. In the Kannada speaking Bellary district, the twice-born was 33%, while the *shudras* and other castes was 63%. And in the Oriya-speaking Ganjam, the twice-born were 35.6% and *shudras* and other castes around 63.5% [p. 22-23].

Quoting from Adam's reports, the author writes that elementary education was not only universal but also extended to all caste people. Even teachers also belonged to several castes. The author quotes the report : "It is true that the greater proportion of the teachers came from the Kayasthas, Brahmins, the Sadgop and the Aguri castes. Yet quite a number came from 30 other caste groups also, and ***even the Chandals had six teachers.*** The elementary school students present an even greater variety and it seems as if every caste group is represented in the student population, the Brahmins and the Kayasthas nowhere forming more than 40% of the total. In the two Bihar districts they together formed no more than 15 to 16%. *The more surprising figure is of 61 Dom, and 61 Chandal school students in the district of Burdwan, nearly equal to the number of Vaishya students,* 126, in that district. While Burdwan, had 13 missionary schools, the number of Dom and Chandal scholars in them were only four and as Adam mentioned, *only 86 of the "scholars belonging to 16 of the lowest castes" were in these missionary schools while 674 scholars from them were in the "native schools"."* [p. 47-48]. The author states that the Indian institutional education was somewhat lagging behind with regard to the education of girls, which quite possibly might have been proportionately more extensive in England in 1800.

- *Causes of the Decay of Indian Education* : Sri Dharampal identifies two major reasons : (i) *Limitless British hunger for revenue* [page 75] which starved Indian education of its resource base. (ii) It is the *"cultural and religious content and structure"* of the indigenous education system, which was perceived to be a threat to the *"maintenance and continuance of British rule"*, that led to deliberate neglect of large scale school education by the rulers.

Source : **Dr. P. Subbanna Bhat's** article Book Review of **Sri Dharampal's** *"The Beautiful Tree"* – published in *"Aseemaa"* English Monthly Journal. 14 May 1998. Pages : 40 - 45.

Chapter 22

SOME SOCIAL PROBLEMS OF INDIA

***1. COMMUNALISM :** Meaning and Definition - Background of the Growth of Communalism - Characteristics and Causes of Communalism - Some Features of Communal Riots Taking Place in India - Suggestions to Control and Eradicate Communalism - Immediate and Long Term Remedial Measures. **2.FUNDAMENTALISM :** Religious Fundamentalism - The Concept of Fundamentalism - Its Origin and Features - Religious Fundamentalism in the Indian Context. **3. CASTEISM :** Meaning and Causes of Casteism - Consequences of Casteism - Solutions to the Problems of Casteism. **4. DOWRY :** Meaning and Definition of Dowry - Dowry As a Social Evil - Causes for Dowry - Arguments in Favour of Dowry - Arguments Against of Dowry - Measures Towards the Abolition of Dowry : Legal and Non-Legal Measures. **5. DIVORCE :** Definition of Divorce - Divorce in India - Some Provisions for Divorce in Ancient India - Divorce Among the Hindus in Modern India - Causes of Divorce - Individual and Social Consequences of Divorce - Remedial Measures for Divorce. **6. CORRUPTION :** Definition of the Concept of Corruption - Main Characteristics - Corruption in Public Life and Among Public Servants - Causes of Corruption - Prevention of Corruption : Legislative Measures to Contain it - The Santhanam Committee and Its Recommendations - Functions of Central Vigilance Committee - Commission Instituted to Probe Charges of Corruption - Introduction of the Lok Pal - Other Measures to Control Corruption. **7. NEPOTISM :** Meaning of Nepotism - Instances of Nepotism - Evil Effects of Nepotism. **8. BLACK MONEY :** Meaning and Causes of Black Money - Effects of Black Money and Measures to Control it. **9. BONDED LABOUR :** Definition and Main Features of Bonded Labour - Extent of Bonded Labour and Its Causes - Abolition of Bonded Labour - Problems Involved in the Effective Rehabilitation of the Bonded Labourers. **10. AIDS :** AIDS at the World Level and In the Indian Context - Causes of AIDS - Control of AIDS : Preventive Method and Curative or Treatment Method - Social Stigma Attached to the AIDS.*

India is known not only for its big size of population but also for the multiplicity of social problems with which it is confronted. Problems are not new phenomena to India. There were problems in India before independence. After independence also these problems continued to grow not only in their size but also in their number. Some of these have economic origin, and some others social origin, while many more have multiple sources. Some of the problems which we find in India are commonly found in many other developing countries; while some are peculiar to India. There is no doubt that these problems are hurdles on the path of India's march towards progress. It is necessary that these problems be tackled and effectively dealt with.

The scientific study of social problems is an essential aspect of the role of sociologists. Sociologists are required to analyse these problems scientifically, find out the causes for them and finally suggest and recommend measures to combat or control them. It is also expected of them to create an awareness among the general public about these problems. It is a matter of pity that the important role of sociology and sociologists in countering and controlling these problems is not yet fully realised by our administrators, political leaders and the public. Our sociologists also have not been able to impress upon them about the importance of sociology in dealing with these problems effectively. *"If sociology and sociologists alienate themselves from the immediate issues and problems of our society, both our discipline and our scholars will render themselves irrelevant to the nation as well as to humanism. It is time that the sociologists develop better predictive capabilities and present the options to the public in a comprehensive manner. This alone will help the society in tackling social problems effectively."*[1]

This chapter provides the reader only a glimpse of some ten social problems which are still holding their sway over the people.

1. COMMUNALISM

Communalism has become one of the biggest menaces of modern India. Problem that arises between the socio-religious relations of the people who belong to various minority communities on the one hand and the majority community on the other, can be referred to as *"communalism"* or *"communal problem."* Communalism and communal riots normally arise when religious matters are politicalised. *Communalism is often understood as an ideology which states that the society is divided into religious communities whose interests differ and are, at times, even opposed to each other.* It is a kind of antagonism which is found between the religious communities.

Definition of *"Communalism"*

1. Bipin Chandra : "......... *the concept of communalism is based on the belief that the religious distinction is the most important and fundamental distinction and this distinction overrides all other distinctions.*"......... He further adds *"since Hindus, Muslims and Sikhs are different religious entities, their social, economic, cultural and political interests are also dissimilar and divergent. As such the loss of one religious group is the gain of another group and vice versa. If a particular community seeks to better its social and economic situation, it is doing at the expense of the other."*[2]

2. Ram Ahuja : *"The antagonism practised by the members of one community against the people of other community and religion can be termed as communalism."*

3. Robert Melson and **Howard Wolpe :** *"Communalism is the political assertiveness of a community to maintain its identity in a plural society undergoing modernisation."*[3]

Communalism denotes antagonism between different religious groups. This antagonism goes to *"the extent of falsely accusing, harming, and deliberately insulting a particular community*

1 **Prof. Ram Ahuja** *"Social Problems in India"* [1992]. Page - 25.

2 **Bipin Chandra** *"Communalism in Modern India."* Page - 2.

3 **Robert Melson** and **Howard Wolpe** in their article in *"American Political Science Review."* Vol. 64, as quoted by **A.P. Avasthi** in *"Indian Government and Politics"* [2001]. Page 578.

and extends to looting, burning down the homes and shops of the helpless and the weak, dishonouring women, and even killing persons." **[Ram Ahuja.** Page - 245.]

Background of the Growth of *"Communalism"* in India

The origin and growth of communalism has its own history in India. In fact, communalism was part and parcel of the British policy of *"divide and rule."* The beginning of communalism can be traced to the pre-independence days. In the first war of independence [1857] the Hindus as well as the Muslims had united to throw the British imperialism out of India. The British suppressed the movement and later on started making use of the policy of *"divide and rule"* to instigate the Muslims against the Hindus and vice versa.

The British Government for quite a long time looked upon the Muslims as untrustworthy and disloyal. In fact, it interpreted the 1857 movement as an attempt by the Muslims to revive the Mughal rule in India. The Muslims were purposefully kept out of the government jobs for the British had continued to nurse a prejudice against them. The Muslims too had their bitter resentment against the British. Later, Lord Minto further contributed to widen the gap between the Hindus and the Muslims. He introduced communal electorate for Muslims but its outcome was disastrous. Muslims were elected to the legislature. In spite of Indian National Congress' opposition to communal politics of the Muslim League, the partition of the country was effected.

Main Characteristics of Communalism

Communalism as a socio-political problem is becoming more and more complex today. Unless we know the real nature of communalism it becomes difficult for us to differentiate between what communalism is, and what it is not. It is important to note that adherence to a religion is not communalism. Attachment to a religious community is not communalism. The religiosity of a community is not communalism. But using a religious community against other communities and against the whole nation is communalism. Let us now discuss the main characteristics of communalism especially in the Indian context.[1]

1. Communalism considers a particular religious community separate from the rest of the communities.
2. It believes that not only religious but also secular interests of that community are separate from similar interests of other communities.
3. Communalism believes that the specific interests of the community can be promoted by maintaining its separate identity and organising it separately for the promotion of those interests.
4. *Communal interests always super impose themselves* on the national interests.
5. Communalism *breeds mutual distrust and disharmony among the communities.* It adopts an attitude of hostility towards other religious communities.
6. Communalism treats some citizens not as citizens *but as members of some specific religious community.*
7. Communalism makes a particular religious community to impose its religious views and *social norms on the members of other religious communities also.* It denies freedom to the members of other religious communities and the right to have their own religious views and social norms. The freedom in religious and social matters is also denied to them.

1 ***Source*** : **A.P. Avasthi** in *"Indian Government and Politics."* Page - 579.

8. *Communalism fails to separate religion from politics.* It tries to conduct government on the basis of religious dogmas.
9. *Communalism leads to the abuse of power.* It seeks to impose the social and religious norms of the community on other communities by several means including force, fraud, economic and other allurements and even assistance from foreign powers.
10. In its extreme form, *communalism claims nationhood for the community concerned* and seeks to raise it to a status of sovereign state.

Causes for the Growth of Communalism

The main factors and forces which have encouraged the growth of communalism in India as listed by **A.P. Avasthi** [Page - 580], can be mentioned below.

1. *Communal political parties and organisations* that have been fanning the fire of separatism.
2. *Minority appeasement policy* which the Indian National Congress and some other political parties have been nursing since decades.
3. The elections which make the political parties and organisations to make a *communal appeal to the voters* and to keep alive the communal feelings.
4. *The media, literature and textbooks that have communal slant* and that give support to communal forces.
5. *Separation and isolationism* found among the Muslims.
6. The economic and educational backwardness found amongst the big minority group that is the Muslims.
7. The *aggressive Hindu chauvinism* championed by a few forces.
8. *Political opportunism* which is found in almost all the political parties in India which makes the political leader to give priority to their partisan political interests rather than to the national interests.
9. *"Divide and rule"* policy which the British had followed caused lot of damage to our national interest. The same type of policy is continued in a surreptitious manner even now.

In addition to the above factors mentioned by **Prof. Avasthi,** we can also list a few other factors which are contributing to the phenomenon of communalism.

10. *Role of foreign forces* which have been instigating communal activities and communal riots in India. The role of these forces in giving training to the communal extremists and in supplying sophisticated technical equipments for fanning the fire of communalism.
11. *Large scale conversion activities taking place in India* are also contributing to communalism. Both the Christian and the Muslim minority forces are indulging in these kinds of conversion activities. These conversions are often made in a forcible manner and sometimes by means of temptations and so on.
12. *The subversion of secularism by the political parties* is also a factor encouraging communalism. Political parties which speak of secularism pay only lip sympathy to secularism but in practice support communalism.
13. *The growing disappointment among the Hindus* who constitute the majority community is also a factor in favour of communalism. The Hindus believe that due to the *"vote bank politics"* of the minority community the larger national interests are sacrificed.

14. *The Hindu militancy* too has added to the problem of communalism. In their attempt to defend Hindu interests and counteract attacks on it, some Hindu organisations have resorted to militant activities. These activities have caused communal frictions and conflicts.

Communal Tensions or Riots

The biggest outcome of the communalism is communal tensions or riots. When religious matters are politicalised it leads not only to communalism but also to the communal riots. *The riots that take place due to clashes of communal interests of two or more communities are regarded as communal riots.*

The concept of communal violence or riot can be defined in the words of **Prof. Ram Ahuja** as follows : *"Communal violence involves people belonging to two different religious communities mobilised against each other and carrying the feelings of hostility, emotional fury, exploitation, social discrimination and social neglect. The high degree of cohesion in one community against another is built around tension and polarisation. The target of attack are the members of the 'enemy' community.......... It could thus be said that communal violence is based mainly on hatred, enmity and revenge."*[1]

The incidences of communal riots are steadily increasing in India. Ever since politics came to be communalised, communal violence has increased quantitatively. According to a study conducted in India in 1966-67, as many as 310 instances of communal riots were reported and the figure increased to 1300 in 1985-86. All the provinces and all the places are not equally sensitive to communal riots. For example, 61 districts out of 350 districts in India were identified as sensitive districts in 1961, whereas 216 districts were identified so in 1979, and 186 were regarded so in 1989. It is reported that property worth Rs.14 crore was damaged in communal riots between 1983 and 1986 [*Times of India* - July 25, 1986]. In the 2086 incidences of communal riots in 3 years between 1986 and 1988, both the years inclusive, 1024 persons were killed and 12352 injured. It is observed that some states are found to be regularly suffering from the problem of recurring communal riots.

Some Features of Communal Riots Taking Place in India

Various studies have been conducted in order to collect enough information about the phenomena of communalism and communal riots. A study instituted to go into the major communal riots that took place in the country for the last five decades has revealed some special features of the communal riots.[2] They can be stated below.

1. Studies of communalism and communal riots have stated that in most of the instances, the communal riots are found to be politically motivated and not instigated by religious factors. Even the **Madan Commission** instituted to look into the communal disturbances in Maharashtra in May 1970 emphasised that *"the architects and builders of communal tension are the communalists and a certain class of politicians.........."*
2. In addition to the political interests, economic interests also play a vital role in augmenting communal clashes.
3. Statistics have revealed that communal riots seem to be more common in north India than in south India.
4. The possibility of recurrence of communal riots in a town where communal riots have already taken place once or twice is greater than in a town in which riots have never occurred.

---

1 **Prof. Ram Ahuja** *"Society in India"* [1999]. Page : 251 - 252.

2 *ibid.* Page : 252 - 253.

5. It is observed that most of the communal riots take place on the occasions of religious festivals.
6. It is also observed that communal riots are found in a larger number in urban areas rather than in rural areas. The concentration of people of the minority communities in urban areas is probably the reason behind this.
7. Normally on the occasion of the communal riots deadly weapons are used by people involved in the communal riots.

Suggestions to Control and Eradicate Communalism

Communalism has been increasing in this country for the past 5 decades. It has impeded the process of development and also has hurt the scientific temper and the secular spirit. *"Communalism emerges in India as the most dangerous threat to the cultural modernisation. It is a complex process but its causes generally subsist in the contradictions generated by the forces of social restructuration."*[1]

A study [conducted by *Mainstream*, Feb. 9, 1988] has revealed that in the time span of 37 years after independence as many as 10,000 communal riots had taken place due to which more than 1,000 people lost their lives and property worth a few crores was damaged. The Ayodhya incident excelled the previous records and a few hundreds lost their lives in 1990s. The communal riot which took place in Gujarat very recently [February - May 2002] cost the lives of more than 800 people and property worth crores of rupees was destroyed.

Communalism is a creeping paralysis which demands solution. Communal riots pose a permanent threat to the religious harmony in this land. They must be effectively dealt with and minimised. A few of the suggestions in this regard may be noted. It is true that giving suggestions is an easy task but putting them into practice is itself a big challenge. **Prof. Ram Ahuja** suggests that the problem of communal riots must be tackled in 2 ways : (A) *undertaking immediate remedial measures,* and (B) *resorting to long term remedial measures.*

(A) Immediate Remedial Measures

1. *Setting up Peace Committee* : In the riot-torn places peace committees consisting of the respected leaders of the different religious communities are to be formed immediately after the outbreak of communal violence. These leaders must exercise their goodwill on the respective communities and persuade them to maintain peace and harmony.

2. *Use of New Strategies and Plans by the State* : Since rioters are making use of modern sophisticated equipments and weapons to spread communal riots everywhere, it is necessary for the State to resort to new strategies and plans to hook and book those rioters and instill confidence in the minds of riot-hit individuals and innocent people.

3. *Supervision of the Media* : The role of the media is very important in the course of communal riots. The media must exercise great restraint in spreading rumours and reports of communal riots. The State must have strict vigilance over the media.

4. *Suppressing the Extremists* : The Government in power must use its authority and power in suppressing the communal riots. It should not hesitate to impose ban on communal organisations directly or indirectly indulging in communal riots. All dangerous and extremist communal leaders must be arrested during the course of communal riots preventing them from fanning the fire of communal riots.

1 Views of **Prof. Yogender Sing** as quoted by **J.L. Kachroo** and **Vijaya Kachroo.** *"Society in India"* [1997]. Page - 282.

5. *Other Measures* :

(i) In the riot-torn areas efficient and secular minded police officials must be posted.

(ii) Special Courts should be established to deal with the cases of communal riots. Speedy disposal of the cases is an essential step in this direction.

(iii) The riot affected people must be given protection immediately and sufficient care should be taken to make arrangements for their rehabilitation if needed.

(iv) Immediate legal action should be instituted against those who instigate communal riots.

(B) Long Term Remedial Measures

1. *To Make the People Free From Communal Frenzies and Passions* : It is necessary to educate the people to become free from communal prejudices, feelings, etc. Steps should be taken to expose the communalist tendencies of the leaders who normally instigate riots.

2. *Preventing Communalisation of the State and the Political Elites in Power* : Communal riots often reach new heights due to the support given to it by the political parties, leaders and some bureaucrats. Hence it is necessary to see that the political elites in power become free from communal attitude. All communal forces to be tackled and treated equally.

3. *Protecting the Civil Society from being Communalised* : Communal riots grow into new proportions when supported by people. Sometimes, ordinary people are also drawn into communal carnage. Hence it is necessary to see that people do not become the victims of communal strategies of the leaders. It is in this regard that the intellectuals, writers, journalists, voluntary organisations freedom fighters and non-controversial political leaders should take a lead in building up public opinion against communalism and communal riots.

4. *Educational System should be Free from Communal Ideas and Ideologies* : It is necessary to see that importance is given to the development of communal harmony at all levels of education. The young minds should not be polluted with the narrow communal ideas. Hence patriotic feelings and sentiments must be strongly encouraged. Extra care should be taken in writing and teaching lessons in History. Distorting historical facts is also unfair.

5. *Role of the Media* : This is an era of publicity and propaganda. The electronic media such as television, radio, newspaper, etc. must play a very responsible role. They must not be allowed to contribute to communal feelings or riots. Communal press must be banned and legal actions must be instituted against communal writers.

6. *Ideology that Economic Development by itself brings down Communalism is not Correct* : Some argue that economic development, industrialisation, growth of capitalism, and the growth of working class would automatically weaken communalism. But our experience has proved to be contrary. Unless special care is taken communal riots cannot be suppressed even in times of economic prosperity. Economic development alone cannot contain communalism. In fact, communal violence is more prevalent in developed states like Maharashtra, Gujarat and also in developed cities like Mumbai, Ahmedabad, Jamshedpur and Kanpur. Hence, separate and well planned efforts are needed to curb the growing disease of communalism.

7. *Legislation against Forcible Conversions* : Since forcible conversion of persons from one religion to another, particularly from Hinduism to Christianity and Islam, is one of the major causes of communal riots. It is necessary that all conversion activities be banned and declared illegal. In fact, a legislation could be introduced in this regard at the all-India level. At the State level, Arunachal Pradesh, Madhya Pradesh, Orissa and Tamil Nadu governments have already made legislations prohibiting conversion activities.

• **Mahatma Gandhiji** was also very much against religious conversions. Long back he wrote : "*.......Every nation considers its own faith to be as good as that of any other. Certainly the great faiths held by the people of India are adequate for her people. India stands in no need of conversion from one faith to another.*"[1] As early as in 19th Jan. 1928 Gandhiji wrote in *"Young India"* that we should not even secretly pray that anyone should be converted, *"but our utmost prayer should be that a Hindu should be a better Hindu, a Mussalman a better Mussalman and a Christian a better Christian. This is the fundamental truth of fellowship."*[2] Gandhiji was totally against the proselytising activities of the missionaries. In his reply to Mahadev Desai's question Gandhiji had once replied : ***"If I had power and I could legislate, I should certainly stop all proselytising. It is the cause of much avoidable conflict between classes and unnecessary heart-burning among missionaries."***[3] On various occasions Gandhiji had expressed his views very strongly against forcible religious conversion.[4]

2. FUNDAMENTALISM

Religious Fundamentalism

"Religious fundamentalism" belongs to the same series of social evils such as *communalism, regionalism, casteism, racism, sexism, ethnicism,* and so on. *Communalism often assumes the form of religious fundamentalism.* It has both national and international dimensions. Religious fundamentalism is posing a new threat to the secular character of the Indian society. Especially after 1980s, it has become more serious a socio-political evil. It is necessary here to know the concepts of *"fundamentalism"* and *"religious fundamentalism"* and their nature.

Concept of *"Fundamentalism"*

1. *"Fundamentalism refers to a firm dogmatic belief in certain principles that are held to be basic or fundamental."*[5]
2. Fundamentalism refers to *"A religious movement that emphasises Biblical literalism and the final authority of the Bible. The term is sometimes applied to all those who have accepted the literal truth of the Bible even in past centuries.........."*[6]
3. *"Fundamentalism is a religious movement that emphasises the absolute truth of essential or "fundamental aspects" of faith, especially those rooted in sacred texts such as the Christian Bible or the Islamic Koran."*[7]

---

1 As quoted by **Prof. K.N. Vaswani** *"Gandhiji on Conversion."* Page - 25.

2 *ibid.* Page - 10.

3 **Gandhiji** in *Harijan* dated 11-5-1935 as quoted by **Prof. K.N. Vaswani.** Page - 21.

4 For example, **Gandhiji** wrote in ***"Young India"*** [23-3-1931] : "I hold that proselytising under the cloak of humanitarianism work is, to, say the least unhealthy..... Conversion now a days has become a matter of business like any other. I remember having read a missionary report saying how much it cost per head to convert and then presenting a budget for "the next harvest"." – Quoted by **Prof. K.N. Vaswani.** Page - 24.

5 **David E. Hunter** and **Phillip Whitten** *"Encyclopaedia of Anthropology."* Page - 182

6 **W.P. Scott** *"Dictionary of Sociology."* Page - 167.

7 **Allan G. Johnson** *"The Blackwell Dictionary of Sociology."*

As it is made clear from the first definition, fundamentalism represents a strong dogmatic belief or an uncompromising belief in some religious, racial, linguistic and other matters. Depending upon the fundamentalist approach, then, we may speak in terms of different types of fundamentalism such as *religious fundamentalism, racial fundamentalism, ethnic fundamentalism, linguistic fundamentalism,* and so on.

Origin of the Concept of Fundamentalism

The origin of the concept of *"fundamentalism"* is to be found in the history of the development of Christianity. Fundamentalism originated in America in the form of a conservative movement in the 19th century emphasising as fundamental to Christianity the literal interpretation of the Bible. *"Christian fundamentalists believe the Bible to be the word of God."*[1] They believe in the explanation given in the Bible regarding the – *"physical second coming of Jesus Christ, the Virgin Birth; Resurrection, and Attainment. Fundamentalism came into its own in the early 20th century in opposition to the Modernist tendencies in both the religious and secular life of America. In the late 20th century the movement was represented by numerous church bodies, educational institutions, and special interest organisations."*[2] However, most of the conservative or orthodox Christians today resent being referred to as *"fundamentalists."* The term should be reserved for those groups and functions that stress the literal truth of the Bible in its entirety.

The term *"fundamentalism"* is now being used in a loose manner with a wide variety of meanings. Sociologically also fundamentalism is important not only because of its unique place among religions, but because it easily extends itself into the political realm. In the Middle East [in Iran, for example] and in Pakistan, Afghanistan and such other countries fundamentalism plays an important role in the conservative political movements and nationalism. But even in India, especially after 1980s, religious fundamentalist trends are slowly spreading.

The main characteristics of religious fundamentalism can be mentioned below.

Features of *"Religious Fundamentalism"*

1. *Dogmatic Belief* : *Fundamentalism is basically a dogmatic belief* in certain principles. Those who justify religious fundamentalism are generally those individuals who are of the very strong opinion that the religious principles, values and ideologies in which they believe are beyond question.

2. *Total Surrender to a Sacred Book and a Religious Leader*: Religious fundamentalists implicitly believe that what is stated in a *"sacred book"* is unchangeable, unquestionable and unalterable. In the same dogmatic manner they submit themselves completely to a religious leader.

3. *Fundamentalism is Opposed to Liberalism* : Liberalism depends upon mutual tolerance of divergent views, opinions and beliefs. But in fundamentalism, there is indifference and even intolerance towards the views of others. It does not accept the stand that differences are probable and are bound to be there. It goes to the extent of suppressing the difference and the opposition. Such tendencies are commonly found in the theocratic states. Some of the Muslim countries such as Pakistan, Iran, Iraq, etc. have become such theocratic states. Pakistan Government's intolerance towards its religious minorities is quite known. Because of its fundamentalist attitude it has been persecuting and torturing its religious minorities [particularly the Hindus and Christians] right from its very inception.

1 *The Blackwell Dictionary of Sociology*. Page - 118.

2 *The New Encyclopaedia Britannica* - Vol.5. Page - 51.

4. ***Religious Fundamentalists Oppose any Change in what is Stated in the Sacred Book or the Tradition They Believe*** : This tendency is opposed to science and modernity. For example, the orthodox Muslims believe that the Islamic law called *"Shariat"* is not created by man, but emerged from God through Mohammad. They also believe that it contains the will of the God; and the terms of law are fixed and unchangeable. It is for this reason, Shariat law became rigid and static. The Talibanese who ruled over Afghanistan for about 10 years had such an uncompromising belief in the divine law for which they were branded as *"fundamentalists."*

5. ***Religious Fundamentalism is Opposed to Secularism*** : Secularism states that religion should not be mixed up with the governance of the state. Since it gives equal importance to all religions, it does not recommend a state religion. On the contrary, fundamentalism does not separate state and religion. It always upholds the supremacy of a particular religious philosophy, principle or tradition.

6. ***Religious Fundamentalism may have its own World View***: Fundamentalism may have a world-view of religion to which all other aspects such as political, cultural, economic, educational, etc. are sub-ordinated. It is for this reason, fundamentalism is opposed to a scientific, rationalist and secular world-view.

7. ***Fundamentalism may Assume the Extreme form of Terrorism*** : Fundamentalists may resort to any type of extreme activity in order to spread their religious views and to suppress the opposition. ***Example***: Muslim fundamentalist organisations such as *Hijbul Mujahiddin, Jaishe Mohammad, Lashkare Toiba, Huriat, I.S.I.* [*Inter Services Intelligence*], etc. have been committing lot of atrocities against the Hindu minorities. It is said that in a time span of about 15-20 years, [that is, since 1980s] these fundamentalists have killed more than 65,000 civilians, police, soldiers, politicians, Government officials with a view to separate Kashmir from India and to establish a separate Muslim State like that of Pakistan.

8. ***Fundamentalism Breeds Separatism*** : Fundamentalism of any type promotes belief in a particular ideology and is unwilling to consider other ideologies or viewpoints. The fundamentalists keep themselves separated from others. ***Example***: Those *racial fundamentalists,* who believe in the supremacy of the white race normally do not want to have links with the people of the Black Race especially in South Africa and America. Similarly, the ethnic fundamentalists have contributed to separatism in Sri Lanka. Muslim fundamentalists have posed a similar problem in Kashmir because of their encouragement of separatism.

9. ***Fundamentalism is a Type of Extreme Ethnocentrism ?*** : Religious fundamentalism gives rise to a feeling among its adherents whatever the things or views they have, are supreme and sacred. Once this feeling enters the mind it draws a black curtain against rationalism and free thinking. Such individuals fail to develop an independent thinking. They try to develop friendship with those who support their views. They tend to develop disrespect and intolerance towards others. They may even go to the extent of attacking their opponents as an attempt to unify all those who share the same views and ideologies.

Religious Fundamentalism in the Indian Context

It should be reckoned here that India as a nation was divided into two / three separate political units [India, Pakistan and the present Bangladesh] because of the fundamentalist approach pursued by some of the political leaders on the eve of independence. The same fundamentalist trends are making their re-appearance today. Pakistan which is known for its fundamentalist approach is trying to give its support to the Muslim fundamentalists found in India. Pakistan which wanted to grab Kashmir politically but failed to do so, is now making fresh attempts in this direction by giving secret support to the pro-Pakistan Muslim fundamentalists to let loose communalism, terrorism, violence, etc. wherever possible. Series of bomb explosions, planned kidnappings, merciless killings of minorities, frequent attacks on military headquarters, etc. that are taking place, especially in the Kashmir region make it evident that religious fundamentalists and fundamentalism pose a serious threat to the integrity and the secular character of our nation. Government alone cannot fightout this problem. People with nationalist fervour and commitment to real and not pseudo-secularism must take an active role in creating an awareness among the people about the dangers of fundamentalism. The Government must also deal stubbornly with these anti-national fundamentalist forces and suppress them with a heavy hand. Those who support fundamentalist forces secretly must also be nabbed and punished.

3. CASTEISM

Casteism is a social problem associated with the caste system. Just as the caste system is exercising its influence in all the fields of social life casteism too has become all pervasive.

What is Casteism ? / Meaning of Casteism

Casteism is understood as a partial or one-sided loyalty in favour of any particular caste. It makes members of the caste to become conscious of their membership of the caste and look at everything from the standpoint of the caste.

1. According to **D.N. Prasad,** *"Casteism is loyalty to the caste translated into politics."*[1]
2. According to **Kaka Kalelkar,** *"Casteism............ is an over-riding, blind and supreme group loyalty that ignores the healthy social standards of justice, fairplay, equity and universal brotherhood."*[2]

It is clear from the above that casteism is a blind group loyalty towards one's own caste or sub-caste which does not care for the interests of other castes and their members.

Causes of Casteism

Casteism which exercises a negative influence on the network of social relations is caused by several factors of which the following may be noted.

1. ***Endogamous Nature of the Caste*** **:** Casteism is often the result of restrictions imposed on the marriage that takes place in the Hindu society. Each caste and sub-caste is endogamous in nature. It means that members of a caste or sub-caste has to marry within his or her own caste or sub-caste. Because of this rule of endogamy, marital relations are confined to a small circle / section of the people. Individuals are more prone to develop their loyalties and admirations to their own caste or sub-caste people. This practice of endogamy makes the people to become somewhat narrow-minded.

2. ***Strong Desire to Enhance Caste Prestige*** **:** People belonging to a particular caste or subcaste have the tendency of developing loyalty to their caste or subcaste and to become more conscious of its relative prestige in society. Every member thus tries his level best to see that his caste prestige is safeguarded and enhanced. This type of loyalty towards the caste makes the members of the caste to favour their own members of the caste wherever they get the opportunity. Excessive caste loyalty tends to keep other caste people at a distance.

3. ***Improvement in the Means of Transport and Communication Leading to a Better Organisation of Caste*** **:** Advancement that has taken place in the field of transport and communication has helped the members of the caste to be in touch with one another regularly. It has also helped them

1 **D.N. Prasad** *"The Myth of Caste System."* Page - 124.

2 **Kaka Kalelkar** - as quoted by **R.N. Sharma** in *"Indian Social Problems."* Page - 47.

to strengthen their caste organisation and conduct activities on caste lines. Caste organisations and caste-get-togethers are on the increase now.

4. *Urbanisation Indirectly Favouring Casteism* : Industrialisation and urbanisation have been attracting people in a large number towards the cities. When the rural people go to the cities they naturally search for their nearer and dearer ones on the basis of the caste. They consider their own caste people as their potential friends and well-wishers. Hence the city atmosphere has also contributed to the strengthening of caste feelings and caste-mindedness.

5. *Powerful Hold of the Caste Over the Members* : Caste is a strong cohesive group. It has a powerful hold over its members. Members of the caste also look to the caste to obtain the needed help and assistance in times of crises, difficulties and emergencies. Dependence of the members on the caste in this way has further added to the problem of casteism.

Consequences of Casteism

Casteism though has certain benefits to the members of the caste on the individual basis, it has several harmful effects on the society as a whole. Some of the major harmful consequences of casteism can be noted here.

1. *Hinderance to the Development of National Feeling* : Members of the caste imbued with the spirit of casteism are more prone to show their loyalty to the caste rather than to the community at large. Casteism divides people in the name of caste and encourages intolerance, jealousy, rivalry and conflicts among members of the caste. Caste clashes and tensions that arise in society for one reason or another wrecks the unity of society and damages social harmony.

2. *Dangerous to Democracy* : Strictly speaking, caste and democracy cannot go together. Caste is based on inequality, whereas democracy assures equality and equal opportunities to one and all. Since democracy and caste system are co-existing in India clashes between them are inevitable. Indian politics has become very much complicated because of the caste interference. Caste plays its role in the processes of selection of candidates to the elections, electioneering, formation of cabinet, distribution of portfolios, and so on. It means at every stage in politics caste creates tensions, misunderstandings, infights, rivalries, etc. It is in this way national interests are undermined and national unity is underscored.

3. *Encourages Moral Degeneration* : Casteism contributes to the moral fall. It encourages nepotism. It makes one go out of the way to help and favour people of one's own caste. People of the same caste also look to the caste leaders to favour them in all the situations. This kind of favour damages the moral values and encourages corruption.

4. *Casteism Leads to the Negligence of Talents and Efficiency* : If candidates are selected and appointments are made on the basis of caste it definitely damages talents, abilities and efficiencies of the people. When unwanted and inefficient people are selected for high offices in the name of caste, honesty, efficiency and duty consciousness become the first causualty.

5. *Casteism may even Lead to Brain-Drain* : It has been observed that some of the most efficient and talented persons have left India and gone abroad for the simple reason that their merits and talents are not properly recognised. Casteism which comes in the way of the recognition of merit and efficiency indirectly promotes brain-drain.

It is clear from the above that casteism has dangerous effects on the society. Though people know casteism is bad they have become the victims of that. Even those who condemn it in public are practising it privately. **Prof. M.N. Srinivas** has rightly said that the caste *"is so tacitly and so* *completely accepted by all, including most vocal elements in condemning it, that it is everywhere the unit of social action."*[1]

More than the common people politicians seem to be contributing much to the survival of casteism. *"Political leaders belonging to different castes seem to secure political and other advantages for themselves at the expenses of others, and to this end they utilise the caste sentiment. Caste consciousness and caste prejudices which exist among the masses are thus turned by politicians into caste passions."*[2]

One of the seasoned politicians of India by name **Namboodiripad** himself has stated *"The existence of caste consciousness, caste prejudices, discontent on the basis of caste inequalities – all these are impediments in the way of the development of the country as a whole, and therefore, of the development of "lower" and "backward" castes themselves. Caste separatism, therefore, rather than helps, the advancement of the "lower" castes themselves."*[3]

Solutions to the Problem of Casteism

Casteism is no doubt a social evil that has to be counteracted and removed. Some have even gone to the extent of telling that even caste system is to be wiped out. But removal of caste and casteism is not an easy thing. Caste has very strong roots in our social set up and hence it cannot be uprooted from our society. It is not the need of the hour; only the ugly face of the caste, that is, casteism, is to be wiped out. We can suggest some solutions in this regard to counteract the problem of casteism.

1. ***Education*** **:** Education seems to be the most ideal solution to the problem of casteism. People must be properly educated about the dangers of practicing casteism. Parents, teachers, elderly people, political leaders should take precautions against contaminating the young minds with casteism.
2. ***Encouragement to Intercaste Marriages*** **:** Marital relations represent the most intimate relations between men and women. Encouragement and promotion of intercaste marriages will help young men and women of different castes to come closer and to develop healthy relations among them.
3. ***Minimum use of the term "Caste"*** **:** Necessary precautions must be taken to see that the word "caste" is used only in limited context. The young generations must be encouraged to give the least importance for it. This is possible only when we make lesser and lesser use of the term "caste."
4. ***Promotion of Economic Equality*** **:** Wide economic gap is found between the upper caste people and the lower caste people. This economic gap widens the social distance and contributes to the development of caste prejudices. Hence, efforts must be made to provide equal economic opportunities for the lower caste people to attain economic prosperity.

4. DOWRY

CAUSES - CONSEQUENCES - SOLUTIONS

Dowry is both a practice and a problem associated with Hindu marriage. Dowry is generally understood as money, goods, estate, ornaments or any other kind of wealth that a woman brings to her husband at the time of marriage. The practice of giving dowry in any of the forms mentioned here,

1 **M.N. Srinivas** in his *"Caste in Modern India."* Page - 225.

2 **A.P. Avasthi** in *"Indian Government and Politics"* [2001]. Page - 576.

3 *ibid.* Page - 577.

is very common among all the people of the world. It exists in all communities and nations of the world in one form or the other. Among Hindus, the girls used to get from their parents as a kind of gift [if not as dowry as it is understood today], all domestic utensils that are necessary to set up a new family.

Meaning of Dowry

1. The dowry refers to *"...... the property which a man receives from his wife or her family at the time of his marriage"* - **Max Radin** in *"Encyclopaedia of Social Sciences."* Vol.5. Page - 240.

2. Dowry is *"......... the property that is given to a woman at the time of her marriage"* - ***Encyclopaedia Britannica.***

3. Dowry may be broadly defined as *"gifts and valuables received in marriage by the bride, the bridegroom and his relatives"* - **Ram Ahuja.**

4. Dowry is defined as *"the money, goods or estate, which a woman brings to her husband in marriage"* - ***The Webster's New International Dictionary.***

Legal Definition of Dowry

The Dowry Prohibition Act, 1961, defines dowry in the following words : "Dowry means any property or valuable security given or agreed to be given either directly or indirectly -

(a) by the party to a marriage to the other party to the marriage; or

(b) by the parents of either party to a marriage or by any other person to either party to the marriage or to any other person;

at or before or after the marriage as consideration for the marriage of the said parties, but does not include dower or *mahr* in the case of persons to whom the Muslim Personal Law [*Shariat*] applies."

Dowry as a Social Evil

The age-old practice of dowry has now assumed the form of a social evil because the bride's family is compelled to give some dowry as a price for marriage. The custom has now taken an acute form and has assumed scandalous proportion. It has become a social bane and a kind of bargain. It has caused unhappiness, misery and ruin of the bride's family. Huge amount of money is demanded at the time of marriage and the failure to give the promised amount would make the bride to suffer the consequences at the hands of her in-laws and also the husband.

It was expected that the problem of dowry would diminish with the spread of education. Much against this expectation, dowry is at its heights at the level of the educated people. We have today relatively a larger number of engineers, advocates, doctors, college / university professors, bank / LIC officers, chartered accountants, government officers, and so on. The extent of dowry depends on the socio-economic status of the bridegroom and differs in different regions and in different caste groups. There are more or less well-defined grades of dowry for men in different professions. For example, men in the IAS, IFS, IPS, and such high cadres belonging to well-to-do families can easily expect 20 to 25 lakh rupees in cash in addition to other items in kind. Business executives and industrialists can also expect lakhs of rupees. Engineers and doctors are also in high demand in the marriage market. Their "dowry price" is also relatively high. **Kapadia** thus remarks that *"the amount of the dowry is generally regulated by the social and economic status of the bridegroom's father, the social prestige of the bridegroom's family, and the educational qualification* *of the bridegroom. A girl's physical beauty or educational qualification may reduce this amount at times, but often this reduction is very meagre."*[1]

Young persons with high qualifications are demanding huge amount of dowry as prospective grooms. Since their price in the marriage market has gone up, the parents who have to give their daughters to such young men, are now faced with difficulties in finding money. In addition to money, these boys also demand jewellery, scooter / motor bike / car, gadgetry, refrigerator, T.V. sets, furniture, clothes, utensils, etc. from the girls' side. In addition to this burden, the girls' family has to spend a huge amount on marriage ceremony. The burden of hospitality is generally heavier on the bride's kinsmen than on the grooms's. The decoration, and wedding dinner expenses which run to thousands of rupees are also to be borne by the bride's parents.

The burden of giving money and other gifts to the groom and to his family does not stop when once marriage is over. On the contrary, the girl's parents have to give gifts to her, her husband and her in-laws long after the marriage on festivals and on varied minor or major occasions. In some castes, [for example, Brahmins of Karnataka] expenses incurred on the married daughter's first pregnancy, delivery and childcare for a couple of months, are to be borne by the girl's parents. Gifts, gold ornaments and clothes are also to be given to the new born infant by its grandparents from the mother's side. It is hence that **Altekar** has rightly said, *"it is now high time for the Hindu society to put an end to this evil custom, which has driven many an innocent maid to commit suicide."* ***The Crime Record Bureau of the Central Home Ministry*** has also reported in 1994 that on an average everyday 17 dowry deaths [6205 deaths in a year] take place.

Causes for Dowry or Motivations for Dowry

Various factors have contributed to the problem of dowry among which the following may be noted.

1. Pressures of the Caste System

Practice of dowry is supported by the caste system sometimes directly and some other times indirectly. Caste is endogamous and sub-castes are also endogamous. Since marriage has to take place within the boundary of sub-caste, the range of selection of life-partners becomes extremely limited. In each caste or sub-caste, there is a paucity of young boys who are highly educated, who have high salaried jobs or promising careers in the profession. They become *"scarce goods"* for whom their parents demand high amount as dowry. Girl's parents who seek a good boy as their son-in-law, are now compelled to pay that amount for they have only a limited range of selection.

2. Aspiration to Establish Marital Relation with Rich Family

Girls' parents are always interested in giving their daughters in marriage to well-to-do families. Many of them do not want to take a risk in arranging the marriage of their daughter with a boy who belongs to a poor family just because the boy is good. They look in to the future prospects of their daughter, her comforts, her pleasures, her satisfaction, and so on. High market value of the boys belonging to rich and high social status families has caused the amount of dowry to go up.

3. False Conceptions of Social Status

Many a time girl's parents themselves offer huge amount of money as *"dowry gift"* just to exhibit their high social status and parade their economic capacity. Jains and Rajputs, for example, spend lakhs of rupees in this way on marriage. Bunts of Dakshina Kannda district [Karnataka],

1 **K.M. Kapadia** *"Marriage and Family in India"* [1966 edition]. Page - 137.

Catholic Christians of Kerala, also spend much either to keep their prestige or to make a show of their status.

4. Hypergamous Marriage System Favouring Dowry

Hypergamous or *Anuloma* system of marriage which is insisted upon by the caste system has also contributed to the practice of dowry. *As per the rule of hypergamy a girl of a higher caste cannot marry a boy of a lower caste. But a lower caste girl marrying an upper caste boy is permitted.* Such marriages often prove to be costlier. Particularly when boys belonging to higher castes marry girls of lower castes, they demand high dowry. Thus, a person often pays a huge amount of dowry to get a son-in-law from a higher caste. Girls' parents also find prestige in arranging their daughter's marriage with a man of higher and prestigious caste.

It is in the context of the practice of dowry on the one hand and hypergamy on the other, **K.M. Kapadia** [Page - 108] commented, "the practice of hypergamy has brought in its train problems of no mean significance. The main concern of the man is found in many of these hypergamous caste, to have been the exploitation of woman and her people economically...... Every parent desired his daughter to be married into the highest social group to keep up or to add to his prestige, and this made him acquiesce in these abuses. When a number of offers were made to a single person, he naturally insisted on his terms and the bridegroom price would go on swelling." **Kapadia** further writes, *"Legislation against dowry will have little effect until it is visualised in this perspective."*

5. Practice of Dowry as a Long Standing Social Custom

Giving dowry and receiving the same has become a matter of *"social custom"* in the Indian social system which consists of innumerable castes and sub-castes. Practice of dowry has a long standing role of its own like that of *"the devadasi system"* and *"child marriage"*. All these had obtained social recognition at one time or the other. Sometimes a religious touch was also given to the dowry and it was regarded as a *"dakshina"* or fees, in addition to the *"Kanyadana"* or the main gift of the girl. The daughter's right to inheritance also helped to make the dowry system rigid among the propertied class of the people. It means many parents felt that it was obligatory for them to give the girl's share of ancestral property in the form of dowry at the time of her marriage. Further, many people give and take dowry only because their parents and ancestors had been practising it. Those who stick to this practice and those who pressurise for the same, are getting financial profit and hence they do not want to do away with it.

6. Impact of the Vicious Circle which Dowry has Created

The practice of dowry has become very dominant because many parents demand dowry on behalf of their sons just to compensate the dowry they have given while celebrating the marriage of their daughters. Sometimes, individuals who are against this system are also compelled to accept a few thousands or lakhs of rupees in cash as dowry only because they have to spend an equal amount or more on their sisters' or daughters' marriage. Thus the vicious circle of dowry starts operating and individuals get entangled with it, whether they desire it or oppose it.

7. Practice of Child Marriage Favouring Dowry

In early times, girls were permitted to marry in their teens, that is, after their puberty. Advanced maidenhood was also tolerated. But when pre-puberty marriages came into existence, the father of the girl became anxious to get her married. being afraid of social ostracism for keeping the girl unmarried, the girl's parents desired to dispose her of within the limited time even with money, which the father of the bridegroom demanded. Practice of taking dowry continued even after the gradual disappearance of child marriages.

• Arguments in Favour of Dowry

Though the practice of dowry is publicly condemned, legally banned and morally despised of, in actuality, it persists. Many people are practising it as though it is a matter of their family tradition. Some people support the practice by citing its advantages. Some of the arguments which the supporters of dowry put forward in defence of it, may be mentioned here.

1. *Dowry helps newly Married Couple to Establish their Family* : The advocates of the practice of dowry say that the dowry money and the utensils and other household articles that are given along with dowry help the newly married couple to establish their new home and to furnish it with necessary accessories.

2. *Provides hopes of Marriage for ugly looking Girls* : Practice of dowry helps to increase the possibility of marriage ugly-looking, uneducated and aged girls. It is normally difficult to get a match for such girls. But if their parents are willing to spend a huge amount in the marriage, it becomes comparatively easier for them to find bridegrooms. In our society it is not difficult to find poor young unmarried men who are waiting for such financial offers as a remedy for the economic problems of their family.

3. *Supports the Higher Education of Poor Boys* : Meritorious boys of poor classes often find dowry as supportive of their higher education. Girl's parents, if they are rich, often make such proposals to prospective bridegrooms. They show their inclination to spend money on the higher education if the grooms, if they are ready to marry their daughters.

4. *Increases the Status of Women in Family* ? : It becomes possible for a lower class / caste woman to marry an upper class / caste boy through which she can increase her status. Further, a woman who brings rich dowry is given greater attention and importance than the woman who belongs to a poor family and brings nothing in cash or in terms of adequate ornaments.

5. *Promotes Intercaste Marriages* : Many a time when parents are not able to get suitable boys for their daughters in their own caste, they seek alliances with other castes. They may take a bold step to violate the caste rule with the sole intention of finding the most suitable match for their daughter.

6. *Other Factors Favouring Dowry* :

(a) It is argued that dowry money can help to reduce the intensity of housing problem by encouraging the new married couple to establish their separate household.

(b) It is said that dowry helps to reduce the difference between sons and daughters in the family. Just as parents spend a huge amount on the education of their sons, they spend almost an equal amount on the marriage of their daughters and also on dowry.

(c) Some people who practise dowry defend it as a kind of future protection assured to the girl at the time of marriage. Girl's parents who put forward this argument also look at the dowry money that they are giving as a kind of *"provident fund"* guaranteed to the girl to face financial hazards.

• Evil Effects of Dowry or Arguments against Dowry

Practice of dowry which assumed the form of an institution over the years has caused lot of hardships to a large number of people in the Indian society. At one time, dowry was being given willingly by the bride's parents, and it was being "accepted" by the groom's party as a kind of voluntary gift. But today, dowry has come to be *"demanded"*. In marriage negotiations, very often dowry considerations become primary ones, and all other considerations become only secondary. Dowry is demanded by the groom's party without taking into consideration the paying capacity of the bride's party. Hence, in many poor families the birth of a child is very much despised. From the day of the birth of the girl, the problem of dowry haunts the minds of the parents. Dowry has virtually become a menace in the Indian society. Its practice leads to various evil consequences among which the following may be noted.

1. Dowry Causes Great Economic Burden on Bride's Family

Dowry has become a great economic burden to the middle and lower-middle class families. People belonging to these classes spend on maintaining the family standard, in providing the necessities of life, educating children, and meeting various social obligations. These people who live from hand to mouth rarely save money. Hence to arrange the marriage of their daughters they have to borrow money or sell a piece of their property and mortgage valuable articles of the family. This incurred debt is passed on from generation to generation which ultimately leads to the total collapse of the family.

2. Dowry Lowers the Status of Woman and Damages Her Dignity

Prevalence of the custom of dowry reflects upon the inferior status of women in the society. In her own natal home, a girl is considered a liability and a drain on the family's resources. This has its effect on the socialisation of children. In respect of food, dresses, medical care, education, etc., in middle class families boy is given more importance than the girl. Particularly when the family income is very less, boy is likely to obtain preference to girls in the matter of education. Dowry is thus a great impediment in the progress of education of girls. Without higher education girls can hardly get into high positions which help them to increase their status. As it is already noted even the education of girls has in no way led to its disappearance.

Dowry lowers the status of women in another way. As every marriage brings a substantial sum, one would naturally be tempted to contract a second and a third marriage just for its monetary benefit. Though such marriages have not become the order of the day, here and there we do hear of such marriages taking place. This naturally affects the status of the wives.

The boy who receives huge amount of dowry may think of himself as more dignified as having a higher status, greater prestige and more respectful than the girl. This may make the married woman to develop a sense of inferiority. It wounds the self-respect of the woman.

3. Dowry Causing Child Marriages

Dowry system is one of the very strong factors leading to the practice of child marriage. Many people arrange the marriage of their daughters in childhood, that is, prior to puberty, in order to escape from dowry. When the boys become mature they often find it difficult to adjust with their wives. Even today child marriages are not completely eradicated.

4. Dowry Harassment and Murders

Women are ill-treated, disrespected, man-handled, tortured and subject to all sorts cruelties in the name of dowry. Very often, our daily papers flash news about the tragic results of the dowry system, in which the newly married girls are always the victims of harassment, violence, murder and suicide. Dowry is demanded as though it is a fundamental right of the bridegroom.[1] Violence against women who bring less dowry or no dowry include – physical battering, emotional neglect / torture, verbal abuse, refusal of sufficient food, imposition of heavy physical work, and so on.

In spite of the legislation against the practice of dowry, it persists. Demands for dowry have even caused dowry deaths. According to an estimate, as many as 4148 dowry deaths were reported in the year 1990 and it increased to 4366 in the year 1993, and to 6205 in the year 1994, that is, at the rate of one dowry death for every 17 minutes.

5. Dowry Leading to Immorality

Practice of dowry is not only regarded as unlawful but even as immoral. Gandhiji, Jayaprakash Narayan and other national leaders condemned it in very strong words. According to **Gandhiji,** one who makes dowry a pre-condition for his marriage, not only shows disrespect to a woman but also humiliates his own nation, education and womanhood. He even said that such young persons should be socially boycotted. Practice of dowry leads to some immoral practices.

***Example*:** (i) In order to escape from the menace of dowry some unmarried young girls take up some petty jobs to earn money in order to reduce the financial burden of their parents / brothers. These young innocent girls are often sexually cheated by young boys who make false promises to marry them. These girls who become pregnant are socially defamed and sometimes foced to commit suicide.

(ii) Some parents who cannot pay substantial dowry to a boy of their selection helplessly decide to give their daughter in marriage to an aged man or physically disabled man or diseased man or to a divorcee. This may make many a girl to become unhappy throughout their lives.

(iii) Further, failure on the part of the parents to arrange the marriage of their daughters because of dowry, sometimes makes the girls to carry on illegal sexual relations which may even cause prostitution.

(iv) Dowry system enhances the importance of male children at home. Due to this, female children are neglected and put to all sorts of hardships. More than that, unwanted female children are killed with the help of modern medical equipments when they are at the stage of foetuses in their mother's womb. These killings have led to an imbalance in the sex ratio.

6. Psychological Crises and Emotional Disturbances in the Family

Practice of dowry may cause emotional upsets within the family. Some such situations may be cited here.

(i) Girls with strong character and self-dignity may refuse to marry a boy who demands dowry. Some of them may be forced to remain spinsters throughout their lives. Forcible suppression of sex urge may make them to become irritable, frustrated, disgusted and pessimistic. They may even develop neurotic diseases and get involved in emotional problems.

(ii) Some courageous women resist the way in which they are treated at the house of their husbands even after the payment of dowry. This type of resistance may spoil their mental peace and cause continuous irritation.

(iii) Even when the boy and girl who love each other are agreeable for marriage, the groom's parents often forcibly arrange the marriage of their son with some other girl with the expectation

---

1 Dowry is demanded in such a manner that a strange incident of a son-in-law going on hunger strike for the pending dowry money has been reported by the press. ***Source*:** **Deccan Herald,** Bangalore dated 14.12.1979.

of high dowry. Marriages arranged in this way against the wishes of its partners on account of dowry rarely bring happiness in the family.

(iv) Practice of dowry creates an unwanted and an unhealthy competition among the brides' parents which ultimately destroys peace and happiness in the family.

(v) Practice of dowry creates misunderstandings, quarrels and conflicts between mother-in-law and daughter-in-law, husband and wife, daughter-in-law and other in-laws at home. These things may become a permanent feature of such families.

Measures Towards the Abolition of Dowry

Legislative Measures : *Dowry Prohibition Act, 1961*

Dowry system and its practices are highly criticised. Social reformers and right thinking persons recommended strong legal measures to remove its practice. Some of the State Governments such as Andhra Pradesh, Kerala, Punjab and Bihar Governments have passed anti-dowry legislations.

The Dowry Prohibition Act, 1961

At the all-India level, *Dowry Prohibition Act* was introduced in the Parliament on 27th April 1959 and was ultimately passed on 20th May 1961. Main provisions of this Act are mentioned below :

1. The Act defines in clear cut terms the meaning of dowry. [*Note* : Refer to Page No.**659** for the legal definition of dowry.]

2. ***Penalty for Giving or Taking Dowry*** : If any person, after the commencement of this Act, gives or takes or abets the giving or taking of dowry, he shall be punishable with imprisonment which may extend to six months, or with fine which may extend to five thousand rupees, or with both.

3. ***Penalty for Demanding Dowry*** : If any person, after the commencement of this Act, demands, directly or indirectly, from the parents or guardian of a bride or bridegroom, as the case may be, any dowry, he shall be punishable with imprisonment which may extend to six months, or with fine which may extend to Rs.5,000/- or with both.

4. ***Dowry to be for the Benefit of the Wife or Her Heirs*** : Where any dowry is received by any person other than the woman in connection with whose marriage it is given that person shall transfer it to the woman —

(a) if the dowry was received before marriage, within one year after the date of marriage; or

(b) if the dowry was received at the time of or after the marriage, within one year after the date of its receipts; or

(c) if the dowry was received when the woman was a minor, within one year after she has attained the age of eighteen years; and pending such transfer, shall hold it in trust for the benefit of the woman.

5. ***Dowry to the Tune of Rs.2,000/= only Permitted*** : The Act permits gifts in the form of ornaments, clothes and other articles not exceeding Rs.2,000/= in value. The Act thus legalises dowry only to the tune of Rs.2,000/=.

6. ***Cognisance of Offences*** : As per the provisions of this Act, no court shall take cognisance of any such offence except on a complaint made within one year from the date of the offence.

This Act which was amended in June 1986, was also made more rigorous and stringent.

Poor Performance of this Legislation

As anticipated this legislation failed to produce the desired results. *"The Committee on the status of women"* in India [1974] reported that *The Dowry Prohibition Act,* 1961 has failed to curb the evils of dowry. In spite of the rapid growth of this evil practice, there are particularly no cases reported under this Act. No law can be enforced without the whole-hearted co-operation of the people. Social reformers were successful in getting the practice of dowry abolished. But they were not successful in persuading the people to accept the legislation in principle and abide by it with the spirit of committment. No one can eradicate this evil unless the people carry the philosophy behind the law much further. Proper efforts are not made to convince people regarding the evils of dowry. As a result, legislation prevails, but its violations take place uninterruptedly. Number of cases taken up under this Act have been awfully insignificant. In fact, **P.N. Sapru,** a former Judge of Allahabad High Court and the then member of Parliament [1960s] had described the Bill as *"ridiculous"* and even went to the extent of suggesting its withdrawal. What he meant was that - it would be meaningless to pass legislations which cannot be enforced. Effective enforcement of legislations such as this obviously demand the willing co-operation of people.

Non-Legislative Measures towards the Abolition of Dowry

Mere legislations cannot do any magic. They are to be accepted and adopted by the people on their own. Sometimes, special efforts are required to persuade them to accept and comply with the legislations. Hence non-legislative measures are also required to face the social menaces like dowry system. Some such measures are worth mentioning here.

1. Propaganda and Publicity against Dowry

Modern media of propaganda including the electronic media such as radio, T.V., movies, dramas, newspapers, internet, etc. must be effectively made use of to convince people that the practice of dowry is not only illegal but also unethical. It is essential to make use of the media in diverse ways and not in a uniform manner taking into consideration the level of education of the people, their rural and the urban background.

2. Creating Public Opinion and Rousing Social Conscience

In marriage negotiations, material considerations such as wealth, ornaments, money, jobs and professional opportunities, etc., have always formed an important incentive. What is deplored in the case of dowry in its compulsive character and material transactions in actual consideration for marriage. Proper measures are to be taken to do away with this. The attack on dowry has to be a multi-pronged. Social legislation alone cannot help in this regard.

(i) A social understanding must be created in the public by bringing to their notice the evils of dowry.

(ii) Social consciousness needs to be aroused, particularly amongst women. They must be educated that their encouragement of dowry will perpetuate the inequality of the sexes.

(iii) Since practice of dowry is at its heights among the higher educated people, formal education alone cannot mitigate this problem. Greater stress is to be laid on moral education and value education. Education that is given to the youths must help to broaden their minds and widen their outlook.

3. Encouraging Inter-Caste Marriages

It is quite known that the endogamous nature of caste and sub-caste restricts the range of selection of life-partners. Hence it is suggested that intercaste marriages must be encouraged among the youths so that they would get a wide range of selection in finding a suitable mate for marriage. This "self-choice" opportunity given to the youths will help them to get out of the vicious circle of dowry. Though this suggestion sounds alright we must not be over-enthusiastic about the outcome of this. Because, the hold of the tradition and the influence of the caste are still powerful in the Indian society.

4. An Appeal to the Idealism of the Youth

Youths are the only ray of hope to combat effectively against the dowry. Youths must be given education and inspired to take initiative towards its actual abolition. Youths are basically idealistic. But only honest and charismatic leaders [like Vivekananda, Gandhiji, Jayaprakash Narayan and others] could appeal to the idealism of the youth and make them committed to the non-acceptance or total rejection of the dowry. In fact, Gandhiji had given a call to socially boycott the supporters of dowry. It may be recalled that **Jayaprakash Narayan** [J.P.] through his theory of *"Samagra Kranti"* [or "Total Revolution"] had made an appeal to the young men and women of the day to take an oath *"that they would never ask for dowry, and reject and boycott those who ask for it."*

5. Role of Voluntary Associations

It is suggested that voluntary associations should take initiative in this regard and make propaganda against the evils of dowry. It is also advocated that such associations should take up the cases of victims of dowry harassment and get them justice with due publicity will definitely create a social wave against the practice of dowry. In fact, organisations such as *"Saheli"* in Delhi, *"Women's Centre"* in Mumbai, *"Sakhi Kendra"* in Kanpur, *"Stree Adhar Kendra"* in Poona, and others are already in the field doing some work in this direction.

Conclusion

It is clear from the above analysis that the dowry system in our country has become a kind of business deal, a big bargain in matrimony. It is unspiritual and is devoid of ethical values. It is a stigma associated with the Indian marital system. It has become equally rampant in the other religious communities of India such as Christians and Muslims. It has made a few young women to remain as spinsters. It is high time that it is stopped.

The successful abolition of the practice of dowry would be a landmark towards social reform. But it is not an easy task. Some of the highly educated and professionally well-placed individuals including the foreign-returned young men are clinging on to it. Determined efforts should be made on an all-India basis to combat this problem. Social and moral consciousness of the people, education and economic independence of women, inter-caste marriages, effective enforcement of legislation against dowry system, establishment of voluntary associations to discourage dowry, civil marriage, arrangement of *"samuhika vivaha"* or community weddings, launching of the youth movements against the dowry system – are some of the means of countering this practice. The sooner it disappears the better it will be for the progress of this society.

5. DIVORCE

Marriage is one of the universal social institutions of mankind. In almost all the societies of the world, both uncivilised and civilised, majority of the people enter into marital relationship at an appropriate age in their own way. Though majority of the people enter into wedlock there is no guarantee that their marriage would ultimately end in success. Many marriages end in failures and wind up with divorce. The rate of divorce is fast increasing in many of the Western countries posing a serious social problem.

Meaning of the Word *"Divorce"*

The English word *"divorce"* is derived from the Latin word *divortium* which again is derived from *dis* which means *"apart"* and *vertere* which means to *"to turn."* Divorce is the dissolution of the tie of marriage.[1] So, *divorce is the turning away of partners from each other. It truly is a complete turn from the way of life the couple had so far.* [**S. Pothen.** Page - 2.]

It is clear from the above description, the term *"divorce"* refers to the complete rupture of the marital bond. The persons thus divorced go back to the original position of being free to marry again. Divorce is the word which is normally given to the legal ending of marriage. In the legal language, it might appear as a simple phenomenon, but in practical life its implications are massive and many-faceted. Divorce represents the end of hopes that husband and wife had for each other; it is the certificate that their relationship failed.

Definition of Divorce

1. ***Ian Robertson*** **:** *"Divorce constitutes official social recognition that a marriage has failed, and it can be a traumatic experience for all concerned".*
2. ***Wallace and Wallace*** **:** *"When a marriage does not have a sufficient base upon which to survive, it may end in divorce".*
3. ***W.P. Scott*** in *'Dictionary of Sociology'* **:** Divorce is *"an institutionalised arrangement for terminating the marriage relationship and allowing each partner the right to remarry".*
4. ***The Hindu Marriage Act,*** **1955** gives the following explanation. According to this Act, *"any marriage solemnised, whether before or after the commencement of this Act, may, on a petition presented by either the husband or the wife, be dissolved by a decree of divorce"* on the grounds mentioned therein.

Divorce, Separation and Desertion

The terms *divorce, separation* and *desertion* are not one and the same and the difference between them must be understood.

• ***Separation*** **:** Separation refers to an informal preliminary step towards divorce for the couple may live separately for a temporary period to lessen the immediate conflict. Separation could also be a legally recognised decision to live separately without divorcing. In any instance of marital separation, the mates are deprived of normal marital association, affecting their health, security and happiness. As far as the children are concerned, there is the loss of daily love and counsel of one parent. *The Hindu Marriage Act,* 1955 also makes provision for judicial separation.

• ***Desertion*** **:** Desertion is often defined as *"deliberate abandonment of conjugal society."* Desertion is an evasion of marital responsibilities and hence, we have no way of ascertaining its true nature. Desertion, as the term is ordinarily employed, means, *"the irresponsible departure from the home on the part of either husband or wife, leaving the family to fend for itself."*

Though instances of desertions are found here and there, they are not always officially recorded. It means a large share of desertions are never broughtout before any public agency. Many wives do not prefer to report about their husbands for they do not want to suffer from the stigma of being abandoned from their husbands. Since divorces are constly and also time-consuming processes, many deserted women do not take the matter to the court to get a permanent relief. Desertion is popularly known as *"the poor man's divorce."* Further, some of the consequences of desertion are similar to those of divorce, for the family may be permanently dissolved.

---

1 *Encyclopedia Britannica,* Vol.III, Cambridge, 1910. Page - 334.

DIVORCE IN INDIA

Divorce is not unfamiliar to modern India. In modern India, divorce rate is found to be higher than what it was a few decades ago. In the absence of the reliable statistics it is very difficult to estimate the actual rate of divorce in India. It could however be generalised that the rate of divorce is higher in the cities and nuclear families than in the villages and undivided families.

Divorce among the Hindus

Hindus, in general, still believe that *"marriages are arranged in heaven."* Hindus consider their marriage irrevocable and indissoluble. According to the traditional Hindu belief, marital bond is said to be inseparable and irrevocable. The parties to the marriage cannot dissolve it at will. They are bound to each other until the death of either of them. The belief states that the wife is supposed to be bound to her husband even after his death.

This concept of marriage that it is indissoluble, is itself a sublime one which makes the husband and the wife to adjust their tastes, tempers, ideals, interests, choices and preferences. It thus involves sacrifices on the part of both the husband and the wife for each is called upon to bear with the other. Each individual is here called upon to make marriage a success by means of compromise and adjustment.

Divorce was almost unknown in the ancient period in India. In spite of having divergent and opposite views, the wife and husband were made to live together. There is no reference to divorce in the whole of Vedic literature. According to ***Manu Smriti,*** Dharma is based on the life long mutual respect for each other by wife and husband. The Puranic writers who popularised the ideal of *"Pativratya"* also expected the Hindu wife to be devoted to her husband and husband alone. Fidelity and modest service to the husband were regarded as the sole duty and main purpose in her life. The ideal of *"pativratya"* gave rise to and glorified the practice of *"sati"* or *"self-immolation"* during the later days.

Some Provisions for *"Divorce"* even in Ancient World ?

Though the Hindu thinkers, in general, were against divorce, some of them had made some provisions for divorce. Even **Manu** had recognised the husband's right to divorce the wife particularly when the bride's basic and irreparable physical and mental defects such as epilepsy, leprosy, adulterous relations with other man, etc., were concealed by the parents prior to marriage.

Kautilya's *"Arthashastra"* also provides some ground for divorce. Accoding to Kautilya, if there is mutual envy or jealousy between the wife and husband, then they can leave each other. However, consent of both is necessary for this. Kautilya mentions four kinds of marriages, such as *Brahma, Prajapatya, Arsha* and *Daiva* in which the question of divorce does not arise at all, because these marriages are subject to the approval and blessings of the father.

Narada and **Parashara,** two other *Shastrakaras* had conferred on the Hindu wife the right to divorce her husband on certain specific grounds such as the following : (i) *the death of first husband;* (ii) *whereabouts of the husband not known for months together;* (iii) *impotency of husband;* (iv) *husband becoming a "sanyasi";* (v) *husband's failure to honour and obey the requirements of Varna Dharma resulting in his outcaste;* (vi) *mutual enmity.*

According to **Valvalkar,** *"divorce is not known to the Hindu institution of marriage."*[1] A married partner, particularly a woman, was expected to undergo any hardship in order to salvage her marriage. The Hindu writers seem to be partial and lenient towards men, right from the beginning.

---

1 **P.A. Valvalkar** *"Hindu Social Institutions"* [1939]. Page - 145.

Strict fidelity and devotion was demanded from a woman, whereas a man could marry again even in the life-time of a wife. In fact, writers during the later days even debased womanhood. Women were pictured as lesser human beings, with only low desires and goals. A woman is depicted as a temptress, who contempts and seduces any man, even the most learned one. Through centuries, Hindu women were suppressed, fettered and ill treated for no fault of theirs. Hindu womanhood was derided and looked down upon. Hence, any attempt to change the nature of Hindu marriage was violently opposed by traditionalists. Vast majority of Indian men were thus not prepared to risk a change even mentally.

Even though some provisions were made by the ancient *Smritikars* for giving divorce, people, on the whole were not in favour of divorce. **Fonseca,** who made a research on the subject under the guidance of eminent sociologist, **Prof. G.S. Ghurye,** came to the conclusion that *"it can be safely asserted that separation, desertion and divorce as they represent various degrees of dissolution of the family are generally not favoured in Indian society."* This is possibly due to the adverse effects of divorce.[1]

Divorce among the Hindus in *Modern India*

Though some ancient *Shastrakaras* did make some provision for divorce under some extra-ordinary circumstances the main stress was in the irrevocability of marital bond only. During the second half of the ancient period, and medieval and early modern period, even those provisions disappeared. Thus Hindu marriage which was regarded as *dharmic* [religious] in the traditional Hindu society did not permit divorce.

Hindu marriage is gradually becoming secularised in the modern period. In spite of the pressure and influence of modernism, the Hindu Law did not permit divorce till 1950s, though some castes did sanction the dissolution of marriage on some grounds.

Legislation to Legalise Divorce

The first legislation in respect of the dissolution of marriage in India was enacted for **Christians** in 1869 called the *"Indian Divorce Act"*, for **Parsis** in 1936 called *"Parsi Marriage Divorce Act"*; and for **Hindus** in **Kolhapur** State in 1920. When the Bombay state passed the *"Bombay Hindu Divorce Act"* permitting divorce on the grounds such as – impotency, lunacy for more than 7 years, leprosy for 7 years, desertion for 4 years, and bigamy, etc. – *as many as 5,500 petitions for divorce were filed within the time span of five years* [1947-52]. This made our legal experts to introduce legislations on an all-India basis permitting the Hindus to avail of the facility of divorce if required.

On an all-India level, *the Special Marriage Act* was passed in 1954, and *the Hindu Marriage Act,* in 1955 which legally permitted divorce to Hindus. The latter one was amended in 1976 and also in 1981 and it provides for judicial separation, divorce, nullity of marriage and annulment of marriage.

Provisions of *"The Hindu Marriage Act, 1955"*

This Act which came into force from May 18, 1955 brought about revolutionary changes not only in the marital relations but also in various other social aspects. This Act applies to the whole of India, except Jammu and Kashmir. The word **"Hindu"** in the Act includes Jains, Sikhs, Buddhists and the Scheduled Castes.

---

1 **S. Pothen** *"Divorce - Its Causes and Consequences in Hindu Society"* [1996]. Page - 7.

Conditions for valid marriage as provided in this Act : (1) neither party has a spouse living; (2) neither party [bridegroom or bride] is an idiot or a lunatic; (3) the groom must have completed 21 years and the bride 18 years of age as per the 1978 Amendement brought to this Act; (4) the parties should not be 'sapindas' of each other unless the custom permits such a marriage.

Section 13 of "The Hindu Marriage Act" lays down various grounds of divorce such as the following [applicable to both the spouses] :

(i) Voluntary sexual intercourse with any person other than his or her spouse;

(ii) Cruel treatment;

(iii) Desertion for two years;

(iv) Ceasing to be a Hindu by conversion to another religion;

(v) Of incurably unsound mind / mental disorder;

(vi) Suffering from a virulent and incurable form of leprosy;

(vii) Suffering from veneral disease in a communicable form;

(viii) Renouncing the world by entering any religious order;

(ix) Has not been heard of as being alive for a period of seven years or more;

(x) No resumption of cohabitation as between the parties to the marriage for a period of one year or upwards after the passing of a decree for judicial separation;

(xi) No restitution of conjugal rights as between the parties to the marriage for a period of one year or upwards after the passing of a decree for restitution of conjugal rights;

(xii) Mutual consent, on the ground that they have been living separately for a period of one year or more, that they have not been able to live together, and that they have mutually agreed that the marriage should be dissolved, on the motion of both the parties made not earlier than six months after the date of the presentation of the petition, and not later than 18 months after the said date.

Causes of Divorce

The phenomenon of divorce is caused by many factors some of which are very general in nature. They may be discussed as below.

1. Stress on the Nuclear Family

The nuclear family has many dysfunctions in modern society. It is highly vulnerable to break up if the bread winner is for any reason unwilling or unable to meet economic obligations. The spouses in a nuclear family have a very strong mutual dependency, especially after the children have left home. They may make extremely heavy demands on one another for emotional support. The failure of one partner to meet the expectations of the other endangers the marriage. But such dangers are not usually seen in the case of the extended family system.

2. The Fading of Romantic Love

The western people are socialised in such a way that they are made to believe that romantic love would make their marriage happy and successful. But the hard realities of life make them understand that the joys of romantic love are usually short-lived. As a result, the excitement of the earlier relationship gets diminished or lost in the daily routines of job and housework. This does not mean that the partners no longer love one another, but their love is likely to be of a different kind.

This could be mature, companionable, and deeply fulfilling, but many people fail to appreciate it. Hence they consider the fading of their romance as a symptom of marital failure. They lose faith in their marriage and may start looking for romance elsewhere.

3. Changing Role of Women

In the past, *"the role of the wife was assumed to be that of housekeeper, child-rearer and nurturant supporter of a husband who was active in the world beyond the home"*. The modern women are rejecting this role, and in doing so, are challenging the established structure of the nuclear family. Women are no longer confined to the home for much of their lives through pregnancy and the care of infants. Women in the modern family is becoming more and more independent. Most of the modern families do not have appropriate norms for the woman who wants an independent career and for the wife who earns more than the husband and becomes the primary bread winner. This situation often develops complexes in men. The growing economic independence of women makes it much easier for them to divorce their mates.

4. Sexual Permissiveness

The widespread availability of contraceptives has separated two different functions of sexual relations - *procreation and recreation.* The use of sex by the marital partners for the purpose of procreation is understandable. But the use of sex for recreational purpose creates problem. Due to the introduction of contraceptives, the danger of pregnancy is removed and hence people feel free to engage in premarital and extramarital sexual intercourse. The nuclear family is built on an assumption of monogamous fidelity, but the growing permissiveness encourages people to search for sexual satisfaction outside their marriage. Sexual permissiveness, thus makes the husband and wife develop mutual distrust, dislike and even contempt. The emotional relationship between them collapses making any one of the two take the earlier opportunity to go away from the other.

Causes of Divorce in the Indian Context

In addition to the general causes of divorce cited above, various other factors have also added to the phenomenon of divorce especially in the Indian context. **Dr. S. Pothen** in her book *"Divorce - Its Causes and Consequences in Hindu Society"* points out at some of the causes, which may be noted below :

1. ***Cruelty*** **:** Cruelty is one of the most important factors responsible for starting serious conflicts between the husband and wife. The complaint of cruelty has been found to be maximum in the lower class than in the middle and upper classes. Physical cruelty like, assaulting and not giving food is more common in the lower classes, but is also found to be present to a certain extent in the middle class. Cruelty may be physical or mental; it may be by words, gestures, or by mere silence.

2. ***Interference by in-laws*** **:** An important problem of the married Hindu women is adjustment with the in-laws, more so in large joint families. In Indian families, a son's loyalty is divided among his parents, his spouse and in the authoritarian joint family, the greater share of his loyalty goes to his kin and not to the spouse. The female spouse finds herself in the midst of strangers, many of whom are hostile. She cannot expect any kind of sympathy, support and understanding from her in-laws, such as – the mother-in-law, father-in-law, sister-in-law, brother-in-law, uncle or aunt-in-law, grand-in-laws, and so on. Pothen's study has revealed that 41.5% of the female spouses have reported that they have had problems with their in-laws.

3. ***Mental Problems*** **:** Modern life brings on us lot of stress and strain. **Reimer** has pointed out that *"neurotic as well as psychotic ailments have been attributed to stresses inherent in the* *urban way of life."*[1] Various pressures such as economic, familial, social and cultural act directly or indirectly on the minds of people. With reference to the changing societies like India, cultural lag and cultural conflict often add to the mental stresses and strains. Dr. Pothen's study has revealed that mental breakdown is one of the causes of marital breakdown in some instances. Both men and women suffer from this problem, though the sufferings of women are comparatively more.

4. *Unplanned and Unthought of Marriage* : It is observed that marital relationship is established without sufficient forethought. In case of arranged marriages, many people do not care to make rational enquiries about the other party. Most of the information given may be only to impress the person at first sight, and unless carefully scrutinised, there can be a lot of discrepancies between the real conditions and the information given. This type of hurried marriages are arranged more in the case of girls than boys. Such hasty marriages can also lead to unpleasant or even shocking discoveries later, which will ultimately shatter the chances of happiness in marriage.

5. *Economic Hardship* : Family life and problems are closely associated with economic hardships and problems. With increasing cost of living, economic problems are soaring high. Such economic problems are more experienced, when the husband is partially or poorly employed or when he is forced to spend his income on certain unwanted things. In such cases, food, clothing, housing and education of the members of the family, particularly the children, are adversely affected. In such a situation, frustrations arise, creating conflicts and tensions in the family. Such state of affairs will also result in desertions and divorce.

6. *Education and Economic Independence of Women* : Emancipation and economic independence of women have been important causes of rapid rise in divorce rate throughout the world. **Fonseca's** study has also showed that *"women today no longer occupy a subordinate position in the family."* Enlightened women are inclined to take advantages of the legal provisions of divorce wherever it is badly and necessarily required. The available data and information are sufficient to conclude that education, employment, emancipation and enlightenment of the Hindu women are causing more and more divorces.

7. *Sexual Maladjustment* : Sexual relationship is considered to be one of the strong bases of any marriage, more so, in the initial stages. Whenever, the spouses are unable to establish satisfying sexual relationship between themselves, marriage is in danger. Physical causes like, impotency of the male and structural malformation of the female sexual organs, may incapacitate the couple to enter into healthy sexual relationships. Further, sexual relationship in human beings is not a mere physical activity. Several physical, psychological and emotional aspects come into play in sexual life. When the favourable circumstances do not prevail in these fields, sex life may be unsatisfying. Sexual maladjustments, thus, can cause divorce.

8. *Other Factors* :

Dr. S. Pothen in her book has also mentioned various other factors contributing to divorce, which may be briefed as follows :

1. Child Marriage, which is still in practice in India, especially among lower castes and classes, contributes to divorce.
2. Marriages, which are arranged against the wishes of the spouses often end in unwanted divorce.
3. Incompatibility of the spouses has been an important cause of divorce in the Indian context. [Sizeable number of individuals (39 husbands and 32 wives) complained of the incompatibility between their temperaments and those of their spouses].

1 **Reimer** *"The Modern City"* as quoted by **Dr. S. Pothen.** Page - 134.

4. Quarrelsome nature of the spouses is another common complaint of men and women of all economic classes. In some cases, the allegation is both ways and in some others it is the one sided allegation.
5. Unhealthy habits like alcoholism, gambling, immorality, often contribute to family tensions, conflicts between husband and wife, and eventually to divorce.
6. Barrenness is considered a curse in the Indian society. A wife, who is found to be barren or infertile, or a husband, who is found to be impotent, often contributes to marital unhappiness and failure. The desire for progeny tempt either one of them to go for divorce.
7. Many a time in our society, there is a tendency to hide physical defects of the parties to marriage before its solemnisation. When the defects are disclosed after the marriage, they get disillusioned.
8. Dowry has become an inseparable part of our marriage system. The husband or his parents would like to extract as much dowry as possible. Unhappiness that is caused because of dowry make the parties to the marriage go apart.
9. A few women have complained of their husbands forcing them to lead an immoral life in order to earn money. These women who belonged mostly to the middle and lower classes were disappointed with their marriage.
10. Lack of affection on the part of spouses towards each other has been found to be one of the causes of divorce. In Dr. S. Pothen's study, around 19.5% of the husbands and 27% wives have complained of lack of affection.

Causes of Divorce : Views of Dr. Damle, Fonseca and Choudhry

The empirical studies undertaken by **Dr. Damle, Fonseca** and **Choudhry** have revealed the following factors contributing to the phenomenon of divorce in the Indian context.[1]

1. Divorce is *not always the result of marital disharmony* especially in the Indian context.
2. Some wives tolerate the alleged neglect, callousness, and even cruelty at the hands of their husbands *but cannot tolerate the trouble, irritation and insult caused by their in-laws.* Such women often seek divorce.
3. Some husbands apply for divorce either because they *doubt the sincerity and single-minded devotion of their wives* towards them or because they find wide intellectual and educational gap between them and their wives.
4. The *failure on the part of the wives coming from the highly orthodox families to keep up with their husbands' social life* - is often the cause. The opposite also sometimes holds good [though less often] where the wife finds life with husband of quiet habits, colourless and dull.
5. In the arranged marriages, where the reason for entering into matrimony is not mutual attraction but a variety of other factors [for example, respect for parents, good dowry, high family connections, etc.] there is less chance for give and take and a low desire for mutual adjustment. People of such *unsatisfying marriage* may often resort to divorce.

Individual and Social Consequences of Divorce

The doubling of the divorce rate since 1950s has meant that many more couples and their children experience the disturbances that frequently accompany divorce. Some of the main consequences or the after-effects of divorce could be listed below.

1 **Prof. Ram Ahuja** *"Indian Social System."* Page - 182.

1. Studies have revealed that divorced men and women experience intermittent *longing for their husbands or wives,* with an accompanying anxiety, even if they themselves had initiated divorce.

2. The immediate *impact of divorce on children is also very severe.* Preschool children experience fright, and bewilderment and tend to blame themselves for separation, while the older children express their anger more directly.

3. *The high divorce rate has created large number of non-traditional single-parent homes.* This is particularly true in the Western context. For example, in 1985, 23.4% of America's 62.5 million children under age 18 lived with only one of their parents [**N.J. Smelser.** Page : 260].

4. *Divorce very badly damages the personality development of children.* In fact, effect upon the children of a dissolved marriage is one of the most forceful arguments against divorce. In these cases where children's parents, with whom they are living, decides to remarry, children face the problem of step-parent. Children also face the social criticism when they are teased and taunted by their playmates. In this way, children face personal disorganisation.

5. *Divorcees often suffer from emotional problems* such as indecision, frustration, disappointment, sleeplessness, mental ambivalence, guilt-consciousness, self-contempt, etc.

6. Divorcees also *face the problem of sex adjustment.* Strong sexual urge on the part of the divorced husband and wife often push them to seek satisfaction in an immoral way.

7. Divorce also *affects the divorcees' habits and regular life.* Duc to thc marital breakdown the routinised habits struggle to find their customary expression, but their failure to do so brings unrest, irritation and dissatisfaction.

8. *Divorce affects the network of social relationships of husband and wife.* It introduces complications into the relations of both husband and wife after separation. Especially in the Indian context, both the individuals become the victims of gossip and irritating comments.

9. Due to *the fear of divorce* many young men and women in the Western countries remain unmarried. Some of them, knowingly or unknowingly, delay it for a long time.

Remedial Measures for Divorce : Avoidance of Family Tensions and Divorce

Various factors discussed above have been causing family tensions, desertions and even divorces. The rate of divorce is slowly increasing in the Indian context. Therefore, steps must be taken to lessen such tensions in the early stages by various means to save marriage and family. Some of the remedial measures can be suggested in this regard.

1. Education About Proper Selection of Mates

Modern young men and women who are very much influenced by movies, T.V. shows, literature, and other media, are more prone to be romantic especially in marital matters. While selecting their life partners, they give more importance to romantic matters rather than to hard reality. Young people must be made aware of the consequences of romantic marriages and need to be advised to become more realistic and to have faith in their parents, who can choose a better companion for them according to their own cultural settings.

Landis P.H. points out, *"many divorces arise because the romantic expectations with which young people often enter marriage, are frustrated by the unromantic realities of the marital* *situation. If these expectations could be modified in the direction of greater realism, large number of marriages might conceivably be saved."*[1]

The caution given by **Eliot** and **Merrill** in this regard is worth considering – *"Men and women are demanding greater personal satisfaction from the estate of matrimony. But then one has to work harder at making marriage a success. Also greater emphasis upon personal happiness in marriage deserves analysis as to its essential validity. Life exacts difficulties as well as pleasures and is full of petty annoyances, disappointments and disillusionments, both in and out of marriage. Probably no married person is completely happy before marriage, nor he can expect to be completely happy after marriage. Many young men nourished in the romantic tradition, may blame their marriage, if they feel unhappy whereas the difficulty may be either within themselves or in situations external to marriage."*[2]

2. Family Counselling Agencies

Family tensions are often due to differences in temperaments, attitudes and social values, economic difficulties, ill health, conflict on child's training, etc. These differences arise due to the lack of understanding between the spouses. Family counselling agencies with trained social workers in family matters can be of great help in mitigating these differences and helping the spouses to develop mutual understanding. Family counselling agencies are commonly found in industrially advanced countries, such as America, Britain, France, Canada, etc. Only recently such agencies have started functioning in India that too in cosmopolitan cities.

Family counselling agencies should be established at all district and taluk centres. They must act as welfare agencies. These welfare agencies which add to the welfare of the family, and ease tensions, agencies rendering financial assistance to economically backward families or family planning clinics should be assisted and encouraged by the state.

3. Family Counselling Courts

When matters relating to family disputes, conflicts, etc. come to the court for divorce, attempt should be made by the concerned authorities to gather facts relating to the cases through the social workers and analyse them properly before giving a decision. The courts should not act just on the basis of statistics, evidences, facts, figures, etc. in a mechanical manner. Its main intention should be to save the marriage and to help the spouses to live together with better understanding and mutual support. *The Family Court Act, 1984* makes provision for that.

4. Help after Divorce

In spite of all the best possible efforts to save a marriage, some cases ultimately end in divorce only. In some cases, that is, constant tension in the family not only affects the life organisation of husband and wife, but also their children. In such cases efforts should be made to provide financial assistance to the forsaken wife and to the maintenance of the children. Divorced women should not be compelled to resort to prostitution if they are not able to secure employment. No other environment has proved so favourable for the upbringing of children as the home, which the parents create. If the home is utterly inharmonious or positively harmful, the state must seek to protect the children in some way or the other.

---

1 **Landis Paul H.** in his article *"Control of the Romantic Impulse Through Education"* as quoted by **G.R. Madan** in *"Indian Social Problems"* Vol.I. [1966]. Page - 386.

2 **Eliot** and **Merrill** quoted by **G.R. Madan.** Page - 386.

Marital Success is Necessary for the Prevention of Divorce

Though marriage is being eulogised on various grounds, we have not been able to stop divorce from taking place. Divorce rate is increasing in the West. The trend towards higher rate of divorce is seen in India too. The main reason for divorce is marital failure. Hence, finding out the secrets of marital success is the best solution for divorce. A great gynecologist **Th.H. Van de Velde** in his book *"Ideal Marriage - Its Physiology and Technique"* [Page : 4] has suggested four important points for attaining happiness in marriage. They are mentioned below:

1. A right choice of marriage partner.
2. A good psychological attitude of partners, both to the world in general and to each other.
3. A solution of the problem of parentage which meets the wishes of both partners, and
4. A vigorous and harmonious sex life.

6. CORRUPTION

Corruption is both Historical and Universal

Corruption as a phenomenon is both universal and historical. It is a fact of history that there existed no society in the past in which corruption was totally absent. At the same time, corruption is practised in one way or another in all the existing societies of the world. Its content and character, its forms and intensity, of course, may differ from society to society.

Corruption as a Social Evil

Corruption is one of the social evils found in all the societies of the world. In some societies, it is more rampant than in some others. Unfortunately, India is regarded as one of the countries where corruption has become very much widespread during the recent years. Corruption is one of the factors that has contributed to the degradation of the Indian politics. Corruption in India has become deep-rooted and its growth is unchecked and unhindered. All those leaders who declared war against corruption have either shamelessly succumbed to corruption or miserably lost the battle. Tall claims made by political leaders to fight out corruption have proved to be shallow.

"Power corrupts and absolute power corrupts absolutely." That is what the events at the national political scene seem to suggest, at least during the last couple of years. Practise of corruption at lower levels by some clerks, peons and attenders for some petty amount, is understandable and tolerable. They may practice it due to tough financial conditions, excessive demands from family, friends or society, health hazards, or some other kinds of pressures. What is more disturbing and dangerous is the corruption at higher levels. Corruption in various forms has become the mainstay of our national polity in the recent past. It is needless to say that the evil of corruption meaning bribery and graft, is not conducive to social stability and equilibrium. It invariably involves negation or betrayal of normative values of society, which are essential for the smooth functioning of society.

Definition of the Concept of Corruption

The meaning of the concept of corruption can be made clearer by means of some definitions.

1. In simple words, corruption refers to *"an act of bribery." It is abuse of political power or public office for personal or private gain brushing aside all formal rules.*
2. The **dictionary** defines corruption as *"an inducement to wrong by bribery or other unlawful means : a departure from what is pure and correct."*

3. According to **D.H. Bailey,** corruption can be understood as the *"misuse of authority as a result of consideration of personal gain which need not be monetary."*
4. **Andriski** considers it as *"the use of public power for private advantage in ways which transgress some formal rule or law."*
5. **Bhargava** says that an *"act of commission or omission by a public servant for securing pecuniary or other material advantage or indirectly for himself, his family or friends is corruption."*

Main Characteristics of Corruption

The above cited definitions point out the following characteristics of corruption.

1. Corruption, as it is understood today refers to an irregular, illegal and immoral practice associated with our public life.
2. An act of corruption involves dereliction of duty, moral and legal lapses.
3. Persons party to corruption tend to neglect their prescribed duty deliberately.
4. Individuals who are charged of corruption are those who deviate from their fixed official duty in order to obtain some economic gains or to provide some physical comfort or convenience to his family members.
5. Corruption involves the practice of receiving bribe not only for getting wrong things done, but also getting right things done at the right time.
6. Corruption involves the abuse of power associated with a public office or public life.

Corruption in Public Life and among Public Servants

Corruption has become a widespread practice today. It has percolated through almost all the fields of our social life. No part of our public life is spared from it. A large number of public servants are guilty of either practising or supporting corruption. The term "corruption" has a very wide meaning, and from the legal point of view, the following behaviour patterns can be dubbed as corrupt practices, according to **Malhotra.**

(1) Receiving some reward on the part of a public servant, for the work done by him in his official capacity. ***Example*:** A doctor in a Government hospital receiving monetary reward from a patient for having treated him.

(2) Obtaining any object or pecuniary advantage illegally. ***Example*:** Police officers receiving *"mamul"* at the hands of small vendors found in footpaths of busy areas of a city.

(3) Misappropriation of public property. ***Example*:** Government officers using their departmental vehicles for their personal tours, family purposes.

(4) Possessing property or financial resources disproportionate to one's declared sources of income. ***Example*:** Clerks and officers in R.T.O. [Regional Transport Office] owning film theatres, hotels, couple of acres of high yielding agricultural lands, etc.

(5) Abuse or misuse of official position. ***Example*:** Police officers misusing their position to get free supply of fruits, vegetables and daily required things from the petty businessmen.

(6) Disregard of rules purposefully to help citizens in avoiding dues / tax / duty due to be paid to the government. ***Example*:** Income tax, sales tax, commercial tax, and other tax officers favouring some people either in reducing dues or in waiving of the same after obtaining some financial benefits from them.

(7) Refusal to do duty on some plea which may benefit the other party. ***Example***: police officer not registering a case to protect a criminal.

(8) Accepting gifts [such as car, gold chain, fridge, colour T.V., etc.] by "persons of positions" from persons with whom they have official dealings. ***Example***: Building contractors giving gifts to the corporation commissioner, businessmen giving gifts to commercial tax officers with the expectation of getting some favours which would cause loss to the government.

(9) Borrowing money for purchasing a costly thing from a person with whom one has official dealings. ***Example***: Income tax officer borrowing money from a businessman to purchase a house, the act of which compels him to do some official favours to the lender of money.

Corruption is so rampant that it is found in all the ministries and departments of the central and the state governments. In some ministries in the union government such as defence, petroleum, power and communication, chances for "making money" through corrupt practices, are more. In the same way, certain departments such as police, transport, income tax, sales tax, commercial tax, revenue department, etc., provide lot of opportunities for the public servants working in them to make money in an illegal way.

Corruption is so widespread today that people have come to accept it as a commonly approved practice. No wonder, if it becomes institutionalised in the days to come.

Causes of Corruption

Corruption is like blood cancer. It has taken deep roots in the country. It has percolated through almost all fields. Corruption in Indian public life is *"all pervasive"* and that businessmen, bureaucrats, contractors, industrialists, entrepreneurs, journalists, vice-chancellors, teachers, doctors, nurses and the politicians all come under suspicion. As the time moves more and more, people are being swept by the move of corruption.

Corruption is a complex phenomenon and various factors and forces have conspired to cause it and spread it everywhere. The causes responsible for corruption as enlisted by **C.B. Mamoria** [Pages : 844 - 847], may be discussed here.

1. ***Economic Insecurity*** **:** This is regarded as the most important cause of corruption. The poor people become corrupt in the hope of becoming rich. The rich indulge in it for fear of losing what they have. The rich have a craving for luxurious goods and imported commodities, such as - dresses, telephone receivers, golden ornaments, cosmetics, transistors, air conditioners, T.V.s, wrist watches, etc. This encourages smuggling on a massive scale.

2. ***High Rate of Income Tax*** **:** Since tax rates are comparatively high in India even the honest people are often tempted to escape from it by making false returns of their property and income. Many of the officers in the Income Tax Department are also equally corrupt and they thrive on bribery. Income tax officers, policemen, sales tax officers, excise inspectors and others started minting money not only from the black marketeers and tax evaders, but also from innocent people who gave bribes in order to avoid suffering and humiliation at the hands of these officials.

3. ***Meagre Salary being Paid to the Government Servants*** **:** Employees in some of the government departments are paid comparatively very less salary. This situation is said to be the cause of corruption in administration. Clerks in the court, peons and attenders in all government departments, police constables and such other employees draw poor salary. They expect tips and bribes even for doing their regular or routine duties. It has been estimated that 60% to 70% of the officers are corrupt in one form or the other. [C.B. Mamoria - Page: 845]

4. ***Emergence of New Sources of Wealth and Power*** **:** The modern political economic set up provides a chance for the politicians in power to make money through illegal means. As **Lincoln Steffens** has said, *"the politicians took bribes because businessmen gave them and businessmen gave them because they had to."* This unholy understanding between the businessmen and the politicians always encourage corruption.

5. ***The System of Democracy*** **:** The present style of functioning of democracy in India, also contributes to corruption. All parties, especially the ruling party spends crores of rupees on each election. This money comes from the big businessmen, industrialists and such other rich men who have their own vested interests in financing the elections. They supply money to the party elections in the form of *"black money."* This in turn, gives them licence a 'moral' justification for accumulating *"number - two"* money [unaccounted money] in different forms.

6. ***The Very Presence of Black Money*** **:** Existence of large amounts of unaccounted black money is one of the main sources of corruption. *"This money is obtained by various ways, namely, tax evasion, smuggling, speculation, in immovable property and shares and stocks, receiving fees and remuneration partly or wholly in cash without showing them in the accounts, trading in licences and permits, ..., etc."* [C.B. Mamoria - Page : 847]

7. ***Social and Economic Modernisation*** **:** It is said that modernisation breeds corruption in industrial society, which *"offers prizes for doing evil; money, position, power",* besides bringing about attitudinal changes in the system. New loyalties and new identifications emerge among individuals and groups. This contributes to an increase in the incidence of corruption. As **Huntington** has said, *"Corruption in a modernising society is in part not so much the result of deviance of behaviour of norms from the established patterns of behaviour."* More than any other thing *"the get-rich quick"* motivation inspires a large number of people both at the top and bottom of the society to become corrupt.

All the factors mentioned above have generated a favourable atmosphere for corruption.

Prevention of Corruption

Legislative Measures to Contain Corruption

Corruption which has become widespread in the Indian society, has to be contained in some way or the other. Legislative measures are very much necessary for this.

1. Prevention of Corruption Act, 1947

Certain sections of the IPC could be used for punishing those who are guilty of taking bribe. The Central Government introduced in 1947 *"The Prevention of Corruption Act"* for the more effective prevention of bribery and corruption. The Act, of course, has been a miserable failure in reaching its target. We know that corruption has increased out of all proportions.

2. Prevention of Corruption Act, 1988

In order to bring all relevant legal provisions relating to the practice of corruption, the Central Government introduced the *Prevention of Corruption Act, 1988.* The Act consolidated the provisions of the Prevention of Corruption Act, 1947, some sections of the Indian Penal Code, the Criminal Procedure Code, and the Criminal Law Act, 1952.

This [1988] Act enlarged the scope of the term "public servant." The Act is now applicable to all the employees of the Central and the Union Territories. The employees of nationalised banks, public undertakings, University Grants Commission [UGC], vice-chancellors, professors, scientists, and others receiving financial aid from the Central and State governments or even local authorities. Office-bearers of the co-operative societies of the central and the state governments, also come under the provisions of this Act. However, M.P.s, M.L.A.s, and M.L.C.s are kept out of the purview of this Act. Offences committed by the public servants, if proved in a court of law are effectively dealt with as per the provisions of this Act.

The Santhanam Committee and Its Recommendations

Corruption which has gone deep into our social life cannot be removed very easily. In fact, it can only be reduced or minimised, and can hardly be stopped altogether. No nation has become successful so far. Even for minimising this problem, both preventive and punitive measures will have to be taken. Thus, the Central Government appointed in 1962, a Committee on "Prevention of corruption" under the Chairmanship of **K. Santhanam.** The Committee gave its report in 1964 in which it recommended various steps to be taken to contain corruption. The Committee observes, *"corruption cannot be eliminated or even satisfactorily reduced unless preventive measures are planned and implemented in a sustained and effective manner. Preventive action must include administrative, legal, social, economic and educative measures"*. [as quoted by **C.B. Mamoria** - Page : 865].

***The Committee recommended the following measures*:**

1. A thorough study of the extent possible, scope and modes of corruption, should be undertaken regarding each department, undertaking or ministry. The study must also suggest preventive remedial measures for the same.
2. Administrative delays should be reduced to the minimum to avoid corrupt practices. For this purpose -
   (a) existing procedures and practices should be reviewed to avoid delays;
   (b) time-limits should be prescribed for dealing with receipts and should be strictly enforced; and
3. Attempts should be made to educate citizens with regard to their rights, responsibilities and the procedures of the government.
4. Improvement must be made to increase the salary of the employees besides making necessary provisions for housing, medical facilities for the government employees, etc.
5. Informal codes of conduct for different categories of employees particularly belonging to the departments dealing with economic affairs must be evolved insisting on them not to avail themselves of entertainment and other facilities provided to them by those with whom they have official dealings.
6. Officials should not have any dealings with a person claiming to act on behalf of an industrial house unless he is properly authorised to do so.
7. Companies and businessmen should be obliged to keep detailed accounts of expenditure.
8. Officers for the administrative posts should be selected with great care. Only those whose integrity is tested to the fullest satisfaction must be appointed for the key posts.
9. There should be a complete ban on government servants accepting private commercial or industrial employment for two years after retirement.

The Central Government established the **Central Vigilance Commission [CVC]** in 1964 itself as per the recommendations of this Committee. The Government also set up three other departments as anti-corruption measures :

1. Administrative Vigilance Division [AVD] in the Department of Personnel and Training.
2. Central Bureau of Investigation [CBI].
3. Domestic Vigilance Units in the Ministries / Departments / Public Undertakings / Nationalised Banks.

Functions of Central Vigilance Commission

The Central Vigilance Commission which is the main legal body for dealing with the cases of corruption, has the following main functions.

(i) to make an inquiry into any complaint of corruption against a public servant;
(ii) to advise appropriate type of proceedings to be initiated against the accused person involved in corruption.
(iii) to give directions to the CBI to register a regular case against the corrupt persons.
(iv) to exercise general check and supervision over the vigilance and anti-corruption work in ministries / departments / banks / public undertakings, etc.

Commissions Instituted to Probe Charges of Corruption against the Politicians and Public Companies

From 1955 to 1999 various commissions were appointed by the Central Government to probe into the charges of corruption made against the politicians. ***Examples*** **:** (1) *Das Commission* against Sardar Pratap Singh Kairan; (2) *Kapur Commission* against Biju Patnaik, Chief Minister of Orissa [1987]; (3) *Sarkaria Commission* against Karunanidhi, Chief Minister of Tamil Nadu [1976]; (4) *Grover Commission* against Devraj Urs, Chief Minister of Karnataka [1977]. Dozens of such Commissions were instituted either by the Central Government or the State Governments to probe into the charges of corruption levelled against politicians, including ministers. It is a pity that none of these Commissions has been able to hold the enquiry successfully and find out the truth.

The Vohra Committee **:** The Government had set up in July 1993 ***The Vohra Committee*** to find out the links between Government functionaries and political personalities and crime syndicates and mafia organisations. The Committee which submitted its report in Oct. 1993 strongly recommended the setting up of an independent agency to probe into corruption cases.

The Lok Pal Bill **:** The Central Government previously tried to introduce the *Lok Pal Bill* in the Lok Sabha several times in the time span of 29-30 years [1968, 1971, 1977, 1985 and 1989] but was not able to pass the Bill for want of consensus. The BJP-led NDA [National Democratic Alliance] Government has also shown great interest in introducing this Bill in the Parliament. At present, there is no substitute for Lok Pal whose jurisdiction is to investigate the charges of corruption made against those holding high offices, including the Prime Minister.

Appointing Lok Pals to look into the charges of corruption at the level of those holding high offices, may prove to be an effective measure in containing corruption. At the States level, the Lok Ayuktas which have been established in as many as 11 states have been proved to be very ineffective for they lacked statutory force. In order to make the Lok Pal an effective agency it is necessary to make it comprise of a single retired judge of the Supreme Court or two or three judges. Such a judge / judges should be selected by a Committee of four persons consisting of the Prime Minister, Chief Justice of India, Speaker of the Lok Sabha and the Leader of the Opposition. The Lok

Pal who should be given final powers must have an independent investigative machinery at his disposal.

Other Suggestions to Contain Corruption

It is to be noted that legal measures alone are not sufficient to contain corruption. As complementary to them, various other measures are to be undertaken to control the practice of corruption. *The Santanam Committee* itself had recommended as early as in 1964 certain measures which may be noted below –

In addition to the above recommendations made by The Santhanam Committee, the following suggestions may be considered with a view to eradicate or minimise corruption :

(a) The taxation laws must be modified, licenses and permit system must be thoroughly reviewed.
(b) The law enforcing authorities must see that the laws are rigorously enforced without any fear or favour.
(c) Mass communication media must play a more positive role in encouraging honesty and discouraging and condemning dishonesty and corruption.
(d) The salaries of government officials and the ministers and legislators must be raised in tune with the price index.
(e) Bureaucratic corruption must be reduced by stringent enforcement of punitive measures against bribe-taking.
(f) Corruption trials should be given the widest possible publicity.

Corruption is a cancer which is eating the vitals of the Indian society. It seems that corruption as such cannot be completely wiped out. At least, it can be minimised and held under control. Time is ripe for controlling it at the earliest. More than the legal measures, the public opinion is to be moulded and mobilised against the practice of corruption. That is the need of the hour. Indian citizens should be encouraged to honour and respect honest and dedicated public servants including political leaders. People, instead of making compromises with corruption must make up their mind to fight it. Only then, the evil practice of corruption could be contained.

7. NEPOTISM

Meaning of Nepotism

Nepotism is a practice associated with the social evil of corruption. Nepotism means *favouritism shown towards one's own relatives.* According to the dictionary meaning, nepotism refers to *"giving undue patronage to one's own relations."*[1]

Nepotism as a Social Evil

Like corruption, nepotism is also a social evil. It is an evil practice in which persons in some public offices bestow patronage on their own relatives in consideration of the family relations and in disregard to merit. In this practice, something is done or undone under the influence of the family relations and in disregard to the accepted norms.

Nepotism due to the New Trend in One's Loyalty ?

Favouring one's own relatives or showing favours to one's own kith and kin is not an uncommon practice. It is not a new trend. It represents one of the oldest forms of corruption. Sociological

1 *Chambers 20th Century Dictionary* [1964]. Page - 715.

analysis reveals that social bonds and kinship play an important role in corruption. There seems to be a change in the individual's primary commitments or loyalty. Today, family considerations, kinship ties, friendship obligations, caste, religious and parochial loyalties get precedence in public servant's mind. One's commitment to rules, regulations, laws, values, ideals, morals become secondary. *"The first obligation of a modern administrator is to his family members, followed by close kin, lineage, or ethnic group. Such ties are more compelling than administrative rules and procedures."*[1] The person in the public office who shows favours to his own kith and kin, does not consider his act as a *"corrupt practice"*, nor as a *"deviation from rules"*, but as *"family obligation."* It appears that nepotism has become widespread today because of this new trend in one's loyalty.

This tendency of nepotism is very much rampant among our administrators, bureaucrats and political leaders. In fact, it is connected with power and authority and originates when it is misused. It has become a common thing for our people to expect favours from their relatives who happen to assume public offices. This explains corrupt actions of many a public servant both at the lower and the higher levels. Hence, men in high and low positions have often indulged in nepotism. Politicians in office, the high-ups in the bureaucracy or officers at lower levels have often been found guilty of nepotism.

Some Instances of Nepotism

Recent history of Indian politics and public life gives ample instances of corruption which could be listed under the heading of "nepotism." There are chief ministers and ex-chief ministers who have openly shown illegal favours to their own sons, daughters, and wives. There are any number of ministers who are protecting their kith and kin who have indulged in immoral and illegal activities, by bestowing on them special favours. There are vice-chancellors who have abused their power and position in giving appointments to their own children and relatives by denying the same opportunity to the more qualified and meritorious persons. At the bureaucratic level, nepotism is not uncommon. Ministers, judges, police inspectors, company directors, deputy commissioners, college principals, vice chancellors, and such other persons occupying responsible public offices, are often found to be guilty of nepotism.

Nepotism as a Common Practice

Nepotism today has become a common practice. *"Nepotism has come to be accepted as a form of prerogative or a privilege inherent in office, and the man in office feels himself free to exploit it to his maximum advantage. Like corruption, if not checked at top, it percolates to the lower levels with sanctity."*[2]

Evil Effects of Nepotism

(i) Nepotism negates talents, abilities, merits and efficiency.

(ii) Practice of nepotism abrogates rules, neglects laws and brushes aside morality.

(iii) It damages the activism and enthusiasm of the really talented people who are discriminated against to favour somebody.

(iv) It spoils the morale of the people, makes them to give up idealism and commitment to values and induces them to become opportunists.

(v) Nepotism adversely affects the general credibility of the public servants and makes the general masses to become cynics.

---

1 **Prof. Ram Ahuja** *"Society in India"* [199]. Page - 403.

2 **Kachroo** and **Kachroo** *"Society in India."* Page - 415.

Thus, it is necessary to contain nepotism. Organised efforts on the part of the people is required to combat nepotism. Strong public opinion is to be created against the practice of nepotism. Modern media should take a leading role in exposing the immoral practice of nepotism. Though it is difficult to root out nepotism, it is possible to control it through collective efforts.

8. BLACK MONEY

'Black Money' which is often referred to as *"parallel economy" or "unrecognised economy"* or *"unofficial economy"* - is both an economic and a social problem. It has both social and economic consequences upon society. Black money is a problem with a difference. If the problem of poverty affects those who are poor, and if the problem of unemployment affects directly those who are unemployed, the problem of black money does not affect those who have ample of black money, but it affects the common man and the society at large. Hence, all the nations are concerned about checking or controlling the growth of black money.

Meaning of Black Money

Black money is that, which is earned or received in contravention of the prevailing Government acts and regulations, or money that has been retained without the payment of taxes, which are due to the Government.

Black money accrues everyday and everywhere and ranges from a few rupees to a few lakhs or crores of rupees. **Example :** (i) It is black money when a minister or a parliament member or an official takes payment for giving a licence or a permit. (ii) It is black money when a cement or steel manufacturer or trader, sells the commodity at a price above the controlled rate without the money appearing in the official records. (iii) When a professor goes to another university to conduct an examination and travels in II class train while claiming I class fare, he also acquires money which is not white, but black. These examples could be multiplied.

In simple words, it can be said that *black money is tax-evaded money.* This kind of money can be earned through either legal or illegal means.

(i) Its legitimate source is that those who earn income through various ways do not reveal their entire income for tax purposes. **Examples :** (i) Teachers earning money through private tuition and book royalty not including it in their income tax returns. (ii) Music artists earning huge amount of money by giving programmes on contract basis and including only a part of it in their income tax returns and retaining with themselves a major portion of their earnings and so on.

(ii) Its illegitimate sources are many. **Examples :** Bribes, black marketing, smuggling, selling commodities at prices higher than the controlled prices, and so on.

Causes of Black Money

According to **Prof. Ram Ahuja**, several factors are responsible for black money. He lists the following factors as important ones.[1]

1. High Rate of Tax : An unrealistic and disproportionate increase in taxes and duties compel some people to evade tax and accumulate black money. As per the present rule [2002-03] the tax free income limit is fixed at Rs.50,000/=. It is a known fact that no man belonging to even the lower middle-class group can run his family smoothly and comfortably in this age of inflation within this income limit of Rs.50,000/=. A mason or a carpenter or a plumber or a painter earns about Rs.200/= to Rs.250/= per day in a city. The yearly income of these people definitely exceed Rs.50,000

1 **Prof. Ram Ahuja** *"Social Problems in India"* - Page : 384 - 387.

But they rarely file their income tax returns and pay their taxes. Similarly, doctors, advocates, chartered accountants, who earn a few lakhs of rupees normally hide their real income to escape paying income tax between 50% to 70% of the total income. There is an argument that if income tax is reduced there is less likelihood of hiding the income and paying more tax.

2. Different Rates of Excise Duty : The Government has fixed different rates of excise duty. On the basis of the quality, the products [such as paints, pipes, textiles, electric wires, etc.] are classified into different grades and tax duties are levied on the basis of the classification made by the manufacturer. Manufacturers, sometimes downgrade a product to pay lower rates of excise, which will help generate black money.

3. Price-control Policy of the Government : The Government often regulates the prices of some commodities [such as sugar, cement, steel, paper, vanaspathi, automobile, tyres, fertilizers, etc.] by following what is known as *"price-control policy"*. Since this policy is comparatively rigid it does not take into account the ups and downs in the market due to the interplay of demand and supply. The private manufacturers and merchants take the undue advantage of this policy and resort to hoarding, fraud, artificial scarcity, etc., which will result in black money.

4. Inflation : Inflationary situation is said to be one of the causes of black money. In this situation, the prices of certain commodities [like petrol] go up and moneyed people start spending their unaccounted money, they may also divert resources from production to speculation. This will cause inflation.

5. Quota System and Scarcity : The Government has fixed quota for import, export and foreign exchange. This quota system is misused to make black money.

When there arises a **scarcity** of essential goods, people are compelled to pay more for them than the controlled prices. This gives scope for black money. *For example,* people are paying now more money than what is fixed as its price for kerosene oil due to its scarcity. The extra payment made by the customer will add to the black money.

6. Elections in a Democratic System : Elections are a part of the democratic process. Electioneering has become a costly affair today. Hence the candidates contesting for elections are bound to spend more than what is legally permissible for them. These elections are generally financed by the black money holders. There is an unholy alliance between the political parties and the business tycoons. These business oriented black money holders expect political patronage and economic concessions. They obtain such concessions from the political leaders by paying them heavy donations through black money. The concessions will help them to generate more and more black money.

7. Real Estate Transactions : People amass black money through real estate transactions. Purchasing a house and / or land at a cheaper rate and selling it at a higher rate by manipulating to pay very less stamp duty has become a profitable business in all major towns and cities. This is also an important source of black money.

The Effects of Black Money

Generation of black money in society will have adverse economic as well as social consequences. Black money damages the economic development of the nation by hampering developmental programmes and plans. Due to tax evasion the exchequer loses huge amount of money which could have been used for developmental activities. It adds to inflation and the government loses its control over the economy. It contributes to economic instability.

The social consequences of black money are also severe. It increases social inequality, creates frustrations among honest people, increases crimes like smuggling, bribery, etc. The government may not get enough revenue to undertake social service programmes for the uplift of the poor and downtrodden. It leads to shifts in income and wealth. It is assumed that black money is mostly transferred from low income groups to the relatively large income groups. It appears that there would be a net loss of money to the poorer sections through black money. Needless to say, it contributes to unemployment and poverty.

Measures to Control Black Money

The problem of *'black money'* has to be tackled in a realistic and at the same time intelligent manner. Since it is not a problem with the poor but with the well to do people, it should be handled carefully. The following measures will be of some help in controlling, if not eliminating this problem.

1. More than any other thing, the standards of public morality must be raised. In this regard, politicians, ministers, senior civil servants, intellectuals and the media people must play an important role. They must set up an example for others to emulate by paying taxes properly.

2. Public expenditure must come down and there must be stringent monitoring of expenditure, especially of public sector projects.

3. There must be much more effective supervision of private sector investment expenditures, particularly where there is greater reliance of development on finance institutions and banks.

4. Tax system must be realistic. Unduly high rates of tax are counter-productive. It would lead to tax evasion - whether it is income tax, wealth tax, capital gains tax or transfer tax on real estate - and at a later stage creating black money.

5. Price controls should be done away with. Exchange rates should be realistic reflecting our comparative prices and competitive position in the world economy.

6. Tax collection machinery must be made more efficient than what it is now. Honest officials in this department must be profusely rewarded.

7. Attractive incentives must be given for voluntary disclosures of income [VDS].

8. A thorough overhauling of the economic intelligence unit must be made. Trusted officials must be recruited for this department.

9. Administrative corruption at different levels must be stopped.

10. Exempting tax on money spent on house construction may help mostly middle class salaried people who are normally made to pay taxes without fail.

With regard to this problem the harsh truth is that the government policies are the biggest sources of black money generation. Hence, the government must take extra precaution in framing its policies to give no scope for black money.

9. PROBLEM OF BONDED LABOUR

"Problem of bonded labour" which is haunting the Indian society is one of the problems of the socio-economic importance. Bonded labour has existed in India for centuries. In fact, *the practice of one man keeping another man in perpetual bondage for his selfish and personal whims and fancies* – seems to be a global phenomenon. It has been in existence for thousands of years, right from the Biblical days to the present era. The system of bonded labour as prevalent in India, appears as a relic of feudal hierarchical society. Social workers, social scientists and the government have evinced a great interest in this phenomenon during the recent years. The magnitude of the problem of bonded labour is also highly distressing for the lakhs of people including men, women and children are condemned to servitude under its yoke.

Definition of Bonded Labour

1. ***The National Commission on Labour*** defines the term *"bonded labour"* as *"labour which remains in bondage for a specific period for the debt incurred."*

2. ***The Commission for Scheduled Castes and Scheduled Tribes*** defines the term *"bonded labour"* in the 24th report of the Commission as – *"persons who are forced to work for the creditors for the loan incurred either without wage or on nominal wages."*

3. ***The Bonded Labour Abolition Act, 1976*** defines bonded labour as – *"the system of forced labour under which a debtor enters into an agreement with the creditor that he would render service to him either by himself or through any member of his family or any person dependent on him, for a specified or unspecified period, either without wages or for nominal wages, in consideration of loan or any other economic consideration obtained by him or any of his ascendants, or in pursuance of any social obligation, or in pursuance of any obligation devolving on him by succession."*

Different Names of Bonded Labourers

Bonded labourers are known by various names in various parts of the country. For example, they are known as *"Jeethadalu"* in Karnataka, *"Jeethams"* in Andhra Pradesh, *"Pandiyals"* in Tamil Nadu, *"Adiyas"*, *"Paniyas"* and *"Kattunaikens"* in Kerala, *"Koltas"*, *"Sevaks"* and *"Haris"* in Uttar Pradesh, *"Halis"* in Gujarat, *"Harwahas"* and *"Halis"* in Madhya Pradesh, *"Kamias"* or *"Kamiantis"* in Bihar, *"Gothees"* in Orissa, and so on.

Main Features of Bonded Labour

Two main features are associated with bonded labour – (i) *indebtedness,* and (ii) *forced labour*.

(i) ***Indebtedness*** **:** The poor economic conditions of some rural people especially those belonging to the lowest castes, force them to borrow money from the landlords or other money lenders. The inability to pay back the borrowed money compel them to bind themselves to work for their landlords or moneylenders for a certain number of years at fixed or unfixed wages in order to repay the money borrowed.

(ii) ***Forced Labour*** **:** Sometimes bonded labourers are forced to work throughout their lives or even for generations. Forced labour can hereditarily descend from father to son or be passed on for generations together. What is important here is, during the period of bondage the debtor or the bonded labourer cannot seek employment with any other person. Speaking in economic terms, this means that he cannot *"sell his labour in the market at market value."*

The bonded labour system as we understand it, is mostly found among agricultural labourers in villages. However, it is often extended to labourers working in various other fields such as beedi factories, glass factories, brick kilns, stone quarries, detergent, carpet and other factories.

Extent of Bonded Labour

There are no reliable statistics relating to the extent of bonded labour in India eventhough the system has been in existence for centuries. However, **Gandhi Peace Foundation** [GPF] and **National Labour Institute** [NLI] conducted a survey of bonded labour for ten major states of India for the year 1978-79. The major findings of the survey of these two institutes can be mentioned below :[1]

1 **Ruddardatt** and **K.P.M. Sundharam.** *"Indian Economy"* [2001] Page - 607.

1. The total number of bonded labourers in the ten states surveyed was estimated to be 26.17 lakhs.
2. For India as a whole, 5.7% of the total agricultural labourers constituted bonded labourers.
3. Uttar Pradesh had the highest number of bonded labourers, that is 5.5 lakhs, followed by Madhya Pradesh [5.0 lakhs], Orissa [3.5 lakhs], and Andhra Pradesh [3.25 lakhs]. These four states accounted for 17.25 lakhs of bonded labourers, that is, about 66% of the total bonded labourers in the country.
4. The most significant aspect of the survey is that about 87% of the bonded labourers belonged to Scheduled Castes and Scheduled Tribes.

Another estimate of the bonded labourers for 12 states was conducted in March 1990 by the State Governments and the total number of bonded labourers was estimated at 2.45 lakhs.]

The **International Labour Organisation** [I.L.O.] also has given an estimate. According to its estimation, there are about 150 lakhs bonded labourers in our country out of which 50 lakhs are children.

Causes of Bonded Labour

Various causes have contributed to the system of bonded labour. These can be grouped into three : (i) *Economic Causes,* (ii) *Social Causes,* and (iii) *Religious Causes.*

(i) *Economic Causes* : The economic factors are the main causes of bonded labour. They include various factors such as extreme poverty of people, heightened unemployment, poor material resources to fall back upon in times of economic crises, lack of alternative small scale loans for the rural and urban poor, extremes of natural calamities such as famines and floods, destruction of men and animals, drying away of wells, soaring prices and inflation, government's inability to rehabilitate the poor whenever they are afflicted with problems, and so on.

(ii) *Social Causes* : Social practices, customs and beliefs of the people also contribute to the problem of bonded labour. The social factors include casteism, caste based discrimination, high expenses on occasions like marriage, religious programmes, feasts, birth of a child, death ceremonies, etc. leading to heavy debts, lack of comprehensive social security measures against all kinds of hazards, non-compulsory and unequal educational system, corruption in governmental machinery, irresponsibility and indifferent attitude of the bureaucrats, and so on.

(iii) *Religious Causes* : Religious factors are also adding to the problem of bonded labour. The illiterate, ignorant and religious minded lower caste people are often made to believe that they have the religious obligation to serve people of high castes. Lack of knowledge, poor living conditions and fear of oppression at the hands of higher caste people make the ignorant people to accept their depressed lot.

It is clear from the above discription that the problem of bonded labour originates mainly from the economic constraints, social pressures and religious commitments.

Misery and Sufferings of the Bonded Labourers

Bonded labourers have been existing in India for the past several centuries. It is a peculiar phenomenon of our agricultural economy. The system grew out of extreme poverty and helplessness of the unprivileged sections of the Indian rural populace such as the Scheduled Castes, Scheduled Tribes and semi-tribal people, who depended upon wage income which they received only for a part of the year. When they needed foodgrains or when they needed money for any kind of an emergency they had to borrow the same at the hands of landlords or moneylenders. Since they had no security to offer in the form of land, jewellery or any other property, they pledged themselves. The moneylenders and the high caste landlords took advantage of their helplessness and ignorance and entered into repressive contracts. The wages were so low and the rate of interest so high - often 25% to 50% - that the total loan got accumulated with the passage of time. The total burden of the loan became so huge that it could not be repaid even with the labour of many generations of the debtors family. Once a landless labourer borrowed money, he and his descendants were doomed to perpetual slavery.

It has been observed that majority of the bonded labourers work as agricultural labourers in villages and belong to the outcaste or tribal communities. Of the total labour force in the rural areas, about 33% are engaged in non-agricultural activities, 42% work as cultivators, and 25% as agricultural labourers. Of those who work as agricultural labourers, 48% belong to SCs and 33% to STs. These labourers are unskilled and unorganised and are forced to sell their personal labour for their livelihood. The bonded agricultural labourers occupy the lowest rung of the rural social ladder. Bonded labourers live in pitiable and miserable conditions. They are socially exploited and made to work sometimes 12 to 14 hours a day, and forced to live with cows and buffaloes in shed. If they fall ill, they may be given medicine collected from the local quacks depending upon the mercy of the employer. In all the possible ways, they are cheated by their employers and maximum labour is extracted from them for minimum remuneration.

Abolition of Bonded Labour

The bonded labour system was abolished throughout the country during the Emergency period with effect from 25th October 1975 under the **Bonded Labour System [Abolition] Act, 1976.** For the first time, the government took swift action against money lenders, building contractors, quarry-owners and others who have been found practising some form of bonded and / or contract labour. The government also took some measures to rehabilitate bonded labourers thus freed.

During the Sixth Plan [1980-85], the maximum cost of rehabilitating a bonded labourer was limited to Rs.4,000/= out of which the state governments were given 50% matching grants. The assistance was given to the freed bonded labourers to help themselves to eke out their livelihood.

As per information available with the **Ministry of Labour** from the State Governments, as many as 2,51,424 bonded labourers were identified and released upto 30th March 1995. Of those freed bonded labourers, 2,27,404 were fully rehabilitated. It implies that nearly 90% of the bonded labourers identified, were rehabilitated. This appears to be encouraging. The government further raised the financial assistance to Rs.10,000/= per bonded labourer with effect from August 1994. It is now known that the total number of bonded labourers released between May 1978 and September 2001 is 2,82,135.[1]

However, it is highly exaggerative on the part of the *Ministry of Labour* to stake that there are only 5,700 bonded labourers who need to be rehabilitated. A general observation of the Indian rural set up gives us an impression that the exact number of the bonded labourers cannot easily be traced out. There is need to have periodic surveys of bonded labour in collaboration with non-governmental organisations such as the Gandhi Peace Foundation. Since the bonded labourers have not been organised as a pressure group they are not able to assert themselves.

Problems Involved in the Effective Rehabilitation of Bonded Labourers

The *Bonded Labour System [Abolition] Act* has not been practically effective in all the places particularly because of the lack of enforcement machinery. Enactment of any legislation

1 *"India Book of the Year* 2002 – *Encyclopaedia Britannica and The Hindu."* Page - 306.

requires dedication and committment. Mere enactment of legislation becomes only a political activity. But its enforcement requires strong will and determination. But this factor has been unfortunately lacking in our country. That is why the system of bonded labour still continues to survive. Some deficiencies are involved in the effective implementation of the legislation and also in the rehabilitation of the bonded labourers.

1. The rehabilitation programme has been dealt with separately. This has often led to its failure. Instead of that it should become a part of rural development programme and there should be a proper co-ordination between their rehabilitation programmes and other programmes.
2. The development departments are overburdened with various schemes like IRDP, JRY, TRYSEM, etc. that they do not find sufficient time and efforts to spare for the rehabilitation programmes.
3. Lack of qualified and committed staff has also contributed to the failure of these programmes.
4. Middlemen are still operating like the parasites and take away the fruits and benefits of the rehabilitation to their advantage. Hence rehabilitation programmes are to be carefully and rationally formulated so as to avoid the interference of the middlemen.
5. The freed bonded labourers who come from the lowest strata of the society are not given freedom to select a scheme of rehabilitation but are forced to accept a particular scheme assigned to them by the bureaucrats. It is necessary that the freedom of choice of particular scheme must be provided to these people.
6. Finally, the attitude of the former bonded labour keepers and employers has not completely changed towards the bonded labourers. They take every chance to suppress the efforts of the freed bonded labourers to move towards progress. Hence, it is the need of the hour that the landlords and other employers change their attitude towards the bonded labourers in view of the changed socio-economic conditions.

10. AIDS

[Acquired Immuno Deficiency Syndrome]

Acquired Immuno Deficiency Syndrome [AIDS] is a fatal disease which is haunting the modern civilised society. AIDS is a viral infection got chiefly by sex with strangers. AIDS is said to be the late stage of infection with the ***Human Immuno Deficiency Virus*** [HIV]. AIDS can take around 7 to 10 years to develop after infection with HIV. *HIV is transmitted through semen and vaginal fluids, infected blood and blood products, infected mother to her baby before birth, during birth or through breast milk.* It can be called our modern pandemic affecting both industrialised and developing countries.

AIDS – At the World Level

The phenomenon of AIDS was traced out in 1980s and soon after that it rapidly spread to various nations of the world. In fact, it evolved from a mysterious illness to a global pandemic which has infected tens of millions in less than 20 years.

"According to the recent **WHO** [World Health Organisation] estimates, at the end of the year 2001, the number of adults and children living with HIV / AIDS worldwide were about 40 million. It is also estimated that during 2001, about 5 million people [including 0.8 million children aged 15 years] became infected, with a prevalence rate of 1.2% and about 3 million died of the disease. HIV infections are now almost equally distributed between men and women [52:48%] with an estimated 17.6 million women aged 15 to 49 years living with HIV / AIDS. At the end of November 2001, a total of 2.78 lakh AIDS cases was officially reported to WHO. This is an increase of about 20% from Nov. 2000."[1]

In South-East Asia Region [**SEAR**], the number of reported cases of AIDS continued to increase even up to the early part of the 21st century. In 1984, Thailand was the first country in the SEAR to report a case of AIDS. In most other countries, HIV infection was not diagnosed till 1986 or later. Since then, HIV infection has spread rapidly and WHO estimates for SEAR countries are shown in ***Table* - 1.**

Table - 1

Reported AIDS Cases and Estimated HIV Infections in the SEAR Countries, as on March 2002

Country	*Reported AIDS Cases*	*Estimated HIV Infections*
Bangladesh	19	13,000
Bhutan	3	< 100
DPR Korea	0	< 100
India	29,007	3,860,000
Indonesia	671	100,000
Maldives	8	< 100
Myanmar	4,598	510,000
Nepal	536	34,000
Sri Lanka	117	73,000
Thailand	181,484	770,000
Total	**216,443**	**5,294,600**

Source **:** WHO [2002], *The Works of WHO in South-East Asia Region,* Report of the Regional Director, 1 July 2001 - 30 June 2002, Regional Office, New Delhi.

AIDS – in the Indian Context

The first case of AIDS in India was reported in 1986 from Chennai. Since then there has been an increase in the number of HIV infections over the years. By March 2002 as many as 29,007 cases of AIDS, and an estimated 38,60,000 cases of HIV infections, were reported in India.

The prevalence of HIV in all parts of the country by 2000 itself highlights the spread of the infection from urban to rural areas. About 3.7 million adults are estimated to be infected. About 89% of the reported cases are in the sexually active and economically productive age group of 18 to 40 years. It is shocking to note that over 50% of the newly infected persons are found to be the youths who are below 25 years. Women who do not have any risk factor other than being married to their husbands, constitute 21% of new infections. More than 80% of all new infections are through sexual transmission, 8% through pre-natal transmission, 6% through injecting drug among users, 4% through blood transfusion.

Various factors contribute to the speedy spread of this disease. *Migration of labour, low literacy levels leading to low awareness, gender disparities, sexually transmitted infections and*

1 **K. Park** *"Text-book of Preventive and Social Medicine"* [2002]. Page - 259.

reproductive tract infections among the population – are some of the factors attributed to the spread of HIV and AIDS in India.

Causes of AIDS

Various causes contribute to this disease. The main causes are – 1. *Infected blood,* 2. *Infected needles,* 3. *Multiple sex partners,* 4. *Infected mother to her baby before birth.*

AIDS virus is generally transmitted through intimate sexual contact. But it is not transmitted from person to person by mere external physical contact or through sneezing, coughing, kissing, embracing, shaking hands, etc. This shows that social contact does not involve any risk factor.

HIV can be passed on by infected people because the virus is present in the sexual fluids, saliva and blood. If infected blood or sexual fluid of the first person gets into the blood of the second person, then the second person becomes infected. If a man or woman with HIV has sex without a condom, infected fluid could pass into their bloodstream through a tiny cut or sour inside the body. This can be so small that the partners can hardly identify or understand it. Other sexual practices are equally at risk infection. If there is any contact with blood during sex, this increases the risk of infection. Recent researches have found that deep kissing where saliva is exchanged, can infect the partner.

Categories of the persons who are most likely to get the AIDS / HIV infection are – 1. Homosexual men, 2. Bisexual men and women having a large number of sex partners, 3. Prostitutes and their male counterparts, 4. Heroine addicts who use a common needle and syringe for injecting drugs, 5. Patients of Sexually Transmitted Diseases [STDs], 6. Professional blood donors, 7. Patients who need repeated blood transfusion, and 8. Children of HIV (positive) mothers.

Early signs and symptoms of the disease are – 1. Significant and unexplained loss of body weight by about 10%, 2. Intermittent low-grade fever, 3. Swollen Iymphatic glands, 4. Persistent watery diarrhoea, 5. Night sweating, 6. Pain all over the body, 7. Formation of white patches or ulcers in the mouth as well as in the food pipe, 8. Itchy skin rashes that appear on many parts of the body, 9. Excessive fatigue after normal daily activities. It may be noted that signs and symptoms of AIDS may appear at any time after 6 months of the entry of HIV virus.

HIV is Not Spread By the Following Ways

Table - 2

Major Information Centres of AIDS

- National Aids Control Organisation [NACO], New Delhi.
- TATA Institute of Social Sciences, Mumbai.
- Indian Health Organisation, Mumbai.
- Voluntary Health Association of India.
- Aids Research Foundation of India, Chennai.
- South India Aids Action Programme, Chennai.
- Child In Need Institute, Calcutta.
- Parivar Seva Samsthan, New Delhi.
- Women and Aids Cell, New Delhi.
- All India Institute of Medical Sciences [AIIMS].
- Human Service Centre, Varanasi.
- Community Medicine Centre [AIDS Section].

There is a lot of misconception about AIDS and the HIV and the way in which they are spread. It should be remembered that ***HIV or AIDS is not spread by the following ways or means or persons*** – 1. Drinking water or eating food from the same utensils - cups, glasses, plates, used by infected persons, 2. Sharing toilets, 3. Shaking hands, 4. Hugging or facial kissing, 5. Donating blood, 6. Working with people who are HIV infected, 7. Massage and rub each others bodies, 8. Swimming in pools used by people with HIV / AIDS. 9. Through mosquito bite, 10. Socialising or casually living with people with HIV / AIDS, 11. HIV is not spread by sitting next to some one who is infected, coughing or sneezing, 12. It is also not spread by travelling with some body in public transportation [bus, train, air, etc.] or taking food with someone in a hotel or using a public telephone, etc.

Control of AIDS ?

The deadly disease of AIDS cannot easily be tackled. We can however suggest two methods of dealing with it : (i) *Preventive Method,* and (ii) *Curative or Treatment Method.*

1. Preventive Method

The popular saying "prevention is better than cure", holds especially true in the case of the horrible disease like AIDS. Until a vaccine or cure for AIDS is found, the only means at present available is health education to create awareness among people to keep themselves away from the reach of the tentacles of AIDS. Certain precautions are necessary in this regard.

The contagious and the deadly disease of the AIDS can be effectively prevented by observing the following methods.

1. Avoiding sex relations with many partners [multiple partners],
2. Keeping away from unknown sexual partners,
3. Keeping away from persons suffering from sexually transmitted diseases [STD],
4. Making it a policy to have sex with one's own spouse, and if this cannot be followed strictly, using good quality condom [nirodh] of ISI standard, whenever the occasion arises,
5. Avoiding kisses with tongue [especially with unknown sex partners],
6. Avoiding sharing of the needles used to inject narcotic drugs,
7. Avoiding homosexual relationship,
8. Avoiding the consumption of marijuana [intoxicating oral drug], alcohol and tobacco,

Table - 3

AIDS Infected Persons in Karnataka : 2002

- By the end of March 2002 there were 1,442 AIDS afflicted persons in Karnataka.
- Number of persons died due to the disease is 146.
- Number of persons newly infected with HIV by the end of March 2002 is 11,583.
- Of the newly traced out cases of infection by the end of March 2002, as many as 2.14% of the cases were found among children.
- In a selected persons survey conducted in **Bijapur,** blood test was held for about 400 pregnant women and of these, 13 persons were found to be infected with HIV.

Source : *Statement issued by the Additional Director [Planning]* ***Dr. D. Thimmaiah,*** *Karnataka State AIDS Prevention Society, and reported in "Udayavani" Kannada daily dated 4-6-2002.*

9. Women suffering from AIDS should decide not to conceive.

It is necessary that educational material and guidelines for prevention should be made widely available. All mass media channels should be involved in educating the people on AIDS, its nature, transmission and prevention, this includes international travellers also.

For the first time, there is a clear sign of reduction in HIV infection rate in a number of developing countries. In USA about 40,000 new HIV infections are reported in 1996 as against 1,00,000 per year a few years ago. In Thailand, there has been a six fold increase in condom usage, and 90% of the sex workers demand the use of condom. The number of men visiting sex workers has gone down and the use of condom has gone up. **Ugandan** cities have also seen a reduction in HIV infection rate. [It should however be noted that there is no guarantee that the use of condoms give full protection.] In Kolkota, India, the Sonagachi health care and education project among sex workers has become a model of successful peer education. The latest data shows that HIV prevalence continues to be low [around 1.4%] and STDs [Sexually Transmitted Diseases] are declining. Community-based treatment approach has been effective in bringing about behavioural changes among injecting drug users in Mynmar and Nepal. This has led to a reduction in HIV infection rates.

2. Curative or Treatment Method

At present, there is no effective vaccine or cure for treatment of HIV infection / AIDS. However, the development drugs, helps the suppression of HIV infection. Though the drugs do not promise a permanent cure, they have proved to be useful in prolonging the life of the severely affected patients. Though medicines such as AZT [Zidovudine] and the PROTEASE - INHIBITOR have been discovered, they are very costly and no person of average income can afford to avail of it. Hence, much stress is laid on preventive method. Still search is on to discover other drugs to control and cure HIV infections / AIDS.

Social Stigma Attached to AIDS

AIDS is said to be the monstrous disease posing a big challenge to the modern civilisation. The haunting disease has threatened the public health security measures of many nations of the world. The disease is not only dreadful but also spreads at an alarming rate.

It is associated with social stigma, AIDS is a disease with a difference. It is not like other contagious diseases. AIDS affected persons are subject to prejudice and discrimination. Those who are the victims of the disease are treated as *"untouchables".* They are branded as people with immoral character. The disease creates lot of social distance between the people who are afflicted by it and those who are not. Even the family members of the diseased person look down upon him / her.

AIDS affected persons are subject to lot of social prejudices and discriminations. There has been a significant increase in the number of medical personnel [doctors and dentists] and institutions such as nursing homes, hospitals, etc., which decline medical services to AIDS affected persons.

AIDS / HIV infected person may face dismissal from work, refusal to work, refusal of admission to medical and educational establishments, refusal of service at boarding and lodging establishments, and so on.

The economic and social costs of maintaining and treating the AIDS affected persons are also very high. No man of average income can afford to pay for the medicine that is required to cure AIDS. If the bread-winner of the family is caught by AIDS, then the entire family collapses economically.

AIDS has posed a big challenge to the modern medical scientists. A large number of scientists are at work to find out an effective and an early cure to this deadly disease. They have not been successful in finding out an effective medicine for AIDS at a reasonable cost, that is, within the reach of an ordinary person. Till it is done, the rapid spread of the disease has to be contained. The best and the most effective strategy to combat AIDS is through education and mass media.

ANNEXURE - 1

Annexure to Chapter – 1

HISTORICAL MOORINGS OF THE INDIAN SOCIETY

1. A BRIEF HISTORICAL SKETCH OF THE INDIAN CIVILISATION

Introduction

Indian society is very ancient and extremely complex. It has a very rich cultural tradition which is said to be at least 5000 years old. India is the 7th largest and the 2nd most populous nation in the world. It has carved a unique place for itself in the midst of the community of nations today.

Our nation which is presently called as ***"Bharatha"*** or ***"India"*** was previously known as *"Bharatavarsha"*, *"Jambu Dvipa"*, and *"Bharata Khanda"*. It was more appropriately and popularly called ***"Bharatavarsha"***, that is, *the country of the king Bharata and his progeny.* King Bharata's name figures prominently in the early Sanskrit texts including the Epics and the Puranas. The British called this land *"India"* and the Muslim invaders, as *"Hindusthan"*.

The Indian society is highly diverse. Several different levels of social evolution co-exist in the contemporary India. Primitive hunters and food-gatherers, shifting cultivators, nomads of different types, settled agriculturists, artisans, landed aristocrats and big industrialists, multi - millionaires and the poorest of the poor - all manage to live together.

India is a land which consists of people who exhibit lot of dissimilarities such as ethnic, linguistic, religious and so on. Despite these diversities, India has never lost the ideal of unity. The bonds of unity are strong enough to hold the Indians together as a nation. It is in this context, the Indian culture developed its unique quality known as *"unity in diversity"*. One finds the reflections of Indian unity in various fields such as religion, language, education, physical territory, political administration, etc. There are forces contributing to strengthen this unity and also to weaken it. The explanation given below provides only a glance of all these aspects.

Origin of Indian Civilisation

India as a nation is said to have a long past which is often stretched from 5000 years to 10,000 years. It is difficult to identify the earliest inhabitants of this nation. Most of the present day historians are of the opinion that the Indian civilisation is at least as old as 3000 B.C. There are enough archaeological and historical evidences to say that around 3000 B.C. a well developed civilisation had flourished on the banks of the rivers Ganga and Sindhu. Archaeological discoveries relating to the Indus Valley Civilisation have now established the view that this civilisation was spread over in the whole of north India, and was not confined to the twin cities of Harappa and Mohen-jo-daro alone. It is now firmly believed that the Indian civilisation virtually originated from here. But the sudden disappearance of this civilisation led to several imaginary views and hypotheses.

Controversies Regarding the Original Homeland of the Aryans

It is a fact of history that the Aryans constituted the originators of Indian civilisation. Whether the Aryans or Indo-Aryans were the original inhabitants of India, or they came from outside - is still disputed. The *"Aryan Invasion Theory"* proposed by **Max Muller** as a hypothesis was made popular by the Western scholars. This view was in currency for a long time. Archaeological investigations that had been taking place for the past 2 decades have established the view that the Aryans and the creators of the Indus Valley Civilisation were the same people and not the two separate groups of people as propagated by the British and some other Western scholars. *"There is no conclusive evidence of Aryans' immigration into India from outside according to the Indian team of historians, archaeologists and linguists."*[1] **Swami Vivekananda** had also challenged this Western view long back.[2]

It is now believed that around 3000 B.C. there were at least two major communities in India, namely, the *Aryans* and the *non-Aryans* between whom politico-cultural clashes must have taken place for a long time. We find the echoes of these clashes in the Rig Veda of the Aryans. The Aryans who were using horses and iron weapons could finally defeat the non-Aryans.

The Beginning of the Aryanisation Process

The Aryans in the beginning preferred to settle in the villages to make their roots very strong. Slowly, they started switching over from cattle-breeding and agriculture to other types of occupations. The socio-economic conditions made intimate social contacts and social harmony [between Aryans and non-Aryans] almost inevitable. Development of social intimacy led to the shaping of the Indian social system. Hence, the prevailing Aryan social institutions, religious beliefs, ways of worshipping, values, ideals, philosophies, etc., underwent changes. The *"give-and-take"*, and *"live-and let-live"* traditions initiated the process of Aryanisation.

Evolution of the Hindu Religious System

Along with the process of Aryanisation, the major religion of India called *"Sanatana Dharma"* or *"Vaidika Dharma"* or *"Hinduism"* also started evolving. *The Vedas, Upanishads, the concept of God, Dharma, Karma, Punarjanma,* [rebirth], *Ashrama* and *Varna* systems came to take shape. The great Epics [Ramayana and Mahabharatha], *Bhagavad Gita, Puranas, Dharmashastras,* the *Hindu moral and value systems*, etc., became inseparable aspects of Hindusim.

The Hierarchical Social System

The *"...... social framework of Indian society began taking shape when the area of interaction between the Indo-Aryans and the earlier inhabitants widened. The Indo Aryans were divided into three groups - (i) the **Rajanya** [warriors and aristocrats]; (ii) the **Brahmins** [priests] and (iii) the **Vaishyas** [cultivators and traders]. ... The **Shudras** were the fourth Varna; they were from outside the Indo-Aryan group..... Outside the four-fold vertical Varna structure, there was a fifth group - **"Avarna"** or the **"Panchama"** whose ethnic status was very low...."*[3]

Emergence of Castes

In the Varna system, in course of time, the Rajanya started losing importance and the Brahmins became more dominant. Varna no more remained as an *"open"* system. When rigidity crept into the Varna system it got degenerated into the caste system. Caste rigidities and cruelties invited rebellions which in due course led to the emergence of new religions.

---

1. **Dr. B.B. Lal** as quoted by **Shriram Sathe** in his *"Aryans : Who Were They ?"* - Page : 5.
2. *"Wherever the Europeans find an opportunity, they exterminate the aborigines and settle down in ease and comfort on their lands; and therefore they conclude that the Aryans must have done the same! But where is your proof ? Guess-work ? Then keep your fanciful ideas to yourselves! In what Veda, in what Sukta, do you find that the Aryans came into India from a foreign country ? Where do you get the idea that they slaughtered the wild aborigines ? What do you gain by talking such non-sense ?"* - **Source** : **Vivekananda** in *"The East and West"* - Page : 104.
3. **S.C. Dube** in *"Indian Society"* - Page : 6.

Origin of New Religions : Buddhism and Jainism : [6th Cen. B.C.]

In the 6th century B.C., Buddhism and Jainism the two new religions were born as a revolt against the rigidity of the caste system. Both the religions became popular in several places of India. Buddhism which became weaker in due course, left India and found acceptance in many other Asian countries [Burma, Ceylone, Tibet, Korea, Japan, China, etc.] On the contrary, Jainism had to confine itself within the borders of India.

The Beginning of the External Invasions and Immigrations

From the 6th century B.C. to 18th century A.D., a large number of foreign invaders and immigrants came to India at different times. The Persians in the 6th century B.C. and the Greeks in the 4th century B.C. invaded some parts of north-west India. But the impact of these two invading communities was very much marginal and short-lived.

The Coming of the Waves of Immigrants

Later waves of immigrants included the ***Scythians, Parthians, Shakas, Huns, Kushans*** who held powers for relatively long periods. But these groups preferred to settle down in India and were willing to be absorbed into the Hindu social system. Since they were aliens, they were treated as *"mlechchhas"*. However, they had power and high status. They wanted to get assimilated into the Hindu society. Thus began the process of assimilation. *The Shakas became "Shaivites", the Huns came to be called the "Rajputs". The Kushans were attracted by Buddhism.* Kanishka, the great Kushan ruler, embraced Buddhism and during his regime, many joined Buddhism.

Though the immigration into India took place from the north-east regions in the form of Mongoloid groups, we do not have much information about such immigrations.

The Islamic Conquests of India [10th to 16th Cen. A.D.]

Islam first came to India through peaceful methods, often with the encouragement of Hindu rulers. The Muslims first appeared in the Sind Province in the 8th century A.D. Thereafter, the *Turks, Afghans,* and *Mughals* came to India as invaders at different times. The defeat of Prithviraj Chauhan the emperor of Delhi, in 1192 A.D. at the hands of Mohammad of Ghor, led to the beginning of the Muslim rule in India.

"As we have already noted, India had known other conquests; the Shaka, the Kushan, and the Huns had come from Central Asia and, after initial confrontation, they were absorbed in Indian society, the confrontation with the Islamic invaders was longer and more bitter as they brought with them their own theology and considered only their religion as true. A divide was thus created ... Some of them [Muslim rulers] took upon themselves the mission of Islamising society more seriously than others; discriminatory practices such as the imposition of "Jizyah" [a poll tax], ... were pursued more vigorously by some rulers, while others were relaxed about them."[1]

The Islamic rule continued in India in one place or the other from the 12th century to 18th century. It may be added that during this period, Hindu rule was never completely wiped out from India. Here and there, the Hindu rulers carried on the independent rule in spite of the Muslim domination. The kingdom of Vijayanagar in the south, for example, was an impressive one. Similarly, the Rajput ruler Rana Pratap in the north, never surrendered to Mughal king Akbar. The defeat of Muslim ruler **Sirajdaul**, the Nawab of Bengal, at the hands of the British in 1757, led to the beginning of the Western imperialistic rule in India.

---

1. **S.C. Dube** - Page : 18.

The Western Rule and the Spread of Christianity

St. Thomas [A.D. 50] and **St. Bartholomew** [same period] are believed to have brought Christianity to India. But Christianity started spreading its religious network in India with a political influence only after the Portuguese navigator **Vasco-da-gama** visited Calicut [Kerala] in 1498. As the Portuguese with their imperialistic agenda started taking roots in Goa, the Dutch, the French and the British followed them in quick succession. For a variety of reasons, only the British became successful in the competition that took place among these forces. The British rule continued to prevail in India for about 150 years. The British rule provided an opportunity for Christianity to spread its influence throughout India. Political backing alone was not sufficient for obtaining acceptance at the hands of the people. Hence, the Christian missionaries resorted to educational and medical services to get immediate support of the people.

The Beginning of the British Rule and the Struggle For Freedom

India came under the direct rule of the British between 1858-1947. The British rule compelled India to come under the heavy influence of the West. The centralised British administration, their political expertise, strict administration, the patriotic spirit of the British officials, and finally their policy of "divide and rule" - helped their cause. Thus, India came under the direct -rule of the British for about 90 years.

India's Successful Struggle Towards Freedom

The British rule created a new awareness among people. Western thoughts, values and ideologies impressed the educated people of India and inspired them to launch a freedom struggle. As the slogan of this struggle echoed and re-echoned throughout India, the British rule started counting its days in the country. The non-violent struggle, revolutionary approach and the military rebellion all proved to be successful in ousting the British. The ungrateful British finally divided this country on the basis of religion in an artificial manner into two nations: India and Pakistan. These two have been at loggerheads ever since the very birth of Pakistan.

India Marches Ahead Facing All the Modern Challenges

Independent India has been marching ahead. By realising its defects and deficiencies it has been trying to come out of the hold of traditionality and conservatism. It has retained its faith in the democratic political system even after 57 years of independent rule. It has successfully faced three wars imposed on it by Pakisthan and the one by China. It is emerging out as one of the strongest forces in the so called *"third world"*. India has attained now political stability and has made impressive achievements in the fields such as education, industry, economy, science, technology, etc. It has carved out a respectable position for itself in the community of the nations. It is now faced with the challenge of forging ahead without making compromises with its national interests.

2. SOCIETY IN CONTEMPORARY INDIA : UNITY AND DIVERSITY

Indian culture consists of both unity and diversity. In fact, *"Unity in diversity"* is our speciality. It is for this unique feature Indian culture stands out as distinct from all the other cultures of the world. We have invited and absorbed the foreign influences and forces and yet maintained our uniqueness. One feature that is most often noticed about India is its *"unity in diversity"*. This catchy phrase has become *a part of India's self-identity*. Even the foreign travellers who visited India from time to time like **Megaasthenese, Huan Tsang, Alberuni** and others also noted and appreciated this.[1] Let us now evaluate the appropriateness of this phrase by examining the nature of diversities in India and the factors that contribute to its unity.

NATURE OF DIVERSITIES IN INDIA

The diversity of India is something unique. India as a huge country with a large population presents endless varieties of physical features and cultural patterns. **Dr. Iravathi Karve** has rightly pointed out that in the whole of the Western world, we do not find a single country which has so extensive and diverse a cultural tradition as India has. Hence, she called *"India – the epitome of the world."*

REFLECTIONS OF INDIAN DIVERSITIES

1. Geographic Diversities

We find in India some extreme diversities in its geographical features. We see here formidable mountains, thick forests, countless hills, steep valleys, innumerable rivers, vast seas, desert land, fertile areas drought-hit places, flood-prone areas and so on. Only in India one can find the world's tallest mountains [the Himalayas] covered with snow throughout the year. The rivers that flow down from the Himalayas have given place to a vast fertile delta area. At the same time, a State like Rajasthan has its desert where water is a scarcity.

It is only in India one encounters different types of climates the cold, the temperate and the tropical. The climate of Kashmir which is cold even in summer, contrasts with that of Kerala which is hot and humid even in midwinter. Wide climatic differences do exist between the North-East States and Rajasthan. Rainfall is very heavy in the North-East [which exceeds even 500 inches a year] whereas it is insignificant in places of Rajasthan like Jaisalmer and Barmer. [it is less than 3 inches a year.].

2. Racial or Ethnic Diversities

India is often called an ethnological museum. Majority of the people of India are descendants of immigrants from across the Himalayas. **Dr. B.S. Guha** identifies six main ethnic groups to which the Indian population belong. They are : *1. The Negrito, 2. Proto-Austroloids, 3. Mongoloids, 4. Mediterranean or Dravidian, 5. Western Brachycephals,* and *6. The Nordics.*

Indian population is a mixture of these different races. None of the above mentioned racial groups is confined to any particular area in its absolute sense. Thus, **S.C. Dube** writes, *"....it is essential to remember that the bulk of the Indian population represents racial admixture in varying degrees.*[2]

3. Linguistic Diversities

Language is yet another source of diversity. It contributes to collective identities as well as conflicts. As **A.R. Desai** remarks *"India presents a spectacle of museum of tongues."*[3] The Constitution of India recognises [up to 1992] as many as **18** major languages. But Indians speak, as reported in 1971 Census, as many as **1652** languages and dialects. Many of them represent

---

1. "In the past, foreign *travellers – among others,* **Megasthenese** [315 B.C], *Fa-Heien* [A.D. 405 - 11], **Huan Tsang** [A.D. 630 - 44], **Alberuni** [A.D. 1030], **Marco Polo** [A.D. 1288, 93], *and* **Ibn Batuta** [A.D. 1325-51]– observed and recorded this. After the partition of India........ this aspect has been passionately articulated both as a reality of the past and as the hope for the future......" - **S.C. Dube** in *"Indian Society."* [1990]. Page 23. *[National Book Trust of India].*
2. **S.C. Dube** in *'Indian Society'* - Page : 23-24.
3. Broadly speaking, the Indian languages belong to five major linguistic families, namely, (*i*) the Indo-Aryan, (*ii*) the Dravidism, (*iii*) the European and (*iv*) the Austric, and (*v*) the Sino-Tibetan.

their mother tongues also. News papers are published in **100** languages and mother tongues. The total number of newspapers and periodicals exceed **50,000** a year. Even tribal languages cannot be dismissed as dialects for many of them have a growing literature.

Hindi, spoken by the majority of people in India [as many as 247.85 million as per 1991 report] though is constitutionally accepted as the national language, it has not been able to replace English. Existence of different languages has often led to conflicts between linguistic groups. The language problem thus has posed a major threat to national integration.

4. Religious Diversities

India is not a theocratic state. It has no state religion. It guarantees freedom to the people to practise or follow religions of their choice. *"Sarvadharma Samabhava"* - equal respect to all religions - has been the cherished value of the Indian society since time immemorial.

India is a land which has given place and protection to several major religions of the world. There are 8 major religious communities in India namely, *1. the Hindus, 2. Muslims, 3. Christians, 4. Sikhs, 5. Buddhists, 6. Jains, 7. Zoroastrians or Persians,* and *8. the Jews.* In addition to these, the tribals follow their own tribal faiths. Each of the major religions has its own sub-divisions and sects.

These diverse religions were seen flourishing in this country; and of these, some were of the foreign origins while many were the offshoots of Hinduism itself. Nevertheless the religious diversity has been a major source of disunity and disharmony in the country. *An attempt to express greater loyalty to one's own religion than to one's own country, always leads to conflicts.* India too has witnessed many such conflicts.

5. Cultural Diversities

In the cultural field also we find innumerable varieties dotted over the length and breadth of this country. Traditional cultural ways and modern thoughts are intermixed here. The food habits, dress styles, folkways, mores, customs and traditions, norms, values, rituals and beliefs, family and marital systems and such other socio-cultural practices of the people are never the same all over India. If one travels from one state to another or from one end of the nation to another one finds such vast diversities.

Further, the historical experiences through invasions and immigrations from time to time, followed by the impact of powerful kingdoms and empires - also added to this socio-cultural diversity.[1] In addition to the influences of ecology and environment, *"powerful kingdoms and empires as also major dynasties, have directly or indirectly contributed to the shaping of cultural regions."* - [S.C. Dube]

6. Stratificational Diversities : Castes / Tribes / Classes

Castes **:** The social stratification system in India also presents differences. India is the only nation in the world where caste as a form of social stratification system is found. Castes are innumerable and their number exceeds even 4000. Each major caste has its own sub-divisions known as *"sub-castes"*. Each caste, and even sub-caste has a way of life of its own. We also find castes among other communities like Muslims, Christians and Sikhs.[1]

---

1. The kings and the dynasties too had their impact on the shaping of the cultural ways. *For example*, "In Kalinga, the consolidation of culture received an impetus under Kharavela. In the North-West, Indo-Greek kings and later the Kushans and the Huns provided an impetus for the emergence of a regional culture... The Cheras influenced the shaping of Kerala society. In other parts of the south, the Pallavas, the Pandyas, the Vatakas, the Chalukyas, the Cholas, and the Vijayanagar kingdom made important contributions to the consolidation of regional cultures. This is only an illustrative list and is by no means comprehensive..." **S.C. Dube** in *"Indian Society"* - Page : 30.

- *Tribal Groups* : Vast tribal groups are also found in India. They are said to be the original inhabitants of India. According to 1991 Census, there are about **7.42** crores tirbals constituting **8.8 %** of our population. Each tribe has a distinctive culture, a way of life of its own adding to the cultural diversity of the land. They are not, however, equally distributed.
- *Social Classes* : India is a caste as well as class-laden society. Vast class differences do exist among the masses. Rich and poor cleavage is very sharp here. As per [10th plan] 1999-2000 estimate, more than 26.1% of the people [260 million] are said to be living below the poverty line. Out of these, 75% [195 million] live in the rural areas and 25% [65 million] live in the urban areas. India accounts for 22% of world's poor.[2] The poor are not equally distributed in all states. States such as U.P., M.P. Maharashtra, West Bengal, Bihar, Tamil Nadu and Orissa account for 199.5 million poor [which is 76.7% of the total 260 million poor estimated for 1999-2000]. In comparison with these, states such as Haryana, Punjab, Gujarat, Himachal Pradesh, Goa and Delhi are found to be relatively rich.

THE IDEAL OF UNITY *OR* BONDS OF UNITY IN INDIA

Despite the widespread differences which one finds in India, it remains as one single nation. India has never lost its ideal of unity. Indian culture possesses a fundamental unity which remained undisturbed in its political history of rise and fall. The imprint of Indian unity can be found in the literature and thoughts of different communities of the country. The fundamental approach to literature, philosophy, tradition and customs is typically Indian. The basis of the social and cultural unity of the country is common to every group.

Unity of India-Not a Gift of the British Rule

It is a historical blunder to say that the unity of India is a gift of British rule. From times immemorial it found noblest expression in the thoughts of our sages and poets. *"The entire country was referred to by the common name "Bharatavarsha" and its people have been referred to as "Bharata Santati" to emphasise the oneness of the country and its people."*[3] Long back, the **Vishnu Purana** reiterated this fundamental unity of India in one of its *slokas.*[4]

FACTORS REVEALING INDIAN UNITY

Of the various factors which manifest the unity of India, the following are of great importance.

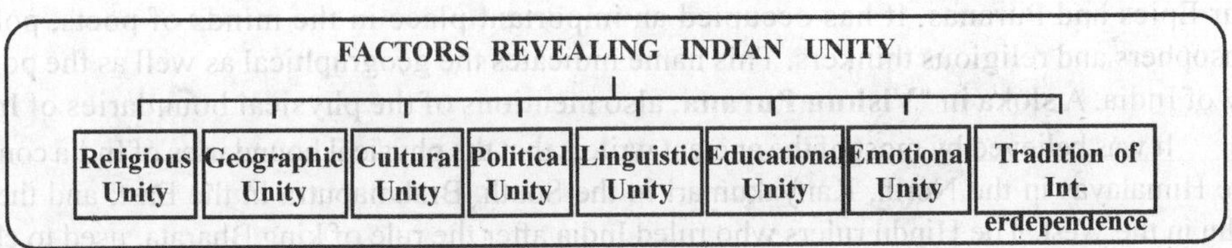

1. *"Among the Muslims we find the hierachy of Sheikhs, Syeds, Mughals and Pathans. Similarly, the Christians also have caste consciousness due to conversion from the Hindu fold. The Sikhs have many castes, the most prominent being the Jat Sikh and the Majuhabi Sikhs..."* - **P.K. Kar** in *"Indian Society"*, (1998) - Page : 10.
2. *Source* : **Ruddar Datt** and **K.P.M. Sundharm** in *"Indian Economy"* - 2005 Edition - Page : 378.
3. **P.R. Rao** in *"Indian Heritage and Culture"* - Page : 4.
4. The meaning of the *sloka* runs like this; "that country which is bounded by the seas on the south and the Himalayas on the north is called Bharatam. There live the progeny of king Bharata."

1. The Religious Basis of Unity

As **Swami Vivekananda** pointed out *"religion is the soul of India"*. Religious unity certainly played a significant role in the history of India. The very spread of Hinduism all over the country has helped the cause of this unity.

- ***Common Gods and Goddesses*** : The worship of main Gods and Goddesses of Hinduism such as - *Ganapathi, Shiva, Vishnu, Sri Rama, Hanuman, Kali, Durgi, Adi Shakti, Saraswathi* and *Laxmi* - and the like is found throughout India.
- ***Common Scriptures of Reverence*** : Religious scriptures, like the Vedas, Upanishads, the Gita, Puranas and the Bhagavata, are given respect throughout India. Similarly, the great Epics, the Ramayana and the Mahabharata are devotionally read by all people. The legends of Rama and Krishna are sung and repeated with equal fervour.
- ***Common Beliefs and Spiritual Ideas*** : Belief in rebirth, *Karma, Moksha, Svarga-Naraka* [Heaven and Hell] immortality of soul, temporary nature of the world, the *'Avataras'* of the Lord, meditation, *yoga* is common to most of the people.
- ***Common Temples and Centres of Pilgrimage*** : India is known for its temple culture which is reflected in various temples and sacred places scattered all over the country. Right from the Amarnath, Vaishnava temple, Badari and Kedarnath in the north, Rameshwar in the South, the Kamarup-Kamakshya in the North-East, Puri in the East, to Dwaraka in the West all provide for religious unity to this country. Adi Shankaracharya's four *mutts* in four corners of India also symbolise its religious unity.

  Pilgrimage to different holy places [especially to Kashi, Ayodhya, Mathura, Puri and Dwaraka] rivers, and mountains plays a definite role in welding people together. It also creates in them a feeling of patriotism.
- ***Common Holy Rivers*** : The Hindu recounts the names of seven holy rivers of the country such as - Ganga, Yamuna, Saraswathi, Godavari, Narmada, Sindhu and Kauvery. Such recountings reveal religious fervour and also cultural unity.

  M.N. Srinivas is also of the opinion that *"the unity of India is essentially religious one."*

2. Physical or Geographical Unity of India

The physical or geographical factors have provided India, a geographical unity. The name *"Bharatavarsha"* or *"Bharata Khanda"* [the *"land of Bharata"*, the founding father of the land] symbolises its historical as well as physical identity. This traditional name also figures in our Epics and Puranas. It has occupied an important place in the minds of poets, political philosophers and religious thinkers. This name indicates the geographical as well as the political unity of India. A sloka in "**Vishnu Purana**, also mentions of the physical boundaries of India.[1]

It was believed by most of the ancient writers that the physical boundaries of India consisted of the Himalayas in the North, Kanyakumari in the South, Brahmaputra in the East, and the river Sindhu in the West. The Hindu rulers who ruled India after the rule of king Bharata, used to cherish this ideal and the ambition of establishing a vast empire. The expressions *"Bharath Mata", "Vande Mataram", "Mother India",* etc. also denote in an emotional manner the geographic unity of India.

3. Cultural Unity of India

India is often called a *'laboratory of cultural experiments'*. In spite of its widespread differences the imprint of cultural unity and in certain respects uniformity, is to be found in several aspects of people's life. This unity finds its expression in literature and thought, in art,

---

1. *"Uttaram yat samudrasya himadrase haiva dakshinam | Varsham tad Bharatam Nama | Bharati yatra santatihi"* - **Vishnu Puranam.**

architecture and sculpture, in philosophy and spirituality, in dance, drama and music. The caste system has also provided a common cultural ideology to the people. Religious rites and ceremonies are also held in more or less the same way everywhere. Festivals such as - *Dasara, Deepavali, Holi, Ganesh Chaturthi, Makarasankramana, Ramanavami, Yugadi, etc.,* are also observed throughout the nation with the same religious fervour. Such festivals also receive international recognition especially when the leading artists give their performances on such occasions in foreign countries. As regards the nature of family, sentiments woven around marriage, respect towards the elders, kitchen norms, sanctity of *samskaras [like namakarana, upanayana, vivaha, anthyakriya, etc.]* caste rules etc. - all the groups seem to have been unanimous in their acceptance.

As early as in 1911 itself the British Census commissioner, **Sir Herbert Risley** had recognised the bonds of unity in relation to Indian cultural heritage.[1]

4. Political Unity

India's political unity is said to be one of the main effects of its religious and cultural unity. India's political unity is as old as its history. In the Rigveda, in Sanskrit literature, in the edicts of Ashoka, in Buddhist *stupas,* pillars and in many other evidences of the ancient eras, the concept of political unity can easily be found.

In the ancient period, king Bharata was able to achieve political unity by esablishing one unified kingdom called *"Bharatvarsha"*. This tradition was followed by the later rulers in the ancient period such as Samrat Sagara, Raja Dilip, Dasharatha, Yudhisthira, Prathu and others. During the historical age also, kings like Ashoka, Chandra Gupta, Samudra Gupta, Prithviraj Chauhan, Shivaji and others also had such intentions. Words such as *"Rajadhiraja", "Samrata", "Chakravarthin", "Sarvabhauma", "Ekachakradhipathi"*, etc., are all evidences of the consciousness of this political, to be more precise, geo-political unity. The practice of conducting sacrifices such as - *Rajasuya, Ashwamedha,* and the grand programmes such as *"Punarabhisheka", "Mahabhisheka", "Pattabhisheka"* - bear testimony to the fact that the idea of universal overlordship had pre-occupied the minds of ancient rulers in India.

India has been struggling to maintain its political unity even after independence [though it lost a part of its territory through partition]. India has shown her political oneness at the time of the attack of China, and three attacks of Pakisthan including the recently concluded Kargil War.

5. Linguistic Unity

Despite the presence of a number of languages India possesses a linguistic unity. The Sanskrit language was a great unifying factor. It was not only the language of religion and scholarship, but also of the royal courts and the law courts. It was the common language in all parts of the country in the past. Sanskrit language and literature reached their heights under the Guptas who maintained political unity in most of the places of India for 200 years.

Sanskrit is the mother of the languages. It has been the source of inspiration for most of the Dravidian languages also. Sanskrit was the root of both Pali and Prakrit the two languages which were used for spreading Buddhism. Sanskrit language served as *"a vehicle of noble thought and expression, and as a repository of our culture"* for more than 3000 years. It is indeed an integral force of unity. What Sankrit had done previously to weld Indians into a unity the present languages such as Hindi and English [one Indian and another foreign] are trying to do at present.

---

1. "Beneath the manifold diversity of physical and social type, language, custom, and religion which strike the observer in India, there can still be discerned....... a certain underlying uniformity of life from the Himalayas to Cape Camorin." - **Sir Herbert Risley** as quoted by **P.R. Rao** in *"Indian Heritage and Culture"* - Page : 4-5.

6. Educational Unity

Educational unity has been observed in India since ancient period. In the learning of *Vedas* and *Shastras,* the same *"guru-shishya parampara"* existed throughout India. Same subjects and topics of study were there throughout India. Sanskrit was the only medium of instruction which facilitated not only the spread of knowledge but also the continuation of studies and teaching in different institutions. *Kashi, Takshashila, Mathura, Kanchipuram, Ujjaini, Nalanda, Udantapuri, Vikramsheela* and other universities spread over in different places were able to attract students. After their studies the students used to carry to their home places the vast knowledge and cultural aspects which they had gathered. **Panini**'s *"Asthadhayayi"* and **Patanjali**'s *"Mahabhashya"* were recommended as the two basic treatises on Sanskrit Grammar in all the institutions from Kashmir to Kanyakumari. *"Pacha mahakavyas"* and *"Panchatantra"* were taught in all institutions.

7. Emotional Unity

The unity of India is essentially emotional or psychological. Nationalistic fervours and patrotic sentiments bind Indians together. Slogans such as *'Vande Mataram', 'Bharathamataki Jai', 'Jai Hind'*, etc., get re-echoed on occasions in different corners of India. The concepts of *'Mother India', 'Motherland'* etc., have further strengthened such sentiments. The government through the institution of national awards and titles for acts of bravery, social service, excellence in art, literature, music, sports and games, etc., tries to promote such emotional unity. The media like the radio, T.V. and the cinema also seek to foster emotional ties.

8. Tradition of Tolerance and Interdependence

Every invader or immigrant to India brought with him his own set of culture, religion, language, etc. Due to the exceptional spirit of tolerance on the part of the Hindus most of these foreigners - the Shakas, Huns, Greeks, Persians, Jews, Muslims and Christians later made India their home and settled here permanently. The *"live-and-let-live"* policy or the process of *"give-and-take relationship"* pursued by the Indians forged a harmonious relationship between the Indians and these one time foreigners.

The tradition of interdependence is also deep rooted in India. In fact, the caste system which is prevalent throughout India used to promote this interdependence through its *"jajmani"* system. This area of interdependence was later on stretched to include the Muslims and Christians also. The traces of this interdependence are still found in the rural areas in some form or the other.

Conclusion : It is clear from the above description that India is a classical land known for *"unity in diversity."* Separatist movements regional feelings and parties, terrorist activities, unhindered conversions that are taking place, inflow of foreign money for sabotage activities, extra-territorial loyalties and such other divisive forces have posed a big challenge to the unity of India. Political attempts to strengthen the national unity have become very weak. Time is ripe to make non-political attempts to preserve the unity of India while ensuring all its positive diversities.

3. NATIONAL INTEGRATION : MEANING-CHALLENGES

Meaning of National Integration

'National Integration' refers to national unity and a sense of belonging to the nation. It is an essential aspect in the making of a nation. Promotion of national integration is regarded as a part and parcel of the policy of any country. In the Indian context, it is a much talked phenomenon for almost all national level leaders gave to it utmost importance. When the nation became independent, they felt the necessity of suppressing the divisive forces and encouraging the unifying factors. They wanted to create conditions which would help people to forget their differences and unite together. It is in this context, the concept of *"national integration"* has assumed importance.

Definition of National Integration[1]

1. **Benjamin** : National integration refers to the *"assimilation of the entire people of a country to a common identity."*
2. ***In simple words,*** national integration refers *to the process wherein a feeling of togetherness, a sense of national unity and above all, a - sense of national belongingness are developed among people.*

Essential Elements of National Integration

A nation is not just a group of people living over a piece of land. Apart from the territorial bond, there are many other ties that bind them together to make them a nation. *A common language, common historic tradition, common cultural heritage, common national values and ideologies* - all play their role in welding people into a unity. The main requirements or elements of national integration may be mentioned below.

1. ***National Attitude*** : National integration is basically an attitude and a kind of broad but self-less feeling. It is a concern with a feeling of national unity and national consciousness.
2. ***Unity in Diversity*** : It implies an attempt to achieve the unity of hearts irrespective of religion, race, creed, language and sex. The purpose here is not just to bring about uniformity but "to achieve unity in diversity". This is especially true in the case of India.
3. ***Supreme National Loyalty*** : It upholds the supremacy of national loyalties and supersedes all other types of affiliations and commitments.
4. ***All-Embrasive*** : National integration is all-inclusive in the sense it covers the wide range of political, economic, social, cultural, emotional and other aspects of life.
5. ***Suppression of Anti-National Forces*** : National integration in order to achieve its purpose suppresses the divisive forces, disruptive elements and disintegrating tendencies.
6. ***Attainment of National Goals*** : The ultimate purpose of national integration is to achieve undisturbed national progress and national glory. In this regard, it struggles for the attainment of ideological goals such as social justice, fraternity, equality, nationalism, secularism, democracy, etc.

Need For National Integration

The unity of a nation depends upon the extent of feeling of national unity on the part of its citizens. National unity does not automatically develop just because its citizens live within the same geographic boundaries. *National integration is basically an emotional integration.*

Just like emotional integration keeps members of a family united, national integration helps the citizens of a nation to get organised to achieve national purposes.

National integration does not emerge on its own automatically. It is only when conditions are created in which people seem to forget their differences and unite together, that national integration emerges. But absolute integration is a myth especially in a country like India which is characterised by widespread heterogeneity. Such heterogeneity tends to reduce the chances of national integration to some extent.

---

1. Two Other Definitions of National Integration

a. "National integration implies ..... the presence of attitudes throughout the society that give preference to national and public interest as distinct from parochial interests." - **Myron Weiner** in *"Politics of Scarcity : Public Pressure and Political Response in India"*.

b. National integration refers to "A socio-psychological and educational process through which a feeling of unity, solidarity and cohesion develops in the hearts of the people and a .... feeling of loyalty to the nation is fostered among them." - **H.A. Gani**

India is a wonderland known for wide differences. One finds here marked differences in the living standards, food habits, dress styles, spoken languages, customary practices, religious beliefs, cultural elements of the various people living in different parts of country. We find extreme poverty on one side, and on the other, we find a small section of the populace rolling in prosperity. There are believers and non-believers in religion; there are highly educated people and also the illiterate masses, there are the most modernised people and at the same time, there are people away from the world of civilization and so on. *These apparent differences imply that we are facing enormous challenges.* These challenges have emanated from various historical, political, cultural, as well as socio-economic factors. *These challenges also emphasise the need for the promotion of national integration.*

CHALLENGES FOR NATIONAL INTEGRATION

Among the various factors that pose serious challenges to the promotion of national integration in India, the following may be noted.

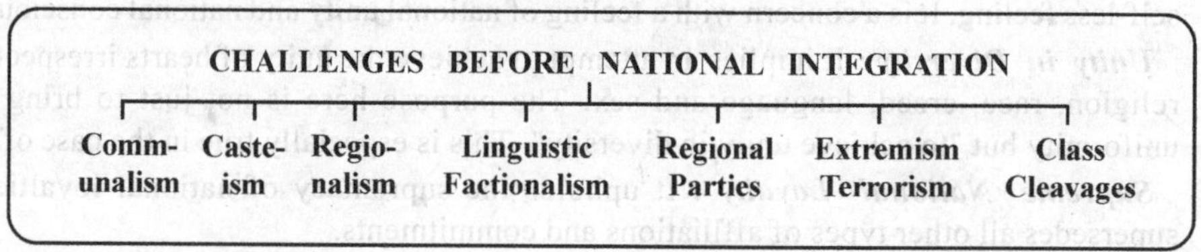

1. Rise of Communalism

- *"The antagonism practised by the members of one community against the people of other community and religion can be called communalism".*[1]

Communalism is responsible for the hatred which one religious group fosters for another. It is a kind of antagonism which is found between religious communities. *Communalism and communal riots normally arise when religious matters are politicalised.* It fails to separate religion from politics. It leads to the abuse of power. Because of communalism communal interests always superimpose themselves on national interests. *Communalism rests on religious prejudices.*

The effects of communalism are disastrous. Communalism causes rivalry and violence among masses. It strikes at the root of secularism and national integration. It leads to mutual distrust, illwill and hatred between the communities. The fire of communalism between different religious groups [mainly between Hindus and Muslims, Hindus and Christians] was kindled by the British. The British policy of *"divide and rule"* caused lot of damage to our national interests. Even after independence we have not been able to deal successfully with the challenge of communalism.

2. Challenge of Casteism

Casteism is understood as *a partial or one-sided loyalty in favour of any particular caste.* As **D.N. Prasad** points out, *"Casteism is loyalty to the caste translated into action."*[2]

Casteism is due to multiplicity of causes. (*i*) The feeling of superiority and inferiority, high and low, sacred and unsacred associated with caste is the main cause of casteism. (*ii*) It is also due to the practice of caste endogamy which unduly restricts one's marital relations. (*iii*) Caste is a strong cohesive group. It has a powerful hold over its members. Hence, its members are hesitant to deal freely with the members of other castes. (*iv*) The practice of untouchability on the one hand, and (*v*) the rise of SCs and the OBCs due to reservation facilities, on the other, have further widened the gap between the castes.

1. **Ram Ahuja** in *"Society in India" (1992)*, Page : 25.
2. **D.N. Prasad** in *"The Myth of Caste System"* - Page : 124.

Consequences of Casteism are many. Casteism hinders the development of national feeling. It is dangerous to democracy for it supports inequality. It is contrary to the spirit of our constitution. It leads to moral degeneration by encouraging nepotism. It ignores the human values and social welfare. It may contribute to the neglect of talents and efficiency. Brain-drain is often the result of casteism. Casteism plays an ugly role in elections. Rise in casteism leads to the weakening of national unity.

3. Challenge of Regionalism

Regionalism refers to *an extreme loyalty or love to a particular region which may undermine the interest of the nation.*

India is a nation with wide regional differences also. When a person goes from one part of the country to another, he often finds himself as a foreigner there. Our imbalanced economic plans also have widened the gap between states. Some states have been greatly benefited by the fruits of industrialisation and mechanisation of agriculture, while on the other hand, some states have miserably lagged behind. It is said that rich states are getting richer, and poor, poorer. People are slowly becoming aware of these disparities. It has now assumed the form of regionalism.

Regionalism is expressed in the desire of people of one region to promote their own regional interest at the expense of the interests of other regions. It has often led to separatism and instigated separatist activities and violent movements. [***Ex.*** : *Kahalisthan Movement in Punjab, Bodoland Movement in Assam.*] It has gained tremendous momentum during the recent years because it is exploited by the selfish politicians. Its linkage with linguism has worsened the situation. Regionalism challenges the primacy of the nationalistic interests and undermines national unity.

4. The Menace of Linguism

Linguism implies an one-sided love and admiration towards one's languages and a prejudice and hatred towards others' languages. It is the prejudice of the speakers of a particular language to develop their language to the detriment of all other languages.

India is a land of many tongues and has been called a *"museum of languages"* and also as a *"linguistic madhouse"*. According to 1961 Census report, there were 1018 different languages including the 18 constitutionally approved languages. This linguistic diversity has led to linguism. It has often been manifested into violent movements posing a threat to national integration. Linguistic tensions are often manifested in the borders which are bilingual. ***Ex*** : *(i) In Karnataka, there is a tug of war between Marathi and Kannada speaking people in Belgaum. (ii) The Goans are divided on the basis of Marathi and Konkani languages. (iii) Assam is confronted with Bengali and Assamese, and so on.*

Consequences of linguism are many. (*i*) Linguism leads to the persecution of linguistic minorities. (*ii*) Linguism begets regionalism and parochialism. (*iii*) It undermines the importance of national issues and makes people to become narrow-minded. (*iv*) It provides fertile ground for regional political parties. (*v*) It causes permanent river-water sharing disputes, border disputes between states, and so on. (*vi*) In its extreme form, it leads to the demand for separate states. In brief, it erodes national feelings and damages national integration.

5. Regional Political Parties

Strong regional feelings, interest in intra-state politics and regional aspirations have given birth to regional political parties. Linguism also encourages the formation and development of regional political parties. Regional political parties confine their interests only to their regions and fail to understand and appreciate things in a larger national perspective. They are narrow-minded and their way of approach may endanger the national interests.

In India, there are some regional parties which are demanding more and more autonomy in their function. ***Examples*** : *Telugu Desham in Andhra Pradesh, D.M.K. and A.D.M.K. in Tamil*

Nadu, Akalidal in Punjab, and Shiv Sena in Maharashtra. Akali Dal and D.M.K. at one time had even demanded not only total autonomy but also the status of an independent nation. Such approaches towards politics can never strengthen national feelings or unity.

6. *Extremism and Terrorism* : Political extremism and terrorism have emerged during the recent years as the most formidable challenges to national integration.

- ***Extremism*** refers to the readiness on the part of an individual or group to go to any extreme even to resort to undemocratic, violent and harmful means- to fulfil one's objectives.
- ***Terrorism*** is a method whereby an organised group or party seeks to achieve its aims by generating fear and horror in the community and through the systematic use of violence.

In fact, terrorism is also a kind of extremism. Extremist and terrorist crimes are taking place in the form of kidnapping and killing of political leaders and government officials, blackmailing the rich and the industrialists, attacking police stations, urban bombings, blasting bridges, T.V. centres, telephone exchanges, microwave stations, looting banks, setting fire to government buses and private vehicles, etc. Various terrorist organisations such as - (*i*) JKLF - *Jammu and Kashmir Liberation Front,* (*ii*) the LTTE - *Liberation of Tamil Tigers Elam,* (*iii*). *All Kaida,* etc. are resorting to very harmful terrorist activities and endangering national integration. (*iv*) *Naxalite terrorism* is also causing new anxieties, tensions, fears and monetary losses now a days.

7. *Class Cleavages* : Though the Indian Constitution assures in its very preamble to all its citizens fundamentals rights, liberties and justice, the Government in reality, has not been able to translate these ideals into actuality. Poverty and illiteracy are the big hurdles on the way.

- ***Illiteracy*** : There exists in India a gap between the literates and illiterates. Even today more than 35 crores of people are illiterate. Among the literates only an insignificant minority is able to avail of higher education. Naturally, the benefits of education are grabbed by this small minority. Rural-urban divide exists even in matters of literacy and illiteracy.
- ***Poverty*** : Economic extremes are very common in India. Wide disparity between the rich and poor exists in both urban and rural areas. Even after **57** years of independent rule, poverty is not wiped out. Around 26.1% of the people live below the line of poverty. [as per 1999 - 2000 estimate]. Economic processes such as liberalisation, privatisation and globalisation let loose by the government have only added to rural poverty and unemployment.

Efforts to Promote National Integration

The importance of the issue of national integration made the Central Government to do something in this regard. The Central Education Ministry organised a *'Committee for National Integration'* in 1961 under the chairmanship of **Dr. Sampurnanand**. The Integration Committee gave some suggestions to promote national integration. Some of them are stated below.

1. ***Reorganisation of syllabi*** at various levels - primary, secondary, college and university level - to promote national integration.
2. ***Giving due encouragement to extra - curricular activities*** besides imparting formal knowledge to the students with the intention of promoting national unity.
3. ***Improvement of textbooks*** helps a great deal in giving a true national perspective to the students. They can be made to understand their rich cultural heritage and feel proud of their nation.
4. ***Conducting community prayers,*** mass meetings, speeches by respected leaders, etc., help to bring the people together.

Other Suggestions

In addition to what the Integration Committee suggested for promoting national integration, we may also consider the following for the same purpose.

1. At the all-India level, one language should be developed as a link language to help proper communication among people.
2. An all-India level educational policy is to be evolved with a view to bring about uniformity and to achieve unity.
3. Special programmes must be chalked out to promote national unity. Cinema, television, radio, drama, dance, art exhibitions, musical concerts and such other media instruments could be made use of in this regard.
4. Role of teachers teaching at all levels and in different fields must be properly made use of in promoting emotional integration.
5. Due importance is to be given to develop inter-cultural understandings [that is, understanding between different religious, linguistic, regional, tribal, caste and other groups] to promote unity.
6. Governmental efforts are also necessary in this regard. It must have sincere dedication towards achieving the goal of national unity. Hence, Government officials should invariably be above all pressures and expressions of linguism, communalism, regionalism, casteism, nepotism, untouchability and so on.

4. DIVERGENT RACIAL GROUPS IN INDIA

India is often regarded as an *"ethnological museum"*. We find here people belonging to different ethnic groups. India in its course of history witnessed the coming of waves of immigrants who belonged to different ethnic or racial stocks. The term ***"race"*** refers to *"the genetically transmitted physical characteristics of different groups."*[1] Those who entered its territory were not driven away but mostly accommodated. Due to this reason, *"Indian population contains many primitive strains of mankind not found elsewhere in the same extent."* **Herbert Risley, Haddon, Eickstedt** and others have given their own classifications of Indian racial groups.

Herbert Risley's Classification of Races

Sir Herbert Risley, a British ethnographer, attempted the first classification of Indian races in the census of 1901. On the basis of the census data, he tried to give on a relatively scientific basis a racial classification in his work *"The Peoples of India"*. According to him, the following are the main ethnic groups at Indian population.

RISLEY'S CLASSIFICATION

Indo - Aryan | **Aryo-Dravidian** | **Mongolo-Dravidian** | **Scythio-Dravidian** | **Turko-Iranian** | **Mongoloid**

Dr. B.S. Guha's Classification of Races

According to **S.C. Dube**, *"the most authoritative and widely accepted classification is by B.S. Guha who identified six major racial elements in the population of India.."*[2] In the Census of 1931 **Dr. Guha** revised earlier classifications of Indian population and presented his own. The six-fold racial classification which he mentioned is given below.

As Dube points out the first three of these are the older residents of the Indian nation. They are confined to small pockets. The second three represent the later arrivals. A breif account of these 6 racial groups is given below.

---

1. **Ian Robertson** in "Sociology".
2. **S.C. Dube** in *"Society in India"* - Page : 2.

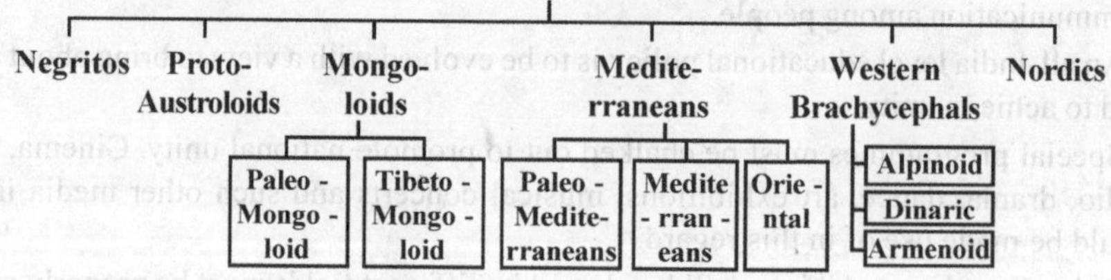

1. The Negritos

The earliest of the Indian racial groups are the Negritos. In the South, the *Kadar,* the *Irula,* the *Paniyan,* and in the Andaman Islands the *Onge* and the *Andamanese* have definite Negrito characteristics. In the North, some traits of this group are found among the *Angami Naga* and the *Bagadi* of the Rajamahal hills. We do not know much about the contribution of this group to the cultural designs of India.

2. The Proto-Austroloids

This group is numerically very significant. Their traces survive in many aboriginal tribes. Most of the tribes of middle India belong to it. These were described by the Indo-Aryans as - *Anas, Dasa, Dasyu,* and *Nishad* - all derogatory terms. It is believed that the Proto-Austroloid group might have followed the first group, that is, the Negritos.

3. The Mongoloid Group

This group has two sub-types; ***a) Paleo-Mongoloid group,*** and ***(b) Tibeto-Mongoloid group.*** Tribes residing in the Himalayan region and also those in the North-East are of Mongoloid stock. This racial element is most visible in Sikkim, Bhutan, and in the whole of the north -eastern region.

4. The Mediterraneans

This racial stock seems to be related with the Caucasian physical type, that is, white race. This is one of the dominant races of India. They normally have a short stature, long head, slender built and dark complexion.

The Mediterranean race has three major subdivisions : ***(a) Palaeo-Mediterranean, (b) Mediterranean*** and ***(c) Oriental.*** Of these three sub-divisions, the Mediterraneans have contributed much the culture of India.

5. The Western Brachycephals [Broad Heads]

It is believed that this racial group came to India from the West and have their association with that of European regions. This has three sub-divisions, namely; (*i*) the ***Alpinoid,*** (*ii*) the ***Dinaric*** and (*iii*) the ***Armenoid.***

6. The Nordics

The Nordics are characterised by - tall stature, long head, fair skin, light hair and blue eyes. They are described as the Aryans and the Sanskrit speaking group. It is also believed that they swept into North India during 2000 B.C. It is said that they contributed much to lay the foundation of the culture and civilisation of India. They have been, in fact, directly or indirectly responsible for the glories of Indian literature and philosophy. They brought horses, iron and best variety of wheat.

Conclusion

It is clear from the above description, that the present population of India is an admixture of almost all the major races found in the modern world. There is, however, a considerable overlapping of races of one area to another. Therefore, no rigid demarcation of race is possible. The only thing we can do is we can demarcate ethnic zones according to the predominance of racial elements.

ANNEXURE – 2

Annexure to Chapter – 5

FAMILY SYSTEM IN INDIA

1. FACTORS AND FORCES THAT SUSTAINED JOINT FAMILIES

Joint families in India continue to be an important social force in our social system. Though they have totally disappeared in the Western societies, around 1/3 of the families in the Indian context still remain as joint families. This proportion is relatively higher in the rural areas. Their very survival in the wake of modern developments gives rise to a basic question as to what factors or forces served to sustain and preserve the joint families. The following explanation is an attempt to answer this question.

1. Functional Advantages of Joint Families

Sociologists very often stress upon a point that no institution survives without a function or purpose. This is true in the case of Indian joint families. They have been fulfilling some vital functions which served to ensure their survival. These functions also proved to be their ***advantages***. ***For example*** : (*i*) Joint family *provides jobs* for a large number of people in an agricultural society; (*ii*) It is *helpful for the religious activities* of the Hindus, (*iii*) It *protected women, children and old people* especially during the period of social upheavals and foreign attacks, (*iv*) It provides the *advantage of division of labour* and fetches more *leisure time* for women and *free recreation* for all. (*v*) It *enjoyed the support of our thinkers,* social reformers and other scholars. (*vi*) It provides *scope for saving and investment* and so on.

2. Role of "Family Adjustments" Made from Time-to-Time

Joint families have been successful in making compromises and adjustments even in the midst of new developments, attractions and divisive and disintegrating forces. This flexibility helped its survival. ***Example*** : Family members want to have their own personal properties. It is a general tendency. *Shastrakaras like* **Manu, Yajnavalkya Kathyayana** and others had recognised this human tendency long back. Hence, they made some provisions in their *Smritis* allowing individual members some right to enjoy some part of the property. Young members of family were also assured of some freedom so that they would stay back in the family. Women were also given some opportunities to take part in the family affairs and so on. For centuries together, family members were successfully prevented from breaking it.

3. No Much Attraction Outside the Family

During the early times, there was no attraction for the members outside the joint family. They never felt the strong need to break it and go away from it. There were reasons for that.

(*i*) "Members were getting married much before they were able to understand and indulge in love-making, romance or courtship. Hence, they never used to feel that *"conjugal love"* is something great. They never felt the urge to go away from the joint family to establish their own household to enjoy marital life exclusively."[1]

(*ii*) During the early times, opportunities were comparatively very less for young men and women to spend time exclusively. Women were never ready for it also. Women surrounded by the in-laws [father-in-law, mother-in-law, sister-in-law] and other members, protected and well taken care of by the elders, never used to feel like going away from the family. They were not prepared to bear the brunt of the family life independently.

---

1. ***Ref*** : **Sri. H.V. Nagesh** in *"Bharateeya Kutumba"* - Page : 16 - Karnataka University Publication.

(*iii*) Ideology of "individualism" had not taken roots in our society. People were more community-minded. Hence, there was no trend in the direction of individual freedom, careerism, exclusive happiness and individual accomplishments.

4. Values that Served to Sustain Joint Families

Ram Ahuja makes a mention of *"the values that nurtured, stabilised and sustained the joint family organisation"* in India.[1] They are stated below.

(i) ***Filial Devotion*** **:** Sentimental forces and parental devotion deterred our youngsters from deserting their parents.

(ii) ***Economic Commitment*** **:** Earning members have the economic obligation towards the needs of all. Economic inability of some brothers to support their wives and children also binds them with the family.

(iii) ***Social Security*** **:** In the absence of state-organised system of social security for the old men, helpless women, childless widows, physically and mutually handicapped members - - joint family used to provide protection and security.

(iv) ***Attraction of the Material Benefit of Physical Labour*** **:** Since joint family served as a centre of economic production, it required relatively a large labour force. Having a larger number of members was an advantage in this regard. Such large families never had to hire the services of outside labourers.

2. NUCLEAR FAMILY : STRUCTURE AND FEATURES

Classification of Families into Joint Family and Nuclear Family

Sociologists have classified families into different types on the basis of different criteria. On the basis of *size or structure, authority pattern* and the *depth of generations,* families can be classified into following two main types :

(*i*) *The Nuclear or the Single Unit Family,* and
(*ii*) *The Joint or the Undivided Family.*

NUCLEAR FAMILY : DEFINITION AND TYPES

Definition of Nuclear Family

1. **Gerog P. Murdock :** *"Nuclear family is one which consists of the husband, wife and their unmarried children."*

2. **Duncan Mitchell :** Nuclear family is *"a small group composed of husband and wife and immature children which constitutes a unit apart from the rest of the community".*[2]

The nuclear family is a small family. Soon after their marriage, the husband and wife leave their parental homes and establish their separate household. Hence, a nuclear family is an autonomous unit free from the control of the elders. Since there is physical distance between parents and their married children, there is minimum interdependence between them. Thus, a nuclear family is mostly independent. The Western family is a typical example of the modern independent nuclear family.

Two Forms of Nuclear Family

T.B. Bottomore makes a distinction between the two types of nuclear family namely; *(i) independent nuclear family*, and *(ii) dependent nuclear family.*

---

1. **Ram Ahuja** in *"Society in India"* - Page : 103.
2. **Duncan Mitchell** in his *"Dictionary of Sociology"*

1. Independent Nuclear Family

As the term indicates, this is a nuclear family system which is relatively independent. It is dominant in modern industrial societies. It has emerged mainly *due to the growth of individualism and intense geographic and social mobility.* The social welfare functions of the modern state have also affected it. The state now comes to the help of the individual to face misfortunes. Hence, he is no longer dependent on his family in times of distress. The modern nuclear family is mostly found in the advanced societies of the West. *Its solidarity largely depends on sexual attractions and companionship between husband and wife and between parents and children.* But the family bonds tend to weaken as the children grow up.

2. Dependent Nuclear Family

The dependent nuclear family is one which is incorporated into or sub-ordinated to a larger group, that is, to the polygamous or the extended family. Among the primitives, and in non-industrial and agriculture dominated societies, dependent nuclear families are found in a relatively larger number. They are normally incorporated into some larger composite family structures.

Is Indian Family - a Joint Family or a Nuclear Family - ?

The Indian family has been pictured as an undivided or joint family since the beginning. Even many of the present day scholars have also expressed the same opinion.

Dr. Iravathi Karve who has made a deep study of the Indian family has also remarked that *family in India is essentially a joint family.* **Kapadia**'s opinion is also not different from that. In a way, it is true. Joint family existed in India even during the Vedic period. It remained so especially at the level of the *"dvija Varnas"* for centuries. Though the family survived as joint family, it was, at times, oscillating between joint families and nuclear families. When the children of the family went out of it - for continuing higher education, to obtain salaried job, or to marry a girl or boy much against the wishes of the elderly members, the family used to get divided into nuclear families. Such nuclear families were again assuming the character of the undivided families especially when children, daughters -in-law, grand children and other relatives were added to it. The proportionate number of such joint families at that time was definitely larger than what it is today. Same situation persisted almost up to the end of the century.

The Changing Nature of Indian Family in the 20th Century and Onwards

The Indian family has been undergoing rapid change especially from the beginning of the 20th century. In 1911 Census report itself there was a reference to the decline of the joint family in India. Studies conducted by scholars like **K.T. Merchant** [1935], **Aileen Ross** [1963], **William J. Goode** [1966], **B.R. Ghosh** and others have also confirmed this view. These studies have drawn our attention to the fact that joint families are slowly getting divided giving place to nuclear families. On the contrary, studies conducted by **K.M. Kapadia** [1956], **I.P. Desai** [1964], **M.S. Gore** [1968] and others have given just the opposite opinion. According to these studies, the Indian joint family still continues to be firmly rooted even though some minor changes are taking place here and there. There are also other studies about family which have given still different opinions. It is in this context of divergent views being expressed by the scholars about the family, we have to analyse the nature and character of the nuclear family in India

NATURE OF INDIAN NUCLEAR FAMILY : SOME OBSERVATIONS AND OPINIONS

No all-India level study has been held so far to study the exact nature and character of the Indian family. In thc absence of such a study, it is difficult to say in exact words about the nature of especially nuclear family which is in a transitional stage in India. In spite of such a handicap, as

Ram Ahuja has pointed out, some considered views could be expressed and observations made about the Indian nuclear family, on the basis of some standard studies made by scholars like - I.P. Desai [1964], K.M. Kapadia [1956], Aileen Ross [1961], A.M. Shah [1955], M.S. Gore [1960], Ramkrishna Mukherjee [1960] Ram Ahuja [1976], Sachidananda [1977], and others.

• Some Views About the Nature of Nuclear Family in India

1. Increasing Number of Nuclear Families

It is a general observation that the number of nuclear families has been increasing during the recent decades. This increase is more intense in the urban areas than in the rural areas.

- ***Views of Some Studies*** :

(*i*) **A.M. Shah** in his studies conducted in a village in Gujarath between 1955-1958 found that 2/3 of the families were simple nuclear families.

(*ii*) **M.S. Gore**'s study conducted in 1960 in the border villages between Delhi and Haryana, revealed the domination of joint families.

(*iii*) **Pauline Kolenda** [1968] who used data from 26 studies conducted by various scholars between 1950-1970, found that majority of the families are nuclear.

(*iv*) **Ram Ahuja** who conducted two studies one in an urban area [1976] and another in a rural area [1988] in Rajasthan, opines that the nuclear families are increasing and this does not indicate the disappearance of the joint family system.

(*v*) **Ramakrishna Mukherjee** in his analysis of 44657 families made in 30 villages and towns in 15 states of India by 18 scholars [like Kapadia, Karve, Kulkarni, S.C. Dube, Kolenda, M.S.A. Rao, I.P. Desai, T.N. Madan, Driver, Bose, Mukherjee and others] found that the percentage of nuclear to total families ranged from **35** to **63**. This indicates though nuclear families are increasing, joint family is still a force to be reckoned with.

2. Element of "Functional Jointness"

In the Indian context, nuclear families are mostly *"dependent nuclear are families"* rather than independent nuclear families. These families are directly or indirectly connected with the original joint family and in times of need, crisis or hardship, obtain all the support from it. They maintain their connection with the original family and on occasions render their help also. They are dependent nuclear families in the sense that they still *"depend"* on the joint family and maintain what is known as *"functional jointness"* with it.

3. Trends Towards Transitional or Nuclear Family

Due to rapid industrialisation, urbanisation, modernisation and an increase in literacy level, there is a greater trend towards nuclear family. The changes from traditional to nuclear or transitional family include trends such as - *establishing separate residence, equality of individuals, equal status to women, functional jointness, better opportunities for individuals to fulfil their aspirations and the weakening of family norms.*

4. Changing Inter-personal Relations Inside the Family

Nuclear families which are getting established due to the disintegration of joint families, are actually the *"conjugal families"*. Such families give much importance to the marital relationship between husband and wife. Kinship relations are either neglected or become very weak. Husband and wife relations are normally established on equalitarian terms. Children are also given much freedom and the interference of the kinsmen is quite less common. Since the married couple have come out of the home of their parents and are living independently, they are not bound by the *"hold of the elders"*. In these families, individuals are given much freedom in *pursuing education, getting into jobs of one's interest and selecting life - partner of one's choice.*

Success of such conjugal families depends much on the nature of understanding and adjustment between husband and wife. As long as balanced emotional relations remain between husband - wife; mother -children and father -children, so long happiness and peace is found in the family. When once this balance is severely upset, clashes and conflicts start taking place in the family. They may ultimately take it towards disintegration.

5. The Decreasing Size of the Joint Family

With an increase in the trend towards nuclear family, the size of the joint families too has started decreasing. Most of the studies held in this connection have pointed out this trend. *For example,* **Ramakrishna Mukherjee**'s survey of 4120 family units in West Bengal as early as in 1960 - 61, revealed that on an average joint family had a size of 4.83 members.

6. Cultural Values Supporting Functional Jointness

Most of the studies have revealed that families in India are changing. But in this changing process they have neither remained as *"full-fledged joint families"*, nor emerged out as *"full-fledged nuclear families"*. They are in a *"transitional stage"*. Though a number of these families exhibit a tendency to move towards nuclear families they seem to continue the character of *"functional jointness"*.

As **Ram Ahuja** point out, *"jointness of family in India is not disappearing"*, ...and at present, such a *"stage can never be envisaged"*. He also says that *"...a nuclear fissioned family [of husband, wife and unmarried children] will not be totally independent but will be functionally dependent on [that is, remain joint with] some primary kin like father or brother, etc."* [1]

The character "functional jointness" is still found due to the cultural values [such as, for example, *religiosity, respect towards parents, commitment towards kinsmen, hospitality towards guests,* etc.] which have been still associated with the family. As long as these values are associated with the family so long it is likely to maintain this character of 'functional jointness'.

Conclusion

"Joint families are fast disintegrating giving place to the nuclear families" - is a general opinion which many people, both scholars and non-scholars hold. *"Statements like these are to be carefully examined"* - opines **Dr. R. Indira**[2] Even at present, members of these nuclear families on occasions like religious ceremonies, *'shraddhas'*, serious illness at home, marriage, death of members, etc., rush to their original joint families and stay over there for sometime. Such gestures or tendencies serve to re-establish the family link. Husband and wife working in offices, factories, etc., in a distant city often call back their aged parents to stay with them to look after their little children when they are away from home. Instances like these help to strengthen the joint family relations.

On the basis of the above discussion, it could thus be concluded that though nuclear families are increasing in number in India, they are not emulating the model of the Western nuclear family. They continue to maintain their connection with the original joint family. Though joint families are slowly decreasing in number there is no immediate threat for their survival.

---

1. **Ram Ahuja** in *"Society in India"* - Page . 101.
2. **Dr. R. Indira** in *"Bharateeya Kutumba"* - Page : 54.

ANNEXURE - 3

Annexure to Chapter – 6

WOMEN IN INDIA

1. ACHIEVEMENTS OF WOMEN IN VARIOUS FIELDS

[Political, Social, Economic, Art, Literature, Sports Bureaucracy, Judiciary, Medicine, Science and Technology]

While speaking about the great achievements of the Indian women we always point out at the achievements of women of the Vedic Age. Through out the Medieval Age women suffered a great deal. But when they entered the modern age things started changing. When India became independent women were given a new lease of life. By making use of the new conditions of life women started slowly exhibiting their talents and efficiency. Those who have not properly recognised this change are still giving a negative picture about women and their role in society. It is a matter of pity that even our mass media - news papers, radio, television and the cinema - are not providing a positive picture about women and what they have been doing. It is, indeed, necessary to take into account the achievements of women in various fields in our study of the status of women in the modern period.

A large number of Indian women have been able to do spectacular achievements in spite of the limitations which the socio-economic and political framework has imposed on them. Four Indian women, for example, have secured, *"Bharata Ratna"*, the highest national award. The receipients of the award are : (*i*) **Indira Gandhi** [1917-1984] awarded in 1971; (*ii*) **Mother Teresa** [Mary Teresa Bojaxhiu [1910-1997] awarded in 1980; (*iii*) **Aruna Asaf Ali** [1909-1996] awarded posthumously in 1997; and (*iv*) **Lata Mangeshkar** [Sushri Lata Dinanatha Mangeshkar - [1929 ...] awarded in 2001.

During the recent time, almost every year along with men, considerable number of women are also getting prestigious national awards such as *"Padma Vibhushana", "Padma Bhushana", "Sangeeta Nataka Akademi Award", "Sahitya Akademi Award"*, etc., for their meritorious performances in specific fields[1] Let us now briefly examine the achievements made by Indian women in such fields as - *political, economic, educational, social, art, literature, medical, sports, bureaucracy, judiciary, science and technology.*

1. Achievements of Women in Political Field

Politics is an important field which plays a vital role in deciding the future of a nation. Women have been playing an active role in politics right from the days of age-old monarchy headed by kings and queens. [***Example*** : The names of Rani Ahalya Bai Holkar, [Poona], Rani Chennamma of Kittur [Karnataka], Rani Lakshmi Bai of Jhansi [U.P.] deserve a special mention here]. In the democratic system of political rule also women never lagged behind. When elections were held to local legislative bodies as early as in 1937, about 56 women including **Kamalabai Chattopadhyaya**, the first woman politician of modern India, were elected.

After independence, from Panchayat to Parliamentary level including the state-level legislative bodies, women have been contesting elections and getting elected. Many assumed offices as state level and central level ministers; and even as chief ministers of states and one as the Prime Minister of the nation also.

Women Who Reached Great Heights in Politics **:** Some women have become memorable because of the great heights they reached in politics. Nehru's daughter **Indira Gandhi** could become

1. ***For example,*** in the year 2003, along with 31 men, 3 women also secured *"Sangeeta Nataka Akademi Award"* They are : 1. **Dr. Kumari Padma Subramanyam**, 2. **Smt. Swapnasundari**, and 3. **Smt. Teejan Bai.**

the Prime Minister of India and lead the nation for about 10-11 years. Nehru's sister **Vijayalakshmi Pandit** was the first woman to become the Central Cabinet minister. She was also the first woman President of UN General Assembly. At the state level, number of women like **Sucheta Kripalani** [U.P.], **Nandini Satpathi** [Orissa], **Shashikala Kakodakar** [Goa]**, Rajinder Kaur Bhattal** [Punjab] **Janaki Ramachandran** [T.N.], **Sushma Swaraj** [Delhi], **Mayavathi,** [U.P.], **Uma Bharathi** [M.P.], **Rabri Devi** [Bihar] and others could rule as Chief Ministers for sometime or the other.

Currently, [2005] **Smt. Vasundhara Raje,** [Rajasthan], **Kumari Jayalalita** [Tamil Nadu] and **Smt. Sheela Deekshit** [New Delhi] are heading their respective States as Chief Ministers. **Smt. Sonia Gandhi** is heading the Congress Party at present [2005] and exercising the highest political influence. In addition to these, a number of other women leaders assumed various types of political offices at different periods as they are doing it now.[1]

2. Women in Economic Field

Women have made sufficient headway in the economic field. They no more remain in the economic field as only the wage-earners, or salaried employees or on honourary remuneration. They have now become owners of property, managers, partners and proprietors in business, directors of companies, and so on.

During the past 30 years women have been able to enter almost all the economic fields for earning income and wealth by giving tough competition to men. They have ventured to step into the fields which were once meant "exclusively for men". [that is, for police, bus drivers, conductors, soldiers, barbers, postmen, pilot officers, judges, etc.] There are banks, educational institutions, Government offices, even police stations [*Ex* : Bhopal Police Station] etc., which are completely managed by women.

3. Women and the Bureaucracy

Women have entered bureaucracies and started working in different capacities, that is, from the bottom most clerical level to the topmost executive level.

- ***Women in I.A.S., I.F.S. and I.P.S.*** : The IAS [*Indian Administrative Service*], the IFS [*Indian Foreign Service*] and the IPS [*Indian Police Service*] represent the three top most bureaucratic offices. Women have entered these prestigious executive posts. Their number in such posts though is not in tune with their share in the population, it is increasing steadily. ***For example,*** in 1948, there was not a single woman in these posts. In 1951, one woman was recruited to the post of I.A.S., it increased to 18 between 1951 and 1960, and then to 339 in 1987 [By then, women IAS officials constituted 7.45% of the total 4548 posts]. By 1993, 17 women IAS officers were working as Deputy Commissioners and around 87 women officers were working in different departments of the Central Government.

- ***Women in IFS and IPS*** : Up to 1993, around 409 people were selected IFS officers out of whom 40 were women. Of these 40 officers, only 6 were selected as Indian ambassadors in foreign countries. **Dr. Kiran Bedi** and **Kanchan C. Bhattacharya** have made name as IPS officers.[2]

---

1. ***For example,*** women leaders like - Rajkumari Amrith Kaur, Sucheta Kripalani, Susheela Nayyar, Sarojni Mahishi, Menaka Gandhi, Margaret Alva, Sushma Swaraj, Mamatha Banarjee, and others served the nation as Central Ministers.

2. ***Achievement of Dr. Kiran Bedi as IPS Officer*** : Dr. Kiran Bedi was the first police officer [in the Cadre of IPS] in the world to enter the police service. When she was posted as the Inspector General of Prisons at the biggest national level jail, namely, **Tihar**, at New Delhi, she resorted to some innovative ways of reforming the jail and its conditions. She sought to breakdown adversarial relations between the police and the community of prisoners. She tried *"to replace the hard hand of punishment with the soft one of correction and rehabilitation"*. In recognition of her yeomen service she was awarded in 1994 ***"Ramon Magsaysay Award"*** which is popularly known as the *"Asian Nobel Prize"*.

   Kanchan C. Bhattacharya has been the first to become the woman DGP [Deputy General of Police] and is currently [2005] serving the State of Uttaranchal.

● ***Women in the Military Forces*** : Women are being recruited to all the three wings of the military forces namely; army, navy and airforce - **Gertrude Ali Ram**, was the first woman major General of the Indian Army who died in Mussoorie in April 2002.

4. Women in the Field of Judiciary

Ever since the ancient period, the judicial system has been under the custody of men. Today women have stepped into this field and are working in a considerable number from magistrate court to the Supreme Court. At present, there are about 19 women judges out of a sanctioned strength of 647 judges in 21 high courts. **Fathima Bibi** of Kerala became the first woman judge in the Supreme Court.

Professional-minded female law- students are found in a large number now a days. They are competing with the boy students to get selected in the prestigious "National School of Law". Women functioning as advocates and judges have made the ordinary women to have greater faith and better hopes in the judicial system.

5. Women in the Educational Field

During the recent years women have been doing exceedingly well in the field of education. The literacy level of women has risen from 39.29% in 1991 to 54% in 2001. From 1980 onwards the performance of girl students in all the public Examinations from SSLC to post-graduation level, has been better than those of boys. They have started entering the prestigious professional courses such as engineering, medical MBA, MCA, MSW, etc. As per the latest information, 1.25 lakh women graduate as doctors every year. This is 50% of the total number. Further, 21% of India's software professionals and 25% of science and engineering graduates are women. More than 50% of the students who pass out every year with a bachelor's degree in humanities are girls.[1] This sudden upsurge of women in the field of education is bound to bring about far reaching consequences in the Indian society.[2]

The grip of women on education is getting tightened year by year. Their number is increasing in the teaching field from primary to post-graduation level. Unlike the situation 20 years ago, we find a large number of women professors, educationists, doctorate holders, educational resource persons, research scholars, scientists, departmental heads, deans, and so on. The only disappointing thing is that the same trend is not found in the case of rural women.

6. Achievements of Women in Medicine, Science and Technology

● ***Medicine*** : India is producing the highest number of women doctors that is, 1.25 lakh, a year in the whole world. They are found today in all the specialised courses of medicine. They are entering the paramedical courses like the pharmacy, nursing, etc., in an equally big number. There are women doctors with great reputation. **Dr. Anupama Niranjan** of Karnataka, for example, made a name not only as a doctor but also as a writer. The number of medical and dental colleges are increasing year by year.[3]

● ***Science and Technology*** : Meritorious girl students have started opting for science subjects today. 21% of the software professionals and 25% of the science and engineering graduates are women. There are today women scientists, technologists, M.Tech degree holders,

---

1. ***Source of these Vital Statistics*** : *"India Today"*, April 4, 2005, Page : 32.
2. ***Mother Recognised*** : In 1996, HRD Ministry issued instructions to include mother's name to students' application forms and certificates issued to them.
3. In Karnataka, for example, in 1998, there were 17 medical colleges and 36 dental colleges and these numbers increased respectively to 29 and 40 in 2004. The same trend is observed in states such as Maharashtra, Tamil Nadu, Andhra and Kerala.

IIT professors, technical advisors, and so on. We no more find the monopoly of men in these fields. Women like **Dr.Kalpana Chavla** have achieved great heights in the most challenging fields such as aeronautical engineering and spacecraft.[1]

7. Women in the Fields of Art and Literature

Women have been providing memorable contributions to the fields of art and literature since centuries. Even in the composition of the RigVedic hymns, it is known that more than 20 women scholars had given their contributions.

Women in the Field of Art : Women have enriched the different fields of art such as - music, dance, drama, cinema, drawing, etc. through talented contributions. Some have carved a permanent niche for themselves in some of the areas of art. Some examples deserve special mention here.

Music : (*i*) **M.S. Subhalakshmi** in Karnataka Music, (*ii*) **Gangubai Hanagal** in Hindusthani music, (*iii*) **Lata Mangeshkar**, the 'Bharata Ratna' award winner, as a playback singer in Hindi films, (*iv*) **Theejan Bai** in the field of folkore, (*v*) **Subhadramma Mansor** in theatre music, and many others have given memorable contributions to the field of music.

Dance : (*i*) Dr. Kumari Padma Subramanya, (*ii*) Jatti Tayamma, (*iii*) Chandrabhaaga Devi, (*iv*) Mallika Sarabai, (*v*) Chandralekha, and others are prominent women artists in the field of dance.

Theatre Artists : (*i*) Jennifer Kapoor, (*ii*) Hamasa Wadkar, (*iii*) B. Jayamma, (*vi*) Usha Ganguli, (*v*) Nagarathnamma - and others have made a mark in the field of theatre art.

- ***Women as Cinema Artists*** : India is a nation which has been producing the highest number of film artists including actors and actresses. We have any number of film actresses in almost all regional language films. Hindi film land is flooded with women actresses some of whom have earned international reputation and admiration.

Women in the Field of Literature

Women writers and poets have never lagged behind in the field of literature. Countless number of women authors have made immense contribution to vernacular languages and also to Hindi and English literature. Some examples;

- Torudatt, Kamaladevi Chattopadhyaya, Sarojini Naidu, Kamala Das and others were famous even during the British period.
- Mahashwethadevi, Mahadevi Varma, Amrith Preetham, Arundhati Roy, Romila Thapar, Vaidehi and others are also famous women writers.
- ***Women Writers in Kannada*** : M.K. Indira, Anupama Niranjana, H.S. Parvathi, Shantadevi Malavada, Jayadevi Tai Ligade, Sara Abubaker, Sudha Murthy, Geetha Nagabhushan and others have earned name and fame as good authors in Kannada Language.

8. Women in Sports Field

Women started taking greater interest in sports only after Independence. We have at present some women atheletes and sports women of national and international reputation. Names of a few such reputed women may be cited here.

1. ***Dr. Kalpana Chavla's Achievements*** : Dr. Chavla [1976-2003] an Indian born American astronaut, obtained her P.G. Degree from the Texas University [U.S.A.] and Doctoral Degree from Colarado University after passing out of Punjab University as an aeronautical engineer. She joined the *"Johnson Space Centre"* at Hooston along with 15 other candidates. She became the first woman of the world to get that opportunity. She became a *"Mission Specialist"* in 1996. She made news by her successful research-oriented space travel in 1997. When she made the second venture in 2003, her spacecraft *"Columbia"* met with the tragedy in which she lost her life [Jan. 16th 2003.

Examples : (*i*) P.T. Usha, (*ii*) Karanam Malleshwari, (*iii*) Bachendri Pal, (*iv*) Ashwini Nachappa, (*v*) Vandana Rao, (*vi*) Rosa Kutty, (*vii*) Nisha Millet, (*viii*) Anjali Vedpathak, (*ix*) Aparna Popat, (*x*) physically handicapped athlete Malathi Holla, (*xi*) swimming expert Meghana Narayan, (*xii*) Shanta Rangaswamy, (*xiii*) Shikha Tandon, (*xiv*) Sania Mirza - and others.

2. HUMAN RIGHTS AND WOMEN

The Concept of Human Rights

The concept of "human rights" did not exist the way it does, until recently. The *"human rights"* refer to all those rights which are common to all human beings. These rights were slowly incorporated into society, in different parts of the world. In the West, the British political thinker **John Locke** gave birth to the concept of *"human rights"* in the 17th century in his book *"The Second Treatise of the Government"*. But the idea of human rights assumed the form of an international movement only in the second half of the 20th century. The human rights movement gained momentum in the decades of 1950, 1960 and 1970. It was during this period that human rights became a major political issue. The UNO took the issue of "human rights" as an article of faith and insisted on all its member countries to make provision for the human rights in their respective territories. The UN General Assembly adopted the *Universal Declaration of Human Rights* [UDHR] a statement of universal goals concerning human rights and freedom. Although it is not legally binding, its content has been incorporated into many national constitutions including ours. People are slowly becoming aware of the human rights. Hence, they have increasingly refused to accept regimes that do not provide for the perfection of human rights.

Meaning and Definition of Human Rights

The concept of 'human rights' does not have one single explanation or definition for it includes a multiplicity of factors that are interlinked. For the purpose of our study we may consider a few of the simple definitions of the concept.

- *"Human rights are literally the rights that one has simply because one is a human being"*. - **Jack Donnelly**. [A leading human rights activist.]
- *"Human rights are those basic rights which everyone inherits the moment one is conceived in the mother's womb."*
- In simple words, it could be said that *"human rights are those basic standards without which men cannot live in dignity"*.

The Main Human Rights

The above definitions or explanations make it clear that human rights are a part and parcel of human life. People, thus, cannot lose their human rights, no matter what they do. These rights constitute the basic requirements of dignified life. Hence, they form a basic framework for the administration of society and political organisation. All civilised societies are expected to protect and ensure these human rights.

- ***Human rights include the following rights -***
  - the right to life
  - the right to food
  - the right to shelter and necessities
  - the right to health
  - the right to education
  - the right to dignity and liberty, and
  - the right to be free.

Main Characteristics of the 'Human Rights'

The 'human rights' mentioned above reveal certain characteristics which may be mentioned below :

1. Human rights are **natural** rights that all human beings possess simply by virtue of being human.
2. Human rights are held by all persons **equally** and **universally.**
3. Human rights are **irrevocable** - they cannot be revoked or suspended for political expediency.
4. Human rights are **inalienable** - one cannot lose these rights any more than one can cease being a human being.
5. Human rights are **indivisible** - one cannot be denied a right because it is *'less important'* or *'non-essential'*.
6. Human rights are **interdependent** - all human rights are part of a complementary framework. ***For example,*** the ability to participate in government is directly affected by the right to express, to get some education, and even to obtain the necessities of life.

HUMAN RIGHTS AND WOMEN

"Human rights" - as the very term indicates represent the rights of all human beings of both the sex, men and women. Individuals of both the sex are born with these rights. Human rights are God-given or Nature-given rights. Both men and women have equal access to these rights. No discrimination be allowed or imposed in the exercise of these rights.

It is a fact of history that women have been denied equal rights for centuries. The *"philosophy of human rights"* became popular only during the second half of the 20th century and the issue of *"gender equality"* and *"equal rights"* for women assumed importance only after 1970's.[1]

Women's Rights and the Declaration of Human Rights

The *"Universal Declaration of Human Rights"* by the UNO on 10th December 1948 both directly and indirectly influenced its member nations to extend these rights to women also. India which joined the UNO after its independence paid sufficient importance to the human rights by incorporating many of these in its constitution. India which adopted a Constitution of its own in 1949 contains several Articles mandating equality and non-discrimination on the ground of sex.

RIGHTS AND PROTECTION GIVEN TO WOMEN BY THE CONSTITUTION OF INDIA

The Constitution of India in its attempts to provide equal rights and opportunities to women, and to ensure protection and justice has made the following provisions.

1. Constitution assures equality to all its citizens including women. [Article - 14].
2. Ensures that no discrimination be made against its citizens on the basis of caste, class, creed, race, sex, place of birth or region [Article - 15(1)].
3. Does not deny or impose sanctions or conditions on its citizens to make use of any public place or institutions on the basis of sex, race, caste, religion, etc., [Article 15 (2)]
4. Recommends the State to make certain special arrangements in order to provide protection to women and children and to promote their welfare [Article - 15(3)]
5. No discrimination be made by the State against its citizens including women while

1. However, the *"Women's Suffrage Movement"* demanding the right to vote during the first phase of the 20th century, proved to be the beginning of women's rights as "human rights".

providing jobs. [Article - 16].

6. To pursue a policy of providing the minimum necessities of life to the citizen without discriminating between men and women [Article 39(a)]
7. Fixing "equal remuneration for equal work" without discriminating between men and women.
8. To provide human conditions for the citizens to fulfil their occupational obligations. The state shall take it as its responsibility to provide maternity benefits for its women employees [Article - 42].
9. Promoting harmony and fraternity among people and doing away with all the humiliating customs in respect of women [Article 51 (A) and (e)]
10. ***1/3 Reservation For Women in the Panchayats*** : Reserving not less than 1/3 of the total number of seats for women in the Panchayats [including the women belonging to the SCs and STs] for which direct elections are held. These reserved seats in the range of the Panchayats are to be kept on rotation basis. [Article - 243 D (3)]
11. ***1/3 of Reservation for women in the Presidential Posts of the Panchayats*** : Reserving not less than 1/3 of the total number of the presidential posts at all the levels of the Panchayat [Gram Panchayat, Thaluk Panchayat and Zilla Panchayat] systems [Article 243 D (4)]
12. ***1/3 of the Reservation for Women in the Municipalities*** : Reserving not less than 1/3 of the total number of seats for women in the town municipalities [including the women belonging to the SCs and STs] for which direct elections are held. These reserved seats in the range of the town municipalities are to be kept on rotation basis [Article 243 (T) 3.]
13. ***Reservation for Women in the Presidential Posts of the Town Municipalities*** : While reserving the presidential posts of the town municipalities for women and also for the SCs and the STs, the relevant law framed by the state legislative body is to be followed.

3. STRATEGIES FOR THE PROTECTION OF WOMEN'S RIGHTSAND REHABILITATION OF WOMEN

The independent Indian Government has undertaken a number of measures with a view to promote the development and welfare of women. Some of them may be briefly mentioned here.

1. Welfare of Women Through Legislations

To ensure equal rights and opportunities for women and to provide for them *'justice'*, the government undertook several legislative measures. ***Examples*** : *(i) The Hindu Marriage Act, 1955; (ii) The Hindu Succession Act, 1956; (iii) The Hindu Adoption and Maintenance Act, 1956; (iv) The Suppression of Immoral Traffic of Women and Girls' Act, 1956; (v) The Dowry Prohibition Act, 1961; (vi) The Equal Remuneration Act, 1976; (vii) The Factories Amendment Act, 1976; (viii) The Family Court Act, 1984; (ix) Medical Termination of Pregnancy Act, 1971; (x) The Muslim Women's Protection of Rights on Divorce Act, 1986. and Iddat.*

2. Legal Assistance to Assure Justice to Women

The government established a special ***'Cell'*** [attached to labour department] in 1976 with a view to provide due assistance to women in distress. The responsibility of this cell is entrusted to the *'Commissioner of Police'*. The central government has also established a separate ministry with a cabinet rank to deal with the issues and problems concerned with women. To assist judiciary in its task of ensuring judicial protection to women *"social vigilance groups"* are established. Family Courts established according to *"the Family Court Act, 1984"*, are giving legal protection to women. The Social Welfare Department has established *"Women's Bureau"* in order to look into the problems of women and to find solutions for the same.

3. Establishment of National Commission for Women

The Central Government established *"the National Commission For Women"* **[NCW]** in 1992 in order to check incidents of violence against women and to promote social, legal and economic equality of women. In addition to the NCW, several states of India established *"State Women's Commissions"* [SWC]. By 2001, there were SWCs in as many as 17 states.

The main function of these Commissions is to inquire into the *"unfair practice"* meted out to women which includes *"mental and physical torture"*. Its other functions include studying inadequacies in laws, monitoring enforcement of laws, inspecting prisons, police stations, lock-ups, refuges for women victims of violence, etc. It makes recommendations for prosecution in individual cases. **Smt. Girija Vyas** is its present national level President.

4. Relief and Rehabilitation

As per ***The Scheduled Castes and Scheduled Tribes [Prevention of Atrocities] Rules, 1989,*** compensation is to be paid to members of those communities who have suffered abuses. This compensation includes Rs. 50,000, to a woman who has had her modesty "outraged" or been sexually exploited, and Rs. **2 lakh** to a woman who has been raped. But it has been observed that proper economic and social rehabilitative facilities are not provided to the victims though such legal provisions are there.

5. Expression of Government's Concern for Women Through the Observance of Women's Day Programmes.

The Government's concern for women has been expressed by means of its observance of *"Women's Day Programmes"*. ***For Example*** : -

(*i*) The ***year 1975*** was observed as ***"International Year of Women"*** as per the call of the UNO. From 1975 onwards, the ***8th Day of March*** is being observed as ***"International Women's Day".***

(*ii*) The year ***1990*** was observed as ***"SAARC year of the Girl Child".***

(*iii*) The Decade between ***1991-2000*** AD was observed as ***"The SAARC Decade of the Girl Child".***

(*iv*) The year ***2001*** was observed as the ***"Year of Women's Empowerment".***

6. Social and Economic Programmes For the Benefit of Women

In order to protect the social and economic interests of women, the Government has undertaken a variety of programmes among which the following may be mentioned.

1. Educational Development Plan for Women - through women study Centres, Human Resources Department, the UNICEF, NCERT, Ford Foundations, and so on.

2. Programmes for Improving Women's Health - through Indian Council of Medical Research, Ministry of Health and Family Welfare, Central Govt. Health Services Scheme, and so on.

3. Economic Development Programmes For Women - Through various schemes such as - Institute for providing vocational training for women, Women's National Training Institute, Working Women's Hostels, the National Committee for Women Welfare, Social Assistance Schemes, The Scheme of Training Cum - Employment, Cum Production Centres, Rastriya Mahila Kosh (1992); Mahila Samriddhi Yojana, Indira Mahila Yojana (1995), Women's

Development Corporation [WDC - 1986-87], Welfare and Support Services, and so on.

- ***Stree Shakti Scheme [Self-Help Groups - SGHs] to Empower Women Economically : Karnataka Model*** : In order to empower rural women economically, the Karntaka Government [under the Chief Ministership of S.M. Krishna] launched the *'Stree Shakti Scheme'* to forge *"Self-help Groups"* among women. ***Purposes*** : (*i*) To strengthen the process of economic development of women. (*ii*) To establish at least **one lakh** SHGs during 2000-2001. (*iii*) To enhance financial stability in rural women by involving them in income generating activities such as producing - detergent powder, cleaning powder, bleaching powder, candle making, coirs, mat-making, tailoring and preparing ready-made clothes, embroidery works, knitting, toy-making, agarbatti making, etc. This scheme was intended to empower at least two million rural women in Karnataka by the end of the year 2002. These SGHs seem to be functioning comparatively well in many of the rural areas of Karnataka at present [2005].

ANNEXURE - 4

Annexure to Chapter - 10

BACKWARD CASTES / CLASSES [OBCs] THEIR PROBLEMS AND WELFARE

BRIEF HISTORY OF BACKWARD CLASSES MOVEMENT IN KARNATAKA

As far as Karnataka is concerned, the *"backward classes movement"* began in the 12th century A.D. due to the efforts of the great socio-religious reformer **Sri Basaveshwara** [or **Basavanna**]. This movement which was launched against the caste rigidities and exploitations, became weaker in course of time. It was once again revived during the British rule by the end of the 19th century, but in a different manner.

Demand For Reservation in Services for Non-Brahmin Castes As the Main Cause For the Backward Classes Movement

In the princely state of Karnataka, Brahmins had an upper hand in the administrative and service positions. Even during the British rule, they were the first to grab the educational opportunities that were newly created.

They also got into various service positions. The non-Brahmins of the Mysore region, finding it difficult to compete with the Brahmins, staged a small movement and urged the government for equality. The Christians and the Brahmo-samajists also supported their cause. Thus was born by the end of the 19th century, *the first backward classes movement in Karnataka* The Government which yielded to the pressure promised to give employment opportunities to the non-Brahmins especially in police and other services. The caste consciousness which this movement created led to the formation of non-Brahmin caste associations such as ***"Veerashaiva Mahasabha"***, ***"Okkaligara Samaja"***, ***"Kurubara Sangha"***, etc., in Mysore region.

Appointment of Millar Committee -Its Report in 1918

The non-Brahmin groups such as Veerashaivas, Okkaligas and Muslims, decided to face the Brahmin domination politically. They formed ***"Prajamithra Mandali"***, a political party on the model of *"Justice party"* of Madras. Prominent leaders of this party such as **M. Basavaiah, H. Chennaiah, C.R. Reddy** and others met Maharaja of Mysore and appealed to him to reserve some seats for the non-Brahmin backward classes in Government jobs, local bodies and educational institutions. In response to their request, the Maharaja of Mysore appointed in 1917 **"Millar Commission"** under the chairmanship of **Leslie Millar,** the chief magistrate of Mysore province. As per the report of the Commission published in 1917, 50% of the higher-level jobs and 2/3 of the lower-level jobs were reserved for the non-Brahmin castes. It also specified that this reservation target to be achieved in a time span of **7** years. **Sir. M. Vishveshwaraiah,** the then Diwan [chief minister] of Mysore, opposed this proposal on merit grounds and on the same issue resigned his post in 1921. In spite of his resignation, the recommendations of the report came into practice and the non-Brahmin backward classes were provided with the recommended reservation facilities. The report was in force almost up to the day of independence.

Nagan Gowda Committee, 1960 :
The First Backward Classes Commission of Karnataka

The Karnataka Government had not taken up the task of identifying the "backward classes" almost up to 1957 general elections. Hence, the Karnataka Government headed by the Chief Minister, S. Nijalingappa appointed in 1960 under the Chairmanship of **Dr. Nagan Gowda** a *"backward classes commission"* first of its kind. It was asked to prepare on a scientific basis a list of backward classes of Karnataka to whom reservation facilities could be bestowed. It gave its final report in 1961 in which it recommended 15% seats to *Scheduled Castes*, 3% to *Scheduled Tribes,* and 50% to *Other Backward Classes* [OBCs], providing for a total of 68% reservation. The Government's attempt to implement the report was stayed by the Supreme Court for it was challenged by Balaji and 22 other students in a writ petition. The Court in its judgement not only nullified the report but also stated that taking only the caste factor into consideration in identifying the backward classes, was unconstitutional. It also stated that economic factor, job, place of residence and such other important factors should also be given due consideration.

However, in 1963, the Nijalingappa Government issued an order guaranteeing 15% reservation to SCs, 3% to STs and 30% to OBCs. It had totally ignored the factor of caste. As per this order, people with an annual income of less than Rs. 1200/-, pursuing agriculture, handicrafts, lower-level jobs and physical work were considered as constituting backward classes. This was in force almost up to 1977.

The Havnoor Commission 1972 :
Submission of Its Report in 1975

The Karnataka Government under the Chief Ministership of Late Devraj Urs appointed in 1972 **the second backward classes commission** headed by **L.G. Havnoor.** The Commission in its report submitted in 1975 stated that though more than 75% of the people in the state belonged to backward classes and deserved reservation facility, there was no constitutional provision for giving it. Hence, it made provision for reservation only up to 50%. The Urs Government, however, issued an order making a provision for 58% reservation.

This order was also challenged in the Supreme Court and when it came up for hearing in 1982, the Karnataka Government gave a written submission to the Court that it was prepared to institute one more commission to decide the issue of identifying the backward classes.

Venkataswamy Commission, 1983 : Its Report in 1986

As per the written promise made to the Supreme Court, the Karnataka Government under the Chief Ministership of Late Ramakrishna Hegde appointed the Venkataswamy Commission in 1983. The Commission gave its report in 1986 making a provision of 18% reservation for SCs and STs and 27% reservation for the OBCs with an overall percentage of 45% reservation.

Since this Comission had kept the Lingayats and Okkaligas, the two dominant castes, outside the purview of the backward classes, wide protests were organised against it especially in old Mysore area. The Government decided not to implement the report but to establish a new commission to find an amicable settlement to this problem.

Chinnappa Reddy Commission and Its Report in 1990

The Janata Government which had the reins of administration in its hands instituted the Chinnappa Reddy Commission in 1990. The Commission which travelled very widely throughout the state for about three years for collecting necessary information from the people and also organisations, finally gave its report in 1990.

● ***Some Special Features of This Commission*** : The report submitted by Chinnappa Reddy Commission has been comparatively more widely welcomed. The commission seems to have tried its best to uphold social justice. The commission in its report has made a distinction between those who have eligibility and deserve reservation and those who do not have eligibility and do not deserve reservation facility. The commission recommend severe punishments to those who produce false certificates to avail of the benefits of reservation.

Present Position of the Report

Significant political developments took place in the state while the Chinnappa Reddy Commission report was being discussed at various platforms. Meanwhile, the state witnessed the rule of Veerendra Patil, Bangarappa, and Veerappa Moiley as Chief Ministers of Karnataka. Though, in 1994 , the Moiley Government issued an order increasing the total quota of reservation to 73% [OBCs - 50%, SCs - 18%, and STs - 5% Total 73%] it could not be enhanced beyond 50% due to Supreme Court verdict dated 1st Aug. 1994. The attempts of the Moiley Government to impress upon the Central Govt. to bring an amendment to the Constitution legalising the increase in the reservation quota even up to 73%, were also not successful.[1] The Government which assumed power after the fall of the Moiley's Ministry did not take up this issue any more. As a result, at present in Karnataka, the SCs and STs together enjoy a reservation of 18%, while the OBC's quota is 32%.

Conclusion

The real progress of the nation lies in the progress of the Backward Classes. Even the great monk Swami Vivekananda had said the same about 100 years ago. But, unfortunately, the issue of reservation has widened the gap between the privileged and the unprivileged. This gap can be lessened and better relations between the two established only if the two communities change their attitude towards each other. The privileged must always consider it as their moral responsibility to allow and encourage the unprivileged to come to their level. The unprivileged and the beneficiaries of the reservation must not develop a vested interest in it. On the contrary, they should make sincere efforts to improve their economic and educational positions so as to stand on their own legs without the support of any type of reservation.

1. The Supreme Court in its 11th Nov. 1994 judgement given in connection with a writ petition had cautioned that for whatever reason the reservation quota should not cross the limit of 50%.

ANNEXURE - 5

Annexure to Chapter - 22

SOME SOCIAL PROBLEMS OF INDIA

(A) PROBLEM OF CHILD LABOUR

Most of the developing countries of the world including India are facing a social tragedy found in the form of *child abuse* and *child labour*. A large number of children below the age of 12-14 are made to work as labourers in many places especially in the agricultural and industrial areas. The physical, emotional, educational and medical needs of these working children are conveniently ignored. These children are made to work for long hours. They are often battered by their employers and harassed by their senior colleagues. Unlike the adult labourers, these child labourers do not have a labour union of their own to fight for their rights and safeguard their interests. Hence, their exploitation continues without any protest. Neither the government nor the public is serious enough to make organised efforts to combat this problem. Even the sociologists and the psychologists have not taken much interest in highlighting this grave problem. The nation is also not aware of the gravity of the problem.

What is Child Labour - ?

The term *'child labourer'* is considered equivalent to the term *"working child"* or *"employed child"*.

1. According to the **Constitution of India**, child labourer may be defined as *a person who is below the age of 14 years and is working for an earning.*
2. According to ***The Concerned for Working Children*** **[*CWC*]** of Bangalore, - a child labourer is *"a person who has not completed his/her fifteenth year of age and is working with or without wages/income on a part-time or a full-time basis".*
3. According to **Home Folks**, *"child labour is any work by children that interferes with their full physical development, their opportunities for a desirable minimum of education or their needed recreation."*

1. NATURE OF CHILD LABOUR

Magnitude of the Problem

The problem of child labour has become a colossal one. India has the largest number of child labourers in the world who are engaged in both organised and unorganised sectors. According to the ***Planning Commission*** estimate, there were around 15.70 million child labourers in the age-group of 10-14, as early as in 1983. Of these, 14.03 million were working in rural areas and 1.67 million were engaged in urban areas.

As per 1990-1991 estimate, India had 827 million population out of which children below 14 years constituted 298 million [36%]. At that time there were about 11.29 million child labourers in the country who constituted 1.34% of the total population. Around 45% of them were girls.

In March 1995, the number of employed children below **14** years of age and engaged in various economic activities constituted **17 million** [9.5 million males and 7.5 million females][1] A large majority of these child labourers are engaged in agriculture and allied sectors, while others are found in urban, semi-urban and industrial areas.

1. The Hindustan Times, March 21, 1995.

DIFFERENT FACETS OF THE PROBLEM

Child labour is a social problem of far-reaching consequences. No outside observer can imagine and understand the complexity and the magnitude of the problem. The problem has different facets also. Without a proper appraisal of the problem its seriousness cannot be understood. The economic, social and the legal facets of the problem may be briefly examined here.

1. Economic Face of Child Labour

In most of the underdeveloped and the developing countries, children of inappropriate age are forced to take part in productive activities due to economic distress. Parents of poor class send their children for work to increase family income while the employers of various business establishments employ children to maximise their profits. The result is economic exploitation of children. This economic exploitation continues both in the ***organised*** and ***unorganised*** sectors.

(A) Child Labour in Unorganised Sector

In the unorganised sector, child labour is mainly found in the rural areas, tea and coffee estates, mining sectors and even in urban areas.

(a) *Child Labour in Rural Areas* : A large number of children are found to be working in rural areas. It is estimated that more than **60%** of them are below the age of **10** years. A study conducted in Western U.P. has revealed that almost **35%** of the girls in **6-11** age-group were engaged in some economic activity. Similarly, over **52%** of the girls in the age-group **11-18** were involved in economic pursuits.

- ***In Tea-gardens and Coffee Estates*** children below 12 years are made to work much against the law. Girls who bring food to their working mothers are often encouraged to stay back and help in the work.
- ***In the Mining Operations*** also, boys below **12** years are preferred to carry things inside the tunnels without bending their head. It is said that in the mining sector, 56% workers are children below **15** years.

(b) *Working Children in Urban Areas* : It is difficult to estimate the number of children struggling to live in urban areas as child labourers. Sizeable number of them work in city canteens, petty shops, restaurants, garages, work shops, etc. ***For example,*** in Delhi alone, 60,000 children work in *dhabas,* [roadside canteens] tea-stalls, restaurants and small eating places on a daily wage of Rs. 8 to 10. They are also found to be picking rags, hawking goods, cleaning private cars, trucks, selling fruits, vegetables, icecandy, news paper, etc., loading and unloading goods for the tempos and trucks, etc. Some of them are working in private houses as domestic servants.

(c) *Child Labourers Working as Bonded Labourers* : Child labour is also associated with bonded labour. It is said that out of the total number of bonded labourers in Karnataka, 10.3% are found to be children. The figure stands at 8.7% for Tamil Nadu and 21% for Andhra Pradesh.

(B) Child Labour in Organised Sector

Studies conducted in several mega cities have revealed some of the shocking facts about child labourers. ***For example,*** **Mumbai** has the largest number of child labourers. In **Varanasi,** more than 5000 children are found working in silk weaving industry alone. Child labourers are found to be working in many factories in several cities much against the prevailing law.

The poor economic conditions of the child labourers are such that they are found even in the so called organised sector that is, in factories and various industrial units.

(c) *Working Children in Industrial Units* : The most pitiable working children are those employed in hazardous industries. Some examples of such industries employing children may be cited here.

(*i*) In the *glass industry* of **Firozabad** in U.P., out of 2 lakh workers, 50,000 [25%] are found to be children.

(*ii*) In the brassware industry of **Moradabad**, [U.P.] about 40000-50000 children [27 to 30%] are working.

(*iii*) In the *fireworks* and *match box units* in **Sivakasi** [Tamil Nadu] 45000 children are employed for work.

(*iv*) In the *slate industry* in **Markapur** [Andhra Pradesh], out of 15000, around 3750 are child workers.

(*v*) In the *carpet-weaving industry* around **Bhadohi** [U.P.], 12500 out of 50000 employees, are children.

(*vi*) In and around **Surat** [Gujarat] many young boys in their teens are engaged in *diamond-cutting* operations.

(*vii*) Small girls are made to work in the back-breaking *carpet weaving industry* in **Kashmir**, and so on.

2. Social Face of Child Labour

The social face of child labour is a horrible one. It leads to several consequences also.

(*a*) ***Parent-Child Relations Become Commercial*** : Child labour tends to disturb the normal family life. It spoils the emotional ties between parents and children and converts them into commercial. Parents tend to look at their children as income-fetching objects rather than as individuals with tender emotions and feelings.

(*b*) ***Child Labour - An Unhealthy Social Practice*** : Compelling the children of inappropriate age to work for a petty amount is a very unhealthy social practice. Because, child labour adversely affects the children's balanced physical growth, spoils their education, and deprives them of their needed recreation. Child labour will have disastrous consequences on the spiritual, moral and emotional make-up of the children.

(*c*) ***No Hope of a Promising Future*** : Child labour makes the future of the children very bleak. It disturbs their family life, hampers their socialisation and stunts their creative ability. Children caught in the vicious circle of working at such tender age can hardly lead a healthy social life in their later adult life.

3. Child Labour and Legal Face

The problem of child labour in India is such that it flourishes in spite of the Constitutional provisions and legislations made against it. ***For Example*** :

(*i*) As per ***Article 24,*** no child below the age of 14 years shall be employed to work in any factory or in any dangerous employment;

(*ii*) According to ***Article 39(f),*** childhood and youth are to be protected against exploitation and moral and physical vices and;

(*iii*) According to ***Article 45,*** the state shall endeavour to provide within a period of 10 years from the commencement of the Constitution free and compulsory education for all children until they complete the age of 14 years.

2. CAUSES OF CHILD LABOUR

Various factors have contributed to the problem of child labour among which the following may be noted.

1. Economic Causes

(a) ***Extreme Poverty*** : Child labour is commonly found in all the developing countries where poverty is usually found. India is a country in which more than 26% of the people are living below the conditions of poverty as per 2001 estimate. Many families with extreme poverty are compelled to send their children for work who contribute something for the family income. Children of poor families are forced to work particularly when the working adult members of the family become disabled due to physical and mental deformities, diseases or accidents.

(b) ***Possibility of Extracting More Work for Less Wages*** : Employers of many enterprises search for child labourers because they can extract more work from them by giving less wages. Child labourers neither have a *"labour union"* of their won, nor the *"bargaining power"* to demand more wages. *It is observed that child labourers are employed in mining, glass-making, carpet-weaving and leather industries mainly with this intention.*

(c) ***To Secure More Profit for Factories*** : Some industrialists [owners of fireworks, match-box units, glass and brassware industries, etc.] believe that their units are able to maximise profits because of the appointment of child labourers whose labour is very cheap. ***For example,*** the carpet industry of U.P. which employs 75000 children earns about Rs. **150/-** crore, a year in foreign exchange. In 1993, its export earnings were estimated to be about Rs. **350/-** crore. These industrialists put forward their own arguments in favour of appointing little children.

2. Familial Factors

Family disorganisation often leads to child labour. Extreme poverty and economic necessity of the family as it is already mentioned, is one of the factors favouring child labour. *Divorce, desertion, rigid family relations, cruelty at home, parent child conflicts, criminal tendencies of the parents* often compel children to run away from the unpleasant family environment. In order to while away their time such children wander here and there as street children and finally get into some jobs. ***Example*** : According to one estimate, of the more than **4** lakh working children in Delhi; nearly **1.5** lakh children are found to be *"street children"*.

A large number of such working children neither have families nor can rely on family support. In these circumstances, if the children do not go for work the alternative left for them is idleness, destitution, or crime.

3. Social and Other Factors

(i) ***Temptation of Bad Habits*** : Children belonging to the poor families often become the victims of certain bad and costly habits such as - *smoking, gambling, purchasing lottery tickets, seeing the movies regularly, consuming alcoholic drinks, etc.* When they don't get enough pocket money from home they often resort to outside work to earn money to satisfy their bad habits.

(ii) ***Justification of Employers of Child Labourers*** : Some employers justify their act of employing little children for work. They argue that work keeps poor children away from starvation. They even say that they are rendering a service to the society by providing some jobs to the wandering children who would otherwise have become criminals or joined the rank of anti-social elements.

(iii) ***Failure of Government Machinery and Legislative System*** : Though the Government has a constitutional obligation and a moral responsibility to promote the welfare of the children, it is not serious about the problem of child labour. The half-hearted legislations undertaken in this regard, are a big failure. The government bureaucracy is also indifferent to the problems of the working children.

- ***Lack of Public Awareness*** : Children constitute the treasury of future wealth of any nation. But unfortunately in India, public awareness is not there regarding the social evils such as child abuse and child labour. No organisation has launched an effective movement at the all-India level to rouse the consciousness of the public regarding its responsibility towards children.
- ***Kidnapping and Blackmailing of Children*** : There are also anti-social forces which often kidnap children and take them to a different place for selling them to some employers who are in search of cheap human labour.

3. WORKING CONDITIONS OF CHILD LABOURERS

Not only working children are found throughout India, but even horrible working conditions exist everywhere. No where in India, the working conditions of children are found to be satisfactory.

1. Horrible Working Conditions in Urban and Industrial Areas

Children who are pushed to the inevitable conditions of physical work in urban and industrial areas suffer from various hardships. They work under intolerable conditions - in private houses as domestic servants; in tea-shops and restaurants as vessel-washers and waiters; in mining and industrial units as young labourers; in garages as cleaners, in shops as salesmen, and so on.

(a) Children Working in Small Industrial Units and Mining Industries are faced with hygienic problems. Some work in dangerously polluted factories while a few others toil near furnaces which burn at a temperature of 1400^0 centigrade. They handle dangerous chemicals like arsenic and potassium. Continuous inhaling of impure air adversely affects their lungs and creates diseases like tuberculosis.

(b) Sad Picture of Working Children in Urban Industrial Units **:** A large number of children working in leather, glass and brassware industries in slate industries and fireworks etc., have sunken chests, and thin bone frames which give them a diseased look. As **Ram Ahuja** writes : *"There are times, when their bodies ache, minds fog, hearts cry, spirits bleed, but on orders of the employer they work for 10 to 11 hours at a stretch."*[1] Any one who visits various factories in Delhi, Andhra Pradesh, Uttar Pradesh, Tamil Nadu and Maharashtra can easily notice child labourers with these characteristics.

(c) Unhygienic Shelters Provided to Working Children **:** These children not only work under insanitary conditions but also are made to stay in unhygienic shelters. A large number of child workers are huddled in small rooms under inhuman conditions. These rooms are compartments of substandard, ill-ventilated, insanitary and poorly lighted shelters. These dwelling places are virtually unfit for human habitation.

(d) Children Becoming Victims of Diseases **:** Child workers who are made to toil for long hours under hazardous conditions hardly maintain good health. Many of them suffer from lung diseases, tuberculosis, chronic stomach pain, eye diseases, asthama, bronchitis, back pain, skin diseases typhoid, decentry, liver complaints, etc. Working conditions of these children are so horrible that some get injured and even disabled in fire accidents. Some of them become so much incapaciated that they are thrown out of work mercilessly to join the rank of the unemployed. Thus, many become unemployed even at the age of 20.

(e) Exploitation at the Hands of the Middlemen **:** Little children are drawn from the rural areas to work as child workers by some agents on some commission basis. These children who earn on an average not more than Rs. 500/- a month have to handover almost the whole money or maximum portion of it to the so called local *"guardians"* or *"dadas"* of that area. Those children who work during night shifts are subject to several hardships.

2. Distressing Conditions of the Child Workers in the Rural Agricultural Areas

Majority of the child workers are found in the rural areas. These children are made to work hard in agricultural related works and also as domestic servants.

(i) Child Workers Mostly Belong to the Landless Families **:** The *National Sample Survey Organisation* [NSSO] which conducted a survey in 1971 revealed that the families to which the child workers belonged did not possess any piece of land worth mentioning. This situation has

1. **Ram Ahuja** in *"Social Problems in India"*.

not improved much even at present.

(ii) The Supportive Rural Environment : Low literacy level of women, poor salary paid to adult workers, presence of large number of landless scheduled caste people, rural indebtedness and other factors in the rural areas have directly or indirectly supported the practice of child labour.

(iii) Child Workers as Domestic Servants : There is a greater demand for girl child workers between 10-14 years to work as maid servants at home while similar demand is there for boy child workers to work outside the family, that is, mostly in paddy fields, gardens, plantations, estates, etc. Studies have revealed that most of these domestic servants are not given reasonable salary and much work is extracted from them.

4. GOVERNMENT MEASURES TO PREVENT CHILD LABOUR AND NATIONAL POLICY OF AMELIORATION

GOVERNMENTAL MEASURES

The problem of child labour has now become a colossal one. Around 15% of the child population [as per 1996 estimate] is found to be child workers in India. The problem is so grave that the government believes that it is not possible to remove the problem completely at a stretch. Hence, it has decided to improve their working conditions, reduce the hours of work, ensure minimum wages and provide facilities for health and education.

1. Legal Measures Against Child Labour

(a) In the very ***Constitution of India*** provisions are made to protect the interests of children. **Article 24** of the Constitution states that children below 14 years shall not be employed in any factory or in any hazardous unit.

(b) ***Directive Principles of the State Policy*** also declare their commitment to safeguard children's interests. Though some legislations were undertaken during the British rule,[1] they were not properly enforced. The fate of a few more legislations undertaken soon after independence was also no better.[2]

(c) ***Legislation at the National Level - The Child Labour [Prohibition and Regulation] Act, 1986*** : The first national level and universally applicable legislation undertaken by the Govt. of India to prevent the appointment of children below 14 years is *"The Child Labour [Prohibition and Regulation] Act, 1986."* This Act insists on providing minimum necessary facilities to the child workers. Other than this national level legislation, different states have their own state-level legislations to control and regulate child labour. ***Example*** : States such as Assam, Andhra Pradesh, Bihar, Kerala, Maharashtra, M.P. Punjab, Tamil Nadu, U.P. and West Bengal, have such legislations.

---

1. *Examples of the Legislations Undertaken During British Rule Affecting Children* :
   1. **The Factories Act, 1881,** which forbids the appointment of children below 7 years.
   2. **Indian Merchant shipping Act, 1923** which prevents appointing children below 14 in ships,
   3. **The Children Pledging of Labour Act, 1933** according to which no children can be pledged for the purpose of getting loan nor for repaying loan.
2. *Examples of the Legislations Undertaken After Independence* :
   1. **The Indian Factories Act, 1948** which forbids appointing children below **14** years for work and fixes the duration of work at $4^1/_2$ hrs per day;
   2. **The Plantations Labour Act, 1951** which forbids appointment of children below **12** years for plantation work;
   3. **The Mines Act, 1952** which prevents the appointment of children below 15 years from working in deep mines.

2. Creation of a National Authority to Eliminate and to Regulate Child Labour in Hazardous Industries - 1993

With the intention of removing the practice of child labour in total especially in the hazardous industries by the end of the 20th century, the Central Govt. constituted a ***"National Authority"*** on 2nd Oct. 1993. The Govt. decided to spend nearly **Rs. 850** crores for the benefit of at least **2** million children out of a total of 17 million child workers. This institute intended to rehabilitate the child workers in at least **15,000** schools spread over the whole nation. The institution had plans to give compensation to the families whose children are taken away for hazardous works. [Though this institute was established with high hopes nothing worth mentioning has been achieved so far].

3. Supreme Court's Order for Setting up Child Labour Rehabilitation Welfare Fund [CLRWF], 1996.

In its judgement to a public interest litigation, the Supreme Court ordered the setting up of *a **Child Labour Rehabilitation Welfare Fund*** [on 10th December 1996] to prevent the exploitation of children and to safeguard their economic interest and humanitarian rights. The Court in its judgement also banned child labour in hazardous industries.[1] Any employer deviating from this order will have to deposit Rs. 20.000/- as compensation for each child in the Fund which could be used for the continuation of his education.

As far as the non-hazardous jobs are concerned, the Court directed the State Govts to establish an appropriate authority to ensure not more than **6 hours** of work a day, and at least **2 hours** of time for the child's education. The Court also directed that the entire cost of education is to be borne by the employer.

NATIONAL POLICY TOWARDS CHILD LABOURERS

The Indian government's approach towards tackling the issue of child labour consists of the following three steps.

(i) ***Resorting to legal actions focusing on the general welfare of the child labourers*** - such as reducing hours of work, ensuring minimum wages, assuring hygienic and sanitary conditions of work, providing for minimum necessary civic facilities. These facilities include - toilets, resting rooms, canteens, reading rooms, periodic medical check-up, entertainment facility, etc.

(ii) ***Undertaking developmental programmes for child workers*** and their families so as to cover their education, health, job prospects, and so on. Much stress is laid on providing educational facilities to the child labourers. Programme of free and compulsory education upto the age of 16, must be extended to these children also. It is believed that only education would fetch them salvation from their present state of affairs.

(iii) ***Launching project-based action plan*** in order to achieve the first two purposes. In the beginning, it was suggested to take up ***ten projects*** to cover areas where child labour was found to be widely prevalent. These projects included - match works in Shivakashi, diamond cutting industry in Surat and Jaipur, carpet-weaving in Mirzapur, brassware industry in Moradabad, glass industry Ferozabad, and so on. Of these ten projects, only three were taken up for implementation.

1. The Court identified 9 industries as the most hazardous ones. They are 1. Match Industry in Shivakashi, TamilNadu; 2. Diamond Polishing Industry in Surath, Gujarath; 3. Precious Stone Polishing Industry Jaipur, Rajastan; 4. Glass Industry in Firozabad, U.P.; 5. Brassware Industry, Moradabad, UP; 7. Lock-Making Industry, Aligarh, UP; 8. Slate-Industry, Markapur, AP; 9. Slate Industry in Mandsaur, MP.

5. GOVERNMENTAL MEASURES :AN EVALUATION

Failure of Legislation : The problem of the child labour continues to exist in spite of the measures of the government to contain it. Legislaions undertaken to cover certain specific areas [***Example*** : *The Indian Factories Act, 1948; The Plantations Labour Act, 1951;* and *The Mines Act, 1952.*] have also not been successful. The much expected and an all-comprehensive national-level legislation such as *the Child Labour [Prohibition and Regulation] Act, 1986* has also not inspired the governmental machinery to take serious steps to remove and to regulate the practice of child labour.

- ***Half - Hearted Welfare Projects Regarding Child Labour*** : Though the Central Labour Ministry made an announcement in Aug. 1987 that it would launch the *project based action plan* as an essential component of the national policy on child labour, it failed to keep up the promise. The Govt. hoped to start 10 projects simultaneously covering vulnerable areas such as glass industry, brassware industry, match-works, diamond-polishing industry, etc. But considering the magnitude of the problem, it decided to take up only the match industry on an experimental basis. Even with regard to this project which would have benefited 30,000 working children, nothing concrete has been done except defining the responsibilities of the States and the Centre in such projects.
- ***Indifferent and Corrupt Enforcement Machinery*** : The 1986 legislation permits the employment of children below 14 years in some selected areas of the non-hazardous organised sector. It, however, insists on some safeguards against their exploitation and provides for educational and recreational facilities. A grave defect of this legislation is that it has to rely on the corrupt and inefficient enforcement machinery. This indifferent and corrupt machinery which is bribed by the industrialists keeps its eyes closed even when the provisions of the legislation are openly violated.
- ***Lack of Clarity in the 1986 Legislation*** : The 1986 Act fails to define properly what constitutes hazardous jobs. A committee which was set up to identify the permissible jobs for working children has also not made much progress.

Some Suggestions to Improve the Present Position of the Child Labourers

It is a matter of disgrace for the society to make the children work as full-fledged employees. Enforcing them to work in conditions dangerous to their health and safety is a crime. Under no circumstances, they be compelled to work before they become matured enough to work.

1. ***Existing Legislations be Made More Effective*** : The government instead of thinking in terms of introducing new legalisations must take necessary steps to implement effectively and strictly the already existing legislations.
2. ***Punishments for Violators*** : To ensure compliance with the 1986 Act, stringent punishments should be given to those who violate its provisions.
3. ***Promotion of the General Welfare of the Child Workers be Insisted Upon*** : It must be made compulsory for all the employers to take proper steps to promote the vocational, educational, medical and intellectual well-being of the child workers whether they are working as domestic servants, factory workers or hotel-workers.
4. ***Law Enforcement Machinery be Instituted*** : Laws and regulations relating to child labour must be backed by effective enforcement machinery with statutary powers to take necessary action. This helps the strengthening of labour inspection and related services.
5. ***Maintenance of Registers be Made Compulsory*** : It should be mandatory for employers to maintain registers and documents indicating the names and age of all the employed children.

6. ***Exploitation of Children be Stopped in the Unorganised Sector Also*** : It is necessary for the government to make proper arrangements and take appropriate precautions to prevent unhealthy and exploitative child labour not only in the organised field but also in *the unorganised sector.*
7. International agencies such as the **World Health Organisation** [WHO], the **United Nations' International Children's Emergency Fund** [UNICEF] and the **International Union for Child Welfare** [IUCW] are also working for promoting child welfare. Due co-operation must be provided to these agencies to obtain their best help.

In conclusion, it could be said that the Government in co-operation with the public should take such appropriate steps with the help of which the child of the 21st century will find himself into the *"heaven of freedom."*

(B) TERRORISM

Terrorism is one of the types of grave violences of the present world. Crossing the national boundaries terrorism has become a global menace. In the recent times, it has affected both the developed and the developing countries. Everywhere, the phenomenon of terrorism is understood as a problem capable of affecting not only national but also international politics. The 11th Sept. 2001 plane attack on the twin towers of the *World Trade Centre* [WTC]. New York, U.S.A. stands out as a powerful evidence to this fact. Progress achieved in the fields of science and technology and particularly in information technology has helped in making terrorism a global phenomena.

Unfortunately, terrorism has assumed catastrophic proportions. It has endangered the World environment of peace and security. Terrorism is totally opposed to democracy and humanity and causes bloodshed, destruction and anarchy all round.

Concept of Terrorism - Its Definition

Terrorism which is a product of the Western civilisation has entered almost all nations including India. Various words such as insurgency, civil war, etc. - are often used to mean terrorism. Terrorist activity is basically a violent activity. It includes - exploding of bombs, kidnapping, setting fire to houses, organising mass murders, blackmailing, highjacking, intimidation, and such other dangerous and extremely violent activities.

Definition of Terrorism

1. According to **Encyclopaedia of Social Sciences,** terrorism is *"a method whereby an organised group or party seeks to achieve its avowed aims chiefly through the systematic use of violence."*
2. **F.R. Scarpitti** and **M.L. Andersen :** Terrorism refers to *"The collective mode of politically oriented violence"*.
3. **Ram Ahuja :** Terrorism can be broadly defined as *"violent behaviour designed to generate fear in the community, or s substantial segment of it for political purposes."*
4. **In simple words,** terrorism can be understood as *a forceful and unlawful method to achieve the desired goal.*

Characteristics of Terrorism

Terrorism is characterised by a deliberate use of violence against civilians, armed personnel, and the state by some group of misguided persons to bring about the desired political intimidation, coercion, or destruction of human lives and property to obtain realistic or illusory goals.

Terrorist activities are carried on in such a way that it is difficult to give an appropriate definition of terrorism. However, its main characteristics can be summed up as follows :

Characteristics

1. Terrorism is basically a form of violence and is manifested in the form of blatant criminal acts such as kidnapping, mass murders, attacks, intimidations, etc..
2. It is directed against civilians, armed personnel, a linguistic, religious, racial, or ethnic or other kind of community, government or state.
3. It is not a sudden outburst or a spontaneous manifestation of wrath. On the contrary, it is an organised, planned and deliberate act of selective violence carried out only by a handful of people.
4. Terrorism of any type is unlawful, illegal, inhuman and anti-democratic. It has no faith in democratic means and has utter disregard for human values. The eternal values of Indian culture such as love, truthfulness and nonviolence are essentially opposed to the gospel of terrorism.
5. Terrorism is mainly politically motivated violence with a sole motive to overthrow or challenge the existing order. Though terrorist type of violence is documented in various civilisations throughout recorded history, it is popularly believed that political terrorism is of recent origin, unique to contemporary society.
6. It is a weapon of blackmail and coercion
7. It uses violence to create a psychological impact for making their demand accepted. It aims at creating impact of fear and panic not only for the victim but also for the people at large.
8. Violent activities branded as "terrorism", are devoid of rational thinking. Such activities are normally indulged in due to emotional outbursts.
9. Terrorism contains arbitrariness in violence. In selecting its victims and in perpetrating violence against them, it does not follow any definite policy and is normally indiscriminate in doing so.
10. Terrorism is frightening that it is normally accompanied by a feeling of helplessness on the part of the general masses.

- Terrorism, however, is not always reactionless. Sometimes, people react strongly to it and fight back. But when it is sudden and strong enough to overpower the masses, they resort to flight.

TERRORISM IN INDIA

India has been witnessing terrorist activities since a long time. Though they are found in various places they can be grouped into four main types. They are as follows.

(a) Naxalite Terrorism found in Bengal, Bihar and Andhra;

(b) Khalistan - Oriented Terrorism in Punjab;

(c) ULFA - Terrorism in Assam; and

(d) Terrorism in Kashmir.

(a) NAXALITE TERRORISM

The Naxalite terrorism which took inspiration from the Chinese Revolution under the leadership of Mao-Tse Tung, first appeared in West Bengal in 1967. This ideology based terrorism later on spread to Andhra Pradesh, Kerala, Orissa, Tripura, and very recently to Karnataka. One of the initial Naxalite leaders by name Charu Mazumdar had declared that *"China's chairman is our chairman, and China's way is our way."* Inspired by the communist thoughts, the Naxalite movement was highly charged by the ideology of violence. Its leaders had given call for the total annihilation of the big farmers, landlords and *jagirdars*.

Though the initial *Naxalbari Movement* [1967 movement] was not successful in reaching its objectives, it was able to create serious law and order problem. It made many idealistic young Naxalite men and women kill landlords, moneylenders and police officers. As many as **2000** persons were killed in between 1969 and 1972. More than **700** cases of looting, and **9000** acts of serious violence by the Naxalites were reported. The police also killed about **400** and arrested more than **6000** terrorists. The movement lost its idealistic flavour when professional criminals also joined it. When the main leaders of the movement [like Charu Majumdar, Kanu Sanyal, Punjab Rao, Panchanama Sarkar, Jungle Santal, and others] were arrested, it switched over to other states such as Bihar, A.P., Tamil Nadu, Kerala, Orissa, Tripura, and so on.

Naxalites believe in violent way of settling problems. They organise killings, blasts, extortions and kidnappings. At present two important left-wing militant organisations namely; (i) *People's War Group [PWG]* and (ii) *Maoists Communist Centre [MCC]* are having their network in different parts of the country. The PWG activists are concentrated in Andhra Pradesh, Chhttisgarh and Orissa, while the MCC is mostly active in Jharkhand and Bihar. The present UPA Government's liberal attitude towards these extremists has given them a new lease of life to spread their tentacles in various parts of the nation.

(b) TERRORISM IN PUNJAB

Terrorism in Punjab is also known as *"Sikh - terrorism"*. This made its appearance in 1980s when some militant groups of Punjab demanded the establishment of an independent sovereign state known as *"Khalistan"*. These militants wanted to make Punjab a *"theocratic state"*. In order to draw the attention of the government and to bring pressure on it to fulfil their demands, these militants resorted to large scale violence. Between 1982 and 1983, its violence continued unabated. The main strategies of the pro-Khalistan militants were as follows:

(*i*) The militants intended to demonstrate that they were more powerful than the political administration,

(*ii*) Claiming themselves to be the champions of Sikhs and Sikh religion.

(*iii*) Killing innocent people, looting banks, and shops and creating a general atmosphere of horror and terror.

(*iv*) Developing their own connections with the smugglers who were made to supply funds for the militant activities inside Punjab.

(*v*) Persecuting the Hindus of Punjab and enforcing them to migrate to other states so that the Sikhs alone could live there.

Militants supporting Khalistan turned places of worship into places of hideouts and anti-national activities. When the violence reached its peak the army conducted what is known as *"Operation Blue Star"* on June 6th 1984 to remove the terrorists from the Golden Temple at Amritsar. During this army operation", leader of the terrorists called **Bhindranwala** was killed and thereafter terrorism in the state slowly subsided.[1] It almost came to an end due to the strict action taken by **K.P.S. Gill** when he was made the Director General of Police, Punjab.

(c) ULFA TERRORISM IN ASSAM

Insurgency in the North-East : Since the days of independence insurgency has been a permanent problem for the nation especially in the North-east. Various ethnic factors, forest cover, hilly terrain, networking among militant groups, involvement of foreign agencies, prevalence of international border especially with Bhutan, Bangladesh, China, have further complicated the situation in this area. The north-eastern states such as Nagaland, Tripura, Manipur, Mizoram, Arunachal Pradesh and Meghalaya land Assam all have been experiencing the problem of insurgency as well as terrorism in one way or the other. Let us now have a glance of ULFA terrorism in Assam.

1. Punjab terrorism however costed the life of Prime Minister Indira Gandhi who was assassinated in the year 1984 by the terrorist instigation. Her assassination immediately led to anti-Sikh riots in Delhi which resulted in the killing of more than **300** Sikhs. This riot itself gave further inspiration for the terrorists to muster mass support.

ULFA Terrorism in Assam

In the North-eastern region, Assam has been the worst sufferer due to various ethnic movements. Its territorial area has been reduced considerably with the creation of the states such as Mizoram, Nagaland, Meghalaya and Arunachal Pradesh. Still Assam has been experiencing terrorism almost since 1980s.

More than any other thing, *"anti-foreigner"* sentiments led to the militant and terrorist activities in Assam. Assamese demand of removing *'foreigners'* [mainly the infiltrators from Bangladesh] and deleting their names from the electoral roles was turned down by the Congress government. When the elections were declared in the midst of agitation in 1983, more than 5,000 persons lost their lives. After a prolonged student - cum peoples' movement fresh elections were held in 1986 in which *Assam Gana Parishad* [AGP] which had the support of the students led by the *All Assam Students' Union* [AASU] came to power. The AGP was, however, a failure and factions in it led to its split. Two militant organisations namely, ***United Liberation Front of Assam*** [ULFA] and the ***United Minorities Front*** [UMF] emerged. Of these, the ULFA became more dominant.

The **ULFA**, born out of *"anti-foreigner sentiments"* has now indulged in selective violent activities. It has resorted to campaign of murder, loot and kidnapping. It has brought the law and order machinery to a grinding halt and has disturbed the state's economy. The army which was called into service conducted *"Operation Bajrang"* (1991) in order to suppress the secessionist and militant activities in Assam. The army was successful in its task and the June 1991 Elections took place without much disturbance.

The Bodo Movement : At the time of the split in the AGP in 1986, yet another student organisation namely *All Bodo Students' Union [ABSU]* also took its birth. It demanded a separate state of Bodoland and indulged in violence. The Bodo movement gave birth to two militant organisation namely : ***(1) National Democratic Front of Bodoland*** **[NDFB]**, and ***(2) Bodoland Liberation Tiger Force*** **[BLTF]** which have caused considerable violence. They continue to indulge in arson, loot, attacks, killings, kidnappings, etc., The Assam problem of is not yet solved.

(d) TERRORISM IN KASHMIR

Ever since the days of partition, Kashmir has been a trouble spot in India. Though Jammu and Kashmir is an integral part of India, Pakistan has illegally occupied a part of it and intends to swallow the whole of it. Pakistan waged twice war with India on the issue of Kashmir and both the times received humiliating defeats. Therefore, Pakistan adopted a new strategy of terrorising the people of Jammu and Kashmir. Its intention is to gain what it has lost in the two battles. Terrorism assumed new proportions in Kashmir especially after 1988. Thousands of people [mostly the Hindus who constitute the minority in this region] have been forced to flee from their homes and they are living the life of refugees in their own homeland in several places. *"It is claimed in one report that nearly 2 lakh Hindus fled Jammu and Kashmir between 1988 and 1991."*[1] Thousands of people including security personnel have been killed. The militants resort to extortion, kidnapping and killing of innocent people to meet their ends.

Innocent Hindus who have been driven away from their original homeland are of the opinion that the Muslim fundamentalists and militants have infilfitrated every sphere of the government in the Kashmir valley. They have also alleged that the government is under the mercy of the militants and the life of the loyalists has been made miserable. According to them, pro-Pakistan forces have overtaken especially the Kashmir valley and there is virtually a total collapse of the administration.

On the contrary, the ordinary civilian Muslims are of the opinion that they are ignorant of what is happening in the valley. They also complain that they are unnecessarily harassed both by the militants and by the security forces. They further claim that they too have become the target of attack of the fundamentalist terrorists.

1. **Ram Ahuja** in *"Social Problems in India"* - Page: 433.

- ***Various Terrorist Organisations*** : Terrorist organisations such as *(i) Hizab - Ul - Mujahedeen, (ii) Jammu and Kashmir Liberation Front [JKLF], (iii) Muslim Janapaez Force, (iv) Iqwan - e - Musalmeen, (v) Allah Tigers, (vi) Lashkar - e - Toiba, (vii) Jaish - e - Mohammad, I.S.I. - sponsored terrorists, etc.*, with thousands of their activist militants are posing a permanent challenge to the security forces on the one hand, and national integrity on the other. The first three of these aim at independent state of Kashmir, some others want the merger of Kashmir with Pakistan.
- ***Role of Muslim Countries in Kashmir Terrorism*** : According to some sources,[1] a large number of terrorists consisting of foreign mercenaries coming from Muslim countries such as Pakistan, Bangladesh, Sudan, Turkey, Libya, Lebanon, Afghanistan are indulged in acts of terrorism in Kashmir. Militants are given training in the camps across the border located in Pakistan and Pakistan Occupied Kashmir [POK]

Main Purpose of Terrorism is to Destabilise India : It is said that the ISI [*Inter Services Intelligence*] of Pakistan is the master brain behind all the terrorist activities going on in Kashmir. The main purpose behind all the militant and terrorist activities has been to destabilise the Indian Union and the state of Jammu and Kashmir. The most dangerous attack of 13th December, 2001 on the India Parliament by these terrorists, is an example in this regard. The latest major terrorist attack that took place on 5th July 2005 on the disputed place at Ayodhya [*Ram Janmasthan*] has also been suspected to be the monstrous handiwork of I.S.I.

IMPACT OF TERRORISM ON SOCIETY

1. *Terrorism Creates Law and Order Problems* : Terrorism has grown into global level and it poses a threat to world peace and order. It creates a serious law and order problem and if unchecked, leads to the disintegration of society.

2. *Leads to Uncertainty* : Life becomes uncertain and it reels under the mercy of terrorists. The horror and terror let loose by the terrorists create an atmosphere of fear and panic all around. In order to spread terror and fear everywhere the terrorists even kill unarmed civilians including women and children. Organised crime and violence cause social disharmony.

3. *Causes Loss of Life and Property* : Terrorists kill people indiscriminately and damage public as well as private property wrecklessly. Conflicts between terrorists and security forces result in enormous loss of life and property.

4. *Encourages Smuggling* : Since terrorism has become a global phenomenon, the terrorists of one country may establish their linkage with other terrorists in a foreign country. Various insurgent groups which have secret connection bring illegal money and encourage smuggling. Terrorism has become almost synonymous with illegal drug trade.

5. *Retards Economic Development* : In an atmosphere of insurgency, uncertainty and terrorism, neither business nor industry flourishes. Terrorists and insurgent groups often collect certain percentage of money from the employees and businessmen on regular basis besides collection through loot, and ransom. People who invest in business or public sectors start to withdraw from the area for safer places. Terrorism, thus demobilises capital and hampers the process of economic development.

6. *All Developmental Activities are Disturbed* : Terrorists very often target their attacks on Government installations like radio and T.V. stations, bus stands, railway stations, aerodromes and harbours, big factories, defence establishments, etc. Disruptions in these only add to the problems of the common man. Condition of the poor becomes pathetic. Governments in power are forced to spend huge amount of money to meet the challenges of terrorism and ensure protection to the people which otherwise could have been spent for developmental works. In brief, because of the menace of terrorism, all developmental activities of the society come to a stand still.

A rich country like America, had to spend heavily to curb terrorism. Small and economically

1. **India Today,** May 15 , 1994.

weaker countries like Afghanistan find it difficult to use its resources to fight terrorism. Developing nation like India is also forced to spend a huge amount of money to curb terrorist activities.

Combating Terrorism

Terrorism has grown into a problem of serious consequences. Politicians alone cannot find a lasting solution for it. To create a general awareness among the masses and to build up strong public pressures to combat terrorism seem to be the only solutions.

The menace of terrorism has been tackled in different ways in different countries. It is not out of place to make a mention of three models of combating terrorism. They are as follows: *(i) the Israeli Model; (ii) the American Model, and (iii) the Indian Model.* Let us now consider in brief each one of these models for the purpose of better understanding of the ways and means of combating terrorism.

1. The Israeli Model : *Counter-Terror and Anti-Terror Model*

Israel has been successfully meeting the challenges of terrorism for the past 50 years. The Palestinian guerillas and terrorists [i.e., the **P.L.O.**: *Palestinian Liberation Organisation* and its supporters] had been causing lot of irritations to Israel right from 1950s. The Israel Government decided to suppress them with a heavy hand. The Israelis sharply reacted to the challenges of the P.L.O. by carrying out air attacks on the P.L.O. camps. They never hesitated to bombard the P.L.O. centres in the neighbouring territory of Jordan. They used tanks to destroy the enemy camps. These attacks caused heavy damage to Jordanian army and property. As a result, the public opinion in Jordan turned against supporting the P.L.O. When the P.L.O. shifted its base towards Lebanon, another neighbouring country, the Israelese turned their attention towards Lebanon. They invaded Lebanon and totally removed the PLO bases in its soil. Israel did the same thing to Arab countries when they intended to protect the terrorists.

The Palestinians later resorted to the tactics of highjacking Israeli civilian aircraft and also kidnapping the Israel civilians. This they did in order to demand the release of their leaders kept in Israeli jails. Israel government instead of yielding to their pressures intensified its attacks on Palestinian camps. It never budged to the criticisms hurled at its policy. It was finally, successful in humbling the Palestinian terrorists through its *"counter-terror"* and *"anti-terror model"* of combating terrorism.

• Main Elements of Israeli Strategy

1. No negotiations be held with the terrorists. If one yields to the pressures and demands of the terrorists they would multiply manifold.
2. Weakening the terrorists by organising calculated raids on their organisational bases.
3. Introducing tight and uncompromising security measures
4. Resorting to open violence against the terrorists and their sympathisers.

2. The American Model : *The Counter - Terror Campaign*

America which has economic supremacy over the world is highly vulnerable to terrorism. It has its economic hold over many nations of the world. Whenever the American economic interests are attacked or endangered, it first resorts to its economic weapon of immediately stopping its trade, technology export and all economic aids to its targeted nation.

When the economic weapon becomes unsuccessful America resorts to bombarding the enemy country and its supporting terrorists. ***Examples***:

(*i*) America resorted to this method for Cuba in 1962 and for Libya in 1986 when its leader **Col. Gaddafi** supported terrorist movements like those of the PLO.

(*ii*) Very recently also America adopted the same method for humbling Afghanisthan which gave shelter for Bin Laden who was instrumental in organising a plane attack on the twin towers of the World Trade Centre [WTO], New York, U.S.A. on 11th Sept. 2001.

(*iii*) Against **Saddam Hussein** - led Iraq also U.S.A. resorted to the same strategy.

As it is made clear from the above, the American model of combating terrorism is basically *"counter terror campaign" and invasion.*

3. The Indian Model : *'Anti - Terror Model'*

Terrorism is not a new phenomenon to India. Ever since 1960s, India has been facing the challenges of violence and terrorism. As early as in 1960s and 1970s the Government had tackled the problem of insurgency and violence in the North-east region and also in Jammu Kashmir through political methods. These methods however, were not successful.

The Indian Government organised a semi-military operation known as ***"Operation Blue Star"*** on June 6th 1984 against the Punjab terrorists. Similarly, it conducted ***"Operation Black Thunder"*** in Assam to counter terrorism. These measures were mainly ***"anti-terrorist measures"*** and not *"counter -terrorist measures"* in which police and military forces had taken part. Unfortunately, both the measures were not successful in either containing or removing terrorism. The Indian model of combating terrorism [as evidenced in the above mentioned measures] consists of the following aspects:

(*i*) Introducing frequent road checks; that is, checking moving vehicles and individuals in strategic places;

(*ii*) Keeping police, military or para-military forces on temporary or permanent basis in sensitive or highly vulnerable areas; and

(*iii*) Providing elaborate security for the VIPs.

Unlike America, India is not able to show its physical power, or at least give a serious warning to those countries which supply the bulk of arms, or give shelter to terrorists or finance terrorism.

On the contrary, the government on several occasions exhibited its weakness in succumbing to the illegal and disastrous demands of the terrorists as happened in Kashmir, Andhra Pradesh and Bihar.

The Israeli Model-More Suitable to India - ?

Of the three models of combating terrorism, the Israeli model seems to be better suited to the Indian conditions. The Israeli model is a combination of *"counter-terror"* and *"anti-terrorist"* measures. Wherever terrorism is found, its support bases are to be destroyed, even if they are found in the neighbouring countries.

Mere police and military operations alone are not sufficient. As revealed in the Israeli model, people's active co-operation is very much needed in effectively dealing with the problem of terrorism.

Sociology of Terrorism

Terrorism as a global phenomenon, has several dimensions. It is both a problem and a challenge for the present world. Since it is spreading its tentacles to the nook and corner of the world, all right thinking people have reasons to be very much concerned about it. Of late, sociologists too have started making their own observations and studies of terrorism. They have now realised the need for developing a new branch of sociology called ***"sociology of terrorism"***. This new specialised field of study is expected to throw more light on the nature and dynamics of terrorism.

Basic Questions Confronting "Sociology of Terrorism"

"Sociology of Terrorism" as a specialised field of study has to address itself to some basic questions such as the following,

(*i*) How exactly "terrorism" or "political terrorism" or "terroristic violence" - originated ?

(*ii*) In what way terrorism disrupt the political as well the social organisation ?

(*iii*) Is terrorism being used as a means or method for bringing about rapid social changes ?

(*iv*) How does terrorism explain the nature of the social relationship prevailing between a frustrated minority which has resorted to violence and insurgency and the ruling political elite which has the monopoly on the use of force ?

Basic Sociological Observations of Sociology of Terrorism

Though sociologists have not yet made any in-depth study of the phenomenon of terrorism they have made some interesting sociological observations about the same. Some such observations are worth mentioning here.

1. ***Terrorism is Not a Special Method for Initiating Historical Changes in Society*** **:** Though terrorism creates serious law and order problem by resorting to killing, attacking, blasting, kidnapping, blackmailing, and such other violent means, it does not proclaim to change the social system as such. Terrorism is not a special method to destroy the existing social order in order to bring a new one. *"No terrorist movement has ever succeeded in achieving its goals. Terrorists, therefore do not shape the course of historical events."*[1]

2. ***Terrorism Sometimes Helps to Unite People*** **:** It is true that terrorism demoralises and demobilises people and disintegrates societies. It is equally true that terrorism in some instances helps to unite people to fight against common enemy. ***Example*** **:** (i) On many occasions, Indians have expressed their solidarity and unity as one national community particularly against Pakistan sponsored insurgent and terrorist activities. (ii) Similarly, the Americans very strongly stood with their national leadership headed by President George Bush in suppressing the terrorist activities supported by Bin Laden of Afghanisthan.

3. ***'Sociology of Terrorism' suggests that Both the Quantitative and Qualitative Aspects of Violence are to be given Importance in our study*** **:** The *quantitative aspect* of violence refers to the amount of violence engaged in by the terrorists, the quantum of force utilised by the security forces, number of persons killed or seriously injured on both the sides etc. It may also include the amount of loss incurred due to terrorist activities and so on. The *qualitative aspect* refers to the effect of terrorist violence on the social order and particularly on people's faith or trust in the existing social order.

Example **:** In the Indian context, a relatively large number of people were killed due to terrorism in Punjab and Kashmir; Naxalite terrorism and ULFA terrorism. Even Indira Gandhi and Rajiv Gandhi were assassinated by the terrorists. In spite of these killings, people's faith in the democratic social order continues to exist. Does it mean that the terrorist activities were unsuccessful . ? We cannot, however, consider them as "unsuccessful" because, the terrorists have been able to shake and loosen the existing order. They have weakened the legitimating capacities of administrative officials and the pioneer elite. They have added much to the seriousness of the security measures and made the government to spend a huge amount on it. These measures have lessened and complicated the opportunities of the ordinary people to approach the leaders. Sociological approach towards terrorism makes us to give more weightage to the social impact of terrorism than to its "success" or "failure".

4. ***Sociology of Terrorism Warns that Terrorism Has to be Contained*** **:** Terrorism and political violence have become the bane of Indian society as they are so in many other countries. Both contribute to anarchy and chaos. Unfortunately, the disappointed and frustrated young people are falling a prey to the temptations of terrorists. It is high time that such deprivation and frustration spreading among the youths be checked. Simultaneously, the government has to take all precautionary steps to suppress terroristic tendencies. Sociology of terrorism suggests that nations of the world must make united efforts to face the challenges of terrorism.

---

1. **Ram Ahuja** in *"Social Problems in India"* - 2001, Page: 446.

(C) PROBLEM OF PROSTITUTION

"Prostitution as a commercialised device and as a profession has existed in the world from times immemorial. As the world's oldest profession prostitution has undoubtedly existed in some form or the other as long as society has attempted to regulate and control sex relationships through the institutions of marriage and family."[1] This institution has existed in all the civilised socieities from the earliest times.

In India also prostitution has a long and an ancient history. There are references in the Vedas of organised prostitution. During the Vedic period, the *"Ganika"* [the courtesan] had her prescribed place and functions in society. It existed in a well established form during the time of Manu and Kautilya. In *Vishnu Samhita, Matsya Purana* and in Vatsayana's *"Kama Sutra"*, we have vast references to prostitution. In Ramayana, Mahabharatha and in Puranas we find references to courtesan women like Rambha, Urvashi, Menaka, Tilothama who used to exhibit their skills and artistic excellence in dance, music, etc., in order to please Gods and the king of Gods, Indra.

The profession of prostitution was so widespread in the ancient period that the Hindu shastrakaras like **Manu**, **Gautama** and **Brihaspati** recommended for suppression of prostitution. During Mohammadan period also, prostitution was much in vogue and many Mohammadan kings had their Harem. However, the rapid urbanization and industrialization during the British period increased this evil, and certain legislative measures were taken to stop it.

The problem of prostitution is becoming more and more acute in the country as the country is getting more and more industrialised. The problem of prostituion as we understand it today, is mostly urban and more particularly metropolitan. Unsatisfactory housing conditions and imperfect family patterns in cities have led to an increase of prostitution in the cities and metropolitan areas.

1. DEFINITION, NATURE AND CHARACTERISTICS OF PROSTITUTION

Definition of Prostitution

1. **Havlock Ellis :** *"A prostitute is a person who makes it a profession to gratify the lust of various persons of the other sex or of the same sex."*
2. **May G. in "Encyclopaedia of Social Sciences" Vol. 12:** Prostitution is *"an act of social intercourse characterised by barter, promiscuity and emotional indifference."*
3. **G.R. Scott :** *"A prostitute is an individual who for some kind of reward or for some other form of personal satisfaction engages in normal or abnormal sexual intercourse with various persons who may be of the same sex or the opposite sex."*
4. **In simple words,** we may define that *Prostitute is a woman who sells her sexual favours indiscriminately and takes money or other valuables for each act of intercourse; and who has no psychic involvement.*

MAIN CHARACTERISTICS OF PROSTITUTION

1. *Prostitution - An Immoral Act* : Prostitution denotes an immoral sex relationship between individuals though it cannot be categorically branded as "illegal relationship". In no society it is justified universally as a moral act. However, there are licensed prostitutes also.

2. *Acceptance to use the Body Against Money / Material Things* : The harlot or female prostitute offers the use of her body to various men whosoever approach her in exchange for money / material things.

3. *Involves Emotional Indifference of the Prostitute in her Act* : Prostitution involves a sexual intercourse characterised by barter, promiscuity and emotional indifference. The woman never

1. G.R. Madan in *"Indian Social Problems"*, Vol. I - Page : 200.

goes through the sexual act devoid of any pleasurable feeling. There is no scope for the expression of real love and affection.

4. *Not a "Volcano of lust"* : A prostitute cannot be regarded as a person having uncontrollable sexual desire. She is not a "volcano of lust" for all the men she attracts. Hence, she cannot be branded as nymphomaniac in characters, she cannot attract all types of persons in spite of her expertise in the art of her profession.

5. *Involves Normal and Abnormal Sex Relationship Also* : A prostitute engages in sexual intercourse - which may be normal or abnormal - with persons of the same or the opposite sex.

6. *May involve Artificial Demonstration of Love* : A prostitute is a professional "love-maker". She has the skill or the attribute of demonstrating her love outwardly. She performs her part in the transaction completely and passionately not out of sensuality or lust, but sheer expertise in the field.

7. *Part-time or a Full Time Job* : Depending upon her objective which she wants to achieve, a prostitute may carry on her profession on a part-time or full-time basis. Her objectives could be monetary gain, mere sexual thrill, or satisfaction of excessive sex lust, etc. In most of the cases, the objective or purpose is found to be nothing other than monetary reward or gain.

8. *Different from Illegitimacy* : According to **Weaver**, prostitution is different from illegitimacy, which invariably involves an *"illicit sex relationship"* which refers particularly to the production of a child outside the socially approved reproduction.

- **Weaver** also says that prostitution is *"different from the broader concept of sexual immorality due to the commercial nature of the relationship."*

TYPES OF PROSTITUTES

G.R. Madan [Page : 206] and **C.B. Mamoria** [Page : 755-756] have mentioned about two general types of prostitutes. They are :

1. ***the overt** or **the professional**,* and
2. ***the clandestine** or **unconventional type***

1. The Overt or Professional Prostitutes

The overt or professional prostitutes include both registered and unregistered prostitutes. In practice, these include two kinds of prostitutes :

(i) *those who operate independently without agents like pimps,* and

(ii) *those who operate through the agents.*

(i) Some prostitutes operate independently without the support of the pimps, brothel-keepers, etc. They are referred to as *"singly operating prostitutes."* It is said that these prostitutes normally get less income and their 'business" is also not prosperous. Their number is rather limited and they carry on their *"trade"* in a secret manner so that *"respectable men"* can visit them without any hindrance. Some of these prostitutes are normally employed at other type of work, notably in personal service or as entertainers like dancers, musicians, etc. Such girls are accustomed to practice prostitution as a more or less regular supplement to their legitimate earnings.

Some of the prostitutes that belong to this category are mostly seen roaming about the cinema houses, restaurants, hotels, public parks and other places of gathering, always looking for customers who may either go to their house or take them to their house or to a hired house.

(ii) Those who operate through the agents such as pimps, brothel-keepers are found to be having good *"business"* taking as much as 10 to 12 men for sex-act. They usually live in *"houses of ill-fame"*, that is cheap brothels attracting customers through agents. It is said that in West Bengal there are **5695** brothels and more than **45000** prostitutes, in Patna and Mirzapur [Bihar] there are **100** brothels, in the cities of Orissa there are more than **200** brothels, and in Mumbai the number of prostitutes exceed **one lakh** and that of the brothels exceed 10,000.[1] Some women themselves attract customers sitting outside their doors or through the windows, settling bargains with the passer by. In big cities like Mumbai, Kolkatta, Lucknow, Kanpur, Nagapur, Hyderbad, Chennai, Delhi, Bangalore, etc. there are thousands of such prostitutes carrying on their business.

2. The Clandestine or the Unconventional Type of Prostitutes

The clandestine prostitutes include a variety of women who carry on their sex trade for monetary considerations. Some such type of women may be identified as follows :

(i) There are ***occasional prostitutes*** who include large number of women belonging to sophisticated class of educated strata and from well-to-do families.

(ii) There are the ***incidental prostitutes*** who want to increase a scanty legitimate income by the sale of sex favour. Girl clerks earning a meagre salary, cast-off mistresses who often enter this profession as a last resort - constitute examples of this kind.

(iii) ***Married women*** on occasions resort to mercenary and adulterous practices and serve a restricted number of clientele.

(iv) ***Concubinage system*** under which the mistress or her guardians enter into an agreement with a male member for a stipulated period. Here the sex relationship is restricted to only two parties and not indiscriminate. *"In India, the mistress mostly belongs to the class of professional singers or temple dancers who performed at the temple ceremonies in the olden days."*[2]

2. CAUSES OF PROSTITUTION

Prostitution as a grave social evil has been haunting many of the civilised countries of the world including India. The problem is becoming more and more rampant in India especially in the urban area. There are many factors and forces causing this problem for it is not an isolated unit. It is indeed, a product of economic, social psychological, pathological and other factors. Here is a brief analysis of the factors contributing to the problem of prostitution.

1. Economic Factors

There is no doubt that poverty or economic necessity is the most important factor behind prostitution. **M. Londres** is of the opinion that *"the foundation of prostitution is hunger."*[3] Studies made by the *League of Nations* in different countries have revealed that *"poverty, overcrowding and low wages are clearly contributory causes of prostitution"*.[4]

It is observed that many women having no other visible means of support in order to eke out a livelihood often resort to prostitution. Most of the prostitutes come from under privileged economic groups. Surveys conducted in 1960s revealed that poverty and lack of employment opportunities are the biggest factors causing prostitution. Over **55.4%** of the prostitutes said that they took up this profession due to poverty. In a sample survey conducted by **Shri Kanga** in the 1990s itself, it was found that **41%** took up this profession because of poverty. **Miss Kamala Rao** and **Dr. Punekar** in their survey held in Bombay found that **71%** of the women took up this profession due to poverty.[5]

In addition to poverty, other economic factors such as - unemployment, under-age employment, unhealthy working conditions, corruption in industrial centres, sexual exploitation in workplace, immoral traffic in women and children, etc. have also contributed to this problem in no small measure.

---

1. ***Source*** : **R.K. Sharma**'s *"Urban Sociology"*, Page : 221 and other sources.
2. **G.R. Madan** - Page : 206.
3. **M. Londres** as quoted by **C.B. Mamoria**, Page : 761.
4. *ibid*, Page : 762.
5. ***Source of statistics*** : **C.B. Mamoria**, Page : 762.

2. Social Factors

Various social factors such as broken home, unsatisfactory marital life, [conflicts between the in-laws], lack of love and affection in the family, cruelty of dowry, evil effects of double standard of morality, polygyny, disintegration of joint family and several others have indirectly instigated a few women to resort to prostitution.

(i) Disintegration of Joint Families and Unhealthy Home Conditions : Family itself is often the starting point of prostitution. Unsatisfactory home conditions. disintegration of joint families, broken homes due to divorce or desertion of the parents, immoral character of either parents or both also breed prostitution. **G.R. Scott** writes, *"In many cases, the mother is a prostitute herself, the father is a pimp and they send their daughters in the streets with the slightest compunction often themselves initiating her in sexual intercourse"*.[1] Lack of understanding, sympathy and affection from the parents during childhood and adolescence, and lack of discipline, marital conflicts and maladjustments, loose habits of the husband all play no mean role in the commission of prostitution.

(ii) Double Standard of Morality : We find double standard of sex morals for men and women in the Indian society. It requires a woman to be chaste and pure but gives free latitude to man for his sexual satisfaction. This is also responsible for lowering the position of women. The erring woman has no other way but to commit suicide or join the rank of the fallen women. Further, a girl who has illicit sex experience because of any reason is often made to feel that she has nothing left to lose for she has already lost all.

(iii) Unhappy Marital Relations : Unhappy marital relationship with the husband, sexual impotency and physical weakness or chronic diseases on the part of the husband, sexual incompatibility between husband and wife, loose sex habits of the husband etc., are also factors driving a woman to such an action.

(iv) Inordinate Sex Desire and Craving for New Sex Experience : Some girls have inordinate sex desire and crave for sex stimulation for its own sake. They do not bother much about sex morals, observing restraints on sex behaviour, etc.

- *Desire for thrilling sex adventure* pushes a few girls to this field. It is also possible that when a girl is under the influence of alcohol she may undergo her first sex relationship. Her continued use of immoderate alcohol may further affect her sexual promiscuity. Childhood assaults also initate many into this profession.

(v) Restrictions on Widow Remarriages and Ill-treatment of Daughters-in-law : In spite of the legislation that is passed permitting widow remarriage, majority of the Hindu widows in India, do not opt for remarriage because of the social disfavour. Young widows who are not ready to re-marry but at the same time, find it difficult to live a life of chastity may fall a prey to seduction. The first instance of seduction may show her a new way of living.

Dowry harassment, ill-treatment of the daughter-in-law either at the hands of the mother-in-law, sisters-in-law or by the husband himself are also factors responsible in driving the woman to lead a life of prostitution.

(vi) Social Customs and Practices Favouring Prostitution : Hindu social customs and practices are also contributory factors. The practice of dowry system makes it almost obligatory for many girls to remain as spinsters, till old age. Child marriage practice still continues, and young widows when forced to live a life of chastity, find it hard to do so, and often fall a prey to seduction. Old maidenhood and enforced widowhood is a rich ground for recruitment to the field of prostitution.

The difference made between sons and daughters in many Hindu homes, the general subjugation of women are also factors conducive to prostitution. Social customs like the *Devadasi* system prevailing among castes in many places, provide excellent opportunities for traffickers to kidnap women.

---

1. **G.R. Scott** as quoted by **R.K. Sharma** in his *"Urban Sociology"* [2007] - Page : 221.

(vii) Kidnapping and Seducing Women : Kidnapping or seducing young girls under the promise of marriage, employment, etc. also contribute to the problem. Procurers, indecent employers, bogus lovers, characterless co-workers, stranger - friends with suspected morals all play their own conspiracy to trap young, innocent and helpless women to lead finally the life of a prostitute.

(viii) Unhealthy Recreation : Dangerous forms of recreation such as drinking, gambling, cabaret dances, dubious clubs, video parlours, amusement parks, sexy films, bad company, etc. may also lead to breakdown of women.

(ix) Hazards of Industrialization and Urbanisation : Rapid industrialisation and urbanisation have brought about the problem of housing in big cities. In Mumbai, for example, it is said that 89% of the people in the city especially in the slum areas live in one room tenements. In Khanpur, Nagpur, Chennai, Ahmedabad, Jabbalpur, Kolkatta, etc. more than 50% of the people live in single room tenements especially in the labour areas. Privacy is badly affected in these areas and healthy sex relationship becomes a casualty.

In all industrial and commercial centres we find an inequality of sexes. This enforced separation of the sexes creates a need for *"red light areas"*. Thus, prostitution flourishes in industrial areas, *busties* and mining areas. They help fill up a *"sexual void"*. Large cities are the "hunting grounds" of prostitutes for customers. It is here, "primarily due to shortage of housing, slum-living, bad and inadequate lighting, lack of healthy outlets and continued deprivation of normal family living", balanced sex life is damaged. As **Dr. Mukherjee** writes *"in thousands of slums of Indian industrial centres manhood is brutalised, womanhood dishonoured and childhood poisoned at its very source."*[1] Prostitution in such areas leads to an increase in the spread of venereal diseases.

Religious Causes

Some of the religious factors are also favourable for prostitution. The prevalence of the practice of *devadasi system* in states like Karnataka, Andhra Pradesh, Kerala, Tamil Nadu, Maharasthra itself reveals that prostitution has been carried on in these areas with the stamp of religion. *Devadasi* has now come to mean a woman prostituting in the name of religion. Under this system, women who are dedicated as *'devadasis'* to Hindu deities at temples are considered unfit to marry later on and this leads them to a life of prostitution.

Some of the socio-religious customs found among the Naiks in U.P., Nambudiris of Malabar, the Kulina system of Bengal were supportive of prostitution. Among the Muslims of Hyderabad a custom known as *"parwardah"* prevailed in which poor families gave their female children to the wealthy families for a consideration, relinquishing all rights over them. These children after their maturity were obliged to serve the needs of the young men of the family.[2]

Physiological and Psychological Causes

Physiological, biological and personal factors also play an important part in causing sex delinquency. Physical deformities, feeblemindedness, adolescent disturbances and unsatisfied sexual desires, desire for enjoying sex varieties, lack of control over sexual impulses and such deficiencies also cause prostitution.

Mental deficiency is yet another cause. A large number of young sex offenders and the common prostitutes show certain deficiency in mental constitution. *The League of Nations' Advisory Committee on Social Questions* found that **1/3** of the women prostitutes studied were found to be either mentally abnormal or subnormal.

1. **Dr. Mukherjee** as quoted by **Mamoria**, Page : 765.
2. ***Source*** : C.B. Mamoria, Page : 764.

Demand and Supply Theory

It is often said that the real cause for the problem is the demand for supply. So long as there is demand, there is bound to be supply. The supply is assured by a prostitute, who absorbs the cosmic passion of man. The demand solely arises because sexual desire is a part of the very nature of man. As **Drzaga** points out "without demand there would be no prostitution...." It is said that man's "passion has to be channelised, controlled and guided properly; and this is not possible by eliminating the institution of prostitutes, call-girls, brothels or red light areas."[1]

Other Factors

The above causes by no means exhaust all the causes of prostitution. There are many "other factors" such as the following :

a) ***Lucrative Business*** : In big cities prostitution is thriving because it has become a very profitable business.

b) ***An accepted practice among some tribals*** : Some tribals have made it their profession for it is not condemned or prohibited among them.

c) ***Society is tolerant towards it*** : Prostitution has been in existence in many places because society has not only tolerated it but also indirectly given support for it.

d) ***Sophisticated medical devices*** have given substantial support for this practice for it can be resorted to without the risk of pregnancy. Effective contraceptive devices have rendered virginity "obsolete" and chastity "outmoded".

e) ***Instigation through pornographic literature, electronic media, etc.*** : Sex hunger in the modern youth of both the sexes hass increased due to these means.

f) ***Favourable modern processes*** : Modern processes such as urbanisation, industrialisation, westernisation, globalisation, cultural invasion - have given impetus to prostitution.

In conclusion, it could be said that prostitution is almost universal. It is observed that different causes work in three different groups of persons to resort to prostitution; *(i) the male and the female unmarried; (ii) the married persons, and (iii) the widows and widowers.* **C.B. Mamoria** [Page : 771] thus concludes : *"the fact is that wherever restless men and money congregate, there are women seeking to sell a "moment of pleasure" for the highest possible price, where there is easy money, women are drawn to the demi-monde[2] of prostitution."*

3. CONSEQUENCES OF PROSTITUTION

Prostitution as a social evil exists in all the countries of the world. The problem has become more intense and widespread in highly industrialised and urbanised countries. It is often treated as a challenge to family norms and values and a stigma attached to the modern civilised society. Problem of prostitution has its own consequences on the society among which the following may be noted.

1. Prostitution - A Disgraceful Profession

Prostitution, as it is already stated, is a black spot on the body politic of the modern civilised society. Though prostitution is found everywhere, in no society of the world prostitution as a profession is held in high esteem, nor prostitutes are respected. It is branded as a disgraceful profession. Prostitution is a sex-specific crime that punishes women not men, for their behaviour. An increase in the number of prostitutes in any society only reveals that it is a society suffering seriously from family disorganisation and sexual deviance. Life also becomes miserable for many women especially during their old age. Studies have revealed that many such women die of exposure, general physical debilitation and infections. Many end their career as drug addicts or alcoholics.

1. "Report of The Advisory Committee of League of Nations" - as quoted by **Mamoria** - Page : 768.
2. **demi-monde** = group considered on the fringe of respectable society / half world.

2. Reflects Personal Disorganisation

Prostitution is a symbol of personal disorganisation and the person involved receives condemnation at the hands of men and women and is excluded from the society. Women suffer great personal deterioration than men due to the double standard of morality. Prostitute's life is very often associated with mental conflict, physical strain and irremediable loss of status. It is also found to be associated with smoking, drug addiction, alcoholism and such other evils.

3. Denotes Family Disorgainsation

Prostitution adversely affects not only the concerned man or woman, but his or her family also. The married person may get some venereal disease from the prostitute which may affect his wife and children. A married person who resorts to prostitution secretly may get the disease from her other client. Studies have revealed that more than *"half of those suffering from venereal diseases have acquired it through promiscuous sex relationships. The other half are innocent victims - the wives and children of men who acquired the disease in premarital or extra-marital contacts."*[1] Illegitimate sex relations of the wife or husband may also be the cause of friction in the family and divorce may even be the ultimate result.

4. Prostitution Leads to Community Disorganisation

Prostitution brings widespread disorganisation of community in which it operates. In two ways it brings harm to the community at large. They are, its commercial aspect and its health aspect.

- ***Its commercial aspect*** makes it commercially exploitative and to become institutionalised. When it becomes institutionalised, it gets deeply rooted and assumes a permanent pattern. In its permanent position especially in towns and cities, it becomes more accessible to the public and as a result many more people get attracted by it and finally become its victims. This situation in turn strengthens the hands of those who are engaged in this business.
- ***Its health aspect*** is still more dangerous. Not only those who are engaged in it suffer from health problems especially venereal diseases, but also, they spread them to all those who come in contact with them.

5. Results in the Degradation and Exploitation of Women

Inequality generally found between men and women is reflected in the profession of prostitution too. It reveals that man makes use of woman like an instrument to satisfy his lust. Woman's helplessness, weaknesses and misfortunes and taken undue advantage of by men.

- ***Exploitation in the Brothel Homes*** : Elderly prostitutes, or *'Gharwalis'*, *'madams'*, or *'mothers'*, who are managing and running the brothels, exploit the new young recruits to the profession. The new recruits are provided with very minimum physical comforts, and only a paltry sum is given as remuneration for their service and a major portion is retained for themselves.
- ***Prostitution is often associated with threats, violence, cruelty, coercion*** : It is especially so in organised prostitution where it is carried on in brothel homes. Rowdies are appointed to keep an eye on the movement of the prostitutes. Those who refuse to give *"satisfactory service"* to the clients are given punishments such as whipping, physical torture, mental torture with abusive and vulgar language, not giving food, locking them in rooms, and so on.
- ***Threat of prisons, hospitals and underground world*** : Wherever it is regarded as illegal, prostitution means for many women frequent jail terms. For some others, it means venereal infections from time to time. Some women are even connected with the underworld, and their association with it, tends to lead them to alcoholic and narcotic addiction. In some cases, a large portion of girl's earnings is paid out in advocate's fees. Much of what is left may be squandered on a succession of pimps and other exploiters. For the poor prostitutes, prisons and hospitals may alternate. With every

1. **Elliot** and **Merrill** as quoted by **G.R. Madan**, Page : 209.

arrest and conviction, they are likely to emerge with a much more hardened and resentful personality. These frustrations and miseries are also conducive to alcoholism and drug addiction.

6. Prostitution Leads to the Spread of Dreadful Venereal Diseases Including AIDS

Prostitution that is carried on in an uncontrolled manner, especially in the big cities is leading to the spread of venereal diseases which brings in train many other social problems. As **Elliot** and **Merrill** observe, *"the venereal diseases - syphilis, chancroid and gonorrhoea - are of vital social concern not only because they are epidemic and devastating diseases but also because they are factors in so many other social problems. Venereal disease produces a large share of insanity. Its victims are particularly likely to commit violent crimes. Children of syphilitic parents are apt to be maimed for life. Many are born blind. The result of syphilitic and gonorrheal infections are so appalling that they rank as the major public health problems in the western world."*[1]

4. PREVENTION AND CONTROL OF PROSTITUTION

The problem of prostitution is not just a problem confronting the prostitutes and their families, but has become a big menace to the public morality and social health. It is necessary to handle this problem in two respects. Two types of measures to deal with the problem are as follows:

A) *Legal measures to control prostitution, and*

B) *Rehabilitative and protective measures to reform them and to help them lead a normal social life.*

(A) Legal Measures

Attempts were made even during the ancient period to control and to remove prostitution. Early *Dharmashastrakaras* like **Manu, Narada, Gautama, Parashara** and others condemned this practice in their treatises and recommended measures to suppress it. During the medieval period, the Muslim rulers made no attempt to curb it, for they were not against the practice. The British made some half-hearted attempts to control it.

Legal Measures taken Before Independence

- The British included in the ***Indian Penal Code*** [IPC] some sections such as 354, 373, 375 and 495 which made the practice of illicit sex relations a "punishable offence". Purchasing of young women below 18 years for prostitution and selling them to national and foreign agencies were declared as punishable offences.
- ***The Bombay Prevention of Prostitution Act, 1923*** was indeed, the first legislation to be undertaken in this regard to prevent prostitution, and to keep women away from taking up this profession.
- Following the example of Mumbai State, the other States such as Madras [1930] Uttar Pradesh [1935] and Punjab [1935] also enacted the same type of legislation. After independence, Bihar [1948], Travancore [1952], and Mysore States also followed the same direction.
- ***Association for Moral and Social Hygiene,*** a non-governmental organisation [N.G.O.] strongly recommended to the Government to take legal steps to stop women's sex trade in order to protect public morality and social health. In fact, on its recommendations, only the Bengal State passed the *Bengal Suppression of Immoral Traffic Act, 1933.*

Governmental Measures After Independence

After the attainment of freedom, the *Association for Moral and Social Hygiene* intensified its campaign for checking this evil. In 1953, at its third All - India Conference, the Association strongly recommended that the individual as well as commercial prostitution should be abolished.

1. **Elliott** and **Merrill** as quoted by **G.R. Madan**, Page : 210.

• ***Appointment of Social and Moral Hygiene Advisory Committee*** : In pursuance of the International convention signed at Geneva in 1950, the Central Social Welfare Board [of the Central Govt.] appointed an *Advisory Committee on Social and Moral Hygiene* in 1954. The Committee headed by **Smt. Dhanawanti Rama Rao** was entrusted the responsibility of investigating the problem in all its aspects throughout India.

• ***Recommendations of the Committee headed by Dhanawanti Rama Rao*** : The committee recommended measures for the suppression of immoral traffic, among which the following may be noted.

(i) It pressed the need for a comprehensive legislation on all - India basis to check prostitution.
(ii) There should be an Inter-state Police Organisation in order to have a strict control over this illicit trade.
(iii) No institution be given permission to take care of and protect such women and girls' unless its bonafides and ability are tested.
(iv) There should be a special police squad for the enforcement of this Act with the squad having a fair proportion of women police.
(v) Special courts should be constituted, consisting of a few trained women to look after the social and human aspects of the problem.
(vi) Those who make use of any brothel or other public or private place for the purpose of prostitution must be severely punished.
(vii) Those women protected from brothel homes or other places of prostitution must be sent to remand homes where they can be contacted by service-minded social workers.

The Suppression of Immoral Traffic in Women and Girls Act, 1956

On the recommendation of the Advisory Committee on Social and Moral Hygiene, the Parliament passed the *Suppression of Immoral Traffic in Women and Girls' Act in 1956*. This Act came into force from Ist May 1958. The main provisions of this Act are mentioned below.

• **Main Provisions of the Act**

(i) The Act prescribes punishments for keeping and managing a brothel home. [Section - 3]
(ii) It prohibits persons from living on the earnings of the prostitutes. [Section - 4 and 5].
(iii) It detains women or girls in premises where prostitution is carried on. [Section - 7].
(iv) It prohibits soliciting in public places [Section -8].
(v) It provides prostitutes right to seek protection in a protective home [Section - 19].
(vi) Provides authority to magistrates to remove any girl or woman carrying on prostitution at any place from there to any other place which they consider proper [Section - 20].

• The Act also envisages setting up of an adequate number of protective homes for the rehabilitation and the educational and vocational training of women and girls recovered and detained under this Act.

(B) Measure for Rehabilitation and Protection of Prostitution

A big social evil like prostitution cannot be completely solved just by legislative measures. In no country of the world legislative measures alone have brought success in solving the problem. Hence, rehabilitative and protective measures are equally needed to deal effectively with the problem.

• **Some Institutional Attempts to Rehabilitate the Prostitutes**

Institutions like *1. The Association for Moral and Social Hygiene,* and, *2. The Central Social Welfare Board* have rendered yeoman service in the task of the rehabilitation of the prostitutes.

1. ***Association for Moral and Social Hygiene*** **:** This non-governmental Organisation has been working actively throughout the country in its task of rehabilitating the prostitutes. It has its branches in 128 districts of 18 states. Its membership exceeds 10,000. Main objectives of this association are mentioned below :

(i) Mobilising public opinion against those who exploit women for sexual purposes;

(ii) Assisting the authorities in effectively implementing *the Suppression of Immoral Traffic in Women and Girls Act,*

(iii) Protecting those women who are already trapped in the trade and rehabilitating them in safe places;

(iv) Helping the prostitutes to get medical aid to get cured of the venereal diseases; and

(v) Conducting surveys and researchers on this issue.

The Association has set up two *"Rescue Homes"*, one at Mumbai, and another at Hyderbad to give protection to prostitutes and is running hospitals to provide treatment to prostitutes suffering from venereal diseases in places such as Delhi, Meerut, Nagpur and Patna. The Association is giving training on issues such as *"family welfare education", "sex education", etc.*

Rescue Homes and Shelters

On the recommendations of the Advisory Committee of the Central Social Welfare Board, the Government decided to launch two centrally sponsored programmes under the head : *"Social and Moral Hygiene and the Aftercare Programmes"*. Under the scheme it was proposed to establish in all, 80 *State Rescue Homes* and 324 *District Rescue Shelters* in different parts of the country to enable the stray women and prostitutes to find a place where they can receive preliminary training for rehabilitation in society.

Rescue Homes and *Protection Centres* established under the Aftercare Programme can also be utilised as Protective Homes. There are about 100 Protective Homes which include Government as well as private ones and they have a total capacity to accommodate around 4420 inmates. In addition to these, there are also other agencies which are active in helping and reforming prostitutes and finding them useful work. ***Examples*** **:** *The Women Home,* Madras; *Shradhanand Ananth Ashram,* Bombay, *The Good Shepherd Home,* Madras, *Christians Home,* Poona; *The Salvation Army Home,* Bengal; *The Feudal Home,* Bengal; *All Bengal's Women's Union Home,* Bengal; *Khushal Bagh Mission Orphange,* Gorakhpur; *Mahila Anathalaya,* Varanasi are some of the important centres for rehabilitation of faller women.

Central Social Welfare Board

The Central Social Welfare Board which is a Central Government established institution has been paying sufficient attention towards the problem of prostitutes also. It conducted a *"National Workshop on Prostitutes and Their Children"* in May 1990 at New Delhi in which social work activists, educationists, doctors, journalists and judges had taken part. The Conference passed a resolution recommending the Government to undertake a comprehensive programme to rehabilitate the prostitutes on a permanent basis.

5. REHABILITATION OF PROSTITUTES : SOME PROPOSALS AND SUGGESTIONS

Legislative measures and governmental efforts are necessary and unavoidable for the control of prostitution. These measures by themselves are not sufficient. Some other measures as mentioned below are also needed to root out the evil.

1. ***Economic Measures*** **:** Sufficient economic provisions must be made, and suitable employment opportunities be created so that young girls and women are not compelled to take to prostitution under the heavy heels of poverty and unemployment. Even the rescued women must also be provided with some decent job, or a remunerative economic task, so that they are not forced to plunge into the same life once again.

2. *Removal of Inhuman Socio-religious Customs that Favour Prostitution* : Various outmoded traditional practices such as *devaadasi* system, *jogathi* system, *kulina* system, child marriage, *nagnika vivaha*, polygyny, bigamy, *"nude service to the God"* [*"bettale seve"* as practiced in a few places in Karnataka] dowry system, restrictions on widow remarriage, etc. have been forcibly pushing many women into this unwanted profession. All these practices should be stopped, and customs outlawed and public opinion must be mobilised against them. Remarriage of young widows be encouraged and dowry system should be suppressed with a heavy hand.

3. *Double Standard of Morality Should be Discouraged* : Men and women should be treated in equal terms in sex matters and there should be no double standards. As **Smt. Ranganayaki** observes; *"It is in reality impossible to have a double standard morality in matters of sex for without male chastity, female chastity is impossible ...."* [1] As long as the double standard continues, so long the *"tolerated vice"* continues to stay.

4. *Sex Education* : To prevent young girls from entering into prostitution, education and character strong enough to resist demoralisation are to be developed. Instructions in religious education will help them to think in the right direction and to reject the immoral behaviour.

Men and women should be educated as to the dangers of venereal diseases and its effects on marriage relations in case of married persons. There is need for educating the public on the seriousness of the consequences of the evils of prostitution both to the individual and to the society as a whole. There should be sex education and some training for family life to young people in schools and colleges.

5. *Severe Action Against those who Kidnap and Sell Women* : All attempts be made to suppress the anti-social activities of those who kidnap the helpless women and children and sell them to anti-social agencies. Those involved in this trade of supplying women for prostitution must be very strictly punished.

6. *Effective Propaganda and Publicity* : The print media and the electronic media must be made use of in an effective manner to give proper information and knowledge to the people about the problems and dangers of prostitution, illicit sexual behaviour, venereal diseases and their horrible consequences, and so on.

The public should be enlightened about the law and to report any such nuisance in their surrounding area to the law enforcing authorities. Blue films be banned, video parlours must be brought under vigilance, and strict censorship be imposed on electronic media so that, it would not tempt young people to go on sex adventure.

7. *Other Suggestions*

(i) Special care should be taken to prevent the children of the prostitutes from taking up the same profession,

(ii) Young men must be encouraged to marry the rescued young girls from the prostitute homes.

(iii) Efforts must be made to assess the implications of providing conditional licenses to prostitutes to run their trade as it has been done in big cities like Bombay, Chennai, Kolkotta and New Delhi.

(iv) Suitable jobs may be offered to prostitutes, their children, the pimps and such other people depending on that profession, so that they may be persuaded to leave that ugly profession once and for all.

---

1. **Smt. Ranganayaki** in her article on *"Can We Prevent Prostitution"* in *"Social Welfare"* April 1958 as quoted by **Madan**.

(D) ALCOHOLISM AND DRUG ADDICTION

Man, like every other living beings on this earth, seeks pleasure in living his life. Seeking pleasure also implies escaping from and reducing pains and sufferings.

Nature has provided means of achieving this goal to all of us. Apart from the pursuits of food and shelter, which help the organism to maintain itself, nature seeks to ensure continuity of life through procreation. Human being, who at present is on the top most step of the evolutionary ladder, is essentially a social animal. Hence, apart from the pleasurable pursuits of food, shelter and sex, he also seeks social security. His social pursuits include interacting with other members of the society, helping other members of the group in achieving their goals, earning a respectable status in the society, maintaining peace and harmony among the members of the group and also between the groups etc. All these biological and social activities are essentially pleasurable and gratifying. But, unlike the other living beings, man has easy access to unnatural means of seeking pleasure and escaping from or reducing physical as well as psychological sufferings. It is this tendency of resorting to easy and artificial means, which has given rise to the phenomenon of dependence on certain substances like *alcohol* and *drugs*. Being unnatural methods, the use of such substances is bound to have adverse effects on one's physical and psychological health as well as social life.

(i) ALCOHOLISM

Alcoholism is a form of individual as well social disorganisation created by the individual's maladjustments with the complex conditions of the modern society. Alcoholism which is basically a human weakness has been widespread in India as a social evil. Three decades ago, there was one alcoholic for every 300 people, and today, we find 10 alcoholics for the same number of people. What is more disturbing and distressing is, an increasing number of youths, women and even school going children are becoming its victims.

1. DEFINITION OF ALCOHOLISM AND ITS NATURE AND TYPES

It was the Sweedish doctor **Magnus Huss** who used the term *"Alcoholism"* in the year **1849** for the first time to denote a disease which is the result of excessive consumption of alcohol. Since then the concept of "alcoholism" has become a popular expression to signify the cases of excessive drinking.

Definition of Alcoholism

1. **Johnson :** *"Alcoholism is a condition in which the individual has lost control over his alcohol intake in that he is constantly unable to refrain from drinking once he begins."*
2. **Collins Dictionary of Sociology :** Alcoholism refers *"to the consumption of alcohol to excess; leading to psychological and physical dependency and addiction."*[1]
3. **Seldon Bacon** defined alcoholism as *"a disease characterised by a compulsion to drink in order to face the ordinary life problems."*

TYPES OF DRINKERS OR ALCOHOLICS

Marshall B. Clinard in his *"Sociology of Deviant Behaviour"*[2] has mentioned about four types of drinkers taking into consideration the type of drinking and the quantity of drinking.

1. ***Moderate Drinkers*** **:** Those who are not drunkards nor or they habituated to it. They drink occasionally in parties, sometimes due to the pressure of the companions or to the special social

1. **David Jarry** and **Julia Jary** in *"Collins Dictionary of Sociology"*, Page : 12.
2. **Marshall B. Clinard** in *"Sociology of Deviant Behaviour"* 3rd Edition, Page : 412-415.

circumstances. Drinking of these people cannot be considered a problem nor a great weakness from the point of view of modern norms.

2. ***Excessive Drinkers*** **:** Some are habituated to drinking. These people drink excessively and experience the compulsion of drinking again and again. Though they have not become the slaves of drinking, they often lose control over their drinking. Even at this stage, these people have sufficient mental stamina to take a firm decision to have control over their drinking.

3. ***Morbid Drinkers*** **:** These are the people who drink excessively and also frequently for they have become the slaves of drinking. They drink for various purposes say, to forget family problems, to run away mentally from the personal economic crises, to overcome physical inabilities and so on. Their excessive drinking may even make them to become diseased.

4. ***Alcoholics or Continuous Drinkers*** **:** Drinking habit reaches its climax in these persons. They consider drinking as their great ideal in life. They believe that they cannot live or survive without drinking. Day in and day-out they think of only drinking. Drinking habit overrules them and in the real sense of the word they become alcoholics or drunkards. They lose their physical, mental and moral health and finally become the victims of drinking.

2. CAUSES OF ALCOHOLISM

A grave social evil like alcoholism is not due to any one single factor. It is the result of the operation of multifarious factors. Further, while analysing the causes of alcoholism one must always bear in mind that *all those who take alcohol or not alcoholics.*

The key to alcoholism is in the motive for continuously repeating the drinking. Hence psychological aspects involved in the habit of excessive drinking must be given due recognition.

Writers like **Catlin, Starling, Bonger, Janet** and others have attributed several reasons for alcoholism. Their views may be summarised in the following manner.[1]

Causes of Drinking Alcohol

1. ***Misery Drinking*** **:** Life proves to be highly miserable and intolerable for some people for it provides them no joy and no contentment, but only hardship and suffering. They find no hopes of fruitful future. In such a life of unending struggles and toils, they find drink as a blessed palliative medicine.

2. ***Bad Housing and Lack of Recreational Facilities*** **:** Poor housing conditions often induce drinking. Some people drink because their houses are so cold, dark, dismal and sordid that they do not feel like staying there for a long time. The house does not provide them mental peace and contentment.

Not only the physical conditions of the house of so many people are poor and distressing even the emotional atmosphere in which they are living is also unfavourable for a safe living. The community fails to provide them sole-elevating recreation. These conditions push a few individuals to become alcoholic addicts.

3. ***Occupational Factor*** **:** Total dissolutionment with the occupation and unsatisfactory conditions of work make a few to become habitual drinkers. Men also drink because their occupation has completely exhausted them. They look forward to get more energy which they believe they would get through drinking.

4. ***For Companionship and Fun*** **:** A large number of young people resort to drinking due to the pressure of the company. Some consume alcohol for fun in the beginning, and in course of time, the fun becomes their permanent habit.

---

1. *Ref* : **G.R. Madan**'s *"Indian Social Problems"* - 1969 (Vol. 1) - Page : 154-157.

5. ***Drinking as a Fashion*** **:** Some pick up the habit of drinking for they consider it as a matter of fashion and an accepted custom in some circles. Drinking also reflects the pathetic attempt of an individual to enter into rapport with his fellows.

6. ***Inherent Nervous Defects*** **:** Some drunkards are often referred to as born drunkards for they have some inherent neurological defects due to which they are unable to face the reality. In their desperate attempts to run away from the real world these unhappy persons become hopeless and helpless alcoholics.

7. ***Ignorance*** **:** Some people who involve themselves in heavy physical work are under the wrong belief that alcohol furnishes them added strength and vigour with which they can pursue their labour. This illusory feeling of vitality after consumption of alcohol is the cause of drunkenness.

8. ***Sudden Success in Business*** **:** When some people become rich suddenly they develop the habit of spending more in arranging parties where alcoholic drinks is the main centre of attraction. They too develop the habit of taking drinks in order to maintain their contacts with people of business magnets.

9. ***Drinking for Business Reasons*** **:** Men also drink for business reasons in the capacity of either potential customers or sellers. When business reverses happen, or uncertainities and tensions involved in business reach their heights, then also some people take recourse to drinking as an escape mechanism.

10. ***Urbanisation and Industrialisation*** **:** Increasing urbanisation, industrialisation, and mechanisation that have been taking place have added additional motivation for drinking. These are the processes that increase worldliness and at the same time increase the weakness towards worldly enjoyments including drinking. When once a person is introduced to that type of material culture, he finds it difficult to come out of it.

11. ***Social Inadequacy*** **:** Human life is subject to joys and sorrows, ups - and downs, pains and pleasures. One must have proper balance of mind to face these realities of life. But there are some persons who are unable to face the hard realities of life and start drinking to overcome their social inadequacy temporarily which later on takes the form of habitual drinking.

It is clear from the above, that drinking alcohol is due to the operation of so many factors. Still the question persists why do certain persons choose drinking as a remedy to environmental pressures and problems while others do not ? Why some who develop the habit of drinking do not get lost in it while a few others make a total surrender to it ? Questions like these throw light on both personality and cultural factors that act as the major conditioning elements in the individual experience. Environmental pressures, cultural norms, individual tendencies, family atmosphere etc. together compel a man to become alcoholic. Thus, one many conclude from this that alcoholism can be explained only on the basis of a holistic approach rather than as a single factor approach.

3. EFFECTS OF ALCOHOLISM

Alcoholism as a social evil is causing lot of damage to the individuals concerned, their families and to the community at large. It brings individual misery, family discord and community disorganisation.

I. Drinking and Individual Disorganisation

Dangerous Effects on the Physical Health **:** The effects of alcohol upon the human organism are many and varied. The effects depend much on the quantity of alcohol and the frequency with which it is consumed. Taken in moderation in the form of wine, or beer, etc., it has not serious or harmful effects on the health of the person. Nor even a periodic dose is permanently injurious to the physical mechanism. It is only acute drinking which carries a train of ill effects. It leads to nervous degeneration, liver cirrhosis, chronic gastritis, high blood pressure and a host of other diseases. The drinker habitually has a shaky hand, and unsteady gait, lack lustre-eye, pale face, haggard look and black expression. He looses memory, becomes rash and violent towards others and becomes a menace to the society. He dies a lingering death or sometimes even a quick death due to heart trouble. Besides these specific diseases, the general resistance to all diseases is considerably reduced by heavy and frequent consumption of alcohol.

Disturbance in the Mental Health : Alcoholism lowers the efficiency of the person who becomes its victim. When the bodily health is damaged and mental ability affected, the fall in efficiency is inevitable. The alcoholic person is whimsical in nature and incapable of sustained attention and concentration. Thus, he cannot pursue any work seriously.

Damages Family and Social Connections : Excessive drinking makes the person to become indifferent in his approach towards others. Drinking makes him to forsake his home, his family and his business. His conversation may seen vulgar to the sober observer. When he is under the grip of alcohol he behaves like a liar, a scoundrel and is prepared to commit any type of crime including murder. A person with such a weakness grows careless, irresponsible, indifferent and even immoral. He fails to make out any difference between morality and immorality. All these individual trends produce personality disorganisation.

II. Drinking and Family Disorganisation

Alcoholism and family disorganisation are very closely linked. More homes are broken due to drinking than any other single cause. Alcoholics directly affect four or five other persons such as wife, parents, children, siblings, close friends and co-workers. An alcoholic shows little or no respect to his wife or children. This often leads to divorce and constant family tension. Family violence and family unrest is also caused by alcoholism.

- ***Alcohol makes domestic relations miserable*** : Liquor has been a traditional enemy of love and marriage, because it often leads to promiscuity and breach of moral standards of the spouses. Domestic unhappiness, moral degradation, divorce and family disorganisation and juvenile delinquency are the resultant consequences.
- ***Negligence towards wife and children*** : Happy family life depends on the harmonious relationship between husband and wife. It is generally said that habitual drinkers feel uneasy in the presence of women. Chronic alcoholics often become completely disinterested in the opposite sex. Hence, even wives, and their basic emotional needs are neglected by the alcoholics.
- ***May lead to divorce*** : A strong prejudice against drink on the part of the husband or wife of one who drinks is a constant source of friction in the family and leads to divorce later on. Wives who are fed up with the excessive drinking habit of their husbands often decide to take divorce to save the good future of the children. In lower class families where people have neither the knowledge of law nor the resources to seek divorce, drunkenness often causes untold misery.

III. Drinking and Community Disorganisation

Economic loss : The effects of alcoholism are far reaching. It disturbs the normal course of community life. Drinking affects the business, the office efficiency and factory productiveness also. Absenteeism, low output and poor judgement leading to work related accidents cost the government crores of rupees.

Damages the moral health of the society : Drinking is associated with cabaret dances, prostitution and gambling especially in public places such as clubs, hotels, public halls, etc. The increased presence of women in such places both as patrons and entertainers, will have the most devastating effect on the public morality. Prostitutes openly solicit in many such places. *"Young girls are often engaged to act as "hostesses" in order to stimulate the consumption of liquor. Such a combination of alcoholic indulgence and sexual licence have disorganising effect both upon the hostess and the patron."*[1]

1. **G.R. Madan** [Vol. 7] Page : 161.

Increase in Crimes : It has been found that there is a close relationship between drinking and crime. *"Partial or complete intoxication is an important element in many types of crimes including arson, stabbing, manslaughter, assaults and sex offences. Drink has a close kinship with cruelty, heinousness and depravity. It is associated with debauchery and prostitution."*[1]

Increases accident proneness : Studies have revealed that *"drink is closely related with increasing accidents which take a heavy toll of human life and maim those who survive."*[2] There is a direct ratio between alcohol and increase in accident proneness.

- ***Drink addiction lowers industrial production.*** Drunkards are often inefficient due to physical weakness. *The Royal Commission on Labour* in India note, *"Alcohol offers its dangerous relief to a fatigued body and believed that a reduction in the consumption of liquor would increase the welfare and efficiency of industrial labour."*[3]

It is clear from the above description that drinkers are a blot upon the society, a stigma upon the community, a shame to their parents and a disgrace to themselves. Hence, judged from any angle - social, economic, moral, spiritual, and even legal - public opinion is to be created and developed against alcoholism and in favour of prohibition.

Enlisting the deadly and disastrous effects of alcoholism **Evangeline Booth**, one time *Head of the Salvation Army,* observed : *"Drink has drained more blood, hung more crape, sold more homes, plunged more people into bankruptcy, armed more villains, stained more children, snapped more wedding - rings, defiled more innocence, blinded more eyes, twisted more limbs, dethroned more reason, wrecked more womanhood, dishonoured more womanhood, broken more hearts, blasted more lives, driven more to suicide, and dug more graves than any other poison scourge that sent its death-dealing waves across the world."* [4]

Sri Bharatan Kumarappa, a reknowned Gandhian, has summed up the evil consequences of alcoholism in the following words : Drinking leads to *".... besides the money loss and food loss, great as they are, we must add to the debit side of drink immorality, murder theft, family squabbles, broken homes, hungry children, and ruined earners - in short, a general lowering of moral sense, judgement and intelligence."*[5]

4. MEASURES TO CONTROL ALCOHOLISM

Alcoholism has been one of the earliest habits of man. Attempts have also been made from the times immemorial to control it. Over the years this habit has grown into a social evil posing a big challenge to public health. It has become necessary for the people vested with authority to introduce various measures to control its practice in some way or the other. Let us now discuss this ways and means of controlling alcoholism.

1. *Not the Removal, but Control of Alcoholic Drinks* : The practice of alcoholism which has been associated with the human life since centuries, cannot be removed immediately. No country has been successful in this regard so far. **Kautilya**, the author of *"Arthashastra"*, had recognised this fact long ago and hence suggested that provision could be made to establish "liquor houses" [*"panagrihas"*] on the outskirts of the towns. He was also of the opinion that men's weakness towards alcohol could never be completely suppressed but only controlled. Since all drinkers are not alcoholics, it is more appropriate to make provision for drinking under vigilance and control, than to make a futile attempt to remove it once and for all.

---

1. **C.B. Mamoria** in *"Social Problems and Social Disorganisation"* Page : 733.
2. *ibid,* Page : 733.
3. *ibid,* Page : 734.
4. *ibid,* Page : 735.
5. *ibid,* Page : 735.

2. *Drinking as a Habit of Physical Labourers and Workers* : 'Liquor shops' are often regarded as *"poor men's club"*. It has been observed that labourers who are engaged in tight hard work want to have some relaxation after their toil. To forget the boredom of work and to relax and refresh, they want to consume alcohol which they believe will be of great help. Thus, it is necessary to provide for good entertainment facilities at affordable cost for the labour class to discourage them to resort to alcohol.

3. *Welfare of People is more Important than Increasing Revenue through the Sale of Alcohol* : The Government should take appropriate legal and administrative steps to introduce prohibition on the sale of liquor. If the supply is not there, one can expect the demand to die down at least gradually. In the Indian context, the state governments are not prepared to introduce prohibition for the simple reason that they get lot of income for the state treasury by way of tax imposed on the sale of liquor. It is difficult to have control over the consumption of alcohol in a nation like India if the state governments are not taking initiative in imposing prohibition. They must understand that promoting people's welfare is the primary duty of the Government. They must make alternative arrangements to collect revenue for the state to make good the loss which they are said to incur due to the introduction of prohibition.

4. *Making Campaign Against Alcoholic Drinks and Creating Awareness About its Evil Effects* : It is necessary to launch a campaign against evil of alcoholism to make the people know about its harmful effects. Government alone cannot do it effectively. Government, non-governmental organisations, private individuals of great repute, religious, political and social leaders should launch a combined campaign against alcoholism.

Modern means of mass media such as radio, television, advertisements, news papers, cinema, etc., can also play an effective role in impressing upon the people about the disastrous effects of the ugly practice of alcoholism.

5. *Introduction of Prohibition Act* : Several nations have tried to stop the practice of taking alcohol by introducing prohibition acts. But the experience of these nations have revealed that legislation alone cannot do any magic here. America, Russia and France, for example, have tried with legislative enactments to stop the practice of taking drinks. Different states in India also have experimented with such legislations. Neither in India nor elsewhere, these legislations have been a total success. This does not mean that legislation in this regard is useless and ineffective. It only means that the legislations have not been implemented honestly and effectively.

In a nation like India where millions of poor people have become the victims of the ugly practice of alcoholism, introduction of legislation against it, is a must. Educated public and non-governmental organisations must give their full co-operation to the Government to implement the legislation.

6. *Need for Widespread Campaign Against Drinking* : Educated and well informed people who have a strong public concern must take initiative in launching campaigns against the practice of drinking. Some such efforts made by some individuals with strong determination have fetched positive results. ***Examples*** : Women of Nellur District of Andhra Pradesh launched such a campaign in their district in 1990s which later on was spread to the whole of Andhra Pradesh. The Telugu Desham Party which supported this campaign was voted to power in 1994 and the party introduced prohibition soon after assuming power.

On the model of the Nellur campaign, if peaceful agitations are organised against alcoholism throughout India, the so-called "liquor kings" are bound to step down. In Karnataka also such campaigns are going on peacefully here and there. For example, under the leadership of Sri Veerendra Heggade, [Dharmadhikari, Dharmasthala] a campaign against alcoholism is silently doing its work in Belthangady thaluk of Dakshina Kannada District. It has been able to persuade successfully as many as 2115 alcoholics to give up the deadly habit of drinking. The campaign has set its target to make Belthangady Thaluk, totally free from the stranglehold of alcoholism.

(ii) DRUG ADDICTION

Drug addiction is a state of indiscriminate use of herbs and herbal preparations, which enslaves the user to them. This is not something new in human society, what is now alarming is the indiscriminate use of drugs on an unimaginably large scale, which may be attributed to breakdown of spiritual and religious value systems that kept man integrated as person and with his family and society.

Drug abuse, instead of leading man towards peace of mind and state of equilibrium throws him into oblivion and causes decay at almost all planes – physical, emotional, psychological, societal and spiritual.

5. MEANING AND NATURE OF DRUG ADDICTION

Drug abuse, drug addiction, drug trafficking, becoming victims of drug addiction - etc., have been the tragedies of the 20th century. They have been passed on with no less vigour to the 21st century. Intoxicating drugs such as *brown sugar, opium, heroin, alcohol, marijuana, ganja, bhang, cocaine, charas, morphine, L.S.D* and such other things are even known to the street children in big cities. Some of them take a chance to taste them. Each year we are adding to more and more such harmful compounds to the already existing ones. What is more distressing today is the abuse of drugs. The abuse of drugs affect adversely the user's mind and body. The victims of the abuse of drugs are also increasing in number.[1] The phenomenon of drug addiction has become a colossal one in a developing nation like India.

Meaning of Drug Addiction

Man has been using or consuming for the past several thousands of years some substances or the other to intoxicate himself for various reasons. More commonly, these substances are used for personal reasons, either to induce states of elevated mood or relieve inner feelings of anxiety, misery and despair. What we presently call *'drugs'* belong to that category of such substances.

Definition of Drug Addiction

- **W.H.O.** *[World Health Organisation]* defines drug addiction as – *"a state of periodic or chronic intoxication detrimental to the individual and to society produced by the repeated consumption of drug, natural or synthetic..."*
- The word *"addiction"* implies physical dependence. *'Drug addiction'* obviously means *the physical dependence of a person/s on the use of some drugs.* The drugs could be any one of the intoxicants such as *heroin, brown sugar, cocaine, bhang, ganja, marijuana, etc.* Addiction involves totally a drug-centred lifestyle. This lifestyle takes an individual to *"a state whereby the body requires continued administration of the drug in order to function."* The functioning of the body is so attuned to the drug, if it is withdrawn the person becomes totally uncomfortable and the *"withdrawal symptoms"* appear. Thus the person helplessly depends on the use of drugs.

Characteristics of Drug Addiction

The W.H.O. in its enlarged definition of drug addiction points out the following important characteristics of drug addiction.

1. ***An Uncontrollable Desire for Drugs*** **:** Drug addiction includes an overpowering desire or need [compulsion] to continue taking the drug or to obtain it by any means. The desire for drug is so

1. A survey report states that in 1990 in America, there were **1.45** crore cocaine addicts and 10 lakh heroin addicts. In the same year, in Pakisthan, the number of registered heroin addicts had reached a mark of 7 lakhs. ***Ref*** : *'Uthana'* Kannada Monthly, Page : 81-85, Sept. 1990.

strong and powerful in the individual that he is prepared to do anything and everything, even if it is immoral and illegal, just for getting and using it.

2. *A Tendency to Increase the Doze* : It involves a tendency to increase the doze. The "thrill" that the consumption of drug creates in the person actually overpowers him and he wants to have it again and again and to increase its doze. In fact, the chronic drug – user develops a feeling that he must constantly increase the doze in order to produce the same effect as that from the initial doze. This phenomenon is called *"tolerance"*. Tolerance represents body's ability to adapt itself to the presence of a foreign substance. This "tolerance" level of the individuals who use drugs, and the tolerance development to the use of different drugs, vary significantly.

3. *Physical and Psychological Dependence on Drugs* : It includes a psychic or psychological; sometimes a physical dependence on the effects of the drug. It means that the body of the drug - user gets conditioned to such an extent he feels that he just cannot do anything without it.

4. *Harmful Effects on the Individual and the Society* : It unavoidably includes an effect that is detrimental to the individual and to the society. Sales and consumption of most of the narcotic drugs are legally banned in most of the countries for they have disastrous effects on the individuals and the society. Drug addiction ultimately destroys the individual, his family relations and social connections. Drug addicts virtually become parasites on society contributing nothing to its effective functioning.

6. SOME BASIC CONCEPTS : DRUG – DRUG ABUSE, DRUG DEPENDENCE

Concepts such as *"drug"*, *"drug abuse"*, *"drug dependence"* etc. are very commonly used in our discussion of the problem of "drug addiction". Hence, it is necessary to clarify the difference in the meanings of these terms.

1. "Drug" and its Meaning

What is Drug ? : It is necessary for us to know the meaning of the word "drug" before we make an attempt to understand *"drug addiction"*.

In an ordinary sense, the word *"drug"* denotes any medicine, solid or liquid prescribed by a physician for the cure of a disease. It is in this sense, equated with medicine. But when used in a specific sense, the word "drug" connotes a different meaning; it represents various narcotic drugs. It is with this meaning the word is analysed here.

- **Joseph Julian** states that drug is *"any chemical substance which affects bodily function, mood, perception or consciousness which has potential for misuse and which may be harmful to the individual or the society."*[1]

Joseph Julian's definition signifies that the frequent use of drug is considered very dangerous and even immoral and anti-social for it arouses a variety of indignant and hostile sentiments on the part of the general public. The use of illegal drugs such as heroin, brown sugar, cocaine, L.S.D. – belongs to that category.

2. Drug Abuse

The word *"abuse"* refers to improper or wrong use of a thing. Obviously, *"drug abuse"* means improper and even illegal use of drugs. It could be more appropriately defined in the following manner.

- **Paul Fuqua** refers to 'drug abuse' as – *"the use of a substance in such a way that it leads to such personal and / or social consequences as impaired physical or mental health, impaired maturation, loss of productivity, and involvement in socially disruptive or illegal activities."*

1. As quoted by **Ram Ahuja** in *"Social Problems in India"* – Page : 387.

- ***In simple words,*** *drug abuse is using natural / and or synthetic chemical substances like alcohol, tobacco, ganja, opium, cocaine, etc., for non-medical purposes to experience pleasure.*

Drug abuse includes, for example, smoking ganja or hashish, taking heroin, cocaine or L.S.D., injecting morphine, drinking alcohol, licking brown sugar, and so on. All these drugs are narcotic in the sense; they give a *'kick'* and psychic ecstasy.

Characteristics of Drug Abuse

As per the above definitions, drug abuse implies the following characteristic features.

1. The use of drugs in any form or style is considered as 'illegal'.
2. The drug is used without proper medical advice and supervision;
3. It is used in excess of accepted standards of self-medication, and
4. The use of drugs in this context leads to loss of control over the user's behaviour.

3. Meaning of "Drug Dependence"

"Drug dependence" is yet another concept associated with the analysis of drug addiction. The term denotes habitual or frequent use of a drug. The use is so frequent that the individual virtually becomes dependent on it. This dependence is of two types : *(i) Physical dependence,* and *(ii) Psychological dependence.*

(i) ***Physical dependence*** refers to the bodily dependence of a person on the use of the drug. Due to the continuous use of the drug, the body becomes so adjusted to the presence of the drug that it will suffer pain, severe discomfort or even illness if the use of the drug is not continued. In a state of drug-addiction of a person, physical dependence reflects the bodily position of a person which requires continued administration of the drug in order to function.

(ii) ***Psychological dependence*** refers to the strong craving for the drug. The craving is so strong that the individual feels that his well-being depends only on its use. Sometimes the word ***"habituation"*** is used to refer to psychic or psychological dependence.

Signs of Drug Dependence

As pointed out by **C.B. Mamoria** drug dependence on the part of the drug addicts reveals certain signs among which the following may be noted.[1]

1. Persons experiencing a static panic and exhibiting anxiety reactions.
2. Impaired judgement and distorted perceptions of space or time.
3. Excessive suspicion of others [or attitudes of paranoia]
4. Occasional convulsions
5. Mental confusion, loss of contact with reality and lapses of memory.
6. Unhealthy physical appearance because of poor diet and personal neglect.
7. Severe drowsiness and finding oneself in sleepy mood.
8. Indifferent, apathetic and sometimes compulsive behaviour.
9. Dilated pupils, a flushed face, and a feeling of being chilly.
10. A deterioration of values.

What is to be borne in mind is that all individuals who suffer from drug dependence need not necessarily exhibit all the above mentioned symptoms. Symptoms also vary with the stage of addiction and the type of the drug used, as well as with the experience of the drug user.

---

1. **C.B. Mamoria** in *"Social Problems and Social Disorganisation in India"* – Page : 719.

7. TYPES OF DRUGS OR NATURE AND IMPACT OF ABUSABLE DRUGS

The conditions of modern society often give scope for drug abuse. These drugs which cause serious health problems to the individuals who use it also lead to some sort of dependence. Hence they are also called *"dependence – producing drugs"*. Though legal restrictions and prohibitions are imposed on these drugs, many individuals are found to be using them escaping the notice of the law enforcement authorities.

The abusable drugs or *"dependence producing drugs"* belong to the following six main categories. They are *(1) alcohol, (2) sedatives, (3) stimulants, (4) narcotics, (5) hallucinogens, and (6) nicotine.* The impact of these drugs on the individual users is not the same, but different.

1. Alcohol

By pharmacological definition, alcohol is a drug and may be classified as a sedative, tranquillizer, hypnotic or anesthetic, depending upon the quantity that is consumed. It relieves tension and lessens aggressive inhibitions. It includes intoxication. Of all the drugs, alcohol is the only drug whose self-induced intoxication is considered as socially acceptable.

Over the 30-40 years increasing percentages of young people have started to drink alcoholic beverages. Their alcohol consumption has increased in quantity and frequency and the age at which drinking starts has declined. This situation is socially disturbing.

Alcohol has a marked effect on the central nervous system. It is not a "stimulant" as it was previously believed, but a primary and continuous depressant. Alcohol produces psychic dependence of varying degrees from mild to strong. Physical dependence develops slowly.

2. Sedatives OR Depressants

Barbiturates, bromides and tranquillizers belong to this category. These drugs are also called *"drowners"*. They act to relax the central nervous system and induce sleep and provide a soothing effect. Medically, these are used in high blood pressure, insomnia, epilepsy and to relax patients before and during surgery.

When these depressants are taken in small quantities, they slow down breathing and heart-beating. Taken in higher doses, their effects resemble alcohol intoxication. Higher doze of its consumption impairs person's ability to think, concentrate and work. His emotional control is also weakened.

3. Stimulants

The most widely known stimulants are *amphetamines* [popularly known as 'pep-pills']. When administered by a medical practitioner, moderate dose of amphetamine can check fatigue and produce feelings of alertness and self-confidence. But the heavy dose of the same may cause extreme nervousness, irritability, head ache, sweating, diarrhoea and unclear speech.

These drugs, however, do not cause physical dependence, though they are psychologically addicting. It is not advisable to take a heavy doze of it for a long time. In such cases, it may cause varying degrees of intellectual, emotional, economic and social deterioration. Sudden stopping of the same is also harmful for it may result in mental illness and a deep suicidal depression.

4. Narcotics

Narcotic drugs are many for they include *opium, marijuana, heroin, morphine, cocaine, codeine, methadone, pithindine and cannabis* such as *charas, ganja, bhang, etc.*

Continued taking of these is regarded as the worst type of addiction because it produces craving and psychic dependence. Narcotic drugs are taken to produce the feelings of pleasure, strength and superiority. They reduce hunger, increase suggestibility and lessen inhibitions.

5. Hallucinogens

These include *mescaline, DMT, STP, MDA* and *LSD* [Lysergic acid diethylamides]. These drugs are called *"psychedelics"*. Their use is not advised by medical practitioners. The well-known drug in this group is LSD which is a man-made chemical. LSD is taken orally and it may also be injected. It is a powerful drug and its effect on the individual lasts for 8 to 10 hours. Any attempt to withdraw from its use leads to panic, depression and permanent severe mental derangement on the part of its addict.

6. Nicotine or Tobacco

This includes *beedi, cigarettes, cigars, snuffs* and *beeda* [which includes tobacco]. This leads to relaxation, stimulates the central nervous system, increases wakefulness, and removes boredoom. The frequent and heavy use of nicotine may cause heart attack, lung cancer, and bronchitis. From the legal point of view this is not a drug.

"Tobacco is in legal use everywhere in the world, yet it causes far more, deaths than all other psychoactive substances[1] combined. About 3 million premature deaths a year [6% of the world total] are already attributed to tobacco smoking. Tobacco is responsible for about 30% of all cancer deaths in developed countries. More people die from tobacco related diseases other than cancer such as stroke, myocardial infarction, …… peptic ulcer …. There is evidence that earlier a person begins to smoke the greater is the risk of life-threatening diseases such as – chronic bronchitis, cardiovascular diseases and lung cancer."[2]

8. CAUSES OF DRUG ADDICTION OR MOTIVATIONS IN DRUG USAGE

Every one knows that drug abuse or addiction has become one of the grave problems of the modern society. The socio-economic conditions of the modern society seem to be favourable for the growth of drug abuse. The questions such as – *why people become drug addicts ? or why drug abuse is found ? what motivations provoke people to become addicts ?* – seem to be tatalising. These questions are to be addressed in order to have a clear picture of the way in which people become the victims of drug abuse.

According to **Ram Ahuja**, the causes of drug abuse may be classified under the following four main heads :

1. *Psychological Causes* : Psychological factors such as – getting *'kicks'* and *'thrills'*, relieving tension, removing inhibitions, avoiding boredom, easing depression, satisfying curiosity, feeling high and confident and intensifying perception, etc. may motivate individuals for drug abuse.

2. *Physiological Factors* like removing pain, getting sleep, heightening sexual experiences, staying awake, getting more physical strength, etc. also induce people to become drug addicts.

3. *Social Causes* that favour drug abuse are -- to become acceptable to friends, the desire to join *"high society"*, facilitating social experiences, challenging social values, to set new social trends, etc.

4. *Miscellaneous Causes* backing the ugly practice of drug abuse include – sharpening religious insight or to get new spiritual light, improving study, solving personal problems, deepening self-understanding, increasing efficiency, to refresh the mind, and so on.

SOME SPECIFIC CAUSES

In addition to four broad categories of factors causing drug abuse, some specific causes may also contribute to it. Among such causes, the following ones deserve a special mention.

---

1. ***Psychoactive substances*** or ***drugs*** include stimulants, depressants, narcotics and hallucinogens.
2. ***Ref*** : **Park**'s *"Textbook of Preventive and Social Medicine"*. [17th Edition, 2007.] – Page : 688.

1. ***Using Drugs for 'Kicks' or 'Thrills'*** **:** Sizeable number of street children, educated and uneducated youths become drug addicts because of their intense eagerness to taste it once. They get initiated to its use in the beginning only for *'fun'*, or for a *'thrill'* or *'kich'*. When such experiences are repeated they find it impossible to come out of the drug trap to which they have already fallen.

2. ***Peer Group Influence*** **:** Peer group influence seems to be very powerful in initiating a new person to drug-taking habit. To get recognition in the company, to satisfy other members of the peer group, to feel superior in the presence of a boy friend or girl friend, to avoid ridicule at the hands of fellow-members – and due to such other factors young people become victims of drug abuse.

3. ***Feeling of Alienation and Lack of Motivation*** **:** The conditions of modern society are such that they may push some mentally. weak or delicate persons towards loneliness. Such persons though live in the midst of people tend to feel that they are alone in the world for they do not have any companions. They are devoid of love, affection, companionship and fellowship. Life becomes monotonous and boring for them. Some of them become introverts by turning increasingly inwards. In order to find a fuller meaning in life some of them resort to drugs.

• ***Lack of motivation*** is another important factor. Many young people fail to get good guidance for setting their aims and missions in life. They find no one to inspire them, correct them, pat them at their back and provide them a model to emulate. They very often experience frustration, disgust and disappointment. To avoid such discouraging things of life, some resort to drugs.

4. ***To Escape from the Pressures and Conflicts of Life*** **:** Our living conditions also impose various pressures, conflicts, tensions and dangers in our life. One requires courage and a realistic approach to face such challenges of life. All are not mentally equipped to face successfully such realities of life. Mentally timid, intellectually average and physically weak individuals may harbour in their mind all negative thinking particularly when they feel that they are incapable of meeting the immediate challenges before them. Some such persons become mentally depressed while a few others exhibit suicidal tendencies. There are also persons of that nature resorting to drugs.

Why Do People Seek Drugs ?

At first, many young people experiment with drugs for which the reasons include ....

- Peer pressure i.e. pressure from friends.
- To feel one with the group in which they live.
- To feel "grown –up"
- To rebel against parents, teachers bosses, and other authority.
- Curiosity to have the experience, i.e. for "kicks".
- To kill boredom
- To escape or reduce unpleasant experiences of life
- As an adventure
- Easy availability of money as well as the "drug"
- Adult examples, i.e., emulating others.

The danger with experimenting is that drugs can become an important part of their daily life. They can also become a means of trying to cope with or avoid problems.

Finally, some people come to need drugs. These hardcore drug users need to continue the drugs because ....

They become physically and / or psychologically dependent on them. i.e. they suffer from the withdrawal effects of the drug even if they miss a single does of it.

9. EFFECTS OF DRUG ADDICTION

Drug addiction is one of the grave social evils of the modern complex society. Unfortunately, it is becoming more and more widespread in the economically and educationally advanced societies.

It is indeed becoming a growing threat to humanity. Some of the disastrous effects of drug abuse may be noted here.

1. *Physical and Mental Decline* : Individuals who become the victims of drug addiction soon deteriorate mentally and physically. Though the consumption of drug gives them 'thrill' or 'kick' in the beginning, its continuous use makes them to become its slave and they get emaciated soon.

2. *The Tragic Dependence on Drugs* : Frequent use of drug makes a person to become 'dependent' on it. In the beginning, he will be intensely aspiring and craving to get it. This is a stage of *"psychological dependence"*. Consistent use of a drug at this stage slowly pushes him to the next worst stage of *"physical dependence"*. At this stage, the individual's body gets so adjusted to the drug that without the drug the body suffers pain, illness, shivering and total discomfort. This is the stage of addiction, a stage in which the drug habit makes the person to dance according to its tune.

3. *Great Damage to Health* : Drug habit at its height is dangerous for health. If the habit becomes a permanent habit then it makes the person to become the victim of many types of diseases and health upsets such as – nervous weakness, bodily weakness, loss of body weight, indigestion, peptic ulcer, liver complaint, sleepiness, higher B.P., and so on.

4. *Moral Degradation* : Drug addiction leads to moral degeneration also. The drug addict gives no respect to moral values and ideals. He does not obey the rules. He is interested in only one thing in life and that is drug. For obtaining it, he is prepared to do anything including the criminal acts such as cheating, stealing, killing, and so on.

5. *Blackmailing the Drug Addicts for Criminal Purposes* : Drug addicts are increasing in number. Huge amount of money is wasted by these drugs addicts for purchasing drugs worth more than Rs. **100** billion dollars every year for their consumption.

Further, anti-social elements and criminals make use of the drug addicts for their criminal activities. They exploit the weakness of the drug addicts and even blackmail them to get their things done.

6. *Other Harmful Effects of Drug Addiction* :

(i) Drug addiction causes waste of huge amount of money on drugs.

(ii) It damages family relations, leads to an increase in divorce, desertion and family disorganisation.

(iii) It spoils human potentiality and prevents a large number of people from utilizing their talents and abilities for their own betterment and for the betterment of the society.

CONTROL OF DRUG ABUSE / ADDICTION

Problem of drug addiction has become one of the serious and pressing social problems of the civilized societies. The problem has to be tackled effectively and the drug addicts are to be persuaded to give up their deadly habits. The programme of prevention of drug abuse / addiction should have realistic aims. Over ambitious hopes of eradicating the drug problem in a short time are likely to lead to policies that are unrealistic and self-discrediting. Changes in cultural attitudes and alteration in relevant aspects of the environment can be brought about only slowly.

1. *Educational Approach* : Imparting education about drugs and the evil effects of their consumption is of great importance. Common approaches here include educational programmes for school children / college and university students and public information campaigns on electronic media. Students and youths who are living away from their parents particularly in hostels/ hotels / private rooms are to be given special attention. People living in slums, industrial workers, street children, truck drivers and autorikshaw pullers must be taken proper care.

• ***All Misleading Knowledge to be Removed*** : General principles of communication can bc applied to increase the effectiveness of educational approach. The method of education should be such people involve themselves actively and there is a free exchange of valuable information. The type of education must be such that all inaccurate information and misleading knowledge that people have about the physical and psychological effects of taking drugs must be removed.

• ***Clear Message to be Given*** : The message should be clear and unambiguous to the intended audience and come from credible source of information. The message should also provide specifice advice, rather than general; and as far as possible the information should be new to the audience and should be capable of provoking discussion or action. Educational approach should not be planned and carried out as an isolated activity. To be effective, such approaches should be regarded as a part of integrated plan of action involving other strategies.

3. *Community Approach* : The rapid changes taking place at the present time in relations between individuals, groups and nations are also reflected in a rapidly changing pattern of drug use in many parts of the world. There should be a strong emphasis on action at the community level to prevent drug abuse. Primary health care centers should be strengthened so as to initiate preventive action that will influence people's every day lives and actions. Action at the community level is also important since communities often bear the brunt of dealing with the harmful use of drugs and drug related problems.

4. *Legal Approach* : The legal control on the distribution of drugs, when effectively applied has been and remains an important approach in the prevention of drug abuse. Controls may be designed to impose partial restrictions or to make a drug completely unavailable. *"Legislation may be directed at controlling the manufacture, distribution, prescription, price, time of sale, or consumption of a substance."*[1]

Legislation restricting or prohibiting advertisements that directly or indirectly promote the use of tobacco and alcohol has been increasingly common in recent years. The minimum age at which minors may legally have access to alcoholic beverages, has been raised in some countries. There is also legislation controlling the distribution of alcohol in some countries. In Inida, in Andhra Pradesh, for example, sale of alcohol is prohibited.

• ***The Narcotic Drugs and Psychotropic Substances Act – 1985*** : The Central Government introduced this Act in the year 1985 to combat trafficking in drugs. It was amended in 1987 to make the legislation still more stringent. The Act provides for a minimum punishment of 10 years rigorous imprisonment for its violation, and it could be extended to 20 years with a fine of 1 to 2 lakh rupees. The courts are also empowered to impose still heavier amount of fines. The Act also lays down imprisonment of one year or fine or both for illegal possession of any narcotic drug or psychotropic substance in small quantity for personal consumption. The Act makes provision for the establishment of as many centers as the government thinks fit for identification, treatment, education, after care, rehabilitation and social reintegration of addicts.

5. *Punishment to Enforcement Agencies Including Police* : No law or legislation is effective by itself. It gets strength only if it is effectively enforced. Police and the enforcement agency play an important role in enforcing the law. When law enforcers are found working in collusion with drug-peddlers, they deserve severe punishment. Corrupt police officials do a great damage in this regard.

6. *Changing the Attitudes of Doctors* : The practising doctors will have to change their approach in prescribing too many and too costly drugs. They have to be careful about the side effects of the drugs which they are prescribing. Though drugs help many, yet there are dangers of over-dependence. Once a patient gets a prescription from a doctor that cures his ailment, he ceases to consult the doctor and continues to use the drugs indiscriminately or excessively whenever he suffers from the same ailment. It is in this way, people often come to depend more on medication than on physician which is a dangerous practice.

---

1. **K. Park** in *"Park's Textbook of Preventive and Social Medicine"* [2007] – Page : 690.

7. ***Follow-up Study of Drug Addicts Under Treatment*** **:** It is necessary to make follow-up study of drug addicts treated under detoxification programmes. This helps the doctors and the consultants to know the effectiveness of the treatment.

8. ***Role of Teachers*** **:** Teachers can play a vital role in the prevention of drug abuse. They can talk openly and freely with the students and can discuss the dangers of drug abuse. They can come to know about their students' interests and activities. They can talk about the problem of adolescence and guide students how to solve them. They can encourage their students to talk freely about their personal problems [in relation to parents, peer groups, money, etc.] and give proper suggestion and advice. Teachers can help the students in selecting career options and setting goals.

9. ***Role of Parents*** **:** Parents' role is no less significant, Drug abuse, at times, may have its roots in parental neglect, over-hostility, rejection, marital disharmony, etc. It is thus necessary that parents have to take more care in keeping the family environment congenial and harmonious. No one becomes an addict overnight. It involves a process of evolution of losing interest in studies, activities and hobbies, indulging in irresponsible behaviour, irritability, impulsive conduct, etc. If the parents are alert and responsible, they can locate these early signs and take proper precaution in protecting their children.

- ***Parents can do a lot in the prevention of drug abuse.*** They could talk to their children openly and affectionately, listen to their problems patiently and suggest them how to handle the problems effectively. Parents need to spare much time to know the activities of their children, their circle of friends, their hobbies, etc. Parents themselves must set a good model for the children by not taking drugs or alcohol. Parents must keep themselves informed about the modern drugs, the drug lobbies, their style of operation, etc. – in order to keep their children away from such influences.

10. ***Providing Alternative Activities*** **:** A popular approach to the prevention of drug abuse is providing for alternative activities which may help to prevent drug abuse. Youth centers and teen centers could provide activities attractive to the adolescents and youths who might otherwise drift in to drug taking subculture. Such activities include the establishment of groups or organizations interested in athletics, sports, music, public policy, religion, artistic activities of various kinds. Non-governmental organizations play a crucial role in the development of such activities and are likely to become important.

• Giving Special Attention to the Teenagers to Prevent Drug Abuse

Choosing the most vulnerable persons i.e., the teenagers, as the target group and giving them proper education regarding the ill effects of alcohol and drug use.

Conclusion **:** Drug abuse today has become a big menace, a threat to humanity. Law enforcement authorities alone cannot do any magic in preventing it. Corrupt police authorities and politicians, mafia gangs, drug lobbies, international terrorist organizations all have added much strength to this menace. Entire society has to take this as a challenge and create awareness among the public. To create awareness among the people, ***"International Day Against Drug Abuse and Illicit Trafficking"*** has been in observance every year on June 26 ever since 1991. Persuasion, motivation coercion, compulsion and punishment are the measures all of which have to be used so that drug-abusers can be made to live a wholesome drug-free life. Prevention, treatment and rehabilitation all require a positive and life-affirming campaign.

Thus, families and voluntary organizations, local agencies, youth forums, women's organizations, religious associations, all must work together not only to prevent people from becoming victims of this problem, but also to bring back the recovered addicts into the mainstream of social life.

❖❖❖❖❖❖❖❖❖

ANNEXURE - 6

Annexure to Chapter - 18

INDIAN POPULATION HIGHLIGHTS AS PER 2011 CENSUS

The first population census in British India was conducted in 1872. Since India's independence in 1947, a census has been carried out every 10 years, starting from 1951. The census in India is carried out by the Office of the Registrar General and Census Commissioner under the Ministry of Home Affairs, and is one of the largest administrative tasks conducted by a federal govenment.

Latest population figures are based on data from the 2011 census of India. During the decade of 2001-2011, India's annual population growth rate has slowed down from 2.15 to 1.76. Based on decennial census data, Dadra & Nagar Haveli shows the highest growth rate 55.5 percent. It is followed by Daman & Diu (53.5 percent), Meghalaya (27.8 percent) and Arunachal Pradesh (25.9 percent), Nagaland recorded the lowest growth rate of 0.5 percent.

2011 Census : This Census 2011 is the 15th census of India since 1872 and conducted in two phases : (i) *houselisting and housing census.* (April to Sept - 2010) and (ii) *population enumeration* (Feb. 9th to 28th - 2011).

The Census covered all 35 states and UTs and cost ₹ 2200 crores. About 27 lakh enumerators were involved in the exercise where 8000 metric tonnes of paper and 10,500 metric tonnes of material moved.

Of the various States and UTs of India, U.P. is the most populous state (199 million) and Lakshadweep is the least populated one (64,429).

- **Increse in the Size of Population :** Total population of India in 2001 was 1027015247 and it increased to 1210193422 in 2011 (Men - 623,724,248 as against 531,277,078 and women - 586469174 as against 493,738,169 in 2001.
- **Decadal Growth Rate :** Population in 2011 registered a decadal growth (2001-2011) of 17.64% as against a decadal growth (2091-2001) of 21.34% in 2001. Fifteen States and

Table 1. Decadal Growth of Population in India from 1901 to 2011

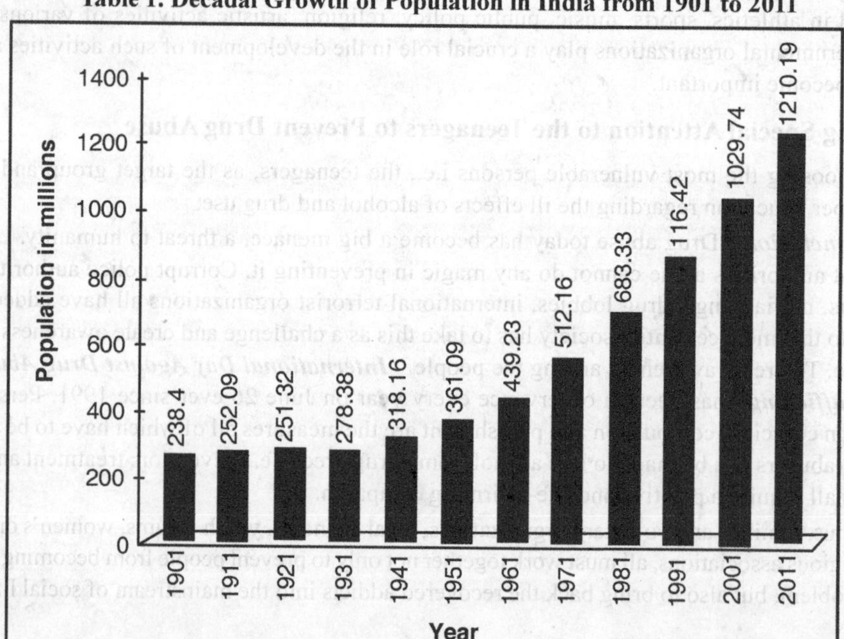

Union Territories have grown by less than 1.5% per annum during 2001-2011, while the number of such states and UTs were only 4 during the previous decade (1991 - 2001)

- **Sex Ratio :** For every 1000 men, there are 940 women as against 933 in 2001. In 13 states, it is above the national average and in 12 states, it is below the national level.
- **Decline in Growth Rate :** Rate of population growth has declined in the country considerably, that is from 21.34% during 1991-2001 to 17.64% between 2001-2011.
- **Retains the Second Position :** India continues to occupy the second position in the world having 17.5% of the total world population next only to China (19.4%).
- **Increase in Literacy :** The average literacy of the nation in 2011 is 74.04% and it was 65.38% in 2001 and this reveals an increase of 8.66% over the previous decade.
- **More Literate Men than Women :** There are 778.4 millions of literate people in the country and out of this, 2 million people are males and 334.2 million people are females. Literacy among males increased from 75.85 % in 2001 to 82.14% in 2011 (registering a differential growth of 6.29%) and in the case of women it increased from 54.16% to 65.46% (registering a decadal increase of 11.3%)
- **Highest and Lowest Literacy :** Highest rate of literacy is found in Kerala (93.91%) followed by States such as Lakshadweep (92.28%) ; Mizoram (91.58%) ; Tripura (87.75%) and Goa (87.40%). In the same way, lowest rate of literacy is found in Bihar (63.82%) followed by states such as Rajasthan (67.06%) ; Jharkhand (67.63%) ; Andhra Pradesh 67.66%) and Jammu and Kashmir (68.74%). ***[See Table No. 7]***
- **11 States with Below Average National Literacy :** In addition to the above mentioned five states (Bihar, Rajasthan, Jharkhand, A.P. and J & K) which have below average national literacy, there are six more states such as Arunachal Pradesh (66.95%) Punjab 68%, Chattisgarh (71.40%) U.P. (69.72%) Madhya Pradesh (70.63%), Orissa (73.45 %) in the same position.
- **Number of Literates in Rural and Urban Areas :** Of the total 778.45 million literate people in the country, 493.02 million are ruralities (men - 288.04 million) and women - 204.97 million)
- **Five Top Most Populous States :** Of the most populous States of India, Uttar Pradesh maintains its top most position with 199.58 million people followed by States such as Maharashtra (112.37 million) ; Bihar (103.8 million) ; West Bengal (91.34 million) and Andhra Pradesh (84.66 million).

Table 2. Population Share of States and Union Territories, India-2011

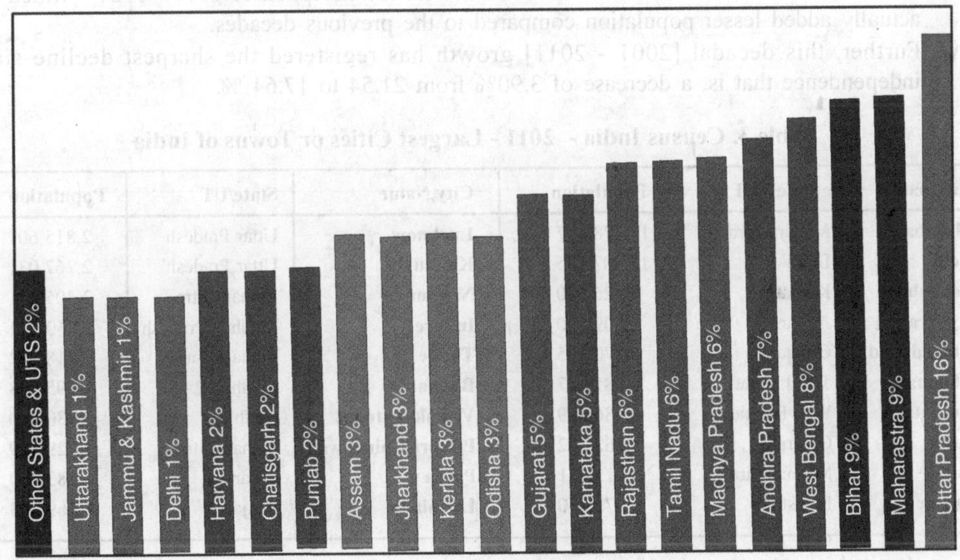

These five states together constitute 49% of the total population of India (U.P. - 16% ; Maharashtra - 9% ; Bihar 9 %, West Bengal - 8% and A.P. 7%).

- **Increase in the Density of Population :** The density of population was 77 in 1901 and 324 in 2001 and it increased to **382** in 2011. Delhi is the most densely populated state with 11297 persons living per square K.M. and Arunachal Pradesh with **17** persons per square K.M., is the least densely populated state. Comparatively, China's density of population is only 135 persons.

Kerala and **Pondichery** are the only two States wherein women out number men and there are 1084 and 1038 women respectively in these two States for every 1000 men.

Sex ratio is lowest in States such as Daman & Diu (618 women per 1000 men) Chandigarh (818), Delhi (866) Sikkim (889) and J & K (803) and Punjab 893.

- **Urban and Rural Sex Ratio :** The total sex ratio for the entire nation stands at 940 (per 1000 men) ; and it is 947 for the rural area and 926 for the urban area.
- **Sex Ratio Between 0 - 6 years :** The total child ratio for the entire nation stands at 914 (per 1000 male children) ; for the rural India it is 919 whereas as for the urban area it is 902.
- **Total No. of Villages, Towns, Districts and States :** As per 2011 census, there are in India at present 35 States (same in 2001); 640 districts as against 593 in 2001 ; 5924 sub districts as against 5463 in 2001, **7935 towns** as against 5161 towns and **640 867 villages** as against 638588 in 2001.
- **Urban and Rural Population :** Of the 120.19 crores of people as per 2011 Census, 833.087 million people (men- 427.917 million, and women - 405.170 million) live in rural area, whereas 377.105 million people (men - 195.807 million and women 181.298 million live in urban area.
- **Decadal Growth in Rural Urban Population :** During the period 2001-2011, Indian population registered a growth of 17.64 % and in this, rural decadal growth was 12.18%, whereas the urban decadal growth was 31.80 %.

During 2001 and 2011 there was 17.19% decadal increase in male population. This decadal increase was 12.12% in the case of rural men and 30.06% in the case of urban men.

For the same period, there was 18.12% decadal increase in female population. This decadal increase was 12.25% in the case of rural women and 33.73% in the case of urban women.

- The population has increased by more than 181 million during the decade 2001 - 2011. This period 2001 - 2011 is the first decade - with the exception of 1911 - 1921 - which has actually added lesser population compared to the previous decades.
- Further, this decadal [2001 - 2011] growth has registered the sharpest decline since independence that is, a decrease of 3.90% from 21.54 to 17.64 %.

Table 3. Census India - 2011 - Largest Cities or Towns of India

City name	State / UT	Population	City Name	State/UT	Population
Mumbai	Maharashtra	12,478,447	**Lucknow**	Uttar Pradesh	2,815,601
Delhi	Delhi	11,007,835	**Kanpur**	Uttar Pradesh	2,767,031
Bengaluru	Karnataka	8,425,970	**Nagpur**	Maharashtra	2,405,421
Hyderabad	Andhra	6,809,970	**Indore**	Madhya Pradesh	1,960 521
Ahmedabad	Gujarat	5,570,585	**Thane**	Maharastra	1,818,872
Chennai	Tamil Nadu	4,681,087	**Bhopal**	Madhya P.	1,795,648
Kolkata	West Bengal	4,486,679	**Vishakapatnam**	Andhra P.	1,730,320
Surat	Gujarat	4,462,002	**Pimpri-Chinchwad**	Maharashtra	1,729,359
Pune	Maharashtra	3,115,431	**Patna**	Bihar	1,683,200
Jaipur	Rajasthan	3,073,350	**Ludhiana**	Punjab	1,769,703

Table 4. Percentage Share of Rural-Urban Child Population in Various States - 2011

States	Share of Rural Child Population in %	Share of Urban Child Population in %
• Uttar pradesh	20.62	13.3
• Bihar	14.37	4.08
• Rajasthan	7.08	5.3
• Madhya Pradesh	6.92	5.86
• West Bengal	6.41	6.26
• Maharashtra	6.33	13.11
• Andhra Pradesh	4.98	6.77
• Gujarath	3.98	6.84
• Karnataka	3.78	6.08
• Orissa (odisha)	3.69	1.7
• Jharkhand	3.61	2.4
• Assam	3.47	1.04
• Tamil Nadu	3.11	7.87
• Chattisgarh	2.44	1.74
• Haryana	1.91	2.56
• Punjab	1.59	2.61
• Kerala	1.49	3.82
• J & K	1.36	1
• Other States / UTs	2.97	2.98

Source : Manorama Year Book - 2012 Page 518

Table 5. Elementary Education in India

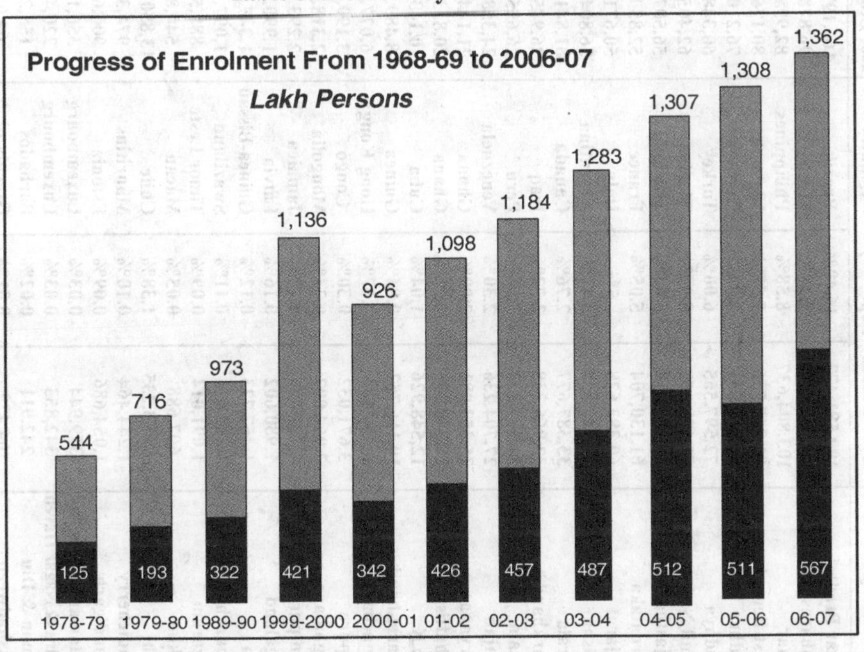

Table 6. 2011 Census : Some Vital Statistics Regarding Indian Population

State or Union Territory	Population 2011 Census	% of Closest Pop.	Comparable Country	Population 2001 Census	% of Pop 2001	% Growth 2001–2011	Decadal Growth 2001–2011	Rural Population	Urban Population	% Urban Population	Sex Ratio
Uttar Pradesh	199,581,477	16.49%	Brazil	166,197,921	16.16%	20.1%	33,383,556	155,111,022	44,470,455	22.28%	908
Maharashtra	112,372,972	9.28%	Mexico	96,878,627	9.42%	16.0%	15,494,345	61,545,441	50,827,531	45.23%	946
Bihar	103,804,637	8.58%	Philippines	82,998,509	8.07%	25.1%	20,806,128	92,075,028	11,729,609	11.30%	916
West Bengal	91,347,736	7.55%	Vietnam	80,176,197	7.79%	13.9%	11,171,539	62,213,676	29,134,060	31.89%	947
Andhra	84,665,533	7.00%	Germany	76,210,007	7.41%	11.1%	8,455,526	56,311,788	28,353,745	33.49%	992
Madhya	72,597,565	6.00%	Turkey	60,348,023	5.87%	20.3%	12,249,542	52,537,899	20,059,666	27.63%	930
Tamil Nadu	72,138,958	5.96%	Thailand	62,405,679	6.07%	15.6%	9,733,279	37,189,229	34,949,729	48.45%	995
Rajasthan	68,621,012	5.67%	Thailand	56,507,188	5.49%	21.4%	12,113,824	51,540,236	17,080,776	24.89%	926
Karnataka	61,130,704	5.05%	France	52,850,562	5.14%	15.7%	8,280,142	37,552,529	23,578,175	38.57%	968
Gujarat	60,383,628	5%	Italy	50,671,017	4.93%	19.2%	9,712,611	34,670,817	25,712,811	42.58%	918
Odisha	41,947,358	3.47%	Argentina	36,804,660	3.58%	14.0%	5,142,698	34,951,234	6,996,124	16.68%	978
Kerala	33,387,677	2.76%	Canada	31,841,374	3.10%	4.9%	1,546,303	17,445,506	15,932,171	47.72%	1,084
Jharkhand	32,966,238	2.72%	Iraq	26,945,829	2.62%	22.3%	6,020,409	25,036,946	7,929,292	24.05%	947
Assam	31,169,272	2.58%	Peru	26,655,528	2.59%	16.9%	4,513,744	26,780,526	4,388,756	14.08%	954
Punjab	27,704,236	2.30%	Venezuela	24,358,999	2.37%	13.7%	3,345,237	17,316,800	10,387,436	37.49%	893
Haryana	25,353,081	2.09%	Ghana	21,144,564	2.06%	19.9%	4,208,517	16,531,493	8,821,588	24.25%	877
Chhattisgarh	25,540,196	2.11%	Ghana	20,833,803	2.03%	22.6%	4,706,393	19,603,658	5,936,538	23.24%	991
J & K	12,548,926	1.04%	Cuba	10,143,700	0.99%	23.7%	2,405,226	9,134,820	3,414,106	27.21%	883
Uttarakhand	10,116,752	0.84%	Guinea	8,489,349	0.83%	19.2%	1,627,403	7,025,583	3,091,169	30.55%	963
Himachal	6,856,509	0.57%	Hong Kong	6,077,900	0.59%	12.8%	778,609	6,167,805	688,704	10.04%	974
Tripura	3,671,032	0.30%	Congo	3,199,203	0.31%	14.7%	471,829	2,710,051	960,981	26.18%	961
Meghalaya	2,964,007	0.24%	Mongolia	2,318,822	0.23%	27.8%	645,185	2,368,971	595,036	20.08%	986
Manipur	2,721,756	0.22%	Jamaica	2,293,896	0.22%	18.7%	427,860	1,899,624	822,132	20.21%	987
Nagaland	1,980,602	0.16%	Latvia	1,990,036	0.19%	-0.5%	-9,434	1,406,861	573,741	28.97%	931
Goa	1,457,723	0.12%	Guinea-Bissau	1,347,668	0.13%	8.2%	110,055	551,414	906,309	62.17%	968
Arunachal	1,382,611	0.11%	Swaziland	1,097,968	0.11%	25.9%	284,643	1,069,165	313,446	22.67%	920
Mizoram	1,091,014	0.09%	Timor Leste	888,573	0.09%	22.8%	202,441	529,037	561,997	51.51%	975
Sikkim	607,688	0.05%	Macau	540,851	0.05%	12.4%	66,837	455,962	151,726	24.97%	889
Delhi	16,753,235	1.38%	Chile	13,850,507	1.35%	21%	2,902,728	419,319	16,333,916	97.50%	866
Pondicherry	1,244,464	0.10%	Mauritius	974,345	0.09%	27.7%	270,119	394,341	850,123	68.31%	1,038
Chandigarh	1,054,686	0.09%	Estonia	900,635	0.09%	17.1%	154,051	2 9,004	1,025,682	97.25%	818
Andaman & Nicobar	379,944	0.03%	Luxembourg	356,152	0.03%	6.7%	23,792	244,411	135,533	35.67%	878
Dadra & Nagar Haveli	342,853	0.03%	Luxembourg	220,490	0.02%	55.5%	122,363	183,024	159,829	46.62%	775
Daman & Diu	242,911	0.02%	Barbados	158,204	0.02%	53.5%	84,707	60,331	182,580	75.16%	618
Lakshadweep	64,429	0.01%	Greenland	60,650	0.01%	6.2%	3,779	14,121	50,308	78.08%	946
India	1,210,193,422	100%	1,028,737,436	100%	17.64%	181,455,986	833,087,662	377,105,760	3,287,240		940

Source : Internet Wikipedia & the free Encyclopedia

Table 7. Literacy Rate in India - 2011

Sl. No.	India/ State/UT	Literate Persons (%)	Males (%)	Females (%)
01	Jammu & Kashmir	68.74	78.26	58.01
02	Himachal P.	83.78	90.83	76.60
03	Punjab	76.68	81.48	71.34
04	Chandigarh	86.43	90.54	81.38
05	Uttarakhand	79.63	88.33	70.70
06	Haryana	76.64	85.38	66.77
07	NCT of Delhi	86.34	91.03	80.93
08	Rajasthan	67.06	80.51	52.66
09	Uttar Pradesh	69.72	79.24	59.26
10	Bihar	63.82	73.39	53.33
11	Sikkim	82.20	87.29	76.43
12	Arunachal	66.95	73.69	59.57
13	Nagaland	80.11	83.29	76.69
14	Manipur	79.85	86.49	73.17
15	Mizoram	91.58	93.72	89.40
16	Tripura	87.75	92.18	83.15
17	Meghalaya	75.48	77.17	73.78
18	Assam	73.18	78.81	67.27
19	West Bengal	77.08	82.67	71.16
20	Jharkhand	67.63	78.45	56.21
21	Odisha	73.45	82.40	64.36
22	Chattisgarh	71.04	81.45	60.59
23	M. Pradesh	70.63	80.53	60.02
24	Gujarat	79.31	87.23	70.73
25	Daman & Diu	87.07	91.48	79.59
26	Dadra & Nagar Haveli	77.65	86.46	65.93
27	Maharashtra	82.91	89.82	75.48
28	Andhra Pradesh	67.66	75.56	59.74
29	Karnataka	75.60	82.85	68.13
30	Goa	87.40	92.81	81.84
31	Lakshadweep	92.28	96.11	88.25
32	Kerala	93.91	96.02	91.98
33	Tamil Nadu	80.33	86.81	73.86
34	Pondicherry	8 6.55	92.12	81.22
35	Andaman & Nicobar	86.27	90.11	81.84
	INDIA	**74.04**	**82.14**	**65.46**

Main Figures at a Glance

No. of States / UT 35 / 35*

No. of Districts 593 / 640*

No. of Sub-Dist. 5,463 / 5,924*

No. of Towns 5,161 / 7,935*

No. of Villages 638,588 / 640,867*

*[2001 - 2011]

Total Population - 2011

Total Persons : 1,210,193,422

	Rural	**Urban**
Male	**427,917,052**	**195,807,196**
Female	**405,170,610**	**181,298,564**

Total Literates - 2011

	Rural	**Urban**
Persons	**493,020,878**	**285,433,242**
Male	**288,047,480**	**156,156,282**
Female	**204,973,398**	**129,276,960**

Languages of India by Number of Native Speakers as per the 2001 Census

Language	Speakers	%
Hindi	422,048,642	41.03%
Bengali	83,369,769	8.11%
Telugu	74,002,856	7.19%
Marathi	71,936,894	6.99%
Tamil	60,793,814	5.91%
Urdu	51,536,111	5.01%
Gujarati	46,091,617	4.48%
Kannada	37,924,011	3.69%
Malayalam	33,066,392	3.21%
Oriya	33,017,446	3.21%
Punjabi	29,102,477	2.83%
Assamese	13,168,484	1.28%
Maithili	12,179,122	1.18%
Bhili/Bhilodi	9,582,957	0.93%
Santali	6,469,600	0.63%
Kashmiri	5,527,698	0.54%
Nepali	2,871,749	0.28%
Gondi	2,713,790	0.26%
Sindhi	2,535,485	0.25%
Konkani	2,489,015	0.24%
Dogri	2,282,589	0.22%
Khandeshi	2,075,258	0.20%
Kurukh	1,751,489	0.17%
Tulu	1,722,768	0.17%
Manipuri	1,466,705*	0.14%
Bodo	1,350,478	0.13%
Khasi - Garo	1,128,575	0.112%
Mundari	1,061,352	0.105%
Ho	1,042,724	0.103%

Note : Figures of the above for 2011 are not available

Table 8. Statewide Distribution of Population as per 2011 Census

SN	Union Territory/ State Name	Total Population	Percent(%) of Total Population	Males	Females
1	Andaman & Nicobar	3,79,944	0.03	2,02,330	1,77,614
2	Andhra Pradesh	8,46,65,533	7.00	4,25,09,881	4,21,55,652
3	Arunachal Pradesh	13,82,611	0.11	7,20,232	6,62,379
4	Assam	3,11,69,272	2.68	1,59,54,927	1,52,14,345
5	Bihar	10,38,04,637	8.48	5,41,85,347	4,96,19,290
6	Chandigarh	10,54,686	0.09	5,80,282	4,74,404
7	Chhattisgarh	2,55,40,196	2.11	1,28,27,915	1,27,12,281
8	Dadra & Nagar Haveli	3,42,853	0.03	1,93,178	1,49,675
9	Daman & Diu	2,42,911	0.02	1,50,100	92,811
10	Delhi	1,67,53,235	1.38	89,76,410	77,76,825
11	Goa	14,57,723	0.12	7,40,711	7,17,012
12	Gujarat	6,03,83,628	4.99	3,14,82,282	2,89,01,346
13	Haryana	2,53,53,081	2.09	1,35,05,130	1,18,47,951
14	Himachal Pradesh	68,56,509	0.57	34,73,892	34,73,892
15	Jammu & Kashmir	1,25,48,926	1.04	66,65,561	58,83,365
16	Jharkhand	3,11,69,272	2.72	1,59,54,927	1,52,14,345
17	Karnataka	6,11,30,704	5.05	3,10,57,742	3,00,72,962
18	Kerala	3,33,87,677	2.76	1,60,21,290	1,73,66,387
19	Lakshadweep	64,429	0.01	33,106	31,323
20	Madhya Pradesh	7,25,97,565	6.00	3,76,12,920	3,49,84,645
21	Maharashtra	11,23,72,972	9.29	5,83,61,397	5,40,11,575
22	Manipur	27,21,756	0.22	13,69,764	13,51,992
23	Meghalaya	29,64,007	0.24	14,92,668	14,71,339
24	Mizoram	10,91,014	0.09	5,52,339	5,38,675
25	Nagaland	19,80,602	0.16	10,25,707	9,54,895
26	Odisha	4,19,47,358	3.47	2,12,01,678	2,07,45,680
27	Pondicherry	12,44,464	0.10	6,10,485	6,33,979
28	Punjab	2,77,04,236	2.29	1,46,34,819	1,30,69,417
29	Rajasthan	6,86,21,012	5.67	3,56,20,086	3,30,00,926
30	Sikkim	6,07,688	0.05	3,21,661	2,86,027
31	Tamil Nadu	7,21,38,958	5.96	3,61,58,871	3,59,80,087
32	Tripura	36,71,032	0.30	18,71,867	17,99,165
33	Uttarakhand	1,01,16,752	0.84	51,54,178	49,62,574
34	Uttar Pradesh	19,95,81,477	16.49	10,45,96,415	9,49,85,062
35	West Bengal	9,13,47,736	7.55	4,69,27,389	4,44,20,347
	TOTAL	**1,21,01,93,422**	**100**	**62,37,24,248**	**58,64,69,17**

Table 9. Population Distribution of the World in Ten Most Populated and Other Countries in Percentage

1.	China - 19.4%	6.	Pakistan - 2.7%
2.	India - 17.5%	7.	Bangladesh - 2.4%
3.	USA - 4.5%	8.	Nigeria - 2.3%
4.	Indonesia - 3.4%	9.	Russia - 2.0%
5.	Brazil - 2.8%	10.	Japan - 1.9%
		11.	Others - 41.1 %

Source : Manorama Year Book - 2012 Page - 513

❖❖❖❖❖❖❖❖❖

BIBLIOGRAPHY

1. Agarwal A.N. - Indian Economy - Problems of Development & Planning
2. Allan G. Johnson - The Blackwell Dictionary of Sociology
3. Altekar A.S. - The Position of Women in Hindu Civilzation
4. Anjana Maitra Sinha - Women in a Changing Society - [1993]
5. Ashwini Mahajan - Globalisation & Small Scale Industries
6. Avasthi A.P. - Indian Government & Politics
7. Bipin Chandra - Modern India - A History Text Book for Class XII
8. Bishwavath Ghosh - Contemporary Social Problems of India
9. Channabassappa .K - Hindulidavaru Yaru ? [Kannada]
10. Chingamani M.A. - Sociology of Indian Society
11. Dara S.S. - A Text Book of Environmental Chemistry & Pollution Control
12. David E. Hunter & Philip Whitten - Encyclopaedia of Anthropology
13. David Jary and July Jary - Collins Dictionary of Sociology
14. Desai A.R. - Rural Sociology in India
15. Devaki Jain - Indian Women [National Book Trust of India]
16. Doshi S.L. & Jain P.C. - Social Anthropology
17. Doshi S.L. & Jain P.C. - Rural Sociology
18. Dube S.C. - Encyclopaedia of Social Work in India - Vol.III
19. Dube S.C. - Indian Society
20. Duncan Mitchel - Dictionary of Sociology
21. Emory S. Bogardus - The Development of Social Thought
22. Fr. Thomas Pazhayampallil SDB - Pastoral Guide : Moral - Canonical - Liturgical - Vol.II [Sacraments Christian Life & Sexuality]
23. Ghurye G.S. - Caste & Class in India
24. Gisbert P. - Fundamentals of Sociology
25. Ian Robertson - Sociology
26. Indira R. - Mahile, Samaja Mattu Samskriti - [2004] [Kannada]
27. Indira R. - Bharateeya Kutumba
28. Jadunath Sarkar - India Through the Ages
29. Jayaram N. - Sociology of Education in India
30. Kachroo J.L. & Kachroo Vijay - Society in India
31. Kapadia K.M. - Marriage & Family in India
32. Kapoor A.C. - Principles of Political Science
33. Kar P.K. - Indian Society
34. Ketkar S.V. - History of Caste in India
35. Kuppuswamy B. - Social Change in India
36. Leah Levin - Human Rights Pub : NBT
37. Leela Dube - Sociology of Kinship
38. Luniya B.N. - Evolution of Indian Culture
39. Majumdar D.N. - Races and Cultures of India
40. Majumdar R.C. - History and Culture of Indian People - Vol. X
41. Mamoria C.B. - Social Problems and Social Disorganisation
42. Mandelbaum David G. - Society in India Vol. I and II
43. Mathur S.S. - A Sociological Approach to Indian Education
44. Misra S.K. & Puri V.K - Indian Economy
45. Moulesh H.K. & Subramanya C. - Sociology of Indian Society
46. Murdock J. - Review of Caste in India
47. Nagesh H.V. - Bharateeya Kutumba [Kannada]
48. Nagesh H.V. - Gramantara [Kannada]

49. Nanjammanni M. - Study of Indian Society
50. Neera Desai and Usha Thakkar - Women in Indian Society - NBT, New Delhi
51. Neera Desai and Vibhuti Patel - Indian Women, Change and Challenge in the Decade - 1975-85
52. Parimal B. Carr - Sociology - The Discipline & Its Dimensions
53. Park K. - Text Book of Preventive & Social Medicine
54. Parvathy A.A. - Secularism & Hinduism - A Discursive Study
55. Pothen S. - Divorce - Its Causes and Consequences in Hindu Society [1996]
56. Prabhu P.H. - Hindu Social Organisation
57. Ram Ahuja - Indian Social System
58. Ram Ahuja - Social Problems in India
59. Ram Ahuja - Society in India
60. Ram Ahuja - Violence Against Women
61. Ram Swarup - Buddhism Vis-a-vis Hinduism
62. Rao P.R. - Indian Heritage & Culture
63. Rebello I. - Indian Culture & Civilisation
64. Richard T. Schaffer - Sociology - International Edition
65. Ruddar Datt & Sundharam KPM - Indian Economy
66. Scarpitti F.R. & Anderson M.L. - Social Problems
67. Scott W.P. - Dictionary of Sociology
68. Shamim Aleem - Women's Development Problems and Prospects - [1996]
69. Shankar Rao C.N. - Samanya Samajashastra [Kannada] for I.A.S.
70. Shankar Rao C.N. - Bharateeya Samaja [Kannada] [1991]
71. Shankar Rao C.N. - Study of Indian Society [1996]
72. Shankar Rao C.N. - Study of Social Thought [2001]
73. Shankar Rao C.N. - Samajashastrada Kiru Vishwakosha [Kannada] [2001]
74. Shankar Rao C.N. - A Study of Contemporary Indian Society [2002]
75. Shankar Rao C.N. - Bharatadalli Samajika Samasyegalu Mattu Samajika Vighatane [Kannada]
76. Sharma B.K & Kaur H - Air Pollution
77. Sharma D.S. - Essence of Hinduism
78. Sharma RN & RK - Indian Social Thought
79. Sheshagiri N. - Pollution
80. Shriram Sathe - Aryans : Who Were They ?
81. Singh K. - Indian Social System
82. Smelser N.J. - Sociology
83. Sreenivas Murthy Dr. A.V. & Kamath Dr. S.U. - Studies in Indian Culture
84. Srinivas M.N. - Caste in Modern India & Other Essays
85. Srinivas M.N. - India's Villages
86. Srinivas M.N. [Ed.] - "Caste - Its 20th Century Avatar"
87. Srinivas M.N. - Social Change in Modern India
88. Swami Shivananda - All About Hinduism
89. Swami Vivekananda - India & Her Problems
90. Swami Vivekananda - Rousing Call to the Hindu Nation [*Ed.* Eknath Ranade]
91. Thomas P. - Indian Women Through the Ages
92. Wallace & Wallace - Sociology
93. William P. Scott - Dictionary of Sociology
94. Yogendra Singh - Modernisation of Indian Tradition

Other Sources

1. Andre Beteille - Article on S.C. Dube in *Economic & Political Weekly*, 20th Mar. 1996
2. Andre Beteille - Article on M.N. Srinivas in *Economic & Political Weekly*, 8th Jan. 2000
3. Antony P. Palatty - Reservation & Its Implementation [*Samaja Shodhana* Vol.I, No.2, Oct. 1992]
4. Apte V.S. - Sanskrit - Hindi Dictionary

5. Chandrashekar Bhat - Article on M.S.A. Rao in *Sociology of Development & Change*
6. Gopala Sarana - Article on D.N. Majumdar *The Eastern Anthropologist,* Vol. XIV, No.2, May - April 1961.
7. Jayaram N. - Article on "Caste & Hinduism : Changing Protean Relationships" in the book *Caste : Its 20th Century Avatar* [*Ed.* M.N. Srinivas]
8. Jeevan Kumar Dr. D. - Article *Understanding Globalisation* in Karnataka Journal of Politics
9. Kranti Kumar Reddy - Article *Globalisation & Environment - A Third World Perspective* in Journal *Third Concept* [Oct. 2001]
10. Leela Dube - Caste and Women [Article in *Caste : Its 20th Century Avatar* (*Ed.* M.N. Srinivas)]
11. Madan T.N. - Article on D.P. Mukerji in *Sociological Bulletin* 43(2), Sept. 1994.
12 Rao M.S.A. - Article on K.M. Kapadia in *Sociological Bulletin* Vol. XVII, Mar. 1968, No.1.
13. Ravindranath Rao - Tribal Social Transformation [Article in *Samaja Shodhana* Vol.I, No.2, Oct. 1992]
14. Romila Thapar - Article *Looking Back in History* in *Indian Women*
15. Sadananda Bhatkal - Article on G.S. Ghurye for Birth Centenary Celebration Committee
16. Saxena R.N. - Article on R.K. Mukherji in *Sociological Bulletin* Vol XVII No.2, Sept. 1968.
17. Srinivas M.N. - Social Structure [Article in Gazetteer of India - Vol.I - 1965]
18. Srinivas M.N. - Sociology in India & Its Future - Article in Souvenir??????
19. Sujith Sikidar & Debabrata Das - Third Concept - Oct. 2001
20. Sunanda Patwardhan - Article on Iravathi Karve in *Sociological Bulletin,* Vol. XIX, No.2, Sept. 1970
21. Collin's Dictionary of Sociology
22. Complete Works of Swami Vivekananda - Ramakrishna Mission Publication
23. Cultural Heritage of India - Vol. I - Ramakrishna Mission Publication
24. Deccan Herald [Bangalore] dated 14.12.1979.
25. Encyclopaedia of Social Work in India - Vol. III
26. Frontline
27. Handbook of Social Welfare Statistics - Ministry of Social Welfare, Govt. of India - 1981
28. Indian Culture [Vivekananda Kendra Prakashana]
29. India Year Book - 1999
30. India Year Book - 2000
31. India Year Book - 2001
32. Indian Book of the Year - 2002 - Encyclopaedia Britannica and The Hindu
33. India Inheritance, Literature, Philosophy & Religion - Vol. I [Bharatiya Vidya Bhavan]
34. Manorama Year Book - 2000, 2001 and 2002
35. Manorama Year Book - 1995, 2004, 2005
36. Manpower Profile, India - 1998
37. *"Selected Reading Material"* issued at National Seminar on Internationalisation of Indian Higher Education - Quality Dimensions, 24 - 25 April, Bangalore.
38. Sociological Bulletin, Vol. 30(1), 1981.
39. Statistical Outline of India - 1999
40. Students' Britannica [India] Vol. - 1 to 5
41. The Gazetteer of India [Vol. 1] - Publications Division, Govt. of India, 1965
42. The Hindusthan Times dated 6th April 1993, 8th July 1995 and 11th July 1995
43. The New Encyclopaedia Britannica - Vol. 22 and Vol. 27
44. Times of India - Editorial - June 1982
45. *Udayavani* Kannada daily dated 27th Feb. 1994
46. *"Viveka Hamsa"* Monthly - Jan. 2003

I.A.S. Examination - Syllabus

Syllabus Prescribed by the U.P.S.C. For Civil Services Examination

SOCIOLOGY [Main]

PAPER - II

Study of Indian Society

1. **Historical Moorings of the Indian Society :** Traditional Hindu social organisation; socio-cultural dynamics through the ages; impact of Buddhism, Islam, and the West - Factors in continuity and change.
2. **Caste System :** Origin of the caste system; cultural and structural views about caste; mobility in caste; caste among Muslims and Christians; change and persistence of caste in modern India; issues of equality and social justice; Views of Gandhi and Ambedkar on caste; caste and Indian polity; Backward Classes Movement; Mandal Commission Report and issues of social backwardness and social justice; Emergence of Dalit Consciousness.
3. **Class Structure :** Class structure in India; Agrarian and industrial class structure; emergence of middle class; Emergence of classes among tribes; Elite formation in India.
4. **Marriage, Family and Kinship :** Marriage among different ethnic groups; its changing trends and its future; Family - its structural and functional aspects - its changing forms; Regional variations in kinship systems and its socio-cultural correlates; Impact of legislation and socio-economic change on marriage and family; Generation gap.
5. **Agrarian Social Structure :** Peasant society and agrarian systems; Land Tenure Systems - historical perspectives; social consequences of land reforms and green revolution; Feudalism - semi-feudalism debates; Emerging agrarian class structure; Agrarian unrest.
6. **Industry and Society :** Path of industrialisation, occupational diversification, trade unions and human relations; Market Economy and its social consequences, Economic Reforms Liberalisation, Privatisation and Globalisation.
7. **Political Processes :** Working of the democratic political system in a traditional society; political parties and their social base; social structural origins of political elites and their orientations; regionalism, pluralism and national unity; decentralisation of power; Panchayath Raj and Nagarapalikas and 73rd and 74th Constitutional Amendments.
8. **Education :** Directive Principles of State Policy and primary education; Educational inequality and change; Education and social mobility; the role of community and state intervention in education; Universalisation of primary education; Total Literacy Campaigns; Educational problems of the disadvantaged groups.
9. **Religion and Society :** Size, growth and regional distribution of different religious groups; educational levels of different groups; Problems of religious minorities; Communal Tensions; assimilation and integration; Issues of tribal identity.
10. **Tribal Societies :** Distinctive features of tribal communities and their geographical spread; Problems of tribal communities - land alienation, poverty, indebtedness; health and nutrition, education; tribal development efforts after independence; Tribal Policy - isolation, assimilation and integration; issues of tribal identity.

11. **Population Dynamics :** Population size, growth, composition and distribution; components of population growth; birth rate, death rate and migration; determinants and consequences of population growth; Issues of age at marriage, sex ratio, infant mortality rate; Population Policy and Family Welfare Programmes.

12. **Dimensions of Development :** Strategy and ideology of planning; poverty, indebtedness and bonded labour; strategies of rural development - poverty alleviation programmes; environment, housing, slums, and unemployment; programmes for urban development.

13. **Social Change :** Endogenous and exogenous sources of change and resistance to change; processes of change - Sanskritisation and Modernisation; Agents of Change, mass media, education and communication; problems of change and modernisation; structural contradictions and breakdowns.

14. **Social Movements :** Reform Movements : Arya Samaj, Satya Shodhak Samaj, Sri Narayanaguru Dharma, Paripalana Sabha, and Ram Krishna Mission. Peasant Movements - Kisan Sabha, Telangana, Naxalbari, Backward Castes Movement; Self respect Movement, Backward castes mobilisation in North India.

15. **Women and Society :** Demographic profile of women; Special Problems - dowry, atrocities, discrimination; existing programmes for women and their impact. Situation analysis of children; child welfare programmes.

16. **Social Problems :** Prostitution, AIDS, Alcoholism, Drug Addiction, Corruption.